Central America
on a shoestring

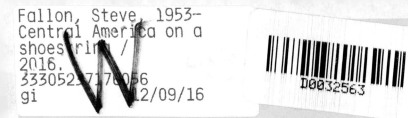

Yucatán &
Chiapas,
Mexico
p48

Belize
p230

Guatemala
p99

Honduras
p351

El Salvador
p286

Nicaragua
p429

Costa Rica
p516

Panama
p621

THIS EDITION WRITTEN AND RESEARCHED BY

Steve Fallon, Bridget Gleeson, Paul Harding, John Hecht, Tom Masters,
Tom Spurling, Lucas Vidgen, Mara Vorhees

PLAN YOUR TRIP

Welcome to Central
America 6

Central America Map 8

Central America's
Top 16 10

Need to Know 18

First Time
Central America 20

If You Like... 22

Month by Month 25

Itineraries 28

Big Adventures,
Small Budgets 36

Outdoor Activities 39

Countries at a Glance . . 44

CRAFT SHOP, CANCÚN,
MEXICO P50

TUUL & BRUNO MORANDI/GETTY IMAGES ©

CATEDRAL DE GRANADA,
NICARAGUA P445

KRYSIA CAMPOS/GETTY IMAGES ©

ON THE ROAD

MEXICO'S YUCATÁN & CHIAPAS 48

The Yucatán. 50
Cancún. 50
Isla Mujeres 56
Puerto Morelos 58
Playa Del Carmen 59
Isla Cozumel 64
Tulum 66
Cobá 68
Laguna Bacalar 69
Mahahual 70
Valladolid 70
Chichén Itzá 72
Mérida 74
Campeche 79
Chiapas 82
San Cristóbal
de las Casas 82
Lagos de Montebello 88
Yaxchilán 88
Palenque 89
Agua Azul & Misol-Ha 93
Understand Mexico's
Yucatán & Chiapas 94
Survival Guide. 95

GUATEMALA 99

Guatemala City 101
Antigua. 114
The Highlands 127
Lago de Atitlán 128
Chichicastenango 144
Santa Cruz del Quiché . . . 147
Nebaj 149
Uspantán 150
Quetzaltenango (Xela) 151
Huehuetenango 161
Todos Santos
Cuchumatán 163
The Pacific Slope 165
Retalhuleu 165

Parque Arqueológico
Takalik Abaj 166
Champerico. 167
Santa Lucía
Cotzumalguapa 167
La Democracia 168
Sipacate 169
Escuintla 169
Monterrico 169
Central Guatemala 172
Salamá & Around 172
Biotopo del Quetzal 172
Cobán 173
El Oriente 179
Chiquimula 179
Esquipulas 180
Quiriguá 183
Lago de Izabal 184
Puerto Barrios 188
Punta de Manabique 189
Lívingston 189
El Petén 193
Sayaxché 193
Ceibal 193
Finca Ixobal 195
Flores & Santa Elena 196
El Remate 201
Tikal 202
Uaxactún 210
Yaxhá 211
El Mirador 211
Understand
Guatemala 213
Survival Guide. 221

BELIZE 230

Belize City 234
Northern Cays. 239
Caye Caulker 239
Ambergris Caye
& San Pedro 243
Northern Belize. 249
Bermudian Landing 249

Contents

Altun Ha.............249
Lamanai.............249
Orange Walk..........250
Corozal.............252
Sarteneja.............254
**Belize City
to Belmopan........255**
**Western Belize
(Cayo District).......255**
Belmopan.............255
Hummingbird Hwy......259
San Ignacio...........260
Mountain Pine Ridge
& Caracol.............265
West to Guatemala....266
Southern Belize.....267
Dangriga.............267
Central Cays..........270
Hopkins
& Sittee Point..........270
Placencia.............272
Punta Gorda..........276
Toledo Villages........279
Understand Belize....280
Survival Guide.......282

EL SALVADOR.....286

San Salvador........290
**Around
San Salvador........304**
Los Planes
de Renderos............305
La Libertad............305
La Costa del Bálsamo...306
Santa Tecla...........309
Western El Salvador...310
Parque Nacional
Los Volcanes...........310
Lago de Coatepeque....311
Santa Ana.............311
Metapán..............314
Chalchuapa...........316
Ruta de Las Flores......316
Sonsonate............322

Tacuba..............322
Parque Nacional
El Imposible...........323
Eastern El Salvador...324
San Vicente...........324
Alegría...............325
Isla Montecristo.......326
Usulután.............326
Bahía de Jiquilisco.....327
San Miguel............327
La Unión..............330
Beaches near La Union...331
Golfo de
Fonseca Islands........332
Morazán..............332
**Northern
El Salvador...........334**
Suchitoto............334
Chalatenango.........336
La Palma.............338
**Understand
El Salvador.........339**
Survival Guide.......345

HONDURAS......351
Tegucigalpa..........353
Western Honduras....365
Comayagua...........365
La Esperanza..........367
Marcala.............368
Lago de Yojoa.........369
San Pedro Sula........371
Copán Ruinas.........374
Copán
Archaeological Site.....380
Gracias..............384
Northern Honduras...388
Omoa...............388
Puerto Cortés.........389
Tela................389
La Ceiba.............392
Trujillo...............400
Bay Islands.........402
Roatán..............402

Utila.................408
The Moskitia.........414
Laguna de Ibans.......414
Reserva de la Biosfera
del Río Plátano........414
Palacios..............415
Brus Laguna..........415
Puerta Lempira........415
**Southern Honduras
& Isla del Tigre.......416**
**Understand
Honduras...........417**
Survival Guide.......423

NICARAGUA......429
Managua............431
**Granada & the
Masaya Region.......444**
Granada..............444
Masaya...............455
Parque Nacional
Volcán Masaya.........456
**Southwestern
Nicaragua...........457**
Rivas.................457
San Jorge.............458
Isla de Ometepe.......458
**Southern Pacific
Coast...............464**
San Juan del Sur......464
**León & Northwestern
Nicaragua...........469**
León.................469
Poneloya & Las
Peñitas Beaches........477
Cosigüina
Peninsula Beaches......477
Northern Nicaragua...479
Estelí................479
Área
Protegida Miraflor......484
Área Protegida Cerro
Tisey-Estanzuela.......485
Somoto.............485
Jinotega.............486

Matagalpa 488

Caribbean Coast 491

Bluefields 491

Pearl Lagoon 494

Corn Islands 495

Bilwi
(Puerto Cabezas) 499

San Carlos & Around . . . 501

San Carlos 501

Islas Solentiname 502

Río San Juan 503

**Understand
Nicaragua** 505

Survival Guide 511

COSTA RICA 516

San José 520

**Central Valley &
Highlands** 533

Alajuela 536

Parque Nacional
Volcán Poás 537

Parque Nacional
Braulio Carrillo 538

Cartago 539

Valle de Orosi 539

Turrialba 540

Caribbean Coast 542

Tortuguero 542

Puerto Limón 544

Cahuita 545

Puerto Viejo
de Talamanca 549

Sixaola 554

**Arenal & Northern
Lowlands** 554

La Fortuna &
Volcán Arenal 554

Tilarán 558

Los Chiles 559

Valle de Sarapiquí 559

**Northwestern
Costa Rica** 561

Monteverde
& Santa Elena 561

Liberia 568

Parque Nacional
Rincón de la Vieja 571

NICK LEDGER/GETTY IMAGES ©

VOLCÁN ARENAL, COSTA RICA P554

Contents

La Cruz 572
Península de Nicoya . . . 573
Playa del Coco 573
Playa Tamarindo 576
Playa Sámara 580
Mal País &
Santa Teresa 582
Montezuma 583
Central Pacific Coast . . . 587
Puntarenas 587
Parque
Nacional Carara 587
Jacó 588
Quepos 590
Manuel Antonio 593
Dominical 595
Uvita 597
**Southern Costa Rica
& Península de Osa . . . 598**
San Isidro de
El General 599
San Gerardo de Rivas . . . 600
Palmar 602
Sierpe 602
Bahía Drake 603
Puerto Jiménez 604
Parque
Nacional Corcovado 606
Golfito 607
Pavones 608
Paso Canoas 609
**Understand
Costa Rica 609**
Survival Guide 613

PANAMA 621

Panama City 623
Around Panama City . . . 641
Panama Canal 642
Isla Taboga 644
Archipiélago
de las Perlas 645
**Pacific Coast &
Highlands 646**

El Valle 646
Chitré 648
Pedasí 649
Sunset Coast 650
Playa Venao 651
Santa Catalina 652
Santa Fé 653
Chiriquí Province 654
David 654
Golfo de Chiriquí 656
Playa Las Lajas 657
Boquete 657
Parque Nacional
Volcán Barú 662
Cerro Punta 663
Parque Internacional
La Amistad 663
**Bocas del
Toro Province 664**
Isla Colón 665
Isla Carenero 673
Isla Bastimentos 673
Almirante 676
Changuinola 676
Colón Province 677
Colón 677
Portobelo 679
Isla Grande 680
**Comarca
de Guna Yala 681**
Darién Province 684
Metetí 688
Yaviza 688
El Real 689
Rancho Frío 689
La Palma 690
Reserva Natural
Punta Patiño 691
Sambú 692
Understand Panama . . 692
Survival Guide 700

UNDERSTAND

Central America
Today 708
History 710
People & Culture 717

SURVIVAL GUIDE

Directory A–Z 724
Transportation 734
Language 739
Index 750
Map Legend 766

SPECIAL FEATURES

Big Adventures,
Small Budgets 36
Outdoor Activities 39
Chichén Itzá,
Mexico in 3D 62
Tikal,
Guatemala in 3D 204

Welcome to Central America

With turquoise seas and lush forests, magnificent Maya ruins, bustling markets and flourishing farms, Central America is packed with opportunities to chill out – or thrill out.

Outdoor Adventure

Eight countries with 300-plus volcanoes and two long tropical coasts make for a pretty big playground. Paddle deep into indigenous territories in a dugout canoe, or explore the remains of Spanish forts on the coast. Zip through rainforest canopies, swim alongside sea turtles or trek to sublime cloud-forest vistas. Everywhere you go, you'll be accompanied by a wild cast of characters: a resplendent quetzal on the highland trail; an unruly troupe of howler monkeys screeching through the canopy; or a breaching whale that turns your ferry ride into an adrenaline-rush event. Your adventures are limited only by your will.

Maya Ruins

The Maya territory sprawled from Mexico to Honduras, with ruins in five present-day Central American countries. Visit them to step into a mysterious, spine-tingling universe. Explore the lost temples of Tikal, soaring above the Guatemalan jungle canopy. Investigate otherworldly Palenque and Tulum, perched above the crashing surf. See jaguars carved to life at Copán, and find out why Chichén Itzá is one of the new seven wonders of the world. Discover a culture that harks back 4000 years – the greatest pre-Columbian civilization – and still persists today.

Diverse Cultures

Central America may be the size of Texas, but its rich mix of people and cultures has created a diverse and dynamic society. With more than 20 Maya languages spoken, Guatemala is the region's indigenous heartland. The Spanish left their mark throughout the region, with majestic colonial plazas, fervent beauty contests and silent hours of siesta. African culture permeates the Caribbean coast, from Congo rebel traditions to Garifuna drumbeats. And the last century brought the rest of the world – Asians, Europeans, North Americans – along with a coat of modernity that dressed up Panama City into a contemporary capital.

Sun & Sea

With chilled-out Caribbean vibes on one side and monster Pacific swells on the other, Central America sits poised to deliver the best of all beach worlds. From deserted *playas* to full-moon parties, this tiny region can deliver just about any sun-soaked experience that your inner beach bum desires. Plus, there's that magnificent, mysterious world that begins at the water's edge. Seize it by scuba diving with whale sharks in Honduras, snorkeling the world's second-largest coral reef in Belize, getting stoked on Costa Rica's world-class surf breaks, or setting sail among Panama's virgin isles. Hello, paradise.

Why I Love Central America

By Mara Vorhees, Writer

On a clear day at the summit of Panama's Volcán Barú, you can see both the Caribbean Sea and the Pacific Ocean in one sweeping, 360-degree vista, from sea to shining sea. (There's a fun fact to impress your trivia team.) I love how this little isthmus – just 50km wide at its narrowest point – contains a whole continent's worth of adventure, history and habitats. Whether you take a week or take a year, you'll only scratch the surface of this rich, varied region.

For more about our writers, see page 768

Above: Woman in traditional Maya clothing, Panajachel (p129), Guatemala

Central America

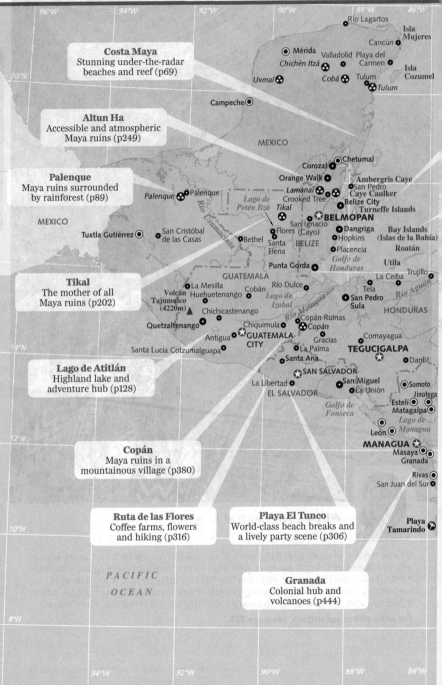

Costa Maya
Stunning under-the-radar beaches and reef (p69)

Altun Ha
Accessible and atmospheric Maya ruins (p249)

Palenque
Maya ruins surrounded by rainforest (p89)

Tikal
The mother of all Maya ruins (p202)

Lago de Atitlán
Highland lake and adventure hub (p128)

Copán
Maya ruins in a mountainous village (p380)

Ruta de las Flores
Coffee farms, flowers and hiking (p316)

Playa El Tunco
World-class beach breaks and a lively party scene (p306)

Granada
Colonial hub and volcanoes (p444)

CARIBBEAN SEA

20°N

Caye Caulker
Idyllic island paradise (p239)

Bay Islands
Scuba-diving paradise (p402)

JAMAICA
KINGSTON

18°N

Islas Santanilla
(Swan Islands, Honduras)

16°N

Guanaja

Laguna de
Caratasca

Río Patuca

The Moskitia

Isla de Ometepe
Lake island packed
with adventure (p458)

Río Coco
(Segovia)

Cayos Miskitos
(Nicaragua)

14°N

**Parque Nacional
Manuel Antonio**
Spectacular beaches (p593)

NICARAGUA

Bilwi
(Puerto
Cabezas)

Isla de
Providencia
(Colombia)

**Archipiélago de
Bocas del Toro**
Turquoise seas and fun (p664)

Isla de
San Andrés
(Colombia)

Boaco

Pearl
Lagoon

Rama

Corn Islands
(Islas del Maíz,
Nicaragua)

Panama City
Cosmopolitan capital and
Panama Canal (p623)

12°N

Lago de
Nicaragua

Bluefields

Bahía
Punta
Gorda

Isla de
Ometepe

San
Carlos

Los Chiles

El Castillo

Liberia Volcán Arenal
(1633m)

El Coco

Tortuguero

Parque Nacional
Tortuguero

Península
de Nicoya

Puntarenas

SAN
JOSÉ

Puerto Limón

10°N

Montezuma

Golfo
de Nicoya

Quepos

COSTA
RICA

San Vito

Cahuita

Volcán
Barú
(3475m)

Bocas del
Toro

Archipiélago
de San Blás

Colón

PANAMA
CITY

Lago
Bayano

Comarca de
Kuna Yala

Golfo de
los Mosquitos

Parque Nacional
Corcovado

Boquete

Bahía de
Panamá

Río Chucunaque

Península
de Osa

David

PANAMA

Penonomé

La Palma

**Reserva Biológica Bosque
Nuboso Monteverde**
Mystical cloud forest (p564)

Golfo de
Chiriquí

Isla de
Coiba

Santiago

Santa
Catalina

Chitré

Península
de Azuero

Archipiélago
de las Perlas

Golfo de
Panamá

Yaviza

COLOMBIA

84°W   82°W   80°W   78°W   76°W

Central America's
Top 16

Bocas del Toro, Panama

1 No wonder this Caribbean island chain (p667) is Panama's number-one vacation spot. 'It's all good,' say the locals. Pedal to the beach on a cruiser bike, hum to improvised calypso on Isla Bastimentos and laze over dinner in a thatched hut on the waterfront. Lodgings range from cheap digs to stunning jungle lodges and luxury resorts on outer islands. Surfers hit the breaks, but there's also snorkeling among dazzling corals and oversized starfish, or volunteering opportunities to help nesting sea turtles.

Tikal, Guatemala

2 The remarkably restored temples (p202) that stand in this partially cleared corner of the jungle still astonish, for both their monumental size and architectural brilliance, as an early morning arrival at the Gran Plaza proves. It's an amazing testament to the cultural and artistic heights scaled by this jungle civilization, which thrived for some 16 centuries. A highlight is the sky-high vantage provided by towering Temple IV, on the west edge of the precinct. Equally compelling is the abundance of wildlife, which you'll see while strolling along ancient causeways between ceremonial centers.

Granada, Nicaragua

3 Granada (p444) is a town of immense and palpable magnetism. At the heart of the city's charms are the picture-perfect cobblestone streets, polychromatic colonial homes and churches, and a lilting air that brings the city's spirited past into present-day focus. Most trips here begin and end on foot; simply dawdling from gallery to restaurant to colonial church can take up the better part of a day. Nearby, myriad wild areas, islands, volcanoes and artisan villages await further exploration of their treasures. Top: Catedral de Granada (p445)

Bay Islands, Honduras

4 Imagine living the Caribbean dream – swimming in balmy, turquoise waters off a white-sand beach, then sipping a sundowner – but on a backpacking budget. Well, Honduras' Bay Islands (p402) offer that opportunity. Blessed with a fascinating British and buccaneering heritage, today these islands are renowned for their fabled coral reefs and terrific scuba diving. Search for the world's biggest fish, the whale shark, off the island of Utila, or explore shipwrecks in Roatán. Then feast on surf-fresh seafood and investigate the islands' surprisingly lively bar scenes. Bottom: Roatán (p402)

Palenque, Mexico

5 Gather all your senses and dive headfirst into these impressive ruins (p89), some of the Maya world's finest. Here pyramids rise above jungle treetops and howler monkeys sound off like monsters in the dense canopy. Wander the maze-like Palacio, gazing up at its unique and iconic tower. Scale the stone staircase of the Templo de las Inscripciones, the lavish mausoleum of Pakal (Palenque's mightiest ruler) and survey the sprawling ruins from atop. Then head downhill, following the Otulum River and its pretty waterfalls, and finish by visiting the excellent museum.

Parque Nacional Manuel Antonio, Costa Rica

6 It's easy to understand why Parque Nacional Manuel Antonio (p593) is Costa Rica's most popular national park: this green gem is blessed with stunning beaches, accessible trails and bountiful wildlife. A perfect day at Manuel Antonio entails a leisurely morning of navigating the trails and scanning the canopy for wildlife, and an even more leisurely afternoon of picnicking under swaying beach palms and swimming in the turquoise Pacific. At day's end, dinner is served at a cliffside restaurant as the sun sets the horizon ablaze. *Pura vida*, indeed.

Bottom: Iguana

Panama City, Panama

7 Panama City (p623) is high-octane Latin America: think crowds, casinos and a stacked skyline. For this city of nearly a million people, transformation is in the air: a new coastal green space, a new biodiversity museum and a new subway system. Also within striking distance: one of the world's great marvels of engineering, the Panama Canal. All this sits next to the atmospheric colonial architecture of Casco Viejo and the romantic ruins of Panamá Viejo. It's incongruous, yet appealing – and undeniably authentic.

Monteverde, Costa Rica

8 To explore the Reserva Biológica Bosque Nuboso Monteverde (Cloud Forest Reserve; p564)) is to arrive at the pinnacle of Costa Rica's continental divide. Warm humid trade winds from the Caribbean sweep up forested slopes, where they cool and condense into clouds that congregate here and over the nearby Reserva Santa Elena. What that means is a blast of swirling misty euphoria as you take in two forests rich in diversity and oxygen, where lichen-draped trees soar, exotic birds sing, and orchids and bromeliads bloom.

Playa El Tunco, El Salvador

9 Playa El Tunco (p306) is the most famous beach in El Salvador. Known for its throbbing weekend party scene, world-class beach breaks and relatively large international crowd, El Tunco delivers in black-sandy spades. But if you'd rather chill out than party down, many surrounding beach hamlets are far less hectic. At the western reaches, Barrio de Santiago is wild and windswept and sea turtles hatch along its shores. Plug further east and find blissful beaches you can have all to yourself.

Lago de Atitlán, Guatemala

10 Possibly the single worthiest destination in Guatemala, Atitlán (p128) elicits poetic outbursts from even the most seasoned traveler. Of volcanic origin, the alternately placid and turbulent lake is ringed by volcanoes and villages such as Santiago Atitlán, with a thriving indigenous culture, and San Marcos La Laguna, a haven for those wishing to plug into the lake's cosmic energy. And there are enough activities – paragliding from Santa Catarina Palopó, kayaking around Santa Cruz La Laguna or hiking the glorious lakeshore trails – to make a longer stay viable.
Top right: Volcán San Pedro (p128)

Costa Maya, Mexico

11 Do yourself a favor and get to this region while the going's still good. Unlike in overdeveloped Cancun and Riviera Maya, you can still find quiet fishing villages on the Costa Maya that put a premium on sustainable development, such as charming Mahahual (p70). This is the place to slow down, lounge on luxurious powder-sand beaches and feast on the freshest of seafood. Offshore, divers and snorkelers can explore Banco Chinchorro – the largest coral atoll in the northern hemisphere – which is teeming with sea life.

JOHN COLETTI/GETTY IMAGES ©

ORLANDO SIERRA/STAFF/GETTY IMAGES ©

Ruta de las Flores, El Salvador

12 Driving through coffee plantations and small mountain villages may seem like a fairly sedate affair, but don't be fooled. Traversing the volcanic Apeneca Range, the Flower Route (p316) is packed with waterfalls, night markets, food fairs and hiking trails. At the northern end of the 60km highway ascent is Tacuba, a gateway town to the spectacular Parque Nacional El Imposible on the Guatemalan border. At the southern tip is the tough city of Sonsonate, but nearby is Lago de Coatepeque, a pristine volcanic lake where the ancients used to swim.
Above: Girl in Juayúa (p320)

Isla de Ometepe, Nicaragua

13 This laid-back island (p458), Lago de Nicaragua's beloved centerpiece, has it all. Archaeological remains, waterfalls, monkeys and birdlife are at your doorstep, as are lapping waves. Activity-seekers can take to the twin volcanoes, zip lines and lush hillsides cut by walking tracks, or kayak, bike and climb their way through this lost paradise. At the heart of the island's charms are the cool hostels, camping areas and peaced-out traveler scenes. Customize your experience, from high-end luxury lodges to groovy-groupie hippie huts: Ometepe is big enough for all kinds. Top right: Volcán Concepción (p459)

Copán, Honduras

14 There may be hundreds of Maya sites dotted around Central America but few can rival the beauty of Copán (p380). Its location in an idyllic river valley, home to scarlet macaws and other outstanding birdlife and surrounded by pine-forested hills, is simply sublime. The site itself is also very special indeed, with a towering hieroglyphic stairway and a great plaza dotted with imposing, fabulously carved stelae and altars. When you've had your fill of exploring Maya temples you'll find the charming little neighboring town of Copán Ruinas a delightful base.

Caye Caulker, Belize

15 Take a plunge into warm waters from island docks, discover the rush of kitesurfing or explore the big blue of Belize's barrier reef. Relaxed Caye Caulker (p239) seduces everyone from backpackers to families with its paradisaical airs. Nearby, the famed Blue Hole is a brilliant sinkhole where divers plunge under the stalactites amid tiger sharks and hammerheads. Diners feast on coconut-fused kebabs and grilled lobster. As destinations around Belize go, it's more central than Placencia and more chilled out than Ambergris Caye.

Altun Ha, Belize

16 Though not the largest Maya site in Belize, Altun Ha (p249) is definitely the country's most well known. An easy trip from Belize City, the 607-hectare site contains a central ceremonial precinct of two plazas surrounded by two temples, including the Temple of the Green Tomb and the Temple of the Masonry Altars (that's the one you'll recognize from both the Beliken Beer label and Belizean bank-note). After a day of exploring, have your weary muscles pampered at the Maruba Spa, 24km north of the site.

15

16

Need to Know

For more information, see Survival Guide (p723)

Boat

Islands and some borders are served by various types of boat.

Bus

The main form of regional transport. Quality ranges from comfortable, air-conditioned, long-haul buses to run-down former school buses.

Car

Rentals are not usually allowed to cross international borders.

Plane

Because of the region's skinny shape, a flight can save several hours of backtracking. Each country has at least one international airport, as well as regional and charter flights via national airlines.

Train

Limited to the Panama City–Colón route in Panama.

When to Go

Cancún
GO Jan–Apr

San Salvador
GO Nov–Apr

Managua
GO Nov–Apr

San José
GO Dec–Apr

Panama City
GO Sep & Dec–Mar

Dry climate
Tropical climate, rain year-round
Tropical climate, wet & dry seasons
Warm to hot summers, mild winters

High Season
(summer: mid-Dec–mid-Apr)

➡ Dry season throughout most of the region.

➡ Higher demand for hotels and rates increase by 25% to 50%.

➡ Significantly more tourists in the most popular destinations.

High Season Peak (holidays)

➡ Includes Christmas, New Year and Easter week.

➡ Hotel rates may be up to double the normal rates.

➡ Resorts, festival towns and beaches are crowded with national vacationers.

Low Season
(winter: mid-Apr–early Dec)

➡ Rainy season in most of the region; hurricane season between June and November.

➡ Many destinations can still be enjoyed – check regional climate charts.

➡ Accommodations and resorts are better priced.

Useful Websites

Planeta (www.planeta.com) Regional articles, events, reference material and links, with an emphasis on sustainable travel.

Authentic Maya (www.authentic maya.com) A trove of articles on all aspects of ancient Maya culture.

OAS (Organization of American States; www.oas.org) Covers regional issues and cultural events.

Lonely Planet (www.lonely planet.com/central-america) The popular Thorn Tree forum, travel news and links to useful sites.

Visas

➡ Generally not required for stays under 90 days. Visitors entering Belize are authorized 30 days.

➡ Centro America 4 (CA-4; p732) is a regional agreement between Guatemala, Nicaragua, Honduras and El Salvador that gives travelers a 90-day stay for all four countries, with extensions possible.

Money

ATMs are widespread (except for remote areas). Credit cards are accepted mainly by midrange/high-end hotels, restaurants and tour operators. Bargaining is OK for informal transactions.

Daily Costs
Budget: US$30–50

➡ Dorm bed: from US$10

➡ Set meals or street food: US$4–8

➡ Public transport: US$5–15

Midrange: US$50–180

➡ Double room in a midrange hotel: from US$30 (from

US$50 in Belize, Costa Rica and Panama)

➡ Restaurant meals: US$8–20

➡ Park fees or surf lessons: US$15–25

Top End: More than US$180

➡ Double room in a high-end hotel, resort or lodge: from US$60 (from US$120 in Belize, Costa Rica and Panama)

➡ Guided hikes and tours: US$30–60

Money-saving Tips

➡ Consider traveling in low season, when rates are cheaper.

➡ Travel by bus and other public transportation.

➡ Go on self-guided hikes and tours, instead of hiring a guide.

➡ Stay in hostels or rooms with shared bathrooms.

➡ Sample street food, pack picnics and cook for yourself.

Arriving in Central America

These are the main airports for the region. See individual country content for other options.

Philip Goldson International Airport Belize (p238)

Aeropuerto Internacional Juan Santamaría San José, Costa Rica (p531)

Aeropuerto Internacional Daniel Oduber Quirós Liberia, Costa Rica (p570)

Aeropuerto Internacional Comalpa San Salvador, El Salvador (p302)

Aeropuerto Internacional La Aurora Guatemala City, Guatemala (p111)

Aeropuerto Internacional Mundo Maya Flores, Guatemala (p201)

Aeropuerto Internacional Ramón Villeda Morales San Pedro Sula, Honduras (p374)

Aeropuerto Internacional Toncontín Tegucigalpa, Honduras (p361)

Aeropuerto Juan Ramón Galvez Roatán, Honduras (p734)

Aeropuerto Internacional de Cancún Cancun, Mexico (p55)

Augusto C Sandino Managua, Nicaragua (p442)

Tocumen International Airport Panama City, Panama (p639)

Aeropuerto Enrique Malek David, Panama (p656)

Responsible Travel

Go overland Take buses, not planes.

Give right Handouts to kids encourage begging; give directly to schools or clinics.

Buy local Eat and stay at family-owned places and use community-owned services.

Volunteer Make a difference by preserving turtle-nesting sights, teaching English or working with reputable nonprofits.

Reduce waste Bring or buy a refillable water bottle.

Respect local traditions Dress appropriately when visiting local churches or traditional communities.

Be curious Interacting and making an effort to use the local language benefits both hosts and travelers.

For much more on **getting around**, see p734

First Time Central America

For more information, see Survival Guide (p723)

Checklist

➜ Make sure your passport is valid for at least six months past your arrival date.

➜ Check the visa situation and government travel advisories.

➜ Organize travel insurance.

➜ Check flight restrictions on luggage and camping or outdoors equipment.

➜ Check your immunization history.

➜ Contact your credit card company to see if your card includes car rental insurance.

What to Pack

➜ Phrasebook

➜ Flip-flops or sandals

➜ Poncho or rain jacket

➜ Binoculars

➜ Bug repellent with DEET

➜ Refillable water bottle

➜ Driver's license (if you plan to rent a car)

➜ Field guide of local fauna and/or flora

➜ Batteries and chargers

➜ Flashlight

Top Tips for Your Trip

➜ Learn as much Spanish as you can – even just basic phrases. It can't hurt, and it might very well help.

➜ Pack half the clothes that you think you'll need: laundry service is cheap in the region.

➜ Don't rely exclusively on email or website booking engines to reserve hotel rooms. If you're not getting a response, make a phone call. (Good practice for overcoming language barriers.)

➜ Visit local *mercados* (markets) – not just to eat fresh food cheaply, but also to sample a lively slice of local life.

➜ Be aware that Belize, Costa Rica and Mexico are significantly more expensive than other parts of the region. The cheapest places to travel here are Guatemala, Honduras and Nicaragua.

What to Wear

Locals rarely wear shorts when they're not at the beach. Bring lightweight pants or skirts and tops with short sleeves.

Dining and nightlife can be formal in the capital cities. Bring proper dress shoes (or sandals for women), and pants and a dress shirt for men or a skirt or dress for women.

A fleece and lightweight shell are necessary for the high-lands. For hiking, long sleeves and quick-drying pants will help keep the bugs away.

Etiquette

➜ **Asking for help** Say *disculpe* to get someone's attention; *perdón* to apologize.

➜ **Personal space** Be aware that Central Americans often have fewer boundaries about personal space than is customary in North America and Europe.

➜ **Visiting indigenous communities** Ask permission to take photos, particularly of children, and dress more modestly than in beachwear. Bargaining may be appropriate for buying crafts but not for lodging and food. The best gifts for children are those that are useful (pens, paper, notebooks, creative games or books).

➜ **Surfing** Novice surfers should be aware of 'dropping in' on more experienced surfers, and of swimmers crossing their path.

Bargaining

It's OK to bargain in markets and at street stalls, but educate yourself first by asking around to get an idea of the pricing of different items and the specific factors that contribute to the quality of what you're bargaining for.

Tipping

➡ **Restaurants** Tip 10% (but check first to see if it's included in the bill).

➡ **Taxis** Tipping is optional but you can round up to leave extra, especially at night.

➡ **Guides** Tip US$1 to US$2 per person for day tours, with more substantial tips for specialized guides.

Sleeping

Booking lodgings ahead is rarely necessary except for during peak seasons – then it's best to book two to six months out, particularly for beach destinations.

➡ **Hotels** Come in every stripe; to save money try private doubles in hostels.

➡ **Camping** Organized campgrounds are not common, though there are facilities in national parks and reserves (particularly in Costa Rica).

➡ **Guesthouses/B&Bs** A good midrange option; usually family-run and small.

➡ **Hostels** Not just for young travelers, hostels range from quiet digs to party central.

➡ **Lodges** Ranging from rustic to high-end, these are good places to commune with nature, mostly in jungle or highland locations.

MATTEO COLOMBO/GETTY IMAGES ©

Uxmal Ruins (p75), Mexico

Central America Soundtrack

Think Central America and salsa, calypso, soca and steel drums may come to mind. But these days, it's a lot more. Reggaetón and *punta* are huge here, and heavily influenced by Afro-Caribbean drumming. Try some music from the following list for a good sampler.

Rubén Blades The Panamanian salsa icon and ex-presidential candidate.

Café Tacvba A Mexican rock band with modern beats.

Gaby Moreno Singer-songwriter from Guatemala with a lush Latin sound.

Sonido Gallo Negro Get entranced by this percussive, psychedelic *cumbia* band.

Rodrigo y Gabriela Fast, rhythmic acoustic guitarists who made their name busking in Europe.

Aurelio Martínez Albums *Garífuna Soul* and *Laru Beya* received rave reviews all over the world.

Language

Beyond English-speaking Belize, Spanish is the primary language of Central America. Knowing some very basic Spanish phrases is not only courteous but also essential. Parts of the Caribbean coast speak English.

If you visit indigenous communities, pick up a few words in the local language beforehand – it's the best way to warm relations.

If You Like...

Snorkeling

Isla Holbox, Mexico An offbeat Gulf island surrounded by sea turtles, manta rays and barracuda. (p57)

Utila, Honduras For the ultimate snorkeling experience seek out the gargantuan whale shark in the big blue. (p408)

Belize Mile upon mile of the Western hemisphere's finest reef makes Belize a snorkeling paradise. (p230)

Parque Nacional Coiba, Panama It's not easy to get here, but this marine park offers pristine conditions. (p653)

Hiking

Volcán Mombacho, Nicaragua Accessible cloud forest with great hiking and even better birdwatching. (p452)

Parque Internacional La Amistad, Panama True wilderness hiking accessible via the highlands or Caribbean coast. (p663)

Parque Nacional Cusuco, Honduras Dramatic and mountainous: trails are laced with giant ferns, dwarf forest and hidden quetzals. (p371)

Parque Nacional Chirripó, Costa Rica Climbing to the top of Cerro Chirripó is a thrilling, chilling adventure. (p601)

Volcán Tajumulco, Guatemala Central America's highest point is a relatively easy climb (especially if you camp overnight). (p153)

Juayúa, El Salvador Perfect for day hikes to coffee plantations and waterfalls with friendly local guides. (p320)

Wildlife Watching

Península de Osa, Costa Rica Monkeys and macaws, sloths and snakes – wildlife is prolific all around the Osa. (p598)

Refugio de Vida Silvestre La Flor, Nicaragua Nesting ground for the olive ridley turtle. (p469)

Isla Bastimentos, Panama From July to August, loggerhead, hawksbill, green and leatherback turtles hatch on the north shore. (p673)

The Moskitia, Honduras Wetlands, savanna and tropical forest – the best place for searching for jaguar and tapir. (p414)

Monterrico, Guatemala Save a turtle, spot a whale or go birdwatching from this Pacific coast village. (p169)

Playa El Cuco, El Salvador Baby turtles hatch in the dry season as dolphin pods and eagles watch. (p331)

Scuba Diving

Roatán, Honduras Outstanding wall dives at the Cayman trench edge feature corals and prolific sea life. (p402)

The Blue Hole, Belize This deep blue sinkhole has you swimming under stalactites with bull sharks and hammerheads. (p246)

Isla Cozumel, Mexico The famed reefs off this island draw diving aficionados from all over the world. (p64)

Isla del Caño, Costa Rica Sea turtles and humpback whales make this a popular destination for dive trips. (p603)

Lago de Atitlán, Guatemala Journey to charming Santa Cruz La Laguna and dive in a gorgeous mountain lake. (p128)

Off the Beaten Track

Pearl Keys, Nicaragua Live out your shipwreck fantasies beneath coconut palms on these tiny, idyllic Caribbean islands. (p494)

Bahía de Jiquilisco, El Salvador Pounding surf, lush mangroves, fishing villages and a biosphere offer *Survivor*-style wonder. (p327)

The Darién, Panama Steeped in indigenous culture and exotic wildlife, this remote province is wild and pristine. (p684)

Mal País, Costa Rica The Nicoya Peninsula's southern tip offers pristine beaches, blood-pumping surf and good vibes. (p582)

La Campa, Honduras A lovely heartland *pueblo* (village); zip-line over canyons, find authentic ceramics and hike the highlands. (p387)

Colonial Cities

Antigua, Guatemala This colonial city is a riot of cobblestoned streetscapes, crumbling ruins and noble churches. (p114)

Granada, Nicaragua This wonderfully preserved colonial show-piece lays on the charm from the moment you arrive. (p444)

Suchitoto, El Salvador A picture-book, historic town littered with art galleries. Festivals reign most weekends. (p334)

Casco Viejo, Panama City Great for night owls: underground bars, brew pubs, wine bars and live-music venues. (p623)

Comayagua, Honduras Relaxed and prosperous, with a historic core of elegant churches and buildings. (p365)

Mérida, Mexico The colonial-era *centro histórico* here is one of the largest in the Americas. (p74)

Surfing

Dominical, Costa Rica Bring your board: you may never want to leave this easygoing hippie haunt. (p595)

Santa Catalina, Panama No souvenir shops in this dusty village – it's all about world-class waves. (p652)

Top: Scarlet macaw, Costa Rica
Bottom: Colonial buildings, Mérida (p74), Mexico

Pavones, Costa Rica Surfers flock here to catch the longest left-hand break on the planet. (p608)

Playa Hermosa, Nicaragua Charge the waves and hang out in one of the best beach hostels around. (p468)

Las Flores, El Salvador Tucked into the untrodden east and as good as anywhere in Latin America. (p331)

Ruins

Tikal, Guatemala This regional superstar is totally worth the visit for its soaring, jungle-shrouded temples. (p202)

Chichén Itzá, Mexico The massive El Castilo pyramid will wow you, especially during an equinox visit. (p72)

Copán, Honduras An exquisite temple acropolis with some of the most intricate Maya carvings anywhere. (p374)

Tulum, Mexico Maya ruins perched atop a cliff offer jaw-dropping views of the Caribbean down below. (p66)

Caracol, Belize The view from the top of the Ka'ana pyramid

alone is worth the journey. (p265)

Tazumal, El Salvador The country's most impressive Maya ruins were once the site of human sacrifices. (p316)

Panamá Viejo This 16th-century city's ruins have been spruced up with walkways and a super new museum. (p628)

Volcanoes

Volcán Rincón de la Vieja, Costa Rica Trails lead to fumaroles, soothing springs, bubbling mud pots and a sputtering *volcancito*. (p571)

Volcán Masaya, Nicaragua Watch parakeets nesting among clouds of sulfuric gases above visible pools of lava. (p456)

Volcán Barú, Panama Steep, foggy and muddy – but the top lets you view both oceans at once. (p662)

Volcán Poás, Costa Rica It's never been easier to peer into the crater of an active volcano. (p537)

El Salvador The land of volcanoes: Santa Ana is the largest; conical-shaped Izalco the most dramatic. (p310)

Beaches

Guna Yala, Panama Known for perfect – and plentiful – postage-stamp islets with turquoise waters. (p681)

Playa Norte, Mexico This gorgeous, swimmable, fine-sand jewel is sometimes called the most beautiful beach in Mexico. (p57)

West Bay, Honduras A classic, white-sand Caribbean beach with the added bounty of a coral reef offshore. (p408)

Little Corn Island, Nicaragua Brilliant turquoise waters meet snow-white sand in secluded coves on this enchanted isle. (p497)

Hopkins, Belize A semi-secret spot with a beautiful beach and rich Garifuna culture. (p270)

Playa El Tunco, El Salvador Chill out by bonfires on black-sand beaches with pro surfers and local revelers. (p306)

Playa Blanca, Guatemala Take a boat from the city to reach this appealing beauty on Amatique Bay. (p190)

Month by Month

TOP EVENTS

Día de los Muertos, November

Carnaval, February or March

Semana Santa, March or April

Bolas de Fuego, August

Garifuna Settlement Day, November

January

The dry season and tourist season are at their peaks, with great kitesurfing and swimming available in warm Pacific waters. Quetzal-viewing season begins in Costa Rica's Monteverde (through July).

☆ Nicaraguan Baseball Championship

The national pastime of Nicaragua culminates in the National Baseball Championship, an action-packed series held in mid-January.

☆ Panama Jazz Festival

The week-long jazz festival is one of the biggest musical events in Panama, drawing top-caliber international musicians from jazz, blues, salsa and other genres. Held around the city; the open-air events are usually free.

February

It's prime time for surfing both on Pacific and Caribbean swells. Carnaval, a feature of all Central American countries, takes place in February or March.

☆ Carnaval, Mexico

A big street bash preceding the 40-day penance of Lent, Carnaval is festively celebrated in Mérida, Campeche and Isla Cozumel with parades, music, dancing and lots o' fun.

☆ Festival de Diablos y Congos, Panama

Held every two years, this festival in Portobelo celebrates rebellious slave ancestors with spirited public dancing, cheeky role-playing and beautiful masks and costumes.

March

Easter celebrations may take place in March or April. Semana Santa (Holy Week) offers re-enactments of the crucifixion and resurrection of Christ. On Good Friday, religious processions are held across Central America.

☆ Desfile de Bufos, Guatemala

Guatemala City university students take to the streets during the Parade of Fools (held on the Friday before Good Friday) to mock the government and make other political statements.

April

The tail end of the dry season for most of Central America. In the jungle lowlands of Guatemala, March and April are scorchers; it's the best time to see whale sharks off Honduras or Belize.

☆ Día de Juan Santamaria, Costa Rica

April 11 commemorates Costa Rica's national hero, who died driving William Walker out of Costa Rica in 1856. The week-long national holiday features parades, parties and other celebrations, especially in Santamaria's hometown of Alajuela.

May

The rainy season is here. May begins a five- to six-month nesting season for both loggerhead and green sea turtles in the Caribbean.

✲ Fería de Cultura de las Flores y las Palmas, El Salvador

In Panchimalco (near San Salvador), this colorful extravaganza stars beauty queens and gauche floral arrangements.

✖ Chocolate Festival, Belize

This festival in mid-May in the southernmost region of Belize brings together folks who grow chocolate, sell chocolate and just plain *love* chocolate. Also showcases the Toledo district's history and culture.

✲ La Feria de San Isidro, Honduras

Honduras' largest fiesta takes place in the streets and clubs of La Ceiba, culminating in late May with 250,000 people attending parades. Costumed dancers and revelers fill the city to bursting.

✲ Palo de Mayo, Nicaragua

Bluefields celebrates fertility with a series of neighborhood block parties leading to the bright and boisterous carnival on the last Saturday of the month. The closing Tulululu features a midnight romp through the streets, complete with brass band.

SEMANA SANTA, GUATEMALA

Although Semana Santa (the Holy Week before Easter) is celebrated all over Guatemala, nowhere comes more alive than Antigua. The faithful dress in purple to accompany revered sculptural images from the city's churches in daily street processions commemorating Christ's crucifixion. Dense clouds of incense envelop them; the streets are covered in elaborate *alfombras* (carpets) of colored sawdust and flower petals. The fervor peaks on Good Friday, when processions depart from La Merced church and Iglesia de la Escuela de Cristo. Smaller-scale processions, *velaciones* (vigils) and other events occur every weekend through Lent, the 40-day period prior to Holy Week.

June

June to November is hurricane season, though big weather events are sporadic and hard to predict. Forty days after Easter, Corpus Christi features colorful celebrations throughout the region, held in May or June.

✖ Lobsterfest, Belize

A celebration of the world's favorite crustacean, along with libations galore. Takes place in San Pedro in mid-June, in Placencia in the last week of June, and then Caye Caulker in early July.

July

Though it's the middle of rainy season, weather is relatively dry on the Caribbean side; Belize can be uncomfortably hot. It's off-peak for visitors and hotels offer better rates.

☆ Rabin Ajau, Guatemala

Guatemala's most impressive indigenous festival, this folkloric gathering takes place in Cobán in late July or early August.

August

Breeding humpback whales can be observed in the Pacific. Rainy season continues.

✲ Festival de Invierno, El Salvador

For the Winter Festival, hip, lefty students flood the small mountain town of Perquín and party like the war has just ended.

☆ Sun Jam, Honduras

In search of the perfect rave? Held in early August, this tech-no-prisoners party, set on a tiny desert island off Utila, features electronic DJs of global repute.

🎆 Bolas de Fuego, El Salvador

Local scallywags paint their faces like devils and throw fireballs at each other – just a bit of (potentially harmful) fun. Held on August 31 in Nejapa.

September

Though it's peak hurricane season further north, rains let up around Panama City. Flooding in Honduras is possible.

🎆 Costa Rican Independence

Action centers on a relay race that passes a 'Freedom Torch' from Guatemala to Costa Rica. The torch arrives at Cartago in the evening of September 14, when the nation breaks into the national anthem.

☆ Festival de la Mejorana, Panama

Panama's largest folk festival, held in Guararé, showcases music and dance by the country's many indigenous and ethnic groups.

October

In most of the region October 12 is Día de la Raza (Columbus Day) – a dubious legacy nonetheless celebrated by every high-school brass band. Loggerhead turtles nest on the Pacific coast from now through March.

☆ Nogapope, Panama

Indigenous Guna people converge on Isla Tigre for three days of tireless traditional dancing. It's visually engaging and fully authentic. Held October 10 to 12, with a three-day fair with art shows and canoe races.

🎆 Noche de Agüizotes, Nicaragua

This spooky festival, held on the last Friday in October in Masaya, brings to life characters from horror stories of the colonial period with elaborate costumes. Keep an eye out for the headless priest.

November

Seasonal rains have tapered off in most of the region, except for Honduras' north coast, where flooding can occur through February. In Panama, the whole country celebrates multiple independence-related holidays.

🎆 Día de Todos los Santos, Guatemala

In Santiago Sacatepéquez and Sumpango, just outside Antigua, celebrations include the flying of huge kites, while in the tiny highlands town of Todos Santos Cuchumatán, November 1 is celebrated with drunken horse races through town.

🎆 Día de los Muertos, Mexico

On November 1 and 2, families build altars in their homes and visit graveyards to commune with their beloved dead, taking garlands and gifts. Theme park Xcaret in the Riviera Maya arranges beautiful altars.

☆ Garifuna Settlement Day, Belize

On November 19, this holiday celebrates the arrival of the first Garifuna people to Belize by boat. The best spots to partake in the three Ds – dancing, drinking and drumming – are Dangriga and Hopkins.

December

December and January are the coolest months on the Pacific coast, from Nicaragua to the jungle lowlands of Guatemala. The Christmas holidays disrupt the region's work schedule – cities empty out and beaches are full.

🎆 Las Fiestas de Zapote, Costa Rica

For one week, this celebration embraces all things Costa Rican – from rodeos to fried food, and a whole lot of drinking – in Zapote, southeast of San José.

Itineraries

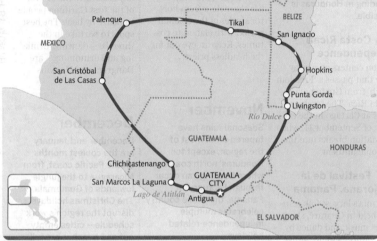

2 WEEKS Northern Loop: Guatemala, Mexico & Belize

In depth on culture and coastline, this route loops through much of the region's northern highlights, including Maya ruins, reef snorkeling and jungle cruising.

From **Guatemala City**, head straight to colonial **Antigua**, fitting in a volcano climb and perhaps a crash course in Spanish. At **Lago de Atitlán** go for a few days of hiking and swimming in the new-age magnet **San Marcos La Laguna**. Then continue on to **Chichicastenango** to see the famous Maya market.

Venture north to Mexico on a Chiapas loop, exploring the colonial city of **San Cristóbal de las Casas** and nearby Maya villages, as well as the jungle-set Maya ruins at **Palenque**. Make your way back to Guatemala to **Tikal,** the mother of all Maya sites.

Bus east to Belize, stopping to go river tubing or caving outside hilly **San Ignacio**, before splashing into the Caribbean – and the barrier reef near **Hopkins**. From **Punta Gorda**, catch a *lancha* (small motorboat) to **Lívingston**, starting point for a serious jungle cruise up the Río Dulce. From there hop a frequent bus back to Guatemala City.

Above:
Chichicastenango
market (p144),
Guatemala

Right: Palenque Ruins
(p89), Mexico

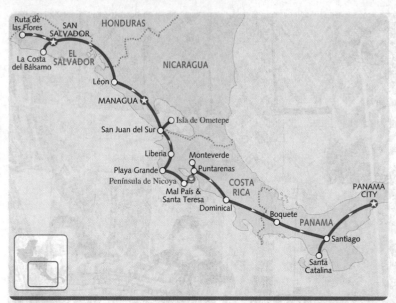

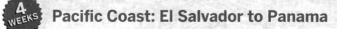

Pacific Coast: El Salvador to Panama

4 WEEKS

This sinuous coastline has something to suit everyone, from insatiable surfers to dedicated beach bums. Inland, there are coffee farms, cloud forests, and even more diverse landscapes. Let your spirit soar on this itinerary that takes in four countries, countless monster curls and infinite adventure. In El Salvador and Nicaragua, peak surf season is March to December, while further south it's February to March.

Arrive in San Salvador and beam to **La Costa del Bálsamo**, home to world-class surf breaks; Playas El Zonte and Sunzal offer reasonable seaside digs and lessons for budding boarders. When you need a break from the waves, take a detour to the **Ruta de las Flores**, where you can hike to hidden waterfalls and discover the region's culinary delights.

Moving east, cross the border(s) to Nicaragua. Stop in offbeat **Léon** for a dose of art and eclecticism. From Managua, catch a shuttle to **San Juan del Sur**, a chilled-out town ringed by beaches with big waves. You're also within striking distance of **Isla de Ometepe**, an island packed with opportunities for adventure.

Continue south to Liberia, Costa Rica, where you'll veer west to hit some surf spots on the Península de Nicoya. **Playa Grande** is a long, pristine stretch of sand where you can catch waves by day and spy on nesting turtles at night. Hardy souls should brave the bumpy ride to the southern tip of the peninsula, where **Mal País and Santa Teresa** offer some of the best breaks in the region. The gorgeous beach and easygoing vibe are beacons for surfers, yogis and free spirits of all types. Nearby **Cabo Blanco** was Costa Rica's first nationally protected nature reserve – still worth a day trip. Take a shortcut to the mainland with a ferry to **Puntarenas**. Hardcore surfers should keep heading south to meet the wicked waves of **Dominical**. Alternatively, an inland jaunt to **Monteverde** offers cooler temperatures, canopy tours and the magic of the cloud forest.

Continue east to Panama. If you missed Monteverde, take a detour to **Boquete**, another mountain town with cool air and strong coffee. Otherwise, make your way to **Santa Catalina**, which claims Hawaii-style waves. From Santiago, you can grab a bus to **Panama City** or David for your homeward journey.

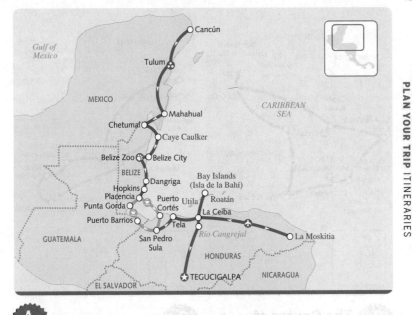

4 WEEKS Caribbean Coast: Mexico to Nicaragua

Explore the 'other side' of Central America – where Spanish is heard less than English or Kriol, where Latin beats give way to reggae rhythms and Garifuna drumming. This east-coast route shows off the rich cultural blend and wild natural scenery that makes the Caribbean unique.

Fly into **Cancún** and start working your way south. Your first stop is **Tulum**, an impressive Maya ruin set on prime beachfront property. Then head south to **Mahahual** to snorkel the largest coral atoll in the northern hemisphere From **Chetumal**, catch a boat to chilled-out, budget-friendly **Caye Caulker**, Belize for some days of sunning, swimming and snorkeling. Then return to the mainland via **Belize City**, perhaps sneaking in a side trip to the **Belize Zoo**. If you're up for some more island-hopping, catch the bus to **Dangriga**, from where you can get a boat to **Tobacco Caye**. Here you can snorkel right off the shore; there are plenty of hammocks to go around afterward. **Hopkins** is also a laid-back Garifuna town with a gorgeous beach, if you prefer to stay on the mainland.

You'll save yourself some time and hassle if you can catch the weekly boat from **Placencia** direct to **Puerto Cortés**, Honduras. Otherwise, continue south through Toledo to **Punta Gorda** to catch a more frequent boat to **Puerto Barrios**, Guatemala. Then take a minibus to the Honduras border at **Corinto**. Buses run to **La Ceiba**, via San Pedro Sula. Along this coastline, there are countless attractions that are unique to this region, including river-rafting on the **Río Cangrejal** and visiting the Garifuna village of **Sambo Creek**. The **Bay Islands** are an absolute must for divers (or would-be divers).

And now, you have reached the final frontier: **The Moskitia**. This huge expanse of untamed wilderness is inhabited in only a few isolated places. If you're curious, consider signing up for a tour to The Moskitia (available in La Ceiba) – there are few roads there and plenty of crime. You've come pretty much as far as you can go. (There is a border crossing into Nicaragua at **Leimus**, but it's a pretty serious slog through jungle – on both sides of the line.) It's time to board the bus to **Tegucigalpa** to travel onwards, leaving behind the fierce and fascinating Caribbean coast.

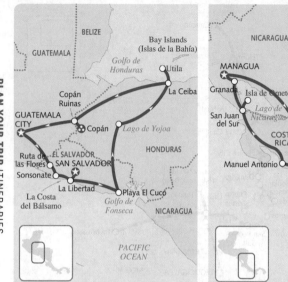

The Center of Central America
2 WEEKS

Southern Loop
2 WEEKS

This route explores the less traveled, less expensive and altogether lesser known countries of central Central America, taking in two coastlines and a wealth of spectacular scenery in between.

From **Guatemala City**, journey east over the El Salvador border to Tacuba, start of the **Ruta de las Flores**, replete with hiking trails and food festivals. From Sonsonate, turn south toward **La Costa del Bálsamo** for a few days of riding waves and catching rays. Stop in **San Salvador** to sample the country's best nightlife. Then continue east to **Playa El Cuco** for a cool and quirky (and eco-conscious) stay at La Tortuga Verde. Turn north and cross into Honduras, heading toward **Lago de Yojoa** to search for a quetzal in the cloud forest. Continue north to **La Ceiba**, jumping-off point for the region's star diving destination – the **Bay Islands**. Utila offers the chance to spot enormous whale sharks suspended in the silent waters of the big blue.

It's time to head back to Guatemala, but not before stopping in the cobblestone town of **Copán Ruinas**, which offers river-tubing trips, horseback rides over mountains, and its namesake ruins.

From volcano climbs to barefoot beach towns, southern Central America offers equal parts adventure and R&R. The green giant, Costa Rica, is flanked by two vibrant countries with colonial character and off-the-beaten-path allure.

Starting in **San José**, journey to the hippie-haven **Puerto Viejo de Talamanca** for good food, great surf and rainforest rich in wildlife. Cross the Panamanian border and hop on a boat to the sugar-sand beaches of **Bocas del Toro**. After a few days in paradise, turn south to the cool cloud forests around **Boquete**, where you can slog up **Volcán Barú** for 360-degree views, including both coasts.

Back in Costa Rica, cut over to the Pacific coast to explore the monkey-crowded trails and picture-perfect beaches in **Manuel Antonio**. Continue up the Interamericana and into Nicaragua. Test the surf and swing in a hammock in kicked-back **San Juan del Sur**. Rest up for your next adventure on **Isla de Ometepe**, a volcano island in a sea-sized lake. Follow up with a trip to admire the colonial architecture in **Granada**, then on to Managua to grab a direct bus back to San José.

Above: Parque
Nacional Manuel
Antonio (p593), Costa
Rica

Right: San Juan del Sur
(p464), Nicaragua

Central America: Off the Beaten Track

SANTA CLARA & DZILAM DE BRAVO

Time seems to stand still on the breezy beaches of Santa Clara and Dzilam de Bravo, east of Progreso. These sands of solitude are a welcome sight in a region where tourist centers abound. (p72)

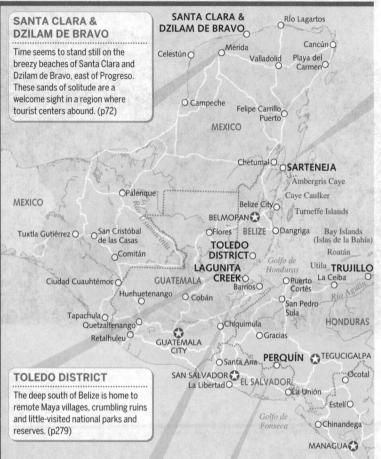

SANTA CLARA & DZILAM DE BRAVO

Río Lagartos

Cancún

Celestún
Mérida
Valladolid
Playa del Carmen

Campeche
Felipe Carrillo Puerto

MEXICO

Chetumal
SARTENEJA
Ambergris Caye
Caye Caulker

MEXICO
Palenque
Belize City
Turneffe Islands
BELMOPAN

Tuxtla Gutiérrez
San Cristóbal de las Casas
Comitán
Flores
BELIZE
Dangriga
Bay Islands (Islas de la Bahía)
Roatán
TOLEDO DISTRICT
Golfo de Honduras
Utila
TRUJILLO

Ciudad Cuauhtémoc
Huehuetenango
GUATEMALA
Cobán
LAGUNITA CREEK
Barrios
Puerto Cortés
La Ceiba
San Pedro Sula
Río Aguán

Tapachula
Quetzaltenango
Retalhuleu
GUATEMALA CITY
Chiquimula
Gracias
HONDURAS

Santa Ana
PERQUÍN
TEGUCIGALPA
Ocotal
SAN SALVADOR
La Libertad
EL SALVADOR
La Unión
Estelí
Golfo de Fonseca
Chinandega
MANAGUA

Rivas

PACIFIC OCEAN

TOLEDO DISTRICT

The deep south of Belize is home to remote Maya villages, crumbling ruins and little-visited national parks and reserves. (p279)

LAGUNITA CREEK

Kayak and swim your way through the turquoise waterways surrounding this remote ecotourism project set in a seriously-hard-to-get-to corner of Guatemala. (p186)

PERQUÍN

Cool mountain air, rugged hiking trails and real war stories await those who make the effort to reach this former guerrilla stronghold near the border in El Salvador. (p333)

PARQUE NACIONAL COIBA

With extraordinary marine wildlife, Panama's newest Unesco World Heritage Site was once its most infamous island prison. Untrampled and pristine, it offers excellent diving and wildlife-watching. (p653)

0 — 200 km
0 — 120 miles

SARTENEJA
Stroll the shoreline to admire the wooden sailboats still constructed here and explore the nearby Shipstern Nature Reserve, a hub of birding, fishing and wildlife-watching. (p254)

TRUJILLO
The best slice of Honduras' Caribbean coastline is a gorgeous place, with lots of history, a delightful end-of-the-road feel, and some of the mainland's best beaches nearby. (p400)

PEARL KEYS
Lush and mostly uninhabited, these coconut islands offer snorkeling in crystalline waters. It's a boat ride away from Bluefields and well worth the splurge. (p494)

CAÑO NEGRO
Not many travelers make it to the far reaches of Costa Rica's northern lowlands. This network of languid lagoons is a birding wonderland, home to some 365 species of birds. (p559)

SAMBÚ
This jungle hub makes a good base for Darién adventures. Guides take visitors up the Río Sambú and its tributaries to Emberá and Wounaan villages, or in search of harpy eagles and petroglyphs. (p692)

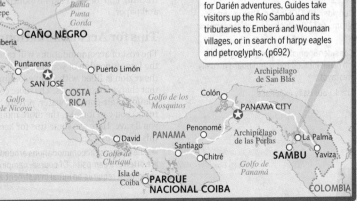

Plan Your Trip

Big Adventures, Small Budgets

The best things in life are free – certainly in Central America, where you don't pay a cent for sand, surf and sun, gorgeous scenery and prolific wildlife. Of course, you have to eat... But you can do a lot with a little if you plan wisely and watch your spending.

Sticking to your Budget

➡ Consider traveling in low season.

➡ Opt for lower-budget destinations (eg lower-cost-of-living countries, non-tourist towns).

➡ Avoid package deals.

➡ Shop online for airfares.

➡ Stay in hostels or rooms with shared bathrooms.

➡ Travel by bus and other public transportation.

➡ Sample street food, pack picnics and cook for yourself.

➡ Snorkel instead of dive.

➡ Get around by bicycle instead of taxi.

➡ Take self-guided hikes and tours, instead of hiring a guide.

➡ Consider WWOOFing or other volunteer programs (p732), which may cover room and board.

➡ Consider Spanish-language programs, which often include room and board (usually homestays).

➡ Track your daily expenses.

Making a Budget

In Central America, shoestringers can skimp by on a budget of US$30 to US$50 per day. This covers the basics: food, shelter, local transportation and a few beers. This budget will vary by season (low vs high), country and popularity of the destination.

In addition to this base rate, factor in the costs of long-distance travel. Add in any special activities, such as diving, canopy tours, surf lessons or guided hikes. Then allow some room for unexpected expenses, and there's your budget.

To stick to your budget, it's important to track your expenses as you go, especially if you're taking a longer trip. Use an expense-tracking app (or good old-fashioned pen and paper).

Tips for Accommodations

The cost of accommodations will take up the largest portion of your budget. Luckily, the region is filled with simple lodgings that charge simple prices. The more creature comforts (air-con, hot water, private bathroom) you can forsake, the more money you'll save. Here are some tips for keeping this line item lean.

➡ The cheapest accommodations around are often in a campsite. Of course, camping equipment requires an initial investment and a fair amount of lugging. But if you're into that, it's often free (or nearly free) to pitch a tent.

➡ Hostels are also great options for budget accommodations – and you don't have to bring your own bed. Many hostels offer community kitchens and low-priced outings catering to their budget clientele.

➡ If you prefer a bit more privacy, most hostels and many guesthouses offer lower-priced private rooms with shared bathrooms.

➡ If the price is too high, ask if the hotel or guesthouse has anything cheaper. Independent businesses often alter their prices.

➡ Except during the low season, most rates are non-negotiable.

➡ Pay per day rather than all at once. This gives you the option of changing hotels if the conditions are unsuitable or if you change plans.

When to Go

Tourist Seasons

Generally speaking, the high tourist season in Central America goes from mid-December to mid-April, while the low tourist season goes from mid-April to mid-December. There are mini peak seasons (higher than high) around major holidays, including the last two weeks of December and the week before Easter.

High season means higher prices for accommodations and for some activities; peak season means *really* high, sometimes double. High season also brings more tourists.

Low season means that prices may be lower – sometimes 25% to 40% – and

crowds are thinner. Traveling during low season is an excellent, easy way to make your money go further.

Meteorological Seasons

Central America has two meteorological seasons: dry and rainy (or 'green,' as some marketers have tried to re-brand it).

Not surprisingly, the high tourist season corresponds roughly with the dry season, which is from January to March or April in most of the region. Likewise, the rainy season generally runs from May to December, with hurricane season making matters worse between June and November.

It should be noted that there are several places where it's pretty rainy all the time, namely the rainforest. This doesn't have to spoil your fun, and it doesn't usually rain all day every day, but travelers should be prepared for wet weather. See the climate chart (p18) for details.

Where to Go

While Central America generally enjoys a lower cost of living than North America or Europe, there are discrepancies within the region: Belize, Costa Rica and Panama are significantly more expensive than the other countries here. Shoestring travelers will find that their money will last longest in Guatemala, Honduras and Nicaragua. Of course, these are more impoverished countries with less tourist infrastructure, so there's a trade-off.

Generally speaking, there's a sort of dual economy everywhere in Central America, where services catering to tourists are more expensive than services used by locals. Fortunately, travelers are not restricted to upscale restaurants, private shuttles and guided tours (or tourist towns, for that matter). The more you can live like the locals (self-catering, local restaurants, public transportation etc), the more you will save. Knowing a bit of Spanish can go a long way toward getting good information in this regard.

Destination Tips

Lonely Planet writers offer their answers to the question 'What is the cheapest place

---

HOW MUCH DOES IT COST?

➡ Bottle of beer US$2–4

➡ Domestic bus ticket US$5–15

➡ Fixed-price meal US$5–8

➡ Hostel bed US$10–18

➡ Domestic flight US$80–150

➡ National park admission US$8–15

➡ Canopy Tour US$40–60

➡ Snorkel Tour US$35–45

in which to have the best time in your country?'

Mexico The Costa Maya (specifically Mahahual and Laguna Bacalar) offers affordable lodging and eats, as well as plenty of low-cost activities, such as swimming in cenotes, snorkeling at Banco Chinchorro and beach-bumming.

Guatemala San Pedro La Laguna is a perfect budget destination: cheap hotels, cheap food and cheap drinks.

Belize The central cays are the best bet for budget travelers. Tobacco Caye is right on the reef, so if you bring your own gear you can snorkel for free just off the island.

El Salvador La Tortuga Verde is a fabulous creative community where you can stay for free (!) if you volunteer for a month. Shuchitoto is a charming, culture-filled town, with the excellent, affordable Pajaro Flor Spanish School and great volunteer opportunities at the Centro Arte Para la Paz.

Honduras The whole country is a great bargain at the moment: the dollar goes a long way and the trickle of visitors means that competition between agencies and hostels is fierce. Utila remains the biggest backpacker destination, beloved for cheap diving. Lago de Yojoa has a brewery, a great hostel and all manner of affordable activities.

Nicaragua San Juan del Sur and the nearby beach towns are prime budget destinations. The outdoor attractions are free, or course, and there are plenty of hostels, cheap places to eat, and services that cater to budget travelers. If you need a guide, those are inexpensive, too (just be sure to tip).

Costa Rica The Caribbean coast is the most affordable part of the country. Puerto Viejo de Talamanca has some great budget lodging. It's free to go to the beach – and you can rent a bicycle to get there. You can also hike for free in the nearby Gandoca-Manzanillo National Wildlife Refuge.

Panama Bocas del Toro and (especially) Boquete offer some excellent budget accommodations – and there's plenty of adventure right on the doorstep.

Packing

Believe it or not, how you pack will have an impact on your budget. Or rather, your budget should decide how you pack.

If you're a shoestring traveler and you're on the move, you'll have to carry your bag everywhere. Make your life simpler by keeping things compact. A smaller bag will better fit into the limited storage area on buses and boats and will make it easier for you to walk through villages in search of the best hostel. Most importantly – you'll be less of a target for touts and troublemakers.

Also, it's cheap to do laundry in Central America. Bring less, wash more.

Gadgets

It's tempting to bring gadgets on your trip – phones, tablets, laptops, cameras – you're going to need them, right? There are several reasons to limit your electronics: first, they take up space; second, the risk of theft or damage is high. Central America is wet and muddy, bags get dropped and tossed, thieves and pickpockets want what you have, and it only takes a short rainstorm to short-circuit your device.

Here are some tips for traveling smartly with technology.

➡ Limit yourself to one or two versatile devices: a tablet with which you can read books and check emails or a smartphone that can do it all.

➡ Store your electronics in dry packs and separate the batteries in case of rain.

➡ Use a volt converter, as some destinations have power surges that can fry sensitive equipment.

➡ USB roaming sticks, available through local cell-phone providers, enable near-universal internet access from your computer.

➡ Look into the international plans offered by your cell-phone provider to avoid expensive roaming charges.

➡ Get a travel insurance policy that covers theft of or damage to your equipment.

Plan Your Trip
Outdoor Activities

Offering two dramatic and diverse coastlines, Central America lures all types of water-lovers with its Pacific swells and Caribbean reef. Meanwhile, the inland terrain is studded with mountains and volcanoes begging for exploration, tropical rainforests are rich with birds and wildlife, and raging rivers crisscross the region. Adventure awaits!

Hiking

Central America's dense forests, steaming volcanoes and abundant wildlife make for great hiking. The terrain ranges from cloud forests and rainforests to tropical dry forest, including river trails and palm-lined beaches.

Most tourist-oriented parks and reserves offer ample day-hike trails that are well maintained and well marked, most of which do not require a guide. Longer-distance hikers can take their pick from several popular, multiday treks. If you really want to get off the beaten track, you can do that, too (though you'll definitely want to hire a guide).

When to Go

In the rainforest (or the cloud forest, for that matter), hiking trails can be muddy. Throughout the region, trails are maintained to varying degrees. They may be reinforced with concrete blocks or wooden supports, but the mud prevails. Trails are obviously firmer and easier to navigate during the dry season, which is when travelers should plan their hiking trips (late December to April).

Some national parks and reserves are closed during the wettest months, such as Chirripó (closed in May and October) and Corcovado (closed in October) in Costa Rica.

Hiking Footwear

Some suggestions for sturdier tropical-hiking footwear, to supplement the flip-flops:

Rubber boots Pick these up at any hardware store (approximately US$10). They're indestructible, protect you from creepy-crawlies and can be hosed off at day's end. Downsides: they're not super comfortable, and if they fill up with water or mud, your feet are wet for the rest of the day.

Sport sandals Great for rafting and river crossings, though they offer minimal foot protection. Closed toes are recommended.

Waterproof hiking boots If you are planning a serious trek in the mountains, it's best to invest in a pair of solid, waterproof hiking boots.

PLAN YOUR TRIP OUTDOOR ACTIVITIES

Where to Go

Belize The jungly terrain and low-lying mountains are studded with Maya ruins. Mountain Pine Ridge (p265) is one of the best places to hike.

Guatemala The most popular hiking destinations are the volcanoes around Antigua (p114). The ultimate is the 60km hike into the Petén jungle to El Mirador (p211), a sprawling, largely unexcavated Maya city.

El Salvador Explore the tropical mountain forests of Parque Nacional El Imposible (p323).

Honduras Spot a quetzal in the cloud forests around Lago de Yojoa (p369) or near the peak of Montaña de Santa Barbara (p370).

Nicaragua Hike to prehistoric petroglyphs on Nicaragua's Isla de Ometepe (p458), or climb a volcano, such as Volcán Mombacho (p452) or the volcanoes near León (p469).

Costa Rica Hike to waterfalls and volcano lakes near Arenal (p554); lose yourself in the clouds at Monteverde (p561). It takes two days to summit Cerro Chirripó (p601), the country's highest peak.

Panama Roam the coffee-scented hills around Volcán Barú (p662), in the Chiriquí highlands.

THE BIG FIVE FOR BIRDERS

The birdlife is rich all around the region, but of course the species vary widely depending on the habitat. Some highlights and where to spot them:

Scarlet macaw Ubiquitous around Corcovado (p606) and Carara, Costa Rica (p587)

Great green macaw Valle de Sarapiquí, Costa Rica (p559)

Resplendent quetzal Monteverde, Costa Rica (p561), Lago de Yojoa, Honduras (p369), Volcán Barú, Panama (p662)

Jabiru stork Crooked Tree, Belize (p251), Caño Negro, Costa Rica (p559)

Ornate hawk eagle Isla de Coiba, Panama (p653)

Wildlife-Watching

The unexpected appearance of a toucan, howler monkey or sloth will surely be a highlight of your trip. Central America is rife with opportunities to spot these kinds of creatures in the wild, thanks to an extensive system of protected areas throughout the region. Often, the best sightings occur when you're not really looking – perhaps in your hotel's garden or on the roadside in a remote area. In short: keep your eyes peeled.

Early morning and late afternoon are the best times to watch for wildlife activity anywhere.

Where to Go

Mexico Howlers are commonly sighted along the Mexico-Guatemala border. Celestún (p75) is a great place to see colonies of flamingos, as well as other bird species and crocodiles.

Guatemala Go whale-watching in Monterrico (p169) or take an early-morning bird hike at Tikal (p202). There's slim chance of seeing manatees (but a very good chance of seeing other wildlife) around Bocas del Polochic (p220).

Belize The black howler monkey lives only in Belize and is practically guaranteed to be seen at the Community Baboon Sanctuary (p249).

Honduras Montaña de Celaque (p388) and Cusuco (p371) are great birding destinations, though mammals are somewhat harder to spot. If you're really up for adventure, venture into The Moskitia (p414).

Nicaragua Take a boat down the jungly Río San Juan (p503) to spot sneaky monkeys, sunbathing caimans and prolific birdlife.

Costa Rica Corcovado (p606) is the ultimate wildlife-watching destination, where you can spot all four species of New World monkeys, the endangered Baird's tapir, kinkajous, sloths, and more. The canals of Tortuguero (p542) and the lazy rivers around Puerto Viejo de Sarapiquí (p560) are also teeming with animals.

Panama Sign up for a boat tour to see some of the 381 bird species and 120 mammal species on Isla Barro Colorado (p644). Alternatively, visit the rainforest of Parque Nacional Soberanía (p643), which is easy to access and brimming with wildlife.

Above: Hiking Volcán Acatenango, near Antigua (p114), Guatemala

Right: Flamingos, Reserva de la Biosfera Ría Celestún (p75), Mexico

TURTLE TOURS

Sea turtles nest on both the Caribbean and Pacific coasts of Central America. During the nesting seasons, travelers can witness various species of turtles returning to their natal beaches to lay their eggs, sometimes in great numbers. It's a truly awe-inspiring experience to watch something that feels at once grandly cosmic and incredibly intimate. Top spots for turtles include Playa Ostional, near Sámara (p580), and Tortuguero (p542) in Costa Rica, Isla Cañas (p649) in Panama and La Flor (p469) in Nicaragua.

Surfing

Surf's up, all across Central America. This sport's popularity is on the rise, with many places offering week-long surf camps, hourly lessons and board rentals.

Costa Rica has the most developed scene and, arguably, the most and biggest waves. But El Salvador, Nicaragua, Panama and even Guatemala have up-and-coming surfing scenes. The waves might not be 'world-class' – at least not all of them – but they're pretty damn good. Plus, there are fewer surfers in these lesser-known spots, so you may have the breaks all to yourself.

When to Go

The surf season varies throughout the region – but there's always a wave to ride somewhere.

On the Pacific side, in Costa Rica, the most consistent surf comes from the southwest between late May and August. Panama's Pacific coast peaks from April to June, with offshore winds and consistent southwesterly swells. In both cases, the surfing is reliably good anytime between February and August. Again, expect more rain (but fewer crowds) starting in May.

El Salvador Along the south-facing coastline, the months from May to August bring the biggest swells, but they also bring massive amounts of rain. Seasoned surfers claim that the tail end of the dry season (late March and early April) offers the best of both worlds, with still-glorious weather and the first southern swells.

Nicaragua The Pacific coast here sees the biggest waves from April to June, thanks to southern swells and offshore winds. The surf is dependable anytime between March and November, though. Again, the rain starts in May, so be prepared.

Costa Rica & Panama These two countries are among a select group of destinations where you can surf two oceans in one day. In both countries, the Caribbean surf season lasts from November to April, with an additional mini season in June and July. You can't really escape the rain on this coast.

Where to Go

Costa Rica Famous for Salsa Brava at Puerto Viejo de Talamanca (p549) and the famous three-minute left at Pavones (p608), for experts only! But the surf is also phenomenal up and down the Pacific coast, including all the beaches around Tamarindo (p576), Santa Teresa and Mal País (p582), and further south at Dominical (p595).

El Salvador There is great surfing all along La Costa del Bálsamo (p306). La Libertad is a shady port town, but the right-hand break at Punta Roca (p305) is tops.

Guatemala Surfing is not as big here as it is further south, but there is a scene growing up near Sipacate (p169), with dedicated surf lodges, classes and board rentals.

Nicaragua The beaches north and south of San Juan del Sur (p464) are the main surf destinations. Find your own private wave at Las Peñitas (p477) or the Tola beaches (p464).

Panama Surfing on both coasts! The waves at Santa Catalina (p652) are among the biggest in the region, while the Bocas del Toro (p664) has mostly reef breaks (ouch!).

Snorkeling & Diving

The Caribbean coast of Central America includes miles and miles of nearly unbroken barrier reef, making this one of the world's superlative spots for diving and snorkeling. Life under the sea is dramatic and diverse, from the fantastic coral formations and the kaleidoscopic fish that feed there to the massive (and sometimes menacing) creatures that lurk in deeper waters. Mexico, Belize and Honduras offer world-class underwater viewing, but there are also snorkeling and diving opportunities further south.

The Pacific coast is also rich with life. There is no reef, but there's still plenty to see, especially from October to February when conditions are normally clearer. There are recommended dive sites near San Juan del Sur (p464), Nicaragua, as well as Playa del Coco (p573), Quepos (p590) and Bahía Drake (p603) in Costa Rica.

Aside from the two great blues, Central America has some intriguing opportunities for inland diving. Mexico offers otherworldly dives in cenotes (freshwater limestone sinkholes); check out some options reachable from Tulum (p66). How about diving in a crater lake? You can do it at the Laguna de Apoyo (p452) in Nicaragua. In Guatemala, you can go high-altitude diving at Lago de Atitlán (p128).

No matter where you intend to dive, don't forget your license. Equipment (for diving or snorkeling) is widely available for rent.

Where to Go

Mexico There is a slew of well-trafficked dive and snorkel sites around Isla Cozumel (p64), while Banco Chinchorro, near Mahahual (p70), is a lesser-known – but no less enticing – underwater hot spot.

Belize The dive-snorkel hub is in the Northern Cays (p239), from where you can access the Blue Hole and the barrier reef. The reef is protected here, so even snorkeling requires a licensed guide. Hopkins (p270) or Placencia (p272) can serve as a base for the central reef. Snorkel right off the beach at Tobacco Caye (p270).

Honduras The Bay Islands (p402) are known for the low cost of open-water certification, though it's perhaps not as cheap as it used to be, due to new tax regulations. Roatán diving is pretty spectacular, but it's only off Utila that you can see whale sharks.

Nicaragua Little Corn Island (p497) offers an atmospheric location and varied dive sites, including underwater caves.

Costa Rica It doesn't really compare to the sites further north, but you can snorkel or dive all along the southern Caribbean coast (p542) in Costa Rica. Conditions are highly variable.

Panama There is plenty of sea life around Bocas del Toro (p664) and Comarca de Guna Yala (p681), but murky conditions make it difficult to see.

White-Water Rafting

Central America offers some of the best white-water rafting in the tropics, including in Guatemala, Honduras, Panama and especially Costa Rica. The Central American rivers offer everything from frothing Class IV white water to easy Class II floats. Most rivers can be run year-round, though more rain brings higher waters.

Where to Go

Honduras Sublime scenery and prolific birdlife along Class III rapids will give you a charge on the Río Cangrejal, near La Ceiba (p392).

Costa Rica Thrilling white water on two rivers near Turrialba (p540), especially the Río Paquare. The Río Sarapiquí (p559) will also get your heart beating fast.

Panama Cruise through narrow canyons and past hidden waterfalls on the Ríos Chiriquí and Chiriquí Viejo, near Boquete (p657).

Cycling

Many shops rent bicycles for casual local exploration, but there are only a few options for cycling tours or other long-distance riding or mountain biking in the region.

Guatemala Several outfits in Antigua (p114) offer mountain-biking trips in the surrounding hills, from half-day to week-long tours.

Costa Rica The Arenal area is a mountain-biking hot spot, with a wide variety of tours and rental offered by Bike Arenal (p555). If you can bring your own bike, **Vuelta al Lago** (www.vueltaal lagoarenal.com; ☺Mar) is an awesome annual two-day ride around Lago de Arenal.

PLAN YOUR TRIP OUTDOOR ACTIVITIES

Countries at a Glance

The green link between North and South America, the seven compact countries that make up Central America, plus the southern strip of Mexico, are a true backpackers' paradise: a complex web of cultures, ancient ruins, tropical wildlife and adventure. For starters, summit a volcano, traipse through jungle to Maya pyramids, or surf the waves crashing on gold-sand beaches. Learn to dive dirt-cheap, take bargain Spanish classes in a cool colonial town, or slow down in a Maya, Miskito or Guna village, where ancient traditions stroll into the present day.

Mexico

Archaeology
Outdoor Activities
Food

Ruin-Hopping

There are so many Maya ruins that you'd need an extended leave of absence to visit them all. World-famous Chichén Itzá is a must-see, but do yourself a favor and get there early, before the tour buses start rolling in.

Adventure

Swim with 15-ton whale sharks, explore some of the world's best coral reefs, spot crocs and flamingos by motorboat, or swim in astonishing cenotes (limestone sinkholes). With so many activities, you might forget what your hotel room looks like.

Cocina Yucateca

Those in the know say the Yucatán is one of Mexico's finest culinary destinations. Sure, you can try classic *yucateco* fare such as *cochinita pibil* (slow-cooked pork) or *sopa de lima* (lime soup) elsewhere, but it won't taste the same.

p48

Guatemala

Archaeology
Nature
History

Maya Mysteries

With a multitude of sites sprinkled across the jungle lowlands, you can delve as deeply as you choose into the mysteries of Classic Maya civilization, from the oft-scaled temples of Tikal to the seldom-seen astronomical observatory of Uaxactún.

Natural Marvels

From lush cloud forests and Caribbean beaches to steamy jungles and dramatic volcanic landscapes, Guatemala's often untamed countryside showcases Central America at its natural best.

Colonial Cities

Whether the architecture crumbles gracefully in places like Guatemala City or Quetzaltenango, or has been gorgeously renovated like much of Antigua, the Spanish legacy offers countless postcard-perfect views – and often a chance to scramble through history.

p99

Belize

Outdoor Activities
Archaeology
Relaxation

Aquatic Adventures

With miles of coastline, uncountable islands and – oh, yeah – the Western Hemisphere's most spectacular reef, this one's a no-brainer. From sailing to kitesurfing, Belize offers endless opportunity for water fun.

Maya Past & Present

This tiny country is packed with Maya archaeological sites: major ruins such as Caracol and Lamanai, and smaller sites around San Ignacio (Cayo) and Toledo. For modern Maya culture, take a week to explore the villages of the deep south.

Take a Break

'Slow Down' reads the sole traffic sign on Caye Caulker, one of the most chilled-out places on the planet. Revel in your R&R in Belize, a country that prides itself on taking it easy.

p230

El Salvador

Landscapes
History
Surfing

Small Packages

The fast track to your Central American fix, El Salvador has black-sand beaches, volcanic lakes, Maya ruins, hip coffee towns and cranking nightlife all within 100km of the capital.

War Stories

See the tide of history turning in remote mountain villages, where the civil war was most fiercely fought. To fill in the blanks, visit excellent regional museums and the galleries of San Salvador.

Wicked Waves

Surf the smoothest and most uncrowded waves in Latin America, from the international flavor of Costa del Bálsamo to the more remote eastern breaks. (The secret may be out, but most folks just don't listen.)

p286

Honduras

Diving
Wildlife
Outdoor Activities

Go Deep for Cheap

Few places are as inexpensive for learning how to dive as the Bay Islands. Boasting outstanding reefs, famous wrecks and bountiful sea life, Utila and Roatán offer memorable marine time.

Call of the Wild

Honduras' national parks are fantastic places to spot elusive wildlife. Look for the resplendent quetzal in the cloud forests of Parque Nacional Cusuco; crocodiles in the wetlands near Tela; and birds and monkeys in The Moskitia.

Endless Adventure

Seek out some adventure in the great outdoors of Honduras. The magical Lago de Yojoa has countless opportunities, including waterfall hikes, birdwatching boat trips, intriguing caves and ancient Lenca ruins.

p351

Nicaragua

Surfing
History
Outdoor Activities

Surf's Up

It's hard to beat Nicaragua for surf. After you hit dawn patrol at legendary spots such as Playas Hermosa and Maderas, you can chill out with waffle breakfasts, cool tunes and friendly companionship in a beachfront hammock paradise.

Colonial Charms

Nicaragua's history is as complex and nuanced as it gets. See the evidence in nearly every corner of intact colonial cities such as Granada and León, and experience it in the festivals, art and living culture.

Secret Spots

Isla de Ometepe and Nicaragua's Caribbean Coast are examples of paradise lost...that have yet to be found. Discover petroglyphs, climb volcanoes, kayak to lost coves and chill out in cool travelers' enclaves on the edge of the wild.

p429

Costa Rica

Surfing
Wildlife
Nature

Catch a Wave

Point and beach breaks, lefts and rights, reefs and river mouths – the warm water and waves available all year round make Costa Rica a legendary surfing destination.

Amazing Animals

The biodiversity astounds: 850 species of birds, 380 kinds of reptiles and amphibians, six species of wild cat, four types of monkey, three of anteater, two species of sloth and one kind of Baird's tapir. How many can you spot?

Cloud Forest

Covering only 0.25% of the planet's land surface, the rare cloud forest is a mysterious Neverland, dripping with mist and mossy vines, sprouting with ferns and bromeliads, gushing with creeks and blooming with life.

p516

Panama

Design
Wildlife
Islands

Engineering Feat

The enlarged locks at this 80km cross-continental cut offer even more reason to see the Panama Canal – a mammoth jigsaw puzzle of engineering. Few know there's also fishing, kayaking and wildlife-watching off the shipping lanes.

Jungle Love

Some of the region's best wildlife-watching happens just outside Panama City. Think canopy towers, rainforest resorts and birding hot spots. For nature on steroids, explore the Darién or Parque Nacional Coiba.

Tropical Paradise

Imagine hundreds of idyllic islands with waters that are Technicolor turquoise. The Panamanian resort islands comprise little more than thatched huts with sandy floors and a few hammocks – but what more do you need?

p621

On the
Road

Yucatán &
Chiapas,
Mexico
p48

Belize
p230

Guatemala
p99

Honduras
p351

El Salvador
p286

Nicaragua
p429

Costa Rica
p516

Panama
p621

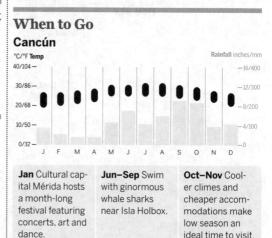

Mexico's Yucatán & Chiapas

🔖 52 / POP 8.9 MILLION

Includes ➡

Cancún..............50
Isla Mujeres.........56
Playa Del Carmen 59
Isla Cozumel........64
Tulum...............66
Chichén Itzá 72
Mérida 74
Campeche..........79
San Cristóbal de
las Casas...........82
Palenque 89
Agua Azul &
Misol-Ha............93

Why Go?

Flanked by the turquoise waters of the Caribbean and the wildlife-rich Gulf coast, the Yucatán Peninsula wows visitors with its Maya ruins, limestone swimming holes, colorful coral reefs and soulful colonial cities. Sure, the Yucatán is Mexico's busiest tourist destination – and, not surprisingly, its most expensive – but you can still score affordable sleeps and eats, even in apparently pricey tourist centers. Exploring the Yucatán pays big rewards: you can delve into Maya culture, chill in tranquil fishing villages, observe a wide variety of nature, and enjoy some of Mexico's finest regional cuisine. Down south in Chiapas, home to the Zapatistas, you'll love San Cristóbal de las Casas, a gorgeous highland colonial city surrounded by pine forest, while in Palenque it's all about the extraordinary ruins set in a celestial jungle. No matter where the road takes you, life is pretty darn sweet in this corner of Mexico.

Best Places to Eat

➡ Nohoch Kay (p70)

➡ Kiosco Verde (p55)

➡ Yerba Buena del Sisal (p71)

➡ Tierradentro (p85)

Best Places to Sleep

➡ Poc-Na Hostel (p57)

➡ Hotel El Rey del Caribe (p50)

➡ Hotel López (p81)

➡ Madre Sal (p89)

➡ L'Hotelito (p67)

When to Go

Cancún

°C/°F Temp   Rainfall inches/mm

Jan Cultural capital Mérida hosts a month-long festival featuring concerts, art and dance.

Jun–Sep Swim with ginormous whale sharks near Isla Holbox.

Oct–Nov Cooler climes and cheaper accommodations make low season an ideal time to visit.

Connections

From Mexico you can loop into Guatemala – from San Cristóbal de las Casas to Quetzaltenango, or to Tikal via Palenque – and into Corozal, Belize, from Chetumal, south of Tulum. Frequent buses run from Chetumal's Nuevo Mercado Lázaro Cárdenas to various destinations in Belize. The best way into Guatemala is at Ciudad Cuauhtémoc, near La Mesilla, Guatemala. Another option is crossing into Guatemala from the Mexican border town of Tapachula, further southwest. For more detailed information, see Survival Guide p98.

ITINERARIES

One Week

Greet the first day with a splash in the turquoise waters of Cancún's Zona Hotelera, then hit downtown for affordable eats and some nocturnal mischief. Cancún makes a good base to visit nearby Isla Mujeres and Isla Blanca, which arguably boast the most beautiful beaches in the Mexican Caribbean. Return to the mainland and head south for Playa del Carmen, where you can catch a ferry to Isla Cozumel, a world-famous diving destination. Next, head on down to Tulum, known for its spectacular oceanfront Maya ruins, and, if time allows, head further south to Mahahual, a laid-back fishing village with excellent dive sites.

Two Weeks

At the start of your second week, return north to catch the turnoff to Valladolid, a colonial city with a small-town feel. West of Valladolid awaits Chichén Itzá, the mother of all Maya ruins. Continue on to the peninsula's cultural capital, Mérida, and spend several days indulging in Yucatecan cuisine and enjoying the city's ample entertainment offerings. From there go south to the immaculately preserved walled city of Campeche. Stop at the archaeological sites of Edzná and Calakmul as you make your way down to the southern state of Chiapas. Even if you're all ruined-out at this point, drop by Palenque, where unforgettable Maya structures sit pretty in a dreamlike forest. For the last leg of the trip, hit San Cristóbal de las Casas, a highland colonial town surrounded by Maya villages.

Essential Food & Drink

→ **Cochinita pibil** Slow-cooked pork marinated in citrus juices and annatto seed spice.

→ **Panuchos** Fried tortilla filled with beans and topped with chicken, lettuce and pickled red onion.

→ **Mezcal** An alcoholic agave drink that packs a mighty punch.

→ **Sopa de lima** Soup with shredded turkey, lime and tortilla strips.

→ **Papadzules** Diced hard-boiled eggs wrapped in tortilla and topped with pumpkin seed and tomato sauces.

AT A GLANCE

Currency Mexican peso (M$)

Language Spanish and Maya

Money ATMs in most towns

Visas Not required for many countries

Time GMT minus six hours

Area Yucatán Peninsula and Chiapas 220,700 sq km

Emergency ☑ 066

Exchange Rates

Australia	A$1	M$13.59
Belize	BZ$1	M$9.15
Canada	C$1	M$14.29
Euro zone	€1	M$20.67
Guatemala	Q$1	M$2.37
Japan	¥100	M$16.96
New Zealand	NZ$1	M$12.92
UK	UK$1	M$26.29
USA	US$1	M$18.11

Set Your Budget

→ **Hostel bed/budget room** M$170/M$550

→ **Evening meal** M$100

→ **Bus ticket** M$190 (three-hour trip)

→ **Ruins admission** M$50 to M$220

Resources

→ **Yucatán Today** (www.yucatantoday.com)

→ **Caribe Mexicano** (www.caribemexicano.gob.mx/en)

→ **Turismo Chiapas** (www.turismochiapas.gob.mx)

THE YUCATÁN

Chock-full of fun and thrilling surprises, the Yucatán is brimming with Maya ruins, Caribbean beaches, old-world colonial cities, famed diving destinations and a host of natural wonders.

Cancún

📞 998 / POP 630,000

Cancún is a tale of two cities. There's the glitzy hotel zone with its famous white-sand beaches, unabashed party scene and sophisticated seafood restaurants. Then there's the actual city itself, which gives you a taste of local flavor at, say, a neighborhood taco joint or a nearby, undeveloped beach.

That's what keeps Cancún interesting. Had your fill of raucous discos in the hotel zone? Escape to a downtown salsa club. Tired of lounging around the pool in Ciudad Cancún? Simply hop on a bus and head for the sapphire waters of the hotel zone.

Or even better, venture out and explore more of Quintana Roo state. Just a day trip away from Cancún, the pristine national park of Isla Contoy beckons with a fascinating variety of bird and plant species. And up north awaits low-key Isla Holbox, where swimming with massive whale sharks has become all the rage.

◉ Sights

Most of Cancun's star attractions – namely its beaches, museum, ruins and water-related activities – are in the Zona Hotelera. If you're staying in Ciudad Cancún, any 'R-1', 'R-2', or 'Zona Hotelera' bus will drop you off at any point along the coast.

WORTH THE SPLURGE

Hotel El Rey del Caribe (📞 998-884-20-28; www.elreydelcaribe.com; Av Uxmal 24; s/d incl breakfast M$900/983; ❄☀🎧🐾; 🚌R-1) is a true ecotel – it recycles, employs solar collectors and cisterns, uses gray water on the gardens, and has some rooms with composting toilets. This beautiful spot has a swimming pool and Jacuzzi in a jungly courtyard that's home to a small family of *tlacuaches* (opossums). All rooms have a fully equipped kitchenette, comfortable beds and fridges. Offers good online deals.

★ **Museo Maya de Cancún** MUSEUM
(Maya Museum; www.inah.gob.mx; Blvd Kukulcán Km 16.5; M$64; ◉9am-6pm Tue-Sun; 🚌R-1) Holding one of the Yucatán's most important collections of Maya artifacts, this modern museum is a welcome sight in a city known more for its party scene than cultural attractions. On display are some 400 pieces found at key sites in and around the peninsula, ranging from sculptures to ceramics and jewelry. One of the three halls shows temporary Maya-themed exhibits.

Cancún's original anthropology museum shut down in 2006 due to structural damage from hurricanes. The new museum features hurricane-resistant reinforced glass. The price of admission includes access to the adjoining San Miguelito archaeological site.

🏃 Activities

Guided tours to Isla Contoy give you several hours of free time to explore the island's interpretive trails, climb a 27m-high observation tower and get in a little snorkeling.

For more information on the island, **Amigos de Isla Contoy** (📞998-884-74-83; www.islacontoy.org; Plaza Bonita Mall) has a website with detailed information on the island's ecology.

Tour operators based out of Cancún and Isla Mujeres run trips to Contoy.

★ **Museo Subacuático de Arte** DIVING, SNORKELING
(MUSA Underwater Museum; www.musacancun.com; snorkeling tour US$41.50, 1-tank dive US$64.50) 🏊 Built to divert divers away from deteriorating coral reefs, this one-of-a-kind aquatic museum features more than 500 life-size sculptures in the waters of Cancún and Isla Mujeres. The artificial reefs are submerged at depths of 4m and 8m, making them ideal for snorkelers and first-time divers. Organize dives through diving outfits; Scuba Cancún is recommended.

Scuba Cancún DIVING
(📞998-849-75-08; www.scubacancun.com.mx; Blvd Kukulcán Km 5.2; 1-/2-tank dives US$62/77, equipment rental extra) A family-owned and PADI-certified dive operation with many years of experience, Scuba Cancún was the city's first dive shop. It offers a variety of snorkeling, fishing and diving expeditions (including cenote and night dives). It also runs snorkeling and diving trips to the underwater sculpture museum, aka MUSA.

Mexico's Yucatán & Chiapas Highlights

1 **Palenque** (p89)
Exploring the astonishing Maya jungle ruins.

2 **Mérida** (p74) Delving into the regional cuisine of the cultural capital.

3 **Mahahual** (p70)
Chilling in this low-key Caribbean town.

4 **Isla Holbox** (p57)
Swimming with massive whale sharks.

5 **Isla Cozumel** (p64)
Immersing yourself in the colorful underwater world.

6 **Valladolid** (p70)
Plunging into crystalline cenotes.

7 **Campeche** (p79)
Embracing the walled city's swashbuckling spirit.

The Yucatán

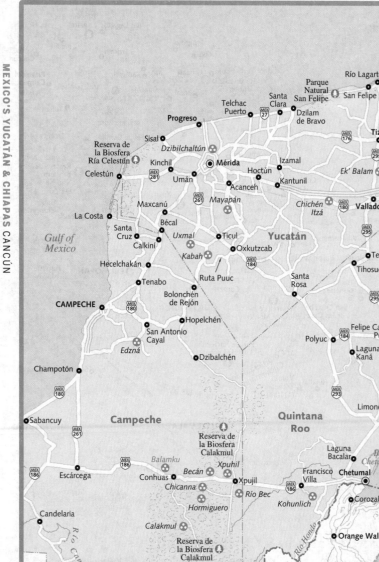

Río Lagartos

Parque Natural San Felipe — San Felipe

Telchac Puerto — Santa Clara — San Felipe

Progreso — MEX 27 — Dzilam de Bravo

Tizimín — MEX 176

Sisal — MEX 295

Reserva de la Biosfera Ría Celestún — Dzibilchaltún

Kinchil — Mérida — Izamal — Ek' Balam

Celestún — MEX 281 — Hoctún

Umán — Acanceh — Kantunil

Maxcanú — Mayapán — Chichén Itzá — MEX 180 — Valladolid

La Costa

Santa Cruz — Bécal — Uxmal — Ticul — Yucatán — MEX 295

Calkiní — Kabah — Oxkutzcab

Hecelchakán — Tepich

Tenabo — Ruta Puuc — MEX 184 — Tihosuco

Bolonchén de Rejón — Santa Rosa — MEX 295

CAMPECHE — MEX 180

Hopelchén

San Antonio Cayal — Polyuc — MEX 184 — Felipe Carrillo Puerto

Edzná — Dzibalchén — Laguna Kaná

Champotón — MEX 307

MEX 180 — MEX 293

Sabancuy — MEX 261 — Campeche — Quintana Roo — Limones

Reserva de la Biosfera Calakmul — Laguna Bacalar — Bahía Chetumal

MEX 186 — Balamku — Becán — Xpuhil — Francisco Villa — Chetumal

MEX 186 — Escárcega — Conhuas — Chicanna — Xpujil — MEX 186

Río Bec — Corozal

Hormiguero — Kohunlich

Candelaria — Río Hondo

Río Candelaria

Calakmul — Orange Walk

Reserva de la Biosfera Calakmul

Reserva de la Biosfera Maya — Parque Nacional El Mirador–Dos Lagunas–Río Azul — BELIZE

GUATEMALA — Belize City

Gulf of Mexico

Isla Holbox

Holbox

Reserva de la Biosfera Río Lagartos

Chiquilá

Parque Nacional Isla Contoy

Isla Mujeres

Punta Sam

Cancún

Kantunilkin

MEX 180

Xcan

El Ideal

MEX 180D

Vicente Guerrero

Puerto Morelos

Chemáx

Cenotes Cristalino, El Jardín del Edén & Azul

MEX 307

Playa del Carmen

Xcaret

Cobá

Paamul

Akumal

Xpu-Há

San Miguel de Cozumel

Xcacel-Xcacelito

Gran Cenote

Xel-Há

Isla Cozumel

Tulum

Tulum

Bahías de Punto Solimán

MEX 307

Punta Allen

Bahía de la Ascención

CARIBBEAN SEA

Reserva de la Biosfera Sian Ka'an

Bahía del Espíritu Santo

Mahahual

Reserva de la Biosfera Banco Chinchorro

Banco Chinchotro

Xcalak

San Pedro

Caye Caulker

0 ——— 80 km
0 ——— 50 miles

Asterix
BOAT TOUR

(☑998-886-42-70; www.contoytours.com; Blvd Kukulcán Km 5.2; adult/child 5-12yr US$109/63; ☉tours 9am-5pm Tue, Thu & Sat) Tours to Isla Contoy depart from Marina Scuba Cancún. They include guide, breakfast, lunch, open bar and snorkeling gear.

🛏 Sleeping

Mezcal Hostel
HOSTEL $

(☑cell 998-1259502; www.mezcalhostel.com; Mero 12; dm/r incl breakfast US$14/45; ☺❊🛜❄; 🚻R-1) Any place with mezcal in its name must be good, or so the logic goes. In this case, it is indeed all good at the Mezcal Hostel, which occupies a beautiful two-story house in a quiet residential area. Private rooms and dorms are kept very clean and weekly Sunday BBQ parties are perfect for sipping smoky mezcal.

Hostal Mayapan
HOSTEL $

(☑998-883-32-27; www.hostalmayapan.com; Blvd Kukulcán Km 8.5; incl breakfast dm M$180-235, r M$850; ☺❊@🛜; 🚻R-1) Located in an abandoned mall, this is a great budget spot in the Zona Hotelera. Thanks to its location just 30m from the beach, it's one of our favorite hostels in town. The rooms are superclean and there's a little hangout area in an atrium upstairs (the old food court?).

Hostel Natura
HOSTEL $$

(☑998-883-08-87; www.hostelnaturacancun.com; Blvd Kukulcán Km 9.5; dm US$26-27, r US$60; ☺❊🛜; 🚻R-1) Up above a health-food restaurant of the same name, this new hostel offers private rooms with lagoon views and somewhat cramped dorms, offset by the airy rooftop common area. The party zone is close by.

🍴 Eating

Eating options in Ciudad Cancún range from your standard-issue taco joints to upscale seafood restaurants. You'll find many restaurants near Parque de las Palapas and along Avenida Yaxchilán. Mercados 23 (Av Tulum s/n; ☉6am-7pm; 🚻R-1) and 28 (Mercado Veintiocho; cnr Avs Xel-Há & Sunyaxchén; ☉6am-7pm) serve up good market food, and there are some food stands (Parque de las Palapas; ☉7:30am-midnight) right on the Palapas plaza. For groceries, try Comercial Mexicana (cnr Avs Tulum & Uxmal; ☉7am-11pm), close to the bus station, or Chedraui Supermarket (cnr Avs Tulum & Cobá; ☉7am-11pm; 🅿; 🚻R-1).

Ciudad Cancún

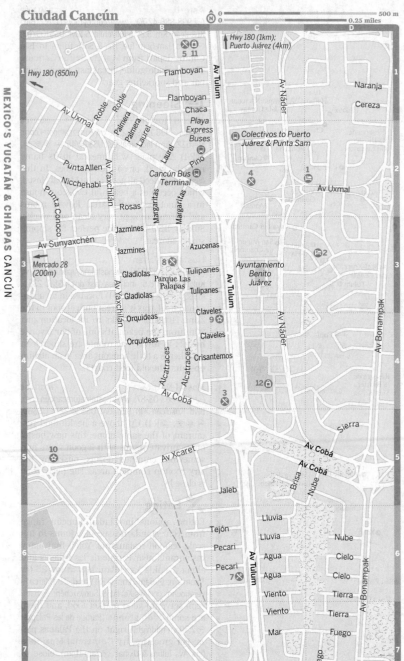

0
0

500 m
0.25 miles

Hwy 180 (1km);
Puerto Juárez (4km)

Hwy 180 (850m)

Naranja

Cereza

Flamboyan

Av Uxmal

Roble

Roble

Palmera

Palmera

Laurel

Laurel

Flamboyan

Chaca

Playa
Express
Buses

Pino

Av Tulum

Av Náder

Colectivos to Puerto
Juárez & Punta Sam

Punta Allen

Av Yaxchilán

Nicchehabi

Punta Conoco

Cancún Bus
Terminal

4

1

Av Uxmal

Rosas

Margaritas

Margaritas

Jazmines

Av Sunyaxchén

Mercado 28
(200m)

Jazmines

Azucenas

2

8

Tulipanes

Ayuntamiento
Benito
Juárez

Gladiolas

Parque Las
Palapas

Tulipanes

Av Tulum

Av Náder

Gladiolas

Av Yaxchilán

Claveles

9

Orquideas

Claveles

Av Bonampak

Orquideas

Crisantemos

Alcatraces

Alcatraces

Av Cobá

12

3

Sierra

10

Av Cobá

Av Xcaret

Av Cobá

Brisa

Nube

Jaleb

Lluvia

Tejón

Lluvia

Nube

Pecari

Agua

Cielo

Av Tulum

Av Bonampak

Pecari

7

Agua

Cielo

Viento

Tierra

Viento

Tierra

Mar

Fuego

6

Fuego

Av Sayil

Ciudad Cancún

🛏 Sleeping
1 Hotel El Rey del Caribe........................D2
2 Mezcal Hostel.................................D3

🍴 Eating
3 Chedraui Supermarket......................C4
4 Comercial Mexicana.........................C2
5 El Paisano del 23.............................B1
6 La Playita.......................................D7
7 Los de Pescado...............................C6
8 Mexican Food Stalls........................B3

🎭 Entertainment
9 11:11...C4
10 Grand Mambo Café.........................A5

🛍 Shopping
11 Mercado 23...................................B1
12 Mercado Municipal Ki-Huic...............C4

El Paisano del 23 MEXICAN $

(cnr Cedro & Cericote, Mercado 23; tortas M$35; ⊗6am-4pm; 📶R-1) A local favorite for more than 40 years, the *paisano* ('fellow countryman' – it's the owner's nickname) marinates *pierna* (pork leg) in red wine and then slow cooks it. The *tortas* (sandwiches) go fast, especially on weekends.

Los de Pescado SEAFOOD $

(www.losdepescado.com; Av Tulum 32; tacos & tostadas M$27-29, ceviche M$86-129, burritos M$39-43; ⊗10am-6pm; 📶R-27) It's easy to order at a place where you have only four choices: *ceviche* (seafood marinated in lemon or lime juice, garlic and seasonings), tacos, *tostadas* (fried tortilla) or burritos. Try the fish and shrimp tacos with fixings from the salad station and you'll understand why locals dig this spot.

★ Kiosco Verde SEAFOOD $$

(www.restaurant-kiosco-verde.blogspot.mx; Av López Portillo s/n, Puerto Juárez; mains M$80-140; ⊗noon-7pm Wed-Mon; 🅿🛜) The Green Kiosk just might be the most underrated seafood restaurant in all of Cancún. It began in 1974 as a grocery store and now it serves elaborate fresh fish and seafood dishes, such as coconut-encrusted shrimp and succulent grilled whole fish. Don't leave without trying the Mexican craft beers or mezcal.

To get here, catch a northbound 'Puerto Juárez' *colectivo* along Avenida Tulum, opposite the bus station.

La Playita SEAFOOD $$

(Av Bonampak 60; mains M$90-170; ⊗11am-2am; 🛜; 📶R-27) Beat the heat with refreshing, light dishes such as seafood cocktails and *ceviche tostadas*. To drink, try the 'frozen miche,' a beer-based cocktail best described as a brain freeze waiting to happen. The daily drink specials and outdoor seating make this one of downtown's most popular bars.

Surfin' Burrito MEXICAN $$

(www.facebook.com/thesurfinburrito; Blvd Kukulcán Km 9.5; burritos M$62-119; ⊗24hr; 📶R-1) Always a crowd-pleaser on the strip, where cheap eats come few and far between, this small joint prepares beef, shrimp, fish and vegetarian burritos with your choice of tasty fixings. It's open 24/7 and makes jumbo margaritas, making it a popular late-night haunt.

🍸 Drinking & Nightlife

★ Grand Mambo Café CLUB

(📞998-884-45-36; www.mambocafe.com.mx; Plaza Hong Kong, cnr Avs Xcaret & Tankah; ⊗10:30pm-5am Wed-Sat; 📶R-2) The large floor at this happening club is the perfect place to practice those Latin dance steps you've been working on. Live groups play Cuban salsa and other tropical styles.

11:11 GAY

(Once Once; cnr Av Tulum & Claveles; ⊗10:30pm-6am Thu-Sat; 📶R-1) The main room in this large house stages drag shows, go-go dancers and the like, while DJs in smaller rooms spin electronica and pop tunes till the sun comes up.

🛍 Shopping

La Europea DRINK

(www.laeuropea.com.mx; Blvd Kukulcán Km 12.5; ⊗10am-9pm Mon-Sat, 11am-7pm Sun; 📶R-1) A gourmet liquor store with reasonable prices, knowledgeable staff and the best booze selection in town, including top-shelf tequilas and mezcals. Most airlines allow you to travel with up to 3L of alcohol, but check first. Salud!

Mercado Municipal Ki-Huic MARKET

(Av Tulum s/n; ⊗9am-9pm; 📶R-1) This warren of stalls and shops carries a wide variety of souvenirs and handicrafts.

ℹ Getting There & Away

AIR

Aeropuerto Internacional de Cancún (CUN; 📞998-848-7200; www.asur.com.mx; Carretera Cancún-Chetumal, Km 22; 🛜) Yellow Transfers shuttles, with ticket offices inside the terminal, cost M$160 per person to Ciudad Cancún or

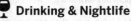

the Zona Hotelera. ADO buses (M$52) go to the downtown bus station. Regular taxis and private vans charge M$450 to M$500.

BOAT

There are several points of embarkation to reach Isla Mujeres from Cancún by boat. From Puerto Juárez it costs M$80; leaving from the Zona Hotelera it runs about M$235.

Puerto Juárez Dock Puerto Juárez is the main port for passenger ferries to Isla Mujeres. Punta Sam, the dock for the slower car ferries to Isla Mujeres, is about 7km north of downtown. Ferry services leave from the Zona Hotelera as well.

BUS

Cancún's modern **bus terminal** (cnr Avs Uxmal & Tulum) occupies the wedge formed where Avenidas Uxmal and Tulum meet. It's a safe area and you'll be fine walking around. Across Pino from the bus terminal, a few doors from Avenida Tulum, is the ticket office and miniterminal of **Playa Express** (Calle Pino), which runs air-conditioned buses down the coast to Playa del Carmen every 10 minutes until early evening, stopping at major towns and points of interest. **ADO** (🕿 800-009-90-90; www.ado.com.mx) covers the same ground and beyond with its 1st-class service.

ADO sets the 1st-class standard, while **ADO Platino** (🕿 800-737-58-56; www.adoplatino.com.mx), **ADO GL** (🕿 800-900-01-05; www.adogl.com.mx) and **OCC** (🕿 800-900-0105; www.occbus.com.mx) provide luxury services. Mayab provides good 'intermediate class' (tending to make more stops than 1st class) to many

points, while Oriente's 2nd-class air-con buses often depart and arrive late.

Isla Mujeres

🕿 998 / POP 16,000

Some people plan their vacation around Cancún and pencil in Isla Mujeres as a side trip. But Isla Mujeres is a destination in its own right, and it's generally quieter and more affordable than the options you get across the bay.

Sure, there are quite a few ticky-tacky tourist shops, but folks still get around by golf cart and the crushed-coral beaches are even better than those of Cozumel and Holbox. As for the calm turquoise water of Isla Mujeres, well, you really just have to see it for yourself.

There's just enough here to keep you entertained: snorkel or scuba dive, visit a turtle farm or put on your sunglasses and settle in with that book you've been dying to finish. Come sunset, there are plenty of dining options, and the nightlife scene moves at a relaxed island pace.

◉ Sights

Isla Mujeres Turtle Farm   FARM
(Isla Mujeres Tortugranja; 🕿 998-888-07-05; Carretera Sac Bajo Km 5; M$30; ⊙9am-5pm; 🚼) 🏊
Although they're endangered, sea turtles are still killed throughout Latin America for their eggs and meat. In the 1980s, efforts

BUSES FROM CANCÚN

DESTINATION	COST (M$)	DURATION (HR)	FREQUENCY (DAILY)
Chetumal	235-456	5½-6	frequent
Chichén Itzá	135-258	3-4	14
Chiquilá	114	3-3½	3 (Mayab)
Felipe Carrillo Puerto	186-248	3½-4	3
Mérida	198-578	4-4½	frequent
Mexico City	1928	27	1 to Terminal Norte; 6:30pm
Mexico City (TAPO)	1904-2160	24½-28	4
Palenque	876-1040	13-13½	3
Playa del Carmen	34-60	1-1½	frequent ADO & Playa Express
Puerto Morelos	22-24	½-¾	frequent ADO & Playa Express
Ticul	220-296	8½	frequent
Tizimín	130-280	3	3
Tulum	92-130	2½	frequent
Valladolid	150-158	2-2¼	8
Villahermosa	550-1480	12¾-14½	frequent

ESCAPE FROM CANCÚN

North of Cancún await several interesting island getaways. To see what Cancún looked like before the development boom, grab a cab from Cancún Centro to Isla Blanca, where you can chill on a beach with affordable cabins.

To swim with 15-ton whale sharks, head to Isla Holbox. Two daily buses depart from the Cancún bus terminal (p56) to Chiquilá, where you can cross on a ferry to Isla Holbox, a laid-back island with sand streets and no cars. Turística Moguel offers tours and Hostel Tribu makes a good spot to crash.

Cabañas Playa Blanca (☑cell 998-2139131; Isla Blanca; beach club admission M$30, cabins M$500-1000; 🅿) A beach club and cabins on a sublime stretch of white-sand beach overlooking Isla Mujeres.

Turística Moguel (☑984-875-20-28, cell 984-1149921; www.holboxislandtours.com; cnr Avs Tiburón Ballena & Damero; per person M$1200) Operating out of the mini-market on the plaza, this is considered one of the best outfits running whale-shark tours. The expedition includes a stop at a beautiful spring (where you can go swimming) and a visit to Isla Pasión, an island that provides great birdwatching.

Hostel Tribu (☑984-875-25-07; www.tribuhostel.com; Av Pedro Joaquín Coldwell; dm/r from M$170/550; 😊❄️🛜) With so many activities available here (from salsa lessons to yoga and kayaking), it doesn't take long to settle in with the tribe. Six-bed dorms and private rooms are clean, colorful and cheerful. Tribu also has a book exchange and a bar that stages weekly jam sessions. From the plaza, it's one block north and two blocks west.

by a local fisherman led to the founding of this *tortugranja* (turtle farm), 5km south of town, which safeguards breeding grounds and protects eggs.

If you're coming from the bus stop, bear right at the 'Y' just beyond Hacienda Mundaca's parking lot (the turn is marked by a tiny sign). The farm is easily reached from town by taxi (M$60).

Playa Norte · BEACH
Once you reach Playa Norte, the island's main beach, you won't want to leave. Its warm, shallow waters are the color of blue raspberry syrup and the beach is crushed coral. Unlike most of the island's east coast, Playa Norte is safe for swimming and the water is only chest deep even far from shore.

Museo Capitán Dulché · MUSEUM, BEACH
(www.capitandulche.com; Carretera a Garrafón Km 4.5; M$65; ⏱10:30am-6:30pm; 🅿) And you thought Isla Mujeres had no culture. Here you get not only a maritime museum detailing the island's naval history but also one of the best beach clubs in town – and we're not just saying that because of the cool boat bar.

🏃 Activities

Fisherman's Cooperative · TOUR
(☑cell 998-1534883; cnr Av Rueda Medina & Madero; snorkeling incl lunch M$350, Isla Contoy tours M$1000, whale-shark tour M$1400; ⏱office 8am-

8pm) The local fisherman's cooperative offers snorkeling tours to various sites, including Isla Contoy and the reef off Playa Garrafón, and it does whale-shark outings as well.

Sea Hawk Divers · DIVING
(☑998-877-02-96; www.seahawkislamujeres.com; Carlos Lazo s/n; 1-/2-tank dives incl equipment US$70/85, resort course US$95, whale-shark tour US$125) Offers reef dives, resort courses, fishing trips and whale-shark snorkeling tours. Rents rooms, too.

🛏️ Sleeping

★ Poc-Na Hostel · HOSTEL $
(☑998-877-00-90; www.pocna.com; Matamoros 15; dm with fan/air-con M$155/195, d with/without bathroom M$430/370, incl breakfast, camping per person M$110; 😊❄️🛜) You can't beat this hostel's common areas. For starters, it's right on a lovely palm-shaded beach, home to one of the town's most happening beach bars at night – and you can also pitch a tent if you bring your own. Guests can chill in a cool *palapa* lobby bar, where breakfast is served and local bands play nightly.

Apartments Trinchan · APARTMENT $
(☑998-877-08-56, cell 998-1666967; atrinchan@prodigy.net.mx; Carlos Lazo 46; r with fan/air-con M$400/450, apt with fan/air-con M$450/500; 😊❄️🛜) Since it has no website, you'll have

to take our word for it when we say this is one of the best budget deals in town – and the beach is right around the corner. If it's available, opt for one of the large apartments with full kitchen.

✗ Eating

Pita Amore
MEDITERRANEAN $

(Guerrero s/n, btwn Morelos & Madero; sandwiches M$35-45; ⊙12:30-10pm Mon-Sat, 6-10pm Sun; 🛜🅿) This unassuming shack does just three varieties of pita sandwiches and does them extremely well. The chicken, beef and vegetarian pitas are the creation of a New York Culinary Institute alum. The secret lies in the homemade sauces and outstanding pita bread, which comes from a Lebanese bakery in Mérida.

Mercado Municipal
MARKET $

(Guerrero s/n, btwn López Mateos & Matamoros; mains M$35-100; ⊙7am-5pm) Inside the remodeled market are several stalls selling cheap hot food, while other vendors offer a variety of produce and fresh juices. Outside the market, four open-air restaurants prepare simple regional fare like *sopa de lima* (lime soup) at decent prices.

Mininos
SEAFOOD $$

(Av Rueda Medina s/n; mains M$90-170; ⊙10am-9pm) A colorfully painted *palapa* restaurant with a sand floor, Mininos dishes up tasty garlic shrimp, fried whole fish and octopus, as well as delicious seafood soups. It's popular with locals and tourists alike.

🍷 Drinking & Nightlife

★T&T Tropical Paradise
LOUNGE

(www.facebook.com/tropicalparadiseislamujeres; Matamoros 20; ⊙5am-2pm) You gotta love a place with sand floors – and unlike some of the nearby bars, T&T dares to play music from the 21st century!

Poc-Na Hostel
BAR

(www.pocna.com; Matamoros 26; ⊙7pm-3am; 🛜) Has a lobby bar with nightly live music and a beachfront bar with bonfires and more hippies than all the magic buses in the world. It's a scene, and an entertaining one at that.

❶ Getting There & Around

There are several points of embarkation from Cancún to reach Isla Mujeres. Most people cross on Ultramar passenger ferries. The R-1 'Puerto Juárez' city bus in Cancún serves all Zona Ho-

telera departure points and Puerto Juárez, in Ciudad Cancún.

Fares for ferries departing from the Zona Hotelera are in dollars. It's much cheaper to leave from Puerto Juárez. Ferries (www.granpuerto.com.mx) depart from the following docks:

Puerto Juárez (4km north of Ciudad Cancún) Leave every 30 minutes; one way M$78.

El Embarcadero (Blvd Kukulcán Km 4) Six daily departures; one way US$14.

Playa Tortugas (Blvd Kukulcán Km 6.5) Eight daily departures; one way US$14.

Playa Caracol (Blvd Kukulcán Km 9.5) Six daily departures; one way US$14.

Puerto Morelos

📞 998 / POP 9200

Halfway between Cancún and Playa del Carmen, Puerto Morelos retains its quiet, small-town feel despite the building boom north and south of town. While it offers enough restaurants and bars to keep you entertained by night, it's really the shallow Caribbean waters that draw visitors here. Brilliantly contrasted stripes of bright green and dark blue separate the shore from the barrier reef – a tantalizing sight for divers and snorkelers – while inland a series of excellent cenotes beckon the adventurous. There's a nice market just a few minutes' walk from the plaza with a good selection of crafts and hammocks.

◉ Sights & Activities

Jardín Botánico Dr Alfredo Barrera Marín
GARDENS

(Jardín Botánico Yaax Che; 📞998-206-92-33; Hwy 307 Km 320; adult/child 3-10yr M$120/50; ⊙8am-4pm Mon-Sat; 🅿) One of the largest botanical gardens in Mexico, this 65-hectare reserve has about 2km of trails and sections dedicated to epiphytes (orchids and bromeliads), palms, ferns, succulents (cacti and their relatives) and plants used in traditional Maya medicine. The garden also holds a large animal population, including the only coastal troops of spider monkeys left in the region.

It's 1.3km south of the Puerto Morelos turnoff.

Aquanauts
DIVING

(📞998-206-93-65; www.aquanautsdiveadventures.com; Hotel Hacienda Morelos, Av Melgar s/n; 1-/2-tank reef dives US$70/90, snorkeling US$30; ⊙office 8am-4pm Mon-Sat) Runs many interesting tours, including drift diving, cenote and shipwreck dives, and lionfish hunting. The dive shop is one block south of the plaza, in Hotel Hacienda Morelos.

Puerto Morelos
Language Center LANGUAGE COURSE
(☑998-871-01-62; www.puertomorelosspanish center.com; Niños Héroes 46; classes per hour/ week US$25/200, homestay per day US$45-60) In addition to hourly and weekly classes of 20 hours, the language center also offers an immersion program with the option of living with a Mexican host family. The school doubles as a travel agency if you're looking to hook up tours and activities.

🛏 Sleeping

Hotel Sevilla HOTEL $
(☑998-206-90-81; pm.h.sevilla@gmail.com; Av Niños Héroes 29; d from M$500; ❄️✳️🛜) The Spanish-run Sevilla is really nothing special but it's one of the only budget options in town during high season. The best bet are the rooftop rooms, which get good natural light and afford partial views of Puerto Morelos.

⭐ **Posada El Moro** HOTEL $$
(☑998-206-90-05; www.posadaelmoro.com; Av Rojo Gómez s/n; r incl breakfast US$69-79, ste US$105-117; P❄️✳️🛜🏊) A well-run property, with cheery geraniums in the halls and courtyard. Some rooms have kitchenettes, all have couches that fold out into futons, and there's a small pool in a tropical garden. Prices drop substantially in low season. It's northwest of the plaza.

🍴 Eating

El Nicho BREAKFAST $$
(www.elnicho.com.mx; cnr Avs Tulum & Rojo Gómez; breakfast M$55-105, lunch M$75-150; ⏱7am-2pm Fri-Wed; 🛜🍴) Puerto Morelos' best and most popular breakfast spot, El Nicho serves organic egg dishes, eggs Benedict, *chilaquiles* (fried tortilla strips in salsa) with chicken, and organic coffee from Chiapas. Vegetarians will find many good options here.

El Merkadito SEAFOOD $$
(www.elmerkadito.mx; Av Melgar s/n, north of the lighthouse; snacks M$48-58, mains M$115-190; ⏱noon-9pm; 🛜) You gotta love a place that serves tortilla chips in a 'Hecho en Mexico' (Made in Mexico) paper bag, even more so when you're sitting in a delightful beachside *palapa* restaurant. The shrimp *aguachile ceviche* is excellent, as are the green mussels in white-wine broth. Top it off with a re-

freshing ice cream served in a hollowed-out orange peel.

🔒 Shopping

Artisans Market ARTS & CRAFTS
(Av Rojo Gómez s/n; ⏱9am-6pm) Find high-quality hammocks, *alebrijes* (colorful, hand-carved wooden animals), handbags, masks, jewelry and more. It's refreshingly low-key and you can often see the craftspeople at work.

ℹ Getting There & Away

Playa Express and ADO buses that travel between Cancún and Playa del Carmen drop you on the highway. Buses and Playa Express vans from Cancún's ADO terminal cost M$22 to M$24. If you're arriving at the Cancún airport, there are frequent bus departures from there to Puerto Morelos for M$90.

Taxis are usually waiting at the turnoff to shuttle people into town; cabs parked at the plaza will take you back to the highway. Some drivers will tell you the fare is per person or overcharge in some other manner; strive for M$25 for the 2km ride, for as many people as you can stuff in.

Playa Del Carmen
☑984 / POP 150,000
With daily cruise-ship visitors, Playa's tourist center now feels like a mass-tourism destination, but it manages to retain its European chic, and one need just head several blocks west of the main strip to catch glimpses of the nontouristic side of things.

🏃 Activities

Flora, Fauna y Cultura de México VOLUNTEERING
(☑984-871-52-44; www.florafaunaycultura.org) Conservation volunteering with turtles on the Caribbean coast.

Scuba Playa DIVING
(☑984-803-31-23; www.scubaplaya.com; Calle 10 s/n; ⏱7:30am-9pm) A PADI five-star instructor development dive resort, with technical diving courses available.

🛏 Sleeping

Hostel Playa HOSTEL $
(☑984-803-32-77; www.hostelplaya.com.mx; Calle 8 s/n; dm/d/tr incl breakfast M$200/490/735; P❄️🛜) This place was made for mingling with its central common area, a cool garden spot and a rooftop terrace. The private

Playa del Carmen

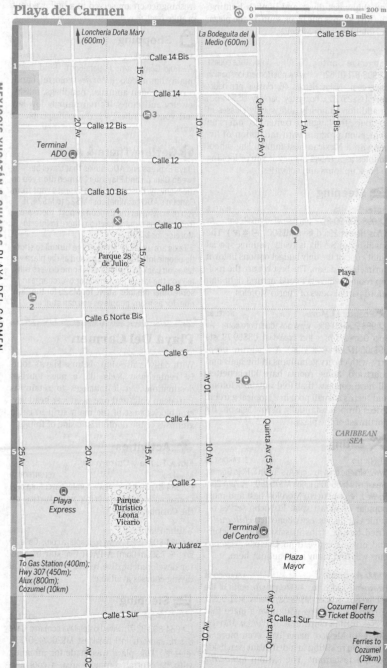

0 _____ 200 m
0 _____ 0.1 miles

Lonchería Doña Mary (600m)

La Bodeguita del Medio (600m)

Calle 16 Bis

Calle 14 Bis

15 Av

Calle 14

Quinta Av (5 Av)

1 Av

1 Av Bis

Calle 12 Bis

10 Av

3

20 Av

Terminal ADO

Calle 12

Calle 10 Bis

4

Calle 10

1

15 Av

Parque 28 de Julio

Playa

Calle 8

2

Calle 6 Norte Bis

Calle 6

10 Av

5

Calle 4

Quinta Av (5 Av)

CARIBBEAN SEA

25 Av

20 Av

15 Av

10 Av

Calle 2

Playa Express

Parque Turístico Leona Vicario

Terminal del Centro

Plaza Mayor

Av Juárez

To Gas Station (400m);
Hwy 307 (450m);
Alux (800m);
Cozumel (10km)

Calle 1 Sur

20 Av

10 Av

Quinta Av (5 Av)

Calle 1 Sur

Cozumel Ferry Ticket Booths

Ferries to Cozumel (19km)

Playa del Carmen

Activities, Courses & Tours
1 Scuba Playa C3

Sleeping
2 Hostel Playa A3
3 Hotel Playa del Karma B1

Eating
4 Kaxapa Factory B3

Drinking & Nightlife
5 Playa 69 .... C4

rooms are simple but decent enough, and the staff are extremely helpful and have great suggestions on what to see and do.

★ **Hotel Playa del Karma** BOUTIQUE HOTEL $$
(☎984-803-02-72; www.hotelplayadelkarma. com; 15 Av, btwn Calles 12 & 14; r from M$1084; P❄✳︎☕️🛜) The closest you're going to get to the jungle in this town; rooms here face a lush courtyard with a small pool. All rooms have air-con and TV, and some come with kitchenette, sitting area and sweet little porches with hammocks. The hotel arranges tours to nearby ruins and diving sites.

✖️ Eating

Kaxapa Factory SOUTH AMERICAN $
(www.kaxapafactory.com; Calle 10 s/n; mains M$50-90; ⊙10am-10pm Tue-Sun; 🛜🍴) The specialty at this Venezuelan restaurant on the park is *arepa*, a delicious corn flatbread stuffed with your choice of shredded beef, chicken or beans and plantains. There are many vegetarian and gluten-free options here and the refreshing fresh-made juices go nicely with just about everything on the menu.

Lonchería Doña Mary YUCATECAN $
(Calle 28 s/n, cnr 30 Av; snacks M$10-35, soups M$30-50; ⊙6pm-1:30am) You'll probably have to wait for a table at this popular eatery and service can be slow. But it's worth the wait when you try Mary's Yucatecan comfort food. All dishes are prepared with chicken: tamales, *panuchos* (fried tortilla with re-fried beans and toppings), *salbutes* (same as *panuchos* sans beans) and a hearty chicken soup, just like Ma used to make.

🍷 Drinking & Nightlife

La Bodeguita del Medio DANCING
(www.labodeguitadelmedio.com.mx; Quinta Av s/n; ⊙1:30pm-2am; 🛜) The writing is literally on the walls, and on the lampshades, and pretty much everywhere at this Cuban restaurant-bar. After a few mojitos you'll be dancing the night away to live *cubana* music. Get here at 7:30pm for free salsa lessons.

Playa 69 GAY
(www.rivieramayagay.com; alley off Quinta Av, btwn Calles 4 & 6; ⊙9pm-5am Tue-Sun) This gay dance club proudly features foreign strippers from such far-flung places as Australia and Brazil, and it stages weekend drag-queen shows.

ℹ️ Information

Banamex (cnr Calle 12 & 10 Av)

ℹ️ Geting There & Away

BOAT
Ferries depart frequently to Cozumel from Calle 1 Sur, where you'll find three companies with **ticket booths**. Barcos Caribe is the cheapest of the bunch. Prices are subject to change. Transcaribe, south of Playa, runs car ferries to Cozumel.

WORTH A TRIP

CRISTALINO CENOTE

Head south of Playa del Carmen for some splish-splashing fun at a swimmable limestone sinkhole. To get there, catch a Tulum-bound **colectivo** (p64).

On the west side of the highway, 23km south of Playa del Carmen, is a series of wonderful cenotes. Among these is **Cristalino Cenote** (Hwy 307 s/n; adult/child 3-10yr M$100/60; ⊙8am-6pm), just south of the Barceló Maya Resort. It's easily accessible, only about 70m from the entrance gate, which is just off the highway. Two more sinkholes, **Azul** and **El Jardín del Edén**, sit just south of Cristalino along the highway. But Cristalino is the best of the three, as you can dive there (or just launch yourself off the rocks into the water below).

Chichén Itzá

It doesn't take long to realize why the Maya site of Chichén Itzá is one of Mexico's most popular tourist draws. Approaching the grounds from the main entrance, the striking castle pyramid **El Castillo** ❶ jumps right out at you – and the wow factor never lets up.

It's easy to tackle Chichén Itzá in one day. Within a stone's throw of the castle, you'll find the Maya world's largest **ball court** ❷ alongside eerie carvings of skulls and heart-devouring eagles at the Temple of Jaguars and the Platform of Skulls. On the other (eastern) side are the highly adorned **Group of a Thousand Columns** ❸ and the **Temple of Warriors** ❹. A short walk north of the castle leads to the gaping **Sacred Cenote** ❺, an important pilgrimage site. On the other side of El Castillo, you'll find giant stone serpents watching over the High Priest's Grave, aka El Osario. Further south, marvel at the spiral-domed **Observatory** ❻, the imposing Nunnery and Akab-Dzib, one of the oldest ruins.

Roaming the 47-hectare site, it's fun to consider that at its height Chichén Itzá was home to an estimated 90,000 inhabitants and spanned approximately 30 sq km. So essentially you're looking at just a small part of a once-great city.

THE LOWDOWN

» **Arrive** at 8am and you'll have a good three hours or so before the tour-bus madness begins. Early birds escape the merchants, too.

» **Remember** that Chichén Itzá is the name of the site; the actual town where it's located is called Pisté.

El Caracol
Observatory
Today they'd probably just use a website, but back in the day priests would announce the latest rituals and celebrations from the dome of the circular observatory.

Edificio de las Monjas (Nunnery)

❻

Akab-Dzib

Entrance

Grupo de las Mil Columnas
Group of a Thousand Columns
Not unlike a hall of fame exhibit, the pillars surrounding the temple reveal carvings of gods, dignitaries and celebrated warriors.

El Castillo
The Castle
Even this mighty pyramid can't bear the stress of a million visitors ascending its stairs each year. No climbing allowed, but the ground-level view doesn't disappoint.

Gran Juego de Pelota
Great Ball Court
How is it possible to hear someone talk from one end of this long, open-air court to the other? To this day, the acoustics remain a mystery.

Entrance

Parking Lot

Visitors Center

Tumba del Gran Sacerdote (High Priest's Grave)

Templo de los Jaguares (Temple of Jaguars)

1

2

3

4

5

Plataforma de los Cráneos (Platform of Skulls)

Cenote Sagrado
Sacred Cenote
Diving expeditions have turned up hundreds of valuable artifacts dredged from the cenote (limestone sinkhole), not to mention human bones of sacrificial victims who were forced to jump into the eternal underworld.

Templo de los Guerreros
Temple of Warriors
The Maya associated warriors with eagles and jaguars, as depicted in the temple's friezes. The revered jaguar, in particular, was a symbol of strength and agility.

BUS & COLECTIVO

Playa has two bus terminals; each sells tickets and provides information for at least some of the other's departures. You can save money by buying a 2nd-class bus ticket, but remember that it's often stop-and-go along the way. A taxi from Terminal ADO to the Plaza Mayor runs about M$25.

Playa Express shuttle buses are a much quicker way to get around the Riviera Maya, or to Cancún.

Terminal ADO (www.ado.com.mx; 20 Av s/n, cnr Calle 12) The Terminal ADO is where most 1st-class bus lines arrive and depart.

Terminal del Centro (Quinta Av s/n, cnr Av Juárez) All 2nd-class bus lines (including Mayab) are serviced at the old bus station, Terminal del Centro.

Playa Express (Calle 2 Norte) Offers quick, frequent service to Puerto Morelos for M$22 and downtown Cancún for M$34.

Colectivos to Tulum & Cancún (Calle 2, cnr 20 Av) *Colectivos* depart from Calle 2 as soon as they fill (about every 15 minutes) from 4am to midnight. They will stop anywhere along the highway between Playa and Tulum, charging a minimum of M$20. Luggage space is somewhat limited, but they're great for day trips. From the same spot, you can grab a *colectivo* to Cancún (M$34).

Isla Cozumel

📞 987 / POP 80,000

Cozumel is too resilient, too proud to let itself become just another cheesy cruise-ship destination. Leaving the tourist area – and the gringo-friendly souvenir shops – behind, you see an island of quiet cool and genuine authenticity. Garages still have shrines to the Virgin, there's a spirited Caribbean energy, and of course there are some holiday things to do, such as diving some of the best reefs in the world.

While diving and snorkeling are the main draws, the town square is a pleasant place to spend the afternoon, and it's highly gratifying to explore the less-visited parts of the island on a rented scooter or convertible bug. The coastal road leads to small Maya ruins, a marine park and captivating scenery along the unforgettable windswept shore.

👁 Sights & Activities

Museo de la Isla de Cozumel   MUSEUM
(📞 987-872-14-34; www.cozumelparks.com; Av Melgar s/n; M$60; ⊙ 9am-4pm Mon-Sat) The Museo de la Isla de Cozumel presents a clear and detailed picture of the island's flora, fauna, geography, geology and ancient Maya history. Thoughtful and detailed signs in English and Spanish accompany the exhibits. It's a good place to learn about coral before hitting the water, and it's one not to miss before you leave the island.

Parque Punta Sur   NATURE RESERVE
(📞 987-872-40-14; www.cozumelparks.com; Carretera Costera Sur Km 27; adult/child 3-11yr M$210/120; ⊙ 9am-4pm Mon-Sat) For the price of admission to this ecotouristic park, you can visit a lighthouse, a small nautical museum and a Maya ruin. About 10 minutes away by car is an observation tower where you can see migratory birds and possibly crocodiles. The park area offers a beach with a shallow reef, a restaurant and three midday boat tours to Laguna Colombia. You'll need your own vehicle or a taxi (M$300 one way) to get here.

Playa Palancar   BEACH
(Carretera Costera Sur Km 19; snorkel-gear rental M$130) About 17km south of town, Palancar is a great beach to visit during the week when the crowds thin out. It has a beach club renting snorkel gear and there's a restaurant. Near the beach, Arrecife Palancar (Palancar Reef) has some excellent diving (it's known as Palancar Gardens), as well as fine snorkeling (Palancar Shallows).

Deep Blue   DIVING
(📞 987-872-56-53; www.deepbluecozumel.com; Calle Salas 200; 2-tank dives incl equipment US$100, snorkeling incl gear US$57; ⊙ 7am-9pm) This PADI and National Association of Underwater Instructors (NAUI) operation has knowledgeable staff, state-of-the-art gear and fast boats that give you a chance to get more dives out of a day. A snorkeling outing visits three sites.

🛌 Sleeping

⭐ **Hostelito**   HOSTEL $
(📞 987-869-81-57; www.hostelcozumel.com; Av 10 Norte s/n, btwn Av Juárez & Calle 2 Norte; dm with/without air-con M$195/180, d M$550, ste from M$600; ⊜ ❋ 🛜) Stay in a fan-cooled or air-conditioned dorm room, or check out the recently remodeled rooms and suites, which have been significantly improved with new beds and furnishings. Hostelito's pleasant open-air kitchen and rooftop sundeck are great spaces for hanging out and exchanging diving stories.

San Miguel de Cozumel

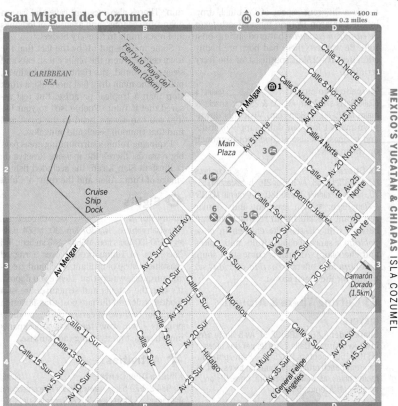

N 0 ———— 400 m
0 ———— 0.2 miles

San Miguel de Cozumel

◎ Sights
1 Museo de la Isla de Cozumel.............C1

◉ Activities, Courses & Tours
2 Deep Blue...C3

🛏 Sleeping
3 Hostelito..C2
4 Hotel Mary Carmen C2
5 Hotel Pepita.....................................C2

✕ Eating
6 La Choza...C3
7 Mercado Municipal.........................C3

Hotel Pepita   HOTEL **$**
(☎ 987-872-00-98; www.hotelpepitacozumel.
com; Av 15 Sur 120; r M$450; ⊝ ❋ 🛜) The HP's
owner, Maria Teresa, takes pride in her work
and it shows, as this is one of the best economical hotels in the city. It's friendly, with

well-maintained rooms grouped around a
garden. All have two double beds, refrigera-
tors and air-con. There's free morning coffee
and wi-fi in the common area.

Hotel Mary Carmen   HOTEL **$$**
(☎ 987-872-05-81; www.hotelmarycarmen.com.mx;
Av 5 Sur 132; d M$790; ⊝ ❋ 🛜) Mary Carmen's
lobby seems a bit odd in a design sense with
its mix of antiques and mismatched modern
furnishings, but it definitely ain't boring.
Clean, colorful rooms overlook a central
courtyard where the owner keeps more than
a dozen turtles, so watch your step! It's just a
short walk from the ferry terminal.

✕ Eating

Camarón Dorado   SEAFOOD **$**
(www.facebook.com/camaron.dorado; cnr Av Juárez
& Calle 105 Sur; tortas M$33-38, tacos M$17-28;
⊙7am-3pm Tue-Sun; 🛜) If you're headed to
the windward side of the island or just want

to see a different aspect of Cozumel, drop by the Camarón Dorado for a superb *torta de camaron capeado* (battered shrimp on a roll). Be warned: these bad boys are highly addictive. It's 2.5km southeast of the ferry terminal.

Mercado Municipal MARKET **$**
(Calle Salas s/n, btwn Avs 20 & 25 Sur; snacks & mains M$25-80; ⊗8am-5pm) Visit this downtown market for your daily supply of fruits and veggies; it's also a good spot to munch on cheap eats.

La Choza MEXICAN **$$**
(☑987-872-09-58; Av 10 Sur 216; breakfast M$52-70, lunch & dinner M$96-180, set menu M$115; ⊗7am-10pm; 🛜) An excellent and popular restaurant specializing in regional Mexican cuisine, with classics like chicken in *mole poblano* (a sauce of chilies, fruits, nuts, spices and chocolate). All mains come with soup. La Choza also offers a *comida corrida* (set menu) for the lunch crowd.

❶ Getting There & Around

BICYCLE

Shark Rider (☑987-120-02-31; Av 5 Norte s/n, btwn Av Juárez & Calle 2 Norte; per day bikes M$100-150, scooters M$250; ⊗8am-7pm) You can rent beach cruisers, mountain bikes and racing bikes, as well as scooters, here. It's on an alley off Avenida 5 Norte.

BOAT

Passenger ferries operated by **México Waterjets** (www.mexicowaterjets.com) and **Ultramar** (www.granpuerto.com.mx) run to Cozumel from Playa del Carmen (one way M$155, hourly 6am to 9pm). See websites for schedules.

To transport a vehicle to Cozumel, go to the Calica car-ferry terminal (officially known as the Terminal Marítima Punta Venado), about 7km south of Playa del Carmen. There are four daily departures Tuesday to Saturday and two on Sunday. See www.transcaribe.net for the schedule. You'll need to line up at least one hour before departure, two hours beforehand in high season. Fares are M$500 to M$1153, depending on the size of the vehicle.

Tulum

☑984 / POP 18,000

Tulum's spectacular coastline – with all its confectioner-sugar sands, jade-green water and balmy breezes – makes it one of the top beaches in Mexico. Where else can you get all that *and* a dramatically situated Maya

ruin? There's also excellent cave and cavern diving, fun cenotes, and a variety of lodgings and restaurants to fit every budget.

Some may be put off by the fact that the town center, where the really cheap eats and sleeps are found, sits right on the highway, making the main drag feel more like a truck stop than a tropical paradise. But rest assured that if Tulum Pueblo isn't to your liking, you can always head to the coast and find that tranquil beachside bungalow.

Exploring Tulum's surrounding areas pays big rewards: there's the massive Reserva de la Biosfera Sian Ka'an, the secluded fishing village of Punta Allen and the ruins of Cobá.

◉ Sights

Tulum Ruins ARCHAEOLOGICAL SITE
(www.inah.gob.mx; Hwy 307 Km 230; M$64, parking M$50-100, tours from M$644; ⊗8am-5pm; 🅿) The ruins of Tulum preside over a rugged coastline, a strip of brilliant beach and green-and-turquoise waters that'll leave you floored. It's true the extents and structures are of a modest scale and the late post-Classic design is inferior to those of earlier, more grandiose projects – but, wow, those Maya occupants must have felt pretty smug each sunrise.

🏃 Activities

Xibalba Dive Center DIVING
(☑984-871-29-53; www.xibalbadivecenter.com; Andromeda 7, btwn Libra Sur & Geminis Sur; 1-/2-tank dive US$85/140) One of the best dive shops in Tulum, Xibalba is known for its safety-first approach to diving. The center specializes in cave and cavern diving, but it also does ocean dives. Xibalba doubles as a hotel and offers attractive packages combining lodging, diving and cave-diving classes.

I Bike Tulum BICYCLE RENTAL
(☑984-802-55-18; www.ibiketulum.com; Av Cobá Sur s/n, cnr Venus; bicycle per day M$100, scooter per day incl insurance M$500; ⊗9am-5:30pm Mon-Sat) Rents a bike with lock and helmet, or if you prefer, a scooter.

Community Tours Sian Ka'an ECOTOUR
(☑984-871-22-02, cell 984-1140750; Osiris Sur s/n, cnr Sol Oriente; tours per person US$75-129; ⊗7am-8pm) 🍃 Runs various excursions to the magnificent Reserva de la Biosfera Sian Ka'an, which include kayaking in canals, birdwatching or visiting Maya ruins. Community Tours is a sustainable tourism project run by locals from Maya communities.

🛏 Sleeping

El Jardín de Frida HOSTEL **$**
(☑984-871-28-16; www.fridastulum.com; Av Tulum s/n, Tulum Pueblo, btwn Av Kukulcán & Chemuyil; dm/r/ste incl breakfast M$200/850/1200; P🌬🐾) 🐾 The main house, dorms and private rooms are painted in colorful Mexican pop-art style at this ecohostel. All rooms are fan-cooled with the exception of the suites, which come with optional air-con. The mixed dorms are clean and cheerful, and the hostel has a fun little bar area.

Cenote Encantado CAMPGROUND **$**
(☑cell 984-1425930; www.cenoteencantado.com; Carretera Tulum-Boca Paila Km 10.5; tents per person M$290; 🚲) A rare budget option near the beach, this new-agey spot gets its name from a pretty cenote right in the campground's backyard. Guests here stay in large furnished tents with beds, rugs and nightstands. It's not in front of the beach, but you can walk or bike there.

You can swim or snorkel in the cenote, but watch out for crocs! It's 6.5km south of the T-junction, near the Reserva de la Biosfera Sian Ka'an entrance.

⭐L'Hotelito HOTEL **$$**
(☑984-160-02-29; www.hotelitotulum.com; Av Tulum s/n; d incl breakfast US$60; 🚲❄@🛜) Wooden boardwalks pass through a jungle-like side patio to generous, breezy rooms at this character-packed, Italian-run hotel. The attached restaurant does good breakfasts, too. Two rooms upstairs come with wide balconies, but they also catch more street noise from the main strip down below.

🍴 Eating

⭐Taquería Honorio TAQUERÍA **$**
(Satélite Sur s/n; tacos M$13, tortas M$28; ☺5:30pm-1:30am Tue-Sun) It began as a street stall and became such a hit that it's now a taco joint with a proper roof overhead. Yucatecan classics like *relleno negro* (shredded turkey in dark sauce) and *cochinita* (pulled pork in annatto marinade) are served on handmade tortillas and *tortas* (sandwiches). You should definitely eat here.

Antojitos la Chiapaneca TAQUERÍA **$**
(Av Tulum s/n, btwn Júpiter & Acuario; tacos & antojitos M$7-10, tortas M$15-20; ☺5:30pm-1am) A good, cheap option to get your late-night taco fix. You'll often have to wait for a table at this popular spot. In addition to *al pastor* (spit-roasted marinated pork) tacos, the Chiapaneca does tasty Yucatecan snacks, such as *panuchos* (fried tortillas with beans and toppings) and *salbutes* (same as *panuchos* sans beans).

Barracuda SEAFOOD **$$**
(www.facebook.com/barracudatulum1; Av Tulum; mains M$80-180; ☺noon-9:30pm Tue-Sun; 🛜) A very popular seafood eatery known for its *parillada de mariscos,* a large platter (for two people) with grilled fish, shrimp, lobster, octopus and squid.

ℹ Getting There & Around

If you're headed for Valladolid, be sure your bus is traveling the short route through Chemax, not via Cancún. *Colectivos* leave from Avenida Tulum for **Playa del Carmen** (M$40, 45 minutes). **Colectivos for Felipe Carrillo Puerto** (Av Tulum

MEXICO'S YUCATÁN & CHIAPAS TULUM

BUSES FROM TULUM

DESTINATION	COST (M$)	DURATION (HR)	FREQUENCY (DAILY)
Cancún	92-130	2	frequent
Chetumal	174-268	3¼-4	frequent
Chichén Itzá	190	2½-2¾	2; 9am, 2:45pm
Cobá	66	1	1; 10:10am
Felipe Carrillo Puerto	54-92	1¼	frequent, consider taking a *colectivo*
Laguna Bacalar	180	3	1; 8:30pm
Mahahual	240	2½	2; 9am, 5:45pm
Mérida	206-298	4-5	frequent
Playa del Carmen	38-62	1	frequent
Valladolid	84-108	2	frequent

s/n; M$50, one hour) depart from a block south of the ADO bus terminal.

Tulum's **ADO bus terminal** (www.ado.com. mx; Av Tulum s/n, btwn Calles Alfa & Júpiter) is toward the southern end of town. **Colectivos** to the beach depart from the corner of Venus and Orión.

Cobá

984 / POP 1300

Though not as large as some of the more famous ruins, Cobá is cool because you feel like you're in an Indiana Jones flick. It's set deep in the jungle and many of the ruins are yet to be excavated. Walk along ancient *sacbés* (ceremonial limestone avenues or paths between great Maya cities), climb up vine-covered mounds, and ascend to the top of Nohoch Mul for a spectacular view of the surrounding jungle.

From a sustainable-tourism perspective, it's great to stay the night in small communities like Cobá.

Sights

Cobá Ruins   ARCHAEOLOGICAL SITE
(www.inah.gob.mx; M$64, guides M$500, bike rentals M$45, parking M$50; 8am-5pm; P) The archaeological site entrance, at the end of the road on the southeast corner of Laguna Cobá, has a parking lot with surrounding eateries and snack stands. Be prepared to walk several kilometers on paths, depending on how much you want to see. If you arrive after 11am, you'll feel a bit like a sheep in a flock.

➡ Grupo Cobá

The most prominent structure in the Grupo Cobá is La Iglesia (the Church). It's an enormous pyramid; if you were allowed to climb it, you could see the surrounding lakes (which look lovely on a clear day) and the Nohoch Mul pyramid. To reach it walk just under 100m along the main path from the entrance and turn right.

➡ Grupo Macanxoc

As you head for Grupo Macanxoc you'll see interesting flora along the 1km-long trail. At the end of the path stands a group of restored stelae that bore reliefs of royal women who are thought to have come from Tikal. You'll find the path to Macanxoc about 200m beyond the *juego de pelota*.

➡ Grupo de las Pinturas

The temple at Grupo de las Pinturas (Paintings Group) bears traces of glyphs and frescoes above its door and remnants of richly colored plaster inside. You approach the temple from the southeast. Leave by the trail at the northwest (opposite the temple steps) to see two stelae. The first of these is 20m along, beneath a *palapa*. Here, a regal figure stands over two others, one of them kneeling with his hands bound behind him.

➡ Grupo Nohoch Mul

Nohoch Mul (Big Mound) is also known as the Great Pyramid, which sounds a lot better than Big Mound. It reaches a height of 42m, making it the second-tallest Maya structure on the Yucatán Peninsula (Calakmul's Estructura II, at 45m, is the tallest). Climbing the old steps can be scary for some. Two diving gods are carved over the doorway of the temple at the top (built in the post-Classic period, AD 1100–1450), similar to sculptures at Tulum.

Activities

Bicycle Rental   BICYCLE RENTAL
(per day M$50; 8am-5pm) If you want to hit the cenotes south of town, you can can rent a bike at this place on the main drag, next to Restaurant La Pirámide. Hotel Sac-Be rents bicycles, too.

Cenotes Choo-Ha,
Tamcach-Ha & Multún-Ha   SWIMMING
(per cenote M$55; 8am-6pm) About 6km south of the town of Cobá, on the road to Chan Chen, you'll find a series of three locally administered cenotes: Choo-Ha, Tamcach-Ha and Multún-Ha. These cavern-like cenotes are nice spots to cool off with a swim, or a snorkel if you bring your own gear.

Sleeping & Eating

Hotel Sac-Be   HOTEL $
(cell 984-1443006; www.hotelsacbe.com; dm M$150, d/tr M$550/650; P 🐕 ❄) The best budget digs in town. Clean and friendly, the Sac-Be is actually two sister properties on the main strip heading into Cobá. It offers air-conditioned dorms with in-room bathrooms and private rooms that sleep up to four people.

Restaurant Ki-Jamal   MEXICAN $$
(mains M$70-160, lunch buffet M$170; 8am-5pm; P 📶) 🍃 Owned by the local Maya community, Ki-Jamal (which means 'tasty food' in Maya) does indeed do some tasty traditional dishes and there's a daily lunch buffet as well. It's a pleasant spot for a meal

when there are no tour buses around. It's in the ruins parking lot.

ⓘ Getting There & Away

Most buses serving Cobá swing down to the ruins to drop off passengers at a small **bus stop**; some only go as far as Hotel El Bocadito, which also serves as a **bus stop**. Buses run six times daily between Tulum and Cobá (M$50 to M$68, 45 minutes). Buses also go to Valladolid (M$60 to M$70, 45 minutes) and Chichén Itzá (M$120, 1½ hours).

Day-trippers from Tulum can reach Cobá by taking **colectivos** (M$50) that depart from Av Tulum and Calle Osiris.

The road from Cobá to Chemax is arrow-straight and in good shape. If you're driving to Valladolid or Chichén Itzá, this is the way to go.

Laguna Bacalar

☏ 983 / POP 11,000

Laguna Bacalar comes as a surprise in this region of scrubby jungle. More than 60km long with a bottom of sparkling white sand, this crystal-clear lake offers opportunities for camping, swimming, kayaking and simply lazing around.

The small, sleepy, lakeside town of Bacalar lies east of the highway, 125km south of Felipe Carrillo Puerto. It's noted mostly for its old Spanish fortress and popular *balnearios* (swimming grounds). There's not a lot else going on, but that's why people like it here. Around the town plaza, you'll find an ATM, a small grocery store, a taxi stand and tourist information office.

◎ Sights & Activities

Fortress   FORTRESS
(cnr Av 3 & Calle 22; M$67; ⊙9am-7pm Tue-Sun) The fortress above the lagoon was built to protect citizens from raids by pirates and the local indigenous population. It also served as an important outpost for the Spanish in the War of the Castes. In 1859 it was seized by Maya rebels, who held the fort until Quintana Roo was finally conquered by Mexican troops in 1901.

Today, with formidable cannons still on its ramparts, the fortress remains an imposing sight. It houses a museum exhibiting colonial armaments and uniforms from the 17th and 18th centuries.

Cenote Azul   SWIMMING
(Hwy 307 Km 34; adult/child under 10yr M$10/free; ⊙10am-6pm) Just shy of the south end of

MAYA-RUN ECOTOURISM PARADISE

About 8km south of Felipe Carrillo Puerto, off Hwy 307, you'll find a 3km dirt road leading to Síijil Noh Há (☏984-834-05-25; siijilnohhankp@gmail.com; off Hwy 307, Laguna Ocom turnoff; admission M$15, kayaks M$50, cabañas M$250; ⊙7am-7pm), a sublime, solar-powered ecotourism center. Run by the local Maya community, the wooded grounds overlook a quiet lake shore. You can rent a kayak, take a dip in a freshwater spring and go hiking or biking along nature trails.

If you like what you see, you can stay in a rustic cabin here. Taxis from town charge M$120 to Síijil, or catch a southbound *colectivo* to the turnoff and walk the 3km.

the *costera* (coast highway) and about 3km south of Bacalar's city center is this cenote, a 90m-deep natural pool with an onsite bar and restaurant. It's 200m east of Hwy 307, so many buses will drop you nearby. You can rent kayaks here.

Balneario   SWIMMING
(Av Costera s/n, cnr Calle 14; ⊙9am-5pm) **FREE** This beautiful public swimming spot lies several blocks south of the fort, along Avenida Costera. Admission is free, but parking costs M$10.

⌖ Sleeping

Hostal Pata de Perro   HOSTEL **$**
(☏983-834-20-62; www.patadeperrobacalar.com; Calle 22 No 63; d from M$510, ste M$750-1560; ✆❊ᢙ) This adults-only hostel on the square houses immaculate rooms, ranging from three-bed setups with shared bathrooms to ample suites with kitchenettes and private bathrooms. Your detail-oriented hosts, Veronica and Alejandro, go out of their way to make sure you have a pleasant stay. Curiously, the 'dog's paw' doesn't accept pets.

Amigo's Hotel Bacalar   HOTEL **$$**
(☏983-107-92-34; www.bacalar.net; Av Costera s/n; d M$900; 🅿✆❊@ᢙ) Right on the lake and about 500m south of the fort, this ideally located property has five spacious guest rooms with king-size beds, hammocks, satellite TV,

terraces and a *palapa*-covered common area with a lake view.

🍴 Eating

Orizaba
MEXICAN **$**
(Av 7, btwn Calles 24 & 26; breakfast M$30-50, set menu M$60; ◷8am-4pm) Highly recommended by locals and expats alike, this place prepares breakfast and a set menu of home-style Mexican favorites such as *poc-chuc* (grilled pork) in a casual setting.

★ La Playita
SEAFOOD **$$**
(www.laplayitabacalar.com; Av Costera 765, cnr Calle 26; mains M$104-159; ◷2-10pm Tue-Sun; 🕾) A sign outside reads, 'Eat, drink and swim' – and that pretty much sums it up. Fish and seafood dishes are tasty, albeit on the smallish side, but the Alipús mezcal and fine swimming certainly make up for that. A large rubber tree, which provides shade in the pebbly garden, was nearly uprooted in 2007 when Hurricane Dean pummeled the coast.

ℹ️ Getting There & Away

Buses don't enter town; however, taxis and most *combis* will drop you at the town square. Buses arrive at the Bacalar's ADO terminal on Hwy 307, near Calle 30. From there it's about a 10-block walk southeast to the main square or you can grab a taxi for M$15.

Mahahual

📞 983 / POP 920

Laid-back fishing town Mahahual is best known for its cool Caribbean vibe, excellent diving and sustainable development.

🎯 Sights & Activities

Banco Chinchorro
DIVE SITE
Divers won't want to miss the reefs and underwater fantasy worlds of the Banco Chinchorro, the largest coral atoll in the northern hemisphere. Some 45km long and up to 14km wide, Chinchorro's western edge lies about 30km off the coast, and dozens of ships have fallen victim to its barely submerged ring of coral.

Mahahual Dive Centre
DIVING
(📞983-102-09-92, cell 983-1367693; www.mahahualdivecentre.com; Huachinango Km 0.7, cnr Cazón; 2-/3-tank dives M$2450/2850, snorkeling M$1650) Does trips to nearby sites as well as Banco Chinchorro and the fishing village of Punta Herrero.

🛏️ Sleeping

Hostal Jardín Mahahual
HOTEL **$**
(✏983-834-57-22; www.facebook.com/hostal.jardin; Sardina s/n, cnr Rubia; dm M$130, r with/without air-con M$620/450; ❄❅🕾) For the price, this is a surprisingly stylish little hostel with five private rooms and an eight-bed coed dorm. Rooms are spotless and the dorms are the best in town by far. It's set back two blocks from the beach, near Calle Rubia.

🍴 Eating

★ Nohoch Kay
SEAFOOD **$$**
(Big Fish; cnr Malecón & Cazón; mains M$125-160, platter per person M$300; ◷1-9:30pm; 🕾) Nohoch Kay, aka the Big Fish, definitely lives up to its name. Don't miss this beachfront Mexican-owned restaurant, where they prepare succulent whole fish in a garlic and white-wine sauce, or opt for the surf-and-turf platter for two, which includes lobster, steak, octopus and shrimp.

Fernando's 100% Agave
MEXICAN **$$**
(Malecón, btwn Calles Martillo & Coronado; mains M$110-180; ◷2-10pm Tue-Sun) With its new smaller boardwalk location, Fernando's feels more intimate now. The restaurant-bar offers up various fish and seafood dishes prepared with sauces ranging from sweet coconut-mango to spicy red. After dinner – or before – try a smooth-tasting Siete Leguas tequila.

ℹ️ Getting There & Away

There's no official bus terminal in Mahahual. At last visit, liquor store **Solo Chelas** (at Calles Huachinango and Cherna) was selling tickets for a daily ADO northbound bus, which departs Mahahual at 5pm for Tulum (M$240, three hours), Playa del Carmen (M$310, four hours) and Cancún (M$370, five hours). A Xcalak-bound Caribe bus (M$50, 1¼ hours) passes through town along Calle Huachinango, usually between 7am and 8am.

Shuttle vans leave hourly from 5:45am to 6:45pm to Chetumal (M$88, 2½ hours), Laguna Bacalar (M$55, two hours) and Limones (M$50, one hour), where you can catch frequent northbound buses. The terminal is on the corner of Calles Sardina and Cherna, on the soccer field's north end.

Valladolid

📞 985 / POP 49,000

Also known as the Sultaness of the East, Yucatán's third-largest city is known for its quiet streets and sun-splashed pastel walls. It's worth staying here for a few days or even a week, as the provincial town makes a great hub for visits to Río Lagartos, Chichén Itzá, Ek' Balam and a number of nearby cenotes. The city resides at that magic point where there's plenty to do, yet it still feels small, manageable and affordable.

◎ Sights

★ Casa de los Venados   MUSEUM
(🖉985-856-22-89; www.casadelosvenados.com; Calle 40 No 204, btwn Calles 41 & 43; admission by donation; ☺tours 10am or by appointment) Featuring over 3000 pieces of museum-quality Mexican folk art, this private collection is unique in that objects are presented in a house, in the context that they were originally designed for, instead of being roped off in glass cases. The tour (in English or Spanish) brushes on the origins of some of the more important pieces and the story of the award-winning restored colonial mansion that houses them.

Templo de San Bernardino   CHURCH
(Church of San Bernardino; cnr Calles 49 & 51; Mon-Sat M$30, Sun free; ☺9am-7pm) The Templo de San Bernardino and the adjacent **Convento de Sisal** are about 700m southwest of the plaza. They were constructed between 1552 and 1560 to serve the dual functions of fortress and church. The church's charming decoration includes beautiful rose-colored walls, arches, some recently uncovered 16th-century frescoes and a small image of the Virgin on the altar. These are about the only original items remaining; the grand wooden *retablo* (altarpiece) dates from the 19th century.

⚹ Activities

★ Hacienda San Lorenzo Oxman   SWIMMING
(off Calle 54; M$30; ☺9am-6pm) Once a *henequén* plantation and a refuge for War of the Castes insurgents in the mid-19th century, today the hacienda's main draw is a gorgeous cenote that's far less crowded than other sinkholes in and around Valladolid, especially if you visit Monday through Thursday.

To get there by bike or car, take Calle 41A (Calzada de los Frailes) past the Templo de San Bernardino along Calle 54A, turn right on Avenida de los Frailes, then hang a left on Calle 54 and head about 3km southwest. A taxi to the hacienda costs about M$70.

Cenote X'Kekén   SWIMMING
(Cenote Dzitnup; 1/2 cenotes M$60/90; ☺8:30am-5:20pm) One of two cenotes at Dzitnup (recently renamed X'Kekén Jungle Park), X'Kekén is a massive limestone formation with stalactites hanging from its ceiling. The pool is artificially lit and very swimmable. Here you can also take a dip in cenote Samulá, a lovely cavern pool with *álamo* roots stretching down many meters.

Shared *colectivos* depart for Cenote X'Kekén from Calle 44, between Calles 41 and 43.

🛏 Sleeping

Hotel Zací   HOTEL $
(🖉985-856-21-67; www.hotelzaci.com.mx; Calle 44 No 191; d M$595; P◉❄🌐☁🏊) Conveniently located one block west of the bus station and a block east of the main plaza, rooms here get the colonial treatment, as does the lobby with its handsome antique furniture. The Zací also runs a 'more austere' budget hotel across the street but we much prefer this one, where you get a pool out back.

Hostel La Candelaria   HOSTEL $
(🖉985-856-22-67; www.hostelvalladolidyucatan.com; Calle 35 No 201F; dm/r incl breakfast M$160/440; ◉@☁) A friendly place right on a quiet little square, this hostel can get a little cramped and hot, but there are two kitchens, a cozy garden area complete with hammocks, a gals-only dorm, and plenty of hangout space, making it one of the best hostels in town. The hostel also rents bikes for M$15 per hour.

★ La Aurora   HOTEL $$
(🖉985-856-12-19; www.hotellaaurora.com; Calle 42 No 192; d M$640; P◉❄☁🏊) If only more economical hotels were like the colonial-style Aurora. Well-appointed rooms overlook a pretty courtyard with a pool and potted plants, and the kicker is the rooftop Jacuzzi and bar. If possible, avoid the noisier street-facing rooms.

🍴 Eating

★ Yerba Buena del Sisal   MEXICAN $
(🖉985-856-14-06; www.facebook.com/yerbabuenadelsisal; Calle 54A No 217; mains M$60-80; ☺8am-5pm Tue-Sun; ☁🍴) Wonderfully healthy and delicious dishes are served in a peaceful garden. Tortilla chips and three delectable salsas come to the table while you look over the menu, which offers many great vegetarian and mostly organic dishes, such

SELDOM-VISITED BEACHES EAST OF PROGRESO

Time seems to stand still on these secluded, breezy beaches – escapists will love the solitude of **Dzilam de Bravo** and **Santa Clara**.

If you don't have wheels, a bus in port town Progreso (30km north of Mérida) departs from Calles 29 and 82 at 7:30am and 2:30pm and goes as far east as Dzilam de Bravo before returning to Progreso.

Hotel Kame House (📞 cell 991-1066847, cell in USA 770-5400509; www.hotelkamehouse. com; Calle 15 No 16, Santa Clara; r M$550-750; 🅿️ ❄️ 🛜) You can either stay in breezy rooms with ocean views in the main house, or just across the beach there's an unusual round building with two fan-cooled rooms, tasteful rustic decor and large showers built from recycled objects. You'll have to head into town for meals, but it's easily walkable. Kame rents bodyboards and snorkeling equipment.

It's on the east end of Santa Clara.

Perla Escondida (📞 cell 991-1079321; miriam_figueroa2@hotmail.com; Calle 11 Km 1; r M$600; 🅿️ ❄️ ❄️ 🛜 🐕) On a quiet white-sand coast just west of Dzilam de Bravo, the Perla Escondida (Hidden Pearl) truly lives up to its name. Rustic cabins sit right on the beach and your hosts can arrange various activities, such as birdwatching, a cenote outing or fishing trips. A sandbar about a half-kilometer offshore makes a relaxing spot to while away the day.

---

as the delightful *tacos maculum* (made with handmade corn tortillas, beans, cheese and aromatic Mexican pepper leaf).

If you're craving meat, try the *tacos de carne ahumada* (smoked pork tacos).

Conato 1910　　　　　　　　　MEXICAN **$$**
(Calle 40 No 226; mains M$60-130; ⏱ 5pm-midnight Wed-Mon; 🛜 🍽) A meeting spot for revolutionaries in the early 20th century, this historic building now houses one of the best restaurants in town in an atmospheric setting with muraled walls. The vegetarian-friendly menu features a wide variety of options, such as salads and pastas, and there are also excellent chicken and beef dishes.

ℹ Getting There & Away

BUS & COLECTIVO

Valladolid's main bus terminal is the convenient **ADO bus terminal** (www.ado.com.mx; cnr Calles 39 & 46). The main 1st-class services are ADO, ADO GL and OCC; Oriente and Mayab run 2nd-class buses.

Buses to Chichén Itzá/Pisté stop near the ruins during opening hours.

Often faster, more reliable and more comfortable than 2nd-class buses are the *colectivos* that depart as soon as their seats are filled. Most operate from 7am or 8am to about 7pm.

Direct services run to **Mérida** (near the ADO bus terminal; M$110, two hours) and **Cancún** (Calle 41, cnr Calle 38; one block east of the plaza; M$170; two hours); confirm they're nonstop. *Colectivos* for **Pisté and Chichén Itzá** (M$30,

one hour) leave north of the ADO bus terminal; for **Tizimín** (Calle 40, btwn Calles 35 & 37; M$40, 40 minutes) from Calle 40 between Calles 35 and 37; and for **Ek' Balam** (Calle 44, btwn Calles 35 & 37; M$50) take a 'Santa Rita' *colectivo* from Calle 44 between Calles 35 and 37.

Chichén Itzá

📞 985 / POP 5500

The Chichén Itzá archaeological site is located in the town of Pisté.

◉ Sights

Chichén Itzá　　　　　　ARCHAEOLOGICAL SITE
(Mouth of the Well of the Itzáes; www.chichenitza. inah.gob.mx; off Hwy 180, Pisté; adult/child under 13yr M$220/free, guided tours M$750; ⏱ 8am-5pm Tue-Sun; 🅿️) The most famous and best restored of the Yucatán Maya sites, Chichén Itzá, while tremendously overcrowded – every gawker and his or her grandmother is trying to check off the new seven wonders of the world – will still impress even the most jaded visitor. Many mysteries of the Maya astronomical calendar are made clear when one understands the design of the 'time temples' here. Other than a few minor passageways, climbing on the structures is not allowed.

➡ El Castillo

Upon entering Chichén Itzá, El Castillo (aka the Pyramid of Kukulcán) rises before you in all its grandeur. The first temple here was pre-Toltec, built around AD 800, but the present 25m-high structure, built over the old one, has the plumed serpent sculpted along the stairways and Toltec warriors represented in the doorway carvings at the top of the temple. You won't see the carvings, however, as ascending the pyramid was prohibited after a woman fell to her death in 2006.

➡ Gran Juego de Pelota

The great ball court, the largest and most impressive in Mexico, is only one of the city's eight courts, indicative of the importance the games held here. The court, to the left of the visitors' center, is flanked by temples at either end and is bounded by towering parallel walls with stone rings cemented up high. Along the walls of the ball court are stone reliefs, including scenes of decapitations of players.

➡ Templo del Barbado

The structure at the ball court's north end, called the Temple of the Bearded Man after a carving inside of it, has finely sculpted pillars and reliefs of flowers, birds and trees.

➡ Plataforma de los Cráneos

The Platform of Skulls (Tzompantli in Náhuatl, a Maya dialect) is between the Templo de los Jaguares y Escudos and El Castillo. You can't mistake it, because the T-shaped platform is festooned with carved skulls and eagles tearing open the chests of men to eat their hearts. In ancient days this platform was used to display the heads of sacrificial victims.

➡ Plataforma de las Águilas y los Jaguares

Adjacent to the Platform of Skulls, the carvings on the Platform of the Eagles and Jaguars depict those animals gruesomely grabbing human hearts in their claws. It is thought that this platform was part of a temple dedicated to the military legions responsible for capturing sacrificial victims.

➡ Cenote Sagrado

From the Platform of Skulls, a 400m rough stone *sacbé* (path) runs north (a five-minute walk) to the huge sunken well that gave this city its name. The Sacred Cenote is an awesome natural well, some 60m in diameter and 35m deep. The walls between the summit and the water's surface are ensnared in tangled vines and other vegetation.

➡ Plaza de las Mil Columnas

Comprising the Templo de los Guerreros (Temple of the Warriors), the Templo de Chac-Mool (Temple of Chac-Mool) and the Baño de Vapor (Sweat House or Steam Bath), this group, behind El Castillo, takes its name (Group of the Thousand Columns) from the forest of pillars stretching south and east.

➡ El Osario

The Ossuary, otherwise known as the Bonehouse or the Tumba del Gran Sacerdote (High Priest's Grave), is a ruined pyramid to the southwest of El Castillo. As with most of the buildings in this southern section, the architecture is more Puuc than Toltec. It's notable for the beautiful serpent heads at the base of its staircases.

➡ El Caracol

Called El Caracol (The Snail) by the Spaniards for its interior spiral staircase, this observatory, to the south of the Ossuary, is one of the most fascinating and important of all Chichén Itzá's buildings (but, alas, you can't enter it). Its circular design resembles some central highlands structures, although, surprisingly, not those of Toltec Tula.

Sleeping

Pirámide Inn HOTEL $

(☎985-851-01-15; www.piramideinn.com; Calle 15 No 30; campsites per person M$50, r M$500; P ⊖ ❄ ☎ ≋ 🐾) Campers can pitch a tent or hang a hammock under a *palapa*, enjoy the inn's pool, have use of tepid showers and

BUSES FROM CHICHÉN ITZÁ

DESTINATION	COST (M$)	DURATION (HR)	FREQUENCY (DAILY)
Cancún	137-258	3-4½	9
Cobá	69	2	1; 7:30am
Mérida	78-144	1¾-2½	frequent
Playa del Carmen	135-282	3½-4	2; 7:30am, 4:30pm
Tulum	100-190	2½-3	3
Valladolid	30	1	8

watch satellite TV in the lobby. Campers also have use of clean shared toilet facilities and a safe place to stow gear. The spacious rooms have decent bathrooms and two spring-me-to-the-moon double beds.

The hotel also has a book exchange and a Maya-style sweat lodge. Located on the main drag in Pisté, this place is as close as you can get to Chichén Itzá for cheap, though it's still a hike of about 1.5km. Animals are welcome.

Hotel Chichén Itzá HOTEL **$$**
(☑985-851-00-22, in USA 800-235-4079; www.mayaland.com; Calle 15 No 45; r/ste M$980/1360; P❄❁🕸🏊) On the west side of Pisté, this hotel has 42 pleasant rooms with tiled floors and old-style brick-tiled ceilings. Rooms in the upper range face the pool and the land-scaped grounds, and all have firm beds and minibars. Parents may bring two kids under 13 years old for free.

✖ Eating

Cocina Económica Fabiola MEXICAN **$**
(Calle 15 s/n; mains M$30-60; ⊙7am-10pm) For a good, honest, cheap meal hit this humble little place at the end of the strip of eateries opposite the church. The *sopa de lima* (lime soup) and *pollo yucateco* (Yucatecan chicken) come highly recommended.

Las Mestizas MEXICAN **$$**
(Calle 15 s/n; mains M$70-100; ⊙8am-10pm; ❄🕸) *The* place to go in town if you're craving decent Yucatecan fare. There's indoor and outdoor seating – depending on the time of day, an outdoor table may mean you'll be getting tour-bus fumes to go along with that *cochinita* (slow-cooked pork).

❶ Getting There & Away

Oriente has ticket offices near the east and west sides of Pisté, and 2nd-class buses passing through town stop almost anywhere along the way. Many 1st-class buses only hit the ruins and the west side of town, close to the toll highway.

Shared vans to Valladolid (M$30, 40 minutes) pass through town regularly.

Mérida

📞999 / POP 780,000

Since the Spanish conquest, Mérida has been the cultural capital of the entire Yucatán Peninsula. At times provincial, at others *'muy cosmopolitano,'* it is a town steeped in colonial history, with narrow streets, broad central plazas and the region's best muse-

ums. It's also a perfect place from which to kick off your adventure into the rest of Yucatán state. There are cheap eats, good hostels and hotels, thriving markets and events happening just about every night somewhere in the downtown area.

Long popular with European travelers looking to go beyond the hubbub of Quintana Roo's resort towns, Mérida is not an 'undiscovered Mexican gem' like some of the tourist brochures claim. Simply put, it's a tourist town, but a tourist town too big to feel like a tourist trap. And as the capital of Yucatán state, Mérida is also the cultural crossroads of the region, and there's something just a smidge elitist about Mérida: the people who live here have a beautiful town, and they know it.

◉ Sights

★**Gran Museo del Mundo Maya** MUSEUM
(Calle 60 Nte No 299E; M$150; ⊙8am-5pm Wed-Mon, light & sound show 8:30pm; P; 🚌R-2) A world-class museum celebrating Maya culture, the Gran Museo houses a permanent collection of more than 1100 remarkably well-preserved artifacts, including a reclining *chacmool* sculpture from Chichén Itzá and a cool underworld figure unearthed at Ek' Balam (check out homeboy's punk-rock skull belt and reptile headdress). If you're planning on visiting the area's ruins, drop by here first for some context and an up-close look at some of the fascinating pieces found at the sites.

★**Parque Santa Lucía** PARK
(cnr Calles 60 & 55) The pretty little Parque Santa Lucía has arcades on the north and west sides; this was where travelers would get on or off the stagecoaches that linked towns and villages with the provincial capital. Today it's a popular restaurant area and venue for **Serentas Yucatecas** (Yucatacen Serenades), a free weekly concert on Thursday at 9pm.

★**Casa de Montejo** MUSEUM
(Museo Casa Montejo; www.casasdeculturabana mex.com/museocasamontejo; Calle 63 No 506, Palacio de Montejo; ⊙10am-7pm Mon-Sat, to 2pm Sun) FREE Casa de Montejo is on the south side of the Plaza Grande and dates from 1549. It originally housed soldiers but was soon converted into a mansion that served members of the Montejo family until 1970. Today it houses a bank and museum with a permanent exhibition of renovated Victo-

WORTH A TRIP

DIY ADVENTURES IN THE YUCATÁN

Reserva de la Biosfera Ría Celestún The 591-sq-km Reserva de la Biosfera Ría Celestún is home to a huge variety of animals and birdlife, including a large flamingo colony. You can see flamingos (via boat tours) year-round in Celestún, but they're usually out in full force from November to mid-March

Uxmal Ruins (Hwy 261 Km 78; adult/child under 13yr M$203/free, light & sound show M$83, parking M$30, guides M$700; ⊘ site 8am-5pm, light & sound show 8pm Apr-Oct & 7pm Nov-Mar; 🚻) Pronounced 'oosh-mahl', Uxmal is one impressive set of ruins, easily ranking among the top Maya archaeological sites. It is a large site with some fascinating structures in good condition and bearing a riot of ornamentation. Adding to its appeal is Uxmal's setting in the hilly Puuc region, which lent its name to the architectural patterns in this area.

Río Lagartos Adventures (📱cell 986-1008390; www.riolagartosadventures.com; Calle 19 No 134; per boat 2hr M$1200, fly-fishing from M$2200) This outfit run by local expert Diego Núñez Martinez does various water and land expeditions, including flamingo- and crocodile-watching, snorkeling to Isla Cerritos, fly-fishing and excursions designed for photography. Diego is a licensed English-speaking guide with formal training as a naturalist and is up to date on the area's fauna and flora, which includes some 400 bird species. He organizes the tours out of Ria Maya Restaurante.

Dzibilchaltún (Place of Inscribed Flat Stones; adult/child under 12yr M$132/free, parking M$20; ⊘ site 8am-5pm, museum 9am-4pm Tue-Sun; 🅿) Lying about 17km due north of central Mérida, Dzibilchaltún was the longest continuously utilized Maya administrative and ceremonial city, serving the Maya from around 1500 BC until the European conquest in the 1540s. At the height of its greatness, Dzibilchaltún covered 15 sq km. Some 8400 structures were mapped by archaeologists in the 1960s; few of these have been excavated. Aside from the ruins, the site offers a lovely, swimmable cenote and a Maya museum.

Ek' Balam (adult/child under 13yr M$181/free, guide M$600; ⊘8am-5pm) The fascinating ruined city of Ek' Balam reached its peak in the 8th century, before being suddenly abandoned. Vegetation still covers much of the archaeological site, but excavations and restoration continue to add to the sights, including an interesting ziggurat-like structure near the entrance, as well as a fine arch and a ball court. Most impressive is the gargantuan Acrópolis, whose well-restored base is 160m long and holds a 'gallery' – actually a series of separate chambers.

---

rian, neorococo and neorenaissance furnishings of the historic building.

Outside, take a close look at the facade, where triumphant conquistadors with halberds stand on the heads of generic barbarians (though they're not Maya, the association is inescapable). Typical of the symbolism in colonial statuary, the vanquished are rendered much smaller than the victors; works on various churches throughout the region feature big priests towering over or in front of small indigenous people. Also gazing across the plaza from the facade are busts of Montejo the Elder, his wife and his daughter.

Plaza Grande   PLAZA
FREE One of the nicest plazas in Mexico, huge laurel trees shade the park's benches and wide sidewalks. It was the religious and social center of ancient T'ho; under the

Spanish it was the Plaza de Armas, the parade ground, laid out by Francisco de Montejo (the Younger).

🏃 Activities

Bici Mérida   BICYCLE RENTAL
(📱cell 999-2873538; Paseo de Montejo s/n, btwn Calles 45 & 47; per hr M$30; ⊘8am-9pm Mon-Fri, to 6pm Sat, 7am-2pm Sun; 🚌R-2) Rents mountain bikes, tandems, bicycles for kids and other cool rides.

Historic Center Tours   WALKING TOUR
(📱999-942-00-00; www.merida.gob.mx/turismo; Calle 62 s/n, Plaza Grande; ⊘walking tours 9:30am Mon-Sat) **FREE** The city tourist office runs free guided walking tours of the historic center departing daily from the Palacio Municipal. You can also rent audio guides here for M$80 if you prefer to go it alone.

Mérida

Fiesta Americana (700m)

Calle 43

Calle 45

Calle 47

Parque Santa Ana 12

Calle 47A

13

Calle 49

14

Calle 49

Calle 74A

Calle 74

Calle 72

Calle 70

Calle 68

Calle 66

Calle 64

Calle 62

Calle 60

Calle 58

Calle 51

9

Calle 51

6

Calle 53

Calle 53

Calle 55

15

Calle 55

Parque Santa Lucía 2

8

Calle 57

10 7

Parque de Santiago

Calle 57

Parque Zoológico del Centenario (950m)

11

Calle 59

Parque de la Madre

Parque Hidalgo

Calle 61

Calle 68

16

3

Calle 64

Calle 63

5

Casa de Montejo 1

Calle 65

Calle 64

17

Calle 62

Calle 60

Calle 70

Calle 68

Calle 66

Calle 58

Calle 56A

(10km)

Calle 67

Terminal de Segunda Clase

Calle 67

Calle 69

Parque de San Juan

CAME Bus Terminal

Calle 69

Calle 71

Mérida

⊙ **Top Sights**
  1 Casa de Montejo C6
  2 Parque Santa Lucía D4

⊙ **Sights**
  3 Plaza Grande C5

⊙ **Activities, Courses & Tours**
  4 Bici Mérida..E2
  5 Historic Center Tours.........................C5

⊟ **Sleeping**
  6 Art Apart Hostel................................D3
  7 Hotel Santa Lucía.............................. D4
  8 Luz en Yucatán.................................. D4
  9 Nómadas Hostel C3

⊗ **Eating**
 10 La Chaya Maya.................................. D4
 11 La Chaya Maya.................................. C4
 12 La Socorrito......................................D2
 13 Manjar Blanco...................................D2

⊙ **Drinking & Nightlife**
 14 La Negrita D2
 15 Orgánico..D3

⊛ **Entertainment**
 16 Centro Cultural Olimpo......................C5

⊟ **Shopping**
 17 Hamacas Mérida................................ C6

🎉 Festivals & Events

Mérida Fest   CULTURAL
(www.merida.gob.mx/festival; ☉Jan) This cultural event held throughout most of January celebrates the founding of the city with art exhibits, concerts, theater and book presentations at various venues.

🛏 Sleeping

Nómadas Hostel   HOSTEL **$**
(☑999-924-52-23; www.nomadastravel.com; Calle 62 No 433; dm from M$169, d M$450, without bathroom M$390; P ⊟ ✳ @ ⊛ ⊠) One of Mérida's best hostels, it has mixed and women's dorms, as well as private rooms. Guests have use of a fully equipped kitchen with fridge, as well as showers and hand-laundry facilities. It even has free salsa and cooking classes, and an amazing pool out back. See the hostel's website for various tours available to nearby ruins.

Art Apart Hostel   HOSTEL **$**
(☑999-923-24-63; www.artaparthostel.com; Calle 60 No 456A; dm with fan/air-con M$135/160, r

WORTH THE SPLURGE

While many much blander hotels are loudly claiming to be 'boutique,' **Luz en Yucatán** (📞999-924-00-35; www.luzenyucatan.com; Calle 55 No 499; r US$59-79, ste US$99, apt US$69-150; 🅿️❄️✳️📶🏊) is quietly ticking all the boxes – individually decorated rooms, fabulous common areas and a wonderful pool-patio area out back. The house it offers for rent across the road, which sleeps seven people and has a hot tub, is just as good, if not better.

with fan/air-con M$400/550; ❄️✳️📶🏊) It's like stepping into a museum at this funky hostel, where you'll find oddball art in every nook and cranny, including the gardens, hallways and pool area. Dorms and rooms vary; some are fairly simple, but all have original artwork. The previous owner was an eccentric collector who was much better at buying than selling the pieces.

Hotel Santa Lucía HOTEL $
(📞999-928-26-72; www.hotelsantalucia.com.mx; Calle 55 No 508; s/d/tr M$450/540/600; 🅿️❄️✳️📶🏊) Across from the park of the same name, this centrally located hotel is clean, secure and popular. The pool is small but clean, and the rooms have TV, phone and just so-so mattresses.

🍴 Eating

⭐ **Wayan'e** TAQUERÍA $
(cnr Calles 59 & 46; tacos M$11-15, tortas M$18-25; ⏰7am-2:30pm Mon-Sat) Popular for its *castacan* (fried pork belly), Wayan'e (meaning 'here it is' in Maya) is one of Mérida's premier breakfast spots. Vegetarians will find options here, such as the *huevo con ixkatic* (egg with chili) taco and fresh juices. But if you eat meat, it's all about the greasy goodness of the *castacan torta* (sandwich).

La Socorrito YUCATECAN $
(Calle 47, btwn Calles 58 & 60; tortas M$17; ⏰7am-2pm; 🚌R-2) These old pros have been slow-cooking *cochinita* in underground pits for more than six decades. You'll find this delightful hole-in-the-wall on the plaza side of the Mercado de Santa Ana.

Manjar Blanco MEXICAN $$
(Calle 47, btwn Calles 58 & 60; mains M$75-140; ⏰8am-6pm; 🚌; 🚌R-2) This family-run restaurant puts a gourmet twist on regional favorites. The *tortillitas tropicales* (fried plantains topped with smoked pork) are delicious, and sweet tooths will love the namesake *manjar blanco* (a coconut-cream dessert).

La Chaya Maya MEXICAN $$
(www.lachayamaya.com; Calle 55 No 510; mains M$67-178; ⏰1-10pm Mon-Sat, 8am-10pm Sun; 🚌) Popular with locals and tourists alike, this restaurant opened a new location in a lovely downtown colonial building. Consider La Chaya your introduction to classic Yucatecan fare like *relleno negro* (black turkey stew) or *cochinita pibil* (slow-cooked pork). The **original location** (cnr Calles 62 & 57; ⏰from 7am daily) opens for breakfast.

🍷 Drinking & Nightlife

La Negrita DANCING
(www.lanegritacantina.com; Calle 62 s/n, cnr Calle 49; ⏰noon-10pm; 🚌) If the live music here doesn't inspire you to get a tropical groove on, it's just a matter of time before the mojitos and mezcals have you dancing the night away. The rear garden makes a nice spot to catch a breather and chat with locals. Groups go on after 5pm from Wednesday to Sunday.

Orgánico CAFE
(Calle 53 No 502, btwn Calles 60 & 62; coffee M$20-42; ⏰8am-4pm Mon, to 11pm Tue-Sat; 🚌) Java junkies will love this place's organic coffee, which is prepared with beans from the highlands of Chiapas, Veracruz and Guerrero. Hungry? You'll find good vegetarian options here.

☆ Entertainment

Centro Cultural Olimpo CONCERT VENUE
(📞999-924-00-00, ext 80152; www.merida.gob.mx/capitalcultural; cnr Calles 62 & 61) Offers something nearly every night: films, concerts, art installations, you name it.

🛍️ Shopping

Hamacas Mérida HANDICRAFTS
(📞999-924-04-40; www.hamacasmerida.com.mx; Calle 65 No 510, btwn Calles 62 & 64; ⏰9am-7pm Mon-Fri, to 2pm Sat) Has a large catalog with all kinds of sizes, shapes and colors, plus it ships worldwide.

ℹ️ Getting There & Away

AIR

Aeropuerto Internacional de Mérida (Mérida International Airport; 📞999-940-60-90;

www.asur.com.mx; Hwy 180 Km 4.5; R-79)
Mérida's airport is a 10km, 20-minute ride
southwest of the Plaza Grande off Hwy 180
(Avenida de los Itzáes). It has car-rental desks,
an ATM, a currency-exchange service and a
tourist information booth.

BUS

Mérida is the bus transportation hub of the
Yucatán Peninsula. Take care with your bags on
night buses and those serving popular tourist
destinations (especially 2nd-class buses); there
have been reports of theft on some routes.

There are a number of bus terminals, and
some lines operate from (and stop at) more than
one terminal. Tickets for departure from one
terminal can often be bought at another, and
destinations overlap greatly among bus lines.
Check out www.ado.com.mx for ticket info on
some of the lines.

CAME Bus Terminal (999-920-44-44; Calle
70 s/n, btwn Calles 69 & 71) Aka the 'Terminal
de Primera Clase,' Mérida's main bus terminal has (mostly 1st-class) buses – including
ADO, OCC and ADO GL – to points around the
Yucatán Peninsula and faraway places such as
Mexico City.

Terminal de Segunda Clase (TAME; Calle 69)
Aka TAME (Terminal de Autobuses de Segunda
Clase), this terminal is just around the corner
from the CAME bus terminal. ADO, Mayab,
Oriente, Sur, TRT and ATS run mostly 2nd-class
buses to points in the state and around the peninsula, including Felipe Carrillo Puerto and Ticul.

Campeche

981 / POP 220,000

Campeche is the least visited of the Yucatán's states, laced through with lonely back
roads, friendly people, quiet coastlines and
a provincial, lost-land charm. It makes a
welcome break from the tourist hordes that
descend on the peninsula's more popular
destinations; here you'll find peace and surprising attractions.

Sights

★ **Centro Cultural
Casa Número 6**   CULTURAL CENTER
(Calle 57 No 6; M$20, audio guide M$15; 9am-
9pm) During the prerevolutionary era, when

BUSES FROM MÉRIDA

DESTINATION	COST (M$)	DURATION (HR)	FREQUENCY (DAILY)
Campeche	202-254	2½-3	frequent
Cancún	198-440	4½-6½	frequent: CAME and Terminal de Segunda Clase
Celestún	56	2½	frequent; Noreste bus terminal
Chetumal	444	6	4
Chichén Itzá	80-144	1½-2	frequent; CAME and Noreste bus terminals
Escárcega	258	4-4½	4; Terminal de Segunda Clase
Felipe Carrillo Puerto	200	6	frequent; Terminal de Segunda Clase
Izamal	27	1½	frequent; Noreste bus terminal
Mayapán	25	1½	hourly; Noreste bus terminal
Mexico City	1582-1882	20	7
Palenque	544-576	7½-10	4
Playa del Carmen	408-450	4-6	frequent
Progreso	19	1	frequent; Progreso bus terminal
Río Lagartos/San Felipe	142-196	3½	3; Noreste bus terminal
Ruta Puuc (round-trip; 30min at each site)	179	8-8½	8am; Terminal de Segunda Clase
Ticul	50-76	1¾	frequent; Terminal de Segunda Clase
Tizimín	105-110	2	frequent; Noreste bus terminal
Tulum	298	4	4
Uxmal	55	1½	5; Terminal de Segunda Clase
Valladolid	95-178	2½-3	frequent

Campeche

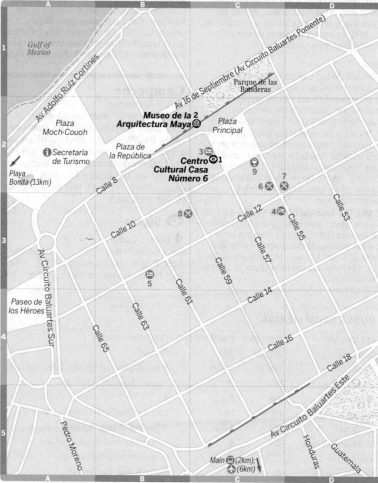

this mansion was occupied by an upper-class *campechano* family, Número 6 was a prestigious plaza address. Wandering the premises, you'll get an idea of how the city's high society lived back then. The front sitting room is furnished with Cuban-style pieces of the period. Inside are exhibition spaces, a pleasant back patio and a gift shop.

⭐**Museo de la
Arquitectura Maya**   MUSEUM
(Calle 8; M$39; ⏰9am-5:30pm Tue-Sun) The Baluarte de Nuestra Señora de la Soledad, designed to protect the Puerta del Mar,

contains the fascinating Museo de la Arquitectura Maya, the one must-see museum in Campeche. It provides an excellent overview of the sites around Campeche state and the key architectural styles associated with them. Five halls display stelae taken from various sites, accompanied by graphic representations of their carved inscriptions with brief commentaries in flawless English.

**Museo Arqueológico de
Campeche & Fuerte
de San Miguel**   MUSEUM, FORT
(Campeche Archaeological Museum; Av Escénica s/n; M$46; ⏰8:30am-5pm Tue-Sun; Ⓟ)

Campeche

⊙ **Top Sights**
1 Centro Cultural Casa Número 6 ....C2
2 Museo de la Arquitectura Maya..........C2

🛏 **Sleeping**
3 Hotel Campeche C2
4 Hotel Guarandocha Inn......................C3
5 Hotel López...B3

✕ **Eating**
6 Café La Parroquia...............................C2
7 Chef Color..C2
8 Luz de Luna B3

🍷 **Drinking & Nightlife**
9 La Casa Vieja......................................C2

MEXICO'S YUCATÁN & CHIAPAS CAMPECHE

🛏 Sleeping

Hotel Campeche HOTEL $
(📞981-816-51-83; hotelcampeche@hotmail. com; Calle 57, btwn Calles 8 & 10; s/d with fan M$280/320, with air-con M$370/450; ✳☎) Not much in the way of frills here, but the plaza-side location and big rooms in this classically crumbling building are about the best budget bet in town. A couple of rooms have little balconies looking out over the plaza.

Hotel Guarandocha Inn HOTEL $
(📞981-811-66-58; rool_2111@hotmail.com; Calle 55, btwn Calles 12 & 14; incl breakfast d M$460-550, tr M$670; ✳@☎) One of the better options in town is at this modest but pleasant hotel. Rooms are nice and spacious, and the newer ones upstairs are brighter and more open (and cost a bit more). A very simple breakfast is included.

★**Hotel López** HOTEL $$
(📞981-816-33-44; www.hotellopezcampeche.com. mx; Calle 12 No 189; s/d/ste M$650/720/980; ✳☎▦) This elegant hotel is one of Campeche's best midrange options. Small but modern and comfortably appointed rooms open onto curvy art-deco balconies around oval courtyards and pleasant greenery. Bring your swimsuit for the lovely pool out back.

✕ Eating

Café La Parroquia MEXICAN $
(📞981-816-25-30; Calle 55 No 8; mains M$60-170, lunch specials M$80; ⊙24hr) Open 24 hours, this casual restaurant appeals to both locals and foreigners with its wide-ranging menu and attentive staff. Order everything from fried

Campeche's largest colonial fort, facing the Gulf of Mexico some 4km southwest of the city center, is now home to the excellent Museo Arqueológico de Campeche. Here you can admire findings from the sites of Calakmul and Edzná, and from Isla de Jaina, an island north of town once used as a burial site for Maya aristocracy.

To get here take a bus or *combi* (minibus; marked 'Lerma') from the market. Ask the driver to let you off at the access road (just say 'Fuerte de San Miguel'), then hike 300m up the hill. Taxis cost M$50.

WORTH A TRIP

EXPLORE MORE OF CAMPECHE STATE

Head out into the less-explored corners of Campeche. **Rio Bec Dreams** (www.rio becdreams.com; Hwy 186 Km 142; 2-person cabañas M$620-1300, extra person M$180; P 🛜) makes a good base for ruin hopping.

Calakmul (admission M$48, road maintance fee per car M$50 plus per person M$30, park fee M$56; ⊙8am-5pm) Possibly the largest city during Maya times, Calakmul was 'discovered' in 1931 by American botanist Cyrus Lundell. The site bears comparison in size and historical significance to Tikal in Guatemala, its chief rival for hegemony over the southern lowlands during the Classic Maya era. It boasts the largest and tallest known pyramid in Yucatán, and was once home to over 50,000 people.

Edzná (M$48; ⊙8am-5pm) Edzná once covered more than 17 sq km and was inhabited from approximately 600 BC to the 15th century AD. Most of the visible carvings date from AD 550 to 810. Though it's a long way from such Puuc Hills sites as Uxmal and Kabah, some of the architecture here has elements of the Puuc style. The causes leading to Edzná's decline and gradual abandonment remain a mystery.

chicken to grilled pork to turkey soup, plus regional specialties and seafood dishes like *ceviche*. Tons of drinks make it all go down easy, and don't miss the creamy flan for dessert.

Chef Color   MEXICAN $
(📞981-811-44-55; cnr Calles 55 & 12; half/full lunch platters M$35/60; ⊙11am-5pm Mon-Sat) This cafeteria-style eatery serves up large portions of tasty Central American–influenced Mexican dishes from behind a glass counter; just point at what you want. The menu changes daily but it's always good, cheap and filling.

★**Luz de Luna**   INTERNATIONAL $$
(📞981-811-06-24; Calle 59 No 6; mains M$90-150; ⊙8am-10pm Mon-Sat) Carved, painted tables and folksy decor add a creative atmosphere to this popular restaurant on a pedestrian street. The menu choices are equally interesting – try the shrimp salad, chicken fajitas, flank steak or vegetarian burritos. There are plenty of breakfast options as well, especially omelettes.

🍷 Drinking & Nightlife

La Casa Vieja   BAR
(Calle 10 No 319A; ⊙8:30am-12:30am) There's no better setting for an evening cocktail than La Casa Vieja's colonnaded balcony overlooking the Plaza Principal. Look for the stairs next to the McDonald's ice-cream counter.

ℹ️ Information

Hospital Dr Manuel Campos (📞981-811-17-09; Av Circuito Baluartes Nte, btwn Calles 14 & 16)

Secretaría de Turismo (📞981-127-33-00; www.campeche.travel; Plaza Moch-Couoh; ⊙8am-9pm Mon-Fri, to 8pm Sat & Sun) Good information on the city and Campeche state.

ℹ️ Getting There & Away

Main Bus Terminal (📞981-811-99-10; Av Patricio Trueba 237) Campeche's main bus terminal, usually called the ADO or 1st-class terminal, is about 2.5km south of Plaza Principal via Avenida Central. Buses provide 1st-class and deluxe service to Mérida, Cancún, Chetumal (via Xpujil), Palenque, Veracruz and Mexico City, as well as 2nd-class service to Sabancuy (M$82), Hecelchakán (M$27), Candelaria (M$138) and points in Tabasco.

CHIAPAS

Chilly pine-forest highlands, sultry rainforest jungles and attractive colonial cities exist side by side within Mexico's southernmost states, a region awash with the legacy of Spanish rule and the remnants of ancient Maya civilization.

San Cristóbal de las Casas

📞967 / POP 170,000

Set in a gorgeous highland valley surrounded by pine forest, the colonial city of San Cristóbal (cris-*toh*-bal) has been a popular travelers' destination for decades. It's a pleasure to explore San Cristóbal's cobbled streets and markets, soaking up the unique ambiance and the wonderfully clear highland light. This medium-sized city also boasts a comfortable blend of city and countryside, with restored century-old houses giving way to grazing animals and fields of corn.

Surrounded by dozens of traditional Tzotzil and Tzeltal villages, San Cristóbal is at the heart of one of the most deeply rooted indigenous areas in Mexico. A great base for local and regional exploration, it's a place where ancient customs coexist with modern luxuries.

The city is a hot spot for sympathizers (and some opponents) of the Zapatista rebels, and a central location for organizations working with Chiapas' indigenous people. In addition to a solid tourist infrastructure and a dynamic population of artsy and politically progressive foreigners and Mexicans, San Cristóbal also has a great selection of accommodations and a cosmopolitan array of cafes, bars and restaurants.

◎ Sights & Activities

★ Na Bolom   HISTORIC BUILDING
(www.na-bolom.org; Guerrero 33; M$40, with tour M$50; ☺7am-7pm) An atmospheric museum-research center, Na Bolom for many years was the home of Swiss anthropologist and photographer Gertrude Duby-Blom (Trudy Blom; 1901–93) and her Danish archaeologist husband Frans Blom (1893–1963). Na Bolom means 'Jaguar House' in the Tzotzil language (as well as being a play on its former owners' name). It's full of photographs, archaeological and anthropological relics and books.

★ Museo de la Medicina Maya   MUSEUM
(Av Salomón González Blanco 10; M$20; ☺10am-6pm Mon-Fri, to 4pm Sat & Sun) This award-winning museum on the northern edge of town introduces the system of traditional medicine used by many indigenous people in the Chiapas highlands. Exhibits include displays of a ritual scene inside a church and a midwife assisting at a birth, a dated video about the work of traditional midwives and a new display about the issue of native plants and corporate biopiracy.

Centro de Textiles
del Mundo Maya   MUSEUM
(Calz Lázaro Cárdenas; M$52; ☺9am-6pm Tue-Sun) Upstairs inside the Ex-Convento de Santo Domingo, this excellent museum showcases over 500 examples of handwoven textiles from throughout Mexico and Central America. Two permanent exhibition rooms display *huipiles* (sleeveless tunics) – including a 1000-year-old relic fashioned

from tree bark. Videos show how materials and clothes are created, and there are some explanations in English. Admission is bundled with the **Museo de los Altos de Chiapas** (Calz Lázaro Cárdenas s/n; M$52; ☺9am-6pm Tue-Sun).

Natutours   OUTDOORS
(☑967-678-12-95; www.natutours.com.mx; Calle 28 de Agosto 4; ☺9am-4pm Mon-Sat) 🖋 Specializes in ecotourism (including intriguing tree-climbing outings), jungle treks and cultural tourism, and also holds workshops to promote recycling and sustainable use in the region.

✯ Festivals & Events

Feria de la Primavera y de la Paz   CULTURAL
(Spring & Peace Fair) Easter Sunday is the start of the weeklong town fair, with parades, musical events and bullfights.

🛏 Sleeping

Hostal Akumal   HOSTEL $
(☑cell 967-1161120; Calle 16 de Sepiembre 33; dm/s/d incl breakfast M$120/210/420; 🛜) Friendly, live-in owners, a decent location and a big free breakfast (a prominent sign quite rightly states 'Continental breakfast is not real breakfast') are some of the winning points at this centrally located hostel. There's a roaring fireplace in the lounge for chilly nights, a funky courtyard hangout area and the rooms and dorms are adequate, if nothing exciting.

Le Gite del Sol   HOTEL $
(☑967-631-60-12; www.legitedelsol.com; Madero 82; s/d M$340/440, without bathroom M$240/305; @🛜) A bountiful breakfast complements simple rooms with floors of radiant sunflower yellow and bathrooms that look a bit like oversized shower stalls, or pleasant rooms with shared facilities in a newer location across the street. French and English spoken, and kitchen facilities available.

Rossco Backpackers   HOSTEL $
(☑967-674-05-25; www.backpackershostel.com.mx; Real de Mexicanos 16; incl breakfast dm M$180-220, d/tr M$550/800; 🅿@🛜) Rossco Backpackers is a friendly, sociable and well-run hostel with good dorm rooms (one for women only), a guest kitchen, a movie-watching loft and a grassy garden. Private upstairs rooms have nice skylights. A free night's stay if you arrive by bicycle or motorcycle!

Chiapas

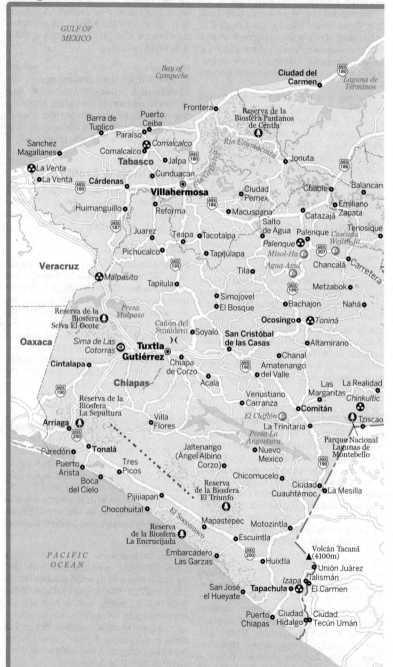

GULF OF
MEXICO

Bay of
Campeche

Ciudad del
Carmen

MEX
180

Laguna de
Términos

Frontera

Reserva de la
Biosfera Pantanos
de Centla

Barra de
Tuplico

Puerto
Ceiba

Paraíso

Comalcalco

Río Usamacinta

Sanchez
Magallanes

Comalcalco

Tabasco

Jalpa

MEX
180

Jonuta

MEX
186

La Venta

La Venta

Cunduacan

Cárdenas

MEX
180

Villahermosa

Ciudad
Pemex

Chable

Balancan

Río Grijalva

Huimanguillo

Reforma

MEX
186

Macuspana

Emiliano
Zapata

Catazajá

Tenosique

MEX
187

Juarez

Teapa

Tacotalpa

Salto
de Agua

Palenque

Cascada
Wejlib-Já

Pichucalco

Tapijulapa

Palenque

MEX
307

Veracruz

Malpasito

MEX
195

Tila

Misol-Ha

Agua Azul

Chancalá

Carretera

Tapilula

MEX
199

Metzabok

Presa
Malpaso

Simojovel

El Bosque

Bachajon

Nahá

Reserva de la
Biosfera
Selva El Ocote

Cañón del
Sumidero

Soyaló

Ocosingo

Toniná

Oaxaca

Sima de Las
Cotorras

Tuxtla
Gutiérrez

San Cristóbal
de las Casas

Altamirano

Chiapa
de Corzo

MEX
190

Chanal

Cintalapa

Chiapas

Acala

Amatenango
del Valle

MEX
190

Reserva de la
Biosfera
La Sepultura

Villa
Flores

Venustiano
Carranza

El Chiflón

Las
Margaritas

La Realidad

Chinkultic

Comitán

Tziscao

Arriaga

MEX
200

Paredón

Tonalá

Jaltenango
(Ángel Albino
Corzo)

Presa La
Angostura

La Trinitaria

Parque Nacional
Lagunas de
Montebello

Puerto
Arista

Tres
Picos

Nuevo
Mexico

MEX
190

Boca
del Cielo

Chicomucelo

Ciudad
Cuauhtémoc

La Mesilla

Pijijiapan

Reserva
de la Biosfera
El Triunfo

El Soconusco

Chocohuital

Mapastepec

Motozintla

Reserva
de la Biosfera
La Encrucijada

Escuintla

Volcán Tacaná
▲(4100m)

PACIFIC
OCEAN

Embarcadero
Las Garzas

MEX
200

Huixtla

Unión Juárez

Izapa

Talismán

San José
el Hueyate

Tapachula

El Carmen

Puerto
Chiapas

Ciudad
Hidalgo

Ciudad
Tecún Umán

Eating

★TierrAdentro MEXICAN **$**

(Real de Guadalupe 24; set menu M$55-130; ⊕8am-11pm; 🛜✍) A popular gathering center for political progressives and coffee-swigging, laptop-toting locals (not that they're mutually exclusive), this large indoor courtyard restaurant, cafe and pizzeria is a comfortable place to while away the hours. It's run by Zapatista supporters, who hold frequent cultural events and conferences on local issues.

La Tertulia CAFE **$**

(Cuathémoc 2; breakfasts around M$38; ⊕9:30am-5pm Sun & Mon, to 10pm Tue-Sat) One of the coolest cafes in town also does great breakfasts, yummy salads and a passable pizza, all served up with ooh-la-la presentation in pleasingly boho surrounds. A little onsite gift store selling local produce and souvenirs rounds out the picture.

★Restaurante LUM MEXICAN **$$**

(Hotel Bo, Av 5 de Mayo 38; mains M$110-200; ⊕7am-11pm) This swanky indoor-outdoor restaurant which serves up the regional cuisines of Chiapas, Veracruz and the Yucatán is in San Cristóbal's first designer hotel. Custom-made lamps, reflecting pools and walls of geometrically stacked firewood create a funky contemporary ambiance.

Drinking & Nightlife

Mezcalería Gusana Grela MEZCALERÍA

(MA Flores 2; ⊕7pm-3am Mon-Sat) Wedge yourself in at one of a handful of tables and try some of the dozen or so artisanal mezcals (M$40 to M$50) from Oaxaca, many which are fruit-infused.

Entertainment

★Cafe Bar Revolución LIVE MUSIC

(www.elrevo.com; Calle 1 de Marzo 11; ⊕1pm-1am) There's always something fun at Revolución, with two live bands nightly (at 9pm and 11pm) and an eclectic lineup of salsa, rock, blues, jazz and reggae. Dance downstairs or order a mojito or caipirinha and chat in the quieter upstairs *tapanco* (attic).

Shopping

Nemi Zapata HANDICRAFTS

(www.nemizapata.com; MA Flores 57; ⊕9am-7pm Mon-Fri,9:30am-3:30pmSat) 🖉 A fair-trade store that sells products made by Zapatista communities: weavings, embroidery, coffee and

San Cristóbal de las Casas

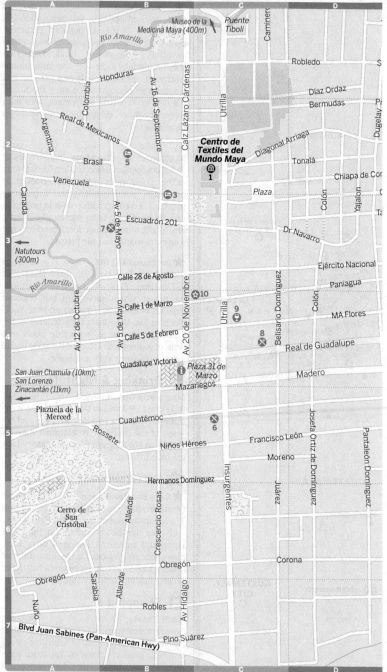

MEXICO'S YUCATÁN & CHIAPAS SAN CRISTÓBAL DE LAS CASAS

San Cristóbal de las Casas

◎ Top Sights
1 Centro de Textiles del Mundo
  Maya C2
2 Na Bolom F2

◎ Sights
  Museo de los Altos de
  Chiapas .... (see 1)

◎ Sleeping
3 Hostal Akumal B3
4 Le Gite del Sol E4
5 Rossco Backpackers B2

◎ Eating
6 La Tertulia C5
7 Restaurante LUM B3
8 TierrAdentro C4

◎ Drinking & Nightlife
9 Mezcalería Gusana Grela C4

◎ Entertainment
10 Cafe Bar Revolución C4

◎ Shopping
11 Nemi Zapata E4

honey, as well as Ejército Zapatista de Libéracion Nacional (EZLN; Zapatista National Liberation Army) cards, posters and books.

ℹ Information

Banamex (Insurgentes btwn Niños Héroes & Cuauhtémoc; ⊙9am-4pm Mon-Sat) Has an ATM; exchanges dollars.

Municipal Tourist Office (☑967-678-06-65; Palacio Municipal, Plaza 31 de Marzo; ⊙9am-9pm) Staff are generally knowledgeable about the San Cristóbal area; English spoken.

ℹ Getting There & Away

The main 1st-class OCC terminal is also used by ADO and UNO 1st-class and deluxe buses, plus some 2nd-class buses. AEXA buses and Ómnibus de Chiapas minibuses share a terminal across the street from the OCC terminal. All *colectivo* vans *(combis)* and taxis have depots on the Pan-American Hwy a block or so from the OCC terminal.

For Guatemala, most agencies offer a daily van service to Quetzaltenango (M$390, eight hours), Panajachel (M$390, 10 hours) and Antigua (M$500, 12 hours); Viajes Chincultik is slightly cheaper, and also has van service to Guatemala City and Chichicastenango. Otherwise, go to Ciudad Cuauhtémoc and pick up onward transportation from the Guatemala side.

BUSES FROM SAN CRISTÓBAL

DESTINATION	COST (M$)	DURATION (HR)	FREQUENCY (DAILY)
Campeche	548	10	6:20pm
Cancún	700-1242	18-19	3 OCC, 1 AEXA
Ciudad Cuauhtémoc (Guatemalan border)	132	3¼	3
Comitán	64	1¾	Frequent OCC & colectivos
Mérida	778	12¾	6:20pm
Mexico City (TAPO & Norte)	1240-1560	13-14	13
Oaxaca	604-726	11-12	3
Ocosingo	52-88	2	7 OCC, 3 AEXA, frequent colectivos
Palenque	122-248	5	6 OCC, 3 AEXA
Pochutla	584	11-12	2
Puerto Escondido	668	12½-13	2
Tuxtla Gutiérrez	52	1-1¼	Frequent OCC; 4 AEXA
Tuxtla Gutiérrez airport (Ángel Albino Corzo)	210	1½	8
Villahermosa	402	5½-7	10am

Lagos de Montebello

The temperate pine and oak forest along the Guatemalan border east of Chinkultic is dotted with more than 50 small lakes of varied hues, known as the Lagos (or Lagunas) de Montebello. The area is very picturesque, refreshing and peaceful. The paved road to Montebello turns east off Hwy 190 just north of La Trinitaria, 16km south of Comitán. It passes Chinkultic after 32km, and enters the Parque Nacional Lagunas de Montebello 5km beyond. A further 800m along is a ticket booth, where you must pay a M$23 park-admission fee. Here the road forks: north to the Lagunas de Colores (2km to 3km) and east to the village of Tziscao (9km), beyond which it becomes the Carretera Fronteriza, continuing east to Ixcán and ultimately circling back up to Palenque.

🛏 Sleeping

Villa Tziscao   CABAÑAS, CAMPGROUND $
(🖉 in Guatemala 502-5780-27-75; www.ecotziscao. com; campsites per person M$60, 1-/2-/3-bed r or cabaña M$450/780/980; 🅿🖻@🛜) By the lake in Tziscao village (2km from the highway turnoff), this medium-sized lakeside complex is run by an *ejido* cooperative. Extensive, grassy grounds include a sandy beach with terrific views across the lake to the foothills of the Cuchumatanes in Guatemala. Comfortable rooms in the main hotel building have new beds and bathroom tiling, plus flat-screen TVs.

❶ Getting There & Away

Public transportation from Comitán is a snap, making it an easy day trip. Vans go to the end of the road at Laguna Bosque Azul and to Tziscao, and will drop you at the turnoffs for Museo Parador Santa María, Chinkultic and the other lakes. The last vehicles back to Comitán leave Tziscao and Laguna Bosque Azul in the early evening.

From San Cristóbal, a number of agencies offer tours that take in the lakes, throw in a visit to El Chiflón and get you back by dinnertime.

Yaxchilán

Yaxchilán   ARCHAEOLOGICAL SITE
(M$55; ⊙8am-5pm, last entry 4pm) Jungle-shrouded Yaxchilán has a terrific setting above a horseshoe loop in the Río Usumacinta. The control this location gave it over river commerce, and a series of successful alliances and conquests, made Yaxchilán one of the most important Classic Maya cities in the Usumacinta region. Archaeologically, Yaxchilán is famed for its ornamented facades and roofcombs, and its impressive stone lintels carved with conquest and ceremonial scenes. A flashlight is helpful for exploring some parts of the site.

ℹ Getting There & Away

To reach Yaxchilán from Palenque, first head to Frontera Corozal. Autotransporte Chamoán runs vans run to Frontera Corozal (M$130, 2½ to three hours, every 40 minutes from 4am to 5pm), leaving from the outdoor *colectivo* terminal near the Maya head statue and south of the bus station.

Lanchas (small motorboats) take 40 minutes running downstream from Frontera Corozal, and one hour to return. The boat companies are in a thatched building near the Frontera Corozal *embarcadero* (wharf), all charging about the same prices for trips (return journey with 2½ hours at the ruins for one to three/four/five to seven/eight to 10 people M$900/1050/1450/1800). *Lanchas* normally leave frequently until 1:30pm or so; try to hook up with other travelers or a tour group to share costs.

Palenque

◢ 916 / POP 43,000

Deservedly one of the top destinations of Chiapas, the soaring jungle-swathed temples of Palenque are a national treasure and one of the best examples of Maya architecture in Mexico. Modern Palenque town, a few kilometers to the east, is a sweaty, humdrum place without much appeal except as a jumping-off point for the ruins and a place to find internet access. Many prefer to base themselves at one of the forest hideouts along the road between the town and the ruins, including the funky travelers' hangout of El Panchán.

⊙ Sights

Combis to the ruins (M$24 each way) run about every 10 minutes during daylight hours. In town, look for 'Ruinas' *combis* anywhere on Juárez west of Allende. They will also pick you up or drop you off anywhere along the town–ruins road.

Palenque Ruins ARCHAEOLOGICAL SITE
(M$51; ⊙ 8am-5pm, last entry 4:30pm) Ancient Palenque stands at the precise point where the first hills rise out of the Gulf coast plain, and the dense jungle covering these hills forms an evocative backdrop to Palenque's exquisite Maya architecture. Hundreds of ruined buildings are spread over 15 sq km, but only a fairly compact central area has been excavated. Everything you see here was built without metal tools, pack animals or the wheel.

MADRE SAL

Drift to sleep pondering the ocean waves at **Madre Sal** (☑ cell 966-6666147, cell 966-1007296; www.elmadre sal.com; Manuel Ávila Camacho; hammock sites M$120, q campsites incl gear M$280, cabañas M$800; ℗), a cooperative-run ecotourism project 25km south of Puerto Arista. Named for a mangrove species, its restaurant (meals M$80 to M$150) and almost 20 thatched two-bed en suite *cabañas* (with mosquito nets) sit astride a skinny bar of pristine land between a lagoon and the Pacific that's reached via *lancha* (M$20 round trip) through dense mangrove forest.

Guests use candles after the 11pm power shutoff, and crabs skitter along the sand when stars fill the night sky. In season, sea turtles come ashore to lay eggs, and the night watchman can wake you if you want to watch or help collect the eggs for the Boca del Cielo hatchery.

From Tonalá, take a taxi (M$60 shared, M$250 private) or *combi* (M$50) to Manuel Ávila Camacho; *combis* charge an extra M$5 to the *embarcadero*, or you can walk five minutes.

➡ Templo de las Inscripciones Group
As you walk in from the entrance, passing to the south of the overgrown **Templo XI**, the vegetation suddenly peels away to reveal many of Palenque's most magnificent buildings in one sublime vista. A line of temples rises in front of the jungle on your right, culminating in the Templo de las Inscripciones about 100m ahead; El Palacio, with its trademark tower, stands to the left of the Templo de las Inscripciones; and the Grupo de las Cruces rises in the distance beneath a thick jungle backdrop.

The first temple on your right is Templo XII, called the **Templo de la Calavera** (Temple of the Skull) for the relief sculpture of a rabbit or deer skull at the foot of one of its pillars. The second temple has little interest. Third is **Templo XIII**, containing a tomb of a female dignitary, whose remains were found colored red (as a result of treatment with cinnabar) when unearthed in 1994. You can look into the Tumba de la Reina Roja (Tomb of the Red Queen) and see her sarcophagus. With the skeleton were found a

MEXICO'S YUCATÁN & CHIAPAS PALENQUE

Palenque Ruins

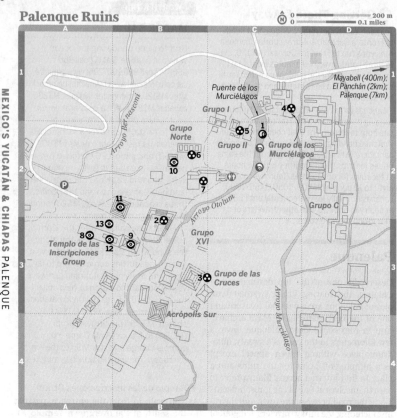

Palenque Ruins

◉ Sights
1 Baño de la Reina C2
2 El Palacio B3
3 Grupo de las Cruces B3
4 Grupo de los Murciélagos C1
5 Grupo II C2
6 Grupo Norte B2
7 Juego de Pelota B2
8 Templo de la Calavera A3
9 Templo de las Inscripciones B3
10 Templo del Conde B2
11 Templo XI B2
12 Templo XIII A3
13 Tomb of Alberto Ruz Lhuillier A3

malachite mask and about 1000 pieces of jade. Based on DNA tests and resemblances to Pakal's tomb next door, the theory is that the 'queen' buried here was his wife Tz'ak-b'u Ajaw. The **tomb of Alberto Ruz Lhuillier,**

who discovered Pakal's tomb in 1952, lies under the trees in front of Templo XIII.

The **Templo de las Inscripciones** (Temple of the Inscriptions), perhaps the most celebrated burial monument in the Americas, is the tallest and most stately of Palenque's buildings. Constructed on eight levels, the Templo de las Inscripciones has a central front staircase rising 25m to a series of small rooms. The tall roofcomb that once crowned it is long gone, but between the front doorways are stucco panels with reliefs of noble figures. On the interior rear wall are three panels with the long Maya inscription, recounting the history of Palenque and this building, for which Mexican archaeologist Alberto Ruz Lhuillier named the temple. From the top, interior stairs lead down into the tomb of Pakal (now closed to visitors indefinitely, to avoid further damage to its murals from the humidity inevitably exuded by visitors). Pakal's jewel-bedecked skeleton and jade mosaic death mask were removed from the tomb to Mexico City, and the tomb was re-created in the Museo Nacional de Antropología. The priceless death mask was stolen in an elaborate heist in 1985 (though recovered a few years afterward), but the carved stone sarcophagus lid remains in the closed tomb – you can see a replica in the site museum.

➡ **El Palacio**

(The Palace) Diagonally opposite the Templo de las Inscripciones is El Palacio, a large structure divided into four main courtyards, with a maze of corridors and rooms. Built and modified piecemeal over 400 years from the 5th century on, it was probably the residence of Palenque's rulers.

➡ **Acrópolis Sur**

In the jungle south of the Grupo de las Cruces is the Southern Acropolis, where archaeologists have made some terrific finds in recent excavations. You may find part of the area roped off. The Acrópolis Sur appears to have been constructed as an extension of the Grupo de las Cruces, with both groups set around what was probably a single long open space.

➡ **Grupo de las Cruces**

(Group of the Crosses) Pakal's son, Kan B'alam II, was a prolific builder, and soon after the death of his father started designing the temples of the Grupo de las Cruces (Group of the Crosses). All three main pyramid-shaped structures surround a plaza southeast of the Templo de las Inscripciones. They were all dedicated in AD 692 as a spiritual focal point for Palenque's triad of patron deities. The 'cross' carvings in some buildings here symbolize the ceiba tree, which in Maya belief held up the universe.

➡ **Grupo Norte**

(Northern Group) North of El Palacio is a **Juego de Pelota** (Ball Court) and the handsome buildings of the Northern Group. Crazy Count de Waldeck lived in the so-called **Templo del Conde** (Temple of the Count), constructed in AD 647.

➡ **Palenque Northeastern Groups**

East of the Grupo Norte, the main path crosses Arroyo Otolum. Some 70m beyond the stream, a right fork will take you to **Grupo C**, a set of jungle-covered buildings and plazas thought to have been lived in from about AD 750 to 800.

If you stay on the main path, you'll descend some steep steps to a group of low, elongated buildings, probably occupied residentially from around AD 770 to 850. The path goes alongside the Arroyo Otolum, which here tumbles down a series of small falls forming natural bathing pools known as the **Baño de la Reina** (Queen's Bath). Unfortunately, you can't bathe here anymore.

The path then continues to another residential quarter, the **Grupo de los Murciélagos** (Bat Group), and then crosses the **Puente de los Murciélagos**, a footbridge across Arroyo Otolum.

Across the bridge and a bit further downstream, a path goes west to **Grupo I** and **Grupo II**, a short walk uphill. These ruins, only partly uncovered, are in a beautiful jungle setting. The main path continues downriver to the road, where the museum is a short distance along to the right.

El Panchán   AREA

(www.elpanchan.com; Carretera Palenque-Ruinas Km 4.5) Just off the road to the ruins, El Panchán is a legendary travelers' hangout, set in a patch of dense rainforest. It's the epicenter of Palenque's alternative scene and home to a bohemian bunch of Mexican and foreign residents and wanderers. Once ranchland, the area has been reforested by the remarkable Morales family, some of whom are among the leading archaeological experts on Palenque. El Panchán has several (mostly rustic) places to stay, a couple of restaurants, a set of sinuous streams rippling their way through every part of the property, nightly entertainment (and daily drumming practice), a meditation temple, a *temascal* (pre-Hispanic steam bath) and a constant stream of interesting visitors from all over the world.

🏃 Activities

Viajes Kukulcán   TOUR

(☑916-345-15-06; www.kukulcantravel.com; Av Juárez 8) Offers transportation packages to Agua Azul and Misol-Ha, to Bonampak, Yaxchilán and Lacanjá Chansayab, and to Flores, Guatemala.

🛏 Sleeping

Yaxkin   HOSTEL $

(☑916-345-01-02; www.hostalyaxkin.com; Prolongación Hidalgo 1; dm M$162, d with/without bathroom M$472/342, r with air-con & bathroom M$586; P ⊕ ✳ @ 🛜) Channeling laid-back El

Panchán from pretty La Cañada, this former disco has been revamped into a modern hostel with a guest kitchen, a ping-pong table, multiple lounges and a swank restaurant-bar and cafe. Rooms without air-con are monastic but funky. The fan-cooled dorms (one for women only) and private rooms with air-con feel more pleasant and comfortable.

Hostal San Miguel   HOTEL $

(☎916-345-01-52; hostalmiguel1@hotmail.com; Hidalgo 43; dm M$150, s/d with fan M$250/380, with air-con M$380/510; ❸❀☎) Who doesn't love a hotel with towel animals? A quiet and clean economical choice; rooms have good light and views from the upper floors. Dark two- and four-bed dorms don't have hot water or air-con, and all air-con rooms have two queen beds.

Margarita & Ed Cabañas   GUESTHOUSE $

(☎916-348-69-90; www.margaritaandedcabanas. blogspot.com; Carreterra Palenque-Ruinas Km 4.5, El Panchán; cabañas M$285, r with fan M$320-410, s/d with air-con M$480/570; 🅿❀) With the most spotless digs in the jungle, Margarita has welcomed travelers to her exceptionally homey place for decades. Bright, clean and cheerful rooms have good mosquito netting, and the more rustic screened cabañas are well kept too, with reading lights and private bathrooms. There's free drinking water, a book exchange, and a lovely newer building with superspacious rooms.

Hotel Maya Rue   HOTEL $$

(☎916-345-07-43; www.hotelmayaruepalenque. com; Aldama s/n; r/tr M$750/900; ❀@☎) Tree-trunk beams and dramatic lighting add un-expected style to this 12-room offering combining traditional materials and industrial chic. Some rooms have shaded private balconies, but all are spacious and come with cable TV. Cafe on premises.

✖ Eating

★ Don Mucho's   MEXICAN, INTERNATIONAL $

(Carretera Palenque-Ruinas Km 4.5, El Panchán; mains M$60-150; ☺7am-11pm) The hot spot of El Panchán, popular Don Mucho's provides great-value meals in a jungly setting, with a candlelit ambiance at night. Busy waiters bring pasta, fish, meat, plenty of antojitos (typical Mexican snacks), and pizzas (cooked in a purpose-built Italian-designed wood-fired oven) that are some of the finest this side of Naples.

Live music – usually andina, cumbia or Cuban – starts around 8pm Friday through Sunday (at 9:30pm other nights), plus there's a rousing fire-dancing show most nights at 11pm.

Café Jade   MEXICAN, CHIAPANECO $

(Prolongación Hidalgo 1; breakfast M$42-68, mains M$53-90; ☺7am-11pm; ☎) A chill indoor-outdoor spot on the ground floor of the Yaxkin hostel, with long sofa seating at tree-plank tables. Good for breakfast, Chiapan specialties and chicken dishes.

★ Restaurant Las Tinajas   MEXICAN $$

(cnr Av 20 de Noviembre & Abasolo; mains M$85-130; ☺7am-11pm) It doesn't take long to figure out why this place is always busy. It slings enormous portions of excellent home-style food – enough to keep you (and possibly

BUSES FROM PALENQUE

DESTINATION	COST (M$)	DURATION (HR)	FREQUENCY (DAILY)
Campeche	382	5-5½	5 ADO
Cancún	630-1040	12-13½	6 ADO
Mérida	576	8	5 ADO
Mexico City (1 TAPO & 1 Norte)	1108-1308	13½	2 ADO
Oaxaca	856	15	ADO at 2:35pm
Ocosingo	76-138	2½	11 ADO, 5 AEXA, very frequent vans
San Cristóbal de las Casas	122-206	5	12 ADO, 5 AEXA
Tulum	524-844	10-11	6 ADO
Tuxtla Gutiérrez	186-324	6½	11 ADO, 5 AEXA
Villahermosa	150-174	2½	frequent ADO & AEXA
Villahermosa airport	278	2¼	5 ADO

another person) fueled up for hours. *Pollo a la veracruzana* (chicken in a tomato, olive and onion sauce) and *camarones al guajillo* (shrimp with a not-too-hot type of chili) are both delicious, as is the house salsa.

La Selva MEXICAN $$
($$916-345-03-63; Hwy 199; mains M$85-220; ☉11:30am-11pm) Palenque's most upscale restaurant serves up well-prepared steaks, seafood, salads and *antojitos* under an enormous *palapa* roof, with jungle-themed stained-glass panels brightening one wall. Try the *pigua* (freshwater lobster) when it's available in the fall. Reserve ahead in high season.

ℹ️ Information

Bancomer (Av Juárez 96; ☉8:30am-4pm Mon-Fri) Also has an ATM.
Clínica Palenque (Velasco Suárez 33; ☉8:30am-1:30pm & 5-9pm) Dr Alfonso Martínez speaks English.

ℹ️ Getting There & Away

It's best to travel the winding stretch of road between Palenque and San Cristóbal during daylight, as highway holdups – though by no means common – do occasionally occur. There have also been recent reports of thefts on the night bus from Mérida. When taking buses along these routes, consider stowing valuables in the checked luggage compartment.

BUS
ADO Bus terminal ($$916-345-13-44) ADO has the main bus terminal in town, with deluxe and 1st-class services, an ATM and left-luggage facilities; it's also used by OCC (1st class) and TRT (2nd class).

Agua Azul & Misol-Ha

These spectacular water attractions – the thundering cascades of Agua Azul and the 35m jungle waterfall of Misol-Ha – are both short detours off the Ocosingo–Palenque road. During the rainy season they lose part of their beauty as the water gets murky, though the power of the waterfalls is magnified.

Both are most easily visited on an organized day tour from Palenque, though it's possible, for about the same price, to go independently. One reason to visit on your own is to spend more time at Misol-Ha, which is usually a shorter tour stop. Agua Azul is especially built-up and crowded with vendors.

👁 Sights

Agua Azul WATERFALL
(M$40) Agua Azul is a breathtaking sight, with its powerful and dazzling white waterfalls thundering into turquoise (outside rainy season) pools surrounded by verdant jungle. On holidays and weekends the place is packed; at other times you'll have few companions. The temptation to swim is great, but take extreme care, as people do drown here. The current is deceptively fast, the power of the falls obvious, and there are many submerged hazards like rocks and dead trees. If you're in decent shape, keep walking upstream – the crowds thin out the further up you go.

The turnoff for Agua Azul is halfway between Ocosingo and Palenque, some 60km from each. A paved road leads 4.5km down to Agua Azul from Hwy 199. A well-made stone and concrete path with steps runs 700m up beside the falls from the parking area, which is packed with food and souvenir stalls. Basic lodging is also available.

Unfortunately, theft isn't uncommon, so don't bring valuables, keep an eye on your belongings and stick to the main paved trail.

Misol-Ha WATERFALL
(total M$35) Just 20km south of Palenque, spectacular Misol-Ha cascades approximately 35m into a wonderful wide pool surrounded by lush tropical vegetation. It's a sublime place for a dip when the fall is not excessively pumped up by wet-season rains. A path behind the main fall leads into a cave, which allows you to experience the power of the water close up. Misol-Ha is 1.5km off Hwy 199 and the turnoff is signposted, and two separate *ejidos* (communal landholdings) charge admission.

🛏 Sleeping

Centro Turístico Ejidal Cascada de Misol-Ha CABIN $
($$916-345-12-10; www.misol-ha.com; d/tr M$330/450, f with kitchen M$580-700; ☉restaurant 7am-7pm, to 10pm high season; 🅿️😊) Has great wooden cabins among the trees near the waterfall, with fans, hot-water bathrooms and mosquito netting, plus a good open-air restaurant (mains M$80 to M$160). Nighttime swims are dreamy.

UNDERSTAND MEXICO'S YUCATÁN & CHIAPAS

Mexico's Yucatán & Chiapas Today

Tourism is one of the driving forces behind life in the Yucatán, Mexico's most visited destination. For better or worse, the industry helps shape politics, economics and many of the region's important social and environmental issues. And because the peninsula is unquestionably one of the safest and most visitor-friendly places in all of Mexico, the tourism economy is thriving like never before.

Yet despite the tourism boom, a broad segment of the population continues to live in poverty and rapid development is causing long-lasting environmental and cultural degradation. A big cause for concern is the gradual disappearance of indigenous languages as more and more hotels and restaurants seek English speakers.

History

The Maya set up many city-states across the broad south of Mexico, though the population and activity had declined before the Spanish arrived. A couple of Spaniards – Diego de Mazariegos in present-day Chiapas, and Francisco de Montejo in the Yucatán – had the area under Spanish control by the mid-16th century. Mexico won independence from Spain in 1821, and pulled in Chiapas from the United Provinces of Central America in 1824.

Long oppressed by Spaniards and *criollos* (Latin Americans of Spanish lineage), the Maya rose in the War of the Castes in 1847, leading to destroyed churches and many massacres. The brimming sense of inequality didn't settle with peace in 1901. As the North American Free Trade Agreement (NAFTA) kicked into effect in 1994, the mainly Maya Zapatistas stormed San Cristóbal de las Casas. Their struggle has since quieted down now that they run autonomous zones (called *caracoles*, literally 'snails') outside San Cristóbal.

Culture

Travelers often comment on the open, gentle and gregarious nature of the people of the Yucatán, especially the Maya. Here, more than elsewhere in Mexico, it seems, you find a willingness to converse and a genuine interest in outsiders. This openness is all the more remarkable when you consider that the people of the Yucatán Peninsula have fended off domination by outsiders for so long. The situation persists today – much of the land is foreign-owned and the Maya generally have no say in the big infrastructure decisions.

Landscape & Wildlife

Separated from the bulk of Mexico by the Gulf of Mexico, and from the Greater Antilles by the Caribbean Sea, the Yucatán Peninsula is a vast, low limestone shelf extending under the sea for more than 100km to the north and west. The eastern (Caribbean) side drops off much more precipitously. This underwater shelf keeps Yucatán's coastline waters warm and the marine life abundant.

The isolation of the Yucatán Peninsula and its array of ecosystems results in an extraordinary variety of plant and animal life, including a number of species that are unique to the region. Whether you like watching birds, following the progress of sea turtles as they nest on the beach, swimming next to manta rays and schools of iridescent fish, or spying wildcats through your binoculars, you'll have plenty of nature activities to do here.

LIONFISH CEVICHE, ANYONE?

There's trouble in the waters of the Mexican Caribbean – invasive lionfish, which are native to the Indo-Pacific region but were introduced to Atlantic waters in the early 1990s, are reproducing at an alarming rate and that's bad news for indigenous fish species. Protected by venomous spines and with no known predators, lionfish have a fierce appetite, making them a serious threat to the balance of reef ecosystems.

In an effort to control the population explosion, fishers are being encouraged to catch lionfish for human consumption. Also, many dive shops now offer lionfish-hunting expeditions, which is capped off with a feast of lionfish *ceviche* at the end of the day.

SURVIVAL GUIDE

❶ Directory A–Z

ACCOMMODATIONS

The Yucatán offers a mixed bag of affordable sleeping options, including hostels, *cabañas* (cabins), campgrounds, guesthouses and economical hotels. Rooms in this category are assumed to have bathrooms, unless otherwise stated. Recommended accommodations in this range will be simple and without frills but generally clean.

Hostels exist in nearly all of the region's most popular tourist destinations. They provide dorm accommodations (for about M$180 to M$220 per person), plus communal kitchens, bathrooms and living space, and often more expensive private rooms. Standards of hygiene and security vary. Always ask if the dorms come with air-con – you might need it on a hot day.

BARGAINING

Most stores and shops have set prices. You can do some friendly haggling in some arts and crafts markets, but don't get carried away – most of the artisans are just trying to make a living. Some hotels are willing to negotiate rates with walk-ins, especially during low season.

CLIMATE

It's always hot in the Yucatán and around Palenque. The wet season, from May to November, makes the air sticky and hot. The hurricane season lasts from June through November.

CUSTOMS

Visitors are allowed to bring the following items into Mexico duty-free:
➡ two cameras
➡ 10 packs of cigarettes
➡ 3L of alcohol
➡ medicine for personal use, with prescription in the case of psychotropic drugs
➡ one laptop computer
➡ one digital music player

See www.sat.gob.mx for more details.

After handing in your customs declaration form, an automated system will determine whether your luggage will be inspected. A green light means pass, a red light means your bags will be searched.

DANGERS & ANNOYANCES

Despite all the grim news about Mexico's drug-related violence, the Yucatán Peninsula remains a safe haven. Most of the killings you hear about happen between rival drug gangs, so tourists are rarely caught up in the disputes – especially in the Yucatán, which keeps a safe distance from the turf wars occurring elsewhere in Mexico. Just to give you an idea of how safe it really is, major US cities such as New York and Chicago

have higher murder rates than the entire state of Yucatán.

Foreign affairs departments can supply a variety of useful data about travel to Mexico.

DISCOUNT CARDS

Reduced prices for students and seniors on Mexican buses and at museums and archaeological sites are usually only for those with Mexican residence or education credentials, but the following cards will sometimes get you a reduction (the ISIC is the most widely recognized). They are also recognized for reduced-price air tickets at student- and youth-oriented travel agencies:

ISIC (www.isic.org) Student card.
ITIC (International Teacher Identity Card) For full-time teachers.
IYTC (International Youth Travel Card) For those under 31 years.

EMBASSIES & CONSULATES

It's important to understand what your own embassy can and can't do to help you if you get into trouble. Generally speaking, it won't be much help in emergencies if the trouble you're in is remotely your own fault. Remember that you are bound by the laws of the country you are in. In genuine emergencies you might get some assistance, such as a list of lawyers, but only if other channels have been exhausted.

Embassy details can be found at **Secretaría de Relaciones Exteriores** (www.sre.gob.mx) and **Embassyworld.org** (www.embassyworld.org).

Many embassies or their consular agencies are in Mexico City (including Australia, Ireland and New Zealand); Cancún is home to several consulates, and there are some diplomatic outposts elsewhere in the region as well.

Belizean Consulate Chetumal (☑ 983-129-3328; conbelizeqroo@gmail.com; Av Juárez 226B, btwn Avs Primo de Verdad & Carranza, Chetumal; ⊙ 9am-noon Mon-Fri)

Canadian Consulate Cancún (☑ 998-883-33-60; www.canadainternational.gc.ca; Blvd Kukulcán Km 12, Centro Empresarial Oficina E7; ⊙ 9:30am-1pm Mon-Fri); **Playa del Carmen** (☑ 984-803-24-11; www.canadainternational.gc.ca; Av 10 Sur, btwn Calles 3 & 5 Sur, in Plaza Paraíso Caribe; ⊙ 9am-1pm Mon-Fri)

Dutch Consulate Cancún (☑998-884-86-72; http://mexico.nlambassade.org; Av Nichupte s/n, in Pabellón Caribe, Cancún; ☺9am-2pm Mon-Fri); **Mérida** (☑999-924-31-22; http://mexico.nlambassade.org; Calle 64 No 418; ☺8am-2pm Mon-Fri)

French Consulate Mérida (☑999-930-15-00; Calle 60 No 385, Mérida; ☺9am-5pm Mon-Fri)

German Consulate Cancún (☑998-884-15-98; Punta Conoca 36, SM24, Cancún); **Mérida** (☑999-944-32-52; Calle 49 No 212, Mérida)

Guatemalan Consulate Ciudad Hidalgo (☑962-698-01-84; 9a Calle Oriente 9, Colonia San José; ☺9am-2pm & 3-5pm Mon-Fri); **Comitán** (☑963-110-68-16; www.minex.gob. gt; 1a Calle Sur Poniente 35, Int.3 4th fl, Comitán; ☺9am-1pm & 2-5pm Mon-Fri); **Tapachula** (☑962-626-12-52; www.minex.gob.gt; Quinta Norte No 3, 3rd fl; ☺9am-5pm Mon-Fri)

Italian Consulate Cancún (☑998-884-12-61; www.ambcittadelmessico.esteri.it; Alcatraces 39)

UK Consulate Cancún (☑998-881-01-00; Royal Sands, Blvd Kukulcán Km 13.5, Cancún; ☺9am-2pm Mon-Fri)

US Consulate Cancún (☑998-883-02-72; Despacho 301, Torre La Europea, Blvd Kukulcán Km 13, Cancún; ☺8am-1pm Mon-Fri); **Mérida** (☑999-942-57-77; http://merida.usconsulate.gov; Calle 60 No 338K, Mérida; ☺9am-1pm Mon-Fri)

EMERGENCY & IMPORTANT NUMBERS

Dial ☑1 before toll-free or long-distance calls. To call cell phones, dial ☑044 and the city code before the cell number; do the same for long-distance cell phone calls, but use ☑045.

Country code	☑52
Directory assistance	☑040
Emergencies	☑066
International access code	☑00;☑011 from USA & Canada
Roadside assistance	☑078

LGBT TRAVELERS

Mexico is more broad-minded about sexuality than you might expect. Gays and lesbians rarely attract open discrimination or violence. Discrimination based on sexual orientation has been illegal since 1999 and can be punished with up to three years in prison. Gay men have a more public profile than lesbians. Cancún has a small gay scene, and there are a number of gay-friendly establishments listed in Mérida at www.gaymexicomap.com.

MONEY

Mexico's currency is the peso, usually denoted by the 'M$' sign.

International credit cards are accepted for payment by mostly midrange and upmarket hotels, and some restaurants. Many businesses take debit cards as well but you'll usually wind up paying the card issuer a 3% international transaction fee.

As a backup to credit or debit cards, always carry cash, especially when visiting remote towns with few or no ATMs available.

OPENING HOURS

Standard hours are as follows:

Archaeological sites 8am-5pm.

Banks 9am-5pm Monday to Friday, 10am-2pm Saturday; some banks do not open Saturday; hours may vary.

Cafes 8am-9pm.

Casas de Cambio (Currency-exchange offices) 9am-7pm, usually daily.

Cenotes 9am-5pm.

Museums Many close on Monday.

Stores 9am-8pm Monday to Saturday; some close from 2pm-5pm.

PUBLIC HOLIDAYS

Banks, post offices, government offices and many shops throughout Mexico are closed on the following national holidays:

Año Nuevo (New Year's Day) January 1

Día de la Constitución (Constitution Day) February 5

Día del Nacimiento de Benito Juárez (Anniversary of Benito Juárez' birth) March 21

Día del Trabajo (Labor Day) May 1

Día de la Independencia (Independence Day) September 16

Día de la Revolución (Revolution Day) November 20

Día de Navidad (Christmas Day) December 25

In addition, many offices and businesses close on the following optional holidays:

Día de la Bandera (National Flag Day) February 24

Viernes Santo (Good Friday) Two days before Easter Sunday

Cinco de Mayo (Commemorates Mexico's victory over French forces in Puebla) May 5

Día de la Raza (Columbus' 'discovery' of the New World) October 12

Día de Muertos (Day of the Dead) November 1 and 2

Día de Nuestra Señora de Guadalupe (Day of Our Lady of Guadalupe) December 12

TOURIST PERMIT & FEE

The Mexican tourist permit (tourist card; officially the *forma migratoria multiple* or FMM) is a brief paper document that you must fill out and get stamped by Mexican immigration when you enter Mexico and keep till you leave. It's available at official border crossings, international airports, ports, and often from airlines and Mexican consulates. At land borders you won't usually be given one automatically – you have to ask for it.

A tourist permit only permits you to engage in what are considered to be tourist activities (including sports, health, artistic and cultural activities).

➡ The maximum possible stay is 180 days for most nationalities but immigration officers will sometimes put a lower number unless you tell them specifically what you need.

➡ The fee for the tourist permit, called the *derecho para no inmigrante* (DNI; nonimmigrant fee), is M$332, but it's free for people entering by land who stay less than seven days. If you enter Mexico by air, however, the fee is usually included in your airfare.

➡ If you enter by land, you must pay the fee at a bank in Mexico at any time before you reenter the frontier zone on your way out of Mexico (or before you check-in at an airport to fly out of Mexico). Most Mexican border posts have on-the-spot bank offices where you can pay the DNI fee. When you pay at a bank, your tourist permit will be stamped to prove that you have paid.

➡ Look after your tourist permit because it may be checked when you leave the country. You can be fined for not having it.

VISAS

Every tourist must have a Mexican government tourist permit, which is easily obtainable. Some nationalities also need to obtain visas.

➡ Citizens of the US, Canada, EU countries, Australia, New Zealand, Iceland, Israel, Japan, Norway and Switzerland are among the dozens of countries whose citizens do not require visas to enter Mexico as tourists.

➡ The website of the **Instituto Nacional de Migración** (☑ toll-free 800-004-62-64; www. inm.gob.mx) lists countries that must obtain a visa to travel to Mexico. If the purpose of your visit is to work (even as a volunteer), to report, to study, or to participate in humanitarian aid or human-rights observation, you may well need a visa whatever your nationality. Visa procedures can take several weeks and you may be required to apply in your country of citizenship or residence.

➡ US citizens traveling by land or sea can enter Mexico and return to the US with a passport card, but if traveling by air will need a passport. Non-US citizens passing (even in transit) through the US on the way to or from Mexico should check well in advance on the US's complicated visa rules. Consult a US consulate, the **US State Department** (www.travel.state.gov), or **US Customs and Border Protection** (www. cbp.gov) websites.

➡ The regulations sometimes change. It's wise to confirm them with a Mexican embassy or consulate. Good sources for information on visa and similar matters are the **London consulate** (consulmex.sre.gob.mx/reinounido) and the **Washington consulate** (consulmex. sre.gob.mx/washington).

VOLUNTEERING

Volunteering is a great way of giving back to local communities. In the Yucatán there are various organizations that welcome any help they can get, from environmental and wildlife-conservation NGOs to social programs. You can always look for opportunities at your local hostel or language school, some of which offer part-time volunteering opportunities. Most programs require a minimum commitment of at least a month, and some charge fees for room and board.

❶ Getting There & Away

AIR

The majority of flights into the peninsula arrive in Cancún or Mérida. The Yucatán's major airports:

Aeropuerto Ángel Albino Corzo (☑ 961-153-60-68; www.chiapasaero.com; Sarabia s/n) Aka Tuxtla Gutiérrez; serves San Cristóbal de las Casas in Chiapas.

Aeropuerto Internacional de Cancún (☑ 998-848-72-00; www.asur.com.mx; Hwy 307 Km 22)

Aeropuerto Internacional de Mérida (Mérida International Airport; ☑ 999-940-60-90; www. asur.com.mx; Hwy 180 Km 4.5; ☒ R-79)

Cozumel Airport (☑ 987-872-20-81; www.asur. com.mx; cnr Av 65 & Blvd Aeropuerto; ☎)

Other cities with airports include Campeche, Chetumal, Ciudad del Carmen, Palenque and Villahermosa.

BOAT

Water taxis depart from Chetumal's *muelle fiscal* (dock) on Boulevard Bahía to San Pedro (Belize). Between the two companies operating water taxis, there's daily service to the island. See www.sanpedrowatertaxi.com and www.belize watertaxi.com for more information.

You can also charter a boat to San Pedro at the **XTC Dive Center** (www.xtcdivecenter.com;

EATING PRICE RANGES

The following price ranges refer to the cost of a main meal.

$	less than M$80
$$	M$80–160
$$$	more than M$160

Coast road Km 0.3; 2-tank dives to Banco Chinchorro US$110, snorkeling trips US$45-75, PADI certification US$529, r US$45-60) in Xcalak for US$300 (minimum of five passengers required).

Mahahual, Puerto Chiapas, Progreso and Isla Cozumel are ports of call for cruise ships. Many cruise-ship lines serve these ports.

BORDER CROSSINGS
Belize
➡ Crossing from Mexico into Belize, at the southern tip of Quintana Roo, is easy for most tourists and there are no special fees for such a visit.

➡ Each person leaving Belize for Mexico needs to pay a US$15 exit fee for visits less than 24 hours and US$19 for longer stays. All fees must be paid in cash, in Belizean or US currency – officials usually won't have change for US currency.

➡ Frequent buses run from Chetumal to the Belizean towns of Corozal (M$40 to M$50, one hour) and Orange Walk (M$75, two hours). The buses depart from the Nuevo Mercado Lázaro Cárdenas and some continue on to Belize City (M$150, four hours).

➡ Car-rental companies do not allow you to cross the Mexico–Belize border with their vehicles.

Guatemala
➡ The borders at La Mesilla/Ciudad Cuauhté- moc, Ciudad Tecún Umán/Ciudad Hidalgo and El Carmen/Talismán are all linked to Guatemala City, and nearby cities within Guatemala and Mexico, by plentiful buses and/or *combis* (minibuses).

➡ Agencies in San Cristóbal de las Casas offer daily van service to the Guatemalan cities of Quetzaltenango, Panajachel and Antigua.

➡ Additionally, there's a daily bus departing from the San Cristóbal de las Casas bus station that goes to the Ciudad Cuauhtémoc border, where you can catch Guatemalan buses on the other side in the border town of La Mesilla.

➡ **Transportes Palenque** (cnr Allende & Av 20 de Noviembre) runs vans out of Palenque to Tenosique (Tabasco), where you'll find onward connections to Guatemala.

➡ Travelers with their own vehicles can travel by road between Tenosique and Flores (Guatemala), via the border at El Ceibo.

➡ Car-rental companies do not allow you to cross the Mexico–Guatemala border with their vehicles.

ⓘ Getting Around

BOAT
Frequent ferries depart from Playa del Carmen to Isla Cozumel, Cancún to Isla Mujeres and

Chiquilá to Isla Holbox. The following prices are one-way fares:
➡ **Isla Holbox** M$80
➡ **Isla Cozumel** M$135 to M$163
➡ **Isla Mujeres** M$78 from Puerto Juárez, about M$230 from Zona Hotelera

Cancún and Chiquilá have long-term parking available near the terminals. For more information about schedules, points of departure and car ferries, see www.granpuerto.com.mx and www.transcaribe.net. The Holbox ferries do not have websites.

To reach the uninhabited island of Isla Contoy, you can hook up with tour operators with boats departing from **Cancún** (p53) and **Isla Mujeres** (p57).

BUS
The Yucatán Peninsula has a good road and bus network, and comfortable, frequent, reasonably priced bus services connect all cities. Most cities and towns have one main bus terminal where all long-distance buses arrive and depart. It may be called the Terminal de Autobuses, Central de Autobuses, Central Camionera or simply La Central (not to be confused with *el centro,* the city center). If there is no single main bus terminal, different bus companies will have separate terminals scattered around town. **Grupo ADO** (☑ 800-900-01-05; www.ado.com.mx) operates most of the bus lines that you'll be using.

COLECTIVOS & COMBIS
On much of the peninsula, a variety of vehicles – often Volkswagen, Ford or Chevrolet vans – operate shared transportation services between towns or nearby neighborhoods. These vehicles usually leave whenever they are full. Fares are typically less than those of 1st-class buses. *Combi* is a term often used for the Volkswagen variety; *colectivo* refers to any van type. *Taxi colectivo* may mean either public or private transportation, depending on the location.

HITCHHIKING
Hitchhiking is never entirely safe in any country and even in Mexico's relatively safe Yucatán region it's best avoided. Travelers who decide to hitchhike should understand that they are taking a small, but potentially serious risk. Keep in mind that kidnappings for ransom can – and do – still happen in Mexico. People who choose to hitchhike will be safer if they travel in pairs and let someone know where they are planning to go. A woman traveling alone certainly should not hitchhike in Mexico, and even two women together is not advisable, especially when traveling near the Mexico–Guatemala border.

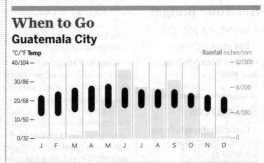

Guatemala

📞 502 / POP 15 MILLION

Includes ➡

Guatemala City	101
Antigua	114
Lago de Atitlán	128
Chichicastenango	144
Quetzaltenango	151
Huehuetenango	161
Cobán	173
Lago de Izabal	184
Lívingston	189
El Petén	193
Flores & Santa Elena	196
Tikal	202

Why Go?

Guatemala is a magical place. If you're into the Maya, the mountains, the markets, kicking back lakeside or exploring atmospheric pre-Columbian ruins and gorgeous colonial villages, you're bound to be captivated.

Want to surf in the morning and learn Spanish in the afternoon? No problem. Descend a volcano, grab a shower and hit the sushi bar for dinner? You can do that. Check out a Maya temple and be swinging in a beachside hammock by sunset? Easy.

Guatemala's got its problems, but they mainly keep to themselves (although if you go looking for trouble, who knows what you'll find). Travel here – once fraught with danger and discomfort – is now characterized by ease; you can do pretty much whatever you want, and your experience will only be limited by your imagination and time.

Best Places to Eat

- ➡ Las Orquídeas (p202)
- ➡ Restaurante Hana (p134)
- ➡ Taberna El Pelicano (p171)
- ➡ Xkape Koba'n (p176)
- ➡ Cactus Grill (p123)
- ➡ Ambia (p107)

Best Places to Sleep

- ➡ La Fortuna (p143)
- ➡ Finca Ixobel (p195)
- ➡ Takalik Maya Lodge (p166)
- ➡ El Hostal (p121)
- ➡ Dai Nonni (p107)

When to Go
Guatemala City

Dec–May Festivities such as Christmas and Easter are celebrated with gusto.	Apr–Sep Prices drop and crowds thin out as the rainy season starts in earnest.	Oct–Nov Rains begin to ease, making for good hiking weather.

GUATEMALA

AT A GLANCE

Currency Quetzal (Q)

Language Spanish (official), 21 Maya languages, Garifuna

Visas Generally not required for stays up to three months.

Money ATMs widely available. Credit cards accepted in higher-end places.

Time GMT/UTC minus six hours

Area 108,890 sq km

Capital Guatemala City

Emergency ☑1500 (English), ☑110 (Spanish)

Exchange Rates

Australia	A$1	Q5.72
Canada	C$1	Q6.03
Euro zone	€1	Q8.73
Japan	¥100	Q7.17
New Zealand	NZ$1	Q5.44
UK	UK£1	Q11.09
US	US$1	Q7.65

Set Your Budget

➡ **Hostel bed** Q80–100

➡ **Set meal** Q30–45

➡ **Three-hour 'chicken bus' ride** Q20

Resources

➡ **Lanic Guatemala** (www.lanic.utexas.edu/la/ca/guatemala)

➡ **EntreMundos** (www.entremundos.org)

➡ **Lonely Planet** (www.lonelyplanet.com/guatemala)

Connections

From Mexico enter Guatemala at Ciudad Hidalgo or Ciudad Cuauhtémoc. From El Salvador enter via Anguiatú; from Honduras via Agua Caliente; and from Belize via Benque Viejo del Carmen. For more detailed information, see Survival Guide p227.

ITINERARIES

One Week

With a week up your sleeve you won't see it all, but you can at least catch the Big Three. Make a beeline for Antigua and spend a couple of days wallowing in colonial glory and climbing volcanoes before heading off to Lago de Atitlán. Choose which village suits you, from bustling Panajachel to out-of-the-way San Juan, and explore the lake and its surrounds by boat, kayak, horseback, bike or whatever else takes your fancy. From there, head back to Guatemala City and catch a bus or plane to Flores, your stepping-off point for the mother of all Maya ruins, Tikal.

Two Weeks

Add another week and you'll have time for a quick dip in the lovely limestone pools at Semuc Champey and a boat ride down the lush Río Dulce. Try to set a day aside for Guatemala City's fantastic collection of museums and galleries.

Essential Food & Drink

➡ **Where to Eat** The cheapest eats are found at food stalls around the central plaza or bus terminal – exercise common sense when buying food at these places. Family-run *comedores* (eating halls) are the next up the budget scale, often serving good-value set meals for a pittance. Towns with large tourist populations, such as Antigua and Panajachel, offer the greatest variety of eats, all the way up to world-class fusion restaurants.

➡ **What to Eat** You won't be able to avoid corn tortillas, and you shouldn't try, either – done right they're delicious. The most common varieties are made with yellow or white corn, but the blue corn and flour ones are worth looking out for, too. The best drinks for miles around are *licuados,* fresh fruit juice blends made with milk or water. Keep an eye out for regional specialties like *tapado* (a seafood stew, found mostly on the Caribbean coast), *pepián* (spicy sesame-seed sauce served with chicken or turkey) and *jocón* (a stew of chicken or pork with green vegetables and herbs), found in the highlands; and *boxbol* (maize dough and chopped meat or chicken), a staple in the Ixil Triangle area.

GUATEMALA CITY

POP 3.4 MILLION / ELEV 1500M

Depending on who you talk to, Guatemala City (or Guate as it's known) is either big, dirty, dangerous and utterly forgettable or big, dirty, dangerous and fascinating. Either way, there's no doubt there's an energy here unlike anywhere else in Guatemala. It's a place where dilapidated buses belch fumes next to BMWs and Hummers, and where skyscrapers drop shadows on shantytowns.

Guate is busy reinventing itself as a people-friendly city. Downtown Zona 1, for years a no-go zone of abandoned buildings and crime hot spots, is leading the way with the pedestrianized 6a Calle attracting bars, cafes and restaurants.

Many travelers skip the city altogether, preferring to make Antigua their base. Still, you may want, or need, to get acquainted with the capital, because this is the hub of the country, home to the best museums and galleries, transportation hubs and other traveler services.

◉ Sights & Activities

The major sights are in Zona 1 (the historic center) and Zonas 10 and 13, where the museums are grouped. If you're in town on a Sunday, consider taking the TransMetro's SubiBaja (Map p104; ◉9am-2pm) FREE hop-on, hop-off self-guided tour – it's an excellent way to see many of the city's sights without worrying about public transportation or taxis.

◉ Zona 1

Parque Central   PLAZA
(Plaza de la Constitución; Map p104; Zona 1) Guatemala City's central plaza is an excellent starting point to begin your journey onto other Zona 1 sights. Parque Central and the adjoining Parque Centenario are never empty during daylight hours, with shoeshine boys, ice-cream vendors and sometimes open-air political meetings adding to the general bustle.

Palacio Nacional de la Cultura   HISTORIC BUILDING
(Map p104; ☑2253-0748; cnr 6a Av & 6a Calle, Zona 1; Q40; ◉9-11:45am & 2-4:45pm Mon-Sat) On the north side of Parque Central is this imposing presidential palace, built between 1936 and 1943 during the dictatorial rule of General Jorge Ubico at enormous cost to the lives of the prisoners who were forced to labor here. It's the third palace to stand on the site.

Centro Cultural Metropolitano   CULTURAL CENTER
(Map p104; 7a Av 11-67, Zona 1; ◉9am-5pm Mon-Fri) To the rear of the ground floor of the *palacio de correos* (post office) you'll find a surprisingly avant-garde cultural center, hosting art exhibitions, book launches, handicraft workshops and film nights.

Casa MIMA   MUSEUM
(Map p104; ☑2253-4020; www.casamima.org; 8a Av 14-12, Zona 1; Q20; ◉10am-5pm Mon-Sat) A wonderfully presented museum and cultural center set in a house dating from the late 1800s. The owners of the house were collectors with eclectic tastes ranging from French neorococo, Chinese and art deco to indigenous artifacts. The place is set up like a functioning house, filled with curios and furniture spanning the centuries.

Museo del Ferrocarril   MUSEUM
(Railway Museum; Map p104; www.museofegua.com; 9a Av 18-03, Zona 1; Q5; ◉9am-4pm Tue-Fri, 10am-4pm Sat & Sun) This is one of the city's more intriguing museums. Documented here are the glory days of the troubled Guatemalan rail system, along with some quirky artifacts, such as hand-drawn diagrams of derailments and a kitchen set up with items used in dining cars. You can go climbing around the passenger carriages, but not the locomotives.

Museo Nacional de Historia   MUSEUM
(Map p104; ☑2253-6149; 9a Calle 9-70, Zona 1; Q10; ◉9am-5pm Mon-Fri) This museum hosts a jumble of historical relics with an emphasis on photography and portraits. Check the carefully coiffed hairstyles of the 19th-century generals and politicos.

◉ Zona 2

Mapa en Relieve   MONUMENT
(Relief Map; www.mapaenrelieve.org; Av Simeón Cañas Final, Zona 2; Q30; ◉9am-5pm) North of Zona 1, Zona 2 is mostly a middle-class residential district, but it's worth venturing along to Parque Minerva to see this huge open-air map of Guatemala showing the country at a scale of 1:10,000. The vertical scale is exaggerated to 1:2000 to make the volcanoes and mountains appear dramatically higher and steeper than they really are.

GUATEMALA GUATEMALA CITY

Guatemala Highlights

1 Tikal (p202) Sidestepping the tour groups to find out for yourself why this is Guatemala's number one tourist attraction.

2 Antigua (p114) Eating, drinking and sleeping well, studying Spanish and climbing volcanoes in this cosmopolitan and picturesque town.

3 Livingston (p189) Seeing another side of Guatemala in this Garifuna enclave.

4 Western Highlands (p127) Hiking the country's best trekking routes.

5 Semuc Champey (p178) Discovering why people call this the most beautiful place in the country.

6 Río Dulce boat tour (p186) Taking a spectacular boat ride through a jungle-walled canyon on the Río Dulce between Río Dulce town and Livingston.

7 San Marcos La Laguna (p141) Exploring Lake Atitlán's prettiest and most laidback village.

8 Santa Lucía Cotzumalguapa (p167) Investigating beguiling stone sculptures from a pre-Maya culture.

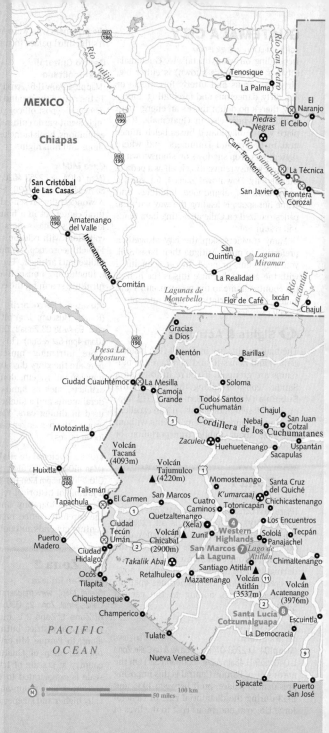

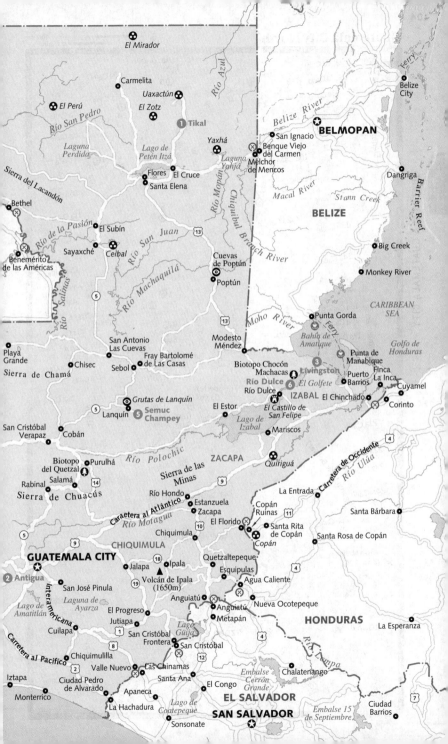

Guatemala City North

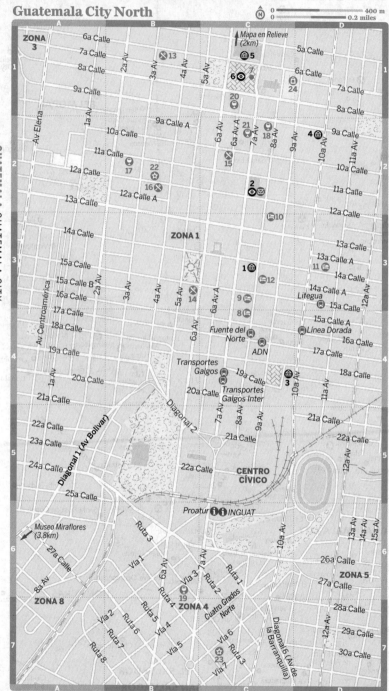

Guatemala City North

◉ Sights
1 Casa MIMA C3
2 Centro Cultural Metropolitano C2
3 Museo del Ferrocarril C4
4 Museo Nacional de Historia D2
5 Palacio Nacional de la Cultura C1
6 Parque Central C1

◉ Activities, Courses & Tours
7 SubiBaja C1

◉ Sleeping
8 Hotel Ajau C4
9 Hotel Clariss C3
10 Hotel Spring C3
11 Posada Belen D3
12 Theatre International Hostel C3

◉ Eating
13 Café de Imeri B1
14 Café-Restaurante Hamburgo B3
15 La Cocina de Señora Pu C2
16 La Majo B2

◉ Drinking & Nightlife
17 Black & White Lounge B2
18 El Gran Hotel C2
19 Genetic B6
20 Las Cien Puertas C1
21 Los Lirios C2

◉ Entertainment
22 La Bodeguita del Centro B2
23 TrovaJazz C7

◉ Shopping
24 Mercado Central C1

Parque Minerva   PARK
(Av Simeón Cañas Final, Zona 2) Minerva, the Roman goddess of wisdom, technical skill and invention, was a favorite of President Manuel Estrada Cabrera. Her park is a placid place, good for walking among the eucalyptus trees and sipping a cool drink. Watch out, however, for pickpockets and purse-snatchers.

◉ Zona 10

Museo Ixchel   MUSEUM
(Map p108; ☎ 2361-8081; www.museoixchel.org; 6a Calle Final, Zona 10; Q35; ☺ 9am-5pm Mon-Fri, to 1pm Sat) This museum is named for the Maya goddess of the moon, women, reproduction and, of course, textiles. Photographs and exhibits of indigenous costumes and other crafts show the incredible richness of traditional arts in Guatemala's highland towns.

Guided tours are available in English (with prior reservation) or Spanish.

Museo Popol Vuh   MUSEUM
(Map p108; ☎ 2338-7896; www.popolvuh.ufm.edu; 6a Calle Final, Zona 10; adult/child Q35/10; ☺ 9am-5pm Mon-Fri, to 1pm Sat) Behind Museo Ixchel, here you'll find well-displayed pre-Hispanic figurines, incense burners and burial urns, plus carved wooden masks and traditional textiles, filling several rooms. Other rooms hold colonial paintings and gilded wood and silver artifacts. A faithful copy of the *Dresden Codex,* one of the precious 'painted books' of the Maya, is among the most interesting pieces.

Pasos y Pedales   FISHING
(Map p108; ☺ 10am-2pm Sun) If you're here on a Sunday, check out a wonderful municipal initiative that sees the Av de las Americas in Zona 10, and its continuation, Av la Reforma in Zona 13, blocked off to traffic for 3km and taken over by jugglers, clowns, in-line skaters, dog walkers, food vendors, tai chi classes, skate parks and playgrounds for kids.

◉ Zona 13 & Around

The attractions here in the city's southern reaches are all ranged along 5a Calle in the Finca Aurora area, northwest of the airport. While here you can also drop into the **Mercado de Artesanías** (Crafts Market; Map p108; ☎ 2475-5915; cnr 5a Calle & 11a Av, Zona 13; ☺ 9:30am-6pm).

Museo Nacional de Arqueología y Etnología   MUSEUM
(Map p108; ☎ 2475-4399; www.munae.gob.gt; 6a Calle, Sala 5, Finca La Aurora, Zona 13; Q60; ☺ 9am-4pm Tue-Fri, 9am-noon & 1:30-4pm Sat & Sun) This museum has the country's biggest collection of ancient Maya artifacts, but explanatory information is very sparse. There's a great wealth of monumental stone sculpture, including Classic-period stelae from Tikal, Uaxactún and Piedras Negras; a superb throne from Piedras Negras; and animal representations from Preclassic Kaminaljuyú.

Museo Nacional de Arte Moderno   GALLERY
(Map p108; ☎ 2472-0467; 6a Calle, Sala 6, Finca La Aurora, Zona 13; Q10; ☺ 9am-4pm Tue-Fri, 9am-12:30pm & 2-4pm Sat & Sun) Here you'll find a collection of 20th-century Guatemalan art including works by well-known Guatemalan artists such as Carlos Mérida, Carlos Valente and Humberto Gavarito.

GUATEMALA GUATEMALA CITY

Museo Nacional de
Historia Natural Jorge Ibarra   MUSEUM

(Map p108; ☑2472-0468; 6a Calle 7-30, Zona 13; Q10; ⊘9am-4pm Tue-Sun) Behind the archaeology museum is this natural history museum, the claim to fame of which is its large collection of dissected animals.

La Aurora Zoo   ZOO

(Map p108; ☑2472-0507; www.aurorazoo.org.gt; 5a Calle, Zona 13; adult/child Q30/15; ⊘9am-5pm Tue-Sun) This is not badly kept as far as zoos in this part of the world go, and the lovely, parklike grounds alone are worth the admission fee.

X-Park   ADVENTURE SPORTS

(☑2380-2080; www.xpark.net; Av Hincapié, Km 11.5; Q15; ⊘10am-6pm) About 10 minutes' drive south of the airport is this very well-constructed 'adventure sports' park. Attractions (they prefer to call them 'challenges') cost from Q20 each and include bouldering and climbing walls, reverse bungees, mechanical bulls, a rope course, zip lines and a playground for kids. A fairly limited range of fast food is available at the cafeteria.

🛏 Sleeping

For budget and many midrange hotels, make a beeline for Zona 1. If you have just flown in or are about to fly out, there are a number of convenient guesthouses near the airport.

🛏 Zona 1

★Theatre International Hostel   HOSTEL $

(Map p104; ☑4202-5112; www.theatreihostel.com; 8a Av 14-17, Zona 1; dm Q60-80, r without bathroom from Q170; 🕸🏊) Zona 1's best hostel is a simple affair, but a welcome sight nonetheless. Rooms and dorms are spacious, the whole place is spotless and the small pool in the patio is a perfect refresher on those muggy city days.

Hotel Clariss   HOTEL $

(Map p104; ☑2232-1113; www.hotelclarissya sociados.amawebs.com; 8a Av 15-14, Zona 1; s/d Q190/240, s/d without bathroom Q145/190; 🅿@) This friendly place is set in a modern building with some good-sized rooms (and other, smaller ones). Those at the front get more air and light, but also the bulk of the street noise.

Hotel Spring   HOTEL $

(Map p104; ☑2230-2858; www.hotelspring.com; 8a Av 12-65, Zona 1; s/d from Q190/235, s/d without bathroom Q140/180; 🅿@🕸) With a beautiful courtyard setting, the Spring has a lot more style than other Zona 1 joints. It has central but quiet sunny patios. The 43 rooms vary greatly, but most are spacious and clean with high ceilings. Have a look around if you can. All rooms have cable TV; some of the more expensive ones are wheelchair accessible.

Hotel Ajau   HOTEL $

(Map p104; ☑2232-0488; hotelajau@hotmail.com; 8a Av 15-62, Zona 1; s/d Q180/230, s/d without bathroom Q110/140; 🅿@🕸) One of the few budget hotels in Guate with any tangible sense of style, the Ajau is a pretty good deal, with lovely polished floor tiles and cool, clean rooms. Room sizes vary and those at the front can get very noisy.

★Posada Belen   BOUTIQUE HOTEL $$

(Map p104; ☑2232-6178; www.posadabelen.com; 13a Calle A 10-20, Zona 1; s/d Q330/420; @🕸) One of Zona 1's most stylish options, this boutique hotel has just 10 rooms, arranged around a couple of lush patios. Rooms are well decorated with *típico* (traditional) furnishings and there's a good restaurant onsite.

🛏 Zonas 10 & 13

Quetzalroo   HOSTEL $

(Map p108; ☑5746-0830; www.quetzalroo.com; 6a Av 7-84, Zona 10; dm/s/d without bathroom Q120/200/280; 🅿@🕸) Guatemala City's best downtown hostel has reasonable rooms and dorms, a cramped kitchen area and a great rooftop terrace. The location's handy for the Zona Viva eating and nightlife scene. Call for free pick-up from the airport or bus terminal.

Hostal Los Lagos   HOSTEL $

(☑2261-2809; www.loslagoshostal.com; 8a Av 15-85 Aurora 1, Zona 13; dm/s/d Q120/170/320, s/d without bathroom Q140/180; 🅿@🕸) This is the most hostel-like of the near-the-airport options. Rooms are mostly set aside for dorms, which are airy and spacious, but there are a couple of reasonable-value private rooms. The whole place is extremely comfortable, with big indoor and outdoor sitting areas.

★Eco Suites Uxlabil   APARTMENT $$

(Map p108; ☑2366-9555; www.uxlabil.com; 11a Calle 12-53, Zona 10; s/d incl breakfast Q395/495; ✳🕸) If you're planning on being in town for a while (or even if you're not) you could do a lot worse than these sweet little apartments decked out in indigenous motifs and tucked away in a leafy corner of Zona 10. Weekly discounts apply.

★ **Dai Nonni** HOTEL $$$
(☑2362-5458; www.dainonnihotel.com; 15 Av A 5-30, Zona 13; s/d Q695/790; ☎) Just south of the Zona 10 action, this small hotel wins points for its eclectic decorations, backyard hangout areas and spacious rooms. Discounts are available for cash payments and longer stays.

✖ Eating

For cheap eats head to Zona 1 – there are little *comedores* around the Mercado Central, and the cheapest of all are inside the market, on the lower floor. Zonas 10 and 14 have the lion's share of upscale restaurants, with a good selection of international cuisines.

North American fast-food chains are sprinkled liberally throughout Zona 1 and across the city. Pollo Campero is Guatemala's KFC clone.

✖ Zona 1

★ **Café de Imeri** CAFE $
(Map p104; 6a Calle 3-34, Zona 1; mains Q40-70; ☺8am-6:30pm Mon-Sat; ☎) Interesting breakfasts, soups and pastas. The list of sandwiches is impressive and there's a beautiful little courtyard area out the back.

Café-Restaurante Hamburgo GUATEMALAN $
(Map p104; 15a Calle 5-34, Zona 1; set meals Q35-55; ☺7am-9:30pm) This bustling spot facing the south side of Parque Concordia serves good Guatemalan food, with chefs at work along one side and orange-aproned waitstaff scurrying about. At weekends a marimba band adds atmosphere.

★ **La Cocina de Señora Pu** GUATEMALAN $$
(Map p104; 6a Av A 10-16, Zona 1; mains around Q80; ☺noon-8pm Mon-Sat) This tiny hole-in-the-wall eatery serves up excellent 'modernized' versions of classic Maya dishes. The menu is impressively wide – featuring beef, chicken, pork, duck, turkey, pigeon, rabbit, fish and shrimp – considering it's all done on a four-burner stove in front of your eyes and the flavors are delicious and sometimes surprising.

La Majo GUATEMALAN $$
(Map p104; 12a Calle 3-08, Zona 1; mains Q50-80; ☺10am-7pm; ✐) Downtown Guatemala City's cultural renovation continues in this pleasing

little boho cafe set in a crumbling colonial house. There's some OK food on offer and a couple of vegetarian and vegan dishes, but the big draw is the events calendar, featuring live music, theater and other local acts.

✖ Zonas 10 & 14

★ **Arbol de la Vida** VEGETARIAN $
(17 Calle A 19-60, Zona 10; mains around Q50; ☺7:30am-6pm Mon & Tue, to 8pm Wed-Fri, to 4pm Sat & Sun; ☎✐) Zona 10's best vegetarian restaurant opens up for early breakfasts and offers a wide menu with tasty soups and mains featuring veg-friendly goodies such as tofu and quinoa.

San Martín & Company CAFE, BAKERY $
(Map p108; 13a Calle 1-62, Zona 10; light meals Q40-60; ☺6am-8pm; ☎) Cool and clean, with ceiling fans inside and a small terrace outside, this Zona Viva cafe and bakery is great at any time of the day. For breakfast try a scrumptious omelet and croissant (the former arrives inside the latter); later there are tempting and original sandwiches, soups and salads.

Pecorino ITALIAN $$$
(Map p108; ☑2360-3035; 11a Calle 3-36, Zona 10; mains Q120-250; ☺noon-1am Mon-Sat, to 6pm Sun; ☎) With a beautiful courtyard setting, this is widely regarded as the city's best Italian restaurant. The menu features a huge selection of antipasto, pizza, pasta, meat and seafood dishes.

★ **Ambia** FUSION $$$
(www.fdg.com.gt; 10a Av 5-49, Zona 14; mains Q150-300; ☺noon-midnight Mon-Sat) As the prices may suggest, this is some of the city's finest dining, with a wide-ranging menu offering some good fusion dishes and leaning heavily on Asian influences. The presentation is fantastic and the ambiance superb. On balmy nights, the outdoor courtyard-lounge area is the place to be.

🍸 Drinking & Nightlife

Zona 1 boasts a clutch of good drinking places, including some Latin music and dance venues, all advantageously within half a block of each other just south of Parque Central.

Zona 10 has a few electronic dance clubs, but many of these have now moved further south to the outskirts of town. Check flyers around town for special nights.

Guatemala City South

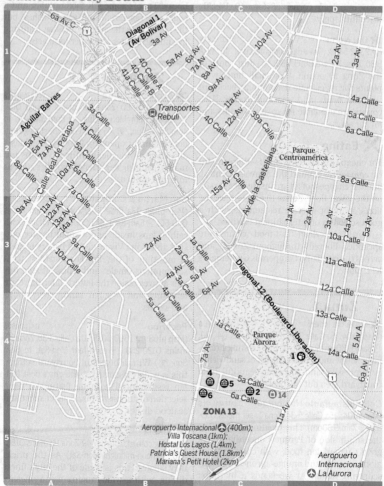

Guatemala City South

◉ Sights
1 La Aurora Zoo		D4
2 Museo de los Niños		C5
3 Museo Ixchel		G2
4 Museo Nacional de Arqueología y Etnología		C4
5 Museo Nacional de Arte Moderno		C4
6 Museo Nacional de Historia Natural Jorge Ibarra		C5
7 Museo Popol Vuh		H2

✪ Activities, Courses & Tours
8 Pasos y Pedales		F2

🛏 Sleeping
9 Eco Suites Uxlabil		H4
10 Quetzalroo		F2

🍴 Eating
11 Pecorino		F4
12 San Martín & Company		F4

🛍 Shopping
13 Centro Comercial Los Próceres		E5
14 Mercado de Artesanías		C5
15 Oakland Mall		G4
16 Sophos		F4

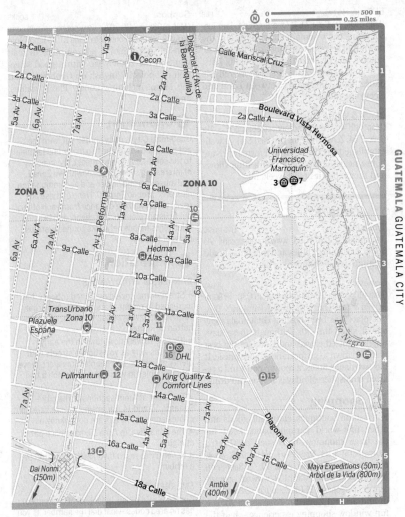

🍸 Zona 1

⭐ **La Bodeguita del Centro** LIVE MUSIC
(Map p104; ☏ 2230-2976; 12a Calle 3-55, Zona 1; ⏰ 9pm-1am Tue-Sat) There's a hopping, creative local scene in Guatemala City, and this large, bohemian hangout is one of the best places to connect with it. There's live music of some kind almost every night from Tuesday to Saturday, usually starting at 9pm, plus occasional poetry readings, films or forums.

Las Cien Puertas BAR
(Map p104; 9a Calle 6-45, Pasaje Aycinena 8-44, Zona 1; ⏰ noon-1am) This superhip (but not studiously so) little watering hole is set in a shabby colonial arcade that's said to have a hundred doors (hence the name) and is sometimes closed off for live bands.

Los Lirios CLUB
(Map p104; 7a Av 9-20, Zona 1; ⏰ 5pm-1am Wed-Sat) With live Latin music and dancing most nights, this is a popular choice for the over-25s crowd.

El Gran Hotel
PUB

(Map p104; 9a Calle 7-64, Zona 1; ⊙6pm-1am Tue-Sun) You can't actually stay here, but the down-market renovated lobby of this classic hotel is one of Zona 1's better-looking bars. It also hosts one of the area's more reliable dance floors, alternating between Latin and electronic music.

Black & White Lounge
GAY

(Map p104; www.blackandwhitebar.com; 11a Calle 2-54, Zona 1; ⊙7pm-1am Wed-Sat) A well-established gay disco-bar in a former private house near the city center with drag shows and theme parties most weekends.

Zona 4

TrovaJazz
LIVE MUSIC

(Map p104; ☑2267-9388; www.trovajazz.com; Vía 6 3-55, Zona 4) Jazz, blues and folk fans should look into what's happening here.

Genetic
GAY

(Map p104; Ruta 3 3-08, Zona 4; from Q30; ⊙9pm-1am Fri & Sat) Formerly called Pandora's Box, this place has been hosting Guatemala's gay crowd since the '70s, although these days it gets a mixed crowd and is one of the best places in town to go for trance/dance music. It has two dance floors, a rooftop patio and a relaxed atmosphere. Friday is 'all you can drink.'

🔒 Shopping

For fashion boutiques, electronic goods and other first-world paraphernalia, head for the large shopping malls such as **Centro Comercial Los Próceres** (Map p108; www. proceres.com; 16a Calle, Zona 10; ⊙8am-8pm) or **Oakland Mall** (Map p108; www.oaklandmall. com.gt; Diagonal 6 13-01, Zona 10; ⊙8am-8pm) in and around Zona 10. Zona 1's 6a Av is a fun window-shopping experience – half the city turns out to check out the shops, eat ice cream and just cruise the pedestrian mall.

Mercado Central
MARKET

(Map p104; cnr 8a Av & 8a Calle, Zona 1; ⊙9am-6pm Mon-Sat, to noon Sun) Until the quake of 1976, Mercado Central, behind the cathedral, was where locals shopped for food and other necessities. Reconstructed after the earthquake, it now deals in colorful Guatemalan handicrafts such as textiles, carved wood, metalwork, pottery, leather goods and basketry, and is a pretty good place to shop for these kinds of things, with reasonable prices.

Sophos
BOOKS

(Map p108; ☑2419-7070; www.sophosenlinea.com; 4a Av 12-59, Plaza Fontabella, Zona 10; ⊙10am-9pm Mon-Sat, to 7pm Sun) A relaxed place to read while in the Zona Viva, with a good selection of books in English on Guatemala and the Maya, including Lonely Planet guides, and maps.

ⓘ Orientation

Guatemala City is quite spread out, with the airport to the south, the two major bus terminals to the southwest and northeast, the majority of interesting sights in the downtown Zona 1, and museums and higher-end accommodation clustered around Zona 10. None of these are really within walking distance from each other, but taxis are plentiful and cheap, and two new, relatively safe bus networks connect various parts of the city.

ⓘ Information

DANGERS & ANNOYANCES

➤ Street crime, including armed robbery, has increased in recent years. Use normal urban caution (behaving as you would in, say, Manhattan or Rome).

➤ It's safe to walk downtown in the early evening, as long as you stick to streets with plenty of lighting and people. Stay alert, leave your valuables in your hotel and catch a taxi after dark.

➤ The more affluent sections of the city – Zonas 9, 10 and 14, for example – are safer, but crimes against tourists are not unknown.

➤ The Zona Viva, in Zona 10, has police patrols at night.

➤ Never try to resist if you are confronted by a robber.

EMERGENCY

Guatemala City (and, in fact, all of Guatemala) has no area codes – just dial the number as you see it.

INGUAT Tourist Information (☑2421-2854)
Tourist Police Liaison (24 hour; ☑1500)

MEDICAL SERVICES

Guatemala City has many private hospitals and clinics. Public hospitals and clinics provide free consultations, but can be busy; to reduce waiting time, get there before 7am.

Hospital Centro Médico (☑2279-4949; 6a Av 3-47, Zona 10; ⊙24hr) Recommended. This private hospital has some English-speaking doctors.

Hospital General San Juan de Dios (☎2232-1187; 1a Av 10-50, Zona 1; ⊗24hr) One of the city's best public hospitals.

MONEY

Card skimming is rife in Guatemala City – try to use ATMs that are under some sort of watch at all times, such as those inside stores or shopping malls.

American Express (☎2331-7422; 12a Calle 0-93, Centro Comercial Montufar, Zona 9; ⊗8am-5pm Mon-Fri, to noon Sat) In an office of Clark Tours.

Banco Agromercantil (7a Av 9-11, Zona 1; ⊗9am-7pm Mon-Fri, to 1pm Sat) Changes US dollars (cash, not traveler's checks).

Banrural (Aeropuerto Internacional La Aurora; ⊗6am-8pm Mon-Fri, to 6pm Sat & Sun) Currency-exchange services. On the airport departures level.

Visa/Mastercard ATM, Zona 1 (18 Calle 6-85; ⊗8am-10pm) Inside the Paiz Supermarket.

Visa/Mastercard ATM, Zona 10 (16a Calle; ⊗10am-8pm Mon-Sat, to 7pm Sun) Inside Los Próceres mall.

POST

DHL (Map p108; ☎2379-1111; www.dhl.com; 12a Calle 5-12, Zona 10; ⊗8am-7:30pm Mon-Fri, to noon Sat) Courier service.

Main Post Office (Map p104; 7a Av 11-67, Zona 1; ⊗8:30am-5pm Mon-Fri, to 1pm Sat) In a huge yellow building at the Palacio de Correos. There's also a small post office at the airport.

TOURIST INFORMATION

Disetur (Tourist Police; ☎2232-0202; 11 Calle 12-06, Zona 1; ⊗24hr) Guatemala's tourist police; travelers are advised to contact their

liaison, **Proatur** (Map p104; ☎toll-free, in English 1500; 7a Av 1-17, Zona 4; ⊗24hr).

INGUAT (Map p104; ☎2421-2800; www.visitguatemala.com; 7a Av 1-17, Zona 4; ⊗8am-4pm Mon-Fri) Main office of the Guatemalan tourism department; has limited handout material, but staff are extremely helpful. There's also a **branch** (☎2322-5055; Aeropuerto Internacional La Aurora; ⊗6am-9pm) at the airport.

ⓘ Getting There & Away

AIR

Guatemala City's **Aeropuerto La Aurora** (Map p104; ☎2260-6257) is the country's major airport. All international flights to Guatemala City land and take off here. The arrivals hall boasts a sometimes-working ATM, sometimes-attended tourist information booth and currency-exchange desks. Various travelers have complained about the rates given at the exchange booth inside arrivals and instead recommend the Banrural bank in the departures hall. There is also a more reliable ATM in the departures hall, helpfully hidden behind the stairs leading up to the mezzanine.

At the time of writing, the country's only *scheduled* domestic flights were between Guatemala City and Flores with **Avianca** (☎2470-8222; www.avianca.com), leaving Guatemala City at 6am and 6:40pm, and **TAG** (☎2380-9494; www.tag.com.gt; cnr Av Hincapie & 18a Calle, Zona 13), which departs at 6:30am and 5:15pm. Domestic flights *may* leave from the domestic terminal, a 15-minute cab ride from the international terminal.

Tickets to Flores cost around Q910/1825 one-way/round-trip with Avianca and Q1065/1825

INTERNATIONAL BUSES FROM GUATEMALA CITY

DESTINATION	COST (Q)	DURATION (HR)	FREQUENCY (DAILY)	COMPANY
San José (Costa Rica)	700-880	40-63	2	Tica Bus
San Salvador (El Salvador)	175-390	5	6	King Quality & Comfort Lines, Tica Bus, Pullmantur
Copán (Honduras)	410-650	5	2	Hedman Alas
La Ceiba (Honduras)	450-690	12	2	Hedman Alas
San Pedro Sula (Honduras)	410-655	8	2	Hedman Alas
Tegucigalpa (Honduras)	305-705	10-35	6	Hedman Alas, King Quality & Comfort Lines, Tica Bus, Pullmantur
Tapachula (Mexico)	175-230	5-7	4	Tica Bus, Línea Dorada, Transportes Galgos Inter
Managua (Nicaragua)	465-625	16-35	2	King Quality & Comfort Lines, Tica Bus
Panama City (Panama)	1040-1350	76	2	Tica Bus

with TAG, but some travel agents, especially in Antigua, offer large discounts on these prices.

Fourteen international airlines also serve Guatemala, flying direct from North, Central and South America and Europe.

BUS

Buses from here run all over Guatemala and into Mexico, Belize, Honduras, El Salvador and beyond. Many bus companies have their own terminals, some of which are in Zona 1. The city council has been on a campaign to get long-distance bus companies out of the city center, so it may be wise to double check with INGUAT or staff at your hotel about the office location before heading out there.

Buses for the Pacific coast mostly leave from the CentraSur terminal in the southern outskirts of town. Departures for central and eastern Guatemala and El Petén mostly leave from CentraNorte in the city's northeast. Second-class buses for the western highlands leave from a series of roadside *paradas* (bus stops) on 41a Calle between 6a and 7a Avs in Zona 8.

International Bus Companies

The following companies offer first-class bus services to international destinations:

Hedman Alas (Map p108; ☑ 2362-5072; www.hedmanalas.com; 2a Av 8-73, Zona 10) Serves multiple destinations in Honduras.

King Quality & Comfort Lines (Map p108; ☑ 2501-1000; www.king-qualityca.com; 4a Av 13-60, Zona 10) Serves most Central American capitals.

Línea Dorada (Map p104; ☑ 2415-8900; www.lineadorada.com.gt; cnr 10a Av & 16a Calle, Zona 1) Has a service to Tapachula, Mexico.

Pullmantur (Map p108; ☑ 2495-7000; www.pullmantur.com; 1a Av 13-22, Holiday Inn, Zona 10) Covers El Salvador and Honduras.

Tica Bus (☑ 2473-3737; www.ticabus.com; Calz Aguilar Batres 18-35, Zona 12) Covers all of Central America and Mexico.

Transportes Galgos Inter (Map p104; ☑ 2232-3661; www.transgalgosinter.com.gt; 7a Av 19-44, Zona 1) Can book connections to Tapachula, Mexico, and as far north as the US. Also goes to El Salvador.

National Pullman Companies

The following bus companies have Pullman services to Guatemalan destinations:

ADN (Map p104; ☑ 2251-0610; www.adnautobusesdelnorte.com; 8a Av 16-41, Zona 1) Flores and Quetzaltenango.

Fortaleza del Sur (☑ 2230-3390; CentraSur, Zona 12) Covers the Pacific coast.

Fuente del Norte (Map p104; ☑ 2251-3817; www.grupofuentedelnorte.com; 17a Calle 8-46, Zona 1) Covers the whole country.

NATIONAL PULLMAN BUSES FROM GUATEMALA CITY

DESTINATION	COST (Q)	DURATION (HR)	FREQUENCY	COMPANY
Antigua	75	1	4 daily	Litegua, Hedman Alas
Chiquimula	60	3	half-hourly 4:30am-6pm	Rutas Orientales
Ciudad Tecún Umán	75	6	4 daily	Fortaleza del Sur
Cobán	60-75	5	hourly 4am-5pm	Monja Blanca
El Carmen (Mexican border)	90	7	hourly 4am-5pm	Fortaleza del Sur
Esquipulas	60	5	half-hourly 4:30am-6pm	Rutas Orientales
Flores & Santa Elena	140-160	8-10	6 daily	Fuente del Norte, Línea Dorada, ADN
Huehuetenango	90-100	5	4 daily	Los Halcones, Línea Dorada
Poptún	120-150	8	3 daily	Línea Dorada
Puerto Barrios	80	5	half-hourly 3:45am-7pm	Litegua
Quetzaltenango	80	4	10 daily	Transportes Galgos, Transportes Alamo, Línea Dorada
Retalhuleu	85	3	5 daily	Fuente del Norte
Río Dulce	70	5	half-hourly 6am-4:30pm	Litegua

Hedman Alas (p112) Daily departures between Guatemala City and Antigua.

Línea Dorada (p112) Luxury buses to El Petén, Quetzaltenango, Huehuetenango, Río Dulce etc.

Litegua (Map p104; 2220-8840; www. litegua.com; 15a Calle 10-40, Zona 1) Covers the east and Antigua.

Los Halcones (2433-9180; Calz Roosevelt 37-47, Zona 11) For Huehuetenango.

Monja Blanca (CentraNorte, Zona 18) For Cobán and points in between.

Rapidos del Sur (2232-7025; CentraSur, Zona 12) For the Pacific coast.

Rutas Orientales (2503-3100; CentraNorte, Zona 18) Covers the east.

Transportes Álamo (2471-8646; 12a Av A 0-65, Zona 7) For Quetzaltenango.

Transportes Galgos (Map p104; 2253-4868; 7a Av 19-44, Zona 1) For Quetzaltenango and Retalhuleu.

Transportes Rebuli (Map p108; 2230-2748; 41a Calle btwn 6a & 7a Av, Zona 8) For Panajachel.

SHUTTLE MINIBUS

Shuttle services from Guatemala City to popular destinations such as Panajachel and Chichicastenango (via Antigua; both around Q260) are offered by travel agencies in Antigua. Quetzaltenango-based travel agents also have shuttles to and from Guatemala City.

ℹ Getting Around

ARRIVING IN GUATEMALA CITY

Aeropuerto La Aurora Guatemala City's international airport is in Zona 13, a Q80 taxi ride to Zona 1 and Q70 to Zona 10. If you're arriving late at night, a popular option is to spend the night in one of the guesthouses close to the airport and get a fresh start the next day.

Bus Arriving from other parts of the country, you'll most likely be coming in on a bus. Guatemala City's bus stations are scattered all over town. Wherever you're going, if it's more than a few blocks away it's a good idea to grab a taxi, which are plentiful (especially around bus stations) and a whole lot cheaper than getting mugged while lugging your backpack around.

BUS

Due to an alarming increase in (often violent) crime on Guatemala City's red city buses, it is pretty much universally accepted that tourists should only use them in case of dire emergency. The major exceptions are the TransMetro and TransUrbano buses, which are most useful for getting to the CentraSur and CentraNorte bus terminals, respectively.

For the thrillseekers out there, listed below are the most useful red bus routes. Buses will stop anywhere they see a passenger, but street corners and traffic lights are your best bet for hailing

2ND-CLASS BUSES FROM GUATEMALA CITY

The services listed below are all 2nd-class bus ('chicken bus') services.

DESTINATION	COST (Q)	DURATION (HR)	FREQUENCY	DEPARTS
Amatitlán	8	30min	every 5min 7am-8:45pm	CentraSur
Antigua	13	1	every 5min 7am-8pm	Calz Roosevelt btwn 4a Av & 5a Av, Zona 7
Chichicastenango	30	3	hourly 5am-6pm	Parada, Zona 8
Ciudad Pedro de Alvarado	55	2½	half-hourly 5am-4pm	CentraSur
Escuintla	25	1	half-hourly 6am-4:30pm	CentraSur
Huehuetenango	65	5	half-hourly 7am-5pm	Parada, Zona 8
La Democracia	30	2	half-hourly 6am-4:30pm	CentraSur
La Mesilla	100	8	hourly 8am-4pm	Parada, Zona 8
Monterrico	45	3	3 daily	CentraSur
Panajachel	40	3	half-hourly 7am-5pm	Parada, Zona 8
Puerto San José	25	1	every 15min 4:30am-4:45pm	CentraSur
Salamá	50	3	half-hourly 5am-5pm	17a Calle 11-32, Zona 1
San Pedro La Laguna	45	4	hourly 2am-2pm	Parada, Zona 8
Santa Cruz del Quiché	45	4	hourly 5am-5pm	Parada, Zona 8
Santiago Atitlán	45	4	half-hourly 4am-5pm	Parada, Zona 8
Tecpán	20	2	every 15min 5:30am-7pm	Parada, Zona 8

GUATEMALA GUATEMALA CITY

ⓘ GETTING TO ANTIGUA

The classic exit strategy on arrival at Guatemala City airport is to make a beeline for elsewhere, usually Antigua. Door-to-door minibuses run to any address in Antigua (usually Q80 per person, one hour). Look for signs in the airport exit hall or for people holding up 'Antigua Shuttle' signs. The first shuttle leaves for Antigua around 7am and the last around 8pm or 9pm, although there's often one hanging around to meet the last flight (around midnight). For groups, the other option is a taxi (around Q250), but if there is only one or two of you, shuttle minibuses are more economical (if a bit slower and less comfortable).

them – just hold out your hand. Buses should cost Q1 per ride in the daytime (but this can as much as quadruple on public holidays or the driver's whim). You pay the driver or his helper as you get on. Don't catch them at night.

Zona 1 to Zona 10 (Bus 82 or 101) Travels via 10a Av, Zona 1, then 6a Av and Ruta 6 in Zona 4 and Av La Reforma.

Zona 10 to Zona 1 (Bus 82 or 101) Travels via Av La Reforma then 7a Av in Zona 4 and 9a Av, Zona 1.

Airport to Zona 1 (Bus 82) Travels via Zonas 9 and 4.

Zona 1 to Airport (Bus 82) Travels via 10a Av in Zona 1 then down 6a Av in Zonas 4 and 9.

TransMetro

In early 2007, in answer to growing concerns about traffic congestion and insecurity on urban buses, Guatemala City inaugurated the Trans-Metro system (http://transmetro.muniguate.com). TransMetro buses differ from regular old, red urban buses because they are prepaid (the driver carries no money, thus reducing the risk of robberies), travel in their own lanes (not getting caught in traffic jams), only stop at designated stops and are new, comfortable and bright green.

There are currently two routes in operation – one connects Zona 1's Plaza Barrios with the CentraSur bus terminal, from where the majority of buses for the Pacific coast now depart. The other runs south from Plaza Barrios through Zonas 9 and 10.

Crime has increased so much on Guate's regular red buses that travelers are advised not to use them, but TransMetro buses are safe, fast and comfortable. All rides cost Q1, payable with a Q1 coin at the bus stop before boarding.

TransUrbano

A more recent improvement to Guatemala City's bus scene is **TransUrbano** (Map p108; www.transurbano.com.gt; cnr Av Reforma & 12a Calle, Zona 10), a much wider network of buses that aren't quite as slick as TransMetro, but are still safe, reliable and comfortable. They're slower because they don't have a dedicated lane, but safer than the old red buses because to board you need a magnetic rechargeable card (card and first ride free), which can only be obtained by showing your passport or Guatemalan ID card. The rechargeable cards are available from special booths, the most useful for travelers being in Zona 1's Plaza Barrios, the CentroNorte bus terminal and the Zona 10 TransUrbano office on Av Reforma.

TAXI

Plenty of taxis cruise most parts of the city. Fares are negotiable; always establish your destination and fare before getting in. Zona 1 to Zona 10, or vice versa, costs around Q50 to Q70. If you want to phone for a taxi, **Taxi Amarillo Express** (☏1766) has metered cabs (figure on Q5 per kilometer) that often work out cheaper than others, although true *capitaleños* (capital city residents) will tell you that taxi meters are all rigged and you get a better deal bargaining.

ANTIGUA
POP 34,685

A place of rare beauty, major historical significance and vibrant culture, Antigua remains Guatemala's must-visit destination.

A former capital, the city boasts an impressive catalog of colonial relics in a magnificent setting. Streetscapes of pastel facades unfold beneath three volcanoes. Many old ecclesiastical and civic structures are beautifully renovated, while others retain tumbledown charm, with fragments strewn about park-like grounds.

Thanks to the dozens of Spanish-language schools that operate here, Antigua is a global hot spot. Yet it remains a vibrant Guatemalan town, its churches, plazas and markets throbbing with activity. Outside the city, indigenous communities, coffee plantations and volcanoes offer ample opportunities for exploration.

Perhaps the real miracle of Antigua is its resilience. Despite earthquakes, volcanic eruptions and floods, followed by virtual abandonment, it has re-emerged with a vengeance, buoyed by the pride of its inhabitants.

History

Founded in 1543, Antigua served as the Spanish colonial capital of Guatemala for 233 years. The capital was transferred to Guatemala City in 1776 after the devastating earthquake of 1773.

The town was slowly rebuilt, retaining much of its traditional character. In 1944 the Legislative Assembly declared Antigua a national monument and in 1979 Unesco declared it a World Heritage Site.

Most of Antigua's buildings were constructed during the 17th and 18th centuries when the city was a rich Spanish colonial outpost and the Catholic church was ascending to power. Many handsome, sturdy colonial buildings remain, and several impressive ruins have been preserved and are open to the public.

◉ Sights

Once glorious in their gilded baroque finery, Antigua's churches and monasteries have suffered indignities from both nature and humankind. Rebuilding after earthquakes gave the churches thicker walls, lower towers and belfries, and unembellished interiors. Furthermore, moving the capital to Guatemala City deprived Antigua of the population needed to maintain the churches in their traditional richness, though they remain impressive.

◉ Parque Central

Palacio de los Capitanes Generales   HISTORIC BUILDING
(Palace of the Captains General; ☑ 7832-2868; www.centroculturalrealpalacio.org.gt; 5a Calle Poniente; ☺ 9am-4:30pm Wed-Sun) FREE Dating from 1549, the palace was colonial headquarters for all of Central America, from Chiapas to Costa Rica, until the capital was relocated in 1776. The stately double-arcaded facade that anchors the south side of the plaza is all that remains of the original complex. Following extensive renovations, the palace now serves as a cultural center with art exhibits and performances.

Catedral de Santiago   CATHEDRAL
(cnr 4a Av Norte & 5a Calle Oriente; ruins Q8; ☺ ruins 9am-5pm, parish 6:30am-noon & 3-6:30pm Mon, Tue, Thu & Fri, 8am-noon & 3-7pm Sat, 5:30am-1pm & 3-7:30pm Sun) Antigua's cathedral was begun in 1545, wrecked by the quake of 1773, and only partially rebuilt over the next cen-

tury. The present sliver of a church – the parish of San José – occupies only the entrance hall of the original edifice. Behind it are the roofless ruins of the main part of the cathedral, which is entered from 5a Calle Oriente.

Antiguo Colegio de la Compañía de Jesús   HISTORIC BUILDING
(☑ 7932-3838; www.aecid-cf.org.gt; 6a Av Norte; ☺ 9am-6pm) FREE Established in 1626, the Jesuit monastery and college was a vital component of Antigua life until the order was expelled in 1767; just six years later, the great earthquake left it in ruins. Rescued from the rubble by the Spanish government, the complex has been reborn as a cultural center, the Centro de Formación de la Cooperación Española.

Palacio del Ayuntamiento   HISTORIC BUILDING
(City Hall Palace; 4a Calle Poniente) This double-decker structure on the north side of the park dates from the 18th century. Besides town offices, the palace houses the Museo del Libro Antiguo (Old Book Museum; ☑ 7832-5511; Q30; ☺ 9am-4pm Tue-Fri, 9am-noon & 2-4pm Sat & Sun), showcasing the early days of Guatemalan printing. The stone benches beneath the lower arcade make a fine people-watching perch.

◉ West of Parque Central

Iglesia y Convento de Nuestra Señora de la Merced   CHURCH
(monastery ruins Q15; ☺ church 6am-noon & 3-8pm, ruins 8:30am-5:30pm) At the northern end of 5a Av is La Merced – a striking yellow building trimmed with plaster filigree. The squat, thick-walled structure was built to withstand earthquakes, and three centuries after its construction it remains in good shape. Only the church is still in use; a candlelit procession, accompanied by bell ringing and firecrackers, starts and ends there on the last Thursday evening of each month.

Iglesia y Convento de la Recolección   RUIN
(Av de la Recolección; Q40; ☺ 9am-5pm) A serene air pervades the remains of the monastery of La Recolección, which stands well west of the center. Erected in the early 1700s by the Récollets (a French branch of the Franciscan order), its church was one of the largest in Antigua at the time. The earthquake of 1773 toppled the structure, of which only the great arched doorway remains intact.

Antigua

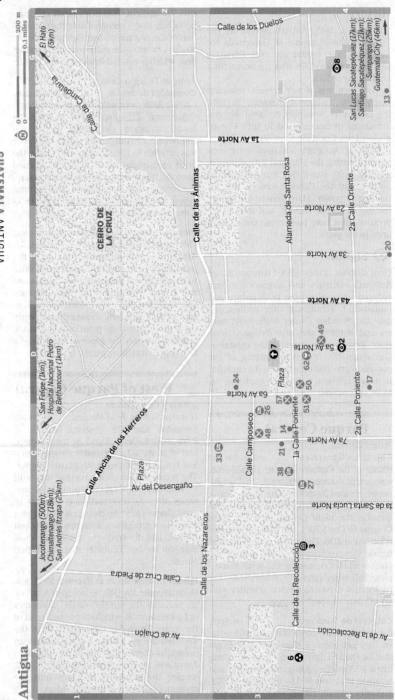

Calle de los Duelos

CERRO DE LA CRUZ

Calle de Candelaria

El Hato (5km)

San Felipe (1km); Hospital Nacional Pedro de Bethancourt (1km)

Jocotenango (500m); Chimaltenango (18km); San Andrés Itzapa (25km)

Calle Ancha de los Herreros

Av del Desengaño

Plaza

Calle Cruz de Piedra

Calle de los Nazarenos

Av de Chajón

Calle de la Recolección

Av de la Recolección

Calle Camposeco

1a Calle Poniente

7a Av Norte

6a Av Norte

5a Av Norte

4a Av Norte

3a Av Norte

2a Av Norte

1a Av Norte

Calle de las Ánimas

Alameda de Santa Rosa

2a Calle Oriente

2a Calle Poniente

Plaza

da de Santa Lucía Norte

San Lucas Sacatepéquez (17km); Santiago Sacatepéquez (21km); Sumpango (26km); Guatemala City (46km)

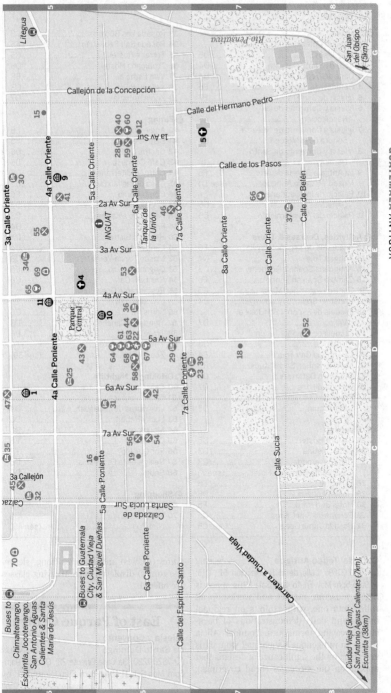

Río Pensativa

Litegua

Callejón de la Concepción

Calle del Hermano Pedro

Calle de los Pasos

San Juan del Obispo (5km)

3a Calle Oriente

4a Calle Oriente

5a Calle Oriente

6a Calle Oriente

7a Calle Oriente

8a Calle Oriente

9a Calle Oriente

Calle de Belén

1a Av Sur

2a Av Sur

3a Av Sur

4a Av Sur

5a Av Sur

6a Av Sur

7a Av Sur

INGUAT

Tanque de la Unión

Parque Central

4a Calle Poniente

5a Calle Poniente

6a Calle Poniente

7a Calle Poniente

Calzada de Santa Lucía Sur

Calle Sucia

Calle del Espíritu Santo

Carretera a Ciudad Vieja

Ciudad Vieja (5km); San Antonio Aguas Calientes (38km) Escuintla

Buses to Guatemala City, Ciudad Vieja & San Miguel Dueñas

Buses to Chimaltenango, Escuintla, Jocotenango, San Antonio Aguas Calientes & Santa María de Jesús

3a Callejón

Calzada

Antigua

◎ Sights
1 Antiguo Colegio de la Compañía de Jesús D5
2 Arco de Santa Catalina D4
3 Casa del Tejido Antiguo B4
4 Catedral de Santiago............................. E5
5 Iglesia de San Francisco F7
6 Iglesia y Convento de la Recolección A3
7 Iglesia y Convento de Nuestra Señora de la Merced D3
8 Iglesia y Convento de Santo Domingo.. G4
9 La Antigua Galería de Arte.................... F5
   Museo del Libro Antiguo...............(see 11)
10 Palacio de los Capitanes Generales... D6
11 Palacio del Ayuntamiento.................... D5

◎ Activities, Courses & Tours
12 Academia de Español Sevilla F6
13 Antigua Tours... G4
14 Antigüeña Spanish Academy................. C3
15 Cambio Spanish School......................... F5
16 Centro Lingüístico Maya........................ C5
17 Christian Spanish Academy.................. D4
18 Escuela de Español San José el Viejo.. D7
19 Escuela de Español Tecún Umán.. C6
20 La Antigua City Tour.............................. E4
21 New Sensation Salsa Studio C3
22 Old Town Outfitters............................... D6
23 Ox Expeditions...................................... D7
24 Proyecto Lingüístico Francisco Marroquín D3

◎ Sleeping
25 Bigfoot Hostel D5
26 Casa Cristina C3
27 Casa Jacaranda C3
   Casa Santo Domingo Hotel...........(see 8)
28 El Hostal... F6
29 Hostal Antigua....................................... D6
30 Hotel Burkhard...................................... F5
31 Posada de San Carlos C6
32 Posada Juma Ocag................................. C5

33 Posada Los Búcaros............................... C3
34 Posada San Sebastián........................... E5
35 Terrace Hostel....................................... C5
36 Tropicana Hostel................................... D6
37 Villa Esthela.. E8
38 Yellow House.. C3
39 Zoola Antigua.. D7

◎ Eating
40 Angie Angie F6
41 Bistrot Cinq F5
42 Cactus Grill.. D6
43 Café Condesa... D5
44 Caffé Mediterráneo............................... D6
45 Casa de las Mixtas................................ C5
46 Como Como.. E6
47 El Viejo Café D5
48 Fernando's Kaffee................................. C3
49 Fridas... D4
50 Hector's Bistro...................................... D3
51 Luna de Miel.. D4
52 Mesón Panza Verde................................ D8
53 Origami.. E6
54 Rainbow Café... C6
55 Restaurante Doña Luisa Xicotencatl E5
56 Samsara.. C6
57 Tienda La Canche.................................. D3
58 Travel Menu... D6
59 Y Tu Piña También F6
   Zoola Antigua..............................(see 39)

◎ Drinking & Nightlife
60 Café No Sé.. F6
61 La Sin Ventura D6
62 Las Vibras de la Casbah D4
63 Lucky Rabbit.. D6
64 Monoloco... D6
65 Ocelot Bar... E5
66 Por Qué No?... F7
67 Reilly's en la Esquina............................ D6
68 Snug... D6

◎ Shopping
69 La Casa del Jade.................................... E5
70 Market... B5
   Nim Po't..(see 49)

Casa del Tejido Antiguo MUSEUM
(☎7832-3169; Calle de la Recolección 51; Q15; ⊙9am-5pm Mon-Fri, to 4pm Sat) This space is like a museum, market and workshop all rolled into one, with exhibits on regional outfits and daily demonstrations of backstrap weaving techniques. Founder Alicia Pérez, an indigenous Kaqchiquel woman, is an expert on the significance of designs that appear on the *tocoyales* (head coverings), *tzutes* (shawls) and *huipiles* (long, sleeveless tunics) displayed here. Weaving classes are offered.

◎ East of Parque Central

Iglesia y Convento de Santo Domingo MONASTERY
(☎7820-1220; 3a Calle Oriente 28; Q42; ⊙9am-6pm Mon-Sat, 11:45am-6pm Sun) Founded by

Dominican friars in 1542, Santo Domingo became the biggest and richest monastery in Antigua. Following three 18th-century earthquakes, the buildings were pillaged for construction material. The site was acquired as a private residence in 1970 by an American archaeologist, who performed extensive excavations before it was taken over by the **Casa Santo Domingo Hotel** (☑7820-1220; www.casasantodomingo.com.gt; 3a Calle Oriente 28A; r from Q1425; P@🛜🞄) 🖉.

La Antigua Galería de Arte   GALLERY
(☑7832-2124; www.laantiguagaleria.com; 4a Calle Oriente 15; ⏱10am-7pm Mon-Sat, noon-6pm Sun) **FREE** Displaying works by more than 70 artists, most Guatemalan, in the halls and patio of a colonial mansion, Antigua's premier art gallery merits an extended visit.

Iglesia de San Francisco   CHURCH, MONASTERY
(☑7882-4438; cnr 7a Calle Oriente & Calle de los Pasos; museum & monastery adult/child Q6/3; ⏱9am-5:30pm) This church is imbued with the spirit of Hermano Pedro de San José de Bethancourt, a Franciscan monk who founded a hospital for the poor in Antigua and earned the gratitude of generations. On the south side are the ruins of the adjoining monastery, with some vivid frescoes still visible amid the rubble.

🏃 Activities

Antigua has a number of professional, established outfits offering a range of activities. Drop into the local offices to chat about possibilities.

Old Town Outfitters   ADVENTURE SPORTS
(☑5399-0440; www.adventureguatemala.com; 5a Av Sur 12C) 🖉 Mountain biking, rock climbing, kayaking and trekking are among the high-energy activities offered by this highly responsible operator, which works with guides from local communities.

It also has a popular range of guided half-day mountain-bike rides (Q400) in the hills around Antigua, at varying levels of difficulty. Its two-day Pedal & Paddle Tour (Q2075 per person with three or more people) includes kayaking and hiking at Lago de Atitlán.

Ox Expeditions   ADVENTURE SPORTS
(☑5801-4301; www.oxexpeditions.com; 7a Calle Poniente 17) Offers rigorous climbing opportunities in the area, plus such adrenaline-fueled activities as paragliding, surfing and zip lining. Part of its profits go to local environmental projects.

Ravenscroft Riding Stables   HORSEBACK RIDING
(☑7830-6669; 2a Av Sur 3, San Juan del Obispo; per hour beginner/experienced riders Q190/230) This outfit, 3km south of Antigua on the road to Santa María de Jesús, offers English-style riding, with scenic rides of two to three hours around the foothills of Volcán Agua.

New Sensation Salsa Studio   DANCE
(☑5033-0921; 7a Av Norte 78; per hour Q85) For those wanting to move to a different beat, this is one of several places around town you can learn to dance. It offers one-on-one instruction in salsa, merengue, *bacchata* and cha-cha.

🎓 Courses

Antigua's Spanish-language schools attract students from around the world. There are dozens of schools to choose from. Price, teaching quality and student satisfaction vary greatly. Often the quality of instruction depends upon the particular teacher, and thus may vary even within a single school. Visit a few schools before you choose and, if possible, talk to people who have studied recently at schools you like the look of – you're bound to run into a few. The INGUAT tourist office (p126) has a list of authorized schools.

Classes start every Monday at most schools, though you can usually be placed with a teacher any day of the week. Most schools cater for all levels and allow you to stay as long as you like. Three or four weeks is typical, though it's perfectly OK to do just one week. The busiest seasons are during January and from April to August, and some schools request advance reservations for these times.

Instruction is nearly always one-on-one and costs Q1000 to Q1800 per week for four hours of classes daily, five days a week. Most schools offer to arrange room and board with local families, usually with your own room and three meals daily (except Sunday), for around Q800 per week (a bit more with private bathroom). Some schools may offer accommodations in guesthouses or their own hostels.

Homestays are meant to promote the total immersion concept of language learning, but this becomes less viable where there are several foreigners staying with one family, or where there are separate mealtimes for students and the family. Indeed, there are so many foreigners about Antigua, it takes some real discipline to converse in Spanish rather than your native tongue. Many enjoy this social scene, but if you think it may deter you, consider studying in Quetzaltenango, El Petén or elsewhere, where there are fewer foreign students.

Academia de Español Sevilla LANGUAGE COURSE
(7832-5101; www.sevillantigua.com; 1a Av Sur 17C) This well-managed institute offers plenty of free activities, and it can arrange volunteer work in local community projects. One-on-one classes are conducted amid the remnants of a colonial monastery. Shared student housing is offered as an accommodation option.

★Proyecto Lingüístico Francisco Marroquín LANGUAGE COURSE
(7832-1422; www.spanishschoolplfm.com; 6a Av Norte 43) Antigua's oldest Spanish school, founded in 1969; run by a nonprofit foundation to preserve indigenous languages and culture, with capacity to teach K'iche' (Quiché) and Kaqchiquel, among other Maya tongues.

Escuela de Español San José el Viejo LANGUAGE COURSE
(7832-3028; www.sanjoseelviejo.com; 5a Av Sur 34) Long-standing school with park-like study environment, complete with tennis court and pool and its own tasteful accommodations. Students may switch teachers each week. Accredited by the Guatemalan Ministry of Education.

Christian Spanish Academy LANGUAGE COURSE
(7832-3922; www.learncsa.com; 6a Av Norte 15) Originally established to train missionaries, this modern outfit is favored by mature language learners with specific professional needs.

Escuela de Español Tecún Umán LANGUAGE COURSE
(5513-4349; www.tecunumanschool.com; 6a Calle Poniente 34A) Long-standing Guatemalan-run outfit with university-trained staff. Classes are held on the pleasant rooftop terrace of a nearby cafe.

Antigüeña Spanish Academy LANGUAGE COURSE
(5735-4638; www.spanishacademyantiguena.com; 1a Calle Poniente 10) Oft-recommended school, authorized by the Ministry of Education. It can arrange volunteer work for social workers at Hermano Pedro hospital on request.

Centro Lingüístico Maya LANGUAGE COURSE
(7832-0656; www.clmaya.com; 5a Calle Poniente 20) Large, professionally managed, pricier institute with 30 years of experience in training diplomatic personnel and journalists.

Cambio Spanish School LANGUAGE COURSE
(7832-8033; www.cambiospanishschool.com; 4a Calle Oriente 28) Supports Niños de Guatemala, an educational program for underprivileged kids.

☞ Tours
INGUAT-authorized guides around Parque Central offer city walking tours, with visits to convents, ruins and museums, for around Q80 per person. Similar guided walks are offered daily by Antigua travel agencies such as Atitrans (p126). Also on offer are trips to the surrounding villages and coffee plantations.

Elizabeth Bell, a local scholar of Antigua history, or her knowledgeable associates lead three-hour cultural walking tours of the town (in English and/or Spanish) on Tuesday, Wednesday, Friday and Saturday mornings. The cost is Q190. Reservations can be made through **Antigua Tours** (7832-5821; www.antiguatours.net; 3a Calle Oriente 22; tour incl museum fees Q190), inside the Café Condesa off Parque Central; groups congregate at the park's fountain at the appointed hour. Bell's book, *Antigua Guatemala: The City and its Heritage,* is well worth picking up: it has extensive descriptions of all the monuments and neatly encapsulates the history and fiestas. Bell and company also do tours to the nearby villages of San Antonio Aguas Calientes and San Andrés Itzapa to investigate weaving workshops and Maya shrines, respectively.

La Antigua City Tour (7832-6151; www.antiguacitytour.com; tours Q200; ⊘9am-5pm) runs a little bus around town, hitting all the key sites from Cerro de la Cruz to Parque Central.

De la Gente (5585-4450; www.dlgcoffee.org; tour per person Q200) offers tours of coffee plantations around San Miguel Escobar, a suburb of Ciudad Vieja, with local growers demonstrating cultivation, harvesting and processing techniques. At the end, participants are guided through traditional roasting methods and share a cup with the family. Tours (three to five hours; minimum two people) depart at 9am or 1pm and should be booked at least a day in advance.

Agencies also offer tours to more distant places, including Tikal, the Cobán area,

Monterrico, Chichicastenango and Lago de Atitlán (although these options often depart from Guatemala City). Two-day trips to Tikal, flying from the capital to Flores and back, start at Q3000 per person. Two-day land tours to Copán (some including Quiriguá and Río Dulce) run around Q1140 per person.

CATours (☑7832-9638; www.catours.co.uk; 6a Calle Oriente 14; ⊙9am-5pm Tue-Sun) offers two-day motorbike tours to Lago de Atitlán or Monterrico from Q1435.

☆ Festivals & Events

Semana Santa   RELIGIOUS
(Holy Week; ⊙ Easter weekend) In the week leading up to Easter, hundreds of devotees garbed in deep purple robes bear revered icons from their churches in daily street processions in remembrance of Christ's crucifixion.

🛏 Sleeping

★Yellow House   HOSTEL $
(☑7832-6646; yellowhouseantigua@hotmail.com; 1a Calle Poniente 24; dm incl breakfast Q70, s/d without bathroom incl breakfast Q110/200; @) 🅿
Thoughtfully designed, ecologically conscious and damn friendly, this makes a fine budget choice. Rooms vary in style and size, but comfy beds, recessed lighting and screened windows are the norm. It can get crowded with just three bathrooms downstairs, but they're kept clean and use solar-heated water. The plant-filled terrace is perfect for enjoying the huge, healthy breakfast served each morning.

★El Hostal   HOSTEL $
(☑7832-0442; www.elhostal-antigua.com; 1a Av Sur 8; dm incl breakfast Q90, s/d/tr without bathroom Q200/270/360; 🕾) Within stumbling distance of the popular Café No Sé, El Hostal is a cordially run budget option with a bit of colonial style. Set around a cheery little patio-cafe are half a dozen neatly kept private rooms and dorms with sturdy single beds or well-spaced bunks, a few sticks of furniture and creatively painted walls.

There's a sparkling guest kitchen and good gas-heated showers.

Tropicana Hostel   HOSTEL $
(☑7832-0462; www.tropicanahostel.com; 6a Calle Poniente 2; dm Q70, r with/without bathroom Q300/200; 🕾🛋) The new standard for party hostels, the Tropicana is a smash hit. Check in any time you like and join the flock of global youth sunning by the poolside bar or soaking in the hot tub against a back-

drop of ruins. Mixed-gender dorms feature as many as 15 beds (on three tiers), each with built-in lockers, privacy curtains and smartphone docks.

Zoola Antigua   HOSTEL $
(☑7832-0364; www.zoolaantigua.wix.com/zoola; 7a Calle Poniente 15; dm/r incl breakfast Q70/180; 🕾) The Antigua branch of the Israeli-run hostel on Lago de Atitlán translates successfully to a colonial setting: sparsely furnished dorms surround an open courtyard where global travelers chill and nosh on healthy Middle Eastern snacks beneath a rainbow canopy. New chillage options include a spectacular roof-terrace bar with hot tub.

Hostal Antigua   HOSTEL $
(☑7832-8090; www.hostalantigua.com; 5a Av Sur 22; dm/d/q Q70/295/340; 🕾🛋) Just a block and a half from Parque Central, this low-key hostel favors cleanliness and comfort over frenetic socializing. Twelve- and four-bed dorms and private rooms, featuring sturdy wood beds and ceiling fans, line up along a pretty leafy corridor. Up above is a roof terrace with guest kitchen and tiled tables.

Bigfoot Hostel   HOSTEL $
(☑7832-0489; www.bigfoothostelantigua.com; 6a Av Norte; dm/d/tr/q Q75/225/275/325; 🛋🕾) Newly renovated by a Nicaragua-based outfit, this place is always hopping, both as a hostel and bar. Though the tall, narrow structure remains cramped, dorms feature comfy carved-wood beds with curtains for privacy and roomy lockers, and air-con is available. Perks for global youth include a pool table, TV lounge, snack bar and the ever-popular Monday pub crawl.

Villa Esthela   HOSTEL $
(☑7832-5162; www.hostelantigua.com; 2a Av Sur 48, Casa A-3; dm/r Q45/150; 🕾) Run by a Dutch expat, this humble but popular hostel is in a quiet part of town five blocks south of Parque Central. Approached down an alley, the old house contains a six-bed dorm with metal bunk beds and several private rooms sharing basic bathrooms. Budget travelers get together in the TV lounge or relax up on the terrace.

Terrace Hostel   HOSTEL $
(☑7832-3463; www.terracehostel.com; 3a Calle Poniente 24; dm incl breakfast Q70, r incl breakfast without bathroom Q200; 🕾) The key feature at this fun-filled establishment is the rooftop terrace, a fabulous perch for both volcano

views and Q10 Brahvas (happy hour starts at noon). Below deck, rooms are fairly bare, but kept tidy. Don't miss the Monday pub crawl, taking off from here at 3pm.

Hotel Burkhard HOTEL $
(✏️7832-4316; hotelburkhard@hotmail.com; 3a Calle Oriente 19A; r Q150; 🖥️) This tiny establishment has a dozen compact, colorfully decorated rooms over two levels.

Casa Jacaranda HOSTEL $
(✏️7832-7589; www.casajacaranda.hotel.com; 1a Calle Poniente 37; dm incl breakfast Q95, s/d incl breakfast without bathroom Q115/230; @🖥️) At this original hostel (not a party center), the rooms (all sharing bathrooms) are simple but display a bit of flair. So does the airy front lounge, with plasma TV and a mural after Klimt (except the female figure is garbed in a *huipil*). If possible, stay out back behind the jacaranda, a tranquil retreat from the traffic. An abundant breakfast is served.

Posada Los Búcaros BOUTIQUE HOTEL $$
(✏️7832-2346; www.hotelbucaros.com; 7a Av Norte 94; s/d Q300/400; 🅿️🖥️❄️) West of La Merced in a quiet zone of pretty cobbled streets, this converted 150-year-old residence strikes a nice balance between colonial splendor and contemporary comfort. Rooms with pastel walls and high wood-beam ceilings open onto three lushly planted courtyards graced with *los búcaros* – semicircular fountains that are set into the walls.

Posada de San Carlos HOSTEL, HOTEL $$
(✏️7832-4698; www.posadadesancarlos.com; 5a Calle Poniente 11; dm/r incl breakfast Q60/300; 🖥️❄️) A hip global inn with an emphasis on comfort, the San Carlos features spacious rooms along a corridor that opens onto a neat patio with fountain. Both private rooms and the seven-bed dorm have colonial flair, with carved wood beds and chests, plus LED TVs. The front cafe whips up tasty natural fare and there are fat-tire bikes on loan.

Posada Juma Ocag HOTEL $$
(✏️7832-3109; www.posadajumaocag.com; Calz Santa Lucia Norte 13; s/d Q150/200; 🖥️) Juma Ocag's seven spotless, comfortable rooms have quality mattresses and traditional appointments including wrought-iron bedsteads, armoires and mirrors crafted in-house, and there's a spiffy little kitchen for guests. Despite the hectic location opposite the market, it remains peaceful – especially the upstairs

rooms – with a rooftop patio and well-tended little garden. Reservations are accepted in person only.

Casa Cristina BOUTIQUE HOTEL $$
(✏️7832-0623; www.casa-cristina.com; Callejón Camposeco 3A; s/d downstairs Q190/230, s/d upstairs Q270/340; 🖥️) There are just a dozen rooms at this hotel on a pretty backstreet near La Merced. Though compact, all are quaintly appointed with *típico* (traditional) bedspreads, brushed-on pastels and wood-stained furniture, and the plant-laden roof terrace makes a nice retreat. *Muy tranquilo.*

Posada San Sebastián GUESTHOUSE $$
(✏️7832-2621; www.posadasansebastian.com; 3a Av Norte 4; s/d/tr Q420/490/570; 🖥️) As carpenter, antique restorer and occasional xylophone player, Luis Méndez Rodríguez is the auteur of this converted mansion. Each of the nine uniquely appointed rooms display his knack for finding and refurbishing art and furniture. Big bathrooms with tub are a bonus, as are the roof terrace, pretty little courtyard garden, and use of a kitchen.

🍴 Eating

For global gourmands, Antigua is a banquet. Within 10 minutes' walk of Parque Central you can dine well and inexpensively on Italian, Belgian, French, Thai, Indian, Irish, Israeli, German, Chinese, Mexican and Salvadoran cuisines.

On Saturday and Sunday, tables are set up in front of Convento La Merced (p115), serving, among other snacks, chicken salad sandwiches, *rellenitos*, *enchiladas*, tamales and *chuchitos* (small tamales) laced with hot sauce and pickled cabbage, along with bowls of *atol blanco* (a corn-based hot beverage). Talk about comfort food!

Note that most formal restaurants in Antigua whack on a 10% tip before presenting the bill. It should be itemized, but if in doubt, ask.

⭐ **Zoola Antigua** ISRAELI $
(www.zoolaantigua.wix.com/zoola; Calle de Santa Lucia 15; salads Q45, sandwiches Q35-50; ⏱️8am-10pm; 🖊️) The restaurant component of Zoola hostel (p121) whips up highly authentic Israeli fare. Nosh on falafels, kebabs or *sabich* – a wrap stuffed with hummus, eggplant and salad. Seating is at low coffee tables surrounded by pillows. On Friday evenings Zoola offers a buffet-style spread of salads.

★**Restaurante Doña Luisa Xicotencatl** CAFE $
(☑7832-2578; 4a Calle Oriente 12; sandwiches & breakfast mains Q20-45; ☺7am-9:30pm) Refreshingly local in character, this is a place to enjoy the colonial patio ambiance over breakfast or a light meal. The selection of pastries are from the attached bakery; banana bread comes hot from the oven around 2pm daily.

Samsara VEGETARIAN $
(☑7832-2200; 6a Calle Poniente 33; salads Q40-50; ☺7am-9pm; 🍴) At this small veggie cafe, fresh organic ingredients are excitingly combined in soups, salads and drinks – how about a kale, peanut butter and avocado smoothie? For breakfast there's quinoa porridge or banana and amaranth-seed pancakes, along with French-press coffee or numerous tea blends. If you don't mind the new-age soundtrack, Samsara can be a culinary thrill.

Y Tu Piña También SANDWICHES $
(www.ytupinatambien.com; 1a Av Sur 10B; sandwiches & salads Q40-50; ☺7am-7pm; 🛜🍴) An international crossroads, this natural-foods cafe does healthy, sophisticated fare for foreign students on the go. There's a tempting array of sandwiches (served on whole wheat, pita or bagel) and salads. It opens early and makes a good breakfast stop, with omelets, abundant fruit salads, and banana pancakes, plus excellent coffee.

Tienda La Canche GUATEMALAN $
(6a Av Norte 42; set lunch Q25; ☺7am-10pm) A hole in the wall if there ever was one, this eatery behind a 'mom and pop' store consists of just two tables. A couple of traditional options are prepared daily, such as *pepián de pollo* (a hearty chicken stew containing chunks of *huizquil*, a yucca-like tuber), accompanied by thick tortillas. *Frescos* (home-squeezed fruit juice beverages) are served alongside.

Café Condesa CAFE $
(☑7832-0038; www.cafecondesa.com.gt; Portal del Comercio 4; cakes & pies Q20-26; ☺7am-8pm Sun-Thu, to 9pm Fri & Sat) Baked goods – pies, cakes, quiches, scones and house-baked whole-wheat sandwich bread – are the strong suit at this grand old cafe set around the patio of a 16th-century mansion off the main square. The lavish Sunday buffet (Q78), from 9am to 1pm, is an Antigua institution.

Fernando's Kaffee CAFE $
(☑7832-6953; www.fernandoskaffee.com; cnr 7a Av Norte & Callejón Camposeco; cinnamon rolls Q10, empanadas Q40; ☺7am-7pm Mon-Sat, noon-7pm Sun; 🛜) Long a draw for coffee and chocolate mavens, this friendly corner cafe also bakes an array of fine pastries, including some delightfully gooey cinnamon rolls. Beyond the counter is an inviting patio ideal for a low-key breakfast and linger.

Luna de Miel CREPERIE $
(☑7882-4559; www.lunademielantigua.com; 6a Av Norte 40; crepes Q34-55; ☺10am-9:30pm Mon & Tue, 9am-9:30pm Wed-Sun; 🛜) Loungey Luna de Miel offers dozens of variations on the classic crepe – try the *chapín* version stuffed with avocado, cheese and fried tomatoes – plus tropical smoothies. As if that weren't enough, the graffitied roof deck makes a remarkably relaxing place to enjoy them.

Casa de las Mixtas GUATEMALAN $
(3a Callejón; mains Q20-30; ☺8am-9pm Mon-Sat) For down-home Guatemalan fare, try this family-run operation on a quiet backstreet across from the market. Aside from its namesake snack (*mixtas* are Guatemalan-style hot dogs, wrapped in tortillas), it also serves a range of set breakfasts. Regulars make for the little terrace upstairs.

Travel Menu INTERNATIONAL $
(☑7832-2937; 6a Calle Poniente 14; mains Q40-50; ☺noon-11pm; 🍴) This recently renovated and expanded restaurant-bar is indeed aimed at travelers (on a budget), serving up a global greatest hits selection (veggie curries, fish burgers, salads) in a relaxed, roomy space.

★**Cactus Grill** MEXICAN $$
(☑7832-2163; 6a Calle Poniente 21; tacos Q45; ☺noon-10pm) Created by a Mexico City native, this colorful little place does a brisk trade in authentic Mexican fare, both traditional and new wave, with superb salsas served in clay bowls. The fish tacos are heartily recommended. It's along the nightlife corridor; start the evening with a chili-fringed margarita or quality mescal from Oaxaca.

El Viejo Café CAFE $$
(☑7832-1576; www.elviejocafe.com; 3a Calle Poniente 12; mains Q50-95; ☺7am-9pm; 🛜🍴) Popular with tourists and *chapines* alike, this atmospheric cafe strewn with antique curios makes an ideal breakfast stop. Choose from an array of fresh-baked croissants and

well-roasted Guatemalan coffees and settle into a window nook.

Hector's Bistro
FRENCH $$
(☑7832-9867; 1a Calle Poniente 9A; mains Q70-175; ☺noon-10pm) This tiny, intimate salon across the way from La Merced has just a few tables, with the kitchen behind the bar. Guatemala City native Hector has garnered acclaim for his versions of *bœuf bourguignon*, grilled duck breast, and so on. There's no proper sign: check the chalkboard for daily specials and the quiche of the week.

Caffé Mediterráneo
ITALIAN $$
(☑7882-7180; 6a Calle Poniente 6A; mains Q90-130; ☺noon-3pm & 6-10pm Wed-Mon) Here you'll find the finest, most authentic Italian food in Antigua in a lovely candlelit setting with superb service. Hailing from Calabria, chef Francesco does a tantalizing array of salads and pasta, using seasonally available ingredients.

Como Como
BELGIAN $$
(☑5514-5014; 2a Av Sur 12; mains Q100-150; ☺noon-3pm & 6-10pm Tue-Sun) Guatemalan ingredients fuse with Euro recipes at this Belgian bistro, popular with the expat crowd. Flemish specialties include *waterzooi* (a creamy fish stew) and *filet americain* (steak tartare). Dining is alfresco in the candlelit courtyard.

Origami
JAPANESE $$
(☑7882-4250; 6a Calle Oriente 6; mains Q50-65; ☺noon-3pm & 6-9pm Mon-Wed & Fri, 6-9pm Sat, noon-4pm Sun; ☑) Rather than striving for authenticity, the Japanese couple who run Origami just serve the sort of things they'd make at home: pulled pork *donburi*, red curry, and wasabi-dressed salad (100% organic) are among the more popular items. It's a cozy place with several salons and some tables in the courtyard. Be sure to try the homemade ginger ale.

🍸 Drinking & Nightlife

The bar scene jumps, especially on Friday and Saturday evenings when the hordes roll in from Guatemala City for some Antigua-style revelry. Besides the watering holes, the restaurants Fridas (☑7832-1296; 5a Av Norte 29; mains Q75-140; ☺noon-midnight) and Bistrot Cinq (☑7832-5510; www.bistrotcinq.com; 4a Calle Oriente 7; mains Q135-175; ☺noon-10:30pm) are at least as popular for cocktails as cuisine. Start drinking early and save: *cuba*

libres (rum and colas) and mojitos are half price between 5pm and 8pm at many bars.

To get an overview of Antigua's nightspots, join the pub crawl that embarks every Monday at 3pm from the Terrace Hostel (p121).

★ Por Qué No?
PUB
(☑4324-5407; www.porquenocafe.com; cnr 2a Av Sur & 9a Calle Oriente; ☺6-10pm Mon-Sat) This alternative cafe is a vertically oriented space that takes up an absurdly narrow corner of an old building (grab the rope to reach the upper level) with vintage bric-a-brac hanging from the rafters and every surface scrawled with guest-generated graffiti. The vibe is relaxed and conversational and a crowd spills out the door each evening.

Ocelot Bar
PUB
(☑5658-9028; 4a Av Norte 3; ☺4:30pm-1am) Just off Parque Central, this Welsh tavern feels like a large living room, with wall-length sofas, murals of literary and sports heroes, and board games, not to mention the best-stocked bar in town. It's highly popular with the mature expat crowd, and the Monday evening pub quiz really packs them in.

Ocelot is part of a nightlife center that consists of at least three other bars, including the Tiki-themed Vudu and game-center Bullseye.

Café No Sé
BAR
(www.cafenose.com; 1a Av Sur 11C; ☺3pm-1am) This downbeat little bar is a point of reference for Antigua's budding young Burroughses and Kerouacs. It's also the core of a lively music scene, with players wailing from a corner of the room most evenings. A semi-clandestine attached salon serves its own brand of mescal, 'smuggled' over from Oaxaca (two-shot minimum). After hours, just bang on the door.

Reilly's en la Esquina
IRISH PUB
(☑7832-6251; 6a Calle Poniente 7; ☺noon-12:30am) Holding the key corner of Antigua's nightlife corridor, the new and improved Reilly's packs in both Guatemalans and gringos on weekends. The sprawling pub counts no fewer than four bars, with most of the action focusing on the central patio. Midweek it's mellower, with the billiard table, pub grub and Guinness on tap pulling in a faithful following.

Snug
PUB
(☑5838-5390; 6a Calle Poniente 14; ☺noon-11pm) It's a tight squeeze, but spirits are high at the

LGBT ANTIGUA

A continuous influx of foreign visitors has granted Antigua a veneer of cosmopolitanism and tolerance beyond that of other similar-sized Guatemalan cities. So despite the strong religious undercurrent, gays and lesbians find a sort of haven here, and the nightlife scene embraces every persuasion. In particular, the restaurant Fridas (p124) hosts a queer gathering with DJs on the final Saturday of each month (upstairs), and the dance club Las Vibras de la Casbah stages alternative events weekly.

aptly dubbed Snug, a new anchor on the expat drinking scene. Live music on Sundays.

Monoloco   PUB

(☑ 7832-4235; 5a Av Sur 6, Pasaje El Corregidor; ☺ 11am-12:45am) As much Guatemala weekender as tourist hangout, the 'wacky monkey' serves up a good blend of comfort foods and local dishes, as well as ice-cold beers, in a relaxed environment with sports TV on dozens of sets.

La Sin Ventura   CLUB

(5a Av Sur 8; ☺ 4pm-1am Tue-Fri, noon-1am Sat, noon-8pm Sun) The liveliest dance floor in town is packed with Guatemalan youth toward the weekend. DJs pump out *cumbias* (Colombian dance tunes) and reggaetón most nights, while musicians play live salsa on Tuesdays.

Las Vibras de la Casbah   CLUB

(☑ 3141-5311; www.lasvibrasantigua.com; 5a Av Norte 30; ☺ 5pm-1am Wed-Sat) It's quite a party most nights at this split-level disco near the Santa Catalina arch: plenty of selfies, vapor shots and EDM form the scene. To take a breather, make your way to the open-air terrace out front.

Lucky Rabbit   BAR

(☑ 7832-5099; 5a Av Sur 8; ☺ 7pm-1am Mon-Sat) A former cinema, this upstairs space favored by Guatemalan youth has morphed into a game room/dance hall, though the movies are still continuously projected throughout the evening.

☆ Entertainment

The Centro de Formación de la Cooperación Española (p115) runs thematic series of documentaries or foreign art-house films on Wednesday night.

Café No Sé (p124), **Angie Angie** (☑ 7832-3352; 1a Av Sur 11A; ☺ noon-11pm Wed-Mon), the **Rainbow Café** (☑ 7832-1919; www.rainbowcafeantigua.com; 7a Av Sur 8; ☺ 8am-11pm; ✐) and **Mesón Panza Verde** (☑ 7832-2925; www.panzaverde.com; 5a Av Sur 19; ☺ 6-10pm Mon, noon-3pm & 6-10pm Tue-Sun) host folk, rock and jazz performances.

🔒 Shopping

Woven and leather goods, ironwork, paintings and jade jewelry are some of the items to look for in Antigua's various shops and markets. For beautiful *típico* fabrics, first get educated at the Casa del Tejido Antiguo (p118), then have a look around Nim P'ot or the big handicrafts markets near the bus terminal and next to Iglesia del Carmen.

Market   MARKET

(Calz de Santa Lucía Sur; ☺ 6am-6pm Mon, Thu & Sat, 7am-6pm Tue, Wed & Fri, 7am-1pm Sun) Antigua's market – chaotic, colorful and always busy – sprawls north of 4a Calle Poniente. The best days are the official market days – Monday, Thursday and especially Saturday – when villagers from the vicinity roll in and spread their wares north and west of the main market building.

La Casa del Jade   JEWELRY

(www.lacasadeljade.com; 4a Calle Oriente 10; ☺ 9am-6pm) More than just a jewelry shop, the Casa has a museum that displays dozens of pre-Hispanic jade pieces and an open workshop where you can admire the work of contemporary craftspeople. It's inside the Casa Antigua El Jaulón shopping arcade.

Nim P'ot   HANDICRAFTS

(☑ 7832-2681; www.nimpotexport.com; 5a Av Norte 29; ☺ 9am-9pm Sun-Thu, to 10pm Fri & Sat) This sprawling hall boasts a huge collection of Maya clothing, as well as hundreds of masks, wood carvings, kites, paintings, refrigerator magnets, and assorted Maximón (a locally worshipped saint) figurines. The *huipiles, cortes, fajas* and other garments are arranged by region, so it makes for a fascinating visit whether you're buying or not.

ⓘ Orientation

Antigua's focal point is the broad Parque Central; few places in town are more than 15 minutes' walk from here. Compass points are added to the numbered Calles and Avs, indicating whether an address is *norte* (north), *sur* (south), *poniente* (west) or *oriente* (east) of Parque Central.

Three volcanoes provide easy reference points: Volcán Agua is south of the city and visible from most points within it; Volcán Fuego and Volcán Acatenango rise to the southwest (Acatenango is the more northerly of the two).

Another useful Antigua landmark is the **Arco de Santa Catalina** (5a Av Norte), an arch spanning 5a Av Norte, two and a half blocks north of Parque Central, on the way to La Merced church.

ⓘ Information

DANGERS & ANNOYANCES

➡ Antigua generally feels safe to walk around, but muggings do occur, so don't let your guard down completely. This holds doubly true after the bars close at 1am; after 10pm, consider taking a taxi back to your accommodations.

➡ Pickpockets work the busy market, doing overtime on paydays at the middle and end of the month. December (bonus time) brings a renewed wave of robberies.

➡ Some of the more remote hiking trails have been the scene of muggings, though stepped-up police patrols have reduced the likelihood of such incidents. If you're planning on hiking independently, check with **Proatur** about the current situation.

EMERGENCY & IMPORTANT NUMBERS

Ambulance (☑128)
Fire (☑123)
Police (☑120)
Tourist Police (☑1500 or ☑2421-2810)

MEDIA

The Antigua-based *Revue Magazine* (www.revuemag.com) runs about 90% ads, but has reasonable information about cultural events; it's available everywhere. *La Cuadra* (www.lacuadraonline.com), published by **Café No Sé** (p124), presents the gringo-bohemian perspective, mixing politics with irreverent commentary; pick up a copy at the cafe.

MEDICAL SERVICES

Farmacia Cruz Verde Ivori (☑7832-8318; 7a Av Norte; ⊗24hr)

Hospital Nacional Pedro de Bethancourt (☑7831-1319; ⊗24hr) Public hospital in San Felipe, 2km north of the center, with emergency service.

Hospital Privado Hermano Pedro (☑7832-1190; www.hospitalhermanopedro.net; Av de la Recolección 4; ⊗24hr) Private hospital that offers 24-hour emergency service and accepts foreign insurance.

MONEY

Banco Agromercantil (4a Calle Poniente 8; ⊗9am-7pm Mon-Fri, to 5pm Sat & Sun) Changes US dollars and euros (cash or traveler's checks). Also houses a branch of Western Union.

Banco Industrial (5a Av Sur 4; ⊗9am-7pm Mon-Fri, to 1pm Sat) Has a reliable ATM and changes US dollars. Another useful BI ATM is inside Café Barista, on the northwest corner of Parque Central.

Citibank (cnr 4a Calle Oriente & 4a Av Norte; ⊗9am-4:30pm Mon-Fri, 9:30am-1pm Sat) Changes US dollars and euros.

Visa & MasterCard ATM (Portal del Comercio) Facing Parque Central.

TOURIST INFORMATION

INGUAT (☑7832-0787; info-antigua@inguat.gob.gt; 5a Calle Oriente 11; ⊗8am-4pm Mon-Fri, 9am-5pm Sat & Sun) The tourist office has free city maps, bus information and helpful, bilingual staff.

Proatur (☑5578-9835; operacionesproatur@inguat.gob.gt; 6a Calle Poniente Final; ⊗24hr) The helpful tourism assistance agency has its headquarters on the west side of town, three blocks south of the market. If you're the victim of a crime, they'll accompany you to the national police and assist with the formalities, including any translating that's needed. Given advance notice, they can provide an escort for drivers heading out on potentially risky roads.

TRAVEL AGENCIES

Atitrans (☑7832-3371; www.atitrans.net; 6a Av Sur 8; ⊗8am-9pm) Multipurpose agency with recommended shuttle service.

LAX Travel (☑7832-2674; laxantigua@hotmail.com; 6a Av Sur 12; ⊗9am-6pm Mon-Fri, to 5pm Sat) International flight specialist.

Onvisa Travel Agency (☑5226-3441; onvisatravel@hotmail.com; 6a Calle Poniente 40) Operates shuttles to Copán and elsewhere.

Rainbow Travel Center (☑7931-7878; www.rainbowtravelcenter.com; 7a Av Sur 8; ⊗9am-6pm Mon-Fri, to 5pm Sat) Specializes in student and teacher airfares.

ⓘ Getting There & Around

BUS

Buses from Guatemala City, Ciudad Vieja and San Miguel Dueñas arrive and depart from a street just south of the market, across from the

Mercado de Artesanías (cnr 5a Calle Poniente & Av de la Recolección). Buses to Chimaltenango, Escuintla, San Antonio Aguas Calientes and Santa María de Jesús go from a lot behind the **main market building** (Av de la Recolección). If you're heading out to local villages, go early in the morning and return by mid-afternoon, as bus services drop off dramatically as evening approaches.

To reach highland towns such as Chichicastenango, Quetzaltenango, Huehuetenango or Panajachel, take one of the frequent buses to Chimaltenango, on the Interamericana Hwy 1, then catch an onward bus. Making connections is easy, as many folks will jump to your aid as you alight from one bus looking for another, but stay alert.

SHUTTLE MINIBUS

Numerous travel agencies and tourist minibus operators offer frequent shuttle services to places tourists go, including Guatemala City and its airport, Panajachel and Chichicastenango. They cost more than buses, but they're comfortable and convenient, with door-to-door service at both ends. Some typical one-way prices include Chichicastenango (Q115), Cobán (Q250), Copán (Honduras; Q270), Guatemala City (Q80), Monterrico (Q115), Panajachel (Q115) and Quetzaltenango (Q195).

Pin down shuttle operators about departure times and whether they require a minimum number of passengers.

TAXI & TUK-TUK

Taxis wait where the Guatemala City buses stop and on the east side of Parque Central. An in-town taxi ride costs Q25 to Q30. *Tuk-tuks* are Q5 to Q10. Note that *tuk-tuks* are not allowed in the center of town, so you'll have to hike a few blocks out to find one; nor do they operate after 8pm.

THE HIGHLANDS

Guatemala's most dramatic region – El Altiplano – stretches from Antigua to the Mexican border. Traditional values and customs are strongest here. Maya dialects are spoken far more widely than Spanish, and over a dozen distinct groups dwell within the region, each with its own language and clothing. Such extraordinary diversity is perhaps most evident in the weekly markets of Chichicastenango and San Francisco El Alto. This is where indigenous tradition blends most tantalizingly with Spanish, and it is common to see Maya rituals taking place in front of and inside colonial churches.

Most travelers spend a spell at volcano-ringed Lago de Atitlán. West of the lake stands Guatemala's second city, Quetzaltenango. Northward spread the Cuchumatanes mountains, where indigenous life follows its own rhythms amid fantastic mountain landscapes. For hikers, this is the promised land.

❶ Getting There & Around

Public transportation connections between towns and villages in the highlands are easy and cheap, accommodation is plentiful, and people are generally welcoming and helpful, making it a cinch to get around.

The meandering Interamericana (Hwy 1), running 345km along the mountain ridges between Guatemala City and the Mexican border at La Mesilla, passes close to all of the region's most important places, and countless buses roar up and down it all day, every day. Two key intersections act as major bus interchanges: Los Encuentros for Panajachel and Chichicastenango, and Cuatro Caminos for Quetzaltenango and

BUSES FROM ANTIGUA

DESTINATION	COST (Q)	DURATION	FREQUENCY	NOTES
Chimaltenango	5	30min	every 10min	
Ciudad Vieja	3	15min	every 15min	Take a San Miguel Dueñas bus.
Escuintla	8	1hr	every 20min	
Guatemala City	10	1hr	every 15min 7am-8pm	A Pullman service (Q45; 9:30am & 4pm) by **Litegua** (☏ 7832-9850; www.litegua.com; 4a Calle Oriente 48) also runs from its office at the east end of town.
Panajachel	36	2½hr	one bus daily at 7am	Transportes Rebulli service, departing from Panadería Colombia on 4a Calle Poniente, half a block east of the market.
San Antonio Aguas Calientes	4	20min	every 10min	

Huehuetenango. If you can't find a bus going to your destination, simply get one to either of those points. Transfers are usually seamless, with not-too-frustrating waiting times and locals who are ready to help travelers find the right bus.

Travel is easiest in the morning and, for smaller places, on market days. By mid- or late afternoon, buses may be scarcer. Further off the beaten track you may be relying more on pick-ups than buses for transportation.

Microbuses – large vans that depart as soon as they fill with passengers – are becoming the dominant mode of transportation along highland routes such as Santa Cruz del Quiché–Nebaj and Chichicastenango–Los Encuentros. They're preferred by many locals for their convenience and are only slightly more expensive than buses.

Otherwise, vans run by tour operators shuttle tourists between the major destinations of the region and beyond. They are faster, more comfortable and more expensive than buses.

Lago de Atitlán

Nineteenth-century traveler-chronicler John L Stephens, writing in *Incidents of Travel in Central America,* called Lago de Atitlán 'the most magnificent spectacle we ever saw,' and he had been around a bit. Today even seasoned travelers marvel at this spectacular environment. Fishermen in rustic crafts ply the lake's aquamarine surface, while indigenous women in multicolored outfits do their washing by the banks where trees burst into bloom. Fertile hills dot the landscape, and over everything loom the volcanoes, permeating the entire area with a mysterious beauty. It never looks the same twice. No wonder many outsiders have fallen in love with the place and made their homes here.

Though volcanic explosions have been going on here for millions of years, today's landscape has its origins in the massive eruption of 85,000 years ago, termed Los Chocoyos, which blew volcanic ash as far away as Florida and Panama. The quantity of magma expelled from below the earth's crust caused the surface terrain to collapse, forming a huge, roughly circular hollow that soon filled with water – the Lago de Atitlán. Smaller volcanoes rose out of the lake's southern waters thousands of years later: Volcán San Pedro (today 3020m above sea level) about 60,000 years ago, followed by Volcán Atitlán (3537m) and Volcán Tolimán (3158m). The lake today is 8km across from north to south, 18km from east to west, and

averages around 300m deep, though the water level has been on the rise since 2009.

Around 900 AD, when the Maya highland civilization was in decline, the region was settled by two groups that had migrated from the Toltec capital of Tula in Mexico, the Kaqchiquel and Tz'utujil. The latter group settled at Chuitinamit, across the way from the present-day village of Santiago Atitlán, while the former occupied the lake's northern shores; this demographic composition persists to this day. By the time the Spanish showed up in 1524, the Tz'utujil had expanded their domain to occupy most of the lakeshore. Pedro de Alvarado exploited the situation by allying with the Kaqchiquels against their Tz'utujil rivals, whom they defeated in a bloody battle at Tzanajuyú. The Kaqchiquels subsequently rebelled against the Spanish and were themselves subjugated by 1531.

Today, the main lakeside town is Panajachel, or 'Gringotenango' as it is sometimes unkindly called, and most people initially head here to launch their Atitlán explorations. Santiago Atitlán, along the lake's southern spur, has the strongest indigenous identity of any of the major lake towns. Up the western shore, the town of San Pedro La Laguna has a reputation as a countercultural party center. On the north side, San Marcos La Laguna is a haven for new-agers, while Santa Cruz La Laguna and Jaibalito, nearer to Panajachel, are among the lake's most idyllic, picturesque locales.

The lake is a three-hour bus ride west from Guatemala City or Antigua. There is an ersatz town at the highway junction of Los Encuentros, based on throngs of people changing buses here. From La Cuchilla junction, 2km further west along the Interamericana, a road descends 12km southward to Sololá, and then there's a sinuous 8km descent to Panajachel. Sit on the right-hand side of the bus for views of the lake and its surrounding volcanoes.

ℹ Information

DANGERS & ANNOYANCES

Although most visitors never experience any trouble, robberies have occurred along the paths that run around Lago de Atitlán. The security situation is forever changing – some months it's OK to walk between certain villages, then that route suddenly becomes dangerous. It's best to check with **Proatur** (p136) about the current situation.

Lago de Atitlán

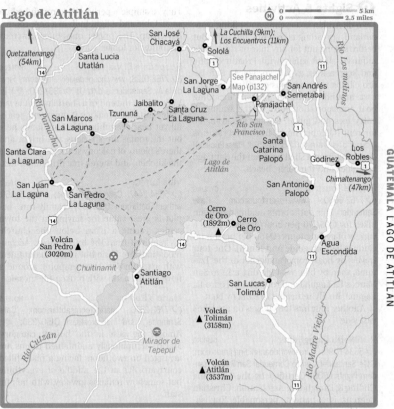

ℹ Getting There & Around

Panajachel is the gateway to Lago de Atitlán and is easily accessed by bus and shuttle from the Interamericana, either directly or by changing at La Cuchilla junction just west of Los Encuentros. There are also direct buses from Quetzaltenango to San Pedro La Laguna on the lake's western shore. Getting around the lake is most rapidly and easily accomplished by frequent motorboat service, though some towns are linked by road as well.

Panajachel

POP 10,238 / ELEV 1584M

The busiest and most built-up lakeside settlement, Panajachel ('Pana' to pretty much the entire country) has developed haphazardly and, some say, in a less-than-beautiful way. Strolling the main street, Calle Santander, crammed with cybercafes, travel agencies, handicraft hawkers and rowdy bars, dodging noisome *tuk-tuks* all the way, you may be forgiven for supposing this paradise lost.

A hike down to the lakeshore, though, will give you a better idea why Pana attracts so many visitors. Aside from the astounding volcano panorama, the town's excellent transportation connections, copious accommodations, varied restaurants and thumping nightlife make it a favorite destination for weekending Guatemalans.

Several different cultures mingle on Panajachel's dusty streets. *Ladinos* (people of mixed indigenous and European heritage) and gringos control the tourist industry. The Kaqchiquel and Tz'utujil Maya from surrounding villages come to sell their handicrafts to tourists. Tour groups arrive by bus for a few hours or overnight. This mix makes Pana a curiously cosmopolitan crossroads in an otherwise remote, rural vicinity. All of this makes for a convenient transition into the Atitlán universe – but to truly experience the beauty of the lake, most travelers venture onward soon after arrival.

◉ Sights & Activities

Lago de Atitlán is a cycling and hiking wonderland, spreading across hill and dale. But before setting out for any hike or ride, make inquiries about safety with Proatur (p136), and keep asking as you go. Volcán San Pedro climbs via numerous operators in town cost around Q700 per person, including boat transportation, taxi to the trailhead, entry fees and guide. Kayaks are available for rent (Q25 per hour) from **Diversiones Acuáticas Balam** (📞5514-8512; Playa Pública), operating from a shed between the Santiago boat dock and the public beach.

Roger's Tours   CYCLING
(📞7762-6060; www.rogerstours.com; Calle Santander) This outfit rents quality mountain bikes for Q35/170 per hour/day and leads a variety of cycling tours (Q460 per person including helmet, guide and lunch). One tour travels by boat from Panajachel to the Tzununá, then by bike west via dirt trail to San Marcos La Laguna and road to San Pedro La Laguna, finally returning to Pana by boat.

Another tour hits the villages on the lake's east side.

RealWorld Paragliding   GLIDING
(📞5634-5699; realworldparagliding.jimdo.com; Calle Santander, Centro Comercial San Rafael; tandem flights Q700) Certified by the US Hang Gliding & Paragliding Association, Christian Behrenz is a patient, personable English-speaking guide who's made more than 2500 tandem flights. If wind conditions are right, you'll take off from above Santa Catarina Palopó and land at Panajachel. Flights last for 20 minutes to an hour, depending on the wind and passenger preferences.

🎓 Courses

Panajachel has a niche in the language-school scene. Two well-set-up schools are **Jardín de América** (📞7762-2637; www.jardindeamerica.com; Calle del Chalí) and **Jabel Tinamit** (📞7762-6056; www.jabeltinamit.com; cnr Avenida de Los Árboles & Callejón Las Armonías). The former is set amid ample gardens while the latter is in the center of town. Four hours of one-on-one study five days per week, including a homestay with a local family, will cost around Q1500 per week.

🛏 Sleeping

Budget travelers will rejoice at the profusion of family-run *hospedajes* (guesthouses).

They're simple – perhaps two rough beds, a small table and a light bulb in a bare room – but cheap. The pricier ones offer generous discounts for longer stays.

Hospedaje El Viajero   HOTEL $
(📞7762-0128; www.hospedajeelviajero.com; Final de la Av Santander; s/d/tr Q100/180/240; 📞) El Viajero is at the end of a short lane off lower Calle Santander, making it quiet and peaceful yet near everything. Nothing fancy here but the rooms are spacious and bright and there's plenty of balcony seating. You can use the kitchen, and there's free drinking water.

Villa Lupita   HOTEL $
(📞5054-2447; Callejón Don Tino; s/d Q75/150, without bathroom Q50/100) Family-run Lupita is great value for staying in the town center. Facing a plaza below the church, it's removed from the tourist drag. Accommodations are basic but nicely maintained, with art from San Juan wrapping around a flower-filled patio with broken-tile mosaic.

Mario's Rooms   HOTEL $
(📞7762-2370; mariosroomsatitlan.com; Calle Santander; s/d incl breakfast Q150/230; 📶) Among the best in the budget category, Mario's scrupulously maintained rooms are arranged on two floors facing a plant-filled courtyard. It's in the middle of everything but somehow remains low-key, with helpful staff.

Hospedaje Sueño Real   HOTEL $
(📞7762-0608; hotelsuenorealpana@hotmail.com; Calle Ramos; s/d from Q150/180; 📶📶📞) Better than most of the budget options along this lane, the Sueño Real has cheerfully decorated, if smallish, rooms with TV and fan. The best are the upstairs triples, opening on a plant-festooned, lake-view terrace.

Hospedaje Casa Linda   GUESTHOUSE $
(📞7762-0386; Callejón El Capulin; r Q180, s/d/tr without bathroom Q80/160/180) Twenty-one spotless little rooms surround a lush garden at this tranquil family-run establishment down a lane off Calle Santander. Upstairs units get a nice breeze and the balconies are good for afternoon siestas. Ask Basilio, the kindly proprietor, for details of his next marimba performance.

Hotel Larry's Place   HOTEL $
(📞7762-0767; www.hotellarrysplace.com; Calle 14 de Febrero; r Q150; 📶) Set back from the road behind a wall of vegetation, Larry's Place of-

fers good-sized, cool rooms in a sylvan setting. Furnishings are tasteful, ceilings high and the balconies welcome. No TV or internet, but who needs 'em anyway?

Hotel Jere
HOTEL **$**

(☑7762-2781; www.jerehotel.com; Calle Rancho Grande; s/d/tr Q100/125/180; [P] [@]) Jere's brick-walled rooms are enlivened with traditional textiles, and some open on to sun-splashed balconies. You can book shuttle buses and lake tours on the spot and rent bicycles.

Hotel Posada Viñas del Lago
HOTEL **$**

(☑7762-0389; braulio.pana@hotmail.com; Playa Pública; s/d/tr Q85/150/200; [P][@][🖂]) Steps from the lakefront, this garishly painted lodging is managed by a Kaqchiquel extended family whose activities are on full view. Mattresses sag and water outages are common but the lake views make up for it, particularly from units 21 to 23.

Hospedaje García
HOTEL **$**

(☑7762-2187; Calle 14 de Febrero; s/d Q130/160, without bathroom Q70/130; [P][🖂]) Located on a side street off Santander, this is a sprawling, airy place with an affable manager and numerous rooms of varying shape and size. If you don't mind the frayed furniture, some of the upper-level units are very good with huge bathrooms and balconies looking out onto the patio.

Jenna's River B&B
B&B **$$**

(☑5458-1984; www.jennasriverbedandbreakfast. com; Calle Rancho; s/d incl breakfast Q350/500; [☺][@][🖂]) You'll feel right at home at Jenna's place, near the lake shore, with seven uniquely decked-out rooms, a studio apartment and a traditional Mongolian yurt that's starlit by night. Jenna and pooches welcome travelers to the tropically abundant garden, gazebo and breakfast room, where the table is set with Jenna's own fresh-baked bread and homemade jams.

Posada Los Encuentros
LODGE **$$**

(☑7762-1603; www.losencuentros.com; Callejón Chotzar 0-41; s/d incl breakfast Q300/335, with kitchen Q380/420; [@][🖂]) Just across the river is this 'ecocultural B&B,' featuring seven cozy rooms in a relaxed home, plus a volcanically heated tub, medicinal plant garden, sunning terrace and fitness center. Owner Richard Morgan is happy to share his encyclopedic knowledge of the lake and offers cultural tours of the area.

Hotel Utz-Jay
HOTEL **$$**

(☑7762-0217; www.hotelutzjay.com; Calle 15 de Febrero 2-50; s/d/tr from Q225/360/495; [P][@][🖂]) These eight adobe cottages stand amid lovely gardens bursting with heliconia, orange trumpet and ferns where no fewer than 46 types of birds have been spotted. Rooms are decorated with traditional fabrics and have cozy porches out front. Good breakfasts are available and there's a *chuj* (traditional Maya sauna).

Posada de los Volcanes
HOTEL **$$**

(☑7762-0244; www.posadadelosvolcanes.com; Calle Santander 5-51; s/d incl breakfast from Q380/460) Sharing the property with its own travel agency, this chalet-style lodging has lovely pine-paneled rooms. On the 4th floor, you'll be rewarded with your own private terrace, suitable for kicking back with cocktails and surveying the lakescape.

Hotel Montana
HOTEL **$$**

(☑7762-0326; atitlanhotelmontana@hotmail. com; Callejón Don Tino; s/d Q175/275; [P]) Down a narrow street near the church, the Montana is an old-fashioned establishment with wonderful plant-laden balconies fronted by pot-bellied railing. Choose a room on the upper level for brilliant views of the mountainside.

🍴 Eating

Near the south end of Calle del Lago, an agglomeration of thatched-roof restaurants crowds the lakefront. All serve lake *mojarra* (bream, Q95) and black bass (Q140), with skinny, bow-tied youths taking your order. Restaurante El Atitlán (p135), the last one on the left, offers the best quality and variety.

Another obvious choice for cheap meals are the myriad taco and fried chicken stalls that proliferate along Calle Santander every afternoon and evening. You might try the appropriately named Humo en Tus Ojos, last spotted near the intersection of Calles Principal and Santander; this is where the cops eat.

For food shopping, there's the **Despensa Familiar**, at the north end of Calle El Amate.

Chero's Bar
SALVADORAN **$**

(Av Los Árboles; pupusas Q10; ⊙12:30pm-1am Tue-Sat) Usefully located in the nightlife zone, Chero's can get pretty lively, with beer-drinking patrons gathering around simple wood tables as *tuk-tuks* zip by. Salvadoran staff slap out *pupusas,* either straight up

Panajachel

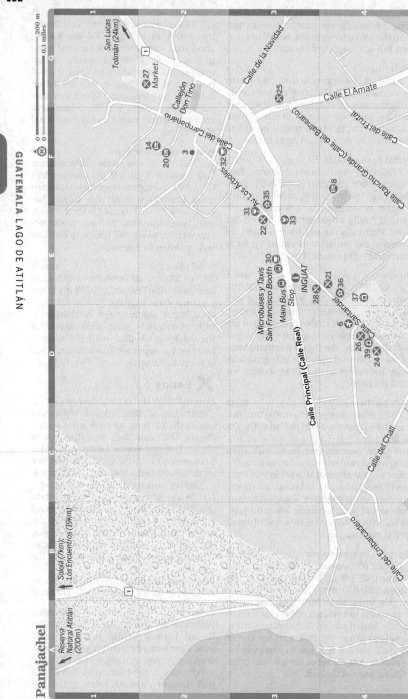

Reserva
Natural Atitlán
(200m)

Solalá (7km);
Los Encuentros (19km)

San Lucas
Tolimán (24km)

Market

Callejón Don Tino

Calle de la Navidad

Calle El Amate

Calle del Frutal

Calle del Campanario

Calle Rancho Grande (Calle del Balneario)

Av Los Árboles

Microbuses y Taxis
San Francisco Booth

Main Bus
Stop

INGUAT

Calle Principal (Calle Real)

Calle Santander

Calle del Chalí

Calle del Embarcadero

200 m
0.1 miles

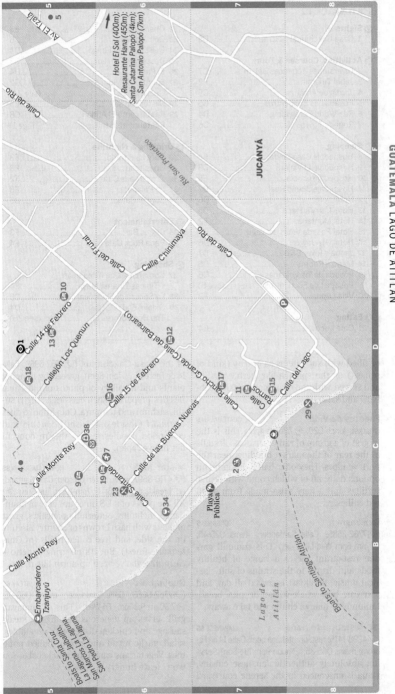

Hotel El Sol (400m);
Resaurante Hana (450m);
Santa Catarina Palopó (4km);
San Antonio Palopó (7km)

AV El Tzalá

● 5

Calle del Río

JUCANYÁ

Río San Francisco

Calle del Frutal

Calle Chinimaya

Calle del Río

Calle 14 de Febrero

● 10

13

Callejón Los Quenun

(Calle del Balneario)

● 12

● 1

18

Calle 15 de Febrero

● 16

Calle Rancho Grande

● 17

Calle Ramos

● 11

● 15

Calle del Lago

Calle Monte Rey

● 38

● 4

● 7

● 9

19

Calle Santander

● 23

Calle de las Buenas Nuevas

● 29

● 2

● 34

Playa Pública

Calle Monte Rey

Embarcadero Tzanjuyú

Boats to 'Santa Cruz
La Laguna, Jaibalito,
La Laguna, La Laguna
San Pedro La Laguna

Lago de
Atitlán

Boats to Santiago Atitlán

Panajachel

⊙ **Sights**
1 Casa Cakchiquel D5

🏃 **Activities, Courses & Tours**
2 Diversiones Acuáticas Balam C7
3 Jabel Tinamit................................F2
4 Jardín de América........................... C5
5 Posada Los Encuentros....................... G5
6 RealWorld Paragliding..........................D4
7 Roger's Tours C6

🛏 **Sleeping**
8 Hospedaje Casa Linda F4
9 Hospedaje El Viajero C5
10 Hospedaje García E5
11 Hospedaje Sueño Real........................ D7
12 Hotel Jere..................................D6
13 Hotel Larry's Place.........................D5
14 Hotel Montana................................F2
15 Hotel Posada Viñas del Lago................ D7
16 Hotel Utz-Jay............................... D6
17 Jenna's River B&B D7
18 Mario's Rooms D5
19 Posada de los Volcanes C6
    Posada Los Encuentros.................(see 5)
20 Villa Lupita F2

🍴 **Eating**
21 Café Loco...................................E4

22 Chero's Bar E3
23 Deli Jasmín..............................C6
24 Deli Llama de Fuego..............................D4
25 Despensa Familiar..............................G3
26 El Patio D4
27 Fuentes de Vida................................G2
    Guajimbo's ....(see 24)
28 Mister Jon's E3
29 Restaurante El Atitlán..........................C8
    Restaurante Hana ....(see 1)

🍸 **Drinking & Nightlife**
30 Café La Parada E3
31 Chapiteau E3
32 Crossroads Café.............................. F2
33 La Palapa E3
34 Sunset Café................................B6

⭐ **Entertainment**
35 Circus Bar F3
36 Pana Rock Café E4

🛍 **Shopping**
37 Comerciales de Artesanías
    Típicas Tinamit Maya........................E4
38 La Señora de Cancuén..........................C5
39 Oxlajuj B'atz'................................D4
    The Book Store............................(see 26)

or filled with such items as *guicoy* (kind of squash) or the spinach-like herb *chipilín*, and served with the customary pickled cabbage and salsa.

Fuentes de Vida   GUATEMALAN **$**
(market; lunch Q20; ⊙ 7.30am-4pm) This is the largest of a group of rather rustic cook stalls at the rear of the market building, near the pork vendors. They offer half a dozen menu options daily, all of which come with beans, tortillas and a fiery salsa made from dried red chilies.

Deli Jasmín   ORGANIC **$**
(☎ 7762-2585; Calle Santander; items Q25-45; ⊙ 7am-6pm Wed-Mon; 🖉) This tranquil garden restaurant serves a range of healthy foods and drinks to the strains of soft classical music. Breakfast is served all day, and you can buy whole-wheat or pita bread, hummus or mango chutney to take away.

⭐ **Restaurante Hana**   JAPANESE **$$**
(☎ 4298-1415; restaurantehana.com; Calle 14 de Febrero; mains Q65-85; ⊙ noon-9pm Tue-Sun) Serving absolutely authentic Japanese cuisine, Hana is ensconced in the serene courtyard of the **Casa Cakchiquel** (☎ 7762-0969; Calle 14 de Febrero; ⊙ 7am-8pm), graced by hanging plants and a gallery of photos of old Pana. Besides preparing such classics as nigiri sushi, sashimi and tempura, Chef Mihoko does *uramaki* ('inside-out' sushi), *donburi* and cold udon noodles just as they're done in her native Japan.

Mister Jon's   NORTH AMERICAN **$$**
(☎ 4710-8697; www.mister-jon.com; Calle Santander; breakfast Q35-50; ⊙ 7am-10pm Tue-Sun; 🖥) All the perks of a US diner are here in abundance, including buttermilk pancakes, great omelets with hash browns or country biscuits on the side, and free coffee refills (of Guatemala's finest). But it's no gringo ghetto – *chapines* who've been up north like it, too.

Guajimbo's   STEAK **$$**
(☎ 7762-0063; Calle Santander; mains Q60-95; ⊙ 7:30am-9:30pm Fri-Wed) This Uruguayan grill serves up generous helpings of steak, sausage and chicken dishes with vegetables, salad, garlic bread and rice or boiled potatoes. Vegetarians can enjoy tofu kebabs. You won't leave hungry.

El Patio
GUATEMALAN $$

([📞]7762-2041; Plaza Los Patios, Calle Santander; mains Q38-60; ⊙7am-9:30pm) This is a locally popular joint for lunch; the front terrace makes an obvious meeting place. Try to make it for Monday lunch when everyone chows down on *caldo de res* (chunky broth), served with all the trimmings.

Deli Llama de Fuego
ORGANIC $$

([📞]7762-2586; Calle Santander; items Q40-55; ⊙7am-9pm Thu-Tue) Offering a variety of healthy food and drink, this natural-foods haven revolves around a *llama de fuego* tree (African tulip).

Restaurante El Atitlán
SEAFOOD $$

(Calle del Lago; black bass Q140; ⊙7am-9pm) The last of a string of thatched-roof restaurants along the lakefront, El Atitlán offers the best quality and variety. The main draw, aside from the stunning setting, is the lake fish, highlighted by *mojarra* (bream) and black bass.

🍸 Drinking & Nightlife

Panajachel's miniature Zona Viva (party zone) focuses on Av Los Árboles.

★Crossroads Café
CAFE

([📞]5292-8439; www.crossroadscafepana.com; Calle del Campanario 0-27; ⊙9am-1pm & 2:30-6pm Tue-Sat) Bay area native Mike Roberts has made Panajachel a major crossroads for coffee aficionados. When he's not roasting beans or working the Cimbali at his narrow cafe near the center of town, Mike spends his time combing the highlands for small estate coffees to add to his roster, now starring the tangy Acatenango Eighth Wonder and smooth Huehue Organic.

La Palapa
PUB

(Calle Principal; ⊙9am-1am) As the name suggests, this party center unfolds beneath a thatched roof shelter (actually two), with a beachy ambiance. It's favored by Peace Corps volunteers and other gringos, but all sorts crowd in for the Saturday afternoon BBQ. There's a convenient hostel round back for those who've neglected to secure a bed (Q61 per person).

Café La Parada
CAFE

(Centro Comercial El Dorado; ⊙6am-7pm; [📶]) Right by the main bus stop (hence the name), this friendly cafe is popular with local travelers, both for its excellent iced coffee and free wi-fi.

Chapiteau
CLUB

([📞]7762-2056; Av Los Árboles; ⊙7pm-1am Wed-Sat) This strobe-lit disco-bar is the anchor of Pana's little Zona Viva. Check out the phantasmagoric marquee before you cross the threshold.

Café Loco
CAFE $

(Calle Santander; ⊙9am-8pm Tue-Sun, 3-8pm Mon) The latest wrinkle in Pana's crazy quilt of storefronts is this Korean-run cafe which has caught the fancy of the travelers who crowd the long counter. The youthful staff set up a formidable range of espresso variations, from a 'Brown Cloud' (small espresso with a bit of milk and foam) to 'Habana Blues' (with brown sugar sprinkled over espresso grounds).

Sunset Café
BAR

(cnr Calles Santander & del Lago; ⊙11am-11pm) This open-air lounge at the end of Calle Santander is the place to enjoy those spectacular volcano sundowns. In high season, there's live music Friday to Sunday evenings.

Circus Bar
LIVE MUSIC

([📞]7762-2056; Av Los Árboles; ⊙noon-midnight) Behind the swinging doors, Circus Bar has a cabaret atmosphere, with live music nightly from 7:30pm to 10:30pm. Flamenco, folk or marimbas nicely complement the cozy atmosphere, as do the substantial list of imported liquors, Q10 cocktails and good pizza.

Pana Rock Café
LIVE MUSIC

([📞]7762-2194; Calle Santander 1-74) Like a Hard Rock by the lake, this lively little pub hosts plugged-in bands nightly from 9pm. It's big with Guatemala City youth, who settle in for the evening with a *cubetazo* (bucket of beer) or two.

🛍 Shopping

Some travelers prefer the Pana shopping scene to the well-known market at Chichicastenango (p144) because the atmosphere is lower key. Calle Santander is lined with booths, stores and complexes that sell (among other things) traditional Maya clothing, jade, Rasta berets with built-in dreadlocks, colorful blankets, leather goods and wood carvings. Otherwise, head for the traditional market building in the town center, busiest on Sundays when every square meter of ground alongside is occupied by vendors in indigenous garb.

La Señora de Cancuén   CLOTHING
(☑7762-2602; Calle Santander; ☺9:30am-7pm)
Displays the innovative clothing and jewelry of Guatemalan designer Ana Kayax, produced by indigenous weavers and craftspeople from around Guatemala. There's a story behind every item sold here.

The Book Store   BOOKS
(Calle Santander, Centro Comercial El Patio; ☺9am-6pm) Eclectic selection of fiction and nonfiction run by a well-read gringo; also features a lending library.

Oxlajuj B'atz'   HANDICRAFTS
(Thirteen Threads; ☑7762-2921; www.oxlajujbatz.org.gt; Plaza Hotel Real Santander; ☺10am-6pm) Supporting an NGO for the empowerment of indigenous women, this fair-trade shop features naturally dyed rugs, handbags, hand-woven goods and beaded jewelry.

Comerciales de Artesanías Típicas Tinamit Maya   HANDICRAFTS
(☺7am-7pm) Be sure to browse the many stalls of this extensive handicrafts market, which has an impressive variety of bags, clothing, blankets, belts and hammocks. More booths line up along the beach end of Calle Santander.

ℹ️ Information

EMERGENCY & IMPORTANT NUMBERS
Proatur (Programa Asistencia al Turista; ☑5874-9450; proatur.solola@gmail.com; Calle Rancho Grande; ☺9am-5pm)

MEDICAL SERVICES
The nearest hospital is at Sololá.
Pana Medic (☑4892-3499; drzulmashalom@hotmail.com; Calle Principal 0-72) Clinic run by an English-speaking doctor.

MONEY
Banco de América Central (Calle Santander, Centro Comercial San Rafael; ☺9am-5pm Mon-Fri, 9am-1pm Sat) ATM; Visa, American Express and MasterCard cash advances; US dollars exchanged.
Banco Industrial (Calle Santander, Comercial Los Pinos; ☺9am-4pm Mon-Fri, 9am-1pm Sat) Visa/MasterCard ATM.

POST
DHL (Calle Santander, Edificio Rincón Sai) Courier service.
Post Office (cnr Calles Santander & 15 de Febrero)

TOURIST INFORMATION
INGUAT (☑2421-2953; info-pana@inguat.gob.gt; Calle Principal 1-47; ☺9am-5pm) is oppo-

BUSES FROM PANAJACHEL

DESTINATION	COST (Q)	DURATION	FREQUENCY & NOTES
Antigua	45	2½hr	A direct bus by Transportes Rébuli departs at 11am Mon-Sat. Alternatively, take a Guatemala City bus & change at Chimaltenango.
Chichicastenango	20	1½hr	Five buses depart between 6:45am & 6pm daily. Alternatively, take any bus heading to Los Encuentros (via Sololá) & change there.
Ciudad Tecún Umán (Mexican border)			By the Pacific route (via Mazatenango) take a bus to Cocales & change there; by the highland route, transfer at Quetzaltenango.
Guatemala City	35	3½hr	Five departures daily from 4:30am to 3pm by Transportes Rebuli. Alternatively, take a bus to Los Encuentros (via Sololá) & change there.
Huehuetenango		3½hr	Take a bus to Los Encuentros (via Sololá), then wait for a Huehue- or La Mesilla–bound bus. Or catch one heading to Quetzaltenango, alight at Cuatro Caminos & change buses there. There are buses at least hourly from these junctions.
Los Encuentros	5.50	40min	Take one of the frequent buses to Sololá, from where there are buses to Los Encuentros every 10min until 6pm.
Quetzaltenango	25	2½hr	Four buses daily starting at 5am, the last leaving at 1pm. Alternatively, take a bus to Los Encuentros (via Sololá) & change there.
Sololá	3	15min	Every 10min from 7am to 7pm.

site the main bus stop on Calle Principal 50m west of Calle Santander. The English-speaking director provides a wealth of information.

❶ Getting There & Away

BOAT
Passenger boats for Santiago Atitlán (35 minutes) depart from the Playa Pública (public beach) at the foot of Calle Rancho Grande. All other departures leave from the **Embarcadero Tzanjuyú**, at the foot of Calle del Embarcadero. Frequent canopied *lanchas* (small motorboats) go counterclockwise around the lake, with direct and local service to San Pedro La Laguna. The local services stop in Santa Cruz La Laguna (15 minutes), Jaibalito, Tzununá, San Marcos La Laguna (30 minutes), San Juan La Laguna and San Pedro La laguna (45 minutes). The first boat to San Pedro departs at 7am, the last around 7:30pm.

One-way passage to San Pedro, Santiago or San Lucas costs Q25 (though local inhabitants are charged less). *Lanchas* are also available for private hire from the Playa Pública or Embarcadero Tzanjuyú: expect to pay around Q400 to San Pedro La Laguna.

BUS
Panajachel's **main bus stop** is at the junction of Calles Santander and Principal, immediately west of the Centro Comercial El Dorado.

SHUTTLE MINIBUS
Tourist shuttle buses take half the time of buses, for several times the price. You can book at a number of travel agencies on Calle Santander. The **Microbuses y Taxis San Francisco booth** (☑7762-0556; mitafsa_56@hotmail.com; Calle Principal) near the main bus stop also sells shuttle-bus seats. Typical one-way fares:

DESTINATION	COST (Q)
Antigua	Q95
Chichicastenango	round trip Thu & Sun; Q95
Guatemala City	Q175
San Cristóbal de las Casas, Mexico	Q280
Quetzaltenango	Q150

Santiago Atitlán
POP 28,665 / ELEV 1606M

Across the lake from Panajachel, on an inlet between the volcanoes of Tolimán and San Pedro, lies Santiago Atitlán, the largest of the lake communities, with a strong indigenous identity. Many *atitecos* (as its people are known) proudly adhere to a traditional Tz'utujil Maya lifestyle. Women wear purple-striped skirts and *huipiles* embroidered

with colored birds and flowers, while older men still wear lavender or maroon striped embroidered pants. The town's *cofradías* (religious brotherhoods) maintain the syncretic traditions and rituals of Maya Catholicism. There's a large art and crafts scene here, too. Boat-building is a local industry, and rows of rough-hewn *cayucos* (dugout canoes) are lined up along the shore. The best days to visit are Friday and Sunday, the main market days, but any day will do.

It's the most workaday of the lake villages, home to the effigy of Maximón, who is ceremonially moved to a new home on May 8 (after Semana Santa). The rest of the year, Maximón resides with a caretaker, receiving offerings. He changes house every year, but he's easy enough to find by asking around.

The Tz'utujil had been in this area for generations when the Spanish arrived, with their ceremonial capital at Chuitinamit, across the inlet. Santiago was established by Franciscan friars in 1547, as part of the colonial strategy to consolidate the indigenous population. In the 1980s, left-wing guerrillas had a strong presence in the area, prompting the Guatemalan army to kill or disappear hundreds of villagers.

◉ Sights

Cojolya Association of Maya Women Weavers   MUSEUM
(☑7721-7268; www.cojolya.org; Calle Real, Comercial Las Máscaras, 2nd fl; donation requested; ⊙9am-5pm Mon-Fri, 9am-2pm Sat) **FREE** This small museum is devoted to the art of backstrap loom weaving. The well-designed exhibit shows the history of the craft and the process from spinning the cotton fibers to the finished textile. There are also daily demonstrations of backstrap loom techniques, and a small shop.

Iglesia Parroquial Santiago Apóstol   CHURCH
The formidable parish church was built by the Franciscans in the mid-16th century. A memorial plaque just inside the entrance on your right commemorates Father Stanley Francis Rother, a missionary priest from Oklahoma. Beloved by the local people, Rother was murdered by ultra-rightists in the parish rectory next door in 1981; the bedroom where he slept remains open to visitors.

Parque de Paz   MEMORIAL
(Peace Park) During the civil war Santiago became the first village in the country to succeed

in expelling the army, following a notorious massacre of 13 villagers on December 2, 1990. The site of this massacre, where troops were encamped, is now the Parque de Paz, about 1km south of the Parque Central along the road toward San Pedro La Laguna.

🏃 Activities

There are several rewarding day hikes around Santiago. Most enticing of all are the three volcanoes in the vicinity: Tolimán, Atitlán and San Pedro. Before attempting a climb, inquire about the current security situation. It's best to go with a guide; the Posada de Santiago can set up a reliable one. Guided volcano climbs run about Q425 for two to five people.

Less daunting a challenge than the massive volcanoes in the vicinity, Cerro de Oro (1892m) still yields great views and features several Maya ceremonial sites. It's some 8km northeast, about halfway between Santiago and San Lucas Tolimán.

Milpas Tours (☎5450-2381; milpastours@ yahoo.es) leads a variety of fascinating tours in and around Santiago Atitlán. They can take you to the Tz'utujil community of Chuk Muk on the slopes of Volcán Tolimán, with an unexcavated archaeological site; show you the temporary shrine devoted to locally worshiped saint Maximón (Q170); or visit the workshops of local weavers, painters and sculptors and chefs.

Another worthy destination is the Mirador de Tepepul, about 4km south of Santiago, near where the inlet ends (four to five hours round-trip, Q225 per person). The hike goes through cloud forest populated with many birds, including parakeets, curassows, swifts, boat-tailed grackles and tucanets, and on to a lookout point with views all the way to the coast.

The pre-Hispanic Tz'utujil capital of Chuitinamit is across the inlet from Santiago. The hilltop archaeological site features some carved petroglyphs as well as some fanciful painted carvings of more recent vintage. From the dock, it's a 20-minute hike to the top, where there are good views of Santiago. Milpas Tours can take you across the inlet by *cayuco* and accompany you up the tenuous trail to the site.

👉 Tours

Dolores Ratzan Pablo   CULTURAL TOUR
(☎5730-4570; dolores_ratzan@yahoo.com) This English-speaking Tz'utujil woman can intro-

duce you to the wonders of Maya birthing and healing, point out examples of Maya-Catholic syncretism at the church and *cofradías,* and describe the incidents that led to the massacre at the Parque de Paz in 1990. Tours typically last two hours and cost Q300 per person.

🛏️ Sleeping & Eating

Hotel Ratzán   HOTEL $
(☎7721-7840; www.hotelyposadaratzan.blogspot. nl; Calle Principal; s/d Q100/200; ☎) This budget option, near the center of town, is a family-run establishment with nice wood-beam ceilings and large, modern bathrooms. Only three of the five rooms have exterior windows but considering it's just down the street from the massive evangelical church, with raucous nightly services, maybe that's a good thing.

Posada de Santiago   LODGE $$
(☎7721-7366; www.posadadesantiago.com; s/d Q235/400, cottages s/d/tr Q500/615/690, ste from Q765; P@🐾🐕🏊) Striking a balance between rustic charm and luxury, the American-owned *posada* makes a great retreat. Seven cottages and five suites, all with stone walls, fireplaces, porches, hammocks and folk art, are set amid rambling gardens. Across the road stretches a lakeside resort with pool and bar. The restaurant serves delicious, natural fare, as well as homegrown roasted coffee.

The *posada* is 1.5km from the town dock. Catch a *tuk-tuk* (Q10) or hire a *lancha* over to the hotel's own dock.

Hotel La Estrella   HOTEL $$
(☎7721-7814; www.hotel-laestrella.blogspot.com; Calle Campo; s/d/t Q175/300/425; P🐕) A short hike north of the ferry dock along the road to San Lucas is this excellent-value option, featuring modern, comfortable units with handsome wood ceilings and locally woven bedspreads. Room 13, adjacent to the top terrace, takes best advantage of the hotel's lakeside position looking straight across the inlet at Volcán San Pedro.

Comedor Santa Rita   GUATEMALAN $
(Calle de Santa Rita 88; lunch Q25-30; ⊙7am-9pm Mon-Fri) The latest incarnation of a generations-old dining hall, this is a good place to try such Maya specialties as *pulique* (a veggie-rich stew) and *patín* (a local lake fish cooked in tomato sauce), served with a stack of tortillas. It's been overseen by doña

Hélida Esther Cabrera, Santiago's resident ethnographer, for the past 40 years; now her granddaughter's the chef. Half a block east of the Parque Central.

ⓘ Information

DANGERS & ANNOYANCES

The road between Santiago and San Pedro La Laguna has a certain notoriety for bandits, carjackers, kidnappers etc. Proatur, the security branch of the tourist board, recommends taking a ferry between the towns instead.

MONEY

G&T Continental (⊘8:30am-5pm Mon-Fri, 9am-1pm Sat) There's a Cajero 5B ATM at G&T Continental, on the south side of the Parque Central.

ⓘ Getting There & Away

Boats leave hourly for San Pedro La Laguna (Q25, 30 minutes). Pick-ups to Cerro de Oro and San Lucas Tolimán depart from in front of the market. Buses to Guatemala City (Q40, 3½ hours) leave every half hour from 3am to 6am, then hourly until 3pm, from the main plaza.

San Pedro La Laguna

POP 10,150 / ELEV 1592M

Spreading onto a peninsula at the base of the volcano of the same name, San Pedro remains among the most visited of the lakeside villages – due as much to its reasonably priced accommodations and global social scene as its spectacular setting. Travelers tend to dig in here for a spell, in pursuit of (in no particular order) drinking, fire-twirling, African drumming, Spanish classes, painting classes, volcano hiking, hot-tub soaking and hammock swinging.

While this scene unfolds at the lakefront, up the hill San Pedro follows more traditional rhythms. Clad in indigenous outfits, the predominantly indigenous *pedranos* (as the locals are called) congregate around the market zone. You'll see coffee being picked on the volcano's slopes and spread out to dry on wide platforms at the beginning of the dry season.

🏃 Activities

Looming above the village, Volcán San Pedro almost asks to be climbed by anyone with an adventurous spirit. It is the most accessible of the three volcanoes in the zone and, classified as a municipal ecological park, regularly patrolled by tourism police.

Another popular hike goes up the hill to the west of the village that is referred to as Indian Nose – its skyline resembles the profile of an ancient Maya dignitary. **Asoantur** (☑4379-4545; asoantur@gmail.com; 4a Av A 3-60; ⊘7am-7pm), an association made up of 16 INGUAT-authorized guides from the local community, leads expeditions to the peak for Q100 per person. They also offer cultural tours of San Pedro and nearby coffee plantations, horseback riding tours, and kayak, bicycle and motorbike rentals. They operate from a hut on the lane up from the Pana dock.

Kayaks are available for hire (Q10 per hour), turning right from the Pana dock. Ask at Natalí hairdressers.

🐾 Courses

San Pedro is making a name for itself in the language game with ultra-economical rates at its various Spanish institutes. The standard price for four hours of one-on-one classes, five days a week, is Q850. Accommodation with a local family, with three meals daily (except Sunday) typically costs Q650. Volcano hikes, Maya culture seminars and dance classes are among the extracurricular activities offered.

Community Spanish School LANGUAGE COURSE
(☑5466-7177; communityspanishschool.com) A professionally managed school staffed by accredited local instructors, who lead one-on-one classes in thatched huts along a strip of garden running down to the lakefront. Arriving at the Pana dock, go 300m left.

San Pedro Spanish School LANGUAGE COURSE
(☑5715-4604; www.sanpedrospanishschool.org; 7a Av 2-20) Well-organized school on the street between the two docks, with consistently good reviews. Classes are held under thatched-roof huts amid an attractive garden setting. The school supports Niños del Lago, an organization that provides education, health care and nutrition for local Tz'utujil children.

Celas Maya LANGUAGE COURSE
(☑5933-1450; www.spanishschool.com.gt) The lake branch of the prestigious Quetzaltenango institute (Map p156; ☑7765-8205; www.celasmaya.edu.gt; 6a Calle 14-55, Zona 1) takes documentaries, news reports and storytelling as the basis for one-on-one classes aimed at building speaking and listening skills. Classes

in Tz'utujil are also offered. It's at the end of the lakefront trail from the Pana dock.

🛏 Sleeping

In many places in San Pedro it is possible to negotiate deals for longer stays and during the low season. It's also possible to rent a room or an entire house in town – ask around.

Hotel Gran Sueño   HOTEL $
(☑7721-8110; 8a Calle 4-40, Zona 2; s/d Q75/150; 🛜) Though this hotel is certainly not in the prettiest part of town, beyond its plant-draped entryway and up a spiral staircase are bright rooms with colorful abstract designs, comfortable beds and uniquely designed bathrooms. Rooms 9 and 11 are fantastic lake-view perches. From the Pana dock, it's a few doors left of the first crossing.

Zoola   HOSTEL $
(☑5847-4857; dm Q50, r Q160, without bathroom Q130) 'Laid-back' best describes this Israeli-run establishment, a place to crash after a Mideast feast at the adjoining restaurant (p141). It's reached down a long, jungly boardwalk opposite the Museo Tz'unun Ya'. Behind the cafe/chill-out lounge, low adobe blocks of dorms extend to the lake, where a canopied swimming pool is the focus of nightly parties. Two-night minimum stay.

Hotel Mansión del Lago   HOTEL $
(☑7721-8124; www.hotelmansiondellago.com; 3a Vía & 4a Av, Zona 2; s/d Q75/150) If you'd just like to drop your bags, this massive L-shaped hotel is just above the Pana dock. Sparkling clean rooms are done up in cloud or dove motifs, with rockers on wide balconies looking right at the Indian Nose.

Mr Mullet's Hostel   HOSTEL $
(☑4419-0566; mrmullets.com; dm Q60, r with/without bathroom Q140/95; 🛜) Word of mouth has ensured the success of the newest party point in lakeside San Pedro, often overflowing with fun seekers who pile into the four-bed dorms (each bed featuring a large locker and essential charging outlet) and cell-like private rooms on two levels or crowd the patio-bar at rear, which shuts at 11pm for those who actually want to sleep.

Hostel Fe   HOSTEL $
(☑3486-7027; www.hostelfe.com; dm/r Q70/200) A runaway smash, this new hostel takes up a massive concrete block 100m south of the Pana dock. It's the destination of choice for global youth, as much for its rockin' waterfront cafe and adjacent sundeck bar (with waterslide) as for the sparely furnished steel-doored rooms and dorms. Local *pedranos* keep the bathrooms and hangout terraces neat and clean.

Hotel Sak'cari El Amanecer   HOTEL $$
(☑7721-8096; www.hotel-sakcari.com; 7a Av 2-12, Zona 2; s/d/tr Q275/305/385; P 🛜 ❄) 🖊 About midway along the trail between the two docks, the ecofriendly Sak'cari (Tz'utujil for 'sunrise') has 20 clean wood-paneled rooms with lots of shelves. Rooms at the rear are best (and priciest), with big balconies overlooking the lake past a landscaped lawn that's a splendid place for hammock swinging. More active guests can grab a kayak and navigate the lake.

Hotel Mikaso   HOTEL $$
(☑7721-8232; www.mikasohotel.com; 4a Callejon A-88; dm/s/d/tr Q80/150/250/300; 🛜) Despite encroaching lake waters, the Mikaso still stands proudly at Atitlán's shores. Big rooms with carved wood furniture and ceiling fans ring a garden bursting with birds-of-paradise; a few have private patios. The rooftop bar-restaurant boasts fantastic lake views and a deck-lounge features a Jacuzzi and pool table.

🍴 Eating

Café La Puerta   CAFE $
(☑4050-0500; 7a Av 2-20; breakfast Q30-40; ⏰7am-5pm; 🖊) The resident cafe for the San Pedro Spanish School (p139), La Puerta is an appealing spot for abundant natural fare. Breakfast on homemade granola, grainy bread, delicious raspberry jam and avocado milkshakes, all served on beautiful mosaic tile tables by the sweetest waitresses ever to wear a *huipil*. Traditional Guatemalan dishes fused with Asian influences are the highlights of the lunch menu.

Shanti Shanti   ISRAELI $
(8a Calle 3-93; mains Q20-30; ⏰7am-11pm; 🖊) With terraced seating cascading down to the lakeside, this makes a pleasant perch for Mideast staples like falafel, baba ghanouj and hummus, plus hearty soups.

Hummus-Ya   ISRAELI $$
(hummus platters Q42-52; ⏰9am-9:30pm) *Sabich,* an Israeli sandwich lovingly stuffed with hard-boiled eggs, hummus and fried

eggplant, is just one highlight on the menu at this cheerful Mideast eatery upstairs midway between the Pana and Santiago docks. Other authentic specialties include *malawach*, a spicy Yemeni dish, and *shakshuka*, a Tunisian combo of poached eggs and stewed tomatoes.

Idea Connection
CAFE $$
(panini & pastas Q30-50; ⏰7am-5pm; 🛜) Yes, you can get connected on one of the computers at this cybercafe along gringo lane, but it's even more appealing as a bakery/garden cafe. Run by Massimo from Milan, it's a real oasis in the shade, with fantastically fresh croissants, cinnamon rolls and muffins, not to mention super smoothies.

D'Noz
INTERNATIONAL $$
(📋7721-8078; 4a Av 8-18; mains Q40-50; ⏰9am-10pm Mon-Sat; 📋) Right up from the Pana dock, Dino's place sports a terrific deck for lake-view dining. The menu spans the globe from tempeh fajitas to Chinese tacos to Tecpán sausage. Other attractions include a lending library and a popular bar.

🍷 Drinking & Nightlife

While many *pedranos* spend their evenings shouting the lord's praises at evangelical congregations, visitors tend to prowl San Pedro's hard-partying bar scene.

D'Juice Girls
JUICE BAR
(⏰7am-11pm) D'Juice Girls are young Hebrew-speaking Tz'utujil women who squeeze the tropical fruits of Guatemala into super-nutritious combos, such as carrot-ginger-beet. Their popular stand is a five-minute walk east of the Pana dock.

Café Las Cristalinas
CAFE
(⏰7am-9pm; 🛜) To savor a shot of the coffee grown on the surrounding slopes (and roasted here), head for this thatched-roof structure on the way up from the Pana dock to the center of town. Be sure as well to try their excellent banana bread, which you may enjoy on various inviting terraces. It also functions as a cybercafe.

Buddha
PUB
(📋5391-5234; thebuddhaguatemala.com; 7a Av 2-24; ⏰noon-1am) The Buddha can be enjoyed on various levels – downstairs there's a boisterous bar with pool table, rock concert videos and sometimes live music, upstairs a restaurant doing convincing versions of Thai, Indian and Mideast fare (Q35 to Q45),

and up top a thatched roof lounge for smoking, conversation and original cocktails.

Zoola
LOUNGE
(⏰11am-midnight; 🛜) Zoola remains San Pedro's premier global chillage venue. Travelers kick back on cushions around low tables, munching scrumptious Mideast fare, grooving on Manu, playing board games and generally unwinding. For serious DJ sessions, follow the cobblestoned path to the sensational lakefront lounge with swimming pool.

Alegre Pub
PUB
(8a Calle 4-10; ⏰9am-1am) Some nights are more *alegre* than others at this long-running upstairs pub at the corner up from the Pana dock, but it remains a watering hole for San Pedro's cast of characters. Shoot pool with the locals (Tz'utujil rules) in the way-laid-back rooftop garden.

❶ Getting There & Away

Passenger boats arrive and depart here for Panajachel and Santiago Atitlán. Boats from San Pedro to Santiago (Q25, 25 minutes) run hourly from 6am to 4pm. Boats from San Pedro to Panajachel (Q25) run every half hour or so from 6am to 5pm. Some go direct; others make stops at San Juan, San Marcos (Q10) and Jaibalito/Santa Cruz (Q20) en route.

San Pedro is connected by paved roads to Santiago Atitlán (although this stretch is plagued by bandits) and to the Interamericana at Km 148 (about 20km west of Los Encuentros), the latter a hair-raising journey with spectacular lake vistas on the way up. A paved branch of the San Pedro–Interamericana road runs along the northwest side of the lake from Santa Clara to San Marcos La Laguna.

Seven buses leave for Quetzaltenango (Q35, three hours) from San Pedro's Catholic church, up in the town center, between 4:45am and 1:30pm Monday to Saturday; there's three on Sunday, including Pullman buses at 8:30am and 1:30pm.

San Marcos La Laguna

POP 2585 / ELEV 1580M

Without doubt the prettiest of the lakeside villages, San Marcos La Laguna lives a double life. The mostly Maya community occupies the higher ground, while expats and visitors cover a flat jungly patch toward the shoreline with paths snaking through banana, coffee and avocado trees. The two converge under the spreading *matapalo* (strangler fig) tree of the delightful central plaza.

San Marcos has become a magnet for global seekers, who believe the place has a spiritual energy that's conducive to learning and practicing meditation, holistic therapies, massage, reiki and other spiritually oriented activities. Whatever you're into, it's a great spot to kick back and distance the everyday world for a spell. Lago de Atitlán is beautiful and clean here, and you can swim off the rocks. Boats put in at a central dock below Posada Schumann. The path leading from there to the village center, and a parallel one about 100m west, are the main axes for most visitors.

It's an outlandish melange of cultures – evangelical Christians, self-styled shamans, Kaqchiquel farmers and visionary artists – against a backdrop of incredible natural beauty. Someone ought to make a movie about it.

Sights & Activities

Cerro Tzankujil   PARK
(admission Q15; ⊙8am-6pm) This nature reserve is on a sacred hill west of San Marcos village. Well-maintained pebbly trails lead to swimming areas with shelters by the bank and a diving platform. The water is crystal clear here. A branch off the main trail ascends to a Maya altar on the summit, while a lower spur reaches a volcano lookout.

Rent kayaks by the entrance (Q20 per hour, available until 11am).

The Yoga Forest   YOGA
(☑3301-1835; www.theyogaforest.org) Up in the hills north of town amid lush forest, this is a blissfully secluded perch to learn and practice shamanic healing and other esoteric arts, with a magnificent yoga platform built into the hillside. A cafe prepares vegetarian food and accommodations are available in shared adobe cabañas with thatched roofs and magnificent lake views.

East-West Center   MEDITATION
(☑3102-4666) Deep tissue massage (Q250 per hour), reflexology, acupuncture and Bach flowers are among the holistic therapies offered here, along with workshops in I-Ching readings, herbal remedies and so on. It's near the top of the main trail from the dock.

Las Pirámides
Meditation Center   MEDITATION
(☑5205-7302; www.laspiramidesdelka.com) San Marcos La Laguna's claim to fame, this retreat by the lake has been providing spiritual guidance for more than two decades. Most structures on the property are pyramidal in shape and oriented to the four cardinal points, including the two temples where sessions are held. A one-month personal development course begins every full moon, with three sessions daily (US$700).

Sleeping

Circles   HOSTEL $
(☑3327-8961; www.circles-cafe.com; dm/r without bathroom Q75/150) Near the top of the path from the dock is this casual cafe-hostel providing the essentials for most of the global seekers who show up here: good espresso and a comfy place to sleep. Upstairs are two private rooms and a thoughtfully designed dorm with curtains on each bunk. A chill-out terrace looks over a garden with cushioned nooks.

Hotel La Paz   HOSTEL $
(☑5061-5316; www.lakeatitlanlapaz.com; dm/r/ bungalow Q60/150/250) 🗲 Along the upper trail that links the two main paths, the holistically minded La Paz has rambling gardens holding bungalows of traditional *bajareque* (a stone, bamboo and mud material) with thatch roofs. A vegetarian restaurant, traditional Maya sauna, Spanish lessons and morning yoga sessions are additional attractions.

★ Hotel Jinava Bay   RESORT $$
(☑5299-3311; en.hoteljinava.com; r with/without bathroom Q350/250; [P][⊛]) Cobbled paths weave through gardens bursting with flowers, coffee, palms and a profusion of hummingbirds at this tropical lakeside spread 300m west of the village. Bungalows are terraced down the hillside, with jaw-dropping views over the bay – though the lower ones are nicer, with stone walls and beds of tropical hardwoods. Children may not stay here.

Dragon Hotel   BOUTIQUE HOTEL $$
(eldragonhotel.com; s/d Q340/565, without bathroom Q215/380; [⊛]) Definitely a work in progress, this lakefront spread created by an American artist could be the wackiest of San Marcos lodgings. Signs of artistic exuberance pop up everywhere, from the dining area with its hanging spheres to the waterfront deck-bar with its trademark serpent. But not at the expense of luxury: uniquely designed rooms feature plasma TVs, loft beds and private terraces.

✗ Eating

Almost all of the above hotels feature their own restaurants.

Allala   JAPANESE **$**
(☑ 5166-8638; mains Q35-45; ⊙ 3-9pm Thu-Tue; 🖊) This groovy little shack can be found by the creek east of the village. Japanese owner Seiko makes a mean miso soup, plus vegetarian sushi and tempura platters, and the plum wine is divine. All this, and complimentary cheesecake for dessert. Service can be slow, but the funky decor gives you something to look at.

Moonfish   ORGANIC **$**
(sandwiches & burritos Q30; ⊙ 7:30am-8pm Wed-Mon; 🖊🖊) Along the main thoroughfare west of the square, Moonfish whips up hippie-friendly fare including tempeh sandwiches, tofu scrambles and mighty fine falafel with ingredients fresh from the garden. Check the bulletin board for upcoming yoga retreats and events.

Restaurante Fé   INTERNATIONAL **$$**
(mains Q55-80; ⊙ 7.30am-10pm; 🖊) Fé, about midway down the main trail, offers informal candlelit dining in a pleasant, open-air hall with a tree in the middle. The pastas, curries and pan-fried fish are all well worth savoring here, and the mulligatawny stew is excellent. A good place to while away the evening.

Blind Lemon's   BURGERS **$$**
(www.blindlemons.com; mains Q55-70; ⊙ noon-10pm; 🖊) This hangout brings the Mississippi Delta to Atitlán, with weekly blues jams by owner Carlos and special guests in a colonial-style mansion. The menu features chicken platters, Cajun-blackened fish, pizza, burgers and other gringo comfort food. It's at the top of the western path.

❶ Getting There & Away

The last dependable boat to Santa Cruz La Laguna and Panajachel departs about 5pm.

A gravel road runs east from San Marcos to Tzununá and a paved one west to San Pablo and Santa Clara, where it meets the road running from the Interamericana to San Pedro. You can travel between San Marcos and San Pedro by pick-up, with a transfer at San Pablo.

Santa Cruz La Laguna

POP 6000 / ELEV 1833M

With the typically dual nature of the Atitlán villages, Santa Cruz comprises both a waterfront resort – home of the lake's scuba-diving

outfit – and an indigenous Kaqchiquel village, about 600m uphill from the dock. The cobblestoned road up is a route villagers customarily take lugging sacks of avocados or firewood. The inaccessibility of the spot – it can only be reached by boat or on foot – may impede its development but also enhances its rugged beauty.

✗ Activities

ATI Divers   DIVING
(☑ 5706-4117; www.atidivers.com) Lago de Atitlán is one of the rare places in the world where you can dive at altitude without using a dry suit. This group leads dive trips from Santa Cruz. On offer is a four-day PADI openwater diving certification course (Q1915), as well as a PADI high-altitude course and fun dives. It's based at La Iguana Perdida hotel.

🛏 Sleeping & Eating

Hotel Isla Verde   BUNGALOW **$$**
(☑ 5760-2648; www.islaverdeatitlan.com; s/d Q375/420, without bathroom Q285/330; 🖊) 🖊 This stylish, environmentally friendly lodging makes the most of its spectacular setting. A mosaic stone path winds through exuberant vegetation to the nine hillside cabins (six with private bathroom); the higher you go, the more jaw-dropping the picture-window views. Simple rooms are tastefully decorated with art and recycled elements. Bathrooms are jungle-chic affairs, and water and electricity are solar powered.

La Iguana Perdida   LODGE **$$**
(☑ 5706-4117; www.laiguanaperdida.com; dm Q45, r from Q270, s/d without bathroom Q95/125; @ 🖊) The first place you see as you step off the dock, La Iguana Perdida makes a great hangout to enjoy the lake views and meet other travelers, go scuba diving or kayaking, learn Spanish or sweat it out in the sauna. Don't miss the Saturday night cross-dressing, fire and music BBQs!

★ La Fortuna   BUNGALOW **$$$**
(☑ 5203-1033; www.lafortunaatitlan.com; bungalows from Q600) 🖊 As luxurious as it is wild and remote, this ecologically outfitted retreat is at Patzisotz, a secluded bay just east of Santa Cruz around a rocky cliff. Four thatch-roof cabins are elegantly constructed of locally forested guanacaste with Asian influences. Each features a porch and upper deck overlooking the lake, mosquito-netted beds and open-air bathrooms with rain showers.

Café Sabor Cruceño
GUATEMALAN $

(mains Q35-40; ⊙8am-3pm Mon-Sat) Up in the village, this innovative *comedor* is run by local students who are learning to make traditional Guatemalan dishes to global tourism standards. Such Kaqchiquel fare as *subanik* (a tomato sauce of ground seeds and chilis accompanied by *tamalitos*) is prepared with locally grown herbs and veggies and served in the bay-view dining hall.

ℹ Getting There & Away
Santa Cruz is a 15-minute *lancha* ride from Panajachel (Q15) or 25 from San Pedro (Q20). The last boat back to Pana passes at around 5:15pm.

Chichicastenango
POP 148,855 / ELEV 2172M

Surrounded by valleys with mountains serrating the horizons, Chichicastenango can seem isolated in time and space from the rest of Guatemala. When its narrow cobbled streets and red-tiled roofs are enveloped in mist, it's downright magical. The crowds of crafts vendors and tour groups who flock in for the huge Thursday and Sunday markets lend it a much worldlier, more commercial atmosphere, but Chichi retains its mystery. *Masheños* (citizens of Chichicastenango) are famous for their adherence to pre-Christian beliefs and ceremonies, and the town's various *cofradías* (religious brotherhoods) hold processions in observance of their saints around the church of Santo Tomás.

Chichi has two religious and governmental establishments. On the one hand, the Catholic church and the Republic of Guatemala appoint priests and town officials; on the other, the indigenous people elect their own religious and civil officers to manage local matters, with a separate council and mayor, and a court that decides cases involving only local indigenous people.

History
Once called Chaviar, Chichi was an important Kaqchiquel trading town long before the Spanish conquest. In the 15th century the group clashed with the K'iche' (Quiché; based at K'um'arkaj, 20km north) and were forced to move their headquarters to the more defensible Iximché. When the Spanish conquered K'um'arkaj in 1524, many of its residents fled to Chaviar, which they renamed Chugüilá (Above the Nettles) and Tziguan Tinamit (Surrounded by Canyons).

These are the names still used by the K'iche' Maya, although everyone else calls the place Chichicastenango, a name given by the Spaniards' Mexican allies.

◎ Sights & Activities
Take a close look at the mural running alongside the wall of the town hall on the east side of the plaza. It's dedicated to the victims of the civil war and tells the story using symbology from the Popol Vuh.

INGUAT-authorized guides in beige vests offer cultural walks of Chichi and up to Pascual Abaj.

Market
MARKET

(Plaza Principal; ⊙Thu & Sun) Some villagers still walk for hours carrying their wares to reach Chichi's market, one of Guatemala's largest. At dawn on Thursday and Sunday they spread out their vegetables, chunks of chalk (ground to a powder, mixed with water and used to soften dried maize), handmade harnesses and other merchandise and wait for customers.

Iglesia de Santo Tomás
CHURCH

(5a Av) This church on the plaza's east side dates from 1540 and is often the scene of rituals that are more distinctly Maya than Catholic. Inside, the floor of the church may be dotted with offerings of maize, flowers and bottles of liquor wrapped in corn husks; candles are arranged in specific patterns along low stone platforms.

Galería Pop-Wuj
GALLERY

(☑ 4629-9327; www.galeriapopwuj.wix.com/galeriapopwuj; Casa 2-27, Calle Pascual Habaj) FREE On the way down the hill to the shrine at Pascual Abaj, you might stop into this interesting gallery. Developed as an art institute for local children with the backing of Project Guggenheim, it holds a small but unique collection of oil paintings by the artist brothers Juan and Miguel Cortéz and their pupils. K'iche' classes are offered.

Pascual Abaj
SHRINE

On a hilltop south of town, Pascual Abaj (Sacrifice Stone) is a shrine to the Maya earth god Huyup Tak'ah (Mountain Plain). A stone-faced idol stands amid a circle of squat stone crosses in a clearing. Said to be hundreds – perhaps thousands – of years old, it has suffered numerous indignities at the hands of outsiders, but local people still revere it.

Chichicastenango

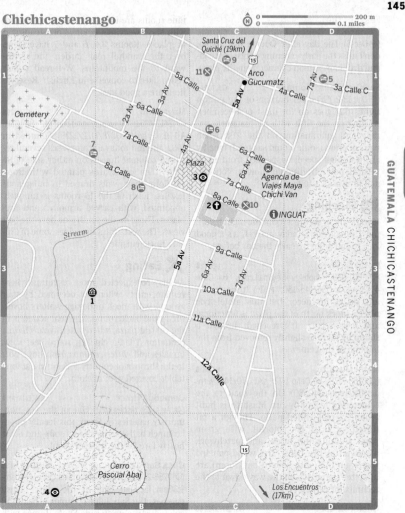

Chichicastenango

◎ Sights
1 Galería Pop-Wuj A3
2 Iglesia de Santo Tomás......................... C2
3 Market.. C2
4 Pascual Abaj... A5

⬚ Sleeping
5 Chalet House.. D1
6 Hotel Girón... C2

7 Hotel Mashito.. A2
8 Mayan Inn... B2
9 Posada El Arco... C1

✖ Eating
10 Casa San Juan C2
11 Comedor Típico C1
    Mayan Inn .... (see 8)

✳ Festivals & Events

Quema del Diablo   CULTURAL
(Burning of the Devil; ⊙ Dec 7) Residents burn
their garbage in the streets and usher a statue

of the Virgin Mary to the steps of the Iglesia
de Santo Tomás. There are lots of incense and
candles, a marimba band and a fireworks
display that has observers running for cover.

**Feast of the
Immaculate Conception** CULTURAL
(☉Dec 8) The day after Quema del Diablo, don't miss the early-morning dance of the giant, drunken cartoon characters in the plaza.

Feast of Santo Tomás CULTURAL
(☉Dec 13-21) The celebration of the patron saint's day goes on for most of December, starting on the fifth with an inaugural parade and culminating on the 21st when pairs of brave (some would say mad) men fly about at high speeds suspended from a tall, vertical pole. Traditional dances, concerts and fireworks also feature.

🛏 Sleeping

If you want to secure a room the night before the Thursday or Sunday market, it's a good idea to call or arrive early the day before.

Hotel Girón HOTEL $
(☎5601-0692; hotelgiron@gmail.com; 6a Calle 4-52; s/d/tr Q85/145/180; P@) It won't win any prizes for decor but this motel-style place a block north of the plaza is functional and feels secure. It's reached through a shopping alley so slightly removed from the hubbub of the center.

Hotel Mashito HOTEL $
(☎5168-7178; 8a Calle 1-72; s/d Q70/140, without bathroom Q40/80) On the road to the cemetery, the family-run Mashito is built around a plant-filled patio. Though a bit frayed, at least it's colorful, with green paint framing the brick, and patchwork blankets on the beds. The wood-paneled rooms up top (with shared bathroom) are in better shape. It's on the way down to the technicolor cemetery.

Chalet House GUESTHOUSE $$
(☎5842-2100; www.chalethotelchichicastenango.com; 3a Calle C 7-44; r incl breakfast Q240) In a quieter residential zone north of the center, this feels like an apartment building, though the rooftop terrace is an exotic extra. Simply furnished rooms have thick *típica* blankets and real solar-powered showers, and there's a guest kitchen. Gregarious owner Manuel has plenty to tell you about his town.

Posada El Arco GUESTHOUSE $$
(☎3469-1590; 4a Calle 4-36; s/d/tr Q225/244/305) 🖉 Near the Arco Gucumatz, this homey, solar-powered spread is one of Chichi's more original accommodations. All nine rooms are idiosyncratically appointed, with Maya weavings, colonial bedsteads and fireplaces. Rooms 3,4, 6 and 7 have views over the tranquil rear garden and northward to the mountains. Well-read owner Pedro likes to converse in English. Reservations are a good idea.

Mayan Inn HOTEL $$$
(☎2412-4753; www.mayaninn.com.gt; 8a Calle A 1-91; ☉s/d/tr Q878/1122/1239) Founded in 1932, the Inn today encompasses several restored colonial houses on either side of 8a Calle, their courtyards planted with tropical flora, their walls draped in indigenous textiles. Each of the 16 rooms is uniquely appointed, with carved armoires and fireplaces. Those on the south side have the best views. The restaurant here does some of Chichi's finest cuisine.

🍴 Eating

As may be expected, most restaurants here remain empty when not occupied by tour groups, with meek underage waiters hovering in the background. The real action is in the central plaza, where attentive *abuelitas* (grandmas) ladle chicken soup, beef stew, tamales and *chiles rellenos* from huge pots to the throngs of country folk sitting at long tables covered with oilcloth.

Comedor Típico GUATEMALAN $
(4a Av 4-23; dishes Q20) One of the few non-touristy eateries in town, this locally popular lunch hall does cow's foot soup and other hearty fare for the traveler's soul.

Casa San Juan GUATEMALAN $$
(☎7756-2086; 6a Av 7-30; mains Q60; ☉10am-9:30pm Tue-Sun) One of the more stylish eateries, the San Juan occupies a beautiful colonial structure beside Santo Tomás with candlelit dining in various salons. Offerings range from burgers and sandwiches to more traditional fare, including good *chiles rellenos* laced with zesty salsa.

Mayan Inn GUATEMALAN $$
(☎2412-4753; 8a Calle A 1-91; mains Q70-125; ☉7am-10pm) The three dining rooms at Chichi's classiest hotel feature colonial-style furnishings and canvases by renowned painter Humberto Garabito. Waiters wear costumes evolved from the dress of Spanish colonial farmers. The food is lavishly presented and abundantly served, with a few traditional options like *pepián* and *jocón*.

❶ Information

Chichi's many banks all stay open on Sunday.

Banco Industrial (6a Calle 6-05) Visa/Master-Card ATM.

INGUAT (☑ 5966-1162; info-quiche@inguat.gob.gt; 7a Av 7-14; ☉ 8am-4pm Sun-Thu) Authorized guides can be hired here for cultural tours of the town and up to Pascual Abaj.

Visa/MasterCard ATM (cnr 5a Av & 6a Calle)

❶ Getting There & Away

Buses heading south to Panajachel, Quetzaltenango and all other points reached from the Interamericana arrive and depart from 5a Calle near the corner of 5a Av, one block uphill from the Arco Gucumatz. Buses approaching from the south go up 7a Av, dropping off passengers two blocks east of the central plaza.

Agencia de Viajes Maya Chichi Van (☑ 5007-2051; mayachichivan@yahoo.es; 6a Calle 6-45) offers shuttles to Guatemala City (Q125), Antigua (Q90), Panajachel (Q55) and Panajachel on Thursday and Sunday at 2pm, plus service to San Cristóbal de las Casas, Mexico, at 7am daily. In most cases they need at least five passengers. They also run tours to K'um'arkaj near Santa Cruz del Quiché, Nebaj and elsewhere.

The hotel **Chalet House** (p146) provides reliable shuttle service to Los Encuentros with connections to Antigua, Lago de Atitlán and Quetzaltenango.

Santa Cruz del Quiché

POP 102,782 / ELEV 1979M

Without Chichicastenango's big market and attendant tourism, Santa Cruz – or just El Quiché – presents a less self-conscious slice of regional life and is refreshingly free of competition for tourist lucre. Just 19km north of Chichi, it's the capital of Quiché department, drawing a diverse populace on business and administrative affairs. The main market days are Thursday and Sunday, boosting the bustle considerably. Travelers who come here usually do so to visit K'um'arkaj, the ruins of the old K'iche' Maya capital, or to change buses en route further north.

The most exciting time to be here is during the **Fiestas Elenas** (www.fiestaselenas.com; ☉ mid-August), a week of festivities and a proud display of indigenous traditions. It all leads up to the *convite feminino,* when El Quiché's women don masks and dance up a storm to marimba accompaniment.

❍ Sights

Most points of interest are within a few short blocks of the tripartite plaza, usually a hive of activity. The top square is flanked on its east side by Gobernación (the departmental government palace), the middle one by the cathedral and *municipalidad* (town hall), and the bottom one by the big domed events hall, in front of which stands a statue of K'iche' warrior Tecún Umán in a fierce posture, though these days sadly engulfed by the stalls of the informal economy. The main market occupies a series of buildings east of the plaza.

K'um'arkaj   ARCHAEOLOGICAL SITE
(Q'um'arkaj, Utatlán; admission Q30; ☉ 8am-4pm) The ruins of the ancient K'iche' Maya capital of K'um'arkaj remain a sacred site for the Maya, and contemporary rituals are customarily enacted there. Archaeologists have identified more than 80 large structures in 12 groups, but only limited restoration has been done. The ruins have a fine setting, shaded by tall evergreens and surrounded by ravines. Bring a flashlight.

BUSES FROM CHICHICASTENANGO

DESTINATION	COST (Q)	DURATION	FREQUENCY & NOTES
Antigua	25	3½hr	Take any bus heading for Guatemala City & change at Chimaltenango.
Guatemala City	30	2½hr	Every 30min from 3am to 5pm.
Los Encuentros	6	30min	Frequent microbuses leave from in front of the Telgua building on 7a Av.
Panajachel	20	2hr	Take a microbus to Los Encuentros & change there.
Quetzaltenango	20	2hr	Every half hour till 3pm. Alternatively, take a microbus to Los Encuentros & change there.
Santa Cruz del Quiché	6	40min	Frequent microbuses from 5a Calle on the west side of 5a Av between 7am & 8pm.

The kingdom of K'iche' was established in late Postclassic times (about the 14th century) by a mixture of indigenous people and invaders from the Tabasco-Campeche border area in Mexico. King Ku'ucumatz founded K'um'arkaj, which owing to its naturally fortified position commanded an extensive valley, and conquered many neighboring settlements. During the long reign of his successor Q'uik'ab (1425–75), the K'iche' kingdom extended its borders to Huehuetenango, Nebaj, Rabinal and the Pacific Slope. At the same time the Kaqchiquel, a vassal people who once fought alongside the K'iche', rebelled, establishing an independent capital at Iximché.

When Pedro de Alvarado and his Spanish conquistadors hit Guatemala in 1524, it was the K'iche', under their king Tecún Umán, who led the resistance against them. In the decisive battle fought near Quetzaltenango on February 12, 1524, Alvarado and Tecún engaged in mortal combat. Alvarado prevailed. The defeated K'iche' invited him to visit K'um'arkaj. Smelling a rat, Alvarado enlisted the aid of his Mexican auxiliaries and the anti-K'iche' Kaqchiquel, and together they captured the K'iche' leaders, burnt them alive in K'um'arkaj's main plaza and then destroyed the city.

The museum at the entrance will help orientate you. The tallest of the structures round the central plaza, the Templo de Tohil (a sky god), is blackened by smoke and has a niche where contemporary prayer-men regularly make offerings to Maya gods. The L-shaped ballcourt alongside it has been extensively restored.

Down the hillside to the right of the plaza is the entrance to a long tunnel known as the *cueva*. Legend has it that the K'iche' dug the tunnel as a refuge for their women and children in preparation for Alvarado's coming, and that a K'iche' princess was later buried in a deep shaft off this tunnel. Revered as the place where the K'iche' kingdom died, the *cueva* is sacred to highland Maya and is an important location for prayers, candle burning, offerings and chicken sacrifices.

If there's anyone around the entrance, ask permission before entering. Inside, the long tunnel (perhaps 100m long) is blackened with smoke and incense and littered with candles and flower petals. Use your flashlight and watch your footing: there are several side tunnels and at least one of them, on the right near the end, contains a deep, black shaft.

The ruins of K'um'arkaj are 3km west of El Quiché. Gray 'Ruinas' microbuses depart from in front of the cathedral in Santa Cruz every 20 minutes (Q1). The last one back is at 6:50pm.

🛏 Sleeping & Eating

The main hotel district is along 1a Av (Zona 5) north of the bus terminal, with at least five hotels within two blocks, and others along 9a Calle.

Hotel Rey K'iche'   HOTEL $
(📞 7755-0827; 8a Calle 0-39, Zona 5; s/d Q100/180; @ 🛜) Between the bus station and plaza, the Rey K'iche' is excellent value with well-maintained, brick-walled rooms around a quiet interior and affable staff. There's free drinking water and a decent cafe upstairs serving breakfast and dinner. All things considered, it's the best place to stay.

El Sitio Hotel   HOTEL $$
(📞 7755-3656; elsitiohotel@gmail.com; 9a Calle 0-41, Zona 5; s/d/tr Q175/300/400; 🅿 🛜) From

BUSES FROM SANTA CRUZ DEL QUICHÉ

DESTINATION	COST (Q)	DURATION	FREQUENCY & NOTES
Chichicastenango	6	40min	Frequent microbuses depart from the corner of 5a Calle & 2 Av, opposite Café San Miguel.
Guatemala City	35	3hr	Every 10min from 3am to 5pm.
Huehuetenango	25	2hr	Microbuses from the south side of the lot depart every half hour from 5am to 6pm.
Nebaj	20	2hr	Every half hour from 6am to 7pm.
Sacapulas	12	1hr	Microbuses depart from 1a Av off the northeast corner of main plaza every half hour till 7:30pm.
Uspantán	30	2-2½hr	Frequent microbuses depart from the west side of the lot from 5:30am to 7pm.

the outside, this business-class hotel two blocks north of the bus terminal resembles a modern evangelical church. Though rather sterile with a cavernous lobby, rooms are modern and well-maintained and have a bit of *típica* decor.

Posada Santa Cecilia   HOTEL $$
(☑ 5180-1194; cnr 1a Av & 6a Calle; s/d Q125/190) Just south of the chaotic main plaza, this modern establishment takes up the top level of a small shopping center. Although the handful of comfortable units have large firm beds with pretty quilts, they're sketchily maintained and unfortunately open to the constant rumble of traffic and car exhaust from the plaza during working hours.

Restaurant El Chalet   STEAK $$
(☑ 7755-0618; 1a Calle 2-39, Zona 5; mains Q60-70; ☺ 7am-9pm) The specialty here is grilled meats, served with homemade salsas. You could make a light meal of the tortilla-sized portions. Dining is beneath an arbor flanked by a strip of garden. It's part of a posh hotel and conference center a few blocks east of the big clock tower.

❶ Getting There & Away

El Quiché is the jumping-off point for the remote reaches of northern Quiché department, which extend all the way to the Mexican border. The main bus terminal, a dusty lot in Zona 5, is located four blocks south and two blocks east of the plaza.

Nebaj

POP 18,484 / ELEV 2000M

Hidden in a remote fold of the Cuchumatanes mountains north of Sacapulas is the Triángulo Ixil (Ixil Triangle), a 2300-sq-km zone comprising the towns of Santa María Nebaj, San Juan Cotzal and San Gaspar Chajul, as well as dozens of outlying villages and hamlets. The local Ixil Maya people, though they suffered perhaps more than anybody in Guatemala's civil war, cling proudly to their traditions and speak the Ixil language. Nebaj women are celebrated for their beautiful purple, green and yellow pom-pommed hair braids, scarlet *cortes* (wraparound skirts), and their *huipiles* (long, sleeveless tunics) and *rebozos* (shawls), featuring bird and animal motifs.

Living in this beautiful mountain vastness has long been both a blessing and a curse. The invading Spaniards found it difficult to conquer, and they laid waste to the inhabitants when they did. During the civil war years, massacres and disappearances were rife, with more than two dozen villages destroyed. According to estimates by church groups and human-rights organizations, some 25,000 Ixil inhabitants (of a population of 85,000) were either killed or displaced by the army between 1978 and 1983 as part of the campaign to expunge guerrilla activity. You may hear some appalling personal experiences from locals while you're here.

The people of the Ixil Triangle are making a heroic effort to build a new future with the help of development organizations and NGOs, whose workers you're likely to encounter during your visit.

◉ Sights & Activities

Centro Cultural Kumool   MUSEUM
(5a Av 1-32; admission Q20; ☺ 9am-noon & 1-6pm Mon-Fri, 8am-1pm Sat) Housed in the Radio Ixil building, this small museum displays a collection of mostly ceramic objects excavated in the Ixil region, all arranged by historical period. Among the more interesting pieces are a ceremonial ax with a skull handle and a giant funerary urn with a jaguar face, plus some well-preserved polychrome vases.

Guías Ixiles   HIKING
(☑ 5847-4747; www.nebaj.com; 3a Calle, El Descanso Bldg, Zona 1; ☺ 8am-12:30pm & 2-5pm) Guías Ixiles offers half-day walks to Las Cataratas (Q55 for one person plus Q25 for each extra person), a series of waterfalls north of town, or around town with visits to the sacred sites of the *costumbristas* (people who still practice non-Christian Maya rites). Guías Ixiles also lead three-day treks over the Cuchumatanes to Todos Santos Cuchumatán.

❧ Courses

Nebaj Language School   LANGUAGE COURSE
(☑ 5847-4747; www.nebaj.com/nls.html; 3a Calle, El Descanso Bldg, Zona 1; 1 week Q615) Offers instruction in Spanish. A package (Q1110) is available, including accommodation with a local family, two meals a day, two guided hikes to nearby villages and internet use. Instruction in the indigenous Ixil language is another option.

You can also learn how to make regional dishes like *boxboles* (corn dough wrapped in squash leaves, served with a spicy peanut sauce).

✦ Festivals & Events

Nebaj's annual festival, coinciding with the Assumption of the Virgin Mary, runs for 10 days in mid-August.

⊨ Sleeping & Eating

Hotel Turansa   HOTEL $
(☑4144-7609; cnr 5a Calle & 6a Av; s/d from Q85/150; P🖥) This friendly, central establishment – just a block from the Parque Principal – has decent-sized rooms with big comfy beds and flat-screen TVs along plant-draped balconies. Top-floor triples open on to a sunny terrace. The only downside is the pervasive engine noise from outside.

Media Luna Medio Sol   HOSTEL $
(☑5749-7450; www.nebaj.com/medialuna.html; 3a Calle 6-25; dm Q35, r per person Q45; 🖥) Nebaj's hostel is around the corner from its parent organization, El Descanso, where you can check in. Two six-bed dorms and a few private rooms with thin mattresses share clean toilets and showers. You're welcome to use the kitchen, though facilities are minimal.

★ Hotel Santa María   HOTEL $$
(☑4212-7927; www.hotelsantamarianebaj.com; cnr 4a Av & 2a Calle; s/d Q150/200; P🖥) Scarlet woven bedspreads, carved wood headboards and other Ixil handicrafts decorate the bright, spotless rooms at this well-maintained property three blocks northwest of the main plaza.

El Descanso   CAFE $
(☑5847-4747; www.nebaj.com; 3a Calle, Zona 1; mains Q28-35; ⊙6:30am-9:30pm) This cozy restaurant features a bar and lounge areas in Nebaj's most alternative ambiance. A range of snacks, salads and soups is served.

Comedor El Si'm   GUATEMALAN $
(3a Av; breakfast Q30; ⊙7am-9pm) This below-street-level place off the main plaza is great for a gut-stuffing *desayuno* (breakfast), served with a bonus bowl of *mosh* (warm cereal) and a freshly baked cookie, and they refill your coffee cup. It's usually crammed with local characters by 8am.

🛍 Shopping

Mercado de Artesanías   HANDICRAFTS
(Handicrafts Market; cnr 7a Calle & 2a Av, Zona 1; ⊙8am-6pm) The numerous vendor stalls here offer well-made *rebozos, cintas* (the pom-pommed braid woven into Ixil women's hair) and *huipiles,* which can cost anywhere from Q300 to Q5000, depending on quality.

ⓘ Information

Banrural (⊙8am-4:30pm Mon-Fri, 7-11am Sat) Changes traveler's checks.

Post Office (5a Av 4-37) One block northwest of the park.

Tourist Office (☑3072-4224; cnr 7a Calle & 2a Av, Zona 1; ⊙8am-6pm Mon-Sat, 8am-noon Sun) The tourist office, inside the Mercado de Artesanías, can answer any question as long as it's posed in Spanish.

ⓘ Getting There & Away

The bus terminal is just below the market. **Microbuses** bound for Santa Cruz del Quiché, via Sacapulas, go every half hour from 4am until 5pm (Q20, two hours), departing from behind the church at the corner of 5a Av and 7a Calle. To head west to Huehuetenango or east to Uspantán and Cobán, change at Sacapulas.

Microbuses to Chajul (Q7, 45 minutes) depart every 20 minutes or so until 6pm from in front of the Hotel Villa Nebaj, on Calz 15 de Septiembre.

The main **bus terminal**, behind the **market**, mainly serves outlying villages such as Tzalbal, Vicalama and Palop; one bus travels all the way to Guatemala City (Q50, 5½ hours) via Chichicastenango, departing at 2am.

Uspantán

POP 41,892

Most travelers who pass through Uspantán are on their way to Cobán. Though the sky-high journey through the Cuchumatanes is reason enough to travel there, Uspantán, a benevolent town halfway between Huehuetenango and Cobán along the 7W road, offers a few attractions of its own.

To get the big picture, hike up to Cerro Xoqoneb', a Maya ceremonial center 1.5km east of town. Signage is sparse; the tourism association ACAT (☑7951-8027; amalia.urizar@yahoo.com) can set you up with a guide.

⊨ Sleeping & Eating

Hotel Posada Doña Leonor   HOTEL $
(☑7951-8041; calutis54@hotmail.com; 6a Calle 4-25, Zona 1; s/d/tr Q80/160/240; P🖥) This well-maintained option a block east of the plaza features 21 rooms around a courtyard with a jacaranda tree in the middle and a cookshack for breakfast and supper. You'll find firm beds, fresh paint, and spotless bathrooms with electric showerheads.

Comedor Yeimy GUATEMALAN $
(7a Calle; meals Q20; ⊗7:30am-8pm) Yeimi's
kitchen is an unusually clean place with silver
tablecloths and several pink-walled salons.
Home-cooked platters of chicken, steak or
eggs are nicely presented and served with a
bowl of pickled carrots and onions. It's one
block south, 1½ blocks east of the plaza.

❶ Getting There & Away

Microbuses for Quiché (Q30, 2½ hours), via
Sacapulas, leave whenever full from Uspantán's
bus terminal on 6a Calle, three blocks west of
the Parque Central, until 7pm. For Cobán (Q30,
three hours), microbuses go hourly from 4am to
3:30pm; a 35km stretch of that journey is over
a perilously unpaved surface. For Nebaj, there
are a couple of direct microbuses (coming from
Cobán), or get a microbus to Sacapulas where
you'll find frequent connections up to the Ixil
triangle.

Quetzaltenango (Xela)

POP 152,743 / ELEV 2367M

Quetzaltenango may well be the perfect Guatemalan town – not too big, not too small,
enough foreigners to support a good range
of hotels and restaurants, but not so many
that it loses its national flavor. The Guatemalan 'layering' effect is at work in the city
center – once the Spanish moved out, the
Germans moved in and their architecture
gives the zone a somber, even Gothic, feel.

Quetzaltenango is big, like its name –
which the locals kindly shorten to Xela
(*shell*-ah), itself an abbreviation of the original K'iche' (Quiché) Maya name, Xelajú – but
by Guatemalan standards, it is an orderly,
clean and safe city. It tends to attract a more
serious type of traveler – people who really
want to learn Spanish and then stay around
and get involved in the myriad volunteer
projects on offer.

Xela also functions as a base for a range of
spectacular hikes through the surrounding
countryside – the ascent to the summit of
Volcán Tajumulco (Central America's highest point) and the three-day trek to Lago de
Atitlán, to name a few.

History

Quetzaltenango came under the sway of the
K'iche' Maya of K'um'arkaj when they began
their great expansion in the 14th century.
Before that it had been a Mam Maya town. It
was near here that the K'iche' leader Tecún

Umán was defeated and killed by the Spanish conquistador Pedro de Alvarado in 1524.

The town prospered in the late 19th-
century coffee boom, with brokers opening
warehouses and *finca* (plantation) owners
coming to town to buy supplies. (Fans of urban decay will appreciate the abundance of
unrestored structures still standing from that
period.) This boom busted when a combined
earthquake and eruption of Santa María in
1902 wreaked mass destruction. Still, the
city's position at the intersection of roads
to the Pacific Slope, Mexico and Guatemala
City guaranteed it some degree of prosperity.
Today it's again busy with commerce, of the
indigenous, foreign and *ladino* varieties.

◉ Sights

Museo de Arte MUSEUM
(Map p152; 4a Calle & 19 Av, Zona 3; donation requested; ⊗9am-1pm & 3-7pm) An interesting if
chaotic collection of some 400 paintings by
Guatemala's leading modernists is exhibited
here, including works by Efraín Recinos,
Jorge Mazariegos and the landscape artist
José Luis Álvarez. Most prominently displayed are the fantastic canvases of Rodrigo
Díaz, who also happens to be the curator.

Museo Ixkik' MUSEUM
(Map p152; ☑5653-5585; 4a Calle 19 & 21 Av, Zona
3; donation requested Q35; ⊗9am-5pm Mon-Fri)
This museum is devoted to Maya weaving,
with traditional outfits arranged by region.
Director Raquel García is an expert on the
symbols and meanings of indigenous clothing and provides interesting commentary.

**Centro Intercultural de
Quetzaltenango** CULTURAL CENTER
(Map p152; 4a Calle & 19 Av, Zona 3) FREE Quetzaltenango's railroad station, 1km east of
the Templo de Minerva along 4a Calle, lay
dormant for years until the city converted it
into this center, which now houses schools
of art and dance, plus three interesting
museums.

Parque Centro América PLAZA
(Map p156) Most of Xela's sights crowd in
and around the broad central plaza. The
original version, designed by Italian architect Alberto Porta in the 1800s, comprised
two separate parks; these were combined
in a 1930s update into the current oblong
shape. Most notable of the monuments scattered along its expanse is a rotunda of Ionic

Quetzaltenango

GUATEMALA QUETZALTENANGO (XELA)

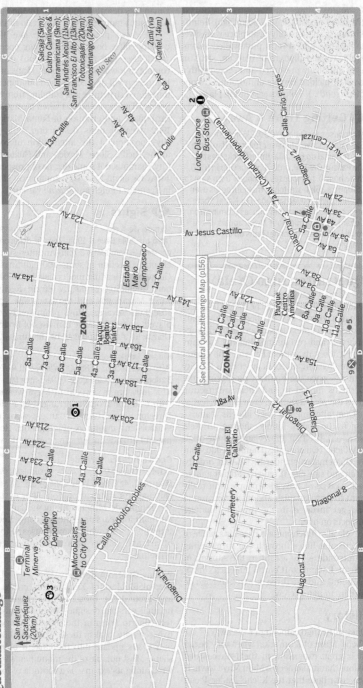

0 __ 500 m
0 __ 0.25 miles

Salcajá (5km);
Cuatro Caminos &
Interamericana (9km);
San Andrés Xecul (11km);
San Francisco El Alto (13km);
Totonicapán (20km);
Momostenango (24km)

Zunil (via
Cantel, 14km)

Río Seco

Calle Cirilo Flores

Av El Cenizal

Long-Distance
Bus Stop

7a Av (Calzada Independencia)

Diagonal 2

2a Av

3a Av

4a Av

5a Av

6a Av

Calle Cirilo Flores

13a Calle

6a Av

4a Av

3a Av

7a Calle

Av Jesus Castillo

Diagonal 3

5a Calle

7

10

9

Estadio
Mario
Camposeco

1a Calle

12a Av

13a Av

14a Av

1a Av

Parque
Centro
América

8a Av

9a Av

8a Calle

9a Calle

10a Calle

11a Calle

5

See Central Quetzaltenango Map (p156)

ZONA 1

1a Calle

2a Calle

3a Calle

4a Calle

12a Av

13a Av

6

8a Calle

ZONA 3

8a Calle

7a Calle

6a Calle

5a Calle

4a Calle

Parque
Benito
Juárez

15a Av

16a Av

17a Av

1a Calle

18a Av

19a Av

20a Av

21a Av

22a Av

23a Av

24a Av

6a Calle

4a Calle

3a Calle

Calle Rodolfo Robles

1

4

18a Av

Parque El
Calvario

Cemetery

Diagonal 12

8

Diagonal 13

Diagonal 8

Diagonal 11

Diagonal 14

San Martín
Sacatepéquez (20km)

Terminal
Minerva

Complejo
Deportivo

Microbuses
to City Center

3

2

Quetzaltenango

⊙ **Sights**
1 Centro Intercultural de
    Quetzaltenango..................................C1
2 Monumento a la Marimba..................G3
    Museo de Arte................................(see 1)
    Museo del Ferrocarril de
    los Altos..(see 1)
    Museo Ixkik'....................................(see 1)
3 Parque Zoológico Minerva..................B1

🟢 **Activities, Courses & Tours**
4 Centro de Estudios de Español
    Pop Wuj..D2
5 El Portal Spanish School....................D4
6 El Quetzal Spanish School..................E4
    Highland Partners......................(see 10)
7 Proyecto Lingüístico
    Quetzalteco de Español...................E4
    Quetzaltrekkers...........................(see 8)

🛌 **Sleeping**
8 Casa Argentina..................................C4

🍴 **Eating**
9 Panorama...D4

🛍 **Shopping**
10 Pixan..E4

columns dedicated to the composer Rafael Álvarez Ovalle.

Parque Zoológico Minerva ZOO
(Map p152; ☎7763-5637; Av Las Américas 0-50, Zona 3; adult/child under 1.2m Q2/free; ⊙9am-4pm Tue-Sun) About 2km northwest of the Parque Centro América is this zoo/city park with spider monkeys, coyotes, turtles, gray foxes and numerous tropical birds, plus a few rides for children. The entrance is around the corner from the Templo de Minerva.

🏃 Activities

There are many exciting walks and climbs to be done from Xela. **Volcán Tajumulco** (4220m), 50km northwest, is the highest point in Central America, and it's a challenging trek of one long day from the city or two days with a night camping on the mountain. This includes about five hours' walking up from the starting point, Tuhichan (2½ hours by bus from Xela).

With early starts, **Volcán Santa María** (3772m), towering to the south of the city, and the highly active **Santiaguito** (2488m), on Santa María's southwest flank, can both be done in long mornings from Xela, though

the tough, slippery trail is recommended only for seasoned hikers. You start walking at the village of Llanos del Pinal, 5km south of Xela (Q5 by bus), from where it's four to five hours up to the summit of Santa María. Getting too close to Santiaguito is dangerous, so people usually just look at it from a point about 1½ hours' walk from Llanos del Pinal.

★**Guate Guides** HIKING
(☎5195-7734; www.guateguides.com) This small, locally run outfit offers tours to area volcanoes, villages and nature reserves with an emphasis on quality equipment and knowledgeable commentary. Experts in hiking and cycling respectively, guides Marvín and Martín are certified in first-aid and survival situations.

Altiplano's Tour Operator CULTURAL TOUR
(Map p156; ☎7766-9614; www.altiplanos.com. gt; 6a Calle 7-55, Zona 1; half-day tours per person Q250-350) This outfit offers some interesting half-day tours to indigenous villages and markets, colonial churches and coffee plantations around Xela, plus reliable shuttle services.

Quetzaltrekkers HIKING
(Map p152; ☎7765-5895; www.quetzaltrekkers. com; Diagonal 12 8-37, Zona 1) Most of the guides at this unique outfit are foreign volunteers (and experienced trekkers can join their ranks). Based at the Casa Argentina hotel, they provide both monetary and logistical support for various social projects.

One-day hikes to Fuentes Georginas and Santa María volcano, three-day trips to Lago de Atitlán (Q750 per person) and six-day treks from Nebaj to Todos Santos Cuchumatán (Q1300) run on a weekly basis; check the calendar to see when they go. Also offered are rock-climbing expeditions to La Muela, a pilgrimage site in the Almolonga Valley where rock pillars rise out of an extinct lava field.

🥾 Courses

Quetzaltenango's many language schools attract students from around the world. Unlike Antigua, it isn't overrun with foreigners, though there is a growing social scene revolving around language students and volunteer workers.

Most schools provide opportunities to get involved in social action programs working with the local K'iche' Maya. The standard weekly price is Q920/1000 for four/five hours of instruction per day, Monday to Friday. Add around Q325 for room and board with a local family. Some places charge up to 20% more for tuition from June to August, and many require nonrefundable registration fees. Extras range from movies and free internet to dancing, cooking classes and lectures on Guatemalan politics and culture.

Proyecto Lingüístico Quetzalteco de Español
LANGUAGE COURSE

(Map p152; ☑ 7763-1061; www.plqe.org; 5a Calle 2-40, Zona 1) This collectively managed and politically minded institute also runs the Escuela de la Montaña, a limited-enrolment language-learning program in a rural zone near the town of Colomba. Courses in K'iche' are also offered.

El Quetzal Spanish School
LANGUAGE COURSE

(Map p152; ☑ 7761-2784; www.elquetzalspanish. com; 7a Calle 4-24, Zona 1) One of the few indigenous-run businesses in town, offering plenty of activities.

El Portal Spanish School
LANGUAGE COURSE

(Map p152; ☑ 7761-5275; www.spanishschoolelpor tal.com; 9a Callejón A 11-49, Zona 1) Small outfit with enthusiastic and supportive atmosphere. Earnings provide scholarships for children of single mothers.

Inepas
LANGUAGE COURSE

(Instituto de Español y Participación en Ayuda Social; Map p156; ☑ 7765-1308; www.inepas.org; 15a Av 4-59) Guatemalan social issues are woven into the Spanish lessons at this Unesco-recognized NGO that promotes educational development in rural communities, and students can participate in a variety of worthy projects. The institute offers a selection of inexpensive accommodations as well as homestays.

Centro de Estudios de Español Pop Wuj
LANGUAGE COURSE

(Map p152; ☑ 7761-8286; www.pop-wuj.org; 1a Calle 17-72, Zona 1) Pop Wuj's profits go to development projects in nearby villages, in which students can participate.

Tours

Highland Partners
VOLUNTEERING

(Map p152; ☑ 7761-6408; 5a Av 6-17, Zona 1) This group seeks to empower Maya women in five rural communities near Quetzaltenango by helping them to become economically

sustainable. You can join a tour to experience life in these villages and learn about their customs, traditions and daily activities. Go further and get involved in special projects such as building fuel-efficient stoves, transplanting trees or teaching art to schoolchildren.

In Xela, Highland Partners runs Pixan (p159), an outlet for weavings made by Maya women.

Festivals & Events

Xela Music Festival
MUSIC

(☉ Nov) Organized by the French Cultural Institute, this performance event features local musicians playing on five or six stages around the city center.

Feria de la Virgen del Rosario
CULTURAL

(☉ Sep/Oct; Feria Centroamericana de Independencia) Held in late September or early October, this is Xela's big annual party. Students create colorful carpets of sawdust upon the streets of the city, taxi drivers shoot fireworks and the sirens of the firetrucks wail. Residents kick up their heels at a fairground on the city's perimeter and there's plenty of entertainment at selected venues around town, including a battle of the brass bands in the Parque Centro América.

Sleeping

With a continual influx of foreign volunteers and language students, Xela counts numerous long-term-stay options. Some guesthouses offer furnished apartments and most language institutes can set up homestays with local families. Look for leads in the classified section of the publication *XelaWho*.

Casa Seibel
HOSTEL $

(Map p156; ☑ 7765-2130; www.casaseibel.com; 9 Av 8-10; dm/r Q50/110; 🕸) Brilliantly incorporated into a vintage Xela house, the recently opened Casa is cozy and comfortable. Set around two plant-fillled courtyards, its dorms and private rooms (sharing two bathrooms, one with tub) have attractive wood floors and painted ceilings and retain some original furniture with plenty of shelves and closet space. Guests can mingle in the shared kitchen and TV lounge.

Hotel Kiktem-Ja
HOTEL $

(Map p156; ☑ 7761-4304; www.hotelkiktem-ja. com; 13a Av 7-18, Zona 1; s/d/tr Q135/180/230; 🅿) Set in a great hundred-year-old house downtown, the Kiktem-Ja is all floorboards at weird angles, stone arches and squiggly wood columns along plant-draped corridors. Rooms are spacious with sturdy bedsteads, fireplaces and pretty tiled bathrooms.

Hostel Nim Sut
HOSTEL **$**

(Map p156; ☑ 7761-3083; www.hostelnimsutquet zaltenango.weebly.com; 4a Calle 9-42, Zona 1; dm Q45, s/d Q100/170, without bathroom Q85/130; ☜) Conveniently placed a block east of the Parque Centro América, this restored colonial relic has plenty of large rooms with basic bedding and clean parquet floors, some considerably brighter than others (room 5 is best). The terrace, from which you can occasionally glimpse the plumes of Santiaguito, is a good place to enjoy an espresso from the cafe downstairs.

Guest House El Puente
HOSTEL **$**

(Map p156; ☑ 7761-4342; celasmaya@gmail.com; 15a Av 6-75, Zona 1; s/d/tr Q75/150/225) The three thoroughly restored rooms here, all with private bathroom, surround a large, well-tended garden. Connected to Celas Maya (p139) Spanish school, it's often occupied by language learners who congregate in the large, well-equipped kitchen.

Black Cat Hostel
HOSTEL **$**

(Map p156; ☑ 7761-2091; 13a Av 3-33; dm incl breakfast Q70, r Q175; ☜) A great place to stay if you're looking to meet up with other travelers, this full-service hostel features a sunny courtyard, a bar-restaurant and a lounge-TV area. Though sparsely furnished, the rooms are done up in soothing colors with nice wood floors.

Casa Argentina
HOSTEL **$**

(Map p152; ☑ 7763-2320; casargentina.xela@ gmail.com; Diagonal 12 8-37, Zona 1; dm Q30, s/d Q60/100 with private bathroom; ☜) This sprawling guesthouse west of the center is a port of call for itinerant quetzal-pinchers. Steer clear of the outrageously overcrowded dorm and opt for the marginally pricier private rooms with cinderblock decor. Overseen by an extended family that is eager to please.

Casa Nativos
HOSTEL **$**

(Map p156; ☑ 7765-4723; casanativos.com; Pasaje Enríquez, 13a Calle, Zona 1; dm Q40, d without bathroom Q125; ☜) One component of a cultural center occupying the rear of the Pasaje Enríquez, this Euro/Guate-run hostel contains basic but stylishly renovated rooms that accent the vintage beauty of the building;

some feature balconies. There's a two-room apartment for long-term stays, including use of a shared kitchen.

★ Casa Renaissance
HOTEL **$$**

(Map p156; ☑ 3121-6315; www.casarenaissance. com; 9a Calle 11-26, Zona 1; r with/without bathroom Q160/125; ☜) This colonial mansion has been reborn as a casual guesthouse with five huge, beautifully restored rooms (two with private bathroom) along a delightful patio. The Dutch-managed place has a relaxed atmosphere: take drinks from the cooler, prepare your own meals in the kitchen or watch videos from a voluminous collection. Rates drop significantly by the week.

✖ Eating

Quetzaltenango has a good selection of places to eat in all price ranges. Cheapest are the food stalls on the lower level of the central market, where snacks and main-course plates are sold for Q10 or less. One popular breakfast spot is **Doña Cristy** (Map p156; ⊙ 7am-7pm), serving *atol de elote* (a hot maize beverage), *empanadas* (turnover stuffed with meat or cheese) and *chuchitos* (small tamales garnished with chopped beets and grated cheese).

Café Nativos
CAFE **$**

(Map p156; ☑ 7765-4723; 13a Calle; breakfast Q25-30; ⊙ 10am-10pm) Part of a hostel/arts center in the Pasaje Enríquez, Café Nativos is an inviting place with good natural fare, espresso, French toast for breakfast, falafel and tofu in *mole*. A terrific balcony terrace, with counter along the edge, looks right at the ex-Gutierrez bank building, a deco wonder, and the burned-out shell of the Café Baviera.

La Chatia Artesano
BAKERY **$**

(Map p156; ☑ 7765-0031; 7a Calle 15-20; sandwiches Q30-40; ⊙ 6.30am-9pm) A good place to stock up for that volcano climb, this craft bakery makes whole-wheat sandwiches (tofu, tempeh, eggplant, cheese), excellent cookies and granola.

Aj de Lunas
GUATEMALAN **$**

(Map p156; ☑ 7761-0097; 9a Calle 11-16; lunch combos Q25; ⊙ 8am-9pm Mon-Sat; ☜✖) This recently upgraded dining hall is a good place to savor Quetzalteco home cooking, with daily specials like *jocón* and *caldo de pata* served with a pile of tortillas and little dishes of lemons and tiny chilies. Vegetarian options are available.

Central Quetzaltenango

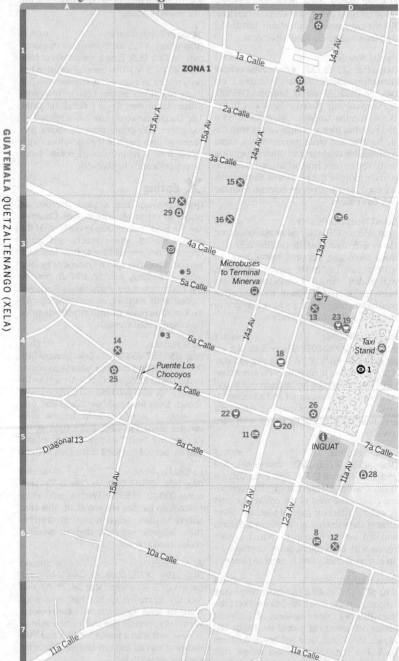

ZONA 1

1a Calle

14a Av

27

24

2a Calle

15 Av A

15a Av

14a Av A

3a Calle

15

17

29

16

13a Av

6

4a Calle

Microbuses
to Terminal
Minerva

5

5a Calle

7

14a Av

13

23 19

3

6a Calle

Taxi
Stand

14

18

1

25

Puente Los
Chocoyos

7a Calle

26

22

11

20

Diagonal 13

8a Calle

INGUAT

7a Calle

11a Av

28

15a Av

13a Av

12a Av

8   12

10a Calle

11a Calle

11a Calle

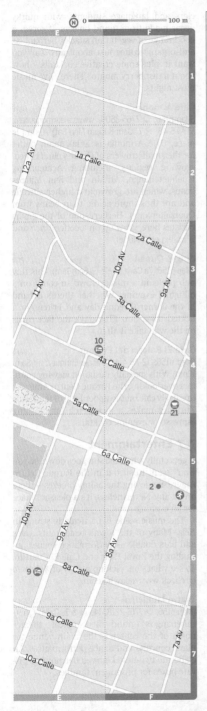

N 0 —————————— 100 m

Central Quetzaltenango

◎ Sights
1 Parque Centro América D4

⊕ Activities, Courses & Tours
2 Altiplano's Tour Operator F5
3 Celas Maya B4
4 EntreMundos F5
5 Inepas B3

🛏 Sleeping
6 Black Cat Hostel D3
7 Casa Nativos D4
8 Casa Renaissance D6
9 Casa Seibel E6
   Guest House El Puente .... (see 3)
10 Hostel Nim Sut E4
11 Hotel Kiktem-Ja C5

✴ Eating
12 Aj de Lunas D6
13 Café Nativos D4
   Doña Cristy .... (see 28)
14 La Chatia Artesano B4
15 Royal Paris C2
16 Sabe Delis C3
17 Sabor de la India B3

⊖ Drinking & Nightlife
18 Café Armonía C4
19 Café El Balcón del Enríquez D4
20 Café El Cuartito C5
21 Café La Luna F4
22 King & Queen C5
23 Salón Tecún D4

✪ Entertainment
24 Bari C1
25 Blue Angel Video Café A4
26 Casa No'j D5
27 Teatro Municipal D1

🛍 Shopping
28 Central Market D5
29 Vrisa Books B3

★ **Sabor de la India**　　　　　　　INDIAN $$
(Map p156; ☎ 7765-2555; 15a Av 3-64; mains Q50-70; ⊙noon-10pm Tue-Sun; 🐾🍴) Authentic South Indian fare is whipped up here by a fellow from Kerala. Servings are huge; the *thalis* – platters of curried veggies, chicken or beef – are highly recommended. Often populated by groups of gringos, the old stone-walled house makes an atmospheric setting for an extended meal.

Sabe Delis　　　　　　　　　CREPERIE $$
(Map p156; ☎ 7761-2635; 14 Av A 3-38; crepes Q35-50; 🐾) Crepes and wood-fired pizzas are the main attractions at this upscale dining

hall, which also prepares exceptionally zesty salads. Popular with both foreigners and *chapines*.

Panorama EUROPEAN $$
(Map p152; ☑7765-8580; www.restaurantepanorama.com; 13a Av A, D16-44; fondue Q80; ☺noon-midnight) A 10-minute hike up the hill at the south end of town with views worthy of its name, Panorama makes a romantic spot for that special night out. Fondues and melted Raclette cheese are the stars of the table at the Swiss-owned establishment.

Royal Paris FRENCH $$
(Map p156; ☑7761-1942; royalparis-quetzaltenango. blogspot.nl; 14 Av A 3-06; salads Q60; ☺noon-10pm Tue-Sun; ☎) Overseen by the French consul himself, this bistro ought to be authentic, and the escargots, baked camembert and filet mignon approach Parisian standards. Check the blackboard for nightly specials. The cozy ambiance is augmented by a sweet terrace and live folk and jazz Wednesday, Friday and Saturday nights.

🍸 Drinking & Nightlife

Coffee plays an important part in Xela's economy, and there are plenty of places to grab a cup.

Xela's Zona Viva revolves around the Teatro Municipal, with discos and clubs popping up along 1a and 2a Calles and up 14 Av.

★Café La Luna CAFE
(Map p156; ☑7761-4354; 8a Av 4-11; ☺11am-9pm Mon-Fri, 4-9pm Sat; ☎) For chocolate aficionados, this is a shrine. Made from scratch on the premises, the chocolate is velvety smooth and served in a variety of beverages: the chocolate cappuccino is mind-blowing. Groups of friends gather in the various salons, which are littered with vintage bric-a-brac.

★Salón Tecún PUB
(Map p156; Pasaje Enríquez; ☺9:30am-12:30am) On the plaza end of the elegant Pasaje Enríquez, alive day and night with a healthy mix of Guatemalans and foreigners quaffing Cabro by the liter, the Tecún claims to be the country's longest-running bar (since 1935). It also serves good pizza and pub food. Don't miss it.

Café El Cuartito CAFE
(Map p156; 13a Av 7-09; ☺8am-11pm; ☎) This offbeat cafe is a point of reference for travelers and language students, with quirky decor made from found objects. It serves a good range of vegetarian snacks, herbal teas and organic coffee just about any way you want it, plus some creative cocktails – how about a raspberry mojito? There's live music most nights.

Café Armonía CAFE
(Map p156; ☑7765-3509; www.cafearmonia.com; 13 Av 5-48; ☺7.30am-8.15pm Mon-Sat) A simple place, Café Armonía is Xela's main outlet for the small growers of Guate's chief coffee-growing regions, including Acatenango, Huehuetenango, Atitlán and San Marcos beans, which are grown at a higher altitude and are thus more acidic than beans from Quetzaltenango. Herbert, one of the smart baristas here, grew up on a coffee *finca* and is an expert roaster.

King & Queen PUB
(Map p156; 7a Calle 13-27; ☺6pm-1am) This tiny pub packs in a mixed crowd so count on a bilingual evening. Whether there's a band in the corner (Wednesday and Friday) or a heated trivia quiz (Tuesday), the face cards on the wall take it all in.

Café El Balcón del Enríquez CAFE
(Map p156; 12 Av 4-40, Pasaje Enríquez; ☺8am-10pm) With specially designed viewing counters overlooking the Parque Centro América, this lively cafe on the upper level of the Pasaje Enríquez makes a nice perch for morning espresso or evening cocktails.

☆ Entertainment

It gets chilly when the sun goes down, so you won't want to sit out in the Parque Centro América enjoying the balmy breezes – there aren't any. Nevertheless, it's a pleasant place for an evening stroll.

The music scene is particularly strong in Xela. Many of the town's restaurants, cafes and bars double as performance venues, including the Royal Paris and Café El Cuartito. To see what's on, pick up a copy of *XelaWho* or check www.xelawho.com.

Teatro Municipal THEATER
(Map p156; ☑7761-2218; 14a Av & 1a Calle) Quetzaltenango's grand neoclassical theater north of the center is the main venue for plays, concerts and dance performances. An elaborate two-tiered curved balcony has private boxes for prominent families.

Casa No'j PERFORMING ARTS
(Map p156; ☑7761-4400; www.centroculturalca
sanoj.blogspot.com; 7a Calle 12-12, Zona 1; ⊙8am-
6pm Mon-Fri) Just off the park's southwest
corner, the 19th-century former Convent of
Bethlehem now houses Xela's premier cultural center. Besides photo and art exhibits,
it stages anything from poetry festivals to
marimba recitals to archaeology conferenc-
es, and occasionally hosts internationally acclaimed artists and literary figures. Regional
food festivals take place here on Sundays.
Check the blog for upcoming events.

Bari LIVE MUSIC
(Map p156; 1a Calle 14-31; ⊙8pm-1am Wed-Sat)
One of several nightspots opposite the
Teatro Municipal, Bari regularly hosts live
trova (Latin American protest folk), rock
and pop.

Blue Angel Video Café CINEMA
(Map p156; 7a Calle 15-79, Zona 1) Maintains an
extensive library of both commercial and
art films that may be viewed upon request,
besides serving a range of vegetarian meals,
herbal teas and hot chocolate.

🔒 Shopping

Pixan HANDICRAFTS
(Map p152; ☑7761-6408; www.amaguate.org; 5
Av 6-17; ⊙9am-5pm Mon-Fri) The fashion outlet for the women's empowerment association AMA (Highland Women's Association),
Pixan sells quality textiles and clothing
produced by Maya weavers in collaboration
with designers from London, New York and
elsewhere.

Central Market MARKET
(Map p156) Xela's central market is three
floors of reasonably priced handicrafts and
souvenirs. Bargain hard.

Vrisa Books BOOKS
(Map p156; 15a Av 3-64) This secondhand bookstore stocks over 4000 titles in English and
will trade used books.

ℹ️ Information

EMERGENCY & IMPORTANT NUMBERS

Proatur (☑1500 or ☑2421-2810)
Bomberos (Fire; ☑7761-2002)
Cruz Roja (Red Cross; ☑7761-2746)
Policía Nacional (national police force;
☑7761-0042)

AROUND QUETZALTENANGO

The beautiful volcanic country around
Xela offers up numerous exciting day
trips. For many, the volcanoes themselves pose irresistible challenges. You
can feast your eyes and soul on the wild
church at San Andrés Xecul, hike to
the ceremonial shores of Laguna Chicabal, or soak in the idyllic hot springs
at Fuentes Georginas. Or simply hop
on a bus and explore the myriad small
traditional villages that pepper this
part of the highlands. Market days are
great opportunities to observe locals
in action, so Sunday and Wednesday in
Momostenango, Monday in Zunil, Tuesday and Saturday in Totonicapán and
Friday in San Francisco El Alto are good
days to visit.

MEDIA
English-language publications are available free
in bars, restaurants and cafes around town.
EntreMundos (Map p156; ☑7761-2179; www.
entremundos.org; 6a Calle 7-31, Zona 1; ⊙2-
4pm Mon-Thu) Publishes a bimonthly magazine,
which has plenty of information on political developments and volunteer projects in the region.
XelaWho (www.xelawho.com) Billing itself as
'Quetzaltenango's leading Culture & Nightlife
Magazine,' this little monthly lists cultural
events in the city, with some irreverent takes
on life in Guatemala in general.

MEDICAL SERVICES
Hospital Privado Quetzaltenango (☑7774-
4700; www.hospitalprivadoquetzaltenango.
com; Calle Rodolfo Robles 23-51) Has 24-hour
emergency service. Usually an English-
speaking doctor on staff.

MONEY
Banco Industrial (4 Calle 11-38, Zona 1; ⊙9am-
6pm Mon-Fri, 9am-1pm Sat), on the north side
of the Parque Centro América, changes US
dollars and euros and gives advances on Visa
cards. There's a Cajero 5B ATM in the Edificio
Rivera just north of the *municipalidad* building.

POST
Main Post Office (Map p156; 4a Calle 15-07,
Zona 1)

TOURIST INFORMATION
There's a plethora of tourist maps circulating;
look for them at internet cafes, language
schools and hotels. Though they're essentially

advertising flyers, the better ones like Xelamap include plenty of useful information.

INGUAT (Map p156; ☑ 7761-4931; vivexela. visitguatemala.com; 7a Calle 11-35, Zona 1; ⊙9am-5pm Mon-Fri, 9am-1pm Sat) Usually staffed by an English speaker, at the southern end of the Parque Centro América.

USEFUL WEBSITES

Xela Pages (www.xelapages.com) Packed with information about Xela and nearby attractions, with a useful discussion forum.

ℹ Getting There & Away

BUS

All 2nd-class buses depart from **Terminal Minerva** (Map p152; 7a Calle, Zona 3), a dusty, crowded yard in the west of town, unless otherwise noted.

Leaving or entering town, buses bound for Salcajá, Cuatro Caminos, San Francisco El Alto and Totonicapán make a **stop** (Map p152) east of the center at the Rotonda, a traffic circle on

Calz Independencia, marked by the **Monumento a la Marimba** (Map p152). Getting off here when you're coming into Xela saves the 10 to 15 minutes it will take your bus to cross town to Terminal Minerva.

Note that service is generally less frequent on Sundays.

SHUTTLE MINIBUS

Most Xela travel agencies, including **Altiplano's** (p153), run shuttle minibuses to such destinations as Antigua (Q195), Chichicastenango (Q195), Panajachel (Q160) and San Cristobal de las Casas, Mexico (Q240).

ℹ Getting Around

Terminal Minerva is linked to the city center by **microbuses** (Map p152), charging Q2 for the 10- to 15-minute ride. From the terminal, walk south through the market to the intersection by the Templo de Minerva, where you'll see the vehicles waiting on the south side of 4a Calle. Going from the center to the terminal, catch **microbuses** (Map p156) on 14a Av north of

BUSES FROM QUETZALTENANGO

DESTINATION	COST (Q)	DURATION	FREQUENCY & NOTES
Almolonga	3	10min	Every 15min, 6am-10pm. Buses depart from the Shell station at the corner of 9a Av & 10a Calle.
Antigua			Take any bus bound for Guatemala City via the Interamericana & change at Chimaltenango.
Chichicastenango	25	2½hr	Every 30min 8am-5pm. Alternatively, take a bus heading to Guatemala City & change at Los Encuentros.
Ciudad Tecún Umán (Mexican border)	40	3hr	Direct buses hourly. Alternatively, take a bus to Coatepeque (every 15min, 4am-5:45pm) & change for Ciudad Tecún Umán.
El Carmen/Talismán (Mexican border)			Take a bus to San Marcos (Q10, 2hr, every 15min), then catch another to Malacatán (Q15, 1hr) where you can find a collective taxi (Q5) to El Carmen.
Guatemala City	35	3½hr	Every 15min 2am-5pm. First-class companies operating between Quetzaltenango & Guatemala City have their own terminals.
Huehuetenango	20	2hr	Every 15min 4am-6:30pm. Alternatively, take a bus to Cuatro Caminos, where you can catch Pullmans by Los Halcones & Velasquez.
La Mesilla (Mexican border)	40	4hr	Four buses 7am-2:15pm. Alternatively, take a bus to Huehuetenango & change there.
Momostenango	7	1½hr	Every 15min 6am-7pm.
Panajachel	30	2hr	Five buses 10am-5pm.
Retalhuleu	13	1hr	Every 10min 5am-7:30pm.
San Andrés Xecul	8	30min	Every half hour 6am-3pm.
San Pedro La Laguna	25	3hr	Six buses 11:30am-5:30pm.
Zunil	5	25min	Every 15min 6am-10pm. Buses depart from the Shell station at the corner of 9a Av & 10a Calle.

5a Calle. **Taxis** (Map p156) await fares at the north end of the Parque Centro América; a ride to the Terminal Minerva should not cost more than Q30 during the day.

The Rotonda bus stop on Calz Independencía is served by 'Parque' microbuses running to the center.

INGUAT (p160) has information on other city bus routes.

Huehuetenango

POP 111,108 / ELEV 1909M

Often used as a stopoff on the journey to or from Mexico, or as a staging area for forays deeper into the Cuchumatanes mountain range, Huehuetenango offers few charms of its own, though some may appreciate its welcoming if scruffy character. Fortunately, 'Huehue' *(way-way)* packs in plenty of eating and sleeping options along with some striking mountain scenery.

Huehuetenango was a Mam Maya region until the 15th century, when the K'iche' (Quiché), expanding from their capital K'um'arkaj (near present-day Santa Cruz del Quiché), pushed them out. But the weakness of K'iche' rule soon brought about civil war, which engulfed the highlands and provided a chance for Mam independence. The turmoil was still unresolved in 1525 when Gonzalo de Alvarado, the brother of Pedro, arrived to conquer Zaculeu, the Mam capital, for Spain.

◎ Sights & Activities

Zaculeu   ARCHAEOLOGICAL SITE
(admission Q50; ⊙8am-4pm) A remnant of the Mam capital, the Zaculeu archaeological zone was restored by the United Fruit Company in the 1940s, leaving its pyramids, ballcourts and ceremonial platforms covered by a thick coat of graying plaster. Though hardly authentic, the work goes further than others in simulating the appearance of an active religious center.

With ravines on three sides, the Postclassic religious center Zaculeu ('White Earth' in the Mam language) occupies a strategic defensive location that served its Mam Maya inhabitants well. It finally failed, however, in 1525, when Gonzalo de Alvarado, aided by Tlaxcalan and K'iche' forces, laid siege to the site for two months. It was starvation that ultimately defeated the Mam.

A small museum at the site holds, among other things, skulls and grave goods found in a tomb beneath Estructura 1, the tallest structure at the site.

Zaculeu is located 4km west of Huehuetenango's main plaza. Buses to the site (Q2.50, 15 minutes) leave about every 30 minutes between 7:30am and 6pm from in front of the school at the corner of 2a Calle and 7a Av. A taxi from the town center costs Q30 one way. One hour is plenty of time to look around the site and museum.

Parque Central   PLAZA
Huehuetenango's main square is shaded by cylindrical ficus trees and surrounded by the town's imposing buildings: the **municipalidad** (Town Hall), with a band shell on the upper floor, and the imposing neoclassical **church**. For a bird's-eye view of the situation, check out the little relief map of Huehuetenango department, which lists altitudes, language groups and populations of the various municipal divisions.

🛏 Sleeping

Hotel Sucot   HOTEL $
(📞7764-2511; Terminal de Buses; s/d Q80/140, without bathroom Q50/80; P🛜) For travelers just needing a sleepover between bus journeys, this is the least scary of the bunch beside the terminal. The beds are decent, showers functional, staff jovial and there's a cafe (and events hall!). It's the next to last one on the right.

Hotel Mary   HOTEL $
(📞7764-1618; 2a Calle 3-52; s/d Q80/130; P) This echoey older hotel has a cafe on the ground floor and a useful map of the province in the lobby. Though drably furnished, rooms do have comfy beds and large tiled bathrooms. At least one – No 310 – features a balcony.

Hotel Zaculeu   HOTEL $$
(📞7764-1086; www.hotelzaculeu.com; 5a Av 1-14; s/d/tr Q125/250/330; P@🛜) The longstanding Zaculeu has loads of character, and despite its advanced age remains quite spiffy. Rooms in the 'new section' (just 20 years old) are a bit pricier but larger and more stylish. The sprawling patio area, overflowing with plants and chirping birds, is conducive to lounging, as is the excellent bar.

Hotel Casa Blanca   HOTEL $$
(📞7769-0777; 7a Av 3-41; s/d Q220/280; P🛜) Hanging ferns and sculpted shrubs grace the attractive courtyard here, ringed by spacious, modern rooms with arched pine

GUATEMALA HUEHUETENANGO

Huehuetenango

Huehuetenango

◎ Sights
1 Catedral de Huehuetenango..............C2
2 Municipalidad.......................................B1
3 Parque Central.....................................C1

🛏 Sleeping
4 Hotel Casa Blanca.............................A2
5 Hotel Mary..C1
6 Hotel San Luis de la Sierra................A2
7 Hotel Zaculeu.....................................B1

✖ Eating
8 Cafetería Las Palmeras......................C2
9 La Fonda de Don Juan........................B1
10 La Tinaja..C2
11 Restaurante Lekaf.............................B3

🍷 Drinking & Nightlife
12 Café Museo...A3

ceilings and good hot showers. The patio restaurant out back serves up good-value set lunches (Q22), and its Sunday breakfast buffet (Q40) is a major deal.

Hotel San Luis de la Sierra HOTEL $$
(☎7764-9217; hsanluis@gmail.com; 2a Calle 7-00; s/d Q135/190/238; 🅿️🛜) The simple, smallish rooms here have pine furniture and homey

touches, and the hotel remains pleasantly aloof from the racket outside. The real attraction, though, is the rambling coffee plantation out back, with paths for strolling.

✖ Eating & Drinking

⭐ **La Tinaja** GUATEMALAN $
(☎7764-1513; 4a Calle 6-51; set menu Q25; ⊙noon-10pm) As much a cultural center as a cafe, the home of historian-gourmand Rolando Gutierréz has an interesting library and a collection of old clocks, radios and namesake *tinajas* (urns), all displayed in a series of inviting salons. Aside from quesadillas and tamales (served with salt from San Mateo Ixtatán), you'll find such local snacks as *sanguichitos* (Huehue-style sandwiches) and *rellenitos*.

Cafetería Las Palmeras GUATEMALAN $
(4a Calle 5-10; mains Q27-50; ⊙7am-8:30pm; 🛜) Popular Las Palmeras features a breezy upper level with views over the Parque Central. The *caldo de pollo criollo* (Q27) is a must, brimming with chicken, *güisquil* and corn. On Saturdays there are tasty tamales.

La Fonda de Don Juan PIZZA $$
(2a Calle 5-35; pizzas Q45-75; ⊙24hr) The place for Huehue's night owls and early risers, La

Fonda serves varied Guatemalan and international fare including good-value pizzas.

Restaurante Lekaf   INTERNATIONAL **$$**
(☑7764-3202; 6a Calle 6-40; mains Q50-100; ⊙10am-11pm) This modern, airy dining hall has a varied menu, including sandwiches, pizza and seafood. Live music (marimbas, folk) attracts a lively crowd nightly from 7pm to 10pm.

Café Museo   CAFE
(☑7764-1101; 4a Calle 7-40; ⊙7am-9:30pm Mon-Sat, 2-9:30pm Sun; 🕸) This 'museum' serves some of Huehue's best coffee, and that's saying something. More than just a place to get a well-prepared cup, it also provides some background on this bewitching bean that has so influenced Guatemala's history. The various salons and delightful patio buzz with java hounds from early morning till late evening.

❶ Information

Banco Industrial (6a Av 1-26) A block west of the main plaza, has a reliable ATM.

❶ Getting There & Away

The bus terminal is in Zona 4, 2km southwest of the plaza along 6a Calle. A number of companies ply the same routes, though information is not posted in any coherent fashion. Microbuses leave from the south end of the station. Another stop, for microbuses to Cobán and Barrillas, via Soloma and San Mateo Ixtatán, is by a gas station at El Calvario, at the corner of 1a Av and 1a Calle, four blocks northeast of the Parque Central.

Todos Santos Cuchumatán
POP 2980 / ELEV 2470M

◉ Sights

Museo Balam   MUSEUM
(admission Q5; ⊙8am-6pm) Todos Santos' museum is in a two-story house along a side street one block east of the plaza. The collection of outfits and masks, traditional kitchen implements, archaeological finds and musical instruments comes to life when Fortunato, its creator and a community leader, is there to provide commentary.

BUSES FROM HUEHUETENANGO

DESTINATION	COST (Q)	DURATION (HR)	FREQUENCY & NOTES
Antigua			Take a Guatemala City–bound bus and change at Chimaltenango.
Barrillas	50	6	Microbuses every half hour 2am-4:30pm.
Cobán	40	7	Microbus at 1pm Mon-Sat from El Calvario gas station.
Gracias a Dios (Mexican border)	50	5	Hourly 3am-1pm by Chiantlequita.
Guatemala City	60	5	Five Pullman buses by Velázquez Plus 5:30am-2:30pm. Two lines run Pullman buses from their own private terminals: Transportes Los Halcones (Q65) leaves seven times a day 1am-3:30pm with deluxe service (Q75) at 7am, 10:30am and 2pm; Línea Dorada departs at 11pm (Q110).
La Mesilla	20	2	Every 15min 3am-7pm by Transportes Los Verdes.
Nebaj			Take a microbus to Sacapulas from where there are frequent connections to Nebaj.
Panajachel			Take a Guatemala City–bound bus and change at Los Encuentros.
Quetzaltenango	20	2	Every 15min 3:30am-7pm.
Sacapulas	20	2	Frequent microbuses 5:30am-5:30pm, via Aguacatán.
Santa Cruz del Quiché	25	2	Frequent microbuses 5am-5pm.
Soloma	25	3	Hourly microbuses 4:30am-2:30pm from El Calvario gas station.
Todos Santos Cuchumatán	20	2	Every 30min 3am-3pm from El Calvario gas station.

TODOS SANTOS' BIG DAY

Todos Santos Cuchumatán is renowned for its wildly colorful horse races, the highlight of **El Día de Todos los Santosa**, a no-holds-barred annual celebration held on November 1. It's the culmination of a week of festivities and an all-night spree of male dancing to marimbas and *aguardiente* (sugar cane liquor) drinking on the eve of the races – which rather than a competitive event is a chance for *todosanteros* to ride up and down as fast as they can while getting progressively drunker the whole day long (with a break for lunch). The authentically indigenous event attracts throngs of inhabitants from surrounding communities who gather on a grassy hillside alongside the sand track or upon the rooftops opposite to observe the riders decked out in their finest traditional garb. Todos Santos, incidentally, is the only place in Guatemala where Day of the Dead is not observed on Nov 1, since that day is reserved for a celebration of autonomy within Huehuetenango province. Instead, the traditional visit to the cemetery is postponed to the following day, when graves are decorated and marimbas serenade groups of mourners as they arrive to pay their respects.

🏃 Activities

January to April are the best months for hitting the trails through Todos Santos' countryside but you can usually walk in the morning, before the weather closes in, year-round.

Red de Turismo Natural y Cultural de Huehuetenango   HIKING

(📞4051-5597; turismoruralguatemala.com/huehuetenango; per person from Q250) This network of ecologically oriented guides throughout the department is locally represented by Roberto Jerónimo Bautista. He leads hikes to the isolated mountain community of San Juan Atitán, where the women wear dazzling *huipiles,* in about six hours, returning by bus to Todos Santos. The trail climbs through old-growth forest to summits that afford views all the way to the Mexican border.

Mam Trekking   HIKING

(📞5206-0916; rigoguiadeturismo@yahoo.com; per person from Q100) Knowledgeable, English-speaking *todosantero* Rigoberto Pablo Cruz leads walks around the Parque Regional Municipal de Todos Santos Cuchumatán, including a climb to the peak of La Torre followed by a descent to La Maceta. In addition, Rigoberto leads walks to Tzunul, a community where men weave women's *cortes* on a loom and women weave men's shirt collars by hand.

🛏 Sleeping & Eating

Hotel Casa Familiar   HOTEL $

(📞5737-0112; hotelyrestaurante_casafamiliar@yahoo.com; s/d Q100/150, without bathroom Q60/90) This cheerfully run lodging just down from the main plaza has four cozy rooms with hardwood floors, traditional textile bedspreads, good hot showers and private terraces. More recently built units on the upper level have less character with tile floors and cheap furniture. Have a breakfast bowl of *mosh* (porridge) or fresh-baked banana bread at the cafe downstairs. Guests may use a *chuj* (Maya sauna) for Q30 per person.

Hotelito Todos Santos   HOTEL $

(📞3030-6950; s/d Q75/150, without bathroom Q45/90) South of the plaza, up a side street that branches left, this backpackers' fave has small and bare but well-scrubbed rooms with tile floors and firm beds. Room 15, one of the four private-bathroom units in the tower, has excellent views over the valley. The casual cafe here is noted for its pancakes.

Tourist Hotel   HOTEL $

(📞4491-0220; r Q75, without bathroom Q50) In a quieter part of town, the Tourist is quite clean and well maintained, with functional hot showers, quality mattresses and plenty of (synthetic) blankets for the evening chill. Around 200m east from the main square, turn left downhill by a shop called La Todosanterita to find the solitary pink concrete structure.

Comedor Katy   GUATEMALAN $

(meals Q20; ⊙7:30am-8pm) Women in traditional garb attend to great vats bubbling over glowing embers at this rustic cookshack just above the central plaza. There are tables on a terrace overlooking the market activity.

ℹ Getting There & Away

Buses depart from the main street between the plaza and the church. About 10 buses leave for Huehuetenango (Q20, two hours) between 4:30am and 2pm. Microbuses going as far as Tres Caminos (the junction with the Huehue-Barillas highway) leave throughout the day, whenever they fill up. There are two buses daily heading northwest to Jacaltenango. A Huisteca bus heads for La Mesilla at 5am.

THE PACIFIC SLOPE

Separated from the highlands by a chain of volcanoes, the flatlands that run down to the Pacific are universally known as La Costa. It's a sultry region – hot and wet or hot and dry, depending on the time of year – with rich volcanic soil good for growing coffee, palm-oil seeds and sugarcane.

Archaeologically, the big draws here are Takalik Abaj and the sculptures left by pre-Olmec civilizations around Santa Lucía Cotzumalguapa.

The culture is overwhelmingly *ladino* (mixed indigenous and European heritage), and even the biggest towns are humble affairs, with low-rise houses and the occasional palm-thatched roof.

Guatemalan beach tourism is seriously underdeveloped. Monterrico is the only real contender, helped along by a nature reserve protecting mangroves and their inhabitants. Sipacate is slowly developing as a surf resort, although serious surfers find more joy in Mexico or El Salvador.

Retalhuleu

POP 34,300

Arriving at the bus station in Retalhuleu, or Reu (*ray*-oo) as it's known to most Guatemalans, you're pretty much guaranteed to be underwhelmed. The neighborhood is a tawdry affair, packed out with dilapidated wooden *cantinas* (canteens) and street vendors.

The town center, just five blocks away, is like another world – a majestic, palm-filled plaza, surrounded by some fine old buildings. Even the city police get in on the act, hanging plants outside their headquarters.

The real reason most people visit is for access to Takalik Abaj, but if you're up for some serious downtime, a couple of world-class fun parks are just down the road.

🛏 Sleeping

Hotel Casa y Campo HOTEL $$
(☑ 7771-3289; 3a Calle 4-73, Zona 1; s/d Q160/300; P ❋ 🛜) Comfortable, good-value rooms a couple of blocks from the plaza. This one books up fast, so it's worth calling ahead.

La Estancia HOTEL $$
(☑ 7771-3053; 10a Calle 8-50, Zona 1; s/d Q120/240; P ❋ 🛜) A good, reasonably priced option is this family-run hotel offering simple, clean rooms a couple of blocks from the bus stop.

Hotel Posada Don José HOTEL $$
(☑ 7771-0180; www.hotelposadadedonjose.com; 5a Calle 3-67, Zona 1; r from Q440; P ❋ 🛜 🏊) A beautiful colonial-style hotel built around a huge swimming pool. Swan dives from the top balcony are tempting, but probably unwise. Rooms are spacious and comfortable – they're slowly remodeling here, so it's worth having a look at a few before deciding.

🍴 Eating

Reu seems to be slightly obsessed with pizza – 5a Av north of the plaza is almost wall-to-wall pizzerias. The dining rooms of the Hotel Posada Don José and the **Hotel Astor** (☑ 7771-2559; 5a Calle 4-60, Zona 1; mains Q60-120; ⊙ 7:30am-11pm) both offer more refined dining options.

Cafetería La Luna GUATEMALAN $
(cnr 8a Av & 5a Calle, Zona 1; mains Q35-75; ⊙ 8am-10pm) In a new location a block off the plaza, this remains a town favorite for simple but filling meals in a low-key environment.

BUSES FROM RETALHULEU

DESTINATION	COST (Q)	DURATION (HR)	FREQUENCY
Champerico	15	1	every few minutes 6am-7pm
Ciudad Tecún Umán (Mexican border)	20	1½	every 20min 5am-10pm
Guatemala City	50-95	3	every 15min 2am-8:30pm
Quetzaltenango	20	1	every 30min 4am-6pm
Santa Lucía Cotzumalguapa	30	2	every 15min 2am-8:30pm

FUN PARKS AROUND RETALHULEU

If you have children along, or your own inner child is fighting to get out, head to one of these two gigantic theme parks next door to one another on the Quetzaltenango road, about 12km north of Retalhuleu.

Both Xocomil and Xetulul are run by Irtra (Instituto de Recreación de los Trabajadores de la Empresa Privada de Guatemala; Guatemalan Private Enterprise Workers' Recreation Institute), which administers several fun sites around the country for workers and their families. Between them, the two sites comprise the most popular tourist attraction in Guatemala, with more than one million visitors a year.

Parque Acuático Xocomil (☎7772-9400; www.irtra.org.gt; Carretera CITO, Km 180.5; adult/child Q100/50; ☺9am-5pm Thu-Sun) With a distinct Guatemalan theme, this world-class water park offers aquatic diversions for all ages (under-fives must have a flotation device; BYO, or hire one for Q20). Among the 14 water slides, two swimming pools and two wave pools are re-creations of Maya monuments from Tikal, Copán and Quiriguá. Visitors can bob along a river through canyons flanked with ancient temples and Maya masks. Three real volcanoes – Santiaguito, Zunil and Santa María – can be seen from the grounds.

Parque de Diversiones Xetulul (☎7722-9450; www.irtra.org.gt; Carretera CITO, Km 180.5; adult/child Q100/50; ☺10am-5pm Fri-Sun) Xetulul is a surprisingly well set-up amusement park, with first-class rides for all ages. Themed areas include representations of a Tikal pyramid, historical Guatemalan buildings, and famous buildings from many European cities. An all-you-can-ride bracelet costs Q50 on top of admission.

Any bus heading from Retalhuleu toward Quetzaltenango will drop you at Xocomil, Xetulul or the Hostales (Q8, 30 minutes).

❶ Information

There is no official tourist office, but people in the **municipalidad** (Town Hall; 6a Av, Zona 1), facing the east side of the church, will do their best to help.

Banco Agromercantil (5a Av, Zona 1) Changes US dollars and traveler's checks and has a MasterCard ATM.

Banco Industrial (cnr 6a Calle & 5a Av, Zona 1) Changes US dollars and traveler's checks and has a Visa ATM.

❶ Getting There & Away

Most buses traveling along the Carretera al Pacífico detour into Reu. Shared taxis (Q9) are the best way to get to El Asintal (for Takalik Abaj). Look for station wagons with 'Asintal' painted on the windscreen around the bus stop and plaza.

Most buses make two stops in town, at the **main terminal** (5a Av, Zona 5) and a smaller **bus station** (10a Calle, Zona 1).

Parque Arqueológico Takalik Abaj

About 25km northwest of Retalhuleu, the **Parque Arqueológico Takalik Abaj** (www.takalikabajpark.com; Q50; ☺7am-5pm) is a fas-

cinating archaeological site set on land now occupied by coffee, rubber and sugarcane plantations. Takalik Abaj was an important trading center in the late Preclassic era, before AD 250, and forms a historical link between Mesoamerica's first civilization, the Olmecs, and the Maya. The Olmecs flourished from about 1200 to 600 BC on Mexico's southern Gulf coast, but their influence extended far and wide, and numerous Olmec-style sculptures have been found at Takalik Abaj.

The city, which had strong connections with the town of Kaminaljuyú (in present-day Guatemala City), was sacked in about AD 300 and its great monuments, especially those in Maya style, were decapitated. Some monuments were rebuilt after AD 600 and the site retained a ceremonial and religious importance for the Maya, which it maintains to this day. Maya from the Guatemalan highlands regularly come here to perform ceremonies.

🛏 Sleeping & Eating

⭐**Takalik Maya Lodge**   HOTEL $$
(☎2334-7693; www.takalik.com; farmhouse/bungalow Sun-Wed Q330/490, Thu-Sat Q400/590) Set on the grounds of a working farm 2km

past the entrance to Takalik Abaj (and on top of a large, unexcavated section of it) this is by far the most comfortable place to stay in the area. Accommodation options include the old farmhouse or newly constructed 'Maya-style' houses set in the middle of the forest.

Check the website for package deals including accommodations, meals and tours of the coffee, macadamia and rubber plantation as well as guided horseback tours of the waterfalls on the property and the archaeological site. Any pick-up from El Asintal passing Takalik Abaj will drop you at the entrance.

ℹ Getting There & Around

To reach Takalik Abaj by public transportation, catch a shared taxi from Retalhuleu to El Asintal (Q9, 30 minutes), which is 12km northwest of Reu and 5km north of the Carretera al Pacífico. Less frequent buses leave from a bus station on 5a Av A, 800m southwest of Reu plaza, about every half hour from 6am to 6pm. Pick-ups at El Asintal provide transportation on to Takalik Abaj (Q5), 4km further by paved road. You'll be shown round by a volunteer guide, whom you will probably want to tip (Q20 per person is a good baseline). You can also visit Takalik Abaj on tours from Quetzaltenango.

Champerico

Built as a shipping point for coffee during the boom of the late 19th century, Champerico, 38km southwest of Retalhuleu, is a tawdry, sweltering, dilapidated place that sees few tourists. Nevertheless, it's one of the easiest ocean beaches to reach on a day trip from Quetzaltenango, and heat-starved students still try their luck here. Beware of strong waves and an undertow if you go in the ocean, and stay in the main, central part of the beach: if you stray too far in either direction you put yourself at risk from impoverished, potentially desperate shack dwellers who live toward the ends of the beach. Tourists have been victims of violent armed robberies here.

🛏 Sleeping & Eating

Hotel Maza   HOTEL **$$**
(☑ 7773-7180; s/d Q180/270; ❄) With large clean rooms just across the road from the beach, the Hotel Maza is a good bet.

7 Mares   SEAFOOD **$**
(mains from Q40; ☺ 8am-7pm) Offers a shaded swimming pool, leafy dining area and up-stairs deck that catches good breezes and views. And the seafood is delicious.

ℹ Getting There & Away

Regular buses connect Champerico with other Pacific Slope towns, Quetzaltenango and Guatemala City. The bus stop is two blocks back from the beach on the road out of town. The last buses back to Quetzaltenango leave at about 6pm, a bit later for Retalhuleu.

Santa Lucía Cotzumalguapa

POP 49,480

Santa Lucía Cotzumalguapa, though benign enough, is unexciting. The region, though, is an important stop for anyone interested in archaeology. In the fields and *fincas* (plantations or farms) near the town stand great stone heads carved with grotesque faces and fine relief scenes, the product of the enigmatic Pipil culture that flourished here from about AD 500 to 700.

In your explorations of the area, you may also get to see a Guatemalan sugarcane *finca* in full operation.

◉ Sights

Museo El Baúl   MUSEUM
(☺ 8am-4pm Mon-Fri, to noon Sat) **FREE** This museum, about 2.75km on foot or 5km by vehicle from the hilltop site of El Baúl, comprises a very fine open-air assemblage of Pipil stone sculpture collected from around Finca El Baúl's sugarcane fields. A large stone jaguar faces you at the entrance.

Other figures include four humans or monkeys with arms folded across their chests; a grinning, blank-eyed head reminiscent of the one at the hilltop site; carvings of skulls; and, at the back, a stela showing a personage wearing an animal headdress, standing over a similarly attired figure on the ground: seemingly winner and loser of a ball game.

El Baúl Hilltop Site   ARCHAEOLOGICAL SITE
With two great carved stones, this archaeological site has the additional fascination of being an active place of pagan worship for local people. Maya people visit regularly, especially on weekends, and make offerings, light fires and candles, and sacrifice chickens. They will not mind if you visit as well, and may be happy to pose with the idols

for photographs in exchange for a small contribution.

Museo Cultura Cotzumalguapa
MUSEUM

(Q30; ⊙8am-1pm & 2:30-4:30pm Mon-Fri, 8am-1pm Sat) At the headquarters of the Finca Las Ilusiones sugarcane plantation, you'll find this museum, which holds a collection of sculptures found around Las Ilusiones' lands. There is some explanatory material and you'll probably be shown around by the caretaker.

The museum includes a reconstruction of a sacrificial altar with the original stones, and photos of some fine stelae that were removed to the Dahlem Museum in Berlin in 1880. The most impressive exhibit, Monumento 21, is actually a fiberglass copy of a stone that still stands in the fields of Finca Bilbao (part of Las Ilusiones' plantations), depicting what may be a shaman holding a sort of puppet on the left, a ball-game player in the middle with a knife in one hand, and a king or priest on the right holding what may be a heart. Another copy of this stone, along with one of Monumento 19, lies on the ground across the street from the museum. Along the road just before the bridge to the *finca* house are copies of some of the sculptures from Museo El Baúl.

To find the museum, head about 1.5km east of the town center on Carretera al Pacífico (Hwy 2). Take a left shortly before the Tecún farm supplies depot and travel about 400m north.

Las Piedras
ARCHAEOLOGICAL SITE

(Bilbao Stones) Monumento 21, a copy of which is in the Museo Cultura Cotzumalguapa, still stands with three other fine sculpted stones in the Finca Bilbao cane fields to the northeast of El Calvario church, on the north edge of town. In the past, tourists have regularly visited these stones, often guided through the tall cane to Las Piedras by local boys, but this is an isolated area and assaults on tourists are not unknown – ask around to find out the current safety situation.

🛌 Sleeping & Eating

Hotel Internacional
HOTEL $

(☎7882-5504; Calle los Mormones; s/d Q130/180; [P][❄]) Down a short lane (signposted) off Carretera al Pacífico is the best budget hotel in town. It has clean, good-sized rooms with fan, cold shower and TV. Air-con is Q70 extra.

Hotel Santiaguito
HOTEL $$

(☎7882-5435; www.hotelsantiaguito.com; Carretera al Pacífico, Km 90.4; s/d Q330/435; [P][❄][≋]) On the highway on the west edge of town, the Santiaguito is fairly lavish for Guatemala's Pacific Slope, with spacious tree-shaded grounds and a nice swimming pool (nonguests Q20). The large rooms have huge, firm beds, and are set around a jungly patio/parking area.

The spacious restaurant is cooled by ceiling fans and serves up good cheeseburgers and slightly overpriced meals (Q30 to Q80).

ℹ️ Information

Banco Industrial (cnr 4a Av & 4a Calle; ⊙9am-5pm Mon-Fri, to 1pm Sat) A block north of the plaza, changes US dollars cash and traveler's checks and has a Visa ATM.

ℹ️ Getting There & Away

As Hwy 2 now bypasses Santa Lucía, a lot of buses do not come into town. Coming to Santa Lucía from the east, you will almost certainly need to change buses at Escuintla (Q12, 30 minutes). From the west you will probably have to change at Mazatenango (Q20, 1¼ hours). At Cocales, 23km west of Santa Lucía, a road down from Lago de Atitlán meets Hwy 2. Eight buses daily run from Cocales to Panajachel (Q30, 2½ hours, 70km; between about 6am and 2pm). Ask about the current situation, as there have been reports of robberies along this stretch of road in the past.

La Democracia
POP 17,500

La Democracia, a nondescript Pacific Slope town 10km south of Siquinalá, is hot day and night, rainy season and dry season. During the late Preclassic period (300 BC to AD 250), this area, like Takalik Abaj to the northwest, was home to a culture showing influence from southern Mexico. As you come into town from the highway, follow signs to the regional *museo*, which is on the plaza. You'll find a 5B ATM there, too.

🛌 Sleeping & Eating

With one vague exception, there are no real 'restaurants' as such in La Democracia. On the up side, the flour tortillas stuffed with meat from the little roadside stands around the plaza are delicious, and a bargain at Q20.

Guest House Paxil de Cayala GUESTHOUSE $
(☑ 7880-3129; s/d without bathroom Q60/120)
Half a block from the plaza, La Democracia's
only place to stay is OK for the night, with
big, mosquito-proofed rooms.

Burger Chops FAST FOOD $
(mains Q25-45; ⊘ 8am-9pm) Just off the
square, this is as close as the town gets to
a restaurant.

❶ Getting There & Away

The Chatía Gomerana company runs buses
every half hour from 6am to 4:30pm, from the
Centra Sur terminal in Guatemala City to La
Democracia (Q25, two hours) via Escuintla. From
Santa Lucía Cotzumalguapa, catch a bus 8km
east to Siquinalá and change there.

Sipacate

An hour and a half down the road from
Santa Lucía Cotzumalguapa is Guatemala's
surf capital. Waves here average 6ft, with the
best breaks between December and April.
The town is separated from the beach by the
Canal de Chiquimulilla.

⌸ Sleeping & Eating

★**Driftwood Surfer** HOSTEL $
(☑ 3036-6891; www.driftwoodsurfer.com; dm/d
Q65/295; ❋❋) The new kid on Sipacate's
block is this excellent little surf hostel right
on the beachfront. The air-conditioned
dorms are a big draw, as is the swim-up bar
in the pool overlooking the beach. Surf classes
and board hire are available.

El Paredon BUNGALOW $
(☑ 4994-1842; www.paredonsurf.com; dm Q85, s/d
from Q270/360) This budget choice is a rustic little surf camp to the east of the village.
It's run by a couple of Guatemalan surfers.
Board and kayak hire, surf lessons and good,
simple meals (Q50 to Q80) are available.
Book in advance.

To get here you can catch the daily bus
from Puerto San José (departs 1pm Monday
to Friday, Q20) or a *tuk-tuk*/pick-up to El Es-
condite pier from Sipacate, then a boat (Q20
one-way) to El Paredon.

❶ Getting There & Away

Buses from Guatemala City's CentraSur terminal
(Q40, 3½ hours) pass through La Democracia
en route to Sipacate every two hours. If you're
coming from Antigua, the easiest way is on the

shuttle (tickets sold in every travel agency in
town), which costs around Q100.

Escuintla

POP 116,000
Surrounded by rich green foliage, Escuintla
should be a tropical idyll where people
swing languidly in hammocks and concoct
pungent meals of readily available exotic
fruits and vegetables. In fact, it's a hot, shabby commercial and industrial city that's inte-
gral to the Pacific Slope's economy, but not at
all important to travelers, except for making
bus connections. Banks are located around
the plaza. There's an ATM in the **Farmacia
Herdez** (cnr 13a Calle & 4a Av; ⊘ 7am-10pm), one
block uphill from the bus terminal.

Accommodations in Escuintla are limited.
For budget digs, try the **Hotel Costa Sur**
(☑ 7888-1819; 12a Calle 4-13; s/d with fan Q90/120,
with air-con Q130/150; ❋), which has decent,
cool rooms with TV and fan. More comfortable is the **Hotel Sarita** (☑ 7888-1959; Av
Centro América 15-32; s/d Q340/380; ❋❋❋),
behind the gloriously air-conditioned restaurant (mains Q60 to Q110) of the same name.

There are simple eateries all along the
main street and around the bus terminal.
For something a little more upscale, head to
Jacobo's (4a Av 14-62; mains Q30-50; ⊘ 11am-
10pm), which offers reasonable Chinese food
in clean and tranquil surrounds.

All buses from the terminal pass along 1a
Av, but if you really want to get a seat, head
to the main bus station in the southern part
of town, just off 4a Av. The station entrance
is marked by a Scott 77 fuel station. If you're
heading to Monterrico and can't find a direct
bus, catch one to Puerto San José or Iztapa
and make a connection there.

Buses coming along the Carretera al Pacífico may drop you in the north of town, ne-
cessitating a sweaty walk through the hectic
town center if you want to get to the main
station.

Monterrico

The coastal area around Monterrico is a
totally different Guatemala. Life here is
steeped with a sultry, tropical flavor, with
rustic wooden-slat and thatched-roofed
architecture and awesome volcanoes that
shimmer in the hinterland. It's fast becoming popular with foreigners as a beach
break from Antigua or Guatemala City. On

weekdays it's relatively quiet, but on weekends and holidays it teems with Guatemalan families.

Monterrico itself is a coastal village with a few small, inexpensive hotels right on the beach, a large wildlife reserve and two centers for the hatching and release of sea turtles and caimans. The beach here is dramatic, with powerful surf crashing onto black volcanic sand at odd angles. This wave-print signals that there are rip tides; deaths have occurred at this beach, so swim with care. Behind the town is a large network of mangrove swamps and canals, part of the 190km Canal de Chiquimulilla.

Sights & Activities

Biotopo Monterrico-Hawaii   WILDLIFE RESERVE
(Reserva Natural Monterrico) This reserve, administered by Cecon (Centro de Estudios Conservacionistas de la Universidad de San Carlos), is Monterrico's biggest attraction. The 20km-long nature reserve of coast and coastal mangrove swamps is bursting with avian and aquatic life. The reserve's most famous denizens are the endangered leatherback and ridley turtles, who lay their eggs on the beach in many places along the coast. The mangrove swamps are a network of 25 lagoons, all connected by mangrove canals.

Boat tours of the reserve, passing through the mangrove swamps and visiting several lagoons, take around 1½ to two hours and cost Q75 for one person, Q50 for each additional person. It's best to go just on sunrise, when you're likely to see the most wildlife. If you have binoculars, bring them along for birdwatching; January and February are the best months. Locals will approach you on the street (some with very impressive-looking ID cards), offering tours, but if you want to support the *tortugario* (which, incidentally, has the most environmentally knowledgeable guides), arrange a tour directly through Tortugario Monterrico.

Some travelers have griped about the use of motorboats (as opposed to the paddled varieties), because the sound of the motor scares off the wildlife. If you're under no time pressure, ask about arranging a paddled tour of the canal.

Tortugario Monterrico   WILDLIFE RESERVE
(Q50; ⊙ 7am-5pm) The Cecon-run Tortugario Monterrico is just a short walk east down the beach from the end of Calle Principal and then a block inland. Several endangered species of animals are raised here, including leatherback, olive ridley and green sea turtles, caimans and iguanas.

There's an interesting interpretative trail and a little museum with pickled displays in bottles. The staff offer lagoon trips, and night walks (Q50) from August to December to look for turtle eggs, and will accept volunteers. Around sunset nightly from September to January on the beach in front of the *tortugario,* workers release baby turtles. For a Q10 donation you can 'buy' a turtle and release it. Despite what everybody else is doing, please refrain from using flash cameras and flashlights.

Parque Hawaii   WILDLIFE RESERVE
(☑ 4743-4655; www.arcasguatemala.com; ⊙ 8am-5pm) This nature reserve operated by Arcas (Asociación de Rescate y Conservación de Vida Silvestre) comprises a sea-turtle hatchery and some caimans, 8km east along the beach from Monterrico. The reserve is separate from the neighboring Biotopo Monterrico-Hawaii, but engages in the same line of conservation. Volunteers are welcome year-round, but the sea-turtle nesting season is from June to November, with August and September being the peak months.

Volunteers are charged Q1330 a week for food and board onsite at the project. Homestays are available with local families for around the same cost. Jobs for volunteers include hatchery checks and maintenance, mangrove reforestation, basic construction and data collection. See the website for the complete lowdown on volunteering here. Most of the egg collection happens at night. It's a way out of town, but there are usually other volunteers to keep you company, and while you're here you can use the kayaks, go on village trips and go fishing in the sea and mangroves.

A bus (Q5, 30 minutes) leaves the Monterrico jetty every couple of hours during the week and every hour on weekends for the bumpy ride to the reserve. Pick-ups also operate on this route, charging Q35 per person.

Tours

Productos Mundiales   BOAT TOUR
(☑ 2366-1026; www.productos-mundiales.com) This outfit offers marine wildlife-watching tours (six hours, from Q1775 per person), leaving from Marina Pez Vela in nearby Puerto Quetzal. Throughout the year you stand a pretty good chance of seeing pilot whales, bottlenose dolphins, spinner dolphins, olive ridley turtles, leatherback

turtles, giant manta rays and whale sharks. From December to May, humpback and sperm whales can also be seen.

Reservations (five days in advance via bank account deposit) are essential; see the website for details. To get to the marina, catch any Guatemala City–bound bus (Q12, one hour) to Puerto Quetzal, then a taxi or *tuk-tuk* from there.

📚 Courses

Proyecto Lingüístico Monterrico   LANGUAGE COURSE
(📞 5475-1265; www.proyectolinguisticomonterrico. com; Calle Principal) About 250m from the beach, this place is quite professional. Classes are generally held outdoors in a shady garden area. You can study in the morning or afternoon, depending on your schedule. Twenty hours of study per week costs Q760, or Q1300 with homestay.

Even if you're not studying here, the school is the best source of tourist information in town.

🛏️ Sleeping & Eating

To save a difficult, hot walk along the beach, take the last road to the left or right off Calle Principal before you hit the beach. Many places offer discounts for stays of three nights or more. Reservations on weekends are a good idea. Midweek, you'll have plenty more bargaining power.

Hotel El Delfin   HOTEL $
(📞 4661-9255; www.hotel-el-delfin.com; dm Q40, s/d from Q125/200, without bathroom Q50/100; 🅿️📶) A humble but sprawling beachside setup that's been slowly improving over the years. Rooms are spacious and well appointed, but the place can get noisy on weekends.

Johnny's Place   HOTEL $
(📞 5812-0409; www.johnnysplacehotel.com; dm Q45, r without bathroom Q145, r with air-con from Q320, bungalows Q550-1200; 🅿️❄️📶) While Johnny's may not be everyone's cup of tea, it's easy enough to find – it's the first place you come to turning left on the beach – and one of the biggest operations here. It's got a decent atmosphere, though, and attracts a good mix of backpackers and family groups.

Brisas del Mar   HOTEL $$
(📞 5517-1142; r per person with fan/air-con Q120/180; 🅿️❄️📶) One block back from the beach, this popular option offers good-sized rooms, a 2nd-floor dining hall with excellent sea views and a large swimming pool.

⭐**Hotel Pez de Oro**   BUNGALOW $$
(📞 2368-3684; www.pezdeoro.com; s/d Q400/500; 🅿️📶) This is the funkiest looking place in town, with comfortable little huts and bungalows scattered around a shady property. The color scheme is a cheery blue and yellow, and the rooms have some tasteful decorations and large overhead fans. The excellent restaurant, with big sea views, serves up great Italian cuisine and seafood dishes.

⭐**Taberna El Pelicano**   ITALIAN, SEAFOOD $$
(mains Q60-150; ⏰noon-2pm & 6-10pm Wed-Sun) By far the best place to eat in town, with the widest menu and most interesting food, such as seafood risotto (Q80), beef carpaccio (Q75) and a range of jumbo shrimp dishes (Q140).

🍷 Drinking & Nightlife

Las Mañanitas   BAR
(⏰noon-late) On the beachfront at the end of the main street, this little bar is what Monterrico really needed – plenty of hammock chairs looking out over the beach, a good range of drinks and low-key music playing in the background.

Playa Club   CLUB
(⏰8am-1am) This venue, located at Johnny's Place, heats up on weekends, with plenty of reggaetón, house music and drinks specials keeping the crowd moving.

ℹ️ Getting There & Away

There are two ways to get to Monterrico. Coming from Guatemala City or Antigua, it's most logical to catch a bus that, with the new bridge at Pueblo Viejo, goes right through to Monterrico. The other option is to head to La Avellana, where *lanchas* (small motorboats) and car ferries depart for Monterrico. The Cubanita company runs a handful of direct buses to and from Guatemala City (Q45, four hours, 124km). Alternatively, you reach La Avellana by changing buses at Taxisco on Hwy 2. Buses operate half-hourly from 5am to 4pm between Guatemala City and Taxisco (Q40, 3½ hours) and roughly hourly from 7am to 4:30pm between Taxisco and La Avellana (Q10, 40 minutes), although taxi drivers will tell you that you've missed the last bus, regardless of what time you arrive. A taxi between Taxisco and La Avellana costs around Q80.

From La Avellana catch a *lancha* or car ferry to Monterrico. The collective *lanchas* charge Q5 per passenger for the half-hour trip along the Canal de Chiquimulilla, a long mangrove canal. They start at 4:30am and run more or less every half hour or hour until late afternoon. You can always pay more and charter your own boat. The car ferry costs Q100 per vehicle.

Shuttle buses also serve Monterrico. The most reliable leaves from outside the **Proyecto Lingüístico Monterrico** (p171) at 1pm and 4pm (Q80/160 to Antigua/Guatemala City); book tickets and inquire about other destinations at the language school. Contact any travel agent in Antigua to arrange a shuttle to Monterrico from Guatemala City or Antigua.

CENTRAL GUATEMALA

Stretching from the steamy lowland forests of El Petén to the dry tropics of the Río Motagua valley, and from the edge of the western highlands to the Caribbean Sea, this is Guatemala's most diverse region.

The Carretera al Atlántico (Hwy 9) shoots eastward to the sea from Guatemala City, passing the turnoffs for the wonderfully preserved ruins of Copán (Honduras), Quiriguá with its impressive stelae and Río Dulce, a favored resting spot for Caribbean sailors and gateway to the Refugio de Vida Silvestre Bocas del Polochic (Bocas del Polochic Wildlife Reserve). While you're here don't miss the gorgeous boat ride down the Río Dulce to Lívingston, the enclave of the Garífuna people.

The north of the region is lush and mountainous coffee-growing country. The limestone crags around Cobán attract cavers the world over, and the beautiful pools and cascades of Semuc Champey rate high on Guatemala's list of natural wonders.

Salamá & Around

A wonderful introduction to Baja Verapaz' not-too-hot, not-too-cold climate, the area around Salamá hosts a wealth of attractions, both postcolonial and indigenous.

The town itself is known for its ornate church (complete with grisly depiction of Jesus), bustling Sunday market and the photogenic ex-sugar-mill-turned-museum and impressive stone aqueduct in the neighboring town of San Jerónimo.

Salamá has some fine accommodations a few blocks from the Plaza, including the **Posada de Don Maco** (2 7940-0083; 3a Calle 8-26; s/d Q120/160; P) and the **Hotel Real**

Legendario (2 7940-0501; www.hotelrealleg endario.com; 8a Av 3-57; s/d Q160/180; P).

There are restaurants and cafes around the plaza. The meat-stuffed flour tortillas at **Antojitos Zacapanecos** (cnr 6a Calle & 8a Av; mains Q25; ⊙ 10am-9pm) are not to be missed.

Salamá also marks the starting point for a back-roads route to Guatemala City, passing **Rabinal**, whose annual fiesta of San Pedro (January 19–25) is a beguiling mix of pre-Colombian and Catholic traditions, and **Cubulco** where the *palo volador* (flying pole) tradition is still observed. There are basic, adequate *pensiones* (family-run guesthouses) in both Rabinal and Cubulco.

From there it's 100km south to Guatemala City, passing the turnoff to **Mixco Viejo**, one of the least-visited and most spectacularly sited Maya sites in the country. The former Poqomam capital, it lies wedged between deep ravines with just one way in and one way out; the Poqomam further fortified the site by constructing impressive rock walls around the city. It took Pedro de Alvarado and his troops more than a month of concerted attacks to conquer it. When they finally succeeded, they furiously laid waste to this city, which scholars believe supported close to 10,000 people at its height. There are several temples and two ballcourts here.

Buses leave Salamá's downtown bus terminal frequently for Cobán (Q30, 1½ to two hours), Guatemala City (Q40 to Q55, three hours) and neighboring villages.

Biotopo del Quetzal

Along Hwy 14, 34km beyond the La Cumbre turnoff for Salamá, is the Biotopo Mario Dary Rivera nature reserve, commonly called **Biotopo del Quetzal** (Hwy 14, Km 161; Q40; ⊙ 7am-4pm), just east of Purulhá village.

You need a fair bit of luck to see a quetzal (Guatemala's national bird), as they're rare and shy, though you have the best chance of seeing them from March to June. Even so, it's well worth stopping to explore and enjoy this lush high-altitude cloud-forest ecosystem that is the quetzal's natural habitat – and you may happen to see one. Early morning or early evening are the best times to watch out for them – they're actually more prevalent around the grounds of the nearby hotels.

The reserve has a visitor center, a little shop for drinks and snacks, and a camping and BBQ area. The ruling on camping changes from time to time. Check by contacting **Cecon** (Centro de Estudios Conservacionistas de la Universidad de San Carlos; Map p108; www.cecon.usac.edu.gt; Av La Reforma 0-63, Zona 10, Guatemala City), which administers this and other biotopes.

Two excellent, well-maintained **nature trails** wind through the reserve: the 1800m **Sendero los Helechos** (Fern Trail) and the 3600m **Sendero los Musgos** (Moss Trail). As you wander through the dense growth, treading on the rich, spongy humus and leaf-mold, you'll see many varieties of epiphytes (air plants), which thrive in the reserve's humid atmosphere. Deep in the forest is **Xiu Gua Li Che** (Grandfather Tree), some 450 years old, which germinated around the time the Spanish fought the Rabinal in these mountains.

Sleeping & Eating

Ranchitos del Quetzal HOTEL $
(4130-9456; www.ranchitosdelquetzal.com; Hwy 14, Km 160.5; r per person from Q100; P) Carved out of the jungle on a hillside 200m away from the Biotopo del Quetzal entrance, this place has good-sized simple rooms with warm (ie tepid) showers in the older wooden building and hot showers in the newer concrete one. Reasonably priced, simple meals (mains from Q30) are served, and there are vegetarian options.

Hotel Restaurant Ram Tzul HOTEL $$
(5908-4066; www.ramtzul.com; Hwy 14, Km 158; s/d Q290/425; P🛜) Quite likely the most beautiful hotel in either of the Verapaces, this place features a restaurant/sitting area in a tall, thatched-roofed structure with fire pits and plenty of atmosphere. The rustic, upmarket theme extends to the rooms and bungalows, which are spacious and elegantly decorated. The hotel property includes waterfalls and swimming spots.

Getting There & Away

Any bus to or from Guatemala City will set you down at the park entrance. Heading in the other direction, it's best to flag down a bus or microbus to El Rancho and change there for your next destination.

Cobán

POP 68,900 / ELEV 1320M

Not so much an attraction in itself, but an excellent jumping-off point for the natural

wonders of Alta Verapaz, Cobán is a prosperous city with an upbeat air. Return visitors will marvel at how much (and how tastefully) the town has developed since their last visit.

The town was once the center of Tezulutlán (Tierra de Guerra, or 'Land of War'), a stronghold of the Rabinal Maya.

In the 19th century, when German immigrants moved in and founded vast coffee and cardamom *fincas* (plantations), Cobán took on the aspect of a German mountain town, as the *finca* owners built town residences. The era of German cultural and economic domination ended during WWII, when the USA prevailed upon the Guatemalan government to deport the powerful *finca* owners, many of whom actively supported the Nazis.

Sights & Activities

Orquigonia GARDENS
(4740-2224; www.orquigonia.com; Hwy 14, Km 206; Q40; 7am-4pm) Orchid lovers and even the orchid-curious should not miss the wonderfully informative guided tour of this orchid sanctuary just off the highway to Cobán. The 1½- to two-hour tour takes you through the history of orchid collecting, starting with the Maya, as you wend your way along a path in the forest. There are sweet little cabins on the grounds where you can stay for Q350 per night.

To get here catch any bus from Cobán headed for Tontem and get off when you see the sign, about 200m up the dirt road off Hwy 14.

Parque Nacional Las Victorias PARK
(3a Calle, Zona 1; Q15; 8am-4:30pm, walking trails 9am-3pm) This forested 82-hectare national park, right in town, has ponds, BBQ and picnic areas, children's play areas, a lookout point and kilometers of trails. The entrance is near the corner of 9a Av and 3a Calle. Most trails are very isolated – consider hiking in a group. You can camp here for Q40 per person.

Templo El Calvario CHURCH
(3a Calle, Zona 1) You can get a fine view over the town from this church atop a long flight of stairs at the north end of 7a Av. Indigenous people leave offerings at outdoor shrines and crosses in front of the church. Don't linger here after 4pm, as muggings are not unknown in this area.

Cobán

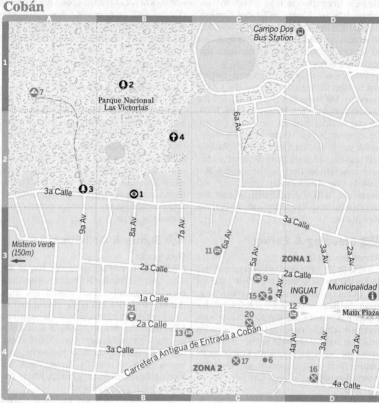

🔊 Tours

Chicoj Cooperative · COFFEE TOUR

(☑ 5524-1831; www.coffeetourchicoj.com; tours Q60) Just 15 minutes out of town by bus, this is a community-tourism initiative offering 2km, 45-minute tours of its coffee farm. Halfway through there's the standard stop for a canopy zip-line tour. The tour winds up with a cup of coffee made from beans grown and roasted at the farm.

Misterio Verde · TOUR

(☑ 7952-1047; 2a Calle 14-36, Zona 1; ⊙ 8:30am-5:30pm) Acts as a booking agent for various community tourism projects in the area, including the Chicacnab cloud forests (near Cobán) and the subtropical rainforests of Rocjá Pomtilá (near Laguna Lachuá) in which participants stay in villages with a Q'eqchi' Maya family. For Q350 to Q450 you get a guide, lodging for two nights, and four meals.

Aventuras Turísticas · TOUR

(☑ 7951-2008; www.aventurasturisticas.com; 1a Calle 4-25, Zona 1) Leads tours to Laguna Lachuá, the Grutas de Lanquín, Rey Marcos and Parque Nacional Cuevas de Candelaria, as well as to Semuc Champey, Tikal, Ceibal, and anywhere else you may want to go; it will customize itineraries. French- English- and Spanish-speaking guides are available.

Finca Santa Margarita · COFFEE TOUR

(☑ 7952-1586; 3a Calle 4-12, Zona 2; tours Q40; ⊙ guided tours 8:30-11am & 2-4pm Mon-Fri, 8:30-11am Sat) This working coffee farm in the middle of downtown Cobán offers stellar guided tours. From propagation and planting to roasting and exporting, the 45-minute tour will tell you all you ever wanted to know about these powerful beans. At tour's end, you're treated to a cup of coffee and you can purchase beans straight from the roaster. The talented guide speaks English and Spanish.

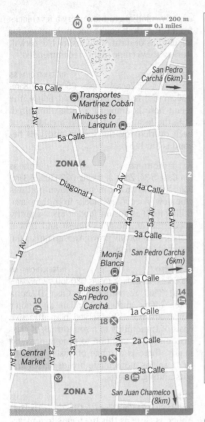

N 0 ____ 200 m
0 ____ 0.1 miles

Cobán

⊙ Sights
1 Ermita de Santo Domingo de
    Guzmán...B2
2 Parque Nacional Las Victorias............B1
3 Parque Nacional Las Victorias
    Entrance...A2
4 Templo El Calvario...........................B2

➌ Activities, Courses & Tours
5 Aventuras Turísticas.........................C3
6 Finca Santa Margarita.......................C4

◉ Sleeping
7 Campground...................................A1
8 Casa Duranta..................................F4
9 Casa Luna......................................C3
10 Hotel Central.................................E3
11 Hotel La Paz..................................C3
12 Hotel La Posada.............................D4
13 Pensión Monja Blanca......................B4
14 Posada de Don Antonio....................F3

⊗ Eating
15 Casa Chavez..................................C3
16 El Bistro.......................................D4
17 Kardamomuss.................................C4
18 La Abadia......................................F4
19 La Casa del Monje...........................F4
20 Xkape Koba'n.................................C4

⊙ Drinking & Nightlife
21 Bohemios......................................B4

🛏 Sleeping

Casa Luna HOSTEL $
(📞 7951-3528; www.cobantravels.com/casaluna; 5a Av 2-28, Zona 1; dm/s/d without bathroom Q50/60/120; @ 🛜) Modern rooms set around a pretty, grassy courtyard. Dorms have lockers and private rooms are well decorated. The shared bathrooms are spotless and the atmosphere is laid-back.

Hotel La Paz HOTEL $
(📞 7952-1358; 6a Av 2-19, Zona 1; s/d Q55/80; 🅿) This cheerful, clean budget hotel, 1½ blocks north and two blocks west of the plaza, is an excellent deal. It has many flowers, and a good cafeteria next door.

Campground CAMPGROUND $
(Parque Nacional Las Victorias; campsite per person Q50) Camping is available at Parque Nacional Las Victorias, right in town. Facilities include water and toilets but no showers.

★**Hotel La Posada** HOTEL $$
(📞 7952-1495; www.laposadacoban.com; 1a Calle 4-12, Zona 2; s/d Q450/490) Just off the plaza, this colonial-style hotel is Cobán's best, though rooms streetside suffer from traffic noise. Its colonnaded porches are dripping with tropical flowers and furnished with easy chairs and hammocks. The rooms are a bit austere, with plenty of religious relics around the place, but they have nice old furniture, fireplaces and wall hangings of local weaving.

Hotel Central HOTEL $$
(📞 7952-1442; 1a Calle 1-79, Zona 1; s/d Q140/200; 🅿🛜) Reasonably sized rooms and lovely outdoor sitting areas make this a decent choice. Try for a room at the back for better ventilation and views out over the town.

Pensión Monja Blanca HOTEL $$
(📞 7952-1712; 2a Calle 6-30, Zona 2; s/d Q185/250, without bathroom Q135/175; 🅿) This place is peaceful despite being on busy 2a Calle. After walking through two courtyards, you come to a lush garden packed with fruit

and hibiscus trees around which the spotless rooms are arranged. Each room has an old-time feel to it and is furnished with two good-quality single beds with folksy covers, and has cable TV.

The hotel's central location and tranquil atmosphere make it a good place for solo women travelers.

Posada de Don Antonio   HOTEL $$

(☑ 7951-1792; 5a Av 1-51, Zona 4; s/d Q270/490; P❋🛜) This atmospheric two-story place provides some of the best value in town. Rooms are spacious with two (or even three!) double beds, high ceilings and loving attention to detail. Breakfast (Q30 to Q50) in the lush patio area is a great way to start the day.

Casa Duranta   HOTEL $$

(☑ 7951-4716; www.casaduranta.com; 3a Calle 4-46, Zona 3; s/d Q310/420; P🛜) Some rooms at this carefully restored, eclectically decorated place are excellent value, while others are a bit cramped for the price. Have a look around if you can.

✗ Eating & Drinking

Most of the hotels in Cobán come with their own restaurants. In the evening, food trucks park around the plaza and offer some of the cheapest dining in town. As always, the one to go for has the largest crowd of locals hanging around and chomping down.

★ Xkape Koba'n   GUATEMALAN $

(2a Calle 5-13, Zona 2; snacks Q25, mains Q50; 🕙10am-7pm) 🍴 The perfect place to take a breather or while away a whole afternoon, this beautiful, artsy little cafe has a lush garden out back. Some interesting indigenous-inspired dishes are on the small menu. The cakes are homemade, the coffee is delectable and there are some interesting handicrafts on sale.

★ La Abadia   FUSION $$

(cnr 1a Calle & 4a Av, Zona 3; mains Q90-160; 🕙6-10pm Mon-Sat) Cobán's dining scene has improved dramatically over the years and this is another welcome addition. The surrounds are refined yet relaxed, the menu offers a great selection of local, international and fusion dishes, and there's a pretty good wine list, too.

La Casa del Monje   STEAK $$

(4a Av 2-16, Zona 3; mains Q60-150; 🕙6:30am-11pm; 🛜) Cobán's best steakhouse is set in

a lovely colonial-era monastery a few blocks from the park. If you're not in the mood for big chunks of meat, local dishes like cack'ik (turkey stew) come highly recommended.

Casa Chavez   INTERNATIONAL $$

(1a Calle 4-25, Zona 1; mains Q50-100; 🕙8am-8:30pm; 🛜) Set in a lovely old house, the menu here is ample if a little uninspired. Still, the location's great, and breakfast out back overlooking the garden and hills beyond is hard to beat.

Kardamomuss   FUSION $$

(3a Calle 5-34, Zona 2; mains Q60-130; 🕙8am-9pm; 🛜) The widest menu in town is at this chic new place a few blocks from the plaza. Billing itself as 'fusion' food, it takes a pretty good stab at Indian, Chinese and Italian dishes, with locally grown cardamom as the featured ingredient.

El Bistro   INTERNATIONAL $$

(4a Calle 3-11, Zona 2; mains Q80-150; 🕙6:30am-10pm) This restaurant, at Casa D'Acuña hotel, offers authentic Italian and other European-style dishes served in an attractive oasis of tranquillity to a soundtrack of classical music. In addition to protein-oriented mains, there is a range of pastas (Q40 to Q65), salads, homemade breads, cakes and outstanding desserts.

Bohemios   CLUB

(cnr 8a Av & 2a Calle, Zona 2; Q15-30; 🕙Thu-Sat) About as close as this town gets to a megadisco, with balcony seating and bow-tied waiters.

ℹ Information

The banks listed here change US-dollar cash and traveler's checks.

Banco G&T (1a Calle) Has a MasterCard ATM.

Banco Industrial (cnr 1a Calle & 7a Av, Zona 1) Has a Visa ATM.

INGUAT (☑ Cell phone 4210-9992; 1a Calle 3-13, Zona 1; 🕙8am-4pm Mon-Sat, 9am-1pm Sun) Has an office a couple of blocks from the plaza. If they can't help you, try the **Municipalidad** (Town Hall; ☑7952-1305, 7951-1148; 1a Calle, Zona 1; 🕙8am-4pm Mon-Sat), where some switched-on young staff work in an office behind the police office.

Lavandería Econo Express (7a Av 2-32, Zona 1; 🕙7am-7pm Mon-Sat) Laundry places are in short supply in Cobán – these folks wash and dry a load for Q50.

Post Office (cnr 2a Av & 3a Calle, Zona 3) A block southeast from the plaza.

ⓘ Getting There & Away

The highway connecting Cobán with Guatemala City and Hwy 9 is the most traveled route between Cobán and the outside world. The road north through Chisec to Sayaxché and Flores is now paved all the way, providing much easier access than before to El Petén. The off-the-beaten-track routes west to Huehuetenango and northeast to Fray Bartolomé de las Casas and Poptún are mostly unpaved and still provide a bit of an adventure (although this second one was being paved at the time of research). Always double-check bus departure times, especially for less frequently served destinations.

Buses leave from Cobán's Campo Dos (Campo Norte) bus terminal. Please be aware that the road to Uspantán and Nebaj is prone to landslides – get the latest before setting out.

Buses leave from a variety of points around town. Minibuses, known as microbuses, are replacing or are additional to chicken buses (former US school buses) on many routes.

Around Cobán

Lanquín

One of the best excursions to make from Cobán is to the pretty village of Lanquín, 61km to the east. People come for two reasons: to explore the wonderful Grutas de Lanquín (p178) cave system just out of town, and as a jumping-off point for visiting the natural rock pools at Semuc Champey.

🛏 Sleeping & Eating

Zephyr Lodge HOSTEL $
(☑ 5168-2441; www.zephyrlodgelanquin.com; dm Q50, r Q150-250; 🛜) Lanquin's party hostel is all class – great rooms with spectacular views, OK dorms and some good hangout areas, including the big thatched-roof bar-restaurant. The river's a five-minute walk downhill.

BUSES FROM COBÁN

Departures from Campo Dos Bus Terminal

DESTINATION	COST (Q)	DURATION
Biotopo del Quetzal	15	1¼hr
Chisec	25	2hr
Fray Bartolomé de las Casas	50	4hr
Nebaj	75	5½-7hr
Playa Grande, for Laguna Lachuá	60	3hr
Raxruhá	35	2½-3hr
Salamá	30	1½hr
Sayaxché	75	4hr
Tactic	10	40min
Uspantán	40	4½hr

Other Departures

Destinations not served by Campo Dos terminal include the following:

DESTINATION	COST (Q)	DURATION	FREQUENCY & NOTES
Cahabón	30	4½hr	Same buses as to Lanquín.
Guatemala City	60-70	4-5hr	Transportes **Monja Blanca** (☑ 7951-3571; 2a Calle 3-77, Zona 4) has buses leaving for Guatemala City every 30 minutes from 2am to 6am, then hourly until 4pm.
Lanquín	30	2½-3hr	**Transportes Martínez** (6a Calle 2-40, Zona 4) has multiple departures throughout the day. Buses to Lanquin (cnr 5a Calle & 3a Av, Zona 4) also depart from 7am to 4pm, some continuing to Semuc Champey. Do check these times, though, as they seem to be fluid.
San Pedro Carchá	5	20min	Every 10 minutes, buses depart from 6am to 7pm from the lot in front of the Monja Blanca terminal.

El Muro
HOSTEL **$$**

(☎ 4904-0671; www.elmurolanquin.net; dm Q50, r Q150-250; 🛜) By far the best option in the town itself, El Muro is a happy little hostel-bar featuring good-sized dorms and rooms. Most have attached bathroom and all have breezy balconies overlooking the hills or garden.

Restaurante Champey
GUATEMALAN **$**

(mains Q30-60; ⊗ 8am-11pm) This large outdoor eatery halfway between town and El Retiro serves up good-sized plates of steak, eggs and rice and gets rowdy and beer-fueled at night.

❶ Getting There & Away

Overnight tours to **Grutas de Lanquín** and **Semuc Champey**, offered in Cobán for Q400 per person, are the easiest way to visit these places, but it's really not that complicated to organize yourself. Tours take about two hours to reach Lanquín from Cobán; the price includes a packed lunch.

Buses operate several times daily between Cobán and Lanquín, continuing to Cahabón. There are eight buses to Cobán (Q35, three hours) between 6am and 5:30pm. Shuttles for Semuc Champey (Q25 one way) leave at 9:30am (book at your hotel) and pick-ups (Q20) leave whenever they are full, half a block from the main square.

If it's raining heavily and you're driving, you'll need a 4WD vehicle. The road from San Pedro Carchá to El Pajal, where you turn off for Lanquín, is paved. The 11km from El Pajal to Lanquín is not. You can head on from Lanquín to Flores in 14 to 15 hours via El Pajal, Sebol, Raxrujá and Sayaxché. The road from El Pajal to Sebol was being paved at time of research. Or you can head from Lanquín to Sebol and Fray Bartolomé de las Casas and on to Poptún.

If you're heading toward Río Dulce, a back road exists, although it's unpaved for most of the way and gets washed out in heavy rains. Transportation schedules along here are flexible at best. Ask around to see what the current situation is. A daily shuttle (Q180, six hours) runs on this road and is the most reliable, easy option. Book at any of the hotels.

Semuc Champey

Eleven kilometers south of Lanquín, along a rough, bumpy, slow road, is Semuc Champey (Q50; ⊗ 8am-6pm), famed for its great 300m-long natural limestone bridge, on top of which is a stepped series of pools with cool, flowing river water good for swimming. The water is from the Río Cahabón, and much more of it passes underground, beneath the bridge. Though this bit of paradise is difficult to reach, the beauty of its setting and the perfection of the pools, ranging from turquoise to emerald-green, make it worth it. Many people consider this the most beautiful spot in all Guatemala.

If you're visiting on a tour, some guides will take you down a rope ladder from the lowest pool to the river, which gushes out from the rocks below. Plenty of people do this and love it, though it is a bit risky.

🛏 Sleeping & Eating

A simple restaurant at the parking area serves OK meals (including *cack'ik*; Q50), but is a long way from the pools. It's a better idea to bring a picnic.

It's possible to **camp** (campsite per tent Q50) at Semuc Champey, but be sure to pitch a tent only in the upper areas, as flash floods are common down below. It's also risky to leave anything unattended, as it might get stolen. The place now has 24-hour security, which may reassure potential campers, but you should keep your valuables with you. If you're looking for a little more comfort, El Portal (☎ 4091-7878; www.elportaldechampey.com; dm Q60, r with/without bathroom Q300/185; 🅿🛜) is located just outside the entrance gates.

★Utopia
HOSTEL **$$**

(☎ 3135-8329; www.utopiaecohotel.com; camping per person Q30, hammock/dm Q35/65, r with/without bathroom Q425/165; 🛜) Set on a hillside overlooking the small village of Semil, 3km from Semuc Chapey, this is the most impressive setup in the area. Every range of accommodation imaginable is available, from luxurious riverside cabins to campsites. The restaurant-bar (serving vegetarian family-style meals) has fantastic valley views and the stretch of river that it sits on is truly idyllic.

The turnoff to Semil is 2km before Semuc Champey. From there it's about 1km to the hotel. Call from Lanquín (or drop into the office at the crossroads where the bus arrives) for free transportation out here.

❶ Getting There & Away

If you're into walking, the 2½-hour trip from Lanquín is a fairly pleasant one, passing through lush countryside and simple rural scenes. If not, there are plenty of transportation options. Pick-ups run from the plaza in Lanquín to Semuc Champey – your chances of catching one are better in the early morning and on market days: Sunday, Monday and Thursday. Expect to pay somewhere between Q15 and Q30. All the Lanquín hotels and hostels run shuttle services out here, too.

Fray Bartolomé de las Casas

This town, often referred to simply as Fray, is a way station on the back route between the Cobán/Lanquín area and Poptún on the Río Dulce–Flores highway (Hwy 13). This route is dotted with traditional Maya villages where only the patriarchs speak Spanish, and then only a little. This is a great opportunity for getting off the 'gringo trail' and into the heart of Guatemala.

Fray is substantial considering it's in the middle of nowhere, but don't let its size fool you. This is a place where the weekly soccer game is the biggest deal in town, chickens languish in the streets and siesta is taken seriously.

Accommodation options are very limited here. Hotel La Cabaña (☑ 7952-0352; 2a Calle 1-92, Zona 3; r per person with/without bathroom Q80/60) is about the best in town.

Eating options are limited here – try Comedor Jireh and Restaurante Doris on the main street. Otherwise, grab a steak (with tortillas and beans, Q20) at the informal BBQ shacks that open up along the main street at night.

At least two daily buses departs from the plaza for Poptún (Q40, five hours). Buses for Cobán leave hourly between 4am and 4pm. Some go via Chisec (Q50, 3½ hours). Others take the slower route via San Pedro Carchá.

EL ORIENTE

Heading east from Guatemala City brings you into the long, flat valleys of the region Guatemalans call El Oriente (the East). It's a dry and unforgiving landscape of stunted hillsides covered in scraggly brush. They breed 'em tough out here and the cowboy hats, boots, buckles and sidearms sported by a lot of men in the region fit well against this rugged backdrop.

Most travelers pass through on their way to Copán in Honduras, or to visit the pilgrimage town of Esquipulas. Further east, the landscape becomes a lot more tropical and you'll see plenty of fruit for sale at roadside stalls. If you've got some time in this area, a quick side trip to the ruins at Quiriguá is well worth your while.

Chiquimula

POP 55,400

Thirty-two kilometers south of Río Hondo on Hwy 10, Chiquimula is a major market town for all of eastern Guatemala. For travelers it's not a destination but a transit point. Your goal is probably the fabulous Maya ruins at Copán in Honduras, just across the border from El Florido. There are also some interesting journeys between Chiquimula and Jalapa, 78km to the west. Among other things, Chiquimula is famous for its sweltering climate and its decent budget hotels (a couple have swimming pools).

🛏 Sleeping

Hotel Hernández HOTEL $
(☑ 7942-0708; 3a Calle 7-41, Zona 1; s/d with fan Q90/140, with air-con Q150/220, without bathroom Q60/100; 🅿❄🛜🏊) It's hard to beat the Hernández – it's been a favorite for years and keeps going strong, with its central position, spacious, simple rooms and good-sized swimming pool.

Hotel Posada Don Adan HOTEL $
(☑ 7942-3924; 8a Av 4-30, Zona 1; s/d Q120/180; 🅿❄) The Don offers the best deal in this price range – neat, complete rooms with TV, fan, air-con, a couple of sticks of furniture and good, firm beds. The doors are locked at 10pm.

Hostal Casa Vieja HOTEL $$
(☑ 7942-7971; www.hostalcasaviejachiquimula.com; 8a Av 1-60, Zona 2; s/d/ste Q200/400/500; ❄🛜) A short walk from the center, this is probably the best hotel in town. Rooms are smallish but delicately decorated and the garden areas are lovely. The whole place radiates a tranquillity sorely missing in the rest of town.

🍴 Eating

There's a string of *comedores* (cheap eateries) on 8a Av behind the market. At night, snack vendors and taco carts set up along 7a Av opposite the plaza, selling the cheapest eats in town.

Corner Coffee CAFE $
(6a Calle 6-70, Zona 1; bagels Q30, breakfast Q30-40; ⊙7am-10pm Mon-Sat, 3-10pm Sun) You could argue with the syntax of the name, but

DEM BONES

Most of the people you hear about who are digging stuff up in Guatemala these days are archaeologists. Or mining companies. But there's another group out there, sifting patiently through the soil in search of treasure – paleontologists.

While it's unclear whether dinosaurs ever inhabited what is now Guatemala, evidence shows that large prehistoric mammals – such as giant armadillos, 3m-tall sloths, mammoths and saber-toothed tigers certainly did. As they migrated southwards from North America they found they could not go much further than present-day Guatemala – back then the landmass stopped at northern Nicaragua, and 10 million years would pass before South and Central America joined, creating the American continents more or less as they are today.

Various theories seek to explain the disappearance of the dinosaurs and other large prehistoric mammals – the most widely accepted one being that a massive meteorite slammed into the Yucatán Peninsula 66 million years ago, causing global climate change.

The great bulk of the fossil and bone evidence uncovered in Guatemala has been in the country's southeast corner, but giant sloth and mastodon remains have been found in what is now Guatemala City. Paleontologist Roberto Woolfolk Saravia, founder of the **Museo de Paleontología, Arqueología y Geología** (Roberto Woolfolk Saravia Archeology & Paleontology Museum; Hwy 10, Estanzuela; ⊙8am-5pm Mon-Fri) **FREE**, claims to have collected more than 5000 fragments and skeletons, and he says there's a lot more out there, just that (you guessed it) the funding isn't available to dig it up.

If you have even a passing interest in prehistoric life, the museum makes for a worthy detour – it's been remodeled recently, and on display are remains of mastodons, giant sloths and armadillos, a prehistoric horse measuring 50cm, and two molar teeth from a mammoth.

---

this air-con haven right on the lovely Parque Calvario serves up the best range of sandwiches, burgers and bagels in town.

Charli's INTERNATIONAL **$$**
(7a Av 5-55; mains Q60-120; ⊙8am-9pm) Chiquimula's 'fine dining' option (tablecloths!) has a wide menu, featuring pasta, pizza, seafood and steaks, all served up amid chilly air-con, with relaxed and friendly service.

Parillada de Calero STEAK **$$**
(7a Av 4-83; breakfast from Q40, mains Q60-110; ⊙8am-10pm) An open-air steakhouse, serving the juiciest flame-grilled cuts in town. This is also the breakfast hot spot – the Tropical Breakfast (pancakes with a mound of fresh fruit) goes down well in this climate.

ℹ Information

Banco G&T (7a Av 4-75, Zona 1; ⊙9am-8pm Mon-Fri, 10am-2pm Sat) Half a block south of the plaza. Changes US dollars and traveler's checks, and gives cash advances on Visa and MasterCard.

Post Office (10a Av; ⊙9am-4pm Mon-Fri, to 1pm Sat) Between 1a and 2a Calles.

ℹ Getting There & Away

Several companies operate buses and microbuses, arriving and departing from the bus station area on 11a Av, between 1a and 2a Calles. **Litegua** (☑7942-2064; www.litegua.com; 1a Calle, btwn 10a & 11a Avs), which operates buses to El Florido (the border crossing on the way to Copán) has its own bus station a half block north. For the Honduran border crossing at Agua Caliente, take a minibus to Esquipulas and change there. If you're headed to Jalapa, you'll need to go to Ipala to make the connection. For Río Dulce, take a Flores bus, or a Puerto Barrios bus to La Ruidosa junction and change there. If you're going to Esquipulas, sit on the left for the best views of the basilica housing the shrine of El Cristo Negro.

Esquipulas

POP 27,400

From Chiquimula, Hwy 10 goes south into the mountains, where it's a bit cooler. After an hour's ride through pretty country, the highway descends into a valley ringed by mountains, where Esquipulas stands. Halfway down the slope, about 1km from the center of town, there is a *mirador* (lookout) from which to get a good view. The reason for a trip to Esquipulas is evident as soon as you catch sight of the place, dominated by the great Basílica de Esquipulas towering above the town, its whiteness shimmering in the sun. The view has changed little in over 150 years since explorer John L Stephens saw it and described it in his book *Incidents of Travel in Central America, Chiapas and Yucatan* (1841).

History

This town may have been a place of pilgrimage before the Spanish conquest. Legend has it that the town takes its name from a noble Maya lord who ruled this region when the Spanish arrived, and who received them in peace.

With the arrival of the friars a church was built here, and in 1595 an image that came to be known as El Cristo Negro (Black Christ) was installed behind the altar. In response to the steady increase in pilgrims to Esquipulas, a huge new church was inaugurated in 1758, and the pilgrimage trade has been the town's livelihood ever since.

◉ Sights & Activities

Basílica de Esquipulas　　BASILICA
(11a Calle) A massive pile of stone that has resisted the power of earthquakes for almost 250 years, the basilica is approached through a pretty park and up a wide flight of steps. The impressive facade and towers are floodlit at night.

Inside, the devout approach the surprisingly small El Cristo Negro (Black Christ) with extreme reverence, many on their knees. Incense, murmured prayers and the scuffle of feet fill the air. When there are

throngs of pilgrims, you must enter the church from the side to get a close view of the famous shrine. Shuffling along quickly, you may get a good glimpse or two before being shoved onward by the crowd behind you. On Sundays, religious holidays and (especially) during the **Cristo de Esquipulas festival** (January 15), the press of devotees is intense. On weekdays, you may have the place to yourself, which can be really powerful and rewarding. On weekends, you may feel rather removed from the intensity of emotion shown by the majority of pilgrims, whose faith is very deep.

Parque Chatún　　AMUSEMENT PARK
(☑ 7873-0909; www.parquechatun.com; adult/child incl lunch Q80/70; ☺9am-6pm Tue-Sat) If you've got kids along (or even if you don't), this fun park 3km out of town should provide some light relief from all the religious business. There are swimming pools, a climbing wall, campgrounds, a petting zoo, a canopy tour and a mini bungee jump. Entry includes the use of all these except the canopy tour.

If you don't have a vehicle, look for the minibus doing rounds of the town, or get your hotel to call it – it will take you out there for Q5.

Centro Turístico Cueva de las Minas　　CAVE
(Q25; ☺8am-4pm) This has a 50m-deep cave (bring your own light), grassy picnic areas and the Río El Milagro, where people come for a dip and say it's miraculous. The cave and river are half a kilometer from the entrance, which is behind the basilica's cemetery, 300m south of the turnoff into town on the road to Honduras. Refreshments are available.

BUSES FROM CHIQUIMULA

DESTINATION	COST (Q)	DURATION	FREQUENCY & NOTES
Anguiatú (El Salvador border)	20	1hr	leaves when full 5am-5:30pm
El Florido (Honduras border)	28	1½hr	leaves when full 5:30am-4:30pm
Esquipulas	25	45min	every 20min 5am-9pm
Flores	120	7-8hr	two daily
Guatemala City	60	3hr	every 30min 3am-3:30pm
Ipala	10	1½hr	hourly 5am-7pm
Puerto Barrios	50	4½hr	every 30min 3:30am-4pm
Quiriguá	35	2hr	every 30min 3:30am-4pm
Río Hondo	18	35min	every 15min 5am-6pm

🛏 Sleeping

Esquipulas has an abundance of places to stay. On holidays and during the annual Cristo de Esquipulas festival (January 15), every hotel in town is filled, whatever the price; weekends are super-busy as well, with prices substantially higher. The rates given here are weekend prices. On weekdays (excluding the festival period), there are *descuentos* (discounts). For cheap rooms, look in the streets immediately north of the towering basilica.

Hotel Portal de la Fe HOTEL $$
(☑7943-4261; 11 Calle 1-70, Zona 1; s/d Q280/500; P✳@🌐🏊) One of the few hotels with any real style in town. Subterranean rooms are predictably gloomy, but upstairs the situation improves considerably.

Hotel Mahanaim HOTEL $$
(☑7943-1131; 10a Calle 1-85, Zona 1; r Q380; P✳@🌐🏊) This establishment is on three levels around a covered courtyard. Rooms are comfortable but plain. It wouldn't be such a good deal if it weren't for the big covered swimming pool out back.

Hotel Monte Cristo HOTEL $$
(☑7943-1453; 3a Av 9-12, Zona 1; s/d Q200/280, without bathroom Q90/120; P) Good-sized rooms with a bit of furniture and super-hot showers. A policy of not letting the upstairs rooms until the downstairs ones are full might see you staying at ground level.

Hotel Vistana al Señor HOTEL $$
(☑7943-4294; hotelvistana@gmail.com; 1a Av 'B' 1-42; s/d Q280/360; 🌐) By far the best deal in

this price range are these sweet little rooms just south of the market. There's a pretty common balcony area with good views upstairs.

🍴 Eating

Restaurants are slightly more expensive here than in other parts of Guatemala. Budget restaurants are clustered at the north end of the park, where hungry pilgrims can find them readily.

Restaurante Calle Real GUATEMALAN $
(3a Av; mains Q40-80; ☺8am-10pm) Typical of many restaurants here, this big eating-barn turns out cheap meals for the pilgrims. It has a wide menu, strip lighting and loud TV.

La Rotonda FAST FOOD $$
(11a Calle; mains Q60-100; ☺8am-10pm) Opposite Rutas Orientales bus station, this is a round building with chairs arranged around a circular open-air counter under a big awning. It's a welcoming place – clean and fresh. There are plenty of selections to choose from, including pizza, pasta and burgers.

City Grill STEAK $$
(cnr 2a Av & 10a Calle, Zona 1; mains Q50-140; ☺8am-10pm) The best steakhouse in town (featuring some of the best steaks for miles around) also serves up some decent seafood and pasta dishes. The pizza is worth a look-in, too.

Restaurant El Angel CHINESE $$
(☑7943-1372; cnr 11a Calle & 2a Av, Zona 1; mains Q50-70; ☺11am-10:30pm) This main-street Chinese eatery does all the standard dishes, plus steaks and a good range of *licuados* (fresh fruit drinks). Home delivery is available.

ℹ Information

Banco Internacional (3a Av 8-87, Zona 1; ☺8am-4pm Mon-Fri, 9am-1pm Sat) Changes cash and traveler's checks, gives cash advances on Visa and MasterCard, is the town's American Express agent and has a Visa ATM.
Post Office (6a Av 2-15) About 10 blocks north of the center.

ℹ Getting There & Away

Buses to Guatemala City (Q60, four hours) arrive and depart hourly from 1:30am to 4:30pm from the **Rutas Orientales bus station** (☑7943-1366; cnr 11a Calle & 1a Av, Zona 1), near the entrance to town.

ℹ GETTING TO EL SALVADOR

Between Chiquimula and Esquipulas (35km from Chiquimula and 14km from Esquipulas), Padre Miguel junction is the turnoff for Anguiatú, at the border with El Salvador, which is 19km (30 minutes) away. Minibuses pass by frequently, coming from Chiquimula, Quetzaltepeque and Esquipulas.

The border at Anguiatú is open 24 hours, but you're best crossing during daylight. Plenty of trucks cross here. Across the border there are hourly buses to the capital, San Salvador, passing through Metapán and Santa Ana.

Minibuses to Agua Caliente (Honduran border; Q25, 30 minutes) arrive and depart across the street, leaving every half hour from 5am to 5pm; taxis also wait here, charging the same as minibuses, once they have five passengers.

Minibuses to Chiquimula (Q20, 45 minutes, every 15 minutes) depart from the east end of 11a Calle.

Transportes Guerra (cnr 5a Av & 10a Calle, Zona 1) goes to Anguiatú (El Salvadoran border; Q20, one hour, every 30 minutes).

There are three buses daily for Flores/Santa Elena (Q130, eight hours) from the **Transportes María Elena** (☑7943-0957; 11 Calle 0-54, Zona 1) office. They pass Quiriguá (Q50, two hours), Río Dulce (Q75, four hours) and Poptún (Q100, six hours).

Quiriguá

POP 4800

Quiriguá archaeological site is only 50km from Copán as the crow flies, but the lay of the land, the international border and the condition of the roads make it a journey of 175km. Quiriguá is famed for its intricately carved stelae – the gigantic brown sandstone monoliths that rise as high as 10.5m, like ancient sentinels, in a quiet well-kept tropical park.

From Río Hondo junction it's 67km along Hwy 9 to the village of Los Amates, where there are a couple of hotels, a restaurant, food stalls, a bank and a small bus station. Quiriguá village is 1.5km east of Los Amates, and the turnoff to the ruins is another 1.5km to the east. The 3.4km access road leads south through banana groves.

History

Quiriguá's history parallels that of Copán, of which it was a dependency during much of the Classic period. Of the three sites in this area, only the present archaeological park is of interest.

Quiriguá's location lent itself to the carving of giant stelae. Beds of brown sandstone in the nearby Río Motagua had cleavage planes suitable for cutting large pieces. Though soft when first cut, the sandstone dried hard in the air. With Copán's expert artisans nearby for guidance, Quiriguá's stone carvers were ready for greatness. All they needed was a great leader to inspire them – and to pay for the carving of the huge stelae.

That leader was K'ak' Tiliw Chan Yo'at (Cauac Sky; r 725–84), who decided that Quiriguá should no longer be under the control of Copán. In a war with his former suzerain, Cauac Sky took Uaxaclahun Ubak K'awil (King 18 Rabbit) of Copán prisoner in 737 and later had him beheaded. Independent at last, Cauac Sky commissioned his stonecutters to go to work, and for the next 38 years they turned out giant stelae and zoomorphs dedicated to his glory.

Cauac Sky's son Sky Xul (r 784–800) lost his throne to a usurper, Jade Sky. This last great king of Quiriguá continued the building boom initiated by Cauac Sky, reconstructing Quiriguá's Acrópolis on a grander scale.

Quiriguá remained unknown to Europeans until the explorer and diplomat John L Stephens arrived in 1840. Impressed by its great monuments, Stephens lamented the world's lack of interest in them in his book *Incidents of Travel in Central America, Chiapas and Yucatan* (1841).

Stephens tried to buy the ruined city in order to have its stelae shipped to New York, but the owner, Señor Payes, assumed that Stephens (being a diplomat), was negotiating on behalf of the US government and that the government would pay. Payes quoted an extravagant price, and the deal was never made.

Between 1881 and 1894, excavations were carried out by Alfred P Maudslay. In the early 1900s all the land around Quiriguá was sold to the US-based United Fruit Company and turned into banana groves. The company is gone, but the bananas and Quiriguá remain. Restoration of the site was carried out by the University of Pennsylvania in the 1930s. In 1981 Unesco declared the ruins a World Heritage Site, one of only three in Guatemala (the others are Tikal and Antigua).

⊙ Sights

Quiriguá

Archaeological Site   ARCHAEOLOGICAL SITE

(Q80; ⊙8am-4:30pm) Despite the sticky heat and (sometimes) bothersome mosquitoes, Quiriguá is a wonderful place. The giant stelae on the Gran Plaza (Great Plaza) are all much more worn than those at Copán. To impede further deterioration, each has been covered by a thatched roof. The roofs cast shadows that make it difficult to examine the carving closely and almost impossible to get a good photograph, but somehow this does little to inhibit one's sense of awe.

Seven of the stelae, designated A, C, D, E, F, H and J, were built during the reign of

Cauac Sky and carved with his image. Stela E is the largest Maya stela known, standing some 8m above ground, with another 3m or so buried in the earth. It weighs almost 60,000kg. Note the exuberant, elaborate headdresses; the beards on some of the figures (an oddity in Maya art and life); the staffs of office held in the kings' hands; and the glyphs on the sides of the stela.

At the far end of the plaza is the Acrópolis, far less impressive than the one at Copán. At its base are several zoomorphs, blocks of stone carved to resemble real and mythic creatures. Frogs, tortoises, jaguars and serpents were favorite subjects. The low zoomorphs can't compete with the towering stelae in impressiveness, but as works of art, imagination and mythic significance, the zoomorphs are superb.

Sleeping & Eating

Hotel y Restaurante Royal HOTEL $
(☎ 7947-3639; s/d Q140/200; P) Of the budget options in town, this is by far the better choice, with spacious clean rooms and a restaurant serving simple, filling meals (Q40 to Q60). Room prices are heavily negotiable.

Getting There & Around

Buses running Guatemala City–Puerto Barrios, Guatemala City–Flores, Esquipulas–Flores or Chiquimula–Flores will drop you off or pick you up here. If you're heading for the hotel, make sure you get dropped at the pasarela de Quiriguá (the pedestrian overpass). They'll also drop you at the turnoff to the archaeological site if you ask.

From the highway it's 3.4km to the archaeological site – Q10 by tuk-tuk (three-wheeled motor taxi), but if one doesn't come, don't fret: it's a pleasant walk (without luggage) through banana plantations to get there.

If you're staying in Quiriguá village or Los Amates and walking to the archaeological site, you can take a shortcut along the railroad that goes from the village through the banana fields, crossing the access road very near the entrance to the archaeological site. A tuk-tuk from Quiriguá village to the site should cost around Q20.

Out on the main highway buses pass frequently for Río Dulce (Q30, two hours), Chiquimula (Q30, two hours) and Puerto Barrios.

Lago de Izabal

Guatemala's largest lake, to the north of Hwy 9, is starting to earn its place on the travelers' map. Most visitors checking out the lake stay at Río Dulce town, by the long, tall bridge where Hwy 13, heading north to Flores and Tikal, crosses the Río Dulce emptying out of the east end of the lake. Downstream, the beautiful river broadens into a lake called El Golfete before meeting the Caribbean at Lívingston. River trips are a highlight of a visit to eastern Guatemala. If you're looking for lakeside ambiance minus the Río Dulce congestion and pace, head to Chapin Abajo, north of Mariscos or El Estor near the west end of the lake, both of which give access to the rich wildlife of the Bocas del Polochic river delta. There are many undiscovered spots in this area waiting to be explored, so don't limit yourself.

Río Dulce

At the east end of Lago de Izabal, this town still gets referred to as Fronteras – a hangover from the days when the only way across the river was by ferry, and this was the last piece of civilization before embarking on the long, difficult journey into El Petén.

Times have changed. A huge bridge now spans the water and El Petén roads are some of the best in the country. The town sees most tourist traffic from yachties – the US coast guard says this is the safest place on the western Caribbean for boats during hurricane season. The rest of the foreigners here are either coming or going on the spectacular river trip between here and Lívingston.

Tours

Ask around at any of the marinas for the latest on which sailboats are offering charter tours.

Aventuras Vacacionales SAILING
(☎ 7873-9221; www.sailing-diving-guatemala.com) This outfit runs fun seven-day sailing trips from Río Dulce to the Belize reefs and islands (from Q3200) and four-day trips to Lago Izabal (from Q1250). The office is in Antigua but you can also hook up with them in Río Dulce. It makes the Belize and lake trips in alternate weeks.

Sleeping

Many places in Río Dulce communicate by radio, but all are reachable by telephone. The bar at Bruno's will radio your choice of place to stay if necessary.

Hotel Vista al Río
HOTEL $

(☑ 7930-5665; dm Q40, r with/without bathroom Q180/120; ❋ 🅟) Under the bridge just south of Bruno's, this little hotel/marina offers spacious, spotless rooms, the more expensive ones with river views. There's a good restaurant here (mains Q60 to Q100), serving juicy steaks, Southern cooking and big breakfasts.

Casa Perico
HOSTEL $$

(☑ 7930-5666; www.casa-perico.com; dm Q60, s/d without bathroom from Q95/140, cabin Q220; @ 🅟) One of the more low-key options in the area, this place is set on a little inlet about 200m from the main river. Cabins are well built and connected by boardwalks. They offer tours all up and down the river and put on an excellent buffet dinner (Q90), or you can choose from the menu (Q50 to Q80).

If you want the one cabin with private bathroom make sure you book ahead.

Hacienda Tijax
HOTEL $$

(☑ 7930-5505; www.tijax.com; s/d from Q334/372, without bathroom Q160/220; 🅟 ❋ 🅟 🏊) This 118-acre hacienda, a two-minute boat ride across the cove from Bruno's, is a special place to stay. Activities include horseback riding, hiking, bird-watching and walking and canopy tours around the rubber plantation and private nature reserve. Accommodations in lovely little cabins are connected by boardwalks. The pricier ones have kitchens and are well set-up for families.

Bruno's
HOTEL $$

(☑ 7930-5721; www.brunoshotel.com; camping per person Q35, dm Q60, s Q110-250, d Q140-350; 🅟 ❋ 🅟 🏊) A path leads down from the northeast end of the bridge to this riverside hangout for yachties needing to get some land under their feet. The dorms are clean and spacious and the new building offers some of the most comfortable rooms in town, with air-con and balconies overlooking the river.

Hotel Backpackers
HOSTEL $$

(☑ 7930-5480; www.hotelbackpackers.com; dm Q60, r with/without bathroom from Q250/160; @ 🅟) Across the bridge from Río Dulce town, this is a business run by Casa Guatemala and the orphans it serves. It's an old (with the emphasis on old) backpacker favorite, set in a rickety building with very basic rooms. The bar kicks on here at night.

✖ Eating

Most of the hotels in town have restaurants. Bruno's serves good breakfasts and gringo comfort food and has a full bar. Hacienda Tijax is a popular lunch spot – give them a call and they'll come pick you up.

★ Sundog Café
INTERNATIONAL $

(sandwiches Q30, meals from Q50; ◷ noon-9pm) Down a laneway opposite the Litegua bus office (200m up the main street past the end of the bridge), this open-air riverfront bar-restaurant makes great sandwiches on homemade bread, a good selection of vegetarian dishes, tasty brick-oven pizzas and fresh juices. It's also the place to come for unbiased information about the area.

ℹ Information

If you need to change cash or traveler's checks, hit one of the banks in town, all on the main road. **Banco Industrial** (◷ 9am-5pm) has a Visa ATM. There's also a trustworthy Visa/Mastercard ATM inside the Despensa Familiar supermarket, also on the main street.

The local online newspaper **Chisme Vindicator** (www.riodulcechisme.com) has loads of information about Río Dulce.

Sundog Café is the place to go for unbiased information about the area.

ℹ Getting There & Away

BUS

The Fuente del Norte and Litegua bus offices are both located on the north side of the bridge, opposite each other.

Beginning at 9:30am, seven Fuente del Norte buses a day head north along a paved road to Poptún (Q40, two hours) and Flores (Q75, four hours). With good connections you can get to Tikal in a snappy six hours. There are also services to San Salvador (El Salvador; Q140) and San Pedro Sula (Honduras; Q150), both leaving at 10am.

At least 11 buses daily go to Guatemala City (Q70, six hours) with Fuente del Norte and Litegua. Línea Dorada has 1st-class buses departing at 1pm for Guatemala City (Q140) and 3pm for Flores (Q140). This shaves up to an hour off the journey times.

Minibuses leave for Puerto Barrios (Q30, two hours) when full, from near the Fuente del Norte office on the main street.

There's a daily shuttle to Lanquín (Q180, five hours), leaving from in front of the **Sundog Café** at 1:30pm.

Minibuses leave for El Estor (Q20, 1½ hours, 7am to 6pm hourly) from the San Felipe and El Estor turnoff in the middle of town.

BOAT

Shared *lanchas* (small motorboats; per person one-way/round-trip Q150/250) go down the Río Dulce (from the new dock) to Lívingston, usually requiring eight to 10 people. The trip is a beautiful one, making a 'tour' of it, with several halts along the way. Boats usually leave from 9am to about 2pm. There are regular, scheduled departures at 9:30am and 1:30pm. Pretty much everyone in town can organize a *lancha* service to Lívingston and most other places you'd care to go, but they charge more.

El Castillo de San Felipe

The fortress and castle of San Felipe de Lara, **El Castillo de San Felipe** (Q25; ⊘8am-5pm), about 3km west of Río Dulce town, was built in 1652 to keep pirates from looting the villages and commercial caravans of Izabal. Though the fortress somewhat deterred the buccaneers, a pirate force captured and burned it in 1686. By the end of the next century, pirates had disappeared from the Caribbean, and the fort's sturdy walls served as a prison. Eventually, though, the fortress was abandoned and became a ruin. The present fort was reconstructed in 1956.

IZABAL BEYOND RÍO DULCE

While Río Dulce town is OK, the best places to stay around here are much further afield. Here's a sampling:

Finca Tatin (☑4148-3332; www.fincatatin.com; dm Q60, s/d Q180/200, without bathroom Q80/130; ☎) This wonderful, rustic B&B at the confluence of Ríos Dulce and Tatin, about 10km from Lívingston, is a great place to experience the forest. Four-hour guided walks and kayak trips, some visiting local Q'eqchi' villages, are offered. Accommodations are in funky wood-and-thatched cabins scattered through the jungle and some rather spiffy new riverfront ones with balconies overlooking the water.

Lagunita Creek (☑4113-0103; dm/r Q100/400) Heading northwest from Lívingston brings you to the Río Sarstun, which forms the border between Belize and Guatemala. Ten kilometers upstream is the small community of Lagunita Creek, where a community-tourism project offers lodging in a simple ecolodge. Simple meals (Q50 to Q70) are available here, or you can bring your own food to cook.

Included in the price is use of kayaks to explore the beautiful, turquoise waters of the river and guided nature walks/bird-watching tours. Transportation isn't complicated but it can be expensive – the only way to get here is by boat. *Lanchas* (small motorboats) from Lívingston charge Q1400 per boatload (up to eight people), with a small discount for smaller groups. **Happy Fish Travel** (p190) in Lívingston offers day/overnight tours here for Q320/560 but require a minimum of six people.

Hotelito Perdido (☑5725-1576; www.hotelitoperdido.com; dm Q60, s/d bungalow Q200/250, without bathroom Q150/200) This beautiful, secluded hideout is a five-minute boat ride from Finca Tatin. The ambiance is superb – relaxed and friendly. The whole place is solar powered and constructed in such a way as to cause minimal impact on the environment.

Hotel Kangaroo (☑5363-6716, in English 4513-9602; www.hotelkangaroo.com; dm Q60, r Q160-200, cabins Q250; @☎) On the Río La Colocha, just across the water from the Castillo San Felipe, this beautiful, simple Australian/Mexican-run place is built on stilts in the mangroves. Its restaurant's beguiling menu (mains Q50 to Q100) features some Aussie classics and probably the best Mexican food you're likely to find outside of Mexico.

Roundhouse (☑4294-9730; www.roundhouseguatemala.com; dm/d without bathroom Q50/110; @☒) Unfortunately closed at the time of writing, this medium-sized hostel, 20 minutes by boat from Lívingston, was one of the best on the river. The 1st floor is a riverfront bar/restaurant/hammock area. On the 2nd floor there's a spacious dorm and some good, simple private rooms.

Today the castle is protected as a park and is one of Lago de Izabal's principal tourist attractions. In addition to the fort itself, there are grassy grounds, BBQ and picnic areas, and the opportunity to swim in the lake. The place rocks during the Feria de San Felipe (April 30 to May 4).

Near the Castillo, Hotel Don Humberto (☏7930-5051; s/d Q60/100; ℗) offers basic rooms with big beds and good mosquito netting. It's nothing fancy, but more than adequate for a cheap sleep.

San Felipe is on the lakeshore, 3km west of Río Dulce. It's a beautiful 45-minute walk between the two towns, or take a minivan (Q15, every 30 minutes). In Río Dulce it stops on the corner of the highway and road to El Estor; in San Felipe it stops in front of the Hotel Don Humberto, at the entrance to El Castillo.

Boats coming from Lívingston will drop you in San Felipe if you ask. The Río Dulce river tours usually come to El Castillo, allowing you to get out and visit the castle if you like, or you can come over from Río Dulce by private *lancha* (small motorboat).

Finca El Paraíso

On the north side of the lake, between Río Dulce and El Estor, Finca El Paraíso (☏7949-7122; Q10) makes a great day trip from either place. This working ranch's territory has an incredibly beautiful spot in the jungle where a wide, hot waterfall drops about 12m into a clear, deep pool. You can bathe in the hot water, swim in the cool pool or duck under an overhanging promontory and enjoy a jungle-style sauna.

If you're coming for the waterfall, head north (away from the lake) where the bus drops you off – you pay the admission fee there, from where it's about a 2km walk to the falls. To get to the hotels, head south (toward the lake) for about 3km.

There are two accommodations options here, both side by side on the lakefront. One is on the grounds of the Finca El Paraíso (☏7949-7122; with fan/air-con Q220/300) and the other is next door, in the humble little cabins at the Brisas del Lago (☏7958-0309; cabin per person Q120).

Both Brisas del Lago and the Finca Paraíso have restaurants. There is no food available at the waterfall, although a *comedor* sometimes operates at the entrance next to the highway.

The *finca* (ranch) is on the Río Dulce–El Estor bus route, about one hour (Q12) from

Río Dulce and 30 minutes (Q10) from El Estor. The last bus in either direction passes at around 4:30pm to 5pm.

El Estor

The major settlement on the northern shore of Lago de Izabal is El Estor, a friendly, somnolent little town with a lovely setting which provides an easy jumping-off point for Bocas del Polochic, a highly biodiverse wildlife reserve at the west end of the lake. The town is also a staging post on a possible route between Río Dulce and Lanquín.

🛏 Sleeping & Eating

There are no upscale hotels here, but there's a good enough range for the short time you're likely to be here.

Restaurante Típico Chaabil apart, the best place to look for food is around Parque Central.

Restaurante Típico Chaabil HOTEL $
(☏7949-7272; 3a Calle; s/d Q150/250; ℗) Although they go a bit heavy on the log-cabin feel, the rooms at this place, at the west end of the street, are the best deal in town. Get one upstairs for plenty of light and good views. The restaurant here, on a lovely lakeside terrace, cooks up delicious food, such as *tapado* (Garifuna casserole).

The water here is crystal clear and you can swim right off the hotel's dock.

Hotel Villela HOTEL $
(☏7949-7214; 6a Av 2-06; s/d Q80/120) The rooms are less attractive than the neat lawn and trees they're set around, but some are airier and brighter than others. All have fan and bathroom.

Hotel Vista al Lago HOTEL $$
(☏7949-7205; 6a Av 1-13; s/d Q180/250) Set in a classic historic building down on the waterfront, this place has plenty of style, although the rooms themselves are fairly ordinary. Views from the upstairs balcony are superb.

ℹ Information

Café Portal (5a Av 2-65; ⊙7am-9pm) Provides information, tours and transportation.

Fundación Defensores de la Naturaleza (☏7949-7130; www.defensores.org.gt; cnr 5a Av & 2a Calle) Administers the Refugio de Vida Silvestre Bocas del Polochic and the Reserva de Biosfera Sierra de las Minas, among other projects.

GUATEMALA LAGO DE IZABAL

❶ Getting There & Away

El Estor is easily reached from Río Dulce.

The road west from El Estor via Panzós and Tucurú to Tactic, south of Cobán, once had a bad reputation for highway holdups and robberies, especially around Tucurú – ask around for current conditions. It's also prone to flooding during the wet season – another reason to inquire. You can get to Lanquín by taking the truck that leaves El Estor's Parque Central at 10:30am for Cahabón (Q50, four to five hours), and then a bus or pick-up straight on from Cahabón to Lanquín the same day. Coming the other way currently involves ungodly departure times and staying the night in Cahabón.

Puerto Barrios

POP 86,400

The country becomes ever more lush, tropical and humid heading east from La Ruidosa junction toward Puerto Barrios.

Port towns have always had a reputation for being slightly dodgy, and those acting as international borders doubly so. Puerto Barrios has an edgy, somewhat sleazy feel; for foreign visitors, it's mainly a jumping-off point for boats to Punta Gorda (Belize) or Lívingston, and you probably won't be hanging around.

⌷ Sleeping

Hotel Ensenada   HOTEL $
(☑ 7948-0861; hotelensenadapuertobarrios@hot mail.com; 4a Av btwn Calles 10 & 11; s/d Q150/200; P ✻) Taking one step up in the budget category gets you these tidy little rooms with good bathrooms and OK beds. Get one upstairs to catch a breeze.

Hotel Europa   HOTEL $
(☑ 7948-1292; 3a Av btwn Calles 11a & 12a; s/d with fan Q80/130, with air-con Q130/170; P ✻ 🛜) The best of the budget options in the port area, this hotel, just 1½ blocks from the Muelle Municipal (Municipal Boat Dock), is run by a friendly family and has clean rooms with TV, arranged around a parking courtyard.

Hotel Lee   HOTEL $
(☑ 7948-0685; 5a Av btwn Calles 9a & 10a; s/d with fan Q80/120, d with air-con Q180; ✻) This is a friendly, family-owned place, close to the bus terminals. Typical of Puerto Barrios' budget hotels, it offers straightforward, vaguely clean rooms. The little balcony out front catches the odd breeze.

Puerto Bello   HOTEL $$
(☑ 7948-0525; www.hotelpuertobello.com; 8a Av btwn Calles 18 & 19; s/d Q230/350; P ✻ @ 🛜 ☲) By far the best-looking hotel in town, marred only by its slightly out of the way location. The rooms are spacious and modern, and the lovely garden and pool area is a blessing year-round.

Hotel del Norte   HOTEL $$
(☑ 7948-2116; 7a Calle; s/d with fan Q100/180, with air-con Q180/300; P ✻ @ 🛜 ☲) A large, classically tropical wooden building with mosquito-screened corridors, the century-old Hotel del Norte is in a class by itself. Its weathered and warped frame is redolent of history and the floorboards go off at crazy angles. Pick a room carefully – some are little more than a wooden box, others have great ocean views and catch good breezes.

✖ Eating

Kaffa   CAFE $
(8a Av btwn Calles 7 & 8; sandwiches & breakfast Q40-60; ⊙ 8:30am-10pm) A hip coffee shop in Puerto Barrios? Well, why not? Let's see how long it lasts. The food's so-so, but the coffee and the breezy deck overlooking the park are both excellent.

Restaurante Morano Calabro   MEDITERRANEAN $$
(11 Calle btwn 7 & 8 Av; mains Q80-160; ⊙ 11am-10pm Mon-Sat) Surprisingly good Italian food (the pizzas are the real winners here, but the pasta rates a mention, too) alongside an interesting selection of tapas items. The great wine list, featuring bottles from Spain and South America, rounds out the picture.

★ Restaurante Safari   SEAFOOD $$
(☑ 7948-0563; cnr 1a Calle & 5a Av; seafood Q70-150; ⊙ 10am-9pm) The town's most enjoyable restaurant is on a thatch-roofed, open-air platform right over the water about 1km north of the town center. Locals and visitors alike love to eat and catch the sea breezes here. Excellent seafood of all kinds including the specialty *tapado* – that great Garifuna casserole.

❶ Orientation

Because of its spacious layout, you must walk or ride further in Puerto Barrios to get from place to place. For instance, it's 800m from the bus terminals by the market in the town center to the Muelle Municipal at the end of 12a Calle, from which passenger boats depart. Very few businesses use street numbers – most just label which street it's on, and the cross streets it's in between.

ℹ Information

Banco Industrial (7a Av; ⊘ 9am-5pm Mon-Fri, 9am-1pm Sat) Changes US dollars and traveler's checks, and has an ATM.

Immigration Office (cnr 12a Calle & 3a Av; ⊘ 24hr) A block from the Muelle Municipal. Come here for your entry or exit stamp if you're arriving from or leaving for Belize. If you're leaving by sea, there is a Q80 departure tax to pay. If you are heading to Honduras, you can get your exit stamp at another immigration office on the road to the border.

ℹ Getting There & Away

BOAT

Boats depart from the Muelle Municipal at the end of 12a Calle.

Regular *lanchas* (small motorboats) depart for Lívingston (Q45, 30 minutes, five daily) between 6:30am and 5pm. Buy your ticket as early as you can on the day (you can't book before your day of departure) – spaces are limited and sometimes sell out.

Outside of these regular times, *lanchas* depart whenever they have six people ready to go and cost Q50 per person.

Most of the movement from Lívingston to Puerto Barrios is in the morning, returning in the afternoon. From Lívingston, your last chance of the day may be the 5pm *lancha*, especially during the low season when fewer travelers are shuttling back and forth.

Lanchas also depart from the Muelle Municipal three times daily for Punta Gorda, Belize (Q220, one hour). The 10am departure arrives in time for the noon bus from Punta Gorda to Belize City. Tickets are sold at the dock. Before boarding you also need to get your exit stamp at the nearby **immigration office** (and pay Q80 departure tax).

If you want to leave a car in Puerto Barrios while you visit Lívingston for a day or two, there are plenty of *parqueos* (parking lots) around the dock area that charge around Q30 per 24 hours. Many of the hotels offer this service, too.

BUS & MINIBUS

Transportes Litegua (📞 7948-1172; cnr 6a Av & 9a Calle) leaves for Guatemala City (Q65 to Q100, five to six hours), via Quiriguá and Río Hondo frequently. *Directo* services avoid a half-hour detour into Morales.

Minibuses for Chiquimula (Q50, 4½ hours), also via Quiriguá, leave every half hour, from 3am to 3pm, from the corner of 6a Av and 9a

Calle. Minibuses to Río Dulce (Q25, two hours) leave from the same location.

Punta de Manabique

The Punta de Manabique promontory, which separates the Bahía de Manabique from the open sea, along with the coast and hinterland all the way southeast to the Honduran frontier, comprises a large, ecologically fascinating, sparsely populated wetland area. Access to the area, which is under environmental protection as the **Área de Protección Especial Punta de Manabique**, is not cheap, but the attractions for those who make it there include pristine Caribbean beaches, boat trips through the mangrove forests, lagoons and waterways, bird-watching, fishing with locals, and crocodile and possible manatee sightings.

The only place to stay here is in the community-run **Ecoalbergue** (📞 5303-9822; www.turismocomunitarioguatemala.com/estero_lagarto.html; Estero Lagarto; per person tent/room Q25/50).

Delicious meals (Q30 to Q60), mostly seafood-based, are prepared by members of the community and served at Ecoalbergue.

To visit, get in touch – a week in advance, if possible – with **Estero Lagarto Community Tourism** (📞 5303-9822; www.turismocomunitarioguatemala.com/estero_lagarto.html).

Lívingston

POP 26,300

Quite unlike anywhere else in Guatemala, this largely Garifuna town is fascinating in itself, but also has the attraction of a couple of good beaches and its location at the end of the river journey from Río Dulce.

Unconnected (for the moment) by road from the rest of the country (the town is called 'Buga' – mouth – in Garifuna, for its position at the river mouth), boat transportation is logically quite good here, and you can get to Belize, the Cayes and Puerto Barrios with a minimum of fuss.

◉ Sights & Activities

Beaches in Lívingston itself are disappointing, as buildings or vegetation come right down to the water's edge in most places. Those beaches that do exist are often contaminated; however, there are better beaches within a few kilometers to the northwest. You can reach Playa Quehueche near the mouth of the Río Quehueche by taxi (Q30) in about 10 minutes. The best beach in the area is **Playa Blanca** (Q15), around 12km from Lívingston. This is privately owned and you need a boat to get there.

Los Siete Altares
WATERFALL

(The Seven Altars; Q25) About 5km (1½-hour walk) northwest of Lívingston along the shore of Bahía de Amatique, Los Siete Altares is a series of freshwater falls and pools. It's a pleasant goal for a beach walk and is a good place for a picnic and swim.

Follow the shore northward to the river mouth and walk along the beach until it meets the path into the woods (about 30 minutes). Follow this path all the way to the falls. Boat trips go to Los Siete Altares, but if you're a walker it's better to go by foot to experience the natural beauty and the Garifuna people along the way. About halfway along, just past the rope bridge is **Hotel Salvador Gaviota** (📞7947-0874; www.hotelsalvadorgaviota.com; Playa Quehueche; per person with/without bathroom Q160/80; 📶), serving decent food and ice-cold beers and soft drinks. You can stay out here, too.

🗺️ Tours

A few outfits in Lívingston offer tours that let you get out and experience the natural wonders of the area. **Exotic Travel** (📞7947-0133; www.bluecaribbeanbay.com; Calle Principal, Restaurante Bahía Azul) and **Happy Fish Travel** (📞7947-0661; www.happyfishtravel.com; Calle Principal, Restaurante Happy Fish) are both well-organized operations. Happy Fish gets extra points for supporting community tourism initiatives in the area and their willingness to share information on how you can visit many of the local attractions without a guide.

The popular Ecological Tour/Jungle Trip (Q70) takes you for a walk through town, out west up to a lookout spot and on to the Río Quehueche, where you take a half-hour canoe trip down the river to Playa Quehueche. Then you walk through the jungle to Los Siete Altares, hang out there for a while, and walk back down the beach to Lívingston. This is a great way to see the area, and the friendly local guides can also give you a good introduction to the Garifuna people who live here.

The Playa Blanca tour goes by boat first to Los Siete Altares and then on to Playa Blanca, the best beach in the area, for two or three hours. This trip goes with a minimum of two people and costs Q100 per person.

Happy Fish offers a return boat trip (Q220) just along the canyon section of Río Dulce (the most interesting and picturesque part) which gives you more time to enjoy the trails, bird-watching and so on than the 'tour' given on the public *lanchas* (small motorboats). They also run tours to Cueva del Tigre, a community-run tourism project 8km from Lívingston (Q180 for a tour, or they'll tell you how to get there on your own) and for transportation to Lagunita Creek (p186), another community-operated tourism initiative.

Also popular are day/overnight trips to the Cayos Sapodillas (or Zapotillas), well off the coast of southern Belize, where there is great snorkeling (Q500/1200 for one/two days). A minimum of eight people is required and exit taxes and national park fees (Q160 in total) are separate.

🍽️ Courses

Rasta Mesa
CULTURAL CENTER

(📞4459-6106; Barrio Nevago; ⏱️10am-2pm & 7-10pm) This is a friendly, informal little cultural center where you can drop in for classes in Garifuna cooking (Q60 per person) and drumming (Q100 per person) or just get a massage (from Q150). It also offers volunteering opportunities.

✨ Festivals & Events

During **Semana Santa** (⊙Easter week) Lívingston is packed with merrymakers. **Garifuna National Day** (⊙Nov 26) is celebrated with a variety of cultural events.

🛏️ Sleeping

Prices in Lívingston hit their peak from July to December – outside of these months many midrange and top-end places halve their rates.

Casa de la Iguana
HOSTEL $

(📞7947-0064; www.casadelaiguana.com; Calle Marcos Sánchez Díaz; hammock/dm Q25/50, cabins with/without bathroom Q160/120; 📶) A five-minute walk from the main dock, this party hostel offers good-value cabins. They're clean wooden affairs, with simple but elegant decoration. Happy hour here rocks on and you can camp or crash in a hammock.

Flowas
BUNGALOW $

(📞7947-0376; infoflowas@gmail.com; per person Q120) An extremely laid-back little backpacker enclave, this place offers rustic wood and bamboo cabins set up on the 2nd floor (catching the odd breeze) right on the beachfront. The atmosphere is relaxed and there's good, cheap food available. A taxi (Q15 from the dock) will drop you within 150m of the front gate.

Hotel Ríos Tropicales HOTEL $$
(☑5755-7571; Calle Principal; s/d Q180/230, without bathroom from Q70/150; ☎) The Ríos Tropicales has a variety of big, well-screened rooms facing a central patio with plenty of hammocks and chill-out space. Rooms with shared bathroom are more spacious, but others are better decorated.

Vecchia Toscana HOTEL $$
(☑7947-0884; www.vecchiatoscana-livingston. com; Barrio Paris; s/d from Q341/488; ❋@☎☎) This beautiful Italian-run place down on the beach has some of the best rooms in town. There's a variety of rooms on offer, going up to apartments that sleep eight comfortably. The grounds and common areas are immaculate and there's a good Italian restaurant with sea views out the front. A taxi here from the dock will cost around Q20.

✖ Eating

Food in Lívingston is relatively expensive because most of it (except fish and coconuts) must be brought in by boat. There's fine seafood here and some unusual flavors for Guatemala, including coconut and curry. *Tapado*, a rich stew made from fish, shrimp, shellfish and coconut milk, spiced with coriander, is the delicious local specialty. A potent potable is made by slicing off the top of a green coconut and mixing in a healthy dose of rum – these *coco locos* hit the spot.

Calle Principal is dotted with many open-air eateries.

Restaurante Gaby GUATEMALAN $
(Calle Marcos Sánchez Díaz; mains Q40-80; ☺8am-9pm) For a good honest feed in humble surrounds, you can't go past Gaby's. She serves up the good stuff: lobster, *tapado*, rice and beans and good breakfasts at good prices. The *telenovelas* (soap operas) come free.

Antojitos Yoli's BAKERY $
(Calle Principal; baked goods Q15-30; ☺8am-5pm) This is the place to come for baked goods. Especially recommended are the coconut bread and pineapple pie.

★**Restaurante Buga Mama** SEAFOOD $$
(Calle Marcos Sánchez Díaz; mains Q70-120; ☺noon-10pm; ☎) This place enjoys the best location of any restaurant in town, and profits go to the Asociación Ak' Tenamit (p192), an NGO with several projects in the area. There's a wide range of seafood, homemade pasta, curries and other dishes on the menu, including a very good *tapado* (Q120).

Most of the waiters here are trainees in a community sustainable tourism development scheme, so service can be sketchy, but forgivable.

Happy Fish SEAFOOD $$
(Calle Principal; mains Q50-120; ☺7am-10pm; ☎) This bustling and breezy main street eatery is always busy with locals and tourists, keeping the food fresh and the service snappy. The requisite *tapado* is here, plus a good range of other options.

🍷 Drinking & Nightlife

Adventurous drinkers should try *guifiti*, a local concoction made from coconut rum, often infused with herbs. It's said to have medicinal properties.

A handful of bars down on the beach to the left of the end of Calle Principal pull in travelers and locals at night (after about 10pm or 11pm). It's very dark down here, so take care. The bars are within five minutes' walk of each other, so you should go for a wander and see what's happening. Music ranges from punta to salsa, merengue and electronica. Things warm up on Friday but Saturday is the party night – often going until 5am or 6am.

Happy hour is pretty much an institution along the main street, with every restaurant getting in on the act. One of the best is at Casa de la Iguana (p190).

☆ Entertainment

Quite often a roaming band will play a few songs for diners along the Calle Principal around dinnertime. If you like the music, make sure to sling them a few bucks. Several places around town have live Garifuna music, although schedules are unpredictable.

Diners in the Hotel Villa Caribe (☑7947-0072; www.hotelvillacaribeguatemala.com; Calle Principal) restaurant can enjoy a Garifuna show each evening at 7pm.

ℹ Information

After being here half an hour, you'll know where everything is. Though there are street names, in reality no one uses them.

For more on Lívingston, check out its **community website** (www.livingston.com.gt).

DANGERS & ANNOYANCES

Lívingston has its edgy aspects and a few hustlers operate here – exercise normal precautions. Use mosquito repellent and other sensible safeguards, especially if you go out into the jungle; mosquitoes here carry both malaria and dengue fever.

IMMIGRATION

Immigration Office (Calle Principal; ⊗ 6am-7pm) Issues entry and exit stamps for travelers arriving direct from or going direct to Belize or Honduras, charging Q80 for exit stamps. Outside business hours, you can knock for attention at any time.

MONEY

Banrural (Calle Principal; ⊗ 9am-5pm Mon-Fri, 9am-1pm Sat) Changes US dollars and traveler's checks and has an ATM.

ℹ Getting There & Away

Frequent boats come downriver from Río Dulce and across the bay from Puerto Barrios. There are also international boats from Honduras and Belize.

Happy Fish (p190) and **Exotic Travel** (p190) operate combined boat and bus shuttles to La Ceiba (the cheapest gateway to Honduras' Bay Islands) for around Q550 per person, with a minimum of four people. Leaving Lívingston at 6am or earlier will get you to La Ceiba in time for the boat to the islands, making it a one-day trip, which is nearly impossible to do independently.

There's also a boat that goes direct to Punta Gorda daily at 7am (Q250, 1½ hours), leaving from the public dock. In Punta Gorda, the boat

RÍO DULCE CRUISES

Tour agencies in town offer day trips up the Río Dulce to Río Dulce town (departing at 9:30am and 2:30pm), as do most local boatmen at the Lívingston dock. Many travelers use these tours as one-way transportation to Río Dulce, paying Q150/250 one way/round trip. It's a beautiful ride through tropical jungle scenery, with several places to stop on the way.

While a boat ride on the Río Dulce is not to be missed, if you're coming from Guatemala City or Puerto Barrios it makes much more sense to catch a boat from Puerto Barrios to Lívingston and do the tour on your way out.

Shortly after you leave Lívingston, you pass the tributary Río Tatin on the right, then will probably stop at an **indigenous arts museum** set up by **Asociación Ak' Tenamit** (📞5908-3392; www.aktenamit.org), an NGO working to improve conditions for the Q'eqchi' Maya population of the area. The river enters a gorge called **La Cueva de la Vaca**, its walls hung with great tangles of jungle foliage and the humid air noisy with the cries of tropical birds. Just beyond that is **La Pintada**, a rock escarpment covered with graffiti. Further on, a **thermal spring** forces sulfurous water out of the base of the cliff, providing a chance for a warm swim. The river widens into **El Golfete**, a lake-like body of water that presages the even more vast expanse of Lago de Izabal further upstream.

On the northern shore of El Golfete is the **Biotopo Chocón Machacas**, a 72-sq-km reserve established within the Parque Nacional Río Dulce to protect the beautiful river landscape, the valuable forests and mangrove swamps and their wildlife, which includes such rare creatures as the tapir and above all the manatee. A network of 'water trails' (boat routes around several jungle lagoons) provide ways to see other bird, animal and plant life of the reserve. You can stay here, at the community-run lodge **Q'ana Itz'am** (📞5992-1853; www.lagunitasalvador.com; r with/without bathroom Q200/70, bungalow Q400) in Lagunita Salvador but you will have to arrange transportation separately.

Boats will probably visit **Islas de Pájaros**, a pair of islands where thousands of waterbirds live, in the middle of El Golfete. From El Golfete you continue upriver, passing increasing numbers of expensive villas and boathouses, to the town of Río Dulce, where the soaring Hwy 13 road bridge crosses the river, and on to El Castillo de San Felipe on Lago de Izabal.

You can also do this trip starting from Río Dulce.

connects with a bus to Placencia and Belize City. The boat waits for this bus to arrive from Placencia before it sets off back for Lívingston from Punta Gorda at about 10:30am.

If you are taking one of these early international departures, get your exit stamp from immigration in Lívingston the day before.

EL PETÉN

Vast, sparsely populated and jungle-covered, Guatemala's largest and northernmost department is ripe for exploration. Whether it's the mysteries of the Classic Maya, the bounty of the jungle or the chance to lounge lakeside that inspires you, it's all here in abundance. How deeply you choose to delve into the Maya legacy will depend on your willingness to get your feet muddy. The towering temples of Tikal can be reached by tour from just about anywhere, while more remote sites such as El Mirador and Piedras Negras require days of planning and further days of jungle trekking. The Reserva de Biosfera Maya (Maya Biosphere Reserve) covers virtually the entire northern third of El Petén, and together with its counterparts in Mexico and Belize forms a multinational wildlife haven that spans more than 30,000 sq km.

ℹ Getting There & Around

El Petén's main tourism node is at the twin towns of Flores and Santa Elena, about 60km southwest of Tikal. The main roads to Flores (from Río Dulce to the southeast, from Cobán and Chisec to the southwest, from the Belize border to the east, and from the Mexican border to the northwest) are now all paved and in good condition, except for a few short stretches. Frequent buses and minibuses carry travelers along these routes. Santa Elena also has the only functioning civil airport in the country aside from Guatemala City.

Sayaxché

Sayaxché, on the south bank of the Río de la Pasión, 61km southwest of Flores, is the closest town to around 10 scattered Maya archaeological sites, including Ceibal, Aguateca, Dos Pilas, Tamarindito and Altar de Sacrificios. Besides its strategic position between Flores and the Cobán area, it has a riverside appeal all its own, with rickety motorboats and funky barges floating trucks

across the broad waterway, the former till sundown, the latter round the clock (pedestrian Q2, car Q15).

Banrural (⊙ 9am-6pm Mon-Fri, 8am-noon Sat, 9am-noon Sun), just below the church toward the river, changes dollars and euros; a nearby branch has a 5B ATM. Get online at **Zona X** (per hour Q6; ⊙ 8am-6pm), three streets up from the dock on the left.

Though the lodges around nearby Laguna Petexbatún make a far more appealing option, Sayaxché has a few laid-back guesthouses by the riverside including the modern, well-appointed **Hotel del Río** (☑ 7928-6138; hoteldelriosayaxche@hotmail.com; s/d Q125/175, with air-con Q150/225; [P][❄][🖥]).

Decent options are limited to the **Café Maya** (Calle del Ferry; mains Q40-50; ⊙ 7am-9pm) and the cookshack at **Hospedaje Yaxkín** (☑ 4913-4879; dm Q30, bungalow per person with/without bathroom Q70/35). River fish may not be available due to unacceptable pollution levels.

Southbound from Sayaxché, four microbuses head for Cobán (Q60, four hours) between 5am and 3pm. Every 25 minutes or so, Raxrujá-bound microbuses go to the San Antonio junction (Q30, 1½ hours), from where there are frequent departures for Cobán. Vehicles depart from a lot just up from the ferry dock. From the north side of the Río de la Pasión, microbuses leave for Santa Elena every 15 minutes, from 5:45am to 6:30pm (Q23, 1½ hours).

For river transportation, contact **Viajes Don Pedro** (☑ 4580-9389; servlanchasdonpedro @hotmail.com).

Ceibal

Unimportant during most of the Classic period, Ceibal (sometimes spelled Seibal) grew rapidly in the 9th century AD. It attained a population of around 10,000 by AD 900, then was abandoned shortly afterward. Its low, ruined temples were quickly covered by a thick carpet of jungle. Excavation of the site is ongoing under the supervision of University of Arizona archaeologist Takeshi Inomata.

Viajes Don Pedro in Sayaxché, on the north side of the river, runs *lanchas* (small motorboats) here (Q600 for up to five passengers). The fee should include a guide, who may actually be the boatman. In high

El Petén

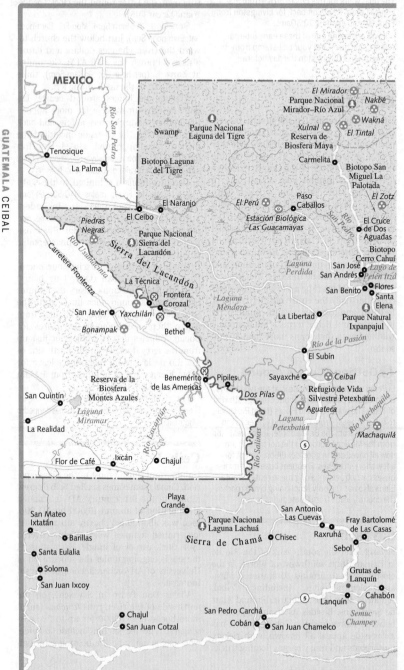

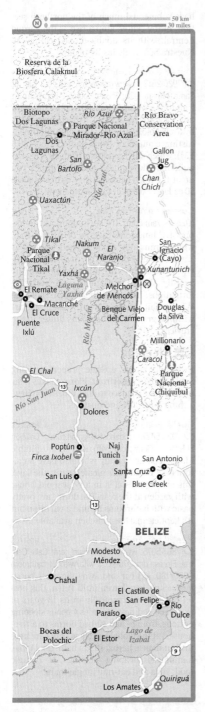

season, ask the *lancheros* about joining a tour group.

The one-hour boat ride up the Río de la Pasión brings you to a primitive dock. After landing, you clamber up a narrow, rocky path beneath gigantic ceiba trees and jumbles of jungle vines to reach the archaeological zone, perched about 100m above the river.

Alternatively, Ceibal can be reached over land: get any bus, minibus or pick-up heading south from Sayaxché on Hwy 5 (toward Raxrujá and Chisec) and get off after 9km at Paraíso, from where it's an 8km walk east down a dirt track to Ceibal. About 2km in, where the road bends left by a small farmhouse, continue straight uphill to enter the park – there's no sign. In the rainy season check first that this stretch is passable.

Finca Ixobal

The **Finca Ixobel** (☎5410-4307; www.fincaixo bel.com; campsite Q35, dm Q50, s/d Q180/315, without bathroom Q85/135, treehouse from Q90/140; 🅿@🛜) 🏊 is an ecological resort/ bohemian hideaway set amid pine forest and patches of jungle between Flores and Río Dulce in southeast Petén. With a friendly, relaxed atmosphere, a wide range of activities, accommodation options and lip-smacking homemade meals, it's a great place to meet fellow travelers.

Everything at Finca Ixobel works on the honor system: guests keep an account of what they eat and drink and the services they use.

If this place suits your style and you want to help/hang out for six weeks minimum, ask about volunteering.

❶ Getting There & Away

Finca Ixobel is 5km south of the regional commercial center of Poptún, from where you can take a taxi (Q30) or *tuk-tuk* (Q20). Otherwise, any bus or minibus along Hwy 13 can drop you at the turnoff, from where it's a 15-minute walk to the lodge. Departing, most buses will stop on the highway to pick you up, but not after dark.

The best way to get to Poptún from Flores/ Santa Elena is to take a minibus from the main terminal (Q30, every 10 minutes, 5am to 7pm); tell the driver where you're heading and he'll drop you at the lodge. Coming from Guatemala City or Río Dulce, all Santa Elena–bound buses make a stop in Poptún.

GUATEMALA FINCA IXOBAL

Flores & Santa Elena

POP 85,000

With its cubist houses cascading down from a central plaza to the emerald waters of Lago de Petén Itzá, the island town of Flores evokes a Mediterranean ambiance. A 500m causeway connects Flores to its humbler sister town of Santa Elena on the lake shore, which then merges into the even homelier community of San Benito to the west. The three towns actually form one large settlement, often referred to simply as Flores.

Flores proper is by far the more attractive base. Small hotels and restaurants line the streets, many featuring rooftop terraces with lake views. Residents take great pride in their island-town's gorgeousness, and a promenade runs around its perimeter. Flores does have a twee, built-up edge to it, though, and some Tikal-bound budget travelers opt for the tranquillity of El Remate, just down the road.

Santa Elena is where you'll find banks, buses and a major shopping mall.

History

Flores was founded on an island *(petén)* by the Itzáes, who came here after being expelled from Chichén Itzá on Mexico's Yucatán Peninsula, probably in the mid-15th century. They called it Tah Itzá ('place of the Itzá'), which the Spanish later corrupted to Tayasal. Hernán Cortés dropped in on King Canek of Tayasal in 1525 on his way to Honduras, but the meeting was, amazingly, peaceable. Cortés left behind a lame horse, which the Itzáes fed on flowers and turkey stew. When it died, the Itzáes made a statue of it, which, by the time a couple of Spanish friars visited in 1618, was being worshiped as a manifestation of the rain god Chac. It was not until 1697 that the Spaniards brought the Itzáes of Tayasal – by some distance the last surviving independent Maya kingdom – forcibly under their control. The Spanish soldiers destroyed its many pyramids, temples and statues, and today you won't see a trace of them, although the modern town is doubtless built on the ruins and foundations of Maya Tayasal.

◎ Sights

Flores is great for strolling, especially now that the lakefront promenade that rings the islet is complete – though rising lake levels have submerged much of the northern section. In the center, atop a rise, is the Parque Central, with its double-domed cathedral, Nuestra Señora de los Remedios.

Museo Santa Bárbara   MUSEUM
(☏7926-2813; www.radiopeten.com.gt; Isle of Santa Bárbara; Q20; ☺8am-noon & 2-5pm) On an islet to the west of Flores, this little museum holds a grab bag of Maya artifacts from nearby archaeological sites, plus some old broadcasting equipment from Radio Petén (88.5 FM), which still broadcasts from an adjacent building. Phone ahead and they'll pick you up at the dock behind Hotel Santana (Calle 30 de Junio, Flores) for Q20 per person.

Cuevas de Ak'tun Kan   CAVE
(Q25; ☺7am-6pm) Try spelunking at the impressive limestone caverns of Ak'tun Kan, which translates from Q'eqchi' Maya as 'Cave of the Serpent.' The cave-keeper provides the authorized interpretation of the weirdly shaped stalagmite and stalactite formations, including the Frozen Falls, the Whale's Tail and the Gate of Heaven, the last within a great hall where bats flutter in the crevices.

🛏 Sleeping

Except for a few upscale properties along Santa Elena's waterfront, Flores makes a far more desirable place to stay, unless you have a thing for traffic and dust.

Hostal Frida   HOSTEL $
(☏7926-5427; fridahostel@gmail.com; Callejón El Rosario, Flores; dm Q45) Run by hospitable Magdalena and family who also have an alternative beauty salon/cafe nearer the lake, this low-key hostel is in a typical old house with garden at the rear. The dorms are pretty basic with bathrooms behind a partition but it's kept clean. Guest kitchen available.

Hostel Los Amigos   HOSTEL $
(☏7867-5075; www.amigoshostel.com; Calle Central, Flores; dm Q70-90, r with/without bathroom Q320/180; @) Far and away the most popular backpackers haven in El Petén, this hostel has grown organically in its 13 years of existence and now includes various sleeping options, from 6- and 10-bed dorms to a treehouse. All the global traveler's perks are here in abundance: herbal steam bath, pool table, hammocks, heaping helpings of organic food, yoga and cut-rate jungle tours.

Hospedaje Doña Goya HOSTEL $
(☑7867-5513; hospedajedonagoya@yahoo.com; Calle Unión, Flores; dm Q40, s/d Q120/160, without bathroom Q90/120; 🛜) This family-run guesthouse makes a fine budget choice. Though it's ultra-basic, the sheets are clean, the fans work, the water's hot and the paint's fresh. Dorms, too, are spacious and spotless. Best of all is the roof terrace with a palm-thatched shelter and hammocks.

Hotel El Peregrino HOTEL $
(☑7867-5701; peregrino@itelgua.com; Av La Reforma, Flores; s/d Q120/160, without bathroom Q70/120; ❄) El Peregrino is an older, family-run place with home cooking in the front *comedor*. Large rooms with tile floors and powerful overhead fans line up along plant-festooned corridors – no views here.

Posada de la Jungla HOTEL $
(☑7867-5185; lajungla@martsam.com; Calle Centroamérica 30, Flores; s/d Q120/180, with air-con Q190/280; ❄🛜) Worth considering is this slender, three-story building with front balconies. Though a bit cramped, rooms are comfortably arranged, with quality beds.

Hotel Aurora HOTEL $
(☑7867-5516; aldeamaya@gmail.com; Calle Unión, Flores; dm/s/d Q40/Q75/150; ❄@🛜) This backpacker haven's got a jungle theme, with banisters made to look like climbing vines. Rooms are plain, airy and well scrubbed, with screened windows, and most have some kind of view. A super roof terrace features an open-air shelter slung with hammocks. Guest kitchen available.

Hotel Flores de Petén HOTEL $
(☑4718-2635; Calle Sur, Flores; s/d/tr Q125/170/200; 🛜) The first hotel you reach coming off the causeway has bright and spacious rooms with cut-rate furniture and a terrace for lake-gazing. The steady flow of traffic from Santa Elena means you'll probably be up early.

Green World Hotel HOTEL $
(☑7867-5662; greenworldhotel@gmail.com; Calle 30 de Junio, Flores; s/d Q125/175, with air-con Q205/275; ❄@🛜) This low-key shoreline property features an interior patio and an upper sundeck overlooking the lake. Compact, low-lit rooms have safes, enormous ceiling fans and good hot showers – number 8, with its rear balcony, is by far the nicest.

Hotel Santa Bárbara HOTEL $$
(☑7926-2813; radiopeten.com.gt; s/d/tr Q200/400/500; ❄🛜) Part of a trio that includes a museum (p196) and cafe, this is a perfect retreat from the hubbub of Flores on an islet just five minutes west by *lancha* (small motorboat; included in price). Three comfy cabins with big beds and tile floors overlook the lake past a garden brimming with coconut palms and a ceiba tree. Highly recommended.

La Posada de Don José HOTEL $$
(☑7867-5298; cnr Calle del Malecón & Calle Fraternidad, Flores; dm Q60, s/d Q175/250, without bathroom Q125/175; ❄🛜) Near the northern tip of the island, this is an old-fashioned establishment (check the lobby for a portrait of the founder) with rocking chairs scattered around a plant-laden patio and a friendly family that knows your name. The lake level has reclaimed the *malecón* (jetty) here, making the rear terrace infinitely more peaceful than further down.

Besides the neat little rooms, there's a spacious fan-cooled dorm in back.

Hospedaje Yaxha HOSTEL $$
(☑5830-2060; www.cafeyaxha.com; Calle 15 de Septiembre, Flores; dm/s/d Q60/150/200) A haven for archaeologists, historians and fans of pre-Hispanic cuisine, Café Yaxha (☑4934-6353; mains Q45-70; ⊙6:30am-10pm) now offers a clean and simple place to lay your head. There's a four-bed dorm, private rooms with bathroom, and an apartment – all with quality mattresses and ceiling fans.

Mayaland Plaza Hotel HOTEL $$
(☑7926-4976; mayalandplaza@yahoo.com; 6a Av & 4a Calle, Santa Elena; s/d/tr Q225/285/375; P❄@❄) The spacious comfortable rooms are set colonial-style around a peaceful courtyard. All services are on hand, including a recommended restaurant and travel agent.

🍴 Eating

As might be expected, Flores is rife with tourist-oriented joints pitching a bland melange of 'international' fare to the package crowd. Nevertheless, a few local gems rise above the pack.

Las Mesitas GUATEMALAN $
(El Malecón, Flores; snacks Q5-10; ⊙3-10pm) Every evening, but especially Sundays, there's a street party on the waterfront promenade, as local families fix *enchiladas* (actually

tostadas topped with guacamole, chicken salad and so on), tacos and tamales, and dispense fruity drinks from giant jugs. All kinds of cakes and puddings are served, too. Everyone sits on plastic chairs or low barrier walls.

Cool Beans
CAFE $
(☑ 5571-9240; Calle 15 de Septiembre, Flores; breakfast Q25-35; ☉ 7am-10pm Mon-Sat; 🛜) Also known as Café Chilero, this laid-back place is more clubhouse with snacks than proper restaurant, featuring salons for chatting, watching videos or laptop browsing. The lush garden with glimpses of the lake makes a *tranquilo* spot for breakfast or veggie burgers. Be warned – the kitchen closes at 9:01pm sharp.

Restaurante El Mirador
GUATEMALAN $
(☑ 7867-5246; Parque Central, Flores; set menu Q25; ☉ 7am-10pm Mon-Sat) Refreshingly not aimed at foreign travelers, this traditional eatery does toothsome home cookin'. You'll find such hearty options as *caldo de res* (beef stew), served with all the trimmings, *fresco* (fruit drink) included, in a bright lunch hall that looks over the treetops. It's next to the basketball court on the Parque Principal.

Café/Bar Doña Goya
CAFE $
(El Malecón, Flores; breakfast Q35-50; ☉ 6:30am-10pm; 🛜) Doña Goya's is good for an early breakfast or sunset snack, with a pretty terrace facing the lake. Toward the weekend, it blends into the nightlife scene along this stretch of the promenade, with occasional live music.

Restaurante Mijaro
RESTAURANT $
(☑ 7926-1615; www.restaurantemijaro.com; 6a Av, Santa Elena; meals Q25-40; ☉ 7am-10pm) You'll find good home cooking at this locally popular *comedor* a few blocks south of the causeway, with an airy thatch-roofed garden area. Besides the grub, it does good long *limonadas* (lime-juice drinks).

★ Terrazzo
ITALIAN $$
(Calle Unión, Flores; pasta Q70-80; ☉ 8am-10pm Mon-Sat) Inspired by a chef from Bologna, this Italian gourmet restaurant covers a romantic rooftop terrace. The fettuccine, tortellini and gnocchi are all produced in-house, the pizzas (made of seasoned dough) are grilled rather than baked, and the fresh mint lemonade is incredible. All this, and the service is the most attentive in town.

Antojitos Mexicanos
STEAK $$
(Calle Playa Sur, Flores; grilled meats Q50-60; ☉ 7-10pm) Every evening at the foot of the causeway these characters fire up the grill and char steak, chicken and pork ribs of exceptional quality. Their specialty is *puyazo* (sirloin) swathed with garlic sauce. Sit outside facing the twinkly lights on the lake or if it's raining inside under a tin roof. Staff behave with all the formality of an elegant restaurant.

Raíces
STEAK $$
(☑ 7867-5743; Calle Sur, Flores; mains Q90-175; ☉ noon-10pm) A broad deck and a flaming grill are the main ingredients at this stylish lakefront restaurant-bar, possibly the prettiest setting in Flores for dinner. Chargrilled meats and seafood are the specialty; they also do wood-oven pizzas.

Restaurante El Peregrino
GUATEMALAN $$
(☑ 7867-5115; Av La Reforma, Flores; mains Q40-60; ☉ 7am-10pm) Part of the hotel of the same name, this humble *comedor* serves heaping helpings of home-cooked fare such as pork-belly stew and breaded tongue. Ask for the daily lunch specials (Q25).

🍸 Drinking & Nightlife

Flores' little Zona Viva is traditionally the strip of bars along Calle Sur, but there's plenty of action around the bend, along the lakefront promenade north of Hotel Santana.

Qué Pachanga
CLUB
(El Malecón, Flores) One of a pair of lively nightspots round the west side of the island, this room gets heavy most evenings, as young Guatemalans decked out in their tightest possible jeans gyrate to a continuous barrage of throbbing reggaetón and *cumbia* (Colombian dance tunes).

El Trópico
BAR
(Calle Sur, Flores; ☉ 4:30pm-1am Mon-Sat) Longest running of the bars along the southern bank, El Trópico supplies tacos and *cerveza* (beer) to a mostly older Guatemalan clientele. The candlelit terrace is a nice spot to start the night, as the lights of Santa Elena reflect pleasingly off the lake. Many Gallos later, the pulse picks up and DJs work the crowd.

Jamming
BAR
(Calle Sur, Flores) One of several nightlife venues along the southern bank, Jamming sports a reggae theme though there's more

Flores

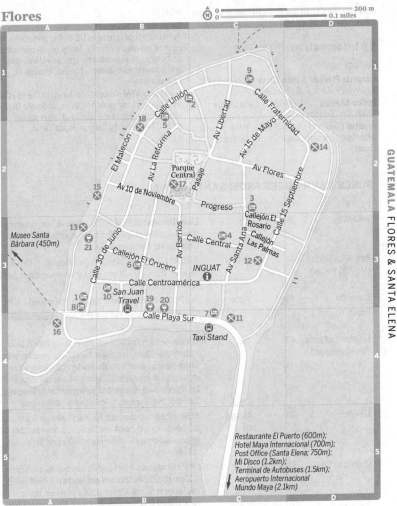

GUATEMALA FLORES & SANTA ELENA

Restaurante El Puerto (600m);
Hotel Maya Internacional (700m);
Post Office (Santa Elena; 750m);
Mi Disco (1.2km);
Terminal de Autobuses (1.5km);
Aeropuerto Internacional
Mundo Maya (2.1km)

Flores

Activities, Courses & Tours
Mayan Adventure ....(see 12)

Sleeping
1 Green World Hotel.................................. A3
2 Hospedaje Doña Goya............................B1
3 Hostal Frida...C2
4 Hostel Los Amigos................................C3
5 Hotel Aurora..B1
6 Hotel El Peregrino..................................B3
7 Hotel Flores de Petén.............................C4
8 Hotel Santana..A3
9 La Posada de Don José..........................C1
10 Posada de la Jungla.............................B3

Eating
11 Antojitos Mexicanos C4
12 Café Arqueológico Yaxha......................C3
13 Café/Bar Doña Goya A3
14 Cool Beans...D2
15 Las Mesitas..B2
16 Raíces...A4
17 Restaurante El Mirador.........................B2
Restaurante El Peregrino....... (see 6)
18 Terrazzo..B2

Drinking & Nightlife
19 El Trópico..B3
20 Jamming..B3
21 Qué Pachanga.......................................A3

beer guzzling than ganja smoking. It attracts a younger set of middle-class Guatemalans.

Information

EMERGENCY

Hospital Privado Santa Elena (☑7926-1140; 3a Av 4-29, Zona 2, Santa Elena)
Police Station (☑7926-1365; Calle Límite 12-28, San Benito)
Proatur (Tourist Police; ☑5414-3594; proatur. peten1@gmail.com; Calle Centro América, Flores)

MONEY

Banrural (Av Flores, Flores) bank, just off the Parque Central, changes US dollar and euros, cash or traveler's checks. Many travel agencies and places to stay will change cash US dollars and sometimes traveler's checks, though at poorer rates.

The only **ATM** (Calle 30 de Junio) in Flores is at the Fotomart convenience store, opposite Capitán Tortuga. There are plenty of other banks with ATMs along 4a Calle in Santa Elena.

BUSES & MINIBUSES FROM SANTA ELENA

DESTINATION	COST (Q)	DURATION	FREQUENCY & NOTES
Belize City	160	5hr	**Línea Dorada** (☑7924-8535) leaves at 7am, returning from Belize City at 1pm. This bus connects with boats to Caye Caulker & Ambergris Caye.
Bethel/La Técnica (Mexican border)	45	4-4½hr	**AMCRU** (☑3127-6684) runs 12 microbuses to Bethel between 4:15am & 4:30pm, eight of which continue on to La Técnica.
Carmelita	40	4½hr	Two Pinitas buses at 5am & 1pm from the market.
Cobán			Take a bus or minibus to Sayaxché, from where connecting microbuses leave for Cobán.
El Ceibo/La Palma (Mexican border)	40	4hr	El Naranjo–bound microbuses depart every 20min, from 4:20am to 6:30pm, stopping at the El Ceibo junction, from where there are shuttles to the border (Q10, 15min). Five of these go all the way to El Ceibo (Q45). At La Palma, on the Mexican side, you can find transportation to Tenosique, Tabasco (1hr), & onward to Palenque or Villahermosa.
El Remate	20	45min	**ATIM** (p209) microbuses leave every half hour from 6:30am to 7pm. Buses & minibuses to & from Melchor de Mencos will drop you at Puente Ixlú junction, 2km south of El Remate.
Guatemala City	130-225	8-9hr	Línea Dorada runs 4 first-class buses between 6:30am & 10pm (Q225). **Autobuses del Norte** (☑7924-8131) has buses at 9pm & 10pm (Q180). Fuente del Norte runs at least 11 buses between 4am & 10:30pm (Q130), including 5 deluxe buses (Q180).
Melchor de Mencos (Belizean border)	50	2hr	Microbuses go about every hour 5am to 6pm. Línea Dorada Pullmans en route to Belize City depart at 7am (Q40).
Poptún	30	2hr	Microbuses, via Dolores, every 10min 5am-7pm.
Puerto Barrios	115	6hr	Take a Guatemala City–bound Fuente del Norte bus & change at La Ruidosa junction, south of Río Dulce.
Río Dulce	100	4hr	Take a Guatemala City–bound bus with Fuente del Norte or Línea Dorada.
San Andrés/San José	8	35-40min	Microbuses depart around every 15min, from 5am-6:40pm, from the left side of the terminal entrance.
Sayaxché	23	1½hr	Microbuses depart about every 15min from 5:35am to 5pm.
Tikal	30	1¼hr	Six microbuses by **ATIM** (p209) between 6:30am & 3pm, the last returning at 5pm. You could also take the Uaxactún-bound bus (Q40) at 2pm, which goes a bit slower.

POST

Post Office (4a Calle & 4a Av; ⊗8am-5pm Mon-Sat)

TOURIST INFORMATION

INGUAT (⌨2421-2800, ext 6303; info-ciudad flores@inguat.gob.gt; Calle Centro América, Flores; ⊗8am-4pm Mon-Sat) The official INGUAT office provides basic information.

INGUAT (⌨7926-0533; info-mundomaya@in guat.gob.mx; Aeropuerto Internacional Mundo Maya; ⊗7am-noon & 3-5pm) Airport-based branch of the official tourist office.

TRAVEL AGENCIES

Martsam Travel (⌨7832-2742, US 1-866-832-2776; www.martsam.com; Calle 30 de Junio, Flores)

ⓘ Getting There & Away

AIR

Aeropuerto Internacional Mundo Maya is on the eastern outskirts of Santa Elena, 2km from the causeway connecting Santa Elena and Flores. **Avianca** (www.avianca.com) has two flights daily between here and Guatemala City. The Belizean airline **Tropic Air** (⌨7926-0348; www.tropicair.com) flies once a day to/from Belize City, charging around Q1500 each way for the one-hour trip.

BUS & MINIBUS

Long-distance buses use the Terminal Nuevo de Autobuses in Santa Elena, located 1.5km south of the causeway along 6a Av. It is also used by a slew of *aka expresos* (microbuses), with frequent services to numerous destinations. Second-class buses and some micros make an additional stop at 5a Calle, in the **market area** (the 'old' terminal) before heading out. You can reduce your trip time by 15 minutes by going straight to the market, though the vehicle may be full by then.

As always, schedules are highly changeable and should be confirmed before heading out.

SHUTTLE MINIBUS

Maayach Expeditions offers a shuttle service at 8am (Q150), picking up passengers from their hotels; purchase tickets at **San Juan Travel** (⌨4068-7616; Calle Playa Sur, Flores). San Juan Travel operates shuttle minibuses to Tikal (one way/return Q50/80). There are five departures between 4:30am and 1pm. Most hotels and travel agencies can book these shuttles and they will pick you up where you're staying. Returns leave Tikal at 12:30pm, 3pm and 5pm. If you know which round-trip you plan to be on, ask your driver to hold a seat for you or arrange one in another minibus. If you stay overnight in Tikal

and want to return to Flores by minibus, it's a good idea to reserve a seat with a driver when they arrive in the morning.

ⓘ Getting Around

A **taxi** from the airport to Santa Elena or Flores costs Q30. *Tuk-tuks* will take you anywhere between or within Flores and Santa Elena for Q5 to Q10; the *tuk-tuk* service stops after 7pm.

El Remate

This idyllic spot at the eastern end of Lago de Petén Itzá makes a good alternative base for Tikal-bound travelers – it's more relaxed than Flores, and closer to the site. Just two roads, really, El Remate has a ramshackle vibe all of its own.

El Remate begins 1km north of Puente Ixlú, where the road to the Belize border diverges from the Tikal road. The village strings along the Tikal road for 1km to another junction, where a branch heads west along the north shore of the lake.

El Remate is known for its wood carving. Some fine examples of the craft are sold from stalls along the main road.

⊙ Sights & Activities

Most El Remate accommodations can book two-hour boat trips for birdwatching or nocturnal crocodile spotting (each Q100 per person). Try Hotel Mon Ami (⌨3010-0284; www.hotelmonami.com; Jobompiche Rd), which also offers sunset lake tours with detours up the Ixlú and Ixpop rivers (Q150 per person).

Asunción, found by the second speed bump from the north shore junction, rents kayaks (Q35 per hour) and bicycles (Q10/70 per hour/day). He also guides horseback rides to Laguna Sacpetén and a small archaeological site there (Q150 per person, 2½ hours).

Biotopo Cerro Cahuí NATURE RESERVE
(Q40; ⊗7am-4pm) Comprising a 7.3-sq-km swath of subtropical forest rising up from the lake over limestone terrain, this nature reserve offers mildly strenuous hiking and excellent wildlife watching, with paths to some brilliant lookout points. As a bonus, there's an adjacent lakeside park with diving docks for a refreshing conclusion to the tour.

More than 20 mammal species roam the reserve, including spider and howler monkeys, white-tailed deer and the elusive Mesoamerican tapir. Bird life is rich and varied, with the opportunity to spot toucans, woodpeckers and the famous ocellated turkey, a big bird resembling a peacock. Trees include mahogany, cedar, ramón and cohune palm, along with many types of bromeliads, ferns and orchids.

A network of loop trails ascend the hill to three lookout points, affording views of the whole lake and Laguna Sacpetén to the east. The trail called Los Escobos (4km long, about 2¼ hours), through secondary growth forest, is good for spotting monkeys.

The admission fee includes the right to camp or sling your hammock under small thatch shelters inside the entrance. There are toilets and showers. The reserve is 1.75km west along the north shore road from El Remate.

🛏 Sleeping & Eating

Most hotels are set up for swimming in – and watching the sun set over – the lake.

Hotel Sun Breeze   HOTEL $
(☑ 5898-2665; sunbreezehotel@gmail.com; Main Rd; s/d Q80/120; ℗) The nearest place to the junction, this excellent-value homey guesthouse has neatly kept and well-ventilated rooms with screened windows and porches. Rear units are best, at the back of a pleasant patio. It's a short stroll to the public beach.

Posada Ixchel   HOTEL $
(☑ 3044-5379;   hotelixchel@yahoo.com;   s/d Q90/120) This family-owned place near the village's main junction is a superior deal, with spotless, wood-fragrant rooms featuring fans and handcrafted mosquito nets. The cobbled courtyard has inviting little nooks with tree-log seats.

Hotel Las Gardenias   HOTEL $
(☑ 5936-6984; www.hotelasgardenias.com; Ruta a Tikal; s/d from Q90/150, with air-con Q150/200; ❀ @ 🛜) Right at the junction with the north shore road, this cordial hotel/restaurant/shuttle operator has two sections: the wood-paneled rooms at the front are bigger, those in the rear are appealingly removed from the road. All feature comfortable beds with woven spreads, attractively tiled showers and porches with hammocks.

Casa de Doña Tonita   HOSTEL $
(☑ 5767-4065;   dm/s/d   Q30/40/80)   This friendly family-run place has four basic, adequately ventilated rooms, each with two single beds and screened windows, in a two-story clapboard *rancho* (small house), plus a dorm over the restaurant, which serves

tasty, reasonably priced meals. There's just one shower. Across the road is a pier's end hut for sunset gazing.

★ Las Orquídeas   ITALIAN $$
(☑ 5819-7232; Jobompiche Rd; pastas Q55-80; ⊗ noon-9pm Tue-Sun) Almost hidden in the forest, a 10-minute walk down the north shore from the Tikal junction, is this marvelous open-air dining hall. The genial Italian owner-chef blends *chaya*, a local herb, into his own tagliatelle and *panzarotti* (smaller version of calzones). There are tempting desserts, too.

ℹ Information

Horizontes Mayas (☑ 5825-8296; www. horizontesmayas.com; Ruta a Tikal) You can change US dollars and euros (at poor rates), or check your email, at this multi-service agency by the junction. It's also a good bet for shuttle services or tours to Tikal, Yaxhá and numerous other destinations.

ℹ Getting There & Around

El Remate is linked to Santa Elena by frequent minibus service (Q20) till around 7pm.

For Tikal, a collective shuttle departs at 5:30am, starting back at 2pm (one way/round trip Q30/50). Any El Remate accommodations can make reservations. Or catch one of the **ATIM** (p209) or **San Juan Travel** (p201) shuttles (Q20) passing through from Santa Elena to Tikal from 5am to 3:30pm.

For taxis, ask at **Hotel Sun Breeze**. A one-way ride to Flores costs about Q300; round trip to Tikal costs Q350.

For Melchor de Mencos on the Belizean border, get a minibus or bus from Puente Ixlú, 2km south of El Remate (Q20, 1¼ hours). Additionally, **Horizontes Mayas** offers daily departures to Belize City (Q150) via Melchor at 5:30am and 8am.

Tikal

The most striking feature of Tikal (☑ 2367-2837; www.parque-tikal.com; Q150; ⊗ 6am-6pm) is its towering, steep-sided temples, rising to heights of more than 44m, but what distinguishes it is its jungle setting. Its many plazas have been cleared of trees and vines, its temples uncovered and partially restored, but as you walk from one building to another you pass beneath the dense canopy of rainforest amid the rich, loamy aromas of earth and vegetation. Much of the delight of touring the site comes from strolling the broad causeways, originally built of packed limestone to accommodate traffic between temple complexes. By stepping softly you're more likely to spot monkeys, agoutis, foxes and ocellated turkeys.

Tikal is a popular day trip from Flores or El Remate, so is much quieter in the late afternoon and early morning, which makes an overnight stay an attractive option.

History

Tikal is set on a low hill, which becomes evident as you ascend to the Gran Plaza from the entry road. Affording relief from the surrounding swampy ground, this high terrain may explain why the Maya settled here around 700 BC. Another reason was the abundance of flint, used by the ancients to make clubs, spear points, arrowheads and knives. The wealth of this valuable stone meant good tools could be made, and flint could be traded for other goods. Within 200 years the Maya of Tikal had begun to build stone ceremonial structures, and by 200 BC there was a complex of buildings on the site of the Acrópolis del Norte.

Classic Period

The Gran Plaza was beginning to assume its present shape and extent by the time of Christ. By the dawn of the early Classic period, around AD 250, Tikal had become an important religious, cultural and commercial city with a large population. King Yax Ehb' Xooc, in power about AD 230, is looked upon as the founder of the dynasty that ruled Tikal thereafter.

Under Chak Tok Ich'aak I (King Great Jaguar Paw), who ruled in the mid-4th century, Tikal adopted a brutal method of warfare, used by the rulers of Teotihuacán in central Mexico. Rather than meeting their adversaries on the plain of battle in hand-to-hand combat, the army of Tikal used auxiliary units to encircle the enemy and throw spears to kill them from a distance. This first use of 'air power' among the Maya of Petén enabled Siyah K'ak' (Smoking Frog), the Tikal general, to conquer the army of Uaxactún; thus Tikal became the dominant kingdom in El Petén.

By the middle of the Classic period, in the mid-6th century, Tikal's military prowess and its association with Teotihuacán allowed it to grow until it sprawled over 30 sq km and had a population of perhaps 100,000. But in 553, Yajaw Te' K'inich II (Lord Water) came to the throne of Cara-

col (in southwestern Belize), and within a decade had conquered Tikal and sacrificed its king. Tikal and other Petén kingdoms suffered under Caracol's rule until the late 7th century when, under new leadership, it apparently cast off its oppressor and rose again.

Tikal's Renaissance

A powerful king named Ha Sawa Chaan K'awil (682–734, also called Ah Cacao or Moon Double Comb), 26th successor of Yax Ehb' Xooc, restored not only Tikal's military strength but also its primacy in the Maya world. He conquered the greatest rival Maya state, Calakmul in Mexico, in 695, and his successors were responsible for building most of the great temples around the Gran Plaza that survive today. King Ah Cacao was buried beneath the staggering height of Templo I.

Tikal's greatness waned around 900, but it was not alone in its downfall, which was part of the mysterious general collapse of lowland Maya civilization.

Rediscovery

No doubt the Itzáes, who occupied Tayazal (now Flores), knew of Tikal in the late Postclassic period. Perhaps they even came here to worship at the shrines of old gods. Spanish missionary friars who moved through El Petén after the conquest left brief references to these jungle-bound structures, but their writings moldered in libraries for centuries.

It wasn't until 1848 that the Guatemalan government sent out an expedition, under the leadership of Modesto Méndez and Ambrosio Tut, to visit the site. This may have been inspired by John L Stephens' bestselling accounts of fabulous Maya ruins, published in 1841 and 1843 (though Stephens never visited Tikal). Like Stephens, Méndez and Tut took an artist, Eusebio Lara, to record their archaeological discoveries. An account of their findings was published by the Berlin Academy of Science.

In 1877 the Swiss Dr Gustav Bernoulli visited Tikal. His explorations resulted in the removal of carved wooden lintels from Templos I and IV and their shipment to Basel, where they are still on view in the Museum für Völkerkunde.

Scientific exploration of Tikal began with the arrival of English archaeologist Alfred P Maudslay in 1881. Others continued his work, Teobert Maler, Alfred M Tozzer and RE Merwin among them. Tozzer worked at

Tikal

SURVEYING THE CLASSIC MAYA KINGDOM

Constructed in successive waves over a period of at least 800 years, Tikal is a vast, complicated site with hundreds of temples, pyramids and stelae. There's no way you'll get to it all in a day, but by following this itinerary you'll see many of the highlights. Before setting out be sure to stop by the visitor center and examine the scale model of the site. The small **Museo Sylvanus G Morley** 1 usually houses a wealth of kings, although the majority of its contents (other than Stela 31) are currently located in the CCIT research center while the museum is indefinitely under restoration. Present your ticket at the nearby control booth and when you reach the posted map, take a left. It's a 20-minute walk to the solitary **Templo VI** 2 . From here it's a blissful stroll up the broad Méndez causeway to the **Gran Plaza** 3 Tikal's ceremonial core, where you may examine the ancient precinct of the **North Acropolis** 4 . Exit the plaza west, and take the first left, along a winding path, to **Templo V** 5 . Round the rear to the right, a trail encircles the largely unexcavated South Acropolis to the **Plaza de los Siete Templos** 6 . Immediately west stands the great pyramid of the **Mundo Perdido** 7 . From here it's a quick stroll and a rather strenuous climb to the summit of **Temple IV** 8 , Tikal's tallest structure.

Templo IV
Arrive in the late afternoon to get magically tinted photos of Temples I, II and III poking through the jungle canopy. If you're lucky you might also get a glimpse of an orange-crested falcon swooping around the treetops.

Mundo Perdido
The smaller temple to the west of the great pyramid may look familiar to those who've visited Teotihuacán near Mexico City, with its elegant stepped *talud-tablero* design, a vivid reminder of that distant kingdom's influence.

TOP TIPS

» Bring food and water.
» If you enter after 3pm, your ticket is good for the next day.
» Stay at one of the onsite hotels to catch the sunset/sunrise.
» To watch the sunset/sunrise from Temple IV, you'll need to purchase an additional ticket (Q100).
» Bring mosquito repellent.

Gran Plaza
Though the surreally tall Templo I, a mausoleum to the Late Classic ruler Ah Cacao, is off-limits to climbers, you're welcome to ascend the almost-as-tall Templo II across the plaza.

North Acropolis
Amid the stack of smaller and much older temples that rise up the hillside north of the plaza, take a peek beneath the two thatched shelters on a ledge to find a pair of fearsome masks.

Museo Sylvanus G Morley
Volumes have been written about the remarkably preserved Stela 31, a portrait of the ruler Stormy Sky crowning himself, flanked by spear-toting warriors in the attire of (ally or overlord?) Teotihuacán.

Ticket Booth 1

Posted Map

Visitor Centre

CCIT

4

2

Templo VI
The secluded temple has a lengthy set of glyphs inscribed on the back of its lofty roof comb, recording the lineage of successive kingdoms. Be patient: the contents of the weathered slab may take some effort to discern.

Plaza de los Siete Templos
Seven miniature temples line up along the east side of this grassy courtyard. Climb the larger 'palace' at the south end to get a sightline along the septet.

Templo V
As steep as it is massive, Tikal's second tallest temple (52m) has unusual rounded corners. Tempting as it may seem to climb, the broad front staircase is off-limits.

Tikal on and off from the beginning of the 20th century until his death in 1954. The inscriptions at Tikal were studied and deciphered by Sylvanus G Morley.

Archaeological research and restoration was carried on by the University of Pennsylvania and the Guatemalan Instituto de Antropología e Historia until 1969. Since 1991, a joint Guatemalan-Spanish project has worked on conserving and restoring Templos I and V. The Parque Nacional Tikal (Tikal National Park) was declared a Unesco World Heritage Site in 1979.

◉ Sights

Gran Plaza

The path comes into the Gran Plaza around the Templo I, the Templo del Gran Jaguar (Temple of the Grand Jaguar). This was built to honor – and bury – Ah Cacao. The king may have worked out the plans for the building himself, but it was actually erected above his tomb by his son, who succeeded him to the throne in AD 734. The king's rich burial goods included stingray spines, which were used for ritual bloodletting, 180 jade objects, pearls and 90 pieces of bone carved with hieroglyphs. At the top of the 44m-high temple is a small enclosure of three rooms covered by a corbeled arch. The sapodilla-wood lintels over the doors were richly carved; one of them was removed and is now in a Basel museum. The lofty roofcomb that crowned the temple was originally adorned with reliefs and bright paint. When it's illuminated by the afternoon sun, it is still possible to make out the figure of a seated dignitary.

Although climbing to the top of Templo I is prohibited, the views from Templo II just across the way are nearly as awe-inspiring. Templo II, also known as the Temple of the Masks, was at one time almost as high as Templo I, but it now measures 38m without its roofcomb.

Nearby, the Acrópolis del Norte (North Acropolis) significantly predates the two great temples. Archaeologists have uncovered about 100 different structures, the oldest of which dates from before the time of Christ, with evidence of occupation as far back as 600 BC. The Maya built and rebuilt on top of older structures, and the many layers, combined with the elaborate burials of Tikal's early rulers, added sanctity and power to their temples. The final version of the acropolis, as it stood around AD 800, had more than 12 temples atop a vast platform,

many of them the work of King Ah Cacao. Look especially for the two huge, powerful wall masks, uncovered from an earlier structure and now protected by roofs. On the plaza side of the North Acropolis are two rows of stelae. These served to record the great deeds of the kings, to sanctify their memory and to add power to the temples and plazas that surrounded them.

Acrópolis Central

South and east of the Gran Plaza, this maze of courtyards, little rooms and small temples is thought by many to have been a palace where Tikal's nobles lived. Others think the tiny rooms may have been used for sacred rites and ceremonies, as graffiti found within them suggest. Over the centuries the configuration of the rooms was repeatedly changed, suggesting that perhaps this 'palace' was in fact a noble or royal family's residence and alterations were made to accommodate groups of relatives. A hundred years ago, one part of the acropolis provided lodgings for archaeologist Teobert Maler when he worked at Tikal.

Templo III & Plaza Oeste

West of the Gran Plaza, across the Calzada Tozzer (Tozzer Causeway) stands Templo III, still undergoing restoration. Only its upper reaches have been cleared. A scene carved into the lintel at its summit, 55m high, depicts a figure in an elaborate jaguar suit, believed to be the ruler Dark Sun. In front of it stands stela 24, which marks the date of its construction, AD 810. From this point, you can continue west to Templo IV along the Calzada Tozzer, one of several sacred byways between the temple complexes of Tikal.

Templo V & Acrópolis del Sur

Due south of the Gran Plaza, Templo V is a remarkably steep structure (57m) that was built sometime between the 7th and 8th centuries AD. It consists of seven stepped platforms and, unlike the other great temples, has slightly rounded corners. A recent excavation of the temple revealed a group of embedded structures, some with Maya calendars on their walls. Tempting as it may seem, you are not allowed to scale the broad central staircase.

Excavation has hardly even begun on the mass of masonry just west of the temple, known collectively as the Acrópolis del Sur (South Acropolis). The palaces on top are from the late-Classic period (the time of

King Moon Double Comb), but earlier constructions probably go back 1000 years.

Plaza de los Siete Templos

To the west of the Acrópolis del Sur is this broad grassy plaza, reached via a path to its southern edge. Built in the late-Classic period, the seven temples with their stout roofcombs line up along the east side of the plaza. On the south end stand three larger 'palaces'; on the opposite end is an unusual triple ballcourt.

El Mundo Perdido

About 400m southwest of the Gran Plaza is El Mundo Perdido (Lost World), a complex of 38 structures with a huge pyramid in its midst, thought to be essentially Preclassic (with some later repairs and renovations). The pyramid, 32m high and 80m along the base, is surrounded by four much-eroded stairways, with huge masks flanking each one. The stairway facing eastward is thought to have functioned as a platform for viewing the sun's trajectory against a trio of structures on a raised platform to the east, a similar arrangement to the astronomical observatory at Uaxactún. Tunnels dug into the pyramid by archaeologists reveal four similar pyramids beneath the outer face; the earliest (Structure 5C-54 Sub 2B) dates from 700 BC, making this pyramid the oldest Maya structure at Tikal.

A smaller temple to the west, dating from the early Classic period, demonstrates Teotihuacán's influence, with its *talud-tablero* style of architecture.

Templo IV & Complejo N

Templo IV, at 65m, is the highest building at Tikal and the second-highest pre-Columbian building known in the Western Hemisphere, after La Danta at El Mirador. It was completed about AD 741, probably by order of Ah Cacao's son, Yax Kin, who was depicted on the carved lintel over the middle doorway (now in a museum in Basel, Switzerland), as the western boundary of the ceremonial precinct. A steep wooden staircase leads to the top. The view east is almost as good as from a helicopter – a panorama across the jungle canopy, with (from left to right) the temples of the Gran Plaza, Temple III, Temple V (just the top bit) and the great pyramid of the Mundo Perdido poking through.

Between Templo IV and Templo III is Complejo N, an example of the 'twin-temple' complexes erected during the late-

Classic period. This one was built in AD 711 by Ah Cacao to mark the 14th *katun* (20-year cycle in the Maya calendar) of *baktún 9*. (A *baktún* equals about four centuries.) The king himself is portrayed on the remarkably preserved stela 16 in an enclosure just across the path. Beside the stela is altar 5, a circular stone depicting the same king accompanied by a priestly figure in the process of exhuming the skeleton of a female ruler.

Templo de las Inscripciones (Templo VI)

Templo VI is one of the few temples at Tikal to bear written records. On the rear of its 12m-high roofcomb is a long inscription – though it will take some effort to discern it in the bright sunlight – giving us the date AD 766. The sides and cornice of the roofcomb bear glyphs as well. Its secluded position, about a 25-minute walk southeast of the Gran Plaza along the Calzada Méndez, make it a good spot for observing wildlife. From here, it's a 20-minute hike back to the main entrance.

Northern Complexes

About 1km north of the Gran Plaza is Complejo P. Like Complejo N, it's a late-Classic twin-temple complex that probably commemorated the end of a *katun*. Complejo M, next to it, was partially torn down by the late-Classic Maya to provide building materials for a causeway, now named after Alfred P Maudslay, which runs southwest to Templo IV. Grupo H, northeast of Complexes P and M, with one tall, cleared temple, had some interesting graffiti within its temples.

Complejo Q and Complejo R, about 300m north of the Gran Plaza, are very late-Classic twin-pyramid complexes with stelae and altars standing before the temples. Complex Q is perhaps the best example of the twin-temple type, as it has been partly restored. Stela 22 and altar 10 are excellent examples of late-Classic Tikal relief carving, dated to AD 771.

Museums

CCIT   MUSEUM
(Centro de Conservación e Investigación de Tikal; ⊘8am-noon & 1-4pm) FREE This Japanese-funded research center is devoted to the identification and restoration of pieces unearthed at the site. The 1300-sq-meter facility has a huge cache of items to sort through, and you can watch the restorers at work. Though not strictly a museum per se, it features

an excellent gallery on the different materials used by Maya craftsmen.

The center will house the **Museo Sylvanus G Morley** (Museo Cerámico; Museum of Ceramics; Q30, also valid for Museo Lítico; ⊘8am-4pm) for an indefinite period while that museum is under restoration.

Museo Lítico MUSEUM
(Stone Museum; Q30, also valid for Museo Sylvanus G Morley; ⊘8am-4:30pm Mon-Fri, 8am-4pm Sat & Sun) The larger of Tikal's two museums is in the visitor center. It houses a number of carved stones from the ruins. The photographs taken by pioneer archaeologists Alfred P Maudslay and Teobert Maler of the jungle-covered temples, in various stages of discovery, are particularly striking. Outside is a model showing how Tikal would have looked around AD 800.

Tours

Archaeologist **Roxy Ortiz** (☑5197-5173; www.tikalroxy.blogspot.com) has 32 years' experience trekking throughout the Maya world and does early-morning tours around Tikal from her base at the Tikal Inn. She also does personalized treks to Uaxactún, Yaxhá and other less-visited sites with her 15-seat military vehicle.

Multilingual guides are available at the information kiosk. These authorized guides display their accreditation carnet, listing the languages they speak. Before 7am, the charge for a half-day tour is Q80 per person with a minimum of five persons. After that you pay Q475 for a group tour.

By the national park entrance **Canopy Tours Tikal** (☑5615-4988; www.tikalcanopy.com; tours Q230; ⊘7am-5pm) offers a one-hour tour through the forest canopy, with the chance to ride a harness along a series of cables linking trees up to 300m apart and to cross several hanging bridges. The fee includes transportation from Tikal or El Remate.

Sleeping & Eating

Staying overnight enables you to relax and savor the dawn and dusk, when most of the jungle birds and animals can be seen and heard (especially the howler monkeys). Other than camping, there are only three places to stay, and tour groups often have many of the rooms reserved. Almost any travel agency in Guatemala offers Tikal tours, including lodging, a meal or two, a guided tour and transportation.

There's no need to make reservations if you want to stay at Tikal's **campground** (campsite per person Q50, hammock with mosquito net Q85), behind the research center. This is a large, grassy area with a clean bathroom block and *palapa* (thatched-roof shelters) for hanging hammocks.

Along the right-hand side of the access road to Tikal stand a series of little *com-*

BIRDWATCHING

As well as howler and spider monkeys romping through the trees of Tikal, the plethora of birds flitting through the canopy and across the green expanses of the plazas is impressive. The ruined temple complexes present ideal viewing platforms for this activity, often providing the ability to look down upon the treetops to observe examples of the 300 or so bird species (migratory and resident) that have been recorded here. Bring binoculars and a copy of *The Birds of Tikal: An Annotated Checklist,* by Randell A Beavers, available at the visitor-center shop. Tread quietly and be patient, and you'll probably see some of the following birds in the areas specified:

Templo de las Inscripciones Tody motmots, four trogon species and royal flycatchers.

El Mundo Perdido Two oriole species, keel-billed toucans and collared aracaris.

Complejo P Great curassows, three species of woodpecker, crested guans, plain chachalacas and three tanager species.

Aguada Tikal (Tikal Reservoir) Three kingfisher species, jacanas, blue herons, two species of sandpiper, and great kiskadees.

Entrance path Tiger herons sometimes nest in the huge ceiba tree located here.

Complejo Q Red-capped and white-collared manakins.

Complejo R Emerald toucanets.

edores (cheap eateries), offering bland versions of standards such as grilled chicken and grilled steak (Q40 to Q50). All are open from 5am to 9pm daily. Another restaurant is in the visitor center, with pastas and hamburgers among the offerings.

Picnic tables beneath shelters are located just off Tikal's Gran Plaza, with soft-drink and water vendors standing by, but no food is sold. If you want to spend all day at the ruins without having to make the 20- to 30-minute walk back to the *comedores*, carry food and water with you.

Tikal Inn   HOTEL **$$**
(☎ 7861-2444; www.tikalinn.com; s/d Q500/730; P @ ☞ ☎) Built in the late '60s, this resort-style lodging offers rooms in the main building and thatched bungalows alongside the pool and rear lawn, with little porches out front. All are simple, spacious and quite comfortable. The most secluded accommodations are the least expensive, in a handful of cabins at the end of a sawdust trail through the forest.

Jungle Lodge   HOTEL **$$$**
(☎ 7861-0446; www.junglelodgetikal.com; s/d Q695/810, without bathroom Q370/385; P @ ☎) Nearest of the hotels to the site entrance, this was originally built to house archaeologists working at Tikal. Self-contained bungalows, plus a bank of cheaper units, are well spaced throughout rambling, jungle grounds. Some newer suites feature jungle-chic decor and outdoor rain-showers. The restaurant-bar (mains Q80 to Q100) serves veggie pastas, crepes and other international dishes in a tropical ambiance.

Jaguar Inn   HOTEL **$$$**
(☎ 7926-2411; www.jaguartikal.com; campsite per person Q50, with tent Q115, s/d/tr Q580/695/925; P ✳ @ ☞) The inn of choice for youthful, independent travelers has duplex and quad bungalows with thatched roofs and hammocks on the porches, plus a smart little restaurant with a popular terrace out front. For those on a tight budget there are tents for rent on a platform.

ℹ Orientation

The archaeological site is at the center of the 550-sq-km Parque Nacional Tikal. The road from Flores enters the park 19km south of the ruins. From the parking lot at the site, it's a short walk back to the junction where there's an information kiosk. Immediately south of this junction, a visitor center sells books, maps, souvenirs, hats, insect repellent, sun block and other necessities; it also houses a restaurant and **museum** (p208). Near the visitor center are Tikal's three hotels, a campground, a few small *comedores* (cheap eateries) and a modern research center containing a second **museum** (p208).

It's a five-minute walk from the ticket control booth to the entry gate. Just beyond, there's a large map posted. From here, it's a 1.5km walk (20 minutes) southwest to the Gran Plaza. From the Gran Plaza west to Templo IV it's over 600m.

ℹ Information

Everyone must purchase a ticket at the entry gate on the road in; tickets purchased after 3pm are valid for the whole next day. Those staying more than one day can purchase additional tickets at the ticket control booth along the path to the site entrance. Seeing the sunrise from Templo IV at the west end of the main site is possible from about October to March, but to enter the park before or after visiting hours you must purchase an additional ticket for Q100, presumably to pay the guide who must accompany you.

The core of the ancient city takes up about 16 sq km, with more than 4000 structures. To visit all the major building complexes, you must walk at least 10km, so wear comfortable shoes with good rubber treads that grip well. The ruins here can be slick from rain and organic material, especially during the wet season. Bring plenty of water, as you'll be walking around all day in the heat.

Please don't feed the coatis *(pisotes)* that wander about the site.

The **Jaguar Inn** will exchange US dollars cash and traveler's checks (at a poor rate).

ℹ Getting There & Away

Six microbuses by **Asociación de Transportistas Imperio Maya** (ATIM; ☎ 5905-0089) depart Flores between 6:30am and 3pm (Q30, 1½ hours), the last returning at 5pm. They return from Tikal at noon, 1:30pm, 3pm and 6pm. You could also take the Uaxactún-bound bus from the market of Santa Elena at 3:30pm, which goes a bit slower. **San Juan Travel** (p201) runs five shuttles daily from Flores (one-way/return Q50/80, including guide Q150) between 4:30am and 1pm, the last returning at 6pm.

From El Remate a collective shuttle departs at 5:30am for Tikal, starting back at 2pm (Q30/50 one way/return). Any El Remate accommodations can make reservations.

If traveling from Belize, get a Santa Elena–bound microbus to Puente Ixlú, sometimes called El Cruce, and switch there to a northbound microbus for the remaining 36km to Tikal.

Heading from Tikal to Belize, start early and get off at Puente Ixlú to catch a bus or microbus eastward. Be wary of shuttles to Belize advertised at Tikal: these have been known to detour to Flores to pick up passengers!

Uaxactún

POP 700

Uaxactún (wah-shahk-*toon*), 23km north of Tikal along an unpaved road through the jungle, was Tikal's political and military rival in late Preclassic times. It was conquered by Tikal's Chak Tok Ich'aak I (King Great Jaguar Paw) in the 4th century, and was subservient to its great sister to the south for centuries thereafter, though it experienced an apparent resurgence during the Terminal Classic, after Tikal went into decline.

Villagers make an income from collecting chicle (a natural gum), *pimienta* (allspice) and *xate* (low-growing palm, exported to Holland for floral arrangements) in the surrounding forest. In the *xate* warehouse on the west end of town, women put together bunches of the plants for export.

Much of the attraction here is the absolute stillness and isolation. Few visitors make it up this way.

At the time of writing there was no cellphone coverage and just one public phone, in an office (⊙to 6pm) on the south side of the airstrip.

◯ Sights

Research performed by the Carnegie Institute in the 1920s and '30s laid the groundwork for much of the archaeological study that followed in the region, including the excavations at Tikal.

The fee of Q50 to enter Uaxactún is collected at the gate to Parque Nacional Tikal, though there is no ticket control at the site itself.

Grupo E

The buildings here are grouped on five low hills. From the airstrip find the sign pointing to Grupo E between the Catholic and Evangelical churches on the right side, from where it's a 10- to 15-minute walk. The most significant temple here is Templo E-VII-Sub, among the earliest intact temples excavated, with foundations going back perhaps to 2000 BC. The pyramid is part of a group with astronomical significance: seen from it, the sun rises behind Templo E-I on the longest day of the year and behind Templo

E-III on the shortest day. The four jaguar and serpent masks affixed to the main temple's staircase were painstakingly restored in 2014 by a group of Slovak archaeologists, but then covered up again for conservation.

Grupos B & A

About a 20-minute walk to the northwest of the airstrip are Grupo B and Grupo A, the latter featuring the more formidable structures around the city's main square. Palacio V, on the east side of the square, is considered a model for Tikal's North Acropolis. In 1916 the American archaeologist Sylvanus Morley uncovered a stela dating from the 8th *baktún* (Maya calendar term) at Grupo A. Thus the site was called Uaxactún, meaning 'eight stone.' Behind Palacio V, along a path back toward the village, is the imposing Palacio A-XVIII, affording the most panoramic view of the site from its summit.

Stela 5, at Grupo B, displays Tikal's signature glyph, from which archaeologists deduced that Uaxactún was under that city's sway by the date inscribed, AD 358.

🛏 Sleeping & Eating

If you arrive here by public bus, you'll need to spend the night, since the only return trip is early in the morning. There are two places to stay, one basic, the other rustic.

A few basic cookshacks provide food, including Comedor Uaxactún (mains Q20; ⊙8am-8pm) and Comedor Imperial Okan Arin (mains Q20; ⊙7am-7pm), and the village's main lodging prepares all meals.

Posada & Restaurante
Campamento El Chiclero   HOTEL $
(☎7783-3931; campamentochiclero@gmail.com; campsite/r per person Q30/Q75) On the north side of the airstrip, this place has 10 spartan, institutional green rooms underneath a thatched roof, with decent mattresses and mosquito-netted ceilings and windows. Clean showers and toilets are in an adjacent outbuilding; lights out at 9pm. Perky owner Neria does the best food in town (Q50 for soup and a main course with rice).

Aldana's Lodge   HUT $
(☎7783-3931; campsite/r per person Q20/Q25) To the right off the street leading to Grupos B and A, the Aldana family offers half a dozen clapboard cabins, with thin mattresses on pallets. Father and son Alfido and Hector Aldaña lead tours to jungle sites, and Amparo prepares good meals.

ℹ Getting There & Away

A Pinita bus leaves the main terminal of Santa Elena for Uaxactún (Q40) at 2:15pm, then migrates to the market terminal, finally leaving town at 3:30pm. This bus passes through El Remate around 4:30pm and Tikal by 5pm. The following day it starts back for Santa Elena from Uaxactún at 7am. This means you'll need to spend two nights in Uaxactún to see the ruins. Otherwise, tours from El Remate to Uaxactún and back by **Casa de Don David** (☏ 5306-2190; www.lacasadedondavid.com; Jobompiche Rd) cost Q615 for up to five persons.

If you're driving, the last chance to fill your fuel tank as you come from the south is at Puente Ixlú, just south of El Remate. During the rainy season (from May to October, sometimes extending into November), the road from Tikal to Uaxactún can become pretty muddy. From Uaxactún, unpaved roads lead to other ruins at El Zotz (about 30km southwest), Xultún (35km northeast) and Río Azul (100km northeast).

Yaxhá

The Classic Maya sites of Yaxhá, Nakum and El Naranjo form a triangle that is the basis for a national park covering more than 370 sq km and bordering the Parque Nacional Tikal to the west. Yaxhá, the most visited of the trio, stands on a hill between two sizable lakes, Lago Yaxhá and Lago Sacnab. The setting, the sheer size of the site, the number of excellently restored buildings and the abundant jungle flora and fauna all make it particularly worth visiting. The site is 11km north of the Puente Ixlú–Melchor de Mencos road, accessed via unpaved road from a turnoff 32km from Puente Ixlú and 33km from Melchor de Mencos.

ℹ Getting There & Away

Agencies in Flores and El Remate offer organized trips to Yaxhá, some combined with Nakum and/or Tikal. **Horizontes Mayas** (p202) in El Remate runs tours (Q125 per person, minimum three persons), including guide and entrance fee, at 7am and 1pm, returning at 1pm and 6:30pm. Otherwise, take a Melchor de Mencos–bound microbus and get off at Restaurante El Portal de Yaxhá, opposite the Yaxhá turnoff, and they can arrange transportation to the site by pick-up truck or motorcycle (Q65 return).

El Mirador

Buried within the furthest reaches of the Petén jungle, just 7km south of the Mexi-

can border, the late-Preclassic metropolis at **El Mirador** (Lookout; www.miradorbasin.com; ⊘24hr) **FREE** contains the largest cluster of buildings of any single Maya site, among them the biggest pyramid ever built in the Maya world. Ongoing excavations have only scratched the surface, so many are still hidden beneath the jungle.

El Mirador was so-named by local *chicleros* (chicle harvesters) for the excellent views provided by some of the pyramids. La Danta (the Tapir) looms 70m above the forest floor. El Tigre is 55m high with a base covering 18,000 sq meters. At its height, the city spread over 16 sq km and supported tens of thousands of citizens. It was certainly the greatest Maya city of the Preclassic era, far exceeding in size anything built subsequently in the Maya world.

ℹ Getting There & Away

A visit to El Mirador involves an arduous jungle trek of at least five days and four nights (it's about 60km each way), with no facilities or amenities aside from what you carry in and what can be rustled from the forest. During the rainy season, especially September to December, the mud can make it extremely difficult; February to June is the best period to attempt a trek.

The trip usually departs from a cluster of houses called Carmelita, 82km up the road from Flores. The **Comisión de Turismo Cooperativa Carmelita** (☏ 7861-2641, 7861-2639; www.turismocooperativacarmelita.com), a group of 16 INGUAT-authorized guides, can make all arrangements for a trek to El Mirador, with optional visits to the Preclassic sites of Nakbé, El Tintal, Wakná and Xulnal. Travelers who participate in these treks should be in good physical shape, able to withstand high temperatures (average of nearly 38°C/100°F) and humidity (average 85%), and be prepared to hike or ride long distances (up to 30km per day).

On the first day of a typical six-day itinerary, you'll hike six hours through mostly agricultural country to El Tintal, where you camp for the night. On the second day, after a look around El Tintal, you proceed through denser forests to El Mirador and set up camp there. The next day is reserved for exploring El Mirador. On day four, you hike four hours southeast to arrive at Nakbé and camp there. The next day the expedition begins the return south via an eastern trail, stopping for the night at the site of La Florida. On day six, you head back to Carmelita.

For a five-/six-/seven-day trip, the cooperative charges Q1915/2300/2700 per person in a group of at least three people. The fee includes tents, hammocks and mosquito netting; all meals and drinking water; Spanish-speaking guide; mules and muleskinners; and first-aid supplies.

Two buses daily travel from Flores to Carmelita, at 5am and 1pm (Q40). Generally you'd take the morning bus and start hiking straight away.

If you'd like to discuss the options and make arrangements, visit the cooperative's **agency in Flores** (☏ 7867-5629; Calle Centro América).

It's also possible to get here from Uaxactún, a longer but gentler approach, since there are fewer *bajos* (seasonal swamps) and it's less affected by agricultural clearing so you're underneath the jungle canopy from the outset. **Posada Campamento El Chiclero** (p210) offers a six-day tour at Q1900 per person per day. The first leg of the journey you're driven in a monster truck to a campground at the former *chiclero* (chicle harvesters) camp of Yucatán, a five-hour journey. The next morning the group is outfitted with mules and proceeds to another camp, La Leontina, a four-hour tramp through the jungle. The following day it's a three-hour walk to Nakbé. After visiting that site, the expedition continues to El Mirador. The journey back follows the same route in reverse.

If expense is not a concern, you can go the easy way: by helicopter. During selected periods throughout the year, **TAG Airlines** (☏ 2380-9400; www.tag.com.gt) offers chopper packages from Flores to El Mirador, including guided commentary by longtime site archaeologist Richard Hansen, plus meals and accommodations for about Q10,340 per person. Contact the airline to find out about the current schedule.

REMOTE MAYA SITES

The Petén region is literally brimming with archaeological sites in various stages of excavation. Some are harder than others to get to; tour operators in Flores and El Remate can help you reach them. Here are a few of the more intriguing ones that you might want to check out:

San Bartolo Discovered in 2003, this site features one of the best-preserved Maya murals with a depiction of the creation myth from the Popul Vuh. It's approximately 40km northeast of Uaxactún, near the Río Azul.

Piedras Negras On the banks of the Río Usumacinta amid black cliffs, these remote ruins boast impressive carvings and a sizable acropolis complex. It was here that part-time archaeologist Tatiana Proskouriakoff deciphered the Maya hieroglyphic system.

La Blanca Located along the Río Mopan near the Belize border, this palatial complex may have flourished as a trading center in the late Classic period. The acropolis is notable for its remarkably preserved stone walls and an abundance of graffiti. Currently under excavation by a Spanish team. The **Mayan Adventure** (☏ 5830-2060; www.the-mayan-adventure.com; Calle 15 de Septiembre), based in Flores, leads tours here.

El Zotz This sprawling site occupies its own biotope abutting Parque Nacional Tikal. Of the three barely excavated temples, one, the Pirámide del Diablo, can be scaled for views all the way to Tikal. Stick around till dusk to see how the place gets its name – 'The Bat' in Maya. Researchers from the University of Southern California are currently uncovering 23 masks within the tombs of the largest pyramid. INGUAT-authorized guides from the community of Cruce dos Aguadas (42km north of Flores) lead tours to El Zotz, a 24km hike east through the jungle.

Río Azul Located up near the corner where the Belize, Guatemala and Mexico borders meet, this medium-sized site fell under the domain of Tikal in the early Classic period and became a key trading post for cacao from the Caribbean. Most notable are the tombs with vibrant painted glyphs inside. **Campamento El Chiclero** (p210) in Uaxactún leads a recommended excursion.

Naranjo Major excavations and restorations are currently going on at this immense site 12km from the Belize border. In the process archaeologists have ascertained that the city was more densely populated than Tikal and possibly larger. Ruled by Princess Six Sky, daughter to a Dos Pilas governor, Naranjo conquered neighboring kingdoms and produced some of the most refined art in the Maya world. Contact **Río Mopan Lodge** (☏ 7926-5196; avinsa@yahoo.com) about visiting the site.

UNDERSTAND GUATEMALA

Guatemala Today

Guatemalans are struggling. Over half the population lives below the poverty line and gang membership is rising as an overwhelmed and under-resourced police force struggles to maintain order. Against this increasingly bleak backdrop, scores of grassroots organizations have sprung up, tirelessly combating Guatemala's many problems. While successive governments continue to make promises, it is Guatemalans themselves who are delivering solutions.

Neither Corrupt nor a Thief

The elections that followed ex-president Otto Pérez Molina's impeachment were won by Jimmy Morales, a popular television comic whose popularity partly stemmed from the fact that he came from outside the country's political elite. Morales ran with the slogan 'Ni corrupto, ni ladrón' (neither corrupt nor a thief), which obviously touched some chords in a country that now had its previous president and vice-president in jail. Morales took office in January 2016. Hopes were high that change was finally in the air, but the new president's ties to the military establishment (themselves seen as the core of the country's real political elite) gave way to concerns that the country was in for more of the same, again.

A Question of Security

Guatemala still struggles with violence. The National Gun Registry campaign started off well, but continues to falter. There are 11 guns for every 100 people in Guatemala, of which only three are registered.

The police force, understaffed and under-resourced, has struggled to keep up with the rise in drug-related crime, particularly in urban areas and most notably in Guatemala City. A measure of their failure to do so is the fact that there are an estimated 150,000 private security guards employed nationwide, compared to just 30,000 police officers. It won't take you too long on your travels before you start spotting heavily armed young (sometimes scarily young) men in official-looking uniforms, guarding everything from private residences to pharmacies and fast-food restaurants.

Global Policy

Global policy continues to affect Guatemala. A possibly unforeseen consequence of the move toward renewable fuels worldwide has seen corn-tortilla prices skyrocket in Guatemala, as the United States uses up to 40% of its corn crop to make biofuel. Corn is a staple in Guatemala – pretty much the one ingredient you are guaranteed to see at every meal – and despite widespread plantations the country pays over US$200 million per year to import corn.

One very touchy subject in rural Guatemala has to do with large (often foreign-administered) projects such as hydroelectric dams and mineral mines. Amnesty International reports state that international companies regularly flaunt human-rights conventions when displacing local communities, and that the worst-affected are impoverished rural indigenous communities.

The Slow Road to Recovery

Guatemala is on the slow road to recovery from its civil war wounds. While this is in part due to the passing of generations who lived through the war, official recognition of some atrocities has been an important step in the recovery process. Though President Morales has stated he does not believe the genocide in the Ixil triangle ever took place, a campaign is underway to exhume clandestine cemeteries used by the military to bury 'disappeared' dissidents and the legal processes have at last begun, with some war criminals being brought to justice. So far the heftiest penalty to be handed down was to ex-military commissioner Lucas Tecún, who was sentenced to 7710 years in prison.

In March 2012, in a move that shocked many hardened cynics, a Guatemalan judge removed the final obstacle barring former dictator Efraín Ríos Montt from facing trial on charges of genocide. At first he was convicted to 80 years in prison, but a later court ruling overturned the conviction, then called for a retrial, citing Ríos Montt's alleged senility.

Grass Roots Movement

In the face of official indifference and/or inability to deal with the country's myriad problems, many community-based organizations and NGOs are moving in to fill the void. Large segments of the Guatemalan population are becoming active in volunteer work, focusing on everything from neighborhood-watch-type programs in areas unpatrolled by police to larger efforts focusing on food security and housing for the poor. This community spirit is also evident after natural disasters hit the country, as citizens band together to deliver aid to affected families.

The mass protests against the Pérez Molina government, mainly non-politically aligned and organized chiefly through social media, seem to have sparked a new interest in politics among young Guatemalans, with alliances being formed from previously disparate groups.

History

Earliest estimates put humans in what is now Guatemala as far back as 11,000 BC. The prevailing theory is that they got here by walking across an ice bridge from Siberia. The development of agriculture and resulting improvement in the stability of the food supply led to population growth, the development of early art forms and a language that is traceable to what many Maya speak today.

Rise & Fall of the Maya

Further developments in agriculture and increases in population gave these early civilizations time and resources to develop artistic and architectural techniques.

Between 800 BC and AD 100, population centers such as El Mirador and Kaminaljuyú grew with trade and conquest and hundreds (if not thousands – many are yet to be uncovered) of temples and ceremonial centers were built. Guatemala's most famous Maya site, Tikal, came into its own around the start of the Classic period – AD 250.

The history of these – and many other – city states was troubled at best, characterized by broken military alliances, food shortages and droughts.

By the early 16th century, Maya civilization was already in trouble. Some centers, such as El Mirador, had already been abandoned and others, such as Tikal and Quiriguá, had shrunk to the size of minor towns. Theories suggest that many abandoned El Petén in favor of the highlands, setting up capitals in K'um'arkaj, Iximché, Zaculeu and Mixco Viejo.

Relocation didn't bring peace, though – soon Toltec tribes, having abandoned the Yucatán, moved in and began to take control. Infighting among tribes, overpopulation and the resulting strain on the food supply combined to make conditions very favorable to the Spanish when they arrived in 1523.

Conquest & Colonization

The Spanish didn't just walk on in, as many think. Spirited resistance was met, most notably from the K'iche' (Quiché; in a famous battle led by Tecún Umán, near present-day Quetzaltenango). Neighboring Kaqchiquel not only refused to join forces with the K'iche', they joined the Spanish and fought against them.

It didn't take long for the Spanish to turn on the Kaqchiquel, though, and pretty soon most of the Maya were under Spanish control, the exceptions being the Rabinal (who have largely maintained their culture) and the Itzáes, who, hidden out on the island of Flores in El Petén were unconquered until 1697.

Independence & the 19th Century

By the time thoughts of independence from Spain began stirring among Guatemalans, society was already rigidly stratified. Angered at being repeatedly passed over for advancement, Guatemalan *criollos* (Guatemalan-born Spaniards) successfully rose in revolt in 1821. Independence changed little for Guatemala's indigenous communities, who remained under the control of the church and the landowning elite.

During the short existence of the United Provinces of Central America, liberal president Francisco Morazán (1830–39) instituted reforms aimed at correcting three persistent problems: the overwhelming power of the church; the division of society into a Hispanic upper class and an indigenous lower class; and the region's impotence in world markets.

But unpopular economic policies, heavy taxes and an 1837 cholera epidemic led to an indigenous uprising that brought conservative Rafael Carrera to power. Carrera ruled until 1865 and undid many of Morazán's achievements.

The liberals regained power in the 1870s under president Justo Rufino Barrios, a coffee-plantation owner who embarked on a program of modernization – constructing roads, railways, schools and a modern banking system – and did everything possible to encourage coffee production, including promoting forced relocation and labor. Succeeding governments generally pursued the same policies, maintaining control by a wealthy minority and repression of opposition.

The Early 20th Century

From 1898 to 1920, Manuel Estrada Cabrera ruled as a dictator, bringing progress in technical matters but placing a heavy burden on all but the ruling oligarchy. He fancied himself a bringer of light and culture to a backward land, styling himself the 'Teacher and Protector of Guatemalan Youth.'

When Estrada Cabrera was overthrown, Guatemala entered a period of instability that ended in 1931 with the election of General Jorge Ubico, who modernized the country's health and social welfare infrastructure but was forced into exile in 1944.

Philosopher Juan José Arévalo came to power in 1945, establishing the nation's social security system, a bureau of indigenous affairs, a modern public health system and liberal labor laws. His six years as president saw 25 coup attempts by conservative military forces.

Arévalo was succeeded in 1951 by Colonel Jacobo Arbenz Guzmán, who looked to break up estates and foster high productivity on small farms. But in 1954 (in one of the first documented covert CIA operations) the US government orchestrated an invasion from Honduras led by two exiled Guatemalan military officers. Arbenz was forced to step down and land reform never took place. Violence, oppression and disenfranchisement ensued, fueling the formation of left-wing guerilla groups.

Civil War

During the 1960s and '70s, economic inequality and the developing union movement forced oppression to new heights. Amnesty International estimates that 50,000 to 60,000 Guatemalans were killed during the political violence of the 1970s. In 1976 an earthquake killed about 22,000 people and left around a million homeless.

In 1982 General José Efraín Ríos Montt initiated a 'scorched earth' policy. Huge numbers of people – mainly indigenous men – from more than 400 villages were murdered in the name of anti-insurgency, stabilization and anticommunism. An estimated 15,000 civilians were tortured and massacred; 100,000 refugees fled to Mexico. In response, four guerrilla organizations united to form the URNG (Guatemalan National Revolutionary Unity).

In August 1983 Ríos Montt was deposed in a coup led by General Oscar Humberto Mejía Victores, but human-rights abuses continued. The US suspended military aid, and 1985 saw the election of civilian Christian Democrat Marco Vinicio Cerezo Arévalo – but the military had secured immunity from prosecution and armed conflict festered in remote areas.

The Signing of the Peace Accords

In 1996 Álvaro Enrique Arzú Irigoyen of the middle-right PAN (Partido de Avanzada Nacional) was elected. In December he and the URNG signed peace accords ending the 36-year civil war – a war in which an estimated 200,000 Guatemalans were killed, a million were left homeless and untold thousands 'disappeared.'

The accords called for accountability for the armed forces' human-rights violations and resettlement of one million refugees. They also addressed the identity and rights of indigenous peoples, health care, education and other basic social services, women's rights, the abolition of compulsory military service and the incorporation of the ex-guerrillas into civilian life.

It's been a rocky road since the war's end. The greatest challenge to peace stems from inequities in the power structure. It's estimated that 70% of the country's arable land is owned by less than 3% of the population. According to a UN report, the top 20% of the population has an income 30 times greater than the bottom 20%. Or, as many Guatemalans will tell you, there are seven families who 'own' Guatemala.

Guatemala in the 21st Century

Any hopes for a truly just and democratic society have looked increasingly frayed in the years since 1996. International organizations regularly criticize the state of human rights in the country and Guatemalan human-rights campaigners are threatened or simply disappear on a regular basis. The major problems – poverty, illiteracy, lack of education and poor medical facilities (all much more common in rural areas, where the Maya population is concentrated) – remain a long way from being solved.

The 1999 presidential elections brought Alfonso Portillo of the conservative Frente Republicano Guatemalteco (FRG) to power. Portillo was seen as a front man for FRG leader, ex-president General Efraín Ríos Montt. Portillo fled the country at the end of his presidency in the face of allegations that he had diverted US$500 million from the treasury to personal and family bank accounts. Having evaded prosecution for years, Portillo was charged by the United States for laundering money using US banks, and looks set to be extradited and put on trial there.

Ríos Montt was granted permission by Guatemala's constitutional court to stand in the 2003 elections, despite the fact that the constitution banned presidents who had taken power by coup in the past, as Ríos Montt had in 1982.

In the end Guatemala's voters dealt Ríos Montt a resounding defeat, electing Oscar Berger of the moderately conservative Gran Alianza Nacional (GANA) as president. Berger managed to stay relatively untouched by political scandal, critics saying this was because he didn't really do anything, let alone anything bad.

The Central America Free Trade Agreement (CAFTA; TLC or Tratado de Libre Comercio, in Spanish) was ratified by Guatemala in 2006. Supporters claim it frees the country up for greater participation in foreign markets, while detractors state that the agreement is a bad deal for the already disenfranchised rural poor.

Another round of elections was held in late 2007, bringing to power Álvaro Colom of the center-leftist Unidad Nacional de la Esperanza (UNE). Colom followed Berger's example of steady, minimalist governance and spearheaded some much-needed improvements to the country's infrastructure. Unfortunately, his entire presidency was dogged by corruption claims, from straight-out vote buying to back-room deals granting contracts to companies who had contributed to his campaign fund.

But probably the most bizarre twist of the Colom presidency happened as he was leaving office. The Guatemalan constitution prohibits members of the president's family from running for the subsequent presidency (supposedly an anti-dictatorship measure), so Colom and his wife filed for divorce in the lead-up to the 2011 elections in an attempt to make her a valid candidate. The Constitutional Court banned her candidature anyway, leaving the door open for hard-line ex-civil war general Otto Pérez Molina to take office in early 2012.

Pérez Molina's election was always going to be controversial – he was a general in Ríos Montt's army in the period where the worst atrocities occurred, in the regions where they occurred. Guatemalans had grown tired of the growing lawlessness in their country, though, and turned a blind eye to history in the hope that Molina would deliver on his two campaign promises – jobs and security.

Despite some heavy-handed reactions to protesters (the army killed seven and wounded 40 in one incident at an anti-dam and anti-mining protest), Pérez Molina did little to combat real crime, and his early presidency was plagued by vague rumors of corruption in the administration. In April 2015, the UN anti-corruption agency CICIG issued a report and things got a whole lot less vague.

The report claimed several senior members of the Pérez Molina administration were involved in taking bribes from importers in return for reduced customs fees. Within days, mass protests were organized over social media and tens of thousands turned out in downtown Guatemala City. Vice president Roxana Baldetti was the first to go – she resigned in early May, unable to explain how she paid for her US$13 million helicopter, among other things.

In the following months more than 20 officials resigned and many were arrested as the scandal snaked its way to the top. Mass protests continued as more findings were released. Baldetti was arrested in August amid calls for Pérez Molina's impeachment. The president hung on for a few weeks more, then resigned in the face of impending impeachment. He was arrested in early September.

Culture

The National Psyche

You'll be amazed when you first reach Guatemala just how helpful, polite and unhurried Guatemalans are. Everyone has time to stop and chat and explain what you want to know. Most Guatemalans like to get to know other people without haste, feeling for common ground and things to agree on.

What goes on behind this outward politeness is harder to encapsulate. Few Guatemalans exhibit the stress, worry and hurry of the 'developed' nations, but this obviously isn't because they don't have to worry about money or employment. They're a long-suffering people who don't expect wealth or good government but make the best of what comes their way – friendship, their family, a good meal, a bit of good company.

Outwardly, it appears that family ties are strong, but beneath the surface you may find that the real reason that three generations live together in one house has more to do with economics than affection.

Guatemalans are a religious bunch – agnostics and atheists are very thin on the ground. People will often ask what religion you are quite early in a conversation. Unless you really want to get into it, saying 'Christian' generally satisfies. Orthodox Catholicism is gradually giving way to evangelical Protestantism among the *ladinos* (persons of mixed indigenous and European race), with the animist-Catholic syncretism of the traditional Maya always present.

Some say that Guatemala has no middle class, just a ruling class and an exploited class. It's true that Guatemala has a small, rich, *ladino* ruling elite; it also has an indigenous Maya population, which tends to be poor, poorly educated and poorly provided for.

But as well as these two groups, there's a large group of poor and middle-class *ladinos,* with aspirations influenced by education, TV, international popular music and North America (of which many Guatemalans have direct experience as migrant workers) – and maybe by liberal ideas of equality and social tolerance. This segment of society has its bohemian/student/artist circles whose overlap with educated, forward-looking Maya may hold the greatest hope for progress toward an equitable society.

Lifestyle

The majority of Guatemalans live in one-room brick or concrete houses, or traditional *bajareque,* with roofs of tin, tiles or thatch. They have earth floors, a stove/fireplace and minimal possessions – often just a couple of bare beds and a few pots. Thus live most of Guatemala's Maya majority, in the countryside, in villages and in towns.

The few wealthier Maya and most *ladino* families have larger houses in towns and the bigger villages, but their homes may still not be much more than one or two bedrooms and a kitchen that also serves as a living area. Middle-class families in the wealthier suburbs of Guatemala City live in good-sized one- or two-story houses with gardens. The elite few possess rural as well as urban properties – for example a comfortable farmhouse on the Pacific Slope, or a seaside villa on the coast.

Despite modernizing influences, traditional family ties remain strong. Extended-family groups gather for weekend meals and vacations. Old-fashioned gender roles are strong too: many women have jobs to increase the family income but few have positions of power. Homosexuality barely raises its head above the parapet: only in Guatemala City is there anything approaching an open gay scene, and that is pretty much for men only.

The CIA's World Factbook states that more than half of all Guatemalans live in poverty. The official national minimum wage is only Q81 (about US$10) per day – and not everyone is entitled even to this. An established school teacher can earn around Q1950 (about US$250) per month. Poverty is most prevalent in rural, indigenous areas, especially the highlands. Wealth, industry and commerce are concentrated overwhelmingly in sprawling, polluted Guatemala City.

People

The great majority of Guatemala's 15 million people live in the highland strip from Guatemala City to Quetzaltenango, the country's two biggest cities. Many towns and large villages are dotted around this region. Some 49% of the population lives in towns and cities, and nearly half are aged under 19.

Some 41% of Guatemalans are indigenous, but this line is blurred as many people

GUATEMALA UNDERSTAND GUATEMALA

have indigenous blood, but some choose not to describe themselves as such. Nearly all of this indigenous population is Maya, although there is a very small population of non-Maya indigenous people called the Chinka' (Xinca) in the southeastern corner of the country. The four biggest Maya groups – the K'iche' (Quiché), Mam, Q'eqchi' (Kekchí) and Kaqchiquel – are most densely concentrated in the highlands. The rest of Guatemala's population is nearly all *ladinos* – descended from both the Maya and European (mostly Spanish) settlers. There are also a few thousand Garifuna (descended from Caribbean islanders and shipwrecked African slaves) around the Caribbean town of Lívingston.

Maya languages are still the way many Maya communicate, with over 20 separate (and often mutually unintelligible) Maya languages spoken in different regions of the country. It's language that primarily defines which Maya people someone belongs to. Though many Maya speak some Spanish, it's always a second language – and there are many who don't speak any Spanish at all.

Religion

Roman Catholicism is the predominant religion in Guatemala, but it is not the only religion. Since the 1980s evangelical Protestant sects, around 58% of them Pentecostal, have surged in popularity, and it is estimated that 30% to 40% of Guatemalans are now evangelicals. These numbers continue to grow as evangelical churches compete hard for further souls.

Catholicism's fall can also be attributed in part to the civil war. Catholic priests were (and still are) outspoken defenders of human rights, and attracted persecution from dictators at the time, especially from Ríos Montt. As a result, many Catholic churches in rural areas simply closed down during this time and evangelical ones moved in to fill the vacuum.

The number of new evangelical churches in some towns and villages, especially indigenous Maya villages, is astonishing. You will undoubtedly hear loud Guatemalan versions of gospel music pouring out of some of them as you walk around, and in some places loudspeakers broadcast the music and its accompanying preaching across entire towns.

Catholicism in the Maya areas has never been exactly orthodox. The missionaries who brought Catholicism to the Maya in the 16th century permitted aspects of the existing animistic, shamanistic Maya religion to continue alongside Christian rites and beliefs. Syncretism was aided by the identification of certain Maya deities with certain Christian saints and survives to this day. A bizarre example is the deity known, among other things, as Maximón.

The Maya still worship at a number of places sacred since ancient times, bringing offerings and sacrificing chickens to gods who predate the arrival of the Spanish. Each place has its own different set of gods – or at least different names for similar gods.

Visitors might also be able to observe traditional Maya ceremonies in places such as the Pascual Abaj shrine (p144) at Chichicastenango, the altars on Laguna Chicabal (p159) outside Quetzaltenango, or El Baúl (p167) near Santa Lucía Cotzumalguapa, but a lot of traditional rites are off-limits to foreigners.

Arts

Literature

Guatemalan writer Miguel Ángel Asturias (1899–1974) won the Nobel Prize for Literature in 1967. Best known for his thinly veiled vilification of Latin American dictators in *El señor presidente,* Asturias also wrote poetry (collected in *Sien de alondra,* published in English as *Temple of the Lark*). Other celebrated Guatemalan writers include poet Luis Cardoza y Aragón (1901–92) and short-story master Augusto Monterroso (1921–2003). Gaspar Pedro Gonzáles' *A Mayan Life* is claimed to be the first novel written by a Maya author.

Music

Music is a very important part of Guatemalan society, and a source of pride is that the marimba (xylophone) may have been invented here (although some claim it was brought from Africa by slaves). The Maya also play traditional instruments including the chirimía (of Arabic origin and related to the oboe) and reed flute.

Guatemalan tastes in pop music are greatly influenced by the products of other Latin American countries. Reggaetón is huge – current favorites being Pitbull, Nicky Jam and J Balvin.

The only record label seriously promoting new Guatemalan artists (mostly in the urban/hip-hop vein) is Guatemala City–based Outstanding Productions.

Guatemalan rock went through its golden age in the '80s and early '90s. Bands from this era such as Razones de Cambio, Bohemia Suburbana and Viernes Verde still have their die-hard fans. The most famous Guatemalan-born musician is Ricardo Arjona.

Weaving

Guatemalans make many traditional *artesanías* (handicrafts), both for everyday use and to sell. Crafts include basketry, ceramics and wood carving, but the most prominent are weaving, embroidery and other textile arts practiced by Maya women.

The *huipil* (a long, woven, white sleeveless tunic with intricate, colorful embroidery) is one of several types of garment that have been worn since pre-Hispanic times. Other colorful types include: the *tocoyal,* a woven head-covering often decorated with bright tassels; the *corte,* a piece of material 7m or 10m long that is used as a wraparound skirt; and the *faja,* a long, woven waist sash that can be folded to hold what otherwise might be put in pockets.

Colorful traditional dress is still predominant generally in the heavily Maya-populated highlands, but you'll see it in all parts of the country. The variety of techniques, materials, styles and designs is bewildering to the newcomer, but you'll see some of the most colorful, intricate, eye-catching and widely worn designs in Sololá and Santiago Atitlán, near Lago de Atitlán; Nebaj in the Ixil Triangle; Zunil near Quetzaltenango; and Todos Santos and San Mateo Ixtatán in the Cuchumatanes mountains.

Landscape & Wildlife

The Land

Consisting primarily of mountainous forest highlands and jungle plains, Guatemala covers an area of 109,000 sq km. The western highlands hold 30 volcanoes, reaching heights of more than 4200m southwest of Huehuetenango. In the Cuchumatanes range, land not cleared for Maya *milpas* (cornfields) is covered in pine forests, although these are dwindling rapidly.

The Pacific Slope holds rich coffee, cacao, fruit and sugar plantations. Down along the shore the volcanic slope meets the sea, yielding vast, sweltering beaches of black volcanic sand.

Guatemala City lies at an altitude of around 1500m. To the north, the Alta Verapaz highlands gradually give way to El Petén, whose climate and topography is similar to the Yucatán: hot and humid or hot and dry. Southeast of El Petén is the banana-rich valley of the Río Motagua, dry in some areas, moist in others.

Guatemala is at the confluence of three tectonic plates, resulting in earthquakes and volcanic eruptions. Major quakes struck in 1773, 1917 and 1976. Its dynamic geology includes a tremendous system of surface-level and subterranean caves. This karst terrain riddles the Verapaces region and has made Guatemala a popular spelunking destination. Surface-level caves have been used for Maya ceremonies since ancient times.

Animals

The country's abundance of animals includes 250 species of mammal, 600 bird species, 200 species of reptile and amphibian, and numerous butterflies and other insects.

The national bird, the resplendent quetzal, is often used to symbolize Central America. Though small, the quetzal is exceptionally beautiful. The males sport a bright red breast, brilliant blue-green across the rest of the body and a spot of bright white on the underside of the long tail.

Other colorful birds include toucans, macaws and parrots. Boasting the ocellated turkey (or 'Petén turkey') – a large, impressive, multicolored bird reminiscent of a peacock – Tikal is a bird-watching hot spot, with some 300 tropical and migratory species sighted to date. Several woodpecker species, nine types of hummingbirds and four trogon species are just the beginning of the list. Also in the area are large white herons, hawks, warblers, kingfishers, harpy eagles (rare) and many others.

Although Guatemala's forests host several mammal and reptile species, many remain difficult to observe. Still, visitors to Tikal can enjoy the antics of the omnipresent *pizotes* (coatis, a tropical mammal related to raccoons) and might spy howler and spider monkeys.

Other mammals deeper in the forest include jaguars, ocelots, pumas, peccaries,

agoutis, opossums, tapirs, kinkajous (nocturnal arboreal mammals), *tepezcuintles* (pacas, white-spotted brownish rodents), white-tailed and red brocket deer, armadillos and very large rattlesnakes. Reptiles and amphibians in the rest of Guatemala include at least three species of sea turtle (leatherback, *tortuga negra* and olive ridley) and two species of crocodile (one found in El Petén, the other in the Río Dulce). Manatees also frequent the waters around Río Dulce.

Plants

Guatemala has over 8000 plant species in 19 different ecosystems, ranging from coastal mangrove forests to mountainous interior pine forests to high cloud forests. El Petén supports a variety of trees, including mahogany, cedar, ramón and sapodilla.

The national flower, the *monja blanca* (white nun orchid), is said to have been picked so much that it's now rare in the wild. Nevertheless, the country has around 600 species of orchid, a third of which are endemic.

Guatemala also has the perfect climate for *xate* (sha-tay), a low-growing palm that thrives in El Petén and is prized in the developed world as a flower-arrangement filler.

Environmental Issues

Environmental consciousness is not largely developed in Guatemala, as vast amounts of garbage strewn across the country will quickly tell you. Despite the impressive list of parks and protected areas, genuine protection for those areas is harder to achieve, partly because of official collusion to ignore the regulations and partly because of pressure from poor Guatemalans in need of land. Deforestation is a problem in many areas, especially El Petén, where jungle is being felled at an alarming rate not just for timber but also to make way for cattle ranches, oil pipelines, clandestine airstrips, new settle-

NATIONAL PARKS & RESERVES

Guatemala has 92 protected areas, including biosphere reserves, national parks, protected biotopes, wildlife refuges and private nature reserves. Even though some areas are contained within other, larger ones, they amount to 28% of the national territory.

Many of the protected areas are remote and hard to access by the independent traveler; the list below outlines those that are easiest to reach and/or most interesting to visitors, but excludes the volcanoes, nearly all of which are protected, and areas of mainly archaeological interest.

Parque Nacional Tikal Diverse jungle wildlife among Guatemala's most magnificent Maya ruins.

Parque Nacional Laguna del Tigre A remote, large park within the Reserva Maya, featuring freshwater wetlands. Wildlife includes scarlet macaws, monkeys and crocodiles.

Parque Nacional Mirador-Río Azul A national park within the Reserva Maya containing the archaeological site of El Mirador.

Parque Nacional Río Dulce The beautiful jungle-lined lower Río Dulce between Lago de Izabal and the Caribbean serves as a manatee refuge.

Parque Nacional Grutas de Lanquín A large, bat-infested cave system 61km east of Cobán.

Biotopo del Quetzal (p172) An easily accessible cloud-forest reserve sheltering howler monkeys and birds (and possibly a quetzal).

Biotopo Cerro Cahuí (p201) A forest reserve beside Lago de Petén Itzá offering abundant wildlife spotting and good walking trails.

Refugio de Vida Silvestre Bocas del Polochic Guatemala's second-largest freshwater wetlands, at the western end of Lago de Izabal. Abundant bird-watching (more than 300 species).

Reserva Natural Monterrico-Hawaii (p170) Covers beach and wetlands, protecting birdlife and marine turtles.

ments and new maize fields cleared by the slash-and-burn method.

On the more populous Pacific side of the country, the land is mostly agricultural or given over to industry. The remaining forests in the Pacific coastal and highland areas are not long for this world, as local communities cut down the remaining trees for heating and cooking fuels.

Nevertheless, a number of Guatemalan organizations are doing valiant work to protect their country's environment and biodiversity. NGOs can be good resources for finding out more about Guatemala's natural parks and protected areas.

SURVIVAL GUIDE

🛈 Directory A–Z

ACCOMMODATIONS

It's generally not necessary to book your accommodations in advance. If, however, you're planning on being in Antigua or down at the beach during Semana Santa, the sooner you book the better.

Hotels From desperate dives out by the bus terminal to fancy-pants boutique numbers, there are no shortage of options.

Hostels Starting to make a dent in the budget accommodation scene, especially in backpacker-favored destinations such as Antigua, Quetzaltenango and around Lago de Atitlán.

Homestays Generally organized through Spanish schools, these are a great way to connect with local culture.

ACTIVITIES

Caving

Guatemala attracts cavers from all around the world. The limestone area around Cobán is particularly riddled with cave systems the full extents of which are unknown. The caves of Lanquín, B'omb'il Pek, Candelaria and Rey Marcos are all open for tourist visits. There are also exciting caves to visit from Finca Ixobel, near Poptún, and some near Flores.

Climbing & Hiking

Guatemala's many volcanoes are irresistible challenges, and many of them can be done in one day from Antigua or Quetzaltenango. There's further great hill country in the Ixil Triangle and the Cuchumatanes mountains to the north of Huehuetenango, especially around Todos Santos Cuchumatán and Nebaj. Lago de Atitlán is surrounded by spectacular trails,

SLEEPING PRICE RANGES

The following price ranges refer to a double room with bathroom in high (but not absolute peak) season. Unless otherwise stated, taxes of 22% are included in the price.

$	less than Q200
$$	Q200–550
$$$	more than Q550

though robberies here have made some routes inadvisable.

Treks of several days are perfectly feasible, and agencies in Antigua, Quetzaltenango and Nebaj can guide you. In the Petén jungles, treks to remote archaeological sites such as El Mirador and El Perú offer an exciting challenge.

Cycling

There's probably no better way to experience the Guatemala highlands than by bicycle. Panajachel, San Pedro La Laguna, Quetzaltenango and Antigua in particular are the best launch points, with local agencies offering trips and equipment.

Horseback Riding

Opportunities for a gallop, a trot or even a horse trek are on the increase in Guatemala. There are stables in Antigua, Santiago Atitlán, Quetzaltenango, El Remate, Laguna Brava and San Pedro La Laguna. **Unicornio Azul** (🖅 5205-9328; www.unicornioazul.com), north of Huehuetenango, offers treks of up to nine days in the Cuchumatanes.

Water Sports

You can dive inside a volcanic caldera at Lago de Atitlán, raft the white waters of the Río Cahabón near Lanquín, or sail from the yachtie haven of Río Dulce. You can also canoe or kayak the waterways of Monterrico, Lago de Atitlán and Lago de Petén Itzá, Lívingston, the Bocas del Polochic or Punta de Manabique.

CHILDREN

Young children are highly regarded in Guatemala and can often break down barriers and open doors to local hospitality. However, Guatemala is so culturally dense, with such an emphasis on history and archaeology, that children can easily get bored. To keep kids entertained, try to make a point of breaking up the trip with visits to places such as Guatemala City's **Museo de los Niños** (Children's Museum; Map p108; 🖅 2475-5076; www.museodelosninos.com.gt; 5a Calle 10-00, Zona 13; Q40; ☺8am-noon & 1-4:30pm Tue-Fri, 9:30am-1:30pm & 2:30-6pm Sat & Sun) and **La Aurora Zoo** (p106); **Autosafari Chapín** (🖅 2222-5858; www.autosafarichapin.com;

Carretera a Taxisco, Km 87.5; adult/child Q60/50; ⊙ 9:30am-5pm Tue-Sun), near Escuintla; and Retalhuleu's **Xocomil** (p166) water park and **Xetulul** (p166) theme park. Most Spanish schools are open to kids, too, and many older children will enjoy activities such as zip lining, kayaking and horseback riding.

For general information on traveling with children, have a look at Lonely Planet's *Travel with Children*.

Practicalities

➤ Facilities such as safety seats in hired cars are rare, but nearly every restaurant can rustle up something resembling a high chair.

➤ If you are particular about brands of diapers and creams, bring what you can with you and stock up in supermarkets.

➤ If your child has to have some particular tinned or packaged food, bring supplies with you.

➤ Fresh milk is rare and may not be pasteurized – again, supermarkets are your best bet. Packet UHT milk and milk powder are much more common.

➤ Public breastfeeding is not common among urban, non-indigenous women and, when done, is done discreetly.

CUSTOMS REGULATIONS

Normally customs officers won't look seriously in your luggage and may not look at all. Guatemala restricts import/export of pretty much the same things as everybody else (weapons, drugs, large amounts of cash etc).

EMBASSIES & CONSULATES

Citizens from countries that do not have embassies generally end up having to go to Mexico City (unless the consulate can be of help).

Australian Honorary Consulate (☑ 2328-0300; sdr@australianconsulate.com.gt; 2a Calle 23-80, Edificio Avante, Oficina 701, Zona 15, Guatemala City)

Belizean Embassy (☑ 2367-3883; www.embajadadebelize.org; 5a Av 5-55, Europlaza 2, Office 1502, Zona 14, Guatemala City)

Canadian Embassy (☑ 2363-4348; www.guatemala.gc.ca; 13a Calle 8-44, 8th fl, Edificio Edyma Plaza, Zona 10, Guatemala City)

French Embassy (☑ 2421-7370; www.ambafrance-gt.org; 5a Av 8-59, Zona 14, Guatemala City)

German Embassy (☑ 2364-6700; www.guatemala.diplo.de; Avenida La Reforma 9-55, Edificio Reforma 10, 10th fl, Zona 10, Guatemala City)

Honduran Consulate (☑ 2332-6281; embhond@intelnet.net.gt; Av La Reforma 6-64, Zona 9, Guatemala City)

Irish Honorary Consulate (☑ 5353-5349; irelandgua@gmail.com; 19a Av, Zona 15, Guatemala City)

Mexican Embassy (☑ 2420-3400; www.embamex.sre.gob.mx/guatemala; 2a Av 7-57, Zona 10, Guatemala City)

Netherlands Consulate (☑ 2296-1490; guatemala@nlconsulate.com; Carretera a El Salvador Km 14.5, Santa Catarina Pinula)

Salvadoran Embassy (☑ 2245-7272; www.embajadaguatemala.rree.gob.sv; 15a Av 12-01, Zona 13, Guatemala City)

UK Embassy (☑ 2380-7300; www.ukinguatemala.fco.gov.uk; 16a Calle 0-55, 11th fl, Torre Internacional, Zona 10, Guatemala City)

US Embassy (☑ 2326-4000; http://guatemala.usembassy.gov; Av La Reforma 7-01, Zona 10, Guatemala City)

FOOD

What you eat in Guatemala will be a mixture of Guatemalan food, which is nutritious and filling without sending your taste buds into ecstasy, and international traveler-and-tourist food, which is available wherever travelers and tourists hang out. Your most satisfying meals in both cases will probably be in smaller eateries where the boss is in the kitchen themselves.

HEALTH

Staying healthy in Guatemala involves some common-sense precautions and a few destination-specific ones.

Discuss your requirements with your doctor, but the vaccines that are usually recommended for travel to Central America are hepatitis A and B and typhoid. If you are planning to spend time handling animals or exploring caves, consider getting vaccinated for rabies.

INTERNET ACCESS

Most travelers make constant use of internet cafes and free web-based email. Most towns have cybercafes with fairly reliable connections. Internet cafes typically charge between Q5 and Q10 an hour.

Wi-fi is becoming readily available across the country, but can only really be counted on in large and/or tourist towns. Most (but not all) hostels offer wi-fi, as do many hotels in the midrange and up category. The best reliable source of wi-fi around the country is at Pollo Campero restaurants – they're in pretty much every town of any size and all offer free, unsecured access.

LEGAL MATTERS

You may find that police officers in Guatemala are, at times, somewhat unhelpful. Generally speaking, the less you have to do with the law, the better.

Whatever you do, don't get involved in any way with illegal drugs – even if the locals seem to do so freely. As a foreigner, you are at a distinct disadvantage, and you may be set up by others. Drug laws in Guatemala are strict, and though enforcement may be uneven, penalties are severe. If you do get caught doing something you shouldn't, your best line of defense is to apologize, stay calm and proceed from there.

While many commentators claim that corruption is rife in Guatemala, don't take this to mean you can buy your way out of any situation. If it does seem that you can 'make everything go away' by handing over some cash, proceed cautiously and tactfully.

LGBT TRAVELERS

Few places in Latin America are outwardly gay-friendly and Guatemala is no different. Technically, homosexuality is legal for persons over 18 years, but the reality can be another story, with harassment and violence against gays too often poisoning the plot. Don't even consider testing the tolerance for homosexual public displays of affection here.

Antigua has a subdued scene; affection and action are still kept behind closed doors. The chief exception is the gay-friendly club Las Vibras de la Casbah. In Guatemala City, Genetic and the Black & White Lounge are the current faves. Mostly, though, gays traveling in Guatemala will find themselves keeping it low-key and pushing the twin beds together.

Gay.com has a personals section for Guatemala, and the Gully (www.thegully.com) usually has some articles and information relevant to Guatemala. The best site, Gay Guatemala (www.gayguatemala.com), is in Spanish.

MONEY

Banks change cash and (sometimes) traveler's checks, but casas de cambio (exchange houses) are usually quicker and may offer better rates.

Cash

Cash is king in Guatemala, although carrying too much of it makes getting robbed a bigger pain than it would otherwise be. Some towns suffer from change shortages: always try to carry a stash of small bills. Keep a small supply of low-denomination US dollars (which are accepted pretty much anywhere, at various rates of exchange) as an emergency fund.

While everybody accepts dollars, you will almost always get a better deal by paying in quetzals.

Currencies other than the US dollar are virtually useless, although a handful of places now change cash euros.

ATMs

You'll find ATMs (cash machines; cajeros automáticos) for Visa/Plus System cards in all but the smallest towns, and there are MasterCard/Cirrus ATMs in many places, too, so one of these cards is the best basis for your supply of cash in Guatemala. The 5B network is widespread and particularly useful, as it works with both Visa and MasterCard cards.

Be aware that card skimming is a problem in Guatemala. Avoid ATMs that are left unguarded at night (ie those in the small room out front of the bank) and look for one that is in a secure environment (such as those inside supermarkets or shopping malls). Failing that, keep your hand covered when entering your PIN and check your balance online.

Tipping

A 10% tip is expected in restaurants (often automatically added to your bill in tourist towns such as Antigua). In small comedores (basic, cheap eateries) tipping is optional, but follow local practice and leave some spare change.

Homestays Better to buy a gift than give cash

Hotels Q10 per bag

Restaurants 10% maximum (if not already included)

Taxis Not customary

Trekking & tour guides Q50 per person per day (extremely optional)

Traveler's Checks

If you're not packing plastic, a combination of Amex US-dollar traveler's checks and some cash US dollars is the way to go. Take some of these as a backup even if you do have a card. Many banks change US-dollar traveler's checks, and tend to give the best rates. Amex is easily the most recognized traveler's check brand. Few businesses will accept traveler's checks as payment or change them for cash.

OPENING HOURS

Hours provided are general guidelines, but there are many variations. Restaurant times, in particular, can vary by up to two hours either way.

The Ley Seca (dry law) stipulates that bars and discotecas must close by 1am, except on nights before public holidays; it is rigidly followed in large cities and universally mocked in smaller towns.

Banks 9am–5pm Monday to Friday and 9am–1pm Saturday

Bars 11am–midnight

Cafes and restaurants 7am–9pm

Government offices 8am–4pm Monday to Friday

Shops 8am–noon and 2–6pm Monday to Saturday

PHOTOGRAPHY

Ubiquitous film stores and pharmacies sell film, though you may not find the brand you like without a hunt. There are quick processing labs in the main cities. Most internet cafes have card readers (lectores de tarjeta), so you can upload your digital photos or burn them onto CD. For tips on taking professional-grade travel pics, hunt down a copy of Lonely Planet's *Travel Photography*.

Photographing People

Photography is a sensitive subject in Guatemala. Always ask permission before taking portraits, especially of Maya women and children. Don't be surprised if your request is denied. Children often request payment (usually Q1) in return for posing. In certain places, such as the church of Santo Tomás in Chichicastenango, photography is forbidden. Maya ceremonies (should you be so lucky to witness one) are off-limits for photography unless you are given explicit permission to take pictures. If local people make any sign of being offended, put your camera away and apologize immediately, both out of decency and for your own safety. Never take photos of army installations, men with guns or other sensitive military subjects.

The Guatemalan postal service was privatized in 1999. Generally, letters and parcels take eight to 10 days to travel to the US and Canada and 10 to 12 days to reach Europe. Almost all cities and towns (but not villages) have a post office where you can buy stamps and send mail. If you want to get a package couriered to you, make sure the courier company has an office in the town where you are staying; otherwise you will be charged some hefty 'handling fees.'

PUBLIC HOLIDAYS

Guatemalan public holidays include the following:

New Year's Day (Año Nuevo) January 1
Easter (Semana Santa; Holy Thursday to Easter Sunday inclusive) March/April
Labor Day (Día del Trabajo) May 1
Army Day (Día del Ejército) June 30
Assumption Day (Día de la Asunción) August 15
Independence Day (Día de la Independencia) September 15
Revolution Day (Día de la Revolución) October 20
All Saints' Day (Día de Todos los Santos) November 1
Christmas Eve afternoon (Víspera Navidad) December 24
Christmas Day (Navidad) December 25
New Year's Eve afternoon (Víspera de Año Nuevo) December 31

SAFE TRAVEL

While crime definitely happens in Guatemala, and definitely happens to tourists, these days the most frequently reported type of nasty incident involves robbery on walking trails.

The days of robbers targeting tourist buses out on the open highway seem to be thankfully in the past, although some tourists in rental cars have been targeted. This information is incredibly fluid – check with **Proatur** (in English 1500) for the latest.

The crime you're most likely to become a victim of involves pickpocketing, bag-snatching, bag-slitting and the like in crowded streets, markets, bus stations and on buses, but also in empty, dark city streets.

Safety Tips

→ It's best to travel and arrive in daylight hours. If that's not possible, travel at night using 1st-class buses and catch a taxi to your hotel once you arrive.

→ Only carry the money, cards, checks and valuables that you need. Leave the rest in a sealed, signed envelope in your hotel's safe, and obtain a receipt for the envelope.

→ Don't flaunt jewelry, cameras or valuable-looking watches. Keep your wallet or purse out of view.

→ On buses keep your important valuables with you, and keep a tight hold on them.

→ Use normal precautions when using ATMs (and be aware that card skimming is a reality here).

→ Hiking in large groups and/or with a police escort reduces the risk of robbery.

→ Resisting or trying to flee from robbers usually makes the situation worse.

→ Hiking on active volcanoes obviously has an element of risk. Get the latest story before you head out. In the wet season, hike in the morning before rain and possible thunderstorms set in.

→ Be careful, especially in rural areas, when talking to small children; always ask permission to take photographs, and generally try not to put yourself in any situation that might be misinterpreted.

Scams

→ One common scenario is for someone to spray ketchup or some other sticky liquid on your clothes. An accomplice then appears to help you clean up the mess and robs you in the process. Other methods of distraction, such as dropping a purse or coins, or someone appearing to faint, are also used by pickpockets and bag snatchers.

→ Regrettably, ATM card cloners have moved into Guatemala, targeting Guatemalans and foreigners alike. They operate by attaching a card reading device to the ATM (often inside the slot where you insert your card) and once they have your data, proceed to drain your account. There have been reports of card cloning in all the major tourist destinations. The only way to avoid it is to use ATMs that cannot be tampered with easily (inside supermarkets or shopping malls). The ATMs most prone to tampering are the ones in the little unlocked room at the front of a bank. Note that you should *never* have to enter your PIN number to gain access to an ATM room.

TELEPHONE

Guatemala has no area or city codes. Calling from other countries, you just dial the international access code (☑ 00 in most countries), then the Guatemala country code (☑ 502), then the eight-digit local number. Calling within Guatemala, just dial the eight-digit local number. The international access code from Guatemala is ☑ 00.

Many towns and cities frequented by tourists have privately run call offices where you can make international calls for reasonable rates.

Don't use the black phones placed strategically in tourist towns that say 'Press 2 to call the United States free!' This is a bait-and-switch scam; you put the call on your credit card and return home to find you have paid between US$8 and US$20 per minute.

Many travelers use an account such as Skype. If an internet cafe does not have Skype installed, it can usually be downloaded in a matter of minutes. If you're planning on using internet cafe computers to make calls, buy earbuds with a microphone attached before you leave – you can plug them into the front of most computers in the country.

Cell Phones

Cell phones are widely used. Roaming is available but expensive. Most travelers buy a local SIM card or a local prepaid phone on arrival.

There are three cell companies in the country – Movistar (www.movistar.com.gt) tends to have the cheapest rates, with coverage limited to not much further than major cities, while Tigo (www.tigo.com.gt) and Claro (www.claro.com.gt) have the best coverage.

It's possible to bring your cell phone from home, have it 'unlocked' for use in Guatemala (this costs between Q50 and Q100 in Guatemala, depending on the make of the phone), then substitute your SIM card for a local one. This works on some phones and not others and there doesn't appear to be a logic behind it.

Guatemalan phone companies work on either 850, 900 or 1900 MHz frequencies – if you have a tri- or quad-band phone you should be OK. Compatibility issues, and the possibility of theft

(cell phones are a pickpocket's delight) makes buying a cheap prepaid phone on arrival the most popular option.

Prepaid phones are available pretty much everywhere and cost around Q100 to Q150, often coming with Q100 or so in free calls. Cards to restock the credit on your phone are sold in nearly every corner store. Calls cost Q1.50 per minute anywhere in the country, the same for calls to the US (depending on the company you're with), and up to five times that for the rest of the world.

Phonecards

The most common street phones (although becoming increasingly rare as everybody goes cellular) are those of Telgua, for which you need to buy a Telgua phonecard *(tarjeta telefónica de Telgua)* from shops, kiosks and the like. Card sales points may advertise the fact with red signs saying *'Ladatel de Venta Aquí.'* The cards come in denominations of Q20, Q30 and Q50: you slot them into a Telgua phone, dial your number, and the display will tell you how much time you have left.

Telgua street phones bear instructions to dial ☑ 147110 for domestic collect calls and ☑ 147120 for international collect calls.

TIME

Guatemala runs on North American Central Standard Time (GMT/UTC minus six hours). The 24-hour clock is often used, so 1pm may be written as 13 or 1300. When it is noon in Guatemala, it is 1pm in New York, 6pm in London, 10am in San Francisco and 4am the next day in Sydney. For more time conversions, see www.timeand date.com/worldclock.

TOILETS

→ You cannot throw *anything* into Guatemalan toilets, including toilet paper. Bathrooms are equipped with some sort of receptacle (usually a small wastebasket) for soiled paper.

→ Toilet paper is not always provided, so be sure to carry some. If you don't have any and need some, asking a restaurant worker for *un rollo de papel* (a roll of paper), accompanied by

---

EATING PRICE RANGES

The following price ranges refer to a standard main course, including taxes but not including tip.

$	less than Q50
$$	Q50–Q150
$$$	more than Q150

a panicked facial expression, usually produces fast results.

➡ Public toilets are rare. Use the ones at cafes, restaurants, your hotel and archaeological sites. Buses rarely have toilets on board and if they do, don't count on them working.

TOURIST INFORMATION

Guatemala's national tourism institute, INGUAT (www.visitguatemala.com), has information offices in major tourist areas. A few towns have departmental, municipal or private-enterprise tourist information offices. **Proatur** (✍ in English 1500), a joint private-government initiative, operates a 24-hour toll-free advice and assistance hotline.

TRAVELERS WITH DISABILITIES

Guatemala is not the easiest country to negotiate for travelers with a disability. Although many sidewalks in Antigua have ramps and cute little inlaid tiles depicting a wheelchair, the streets are cobblestone, so the ramps are anything but smooth and the streets worse!

Many hotels in Guatemala are old converted houses with rooms around a courtyard; such rooms are wheelchair accessible, but the bathrooms may not be. The most expensive hotels have facilities such as ramps, elevators and accessible toilets. Transportation is the biggest hurdle for travelers with limited mobility: travelers in a wheelchair may consider renting a car and driver as the buses will prove especially challenging due to lack of space.

Mobility International USA (www.miusa.org) advises travelers on mobility issues, runs exchange programs (including in Guatemala) and publishes some useful books. Also worth consulting are Access-Able Travel Source (www.access-able.com) and Accessible Journeys (www.disabilitytravel.com).

Antigua-based Transitions (www.transitionsfoundation.org) is an organization aiming to increase awareness and access for people with disabilities in Guatemala.

VISAS

Many nationalities do not require tourist visas and will be given a 90-day stay upon entry, though citizens of some countries do need visas.

VOLUNTEERING

If you want to get to the heart of Guatemalan matters, consider volunteer work. Opportunities abound, from caring for abandoned animals to writing grant applications to tending fields. Travelers with specific skills such as nurses, doctors, teachers and website designers are particularly encouraged to investigate volunteering in Guatemala.

Most volunteer posts require basic or better Spanish skills and a minimum time commitment. Depending on the organization, you may have to pay for room and board for the duration of your stay. Before making a commitment, you may want to talk to past volunteers and read the fine print associated with the position.

An excellent source of information on volunteer opportunities is Quetzaltenango-based **EntreMundos** (Map p156; ☎ 7761-2179; www.entremundos.org; 6a Calle 7-31, Zona 1; ⊙ 2-4pm Mon-Thu). You only have to visit their website to see the huge range of volunteer opportunities that exist. Many language schools have close links to volunteer projects and can introduce you to the world of volunteering – this is often the best option if you are only looking to commit for a few weeks. The best worldwide site for volunteer positions (with many Guatemala listings) is www.idealist.org.

WOMEN TRAVELERS

Women should encounter no special problems traveling in Guatemala. The primary thing you can do to make it easy for yourself while traveling here is to dress modestly. Modesty in dress is highly regarded, and if you practice it, you will usually be treated with respect.

Specifically, shorts should be worn only at the beach, not in town, and especially not in the highlands. Skirts should be at or below the knee. Going braless is considered provocative. Many local women swim with T-shirts over their swimsuits.

Women traveling alone can expect plenty of attention from talkative men. Often they're just curious and not out for a foreign conquest. It is, of course, up to you how to respond, but there's no need to be intimidated. Consider the situation and circumstances, and stay confident. Try to sit next to women or children on the bus. Local women rarely initiate conversations, but usually have lots of interesting things to say once the ball is rolling.

While there's no need to be paranoid, the possibility of rape and assault does exist. Use your normal traveler's caution – avoid walking alone in isolated places or through city streets late at night, and skip hitchhiking.

WORK

Some travelers find work in bars, restaurants and places to stay in Antigua, Panajachel or Quetzaltenango, but the wages are just survival pay. If you're looking to crew a yacht, there's always work being offered around the Río Dulce area, sometimes for short trips, sometimes to the States and further afield. Check noticeboards and online forums for details.

ⓘ Getting There & Away

AIR

There are direct flights from the USA with a variety of airlines, including Avianca (www.avianca.com). AeroMexico (www.aeromexico.com) and Interjet (www.interjet.com.mx) fly direct from Mexico City. Avianca and Alternative Airlines (http://taca.alternativeairlines.com) have flights from most Central American capitals. If you are coming from elsewhere, you will almost certainly be changing planes in the US, Mexico or elsewhere in Central America.

LAND

Guatemala has official border crossings with all of its neighboring countries. Check visa requirements (p226) before arrival.

Belize
➡ Melchor de Mencos (GUA) – Benque Viejo del Carmen (BZE)

El Salvador
➡ Ciudad Pedro de Alvarado (GUA) – La Hachadura (ES)
➡ Valle Nuevo (GUA) – Las Chinamas (ES)
➡ San Cristóbal Frontera (GUA) – San Cristóbal (ES)
➡ Anguiatú (GUA) – Anguiatú (ES)

Honduras
➡ Agua Caliente (GUA) – Agua Caliente (HND)
➡ El Florido (GUA) – Copán Ruinas (HND)
➡ Corinto (GUA) – Corinto (HND)

Mexico
➡ Ciudad Tecún Umán (GUA) – Ciudad Hidalgo (MEX)
➡ El Carmen (GUA) – Talisman (MEX)
➡ La Mesilla (GUA) – Ciudad Cuauhtémoc (MEX)

RIVER

There are two possible crossings from Mexico's Chiapas State to El Petén – the most commonly used one crosses at the Mexican town of Frontera Corozal to either La Técnica or Bethel in Guatemala. Frontera Corozal has good transportation connections to Palenque in Mexico and there are regular buses from La Técnica and Bethel to Flores/Santa Elena, Guatemala.

The other river route from Mexico into Guatemala's Petén department is up the Río de la Pasión from Benemérito de las Américas, south of Frontera Corozal, to Sayaxché, but there are no immigration facilities or reliable passenger services along this route.

SEA

Public boats connect Punta Gorda in Belize with Lívingston and Puerto Barrios in Guatemala. The Punta Gorda services connect with bus services to/from Belize City.

There is a Q80 departure tax when leaving Guatemala by sea.

ⓘ Getting Around

AIR

At the time of writing the only scheduled internal flights were between Guatemala City and Flores, a route operated daily by Avianca (www.avianca.com) and TAG (www.tag.com.gt).

BICYCLE

Guatemala's mountainous terrain and occasionally terrifying road conditions make for hard going when it comes to intercity pedaling. That said, if you have your wits about you, cycling is a great way to get around smaller towns – Antigua, Quetzaltenango and San Pedro La Laguna are among the towns where you can rent reasonable mountain bikes (you don't want skinny wheels here) by the hour, day, week or longer. There are bike shops in almost every town where you can buy a new bike starting from around Q800.

BOAT

The Caribbean town of Lívingston is only reachable by boat, across the Bahía de Amatique from Puerto Barrios or down the Río Dulce from the town of Río Dulce – both great trips. In Lago de Atitlán fast fiberglass launches zip across the waters between villages – by far the best way to get around.

BUS

Buses go almost everywhere in Guatemala, and the buses will leave you with some of your most vivid memories of the country. Most of them are ancient school buses from the US and Canada. It is not unusual for a local family of five to squeeze into seats that were originally designed for two child-sized bottoms. Many travelers know these vehicles as chicken buses, after the live cargo accompanying many passengers. They are frequent, crowded and cheap. Expect to pay Q10 (or less!) for an hour of travel.

Chicken buses will stop anywhere, for anyone. Helpers will yell 'hay lugares!' (eye loo-gar-ays), which literally means 'there are places.' Never mind that the space they refer to may be no more than a sliver of air between hundreds of locals mashed against one another. These same helpers will also yell their bus's destination in voices of varying hilarity and cadence; just listen for the song of your town. Tall travelers will be especially challenged on these buses. To catch a chicken bus, simply stand beside the road with your arm out parallel to the ground.

Some routes, especially between big cities, are served by more comfortable buses with the luxury of one seat per person. The best buses are labeled 'Pullman,' *'especial'* or *'primera clase.'* Occasionally, these may have bathrooms (but don't count on them working), televisions and even food service.

Pullman routes always originate or end in Guatemala City.

In general, more buses leave in the morning (some leave as early as 2am) than the afternoon. Bus traffic drops off precipitously after about 4pm; night buses are rare and not generally recommended. An exception are the overnight buses from Guatemala City to Flores, which have been relatively drama-free for some years now.

Distances in Guatemala are not huge and, apart from the aforementioned Guate–Flores run, you won't often ride for more than four hours at a time. On a typical four-hour bus trip you'll cover 175km to 200km for Q60 to Q100.

For a few of the better services you can buy tickets in advance, and this is generally worth doing as it ensures that you get a place.

On some shorter routes, minibuses, usually called 'microbuses,' are replacing chicken buses. These are operated by the same cram-'em-all-in principle and can be even more uncomfortable because they have less leg room. Where neither buses nor minibuses roam, pick-up *(picop)* trucks serve as de facto buses; you hail them and pay for them as if they were the genuine article.

At least a couple of times a month, a chicken bus plunges over a cliff or rounds a blind bend into a head-on collision. Newspapers are full of gory details and diagrams of the latest wreck, which doesn't foster affectionate feelings toward Guatemalan public transportation.

GOVERNMENT TRAVEL ADVICE

The following government websites offer travel advisories and information on current hot spots. Please bear in mind that these sites are updated occasionally and are obliged to err on the safe side – many, many travelers visit Guatemala and don't experience any of the reported problems.

Australian Department of Foreign Affairs (www.smartraveller.gov.au)

British Foreign Office (www.fco.gov.uk)

Canadian Department of Foreign Affairs (www.dfait-maeci.gc.ca)

US State Department (http://travel.state.gov)

ⓘ DEPARTURE TAX

Guatemala levies a departure tax of US$30 on outbound air passengers, which is nearly always included in your ticket price. If it's not, it has to be paid in cash US dollars or quetzals at the airline check-in desk.

SHUTTLE BUS

Shuttle minibuses run by travel agencies provide comfortable and quick transportation along the main routes plied by tourists. You'll find these heavily advertised wherever they are offered. With a few notable exceptions, they're much more expensive than buses (anywhere between five and 15 times as expensive), but more convenient – they usually offer a door-to-door service, with scheduled meal and bathroom breaks. The most popular shuttle routes include Guatemala City airport–Antigua, Antigua–Panajachel, Panajachel–Chichicastenango and Lanquín–Antigua.

CAR & MOTORCYCLE

You can drive in Guatemala with your home-country driver's license or with an International Driving Permit (IDP). Guatemalan driving etiquette will probably be very different from what you're used to back home: passing on blind curves, ceding the right of way to vehicles coming uphill on narrow passes and deafening honking for no apparent reason are just the start. Expect few road signs and no indication from other drivers of what they are about to do. Do not pay any attention to turn signals – they are rarely used and even more rarely used to indicate a turn in the direction they would seem to be. Hazard lights generally mean that the driver is about to do something foolish and/or illegal.

A vehicle coming uphill always has the right of way. *Túmulos* are speed bumps that are generously (sometimes oddly) placed throughout the country, usually on the main drag through a town. Use of seat belts is obligatory, but generally not practiced.

In Guatemala driving at night is a bad idea for many reasons, not the least of which are armed bandits, drunk drivers and decreased visibility.

Every driver involved in an accident that results in injury or death is taken into custody until a judge determines responsibility.

If someone's car breaks down on the highway (particularly on curvy mountain roads), they'll warn other drivers by putting shrubs or small branches on the road for a few hundred meters beforehand. Annoyingly, they rarely pick them

---

up afterward, but if you're driving and you see these, it's best to be cautious and slow down.

HITCHHIKING

Hitchhiking in the strict sense of the word is generally not practiced in Guatemala because it is not safe. However, where the bus service is sporadic or nonexistent, pick-up trucks and other vehicles may serve as public transportation. If you stand beside the road with your arm out, someone will stop. You are expected to pay the driver as if you were traveling on a bus and the fare will be similar. This is a safe and reliable system used by locals and travelers, and the only inconvenience you're likely to encounter is full-to-overflowing vehicles – get used to it.

Any other form of hitchhiking is never entirely safe, and we don't recommend it. Travelers who hitch should understand that they are taking a small but potentially serious risk.

LOCAL TRANSPORTATION

Bus

Public transportation within towns and cities outside of Guatemala City is chiefly provided by newish, crowded minibuses. They're useful to travelers chiefly in the more spread-out cities such as Quetzaltenango and Huehuetenango. Guatemala City has its own forms of bus services – the old red buses that are not recommended for safety reasons and the newer fleets of TransMetro and TransUrbano buses.

Taxi

Taxis are fairly plentiful in most significant towns. A 10-minute ride can cost about Q60, which is relatively expensive – expect to hear plenty of woeful tales from taxi drivers about the price of gasoline. Except for some taxis in Guatemala City, they don't use meters: you must agree upon the fare before you set off – best before you get in, in fact.

If you feel reluctant to take on the Guatemalan roads, an interesting alternative to car hire can be to hire a taxi driver for an extended time. This often works out only slightly more expensive than renting and gives you all the freedom and comfort without the stress of having to drive.

Tuk-Tuk

If you've spent any time in Asia, you'll be very familiar with the *tuk-tuk*, a three-wheeled mini-taxi nominally seating three passengers and a driver, but obviously capable of carrying twice that amount.

Named for the noise their little lawnmower engines make, *tuk-tuks* are best for short hops around town – expect to pay somewhere around Q5 per person. Hail them the way you would a normal taxi.

GUATEMALA SURVIVAL GUIDE

229

Belize

☏ 501 / POP 370,300

Includes →

Belize City 234
Caye Caulker. 239
Ambergris Caye &
San Pedro 243
Orange Walk 250
Corozal. 252
Western Belize 255
Belmopan 255
San Ignacio 260
Dangriga 267
Placencia. 272
Punta Gorda 276

Best Places to Eat

➡ Nerie's II Restaurant (p235)

➡ Farmers Market, San Ignacio (p263)

➡ Mojo Lounge & Bartique (p274)

➡ Cocina Sabor (p251)

➡ Habaneros (p242)

Best Places to Sleep

➡ Sea Dreams Hotel (p241)

➡ Tobacco Caye Paradise (p270)

➡ Funky Dodo (p271)

➡ Crooked Tree Lodge (p251)

➡ Ak'bol Yoga Retreat (p246)

Why Go?

Tiny Belize doesn't quite fit the mould of Latin America or the Caribbean, but proudly considers itself both. English, rather than Spanish, is the official language, and Central America's youngest nation dances to its own beat with a diverse and laid-back culture that encompasses Garifuna, Maya, Creole and Mestizo influences, as well as Mennonite and expatriate communities. With 240 miles of Caribbean coastline, endless island cays and the barrier reef (the northern hemisphere's largest), diving, snorkeling, swimming and slacking is world class. Inland, Belize's thick jungles are dotted with ancient Maya structures, along with incredible caves, wildlife-filled sanctuaries and adventure activities.

Though among the pricier destinations in Central America, for cuisine, diversity and culture, Belize still offers more than enough bang for your buck to make it worth the trip.

When to Go
Belize City

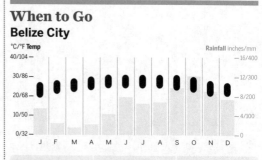

Mid-Dec–Apr Higher prices and drier weather; ideal for beach, diving and wildlife.

May–Nov Discounts abound for those willing to brave the heat and rains.

Sep National holidays spark two festive weeks of music, dancing and parades.

Connections

The Mexican border town of Chetumal has good connections into Belize, both overland into Corozal and by boat into Ambergris and Caye Caulker. The other popular entry point is Benque Viejo del Carmen on the Guatemalan border on the road from Tikal. A southern road from the Toledo district into Guatemala is almost complete and the new crossing may open in 2016. For more detailed information, see Survival Guide p285.

ITINERARIES

One Week

Starting at the western border (from Guatemala), visit Xunantunich before heading into San Ignacio. From there, your choices for exploration within the Cayo region are limited only by time and budget, and jungle activities abound. Caracol and ATM cave are highlights. With a few days left, head to Caye Caulker or San Pedro to spend a few days swimming, snorkeling, eating great seafood or just lazing in a hammock.

Two Weeks

Head in through Corozal (from Mexico) before heading deeper into nature at Crooked Tree or the Community Baboon Sanctuary. The views along the Hummingbird Hwy make the trip from north to south well worth it.

Dangriga, a centre for Garifuna culture, is the jumping-off point for Belize's central Cayes, including Tobacco and Glover's Reef. If you want to keep on the terrestrial tip, continue south to either Hopkins or Placencia for a few days on the beach. When you're beached out, make the trek south to Punta Gorda to get the latest information on Maya Village guesthouses and learn Garifuna drumming from the masters. Next, head to the Maya villages of the Deep South – Big Falls, San Pedro Columbia and Blue Creek – to explore ruins and hike or swim at beautiful Río Blanco National Park.

Essential Food & Drink

Rice and beans prevail on Belizean menus and plates. They're usually served with other ingredients – chicken and beef (and sometimes more exotic items like *gibnut;* a type of rodent found in South and Central America) are the usual suspects – plus some spices and condiments, such as coconut milk.

But Belizean cuisine is so much more than this ubiquitous rice-based dish. Seafood abounds everywhere on the coast. Lobster – in season (June to February) – is always excellent, and conch fritters are a must-try. Expect to find plenty of Mexican dishes like *salbutes, garnaches* and *ceviche.* And of course, no visit to Dangriga or Hopkins would be complete without tasting hudut, a beloved Garifuna dish.

AT A GLANCE

Currency Belize dollars (BZ$); US dollars (US$) accepted everywhere

Languages English, Spanish, Kriol, Garifuna

Money ATMs are widely available

Visas Generally not required for stays of less than 30 days

Time GMT minus six hours

Area 8875 sq miles (22,966 sq km)

Capital Belmopan

Emergency ☎ 911

BELIZE

Exchange Rates

Australia	A$1	BZ$1.49
Canada	C$1	BZ$1.57
Europe	€1	BZ$2.27
Guatemala	Q1	BZ$0.26
Japan	¥100	BZ$1.90
Mexico	M$1	BZ$0.11
New Zealand	NZ$1	BZ$1.41
UK	UK£1	BZ$2.85
USA	US$1	BZ$2.01

Set Your Budget

➡ **Budget hotel** US$30

➡ **Bottle of beer** US$2

➡ **Set lunch** US$5

➡ **Three-hour bus ride** US$6

Resources

➡ **Belizean Journeys** (www.belizeanjourneys.com)

➡ **Belize Tourism Board** (www.travelbelize.org)

➡ **Belize Forums** (www.belizeforum.com/belize)

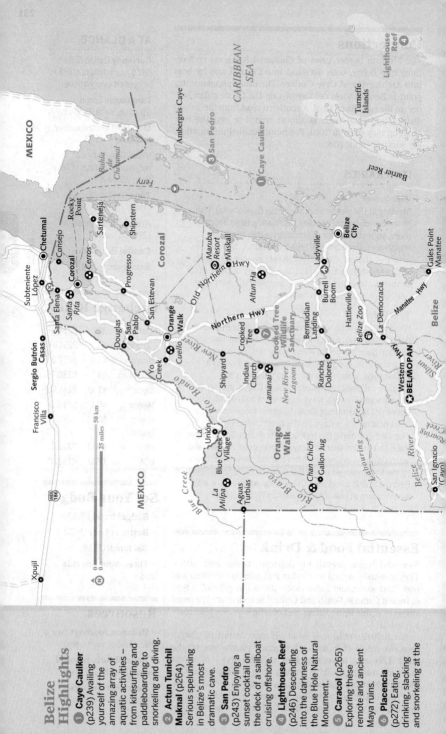

Belize Highlights

1 **Caye Caulker** (p239) Availing yourself of the amazing array of aquatic activities – from kitesurfing and paddleboarding to snorkeling and diving.

2 **Actun Tunichil Muknal** (p264) Serious spelunking in Belize's most dramatic cave.

3 **San Pedro** (p243) Enjoying a sunset cocktail on the deck of a sailboat cruising offshore.

4 **Lighthouse Reef** (p246) Descending into the darkness of the Blue Hole Natural Monument.

5 **Caracol** (p265) Exploring these remote and ancient Maya ruins.

6 **Placencia** (p272) Eating, drinking, slacking and snorkeling at the

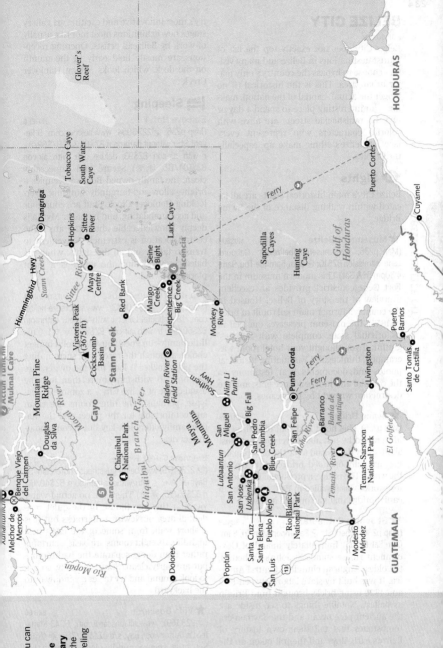

mainland 'cay you can drive to:

7 Crooked Tree Wildlife Sanctuary (p251) Cruising the lagoon and marveling at the birdlife.

BELIZE CITY

POP 60,963

Belize City does not exactly top the list of tourist destinations in Belize and many visitors choose to bypass the country's only major urban area. This is the historical (if no longer the actual) capital of the nation, making it an interesting place to spend a day or two. Its ramshackle streets are alive with colorful characters who represent every facet of Belize's ethnic make up, especially the Creoles.

◉ Sights

Belize City's main historical sights are all located within walking distance of the Swing Bridge.

★ Museum of Belize   MUSEUM

(Map p236; www.museumofbelize.org; Gabourel Lane; admission BZ$10; ⊙9am-5pm Tue-Thu, 9am-4:30pm Fri & Sat) This modern museum in the Fort George district provides an excellent overview of the story of Belize. Housed in the country's former main jail (built of brick in 1857), the museum preserves one cell in its original state, complete with inmates' graffiti; if you thought your hotel room was cramped, think again! Fascinating historical photos and documents bear testimony to the colonial and independence eras, and the destruction wrought by hurricanes.

★ Swing Bridge   LANDMARK

(Map p236) This heart and soul of Belize City life, crossed by just about everyone here just about every day, is said to be the only remaining manually operated bridge of its type in the world. The bridge, a product of Liverpool's ironworks, was installed in 1923, replacing an earlier bridge that had opened in 1897.

★ St John's Cathedral   CHURCH

(Map p236; Albert St; ⊙8am-noon Mon-Fri, 8am-6pm Sat & Sun) Immediately inland of Government House stands St John's Cathedral, the oldest Anglican church in Central America. It was built by slave labor between 1812 and 1820 using bricks brought from Britain as ballast. Notable things to see inside are the ancient pipe organ and the Baymen-era tombstones that tell their own history of Belize's early days and the toll taken on the city's early settlers.

Image Factory   GALLERY

(Map p236; www.imagefactorybelize.com; 91 North Front St; ⊙9am-5pm Mon-Fri) FREE The country's most innovative and exciting art gallery stages new exhibitions most months, usually of work by Belizean artists. Opening receptions are mostly held early in the month on the deck, which looks out on Haulover Creek.

⊨ Sleeping

Belcove Hotel   HOTEL $

(Map p236; ☑227-3054; www.belcove.com; 9 Regent St; r without bathroom BZ$65, s/d BZ$69/81, r with air-con BZ$93, deluxe d/tr with air-con BZ$104/115; ❋ 🖳) Secure and impeccably clean, the family-owned Belcove occupies a bright-yellow-and-burgundy building overlooking Haulover Creek. Staff are courteous and accommodating, and manager Myrna is deeply knowledgeable about the area. The central location is extremely convenient to transportation and all the sights, while the balcony overlooking the creek is a great place to unwind.

Sea Breeze Guesthouse   GUESTHOUSE $

(Map p236; ☑203-0043; www.seabreeze-belize.com; 18 Gabourel Lane; r with/without bathroom BZ$60/50, tr with air-con BZ$80; ❋ 🖳) This little family-run guesthouse is a solid budget choice, although the razor wire surrounding the place makes it look like the owners are planning to withstand more than just the usual crime of Belize City – a zombie apocalypse, perhaps? The nine rooms are clean and comfortable for the price; and the Kalam family offers low-key but accommodating service.

Bayview Guest House   GUESTHOUSE $

(☑223-4179; www.belize-guesthouse-hotel.com; 58 Baymen Ave; s with/without bathroom BZ$40/60, d BZ$55/70; ❋ 🖳) There are no actual water views at this guesthouse in the quiet residential area of Newtown Barracks but it is a short walk from some of the city's best nightlife. Its eight rooms are basic – curtains rather than doors separate the bathroom – but are fairly clean. Some are poky, so ask to look around and try to get a window onto the backyard.

★ Villa Boscardi   B&B $$

(☑223-1691; www.villaboscardi.com; 6043 Manatee Dr, Buttonwood Bay; s/d BZ$185/225; ❋ @ 🖳) Set in a secure middle-class suburb, this guesthouse and its charming hosts will smooth away any stresses that Belize City's rougher edges might induce. The eight rooms are large and elegant, built with Belizean materials and decorated with fresh, bold colors and prints. Some rooms have kitchen facilities, while guests of the other rooms have access to a shared kitchen.

D'Nest Inn   B&B **$$**

(📞 223-5416; www.dnestinn.com; 475 Cedar St, Belama phase 2; s/d/tr from BZ$144/179/214; ❄️ 🐾 🛜)
Your hosts Gaby and Oty have evidently put a lot of care into this retreat on the northern edge of town. The individually decorated rooms have four-poster beds and other Victorian-era antiques, handmade quilts and floral wallpaper. Even more enticing, a lush garden beckons with blooming orchids and allamandas, singing birds and quiet corners.

✖ Eating

★ Nerie's II Restaurant   BELIZEAN **$**

(Map p236; cnr Queen & Daly Sts; mains BZ$10-18; ⏰ 7am-9pm, closed Sun) Nerie's offers most accompaniments imaginable to rice and beans, including curried lamb, stewed cow foot, lobster, *gibnut* and deer. Begin with a choice of soups, including chicken, *escabeche* (with chicken, lime and onions), *chirmole* (with chicken and a chili-chocolate sauce) or cow foot, and finish with cassava pudding. Nerie's has another outlet – **Nerie's I Restaurant** (Douglas Jones St; mains BZ$10-18; ⏰ 7am-9pm, closed Sun) – on the north side.

The Ice Cream Shoppe   ICE CREAM **$**

(Map p236; 📞 223-1965; 17 Eve St; ⏰ 11am-7pm Mon-Thu, 11am-9pm Fri-Sun) When the heat hits unbearable head to this boutique ice-cream parlor and cool off with delicious homemade ice cream in a variety of great flavors, including some starring local fruits. Order a few scoops and sit back and enjoy the air-con and fast wi-fi.

Dario's Meat Pies   BELIZEAN **$**

(Map p236; 📞 203-5197; 33 Hydes Lane; meat pies BZ$1; ⏰ 5am-3pm) Ask any local who makes the best meat pies and they'll tell you without hesitation, Dario's. Get in line and choose from beef or chicken. They're also resold all over the country but it's best to buy them oven fresh at the source. The fillings are piping hot – take care when biting through the crust.

Celebrity Restaurant   INTERNATIONAL **$$**

(Map p236; 📞 223-7272; www.celebritybelize.com; cnr Marine Parade Blvd & Goal Lane; mains BZ$16-40; ⏰ 11am-11pm) We love Celebrity because it is a semi-swanky place that is not inside a hotel. The place has an extensive menu that

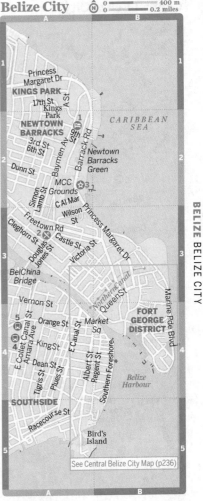

Belize City

🛏 **Sleeping**
1 Bayview Guest House A2

🍴 **Eating**
2 Nerie's I Restaurant..........................A3

🎭 **Entertainment**
3 Princess Cinema...............................A2

ℹ **Transport**
4 Main Bus Terminal.............................A4
5 Pound Yard Bus Stop........................A4

Central Belize City

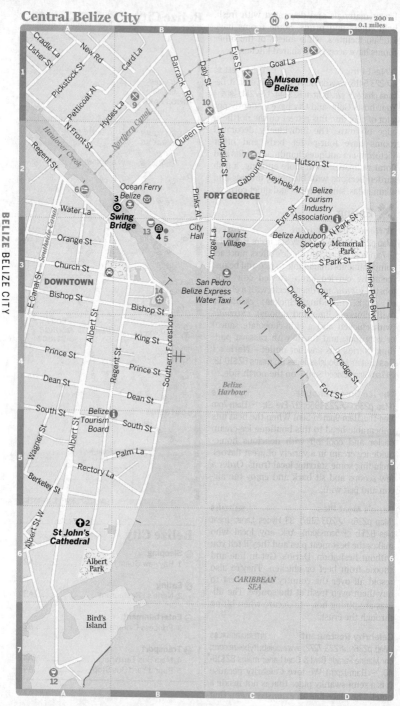

Central Belize City

◎ Top Sights
1 Museum of Belize C1
2 St John's Cathedral............................A6
3 Swing Bridge B2

◎ Sights
4 Image Factory B3

● Activities, Courses & Tours
5 S&L Travel B3

● Sleeping
6 Belcove Hotel A2
7 Sea Breeze Guesthouse C2

● Eating
8 Celebrity Restaurant.........................D1
9 Dario's Meat Pies B1
10 Nerie's II Restaurant..........................C1
11 The Ice Cream Shoppe C1

● Drinking & Nightlife
12 Bird's Isle Restaurant........................A7
13 Spoonaz B3

● Entertainment
14 Bliss Centre for the Performing
Arts B3

includes North American favorites such as steaks and sandwiches, Mexican fare like fajitas and quesadillas, plenty of pasta dishes and a few Mediterranean surprises like hummus, kofta and kebabs.

🍷 Drinking & Entertainment

★Spoonaz   CAFE
(Map p236; 223-1043; North Front St; noon-10pm Wed, 3pm-midnight Thu & Fri, noon-midnight Sat) An oasis in downtown Belize City, this cosmopolitan cafe serves quality coffee as well as paninis and sandwiches. There is a smart air-conditioned lounge area inside but you really want to be under the green cloth umbrellas out the back watching the sailboats bobbing on Haulover Creek and working your way through the cocktail list.

Bird's Isle Restaurant   BAR
(Map p236; Bird's Island; 10:30am-2:30pm & 5:30pm-late Mon-Fri, 10:30am-10pm Sat) Bird's Isle may be the best that Belize City has to offer. An island oasis at the southern tip of town, it manages to defy the urban grit that lies just a few blocks away. Locals and tourists alike flock to the open-air *palapa* to partake of sea breezes, fresh-squeezed juice and cold beers.

Bliss Centre for the Performing Arts   PERFORMING ARTS
(Map p236; 227-2110; www.nichbelize.org; Southern Foreshore) Operated by the Institute for Creative Arts, the revamped Bliss Centre has a fine 600-seat theater that stages a variety of events throughout the year. Look for concerts of traditional Belizean music and shows celebrating Belize and its culture. Annual events include the Belize Film Festival and the Children's Art Festival in May.

Princess Cinema   CINEMA
(223-2670; Princess Hotel & Casino, Newtown Barracks, Kings Park; admission BZ$15) The two-screen Princess cinema shows first-run Hollywood films, though usually a bit later than their US release dates.

ℹ Information

DANGERS & ANNOYANCES
Belize City isn't exactly the relaxed place the rest of the country is. While you are likely to spend most of your time in the commercial district (east of Southside Canal around Albert and Regent Sts) and in the Fort George district, both of which are safe during daylight hours, it's worth remaining vigilant.

After dark, it's best to take a taxi anywhere you go in the city. If you must walk, stay on better-lit major streets and don't go alone if you can help it. Get advice from your hotel about safety in specific neighborhoods.

INTERNET ACCESS
King Internet Service (16 King St; per hr BZ$3; 9am-7pm Mon-Sat) Downtown Internet access.

S&L Travel (Map p236; 227-5145, 227-7593; www.sltravelbelize.com; 91 North Front St) Aircon internet near the water-taxi docks

MEDICAL SERVICES
Karl Heusner Memorial Hospital (223-1671, 223-1548; www.khmh.bz; Princess Margaret Dr; emergency services 24hr) A public hospital in the north of town.

MONEY
All banks exchange US or Canadian dollars, British pounds and, usually, euros. Most ATMs are open 24 hours, though it's highly recommended that you visit them during daylight hours.

Belize Bank (60 Market Sq; 8am-3pm Mon-Thu, 8am-4:30pm Fri) The ATM is on the north side of the building. There is another **Belize Bank ATM** (North Front St) that is convenient for water taxis.

First Caribbean International Bank (21 Albert St; 8am-2:30pm Mon-Thu, 8am-4:30pm Fri)

Scotiabank (cnr Albert & Bishop Sts; ⊗8am-3pm Mon-Thu, 8am-4:30pm Fri)

POST

Main Post Office (Map p236; North Front St; ⊗8am-5pm Mon-Thu, 8am-4:30pm Fri)

TELEPHONE

BTL (☑227-7085; 1 Church St; ⊗8am-6pm Mon-Fri) Pick up SIM cards for cell devices at this downtown shop.

TOURIST INFORMATION

Belize Tourism Board (BTB; Map p236; ☑227-2420; www.travelbelize.org; 64 Regent St; ⊗8am-5pm Mon-Thu, 8am-4pm Fri) Pick up maps, magazines and all sorts of information relating to travel around Belize. This is also where you will find the cruise-ship schedule, which is published in a handy booklet.

Belize Tourism Industry Association (BTIA; Map p236; ☑227-1144; www.btia.org; 10 North Park St, Belize City; ⊗8am-noon & 1-5pm Mon-Fri) The BTIA is an independent association of tourism businesses, actively defending 'sustainable ecocultural tourism'. The office provides leaflets about the country's regions, copies of its *Destination Belize* annual magazine (free), and information on its members, which include many of Belize's best hotels, restaurants and other tourism businesses. The website has a plethora of information.

❶ Getting There & Away

AIR

Belize City has two airports: Philip Goldson International Airport (BZE), which is 11 miles northwest of the city center off the Philip Goldson Hwy; and the Municipal Airstrip (TZA), around 2 miles north of the city center. All international flights use the international airport. Domestic flights on both local carriers are divided between the two airports, but those using the Municipal Airstrip are cheaper (often significantly).

The following domestic airlines fly from Belize City:

Maya Island Air (☑223-1140, 223-1362; www.mayaislandair.com) Operates domestic flights to Caye Caulker, Dangriga, Placencia, Punta Gorda, and San Pedro on Ambergris Caye.

Tropic Air (☑226-2012; www.tropicair.com) Domestic flights from Belize City to Caye Caulker, Dangriga, Placencia, Punta Gorda, San Ignacio and San Pedro. Also serves Flores, Guatemala; Roatan, Honduras; and Cancún and Merida in Mexico.

BOAT

There are two water-taxi companies on North Front St offering similar services to Caye Caulker and San Pedro:

San Pedro Belize Express Water Taxi (Map p236; ☑223-2225; www.belizewatertaxi.com; Brown Sugar Mall, Front St) Professionally run water-taxi service with nine departures a day (approximately every hour from 8am to 5pm) to Caye Caulker (one way/return BZ$30/50, 45 minutes) and San Pedro (one way/return BZ$40/70, 1½ hours). Also operates one daily boat to and from Caye Caulker to Chetumal, Mexico (via San Pedro).

Ocean Ferry Belize (Map p236; ☑223-0033; www.oceanferrybelize.com; North Front St) New company running boat services to Caye Caulker (one way/return BZ$19/29, 45 minutes) and San Pedro (one way/return BZ$29/49, 1½ hours) out of the old Caye Caulker Water Taxi terminal. Leaves Belize City for both destinations at 8am, 10:30am, 1:30pm, 3pm and 5pm.

BUS

Belize City's **main bus terminal** (West Collett Canal St) is the old Novelo's terminal next to the canal which now sports a faded Rastafarian red, gold and green paint job. Most buses leave from here, although local buses within Belize District to destinations such as Ladyville and Burrell Boom leave from around the corner at the **Pound Yard bus stop** (Cemetery Rd).

❶ Getting Around

TO/FROM THE AIRPORT

Philip Goldson International Airport The taxi fare to/from the international airport is BZ$50 for one to two passengers and BZ$60 for three to four passengers. Alternatively, walk the 1.6 miles from the airport to the Philip Goldson Hwy, where fairly frequent buses pass heading to Belize City.

Municipal Airstrip Taxis cost around BZ$10 to the center of town.

Main Bus Terminal Taxis line up outside the bus terminal. They supposedly work on a turn basis but there always seems to be plenty of debate among drivers.

TAXI

Cabs cost around BZ$7 for rides within the city, give or take; if it's a long trip from one side of town to the other, expect to be charged a bit more. Confirm the price in advance with your driver. Most restaurants and hotels will call a cab for you.

NORTHERN CAYS

If you imagined stringing up a hammock on a deserted beach, there is an outer atoll with your name on it. Pining to be pampered? You can choose from an ever-growing glut of ritzy resorts on Ambergris Caye. San Pedro is prime for dancing the night away to a reggae beat, while Caye Caulker moves at a slower pace.

But the islands are only the beginning: the northern cays' richest resource lies below the surface of the sea. Only a few miles offshore, the barrier reef runs for 80 miles, offering unparalleled opportunities to explore canyons and coral, to face off with nurse sharks and stingrays, and to swim with schools of fish painted every color of the palette.

Caye Caulker

POP 1763

On Caye Caulker, there are no cars, no fumes and no hassles, just balmy breezes, fresh seafood, azure waters and a fantastic barrier reef at its doorstep. The easygoing attitude is due in part to the strong Creole presence on the island, which pulses to a classic reggae beat and is home to a small community of Rastafarians.

🏃 Activities

Activities on the island focus on water sports and sea life.

★ Stressless Tours   SNORKELING, FISHING
(☑ 624-6064; www.stresslesstours.com; Dock St)
🦯 This professional new operation stands out in the crowded snorkeling market for its great customer service, focus on sustainability and passionate guides. It offers a condensed version of the classic Hol Chan/Shark Ray Alley trip with a focus on exploring a variety of experiences in the water rather than non-snorkeling extras. It also runs fishing trips and charter excursions.

★ Contour   WATER SPORTS
(☑ 653-8515; www.contourbelize.com; Front St; rentals per hr/half-day/full day BZ$30/80/120; ⊙8am-6pm) This well-run shop brings something different to the world of Caulker aquatic recreation: taking visitors through mangroves or on sunset tours on paddleboards. It also runs scenic yoga sessions on paddleboards and rents out its quality equipment.

Belize Diving Services   DIVING
(☑ 226-0143;   www.belizedivingservices.net;
Chapoose St) Professional and highly recommended dive shop that runs PADI-certification courses and offers immersions around the local reefs, as well as offshore dives at Turneffe Elbow and the Blue Hole. It also offers advanced technical dive training and organizes trips to local cave systems.

Kitexplorer   KITESURFING
(☑ 626-4613; www.kitexplorer.com; Front St; equipment rental per hr/half-day/day BZ$120/200/300; ⊙8am-6pm) Offers a two-hour introductory course (BZ$360) or a six-hour basic course (BZ$980), as well as equipment rental. Also offers windsurfing classes and has SUP boards. Located at the northern end of the island near the Split.

👉 Tours

Blackhawk Sailing Tours   SAILING
(☑ 607-0323; www.blackhawksailing.com; Front St) Locally owned and operated, Blackhawk offers sailing/snorkeling tours; overnight sailing trips, where guests sleep under the stars on sandy isles; and sunset reggae cruises complete with fresh *ceviche*.

★ Caveman Tours   SNORKELING
(☑ 226-0367;   www.cavemansnorkelingtours.com;
Front St;   ⊙8:30am-5:30pm) Larger-than-life Captain Caveman offers extremely popular snorkeling trips throughout local waters, as well as manatee-watching expeditions to Swallow Caye and visits to sandy Goff Caye. He is serious, safety conscious and very attentive to customer needs. His office is inside the handicraft market.

Raggamuffin Tours   BOAT TOUR
(☑ 226-0348; www.raggamuffintours.com; Front St) Runs popular three-day sailing and camping trips to Placencia departing every Tuesday and Friday that pass through some less-visited islands and areas of reef. Advance reservations are essential. Also runs snorkeling tours to Hol Chan and sunset sailing cruises.

🛏 Sleeping

Ocean Pearl Royale Hotel   HOTEL $
(☑ 226-0074; oceanpearl@btl.net; Park St; r with/without air-con BZ$90/65, cabaña BZ$100; ❄🐾) Located on a quiet side street, this small hotel is surrounded by sandy grounds strewn with palms and flowering trees that attract hummingbirds and other beauties. The 10

Caye Caulker

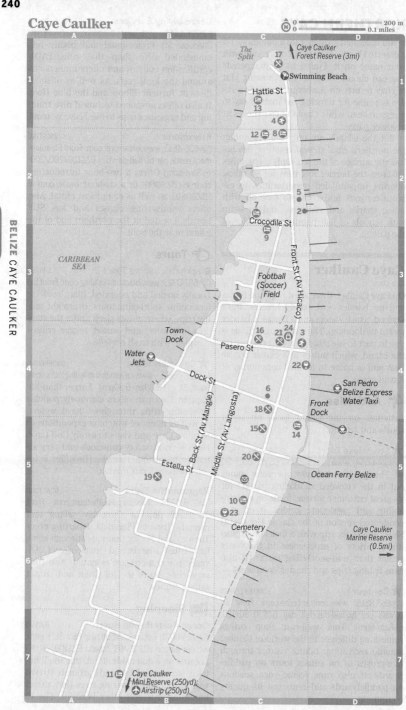

The Split

17

Caye Caulker Forest Reserve (3mi)

Swimming Beach

Hattie St

13

4

12   8

5

2

7

Crocodile St

9

CARIBBEAN SEA

Football (Soccer) Field

1

Town Dock

16   21   24

3

Pasero St

Water Jets

22

Dock St

San Pedro Belize Express Water Taxi

6

Front Dock

18

Front St (Av Hicaco)

15

14

Back St (Av Mangle)

Middle St (Av Langosta)

20

Estella St

Ocean Ferry Belize

19

Cemetery

10

23

Caye Caulker Marine Reserve (0.5mi)

11

Caye Caulker Mini Reserve (250yd); Airstrip (250yd)

0   200 m
0   0.1 miles

Caye Caulker

🔵 Activities, Courses & Tours
1 Belize Diving Services	C3
Blackhawk Sailing Tours	(see 8)
2 Caveman Tours	C2
3 Contour	C4
4 Kitexplorer	C1
5 Raggamuffin Tours	C2
6 Stressless Tours	C4

🔵 Sleeping
7 Bella's Hostel	C2
8 Caye Reef	C2
9 Dirty McNasty's Hostel	C3
10 Juan in a Million	C5
11 Oasi	B7
12 Ocean Pearl Royale Hotel	C2
13 Sea Dreams Hotel	C1
14 Seaside Cabanas	C5

🔵 Eating
15 Amor Y Café	C5
16 Errolyns House of Fry Jacks	C4
17 Gelato Italiano	C1
18 Habaneros	C4
19 Little Kitchen Restaurant	B5
20 Pasta per Caso	C5
21 Roy's Blue Water Grill	C4

🔵 Drinking & Nightlife
22 Barrier Reef Sports Bar & Grill	C4
23 I&I Reggae Bar	C5

🔵 Shopping
24 Little Blue Gift Shop	C4

clean rooms are remarkably good value, with brightly painted walls and simple wood furnishings. A big, airy lobby offers space for guests to congregate and swap island stories.

Juan in a Million   GUESTHOUSE **$**
(Pirates of the Caribbean; Front St; dm BZ$15, s with/without air-con BZ$44/39, d with/without air-con BZ$49/44) On the quiet southern end of Front St, this small, friendly guesthouse is popular with budget travelers thanks to its cheap, comfortable air-conditioned dorms and neat private rooms. For value its hard to beat.

Bella's Hostel   HOSTEL **$**
(✎635-4265; bellas.hostel@yahoo.com; Crocodile St; dm with/without air-con BZ$35/25, s/d/t BZ$35/60/75; 🛜) On the back side of the island, Bella's is a hideaway for the backpacker set, who appreciate the good-value dorms in the elevated wooden house. There is a chilled-out vibe here aided by laid-back management and good tunes. You are likely to see travelers sharing a meal in the kitchen, playing cards on the balcony and taking advantage of free rentals, such as canoes and bikes.

Dirty McNasty's Hostel   HOSTEL **$**
(✎636-7512; Crocodile St; dm with/without air-con BZ$43/32, d BZ$76; 🛜) The ongoing construction work at this large hostel takes away from the paradise vibe, and many of the rooms feel like budget university dorms or even a bush penitentiary, with the only decoration being the fire extinguishers. Even so, the place remains popular for its free breakfast and rum punch, which guarantees a social atmosphere.

⭐ **Sea Dreams Hotel**   B&B **$$**
(✎226-0602; www.seadreamsbelize.com; Hattie St; r BZ$230, apt BZ$330-430; ❄🛜) A lovely guesthouse on the north side of the island, Sea Dreams offers a rare combination of easy access and sweet tranquillity. Spend the day lounging around the Split, then retreat to the cozy accommodation just a few steps away. Original paintings by local artists adorn the colorful walls of the rooms and apartments, which are elegant and comfortable.

⭐ **Oasi**   GUESTHOUSE **$$**
(✎623-9401; www.oasi-holidaysbelize.com; Back St; apt BZ$190-210; ❄🛜🞿) Set around blooming tropical gardens featuring an inviting pool, this excellent guesthouse has just four elegant apartments with lovely wide verandas (hung with hammocks, of course). Woven tapestries and warm hues enrich the interiors, which are equipped with full kitchens, sofas and quality bathrooms. There's also a small bar that hosts regular low-key concerts and a fine BBQ area.

Seaside Cabanas   RESORT **$$**
(✎226-0498; www.seasidecabanas.com; Dock St; r BZ$258-358, ste BZ$398; ❄🛜🞿) Sun-yellow stucco buildings shaded by thatched-palm roofs exude a tropical atmosphere at this beachfront beauty. The interior decor features desert colors, rich fabrics and plenty of pillows. Most of the rooms occupy the main building facing the ocean; closer to the sea, the comfortable *cabañas* take advantage of the location with private rooftop decks and terrace hot tubs.

⭐ **Caye Reef**   BOUTIQUE HOTEL **$$$**
(✎226-0381; www.cayereef.com; Front St; 1-bedroom apt BZ$346-420, 2-bedroom apt BZ$420-

494; ✻🔊🖥) The six apartments at Caye Reef have been designed with the utmost attention to detail – from the original artwork hanging on the walls to the swinging hammocks hanging on the private balconies. Room prices rise with the floor, with the most expensive rooms being on the 3rd floor.

🍴 Eating

Amor Y Café   BREAKFAST $
(Front St; breakfast BZ$6-12.50; ⊙6am-noon; 📶) There's no contest when it comes to the most popular breakfast spot on the island – this place is always busy, but you won't have to wait long for a table on the shaded porch overlooking Front St. Take your pick from freshly squeezed juices, scrambled eggs or homemade yogurt topped with fruit – and don't miss out on the freshly brewed coffee.

Errolyns House of Fry Jacks   BELIZEAN $
(Middle St; BZ$1.50-5; ⊙6am-3pm & 6-9pm Tue-Sun) Who said Belize had to be expensive? Locals and travelers alike descend on this neat, board takeout hut to chow down on the island's best-value breakfast – delicious golden fry-jacks (deep-fried dough) filled with any combination of beans, cheese, egg, beef or chicken. Cheap, filling and delicious.

Gelato Italiano   ICE CREAM $
(The Split; ice cream BZ$5-10; ⊙11am-6pm) Long overdue on Caye Caulker, Gelato Italiano has brought first-class ice cream to the island. Choose from over a dozen varieties of genuine Italian gelato and head outside to pull up a stool on the long balcony overlooking the vivid blue Caribbean. The perfect way to cool off.

Little Kitchen Restaurant   BELIZEAN $$
(📶667-2178; off Luciano Reyes St; mains BZ$15-25; ⊙noon-10pm) Elisia Flower's Little Kitchen is a 3rd-floor, open-air restaurant on Caulker's southwestern side serving traditional (yet artfully done) Belizean dishes such as curry shrimp, coconut red snapper and excellent conch fritters (just to name a few). Portions are big and it's outstanding value, although we have some concerns about immature lobsters on the menu – make sure yours is legal size.

Pasta per Caso   ITALIAN $$
(Front St; mains BZ$25-27; ⊙6-9pm Mon-Thu) Pull up a stool at one of the long tables on the deck and dig into some of the best pasta in Belize, prepared the traditional way by the Milanese owners. There is usually just one vegetarian and one non-veg sauce served with a healthy portion of one of the many varieties of fresh pasta made onsite. Garden fresh salads also make an appearance.

Roy's Blue Water Grill   BELIZEAN $$
(Pasero St; mains BZ$18-25; ⊙6-10pm) Former Habaneros chef Roy has branched out on his own with this simple open-air restaurant just off the main drag. The menu features plenty of fresh seafood, but there are also interesting chicken and pork dishes, all of which are imbued with rich Caribbean flavors.

⭐Habaneros   INTERNATIONAL $$$
(📶626-4911; habanerosdream@gmail.com; cnr Front & Dock Sts; mains BZ$32-58; ⊙6-11pm) Caulker's 'hottest' restaurant, named for the habanero chili, is located in a brightly painted clapboard house in the center of town. Here chefs prepare gourmet international food, combining fresh seafood, meat and vegetables with insanely delicious sauces and flavors. Wash it down with a fine wine or a jug of sangria.

🍷 Drinking & Nightlife

Barrier Reef Sports Bar & Grill   SPORTS BAR
(Front St; ⊙9am-midnight) Perennially popular with expats and international visitors alike, this waterfront beach bar serves fantastic international food and all kinds of drinks. There is often live music and major sporting events are shown on the many flat-screen TVs. It's pretty much the only place on the island that you are always guaranteed to find a social atmosphere.

I&I Reggae Bar   BAR
(Luciano Reyes St; ⊙6pm-midnight) I&I is the island's most hip, happening spot after dark, when its healthy sound system belts out a reggae beat. Its three levels each offer a different scene, with a dance floor on one and swings hanging from the rafters on another. The top floor is the 'chill-out zone,' complete with hammocks and panoramic views. A great place for a sunset drink.

🛍 Shopping

Little Blue Gift Shop   GIFTS
(Front St; ⊙9am-4pm Mon-Sat) This excellent gift shop near the dock sells handcrafted artisanal products made from local ingredients, including non-chemical bug spray

made with coconut oil, and a variety of interesting works by local artists.

ℹ️ Information

There is a basic health center on the island but if you really need medical attention you're better off heading directly to Belize City.

Atlantic Bank (Middle St; ⊗8am-2pm Mon-Fri, 8:30am-noon Sat) Has a pair of fairly reliable ATMs, although make sure you have some cash before you arrive in case they are out of service.

Caye Caulker BTIA (www.cayecaulkervacation.com) The official site of the Caye Caulker branch of the Belize Tourism Industry Association (BTIA).

Caye Caulker Health Center (☑226-0166, emergency 668-2547) Just off Front St, two blocks south of Dock St.

GoCayeCaulker.com (www.gocayecaulker.com) General information for visitors.

Post Office (Estella St, Caye Caulker Health Center Bldg; ⊗8am-noon & 1-4:30pm Mon-Thu, to 4pm Fri)

ℹ️ Getting There & Away

AIR

Both **Maya Island Air** (☑226-0012; www.mayaislandair.com) and **Tropic Air** (☑226-0040; www.tropicair.com) connect Caye Caulker with San Pedro and Belize City. The airline offices are at Caye Caulker's newly renovated airstrip at the southern end of the island.

BOAT

There are two companies running boats from Caye Caulker to Belize City and San Pedro.

Ocean Ferry Belize (☑226-0033; www.oceanferrybelize.com) boats depart for Belize City (one way BZ$19, round trip BZ$29, 45 minutes) at 6:30am, 8:30am, 10:30am, 1:30pm and 4:30pm, and for San Pedro (one way BZ$19, round trip BZ$29, 40 minutes) at 8:45am, 11:15am, 2:15pm, 3pm and 5pm.

San Pedro Belize Express Water Taxis (☑226-0225; www.belizewatertaxi.com) depart for San Pedro (one way BZ$30, round trip BZ$50) at 7am, 8:45am, 9:45am, 11:15am, 12:45pm, 2:15pm, 3:45pm, 4:45pm, 5:15pm and 6:15pm, and Belize City (one way BZ$30, round trip BZ$50) at 6:30am, 7am, 8am, 9am, 10:30am, noon, 1:30pm, 3:30pm and 5pm.

The docks are a couple of blocks apart on the reef side of the island.

San Pedro Belize Express Water Taxis also runs a daily service to Chetumal, Mexico via San Pedro. **Water Jets** (☑226-2194; www.sanpedrowatertaxi.com; lagoon dock) runs the same service on alternate days.

ℹ️ Getting Around

Caulker is so small that most people walk everywhere. A couple of golf-cart taxis hang out around Front St and charge BZ$5 to BZ$7 per short trip around town.

You can rent a golf cart at **Buddy's Golf Cart Rentals** (☑628-8508; buddys_carts@hotmail.com; Middle St; per hr/day/24hr BZ$25/100/150) but bicycle rental is far cheaper and just as fast a way to get around. You can rent bikes at grocery stores, tour operators and hotels.

Ambergris Caye & San Pedro

POP 16,444

The undisputed superstar of Belize's tourism industry, 'La Isla Bonita' is an enigma that continues to defy the odds by somehow balancing large-scale tourism development with a fun, laid-back atmosphere.

Ambergris Caye remains for many visitors the archetypal tropical paradise where sun-drenched days are filled with fruity drinks and water sports. There are plenty of simple pleasures to be had here from riding a bike along a windswept beach path under the shade of coconut trees to snorkeling in crystal clear waters.

Though the entire island is often called San Pedro, technically that is the name of the town that dominates the southern half.

🏃 Activities

If you're into water sports, you'll be in ecstasy on Ambergris. San Pedro is awash with tour companies and individuals organizing scuba diving, snorkeling, windsurfing, sailing, kitesurfing, swimming and fishing trips.

★**Hol Chan Marine Reserve** DIVE SITE (www.holchanbelize.org; admission BZ$20) At the southern tip of Ambergris, the 6.5-sq-mile Hol Chan Marine Reserve is probably Belize's most oft-visited diving and snorkeling site due to its spectacular coral formations, and abundance and diversity of marine life – not to mention its proximity to the cays. Hol Chan is Maya for 'Little Channel,' which refers to a natural break in the reef known as **Hol Chan Cut**. The channel walls are covered with colorful corals, which harbor an amazing variety of fish life, including moray eels and black groupers.

San Pedro (Ambergris Caye)

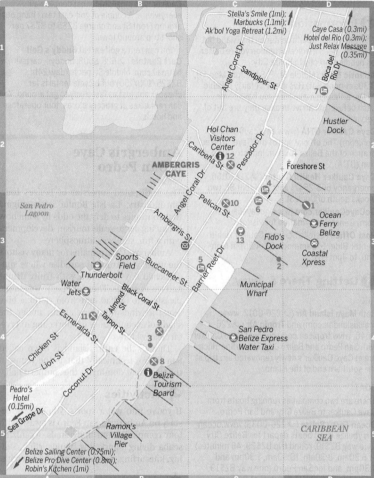

Stella's Smile (1mi);
Marbucks (1.1mi);
Ak'bol Yoga Retreat (1.2mi)

Caye Casa (0.3mi);
Hotel del Rio (0.3mi);
Just Relax Massage
(0.35mi)

Hustler
Dock

AMBERGRIS
CAYE

Hol Chan
Visitors
Center

Foreshore St

San Pedro
Lagoon

Ocean
Ferry
Belize

Fido's
Dock

Coastal
Xpress

Sports
Field

Thunderbolt

Water
Jets

Municipal
Wharf

San Pedro
Belize Express
Water Taxi

Belize
Tourism
Board

Pedro's
Hotel
(0.15mi)

Ramon's
Village
Pier

CARIBBEAN
SEA

Belize Sailing Center (0.75mi);
Belize Pro Dive Center (0.8mi);
Robin's Kitchen (1mi)

Belize Pro Dive Center   DIVING
(☏ 226-2092; www.belizeprodivecenter.com; Sea Grape Dr; ☺ 7am-6pm) Professionally run dive shop with two-tank reef dives and Hol Chan trips departing every morning, as well as offshore dives and dive courses.

Belize Sailing Center   WATER SPORTS
(☏ 632-4101; www.belizesailingschool.com; Caribbean Villas Hotel, Sea Grape Dr) Sign up for sailing lessons for BZ$90 per hour, or if you're already your own captain, rent a Laser Pico or a Hobie and set sail. You can also go kitesurfing – a basic three-hour instructional course costs BZ$400, while rental equip-

ment runs at BZ$240 per half day. Instructors are enthusiastic and highly qualified.

★ Ecologic Divers   DIVING
(☏ 226-4118; www.ecologicdivers.com; single-/double-/triple-tank dives BZ$112/180/247) High-end dive shop with great customer service and solid environmental credentials. It offers all of the local dives, multiday dive charters on luxurious catamarans, fishing expeditions and boat cruises. Management promises small groups with one dive master to every six divers on all immersions. Also recommended for dive courses.

San Pedro (Ambergris Caye)

⊕ **Activities, Courses & Tours**
1 Ecologic Divers.....................................D3
2 Island Dream Tours.............................C3
3 Seaduced by Belize............................B4

⊛ **Sleeping**
4 Conch Shell Inn...................................C2
5 Hostel La Vista.....................................C3
6 Hotel San Pedrano..............................C3
7 Sandbar..D1

⊗ **Eating**
8 Belize Chocolate Company................B4
9 Celi's Deli..B4
10 DandE's Frozen Custard....................C3
11 El Fogón..A4
12 My Secret Deli.....................................C2

⊙ **Drinking & Nightlife**
13 Fido's...C3

⊛ **Shopping**
Belizean Arts Gallery.................(see 13)

Packages to the Blue Hole including breakfast, lunch, drinks and park fees run at BZ$697 while Turneffe Atoll trips are BZ$540.

Just Relax Massage MASSAGE
(666-3536; Boca del Rio beachfront) Certified massage therapist Shirlene Santino runs a small beachfront day spa out of a lovely cloth *palapa* tent. Shirlene specializes in Swedish, deep tissue and Belizean-style massage (using coconut oil and incorporating a variety of deep tissue toxin-releasing techniques). Beachfront massages are BZ$80 to BZ$100 per hour, and house calls are BZ$120 to BZ$140.

Ak'bol Yoga Retreat YOGA
(☑626-6296, 226-2073; www.akbol.com; North Island) With two open, thatch-roof yoga studios (one at the end of the dock), Ak'bol offers daily walk-in classes (BZ$30), in addition to the week-long yoga retreats that are scheduled throughout the year. It's 1 mile north of the bridge.

☞ Tours

Island Dream Tours BOAT TOUR
(www.islanddreamtours.com; Fido's Dock) Offers a variety of trips aboard a spacious motorized catamaran including snorkeling trips and an epic sunset cruise that morphs into a full dinner on the water.

Seaduced by Belize BOAT TOUR
(☑226-2254; www.seaducedbybelize.com; Tarpon St, Vilma Linda Plaza; ⊙8am-6pm; 🚻) Offers a range of sailing trips, including a sunset cruise and a full-day trip to Caye Caulker. Also runs good-value outings to spot manatees at Swallow Caye (BZ$210), including lunch at Goff's Caye and snorkeling. Other tours include visits to Bacalar Chico and a recommended full-day trip to Robles Beach, complete with snorkel stops and beach BBQ.

El Gato BOAT TOUR
(☑602-8552, 226-2264; www.ambergriscaye.com/elgato; half-/full-day cruise BZ$120/160) Sail to Caye Caulker aboard the *El Gato,* stopping to snorkel if you like. Also offers sunset cruises.

🛏 Sleeping

Reservations are recommended for the high (winter) season, between December and May. Almost all hotels accept major credit cards, though you may pay a steep surcharge. For apartments, suites and condominiums, check www.ambergriscaye.com.

Hostel La Vista HOSTEL $
(☑627-0831; www.hostellavista.com; Barrier Reef Dr; dm BZ$30-36, r BZ$100-120; 🟦) On the site of one of San Pedro's original hotels, in front of the park right in the middle of town, this friendly new hostel has clean and comfortable rooms with air-conditioning. Dorms are fairly spacious while private rooms can fit up to five guests, making them a good deal if you get a group together.

Hotel San Pedrano GUESTHOUSE $
(☑226-2054; sanpedrano@btl.net; Barrier Reef Dr; s/d BZ$75/85, with air-con BZ$95/105; 🟦🔲) There are no views from this 2nd-story, streetside hostelry, but you might catch the breeze from the balcony. Relatively spacious rooms have two or three beds.

Pedro's Hotel HOSTEL, HOTEL $
(☑226-3825, 206-2198, 610-5526; www.pedroshotel.com; Sea Grape Dr; s/d without bathroom BZ$30/60, r with air-con BZ$120, deluxe BZ$140; 🟦🔲🟦) One of the cheapest budget options on the island, Pedro's is a longtime San Pedro party hotel favorite. The original 'hostel' has tiny cell-like rooms with thin walls and shared bathrooms. The best accommodations are near the pool in the deluxe annex, which has 12 rooms featuring flat-screen TVs with 110+ channels, air-con and en suite bathrooms with hot showers.

BELIZE AMBERGRIS CAYE& SAN PEDRO

Sandbar
HOSTEL $$

(📞 226-2008; www.sanpedrohostel.com; Boca del Rio; dm/r BZ$30/120; ✳🛜) Rejoice! A tight budget no longer means having to bed down in a stifling room on a back street. San Pedro's only waterfront hostel is also easily its best. The bright private rooms have big sliding doors leading onto a balcony with fine Caribbean vistas, while the air-conditioned dorms are well designed with privacy curtains and individual power sockets for each bed.

★ Caye Casa
BOUTIQUE HOTEL $$

(📞 226-2880; www.cayecasa.com; Boca del Rio; r BZ$250, ste BZ$300, villa from BZ$480; ✳🛜🏊) At the quiet northern end of San Pedro town, Caye Casa stands out for its simplicity, sophistication and utter loveliness. The sweet colonial-style *casitas* and villas offer thatched-roof porches with wonderful sea views, fully stocked kitchens with stainless-steel appliances and limestone countertops, spacious tiled bathrooms and inviting king-and queen-sized beds.

★ Ak'bol Yoga Retreat
RESORT $$

(📞 626-6296, 226-2073; www.akbol.com; North Island; s/d BZ$70/100, cabaña BZ$290-330; 🏊) Yogis, rejoice! Ak'bol, or 'Heart of the Village,' is a sweet retreat in a near-perfect location about 1 mile north of town on the North Island. The seven colorful *cabañas* have delightful details, such as handcrafted hardwood furniture and mosaic sinks with conch shell faucets. Enjoy plantation-style shutters that open to the sea and mosaic-tiled showers that are open to the sky.

Conch Shell Inn
HOTEL $$

(📞 226-2062; 11 Foreshore St; r downstairs/upstairs BZ$148/188; ✳🛜) This pink-and-white beauty on the beach offers excellent value smack dab in the middle of town. Recently revamped, the 10 brightly tiled rooms are spacious and comfortable, and the upstairs ones have kitchenettes and hammocks hanging on the shared balcony. The sandy beach area is not great for swimming, but it is decked out with hammocks and lounge chairs from which to watch the comings and goings.

Hotel del Rio
GUESTHOUSE, CABINS $$

(📞 226-2286; www.hoteldelriobelize.com; Boca del Rio; r BZ$120-150, cabaña BZ$180-300; ✳🛜) Just south of San Pedro River, this little lodge is in a perfect spot on a quiet stretch of beach, and provides easy access into town.

WORTH A TRIP

BLUE HOLE NATURAL MONUMENT

At the center of Lighthouse Reef is the world-famous Blue Hole Natural Monument (www.belizeaudubon.org; entrance fee BZ$60; ⊙ 8am-4:30pm), an incomparable natural wonder and unique diving experience. It may not be the best dive in Belize, but it certainly ranks among the most popular. The image of the Blue Hole – a deep blue pupil with an aquamarine border surrounded by the lighter shades of the reef – has become a logo for tourist publicity and a symbol of Belize.

Deep blue in the center, the hole forms a perfect 1000ft-diameter circle on the surface. Inside, it is said to be 430ft deep, but as much as 200ft of this may now be filled with silt and other natural debris.

Note: this trip involves two hours each way by boat in possibly rough, open waters. Also, there's a BZ$60 marine-park fee for diving or snorkeling at the Blue Hole, that is usually on top of the dive fees.

Rooms vary in size and layout: most enticing are the fan-cooled, thatched-roof *cabañas* (sleeping two to four people) that are clustered around the sandy grounds, which have a central *palapa* that's ideal for socializing or swinging in a hammock.

★ Victoria House
RESORT $$$

(📞 226-2067, in USA 800-247-5159; www.victoriahouse.com; Sea Grape Dr; r from BZ$400, casitas BZ$670, villas BZ$1950-3950; ✳🛜🏊) This elegant beach resort is one of the oldest on the island, but is meticulously maintained and shines like new. It is fronted by a beautiful, wide beach shaded by a healthy stand of palms, while the grassy grounds center around two excellent pools. Rooms are in thatched-roof *casitas*, or colonial-style 'plantation' houses, with a sophisticated white-on-white scheme that oozes luxury.

🍴 Eating

Although there are plenty of options for cheap street food, tacos and fry-jacks, it's hard to sit down at a San Pedro restaurant without paying as much as BZ$50 per person.

★ DandE's Frozen Custard ICE CREAM $

(www.dande.bz; Pescador Dr; ice cream from BZ$6; ⊘2-9pm; ⚑) Don't be confused by 'frozen custard.' It's basically high-quality ice cream, made with eggs for extra richness, then churned as it freezes for extra dense creaminess. The flavors change frequently, often featuring local fruity flavors such as coconut, sour sop and mango. Alternatively, you can't go wrong with 'not just' vanilla. DandE's also makes sorbet, but you're a fool if you forgo the frozen custard.

My Secret Deli BELIZEAN $

(Caribeña St; meals BZ$8-12.50; ⊘8am-9pm Mon-Sat) This is one secret too good to keep, especially for the budget-conscious traveler looking for good bargain eats. This family-run eatery serves filling Belize favorites such as stew chicken, steak and rice, and chunky chicken vegetable soup. It gets busy but is worth waiting for a table.

Celi's Deli FAST FOOD $

(Barrier Reef Dr; deli items BZ$1-8; ⊘5am-5pm) A fantastic find for breakfast or lunch, Celi's Deli serves great food to go – sandwiches, meat pies, tacos, tamales and homemade cakes.

Belize Chocolate Company SWEETS $

(www.belizechocolatecompany.com; Barrier Reef Dr; chocolates BZ$2.50-4; ⊘9am-7pm; ⚑🛜) Run by Chris and Jo Beaumont, the same couple who manufacture the amazing (and Ambergris-produced) Kakaw brand chocolate, this newly opened cafe serves up the finest cacao products on the island.

El Fogón BELIZEAN $$

(📞206-2121; Trigger Fish St; mains BZ$25-40; ⊘11am-9pm) At first glance the ambiance doesn't seem to match the price tag at this backstreet eatery, but once the food arrives you'll not be too worried about the lack of chic design. El Fogón serves up wonderfully prepared classic Belizean Creole cuisine including plenty of fresh seafood cooked to perfection. The conch is especially tasty.

★ Robin's Kitchen JAMAICAN $$

(📞651-3583; Sea Grape Dr; mains BZ$15-20; ⊘11am-9pm Sun-Fri, 6-9pm Sat) At his simple, small roadside restaurant south of town, Jamaican BBQ king Robin prepares the best jerk chicken and fish this side of Kingston. Dishes are spicy without overbearing the subtle flavors, and his sauces are also to die for. If you catch your own fish, Robin will prepare it for you any way you like and will only charge for sides.

★ Palmilla Restaurant INTERNATIONAL $$$

(📞226-2067; www.victoria-house.com; Coconut Dr; mains BZ$40-78; ⊘7am-10pm; ⚑📶) The classy, candlelit restaurant at Victoria House is overseen by New York–trained chef José Luis Ortega, who prepares high-quality cuisine for his discriminating guests. At lunchtime, you might prefer Admiral Nelson's Beach Bar, the hotel's casual, open-air cafe on the beachfront.

★ Hidden Treasure CARIBBEAN $$$

(📞226-4111; www.hiddentreasurebelize.com; 4088 Sarstoon St; mains BZ$29-68; ⊘5-9pm Wed-Mon; 📶) Living up to its name, Hidden Treasure is a gorgeous open-air restaurant set in an out-of-the-way residential neighborhood (follow the signs from Coconut Dr). Lit by candles, the beautiful bamboo and hardwood dining room is the perfect setting for a romantic dinner, which might feature almond-crusted grouper, snapper wrapped in a banana leaf, or spare ribs marinated in a Garifuna spice rub.

🍷 Drinking & Nightlife

Stella's Smile WINE BAR

(📞602-6574; Mile 1, Tres Cocos, North Island; ⊘4-9pm Wed-Sat, 8am-2pm Sun) A fantastic addition to the North Island entertainment scene, Stella's is a classy but unpretentious wine bar set in a lovely garden on the edge of the San Pedro Lagoon that affords fine sunset views. Sit on lounge chairs under the trees or at a table in the open-air *palapa* and work your way through the 14 reds and 14 whites on the menu.

Marbucks COFFEE

(coffee BZ$4-15) The North Island's only real coffee shop serves up all kinds of caffeinated beverages – both hot and cold – using quality Guatemalan beans. Also sells excellent breakfasts. It's just off the main road at the Palapa Bar turnoff.

Fido's CLUB

(www.fidosbelize.com; 18 Barrier Reef Dr; ⊘11am-midnight) This enormous *palapa* – decorated with seafaring memorabilia – attracts crowds for drinking, dancing and hooking up. There's plenty of seating, an extensive food menu and an ample-sized dance floor. Live music is on every night at 8pm – classic and acoustic rock, reggae and the occasional record spin.

248

🛍 Shopping

Belizean Arts Gallery   ARTS
(www.belizeanarts.com; 18 Barrier Reef Dr; ⊙9am-
10pm Mon-Sat) This is one of the country's
best shops for local art and handicrafts,
selling ceramics, wood carvings, Garifuna
drums and antiques alongside affordable
and tasteful knickknacks. You'll also find a
decent selection of paintings by local and
national artists. Rainforest-flora beauty
products, including soaps, are on sale, too.
It's inside Fido's.

❶ Information

You can exchange money easily in San Pedro,
and US dollars are widely accepted. Most accommodations accept card payment.

San Pedro has both private and public health
facilities, but for serious conditions you would
want to get to Belize City.

Ambergris Caye (www.ambergriscaye.com)
Excellent island information and a lively mes-
sage board.

Atlantic Bank (Barrier Reef Dr; ⊙8am-3pm
Mon-Fri, 8:30am-noon Sat)

Belize Bank (Barrier Reef Dr; ⊙8am-3pm
Mon-Thu, to 4:30pm Fri)

Belize Tourism Board (☑226-4532; Barrier
Reef Dr; ⊙8am-5pm Mon-Fri) Goverment tourism office with limited practical information.

Hol Chan Visitors Center (Caribeña St;
⊙9am-5pm) Information and displays on
marine life.

Hyperbaric Chamber (☑226-3195, 684-8111,
226-2851; Lion St; ⊙24hr) Center for diving
accidents – it's in front of the Maya Island Air
terminal.

Post Office (Pescador Dr; ⊙8am-5pm Mon-
Thu, to 4pm Fri)

**San Carlos Medical Clinic, Pharmacy &
Pathology Lab** (☑226-2918, emergencies 614-
9251; 28 Pescador Dr; ⊙24hr) Private clinic
treating ailments and performing blood tests.

San Pedro Policlinic (☑226-2536; Sea Grape
Dr; ⊙24hr) A 24-hour public health clinic.

❶ Getting There & Away

AIR

The San Pedro airstrip is just south of the town
center on Coconut Dr.

Tropic Air (☑226-2012; www.tropicair.com;
Coconut Dr) Operates around 20 flights a day
to Belize City's Philip Goldson International Airport (one way BZ$178, return BZ$315, 20 minutes), as well as around a dozen flights to the
Belize City Municipal Airstrip, 12 miles closer to
town (one way BZ$109, return BZ$192, 20 minutes). There are also four flights a day to Caye

Caulker (one way BZ$106, return BZ$186, five
minutes, six daily). Other destinations include
Corozal, Orange Walk and San Ignacio.

Maya Island Air (☑226-2485; www.maya
islandair.com) Runs regular flights to Belize
International (one way BZ$169, return BZ$306,
20 minutes) and Belize Municipal (one way
BZ$102, return BZ$186, 20 minutes) airports
with some services stopping on Caye Caulker.
Also has four flights daily to Corozal and two to
Orange Walk.

BOAT

There are two water-taxi companies running
the route between San Pedro and Belize City via
Caye Caulker, both departing from docks on the
reef side of the island.

San Pedro Belize Express Water Taxi (☑226-
3535; www.belizewatertaxi.com; Black Coral
St) Departs San Pedro for Caye Caulker (one
way BZ$30, round trip BZ$50, 40 minutes) and
Belize City (one way BZ$40, round trip BZ$70,
1½ hours) at 6am, 6:30am, 7:30am, 8:30am,
10am, 11:30am, 1pm, 3pm and 4:30pm.

Ocean Ferry Belize (☑226-2033; www.ocean
ferrybelize.com; Caribeña St) Leaves San Pedro
for Caye Caulker (one way BZ$19, round trip
BZ$29, 40 minutes) and Belize City (one way
BZ$29, round trip BZ$49, 1½ hours) at 6am,
8am, 10am, 1pm and 4pm.

Thunderbolt (☑631-3400; Black Coral St; one
way/return BZ$50/90) Operates a daily service
between San Pedro and Corozal in northern
Belize (one way BZ$50, round trip BZ$90, two
hours) departing from behind the football field
on the lagoon side of the island.

There are also departures every morning at
8am for Chetumal, Mexico (one way BZ$100
to BZ$110, two hours) from the **International
Departures Dock** on the lagoon side of town
with companies **Water Jets** (☑226-2194; www.
sanpedrowatertaxi.com; Tarpon St) and San
Pedro Express taking turns to make the run.

❶ Getting Around

You can walk into the center of town from the
airport terminals in five minutes and the walk
from the boat docks is even shorter.

Minivan taxis ply the streets looking for
customers. Official rates are BZ$7 during the
day and BZ$10 at night to anywhere in the town
center. For hotels outside the center negotiate
the rate before hopping in.

There is a small **toll bridge** over the San Pedro
river. Pay a ridiculous BZ$5 for each 20m cross-
ing on a golf cart. Bicycles cross for free.

Beach Cruiser (☑651-1533; solenyancona@
gmail.com; Pescador Dr; per day BZ$18;
⊙9am-7pm Mon-Thu, to 9pm Fri & Sat) Rental
place with a plenty of rides.

Coastal Xpress (☑ 226-2007; www.coastal press.com; Caribeña St; per trip BZ$10-28, day pass BZ$50, week pass BZ$250; ⊙5am-10pm) Runs a regular scheduled passenger boat service between San Pedro town and the resorts on the northern island. Boats leave from the Amigos del Mar pier roughly every two hours from 5:30am to 10pm. Charter services are also available to destinations outside their normal route or schedule.

Gulf Karts (☑ 615-5278; www.belizebuggies. com; Lion St; ⊙8am-6pm) This new outfit on the lagoon side of the airport offers good prices and top customer service.

NORTHERN BELIZE

Northern Belize comprises two districts: Corozal and Orange Walk, both traversed by the straight, flat Philip Goldson Hwy. Off the main road, adventurous travelers will find pretty fishing villages, pristine jungles, ancient Maya cities and anachronistic Mennonite communities.

Bermudian Landing

No real baboons inhabit Belize; but Belizeans use that name for the Yucatan black howler monkey *(Alouatta pigra)*, an endangered species that exists only in Belize, northern Guatemala and southern Mexico and is one of the largest monkeys in the Americas. The **Community Baboon Sanctuary** (CBS; www.howlermonkeys.org; $BZ10; ⊙8am-5pm) is an amazing community-run, grassroots conservation operation that has engineered an impressive increase in the primate's local population.

CBS occupies about 20 sq miles, spread over a number of Creole villages in the Belize River valley. More than 200 landowners in seven villages have signed pledges to preserve the monkey's habitat, by protecting forested areas along the river and in corridors that run along the borders of their property. The black howlers have made an amazing comeback in the area, and the monkeys now roam freely all around the surrounding area.

The **CBS Museum & Visitor's Center** (☑ 622-9624, 245-2007, 245-2009; cbsbelize@ gmail.com; Bermudian Landing; admission BZ$14; ⊙8am-5pm; P) has a number of good exhibits and displays on the black howler, the history of the sanctuary and other Belizean wildlife. Included with the admission fee is a

45-minute nature walk on which you're likely to get an up-close introduction to a resident troop of black howlers. Along the way the trained local guides also impart their knowledge of the many medicinal plants.

🛏 Sleeping & Eating

Nature Resort   CABAÑAS $$
(☑ 223-6115; naturer@btl.net; Bermudian Landing; cabañas s/d BZ$130/150, r with fan BZ$90; P ❋) Right next to the CBS Museum & Visitor's Center, this little resort has six comfortable *cabañas* in a lovely natural setting. It is managed remotely from Belize City and there is not always staff onsite, but you can make bookings through the Visitor's Center.

ℹ Getting There & Away

Bermudian Landing is 28 miles northwest of Belize City and 9 miles west of Burrell Boom. Buses depart from the CBS Museum & Visitor's Center to Belize City (BZ$5, one hour) very early in the morning with an additional departure at 3:30pm from Monday to Saturday. Buses leave Belize City from the corner of Amara Ave and Cemetery Rd at 12:20pm, 3:30pm, 5pm, 5:20pm and 8pm.

Altun Ha

Altun Ha   RUIN
(www.nichbelize.org; admission BZ$10; ⊙8am-5pm) Altun Ha, the Maya ruins that have inspired Belikin beer labels and Belizean banknotes, stands 34 miles north of central Belize City, off the Old Northern Hwy. While smaller and less imposing than some other Maya sites in the country, Altun Ha, with its immaculate central plaza, is still spectacular and well worth the short detour to get here.

The original site covered 1500 acres, but what visitors today see is the central ceremonial precinct of two plazas surrounded by temples.

The ruins were originally excavated in the 1960s and now look squeaky clean following a stabilization and conservation program from 2000 to 2004. The largest and most important temple is the Temple of the Masonry Altars (B-4) also known as the Temple of the Sun God.

Lamanai

Lamanai   ARCHAEOLOGICAL SITE
(www.nichbelize.org; admission BZ$10; ⊙8am-5pm) Perhaps the most fascinating Maya site in northern Belize, Lamanai lies 24 miles

south of Orange Walk Town up the New River (or 36 miles by unpaved road). The ruins are known both for their impressive architecture and marvelous setting, surrounded by dense jungle overlooking the New River Lagoon. Climbing to the top of the 125ft High Temple to gaze out across the vast jungle canopy is an awe-inspiring experience that is not to be missed.

Most visitors approach Lamanai by guided river trip from Orange Walk not just to avoid the long and bumpy road, but to take advantage of the river trip itself, which goes deep into the home of the countless colorful and unusual birds that live in the area. Many guides who do the 1½-hour river trip are experts in both archaeology and the area's wildlife, making it an especially worthwhile experience. The river voyage passes through some of the most beautiful jungle and lagoon country in northern Belize, and the Mennonite community of Shipyard, before reaching Lamanai itself. There are a number of excellent tour guides in Orange Walk who specialize in the journey.

Sleeping

Guesthouse Olivia GUESTHOUSE $
(☎668-8593; Indian Church; r per person BZ$40) This no-frills guesthouse has the only cheap beds near the Lamanai site. Don't expect luxury, but rest easy knowing you'll have the archaeological site all to yourself in the morning. Call first to make sure there is a room ready. It's next to the Gonzalez Store in the heart of Indian Church.

Getting There & Away

If you decide to go without a guide, you can get to the village of Indian Church (next to Lamanai) from Orange Walk, but the bus goes only twice a week on Monday and Friday. You'll need to find somewhere to spend a few nights while waiting for your return bus.

Orange Walk

POP 13,687

Orange Walk Town is many things to many people: agricultural town, economic hub, Mennonite meeting place, street-food paradise...but it is not generally considered a tourist town. And the chances are pretty good that this won't change any time soon. This town of 14,000 souls – just 57 miles from Belize City – doesn't have much to keep travelers around for more than a day or two.

Sleeping

St Christopher's Hotel HOTEL $
(☎302-1064; www.stchristophershotelbze.com; 10 Main St; r with fan/air-con BZ$80/110; P ❄ @ ≋) The flowering gardens and riverside setting make this otherwise nondescript hotel an attractive place to stay. The rooms themselves are spacious but plain. River-boat trips to Lamanai pick up right from the hotel grounds and your hosts – the Urbina family – are attentive and welcoming, in a low-key, unassuming sort of way.

Orchid Palm Inn HOTEL $
(☎322-0719; www.orchidpalminn.com; 22 Queen Victoria Ave; s/d BZ$77/94; P ❄ @ ≋) Set on a busy corner in the center of all the action, the friendly Orchid Palm Inn is a tiny island of tranquillity. It has eight well-furnished and nicely decorated rooms that offer excellent value. Avoid Room One if you need wi-fi.

El Gran Mestizo CABAÑAS $$
(☎322-2290; www.elgranmestizo.com; 1 Naranjal St; r BZ$130-150; P ❄ ≋) Perched on the banks of the New River south of town, these new *cabañas* are a great choice for those looking to be surrounded by nature but want to be close to town. On the far side of the river there is a wall of jungle that is a riot of birdlife and iguanas laze around on the hotel grounds.

Hotel de la Fuente HOTEL $$
(☎322-2290; www.hoteldelafuente.com; 14 Main St; r BZ$80-170, ste BZ$130-170; P ❄ @ ≋) This family-run hotel is smack dab in the center of Orange Walk, but most of the rooms are in a brand-new building set back from the hustle and bustle (and noise) of the road. The clean, cozy rooms – all equipped with fridge and coffee maker – are probably the best in town, while the suite has a full kitchen.

Eating & Drinking

Maracas Bar & Restaurant BELIZEAN $
(☎322-2290; 1 Naranjal St; mains BZ$8-22; ⏲11:30am-10pm Thu & Sun, til midnight Fri-Sat) For good eats in a fantastic natural setting, take a taxi down to this restaurant at the El Gran Mestizo on the banks of the New River south of town. For the full experience pick a table in one of the waterside *palapas* and choose from Belizean- and Mexican-inspired dishes on the ample menu.

Come n' Dine Restaurant BREAKFAST, BELIZEAN $
(Philip Goldson Hwy; dishes BZ$8-30; ⏲7am-10pm) Unassuming and unexpected, this

roadside restaurant serves some of the best Belizean food around. Located right next to the gas station on a crook on the Philip Goldson Hwy just a couple of miles south of town, it's well placed for road-trippers (but also worth the trip if you are staying in town). Look for excellent stews, steaks and stir-fries.

★**Cocina Sabor**   BELIZEAN $$
(☑322-3482; Philip Goldson Hwy; mains BZ$18-40, light meals BZ$12-25; ⊙11am-10:30pm, closed Tue) Hugely popular among expats, this welcoming place on the highway has a large menu of local and international fare, including good pasta and steak served in the spotless air-conditioned wooden dining room. During the day it serves light meals, such as tasty burgers and wraps. Service is prompt and courteous, and there's a well-stocked bar.

Nahil Mayab   BELIZEAN, MEXICAN $$
(www.nahilmayab.com; cnr Santa Ana & Guadalupe Sts; mains BZ$14-25; ⊙11am-3pm Mon, 11am-10pm Tue-Thu, 11am-2am Fri & Sat; 🛜☑) Decked in exotic greenery and faux Maya carvings, the dining room evokes the district's surrounding jungles, as does the pleasantly shaded patio. It's a fun, kitschy atmosphere in which to sample some Yucatecan-inspired food, like Ke'Ken (salt pork in tomato sauce) or Cham Cham (empanadas).

ℹ Information

Belize Bank (34 Main St) ATM accepts all major credit cards.

Post Office (cnr Queen Victoria Ave & Arthur St; ⊙8am-5pm Mon-Thu, until 4pm Fri)

Scotiabank (cnr Park & Main Sts) Accepts all cards.

ℹ Getting There & Away

Orange Walk is the major northern Belize bus hub for buses plying the Corozal–Belize City route. There are half a dozen companies servicing this route and around 30 buses a day going in each direction. All long-distance buses, including services to Belize City, Corozal, Chetumal and Sarteneja, stop at the **makeshift bus terminal** (Temporary Bus Station; Dunn St) west of the cemetery. It is supposed to be a temporary facility but it has an air of starting to

---

CROOKED TREE WILDLIFE SANCTUARY

Between December and May, migrating birds flock to the lagoons, rivers and swamps of the massive Crooked Tree Wildlife Sanctuary (CTWS; www.belizeaudubon.org; admission BZ$8; ⊙8am-4:30pm), which is managed by Belize Audubon. The best birdwatching is in April and May, when the low level of the lagoon draws thousands of birds into the open to seek food in the shallows. That said, at any time between December and May, birdwatchers are in for hours of ornithological bliss.

Boat-billed, chestnut-bellied and bare-throated tiger herons, Muscovy and black-bellied whistling ducks, snail kites, ospreys, black-collared hawks and all of Belize's five species of kingfisher are among the 276 species recorded there. Jabiru storks, the largest flying bird in the Americas, with wingspans of up to 12ft, congregate here in April and May, and a few pairs nest in the sanctuary in the preceding months.

At the entrance to the village, just off the causeway, stop by the CTWS Visitor Center (⊙8am-4:30pm) to browse the interesting displays.

Tillett's Village Lodge (☑607-3871, 245-7016; www.tillettvillage.com; r BZ$60-120, lakeside cabin BZ$200; P❄) The Tilletts are a local Crooked Creek clan who have reared some of the most celebrated bird guides in the country. Their welcoming guesthouse is a good option for those that want to immerse themselves in village life. It has five simple rooms (some with air-con), with comfortable beds, hot showers and an assortment of original artwork featuring the local birdlife.

Crooked Tree Lodge (☑626-3820, 636-3396; www.crookedtreelodgebelize.com; campsite per person BZ$20, 1-bedroom cabaña BZ$140-200, 2-bedroom cabaña BZ$400; P🛜) Mick is a British pilot who served for years in Belize; Angie was born and bred in Crooked Tree. This delightful couple has found their little plot of paradise and they welcome visitors! The beautifully crafted wood *cabañas* all have private porches that overlook the lagoon, providing perfect sunrise views. The self-service waterfront bar and open-plan dining room are wonderful and welcoming.

feel permanent as there has been no progress on a replacement.

Buses heading north from Orange Walk begin at 6:45am and run until around 9:15pm. Heading south to Belize City, buses begin at 4:45am and run until 8:30pm. The trip to Belize City takes around two hours, and costs BZ$5 to BZ$7; the trip to Corozal is slightly quicker and cheaper.

Corozal

POP 11,722

Just 9 miles south of Mexico and 29 miles north of Orange Walk Town, Corozal has a vibe different from any other town in Belize. The Mexican influence is palpable on the streets of this provincial town, where you are likely to hear Spanish and eat tacos. Though it feels prosperous (especially by Belizean standards), most of the town's wealth comes from its position as a commercial and farming center – not from tourism. In fact, the town's fledgling tourism sector has been hit hard by the direct boat service between San Pedro and Chetumal, which has seen many travelers bypass Corozal altogether and several tourist-orientated businesses close.

◉ Sights

★ Old Customs House   HISTORIC SITE

(cnr 2nd St South & 1st Ave; ⊙9am-5pm Mon-Fri) **FREE** Built in 1886, this fine old Spanish Colonial building once housed a bustling market and customs house. It was one of only 11 buildings spared by Hurricane Janet in 1955. Today the historic building houses a cultural center and museum with exhibits of local artifacts. It's a good place to catch up on what's going on in Corozal during your visit.

Santa Rita   RUIN

(admission BZ$10; ⊙8am-6pm) Santa Rita was an ancient Maya coastal town that once occupied the same strategic trading position as present-day Corozal Town, namely the spot between two rivers – the Río Hondo (which now forms the Belize–Mexico border) and the New River (which enters Corozal Bay south of town). Much of Santa Rita remains unexcavated, but it's worth a short excursion out of town to explore the site.

Cerro Maya   RUIN

(Cerros; admission BZ$10; ⊙8am-5pm) The ruin at Cerro Maya is the only Maya site in Belize that occupies beachfront property. It is composed of a series of temples built from

about 50 BC. While the site is mostly a mass of grass-covered mounds, the center has been cleared and two structures are visible. Be warned: Cerro Maya can get very buggy, especially during the rainy season; cover up and don't skimp on the bug spray!

⌁ Sleeping

Bayside Guesthouse   GUESTHOUSE $

(☑625-7824; baysideguesthouse@live.com; 31 3rd Ave; s/d/tr BZ$80/90/100, d with air-con BZ$105, incl breakfast) A welcoming and homey option just off the waterfront with just four big, well-equipped rooms and an ample terrace upstairs offering bay views. Everything here is spotless and well maintained. Breakfast is included and other meals are available on request.

Hotel Maya   HOTEL $

(☑422-2082; hotelmaya@btl.net; 7th Ave, South End; s/d BZ$70/85, with air-con BZ$85/95; ❄⊛⊚) Run by the very friendly Rosita May, the Hotel Maya is a long-time favorite of budget-conscious travelers. Rooms are clean and homey, and enlivened by colorful bedspreads and paintings done by local artists. Apartments are available for long-term rentals. In addition to being a licensed travel agent, Rosita is also a great source of local information.

★ Serenity Sands   B&B $$

(☑669-2394; www.serenitysands.com; Consejo Rd; d BZ$190-200, house BZ$220; ℙ⊛@⊚) ◈ Located about 3 miles north of Corozal Town, this B&B is off the beaten track, off the grid and out of this world. The remote beachside setting offers the perfect combination of isolation and accessibility (though you'll need a vehicle to get here), and the four spacious tiled rooms are decorated with locally crafted furniture and boast private balconies.

Hok'ol K'in Guest House   GUESTHOUSE $$

(☑422-3329; www.corozal.net; 89 4th Ave; s/d with fan BZ$77/104, with air-con BZ$92/120; ⊛@⊚) With a Maya name meaning 'rising sun,' this modern, well-run, small hotel overlooking the bay may well be the best value in town. The large, impeccably clean rooms are designed to catch sea breezes. Each has two double beds, a bathroom and a balcony with hammock. Hok'ol K'in also serves meals at reasonable prices (breakfasts are particularly good).

Corozal Town

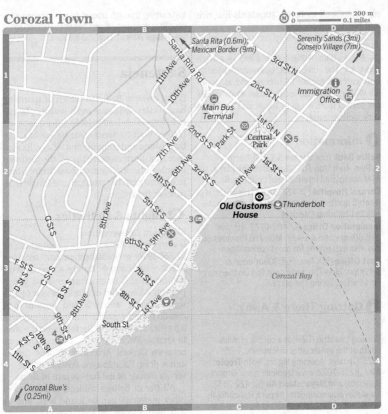

Map labels: Santa Rita (0.6mi); Mexican Border (9mi); Serenity Sands (3mi); Consejo Village (7mi); 3rd St N; 2nd St N; Immigration Office; 2; Santa Rita Rd; 11th Ave; 10th Ave; Main Bus Terminal; 2nd St S; Park St; 1st St N; Central Park; 5; 7th Ave; 6th Ave; 3rd St S; 1st St S; 4th St S; 4th Ave; 5th St S; 1; Old Customs House; Thunderbolt; 8th Ave; G St S; 6th St S; 5th Ave; 6; Corozal Bay; F St S; E St S; D St S; C St S; B St S; 7th St S; 8th St S; 1st Ave; 7; 9th St S; A St S; 10th St S; South St; 11th St S; Corozal Blue's (0.25mi); 3

0   200 m
0   0.1 miles

BELIZE COROZAL

Corozal Town

◎ Top Sights
1 Old Customs House C2

🛏 Sleeping
2 Bayside Guesthouse D1
3 Hok'ol K'in Guest House C3
4 Hotel Maya..A4

❌ Eating
5 The 1 ....D2
6 Venky's Kabab Corner B3

🍸 Drinking & Nightlife
7 Jamrock B3

❌ Eating & Drinking

The 1 MEXICAN $
(4th Ave; tacos BZ$2; ⊘8am-8pm) Right on the corner of Central Park, this popular little shop serves authentic Mexican-style tacos and *tortas* (Mexican pressed sandwiches) with a great variety of sauces.

Venky's Kabab Corner INDIAN $
(☑402-0546; 5th St South; dishes BZ$10-15; ⊘9am-9:30pm) Chef Venky is the premier – and, as far as we know, only – Hindu chef in Corozal, cooking excellent Indian meals, both meat and vegetarian. The place is not much to look at on the inside, in fact there is just one table that is usually covered in assorted clutter, but the food is excellent and filling.

Corozo Blue's PIZZA, BELIZEAN $
(Philip Goldson Hwy; mains BZ$12-24; ⊘10am-midnight Sun-Thu, 10am-2am Fri & Sat; ☑) Located on an inviting curve of beach just where the road turns south out of town, this semi-enclosed restaurant has indoor and beach-front seating with a spectacular view of the bay. (On a clear day you can see the ruins at Cerros!) It has an outdoor stone oven for

pizzas, as well as Belize standards like rice and beans and *ceviche*.

Jamrock BAR
(1st Ave; ⊘ 11am-midnight, closed Tue) In a park right by the bay, this open-air watering hole catches plenty of breeze and is popular with expats and locals alike. Tasty meals are served from noon to 10pm and the bar is very well stocked.

ⓘ Information

Belize Bank (cnr 5th Ave & 1st St North; ⊘ 9am-4pm Mon-Fri) Situated on the plaza; ATM accepts all international credit cards.

Corozal Hospital (☑ 422-2076) This hospital is located northwest of the center of town on the way to Chetumal (Mexico).

Immigration Office (☑ 402-0123; 4th Ave; ⊘ 8:30am-noon & 1-4pm Mon-Fri) Provides 30-day visa extensions for most nationalities.

Post Office (5th Ave; ⊘ 8:30am-noon & 1-4:30pm Mon-Thu, until 4pm Fri) On the site of Fort Barlee, facing the plaza.

ⓘ Getting There & Away

AIR
Corozal's airstrip (CZH) is a couple of miles south of the town center in Ranchito. Taxis (BZ$10) meet incoming flights. Both **Tropic Air** (☑ 226-2012; www.tropicair.com; Airport, Ranchito) and **Maya Island Air** (☑ 422-2333; www.mayaislandair.com; Airport, Ranchito) fly in and out of Corozal with direct flights to San Pedro.

BOAT
Corozal is the natural jumping-off point for trips to Cerros, Sarteneja and San Pedro, and the town's only water-taxi service is **Thunderbolt.** (☑ 631-3400, 610-4475; 1st Ave) The advent of the Chetumal to San Pedro boat has made this journey less popular but crossing the border by bus and taking this boat is significantly cheaper.

It leaves Corozal at 7am, returning from San Pedro at 3pm. It stops at Sarteneja (upon request). The trip to Sarteneja takes 30 minutes and costs BZ$25/50 one way/return; San Pedro is two hours away and will cost you BZ$50/90 one way/return.

BUS
Corozal's **main bus terminal** is a key stop for nearly all of the myriad bus lines that ply the Philip Goldson Hwy down to Orange Walk and Belize City. At last count, 30 buses daily were doing the 2½-hour run from Corozal Town to Belize City, from 3:30am until 7pm; there are half a dozen buses in the other direction on the 15-minute run to the Mexican border, with the

last coming through around 4pm. There are a couple of very early direct buses to Belmopan via Orange Walk at 3am and 3:30am.

Sarteneja
POP 2000

If you came to Belize in search of sparkling blue waters, delicious fresh seafood, fauna-rich forests and affordable prices, look no further than Sarteneja (sar-ten-*eh*-ha). The tiny fishing and shipbuilding village, located near the northeastern tip of the Belizean mainland, is a charming base from which to explore both the nautical and jungle treasures of the region.

⦿ Sights & Activities

Shipstern Conservation Management Area NATURE RESERVE
(☑ 660-1807; www.visitshipstern.com; admission BZ$10; ⊘ 8am-5pm) 🐾 Run by a nonprofit organization, this large nature reserve, which protects 43 sq miles of semideciduous hardwood forests, wetlands and lagoons and coastal mangrove belts, has its headquarters 3.5 miles southwest of Sarteneja on the road to Orange Walk. Lying in a transition zone between Central America's tropical forests and a drier Yucatán-type ecosystem, the reserve's mosaic of habitats is rare in Belize.

All five of Belize's wildcats and scores of other mammals can be found here, and its 250 bird species include ospreys, roseate spoonbills, white ibis and a colony of 300 pairs of American woodstorks, one of this bird's few breeding colonies in Belize.

🛏 Sleeping

Shipstern Nature Reserve Bungalows LODGE $
(☑ 660-1807; www.visitshipstern.org; Shipstern Conservation Management Area; dm/s/d BZ$40/78/98) Located at the Shipstern Nature Reserve headquarters 3 miles out of town, these four new bungalows are a great choice for visitors intending to take early nature tours or looking to be surrounded by wilderness. The air-con rooms have private bathroom and open out onto a screened porch to enjoy the sounds of the jungle.

Backpackers Paradise CABAÑAS, CAMPGROUND $
(☑ 607-1873, 423-2016; cabanasbelize.wordpress.com; Bandera Rd; camping BZ$12, s/d BZ$30/40, s/d without bathroom BZ$26/34, little house BZ$50-60, family house BZ$60-80, breakfast

BZ$10, lunch & dinner BZ$20; 🐾) Peaceful, sustainable and affordable, this laid-back spot set on lush grounds is a bit of a hike from the beach but is one of the best bases for budget travelers in northern Belize. All sorts of travelers (not just backpackers) will enjoy spending a few days here, walking on jungle trails, swimming in the nearby ocean, or just lounging in the comfy communal spaces.

BELIZE CITY TO BELMOPAN

Formerly the Western Hwy and still referred to as such by many locals, the George Price Hwy stretches from Belize City through the village of Hattieville, and on to Belmopan and Cayo District.

◉ Sights & Activities

**Monkey Bay
Wildlife Sanctuary**   WILDLIFE RESERVE
(🖉 822-8032; www.belizestudyabroad.net; Mile 31.5 George Price Hwy) 🏝 A natural wonderland located just off one of the country's main highways, this 1.7-sq-mile wildlife sanctuary and environmental education center offers lodging and activities for casual travelers, as well as internship activities for those with a more long-term interest in Belize. A well-stocked library provides plenty of reference and reading matter on natural history and the country.

★Belize Zoo   ZOO
(🖉 822-8000; www.belizezoo.org; Mile 29 George Price Hwy; adult/child BZ$30/10; ⊙ 8am-5pm) If most zoos are maximum-security wildlife prisons, then the Belize Zoo is more like a halfway house for wild animals that can't make it on the outside. A must-visit on any trip to Belize District, the zoo has many animals you're unlikely to see elsewhere – there are nine fat tapirs (a Belizean relative of the rhino), *gibnuts,* a number of coatimundi (they look like a cross between a raccoon and a monkey), scarlet macaws, white-lipped peccaries, pumas and many others.

**★Nohoch Che'en Caves
Branch Archaeological Reserve**   CAVE
(park admission BZ$10; ⊙ 7am-4pm) This extensive network of limestone caves northwest of Belmopan is super-popular for cave-tubing, kayaking and spelunking. The Caves Branch River flows through nine caves, providing ideal conditions for floating through on a rubber tube or allowing for exploration of side passages, which lead to other caves, such as the spectacular Crystal Cave.

Vital Nature & Mayan Tours   CAVE ACTIVITIES
(🖉 602-8975; http://cavetubing.bz; per person from BZ$90, with zip-lining BZ$130) One of the pioneers of cave-tubing in Belize, Vitalino Reyes is still a reliable and recommended operator. There are a variety of cave-tubing trips (including equipment and lunch), up to the full-day Crystal Cave (BZ$180) and 'sunset tubing' (last entry is at 4pm). Vital also has a zip-line course and ATVs (quad bikes).

A combo with all three activities is BZ$200 per person. Add BZ$40 per person for transfers from Belize City or Belmopan.

WESTERN BELIZE (CAYO DISTRICT)

Cayo District is Belize's premier adventure and eco-activity region. The lush environs of the Wild West are covered with jungle, woven with rivers, waterfalls and azure pools, and dotted with Maya ruins ranging from small, tree-covered hills to massive, magnificent temples. Cahal Pech, Xunantunich, El Pilar and the mother of all Belizean Maya sites, Caracol, are all in Cayo.

Belmopan

POP 19,460

Like many purpose-built capital cities around the world, Belmopan can seem a bit dull at first glance. Ordered streets, empty urban parklands and drab government buildings conspire to give it a desolate feel. The exception is the vibrant central market area, where cheap food stalls and incoming buses provide some welcome activity.

But this is the national capital, a major transportation hub, a place to extend your visa and an easygoing university city with a decent range of restaurants and shopping. More importantly, it's a useful base for exploring nearby caves, national parks, the Hummingbird Hwy and most of the attractions in eastern Cayo.

◉ Sights & Activities

The main market days are Tuesday and Friday, when stallholders come from all over the district to sell produce.

BELIZE BELMOPAN

Western Belize

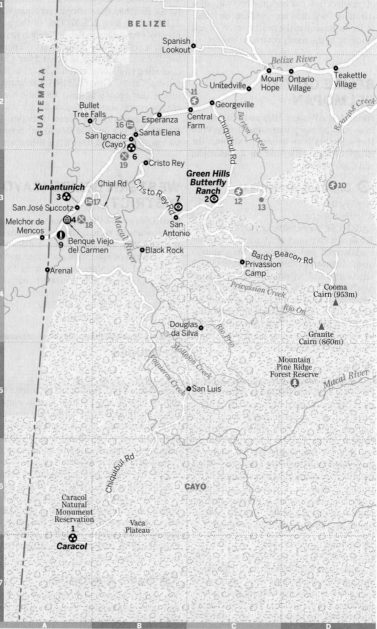

BELIZE

GUATEMALA

Spanish Lookout

Belize River

Teakettle Village

Unitedville

Mount Hope

Ontario Village

Bullet Tree Falls

11

Georgeville

Esperanza

Central Farm

Barton Creek

Roaring Creek

16

San Ignacio (Cayo)

Santa Elena

6

19

Cristo Rey

Chiquibul Rd

Green Hills Butterfly Ranch

10

Xunantunich

3

Chial Rd

Cristo Rey Rd

2

12

13

San José Succotz

17

7

Melchor de Mencos

4

18

San Antonio

9

Benque Viejo del Carmen

Macal River

Black Rock

Baldy Beacon Rd

Arenal

Privassion Camp

Privassion Creek

Cooma Cairn (953m)

Rio On

Douglas da Silva

Rio Prio

Granite Cairn (860m)

Mollejon Creek

Mountain Pine Ridge Forest Reserve

Macal River

Vaqueros Creek

San Luis

Chiquibul Rd

CAYO

Caracol Natural Monument Reservation

1

Vaca Plateau

Caracol

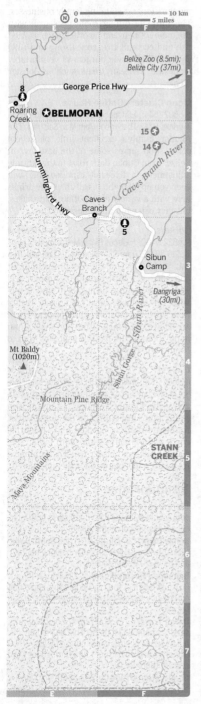

Western Belize

◎ Top Sights
1 Caracol A7
2 Green Hills Butterfly Ranch C3
3 Xunantunich A3

◎ Sights
4 Benque Viejo House of Culture A3
5 Blue Hole National Park F3
6 Cahal Pech B2
7 García Sisters' Place B3
8 Guanacaste National Park E1
9 Poustinia Land Art Park A3

◎ Activities, Courses & Tours
10 Actun Tunichil Muknal D3
11 Belize Wildlife & Referral
   Clinic C2
12 Calico Jack's C3
13 Mike's Place C3
14 Nohoch Che'en Caves Branch
   Archaeological Reserve F2
15 Vital Nature & Mayan Tours F2

◎ Sleeping
Benque Resort & Spa .... (see 4)
16 Midas Resort B2
17 Trek Stop A3

◎ Eating
18 Benny's Kitchen A3
19 Cahal Pech Restaurant B3

BELIZE BELMOPAN

**George Price Center for
Peace & Development** MUSEUM
(☎822-1054; www.gpcbelize.com; Price Blvd;
⊙8am-6pm Mon-Thu, 8am-5pm Fri, 9am-noon Sat)
FREE This museum and conference center
celebrates the life of Belize's beloved states-
man and first prime minister after independence, George Price, who passed away in
2011. As well as photographs and information panels, there's an archive of documents
and letters written by Price.

Guanacaste National Park NATIONAL PARK
(George Price Hwy; admission BZ$5; ⊙8am-
4:30pm) Belize's smallest national park was
declared in 1990 and is named for the giant
guanacaste tree on its southwestern edge.
The tree survived the axes of canoe-makers
but has now died naturally, though it still
stands in its jungle habitat. The 250,000-sq-
yd park, off the highway at the Belmopan
turnoff, is framed by Roaring Creek and the
Belize River, with 2 miles of hiking trails
that will introduce you to the abundant local trees and colorful birds.

Belize Inland Tours ADVENTURE TOUR
(http://belizeinlandtours.com; Mile 42 Humming-bird Hwy, Armenia) Based just out of Belmo-pan in Armenia, Belize Inland Tours runs cave-tubing trips, guided tours of Blue Hole National Park and tours all over the Cayo District.

🛏 Sleeping

★**El-Rey Hotel** HOTEL $
(☑822-3438; www.elreyhotel.com; 23 Moho St; r BZ$80, with air-con BZ$120-160; P❄🛜) North-east of town, El-Rey is Belmopan's best budget offering, an affordable and welcom-ing place with 12 plain, clean ground-floor rooms equipped with private bathrooms, TVs, wi-fi and fans. All rooms have air-con but you can pay the budget price not to use it. Tours can be booked here.

★**Hibiscus Hotel** HOTEL $$
(☑822-0400, 633-5323; www.hibiscusbelize.com; Market Sq; s/d BZ$110/120; ⊘reception from 11am; P❄🛜) 🖉 Close to Belmopan's lively market place, this neat little place has just six chalet-style rooms. Comforts include king and twin-sized beds, flat-screen cable TV, bath tubs, and tea and coffee facilities. There's an eco angle – some of the profits go to support local avian conservation and rescue projects – and the excellent Corkers restaurant and bar is upstairs.

Bull Frog Inn HOTEL $$
(☑822-2111; www.bullfroginn.com; 25 Half Moon Ave; s/d BZ$180/213; P❄🛜) The Bull Frog is a cheerful, if nondescript, place on the eastern edge of town. The 26 rooms are spa-cious and comfortable enough with cable TV, fridge and two double beds (kids under 12 years stay free). There's a playground and a popular restaurant and bar.

🍴 Eating

★**Market Food Stalls** MARKET $
(Market Sq; from BZ$2; ⊘6am-6pm) For a cheap meal, you can't beat the food stalls in the market square. They serve quick-fire Mexi-can snacks such as burritos and *salbutes* (mini-tortillas, usually stuffed with chicken), as well as Belizean standards such as beans and rice and cow-foot soup, or omelettes and fry-jacks for breakfast.

Caladium Restaurant BELIZEAN, SEAFOOD $
(☑822-2754; Market Sq; mains BZ$8-12; ⊘7:30am-8pm Mon-Fri, 7:30am-7pm Sat; ❄) In the market area, the Caladium is one of Bel-

mopan's longest-standing family businesses. The intimate dining room goes well with the menu of Belizean favorites, such as fried fish and coconut rice, conch soup and BBQ chicken. Well-made burgers sit comfortably alongside Belizean treats such as lobster creole.

Moon Clusters Coffee House CAFE $
(☑602-1644; 4 Shopping Center, E Ring Rd; coffee & drinks BZ$3-11; ⊘noon-7pm Mon-Sat; ❄) The Aguilar family's excellent little old-school coffee shop serves some of the best Java in Belize, from Cuban dark roast to the attitude adjustment, a five-shot espresso that will keep you up all night. It's all about the drinks here with a variety of smoothies and shakes, but they can whip up a quesadilla too.

Corkers INTERNATIONAL $$
(☑822-0400; Hibiscus Plaza, Melhado Pde; mains BZ$16-30; ⊘11am-9pm Mon-Wed, 11am-late Thu-Sat; 🛜🖉) This breezy upstairs restaurant and bar has a 'Brit pub in the tropics' feel with a welcoming atmosphere and a me-lange of seafood, meat and pasta dishes from tortillas to steak and veggies. There are good-value lunch dishes and snacks, and happy hour at the bar is a generous 4pm to 10pm Thursday to Saturday.

Everest NEPALESE $$
(☑662-2109; mains BZ$15-20; ⊘8am-9am Mon-Sat, 9am-6pm Sun; 🖉) Belmopan's (and prob-ably Belize's) only Nepalese restaurant is in a cute blue shack opposite the market area. Authentic mutton, chicken and vegetarian curries and biryanis, along with Indian spe-cialties such as masala tea. The laminated menu even has pictures for the uninitiated.

ℹ Information

There are a couple of internet places in town. **PC.com** (per hr BZ$5; ⊘8am-8pm) offers both inter-net access and computer repairs.

Belize Bank (Constitution Dr) and **Scotiabank** (Constitution Dr) keep regular banking hours and have 24/7 ATM access.

Belmopan Hospital (☑822-2264; off N Ring Rd) Just north of the city center, this is the only emergency facility between Belize City and San Ignacio.

Darah Travel (☑822-3272; www.belizetravelservices.com; 23 Moho St) This Belmopan-based travel agency can organize flights, transfers and adventure tours throughout Cayo and southern Belize.

Immigration Office (☑822-3860; Dry Creek St; ⊘8am-noon & 1-5pm Mon-Thu, to 4:30pm

Fri) Cayo's only immigration office offers 30-day visa extension stamps for BZ$50. It's in the green building down a side street just off South Ring Rd and gets busy, so arrive early.

Post Office (⊙ 8am-noon & 1-5pm Mon-Thu, to 4:30pm Fri)

US Embassy (✆ 822-4011; http://belize.us embassy.gov; Floral Park Rd; ⊙ 8am-noon & 1-5pm Mon-Fri) From visa and passport information to marriage advice and hurricane preparedness tips, the US embassy can help. The website is comprehensive and easy to navigate.

ⓘ Getting There & Away

AIR

Belmopan's tiny airstrip is just a few miles east of the city.

Tropic Air (✆ 226-2012; www.tropicair.com) has four daily flights to San Pedro (BZ$243, 55 minutes), Belize City Domestic (BZ$134, 25 minutes) and Belize City International (BZ$178, 25 minutes).

BUS

Belmopan's **bus terminal** (✆ 802-2799; Market Sq) is Cayo's main transit hub, and all buses (regardless of company) heading south or west from the Belize District, as well as north and west from Dangriga (and points south), stop in Belmopan. Along the George Price Hwy, buses head east to Belize City (BZ$5, one hour) and west to San Ignacio (BZ$5, one hour) and Benque Viejo del Carmen (BZ$6, 1½ hours) every half-hour from 6am to 7pm. Along the Hummingbird Hwy, buses go south to Dangriga (BZ$6, two hours) once or twice an hour from 6:45am until 7:15pm. From Dangriga, most buses continue on to Punta Gorda (BZ$19, 5½ hours).

ⓘ Getting Around

The city center, within the ring road, is compact and easily negotiated on foot. Taxis gather outside the bus terminal. A short fare around town is BZ$5.

Hummingbird Hwy

The lyrically named Hummingbird Hwy is one of the prettiest drives in Belize, winding its way through jungle and citrus orchards and impossibly small villages as it skirts the northern edges of the Maya Mountain range between Belmopan and Dangriga. Passing caves and jungle adventures, on a clear day the road affords plenty of postcard-perfect vistas. You can drive the 55-mile length of it in two hours but along the way are some excellent ecolodges and budget accommodations, just begging for an overnight stay.

⊙ Sights & Activities

Blue Hole National Park   NATIONAL PARK
(admission BZ$8; ⊙ 8am-4:30pm) The 575-acre Blue Hole National Park contains St Herman's Cave, one of the few caves in Belize that you can visit independently. The visitors center (where flashlights can be rented for BZ$3) is 11 miles along the Hummingbird Hwy from Belmopan. From here a 500yd trail leads to St Herman's Cave. A path leads 200yd into the cave alongside an underground river – to go any further you'll need a guide.

Caves Branch Adventures   ADVENTURE TOUR
(✆ 610-3451; www.cavesbranch.com; Mile 41½ Hummingbird Hwy; tours per person BZ$150-500) At Ian Anderson's the signature adventures include jungle treks, river caves and waterfall caves expeditions, and the Black Hole Drop. Adventure activities are exclusive and depart from the excellent lodge just off the Hummingbird Hwy.

Maya Guide Adventures   TOUR
(✆ 600-3116; www.mayaguide.bz; overnight tours from BZ$320) Highly experienced Kekchí Maya guide Marcos Cucul runs jungle survival tours ranging from overnight to multiple nights. Tours feature trekking, leadership and survival skills with the night spent suspended in Hennessy hammocks. With over a decade's experience as an area guide, Cucul enjoys an excellent reputation.

🛏 Sleeping & Eating

Hummingbird Haven
Lodge & Hostel   HOSTEL $
(✆ 626-4599; www.hummingbirdlodge.com; Mile 29.5 Hummingbird Hwy; camping BZ$20, dm/d BZ$30/80, 2-bedroom lodge BZ$150; P 🐾 🎧) 🐾
Hummingbird Haven enjoys a sublime location in a quiet patch of forest just off the highway and surrounded by a split in the creek. The 100-acre property features a double-story timber lodge with two large dorms, and a few private rooms in another building, as well as plenty of space to camp.

T.R.E.E.S   CABIN $
(Toucan Ridge Ecology & Education Society; ✆ 669-6818, 665-2134; www.treesociety.org; Mile 27.5 Hummingbird Hwy; bunkhouse BZ$30, s/d cabin BZ$125/140, without bathroom BZ$85/100; 🎧)
🐾 T.R.E.E.S is part field station and part ecofriendly lodge, welcoming research students, interns, birders and passing backpackers alike. The operation is nonprofit,

with proceeds going into community conservation projects and ecotourism. There are lectures in biodiversity, field courses and guided activities, along with yoga, hiking and village tours.

Yax'che Jungle Camp   CABAÑAS **$**
(☑600-3116; www.mayaguide.bz; Hummingbird Hwy; camping BZ$20, bunkhouse BZ$30, d cabañas BZ$140; ⓟ⏏) 🍴 Adventure guide Marcos Cucul runs this little camp just off the highway. Spacious *cabañas* on stilts have sunken bathrooms and verandas. There's a communal dining area and a great range of jungle activities on offer.

San Ignacio

POP 20,580

San Ignacio is the heart and soul of the Cayo District, a vibrant traveler center from where all roads and activities fan out. Together with twin-town Santa Elena, on the east bank of the Macal River, this is the main population center of Cayo, with lots of good budget accommodation, decent restaurants and frequent transportation.

But San Ignacio is no inland San Pedro, existing only for tourism. It has a very positive and infectious local vibe, with a bustling market and a steady influx of immigrants. Residents are Mestizos, Maya and Garifuna, as well as a bunch of free-spirited expats from Europe and North America. San Ignacio is on the west bank of the Macal River, a couple of miles upstream from its confluence with the Mopan River – a meeting of waters that gives birth to the Belize River.

◎ Sights & Activities

Cahal Pech   RUIN
(☑824-4236; admission BZ$10, 2hr tours BZ$20; ⏲6am-6pm) High atop a hill about a mile south of San Ignacio, Cahal Pech is the oldest-known Maya site in the Belize River valley, having been first settled between 1500 and 1000 BC. Less impressive than Xunantunich and Caracol, it's still a fascinating example of Preclassic Maya architecture and an easy uphill walk from town. It was a significant Maya settlement for 2000 years or more. Drop into the small visitors center, which explains some of the history of Cahal Pech.

Cahal Pech (kah-hahl pech) is Mopan and Yucatec Maya for 'Place of Ticks,' a nickname earned in the 1950s when the site was surrounded by pastures grazed by tick-infested cattle. Today it's a pleasantly shady site with plenty of trees and few tourists. Its core area of seven interconnected plazas has been excavated and restored since the late 1980s. Plaza B is the largest and most impressive complex; Structure A-1, near Plaza A, is the site's tallest temple. Two ballcourts lie at either end of the restored area.

★**Green Iguana**
Conservation Project   GARDENS
(☑824-2034; www.sanignaciobelize.com; 18 Buena Vista St; tour BZ$18; ⏲8am-4pm, tour every hour; 🛈) 🍴 On the lush Macal Valley grounds of the San Ignacio Resort Hotel, this excellent program collects and hatches iguana eggs, raising the reptiles until they are past their most vulnerable age. The iguanas are then released into the wild. On the guided tour you'll get plenty of opportunities to stroke and handle the adorable iguanas and learn much about their habits and life cycle. The tour also follows the medicinal jungle trail that winds through the forest.

★**Ajaw Chocolate**   TOUR
(☑635-9363; ajawchocolatebze@gmail.com; Victoria St; demonstration only per person BZ$24, with farm tour BZ$50; ⏲9am-6pm Mon-Sat, tours hourly; 🛈) Adrian and Elida, Kekchí Mayas from Toledo, bring their chocolate-making expertise to San Ignacio with excellent demonstrations that can be combined with a tour of their small cacao farm. The tour includes grinding and creating your own chocolate drink and chocolate bar from roasted beans.

☞ Tours

San Ignacio, or the lodges around it, are the natural base for visiting the cultural and natural riches of the Cayo region. Trips to Actun Tunichil Muknal and Barton Creek Cave can only be done with a guide, while Caracol must visited by vehicle convoy.

David's Adventure Tour   ADVENTURE TOUR
(☑804-3674; www.davidsadventuretours.com; Savannah St; canoe tours BZ$40-90) Based just across the street from the Saturday market, David's is an experienced operator offering ecofriendly tours to sites throughout the area, specializing in river canoe trips, cave adventures and overnight jungle treks.

Belize Nature Travel   CAVE TOUR
(☑824-3314; www.experiencebelize.com; Santa Elena) Belize Nature Travel specializes in cave tours such as Actun Tunichil Muknal

and Barton Creek, and trips to Caracol. Check the website for other tour packages.

Pacz Tours
TOUR

(📞824-0536; www.pacztours.net; 30 Burns Ave; tours BZ$80-290) Offers reliably excellent service and knowledgeable guides to Actun Tunichil Muknal and Tikal, as well as shuttle transfers all over Cayo.

Mayawalk Tours
ADVENTURE TOUR

(📞824-3070; www.mayawalk.com; 19 Burns Ave) One of San Ignacio's original tour companies does recommended trips to Caracol (BZ$190), Actun Tunichil Muknal (BZ$190), Tikal (Guatemala) and many other adventure tours geared toward travelers of all levels and interests. Also operates a shuttle service all over Belize.

River Rat Expeditions
ADVENTURE TOUR

(📞661-4562; www.riverratbelize.com; Burns Ave) Specialist in kayaking, river-tubing and cave trips, including Che Chem Ha near Benque Viejo del Carmen. Enjoy a relaxing paddle down the Mopan River near Clarissa Falls, or take on some white water near Paslow Falls.

🛏 Sleeping

San Ignacio has the best range of good-value budget accommodation (including camping) in Belize.

Casa Blanca Guest House
GUESTHOUSE $

(📞824-2080; www.casablancaguesthouse.com; 10 Burns Ave; s/d/tr BZ$50/65/80, with air-con BZ$80/100/120; ❄🛜) Intimate, immaculate and secure, the Casa Blanca is everything you need from a budget guesthouse. Decent-sized rooms have clean white walls and crisp fresh linens. Guests have a comfy sitting area, a clean kitchen and a breezy balcony from which to watch the world go by.

Old House Hostel
HOSTEL $

(📞623-1342; www.facebook.com/hostelbelize; 3 Buena Vista St; dm/d BZ$25/70) There's a lot to like about this hostel above the sometimes-happening Soul Project. The two eight-bed dorms are clean and spacious with lockers and wi-fi, and there's a neat common room, self-catering kitchen and street-view balcony. There's only one private double room so book ahead.

Bella's Backpacker's
HOSTEL $

(📞824-2248; www.bellasinbelize.com; 4 Galvez St; dm BZ$25, d with/without bathroom BZ$66/60; 🛜) Bella's is a classic backpackers, with rustic charm, bohemian travelers of all ages floating about and a sociable rooftop chill-out area with hammocks and couches. Well-laid-out dorms with sturdy timber bunk beds and bathrooms are complemented by a few private rooms with screened-in windows and a rock-motif bathroom. Breakfast is available for BZ$10. Bella also has a farm at Cristo Rey.

Venus Hotel
HOTEL $

(📞824-3202; 29 Burns Ave; d/tr BZ$66/82, with air-con BZ$93/115; P❄🛜) The three-story Venus is something of a landmark on Burns Ave, drawing in wandering travelers like a tractor beam. It's not flash but it's friendly and good value and the variety of rooms are clean and comfy – the best are the spacious air-con rooms with shared balcony overlooking the marketplace. A bonus is free use of the large adjacent car park.

Mana Kai Camp & Cabins
CAMPGROUND $

(📞624-6538; http://manakaibelize.weebly.com; Branch Mouth Rd; camping per person BZ$10, s/d cabin BZ$30/40, with bathroom BZ$50/60, with air-con BZ$100/110; P❄🛜) One of the best urban camping grounds in Belize, Mana Kai is a big swath of flat grassy land with an open-air communal kitchen, *palapa* with hammocks and free wi-fi. Even if you're not camping there are several log cabin-style cottages, some with air-con. There's a great feeling of space here, just a short walk from the town center.

Western Guesthouse
GUESTHOUSE $

(📞824-2572; www.westernguesthousebelize.com; 54 Burns Ave; s/d with fan BZ$66/76, with air-con BZ$86/106, family ste BZ$152; P❄🛜) The Urbina family's guesthouse is above a hardware store on San Ignacio's quiet west side. Big pluses are the family atmosphere and access to a fully furnished kitchen. The eight clean and comfortable guestrooms each have two beds, TV and hot shower, and there is also a large family suite with three double beds and full bathroom.

Midas Resort
HOTEL $$

(📞824-3172; www.midasbelize.com; Branch Mouth Rd; cottage/cabaña/casita BZ$152/166/370, d/f BZ$235/320; P❄🛜🏊) In a budget town, Midas stands out as one of San Ignacio's better midrange choices. The large pool, funky bar and friendly staff complement an interesting array of accommodations from hotel-style rooms in the main building to cottages, *cabañas* and a two-bedroom *casita* at the

San Ignacio

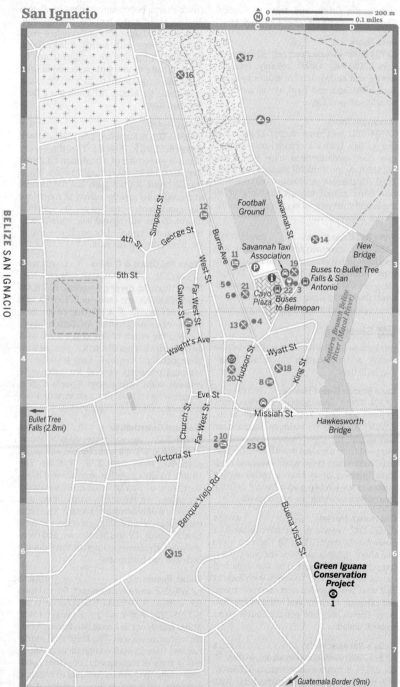

N 0 — 200 m
0 — 0.1 miles

17

16

9

Simpson St

4th St
George St

Burns Ave

Football
Ground

Savannah St

Savannah Taxi
Association

14

New
Bridge

5th St

West St

12

11

19

Buses to Bullet Tree
Falls & San
Antonio

Far-West St

Galvez St

5
6
21

22 **3**
Cayo
Plaza
Buses to Belmopan

Eastern Branch Belize
River (Macal River)

7

13 **4**

Waight's Ave

Hudson St

Wyatt St

King St

20

18

8

Eve St

Church St

Far-West St

Missiah St

Hawkesworth
Bridge

← Bullet Tree
Falls (2.8mi)

2 **10**
Victoria St

23

Benque Viejo Rd

Buena Vista St

15

Green Iguana
Conservation
Project
1

↗ Guatemala Border (9mi)

San Ignacio

◎ Top Sights
1 Green Iguana Conservation
  Project...D6

◈ Activities, Courses & Tours
2 Ajaw Chocolate......................................C5
3 David's Adventure Tour........................C3
4 Mayawalk Tours.....................................C4
5 Pacz Tours..C3
6 River Rat Expeditions...........................C3

◉ Sleeping
7 Bella's Backpacker's.............................B4
8 Casa Blanca Guest House....................C4
9 Mana Kai Camp & Cabins.....................C2
  Old House Hostel..........................(see 23)
10 Rainforest Haven Inn............................C5
  San Ignacio Resort
  Hotel..(see 1)

11 Venus Hotel..C3
12 Western Guesthouse............................B2

◈ Eating
13 Eva's...C4
14 Farmers Market.....................................D3
15 Great Mayan Prince..............................B6
16 Guava Limb Cafe...................................B1
17 Hode's Place...C1
18 Ko-Ox Han-nah......................................C4
19 Mike's..C3
20 Pop's Restaurant...................................C4
21 Serendib...C3

◉ Drinking & Nightlife
22 Bamboo Bar...C3

◈ Entertainment
23 Soul Project..C5

BELIZE SAN IGNACIO

back of the property. It's in a quiet location a five-minute walk north of the market.

Rainforest Haven Inn HOTEL $$
(☑674-1984; www.rainforesthavens.com; 2 Victoria St; r & cabaña BZ$100, 2-bedroom apt BZ$130; ✳@☎) Rainforest Haven is a good find if you're looking for midrange comfort at an almost budget price. The five rooms have air-con, flat-screen TVs with cable, fridges, wi-fi and hot-water showers. The *cabaña* has a kitchenette and the two-bedroom apartment boasts a full kitchen – a steal for families or groups. There's a cool chill-out spot on the 2nd floor.

San Ignacio Resort Hotel HOTEL $$$
(☑824-2034; www.sanignaciobelize.com; 18 Buena Vista St; s/d from BZ$336/382, s/d regal BZ$368/442, family ste BZ$550; P✳@☎☀) The most upscale hotel in San Ignacio by a considerable margin (Queen Elizabeth stayed here in 1994, as the photos in the lobby attest), this is boutique luxury but with welcoming, professional staff and a serene location just uphill from the town center. Beyond the pool area the property is backed by jungle and home to the excellent Green Iguana Conservation Project.

✖ Eating

Farmers Market MARKET $
(⊙from 5am Sat) Saturday is the big market day in San Ignacio when traders come from all over Cayo to sell fresh bargain produce, handicrafts and clothing. The dozen or so food stalls set up in the middle of the ac-

tion serve quick-fire street food – cheap and tasty. Smaller versions of the market happen most other days of the week.

Pop's Restaurant DINER $
(West St; breakfast BZ$4-13; ⊙6.30am-2pm) You may feel like you're in a *Seinfeld* episode at this friendly six-booth, hole-in-the-wall diner. Best omelets in town and bottomless cups of coffee make this San Ignacio's worst-kept breakfast secret and a great place to meet other diners. Good burritos at lunchtime.

Mike's BREAKFAST $
(dishes BZ$3-8; ⊙5-9am) This unsignposted green shack opposite the market is a local legend for breakfast and fresh Johnnycakes (cornmeal flatbread). Go early or miss out.

Great Mayan Prince BELIZEAN $
(☑824-2588; 28 Benque Viejo Rd; mains BZ$8-15, Sunday brunch adult/child BZ$15/7; ⊙7am-9pm Mon-Thu, 7am-10pm Fri & Sat, 7am-3pm Sun; ☎☀) Great Mayan Prince is worth the short hike up Benque Viejo Rd for the sweeping balcony view of San Ignacio and an honest (not overpriced) menu of Belizean and Mexican dishes. A good spot for breakfast and Sunday brunch.

Eva's BREAKFAST, BELIZEAN $$
(Burns Ave; mains BZ$10-24; ⊙6am-10pm) Open early for breakfast, Eva's is a popular traveler hangout on Burns Ave, serving good breakfast and tasty Belizean and Western favorites. Tex-Mex, rice and beans, burgers, steaks and curries.

Cahal Pech Restaurant
BELIZEAN $$

(☎824-3740; Cahal Pech Village Resort, Cahal Pech Hill; mains BZ$5-22; ⊙7am-10pm; 🤏🍴) If it's food with a view you're after, you won't get better than this unless you have your own chef and a Zeppelin. From the dining room, with its Maya jungle motifs, you can enjoy sweeping views over San Ignacio and Cayo while enjoying a menu of Belizean faves, such as Maya pork chops, or burgers and pasta.

Ko-Ox Han-nah
BELIZEAN, INDIAN $$

(☎623-0019; 5 Burns Ave; breakfast BZ$8-12, Belizean mains BZ$10-12, Indian mains BZ$28-32; ⊙6am-9pm; 🥄) The name means *let's go eat* in Maya, but Han-nah's is far from just another Belizean restaurant. The schizophrenic menu features an intriguing range of Indian dishes, such as lamb curry and the likes of Mozambique peri-peri chicken, with all food sourced from local farms. Breakfasts are good, while lunch and dinner are a mix of Mexican, burgers and Indian.

Serendib
SRI LANKAN $$

(☎804-2302; Burns Ave; mains BZ$14-22; ⊙11am-10pm) San Ignacio's only Sri Lankan restaurant serves excellent curries with a choice of yellow, fried or savory rice, spicy chicken tandoori, and other delicacies from the Indian subcontinent. Friendly owners, sensational food and streetside or peaceful courtyard dining areas.

Hode's Place
BELIZEAN, AMERICAN $$

(Branch Mouth Rd; mains BZ$10-28; ⊙9am-10pm; 🤏🍴) Locals love this rambling barn-sized place north of the city center. A large terrace restaurant opening onto a citrus orchard and kids' playground, it's a popular spot with families or for an evening drink. Friendly service and satisfying food – from burritos and fajitas to steaks, seafood and rice and beans – complete the recipe.

★ Guava Limb Cafe
INTERNATIONAL $$$

(☎824-4837; 79 Burns Ave; mains BZ$14-38; 🤏🥄) 🍴 One of San Ignacio's newest and trendiest restaurants, boutique Guava Limb is set in an adorable turquoise two-story building with a serene outdoor garden area. Fresh organic ingredients are sourced from the owners' farm or local providers to create an eclectic international menu that might include Indonesian *gado gado,* Thai chicken and lettuce wraps, or Hawaiian teriyaki chicken burgers.

◗ Drinking & Entertainment

Bamboo Bar
BAR

(South side, Market Sq; ⊙9am-midnight; 🤏) In a town with low-key nightlife, Bamboo Bar is a standout, smack in the market square and

---

ACTUN TUNICHIL MUKNAL CAVE

Actun Tunichil Muknal (admission BZ$30) – the Cave of the Stone Sepulchre – is one of the most unforgettable and adventurous underground tours you can make in Belize. The guided trip into ATM takes you deep into the underworld that the ancient Maya knew as Xibalba. The entrance to the 3-mile-long cave lies in the northern foothills of the Maya Mountains.

The experience is moderately strenuous, starting with an easy 45-minute hike through the lush jungle and across Roaring Creek (your feet will be wet all day). At the wide, hourglass-shaped entrance to the cave, you'll don your helmet, complete with headlamp. To reach the cave entrance, you'll start with a frosty swim across a deep pool (about 15ft across), so you must be a reasonably good swimmer. From here, follow your guide, walking, climbing, twisting and turning your way through the blackness of the cave for about an hour.

Giant shimmering flowstone rock formations compete for your attention with thick, calcium-carbonate stalactites dripping from the ceiling. Phallic stalagmites grow up from the cave floor. Eventually you'll follow your guide up into a massive opening, where you'll see hundreds of pottery vessels and shards, along with human remains. One of the most shocking displays is the calcite-encrusted remains of the woman for whom Actun Tunichil Muknal is named.

The trip takes about 10 hours from San Ignacio, including a one-hour drive each way. A number of San Ignacio–based tour companies do the trip for BZ$180 per person, including transportation, admission, lunch and equipment. You must be accompanied by a licensed guide, and cameras are not permitted inside the cave.

with welcoming staff, regular live music and a guaranteed crowd most nights.

Soul Project PERFORMING ARTS
(📋 653-1855; Buena Vista Rd; ⊘ 4-10pm Wed, 6-11pm Fri; 🐾) 🎵 Soul Project is a sweet bar and venue where local artist, filmmaker and conservationist Daniel Velazquez works hard to create a space for local and visiting artists and musicians. And he makes his own herbal fruit wine. At the time of writing it was only open Wednesday and Friday, but with a hostel upstairs and a bit of prodding, this may change.

ℹ Information

Belize Bank (16 Burns Ave), **Scotiabank** (cnr Burns Ave & King St) and **Atlantic Bank** (Burns Ave) have ATMs that accept international Visa, MasterCard, Plus and Cirrus cards.
Cayo Welcome Center (📋 634-8450; Savannah St, Cayo Plaza; ⊘ 8am-5pm Mon-Fri, 8am-4pm Sat) The only tourist office in the Cayo District, this is a helpful, air-conditioned modern place in the central plaza opened in 2013. As well as some local exhibits, a short film about the region runs on a loop.
Post Office (📋 824-2049; West St)

ℹ Getting There & Away

San Ignacio (surprisingly) has no bus station. Buses stop in the market plaza en route to/from Belize City (regular/express BZ$9/10, two hours), Belmopan (BZ$5, one hour) and Benque Viejo del Carmen (BZ$2, 30 minutes). Buses run in both directions about every half-hour from 3:30am to 7pm, with a less frequent service on Sunday.

From a vacant lot on Savannah St, buses leave for Bullet Tree Falls (BZ$1, 15 minutes) roughly hourly from 10:30am to 5pm Monday to Saturday. From the same spot, buses go to San Antonio (BZ$3, 35 minutes) five or six times a day, Monday to Saturday.

Several tour companies also run charter shuttle buses around Cayo and further afield. Sample fares include Guatemala border (BZ$50) and Belize City (BZ$150).

To really explore Cayo, a car is useful, preferably with good off-road capabilities and high clearance. Don't even think about heading to Caracol without a 4WD. Try **Cayo Auto Rentals** (📋 824-2222; www.cayoautorentals.com; 81 Benque Viejo Rd).

Several taxi stands are dotted around the town center; **Savannah Taxi Association** (📋 824-2155; ⊘ 24hr) is San Ignacio's main central taxi stand. Sample fares are BZ$25 to the Guatemalan border (9 miles), BZ$60 round-trip to

Xunantunich, and BZ$80 to BZ$100 one way to the Mountain Pine Ridge lodges. Taxis to Bullet Tree Falls (*colectivo*/private BZ$4/20) go from **Wyatt St**, just off Burns Ave.

ℹ Getting Around

San Ignacio is small enough that you can easily walk to most places of interest. If you're driving, note that parking can be difficult in the city center. Also pay attention to the one-way traffic system; Hawkesworth Bridge is one-way leaving San Ignacio while New Bridge enters town north of the market.

Short taxi rides around town cost BZ$5.

Mountain Pine Ridge & Caracol

Southeast of San Ignacio, the land begins to climb toward the heights of the Maya Mountains, whose arching ridge forms the border separating Cayo District from Stann Creek District to the east and Toledo District to the south.

In the heart of this highland area, 200 sq miles of submontane pine forest is the **Mountain Pine Ridge Forest Reserve**. The reserve is full of **rivers, pools, waterfalls** and **caves**; the higher elevation means relief from both heat and mosquitoes. Beyond Mountain Pine Ridge is the spectacular Maya ruin of Caracol.

◉ Sights & Activities

★**Caracol** ARCHAEOLOGICAL SITE
(admission BZ$30; ⊘ 8am-4pm, convoy departs 9am) Once one of the most powerful cities in the entire Maya world, Caracol now lies enshrouded by thick jungle near the Guatemalan border, a 52-mile, roughly two-hour drive from San Ignacio. Sitting high on the Vaca Plateau, this is the largest Maya site in Belize, having stretched over possibly 70 sq miles at its peak around AD 650. Nearly 40 miles of internal causeways radiate from the center to large outlying plazas and residential areas.

At its height, the city's population may have approached 150,000, more than twice as many people as Belize City has today. Though they had no natural water source, the people of Caracol dug artificial reservoirs to catch rainwater and grew food on extensive agricultural terraces. Its central area was a bustling place of temples, palaces, busy thoroughfares, craft workshops and markets. Caracol is not only the pre-eminent archaeological site in Belize but also exciting for its jungle setting and prolific bird life. At the ticket office, a small visitors center outlines Caracol's history and has a helpful scale model, while a museum houses much of the sculpture found at Caracol. There are toilets, picnic tables and a small gift shop. Be sure to bring food, water and, if you're driving, a spare tire. Overnight stays are not permitted.

García Sisters' Place CULTURAL CENTER
(☑669-4023; artistmai1981@gmail.com; Cristo Rey Rd, San Antonio; ☉7am-6pm) The García sisters display and sell a wide assortment of beautiful black-slate carvings. These five sisters – born and raised near San Antonio – developed this craft, which is now widely imitated around Belize. Their carvings, selling for between BZ$10 and BZ$200, depict a variety of subjects, including local wildlife and Maya deities and calendars.

★ Green Hills Butterfly Ranch FARM
(☑834-4017; http://biological-diversity.info/greenhills.htm; Mile 8 Chiquibul Rd; adult/child BZ$20/10; ☉8am-4pm, last tour 3:30pm) This amazing butterfly ranch offers a unique opportunity to see 50-plus exquisite native species in flight. Biologists Jan Meerman and Tineke Boomsma breed the butterflies for research and educational purposes, with research activity including tracking interaction between different species and compiling a field guide, as well as cultivating a botanical garden that supports the butterfly population. The ranch also boasts 13 species of hummingbird. Guided tours are hourly, with a minimum of two people required.

Calico Jack's ADVENTURE SPORTS
(☑820-4078, in USA 301-792-2233; www.calicojacksvillage.com; 7 Mile El Progresso; per person BZ$80-170; ☉8am-4pm) This 365-acre property boasts the largest state-of-the-art zip-lining set-up in Western Cayo, a nine-run 15-platform zip line; various packages take you on different runs ranging from a 45-minute 'explorer' to a 90-minute 'ultimate adventure.' Adventurous visitors can try the jungle swing (BZ$50), which offers a trip across a canyon combined with a 55ft free-fall, or the cable walk.

Mike's Place TOUR
(☑670-0441; www.bartoncreekcave.com; Barton Creek Cave; cave tour adult/child BZ$260/130) Mike's is based near Barton Creek Cave and offers guided canoe trips into the cave, as

well as rock climbing and a short zip-lining course. You can camp here for BZ$20, and there's a restaurant serving burritos and Belizean rice and beans. Transfers are available from San Ignacio for an extra BZ$60. The steep road here is atrocious.

West to Guatemala

Southwest from San Ignacio, the George Price Hwy runs across rolling countryside toward Benque Viejo del Carmen and the Guatemalan border. There is a variety of places to stay strung out along the highway and along diversions such as Chial Rd.

◎ Sights & Activities

★ Xunantunich RUIN
(San Jose Succotz; admission BZ$10; ☉7:30am-4pm) Set on a leveled hilltop, Xunantunich (shoo-nahn-too-neech) is one of Belize's most easily accessible and impressive Maya archaeological sites. Getting here is half the fun with a free hand-cranked cable ferry taking you (and vehicles) across the Mopan River. Xunantunich may have been occupied as early as 1000 BC but it was little more than a village. The large architecture that we see today began to be built in the 7th century AD.

You can climb to the top of El Castillo to enjoy a spectacular 360-degree view. Its upper levels were constructed in two distinct phases. The first, built around 800, included an elaborate plaster frieze encircling the building; the second, built around 900, covered over most of the first and its frieze.

To reach the ruins, take the ferry in San Jose Succotz village, then it's about 1 mile uphill to the parking lot and ticket office. Any bus from San Ignacio can drop you at the ferry point.

Poustinia Land Art Park SCULPTURE
(☑822-3532; Mile 2.5 Mollejon Rd; admission by appointment only BZ$20) Created by Benque brothers Luis and David Ruiz, this highly unexpected avant-garde sculpture park is one of the hidden artistic gems of Western Belize. Set in 60 acres of rainforest about 2 miles southeast of Benque, the park displays some 35 works by Belizean and international artists.

⌂ Sleeping & Eating

★ Trek Stop LODGE, CAMPGROUND $
(☑823-2265; www.thetrekstop.com; Mile 71 Western Hwy; camping per person BZ$14, s/d without

bathroom from BZ$30/48, d/tr/q with bathroom BZ$76/100/120; P@🛜) 🏊 Trek Stop is a great option if you want to get out of San Ignacio on a budget and be close to Xunantunich. The ecolodge and backpackers' outpost consists of well-made timber cabins in a jungle setting just off the highway. There's an eco-vibe but it has mains electricity and wi-fi. Plenty of hangout space, a self-catering kitchen and a cool little restaurant.

Benque Resort & Spa   HOTEL $
(📞 632-0688; www.benque-resort.com; 22 Riverside; dm BZ$35, s/d BZ$60/80, d with air-con BZ$100; ❄🛜) This charming three-story home on the south bank of the Mopan River offers unexpected B&B-type amenities, including beautiful woodwork and colorful tiled bathrooms with hot showers, as well as popular budget dorm accommodation. There's a professional-quality onsite massage studio. Larger rooms offer more space and a veranda with a river view.

Benny's Kitchen   BELIZEAN $
(📞 823-2541; Mile 72 Western Hwy; meals BZ$10-16; ⊙8am-9pm Mon-Thu, 8am-11pm Fri & Sat, 8am-10pm Sun; 🛜🍴) Benny's is a local institution in San Jose Succotz – the turnoff is opposite the Xunantunich ferry so it's convenient for a post-ruin meal. Local specialties include tangy *escabeche* (spicy chicken with lime and onions), fiery BBQ and cow-foot soup. The semi-open-air dining area has a bar, a gift store, a children's playground and an internet cafe.

SOUTHERN BELIZE

Southern Belize is the country's most absorbing cultural melting pot, with a strong Garifuna influence around Dangriga and Hopkins, and Belize's largest Maya population down in Toledo. Nature is rich here too, where open savannah and citrus-filled farmland give way to forested hills dotted with Maya villages and ruins.

Dangriga

POP 10,100

Dangriga is the largest town in southern Belize, and the spiritual capital of the country's Garifuna people. It has a funky coastal vibe about it – tumbledown and mildly untidy. Despite sharing a similar ramshackle exterior with Belize City, Dangriga doesn't have a big-city feel and is generally a safe place to explore.

👁 Sights

Gulisi Garifuna Museum   MUSEUM
(📞 669-0639; www.ngcbelize.org; Hummingbird Hwy, Chuluhadiwa Park; admission BZ$10; ⊙10am-5pm Mon-Fri, 8am-noon Sat) This museum, operated by the National Garifuna Council (NGC), is a must for anyone interested in the vibrant Garifuna people. The museum is 2 miles out of town; ask any bus heading out of Dangriga to drop you here or hire a bicycle. It brings together artifacts, pictures and documents on Garifuna history and culture, including an exhibit on the life and music of the late Garifuna musician Andy Palacio. A free guided tour is included with admission.

Pen Cayetano Studio Gallery   GALLERY
(📞 628-6807; www.cayetano.de; 3 Aranda Cres; adult/student BZ$5/3; ⊙9am-5pm Mon-Fri, weekends by appointment) Renowned throughout Belize for his art and music, Pen Cayetano's workshop and gallery displays Garifuna artifacts and crafts. It also has works of art and music by Pen, and the textile artwork of his wife, Ingrid, available for sale. Among the most unique items are drums made of turtle shells, which sell for around BZ$50.

Marie Sharp's Factory   FACTORY
(📞 532-2087; www.mariesharps-bz.com; 1 Melinda Rd; ⊙7am-4pm Mon-Fri) The super-hot bottled sauces that adorn tables all over Belize and beyond are made from habanero peppers here at Marie Sharp's Factory, 8 miles northwest of town on Melinda Rd. Free tours are usually offered during business hours (by advance reservation), and the factory shop sells hot sauces and jams at outlet prices. If you can't make it to the factory, Marie Sharp's also has a store (📞 522-2370; 3 Pier Rd; ⊙8am-noon & 1-5pm Mon-Fri) in Dangriga.

🎉 Festivals & Events

Garifuna Settlement Day   CULTURAL
On November 19 Dangriga explodes with celebrations to mark the arrival of Garifuna in Dangriga in 1832. Dangrigans living elsewhere flock home for the celebrations. Drumming, dancing and drinking continue right through the night of the 18th to the 19th, while canoes reenact the beach landing in the morning. Book ahead for accommodation.

BELIZE DANGRIGA

Dangriga

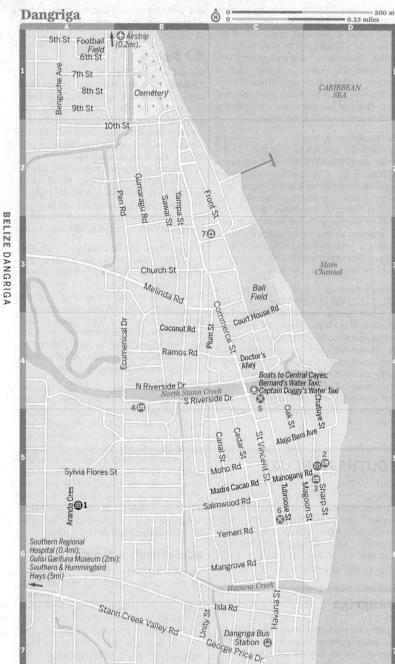

N
0   500 m
0   0.25 miles

BELIZE DANGRIGA

5th St
Football Field
6th St
7th St
8th St
9th St
Cemetery
Airstrip (0.2mi)
10th St

Benguche Ave

CARIBBEAN SEA

Gumaragu Rd
Sawai St
Yampa St
Front St
Pen Rd

7

Church St
Melinda Rd

Ball Field

Main Channel

Ecumenical Dr
Coconut Rd
Plum St
Commerce St
Court House Rd
Ramos Rd

Doctor's Alley

N Riverside Dr
North Stann Creek
S Riverside Dr

Boats to Central Cayes;
Bernard's Water Taxi;
Captain Doggy's Water Taxi

4
5

Oak St
Chatuye St
Alejo Beni Ave

Cedar St
Canal St
St Vincent St

Sylvia Flores St

2
3

Moho Rd
Madre Cacao Rd
Mahogany Rd
Tubroose St
Magoon St
Sharp St

Salmwood Rd

6

Aranda Cres

1

Yemeri Rd

Southern Regional
Hospital (0.4mi);
Gulisi Garifuna Museum (2mi);
Southern & Hummingbird
Hwys (5mi)

Mangrove Rd

Havana Creek

Havana St

Stann Creek Valley Rd
Isla Rd
Unity St

Dangriga Bus Station
George Price Dr

Dangriga

⊙ Sights
1 Pen Cayetano Studio Gallery..............A5

⊟ Sleeping
2 Bonefish Hotel......................................D5
3 D's Hostel..D5
4 Jungle Huts Hotel B4

⊗ Eating
5 Riverside Café C4
6 Steph's C6

⊟ Shopping
7 Marie Sharp's Factory Store..............C3

🛏 Sleeping & Eating

D's Hostel   HOSTEL $
(📞502-3324; 1 Sharp St; dm/d BZ$25/100; @🏠)
Dangriga's one and only hostel (formerly
Val's) is a local institution. A large porch
faces a desolate park with views to the sea
and leads to an eight-bed dorm and two spacious, hotel-quality private rooms sleeping
up to three, with TV and fridge.

Jungle Huts Hotel   HOTEL $$
(📞665-8966, 522-0185; junglehutsresort@gmail.
com; 4 Ecumenical Dr; d from BZ$86, cabañas &
suites BZ$158; P❄🏠) Philip Usher's river-
side resort is just a little way out of town but
its location is a blessing, offering a peaceful
(even jungle) vibe away from the Commer-
cial Rd scene. There are good-value rooms,
suites and three *cabañas*, all with one dou-
ble and one single bed, en suite bathrooms
with showers, and air-con. Only suites and
cabañas have TV with cable.

Bonefish Hotel   HOTEL $$
(📞522-2243; www.bluemarinlodge.com/bonefish-
hotel; 15 Mahogany Rd; r BZ$180-210; P❄🏠)
Upper floors are not without charm, but the
ones on the lower floor are darker and somewhat less cheery, though no less functional.
All rooms have two double beds, fan, air-con
and cable TV. Pay a bit extra for breakfast or
a lot more for full board.

Steph's   BELIZEAN $
(St Vincent St; mains BZ$5-10; ⊙7am-10pm Wed-
Mon) There's no menu but tasty Belizean
classics such as baked pork or chicken with
rice and beans are a steal at this clean shack
restaurant on the main street.

Riverside Café   SEAFOOD $
(S Riverside Dr; mains BZ$8-15; ⊙7am-9pm) Just
east of the Stann Creek bridge, this cafe is the

place to meet fishers and the boat captains
who offer tours and transportation to the
outlying cays. The food is inexpensive, the
fish is always fresh and the Belikin is cold.

ℹ Information

Belize Bank (St Vincent St), **Scotiabank** (St
Vincent St) and **First Caribbean International
Bank** (Commerce St) all have 24-hour ATMs
that accept international Visa, MasterCard,
Plus and Cirrus cards. The latter charges an
outrageous US$5 fee for transactions.
Immigration Office (📞522-3412; St Vincent
St; ⊙8am-5pm Mon-Thu, 8am-4:30pm Fri) Of-
fers 30-day visa extension stamps for BZ$50.
Post Office (📞522-2035; Mahogany Rd) Next
to Bonefish Hotel.

ℹ Getting There & Away

AIR
From Dangriga airport (DGA), **Maya Island Air**
(📞522-2659; www.mayaislandair.com) and
Tropic Air (📞226-2012) fly direct to Belize City,
Placencia and Punta Gorda several times daily.

BOAT
Dangriga is the departure point for trips to
Belize's central cays, as well as for chartered
trips up and down the coast. The best spot to
arrange **boat transportation** is just outside the
Riverside Café on South Riverside Dr. Stop by
before 9am, or the afternoon before, to check
when boats will be leaving. The more people you
can get for one trip (within reason), the cheaper
it works out per person.

Boats usually go daily to Tobacco Caye (BZ$40
per person) but can also be chartered to Thatch
Caye, South Water Caye and Glover's Reef; the
upmarket lodges on these islands will organize
your boat for you.

The colorful Captain Doggy's 25ft **boat**
(📞627-7443; captaindoggy@gmail.com) travels
between Dangriga and all of the cays. He also
does custom day trips with spearfishing, island
stops and lunch for BZ$100.
Bernard's Water Taxi (📞633-0160; dalila56@
yahoo.com) also offers trips out to all the cays,
as well as fishing and other privately chartered
trips.

BUS
A major transit point for all bus companies servicing southern Belize, Dangriga's main **bus station**
(St Vincent St) is near the roundabout at the southern end of town. There are frequent buses to Belize
City (regular/express BZ$10/12, two hours), Bel-
mopan (BZ$6, 1½ hours), Punta Gorda (BZ$13, 2½
hours) and San Ignacio (BZ$11, 2¼ hours), and a
few direct services to Hopkins (BZ$5, 30 minutes)
and Placencia (BZ$10, 1½ hours).

Central Cays

Less crowded, lesser known and often less costly than the cays in the north, the central cays – most of them private islands – off Belize's central coast are smack in the middle of some of the country's most amazing diving, snorkeling and fishing sites.

South Water Caye and Thatch Caye are home to fancy all-inclusive resorts, but some good deals can be found on Tobacco Caye and Glover's Reef Atoll.

In most cases the resorts will arrange boat transfers. The central cays are best reached from Dangriga, but charters also run from Hopkins and Placencia.

🛏 Sleeping

Tobacco Caye Paradise CABIN $
(☑ 532-2101; http://tobaccocaye.com; cabañas per person BZ$70; 🛜) This is the best deal on Tobacco. Paradise has six lovely *cabañas* perched on stilts over the water with private bathrooms and cold-water showers. Verandas, with chairs and hammock, look out toward the reef where the water is shallow enough to wade right in. Meals are served in the classroom-like dining room (breakfast/lunch/dinner BZ$20/20/30). Wi-fi is BZ$5 per day, per cabin.

★ Glover's Atoll Resort CABIN $
(☑ 520-5016; www.glovers.com.bz; per person per week camping BZ$198, dm & onsite tents BZ$298, cabins BZ$498-598; 🛜 🚌) Occupying the Glover's northeast cay, this ramshackle backpackers' paradise is the perfect, affordable island getaway. The private 10-acre island has 16 cabins (over the water and on the beach), a basic dorm and eight private campgrounds. Most travelers take the weekly deal, which includes boat transfers from Sittee River, but nightly 'drop-in' rates are also available, starting from BZ$24 for camping.

Hopkins & Sittee Point

POP 1500

The friendly, slightly scruffy, coastal village of Hopkins attracts travelers looking to soak up sea breezes and Garifuna culture. It's an unpretentious place to meet other travelers and makes a good base for explorations of the cays, reefs and islands to the east, and the jungles, mountains and parks to the west.

About 1.5 miles south of Hopkins, Sittee Point is a small community where high-end beachfront resorts and a few interesting independent restaurants gather.

🏃 Activities

Hopkins is a fine place from which to access some of Belize's best dive sites. The barrier reef is less than a 40-minute boat ride away, and Glover's Reef is about 90 minutes on a fast skiff. Diving and snorkeling can be arranged through several outfits in Hopkins and nearby Sittee Point.

Lebeha COURSE
(☑ 665-9305; North Side; lessons per hr BZ$30) Set up by local drummer Jabbar Lambey and his wife Dorothy, Lebeha functions both as an educational and cultural center for locals and as a general happening spot for travelers interested in Garifuna drumming. Lessons for individuals and groups are available, and there's drumming most nights from 7pm. Full-moon drumming parties are an especially great reason to visit.

Motorbike Rentals & Alternate Adventures TOUR
(☑ 665-6292; www.alternateadventures.com; South Side) MR&AA rents 200cc dirt bikes (BZ$118 per day, BZ $598 per week) and 250cc cruiser motorcycles (BZ$150 per day, BZ$750 per week) for self-guided motorcycle touring. Emma, the owner, offers helpful suggestions for independent-minded travelers and is a wealth of local knowledge.

Hopkins

Standup Paddleboard WATER SPORTS
(☑ 650-9040; www.suphopkins.com; Sittee Point; paddleboarding tours BZ$110-150) Stand-up paddleboarding has arrived in Sittee Point in a pretty special way. This outfit offers SUP tours on the Sittee River with a mind-blowing two-hour evening bioluminescence paddle or a half-day paddle in search of wildlife. Combination paddle and snorkel tours are also available. The office is at the junction at Sittee Point.

Happy Go Luckie Tours BOAT TOUR
(☑ 635-0967; www.hgltours.com; half-/full-day charters BZ$470/700) Happy Go Luckie offers custom half- and full-day boat charters for up to five people, including snorkeling, fishing and island-hopping. Also does transfers to the southern cays and Glover's Reef. The office is in Hopkins village but the boats leave from Sittee Point marina.

Belize Underwater DIVING
(⌨ 633-3401; www.hopkinsunderwateradven
tures.com; Sittee Point) Belize Underwater is
a PADI-certified dive shop offering scuba
instruction and trips to South Water Caye,
Thatch Caye and Glover's Reef.

Seemore Adventures DIVING, SNORKELING
(⌨ 602-4985, 667-6626; http://seemoreadven
tures.com) Run by local dive instructor Elmar
'Boo' Avila, Seemore offers customized snorkeling, fishing or just cruisey trips out to the
reef, as well as scuba-diving trips.

🛏 Sleeping

★**Funky Dodo** HOSTEL $
(⌨ 676 3636; www.funkydodo.bz; South Side;
dm/d with shared bathroom BZ$22/51, d/tr/q with
bathroom BZ$66/90/120; 🛜) Hopkins' only
hostel is indeed a funky place, with a tightly
packed village of rustic timber cabin rooms
and dorms inhabiting a leafy garden. Backpackers swing in hammocks reading books,
while others roll out the yoga mats. Upstairs
the Tree Top Bar is a good place to socialize
or find a cheap meal. There's also a communal kitchen and tour desk.

Solution Guest House GUESTHOUSE $
(⌨ 668-7594; elaineortiz_37@yahoo.com; r with/
without bathroom BZ$66/56; Ⓟ🛜) Across the
road from the Funky Dodo, this five-room
guesthouse is an excellent deal if you're after
a clean, private room in the village center.
Elaine is a cheerful host who can book tours
and cook meals, and will let you use the
downstairs kitchen.

Windschief Cabanas CABIN $
(⌨ 523-7249; www.windschief.com; South Side;
small/large cabaña BZ$60/90; Ⓟ@🛜) There are
just two basic but comfy stilted *cabañas* with
private bathrooms and hot showers here in
this seafront location. Oliver and Pamela's
beachfront bar is a happening spot on Friday and Saturday. Oliver was busy building
a minigolf course out front when we visited.

Castille Beach CAMPGROUND $
(⌨ 660-2413; per tent BZ$10) You can pitch a
tent on this private bit of beach between
Hopkins and Sittee Point. Shared bathrooms
and canoes available.

★**Coconut Row**
Guesthouse GUESTHOUSE $$
(⌨ 670-3000, in USA 518-223-9775; www.coco
nutrowbelize.com; beachside; d BZ$230, cabins

BZ$250, apt BZ$260; Ⓟ❋🛜) The colorfully
painted Coconut Row boasts some of the
finest beachfront rooms in Hopkins. The
five main rooms are spacious and spotless,
and come with air-conditioning, fridge and
coffee-maker, and two of them are full two-
bedroom apartments. Rooms are beautifully
designed for maximum comfort with tile
floors and king-sized beds. In the adjoining
property are three free-standing beachfront
log cabins.

★**All Seasons**
Guest House GUESTHOUSE $$
(⌨ 523-7209; www.allseasonsbelize.com; South
Side; r BZ$86-150, family cabins BZ$196; Ⓟ❋🛜)
With its colorful two-bedroom *cabañas* and
cozy guesthouse rooms, All Seasons may just
be the cutest accommodations in town. All
rooms have air-con, coffee-makers and hot
showers. There's a great patio out front with
a grill and picnic area. The location is good,
at the south end of town and a short walk
over the road to the beach.

Tipple Tree Beya HOTEL $$
(⌨ 615-7006; www.tippletreebelize.com; South Side;
r BZ$80-110, 1-/2-bedroom apt BZ$196/360; 🛜) 🏖
This sturdy wooden beachside place rents
three cozy, clean, fan-cooled rooms sharing a
sociable veranda beneath the owner's quar-
ters upstairs. In an adjacent buildings are
some excellent self-contained apartments
that would suit a family or group. The owner,
Tricia, implements a number of sustainable
practices including composting, recycling
and keeping the place as energy efficient as
possible.

🍴 Eating & Drinking

Gecko's BELIZEAN $
(⌨ 629-5411; North Side; mains BZ$6-15; ⏲ noon-
9pm Mon & Wed-Sat; 🛜🍴) One of Hopkins'
newer places, Gecko's gets ticks for cheap
tacos; vegetarian, vegan and gluten-free
dishes; an interesting range of specials; and
a breezy open-air dining space located just
north of the main intersection.

★**Loggerheads Pub & Grill** BURGERS $$
(⌨ 650-2886; burgers BZ$12-20; ⏲ 11am-10pm
Thu-Mon) The best burgers in town are served
here on homemade rolls. Try the pulled pork
or the gorgonzola-stuffed beef burger with
bacon. The breezy upstairs dining area is the
place for a cold beer.

★ **Driftwood Beach**
Bar & Pizza Shack PIZZA $$
(North Side; pizza BZ$16-25, tacos BZ$10; ⊙ 11am-10pm Thu-Tue) On a decent stretch of beach at the northern end of Hopkins, Driftwood serves excellent pizza and tacos beneath a thatched roof. This is a popular social hub and party place: Tuesday is the big night with Garifuna drumming, but there are also weekend events and beach BBQs.

★ **Swinging Armadillo** SEAFOOD $$
(☑ 635-5404; North Side; mains BZ$12-25; ⊙ 10am-10pm Sun-Fri) The Swinging Armadillo has one of the most enviable locations in Hopkins with a sweet little veranda hanging over the water. Ted and his crew back it up with generous portions of superb fresh seafood and an ever-changing blackboard menu.

Thongs Cafe CAFE $$
(Main St; mains BZ$7-22; ⊙ 7am-3pm Wed-Sun) This cute Euro-style cafe is a cool spot for breakfast or a light lunch of salad, wraps and specials such as quesadillas or meatballs. Smoothies are good – if you're detoxing try the Green Fusion with spinach, cucumber and pineapple. Service can be slow, so browse the gift shop with designer T-shirts and vintage clothing while you wait.

ℹ Information

There's a **Belize Bank ATM** (⊙ 24hr) at the main intersection in the town center.

ℹ Getting There & Away

Two buses a day leave Hopkins for Dangriga (BZ$5, 30 minutes) from Monday to Saturday from the main intersection in town. Many travelers hitch or take a taxi (BZ$20) the 4 miles to the Southern Hwy junction and pick up any passing bus going north or south from there. A taxi to Hopkins from Dangriga costs BZ$80.

Placencia

POP 1500

Placencia, a true beach-holiday strip on the mainland, is enduringly popular with North American expats and tourists. Perched at the southern tip of a long, narrow, sandy peninsula, the village has long enjoyed a reputation as 'the cay you can drive to' – a fully-paved 27-mile road heads off the Southern Hwy via Maya Beach and Seine Bight to the tip of the peninsula.

The village of Placencia occupies the southernmost mile of the peninsula. On the eastern side is a sandy beach; between the beach and the road is a narrow, pedestrian-only footpath known as the Sidewalk.

🏃 Activities

Diving, snorkeling, fishing, kayaking and trips to inland adventures are all available from Placencia and there are plenty of operators who can organize activities.

★ **Splash Dive Center** DIVING, TOURS
(☑ 523-3058; www.splashbelize.com; Main St) Splash teaches PADI courses to divers of all levels, as well as offering diving and snorkeling tours to islands and reefs throughout the area. Owner Patty Ramirez is a patient and professional instructor, making her suitable for first-time divers and experts alike. As Quest Tours, Patty and partner Ralph also lead tours inland, including trips to Maya ruins and jungles.

🧭 Tours

Joy Tours TOUR
(☑ 523-3325; www.belizewithjoy.com; Main St) Joy is a reliable outfit offering a variety of local fishing, snorkeling and diving activities, as well as arranging hiking tours to Maya ruins around southern Belize.

Ocean Motion Services TOUR
(☑ 523-3162, 523-3363; www.oceanmotionplacencia.com; Sidewalk; tours BZ$70-400; ⊙ 7.30am-6pm Mon-Sat, 7.30am-5pm Sun) Arranges fishing and snorkeling trips, as well as cave tubing.

Trip 'n Travel TOUR, FISHING
(☑ 523-3205; www.tripntravel.bz; Main St; tours BZ$140-450; ⊙ 8am-6pm Mon-Fri, 8am-2pm Sat) Reliable company offering all the usual tours, plus fly-fishing and regular tours into Maya country in Toledo. Most tours will go with only two people.

🛏 Sleeping

★ **Anda Di Howse** HOSTEL $
(☑ 523-3306, 631-1614; pandora_gaudino@yahoo.com; dm BZ$25; 🛜) 'Under the House' is Placencia's only genuine hostel. Owner Pandora has designed a beautiful 10-bed dorm beneath her stilt home, with timber floors, spring mattresses, individual fans, lockers and spotless bathrooms. Best of all, it's right on the beach at the southern end of the Sidewalk.

Placencia

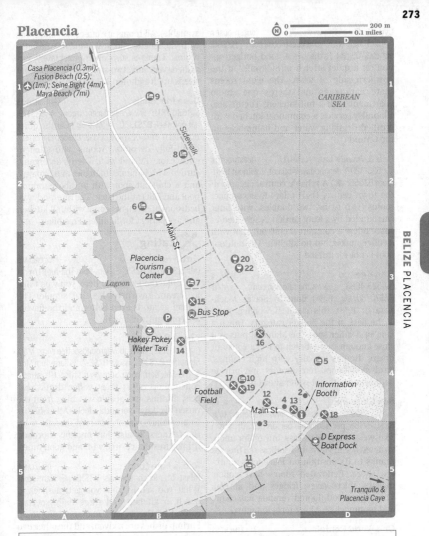

Placencia

🜚 Activities, Courses & Tours
Book it @ Barefoot........................(see 20)
1 Joy Tours B4
2 Ocean Motion Services.......................D4
3 Splash Dive Center C5
4 Trip 'n Travel...C4

🛏 Sleeping
5 Anda Di Howse D4
6 Captain Jak's B2
7 Deb & Dave's Last Resort....................B3
8 Lydia's Guesthouse B2
9 Manatee Inn...B1
10 One World Rentals C4
11 Sea Glass Inn..C5

🍴 Eating
12 Above Grounds.......................................C4
13 Mojo Lounge &
    Bartique..C4
14 Omar's Creole Grub B4
15 Radi's Fine Food B3
16 Rick's Cafe..C4
17 Rumfish...C4
18 Shak D4
19 Tutti Frutti..C4

🍸 Drinking & Nightlife
20 Barefoot Bar...C3
21 Brewed Awakenings...............................B2
22 Tipsy Tuna Sports Bar...........................C3

Lydia's Guesthouse
GUESTHOUSE $

(☑ 523-3117; www.lydiasguesthouse.com; r BZ$60, apt BZ$70; ☞) Lydia's is a good budget option on a quiet stretch of Sidewalk on the northern side of town. The eight rooms share bathrooms and there's one studio apartment with a full kitchen. There's also a laundry service, a communal kitchen with purified drinking water and hammocks on the veranda.

Deb & Dave's Last Resort
GUESTHOUSE $

(☑ 523-3207; debanddave@btl.net; r without bathroom BZ$55; ☞) A reliable central cheapie in the town centre, D&D offers four compact rooms (two twins, two doubles) with fans, surrounded by a leafy garden. A screened-in space offers a communal chill-out spot with a coffee-maker, but no kitchen. The outdoor pool is not for guests!

Manatee Inn
HOTEL $

(☑ 523-4083; www.manateeinn.com; s/d/tr BZ$70/80/90; P☞) Built by Slavek Machacka in 1999, this classical wooden hotel is the best in the budget category. Down a lane in a quiet spot, the Manatee puts you close enough to the beach to feel a constant breeze. Rooms are airy with high ceilings, hardwood floors, refrigerators and private bathrooms with hot-water showers.

Sea Glass Inn
HOTEL $$

(☑ 523-3098; www.seaglassinnbelize.com; d/tr BZ$158/188, per additional person BZ$20; ✳☞) The welcoming Sea Glass Inn offers unobstructed ocean views and endless sea breezes thanks to its position on Placencia's southern shore. Renovated rooms have coffee-makers, microwaves, fridges and air-con. The wide, wood-floored veranda has chairs and hammocks for long-term lounging.

One World Rentals
APARTMENT $$

(☑ 620-9975, 523-3103; www.oneworldplacencia.com; Main St; studios from BZ$130, cabaña BZ$180, apt from BZ$200; P✳☞) These clean, colorful, fully equipped studios and apartments come with kitchenettes, ample parking and a leafy central courtyard. Run by a gregarious Swiss woman named Claudia, it's behind the gift shop of the same name, and there's also a laundry onsite.

Captain Jak's
CABIN $$

(☑ 628-6447; www.captainjaks.com; Main St; cabaña BZ$190, cottage BZ$250; P☞) The Captain offers three cabañas and two larger cottages surrounding a quiet garden (weekly rates are available). All rooms are fan-cooled and come with kitchenettes, hot water and private bathrooms. There is also an immaculately furnished, very airy, two-story private villa that sleeps up to eight for BZ$630 a night.

Casa Placencia
APARTMENT $$

(☑ 630-7811; www.casaplacencia.com; r BZ$110, apt per week BZ$1300; P✳☞☀) On the quiet northern end of town, Casa Placencia offers beautifully decorated rooms with kitchenettes, cable TV and wi-fi. There's an organic garden with bananas, mangoes and papayas, and a chill-out spot with an above-ground pool and BBQ at the back. The one- and two-bedroom apartments come with full kitchen and are perfect for families. Free bikes.

✕ Eating

Tutti Frutti
ICE CREAM $

(Main St; from BZ$5; ⊙ 9am-9pm Thu-Tue) If you don't like the ice cream here, you won't like ice cream anywhere. It's that simple. The Italian gelato is even better and the flavors are constantly changing.

Above Grounds
CAFE $

(☑ 634-3212; www.abovegroundscoffee.com; Main St; coffee BZ$3-5, snacks BZ$2-7; ⊙ 7am-4pm Mon & Thu-Sat, 8am-noon Sun; ☞) This stilt shack coffee shop offers great coffee drinks, bagels, muffins and people-watching from the raised wooden veranda deck. All coffee is Guatemalan organic, sourced directly from the farmers. It also has organic chocolate drinks, fresh juice, free wi-fi and good tunes.

Radi's Fine Food
BELIZEAN $

(Main St; lunch specials BZ$10; ⊙ 11am-3pm) What you see is what you get: a shack, a porch, a kitchen and three daily specials cooked by Creole chef Radiance, aka Radi. Shrimp dishes are a given, and the other two dishes can be anything from conch soup to meatloaf. All are delicious, and portions are always more than ample.

Shak
CAFE $

(☑ 622-1686; dishes BZ$10-15; ⊙ 7am-6pm Sun & Mon, 7am-9pm Wed-Sat) This ocean-facing restaurant is one of the best places in town for a healthy smoothie – there are 28 varieties – or an all-day breakfast. It also serves seafood, tacos and other Mexican dishes. The vibe is mellow and the people-watching fine.

★ Mojo Lounge & Bartique
CAFE $$

(☑ 628-7974; www.mojoloungeplacencia.com; Main St; starters BZ$10-12, mains BZ$24-30;

5-9pm Mon-Sat; ✺ 📶) Since opening in 2013 little Mojo has made a big name for itself with an imaginative menu, fresh local ingredients, impressive cocktails and the ultimate in cozy lounge vibe. From 5pm till 6pm it's happy hour, so get in early and grab a space on the balcony for half-price cocktails and starters.

★ **Rumfish**   FUSION $$
(📋 523-3293; www.rumfishyvino.com; Main St; tacos BZ$9, mains BZ$22-38; ⊙noon-midnight, kitchen closes at 10pm) Rumfish is a gastro-style wine bar done Central American style. Head up to the balcony of the beautiful old timber building and enjoy simple starters such as Peruvian *ceviche* or specialty mains such as Yucatan chicken or Caribbean fish stew. Gourmet tacos are BZ$9 a pop. Imported wines, beers and cocktails, and a breezy colonial veranda complete the picture.

★ **Omar's Creole Grub**   SEAFOOD $$
(📋 605-7631; Main St; mains BZ$10-45; ⊙7am-9pm Sun-Thu, 7am-5pm Fri, 6-9pm Sat) Omar's has been around a long time and still serves some of the freshest seafood in town. Step into the small and rustic streetside shack and choose from crab, lobster, shrimp or conch prepared either traditional Creole, Caribbean curry or coconut curry. There's also burgers and burritos. No alcohol.

Rick's Cafe   PIZZA $$
(Sidewalk; mains BZ$14-32; ⊙11am-9:30pm; 📶) This cool little veranda cafe on the Sidewalk is best known for its pizza and pasta, but Rick also whips up sandwiches, quesadillas and *ceviche*.

🍷 Drinking & Nightlife

Barefoot Bar   BAR
(📋 523-3515; Sidewalk; ⊙11am-midnight; 📶) Occupying prime beach real estate, Placencia's most happening spot for drinking and entertainment has live music five nights a week, fire dancing on Wednesdays, full-moon parties and more. Happy hour is from 5pm to 6pm, with bitters and cheap rum. The menu has a big range of Mexican snacks, pizza and burgers.

Tipsy Tuna Sports Bar   BAR
(www.tipsytunabelize.com; Sidewalk; ⊙11am-midnight) Brightening up the beach with its multicolored sun loungers, Tipsy Tuna provides occasional action with live music (Garifuna drumming on Wednesday), along with big-screen TV, pool tables, rooftop deck

and happy hour from 5pm to 7pm. The food is reasonably priced: standard-issue burgers, tacos, wings and the like.

Brewed Awakenings   CAFE
(Main St; coffee BZ$3.50-6.75, shakes BZ$7-8; ⊙6am-5pm Mon-Sat) The imaginative name extends to the drinks with perfectly brewed espresso coffee and a range of flavored seaweed shakes (the seaweed acts as a thickener and is said to contain various healthy vitamins). Great for an early-morning caffeine fix.

ℹ Information

Belize Bank and **Scotiabank** (⊙8:30am-2:30pm Mon-Thu, to 4pm Fri) are both on the main drag and have 24/7 ATM access. There's an Atlantic Bank branch on the far north end of town.

There's no shortage of info on Placencia, both on the web and around Belize. In town, head to the **Placencia Tourism Center** (📋 523-4045; www.placencia.com; ⊙8am-5pm Mon-Fri), down a lane opposite Scotiabank (look for the sign). This private BTIA (Belize Tourism Industry Association) office has friendly staff who can offer local information such as transportation info. While you're there, pick up a copy of the monthly *Placencia Breeze* (also online at www.placenciabreeze.com). Or try your luck at the erratically staffed **Information Booth** (Main St; ⊙9-11am & 2-4pm Mon-Fri).

ℹ Getting There & Around

The **Hokey Pokey Water Taxi** (📋 665-7242; one way BZ$10; ⊙ approx hourly from 6:45am to 6pm, or 5pm Sunday) runs skiffs between the southern tip of Placencia and the town of Independence/Mango Creek; from Independence bus station you can connect with any of the buses that traverse the Southern Hwy (to Punta Gorda, for instance).

The 45-passenger **D Express** sails from Placencia municipal pier to Puerto Cortés, Honduras (BZ$130, 4½ hours including immigration time) at 9am on Friday. Tickets are sold at **Book it @ Barefoot** (📋 523-3515). The return trip leaves Puerto Cortés at 11am on Monday.

Ritchie's (📋 523-3806; www.ritchiesbusservice.com) bus line has one daily bus to Belize City at 6:15am (BZ$20, 4½ hours) and three buses to Dangriga (BZ$10, 1¾ hours) Monday to Saturday, from where you can transfer to Belmopan and points beyond. Buses to Dangriga leave at 7am, 12:45pm and 2:30pm (2:30pm only on Sunday) from the **bus stop** on Main St opposite the Hokey Pokey Water Taxi.

To get to Hopkins, ask to be let off at the Hopkins junction and hitch or call a taxi from there.

Cars, motorbikes and golf buggies can be hired along the Placencia peninsula; try **Barefoot Services** (☑ 523-3066; www.barefootservicesbelize. com; ☺ 8am-5:30pm Sun-Fri), near the airport.

Punta Gorda

POP 5910

Punta Gorda (or PG as it's known) is a slightly ramshackle coastal settlement down in the Deep South of Toledo. Once known to travelers mainly as a port to get the boat across to Guatemala, it's increasingly attracting visitors looking to chill out in the south and as a base for exploring surrounding Maya villages and culture, and the remote Southern Cayes.

🏃 Activities

Ixcacao Maya Belizean Chocolate FOOD

(☑ 742-4050; www.ixcacaomayabelizeanchoco late.com; San Felipe village; tours from BZ$60 per person; ☺ 9am-5pm) 🥾 Learn all about the Maya chocolate-making process at Juan and Abelina's beautiful cacao farm and chocolate factory in the off-track village of San Felipe, 10 miles from PG. There's a variety of tour options, including farm tours, factory tours and traditional Maya lunch. Juan will walk you through the traditional chocolate-making process – from harvest and fermentation to drying and roasting, to deshelling and grinding, tasting as you go.

The family also has a small homestay bunkhouse next to the factory (BZ$50 per person including breakfast and dinner) as well as camping (BZ$10) and farmstay (BZ$50).

★ Cotton Tree Chocolate Factory FOOD

(www.cottontreechocolate.com; 2 Front St; ☺ 8am-noon & 1:30-5pm Mon-Fri, to noon Sat) 🥾 FREE Cotton Tree is a good opportunity to buy some local chocolate and learn a bit about the process. Beans are sourced from Toledo Cacao Growers Association, promoting both fair trade and local production. The owner happily offers tours of the small factory, and there's a gift shop selling only locally made (and some chocolate-themed) handicrafts, including soaps, cacao-bean jewelry and, obviously, chocolate bars.

Maroon Creole Drum School COURSE

(☑ 668-7733, 632-7841; methosdrums@hotmail. com; Joe Taylor Creek; ☺ by appointment) Those looking to study with a master will find the trip to Emmeth Young's drum school well

worth it. When he's not touring the country performing, one of Belize's most respected Creole drummers hosts drum-making workshops and group presentations. It costs BZ$25 an hour for drum lessons, or for around BZ$250 you can spend a few days learning both drumming and drum-making, leaving with your own handcrafted drum.

Warasa Garifuna Drum School COURSE

(☑ 632-7701; www.warasadrumschool.com; New Rd; drum lessons BZ$25, half-day package BZ$125; ☺ by appointment) Local drummer Ronald Raymond (Ray) McDonald teaches Garifuna beats at his Warasa Garifuna Drum School on New Rd (about 15 minutes' walk out of town). There are one-on-one classes and group lessons. McDonald also performs and lectures about Garifuna culture at **Hickatee Cottages** (☑ 662-4475; www. hickatee.com; cottages BZ$130-200, d BZ$160, ste BZ$240-260; 🅿🛜❄).

Garbutt's Marine & Fishing Lodge FISHING, DIVING

(☑ 722-0070; www.garbuttsfishinglodge.com; Front St; fishing charters per day US$450) Garbutt's is an experienced and highly professional fishing charter company and dive outfit, with exclusive access to private island Lime Caye in the Sapodillas and accommodation and kayak rental in Punta Gorda.

🛏 Sleeping

A Piece of Ground HOTEL $

(☑ 665-2695; www.apieceofground.com; 1050 Pelican St; dm/d BZ$30/70; ❄🛜) Better known locally as Backa Jama's, this funky, sociable four-story place has a new ground-floor hostel with two dorms (one with air-con) and four spotless guesthouse rooms with attached bathroom on the 2nd floor. Keep going up the stairs to the popular restaurant, serving chicken dishes and American-style burgers and fries, and the rooftop bar with pool table.

Tate's Guest House GUESTHOUSE $

(☑ 722-0147; tatesguesthouse@yahoo.com; 34 Jose Maria Nunez St; r BZ$70-80, unit BZ$125-150; 🅿❄🛜) Former postmaster Mr Tate keeps his guesthouse in immaculate condition and it's the best budget deal in the town center. The six rooms inside the mauve two-story facade, set in a little garden with a gazebo, are good value at these rates. Two are self-contained, with kitchenettes and air-con, and all come with cable TV and hot showers.

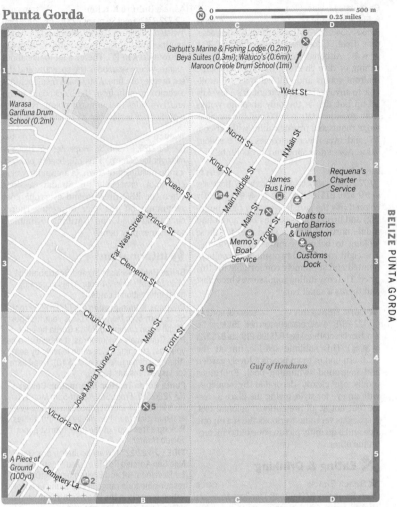

Punta Gorda

BELIZE PUNTA GORDA

Punta Gorda

◎ Activities, Courses & Tours
1 Cotton Tree Chocolate Factory..........D2

⊜ Sleeping
2 Coral House Inn.....................................A5
3 Nature's Way Guest House B4
4 Tate's Guest House C2

⊗ Eating
5 Asha's Culture Kitchen B4
6 Gomiers...D1
7 Snack Shack...C2

Nature's Way Guest House   GUESTHOUSE $
(☏ 702-2119; natureswayguesthouse@hotmail.com;
82 Front St; dm BZ$18, s/d/tr/q BZ$28/38/48/58,
s/d with bathroom BZ$30/40) Rustic and ram-
shackle, this place has been a longtime backpacker bolthole in Punta Gorda. Simple,
screened-in, ocean-breeze–cooled wooden
rooms are upstairs, and a large sociable communal area with TV, music and free wi-fi is
below. Nature's Way also rents bikes and
kayaks for BZ$15 per day.

Garbutt's Marine & Fishing Lodge
CABIN **$$**

(☑ 604-3548, 722-0070; www.garbuttsfishinglodge. com; Front St, Joe Taylor Creek; r BZ$160-200; P❋🛜) Although primarily for guests on fishing or dive charters, Garbutt's awesome seafront rooms and stilt cabanas are available to anyone if they're vacant. It's a low-key set-up but this is the only absolute waterfront accommodation in PG and the spacious lodge rooms and private cabins with air-con, TV and over-water balconies are excellent value. Also a dive shop and kayak rental.

Beya Suites
HOTEL **$$**

(☑ 722-2188; www.beyasuites.com; 6 Hopeville; s/d/tr from BZ$142/175/208; P❋🛜) Brightly colored (it's the garish two-story pink building) and breezy, this seaside hotel about half a mile north of PG is a good find for those looking to balance comfort and economy. The eight rooms and two suites are well appointed and supremely comfortable for this price. The cozy dining room serves breakfast and there's a small bar.

★ Coral House Inn
BOUTIQUE HOTEL **$$**

(☑ 722-2878; www.coralhouseinn.net; 151 Main St; d incl continental breakfast BZ$196-218, ste BZ$272; ❋🛜🏊) This sublime seaside inn at the southern end of town boasts a lovely garden and in-ground swimming pool. Enormous rooms are clearly decorated by someone with an eye for style, giving the place a classic (but not at all pretentious) colonial feel. A spacious veranda overlooks the sea on one side and a quaintly picturesque old cemetery on the other.

🍴 Eating & Drinking

★ Snack Shack
CAFE **$**

(Main St; mains BZ$6-12; ⊙7am-3pm Mon-Sat) Tucked away off the main street among a group of shack restaurants, this is the best spot in town for Western or Belizean breakfasts. Lunchtime is 'build your own burrito' served alongside brain-freezing slushies. The open-air deck is breezy and inviting.

★ Gomiers
VEGETARIAN **$**

(☑ 620-1719; 5 Alejandro Vernon St; meals BZ$6-17; ⊙8am-10pm; 🛜🍴) There's a laid-back bohemian vibe at this small open-air restaurant where excellent organic vegetarian cuisine, veg and conch fritters, fresh juices and a variety of tofu-based creations are the order of the day. Friday night's live reggae is a PG institution.

Asha's Culture Kitchen
SEAFOOD **$$**

(☑ 722-2742; Front St; mains BZ$15-30; ⊙4-10pm) Twisted lobster, baked barracuda, whole snapper and lionfish finger – and the best waterfront deck in PG. There's a lot to like about Asha's, where seafood is the specialty and the sea breezes are fine. A standard meal includes a choice of main from the blackboard menu and two sides (garlic mash potato is a winner). Service is slow but it's worth the wait.

Waluco's
BAR

(☑ 702-2129; Front St, Hopeville; ⊙11:30am-midnight Tue-Sun; 🛜) This big, breezy *palapa*, a mile northeast of town, is a popular weekend spot, especially for Sunday sessions when the BBQ fires up and everyone goes swimming off the pier opposite. There's cheap bar food and Garifuna drummers sometimes play here.

ℹ️ Information

Belize Bank (30 Main St) and **Scotiabank** (1 Main St) both have 24-hour ATMs accepting most international cards.

Customs & Immigration (☑722-2022; Front St; ⊙9am-5pm Mon-Fri) This is your first port of call when coming to Punta Gorda by boat from Guatemala or Honduras; it should also be your last stopping place when leaving by sea (there's a departure tax of BZ$40). Head here for visa extensions too.

Punta Gorda Tourism Information Center (☑722-2531; Front St; ⊙8am-5pm Mon-Fri) PG's little BTIA tourist office can answer general questions and has village bus timetables. Pick up a free copy of the local tourist paper *Toledo Howler*.

TIDE (☑722-2274; www.tidebelize.org; One Mile San Antonio Rd) The Toledo Institute for Development and Environment (TIDE) is responsible for a range of community conservation projects in the Deep South, both in the inland forests and the marine parks.

ℹ️ Getting There & Away

There are four daily **boat services** to Puerto Barrios in Guatemala, at 9.30am, 1pm, 2pm and 4pm. There is also one daily boat to Livingston. Boats depart from the municipal pier in front of the Customs & Immigration office.

Requena's Charter Service (☑722-2070; 12 Front St) operates the *Mariestela*, departing Punta Gorda at 9.30am daily for Puerto Barrios, Guatemala (BZ$50, one hour), and returning at 2pm. Tickets are sold at the office and the **customs dock** down the street.

Memo's Boat Service (☑651-4780; memos boatservicandtours@yahoo.com; Front St) departs Punta Gorda daily at 12:45pm for

Livingston (BZ$50, 30 minutes) and Puerto Barrios, Guatemala (BZ$60, 45 minutes). Returning, Memo's boat leaves Livingston at 2pm and Puerto Barrios at 3pm, with identical prices. The office is across from Customs & Immigration.

James Bus Line (☑702-2049, 722-2625; King St) has hourly buses from Punta Gorda to Belize City (regular/AC BZ$22/24, seven hours) from 4am to 4pm. Buses stop at Independence (BZ$9/11, two hours), Dangriga (BZ$13/15, 3½ hours) and Belmopan (BZ$19/22, 5½ hours). All buses leave from the main bus station on King St and cruise around PG a bit before heading north.

Toledo Villages

Visitors to Belize's Deep South have a unique opportunity to simultaneously experience both ancient and contemporary Maya culture. Over 60% of the population of Toledo District is Maya and these people, with more than 30 villages, have done a great deal to keep their culture alive and intact. The sealing of the Southern Hwy through to Guatemala has made this area much more accessible and many villages can be visited without leaving the main road, but you'll need to delve a little further to experience the best of the Deep South.

Big Falls & Around

On the Southern Hwy, about 20 miles from Punta Gorda, Big Falls is a small village with a number of cultural and adventure attractions. This is a good starting point for the Toledo cultural circuit taking in San Miguel and San Pedro Columbia.

★ **Living Maya Experience** CULTURAL CENTER
(☑Chiacs 632-4585, Cals 627-7408; livingmaya experience@gmail.com; Big Falls; tours per person BZ$20-30; ☺by appointment) Two Kekchi families in Big Falls village have opened up their homes as a cultural experience for visitors and both are excellent. The Cal family demonstrates ancient Maya lifestyle from tortilla- and chocolate-making to traditional instruments and an exploration of their self-sufficient garden. With the Chiac family, you can learn to make woven Maya crafts – baskets, hammocks or bags.

Nim Li Punit RUIN
(☑822-2106; admission BZ$10; ☺8am-5pm) The Maya ruins of Nim Li Punit stand atop a natural hill half a mile north of the Southern Hwy, near the village of Indian Creek. The site is notable for the 26 stelae found in the southern Plaza of the Stelae. Four of the finest are housed in the stela house beside the visitors center.

San Pedro Columbia

Around 20 miles northwest of Punta Gorda is the village of San Pedro Columbia, the largest Kekchi Maya community outside Guatemala.

◉ Sights & Activities

Lubaantun RUIN
(admission BZ$10; ☺8am-5pm) The Maya ruins at Lubaantun, 1.3 miles northwest of San Pedro Columbia, are built on a natural hilltop and display a construction method unusual in the ancient Maya world of mortar-less, neatly cut, black-slate blocks. Archaeologists postulate that Lubaantun, which flourished between AD 730 and 860, may have been an administrative center regulating trade, while nearby Nim Li Punit was the local religious and ceremonial center. The Maya site comprises a collection of seven plazas, three ballcourts and surrounding structures.

Eladio's Chocolate Adventure FOOD
(☑624-0166; eladiopop@gmail.com; per person BZ$60) In San Pedro Columbia village, Eladio Pop will take you on a tour of his cacao farm, followed by a traditional chocolate-making demonstration and Maya lunch.

BELIZE TOLEDO VILLAGES

TEA GUESTHOUSES

A unique opportunity to be welcomed into local villages and experience village life firsthand is provided by the Toledo Ecotourism Association (TEA; ☑702-2119; www.teabelize.org). TEA is a community organization that manages guesthouses in several Maya villages. Currently, villages with TEA guesthouses are San Jose, Santa Elena, San Antonio, Laguna and San Miguel.

Although these are guesthouses, not homestays, you get the opportunity to mix with local families by having meals in different village homes. Rates vary depending on the guesthouse, starting from BZ$25 per person, and meals are around BZ$10. To get specific contact information for key people in individual villages, call Reyes Chun or stop by Nature's Way Guest House (p277) in Punta Gorda, which has a booking desk.

San Antonio

The largest Mopan Maya community in Belize, San Antonio was founded in the mid-19th century by farmers from San Luis Rey in the Petén, Guatemala.

Río Blanco National Park   NATIONAL PARK
(admission BZ$10; ☺7am-5pm) The 105-acre Río Blanco National Park is a compact protected wildlife area that's home to a variety of flora and fauna. The highlight for visitors is definitely Río Blanco Falls, a beautiful 20ft-high waterfall leading into a clear swimming hole just a five-minute walk from the ranger station. Other attractions include birdwatching, hiking and kayaking (the ranger station has one kayak at BZ$5 per hour).

There's also a basic dorm bunkhouse at the ranger station (BZ$20), which has a small stove for cooking, or you can camp in the park itself (BZ$10).

Blue Creek

This village, part Kekchi and part Mopan, is split by the pretty, blue-green–tinted namesake river. Howler monkeys inhabit the surrounding hilly jungles, otters live along the creek and green iguanas are plentiful. For travellers Blue Creek is an appealing destination for its cave, zip lining and jungle walks.

Blue Creek Canopy Tours   ADVENTURE SPORTS
(☏653-6533; www.bluecreekbelize.com; Blue Creek; per person BZ$130, per person with group BZ$110) One of Belize's more remote zip-lining adventures has nine lines and 15 platforms traversing thick jungle over the namesake Blue Creek. Numbers are limited to 35 per day so book ahead.

UNDERSTAND BELIZE

Belize Today

To the casual observer Belize seems to be flourishing, with compulsory primary education, a relatively stable democracy, a thriving tourism industry and an economy that is plugging along. Indeed a sufficient proportion of Belizeans were pleased enough with the way the country is being run to re-elect the government for a third time in 2015. However, not everyone in Belize has seen the benefits of this progress and poverty remains widespread, especially in rural areas.

Tourism is the country's top source of employment and investment, though the discovery of crude oil has been a boost to the export economy. The challenge moving forward seems to be one of balancing the needs of the tourism industry with Belizeans' desire – expressed time and again – to protect the environment.

While the benefits of tourism for the country as a whole are acknowledged by Belizeans at nearly every level of society, Belize does not yet have the infrastructure to support the massive numbers of tourists that arrive each year. The most contentious tourism-related issue today concerns cruise-ship passengers.

History

Belize Before Columbus

Belize certainly earns its place on the Ruta Maya – ruins are everywhere and the Maya population is still thriving, particularly in the southwest. The Maya have been in Belize since the first human habitation. One of the earliest settlements in the Maya world, Cuello, was near present-day Orange Walk. Maya trade routes ran all through the country, and the New River, Río Hondo and Belize River all played an important role in early trade and commerce. Important archaeological sites such as Cahal Pech, near San Ignacio and Lamanai, date from this period.

Pirate's Paradise

Lack of effective government and the onshore safety afforded by the barrier reef attracted English and Scottish pirates to Belizean waters during the 17th century. They operated freely, capturing booty-laden Spanish galleons. In 1670, however, Spain convinced the British government to clamp down on the pirates' activities. Most of the unemployed pirates went into the logwood business.

During the 1780s the British actively protected the loggers' interests, at the same time assuring Spain that Belize was indeed a Spanish possession. But this was a fiction. By this time, Belize was already British by tradition and sympathy, and it was with relief and jubilation that Belizeans received the news, on September 10, 1798, that a British force had defeated the Spanish armada off St George's Caye.

Into the 19th Century

With the diminishing importance of logging, Belize's next trade boom was in arms, ammunition and other supplies sold to the Maya rebels in the Yucatán who fought the War of the Castes during the mid-19th century. The war also brought a flood of refugees from both sides to Belize.

In 1859 Britain and Guatemala signed a treaty that gave Britain rights to the land provided that the British built a road from Guatemala to the Caribbean coast. The treaty still stands, and the road, long ignored, is only now being constructed. Many Guatemalan-made maps show most of Belize south of the Hummingbird Hwy as being part of Guatemala.

Independence & Beyond

The country's first general election was held in 1954, and the People's United Party (PUP) won handsomely on leader George Price's pro-independence platform. On September 21, 1981, the colony of British Honduras officially became the independent nation of Belize.

Since independence, the political landscape has been one of one-term governments (the United Democratic Party, or UDP, being the other player there), corruption scandals, power struggles and broken electoral promises. In 2003 PUP won an unprecedented second term. But it has been the UDP that has bucked the trend over the past decade, winning three consecutive terms in 2007, 2012 and most recently in 2015 in the face of a stable economy.

Culture

The National Pysche

Rule number one in Belize: give respect and you'll get respect. Belizeans are friendly and curious by nature, but often wait to see what you're like before deciding how they're going to be.

Belize's long association with the UK has left some odd legacies. Perhaps because of this (and the language thing), the country is more closely aligned with the USA than with other Central American countries. Many Belizeans also identify more closely with the Caribbean than they do with Central American culture.

People

Belize is a tiny country (population around 370,300), but it enjoys a diversity of ethnicities that is undeniably stimulating and improbably serene. Four main ethnic groups – Mestizo, Creole, Maya and Garifuna – comprise 76% of the population. The remaining 24% includes East Indians (people of Indian subcontinent origins), Chinese, Spanish, Arabs (generally Lebanese), the small but influential group of Mennonites, and North Americans and Europeans who have settled here in the last couple of decades.

The Maya people of Belize make up about 10% of the population and are divided into three linguistic groups. The Yucatec live in the north near the Yucatán border, the Mopan live in western Belize around the border town of Benque Viejo del Carmen, and the Q'eqchi' inhabit far southern Belize in and around Punta Gorda.

Southern Belize is the home of the Garifuna (or Garinagus, also called Black Caribs). The Garifuna are of South American indigenous and African descent.

Music

Music is by far the most popular art form in Belize, from the reggae-soaked cayes to the ribcage-rattling tunes pumped out on every bus in the country. Styles are much more Caribbean than Latin – after a few weeks you'll be an expert on calypso, soca, steel drums and, quite possibly, reggae.

Punta rock is the official musical style of Belize. Its origins are from the music of the Garifuna – drum heavy with plenty of call and response. This music is designed to get your hips moving. Probably the most famous punta rocker is Pen Cayetano, who has a studio and gallery in Dangriga.

The parranda style, which owes its roots to more traditional Garifuna arrangements with acoustic guitar, drums and shakers, is most widely associated with artists such as Paul Nabor and the late Andy Palacio.

Brukdown, another Belizean style, was developed by Creoles working in logging camps during the 18th and 19th centuries. It involves an accordion, banjo, harmonica and a percussion instrument – traditionally a pig's jawbone is used, the teeth rattled with a stick.

The Maya of Belize are off on their own tangent when it comes to music. Most notable here is the flute music of Pablo Collado and the traditional marimba (played with large wooden xylophones, double bass and drum kit) of Alma Beliceña.

Landscape & Wildlife

The Land

Belize is mostly tropical lowland, typically hot and humid for most of the year. Rainfall is lightest in the north, heaviest in the south. The southern rainforests receive almost 4m of precipitation annually, making the south the country's most humid region.

An exception to Belize's low-lying topography and hot, sticky climate can be found in the Maya Mountains, which traverse western and southern Belize at elevations approaching 1000m. The mountains enjoy a more pleasant climate than the lowlands – comfortably warm during the day, cooling off a bit at night.

The country's coastline and northern coastal plain are largely covered in mangrove swamp, which indistinctly defines the line between land and sea. Offshore, the limestone bedrock extends eastward into the Caribbean for several kilometers at a depth of about 16.5ft (5m). At the eastern extent of this shelf is the second-longest barrier reef in the world (after Australia's Great Barrier Reef).

Wildlife

The lush tropical forests contain huge ceiba trees as well as mahogany, guanacaste and cohune palms, all festooned with orchids, bromeliads and other epiphytes and liana vines. Much of the shorelines of both the mainland and the islands are cloaked in dense mangrove.

Baird's tapir is Belize's national animal. The *gibnut* or *tepezcuintle* (paca), a rabbit-size burrowing rodent, is abundant. Other tropical animals include the jaguar, ocelot, howler monkey, spider monkey, peccary, vulture, stork and anteater.

There are 60 species of snake in the forests and waters of Belize, but only a handful are poisonous: the fer-de-lance, the coral snake and the tropical rattlesnake are especially dangerous.

Belize's birdlife is varied and abundant, with hummingbirds, keel-billed toucans, woodpeckers and many kinds of parrots and macaws.

National Parks & Protected Areas

Nearly 40% of land in Belize is protected, either by national organizations or private trusts. Much of the Maya Mountain forest south of San Ignacio is protected as the Mountain Pine Ridge Forest Reserve and Chiquibul National Park. There are smaller parks and reserves, including marine reserves, throughout the country.

Environmental Issues

Belize takes environmental issues quite seriously, and much has been done to protect the endangered species that live within its borders. Species under threat include the hawksbill, green and leatherback sea turtles, the Morelet's and American crocodiles, the scarlet macaw, the jabiru stork and the manatee.

Deforestation for farmland is becoming an issue, leading to loss of habitat, soil erosion and salination of waterways.

Continuing oil drilling in the Cayo district, as well as new exploration in other parts of the country, is also an environmental concern.

SURVIVAL GUIDE

❶ Directory A–Z

ACCOMMODATIONS

Budget Within this range the best value is usually provided by small, often family-run guesthouses. Only the cheapest budget options have shared bathrooms or cold showers. This also includes the few backpacker hotels providing dorm accommodations, and camping.

Midrange Midrange embraces many hotels, more-comfortable guesthouses, and most of the small-scale lodges and resorts. Many places in this range have their own restaurants and bars, and offer arrangements for activities, tours and other services. The range of accommodations and service is wide within this category.

Top End Top-end accommodations can be seriously sumptuous. These are resorts, lodges and classy hotels with large, well-appointed rooms and plenty of other facilities, from restaurants and bars to private beaches, spas, pools, horse stables, dive shops and walking trails. Many have their own unique style and atmosphere created with the help of architecture, decor, location and layout.

EMBASSIES & CONSULATES

Australian Embassy (📞 55-1101-2200; www.mexico.embassy.gov.au; Rubén Darío 55,

Mexico City) The Australian embassy in Mexico handles relations with Belize.

Canadian Honorary Consulate (☎ 223-1060; cdncon.bze@btl.net; 80 Princess Margaret Dr, Belize City; ◷ 9am-2pm Mon-Fri)

German Honorary Consulate (☎ 222-4369; seni@cisco.com.bz; Mlle 3.5 Western Hwy, Belize City)

Guatemalan Embassy (☎ 223-3150; embbe lice1@minex.gob.gt; 8 A St, Kings Park, Belize City; ◷ 8:30am-12:30pm Mon-Fri)

Honduran Embassy (☎ 224-5889; embajada honduras.belice@gmail.com; 6 A St, Kings Park, Belize City; ◷ 9am-noon & 1-4pm Mon-Fri)

Mexican Embassy (☎ 822-0406; www.sre.gob. mx/belice; Embassy Sq, Belmopan; ◷ 8am-5pm Mon-Fri)

Mexican Consulate (☎ 223-0193; consular@ embamex.bz; cnr Wilson St & Newtown Barracks Rd, Belize City)

Netherlands Honorary Consulate (☎ 223-2953; mchulseca@btl.net; cnr Baymen Av & Calle Al Mar, Belize City)

UK High Commission (☎ 822-2146; http:// ukinbelize.fco.gov.uk; Embassy Sq, Belmopan; ◷ 8am-noon & 1-4pm Mon-Thu, 8am-2pm Fri)

US Embassy (☎ 822-4011; http://belize. usembassy.gov; Floral Park Rd; ◷ 8am-noon & 1-5pm Mon-Fri)

INTERNET ACCESS

Belize has plenty of internet cafes, with typical rates ranging from BZ$4 to BZ$8 per hour. Many hotels and lodges also provide computers where their guests can access the internet. Most accommodations also have wireless access in the rooms or in common areas.

LGBT TRAVELERS

LGBT travelers should be aware that male homosexuality is illegal in Belize, although female homosexuality is legal. Tourists have not been prosecuted for homosexuality, but local people have been arrested and jailed. Generally speaking, Belize is a tolerant society with a 'live and let live' attitude. But underlying Central American machismo and traditional religious belief, as well as legal prohibitions, mean that same-sex couples should be discreet.

Gay Travel Belize (☎ 635-0518) A LGBT-focused travel agency based in San Pedro. Its Facebook page has useful tips for LGBT travelers.

MEDIA

➻ **Newspapers** Belize's most-read paper is *Amandala*, a twice-weekly publication with a left-wing slant.

➻ **Radio** Love FM is Belize's most widely broadcast radio station, with spots at 95.1MHz and 98.1MHz, while KREM FM (www.krembz.com) plays a modern selection of music at 91.1MHz and 96.5 MHz.

➻ **TV** There are two main commercial TV stations: Channel 5 (www.channel5belize.com) and Channel 7 (www.7newsbelize.com).

MONEY

The Belizean dollar (BZ$) is pegged to the US dollar at two to one (BZ$1 = US$0.50). Nearly every business in Belize accepts US dollars and prices are sometimes quoted in US dollars at upscale resorts and hotels.

ATMs & Credit Cards

ATMs are widely available; credit cards are accepted at most hotels, restaurants and shops.

Tipping & Bargaining

Tipping is not obligatory but is always appreciated if guides, drivers or servers have provided you with genuinely good service. Some high-end hotels and restaurants add an obligatory service charge to your check (usually 10%), in which case you definitely don't need to tip.

Bargaining is not common in Belize, with the notable exception of outdoor souvenir markets where everything is negotiable.

OPENING HOURS

Banks 8am to 3pm Monday to Thursday and 8am to 4pm or 4:30pm Friday

Pubs and Bars noon to midnight (or later)

Restaurants and Cafes 7am to 9:30am (breakfast), 11:30am to 2pm (lunch) and 6pm to 8pm (dinner)

Shops 9am to 5pm Monday to Saturday, some open Sundays

POST

The Belize postal service has branches all over the country and offers fairly slow normal mail and a far better express service. Express mail sometimes needs to be sent from a different counter or office.

PUBLIC HOLIDAYS

Many of Belize's public holidays are moved to the Monday nearest the given date in order to make a long weekend. You'll find banks and most shops and businesses shut on these days. Belizeans travel most around Christmas, New Year and

---

SLEEPING PRICE RANGES

The following price ranges refer to a double room with bathroom during high season. Unless otherwise stated, a tax of 9% is added to the price.

$	less than BZ$100
$$	BZ$100–$300
$$$	more than BZ$300

Easter, and it's worth booking ahead for transportation and accommodations at these times.

New Year's Day January 1
Baron Bliss Day March 9
Good Friday March or April
Holy Saturday March or April
Easter Monday March or April
Labor Day May 1
Sovereign's Day May 24
National Day September 10
Independence Day September 21
Day of the Americas October 12
Garifuna Settlement Day November 19
Christmas Day December 25
Boxing Day December 26

SAFE TRAVEL

Belize has fairly high levels of violent crime but most areas frequented by travelers are safe and by taking basic precautions visitors are unlikely to experience any serious problems. The most likely issues for travelers involve opportunistic theft both while out and about and from hotel rooms.

TELEPHONE

Belize has no regional, area or city codes. Every number has seven digits, all of which you dial from anywhere in the country. When calling Belize from other countries, follow the country code with the full seven-digit local number.

Cell Phones

Local SIM cards can be used in most unlocked international cell phones, with the notable exception of phones from some operators in the US. You can buy a SIM pack for US$10 from DigiCell distributors around the country.

TOURIST INFORMATION

Belize Tourism Board (BTB; www.travelbelize.org) The official tourist agency has information offices in Belize City and San Pedro.
Belize Tourism Industry Association (BTIA; www.btia.org) An independent association of tourism businesses, actively defending 'sustainable ecocultural tourism.'

EATING PRICE RANGE

The following price ranges refer to a standard meal – rice, beans, meat or fish and a side. Only the fanciest places tend to have service charges, but tipping is always appreciated.

$	less than BZ$15
$$	BZ$15–35
$$$	more than BZ$35

VISAS & DOCUMENTS

At the time of writing, visas were not required for citizens of EU, Caricom (Caribbean Community) and Central American countries, nor Australia, Canada, Hong Kong, Israel, Mexico, New Zealand, Norway, Singapore, Switzerland and the USA. A visitor's permit, valid for 30 days, will be stamped in your passport when you enter the country. In most cases this can be extended by further periods of one month (up to a maximum of six months) by applying at an immigration office (there's at least one in each of Belize's six districts). For further information you can contact the **Immigration & Nationality Department** (p258) in Belmopan.

VOLUNTEERING

There are a lot of opportunities for volunteer work in Belize, especially on environmental projects. In some cases, you may have to pay to participate (costs vary).

Belize Audubon Society (Map p236; 223-4987, 223-5004; www.belizeaudubon.org; 16 North Park St) Invites volunteers who are available to work for at least three months to assist in the main office or in education and field programs. Divers can volunteer for marine research projects. For rural sites, volunteers should be physically fit and able to deal with rustic accommodations.

Belize Wildlife & Referral Clinic (632-3257; www.belizewildlifeclinic.org) Offers short-term internships in wildlife medicine for veterinary and non-veterinary students. Various scholarships and work exchanges are available for students with sincere interests and skills, and the clinic is flexible and always interested in speaking with potential interns and long-term volunteers.

Oceanic Society (in USA 800-326-7491; www.oceanic-society.org; Blackbird Caye; 5-day research programs BZ$5400) Paying participants in the society's expeditions assist scientists in marine research projects at the society's field station on Blackbird Caye and elsewhere.

Cornerstone Foundation (www.cornerstonefoundationbelize.org) This NGO, based in San Ignacio, hosts volunteers to help with AIDS education, community development and other programs. Most programs require a two-week commitment, plus a reasonable fee to cover food and housing.

Monkey Bay Wildlife Sanctuary (p255) Monkey Bay's programs provide opportunities in education, conservation and community service. It also has many links to other conservation organizations in Belize.

Maya Mountain Research Farm (630-4386; www.mmrfbz.org) The 70-acre organic farm and registered NGO in Toledo offers internships for those interested in learning about organic farming, biodiversity and alternative energy.

Plenty International (www.plenty.org) Opportunities for working with grassroots organizations (such as handicraft cooperatives) and schools, mostly in Toledo District.

The imperial system is used. Note that gasoline is sold by the (US) gallon.

Getting There & Away

AIR

Belize City has two airports. All international flights use Philip SW Goldson International Airport (BZE), 9 miles (16km) northwest of the city center.

Non-Belizeans must pay fees that total US$39.25 when flying out of Belize City on international flights. Most major carriers now include this tax in the price of the ticket. Many travelers save money by flying into Cancún and taking an ADO bus south to Chetumal, crossing into Corozal by land or San Pedro by sea.

LAND

When departing Belize by land, non-Belizeans are required to pay fees that total BZ$37.50 (US$18.75) in cash (Belizean or US dollars).

Mexico

There are two official crossing points on the Mexico–Belize border. The more frequently used is at Subteniente López–Santa Elena, 9 miles from Corozal Town in Belize and 7 miles from Chetumal in Mexico. The all-paved Philip Goldson Hwy runs from the border to Belize City.

The other crossing is at La Unión–Blue Creek, 34 miles southwest of Orange Walk Town near the Rio Bravo Conservation and Management Area. The road between Blue Creek and Orange Walk was under construction at the time of research and should be a nice, wide paved highway by the time you read this.

Mexican bus company ADO runs excellent air-conditioned express bus services nightly from Cancún (BZ$102, 10 hours) and four times a week from Merida (BZ$102, 10 hours) to Belize City via Corozal and Orange Walk. The Cancún bus stops in Playa del Carmen and can drop passengers directly at Cancún airport on the return leg. The buses do not enter Chetumal town in either direction.

Many regular Belizean buses ply the Philip Goldson Hwy between Belize City and Chetumal. In Chetumal, buses bound for Corozal Town (BZ$4, one hour), Orange Walk Town (BZ$8, two hours) and Belize City (BZ$14 to BZ$16, four hours) leave from the north side of Nuevo Mercado, about 0.75 miles north of the city center. Leaving from Belize buses mostly depart in the morning, while from Chetumal afternoon departures are more common.

Additionally, an air-conditioned tourist bus (BZ$50, three hours) runs daily between the San Pedro Beilze Express Water Taxi Terminal and Chetumal.

Guatemala

Although a new southern border crossing was due to open in 2016, the main land crossing between Belize and Guatemala is a mile west of the Belizean town of Benque Viejo del Carmen at the end of the all-paved George Price Hwy from Belize City. The town of Melchor de Mencos is on the Guatemalan side of the crossing.

Two companies run express buses to/from Guatemala. From the San Pedro Belize Express Water Taxi terminal in Belize City, you can go to Flores (BZ$50 to BZ$60, five hours) at 10am and 1pm. From Flores there are frequent connections to Guatemala City.

You can also take any of the frequent westbound Belizean buses to Benque Viejo del Carmen and then use the local service to the border.

SEA

It's now possible to arrive in Belize by boat from all three of its neighboring countries.

The only fee you have to pay when leaving Belize by sea from Placencia is the BZ$7.50 (US$3.75) Protected Areas Conservation Trust (PACT) fee. It's payable in cash (Belizean or US dollars).

Those leaving from Punta Gorda or using the water-taxi service from Caye Caulker/San Pedro to Chetumal are required to pay the regular departure tax of BZ$37.50 plus a BZ$2.50 facility fee before leaving Belize.

Getting Around

Transportation in Belize is cheap and occasionally efficient. A useful website offering updated schedules and other transport-related info is http://belizebus.wordpress.com.

Air Two companies (Maya Island and Tropic Air) fly between all major towns in Belize. Planes are small, flights are short and fairly affordable, although ticket prices are on an upward trajectory. Both companies enjoy good safety records.

Boat Caye Caulker and Ambergris are serviced by ferries from Belize City, and there is also a boat from Corozal to Ambergris with a possible Sarteneja stop. No regular boats to the smaller islands and cayes, but passage can be arranged with a private boatman from Dangriga, Hopkins or Placencia, or through resorts and hotels.

Bus Most travel in Belize is done by bus. All towns from Corozal to Punta Gorda are serviced by one or more of a bewildering variety of private bus services, and you can usually flag down a bus on the highway.

Car Belize drives on the right side of the road. All major highways are paved, but few have decent shoulders and painted dividing lines. Speed bumps are common but not all are marked.

El Salvador

📞 503 / POP 6.4 MILLION

Includes ➜
San Salvador 290
La Libertad 305
La Costa
del Bálsamo 306
Santa Ana 311
Ruta de Las Flores . . . 316
Parque Nacional
El Imposible 323
San Miguel 327
La Unión 330
Morazán 332
Suchitoto 334
Chalatenango 336
La Palma 338

Best Places to Eat

➜ Beto's, Zona Rosa (p300)

➜ R&R (p321)

➜ Balompie Sports Bar & Cafe (p315)

➜ Sharky's (p308)

Best Places to Sleep

➜ La Tortuga Verde (p331)

➜ Hostal Cumbres del Volcan (p294)

➜ Hotel Mopelia (p307)

➜ Los Almendros de San Lorenzo (p336)

➜ Hotel Anáhuac (p321)

Why Go?

Wanted: public relations expert to rebrand Central America's most underrated country. Criteria: passion for adventure and dispelling travel myths. Salary: the honor of righting a travel wrong.

El Salvador suffers horribly from bad press. While gang violence still dominates international headlines – and keeps so many adventurous travelers at bay – the vast majority of this beautiful country remains untouched by 'the troubles.'

Those visitors who do make the effort are invariably impressed by just how much this tiny country has to offer: world-class surfing on empty, dark-sand beaches; coffee plantations clinging to the sides of volcanoes; colorful Spanish colonial towns; and sublime national parks. There are few crowds outside the capital, San Salvador, which itself boasts more swagger than its Central American counterparts. There is only so much encouragement we can give; it's now up to you. Please inquire within.

When to Go
San Salvador

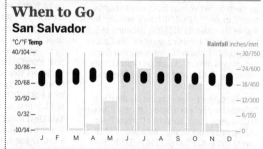

Dec–Jan The landscape is lush and green after the rainy season and the weather is perfect.

May–Aug The surf gets heavy, early August brings a week-long celebration of El Salvador's patron saint.

Jul–Nov It's turtle-nesting season right along the 300km Pacific Ocean coastline.

Connections

From Guatemala, enter through Anguiatú, San Cristóbal or La Hachadura. From Honduras, El Poy or El Amatillo are your two official options. Many operators are now offering boat transfers from La Unión, El Salvador, to Potosí, Nicaragua. The best of these are La Tortuga Verde (p331) in El Cuco and Suchitoto Adventure Outfitters (p335) in Suchitoto. This is a both a time- and cost-effective way to continue your travels through Central America. For more detailed information, see Survival Guide p349.

ITINERARIES

One Week

El Salvador is small; this itinerary can you get across the whole country in a week. Let's assume you enter from Guatemala. Head straight along the Costa del Bálsamo, sleeping in either Playa El Tunco or Playa El Zonte, depending how much rest you need. Head north to Ruta de las Flores to sample coffee and culture in small artisanal towns. Sleep in Juayúa. Spend a day hiking nearby Cerro Verde or visit the Maya pyramids at Tazumal. Sleep in San Salvador, then explore the capital's galleries and museums.

Two Weeks

Now you have a choice (if you didn't already). Head to the mountains and visit La Palma and Suchitoto then return to San Salvador. If you are bound for Nicaragua, scoot east along the highway. Alternatively, Playa El Cuco is a relaxing base for exploring the islands in Golfo de Fonseca, the volcanoes around San Miguel and even further north to the ex-guerrilla stronghold of Morozán. Exit the country via La Unión.

Essential Food & Drink

➡ A typical breakfast includes eggs, beans or *casamiento* (rice and beans mixed together), fried plantains, cheese, tortillas and coffee or juice. *Panaderías* (bakeries) usually offer a selection of morning cakes and coffee.

➡ El Salvador's most famous food by far is the *pupusa*, round cornmeal dough stuffed with a combination of cheese, refried beans, wild vegetables such as *ayote* and *mora*, *chicharrón* (pork rinds), or *revuelta* (mixed filling), then grilled. *Curtido*, a mixture of pickled cabbage and vegetables, provides the final topping.

➡ *Licuados* (fruit drinks made with water or milk) are perfectly suited to El Salvador's climate. Note that *refresco*, which means soft drink in many countries, means lemonade here. *Horchata* (rice milk and cinnamon) and *chilate* (roasted corn drink with other natural ingredients) are popular alternatives found at street stalls and most restaurants. A *refresco de ensalada* is not coleslaw puree, but a mixed fruit juice served with a spoon for the fruit salad floating on top, sangria style.

AT A GLANCE

Currency US dollar (US$)

Language Spanish, Nahuat

Money ATMs are plentiful, and credit cards widely accepted

Visas Tourist cards for citizens of most countries cost US$10 and are valid for up to 90 days

Time Central Standard Time (GMT/UTC minus six hours)

Area 21,040 sq km

Capital San Salvador

Emergency 911

Exchange Rates

Australia	A$1	US$0.74
Canada	C$1	US$0.78
Euro zone	€1	US$1.13
Japan	¥100	US$0.94
New Zealand	NZ$1	US$0.70
UK	UK£1	US$1.42

Set Your Budget

➡ **Dorm bed** US$7–10

➡ **Bottle of beer** US$1.50

➡ **Three-hour bus ride** US$1.50

➡ **Bean-and-cheese pupusa** US$0.25

➡ **Surfboard rental** US$10

Resources

➡ **Ministry of Tourism** (www.elsalvador.travel)

➡ **SalvaNATURA** (www.salvanatura.org)

➡ **Search Beat** (www.search-beat.com/elsalvador.htm)

➡ **Lonely Planet** (lonelyplanet.com/el-salvador)

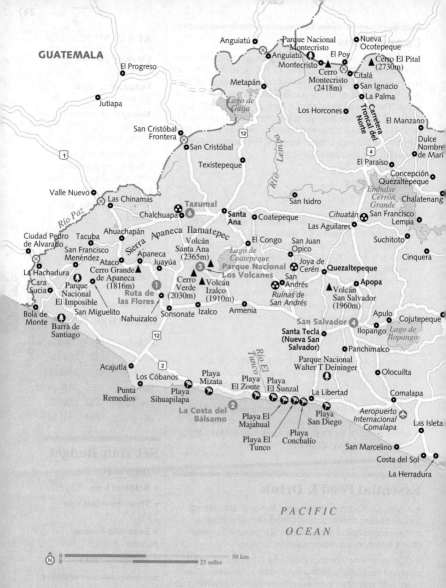

El Salvador Highlights

1 Ruta de las Flores (p316) Tracking your gourmet coffee from plantation to cup, swimming in natural springs and hanging out at weekend food fairs.

2 La Costa del Bálsamo (p306) Kicking back at Playa El Tunco: surf, party, repeat.

3 Parque Nacional los Volcanes (p310) Getting steamy hiking the park's active peaks.

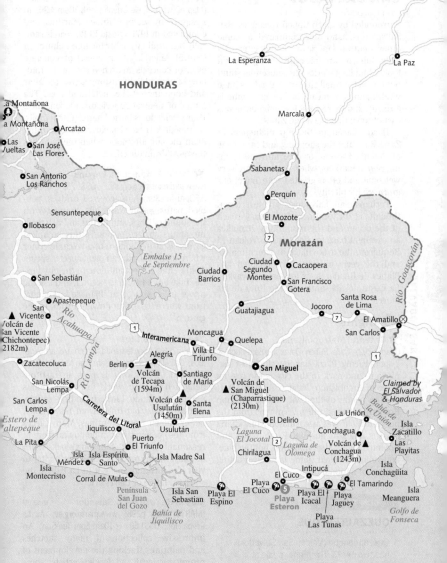

HONDURAS

La Esperanza
La Paz

Marcala

Sabanetas

Perquín

El Mozote

Morazán 7

Ciudad
Segundo
Montes
Cacaopera

San Francisco
Gotera

Santa Rosa
de Lima

Jocoro

El Amatillo

San Carlos

La Montañona
Montañona
Las
Vueltas
San José
Las Flores
Arcatao

San Antonio
Los Ranchos

Sensuntepeque

Ilobasco

Embalse 15
de Septiembre

Ciudad
Barrios

Guatajiagua

San Sebastián

Apastepeque

San Vicente
Volcán de
San Vicente
(Chichontepec)
(2182m)

Río
Acahuapa

Río Lempa

Interamericana

Moncagua

Quelepa

Zacatecoluca

Alegría

Berlín

Villa El
Triunfo

Volcán de
Tecapa
(1594m)

Santiago
de María

San Miguel

San Nicolás,
Lempa

Volcán de
Usulután
(1450m)

Santa
Elena

Volcán de
San Miguel
(Chaparrastique)
(2130m)

San Carlos
Lempa

Carretera del Litoral

El Delirio

La Unión

Estero de
altepeque

Jiquilisco

Usulután

Laguna
El Jocotal

Conchagua

Volcán de
Conchagua
(1243m)

Isla
Zacatillo

La Pita

Puerto
El Triunfo

Chirilagua

Laguna de
Olomega

Claimed by
El Salvador
& Honduras

Isla Espíritu
Santo

Isla
Méndez

Isla Madre Sal

Intipucá

El Cuco

Las
Playitas

Isla
Montecristo

Corral de Mulas

Playa
El Cuco

Playa
Esteron

Playa El
Icacal

El Tamarindo

Playa
Jaguey

Isla
Conchagüita

Península
San Juan
del Gozo

Isla San
Sebastian

Playa El
Espino

Isla
Meanguera

Bahía de
Jiquilisco

Playa
Las Tunas

Golfo de
Fonseca

Río Goascorán

Bahía
de
la Unión

4 San Salvador (p290)
Gallery-hopping and rubbing
shoulders with the young
party set in flash Zona Rosa.

5 Playa Esteron (p331)
Tackling the wild east, starting
in the poorly kept secret of
Playa Esteron, before venturing
by boat to the deserted islands
near Nicaragua.

6 Tazumal (p316)
Enjoying Maya ruins all to
yourself, then gazing at the
finest architecture in the
country at nearby Santa Ana.

SAN SALVADOR

POP 1.1 MILLION

Surrounded by green-tipped volcanoes, San Salvador is handsome compared to some other Central American capital cities. Its leafy suburbs are pleasant to explore on foot, while its galleries and museums stand out for such a small city. San Salvador's huge wealth gap does mean that violent crime is a reality, and there are a few neighborhoods east of town that are no-go zones.

Head instead to the hip nightspots of Zona Rosa and the shopping and cafe scene of Colonia Escalon, or dive into the teeming *centro* markets, where travelers are very welcome and often greeted with infectious *guanaco* hospitality.

Perhaps San Salvador's greatest asset, though, is its location within easy reach of the ocean and the mountains. It makes an excellent base for day trips to Volcan El Boquerón, the arts village of Panchimalco, and the eerie hillside district called Los Planes de Renderos, or for longer forays to La Costa del Bálsamo and the Ruta de las Flores.

⊙ Sights

★ Catedral Metropolitana   CATHEDRAL
(Map p292; Calle Rubén Darío; ⊙8am-noon & 2-4pm) Facing Plaza Barrios, the most significant landmark in the city is the resting place of Archbishop Oscar A Romero. During the height of the civil war, Archbishop Romero criticized the government from the pulpit until he was assassinated while giving mass at a nearby hospital. Earthquakes and fire have shaken its foundation, but the blue-and-yellow-checked dome is an everlasting symbol of national pride.

DON'T MISS

QUEZALTEPEQUE

Quezaltepeque (Volcán San Salvador) has two peaks. The higher peak, at 1960m, is called Picacho. The other, Boquerón (Big Mouth), is 1893m high and has a second cone within its crater – 45m high and perfectly symmetrical – formed in 1917. A paved road affords an easy climb to top, from where the view of San Salvador is unbeatable. Entry to the park costs US$3. Bring a bag for your litter.

★ Iglesia El Rosario   CHURCH
(Map p292; 4a Calle Oriente; ⊙8:30am-4:30pm) Designed by sculptor Ruben Martinez and completed in 1971, Iglesia El Rosario is radically beautiful. Arguably the finest church in Central America, its nondescript concrete exterior conceals an arched roof and a rainbow of natural light rushing across the altar and bouncing off the metal and rock. The father of Central American independence, Padre Delgado, is buried here, quite happily, we imagine. Try to visit early in the morning or in the late afternoon when the light has the most dramatic effect.

★ Jardín Botánico La Laguna   GARDENS
(www.jardinbotanico.org.sv; US$1.25; ⊙9am-5:30pm Tue-Sun) Moss-covered bridges, pebbled paths, small waterfalls running with the sound of frogs, and turtles and fish feeding at the surface of ponds, this botanical garden is at the bottom of a volcanic crater where many Salvadoran plant species spring to life – the perfect antidote to the city bustle. Take bus 44 from the center, and ask the driver to let you off at 'Plan de la Laguna', from where it's a 1km downhill walk to the garden.

★ El Arbol de Dios   GALLERY
(Map p298; www.fernando-llort.com/el-arbol-de-dios; Calle la Mascota; ⊙8am-7pm Mon-Fri, 9am-6pm Sat) FREE 'God's Tree' is an institute dedicated to the work of world-famous painter Fernando Llort, including sophisticated pieces that differ from his simpler, better-known wood paintings. Many pieces from his cooperative can be bought here at reasonable prices. It's four long blocks south of Plaza Masferrer. It is particularly vital to visit if you cannot make it to La Palma, the spiritual home of Llort's art.

Museo de Arte de El Salvador   MUSEUM
(MARTE; Map p298; www.marte.org.sv; Av La Revolución; US$1.50; ⊙10am-6pm Tue-Sun) An impressive collection of many sketches and paintings tracking the development of prominent local and foreign artists; some of the larger contemporary sculptures are outstanding. It's up the hill behind the large Monumento a la Revolución. There is also a small restaurant onsite. The museum is free on Sundays.

Museo de la Palabra y La Imagen   MUSEUM
(Map p296; www.museo.com.sv; 27 Av Norte 1140; US$2; ⊙8am-noon & 2-5pm Mon-Fri, 8am-noon Sat) This innovative museum documents

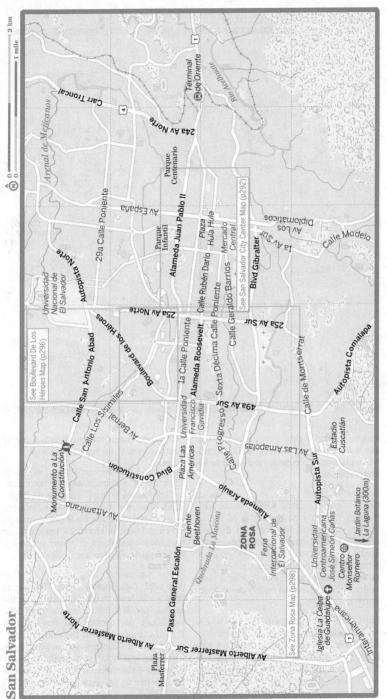

San Salvador

1 mile

2 km

N

Arenal de Mejicanos

Carr Troncal

24a Av Norte

Terminal de Oriente

Río Acelhuate

Parque Centenario

29a Calle Poniente

Av España

See Boulevard De Los Héroes Map (p296)

Universidad Nacional de El Salvador

Autopista Norte

Parque Infantil

Alameda Juan Pablo II

Plaza Hula Hula

Mercado Central

Calle Rubén Darío

See San Salvador City Center Map (p292)

Blvd Gibralter

Av Los Diplomáticos

1a Av Sur

Calle Modelo

25a Av Norte

1a Calle Poniente

Francisco Gavidia

Alameda Roosevelt

Sexta Décima Calle Poniente

Calle Getaldo Barrios

25a Av Sur

Calle San Antonio Abad

Calle Los Símiles

Av Bernal

Boulevard de los Héroes

Universidad

Plaza Las Américas

49a Av Sur

Calle Progresso

Av Las Amapolas

Calle de Montserrat

Autopista Comalapa

Monumento a La Constitución

Av Altamirano

Blvd Constitución

Alameda Araujo

Estadio Cuscatlán

Autopista Sur

Fuente Beethoven

ZONA ROSA

Feria Internacional de El Salvador

See Zona Rosa Map (p298)

Quebrada La Mascota

Universidad Centroamericana José Simeón Cañas

Centro Monseñor Romero

Jardín Botánico La Laguna (300m)

Paseo General Escalón

Av Alberto Masferrer Norte

Av Alberto Masferrer Sur

Plaza Masferrer

Iglesia La Ceiba de Guadalupe

Interamericana

San Salvador City Center

various human rights campaigns through visual and audiovisual means. Black-and-white photographs complement more interpretive pieces.

Palacio Nacional   PALACE
(Map p292; Av Cuscatlán; US$3; ⊙9am-5pm) Built in the early 20th century of Italian marble, the Palacio Nacional was the government headquarters until the 1986 earthquake. Many of the rooms now preserve remnants of the country's early governance, but it's the courtyard that will delight most visitors. It occupies the west side of Plaza Barrios.

Centro Monseñor Romero   MUSEUM
(www.uca.edu.sv/cmr; Calle de Mediterraneo; ⊙8am-noon & 2-6pm Mon-Fri, 8-11:30am Sat) FREE At Universidad Centroamericana José Simeón Cañas (La UCA), the Centro Monseñor Romero pays homage to the martyred

Archbishop Oscar Romero. This is a highly informative and moving place to visit.

Hospital La Divina Providencia   HISTORIC SITE
(El Hospitalito; www.hospitaldivinaprovidencia.org; cnr Calle Toluca & Av Rocio; ⊙8am-noon & 2-5pm) FREE Monseñor Romero was assassinated by government agents while giving mass in the chapel here on March 24, 1980. You can tour his modest quarters, where his blood-soaked shirt and robes are displayed.

Teatro Nacional   THEATER
(Map p292; Calle Delgado) FREE This ageing beauty still hosts major productions in the capital. Located east from Catedral Metropolitana, the theater was renovated in French Classical style in the mid-20th century. Opening times are not particularly reliable, but it is worth persevering to get in, especially if you cannot make it to Santa Ana. Entry is free unless you want to see a show.

San Salvador City Center

◎ Top Sights

1 Catedral Metropolitana........................D3
2 Iglesia El Rosario...............................E3

◎ Sights

3 Biblioteca Nacional............................D3
4 Iglesia El Calvario.............................D3
5 Palacio Nacional................................D3
6 Teatro Nacional.................................E3

⊨ Sleeping

7 Hotel Villa Florencia Centro
   Historico..B2

⊗ Eating

8 Restaurante Hong Kong C3
9 Sidewalk Comedores D3

⊟ Shopping

10 Mercado Central...............................C4
11 Mercado Ex-Cuartel F3

🏃 Activities

EC Tours   WALKING TOUR
(☎7842-4708; www.ectourselsalvador.com) This friendly new company runs highly recommended walking tours of downtown El Salvador.

Akwaterra   ADVENTURE SPORTS
(☎2263-2211; www.akwaterra.com) Friendly and bilingual Julio and Gabi De Vega of Akwaterra offer tailor-made land- and water-based ecotours, including horseback riding, mountain biking, surfing and kayaking. They also arrange recommended trips throughout Central America.

El Salvador Divers   DIVING
(Map p298; ☎2264-0961; www.elsalvadordivers. com; 3a Calle Poniente; ⊙9am-6:30pm Mon-Fri, to 1pm Sat) This professional dive shop offers dives in Lago Ilopango and in the Pacific near Los Cóbanos. Open-water courses cost US$365, two-tank fun dives US$75.

Centro de Intercambio y Solidaridad   VOLUNTEERING
(CIS; Map p296; ☎2235-1330; www.cis-elsalvador. org; Av Bolivar 103, Colonia Libertad) This center for peace and social justice provides opportunities for volunteers to help teach English to low-income Salvadorans and in the process learn Spanish. The program is an entry point into local life, with an emphasis on political awareness. There's a 10-week minimum commitment and teachers get half-price Spanish

Museo Nacional de Antropología David J Guzmán   MUSEUM
(Map p298; Av La Revolución; US$3; ⊙9am-5pm Tue-Sun) This small museum has an excellent range of Maya and Olmec (pre-Maya) statues and relics from ancient Cuscatlan. The traditional crafts displays are also enlightening, especially if you plan to purchase during your visit to an artisan village. All explanations are in Spanish.

Iglesia El Calvario   CHURCH
(Map p292; 6 Calle Poniente) West from Biblioteca Nacional, and surrounded by aggressive touts, you'll find the Gothic towers of the decaying Iglesia El Calvario. Walk inside to experience its real beauty.

Biblioteca Nacional   LIBRARY
(Map p292; 4a Calle Oriente; ⊙8am-4pm Mon-Fri) The imposing Biblioteca Nacional is on the south end of Plaza Barrios. It is a spacious and comfortable place to escape the hot city.

A FESTIVAL FOR EVERY OCCASION

For a conservative Catholic country, El Salvador knows how to get its groove on.

Fería Gastronómica (p321) Every weekend is worth celebrating, so go to Juayúa: everyone's there eating lizard and dancing.

Dia de Indepencia (☉15 Sep) FREE September 15 commemorates one of El Salvador's many political struggles with nationwide bipartisan panache, lest it disappear.

Carnaval de San Miguel (p329) A riot of color, merengue, drinking, scantily clad dancers and Mardi Gras–style floats.

Suchitoto (p334) Every weekend in February, Suchitoto celebrates its artistic temperament with stunning performances across a range of pursuits.

Bolas de Fuego (p304) Mask-wearing locals throw fireballs at each other to honor a saint, or possibly settle a score.

Fiestas Agostinas (☉1-6 Aug) Celebrates El Salvador's patron saint. All cities have festivities; San Salvador's is the biggest.

classes in return. It can also arrange affordable homestays.

🛏 Sleeping

Zona Rosa and Colonia Escalón have the city's best hotels, big or small. Safe and convenient, the Blvd de los Héroes area offers reasonable lodgings close to the Universidad Nacional where lots students mingle during the day. The shaded streets around the Universidad Tecnológica (south of the Puerto bus terminal) offer easy access to the airport shuttle and international buses. The city center (*el centro*) is convenient for markets, but avoid sleeping here.

⭐**La Zona Hostal**　　　HOSTEL $
(Map p298; ☎6200-4085; Blvd del Hipódromo 436, Colonia San Benito; dm US$8, s/d US$12/24; ❄🛜) This new self-styled 'travelers spot' is a welcome addition to the capital's budget accommodation stocks. Perfectly located for the Zona Rosa action, and in a safe, prosperous neighborhood, La Zona has colorful, spotless dorms, comfortable communal areas, and attracts a more understated solo traveler.

⭐**Hostal Cumbres del Volcan**　　HOSTEL $
(Map p298; ☎2207-3705; www.cumbresdelvolcan. com; 85a Av Norte 637; dm $8-10, r US$20-45; ❄🛜) 'Volcano Summit,' managed by the knowledgeable Walter, offers popular dorm rooms and four color-themed private rooms (downstairs '*naranja*' is the most basic, while '*roja*' has the best views). The communal lounge is large and quiet, and the shared kitchen and terrace are ideal for meeting

other independent travelers. The owners are also opening a new premises in Colonia Flor Blanca.

Ali's Downtown　　　　HOSTEL $
(☎7170-3262; www.ectourselsalvador.com; 17 Calle Oriente 283; per person incl breakfast US$10; P❄🛜) This lovely house with bright, tiled interiors and a beautiful urban garden is by far the best accommodation in the vicinity of downtown. The three bedrooms have twin beds and all are spotless. Free pick-up from bus stations, strong wi-fi and complimentary walking tours for guests who stay longer than two nights round out the experience.

La Almohada　　　　　HOSTEL $
(Map p296; ☎2260-7380; www.la-almohada.com; Calle Berlín 220; dm US$10; 🛜) 🞡 The socially conscious Almohada hostel supports a local kids charity by selling a cheap place to rest in a friendly, communal atmosphere. The quiet suburban location is safe for walking and there are a few restaurants within easy reach, though many guests will happily settle for the large shared kitchen and common areas to plan their assault on the city.

Ximena's Guest House　　　HOSTEL $
(Map p296; ☎2260-2481; www.ximenasguesthouse.com; Calle San Salvador 202; dm US$7-9.50, d US$19-35, tr US$45; P❄@🛜) Ximena's has been serving the travel community for nearly two decades, and it is starting to show in some of the more tired rooms. Still, it's located in a leafy suburb of San Salvador and is run by a Norwegian woman who knows her adopted city backwards and forwards.

It's also a great place for meeting people, but it's not all that easy to find alone.

International Guest House
HOTEL **$**

(Map p296; ☑ 2226-7343; i_guesthouse@hotmail. com; 35a Av Norte 9 Bis; s/d US$18/25; @ 🛜) Competition for customers brings out the best in the International, signposted by various national flags, and overseen by a charmingly effusive host. Wi-fi is super-fast, beer is chilled, and the beds are just right. Overall, it's solid, if unspectacular.

Hostal Armonía
BOUTIQUE HOTEL **$$**

(Map p296; ☑ 2225-6124; www.armoniahostal. com; 35a Av Norte; r US$35; P ✸ 🛜) This new guesthouse has surpassed its rivals in the neighborhood thanks to its excellent value and prompt, courteous service. A smart option for those wanting a little peace and convenience; look for the white arches.

Hotel Villa del Angel
BOUTIQUE HOTEL **$$**

(Map p298; ☑ 2223-7171; www.villadelangelhotel. com; 39a Av Norte 219; d incl breakfast US$65-75; P ✸ 🛜) The Angel has really taken on the competitors since appearing a few years ago with its range of bright, oversized rooms at a decent price point. Service is discreet and assured and the location is very safe and convenient for accessing Galerias Escalon. English is widely spoken.

Arbol de Fuego
HOTEL **$$**

(☑ 2557-3601; www.arboldefuego.com; Av Antiguo Cuscatlan, Colonia La Sultana; s US$60-70, d US$70-80; ✸ @ 🛜) 🍴 'Fire Tree' is the pick of the hotels in the quieter Antiguo Cuscatlan area south of the city. The rooms are all impeccably presented, featuring colorful local fabrics and natural soaps. Most of the rooms face internally, so it can feel a little cramped, but the breakfast garden is an oasis and the service is warm and friendly.

Hotel Villa Florencia
Zona Rosa
BOUTIQUE HOTEL **$$**

(Map p298; ☑ 2243-7164; www.hotelvillafloren cia.com; Av La Revolución; s/d/tr incl breakfast US$55/68/85; P ✸ @ 🛜) A number of excellent cultural and dining options within close walking distance make this small hotel a favorite among return travelers to San Salvador. It isn't particularly cheap, but the small rooms are modestly lavish and the stone courtyard is a refuge from the heat. It's also close to the bus stop for buses to Guatemala and Honduras.

Hotel Villa Florencia
Centro Historico
HOTEL **$$**

(Map p292; ☑ 2221-1706; www.hotelvillaflorencia. com; 3a Calle Poniente 1023; s/d US$25/35) The majority of cheap hotels in San Salvador are bland in their presentation, but the Florencia Centro is refreshingly unorthodox. Antiques abound and the terracotta-tiled internal courtyard adds a sense of space and old-world charm. There is no hot water and little English spoken; however, a new cafe has opened onsite.

Hotel Morrison
HOTEL **$$**

(Map p298; ☑ 2223-7111; www.hoteldelaescalon. com; 1 Calle Nueva 3999; s/d/tr incl breakfast US$59/73/83; P ✸ 🛜 ⛱) The Morrison is a professional operation that can soften the landing or energize your departure. The tidy rooms are on the small side, but everything is in its right place. The real boon is the courtyard and lounge area where breakfast is served beside a plunge pool. The location is handy for walks around Colonia Escalón.

La Posada del Rey I
HOTEL **$$**

(Map p298; ☑ 2264-5245; www.laposadadel reyprimero.com; Pasaje Dordely, Colonia Escalón; s/d/tr US$59/80/95; ✸ @ 🛜 ⛱) This stalwart of Colonia Escalón still churns out well-sized rooms with plush beds to tour groups,

---

WRITING ON THE WALL: EL SALVADOR'S MURALS

The murals that grace El Salvador's many towns and villages are synonymous with the country's transition to postwar stability. They are both primary and secondary sources of recent historic events and often serve to raise awareness of current social issues.

The destruction in late 2012 of a facade at San Salvador's Catedral Metropolitana was an unexpected move by the Catholic Church that triggered concerns for the country's rich artistic heritage. That the facade was created by national icon Fernando Llort only exacerbated the shock.

Passionate local advocacy groups – and increasing international interest in the murals – should ensure their long-term survival as part of the national story. Towns such Perquín, La Palma and Suchitoto boast the best examples outside the capital.

Boulevard De Los Héroes

See Zona Rosa Map (p298)

N 0 _____ 400 m
0 _____ 0.2 miles

EL SALVADOR SAN SALVADOR

Av Washington
Calle Los Pinos
39a Av Norte
Av Sucre
Av Aguilares
Av Bolivar
Av José Marti
Av Libertad
Calle Principal
Calle 2c
Calle Los Lirios
39a Av Norte
Av Los Lirios
37a Av Norte
Av Central
33a Av Norte
Calle Las Violetas
Av Don Bosco
Av Los Cedros
Calle Las Palmas
Blvd Universitario
Av A
Universidad Nacional de El Salvador
Avizalco
Pasaje 2a
Parque San José
39a Av Norte
Blvd Universitario
Av C
Calle 4a
Av B
Calle 2a
Calle San Antonio Abad
Calle El Quetzal
Av San José
Av Izalco
Calle San Antonio Abad
Pasaje Italia
Av Alvarado
Av Santa Victoria
Calle Centro America
Calle Guatemala
Calle San Salvador
Calle Managua
Calle Aurora
Calle Gabriela Mistral
Calle Berlin
Av Cañales
Av Boriquen
Av 4 de Mayo
Pasaje Plat
29a Av Norte
27a Av Norte
Calle Los Sisimiles
Calle Talamanca
Av Cortés
Boulevard de los Héroes
Pasaje Los Angeles
Pasaje San Carlos
Pasaje Las Palmeras
Calle Lamatepec
Blvd Tutunichapa
25a Av Norte
Calle Andes
Metrocentro
Alameda Juan Pablo II (Tercera Séptima Calle Poniente)
39a Av Norte
33a Av Norte

Boulevard De Los Héroes

◎ Sights
1 Museo de la Palabra y La Imagen.......D5

◎ Activities, Courses & Tours
2 Centro de Intercambio y
  Solidaridad.. B1

◎ Sleeping
3 Casa de Huéspedes Tazumal..............C2
4 Hostal Armonía C2
5 Hostal San José B3
6 International Guest House C2
7 La Almohada C4
8 Ximena's Guest House........................B5

◎ Eating
9 Café Maquilishuat................................B6
10 Las Fajitas..B3
11 Pupusería La Ceiba............................B4

◎ Entertainment
12 Café La 'T'...B3
13 CineMark...B6
14 Multicinema Reforma.........................C3
15 Teatro Luis Poma................................B6

◎ Shopping
16 La Ceiba Libros B6

business folk and random solo travelers. Rooms are overstocked with wooden furniture, but the numerous staff are always smiling and the paint job will cheer the jet lag. The surrounding area is pleasant for walking.

Hostal San José   HOTEL $$
(Map p296; ☑2226-4603; www.sanjosehostal. com; Blvd Universitario 2212; s/d/tr incl breakfast US$32/50/60; @🛜) A little pricey for the humble location, but nonetheless convenient for exploring the northern part of town. The San José has an efficient motel feel, with a pleasant patio for breakfast. Ask for a room with a window. There's a free bus pick-up service if you call ahead.

Casa de Huéspedes Tazumal   HOTEL $$
(Map p296; ☑2235-0156; www.hoteltazumal house.com; 35a Av Norte 3; s/d/tr incl breakfast US$35/45/55; @🛜) In an area with numerous small hotels offering similar rooms, Tazumal stands out for its homely communal spaces, natural light and pretty courtyard. Not much English is spoken, so dust off the phrasebook.

★**Casa ILB**   BOUTIQUE HOTEL $$$
(Map p298; ☑2528-4200; www.casailb.com; Blvd del Hipódromo 605, Colonia San Benito; s/d incl breakfast from US$110/120; 🅿❄🛜) Zona Rosa is rosier for Casa ILB, the most upscale boutique hotel in the country. The five rooms are minimalist in design, yet spacious enough to swing a yoga mat. The stone floors, sheltered lawn garden and pure cotton sheets cancel out the need for a swimming pool, while the furniture and art selections create a sanctuary of good taste.

Suites Las Palmas   APARTMENT $$$
(Map p298; ☑2250-0800; www.hotelsuiteslas palmas.com.sv; Blvd del Hipódromo, Colonia San Benito; r/ste incl breakfast US$75/90; ❄@🛜) Verging on slightly overpriced, but still the ideal choice for a group looking to party in Zona Rosa across the road. Big beds, large fridges, discreet staff, space to dance and a rooftop pool. Gotta feeling that tonight's gonna be a good night?

✖ Eating

San Salvador has the country's most cosmopolitan restaurants by a mile, and real variety across all tastes and budgets. Zona Rosa has plenty of well-patronized restaurants, especially at night, and Colonia Escalon has a decent cafe scene.

The center has plenty of eateries, but few standouts.

Pupusería La Ceiba   PUPUSERÍA $
(Map p296; Calle San Antonio Abad; mains US$1-3; ◷7-11am & 4-9pm) Named after the port town in Honduras, this place is totally Salvadoran. A plate of these *pupusas* can solve your problems.

Café Maquilishuat   SALVADORAN $
(Map p296; Av Los Andes, Metrocentro; mains US$2-6; ◷7:30am-7pm; 🍴) Named after the pinkish national tree of El Salvador, this *típico* train is a very clean and reliable option. The menu changes daily through the local staples, with plenty of vegetarian options.

Sidewalk Comedores   SALVADORAN $
(Map p292; 1a Av Sur; mains US$1-3; ◷8am-10pm) If in the city on foot, you'll probably be drawn to the smells on the sidewalk *comedores* a block west of Plaza Barrios. The *panes de carnes* (beef sandwiches) are slightly toasted and sprinkled with peppercorns.

EL SALVADOR SAN SALVADOR

EL SALVADOR SAN SALVADOR

Zona Rosa

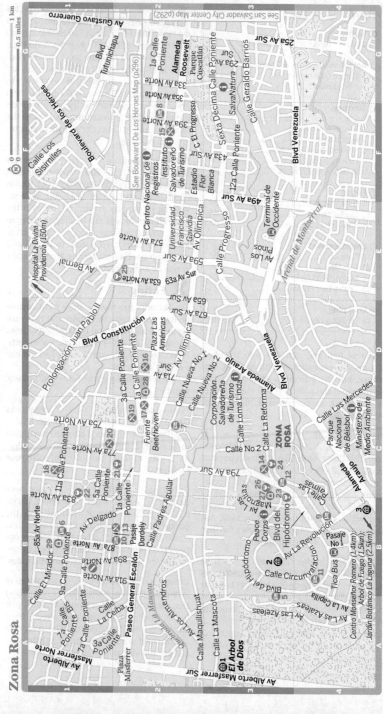

0 | 0.5 miles
0 | 1 km

See San Salvador City Center Map (p292)

See Boulevard De Los Héroes Map (p296)

Av Gustavo Guerrero

Blvd Tutunichapa

Boulevard de los Héroes

Calle Los Sisimiles

Hospital La Divina Providencia (150m)

Av Bernal

Prolongación Juan Pablo II

Blvd Constitución

63a Av Norte

63a Av Sur

65a Av Sur

67a Av Sur

59a Av Sur

57a Av Norte

Centro Nacional de Registros

Instituto Salvadoreño de Turismo

1a Calle Poniente

Alameda Roosevelt

Parque Cuscatlán

33a Av Norte

35a Av Norte

39a Av Norte

29a Av Sur

Calle Geraldo Barrios

25a Av Sur

Calle Geraldo Barrios

Sexta Décima Calle Poniente

SalvaNatura

C El Progresso

Estadio Flor Blanca

Universidad Francisco Gavidia

Av Olímpica

43a Av Sur

12a Calle Poniente

49a Av Sur

Terminal de Occidente

Blvd Venezuela

Calle Progresso

Av Los Pinos

Arenal de Montserrat

Plaza Las Américas

Av Olímpica

Calle Nueva No 1

Calle Nueva No 2

Corporación Salvadoreña de Turismo

Alameda Araujo

Blvd Venezuela

Calle Loma Linda

Calle La Reforma

ZONA ROSA

Parque Nacional de Béisbol

Calle Las Mercedes

Ministerio de Medio Ambiente

Calle No 2

79a Av Sur

Calle Las Palmas

Alameda Araujo

71a Av Sur

3a Calle Poniente

1a Calle Poniente

Fuente Beethoven

75a Av Norte

77a Av Norte

3a Calle Poniente

Blvd del Hipódromo

Blvd del Hipódromo

Av La Revolución

Peace Corps

Av Las Magnolias

Calle Circunvalación

Pasaje No 1

Tica Bus

Pasaje Dordely

Calle Padres Aguilar

85a Av Norte

Calle El Mirador

83a Av Norte

87a Av Norte

89a Av Norte

91a Av Norte

Av Delgado

5a Calle Poniente

11a Calle Poniente

9a Calle Poniente

7a Calle Poniente

7a Calle Bis

Paseo General Escalón

Calle La Ceiba

3a Calle Poniente

Calle La Mascota

Quebrada La Mascota

Av Los Almendros

Calle Maquilishuat

Plaza Masferrer

Av Alberto Masferrer Norte

Av Alberto Masferrer Sur

El Árbol de Dios

Av Las Azaleas

Av Las Azaleas

Jardín Botánico La Laguna (2.5km); Árbol de Fuego (1.5km); Centro Monseñor Romero (1.4km)

1 2 3 4 5 6 7 8 9 10 11 12 13 14 15 16 17 18 19 20 21 22 23 24 25 26 27 28 29

Zona Rosa

⊙ Top Sights
1 El Arbol de Dios A3

⊙ Sights
2 Museo de Arte de El Salvador B3
3 Museo Nacional de Antropología
   David J Guzmán B4

⊕ Activities, Courses & Tours
4 El Salvador Divers B1

⊜ Sleeping
5 Casa ILB..A3
6 Hostal Cumbres del Volcan................B1
7 Hotel Morrison C2
8 Hotel Villa del Angel..........................F2
9 Hotel Villa Florencia Zona Rosa B4
10 La Posada del Rey I............................B2
11 La Zona Hostal B4
12 Suites Las Palmas C3

⊗ Eating
13 Beto's B2
14 Caminito Chocos C3
15 El Cafe de Don Pedro F2
16 El Sopón Típico D2
   Koi Sushi ....(see 29)
17 Le Croissant C2
18 Mile Time..C1
19 Rustico Bistro C2
20 Típicos Margoth C1

⊙ Drinking & Nightlife
21 Barbass...C2
22 La Ventana..C1
23 Los Rinconcitos...................................B3
24 Republik C3
25 Scape..E2
26 Zanzibar..C3

⊜ Shopping
27 Bookmarks..C3
28 Galerías Escalón.................................D2
29 La Gran Vía B1

Le Croissant   BAKERY $
(Map p298; 1a Calle Poniente 3883, Colonia Escalón; pastries US$1-3; ⊙7:30am-6:30pm) Chain patisserie with an excellent option in Escalón. The coffee is decent.

★**Rustico Bistro**   BURGERS $$
(Map p298; ☑2224-5656; 3a Calle Poniente; burgers US$10-12; ⊙11am-4pm) Rustico rivals any burger place in the world as far as we're concerned. The bread is chunky and fresh and the meat must weigh half a cow. Try the pulled-pork sandwiches with tamarindo sauce and wash it all down with a jar of fruit juice.

★**El Sopón Típico**   SALVADORAN $$
(Map p298; Paseo General Escalón; mains US$5-8; ⊙10:30am-9pm; 🖐) Simple, fresh and delicious local food is the order of the day at this famous *típico* restaurant on a busy corner beside Galerias Escalón. Winning dishes include *marisco en crema* and *sopa de chorizo*, but it's hard to fault much. The popular yuca dishes come out at night as families arrive en masse.

Mile Time   VEGETARIAN $$
(Map p298; ☑2264-9980; cnr 11a Calle Poniente 4134 & 81a Av Norte, Colonia Escalón; mains US$4-8; ⊙7am-10pm; 🖐) Faux-meat never tasted so good. The full gamut of Asian and Western vegetarian dishes is served at this impressive restaurant in Escalón. The *empanada en sopa agripicante* (US$7) is divine, and the dessert menu is extensive.

Koi Sushi   JAPANESE $$
(Map p298; ☑2264-4294; Calle El Mirador, Plaza Futura, Colonia Escalón; ⊙noon-11pm) Okay, so it's a Japanese restaurant in a mall in Central America. Still, sometimes you need fresh sushi with a twist of salsa. And this is a pretty fancy mall.

El Cafe de Don Pedro   SALVADORAN $$
(Map p298; ☑2260-2011; cnr 39a Av Norte & Alameda Roosevelt; mains US$4-8; ⊙7am-4pm) The *pinchos* (skewered meat and vegetables) and breakfast specials are the highlights of this 24-hour family-run restaurant with four branches across the city. The Roosevelt branch features bubbly waitstaff, ample parking and dirt-cheap beer.

Caminito Chocos   ARGENTINE $$
(Map p298; ☑2223-6807; Calle La Reforma; mains US$7-9; ⊙noon-10pm) The pseudo-Argentine food here is really just heart-stopping BBQ, burgers and fries; you won't see your personal trainer here, unless they are among the young crowd necking huge beers on weekends.

Las Fajitas   MEXICAN $$
(Map p296; Blvd Universitario; mains US$4-8; ⊙noon-midnight) The secret is in the five spicy sauces you can choose from to douse your nachos at this dependable Mexican joint.

Típicos Margoth   SALVADORAN $$
(Map p298; ☑2263-3340; 77a Av Norte, Colonia Escalón; mains US$5-8; ⊙7am-9:30pm; 🖐) While service is not always as *margoth* (bubbly and extroverted) as advertised, this self-serve

family-run restaurant is a tasty initiation into Salvadoran cuisine. The *antojitos* (small dishes) are a good place to start; finish with *plátanos* (plantain) and cinnamon cream.

Restaurante Hong Kong
CHINESE $$

(Map p292; 9a Av Sur; mains US$4-9; ⊙11am-9pm) There's no Chinatown in San Salvador, so this long-standing, cavernous southern 'Chinese' restaurant will have to do. Expect your noodles oily and your spring rolls dripping in soy sauce.

★Beto's
SEAFOOD $$$

(Map p298; ☑2263-7304; www.betosrestaurante. wix.com/betosrestaurante; cnr 85a Av Norte & Pasaje Dordely, Colonia Escalón; mains US$7-18; ⊙noon-10pm; P🖘) Colonia Escalón is the place to be seen lingering over crustaceans, and Beto's has the perfect mix of lunchtime work crowd and Salvadoran elite dining on anything that moves under the sea. Service is disarmingly good.

🍷 Drinking & Nightlife

San Salvador has a healthy and diverse nightlife. Zona Rosa is the most popular locale, with plenty of smoky dance floors and live bands jamming until well after midnight, while a more refined crowd can be found around Colonia Escalon. Outside town, Paseo El Carmen in Santa Tecla is the nightspot à la mode, with alfresco cafes and thumping bars on weekends.

★La Ventana
BAR

(Map p298; ☑2264-4885; www.laventana.com. sv; 83a Av Norte 510; ⊙noon-midnight Mon-Thu, to 1am Fri & Sat, 8am-10pm Sun) The dimly lit Ventana has been functioning as a gallery-restaurant for nearly two decades, which is some achievement in a city like San Salvador. The beer comes first though, with a huge list of ales to choose from to accompany a solid pub-style menu (mains US$5 to US$12). A variety of crepes make for a point of difference.

Barbass
BAR

(Map p298; 79a Av Norte 725, Colonia Escalón; ⊙7pm-late) Rock and roll ain't noise pollution at this reverberating den, which hosts local guitar heroes and a friendly all-ages crowd. The walls are covered in interesting street art. Tattoos are not a prerequisite for entry, though they will be appreciated.

Republik
BAR

(Map p298; ☑2240-0041; Calle La Reforma 243-247; ⊙3pm-1am Wed-Sun) Irish bar Republik is the most consistently lively venue in Zona Rosa. Live cover bands and CD-spinning DJs entertain a well-dressed crowd who dance in groups and drink mojitos (US$5) and buckets of bottled beer on reserved tables.

Scape
GAY

(Map p298; Prolongación Juan Pablo II; ⊙9:30pm-1am Thu-Sat) Gay disco heaven on weekends.

Zanzibar
COCKTAIL BAR

(Map p298; ☑2279-0833; Blvd del Hipodrómo, Centro Commercial Basilea; ⊙11am-1am) Better-than-average cocktail bar in an elevated location on the Hippodrome.

Los Rinconcitos
BAR

(Map p298; Blvd del Hipódromo 310; ⊙6pm-1am Wed-Sat) Karaoke is a universal language and Salvadorans love to lip-synch. While not the classiest place you'll drink in, the business model appears to be working. Foreigners are encouraged to sing.

☆ Entertainment

★Café La 'T'
LIVE MUSIC

(Map p296; Calle San Antonio Abad 2233; ⊙10am-9:30pm Mon-Wed, to 11pm Thu-Sat) The country's finest musicians appear intermittently at this down-tempo cafe set aside from the hullabaloo. Ska, jazz, blues: just turn up and try your luck. There's light food, booze and particularly good coffee.

Teatro Luis Poma
THEATER

(Map p296; ☑2261-1029; Blvd de los Héroes, Metrocentro; US$5) Contemporary performances across genres at San Salvador's most respected theater. Naturally, it's at the mall.

Multicinema Reforma
CINEMA

(Map p296; ☑2225-9588; Blvd Universitario; US$2.50) Discounts on Tuesdays.

CineMark
CINEMA

(Map p296; ☑2261-2001; Blvd de los Héroes, Metrocentro, 3rd fl; US$3) Our favorite of the big cinema groups.

🛍 Shopping

San Salvador has a string of shiny malls, where all the international brands are available; Colonia Escalon has some good local boutique stores. Mercado Centro is the place for cheap clothes and electronics, while Mercado Ex-Cuartel is a veritable emporium for traditional handicrafts, including amazing hammocks.

The country's most definitive artist is La Palma painter Fernando Llort. His iconic, colorful wares are ubiquitous; for an extensive collection, visit El Arbol de Dios (p290).

La Gran Vía   MALL
(Map p298; 87a Av Norte) A pleasant mall experience, with good nightclubs and restaurants.

Mercado Central   MARKET
(Map p292; 6 Calle Ote; ⊙7:30am-6pm Mon-Sat, to 2pm Sun) Salvadoran city life at full throttle, the Mercado Central is the locals' favorite for clothes and electronics.

Mercado Ex-Cuartel   MARKET
(Map p292; Calle Delgado; ⊙7:30am-6pm Mon-Sat, to 2pm Sun) The Mercado Ex-Cuartel is a difficult place to navigate, but be patient, go with a friend, and find handmade hammocks and embroidered fabrics from across the country.

Bookmarks   BOOKS
(Map p298; www.bookmarks.com.sv; Blvd del Hipódromo, Centro Commercial Basilea; ⊙10am-9pm) Good range of English-language fiction and guidebooks (including Lonely Planet).

Galerías Escalón   SHOPPING CENTRE
(Map p298; Paseo General Escalón; ⊙8am-8pm) Galerías Escalón boasts three air-conditioned levels of upscale clothing and jewelry stores, electronics stores, cell-phone offices and banks. Grab some sushi at the swish food court then catch a movie at the Cinépolis mega-cinema.

La Ceiba Libros   BOOKS
(Map p296; Blvd de los Héroes, Metrocentro, 1st fl; ⊙9am-7pm Mon-Sat, 10am-5pm Sun) Stock up on Salvadoran history and literature in Spanish. There are four branches in the capital.

ℹ Information

EMERGENCY
Police (☎2261-0630; Calle Berlín; ⊙24hr)
Tourist Police (☎2298-9983)

IMMIGRATION
Immigration Office (☎2221-2111; cnr 9a Calle Poniente & 15a Av Norte, Centro de Gobierno; ⊙9am-5pm Mon-Fri, to 1pm Sat) Visa renewals and other immigration matters.

LAUNDRY
Lavapronto (Calle Los Sisimiles 2944; ⊙7am-6pm Mon-Fri, to 5pm Sat) Same-day laundry service available.

MEDICAL SERVICES
Pollution is a consistent pest, seemingly set in place by the surrounding mountains. Thick vehicle exhaust, especially from buses, can leave you with runny eyes and a sore throat.
Hospital Bloom (☎2225-4114; cnr Blvd de los Héroes & Av Gustavo Guerrero; ⊙24hr) Public hospital with long lines. Specializes in children's treatment.
Hospital Diagnóstico Escalón (☎2264-4422; 3a Calle Poniente; ⊙24hr) Recommended by the US embassy.

MONEY
Dispensa de Don Juan (2a Calle Poniente; ⊙9am-8pm) Near Plaza Barrios, has several ATMs and is probably the most secure place to withdraw money in the centro.

POST
Correos Central (Map p296; Blvd de los Héroes, Metrocentro; ⊙7:30am-5pm Mon-Fri, 8am-noon Sat) The most convenient branch.

TOURIST INFORMATION
Centro Nacional de Registros (IGN; Map p298; www.cnr.gob.sv; 1a Calle Poniente, 2nd fl; ⊙8am-12:30pm & 2-5pm Mon-Fri) One of the best places to find city maps.
Corporación Salvadoreña de Turismo (Corsatur; Map p298; ☎2243-7835; www.elsalvador.travel; Alameda Araujo; ⊙8am-12:30pm & 1:30-5:30pm) Has an excellent website.
Entre Amigos (☎2206-8400; entreamigos@salnet.net; 17a Calle Poniente 142, Barrio San Miguelito; ⊙10am-4pm Mon-Fri) This organization promotes LGBT rights.
Instituto Salvadoreño de Turismo (ISTU; Map p298; ☎2260-9249; istu@mh.gob.sv; 41a Av Norte; ⊙8:30am-noon & 1-4pm Mon-Sat) General information about El Salvador's national parks and turicentros.
Ministerio de Medio Ambiente (Map p298; ☎2267-6276; www.marn.gob.sv; Alameda Araujo/Carretera Santa Tecla Km 5.5; ⊙7:30am-4:30pm Mon-Fri) Manages the Parque Nacional Montecristo-El Trifinio near Metapan. You need permission to stay overnight in the park, and even day-trippers should call ahead to be sure there isn't a big group headed there at the same time. Permits are issued in person or by fax.
Peace Corps (Map p298; ☎2207-6002; www.peacecorps.gov; Av Las Dalias 3; ⊙9am-4:30pm Mon-Fri) If you want to get off the beaten track, this US-based organization may

be a good resource. Volunteers are very receptive to visitors.

SalvaNatura (Map p298; ☑2202-1515; www.salvanatura.org; 33 Av Sur 640; ☺8am-12:30pm & 2-5:30pm Mon-Fri) Friendly and helpful staff manage Parque Nacional El Imposible and Parque Nacional los Volcanes. Call before visiting either park.

🛈 Getting There & Away

AIR

Aeropuerto Internacional Comalpa (☑2339-8264; www.aeropuertoelsalvador.gob.sv), a major Central American hub, is located 50km southeast of San Salvador.

American Airlines (☑2298-0777; www.aa.com; cnr 89a Av Norte & Calle del Mirador, World Trade Center I; ☺9am-7pm Mon-Fri, to 1pm Sat)

Avianca (☑2247-3263; www.avianca.com; Paseo General Escalón, Galerías Escalón; ☺9am-7pm Mon-Fri, to 5pm Sat, to 1pm Sun)

Copa Airlines (☑2209-2672; www.copaair.com; cnr 89a Av Norte & Calle del Mirador, World Trade Center I; ☺ 8am-6pm Mon-Fri, to noon Sat)

Delta Airlines (☑2275-9292; www.delta.com; cnr 89a Av Norte & Calle del Mirador, World Trade Center I; ☺8am-6pm Mon-Fri)

United Airlines (☑2283-4000; www.united.com; Av de la Revolución, Sheraton Presidente Hotel; ☺8am-6pm Mon-Fri, to noon Sat)

BUS

International buses leave from **Terminal Puerto Bus** (Map p292; cnr Alameda Juan Pablo II & 19a Av Norte). Take city bus 29, 101D, 7C or 52 to get there.

Platinum (Map p292; ☑2281-1996; www.platinumcentroamerica.com; 19a Av Norte) offers deluxe service to Guatemala City featuring air-con, movies and a meal (US$35, five hours), departing at 6:30am from the Terminal Puerto Bus. It also has daily services to San José (US$67, 18 hours) leaving at 3am. For Honduras, air-conditioned buses leave every day for Tegucigalpa at 5:30am (US$44 to US$56, six hours) and San Pedro Sula at 7am (US$35, six hours). It leaves for Managua, Nicaragua at 11:30am (US$51, 10 hours)

Tica Bus (Map p298; ☑2243-1188; www.ticabus.com; Blvd El Hipodrómo, Colonia San Benito; ☺8am-4:30pm) has services to Guatemala City at 6am and 2pm (US$18, five hours) from the Hotel San Carlos. Reserve one to two days in advance and arrive at the San Carlos a half-hour early. Tica Bus is inside the hotel. From Guatemala City it continues to the Mexican border at Tapachula, Chiapas (US$19, seven hours).

Tica Bus leaves the Hotel San Carlos at 5am and arrives in Managua, Nicaragua, at 3:30pm (US$30). The bus arrives in San José, Costa Rica, between 3pm and 4pm (US$56). It then leaves at 10pm for Panama (US$96), where you arrive between 3pm and 4pm on the third day.

San Salvador has three main terminals for national long-distance buses.

🛈 Getting Around

TO/FROM THE AIRPORT

Shuttle Shuttles operated by **Taxis Acacya** (p304) offer the best way to/from the airport (45 minutes). You can take two suitcases. In San Salvador, shuttles leave from Taxis Acacya behind the Puerto bus terminal, from 8am, on the hour. From the airport, they depart at 9am, 1pm and 5:30pm.

Microbus Microbus 138 (US$0.60, 45 minutes to one hour, every 10 minutes) passes the airport – if you remind the driver – traveling to and from the city center. Pick it up just south of Plaza Barrios in town. If heading into town, cut through the parking lot to reach the highway (a 75m walk) and a bus shelter.

Taxi A taxi between San Salvador and the airport costs US$30 to US$35.

BUS

San Salvador's bus network is extensive, from large smoke-spewing monsters to zippy microbuses. Fares are US$0.30 to US$0.35.

Buses run frequently from 5am to 7:30pm daily; fewer buses run on Sunday. Services stop between 7:30pm and 8:30pm; microbuses run later, until around 9pm. After 9pm you'll have to take a taxi.

In the center, it is fastest to walk a few blocks away from Plaza Barrios to catch your bus. Key routes:

Bus 9 Goes down 29a Av Norte alongside the Universidad de El Salvador. Then it turns east toward the city center, heading past the cathedral and up Independencia past Terminal de Oriente.

Bus 26 Passes Plaza Barrios and Parque Zoológico on its way to Terminal de Sur.

Bus 29 Goes to Terminal de Oriente via the center. Buses stop between Metrocentro and MetroSur.

Bus 30 Heads downtown and is the best way to get to and from bus 138 to the airport. Pick it up behind Metrocentro or at Parque Libertad in the center.

Bus 30B A very useful route, especially from Blvd de los Héroes. The bus goes east on Blvd Universitario, then southwest along Blvd de los Héroes to Metrocentro. From there, it goes west along Alameda Roosevelt. It then turns south at 79a Av and continues along Blvd del

303

BUSES FROM SAN SALVADOR

Terminal de Oriente

Buses serving all points east and a few northern destinations arrive and depart from the **Terminal de Oriente** (Alameda Juan Pablo II), on the eastern side of the city. To get to the terminal, take bus 9, 29 or 34 from the city center; bus 29 or 52 from Blvd de los Héroes; bus 7C or 34 from Terminal de Occidente; or bus 21 from Terminal de Sur. Frequent departures are as follows; note that faster especial services are available for La Unión and San Miguel.

DESTINATION	BUS	COST (US$)	DURATION (HR)
Chalatenango	125	1.10	2
El Poy (Honduran border)	119	1.75	3
Ilobasco	111	1.10	1½
La Palma	119	1.80	2¾
La Unión	304	3.25	4
San Miguel	301	1.25-2.50	3
San Vicente	177	1	1½
Suchitoto	129	0.90	1½

Terminal de Occidente

Buses serving all points west, including the Guatemalan border, arrive and depart from the **Terminal de Occidente** (Map p298; Blvd Venezuela, near 49a Av Sur). To get here, take bus 34 from the city center; bus 44 from Blvd de los Héroes (get off at Blvd Venezuela and walk a few blocks west to the terminal); or bus 7C or 34 from Terminal de Oriente. Frequent departures:

DESTINATION	BUS	COST (US$)	DURATION
Ahuachapán	205	1.10	2¼hr
Cerro Verde	Santa Ana to El Congo, then 246	0.90	40min
Joya de Cerén	108 to San Juan Opico	0.65	1¾hr
La Hachadura	205 to Sonsonate then 259	1.55	3½hr
La Libertad	102	0.70	1hr
Lago de Coatepeque	Santa Ana to El Congo then 248	0.90	40min
Las Chinamas	202 to Ahuachapán then 263	1.60	2½hr
Los Cóbanos	205 to Sonsonate then 257	1.30	2½hr
Metapán	201A	2.50	1¾hr
Ruínas de San Andrés	Santa Ana bus 201	0.80	40min
San Cristóbal	498	1.30	3hr
Santa Ana	201	0.90	1¼hr
Sonsonate	205	1	1¼hr

Terminal de Sur

In the south of the city, **Terminal de Sur** (Autopista a Comalapa), also called Terminal San Marcos, serves destinations to the south and southeast. To get here take bus 26 or microbus 11B from the city center or bus 21 from Terminal de Oriente. Departures include the following; note that a faster especial service is available for Usulután.

DESTINATION	BUS	COST (US$)	DURATION (HR)
Costa del Sol	495	1.25	2½
Puerto El Triunfo	185	1.60	2
Usulután	302	1.70	2½

Hipódromo to Av Revolución, then returns on Alameda Araujo, Roosevelt, and 49a Av Sur back to Metrocentro.

Bus 34 Runs from Terminal de Oriente to Metrocentro then down to the Zona Rosa, turning around right in front of MARTE art museum. Passes Terminal de Occidente on return.

Bus 42 The bus goes west along Calle Arce from the cathedral and continues along Alameda Roosevelt. At El Salvador del Mundo, it heads southwest along Alameda Araujo, passing the Mercado de Artesanías and Museo Nacional de Antropología David J Guzmán, and continues down the Carretera Interamericana, passing La Ceiba de Guadalupe.

Bus 101 Goes from Plaza Barrios in the center, past Metro Sur, the anthropology museum, La Ceiba de Guadalupe and on to Santa Tecla.

CAR & MOTORCYCLE

Avoid driving through the city center. The traffic gets snarled in daytime and the area is unsafe at night. It's quickest to take major thoroughfares. One-way streets have signage or an arrow painted on the pavement.

Alamo Rent a Car (☑ 2367-8000; www. alamoelsalvador.com; Blvd del Hipódromo 426; ☺ 5:30am-7:30pm)

Avis (☑ 2500-2800, airport 2339-9268; www. avis.com.sv; 43a Av Sur 127; per day US$40; ☺ 7:30am-6:30pm Mon-Sat, to 5pm Sun)

Budget (☑ 2264-3888; www.budget.com.sv; 85a Av Norte 648, Colonia Escalón; per day US$35; ☺ 8am-5pm Mon-Fri, to noon Sat)

Quick Rent a Car (☑ 2229-6959; www.quick rentacar.com.sv)

TAXI

Taxis are plentiful, but unmetered, so negotiate a price in advance. A ride in town should cost between US$5 and US$10 during daytime. Rates go up a few dollars late at night. License plates beginning with 'A' indicate a registered taxi; in theory they can be held accountable for problems. If you don't spot a passing taxi, call **Taxis Acacya** (☑ 2271-4937, airport 2339-9282; cnr 19a Av Norte & 3a Calle Poniente; US$5) or **Acontaxis** (☑ 2523-2424).

AROUND SAN SALVADOR

San Salvador lies in the 'valley of the hammocks', skirted by makeshift communities clinging precariously to sloping land and with Maya ruins dotted at its fringe. It is also surrounded by steep volcanic peaks which offer hiking opportunities and visits to small artists' towns and coffee *fincas* (plantations) elevated from the heat. The coast is a short drive to the south; La Libertad, the main port, marks the start of a world-class surf voyage.

◉ Sights

The area around San Salvador is awash with historic ruins and grand *miradors*.

Joya de Cerén   RUIN
(admission US$3; ☺ 9am-5pm Tue-Sun) Called the Pompeii of America, Unesco World Heritage Site Joya de Cerén was a small Maya settlement buried under volcanic ash when the Laguna Caldera Volcano erupted in AD 595. The small museum offers a good collection of artifacts and models of the villages. One compelling piece is a small dish showing fingerprints smeared in the remains of an interrupted meal.

The site is 36km west of San Salvador – take bus 108 from Terminal de Occidente and get off after crossing the bridge over the Río Sucio.

Cihuatán   RUIN
(www.cihuatan.org; admission US$3; ☺ 9am-4pm Tue-Sun) The modest ruins of Cihuatán were once an immense urban area alongside the Río Guazapa, possibly the largest pre-Columbian city between Guatemala and Peru. Today Cihuatán makes a convenient history excursion for those staying in the capital and helps to contextualize San Salvador's modern-day urban settlement.

From San Salvador's Terminal de Oriente, take bus 119 toward Chalatenango and get off about 4km beyond Las Aguilares; ask the driver to let you off at the ruins. It's a 900m walk to the site.

Ruinas de San Andrés   RUIN
(admission US$3; ☺ 9am-5pm Tue-Sun) In 1977 a step pyramid and a large courtyard with a subterranean section were unearthed at this site, inhabited by Maya between AD 600 and AD 900. Experts believe that up to 12,000 people lived here. The peaceful ruins are 300m north of the highway and 33km west of San Salvador in the Valle de Zapotitán. Take the Santa Ana bus 201 from San Salvador's Terminal de Occidente and get off at Km 33, at a small black sign for the ruins.

★ Festivals & Events

Bolas de Fuego   CULTURAL
(☺ 31 Aug) To commemorate an eruption of Volcán San Salvador that destroyed the original town, Nejapa residents spar by throwing balls of fire then dancing till dawn around street bonfires.

Los Planes de Renderos

This hillside district, 12km to the south of San Salvador, is famous for **Puerta del Diablo** (Devil's Door). Two towering boulders, reputedly one single stone split in two, form a lookout with fantastic views. During the war this place was an execution point, the cliffs offering easy disposal of the bodies.

◎ Sights

Parque Balboa   PARK
(admission US$0.80) The *pupusas* here are famous in San Salvador. Can you make it to double figures? If you're not hungry, it's still a pleasant place to hang out and is often filled with children.

❶ Getting There & Away

The boulders are 2km past the family-friendly **Parque Balboa**. Take bus 12, 'Mil Cumbres', from the east side of the Mercado Central, at 12a Calle Poniente. If you're driving, head down Av Cuscatlán until you see the signs.

La Libertad

POP 16,885
La Libertad is the first port of call for many travelers fleeing the capital in search of Pacific Coast surf beaches and all the misadventure that entails. Its no picture postcard, but the notorious **Punta Roca** wave breaking before a bustling fish market and *malecón* creates a striking urban image hard to manufacture elsewhere in the world. Its reputation as dangerous is not unfounded, but it's hardly the wild west many pundits suggest.

Beyond the beach, La Libertad is an important commercial center – thanks mostly to the port – with more energy, souped-up buses and loud-mouthed touting than you'd expect for a town of such modest proportions. Most travelers bypass it for the more chilled-out beaches to the west, or the Deininger national park to the east, but it's an ideal stop to stock up on supplies, or to experience a midsize, working-class Salvadoran city within minutes of your hammock.

◎ Sights

Parque Nacional Walter
T Deininger   NATIONAL PARK
(admission US$1, guides US$12; ⊙8am-5pm) About 4km north of La Libertad, along the Comalapa road, Parque Nacional Walter T

Deininger is named for the German settler who donated the land. It includes two types of forest: *caducifolio*, which sheds its leaves in summer, and *galería*, which retains its foliage year-round.

To visit, you supposedly must obtain a permit from ISTU in San Salvador five days prior to arrival. You might try just showing up and talking with the guard. It's a 15-minute ride from La Libertad – catch bus 187.

✦ Activities

Hospital de Tablas de Surf   SURFING
(☏ 2335-3214; 3a Av Norte 28-7) Surf Doctor Saul has expanded Hospital de Tablas de Surf into the neighboring premises, so there's even more space for repairing, renting and selling boards; in addition, surfing lessons are also offered. Just knock if it appears closed.

⌂ Sleeping

La Libertad has a few rough motels which are best avoided unless you really can't make it slightly further west to Playa El Tunco and beyond.

Hotel Renacer   HOTEL **$**
(☏ 7027-2899; Calle 4a Poniente 3 Av Sur; per person with/without air-con US$20/15; ✲) In a town notoriously low on sleeping options, Renacer just squeaks into the upper ranks. Its seven rooms with private bathrooms are popular with long-term surfers and not many others.

OFF THE BEATEN TRACK

PANCHIMALCO

Set on the green slopes of Cerro Chulo, Panchimalco is a small town renowned for its religious festivals, particularly Palm Sunday, when residents march through the streets bearing decorated palm fronds. Early May's **Fería de Cultura de las Flores y las Palmas** features palm artistry, folk dancing and fireworks.

Inhabited by descendants of the Pipils, Panchimalco has reinvented itself as an artists' enclave. You can visit a number of working galleries here and purchase work from leading national artists at reasonable prices.

Hotel Rick
HOTEL **$**

(☎ 2335-3542; 5a Av Sur; d US$25; ❄) Even the grottiest surfers agree that Hotel Rick is pretty shady, but rooms on the 2nd floor at least get more sunlight. Bathrooms are clean.

Punta Roca Surf Resort
RESORT **$$**

(☎ 2352-4628; Playa El Cocal; d US$40; ❄) Run by the same couple who own the famous restaurant on the point in La Libertad city, this popular local resort is a day-tripper's delight for the spacious pool area, and a quiet, low-key resort by night. Nothing fancy, but the sincere hospitality and the comfortable beds make it work.

Sol Bohemio
HOSTEL **$$**

(☎ 7262-0497; www.solbohemio.com; Playa San Blas; d US$54) Not the cheapest place, but very peaceful and it definitely beats staying in La Libertad. The restaurant fills with day guests on weekends, but the four-room guesthouse is ghostly quiet on a beautiful beach.

✖ Eating

A number of excellent seafood restaurants line the *malecón*.

★ Punta Roca
SEAFOOD **$$**

(cnr 5a Av Sur & 4a Calle Poniente; mains US$4-14; ⊙ 8am-8pm Sun-Thu, to 10pm Fri & Sat) Overlooking the point is the pride of expatriate surfer Robert Rotherham, who has been feeding the notoriously fussy surf community for decades. The *gringo frijolero* (grilled fish or meat with beans, vegetables, avocado and tortillas, $11) will satisfy a whole gang of grommets. The generous shakes, smoothies and cocktails (US$4 to US$5) are best taken at sunset.

Nuevo Altamar
SEAFOOD **$$**

(4a Calle Poniente; mains US$6-15; ⊙ 11am-11pm) If you're passing through La Libertad, it's worth stopping for the white-tablecloth service and exquisite *ceviche* and *cazuela* (seafood soup) at this institution. Many San Salvadorans make the trip down for special occasions.

La Dolce Vita
ITALIAN **$$**

(☎ 2335-3592; Calle San Diego; mains US$9-12; ⊙ 9am-10pm) Near the water are a series of restaurants with vocal staff trying to win your business. La Dolce Vita doesn't need to shout too loud; its pizza and pasta are pretty much spot on.

ℹ Information

Banco Agrícola Branches are located east of the market in Barrios and in El Faro mall. Changes traveler's checks; there's a new 24-hour ATM at El Faro mall.

Post Office (2a Calle Oriente; ⊙ 8am-5pm Mon-Fri, to 1pm Sat) Near 2a Av Norte.

ℹ Getting There & Away

There is no bus terminal. Bus 102 goes to and from San Salvador (US$0.70, one hour). In San Salvador, catch it at its terminal behind Parque Bolivar or at Terminal de Occidente. In La Libertad, buses leave from the corner of 4a Av Norte and Calle Gerardo Barros.

To Sonsonate, take bus 287 (US$1.25, 2½ hours, 1:45pm only) from the bus stop at 2a Calle Poniente, or take bus 192 to Playa Mizata and change.

You can also go directly from the airport to La Libertad – it's about the same distance as San Salvador. Take bus 133 to the puente a Comalapa (Comalapa overpass) a few minutes away. A path leads up onto the intersecting road; from there it's 100m to the town of Comalapa, where bus 187 or 495 goes every 20 minutes to La Libertad (US$0.40).

La Costa del Bálsamo

Welcome to surfing paradise, El Sal style. Starting at the tough port city of La Libertad, the coastal highway glides west past tiny two-break, black-sand beaches in the one part of El Salvador that young travelers and ocean lovers gravitate toward without exception.

Playa El Tunco really parties hard on weekends, but press on a few clicks away from the city, circle down like an eagle and you'll soon have the glistening ocean, awash with turtles, dolphins and huge leaping fish, all to your beautiful self. Playa El Zonte is the best place to learn surfing or rent a fisher's boat for the morning.

Los Cóbanos is essentially a fishing village on a secluded reef at the western tip of La Costa del Bálsamo. It boasts the country's best snorkeling and diving.

The region takes its name from the valuable aromatic oil extracted here by burning the bark of live balsam trees. Today only a handful of trees remain and cotton has become the main cash crop.

🛏 Sleeping

Some of the country's best budget accommodation is located in the beach hamlets west of La Libertad.

Papaya's Lodge
HOSTEL $

(☑2389-6027; www.papayalodge.com; Playa El Tunco; dm with/without air-con US$10/8, r with/without air-con US$25/20) Papaya's is a no-frills big-hearted hostel which has seen the township expand astronomically since 2000. The cement dorms are nothing special, but the best have bathrooms and all are clean.

The property is set back slightly from the party scene, but the enthusiastic surf community can raise the decibels when trading stories. The river deck makes a welcome change from the norm.

Sombra
HOSTEL $

(www.surflibre.com; Playa El Tunco; dm/d without bathroom US$7/18, dm/d/tr with bathroom US$18/22/30; ☎☀) Sombra is an upbeat little hostel that punches above its weight. Tidy dorm rooms are the best in El Tunco and the small pool does the trick, but it's the little things that make a difference: bus pickup in San Salvador, outdoor shower, free water, working wi-fi and BYO booze!

El Balsamo
HOSTEL $

(☑2389-6140, 7404-8117; www.elbalsamo.com; Playa El Sunzal; dm US$7, s/d without bathroom US$10/15, with bathroom US$20/25) The double and dorm rooms here are clean and good value, with plenty of greenery outside your window; the upstairs rooms take advantage of sea breezes. El Balsamo is not right on the beach though, so be prepared to walk 300m (not ideal for solo women). If there's no swell, you can get your kicks on a skate ramp.

Canegue Hostal
HOSTEL $

(☑7598-6913; Playa El Zonte; dm/r US$7/20, hammocks & camping US$3) Canegue is a no-frills hostel run by funny local surfer Zancudo, who loves to chat with guests at his notorious bar. The two private rooms are nothing special, but the location is very quiet and the hammocks, right next to the water, are a good deal.

Sunzal Point Surf Lodge
LODGE $

(☑2389-6070; www.surfsunzal.com; Carretera Litoral Km 44, Playa El Sunzal; dm US$8, d with/without air-con US$30/16; ☀@) Oldest of the old school, Sunzal Point was given a modest revamp a few years ago. Today's it's a basic backpacker joint catering predominantly to the surfer crew. The sprawling garden property is its greatest asset.

El Palmarcito Hotel
HOSTEL $

(☑2305-7900; Playa El Palmarcito; d from US$12; P@☀) There's nothing much in El Palmarcito except for a few shacks and a beautiful beach. Oh, and this friendly, welcoming surfer hangout, which rents out comfortable rooms and serves huge portions of local seafood (US$4 to US$10). It's 5km west of Sunzal.

★Hotel Mopelia
BOUTIQUE HOTEL $$

(www.hotelmopelia-salvador.com; Playa El Tunco; s/d from US$15/20, with air-con US$35/40; ☀) This large property is a magnet for travelers who appreciate the thoughtfulness and space afforded by the owner's business model. Now upgraded to 12 rooms, at a variety of price points, Mopelia moves at whatever pace you want.

There's also the town's best pizza onsite at Tunco Veloz, and one of the most extensive beer menus in El Salvador.

★Eco del Mar
BOUTIQUE HOTEL $$

(www.ecosurfelsalvador.com; Playa El Tunco; r US$44-66, with air-con US$54-86; ☀) Next to the police station and the beach is one of Tunco's more discreet places, the Eco del Mar. This two-story building uses plenty of wood, including for its pleasant veranda, sitting area and external staircases. The rooms are larger than average and feature breakfast tables, cooking facilities and televisions. Excellent value for a small family. Cash only.

Tekuani Kal
BOUTIQUE HOTEL $$

(☑2389-6388; www.tekuanikal.com; Playa El Tunco; s/d incl breakfast US$60/75; ☀☀) Pushing the higher end for Tunco, and you pay mostly for the view. Popular with a slightly more reserved crowd.

El Sunzalito
HOSTEL $$

(☑7211-9519; Playa El Tunco; dm/s/d US$5/25/50) Welcome new addition to El Tunco, close to the town entrance.

El Dorado
BOUTIQUE HOTEL $$

(☑7859-4212; www.surfeldorado.com; Playa El Zonte; dm/s/d from US$28/40/55; P☀☀) Across the river from the main 'drag' is El Dorado, a stylish resort run by an enterprising French-Canadian couple and staffed by a tightly knit team of locals. Direct access to the waves will get you out of bed, while the presentation of the rooms with bamboo artworks, quality linens and stone showers will keep you primed for the next session.

La Guitarra
BOUTIQUE HOTEL **$$**

(☎2389-6388; www.surfingeltunco.com; Playa El Tunco; s/d/tr with fan from US$20/30/36, with air-con US$30/55/75; ✳@☀) The beachside rooms are a tad overpriced at this rock-music-themed Tunco sleep-easy, but the garden rooms (both quieter and closer to reception) are still decent value. Management is somewhat aloof, but the grassy area by the pool and the indoors TV lounge encourage interactivity between guests. Live music fills the bar on weekends, so be prepared.

Esencia Nativa
HOSTEL **$$**

(☎7737-8879; www.esencianativa.com; Playa El Zonte; dm/d/tr US$15/25/30, r with bathroom & air-con US$35; P✳☀) El Zonte's one road leads to Escencia Nativa, and rightly so. This low-key hostel is where most travelers linger, irrespective of where they choose to sleep. The pool is a winner and it will take some serious swell to get you away from your pizza at the 'munchie shack' replete with ocean views. Long-time local Alex is your fount of knowledge.

Casa Garrobo
HOTEL **$$**

(www.casagarrobo.com; Los Cóbanos; s/d US$20/30; P✳☀) 'Iguana House' is heaven for beach bums, its golden-sand path leading to nutrient-rich, rocky shallows in front (known as Playa La Amor), and to a string of beaches to explore further west. The property itself contains three large rooms, 10 beds, tiled floors and lukewarm showers. The landing is strewn with hammocks, comfortable furniture and a small book collection.

The small kidney-shaped pool and shared open-plan kitchen round out your low-rent holiday home for a few lazy days.

B Boutique Hotel
BOUTIQUE HOTEL **$$$**

(☎7210-9258; www.bbboutiquehotel.com; 45.9 Carretera Litoral; d US$350; P✳☎☀) Just outside Playa El Sunzal is the finest upmarket accommodation in El Salvador. This small hotel is remarkably discreet, with only four rooms overlooking an infinity pool and the Pacific Ocean beyond. The fabulous seafood restaurant, Beto's, is on the premises.

Boca Olas
BOUTIQUE HOTEL **$$$**

(☎2389-6333; Playa El Tunco; d US$100-140; ☀) Little El Tunco has grown up! Boca Olas has lifted the sophistication of the beach hamlet with this manicured, high-end offering, which has a fine pool and professional service. The two-bedroom suites (US$150) are ideal for small groups.

✗ Eating

Playa El Tunco is the star of the culinary scene here, offering a huge variety of surf-inspired cafes, seafood restaurants and relaxed bar meals.

Cojo Coyote
CAFE **$**

(Playa El Tunco; mains $3-6; ⊙6.30am-5pm) A funky fresh new cafe just before the end of the sandy road, Cojo Coyote serves moreish breakfasts, smoothies, coffee and in-between-surf food.

★ Sharky's
TEX-MEX **$**

(Playa El Sunzal; mains US$3-6; ⊙7am-3pm) So this ex-pilot turns up in Playa El Sunzal,

---

SURFING EL SAL

With 16 right-hand point breaks and 28°C (82°F) water swarming with sea turtles, what's not to love? Our favorites:

Punta Roca Iconic for a reason. Central America's best wave is often compared to South Africa's J Bay. A rocky bottom makes it fast and strong. Bring just your board – theft is common on the walk to the point.

Las Flores A fast sandy point break best at low tide. Picture a hollow take-off ending on a black-sand beach. A 300m ride is possible – welcome to the Wild East. From here you can also reach the infamous Punta Mango by boat. Don't drop in!

Playa El Sunzal The most popular wave in El Salvador; fun, consistently big right-hander with a seasoned surf crowd.

Playa El Zonte Oodles of foam and plenty of instructors on hand make this pretty, largely protected beach an ideal place to learn.

Playa El Palmarcito A bit of a secret, this little beauty can serve up tasty waves for all levels when conditions are right.

and decides to open a small cafe because he is always so wiped out from surfing (and he needs something to do when the surf is flat). Just the basics, nothing special. Sure, Richard, good luck with that. The outcome? You'd walk across broken beer bottles for the breakfast burritos (and for pretty much anything else).

★ **Take a Wok**   NOODLES **$$**
(Playa El Tunco; mains US$6-8; ⊗5pm-10pm) The best noodles in El Salvador (trust me, we looked hard) are found at this little booth on the road into El Tunco. You don't need to ask where it is because it is always packed with surfers and stoners shouting out the combo they want, then tapping their feet until it's ready.

Comedor La Esquina   SALVADORAN **$$**
(Playa El Tunco; mains US$4-8; ⊗7am-9pm) Still punching out burritos on big colorful plates to all who stop by the famous 'corner.'

La Bocana   SEAFOOD **$$**
(Playa El Tunco; mains US$6-16; ⊗8am-11pm) It's on the beach, seats a hundred-plus people, has an oversupply of waiters and a long menu of pretty much anything you feel like. Gets raucous once the sun sets, but then again, so do you after a six-hour lunch.

Dale Dale Cafe   CAFE **$$**
(☑7080-0263; Playa El Tunco; sandwiches US$5-7; ⊗6.30am-5pm) If you crave a less Latin American start to the day, then try a smoothie, herbal tea, mug of Americano or stack of fluffy pancakes at this moderately upscale place on the main drag. Go on! (*Dale dale!*)

Soya Nutribar   JUICE BAR
(☑7887-1596; Playa El Tunco; ⊗8.30am-3pm) *Deliciosa* juices, shakes, and probiotic liquid meals. The customers shine coming out of this place. Take an energy ball for the road.

🍷 **Drinking & Nightlife**

★ **Monkey Lala**   BAR
(Playa El Tunco) Everyone's new favorite Tunco sunset spot, this gorgeous cocktail bar is to the left of the main beach. Crisp electronic beats are the default sound, as well-heeled locals and savvy travelers mingle above the sand. Karaoke every Friday, BBQ on Sundays and a few surprises in between, Monkey Lala should be the sign of things to come.

D'Rocas   CLUB
(☑2389-6313; Playa El Tunco; ⊗noon-2am Fri & Sat) Love it or not quite sure what you're

doing here yet again, D'Rocas converts from a hotel to a rowdy nightclub on weekends, when Salvadorans descend on El Tunco, dance to Latin anthems and drink stiff spirits poured into plastic cups by gorgeous staff.

Lab   BAR
The Lab staff concoct natural fruit-flavored alcoholic shots (US$1 to US$2) and invite leading DJs and Latin groups from across the country to test the dance-ability of each mix. It's a lot of fun in the dark.

ℹ **Getting There & Away**

Bus 80 from La Libertad goes as far as Playa El Sunzal. Beyond that, take the less frequent bus 192.

Santa Tecla

POP 133,601

As San Salvador has started to creak under social and infrastructure difficulties, the city of Santa Tecla (or Nueva San Salvador), 15km southwest, has ever so slowly gentrified, particularly in the area around Paseo El Carmen. This pedestrian-only strip turns into a market each weekend and every day during summer, then into a happening nightspot, with cafes, bars, restaurants and even furniture stores serving a noticeably relaxed crowd.

Taxis cost around US$12 one way from San Salvador.

🛏 **Sleeping**

Santa Tecla has a number of guesthouses popping up around Paseo El Carmen.

Hotel El Portal De Las Colinas   HOTEL **$**
(☑2287-2544; Calle Poniente 5-4; s/d US$10/13) This brand new hotel and restaurant is a gregarious establishment where acoustic music plays live on weekends. The rooms have wooden floors and attractive greenery. Excellent value for a location close to the action.

Hotel Jardin del Carmen   HOTEL **$$**
(☑2519-6487; www.hoteljardindelcarmen.com; 7a Calle Oriente 7-8; s/d US$28/35; P❄🛜) Carmen is the pick of the hotels near the eponymous pedestrian-only area and the most experienced at dealing with travelers. The tiled rooms are tasteful and spacious. There are generous discounts for longer stays.

✗ Eating

Eating options are quite varied in Santa Tecla, with many restaurants getting especially busy on weekends.

Cafe Caracol   INTERNATIONAL $$

(☑ 7730-6502; Paseo El Carmen; $8-12; ☉ 4-11pm) This classy cafe in the heart of Paseo El Carmen personifies the weekend demographic of Santa Tecla. The international menu is accompanied by a fine wine list, and an extensive range of coffee-infused drinks and cocktails.

Teklebab   MIDDLE EASTERN $$

(☑ 7910-1482; 5a Av Norte 2-13; mains US$6-14) Expect excellent Turkish-influenced cuisine in this hip restaurant and bar with the requisite hookah lounge.

Happy Coffee   CAFE $$

(☑ 2532-9918; Av Rio Amazonas 3, Antiguo Cuscatlan; burgers US$5-6, espresso US$1.50; ☉ 8am-5pm) This modern American-style coffee shop is the successful venture of a couple of young friends who love roasting the beans of their homeland. Coffee culture is slowly brewing in El Salvador, thanks to places like Happy.

🍷 Drinking & Nightlife

Santa Tecla is the place to be on Friday night for the hip young folks from San Salvador. Venues seem to alternate annually, but you won't go thirsty looking for the perfect place.

Hard Bar   BAR

(☑ 7468-2552; Calle Oriente 1, Paseo El Carmen; ☉ 3pm-late Thu-Sat) On a Friday night you won't go far wrong in any of the packed music venues along Paseo El Carmen; Hard Bar stood out to us for the bling factor.

ℹ Getting There & Away

Bus The 102 from La Libertad costs US$1 and takes 45 minutes.

Taxi To/from San Salvador costs about US$12.

WESTERN EL SALVADOR

Western El Salvador is a small region that somehow contains the majority of the country's attractions. The cloud forest and conical splendor of Parque Nacional Los Volcanes, the mysterious and at times unvisited Maya ruins at Tazumal, the Ruta de las Flores and a volcanic lake are all within a 90-minute drive of Santa Ana, the charming provincial capital with the finest plaza in El Salvador.

From the wilds of Parque Nacional El Imposible near the Guatemalan border – where you can find pumas, boars and tigrillos – traverse waterfalls until you pick up the famed Flower Route, a pin-up region of hot springs, food fairs and artisan villages.

Indeed, if you fly into San Salvador, you can reach it all in a day and end at the far western tip at Barrio de Santiago, a windswept beach with massive surf where turtles lay eggs by moonlight.

Parque Nacional Los Volcanes

With three major volcanoes in hiking distance – one prehistoric, one impossibly steep and one recently exhausted – the burning heart of El Salvador is justifiably a highlight for many travelers to the country.

Active Volcán Izalco is the youngest in the group. Its cone began forming in 1770 from a belching hole of sulfuric smoke and today stands 1910m high. Izalco erupted throughout the 20th century, spewing smoke, boulders and flames and earning its reputation as 'the lighthouse of the Pacific.' Today, this bare, perfect cone stands devoid of life in an otherwise fertile land.

Without Izalco's stark drama but 400m higher, Santa Ana (also known as Ilamatepec) is El Salvador's third-highest point. Its eruption in October 2005 triggered landslides that killed two coffee pickers and forced the evacuation of thousands. The barren and windy summit affords spectacular views of a steep drop into the crater on one side and Lago de Coatepeque on the other.

👁 Sights

Parque Nacional
Los Volcanes   NATIONAL PARK

(admission US$3, guide US$8; ☉ 8am-5pm) Alongside volcanoes in triplicate, Parque Nacional Los Volcanes boasts hectares of lush forest that provide sanctuary for hundreds of migrating bird species, including emerald toucanets, woodpeckers and 17 species of hummingbird. The national park is easily accessible via a paved road that leads all the way to the visitor center.

★ Activities

Four-hour guided hikes to either volcano (Izalco US$1, Santa Ana US$2) leave at 11am sharp; this means you can't do both in one day. Wear sturdy shoes. A short alternative is a 40-minute nature trail that offers views of the lake and Volcán Santa Ana. All hikes start from the carpark, near the park entrance.

🛏 Sleeping

Campground CAMPGROUND **$**
(☑2483-4713, 2483-4679; campsite per person US$2) A local cooperative manages a rustic campground, 13km from San Blas heading toward Los Andes. Los Andes has a ranger who can also guide Santa Ana hikes (US$35 for a two-person hike). For information, contact SalvaNatura (p302) in San Salvador.

Casa de Cristal CABINS **$$**
(☑2483-4713; jm78755@gmail.com; cabins per person US$12-18) Casa de Cristal has rustic *cabañas* and is a popular meeting point for hikes. Call ahead for availability.

Campo Bello CABINS **$$**
(☑2271-0853; r US$25-60) Wake up in a concrete igloo surrounded by volcanoes. Bizarrely beautiful.

❶ Getting There & Away

Arrive by 11am as the guided hikes leave just once a day. The easiest, surest route is to come from Santa Ana, where bus 248 goes all the way to the entrance. The last bus leaves the park at 5pm, but verify times with the driver who drops you off.

Leave early from San Salvador to make connections. Take any bus to Santa Ana and disembark at El Congo on the Carretera Panamericana; walk uphill to the overpass and catch bus 248.

If you're driving, Parque Nacional Los Volcanes is 67km from San Salvador via Sonsonate or 77km by the more scenic route toward Santa Ana.

Lago de Coatepeque

Approaching Lago de Coatepeque via road, visitors are surprised at the dramatic beauty of the 6km-wide sparkling blue caldera. You'll notice many cars slowing down at the *mirador* when the lake first comes into view. It's also remarkably free of crowds – mostly as the majority of properties dotting the lake's edge are privately owned by San Salvador's elite – and you can swim, dive or splash about in a boat without fear of the dreaded blue-green algae.

For around US$5, day-trippers can enjoy lake access at one of the hotels on the northeast shore. For US$20 you can rent a boat for a couple of hours.

🛏 Sleeping

Hostal Amacuilco HOSTEL **$**
(☑7834-9843; hostalamacuilco@hotmail.com; El Congo; dm US$8, d US$20-30; ❇@❇) This popular hostel has moved to the small village at the top of the road into Coatepeque. The sleeping options include tidy dorms and five double rooms. There's a compact pool in a tropical garden, a book exchange, a free shuttle to the lake, and highly recommended Spanish lessons onsite.

Rancho Alegre HOTEL **$$**
(☑7888-0223; Carretera al Cerro Verde Km 53.5; q US$40; ❇) One of the few public places with a lakeside setting, Rancho Alegre can get busy on weekends with its seafood restaurant and cheesy poolside 'day-club.' There are some neat bungalows close to the road, but you need a group to make it worth the price.

Hotel Torremolinos HOTEL **$$**
(☑2441-6037; r from US$30) You can usually get a bed at this crumbling old dame, which is about all it has going for it other than the lakeside location. The restaurant makes delicious seafood pastas (US$8).

🍴 Eating

El Gran Mirador SEAFOOD **$$**
(☑7822-4251; mains US$5-10) Eat fresh *mojarro* fish from the lake at this seafood restaurant with 'the view.' It's on your left, just past El Congo village, about halfway down the road from Santa Ana.

❶ Getting There & Away

Buses 220 and 242 depart Santa Ana for the lake every half-hour (US$0.50, 45 minutes). The last return bus to Santa Ana leaves at 6pm.

Santa Ana

POP 176,660

Only 65km from the capital, Santa Ana is a mid-sized El Salvadoran city, the longstanding coffee wealth of which is reflected in its architecture, some of the most magnificent in Central America. There's a relaxed confidence in the wide, tree-lined streets

Santa Ana

Santa Ana

◎ **Sights**
1 Catedral de Santa Ana C1
2 Iglesia El Calvario B1
3 Iglesia El Carmen C2

🛏 **Sleeping**
4 Casa Verde B2

🍽 **Eating**
5 Café Expresión Cultural B3
6 Cafe Santaneco C1
7 El Sin Rival D2
8 Food Stands C1
9 Pastelería Ban Ban C1

🍸 **Drinking & Nightlife**
10 Los Cuñados B1
11 Simmer Down C1

🎭 **Entertainment**
12 Teatro de Santa Ana C1

and colorful houses, and Santanecos are genuinely proud of their growing cultural scene. Smart travelers are choosing Santa Ana as an alternative base to the capital for exploring Lago de Coatepeque, the Maya ruins at Tazumal or the Ruta de las Flores.

◎ **Sights**

Catedral de Santa Ana CATHEDRAL
(1a Av Norte; ⊙7am-12:30pm & 2:30-7pm) The most notable sight in Santa Ana is its large neo-Gothic cathedral, which was completed in 1913. Exquisite ornate moldings cover the church's front, while interior pillars and high archways are painted in slate and pink stripes, enhancing a sense of stillness and spaciousness. A spooky figure of the city's patron saint, Nuestra Señora de Santa Ana, greets you as you enter.

Iglesia El Carmen
CHURCH

(7a Calle Oriente; ⊙7am-7pm) Santa Ana's trifecta of Catholic churches is rounded out by El Carmen, which was damaged during the 2001 quake after nearly two centuries of fortitude. Visitors are welcome.

Iglesia El Calvario
CHURCH

(10a Av Norte; ⊙7am-6pm) El Calvario has undergone numerous hardships and catastrophes since its initial construction in the early 19th century. Today, it's a pensive place that serves the community. Visitors are welcome.

🛏 Sleeping

★Casa Verde
HOSTEL $

(✉English 7856-4924, Spanish 7840-4896; www.hostalcasaverde.com; 7a Calle Poniente; dm/r incl breakfast US$10/25; P❋🛜🏊) Carlos and his team at Casa Verde display the kind of resourceful, conscientious hospitality that makes this country such a joy to visit. From the roof terrace, all post-travel calm will be restored, particularly at sunset. Dorm rooms are generously sized, with single-level beds, small tables and ample storage, plus there are two spotless kitchens and a lounge area to meet other travelers.

Hostal Vital Yek
HOSTEL $

(✉2455-4899; realtripses7@outlook.es; 15a Av Norte, Barrio Santa Cruz; dm/d US$8/16) Grungy little Vital Yek is a fun addition to the Santa Ana travel scene – don't be put off by the crumbling exterior. Popular with local musicians and artists, the narrow hang-out area is covered in graffiti and plant life. The double rooms are very clean and comfortable, the kitchen is big enough to cater for a party and there's talk of a bar.

Casa Frolaz
B&B $

(✉2440-5302; 29a Calle Poniente; per person US$8) Francisco is a cultured gentleman who politely scrutinizes travelers' itineraries from the comfort of his splendid open home. Each double room has a small balcony and guests can enjoy the kitchen and garden. It's located in a quiet street near a supermarket.

Villa Napoli
B&B $$

(✉7985-6021; www.villanapoli.hostel.com; Quinta del Moral Km 62-63; d US$20-30; P❋🛜🏊) Rosa is a natural host and the Napoli is a restful, stylish guesthouse on the road out of Santa Ana, where the gardens grow wilder and the houses were built for an extended family. The pool area will lure you in for the long term. Guests can be picked up at Café Expresión – a good idea, as signs are hard to follow.

🍴 Eating

El Rincon Tipico de El Sopón
SALVADORAN $

(✉2440-5697; 3a Av Sur; mains US$3-5; ⊙11am-10pm; 🛜) This is a terrific place to try hearty Salvadoran stews, barbecued meats and fresh salads. The homemade soft drinks are a hit. There is often live music on weekends.

Pastelería Ban Ban
BAKERY $

(Av Independencia Sur; pastries US$0.50-2.50; ⊙8am-7pm) Ban Ban is all over the country, but it started in Santa Ana and the locals like to celebrate their hometown each mid-afternoon over sublime cakes and pastries.

El Sin Rival
ICE CREAM $

(Calle Libertad Oriente; cones US$0.50-1; ⊙9am-9pm) This outfit has been making ice cream and sorbet (and amazing fruit cones) for decades. Try the tart *arrayán* (a bittersweet local fruit) or *mora* (blackberry).

Cafe Santaneco
SALVADORAN $

(✉2447-8431; Calle Libertad Poniente; mains US$2-4; ⊙7am-4pm) Every Santaneco and his dog tuck in to fresh *comida a la vista* at this inner-city eatery with green and yellow walls.

Food Stands
FAST FOOD $

(1a Av Norte; mains US$1-2; ⊙7am-8pm) Hit the row of food stands on the plaza for enormous chicken sandwiches in soft bread, burgers and greasy fries.

★Inna Jammin
INTERNATIONAL $$

(✉2400-5757; Av Indepencia Sur; pizzas small/large US$3/10; ⊙11am-11pm; P🛜🍽) The Rasta vibe flows over two levels in this happening new restaurant with a broad international menu. The pizzas rate highly, but the Salvadoran grills are exceptional and the cocktails are generously poured. The atmosphere, though, is reason enough to come; cool young staff flit about, reggae tunes blast (occasionally live) and Santanecos celebrate life for the sake of it.

★Café Expresión Cultural
CAFE $$

(✉2440-1410; 11a Calle Poniente, btwn 6a & 8a Av Sur; mains US$4-8; ⊙7am-6pm Mon-Sat; 🛜🚻) This versatile establishment is a favorite among intellectuals and artists who come for the live music and the well-stocked bookshop. Tourists and young lovers enjoy the big breakfasts, fine coffee and accessible art. Ignore the nefarious street life and take refuge in the outside garden.

🍷 Drinking & Nightlife

★ Trenchtown Rock   CLUB
(Carretera Panamericana desvío a Chalchuapa; ☺7pm-late Wed-Sat) This thumping outdoor club on the outskirts of Santa Ana is spontaneous and friendly and can bob up as a highlight of a trip to the whole country for those who like to dance to reggae and ska. There's a shop selling handicrafts, a beer-friendly menu including killer baked potatoes, and a sound system to chant down Babylon. Ja! Ja!

Simmer Down   BAR
(☑2484-7511; 1a Av Norte; ☺10am-2am) Overlooking the cathedral, this busy bar serves ice-cold beer and creates a festive atmosphere week-round. The natural wooden furniture belies the urban setting.

Los Cuñados   BAR
(cnr Calle Libertad Poniente & 10 Av Sur 25; ☺8am-9:30pm) Drink tall glasses of freezing beer at this downtown watering hole with sticky floors and big-screen TVs.

☆ Entertainment

Teatro de Santa Ana   THEATER
(☑2447-6268; cnr Av Independencia Sur & 2a Calle Poniente; US$1.50; ☺8am-noon & 2-6pm Mon-Fri, 8am-noon Sat) The Teatro de Santa Ana is an opulent renaissance-style building constructed using funds from an export tax on coffee beans. The epitome of wealth, excess and culture, it features stained-glass windows, marble staircases and immaculate detail. In 1933, it was converted into a movie house, and, after a hefty facelift, is now a theater again (tickets around US$5).

Cinemark   CINEMA
(www.cinemark.com.sv; cnr Av Independencia & 35a Av Poniente; US$3; ☺10am-10pm) For Hollywood action flicks and the occasional tear-jerker.

ℹ Information

Ciberworld (Av Independencia Sur, btwn 9a & 11a Calle Poniente; per hour US$1; ☺8am-7:30pm Mon-Sat, 9am-6pm Sun) Friendly service.

Citibank (cnr Independencia Sur & 3a Calle Oriente; ☺8am-4:30pm Mon-Fri, to noon Sat) Has an ATM.

Post Office (Av Independencia Sur; ☺7:30am-5pm Mon-Fri, to noon Sat)

Red Cross (☑2441-2645, 2447-7213; cnr 1a Av Sur & 3a Calle Oriente; ☺24hr)

ℹ Getting There & Away

Central Bus Terminal (cnr 10a Avenida Sur & 15a Calle Poniente)

Metapán
POP 19,145

A new freeway connecting Metapán to La Palma may see more travelers discovering this hot agricultural capital, which makes a charming detour from the wilds of the bigger cities.

Metapán is a comfortable and convenient base for forays into Parque Nacional Montecristo, the country's most inaccessible and exotic national park. The park is closed from May to November to let the wildlife breed in peace; when it is open you need a 4WD vehicle to get there.

🏃 Activities

Apuzunga Water Park   RAFTING
(☑2483-8952; www.apuzunga.com; entry US$3, rafting trips per person US$50) Apuzunga is one

BUSES FROM SANTA ANA

DESTINATION	BUS	COST (US$)	DURATION
Ahuachapán	210	0.75	1hr
Lago de Coatepeque	220, 242	0.40	1¼hr
San Cristóbal (Guatemalan border)	236	0.50	1hr
San Salvador directo	201	1	1½hr
San Salvador especial	201e	1.30	1¼hr
Sonsonate	216	0.75	1¼hr
Tazumal, Chalchuapa	218	0.25	30min

ROCK THE VOLCANO

Strato-, lava-domed, shield or conical, dormant or active or just a casual smoker, there's a volcano type for every budding geologist in El Salvador, often within easy reach.

Parque Nacional Los Volcanes (p310) Less than hour from the capital, three significant volcanoes vie for your attention in this lush national park.

Volcán Izalco (p310) Otherworldly Izalco snakes to the sky. Climb Santa Ana to see it rise through the clouds, with the Pacific Ocean in the background.

Quezaltepeque (p290) When life in the big city gets you down, look up to see San Salvador's highest point; juvenile El Boquerón volcano peeks through its top.

Volcán Chaparrastique (p329) This eastern beauty looms large over the city of San Miguel and can be climbed in a day.

Lago de Coatepeque (p311) A crystal-blue caldera, ideal for swimming or fishing for sweet *mojarro*.

of the better known and most developed of the thermal-springs resorts in El Salvador. The real plus here are the rapids running below the bar-restaurant (mains US$5 to US$12). They are surprisingly fast after the wet season.

🛏 Sleeping

Hostal de Metapan HOSTEL $
(☑2402-2382; 2 Calle Oriente; d incl breakfast US$20; P🅿❄🛜) The owners make every effort to make out-of-towners feel welcome in this functional small hotel that opened a few years ago. The interior design feels like the set of a 1990s TV romance.

★Hostal Villa Lemon HOSTEL $$
(☑2442-0149; cottages US$55; P🅿) Hostal Villa Lemon is a collection of three forest cottages that can each sleep four people comfortably, possibly more. It is located 14km north of Metapán near a spectacular waterfall at Reserva Ecologica El Limo. Call ahead to arrange pick up from Metapán; if driving, take the dusty road toward Frontera Anguiatú then continue straight until you see the signs.

Hostal Villa Blanca BOUTIQUE HOTEL $$
(☑2402-3383; www.hostalvillablanca.com; Av Isidro Menendez 4; s/d US$30/45; P🅿❄🛜) The smartest choice in town is this new hotel in the quaint old quarter. The pristine tile floors keep the place cool, while the spacious rooms are brightened up with colorful furniture. It is popular with honeymooners and hikers.

🍴 Eating

El Portal Colonial SALVADORAN $
(mains US$3-6) Next to Iglesia San Pedro you will find this thriving, friendly *típico* restaurant that does top-value lunch deals for under US$4, including a drink and tortillas. Recommended are the *pollo al horno* (baked chicken) or *carne a la parilla* (grilled meat), which come direct from the farm butcher.

★Balompie Sports Bar & Cafe CAFE $$
(☑2402-3567; 3 Av Norte 17; pupusas US$1-2, mains US$4-8; ⏰10am-1pm Wed-Sun) Fronting the town square and backing onto Metapán's football stadium, this incongruously good sports bar is more than a place to sink beers and cheer on *Los Caleros*. Here you can sit on a sunny terrace and enjoy authentic Salvadoran food and agreeable service. Entrance is via a concrete arch leading to a staircase.

ℹ Information

Scotiabank (Av Ignacio Gómez; ⏰8am-4:30pm Mon-Fri, to noon Sat) Exchanges traveler's checks and has a 24-hour ATM.

ℹ Getting There & Away

The bus terminal sits on the highway facing the entrance to town. For Santa Ana, take bus 235 (US$0.90, 1½ hours) or a *directo* (US$2.50, one hour). San Salvador bus 201A (US$2.50, 1¾ hours) departs seven times daily. Bus 235 and microbuses go to the Guatemalan border at Anguiatú (US$0.50, 30 minutes); the last leaves at 6:30pm. Bus 463 departs at 5:30am and noon daily for the gorgeous and hair-raising haul over

EL SALVADOR METAPÁN

the mountains to Citalá (US$2, three hours), close to the Honduran border crossing at El Poy.

Agencia Puerto Bus (🖉 2440-1608; 25a Calle Poniente)

Chalchuapa

POP 83,060

The plains town of Chalchuapa is known as the home of Tazumal, a pre-Columbian settlement featuring the finest ruins in El Salvador. The friendly central neighborhood of low-rise multi-colored houses with crumbling colonial exteriors is pleasant to walk around.

In the nearby suburbs, Laguna Cuzcachapa is a natural sulfur pond and a mystical place of great significance in Maya culture. Locals suggest coming here when faced with difficult decisions, but beware the *siguanaba* (a mythical creature that poses as a beautiful woman to lure solo male travelers)! You can swim in natural springwater pools at El Trapiche (location of the first Maya settlement in 2000 BC) or jump into a waterfall in Salto El Espino.

◉ Sights & Activities

Tazumal   RUIN
(US$3; ⊙ 9am-5pm Tue-Sun) Archaeologists estimate that the verdant Tazumal area was first settled around 5000 BC. Part of a 10-sq-km zone, much is still buried under Chalchuapa's more basic housing. The latest restoration, inaugurated in December 2006, restored the original stone-and-mortar construction in much of the ruins. A chain-link enclosure prevents visitors walking on the pyramids, but their close proximity to everyday Salvadoran life connect the site to the present in a powerful way.

Casa Blanca   RUIN
(US$3; ⊙ 9am-5pm Tue-Sun) Across the highway from the Tazumal site sits Casa Blanca, home to some Preclassic ruins and an indigo workshop where you can dye your own fabrics.

Rasta Maya Tours   TOUR
(🖉 2408-0344; www.rastamaya.com; 5 Av Sur Casa 6, Barrio Apaneca, btwn Calles 1 & 3 Oriente) Based near the ruins of Tazumal, former English teacher Jorge and his vibrant young team put real heart into curating offbeat adventures. Tours like Aguas Termales (Hot Springs) and Ruta Ancestral are unique and a lot of fun.

🛌 Sleeping

There are a few cheap (and nasty) places to stay, plus one decent guesthouse. Most folk opt for Santa Ana.

Hostal Las Flores   GUESTHOUSE **$$**
(🖉 2408-1098; Av 2 de Abril; r US$25-35; ❋) The only real choice in town is luckily more than satisfactory. The former colonial residence of a wealthy Santaneco, this boutique hotel consists of a dozen bright rooms, a yellow tiled internal courtyard and flourishing garden, and fastidious staff. It's walking distance to Tazumal.

✖ Eating

The town is known for the prevalence of *chilate,* a nourishing drink made of corn, served with *camote* (sweet potato) and sugary *buñuelos* (cassava), as well as its *yuka* (yam) with roasted pork – a national delicacy. The stalls lining the road into Tazumal serve excellent *comida típica*.

La Rinconchita   SALVADORAN **$$**
(cnr Av 2 de Abril & 6a Calle Poniente; mains US$5-9; ⊙ noon-10pm Sat, to 6pm Sun) This bar-restaurant on a popular corner serves *pupusas* and spicy *ceviches* alongside contemporary cocktails to a predominantly younger crowd.

❶ Getting There & Away

Bus 218 comes from Santa Ana, 14km (30 minutes) away. A sign on the main road through Chalchuapa points toward the ruins, about a five-minute walk from the highway. If driving from Santa Ana, stay right at the fork in the road, continuing toward Ahuachapán, then turn left at the Texaco station in Chalchuapa. The ruins are at the end of the road.

Ruta de las Flores

Traveling the La Ruta de las Flores, slowly and purposefully, is like a meander through the story of El Salvador. It's a searingly beautiful series of villages, each with a mix of colonial architecture in indigenous tones. Those who like the good life can feast on local food, particularly at the weekend markets, browse the craft *tiendas,* or undertake firsthand research into why El Salvadoran coffee is renowned across the world. If the pace is too slow, you can hit the Cordillera Apaneca, a volcanic mountain range filled with waterfalls, mountain-bike trails, and pine forest hikes where white flowers bloom in May.

In 1932 this region witnessed the horrible Peasant Massacre, when mostly Nahuatl coffee farmers were slaughtered by government troops for an attempted insurrection and mass protest. The actual number of deaths still varies, but 30,000 people is a close estimate.

ℹ Getting There & Away

Bus 249 runs frequently between Sonsonate and Ahuachapán, stopping in all the towns along the way, including Juayúa, Apaneca and Ataco.

Ahuachapán

POP 38,110

Ahuachapán is either the beginning or end of the Ruta de las Flores, depending on which direction you roll. Either way, it's a prosperous, small provincial capital that supplies 15% of the country's electrical power thanks to the wonders of geothermal energy. There are some attractive colonial buildings, but for travelers it's mostly a jumping-off point for trips to Parque Nacional El Imposible or Ataco.

◉ Sights

Nuestra Señora de Asunción   CHURCH
This church east of Plaza Concordia has pretty *azulejo* floors and a stained-glass Virgin.

Plaza Concordia   PLAZA
Green gardens and palms make Plaza Concordia an agreeable stop to catch a breeze. The kiosk occasionally holds concerts and free events.

⌷ Sleeping

Termales de Santa Teresa   RESORT $
(☏2423-8041; www.termalesdesantateresa.com; r Spanish/French/Japanese-themed US$25/45/50) In a region famed for its hot springs, Santa

Teresa surpasses expectations. You can opt for the bathing only (US$10), or sleep it off in kitsch splendor. Coffee plantation tours can be arranged. To get here, take the road toward Ataco for 2km, then turn left (it's signed) and drive for another 2km.

Hotel Casa Blanca   HOTEL $$
(☏2443-1505; cnr 2a Av Norte & Calle Barrios; s/d with fan US$25/35, with air-con US$35/65; P❋@☀) Set inside an old mansion filled with colonial-style furniture, this slightly ostentatious hotel is a fine choice to start your journey down the Ruta de las Flores. The eight rooms are a little cluttered and the color schemes disarming, but the beds are heavenly and every piece serves a purpose. Take your coffee in the internal courtyard, which speaks to an earlier time.

La Casa de Mamapan   B&B $$
(☏2413-2507; www.lacasademamapan.com; cnr 2a Ave Sur & Pasaje La Concordia; s/d US$26/52; P❋🛜) Mamapan is a 19th-century house opposite Plaza Concordia that celebrates authentic Salvadoran life in the food, artwork and quiet respectfulness of the owners. The rooms are modest and functional, with comfortable, dark wooden beds and very clean bathrooms.

✖ Eating

Las Mixtas   SALVADORAN $
(cnr 2a Av Sur & 1a Calle Poniente; mains US$4-5; ⊙8am-9pm) Colorful and friendly and teeming with young couples, Las Mixtas serves, you guessed it, *mixtas,* which is basically a sloppy sandwich filled with too much of everything, including pickled vegetables. Locals rave about the ice-cold *licuados* (fresh fruit drinks).

La Casa Grande   SALVADORAN $
(Av Norte 4a; mains US$4-6; ⊙noon-10pm) Rabbit and venison head the otherwise standard

EL SALVADOR RUTA DE LAS FLORES

BUSES FROM AHUACHAPÁN

DESTINATION	BUS	COST (US$)	DURATION
Las Chinamas	263	0.60	40min
San Salvador	202	1.25	3hr
San Salvador especial	202e	2	1¼hr
Santa Ana	210	0.75	1hr
Sonsonate directo	23	1.25	1½hr
Sonsonate via Apaneca & Juayúa	249	0.95	2hr
Tacuba	264 or Ruta 15	0.70	45min

menu at this only real 'nightspot' in town; there are cheap-ish beds (US$12) out the back, but only stay if you must.

La Estancia
SALVADORAN $

(1a Av Sur btwn Calle Barrios & 1a Calle Oriente; mains US$2-4; ⊘7am-6pm Mon-Sat) Seats for the *típico* buffet lunch at this colonial-era building fill with business folk during the week and young families on weekends. Enjoy eating among the stuffed animals.

ⓘ Information

Banco de America Central (3a Calle Oriente; ⊘8am-5pm Mon-Fri, to noon Sat) Changes Amex and Visa traveler's checks.

Ciber Café Cetcomp (cnr 2a Av Sur & 1a Calle Poniente; per hour US$0.60; ⊘9am-8pm Mon-Fri, 9:30am-8:30pm Sat, 10am-9pm Sun)

ⓘ Getting There & Away

Buses line Av Menéndez at 10a Calle Oriente, one block north of Parque Central. Buses for the Guatemalan border at Las Chinamas leave from 8a Calle Poniente, at the northwest corner of Parque Menéndez. Note that for Santa Ana you can also take the faster San Salvador bus, get off at Metrocentro and catch a local bus into town.

Apaneca

POP 8460

Apaneca means 'river of the wind' in Nahuatl, and there is a definite cooling in the air in El Salvador's second-highest town (1450m). One of the country's prettiest places to visit, its cobbled streets and colorful ado-

---

AGUA TERMALES
....

El Salvador's volcanic activity is always bubbling just beneath the surface in the hot or cold *aguas termales* (thermal springs). Apart from the restorative benefits of swimming in the clean, clear water, these natural pools provide a charming entrée into local life where families and teenagers gather to natter and relax. Most are (moderately) supervised and you can usually buy drinks and snacks inside. Entry is around $1. There are dozens scattered around the country, but they are especially prominent around Ahuachapán, Santa Ana, Metapan and San Miguel. Look for a squiggly whirlpool sign off any main road...and jump right in!

---

be houses are largely untouched by tourism, while its cottage craft industry is highly revered. The surrounding Sierra Apaneca Ilamatepec is a hiker's paradise.

The beautiful Iglesia San Andres was one of the oldest churches in the country until the 2001 earthquake reduced it to rubble, but it has been rebuilt with a similar appearance.

◎ Sights

Finca Santa Leticia
FARM

(☑2433-0357; www.hotelsantaleticia.com; Km 86.5) Finca Santa Leticia is a coffee farm and restaurant just south of Apaneca. The highlights of the small onsite archaeological park (admission US$5) are two pot-bellied figures carved from huge basalt boulders, weighing between 6350kg and 11,000kg. Experts speculate that these 2000-year-old chubbies were created by early Maya in deference to their rulers. The attached hotel is overpriced, but may suit families or groups.

🏃 Activities

Vivero Alejandra
TOUR

(⊘7am-4pm Wed-Sun) FREE *Vivero* (nursery) tours make for a relaxed afternoon of strawberries, strong coffee and rare plants. Vivero Alejandra is a short walk from the center (toward Juayúa) and is the pick of the few.

Apaneca Canopy Tours
ADVENTURE TOUR

(☑2433-0554; 2hr tour US$35) An excellent zip-line experience covering a dozen cables and 2.5km of mountain forest. Tours leave daily at 9:30am, 11:30am, 2pm and 4pm.

Apaneca Aventura
ADVENTURE TOUR

(☑2612-7034; www.503apanecabuggies.wix.com/ apanecaadventure; 4a Av Norte; 2hr tour for 2 people US$60) A convoy of dirt buggies in the quiet village of Apaneca jolts the senses, but it is good, honest, dirty fun to roar down to Laguna Verde with this popular outfit.

🛏 Sleeping

Hostal II Piemonte
HOSTEL $

(☑7739-5830; Av 2 Sur 4; dm/d US$8/15; ❋🅿) Italian Massimo has opened his home (and his action-figurine collection) to budget travelers, and the town is better for it. Natural light fills the well-kept rooms and hikers will appreciate the homemade pasta.

Laguna Verde Guest House
CHALET $

(☑7859-2865, 2102-8575; gpssal@intercom.com. sv; dm/d $15/35) For those wanting a more

BEAN TO CUP: EL SALVADOR'S GOURMET COFFEE SCENE

Coffee beans from El Salvador are revered across the globe. Yet with the world's middle class largely obsessed with coffee, it can be surprising to the visitor just how complacent the average Salvadoran is toward their daily brew. In short, it's hard to find a decent latte in the country, despite its leading producers exporting such a high quantity per capita. This may be slowly changing due to the global interest in carefully sourcing each bean, as boutique coffee roasters try to distinguish their drink from the competition and lessen the exploitation of the 'middle man.'

In towns like Juayúa, Ataco, La Palma, Metapán and Alegría, the next generation of coffee plantation owners are leading a vanguard in coffee culture. Rather than settling for the mass market, where wages are low, work is steady, and the beans are torn green from the tree, many Salvadorans are responding to an increasing demand, both here and abroad, for an authentic, nuanced blend of beans that reflects the quality of the volcanic soil, high altitude and hot climate.

Perhaps the watery cup you are served in El Salvador will soon be tipped down the sink, for everyone's economic, social and culinary benefit. Hipsters of the world unite!

rural setting, but don't want to be too far from civilization, Laguna Verde is an easy compromise. It's 3km from Apaneca near the volcanic Cuyanausal Range. Choose between a dormitory or a larger chalet, each in its own clever log structure. Hiking options abound; call ahead to arrange pick-up.

Solvang Hostal HOSTEL $$
(📞7025-5862; jc_artero1923@hotmail.com; Av 15 de Abril Norte; s/d US$20/40; 🛜) More like a house than a hostel, this mustard-colored corner building in the center of town has been fitted anew, from the kitchen appliances to the dining set. It feels like a sharehouse for 20-somethings, decorated by one of their mothers. Still, it's a good place to self-cater while on the Flower Route.

Hostal Colonial HOSTEL $$
(📞2433-0662; hostalcolonial_apaneca@hotmail.com; cnr 1a Av Sur & 6a Calle Poniente; d US$20-30; 🅿) Hostal Colonial has let sleeping travelers lie for longer than other small hostel operators in Apaneca, so gets a tick for longevity alone. The nine double rooms have colorful murals and open onto a bucolic garden.

🍴 Eating

Mercado Saludable MARKET $
(mains US$2-3; ⊙6:30am-8pm) Cheap eats deluxe, this market facing the park offers good little eateries serving ham, eggs and beans, and *atole* (a corn-based drink), as well as chicken dishes and *pupusas*.

⭐**El Jardin de Celeste** INTERNATIONAL $$$
(📞2433-0281; www.eljardindeceleste.com; mains US$8-17; ⊙9am-9pm; 🛜) This heavenly garden venue is one of the culinary highlights of the region and warrants a stay or, at the very least, a coffee and cake. Located between Apaneca and Ataco, Celeste is best enjoyed with friends, laughing and eating and celebrating the sub-tropical splendor. The log cabins (US$30 to US$50) are more than comfortable for your gang to lay flat in.

ℹ Getting There & Away

Buses drop off and pick up on the main street, right in front of the market. Bus 249 plies the route between Ahuachapán and Sonsonate, stopping in Apaneca every half-hour. The last bus runs between 7pm and 8pm. Ask a local to be sure.

Ataco
POP 12,910
Many people leave Ataco with a new favorite village in El Salvador. Brightly colored murals and artisan markets, cobblestone streets and colonial-era buildings, a congenial mountain setting and excellent, cheap dining and sleeping options, the sleepy Flower Route destination even gets a little festive on Saturday nights with live music spilling into the streets.

Water is a valuable resource in this mountainous region, and efforts are slowly being made to protect it; the discovery of decent ruins nearby may exacerbate the need to safeguard the town's charms for posterity.

Founded by the pre-Columbian Pipils, the next town along, Salcoatitán, has lots of tiny art galleries down cobblestone streets.

🛏 Sleeping

Meson de San Fernando   HOSTEL $
(☎7871-2126; Calle Poniente 1; dm/d US$10/20; P❉) The price is low and the service is satisfactory at San Fernando, but the walls are thin and the welcome can be perfunctory. The garden is well shaded.

Segen Hostel   HOSTEL $$
(☎2450-5832; alicanteapaneca@hotmail.com; Calle Poniente 3; dm/d $15/30; P❉🛜) Not much has changed in recent years at one of Ataco's best little hostels. Rooms are adequate for the price, the rooftop balcony is still a great place to watch the village go about its business, and the hosts still fuss over their guests. Entrance is via a locked gate; don't worry, someone's always home, usually Eduardo, the English-speaking owner.

Quinta El Carmen   BOUTIQUE HOTEL $$
(☎2243-0304; www.elcarmenestate.com; q incl breakfast from US$70; P❉🛜) The ubiquitous Cafe Ataco brand hails from this charming *finca,* which has been operating since the 1930s. Tours (US$5) are interesting, particularly walking through the plantations themselves, but the smart hotel is also a fabulous option for families, or for friends who overdo lunch in the popular restaurant (mains US$6 to US$12).

Raíces Hostal   GUESTHOUSE $$
(☎2512-4331; cnr Av Central & Calle Poniente 6; r from US$25; ❉🛜) This sparkling new guesthouse is dead quiet, even when busy, due to a lack of communal areas. Suits couples.

Villa Santo Domingo   HOSTEL $$
(☎2450-5442; hotel.villasantodomingo@gmail.com; d US$30; @) Beautiful gardens and a spread of local antiques and artworks round out a very pleasant hotel experience hidden inside this red-brick building.

🍴 Eating

KáfeKali   SALVADORAN $
(Parque Concepcion de Ataco; mains US$4-6; 🕘9am-9pm) This cafe rates as one of the best and most affordable places to eat in Ataco. Sit upstairs for views of the square while you feast on grilled meats, rice dishes, sticky puddings and chilled wine. It's on the western side of the *parque.*

★Café Tayua   CAFE $$
(1a Calle Poniente; meals US$5-12; 🕘8am-10pm Sun-Thu, to 11pm Fri & Sat) 'The night' just keeps on getting better. Homemade pizza, salads and gourmet sandwiches use fresh herbs from the garden out back, while the decadent sweet pastries are perfect for dunking in coffee. Live music bobs up on occasions, and purchasable artwork adorns the walls.

House of Coffee   CAFE $$
(☎2450-5353; Av Central; meals US$2-10; 🕘9am-7pm Mon-Fri, to 10pm Sat & Sun) All the fuss about the dark brown liquid comes to fruition at this simple outdoor cafe with black rattan chairs and a small coffee 'bar.' Plenty of decadent sweets to accompany your perfect espresso, but avoid the mains if possible.

La Caretta   SALVADORAN $$
(☎2450-5369; cnr Av Central & 4a Calle Poniente; mains $3-9) A fine *comida típica* place that also trades in colorful handicrafts. The *gallo en chicha* (rooster in corn liquor) is the best in town.

🛍 Shopping

Market   MARKET
(2a Av Sur; 🕘8am-5pm) Ataco's rambling market makes for a fascinating walkabout.

Diconte-Axul   CRAFTS
(cnr 2a Av Sur & Calle Central; 🕘8am-6pm) This store is popular for its homemade textiles, tie-dyes and hand-painted objects.

ℹ Information

Tourist Information Kiosk (🕘7am-7pm Sat & Sun)

ℹ Getting There & Away

Bus 249 stops on the corner of 2a Calle Oriente and 4a Av Sur. It heads north to Ahuachapán (US$0.35, 15 minutes); and south to Apaneca (US$0.25, 10 minutes), Juayúa (US$0.70, 30 minutes) and Sonsonate (US$0.80, one hour). Frequency is every 15 minutes.

Juayúa

POP 9935

Juayúa (why-ooh-ah) is the most-visited town on Ruta de las Flores due to its attractive cobbled streets, weekend food fair, and nearby waterfalls and hot springs. The fresh mountain air led to a rich indigenous settlement in the town where Nahuatl roots can still be seen in the craft aesthetic and high cheekbones.

Cristo Negro, or Black Christ, an important religious statue carved by Quirio Cataño in the late 16th century and housed in the church, is as significant as a symbol of change as for its obvious beauty.

Juayúa has a tumultuous past. Indigenous uprisings in the region ignited the revolutionary movement of 1932. Backed by the coffee elite, government forces brutally quelled the ill-organized insurrection.

A recommended hike and swim is to Los Chorros de Calera, a series of falls spewing from fractured cliffs to form large, cold pools. The Ruta de las Seite Cascadas follows the Río Bebedero over seven scenic drops. Consult Hotel Anáhuac or Casa Mazeta for directions or guides; a guide is recommended due to reported robberies en route. Other guided excursions include lake visits, coffee tours and waterfall rappels.

⚜ Festivals & Events

Fería Gastronómica FOOD
A popular food fair held every weekend.

🛏 Sleeping

★Casa Mazeta Hostal HOSTEL $
(⌨ 7252-8498; www.casamazeta.com; 1 Calle Poniente 22; dm/s/d US$9/20/25; 🅿 ❄ @) Mazeta is a superlative small hostel overseen by dashing owners who have decorated this converted home with panache. The double rooms are festooned with local fabrics and antique furniture, and the dorms are the stuff of guidebook legend, filled with character and free from dust.

★Hotel Anáhuac HOSTEL $
(⌨ 2469-2401; www.hotelanahuac.com; dm/s/d US$9/17/25; @) To many travelers, Hotel Anáhuac is synonymous with Juayúa. Space is used effectively throughout, from the internal breakfast garden to the upstairs double room above the trees to the spare bathroom near the entrance. Owner César is incredibly knowledgeable about the region and knows even more about coffee; do not miss the tour of his plantation and roastery (US$20), which includes unlimited incredible coffee.

Hotel Juayúa BOUTIQUE HOTEL $$
(⌨ 2469-2109; www.hotel-juayua.com; Final Av 6; r US$30-50; 🅿 ❄ 🛜 ☒) This charming property is perfect for families looking for a little run-around room. Lounging on the

manicured lawn by the sparkling swimming pool with flowering coffee plantations in the background is pretty easy to get used to. Some rooms are brighter than others (try number four or five), but all are spacious and stylish in a rustic kind of way.

Portezuelo Mountain LODGE $$
(⌨ 2265-1111; www.elportezuelo.com; Cantón San Juan de Dios; campsites US$5, raised tents d US$35, r/ste sleeping 4 US$55/65) If you're camping – or want to launch into nature from your backdoor – don't go past this funky lodge 6km from Juayúa. Loads of activities are on offer, including a ropes course, hiking, mountain biking and horse riding.

✖ Eating

Taquería la Guadalupana MEXICAN $
(2a Calle Oriente; mains US$2-7; ⊙ 11am-9pm Tue-Sun) Gaudy and loud, Guadalupana serves upstanding Mexican food, without much fanfare.

Tienda San José FAST FOOD $
(mains US$2-7; ⊙ 8:30am-11pm) This mini-mart doubles as a late-night grease joint. It's an inspired business model on the main plaza.

★R&R SALVADORAN, FUSION $$$
(⌨ 2452-2083; Calle Mercedes Caceres 1-4 Poniente; mains US$7-17; ⊙ 11am-10pm Tue-Sun) R&R is still the finest restaurant in Juayúa, and possibly in the whole Ruta de las Flores. The chef, Carlos, puts a twist on steaks, salads and Mexican food. Even when Juayúa is dead, the tables at this small, brightly painted corner building are filled with happy diners.

🍷 Drinking & Nightlife

★El Cadejo BAR
(⌨ 7603-5306; 3a Av Norte; mains US$4-10; ⊙ 11am-late Wed-Sat) Cadejo Brewery continues to grow its profile in El Salvador, and this hip cafe-bar does the reputation no harm whatsoever. All the Cadejo staples are matched by a creative food and cocktail menu. The real highlight though is the live-music scene, with lots of jazz, funk and experimental sounds cropping up in the art-laden courtyard. Worth the trip to Juayúa alone.

ℹ Information

Juayutur (Plaza de Juayúa; ⊙ 9am-5pm Sat & Sun) Juayúa's tourist agency dispenses information about the town and area excursions from its kiosk on the east side of the plaza.

Scotiabank (Calle Monseñor Óscar Romero) Exchanges traveler's checks, gives Visa advances and has an ATM.

❶ Getting There & Away

Bus 249 has services northwest to Apaneca (US$0.60, 20 minutes), Ataco (US$0.70, 30 minutes) and Ahuachapán (US$0.90, one hour) and also south to Sonsonate (US$0.80, 45 minutes) during daylight. Buses leave every 15 minutes from the park, or from four blocks west on weekends. For Santa Ana, bus 238 (US$0.75, 40 minutes) goes direct, leaving a few blocks west of Parque Central six times daily.

Sonsonate

POP 59,470

Sonsonate is a dusty city at the foot of Ruta de las Flores, which many travelers will pass through en route to beaches and volcanoes. There's a slightly rural feel in the jeans and boots of the cattle men, and a few attractive colonial-era buildings. There's not much need to hang about in 'Cincinatti' though, particularly at night, unless you're in town during Semana Santa, when half the province descends.

🛏 Sleeping

Hotel Orbe   HOTEL **$**
(☑ 2451-0469; cnr 4a Calle Oriente & 2a Av Flavian Muchi; s/d US$14/18, with air-con US$20/24; ❄) In a city low on accommodation options, Orbe is satisfactory, due mostly to the friendly faces and cleanliness. It's right downtown.

Hotel Plaza   HOTEL **$$**
(☑ 2451-6626; cnr 9a Calle Oriente & 8a Av Norte; s/d US$40/50; P❄⊠) This yellow, flat-roofed property has a good swimming pool and a restaurant. Its rooms are an ode to 1980s creature comforts, which appeal when darkness encroaches, and you can simply travel no further.

🍴 Eating

Food Stands   FAST FOOD **$**
(cnr 7a Calle Oriente & 10a Av Norte; ⊙5-10pm) For junk-food feasting, try these food stands where you can grab burgers, sandwiches, fries and *pupusas*.

La Casona   PUPUSERÍA **$**
(3 Calle Poniente btwn 1 & 3 Av Norte; mains US$1.50-4; ⊙8am-4pm Mon-Sat) *Comida a la vista* is dished up fresh and *pupusas* sizzle and steam in the city's best bargain restaurant, located in an antiquated building.

LA COCOTERA

El Salvador's only real luxury resort outside San Salvador, La Cocotera (☑2245-3691; www.lacocoteraresort. com; Barra de Santiago; d per person incl meals from US$128; @⊠) easily trumps those for conscious living and solitude. Located on the rugged oceanfront of Barra de Santiago, near the Guatemalan border, these six apartment-style rooms with king-sized beds open onto a long, empty beach surrounded by coconut and mango trees.

Only 4WDs can make it here, or you can approach by boat if you request it. Silence descends once the sun sets; there's no TVs or internet or, sometimes, any other people besides the attentive staff. The attention to locally sourced, environmentally sustainable materials throughout the property is exemplary.

❶ Information

Citibank (cnr Calle Marroquín & 4a Av Norte; ⊙8am-4:30pm Mon-Fri, to noon Sat) Has a 24-hour ATM.

Post Office (1a Av Norte, btwn 1 & 3 Calles Poniente; ⊙8am-5pm Mon-Fri, to noon Sat)

❶ Getting There & Away

Take a taxi or bus 53C from the central park to the bus station, 2km east of the city center. Buses to San Salvador leave from outside the terminal.

The terminal also serves Izalco (bus 53A), Nahuizalco (bus 53D) and Acajutla (bus 252). For Parque Nacional El Imposible take any La Hachadura bus to Puente Ahuachapío or Cara Sucia (US$0.50, 30 minutes). An alternative for Barra de Santiago is to take bus 259 to the turnoff and catch a pick-up.

Tacuba

POP 31,210

Tacuba is a small, pretty mountain outpost known to travelers as the access point for the wilds of Parque Nacional El Imposible (p323). At 680m and atop a one-way road, the lush, green setting mesmerizes first-time visitors, but its isolation is a double-edged sword. Tacuba is known in left-wing political circles as the site of the Americas' first communist revolution in 1932; today, sustainable tourism appears a more likely long-term hope to lift the town's economic fortunes.

✦ Activities

★ Imposible Tours   ADVENTURE TOUR
(☑ 2417-4268; www.imposibletours.com; Hostal de Mamá y Papá; hot pools tour US$20, waterfall tour US$30, 2-day Barria de Santiago tour US$65) It's worth going far out of the way for an Imposible Tour. Effervescent Manolo knows this land backwards and forwards and his passion for his backyard is infectious. Tours run from two hours to three days, depending on how deep into Imposible you are willing to venture.

🛏 Sleeping

Hostal de Mamá y Papá   HOSTEL $
(☑ 2417-4268; www.imposibletours.com; dm/d US$7/14; ☎) Mama runs Tacuba's best hostel, and luckily it exceeds all expectations for such a remote town. All the action takes place in the trellised garden where guitar music accompanies delicious home-cooked food (meals US$4). Rooms are large, clean and well priced, and include hot showers. There's an upstairs chill-out area with sublime views, while Manolo from Imposible Tours will attend to your every need.

La Cabaña   CABIN $$
(☑ 2417-4332; r US$30; ☎) Rustic cabins and big grounds; downhill from the square.

ℹ Getting There & Away

Bus 264 and Ruta 15 (US$0.70, 45 minutes, every 30 minutes 5:30am to 7pm) go to Ahuachapán from the main plaza.

Parque Nacional El Imposible

Parque Nacional El Imposible is the largest park in El Salvador and is named for the perilous gorge that claimed the lives of farmers and pack mules transporting coffee to the Pacific port. Decreed a national park in 1989, it sits in the Apaneca Ilamatepec mountain range between 300m and 1450m above sea level, and includes eight rivers that feed the watershed for Barra de Santiago and the mangrove forests along the coast.

⊙ Sights

Parque Nacional El Imposible   NATIONAL PARK
(US$6) Edging Guatemala, the mostly primary forest of Parque Nacional El Imposible shimmers with rivers and beautiful waterfalls. Hiking can get muddy and steep, but

offers grand vistas of misty peaks and the gleaming Pacific Ocean. The best time to visit is October to February, as the rainy season hinders travel. Entry is via one of two points – either from the north or the southeast.

The main San Benito entrance is on the southeast side, beyond the hamlet of San Miguelito. In theory you need to visit the San Salvador office of the park's administrators, SalvaNatura (p302), to pay the entry fee and arrange for guide service (there is no guide fee, but a US$5 tip is customary), however the reality is you can just turn up and pay. Otherwise, if entering from the north via Tacuba, you don't need to pay, but should ideally be with a guide as it gets dense pretty quickly. Try Imposible Tours for a range of excellent options.

Patient wildlife spotters can eye pumas, tigrillos, wild boars, antelope and anteaters, while twitchers will thrill to black-crested eagles, king hawks, motmots and hundreds of other bird species. Butterflies are also in abundance.

✦ Activities

Piedra Sellada   HIKING
A 4km trail to a swimming spot and a stone etched with Maya writings. Take the Los Enganches trail; just before the end another trail cuts upriver 1km to Piedra Sellada.

Los Enganches   HIKING
An ideal picnic spot, this big swimming hole is reached by a trail (3.5km one way), which passes Mirador El Mulo and descends steeply. Along the way you'll pass Mirador Madre Cacao, with views of the southeastern part of the park. Look for agoutis and coatis.

Cerro El Leon   HIKING
A tough 8km circuit topping out on one of the park's highest peaks (1113m), starting in a lush, humid gorge and climbing through dense forest. This trail offers terrific panoramic views. Allow several hours and bring plenty of water.

🛏 Sleeping

Hostal El Imposible   LODGE $$
(☑ 2405-6505;   www.hostalelimposible.com; s/d US$25/40, extra person US$10; ☎) This ecolodge is a good choice if you want to settle into park life or break up a couple of different hikes over two days. Each well-kept cabin can sleep up to six people. Coffee on the stone terrace or in a hammock after overcoming the Imposible is a must. It's 1km

from the park entrance and there's an organic restaurant that's popular with groups.

❶ Getting There & Away

From Sonsonate catch bus 259 toward La Hachadura and get off at Cara Sucia (US$1.75). From there, a bus leaves at 11am and a pick-up at 2pm (both US$2, one hour) for the main entrance. The trucks return to Cara Sucia every morning at 5:30am and 7:30am. If you think you might miss the pick-ups in Cara Sucia, you may be able to cut them off at Puente Ahuachapío (bridge), a few kilometers short of Cara Sucia. If the pick-ups have already passed, you may be able to hitch a ride (13.5km).

You can also visit the park from the northern side via Tacuba.

EASTERN EL SALVADOR

Most travelers race down the Carretera Interamericana in search of El Salvador's western attractions or, if heading east, the Nicaraguan border. However, the wild east of the country is a diverse geographical region that warrants greater consideration.

The quaint village of Alegría, the visceral war history around Morazán, and the long, sandy surf beaches near El Cuco and Las Flores will give even the most worldly traveler something to savor. They see only fleeting traffic from nearby cities such as San Miguel, the working-class capital with a distinctly cavalier attitude. Real off-the-beaten-track coastal adventure is found at Bahía de Jiquilisco, where birdlife soars, and in tiny fishing villages with little contact with the outside world.

Prior to the war, subsistence farming was long the primary means of survival here. The inevitable demand for nationwide land reform resonated throughout the poorer communities, and the northeast in particular became a fierce guerrilla stronghold. Far from the capital, these mountainous areas witnessed horrific atrocities – none worse than at El Mozote – but barely a village was spared from

the fighting, and the resilience of the locals will stir visitors for generations to come.

There are two ways to travel east – along the Carretera Interamericana or along the Carretera del Litoral (CA2); the latter accesses the beaches, and the former the northern reaches. The Ruta de La Paz (peace route; CA7) runs north from San Miguel.

San Vicente

POP 53,213

San Vicente is dwarfed by pointy Volcán Chichontepec in the Jiboa Valley. Look out for the equally dramatic behemoth of Torre Kiosko, an otherworldly clock tower that juts from the farmland like some Disneyland ride gone haywire. Home to many musicians, San Vicente is also very gay-friendly – come July, the annual Miss Gay San Vicente draws quite the crowd (and contestants!).

El Pilar, a beautiful colonial church built in the 1760s, was badly damaged by an earthquake; despite renovations, it remains closed.

🛏 Sleeping

Hotel Central Park HOTEL $
(☑ 2393-0383; r with fan/air-con US$10/15; ❋) New management have made some improvements at the only real sleeping option we could find. Come for the 2nd-floor terrace, if nothing else. The small bar is popular and the restaurant (open 6:30am to 10pm) below the hotel serves decent *típico* (regional specialties).

🍴 Eating

Jarro Cafe SALVADORAN $
(3a Calle Oriente; US$5-7; ⊙11am-10pm) Regular drinks specials, BBQ meats with rice and salad and a prime location on the park square make Jarro an amiable spot to while away an afternoon.

Comedor Rivolí SALVADORAN $
(1 Av Sur; mains US$2-4; ⊙7am-8:30pm) We ate ourselves silly at the Rivolí and laughed with

BUSES FROM SAN VICENTE

DESTINATION	BUS	COST (US$)	DURATION	DEPARTURES
Ilobasco	530	0.60	1hr	6:50am, 11am, 4pm
San Miguel	301 from the turnoff at the highway	1.50	1½hr	last bus 6pm
San Salvador	116	1	1½hr	last bus 6pm
Zacatecoluca	177	0.60	50min	

hedonistic delight at the taste and value of the *comida a la vista*, while seated beside rose gardens. How many *licuados* is too many *licuados?* Four.

ℹ Information

Citibank (2a Av Sur; ⏱8am-4:30pm Mon-Fri, to noon Sat) Cashes traveler's checks and has a 24-hour ATM.

Police (☎2303-7300, 2396-3353; cnr 1a Av Norte & 3a Calle Poniente) Can arrange for an escort up the volcano.

ℹ Getting There & Away

All buses pass by the Parque Central after leaving the bus terminal up the hill on 6a Calle and 15 Av. Beat the crowds at the park without hoofing it to the terminal by catching buses at 6a Calle and 2a Av. For Alegría, catch an eastward bus from the Carretera Interamericana and transfer at Villa El Triunfo.

Alegría

Happiness is an elusive state, but at least towns like Alegría exist to remind us to stop and smell the rose bushes in the town square. Arriving via a slow mountain pass, visitors are struck by the tranquillity of the place, that a *mirador* so grand could be seen from a family's kitchen table. There's not much to do per se – you can walk the town in half an hour – but a day at the lagoon, or an afternoon cafe-hopping, buying flowers and local crafts, could make for a wonderful rest day between hikes in the surrounding area.

The friendly tourist agency has a municipal office and a booth on the Parque Central. It also offers some worthy guided hikes (US$10 to US$15 per half day) to coffee plantations, geothermal plants and sites related to philosopher and native Alegrían, Alberto Masferrer.

◎ Sights

La Laguna de Alegría　　　　　　　　LAKE
(admission US$0.25) The scenic crater lake La Laguna de Alegría is a 2km downhill walk from town. Its icy waters are said to be medicinal. Don't miss the beautiful view from the **Mirador de las Cien Grados** – a vista point at the top of 100 steps. You can also take the road toward **Berlín**, another pretty mountain village.

▦ Sleeping

Cabanas La Estancia de Daniel　　　CABIN $
(☑2628-2030; 1a Av Norte; per person US$10; **P⏏**) The best value in Alegría is found at this friendly house a block south of the plaza, which has five *cabañas* in a flowery garden. It's close to the lake and the owners are very accommodating.

Casa del Huéspedes la Palma　　　B&B $
(☑2628-1131; 1a Av Norte, near Calle Alberto Masferrer; per person US$10; **@**) This eccentric family home cluttered with religious carvings, photos and bric-a-brac serenades as an informal hostel with spare, tiled rooms. Coffee is served on the plaza, which is just about the order of the day.

★**Entre Piedras Hotel**　　　　　　HOTEL $$
(☑2313-2812; entrepiedras.alegria@hotmail.com; Av Camilo Campus; s/d US$16/32; **✳@**) Easily the best digs in Alegría, Entre Piedras uses cooling slate tile to perfection, offset by wood-paneling and slick bathrooms. There's a charming courtyard cafe where you can try one of the specialty chocolate dishes or panini (US$5). Book ahead on weekends.

La Casa Mia　　　　　　　　　　HOTEL $$
(☑2634-0608; www.berlinlacasamia.com; 2a Av Norte, Berlín; d US$33) The next village around from Alegría is Berlín, which is just as beautiful but much smaller. If you want real solitude, or Alegría is full, try this dependable family hotel.

✕ Eating

Merendero Mi Pueblito　　　　SALVADORAN $
(Av Camilo Campus; mains US$2-6; ⏱8am-7pm) Huge plates of chicken, rice, beans and salad are served at this old staple run by an industrious family. It's south of the park and there are stirring views to the border.

Cartagena　　　　　　　　SALVADORAN $$$
(mains US$10-12; ⏱10am-8pm) Ignore the overpriced rooms, but come instead for the view. The beer is cold and the lunch servings of grilled meat and sides can be easily shared. It's a couple of blocks downhill from the plaza.

☕ Drinking & Nightlife

El Portal　　　　　　　　　　　　CAFE
(Av Camilo Campus; ⏱11am-9pm) The pick of the park cafes for an evening beer (US$1) and a slice of game meat.

ℹ Information

Tourist Agency (☑ 2628-1087; 1a Av Norte at 1a Calle Poniente)

ℹ Getting There & Away

Alegría sits between the Interamericana and Litoral highways and is accessible from either side. From Carretera Interamericana, catch a minibus from Villa El Triunfo to Santiago de María (US$0.30, 15 minutes), where buses leave hourly for Alegría (US$0.60, 45 minutes).

Isla Montecristo

A steamy, pristine sanctuary for hundreds of pelicans and egrets, this island and estuary sit where the Río Lempa meets the Pacific Ocean. During the war, the island and its cashew plantation were abandoned and taken over by the FMLN. After 1992 it was resettled by local farmers taking advantage of the postwar land transfer program. These days there are a number of families growing organic cashews as an export crop.

🛏 Sleeping

Hostal Lempa Mar HOSTEL $$
(☑ 2310-9901; www.gbajolempa.net; La Pita; r US$25) Operated by a local development group, this pleasant premises has cabins with basic rooms, shared bathrooms and a comfortable terrace. Meals are available in the restaurant.

ℹ Getting There & Away

La Pita and Montecristo are at the end of a 22km road which connects the Carretera del Litoral to

SEXY SURPRISES

Sorpresas (surprises) are little scenes and figures hidden in egg-sized shells, pioneered by folk artist Dominga Herrera of Ilobasco. Underneath a bulbous papaya or white chapel you'll find a charming microsized scene of village life – usually. One local artist got sassy and sculpted a couple in the giddy throes of sex. The illicit art was condemned by the town priest and briefly removed from stores. But prosperity may have beat out piety. *Pícara* (sinful) *sorpresas*, now available as matchbox copulation scenes, continue selling strong. Expect yours to come discreetly wrapped.

the coast. The road can be rough in rainy season. Take bus 155 (US$0.75, 40 minutes) or a pick-up from the Texaco in San Nicolás Lempa, with departures between 6am and 5:30pm.

From La Pita, *lanchas* (small motorboats; US$20 round trip) or canoes (US$4 one way) can take you out to the island.

Usulután

POP 51,910

The eponymous capital of Usulután Department is a noisy market town at the foot of 1450m Volcán de Usulután. For travelers Usulután will probably serve as a way station to Bahía de Jiquilisco and the lovely Playa El Espino. You can also easily reach the mountain hamlet of Alegría from here.

🛏 Sleeping

⭐**La Posada de Don Quijote** HOTEL $
(☑ 2635-9792; cnr 1a Calle Poniente & 1a Av Sur; s/d US$12/24; ❄) Hidden on the 1st floor of a small shopping complex, Don Quijote has hot showers, a minigym, excellent self-catering facilities and sturdy beds. It's 'downtown' so there are plenty of options for eating or picking up supplies to break up the road trip.

Hostal Dona Consuelo BOUTIQUE HOTEL $$
(☑ 2627-5254; info@hostaldonaconsuelo.com; Barrio La Parroquia, Jucuarán; s/d/t US$40/60/80; P❄🌐🏊) This wonderful city escape is in the village of Jucuarán, 30km southwest of Usulután. The property is professionally managed and each room is presented with great attention to detail. There's a lovely pool, a restaurant and views all the way to Bahía de Jiquilisco, which you can reach in 20 minutes by car. It's popular with couples and families.

🍴 Eating

Mercado Central FAST FOOD $
(4a Av Norte; ⊙7am-6pm) The Mercado Central is a hit with street-food aficionados.

L'Azteca MEXICAN $
(cnr Calle Dr Federico Penado & 1a Av Norte; mains US$2-3; ⊙10am-8pm) Large Mexican place with open windows, long wooden benches and a sizzling BBQ. The *tortas* cooked out front are delicious, as are the sizable tacos.

Pastelería Trigo Puro BAKERY $
(Calle Dr Penado; mains US$2-3; ⊙7am-5pm Mon-Sat) Fat cinnamon rolls, doughnuts and coco-

nut cookies beckon from the glass case of this popular bakery, which also serves cafeteria-style *típico*. It's one block west of the park.

ℹ Information

Citibank (2a Calle Oriente, near Av Dr Guandiquil) On the Parque Central; cashes traveler's checks and has a 24-hour ATM.

Cyber Start (4a Calle Oriente, btwn 2a & 4a Avs Norte; per hr US$0.50; ☉8:30am-6pm Mon-Sat, to noon Sun)

ℹ Getting There & Away

Usulután's main bus terminal is 1.5km east of the Parque Central (taxi US$3). The San Miguel terminal is west of town, but passengers can board along 1a Calle Oriente, a block south of the Parque Central. The San Miguel bus is number 373 (US$0.80, 1½ hours); take it to connect to La Unión.

Buses to Alegría, Puerto El Triunfo and San Salvador all take 4a Calle west through the center of town. Since most buses travel this way through town you don't necessarily have to go to the terminal (unless you want a seat).

For Playa El Espino, buses 351 and 358 (US$1.25, 1½ hours) leave from a small lot 100m west of main terminal, across from a supermarket. For Puerto El Triunfo take bus 363 (US$0.55, one hour) from a lot along the highway.

Bahía de Jiquilisco

With kilometer after kilometer of white sand pounded by surf, and inland mangroves facing the volcanoes, the Península San Juan del Gozo beckons. The inland sector is a habitat for gray egrets, pelicans and other waterbirds. Fishing towns include Corral de Mulas and Isla Méndez. Other less accessible beaches are at Punta San Juan on the peninsula's east end and Isla Madre Sal. Also called Isla Jobal, Isla Espíritu Santo has endless coconut groves and a coconut-oil processing plant, but the beaches are no big deal. The Pacific side has strong, powerful and unguarded surf, so be careful.

🛏 Sleeping

★**Hotel Solisal**   RESORT $$
(☑7890-2638, 2243-2290; www.hotelsolisal.com; San Juan del Gozo; r for 3/5 people max US$35/55, house US$80) Highly recommended for groups (though solo travelers could make it work at a price), the Solisal is famed for its floating restaurant on the calm peninsula

of San Juan del Gozo. Lodge in a variety of wooden rooms on stilts, where the birdlife will flash by your window and the fish will dance by your back door.

The accommodation and activity offerings are impressive for such a remote and spectacular part of the world. Green mangroves and volcanoes round out a classic Central American landscape.

Puerto Barillas   RESORT $$$
(☑San Salvador head office 2632-1802; www.puertobarillas.com; tree houses/apt US$118/236) Puerto Barillas is in the heart of a unique biosphere, where some of El Salvador's flashiest boats moor in search of solitude. The hotel works closely with environmental groups to protect hawksbill turtle nesting sites and monitor migratory birds.

If arriving by car, exit the Carretera Litoral (CA2) at KM 108.5. If arriving by bus, change at Usulután or pick up a minibus (US$0.50) or taxi (US$5) at the turnoff.

The posh tree houses here have good novelty value if you decide to sleep over, but they aren't cheap, so you may prefer to seek nourishment in the restaurant (burgers US$7), grab a boat tour, and move on. Accommodation rates are half price for members paying an annual fee of US$600.

La Familia Flores   HOMESTAY $
(r US$15) La Familia Flores is a unique family home made entirely from coconut husks, a potentially lucrative building material. Ask at the bus stop for directions.

🍴 Eating

El Cangrejito Playero   SEAFOOD $$
(☑7567-4603; mains US$4-10) The best seafood restaurant on the mainland side, specializing in prawn dishes.

ℹ Getting There & Away

The gateway to Bahía de Jiquilisco, seedy Puerto El Triunfo, is best sped through, preferably by boat. The last bus to Puerto El Triunfo from Usulután is at 4:40pm; the last one back to Usulután is at 5:30pm. From the highway turnoff, take bus 377 to San Miguel (US$1.40, 2½ hours, last bus 2:50pm) or bus 185 to San Salvador (US$1.65, two hours, every 30 minutes, last bus 2:50pm).

San Miguel

POP 249,638

Founded in 1530 and dwarfed by Volcán Chaparrastique, San Miguel is El Salvador's

San Miguel

San Miguel

◎ Sights
1 Antiguo Teatro Nacional.....................C2
2 Catedral Nuestra Señora de la Paz C2
   Museo Regional del Oriente ....(see 1)

🛏 Sleeping
3 Hotel Caleta.....................................C4
4 Hotel Inn El Guanaco.........................D2
5 Hotel Plaza Floresta A3

🍽 Eating
6 Comedor Chilita.................................D2
7 Pastelería Lorena..............................C3

🍸 Drinking & Nightlife
8 Melodia..A3

second-largest city and a provincial capital with plenty of swagger. For the traveler, there are some colonial-era buildings in the center, though it remains mostly an important transportation hub, halfway point between the mountains of Morazán and the Pacific Ocean beaches, and a base for excursions up (and even into) the volcanic hinterland.

San Miguel is best known for the biggest party (p329) in El Salvador. For the rest of the year, nightlife returns to normal, but as San Miguel has more strip clubs per capita than any other city in Central America, most visitors stick to the flash new malls along Av Roosevelt for their entertainment fix.

Parque David J Guzmán is Parque Central, with the cathedral to the east. This area can get busy with traffic by day and a little sketchy at night; west of central park is quieter and more secure. Av Roosevelt (Carretera Interamericana) skirts the southwestern edge of town.

◎ Sights

Ruinas de Quelepa ARCHAEOLOGICAL SITE
Archaeology buffs will appreciate the Ruinas de Quelepa, grassy mounds covering 40 ter-

raced ceremonial platforms, largely unexcavated. Lenca inhabited the site between the 2nd and 7th centuries AD, trading with Copán in Honduras as well as Mexico. Stone sculptures uncovered here are on display in the Museo Regional del Oriente.

The ruins are 8km west of San Miguel off the Interamericana. From the cathedral, bus 90 to Moncagua (US$0.60, 30 minutes) passes them.

Laguna de Olomega   LAKE
About 40km southeast of San Miguel is a pretty lake on which you can catch a small boat (US$5 round trip) to minuscule Los Cerritos Island. It's great for swimming and fishing in a place of great significance to the area's original inhabitants. A taxi (around US$15) is your best chance of making the 30-minute trip.

Museo Regional del Oriente   MUSEUM
(2a Calle Oriente; ⊙10am-5pm Mon-Sat) FREE
Opened in 2007, the Museo Regional del Oriente is in the same building as the Antiguo Teatro Nacional, on the 2nd floor. The collection of pottery and photos is meager but well thought out, and probably the best attraction in the city itself.

Antiguo Teatro Nacional   THEATER
(2a Calle Oriente; ⊙10am-5pm) FREE A neoclassical gem which functioned as a cinema during the silent-film era and later as the Telecom headquarters and a public hospital.

**Catedral Nuestra
Señora de la Paz**   CATHEDRAL
Facing Parque David J Guzmán, San Miguel's cathedral dates from the 18th century.

🏃 Activities

Volcán Chaparrastique   HIKING
Strong hikers can tackle 2130m Volcán Chaparrastique, aka Volcán de San Miguel, a towering cone southwest of the city. Arrange police escorts through the Chinameca Police Station (p330), with at least a few days' notice. Get there with a rental car, or take the Placitas bus from San Miguel at the corner of Calle Chaparrastique and 7a Av Sur and then arrange a taxi.

The top of the volcano affords gaping views of the coast and a patchwork of rolling farmland. The crater is hundreds of meters deep, with a jumble of boulders and Virgins at the bottom.

🎊 Festivals & Events

Carnaval de San Miguel   CARNIVAL
(⊙Nov) The biggest party in the country takes place in the second-largest city in the final week of November.

Fiestas Patronales   RELIGIOUS
(⊙Nov) Every November San Miguel honors the Virgen de la Paz with Fiestas Patronales, marking the occasion with holy processions and enormous, colorful sawdust carpets.

🛏 Sleeping

Hotel Plaza Floresta   B&B $$
(☑2640-1549; Av Roosevelt 704; s/d US$25/50; P❋🛜🏊) A welcoming local family do a fine job of managing this 'boutique' hotel on Av Roosevelt. The internal courtyard with swimming pool is perhaps the most relaxing place to hang out in San Miguel. The standard, tiled rooms across two levels are airy, clean and surprisingly quiet.

Hotel Caleta   BOUTIQUE HOTEL $$
(☑2677-0091; 3a Av Sur, Barrio San Nicolas; d US$25) With a tropical garden, a hammock-strewn landing, a tasteful maroon-and-mustard color scheme and neat, affordable rooms, Caleta is the standout midrange option in San Miguel.

Hotel Inn El Guanaco   HOTEL $$
(☑2661-8026; cnr 8a Av Norte & Pasaje Madrid; s/d US$20/30; ❋) Small and welcoming, El Guanaco has enormous spotless rooms with hot-water bathrooms and cable TV. For something quiet and removed, choose the 3rd floor. There's a pool table and a small restaurant on the ground floor.

🍴 Eating

★Comedor Chilita   CAFE $
(cnr 8a Calle Oriente & 6a Av Norte Bis; mains US$2-3; ⊙7am-10pm) This buzzing cafeteria spoons up a happy, huge variety that includes steamed veggies, spaghetti and roasted pepper chicken. After 4pm, it's all *pupusas* – use the side entrance on 8a Calle Oriente.

Pastelería Lorena   BAKERY $
(3a Calle Poniente 21; cakes US$0.20-3; ⊙7am-7pm) El Salvador's most famous bakery started here. A glass of *horchata* and a slice of *Maria Luisa* (jam cake) are the business.

La Pema   SALVADORAN $$
(mains US$7-15; ⊙10:30am-4:30pm) This churchlike structure is home to one of the

country's most enjoyable gastronomic experiences. Located 5km out of town on the road to Playa El Cuco, La Pema is famous for its creamy soups and long lunches. Don't miss the *mariscada* (creamy seafood soup), served up with thick cheese tortillas. The service is earnest and quick and the crowd comes in from afar. Taxis know where to go.

Drinking & Nightlife

Melodia CLUB
(Av Roosevelt Sur, Plaza Chaparrastique; ⊙10pm-5am Fri-Sat) They should make all *discotecas* like this – a booming, cheesy, high-heeled and high-octane Latin pop paradise where large contingents of well-heeled students compete for attention. Drinks are cheapest before midnight, but it's empty till 1am.

Information

Banco Cuscatlán (cnr 4a Calle Oriente & Av Barrios) Exchanges traveler's checks and foreign currency, and has a 24-hour ATM.

Banco Salvadoreño (cnr Av Barrios & 6a Calle Poniente) Cashes traveler's checks, does Visa cash advances and has a 24-hour ATM.

Chinameca Police Station (☎2665-0074; fax 2665-1014) Contact Chinameca police station for a police escort to Chaparrastique.

Immigration Office (Migración; ☎2660-0957; cnr 15a Calle Oriente & 8a Av Sur; ⊙8am-4pm Mon-Fri)

Post Office (cnr 4a Av Sur & 3a Calle Oriente; ⊙ 8am-5pm Mon-Fri, to 1pm noon)

Getting There & Away

San Miguel's **Bus Terminal** has clearly marked bus lanes but ask around for schedules. Take a taxi to your hotel if you arrive at night.

For the Honduran border, the El Amatillo bus 330 (US$2, 1½ hours) leaves at 10-minute intervals from 4am to 6pm. For Perquín, bus 332 (US$1.75, three hours) leaves at 6:20am, 9:50am, 10:20am, 12:40pm and 3:20pm. Alternately, take 328 to San Francisco Gotera and transfer to a pick-up.

Getting Around

Alamo Rent A Car (☎2661-0344; Av Roosevelt Sur)

La Unión

POP 26,739

While some pockets retain a salt-crusted colonial charm, La Unión is the kind of town even the saltiest sea dogs are keen to avoid. It's hot and downright dirty, with little to keep you here but an overdue boat headed for Nicaragua. The heat can be brutal too; even dogs whimper at noon.

Playa Las Tunas and Playa Jaguey are good beaches on the coast west of La Unión. For some respite from the heat, and views of the gulf, head to Conchagua, at the base of the imposing volcano of the same name. The views are knee-trembling.

Sleeping

Comfort Inn MOTEL $$
(☎2665-6565; Km 2.8 Calle a Playitas Carretera Panamericana; r with breakfast US$75; ❉@☒) On the highway out of town is the best hotel you'll find for miles. It's a somewhat uninspiring setting, but there's a wonderful pool and the rooms are better than your average three-star chain motel.

Hotel San Francisco HOTEL $$
(☎2604-4159; Calle San Carlos, btwn 9a & 11a Avs Sur; s/d US$20/40; ❉) Rooms are a little damp at this rough motel with a half-decent facade, but the street itself is okay and there are very few options in town to keep up the competition.

Eating

Cappucino's CAFE $
(cnr 1a Calle Oriente & 3a Av Norte, Barrio El Centro; coffee US$2, snacks US$2-5; ⊙8am-7pm) Cappucino's is a brightly lit, professionally run operation which will surprise you with its

BUSES FROM SAN MIGUEL

DESTINATION	BUS	COST (US$)	DURATION (HR)	FREQUENCY (DAILY)
El Cuco	320	1	1½	every 30min
La Unión	324	1.50	1¼	hourly
Marcala, Honduras	426	4	5½	4 daily
Puerto El Triunfo	377	1.60	2	3 daily
San Salvador	301	2.20	3	every 30min
San Salvador *especial*	301	4	2	hourly

genial atmosphere and tasty cafe fare, including breakfast sandwiches (US$4) and apple pie (US$1).

Pupusería Mayra
SALVADORAN $
(Calle San Carlos; mains US$1-2; ⊙5-10pm) Get your fill of *panes de pollo* (chicken sandwiches) and fresh *pupusas* before they run out, which happens often.

ℹ Information

Cyber Cafe (1 Calle Poniente Comercial Flores, Comercial Flores; per hr US$0.50)

Immigration Office (☑2604-4375; cnr Av General Cabañas & 7a Calle Poniente; ⊙6am-10pm Mon-Sat) Next door to the post office; the sign says *Control Migración*. You must stop by here if you're arriving or departing by boat from Nicaragua or Honduras.

Plaza Médica Vida (☑2604-2065; Calle General Menénde, btwn 7a & 9a Avs Sur; ⊙24hr) A decent hospital near the center.

Scotiabank (3a Calle Oriente, near 1a Calle Sur; ⊙8am-5pm Mon-Fri, to noon Sat) Changes traveler's checks and has a 24-hour ATM.

ℹ Getting There & Away

The bus terminal is on 3a Calle Poniente between 4a and 6a Avs Norte. For El Amatillo at the Honduran border take Santa Rosa de Lima bus 342 (US$1, one hour) to San Carlos and transfer to bus 330 at the turnoff.

Boat service from La Unión to Coyolitos, Honduras, and the port of Potosí, Nicaragua, is very infrequent. Ask a navy officer at the pier. You could also try calling **Hotel La Joya del Golfo** (p332) on Isla Meanguera to see if it has a trip planned. Prices vary widely. The land route may not be too exciting, but neither is hanging out in La Unión.

Beaches near La Union

Southwest of the unspoiled coastal forest of Bosque Conchagua sits a long, sweeping stretch of sandy beach once the sole preserve of surfers, San Miguelites and sea turtles.

Playa Esteron is the pick, partly due to its accessible, clean surf and coconut trees. It's also home to the most talked about retreat in Central America.

About 3km west of Esteron is **Playa El Cuco**, which is popular with weekenders from San Miguel. Be aware of potential jellyfish and manta rays – shuffle while walking out. There are plenty of good, cheap seafood restaurants in the sandy town square and a sizable surf break out front.

Further west, **Las Flores** is a prime surfing point suitable for beginners from December to February. The rest of the time it's best left to the pros. You can access the famed Punta Mango break by boat from either Las Flores or El Cuco.

Broad and sandy **Playa Jaguey** is another good beach between El Tamarindo and El Cuco, with moderate surf. Private homes front the beach but you can still use it. There are no facilities. **Playa Las Tunas** is also pleasant enough, with a wide, flat beach reaching 100m to an estuary. The seafood restaurants get rowdy on weekends.

🛏 Sleeping

Cuartos Mama Cata
HOTEL $
(☑2619-9173; casacata1@hotmail.com; Playa Las Flores; r US$15) Mama Cata will sort you out for a cheap, clean room by the breaks. She will also cook, and treat you like the reckless young person you have become.

★ La Tortuga Verde
RESORT $$
(☑7774-4855 7338-9646; www.latortugaverde.com; Playa Esteron; dm/s/house US$10/18/200, d US$25-70; ❋❋) ⊘ Hidden across three beachfront properties covered in coconut trees, green vegetation, found objects and sandy, low-lit paths, all rooms at La Tortuga Verde induce relaxation through natural light and airflow. Whether it's a dorm room or a five-bedroom house, only quality linen and organic soaps are used.

For over six years now Tom Pollack has been creating his dream community by the ocean. With an open heart, an open checkbook, and the help of the hundreds of locals he now employs, the New York native has designed a *ridiculously* enjoyable eco-resort to suit all budgets. There's a sparkling swimming pool (and a second under construction), happening sunset bar, yoga studio, turtle hatchery, 'cosmic' cafe for killer vegetarian food, day spa (best massage for miles!), and large self-catering kitchen.

The reputable onsite restaurant serves hundreds of meals to locals and gob-smacked travelers who can't quite believe what they've stumbled into, while a volunteer program enables some to trade their services for free board. Various boat trips, excursions, parties and spontaneous activities take place at your desire; just enter into the spirit of the place, smile and wave to the ever-present camera. If traveling to/from Nicaragua, you can catch a fast boat for US$75, which is a glorious way to cross a border.

La Tortuga Verde is 3km east of El Cuco. Once you reach El Cuco, turn left and follow the gravel road for roughly 3km. La Tortuga Verde is on the right.

Hotel Miraflores   HOTEL **$$**

(🖉 7890-4751; www.elhotelmiraflores.com; Playa Las Flores; s/d/tr US$70/82/95) Hotel Miraflores has elevated views of the famed Las Flores wave and respectable rooms in a red adobe building with a huge interior courtyard.

Azul Surf Club   RESORT **$$**

(🖉 2612-6820; www.azulsurfclub.com; Playa El Cuco; dm/r US$10/25, d incl breakfast from US$75; ❅ @ ☎) Azul Surf Club is an attractive family-run surf resort with a range of accommodation options right on the beach. The dormitory is new and well laid out, but is in El Cuco town. Owner Lisette is passionate about her community and runs service projects in the area.

❶ Getting There & Away

La Unión Bus 383 takes a circular route to El Tamarindo; it passes Las Tunas and Jaguey on the way. For a breezy shortcut, take the same bus only as far as Buenavista, catch a *lancha* across the inlet to El Tamarindo (US$0.40) and hop on bus 383 returning to La Unión via Jaguey and Las Tunas.

San Miguel Catch bus 320 to Playa El Cuco (US$1, 1½ hours, every 30 minutes, 5.30am to 4pm).

Golfo de Fonseca Islands

This archipelago near the coast of Nicaragua was once the playground of 17th-century pirates. Today it is home to small fishing villages, pretty pepper-colored coves and warm, abundant waters. The raw ocean setting is memorable, particularly if you are whizzing to the border, or just cruising about in a speedboat chartered from El Cuco in search of a seafood lunch at Isla Meanguera.

The nearest island, Isla Zacatillo, has the largest community, and numerous coves with sandy beaches can be explored here. The principal village has a few stores and lodgings in a wooden shack over the bay.

For solitary beaches, head for Isla Martín Pérez, just south of Zacatillo. More mountainous Isla Conchagüita offers hiking opportunities. Fishing boats are neatly lined

up under *enramadas* (arbors or protective awnings, typically made of wood or branches) along the beachfront of the main village. There are prehistoric rock carvings on the way out to Playa Brava, a black-sand beach an hour's walk from the village.

The pick of the islands is the furthest from the mainland. Isla Meanguera was long the subject of territorial disputes with Honduras and Nicaragua, until an international court declared it part of El Salvador in 1992. Aside from a small, friendly village, the island boasts Playa Majahual, a spectacular black-sand beach with warm, calm waters perfect for swimming. It's a 45-minute walk from the ferry landing; shuttles (US$1) depend on availability.

🛏 Sleeping

Hotel La Joya del Golfo   HOTEL **$$**

(🖉 2648-0072; www.hotellajoyadelgolfo.com; Isla Meanguera; d US$79-89, extra person US$10; ❅ @) Hotel La Joya del Golfo is a boutique hotel nestled in a picturesque bay. The rooms are large, with gilt-edged bathrooms, cable TV and clear views of 'Bird Island.' Call before arriving or to arrange pick-up.

❶ Getting There & Away

La Unión has services to Zacatillo (US$2, 20 minutes) and Meanguera (US$2.50, 1½ hours) from the pier. Departure times vary, but are generally from 10:30am, returning at 5am the next day. Day-trippers have to arrange a private pick-up.

A private 'express' *lancha* costs US$60 round trip to Meanguera. Agree on a price before the journey starts, and pay only half up front to ensure your return trip. Ferries for the islands also depart from Las Playitas, further down the coast.

Morazán

The northeastern Morazán Department is a small agricultural region interspersed with rugged mountain forest. The cooler climate attracts visitors from San Miguel, as does the country's cleanest river, the Río Sapo, and the opportunity for countless hikes to waterfalls and old hideaways from the civil war. The museum in Perquín and a memorial in El Mozote are powerful displays of reconciliation and remembrance, while indigenous traditions survive in villages around San Francisco Gotera, the department capital.

◉ Sights

Cacaopera Museum   MUSEUM
(Cacaopera; admission US$1; ⊘9am-noon & 2-5pm Mon-Fri) The village of Cacaopera (bus 337 from San Francisco Gotera, 15 minutes, US$0.20) has a small ethnographic museum with photo exhibits and artifacts from the local Kakawira indigenous community. Through the museum you can also arrange guided hikes in the dry season (December to April) to pre-Columbian petroglyphs (US$15 per group).

🛏 Sleeping

Cacaopera Hostel   HOSTEL $
(☑2651-0251; Cacaopera; dm US$5) The Cacaopera Museum maintains a rustic hostel, without electricity or running water. You can bathe in the nearby Río Torola and cook on the wood-burning stove. Sure, it's roughing it, but the experience is undoubtedly unique.

🔒 Shopping

Cedart   CRAFTS
(Calle Principal; ⊘8am-5pm Mon-Fri, to noon Sat) The community at Guatajiagua produces quality black pottery in the Lenca tradition. Cedart is a simple craft shop which can also point you in the direction of local artist workshops.

Perquín

POP 5500

A visit to the former FMLN headquarters in the mountain town of Perquín is paramount to understanding El Salvador's brutal civil war. It was in these hills that the opposition garnered its most loyal support, and despite vigorous bombing campaigns, the military was unable to dislodge the guerrilla forces. The town itself is small but the stunning pine forest surroundings can be seen at every turn, the mountain climate is agreeable and the war museum makes a trip here the highlight of El Salvador for many visitors.

◉ Sights

Museo de la Revolución Salvadoreña   MUSEUM
(Calle Los Héroes; admission US$1.25; ⊘8:30am-4:30pm Tue-Sun) A few blocks north of the park, this museum charts the causes and progress of the armed struggle. Highlights include the collection of antiwar posters from throughout the world, the stark color photos of life inside guerrilla camps, the incredible assortment of Soviet weapons and some histories of those who died in action. It makes for a somber, stirring visit.

El Campamento Guerrillero Simulado   MUSEUM
(Calle Los Héroes; admission US$0.50, guided trips per group US$20; ⊘8:30am-4:30pm Tue-Sun) This reconstructed guerrilla camp is connected by swing bridges and dirt tracks in a patch of partially cleared woodland. The museum is also the contact point for ex-guerrilla guides who can take visitors on fascinating guided trips throughout the war zone. The most popular destination is El Mozote.

Sites within the camp include the remains of the downed helicopter that carried Lieutenant Colonel Domingo Monterrosa, head of the notorious Atlacatl Battalion, to his death. You'll see the studios of the FMLN's clandestine station Radio Venceremos (We Will Win Radio), part of an elaborate hoax that used a radio transmitter rigged with explosives to bring Monterrosa's helicopter down.

🏃 Activities

Prodetur   TOUR
(☑2680-4086; prodeturperquin.tripod.com; Parque Central; ⊘8am-5pm Mon-Fri, to 2pm Sat) Perquín's helpful tour office organizes guided tours and hikes (US$15) with a day's notice. Some English is spoken.

✨ Festivals & Events

Festival del Invierno   ART
(⊘Aug) Perquín's art and music festival is popular with the boho crowd and college students.

Tours Ciclista de Montaña   SPORTS
(⊘Nov) Major cycling race.

Festival de Montaña   CULTURAL
(⊘late Dec) A week-long cultural festival.

🛏 Sleeping

La Posada de Don Manuel   B&B $
(☑2680-4037; s/d US$10/20; 🅿🛜) Manuel and his wife Corinal oversee this converted lumber mill tucked away 500m to the left of town as you enter. The rooms are fairly dire, but there is hot water, delicious home-cooked meals and a strong wi-fi connection. Their tours are recommended.

Hostal Perquín Real   HOSTEL $
(☑2680-4158; s US$8) In a prime location in Perquín proper, this humble hostel charges

fairly for clean rooms and a relaxing landing which backs onto the best restaurant in town, Cocina de Mama Toya y Mama Juana. The showers are icy cold though, so be prepared. It's located at the south entrance of town.

Eco Albergue Río Sapo   CABIN $
(☑ 2680-4087, 2680-4086; campsites/dm per person US$4/7) Access to a swimming hole and a dozen hikes is the best reason for staying at these rustic dorm-style cabins at Area Natural Protegida Río Sapo. There's no electricity and limited water; bring your own food and flashlights. You can rent a tent (US$3) or sleeping bag (US$1) if you don't have your own. It's operated by Prodetur.

Hotel Perkin Lenca   HOTEL $$
(☑ 2680-4046; www.perkinlenca.com; s/d incl breakfast US$40/50) On the road into Perquín is a reputable and attractive mountain retreat hand-built by an American expatriate who excels in community projects. Finished in pine oak, the rooms are wholesome and spacious, all with hot water. Hiking and cultural tours are readily available. The views from the restaurant are superb.

✗ Eating

La Cocina de la Abuela   SALVADORAN $
(mains US$2-4; ⊗ 8am-8pm) The pick of the cheap *comedores* on the town square.

La Cocina de Ma'Anita   SALVADORAN $$
(Hotel Perkin Lenca; mains US$5-10; ⊗ 7am-8pm; 🖥🖉📶) Mostly organic, always tasty, Anita's kitchen is an all-day affair which, aside from the usual breakfast and lunch spread, serves heartier meals such as the Perkin *parillada* (BBQ, US$8.50), which could feed a mountain goat, and *churrasco de la casa* (house steak, US$8), which is far too delicious to be mere mountain goat. Diners also enjoy wall-length windows and homemade preserves.

❶ Information

Cyberspace (per hr US$1; ⊗ 8am-9pm Sat-Thu, to 6pm Fri)

❶ Getting There & Away

The CA7 north of San Miguel to the Honduran border is in good shape. Bus 332 runs from San Miguel to Perquín (US$2.50, three hours) at 6am, 7am, 9:50am and 12:40pm. Alternatively, there's the more frequent bus 328 to San Francisco Gotera (US$1, two hours), from where pick-ups go on to Perquín (US$0.70, one hour).

The last bus back to San Miguel is at 4pm; the last pick-up to Gotera leaves at 5:40pm, but you have to catch the 5pm to make the last Gotera–San Miguel bus.

NORTHERN EL SALVADOR

The small province of Chalatenango constitutes the northern region of El Salvador, where mountains run to the Honduran border. It's a very pretty, peaceful area, easily accessible from San Salvador and, the more so since the construction of a new freeway, the Honduran border too.

Suchitoto – everyone's favorite Salvadoran colonial town – is deservedly the area's most well-known attraction. On some weekends it can feel like the cultural center of Central America, and it makes a fabulous base for a visit to the country.

La Palma is a unique artists' hangout, famous for naïve art which continues to capture the world's imagination, while hiking trips from San Ignacio and Miramundo are world class. The commercial hub of Chalatenango – the center of what is now El Salvador's safest province – is a proud farming town with a strong community spirit, as seen in an ongoing dispute with international mining companies.

The Chalatenango district bore the brunt of the military's *tierra arrasada* (scorched land) tactics, which burned fields and killed livestock as a form of combat. The main provider of water and hydroelectric power for El Salvador, the district faces a serious deforestation problem.

Suchitoto

Located 50km northeast of San Salvador, wondrous little 'Suchi' is the cultural capital of the country. Every weekend the cobbled streets come alive for an arts and food festival in a grand celebration of *guanaco* pride. In February, the entire month celebrates the town's resident artists and the small galleries swell with domestic tourists. None of this is new, however; when indigo ruled the marketplace and the beautiful Spanish church was packed daily, Suchitoto was the pride of the province.

Architecture buffs will love the colonial buildings, while outdoor types can choose between numerous hikes to waterfalls, caves and beautiful Lago Suchitlán that begin and end just meters from town. Suchitoto is also a bird migration zone with over 200 species. Thousands of hawks and falcons fill the skies as the seasons change, and birds of all sorts nest in the relative safety of the lake islands.

It is presumed that Yaqui and Pipil peoples settled in the area some 1000 years ago. El Salvador's capital was established near here in the early 16th century. More recently, some of the earliest fighting of the civil war began in Suchitoto, accompanied by much destruction and emigration. Today the town has rebounded to become the highland seat of national tourism.

◉ Sights

★ **Centro Arte para la Paz** CULTURAL CENTER
(☑ 2335-1080; www.capsuchitoto.org; 2a Calle Poniente 5) FREE Opened in 2000 as a charitable initiative to support victims of domestic violence, the Centro Arte para la Paz now organizes a range of cultural activities from its premises in a beautiful, old Dominican convent. There's a small museum and gallery, and even a self-catering dorm (US$7) with respectable facilities. The community spirit alone makes it a lovely place to visit.

✦ Activities

★ **Suchitoto Adventure Outfitters** TOUR
(☑ 2335-1859, 7921-4216; www.elsalvadoradventures.com) There really aren't many places left in El Salvador where René Barbon has not roamed firsthand. Kayaking, fishing and physical pursuits are his strength, but he is equally knowledgeable about history and culture. A new day trip includes a visit to Lago de Ilopango to the east of San Salvador, and to the war history and rainforest park at Cinquera (US$55).

The Maya Grouper is his new bed and breakfast; book through the website.

Pajaro Flor
Spanish School LANGUAGE
(☑ 7230-7812, 2327-2366; www.pajaroflor.com; 4a Calle Poniente 22) Pajaro Flor Spanish School offers 20 hours of accomplished private instruction for US$160; homestays can be arranged for about US$10 per day.

IPES VOLUNTEERING
(☑ 2335-1891; www.permacultura.com.sv; 2a Av Sur 38, Barrio El Cavario) An opportunity to volunteer in grassroots permaculture projects on a purpose-built site 15km outside Suchitoto, where local farmers complete formal studies in sustainable farming. For US$400 a month volunteers receive lodging onsite, immersion in the local community and access to experienced instructors.

El Tejado SWIMMING
(☑ 2335-1769; 3a Av Norte 58; pool admission US$3; ☺9am-6pm) To escape the heat, swim in the huge pool with a view at this hotel (double US$65), owned by an evangelical church. It's also a good spot for a beer.

Global Platform LANGUAGE COURSE
(☑ 2340-6301; globalplatform-elsalvador@ms.dk; 2a Av Sur 39, Barrio El Cavario) Global Platform is a Danish NGO that offers Spanish lessons in conjunction with grassroots development projects around Suchitoto. Non-Danes are welcome to apply; a month costs roughly US$400, which includes basic lodging, food and various excursions.

✦ Festivals & Events

Festival de Maíz CULTURAL
(☺Aug) Suchitoto's corn-harvest festival has religious processions and street parties.

🛏 Sleeping

Posada Blanca Luna HOSTEL $
(☑ 2335-1661; 1a Calle Oriente; r per person US$8) A small, peaceful hotel tucked away a block behind the church. The six tidy, simple rooms, all with private bathroom (no hot water), are elevated so you can enjoy lovely views of the sunset over Suchi. The spacious terrace is the place to congregate.

El Gringo HOSTEL $
(☑ 2327-2351; www.elgringosuchitoto.com; Calle Francisco Morazán 27; dm/s/d US$7/12/18; P❄️🎧) For a low-key, informed and affordable stay in Suchitoto, expatriate Robert oversees a colorful hotel and Tex-Mex restaurant west of the square. Rooms are basic but very comfortable. Local art is on display and the excellent book exchange is welcome in these parts.

Hostal Vista al Lago HOSTEL $$
(☑ 2335-1357; 2a Av Norte 18; dm/d US$8/30) The views at this leafy premises are simply incredible. Enter through an unremarkable reception area, where the dorms are also a little gloomy. But press on into the garden and check out the newer double rooms, which boast the vista taken for the name. The owners are cheerful and happy to leave you to your own electronic devices.

★**Los Almendros
de San Lorenzo** BOUTIQUE HOTEL **$$$**
(☑2335-1200; www.hotelsalvador.com; 4a Calle
Poniente; d/ste US$93/120; ❉@❉) Without a
doubt this posh, boutique hotel set in a re-
stored 200-year old home is one of the best
places to stay in El Salvador. High-end Salva-
doran art, antique and modern furnishings,
custom-made doors and several gurgling
fountains set the scene for six immaculate
rooms. All have high ceilings, large tile bath-
rooms and classy, simple decor.

The suites – one with its own fountain,
the other distributed over two floors – are
worth every extra cent.

In addition to enjoying rooms that are
hard to leave, guests can lounge in a luxu-
rious library, at the well-tended pool, or in
the lush garden. A fine restaurant and hip
lounge-bar complete the experience.

✖ Eating

★**La Lupita del Portal** INTERNATIONAL **$**
(☑2335-1429; mains US$3-8; ⊗8am-10pm) Now
flanked by pop-up *pupusa* joints, Lupey's is
still Suchi's best-value restaurant and drink-
ing spot. Generous meal deals feature sand-
wiches, pizza and grills, alongside large fruit
shakes. Good fun all round.

La Posada Suchitatlan SALVADORAN **$$**
(☑2335-1064; Barrio San José; mains US$6-12;
⊗11am-8pm) On lush, sprawling grounds
overlooking the lake, you'll find typical Salvadoran food in an atypical setting.

Xela's Pizza PIZZA **$$**
(☑2335-1397; pizza US$6-10; ⊗noon-9pm) This
smart little pizza joint is growing in popular-
ity. Perfect date place; follow the signs from
the plaza.

🍷 Drinking & Nightlife

El Necio BAR
(4a Calle Oriente No 9; ⊗4pm-1am) Straight up
drinking den with a revolutionary flavor
in the stiff drinks. Jerry and friends rotate
the political paraphernalia with great zeal.
You can learn as much about the country's
history in a night as in a three-year under-
graduate degree.

🔒 Shopping

Casa de la Abuela HANDICRAFTS
(☑2335-1227; www.suchitotoelsalvador.com; cnr 1
Av Norte & 2 Calle Oriente; ⊗9am-7pm) If you are
short on time, but light on luggage, then stop

by this ever-expanding store which stocks
handicrafts and artwork from the region.

ℹ Information

Banco ProCredit (cnr 2a Av Norte & 2a Calle
Poniente; ⊗8am-4:30pm Mon-Fri, to noon Sat)
Tourism Office (☑2335-1739; Calle San Mar-
tin 2; ⊗8am-4pm) Professional and friendly
office, with information on sights, activities and
cultural events in Suchitoto.
X-Streme Speed Cyber Cafe (☑2235-1722; 1a
Calle Poniente; per hr US$1; ⊗8am-8pm)

ℹ Getting There & Away

From San Salvador's Terminal de Oriente take
bus 129. To return, the same bus departs from
the corner of 1a Calle Poniente and 4a Av Sur,
a block west of Parque Centenario. By car, go
toward Cojutepeque on the Interamericana.
When you get to San Martín, turn left at the
Texaco sign.

If you're headed north, catch bus 163 to Las
Aguilares (US$0.80, one hour), where buses
pass for Chalatenango, Las Palma and the El
Salvador–Honduras border. A slower but more
scenic option is to take a boat (per person US$6,
20 minutes) or car ferry (per person US$1, per
car US$4) across Lago de Suchitlán to San
Francisco Lempa and from there catch a bus to
Chalatenango. The last one leaves at 3pm.

Chalatenango
POP 21,102
'Chalate' is the capital of the mountainous
Chalatenango province in the country's
north. There's a lovely daily rhythm here,
as the narrow streets fill with farm trucks
laden with fruit, sugarcane, indigo and cof-
fee en route to the morning market on Calle
San Martín, where you might just meet a
cowboy. Colorful buses are stacked with
friendly locals selling DVDs, toiletries and
glittery sequined dresses; locals will strike
up conversation in no time.

It's a pleasant place to walk around as
you catch glimpses of the spectacular La
Peña mountains and the Cerro Verde fur-
ther west, both likely destinations if you've
made it this far. Another popular day trip is
to Lago de Suchitlan to the east.

The stains of history are hard to erase
here. There's a real contrast between the
ambitious, city-bound youth and a genera-
tion of leather-skinned subsistence farmers
recounting tales of FMLN might. The large
military garrison on the plaza was built dur-

ing wartime to rein in revolutionary activity in this FMLN stronghold.

⊙ Sights

Turicentro Agua Fría   PARK
(admission US$1; ⊙ 8am-5pm) A 20-minute walk from the Parque Central, Turicentro Agua Fría has a lush park with picnic tables, but the main draw is the pools set with an artificial rock island topped by a waterslide. Dry season means water shortages – expect an overdose of chlorine. A cafeteria serves beer and meals. To get here, go up Calle Morazán (east) about 400m, and turn left at the big sign.

Iglesia de Chalatenango   CHURCH
The Iglesia de Chalatenango, with its squat bell tower and bright chalky facade, sits on the east side of the Parque Central, a stone's throw from the military garrison.

🕇 Activities

Cerro La Peña   HIKING
For panoramic views of the Cerrón Grande reservoir, climb Cerro La Peña, a 1½-hour hike starting at a trailhead before the *turicentro*. A number of roads and paths reach the top; ask passersby for directions.

🛌 Sleeping

Hotel La Ceiba   HOSTEL $
(☑ 2301-1080; 1a Calle Poniente; s US$10) This is an old-fashioned cheap sleep behind the garrison building.

La Posada del Jefe   HOTEL $
(☑ 2335-2450; Calle el Instituto, Barrio El Calvario; s/d US$16/25; ❄) It's a tough climb with your backpack to this white concrete hotel, and the interior decorating is not really worth the effort. There is a little convenience store out front, though, and a friendly owner who will point you in the direction of the hiking trails.

🍴 Eating

Comedor Carmary   SALVADORAN $
(3a Av; mains US$2-3; ⊙ 7am-5pm Mon-Sat) This tidy cafeteria packed with bus-stop patrons serves tasty *comida a la vista,* which might include stewed chicken in tomatoes, plantains and the ubiquitous beans and rice, alongside tall glasses of fresh juice.

Market   MARKET $
(⊙ 5am-1pm) The open-air market offers a visual feast of veggies, fruits and grains, as well as stock to replenish your toiletries. It's

just east of Av Fajardo. Another cacophonous market is also held on Tuesday and Sunday in the town center.

Cafe Colombia   CAFE $
(4a Calle Poniente; coffee US$1; ⊙ 8am-5pm) Big ham, cheese or chicken sandwiches are served at this makeshift cafe which serves strong local coffee to student-types. Seating is on large hessian coffee sacks.

🛈 Information

Cibercafé@halate Online (1a Calle Oriente, at 5a Av Norte; per hr US$1; ⊙ 8am-9:30pm Mon-Sat, 9am-1pm Sun)

Citibank (4a Calle Poniente, near 6a Av Sur; ⊙ 8am-4:30pm Mon-Fri, to noon Sat)

🛈 Getting There & Away

Bus 125 runs regularly from San Salvador (US$1, two hours) and terminates on 3a Av Sur, a few blocks south of the church. To La Palma and El Poy, take bus 125 toward El Amayo (the highway intersection) and transfer to bus 119 (1½ hours) heading north.

Around Chalatenango

The countryside around Chalatenango climbs into dry forest studded with toothy peaks and rugged tawny hills. The small villages in this remote area have stunning landscapes and interesting histories. La Montañona is a pine-forest reserve at 1600m with prime views and pre-Columbian rock carvings. The civil war left several *tatús* (cave hideouts), including one used by clandestine guerrilla radio station Radio Farabundo, as well as an underground guerrilla hospital. Beyond the Río Sumpul, Arcatao is a beautiful village in the mountains bordering Honduras. Northwest of Chalate, Concepción Quezaltepeque is a hammock-making center. You'll see women threading them along the side of the road.

🎉 Festivals

Festival de Hamacas   FAIR
(⊙ mid-Nov) Hammocks fill the streets of Concepción Quezaltepeque during this street fair.

🛌 Sleeping

La Montañano   LODGE $
(☑ 7723-6283; r US$5) You can stay in the small village of La Montañona – a rustic cabin has beds and a shared bathroom.

La Palma

Starring murals upon murals in the rainbow-colored, naïve art–style made famous by local boy Fernando Llort, La Palma is a tiny village which makes a big splash of paint. A two-hour drive north of San Salvador, the clean mountain air and access to exceptional hiking trails is reason enough to visit, but given every bus stop, spare wall and park bench screams at you in thick pastel daubs, the playful irreverence keeps you happily grounded.

These bright, primitive images of mountain villages, *campesinos* (farmers) or Christ are synonymous with the modern Salvadoran art movement. Llort taught local residents how to create the same images and started a successful cooperative. Today 75% of the village makes a living by mass-producing these bright motifs.

When it is time to move on, there are challenging peaks to test most. Serious hikers often prefer lodging in the neighboring village of San Ignacio as it's closer to the main trails.

◎ Sights

★ La Semilla de Dios   ARTS CENTER
(cnr 3a Calle Poniente & 5a Av Norte; ⊙10am-6pm) Local cooperative La Semilla de Dios, founded in 1977 by Fernando Llort himself, crafts quality products in workshops behind the store. If you ask permission you can wander through the workshops and watch the painters and woodworkers at work.

Copapase   ARTS CENTER
(⌨2305-9376; ⊙8am-5pm Mon-Fri, to noon Sat & Sun) Copapase is the most established artists cooperative in the area – it even has a small museum.

🏃 Activities

Cerro El Pital (2730m) is the highest peak in El Salvador, but thanks to an access road it is also one of the easiest to hike. From nearby San Ignacio, bus 509 to Las Pilas leaves you at Río Chiquito near the trail. It's about 1½ hours to the top, where spectacular views await. You will know you've reached the summit when you find the cement block marking it. It is private property, so bring US$2 to cover admission.

Once there, ask for directions to Piedra Rajada, a huge cloven rock a half-hour walk from the summit, accessed by a nerve-racking log bridge spanning a 25m drop. Don't try this one in wet weather.

The pinnacle of awesome forest views is in Miramundo, a small, aptly named community perched on a steep hillside. Back at Río Chiquito, follow the right-hand fork for about an hour to Miramundo. Right on the trail is the ridgetop Hostal Miramundo.

San Ignacio is a great base for hardcore hiking enthusiasts. For a guide, contact José Samuel Hernández, the owner of Comedor y Artesanías El Manzana, outside La Palma, or Humberto Regalado (⌨2352-9138), who owns and maintains the trail to Peña Cayaguanca.

Buses to Las Pilas, passing through Río Chiquito, leave San Ignacio at 7am, 9:30am, 12:30pm, 2:30pm and 4:30pm and return at the same times.

Comedor y Artesanías El Manzana   HIKING
(⌨2305-8379; Carretera La Palma–El Poy km 85) Tiny San Ignacio's answer to the *cooperatif* also serves basic meals and provides information for hikers.

🛏 Sleeping

Hotel La Palma   HOTEL $
(⌨2305-9344; www.hotellapalma.com.sv; r per person US$14-18; @☎) A long-standing retreat catering to large groups, this mountain getaway bordered by the Río La Palma is nonetheless a decent choice for individuals due to a yummy restaurant and well-kept grounds.

Hotel Posada Real   HOTEL $
(⌨2335-9009; r per person US$10) Has a nice location and a cute little snack bar, but there's not much character in these cinderblock rooms. The price is good though, plus it has hot water.

Hostal Miramundo   HOTEL $$
(⌨2219-6252; www.hotelmiramundo.com; San Ignacio; 4-person cabins US$65) This smart cabin in the woods in near San Ignacio is a good choice if you have a small group of would-be hikers. You can walk to Río Sumpul and El Pital from the doorstep then sleep in lovely, firm beds.

Hotel de Montaña El Pital   HOTEL $$$
(⌨2221-6954, 7894-4349; www.elpital.com.sv; cabins from US$90; ❋☎) If you need a little more comfort when bracing for the great outdoors – and you're not alone – then this mountain resort is a reasonable deal. New cabins and a fine restaurant make it worth-

CINQUERA

The former FMLN stronghold of Cinquera has transformed itself into a successful example of grassroots tourism. The friendly community has initiated a series of projects that have helped it to rebound from the horrors for the civil war. Ex-guerrillas share firsthand accounts of the conflict at a **war museum**. A terrific little **rainforest park** is great for a short hike and waterfall swim, and there's a sustainable **iguana farm** for the herpetophiles.

The **ARDM Hostel** (📞2389-5732; ardmcqr@yahoo.es; cabins US$20), run by the Association for Reconstruction and Municipal Development (ARDM), is a noble and comfortable place to stay. The spartan rooms are in faux-cabins (pine on concrete) and there's a decent restaurant onsite. It is always seeking volunteers for community and ecotourism projects.

The road into Cinquera is terrible. Bus 482 (US$0.80, one hour) leaves Suchitoto at 9.15am and 1.30pm.

while, and the location, well, it's truly remarkable. It has an office in San Salvador.

✖ Eating

★ **Ola Cafe**   CAFE $
(coffee US$1-2, cake US$1-2; ⊙8am-6pm) Hipster coffee has arrived in La Palma! This small, incongruously good coffee shop on the square roasts its own beans and serves homemade cakes to tables of very relieved local folk and out-of-town connoisseurs.

Restaurante del Pueblo   SALVADORAN $
(mains US$2-6; ⊙7am-9pm) Behind the town's wildest mural lies chunky beef sandwiches outdone only by a sausage- and steak-laden *plato típico* (grilled meat, bananas, beans, cheese and cream).

Cafe de Cafe   CAFE $
(📞2335-9190; Calle El Principal; mains US$3-7; ⊙11am-7pm) Expect top food at this popular cafe on the town square, namely steak, vegetable grills and various desserts. Coffee is strong and hot.

Cartagena Pizza   PIZZA $$
(📞2305-9475; Barrio el Centro; pizzas US$3-12; ⊙11am-9pm) These delicious thin-based pizzas make a welcome change from the standard Central American fare.

❶ Information

Citibank (cnr Calle Barrios & 1a Calle Poniente; ⊙8am-4:30pm Mon-Fri, to noon Sat) Twenty-four-hour ATM on the northeast corner of Parque Centro.

Palma City Online (Calle Principal; per hr US$0.80; ⊙8am-7pm)

Tourist Office (📞2335-9076; Parque Municipal; ⊙8am-4pm Mon-Fri, 9am-1pm Sat & Sun) Very helpful; Spanish only.

❶ Getting There & Away

Bus 119 runs every half-hour from San Salvador's Terminal de Oriente to the El Salvador–Honduras border at El Poy, stopping at La Palma (US$1.70, 2¾ hours). Some enter San Ignacio, 3km to the north; others drop you off at the entrance.

A shuttle bus runs half-hourly between La Palma and San Ignacio (10 minutes, US$0.25). From San Ignacio you can catch the bus to El Pital and its environs.

UNDERSTAND EL SALVADOR

El Salvador Today

El Salvador has been in the international spotlight due to a recent surge in gang-related violence. This disturbing trend overshadowed a positive first year in office for former guerrilla soldier President Salvador Sanchez Ceren, who oversaw a number of well-received social-welfare initiatives and education reform. The marginal victory by his leftist Frente Farabundo Martí para la Liberación Nacional (FMLN) party in 2014 was viewed as a triumph for democratic process, although the right-wing ARENA party continues to cry foul.

The El Salvadoran economy is still too reliant on remittances from abroad (one-fifth of the national economy), with Salvadorans now the third-largest Latino group in the US, behind Mexicans and Puerto Ricans. Some commentators have also suggested that President Ceren has been too cozy with struggling socialist countries such as Venezuela, to the detriment of long-term economic progress.

While the military has kept a healthy distance from political proceedings, corruption continues to cast a shadow over El Salvador's international standing. Even the beloved football team has been unable resist: in 2013, 14 players received life bans for match fixing. The revelation appeared to unite both parties in their condemnation of foul play, including the 2015 murder of disgraced star Alfredo Pacheco. Observers wonder if similar solidarity can be found in the political arena.

History

Traders & Raiders

Paleo-Indian peoples populated El Salvador as early as 10,000 years ago, literally leaving their mark with cave paintings in modern Morazán. Around 2000 BC the Olmecs followed, leaving as their legacy the Olmec Boulder, a giant head sculpture similar to those from Mexico, found near Casa Blanca.

El Salvador was once a key regional trading center. Archaeological remains reveal diverse influences, from Pipil, Teotihuacan and Maya in the west to Lenca, Chorti and Pok'omama in the east. The step pyramid ruins at Tazumal, San Andrés and Casa Blanca show 3000 years of nearly constant pre-Hispanic habitation.

When Spanish conquistador Pedro de Alvarado arrived in 1524, he saw a country dominated by Pipils, descendants of Toltecs and Aztecs. These northern peoples (from modern-day Mexico) dubbed their home Cuscatlán, 'Land of Jewels.' Their maize-based farming economy flourished enough to support several cities and a sophisticated culture with pursuits that included hieroglyphics, astronomy and mathematics. Their dialect is related to modern Nahuat.

From Indigo to Independence

Spanish rule started with a year-long struggle against the Pipil. The Spaniards prevailed and laid claim to the land, transforming it into plantations of cotton, balsam and indigo. Agriculture boomed throughout the 1700s, with indigo the number-one export. A small group of Europeans, known as the '14 families,' controlled virtually all of the colony's wealth and agriculture, enslaving indigenous peoples and Africans to work the land.

Conflict simmered under this gross imbalance of power. A revolt against Spain in 1811 was led by Padre (Father) José Delgado. While it failed, it planted a seed of discontent. Independence was gained 10 years later, on September 15, 1821, when El Salvador became part of the Central American Federation.

Pushing for land reform, Anastasio Aquino led an indigenous rebellion in 1883. Though it was subdued and Aquino was executed, he became a national hero. El Salvador withdrew from the Central American Federation in 1841, but Independence Day continues to be celebrated on September 15.

In Comes Coffee

In the late 19th century, synthetic dyes undermined the indigo market, and coffee took the main stage. A handful of wealthy landowners expanded their properties, displacing indigenous people. Coffee became the most important cash crop and *cafetaleros* (coffee growers) earned purses full of money that was neither taxed nor redistributed at reasonable wages to the workers. By the 20th century, 95% of El Salvador's income derived from coffee exports, but only 2% of Salvadorans controlled that wealth.

The 20th Century

The government vigorously eradicated union activity in the coffee industry during the 1920s. In January 1932 Augustín Farabundo Martí, a founder of the Central American Socialist Party, led an uprising of peasants and indigenous people. The military responded brutally by systematically killing anyone who looked indigenous or supported the uprising. La Matanza (the Massacre) resulted in the death of 30,000 individuals, including Martí, who was killed by firing squad. The FMLN (Frente Farabundo Martí para la Liberación Nacional) revolutionary army would later take up his name in his honor.

Over the course of the 1970s, landlessness, poverty, unemployment and overpopulation became serious problems. In government, the polarized left and right tangled for power through coups and electoral fraud. In 1972 José Napoleon Duarte, cofounder of the Christian Democrat Party (Partido Democrático Cristiano; PDC), ran for president supported by a broad coalition of reform groups. When his victory was denied amid allegations of fraud, protests followed. The military averted an attempted coup, and the right responded to increasing guerrilla activity by creating 'death squads.' Thousands of Salvadorans were kidnapped, tortured and murdered.

In 1979 a junta of military personnel and civilians overthrew President Carlos Humberto Romero and promised reforms. When promises were not met, opposition parties banded together as the Frente Democrático Revolucionario (FDR) and allied with the FMLN, a revolutionary army composed of five guerrilla groups for whom armed struggle appeared to be the only means of change. The successful revolution in Nicaragua in 1979 had encouraged many Salvadorans to demand reforms. One of them was Monsignor Oscar Romero, a formerly conservative priest who took up the cause of the people.

On March 24, 1980, outspoken Archbishop Romero was assassinated while saying Mass in the chapel of the San Salvador Divine Providence Cancer Hospital. His murder ignited an armed insurrection that same year that was to turn into a civil war.

Civil War

The rape and murder in late 1980 of four US nuns performing relief work in El Salvador prompted the Carter administration to suspend military aid. But in 1981 the newly elected Reagan administration, bristling from the threat of Nicaragua's socialist revolution, pumped huge sums into the moribund Salvadoran military. Uncle Sam's support would effectively prolong the conflict. When guerrillas gained control of areas in the north and east, the Salvadoran military retaliated by decimating villages. In 1981 the US-trained elite Atlacatl Battalion killed more than 700 men, women and children in El Mozote, Morazán. As many as 300,000 citizens fled the country.

In 1982 Major Roberto D'Aubisson, founder of the extreme-right ARENA party, became president of the legislative assembly and enacted a law granting the legislative body power over the president. D'Aubisson created death squads targeting, among oth-

ers, trade unionists and agrarian reformers. In response, the FMLN offensive blew up bridges, cut power lines and destroyed coffee plantations and livestock – anything to stifle the economy. When the government ignored an FMLN peace proposal, the rebels refused to participate in the 1984 presidential elections, in which Duarte won over D'Aubisson. For the next few years the PDC and FMLN engaged in peace talks unsuccessfully. Death squads continued pillaging, and the guerrillas continued to undermine military powers and jeopardize municipal elections.

The Price of Peace

Hopes for peace rose in 1989, when the FMLN offered to participate in elections if the government agreed to a postponement to ensure democratic polls. Its calls were ignored and Alfredo Cristiani, a wealthy ARENA businessman, was elected president. The FMLN's response was a major attack on the capital. In retaliation the military killed an estimated 4000 'leftist sympathizers.'

UN-mediated negotiations began between the government and FMLN in April 1990. Among the first agreements was a human-rights accord signed by both parties. Yet violent deaths actually increased in 1991 when a UN mission arrived to monitor human rights.

On January 16, 1992, a compromise was finally signed. The FMLN became an opposition party, and the government agreed to various reforms, including dismantling paramilitary groups and death squads, replacing them with a national civil police force. Land was to be distributed to citizens and human-rights violations investigated. But instead, the government gave amnesty to human-rights abusers.

During the course of the 12-year civil war, an estimated 75,000 people were killed.

Modern Currents

The FMLN has mostly proven to be a model example of a former guerrilla organization transitioning to mainstream politics. Sceptics argued that Salvadorans would always prefer conservatives. However, this all changed in 2009 when Mauricio Funes led the FMLN to power in a popular victory. The FMLN narrowly achieved re-election in 2014 under the leadership of Salvador Sanchez Ceren.

An ongoing issue for the ruling administration has been how to deal with the two major criminal gangs in the country. Also known as M-13, or Mara Salvatrucha (*mara* means 'gang', *trucha* means 'clever trout'), and Barrio 18, these gangs of roughly 100,000 across Central America were formed in the US in response to orchestrated attacks by Mexicans. Deported en masse from the US between 2000 and 2004, the *maras* became heavily involved in drug cartels, guns, the sex trade and illegal immigration.

Both the carrot and the stick have failed to have a lasting impact on the gang problem, as successive governments have struggled to curtail the violence. A heavy-handed approach by the right-wing ARENA party in the 2000s led to numerous high-profile arrests but arguably exacerbated the retaliation, while a carefully brokered 'truce' between the rival gangs in 2012 proved only a temporary reprieve.

Record body counts in 2015 earned El Salvador the distinction of the world's 'highest murder rate'. International media continues to frame the progress of the country in relation to this damning statistic. However, there remains cautious optimism that Ceren's wide-reaching social reforms will bring about an increase in public safety.

Culture

The National Psyche

Salvadorans are strong-willed people who are very welcoming to travelers. With an estimated third of the population residing in the US, they are nostalgic for their country of birth and often fiercely idealistic about the future. There is at times a palpable frustration with the progress of the nation.

The civil war still looms large in the national psyche, as it must – not only are the memories too searing to forget, but the ruling party itself was borne out of the guerrilla movement. At the same time, Salvadorans are genuinely dismayed to learn that many foreigners know little about El Salvador beyond the war. They will eagerly volunteer information and assistance.

Lifestyle

Remittances sent home from the roughly two million Salvadorans living abroad, which annually total US$3 billion (20% of national GDP), provide a measure of stability to the economy and greatly influence how people live. Poverty and unemployment persist, with about 30% of the population below the poverty line, mostly in rural areas. That said, El Salvador enjoys the highest minimum wage in Central America (about US$150 per week) and is notably more prosperous than neighboring Honduras and Nicaragua.

Religion

El Salvador is a very religious country. Once staunchly Catholic, like the rest of Latin America, El Salvador is experiencing an explosive growth of evangelical churches. Their fiery services seem to have brought fresh energy to faith. Town-square services with booming speakers are becoming an

---

BEHIND THE SCENES OF NAÏVE ART

Holy scenes, strange birds, unabashed rainbow colors: the childlike images of Fernando Llort have come to symbolize hope in a war-torn Central America. Compared to Miró and Picasso, Llort differs with earnest iconography and flat tropical hues in a style dubbed primitive modern.

Ironically, this strong Latin American identity was forged when Llort went to France to study architecture and then theology. Religious symbols are recurring motifs in his artwork. He prefers the rough and everyday to the exalted.

When Llort returned to El Salvador in the early 1970s, he arrived to the tensions and violence leading up to the civil war. Llort moved to La Palma, a distant mountain town in the north, to take refuge. The apparent simplicity of a life in harmony with nature further informed his style. He started La Semilla de Dios (God's Seed), a workshop to teach others his craft and professionalize local artisans.

Llort has since lived in San Salvador and abroad, but the workshop is still going strong in his former studio. You can find his work in the White House, MoMA and the Vatican.

all-too-typical way of spreading 'the word.' Protestant churches now account for almost 50% of believers, which speaks of frustration with the traditional Catholic church. Before and during the war, priests and missionaries were often outspoken critics of government repression – many, such as Archbishop Oscar Romero, were killed for their stands.

Arts

El Salvador's artisan products can be innovative and high quality. Fernando Llort's naïve art inspired an industry of brightly painted crafts in childlike motifs in the community of La Palma. Guatajiagua in Morazán produces unique black pottery with a Lenca influence and Ilobasco is known for its *sorpresas,* intricate miniatures hidden in ceramic shells.

Poetry is beloved in El Salvador. Iconoclast poet Roque Dalton was exiled for radical politics. He eventually returned home to aid the guerrilla cause but was executed by his own side due to suspicion that he was a CIA operative. Notable works include *Taberna y otros lugares* (1969), a political vision in verse, and *Miguel Marmol.* Progressive poet Claudia Lars wrote spare, bold erotic poetry and is considered one of the country's foremost writers.

Written under the pen name Salarrué, lauded writer Salvador Efraín Salazar Arrué's *Cuentos de barro* (Tales of Mud), published in 1933, marks the beginning of Central America's modern short-story genre. Likewise, Manlio Argueta's *One Day of Life* (1980), a tale of a rural family with the backdrop of the civil war, is considered a modern classic. Matilde Elena Lopez is a playwright who wrote a compelling 1978 play based on the life of indigenous leader Anastasio Aquino.

One of the more interesting contemporary Salvadoran novelists is Horacio Casellanos Moya. His translated *Senselessness* (2004) is a burning black comedy about government-sponsored violence.

Films *Romero,* produced by Ellwood Kieser in 1988, and *Salvador,* directed by Oliver Stone, offer Hollywood versions of the civil war. *Innocent Voices* (2004) looks at the civil war from a child's perspective and was nominated for an Oscar.

In 2015 El Salvador cohosted the prestigious Mexican documentary film festival, Ambulante.

Landscape & Wildlife

The Land

The Land of Volcanoes, El Salvador has two volcanic ranges spanning east to west, spicing the views, as well as daily life, with a little drama. Much of the land is deforested but mountains in the far north are blanketed in pine and oak, jagged rock formations and cloud forests. The Río Lempa bisects the country with a fertile swath of land. While El Salvador is the only Central American country not to have a Caribbean coast, there is over 300km of Pacific coastline bordering mangroves, estuaries and tropical dry forest. Lakes and freshwater lagoons provide drinking water and recreation.

Wildlife

El Salvador was drastically deforested over the 20th century. As a result, many species of plants and animals ceased to exist in the country. However, national parks and protected lands still maintain good biodiversity.

NATIONAL PARKS & RESERVES

El Salvador has only four official national parks, but there are a number of locally or privately administered reserves.

Barra de Santiago (p322) A remote bar of mangrove-fringed estuaries and beaches on the Pacific coast.

Cerro El Pital (p338) El Salvador's highest peak. *Torogoz* (blue-crowned motmots) and quetzals can be observed on its piney slopes.

La Laguna de Alegría (p325) An emerald-green lake fed by hot springs, in the crater of dormant Volcán de Tecapa. Ocelots and coatis are among the wildlife inhabiting primary-growth forest surrounding the lake. In 2015 the lake receded to record low water levels.

Laguna El Jocotal This freshwater lagoon east of Usulután is an important sanctuary for migratory birds from October to March.

Parque Nacional El Imposible (p323) Near El Salvador's western limit; one of the country's last remnants of original tropical forest with waterfalls, views and numerous endangered plant and animal species.

Parque Nacional Los Volcanes (p310) A volcano-crater forest with amazing views of nearby Izalco and Santa Ana volcanoes. Highlights include emerald toucanets, motmots and hummingbirds.

Parque Nacional Montecristo–El Trifinio A mountainous cloud-forest reserve at the borders of El Salvador, Honduras and Guatemala. Wildlife includes pumas, spider monkeys and agoutis. Giant ferns, orchids and bromeliads are abundant.

Parque Nacional Walter T Deininger (p305) This dry tropical forest on the Pacific coast is the habitat for 87 bird species, deer and pacas.

The country has over 800 animal species. Almost half are butterflies; bird species are second in number, with about 330 resident species (and 170 migratory), including quetzals, toucans, herons, kingfishers, brown pelicans, egrets, parakeets and sandpipers. Illegal bird trafficking continues to pose a problem, in particular macaws from Nicaragua.

The remaining mammal species number around 200 and can be seen mostly in reserves. They include opossums, anteaters, porcupines, agoutis, ocelots, spider monkeys and white-tailed deer.

In all, about 90 animal species are in danger of extinction, including marine turtles, armadillos and over 15 types of hummingbird.

With so much of the land cultivated, few original plants still exist. Small stands of balsam trees survive along the western Pacific coast (dubbed the Costa del Bálsamo) and mangroves line many estuaries. Bosque Montecristo and El Imposible offer the widest variety of indigenous plants, and Parque Nacional Los Volcanes offers good vegetation. Plants in these areas include mountain pines, oaks, figs, magueys, ferns and orchids.

Environmental Issues

The latest high-profile environmental case in the country revolves around an Australian-owned gold-mining operator, Pacific Rim, which is facing fierce community opposition to its plans to extract gold from the La Cabanas region in the north. Pacific Rim subsequently sued the El Salvadoran government for US$300m. In late 2015 the international community was awaiting the outcome of the case, which will have serious ramifications for land rights and community activism across the globe.

Deforestation is a major cause for concern, coupled with relatively high population density which disrupts the regeneration of ecosystems. Today, a mere 14% of the country is forested, with only a minuscule 2% to 5% of that primary forest. As a result, many native species have become endangered or extinct.

El Salvador has also copped the brunt of many natural disasters in recent years. Earthquakes in 2001 brought on landslides and destroyed buildings, killing 1159 people; the eruption of Santa Ana volcano in October 2005, coupled with Hurricane Stan's torrential rains, unleashed scores of landslides, with the largest loss of life occurring in poor areas built on steep slopes or riverbanks. In 2009 massive floods killed 200 people and devastated large tracts of land and housing within 50km of the capital.

Another particularly volatile year for seismic activity was 2012, while 2015 saw the San Miguel volcano spew gas above the second-largest city in the land.

Río Lempa, a crucial watershed for the country, suffers from pollution due to decades of pesticide use and the destabilizing effects of global warming. Community leaders have labelled damage to the protected biosphere around Bahía de Jiquilisco an environmental emergency and a government response is being closely monitored by climate-change watchdogs.

SURVIVAL GUIDE

🛈 Directory A–Z

ACCOMMODATIONS

El Salvador has an excellent range of small hotels and backpacker hostels, particularly in San Salvador, and the busier tourist areas such as Playa El Tunco, Suchitoto and the Ruta de las Flores. We seek out the safest and most secure options for travelers here.

Camping and *eco-albergues* (ecohostels; basic shared cabins, some with modest kitchen facilities) are found around popular outdoor destinations. Bring your own camping equipment.

Room rates are stable season to season, except during the first week of August (summer holidays) and the Semana Santa (around Easter), when hotels can fill up quickly. The average rate for dorms is around US$10, and for doubles US$35.

BARGAINING

Bargaining is less common here than it is in other Central American countries. A little back-and-forth is common with taxi drivers and market shopkeepers, but hard bargaining can seem a bit rude.

CLIMATE

The *invierno* (wet season) is from May to October, and the *verano* (dry season) is from November to April. During the rainy season, it usually only rains at night.

In San Salvador the maximum temperature varies from 27°C (80°F) in November to 30°C (86°F) in March and April; the minimum temperatures range from 16°C (61°F) in January and February to 20°C (68°F) in March. The coastal lowlands are the hottest region.

DANGERS & ANNOYANCES

Crime shouldn't deter travelers from El Salvador any more than it does from the rest of Central America. Despite the country's reputation for violence, attacks on tourists are rare.

Of course, violence does occur. Two major *maras* (gangs) operate in the country, but travelers are unlikely to have encounters with a gang member as groups concentrate in neighborhoods with no outside appeal, and also because the police control most tourist areas. Still, visitors should avoid traveling at night. Weapons are widespread, so never resist a robbery – it's not worth it.

Take commonsense precautions: carry as little as possible on day trips, be aware of your bags on buses, and avoid toting expensive items. Before traveling, make copies of your credit cards and important documents; carry a copy with you and leave one with someone at home who could fax them to you in a pinch. After dark it's best to take a taxi, even if the rates can be a little steep. This is particularly important in San Salvador, San Miguel, Sonsonate, La Unión and La Libertad.

Most volcano climbs are best done with a police escort, partly for your safety and partly so you won't get lost on unmarked and intersecting trails. The service is free, but you must request it by phone or in person at least a day in advance (and preferably more). Officers are friendly and trustworthy.

EMBASSIES & CONSULATES

Australian Consulate (☎ 2298-9447; consuladohonorarioelsalvador@gmail.com; 12a Calle Poniente 2028, Colonia Flor Blanca)

Canadian Embassy (☎ 2279-4655; www.canadainternational.gc.ca/el_salvador-salvador; 63a Av Sur, Alameda Roosevelt, Torre A; ⊙ 8:30am-noon Mon-Fri) Also welcomes Australians.

Dutch Consulate (☎ 2264-8449; info@recusa.com.sv; 75 Av Sur 9a, Pasaje C, Colonia Escalón; ⊙ 9am-1pm Mon-Fri)

SLEEPING PRICE RANGES

The following price ranges refer to a double room with bathroom. Unless otherwise stated, breakfast is not included in the price.

$	Less than US$25
$$	US$25–80
$$$	More than US$80

French Embassy (☎2279-4016; www.emba francia.com.sv; 1a Calle Poniente 3718; ⊙8am-noon Mon-Fri)

German Embassy (☎2247-0000; www. san-salvador.diplo.de; 7a Calle Poniente 3972; ⊙8am-11:30am Mon-Thu, to 11am Fri)

Guatemalan Embassy (☎2271-2225; 15a Av Norte, btwn Calles Arce & 1a Calle Poniente, Colonia Escalón; ⊙8am-noon Mon-Fri)

Honduran Embassy (☎2263-2808; 89a Av Norte, btwn 7a & 9a Calle Poniente, Colonia Escalón; ⊙8am-noon Mon-Fri)

Irish Consulate (☎2263-8236; rmurray@ agrisal.com; Pasaje Francisco Campos 160, Colonia Escalón)

Mexican Embassy (☎2243-0445; http://em bamex.sre.gob.mx/elsalvador; cnr Calle Circun-valación & Pasaje 12, Colonia San Benito)

New Zealand Consulate (☎2278-3372; acabrales@fusades.com.sv; Edificio Fusades, Boulevard y Urbanizacion Santa Elena, Antiguo Cuscatlan)

Nicaraguan Embassy (☎2263-8770; 7a Calle Poniente, Colonia Escalón; ⊙9am-4:30pm Mon-Fri)

US Embassy (☎2501-2999; http://sansalvador. usembassy.gov; Blvd Santa Elena; ⊙9am-4pm Mon-Fri)

UK Consulate (☎2511-5757; www.gov.uk/ government/world/el-salvador; Torre Futura, 14th fl, Colonia Escalón; ⊙7:30am-4:30pm Mon-Thu, to 11:30am Fri)

EMERGENCY
Emergencies ☎911

ENTRY & EXIT FORMALITIES
➡ Salvadoran border officials are among the most scrutinizing in the region. They check for previous entry and exit stamps. If you're entering on an international bus, your bags may well be searched.

➡ Carry your passport with you in all border regions, regardless of whether you're leaving the country, since there are a lot of police checkpoints (mostly searching for drugs).

Visas
Citizens of the USA, Canada, Australia, New Zealand, South Africa, Switzerland, Norway, Japan, Taiwan, Brazil, Argentina, Mexico, other Central American countries, Israel and EU member countries do not need a visa, but must purchase a single-entry tourist card for US$10 when entering the country. For those who do need a prearranged visa, the cost is US$30. The standard length of stay is 30 days, but you can request up to 90 days – do so quickly before the official stamps your passport! If you leave and return within the allotted time, you can use the same tourist card.

The Central America-4 agreement allows for travel between the borders of Guatemala, Honduras, El Salvador and Nicaragua with one entry fee and one passport stamp (in this case, be sure you ask for the 90-day option). If you are traveling overland, please note the change; it's possible you will have to 'remind' some border guards about the agreement.

For up-to-date visa information visit http:// www.lonelyplanet.com/el-salvador/practical-information/visas.

No vaccinations are required unless you are coming from an area infected by yellow fever (some are recommended, however).

HEALTH
El Salvador has a burdened public health system, and an excellent private system with well-trained professionals. Vigilance is required in mosquito-prone areas near the coast and during the rainy season when dengue fever outbreaks can occur. Keep up to date with the status of the Zika virus.

Availability & Cost of Healthcare
You can easily get access to a top doctor in San Salvador, but you will have to pay significant fees up-front.

Health Insurance
Health insurance is highly recommended and necessary for the better hospitals.

Tap Water
Tap water is generally very good in El Salvador; however, in poorer areas it is best to always boil before drinking.

INTERNET ACCESS
The internet is easy to access at internet cafes across the country, though speeds vary considerably. Expect to pay between US$0.50 to $1 per hour.

LANGUAGE
Spanish is the national language. In a few indigenous villages just a handful of people still speak the Nahuat language of the Pipil, but there is increasing interest in preserving it. Many Salvadorans pick up some English working in the USA, Australia and elsewhere, which means you are

---

EATING PRICE RANGES

The following price ranges refer to a standard meal. Unless otherwise stated, tax is included in the price.

$	Less than US$5
$$	US$5–15
$$$	More than US$15

more likely to meet English speakers here than in neighboring countries.

Courses

SalvaSpan have a range of reputable homestays throughout the country, while **Centro de Intercambio y Solidaridad** (p293) also offers Spanish classes with progressive sensibilities. Suchitoto has two excellent schools and locals there are used to conversing with traveling language students. Luis from Spanish S-Cool in Playa El Zonte is one of the best of language tutors/surf instructors along the Costa del Bálsamo. Playa El Tunco is also a pretty good place to find a qualified language tutor.

LEGAL MATTERS

Law enforcement is strict and effective, from beat cops to border officials. Police are entitled to stop buses and search people and bags, and do so with some frequency, often helped by army soldiers. Bribes are generally not expected, though can assist in minor indiscretions. If arrested, cooperate and call your embassy, although if you have committed a crime there's little your embassy can do. Even minor offenses require jail time.

LGBT TRAVELLERS

Gay people receive little tolerance. Numerous recent attacks on members of the gay community have gone unpunished. Some hotels refuse to rent a room with one bed to two men; women will encounter less scrutiny. In San Salvador, the area around Blvd de los Héroes has cultural centers and clubs that are gay friendly. Gay organization **Entre Amigos** (p301) is the most established in the country, dedicated mostly to HIV/AIDS outreach.

MAPS

➜ Corsatur and the Ministry of Tourism offer glossy maps of El Salvador and the capital, available at some hotels and tour offices.

➜ Simple maps of hiking trails are sometimes available at visitor centers.

MEDIA

San Salvador's main newspapers are *La Prensa Gráfica* and the conservative *El Diario de Hoy;* check them for domestic and international news, plus entertainment listings. *El Mundo* and *El Latino* are thinner afternoon papers. *El Faro* is a respected and often controversial online journal.

MONEY

El Salvador's official currency is the US dollar. ATMs are plentiful, and credit cards, particularly visa cards, widely accepted.

ATMs

ATMs are found in most cities and towns. Citibank, Scotiabank and Banco Atlántida have the largest networks of ATMs. Plus/Visa and Cirrus/MasterCard cards generally work well, but try more than one machine should your initial attempt fail. Look for safer locking cabins when withdrawing money, and avoid taking out cash at night.

Tipping

➜ **Restaurants** Tip 10%

➜ **Taxis** It is not customary to tip taxi drivers, though rounding up the amount is appreciated

Cash

On January 2001, El Salvador adopted the US dollar as its official currency, replacing the colón. Bring some US dollars with you, preferably in US$20 bills and smaller. The border crossings have money changers.

Credit Cards

Credit cards are quite widely accepted, though many establishments add a surcharge. Visa cards encounter the least resistance. MasterCard is becoming more widely accepted while American Express is less common.

OPENING HOURS

Some offices and stores close at lunchtime, between noon and 2pm, but this practice is fading.

Businesses & stores 9am to 6pm weekdays

Government offices 8am to 4pm weekdays

Banks 8am to 4pm or 5pm weekdays; most open Saturday morning as well

Restaurants Dinner is early; 4pm is *pupusa* hour.

POST

There are two rates for sending international mail: airmail and express mail. Letters sent by airmail to the USA should arrive in 10 days (US$0.50), to Europe and Asia in up to 15 days (US$0.65). Letters sent express to the USA should take five days (US$1), to Europe and Australia 10 days (US$1.20). FedEx and DHL have offices in large cities.

PUBLIC HOLIDAYS

January 1 New Year's Day

Easter Semana Santa

May 1 Labor Day

June 17 Fathers Day

August 6 Feast of San Salvador

September 15 Independence Day

November 2 All Souls' Day

December 25 Christmas Day

RESPONSIBLE TRAVEL

Many travelers come to El Salvador with a notion of which 'side' they supported in the civil war (usually the FMLN). In fact, both sides committed

terrible atrocities and in 12 years of war, neither came to fully represent (or betray) the ideals of the majority of Salvadorans. Visitors should not be hesitant to discuss the war, but should honor the personal experiences of everyday Salvadorans.

Tourism is starting to make itself felt but Salvadorans remain relatively unjaded toward backpackers. Hard bargaining, whether in taxis or in markets, is rare. It may be too late to reverse the unpleasant wheeling and dealing of Guatemala and elsewhere, but in El Salvador, an honest price and a friendly transaction are still the norm.

SMOKING

Smoking is still very common; banned in closed public places.

TAXES & REFUNDS

A VAT of 13% applies to all goods and services; it is usually factored into prices.

TELEPHONE

➡ The country code when calling El Salvador from abroad is ☑ 503.

➡ Phone numbers usually have eight digits; there are no internal area codes.

➡ Telecom and Telefónica payphones accept their respective phone cards. Buy prepaid phone cards (in US$3, US$5 and US$10 denominations) at pharmacies and corner stores.

➡ Phone booths post local and international dialing instructions in English and Spanish.

➡ Some internet cafes offer web-based calling.

Cell Phones

Claro, Tivo, Digicel and Movistar all provide decent service and affordable, ubiquitous prepaid SIM cards which work in Australian and European phones. You will need a passport to sign up initially.

US travelers should be aware that CDMA-only phones cannot use GSM SIM cards.

TIME

El Salvador has one time zone – Central Standard Time (CST).

CITY	DIFFERENCE TO EL SALVADOR TIME
Sydney	+17hr
Tokyo	+15hr
Dubai	+10hr
London	+6hr
New York	+1hr

TOILETS

➡ Toilets are sit-down, not squat.

➡ Usually free, but sometimes a small charge (US$0.10).

TOURIST INFORMATION

➡ El Salvador has decent tourist offices in the more popular areas, including Suchitoto, Ruta de las Flores, La Libertad and Perquín; however, hotel owners are often the best resources.

➡ In the capital you'll find the office of **Corporación Salvadoreña de Turismo** (p301), offering brochures and fliers.

➡ The **Instituto Salvadoreño de Turismo** (p301) has very general information about El Salvador's national parks and *turicentros*.

TRAVEL WITH CHILDREN

El Salvador is a very Catholic/Christian, family-centered society, so children are always welcomed. Some tips:

➡ Avoid San Salvador; it can be overwhelming for kids.

➡ La Costa del Bálsamo has fabulous beaches, but the ocean is not good for weak swimmers.

➡ Suchitoto, Ruta de Las Flores and Alegría are gentle alternatives.

➡ Camping is potentially excellent, but some experience is needed as facilities are not great.

TRAVELLERS WITH DISABILITIES

There are many people with disabilities in El Salvador – most victims of war-related violence – but there are still limited services or amenities to make their lives easier. There are few well-maintained ramps and handrails, and few services for the visually and hearing impaired. However, all travelers, including those with disabilities, will find Salvadorans extremely friendly and eager to help.

VOLUNTEERING

In San Salvador's Blvd de los Héroes area, **Centro de Intercambio y Solidaridad** (p293) offers Spanish classes to tourists and English classes to low-income and activist Salvadorans, always with a strong emphasis on progressive politics. A friendly place to visit, the CIS has positions for volunteer English teachers (10-week minimum), and information about NGOs working on various issues, including community development, gang intervention, the environment and more. CIS cannot arrange an actual volunteer position, but can point you in the right direction. During national elections you can volunteer with CIS's well-respected international election-observer mission.

Global Platform (p335) is a Danish NGO based in Suchitoto that offers Spanish lessons and lodging in return for assistance on community projects in the surrounding area. A month costs roughly US$400 all-inclusive.

WEIGHTS & MEASURES

The metric system is used.

WORK

There are no publicized working opportunities in El Salvador for travelers, though teaching English or surfing is sometimes done on an ad hoc basis. Those looking to stay longer term are invariably involved in volunteer community projects.

ℹ️ Getting There & Away

El Salvador's discerning immigration officials scrutinize entry and exit stamps, so avoid cutting corners. Request a 90-day tourist card in advance if you'd like one, otherwise you may be given less time.

AIR

Flights to and from the US sell out quickly around Christmas and Easter so book well in advance to avoid excessive costs.

La Costa del Bálsamo is as close to the airport as San Salvador, so it is easy to avoid the capital if you so desire.

Airports & Airlines

The **Aeropuerto Internacional Comalpa** (p302) is located 44km south of San Salvador. A major Latin American hub, it is also a gateway to North American cities.

Buses run to the city center every 60 minutes, but it can be stressful finding the location, especially with luggage. Taxis cost about US$30 to US$35 (45 minutes) and are plentiful, but negotiate beforehand. Taxis Acacya (US$5) run a smart shuttle service to downtown, but you'll most likely need a second cab as they terminate in a dangerous area. Hotels arrange pick-ups.

Avianca, American Airlines, United Airlines, Delta Air Lines and Copa Airlines are among those providing services to El Salvador.

LAND

El Salvador has excellent bus networks and most travelers happily bounce between long-distance coaches and souped-up old American school buses. There are no trains, and few travelers bother renting a car.

Border Crossings

Unless you arrive by plane, you will already have the CA-4 visa (p732) when you arrive at an El Salvadoran border. There's no need to pay anything, unless you are an American entering/exiting Nicaragua (US$12); don't let the guards tell you otherwise.

Costa Rica & Nicaragua

El Amatillo Microbuses run from 5:30am to 5pm across the southern tip of Honduras to the Nicaraguan border town of Guasaule (US$5 depending on number of passengers, two hours). Walk 200m for the connections which

reach León and Managua. Note that Americans must pay US$12 to enter Nicaragua.

San Miguel Managua can be reached by a Platinum bus (www.platinumcentroamerica.com; US$30, nine hours) from San Miguel that continues on to San José, Costa Rica (US$67, 19 hours). It stops at San Miguel's Esso gas station (corner Av Roosevelt and Ruta Militar) at about 7:30am and 1:30pm.

Guatemala

Ahuachapán The Las Chinamas–Valle Nuevo border is open 24 hours but it's best to cross in daylight. Buses leave Ahuachapán from Parque Menéndez every 15 minutes (US$0.50, 5am to 7:30pm) for the Guatemalan border. After crossing the border it's 300m to the bus stop for service to Guatemala City via Cuilapa. Tica bus (US$3) passes every half-hour and is safer than 2nd-class service. The last bus from the border to Ahuachapán is at 5:45pm.

Metapán Ordinary and *especial* services to Guatemala City via Las Chinamas–Valle Nuevo are offered by **Agencia Puerto Bus** (p316). Ordinary buses (US$9, four hours) leave hourly 5am to 4pm, except 7am. *Especial* buses (a well-spent US$11.50, 3½ hours) leave at 7am and 5:30pm. Another option is to catch a 1st-class bus at Las Chinamas. From Metapán, microbuses also run every half-hour to the Anguiatú–Chiquimula border (open 24 hours but more reliably from 6am to 7pm). On the Guatemalan side, buses run frequently to Chiquimula (one hour, last bus at 5:30pm) and onward to Guatemala City (three hours, last bus from Chiquimula at 3:30pm). This is the quickest route to Nueva Ocotopeque or Copán Ruínas, Honduras. In El Salvador, the last bus from the border to Metapán is at 6:30pm.

Santa Ana The San Cristóbal–El Progreso border is open 24 hours but you should cross during daylight hours. From Santa Ana, take bus 236 to San Cristóbal (US$0.50, one hour, every 20 minutes 5:30am to 9pm). Buses on the other side of the border go to El Progreso. The last bus back from San Cristóbal is at 6pm.

Sonsonate The La Hachadura–Ciudad Pedro de Alvarado border is open 24 hours, but it's

DEPARTURE TAX

US citizens and some other nationalities are required to pay for a US$10 tourist card upon arrival to El Salvador's airport. The Central America-4 agreement allows for travel between the borders of Guatemala, Honduras, El Salvador and Nicaragua with one entry fee.

Departure tax is included in the price of tickets.

best to cross in daylight. Bus 259 from Sonsonate drops you right at the border; Salvadoran and Guatemalan immigration posts are at the far side of the complex. In Guatemala, the bus stop is 1km away; bicycle taxis cost US$0.50. Buses for Guatemala City (US$5, four hours) leave every half-hour via Chiquimulilla and Escuintla. The last bus from La Hachadura to Sonsonate is at 6pm.

Honduras

La Palma The bus from La Palma drops you about 100m from the El Salvador–Honduras border (open 24 hours) at El Poy, where you pay US$3 to enter Honduras. From El Poy, you can take a bus or *colectivo* (shared taxi) to Nueva Ocotepeque, Honduras. From there buses leave hourly for San Pedro Sula. For Copán Ruinas, transfer at La Entrada. The last bus to El Poy from La Palma (bus 119, US$0.50, 30 minutes) leaves at 7pm. The last bus south from El Poy to San Salvador leaves around 4:15pm.

San Miguel For Tegucigalpa (US$56, five hours), 1st-class Platinum buses stop at San Miguel's Esso gas station (corner Av Roosevelt and Ruta Militar) at around 8am and 3:30pm daily – be early just in case. Buy tickets at the gas station one day in advance. Otherwise, bus 330 drops you 50m from El Amatillo on the Salvadoran border where a bridge crosses into Honduras. Honduran buses then go to Choluteca (US$2.10, 1½ hours) and on to Tegucigalpa (US$2.50, 3½ hours); the last bus for both leaves at 5:30pm. The last bus from El Amatillo to San Miguel goes at 6:30pm.

CAR & MOTORCYCLE

If you drive into El Salvador, you must show a driver's license (an international driving permit is accepted) and proof that you own the vehicle. You must also fill out extensive forms. Car insurance is available and advisable but not required. Vehicles may remain in El Salvador for 30 days. If you wish to stay longer, it's best to leave the country and drive back in rather than attempt to deal with the Transport Ministry.

SEA

El Salvador shares the Golfo de Fonseca with Honduras and Nicaragua. Boats occasionally ferry passengers between La Unión (El Salvador), Coyolito, Amapala or San Lorenzo (Honduras), and Potosí (Nicaragua). Going by sea does not save time since there are no scheduled passenger boats and land crossings are relatively close.

❶ Getting Around

El Salvador is small and pretty easy to get around by bus, car and taxi.

AIR

Flying within El Salvador is neither cost effective nor easily accessible. Some well-heeled execs fly private planes between San Miguel and San Salvador, and Puerta Barillas in Bahía de Jiquilisco has a helicopter pad, but most folk here stay grounded.

BOAT

You'll need to use a boat to get around the Bahía de Jiquilisco in eastern El Salvador and for any trips in the Golfo de Fonseca, near La Unión. Otherwise, water transportation is rare.

BUS

➧ Hypercolored American school buses run frequently to points throughout the country and are very cheap (US$0.25 to US$5). Some weekend fares increase by up to 25%.

➧ Routes to some eastern destinations have different categories: *ordinario*, *especial* and *super especial*. The last two options cost more, but they are faster and more comfortable.

➧ Most intercity bus services begin between 4am and 5am and end between 6pm and 7pm.

CAR & MOTORCYCLE

Most roads in El Salvador are paved, but traffic is not easy to negotiate and roads are not particularly well signed. A gallon of regular unleaded costs about US$2.50.

Police set up checkpoints, especially on roads to border crossings. Carjacking is a problem, as is getting parts stolen off your parked car. Don't drive alone in areas of ill repute and park in safe places. Car insurance is a good idea, but not required.

Rental cars are available in San Salvador and San Miguel and can be delivered elsewhere. In San Salvador you'll find Alamo, Avis, Budget and Quick Rent a Car.

HITCHHIKING

Buses or collective pick-ups go just about anywhere you could want to go, so hitchhiking isn't usually necessary. Both men and women usually hop in the back of pick-up trucks, but women might think twice before climbing into a car of only men. Hitchhiking is never entirely safe, and we don't recommend it. Travelers who hitch should understand that they are taking a small but potentially serious risk.

Santa Clara County Library District

408-293-2326

Checked Out Items 6/16/2018 11:24
XXXXXXXXXX3106

Item Title	Due Date
1. The sting 33305226918039	6/23/2018
2. Central America on a shoestring 33305237176056	7/7/2018

No of Items: 2

24/7 Telecirc: 800-471-0991
www.sccl.org
Thank you for visiting our library.

Honduras

♪ 504 / POP 8.1 MILLION / ELEV 975M

Includes ➡

Tegucigalpa	353
Comayagua	365
Lago de Yojoa	369
San Pedro Sula	371
Copán Ruinas	374
Gracias	384
Tela	389
La Ceiba	392
Trujillo	400
Roatán	402
Utila	408
The Moskitia	414
Isla del Tigre	416

Best Places to Eat

➡ Roatán Oasis (p405)

➡ Restaurante El Estoraque (p370)

➡ Galeano Cafe (p357)

➡ Café Honoré (p357)

➡ El Jardín de Susana (p395)

Best Places to Sleep

➡ D&D Brewery (p369)

➡ La Madrugada (p372)

➡ Roatán Backpackers Hostel (p407)

➡ La Casa de Café (p377)

➡ Hotel Guancascos (p385)

Why Go?

Honduras, so often hurried through or avoided entirely due to its dangerous image, is actually a vibrant and fascinating place with an enormous amount to offer intrepid travelers. After a decade in which the country spiraled into a whirlwind of terrible violence, Honduras has very definitely begun the journey back from the abyss, and while the challenges ahead are still significant, things haven't looked this positive for years.

Attractions include the Maya ruins of Copán, the pristine diving of the Bay Islands and the majestic scenery of over a dozen national parks. Need another reason to come here? It's also one of the cheapest countries in the region, and you'll be able to do activities for a fraction of the price you'll pay in its neighbors. It's important to take care in the cities, but other than that, Honduras is back open for business and just waiting to be discovered.

When to Go
Tegucigalpa

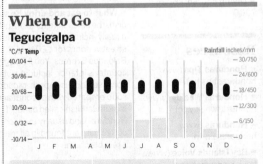

Oct–Feb Rainy season on the north coast and islands but dry in the interior.

Mar–Apr Hot and dry everywhere, with temperatures soaring inland.

Jun–Sep Peak season for viewing whale sharks in Utila.

AT A GLANCE

Currency Lempira

Language Spanish (and some English)

Money ATMs are widespread

Visas Not needed for most nationalities

Time GMT minus six hours

Area 112,090 sq km

Capital Tegucigalpa

Emergency ☏199

Exchange Rates

Australia	A$1	L16.79
Canada	C$1	L17.73
Euro zone	€1	L25.67
Japan	¥100	L21.42
New Zealand	NZ$1	L16.01
UK	UK£1	L32.30
USA	US$1	L22.73

Set Your Budget

➡ **Dorm bed:** L200

➡ **Simple meal:** L80–120

➡ **Diving course:** L6000–7000

Resources

➡ **Honduras Tips** (www.hondurastips.hn)

➡ **Honduras Weekly** (www.hondurasweekly.com

➡ **Honduras** (www.honduras.com)

➡ **Bay Islands Voice** (www.bayislandsvoice.com)

Connections

It's possible to enter Honduras from all three of its neighbors. Border crossings include Corinto and El Florido (Guatemala), El Amatillo and El Poy (El Salvador), and Guasaule and Las Manos (Nicaragua). For more detailed information, see Survival Guide p427.

ITINERARIES

One Week

Entering Honduras at the El Florido border, you'll hit a key attraction immediately: the stunning ruins of Copán. Budget at least a couple of days in the area taking in the temples and surrounding sights before making a short hop west to the atmospheric highland town of Gracias with its hot spring and Lencan villages. Then it's a long day on the road to the coastal city of La Ceiba. Set sail from here for either Roatán or Utila and indulge in some serious beach and reef time, snorkeling, diving and living the dream.

Two weeks

Back on the mainland, sign up for a rafting trip down the exquisite Río Cangrejal then it's south to Lago de Yojoa for an artisan brew or two, hiking and boat trips. Finish off with a night in either colonial, tranquil Comayagua or the bustling capital of Tegucigalpa.

Essential Food & Drink

➡ **Where to eat** To keep costs down head to *comedores* (simple eateries) where a two- or three-course meal is virtually certain to be under L70. Buy snacks from *panaderías* (bakeries) and markets. Cafes and restaurants in tourist towns have plenty of international dishes on their menus, including vegetarian choices.

➡ **What to eat and drink** Be sure to try Honduras' national dish, the *baleada* (a tortilla stuffed with myriad fillings, usually including refried beans and salad) available from street vendors for L20 to L50, and also from national chain Baleadas Express. You'll find great grilled meats in the country's interior, including lots of *pinchos* (kebabs). On the coast seafood is superb: *tapado* is a legendary Garifuna fish soup prepared with coconut and spices; in the Bay Islands is a similar dish called *bando*. Fresh juices are ubiquitous in Honduras and usually excellent and affordable. Espresso coffee bars are found in all main towns; American Espresso is a reliable chain.

TEGUCIGALPA

POP 1.13 MILLION

Ringed by forested hills in a highland valley, sprawling Tegucigalpa enjoys a relatively fresh, mild climate and a spectacular setting. It's a bustling and dynamic place, but one that many travelers minimize their time in or skip over entirely. This is a shame, as while Tegus (as all locals call it) is no beauty – streets are choked with traffic and its resultant pollution, and crime stats are high – it's a fascinating place, with some good museums, restaurants and the air of a place on the up. Keep your ear to the ground and you'll discover a dynamic young urban scene led by emerging artists, musicians, DJs and designers.

⊙ Sights

Downtown Tegus is the neglected heart of the nation, a cluster of once elegant but now faded streets where *ropa americana* (used clothing) outlets have replaced department stores. For a feel of the city, stroll the pedestrianized Calle Peatonal, visit a couple of the city's decent museums and grab a snack at the market.

★ Museo para la Identidad Nacional   MUSEUM
(MIN; Map p362; www.min.hn; Av Miguel Paz Barahona; L70; ⊙9am-5pm Tue-Sat, 11am-5pm Sun) If you hit only one sight in Tegus, head here. The capital's finest museum is housed in an expertly renovated 19th-century edifice, the former Palace of Ministries. It provides a superb, comprehensive overview of the nation's history and identity through a series of modern exhibits. Displays are in Spanish, but free guided tours in English are given four times a day. The masterstroke is a 3D-film tour of the Copán ruins (L35), shown four times per day.

Plaza Morazán   PLAZA
(Map p362; Av Miguel de Cervantes) At the center of the city is the Plaza Morazán, often called Parque Central by locals – this is Tegucigalpa's hub. A statue of former president Francisco Morazán on horseback sits at its center. An elaborate baroque cathedral dating from the 18th century overlooks the square: step inside and you'll find an intricate altar of gold and silver.

Iglesia Los Dolores   CHURCH
(Map p362; Av Máximo Jeréz) This striking church, which dominates an otherwise unremarkable plaza, has some attractive religious art. Its facade contains figures representing the Passion of Christ – his unseamed cloak, the rooster that crowed three times – all crowned by the more indigenous symbol of the sun.

Basílica de Suyapa   CHURCH
(Anillo Periferico 2) The most important church in Tegucigalpa – and therefore in Honduras – is the Gothic Basílica de Suyapa. La Virgen de Suyapa is the patron saint of Honduras; in 1982 a papal decree made her the patron saint of all Central America. Construction of the basilica, which is famous for its large stained-glass windows, began in 1954; finishing touches were still being added when we visited.

Centro de la Cultura Garinagu de Honduras   CULTURAL CENTER
(Map p362; ☎2222-0511; Plaza Morazán; ⊙8am-5pm Mon-Sat) FREE It's well worth dropping by this cultural center, situated right on the Parque Morazán, which has handicrafts, clothing and tools on display, as well as a library and information about the Garifuna people. Employees will also be able to tell you where you can see Garifuna dance troupes performing their incredibly athletic and sensual dance moves.

Monumento a La Paz   MONUMENT
(Map p358) This monument, inside Tegucigalpa's largest park, was erected in 1996 in the name of eternal peace between the 'fraternal nations of Central America.'

Palacio Legislativo   BUILDING
(Map p362; Calle Bolívar) This unusual modern building on stilts (next door to the Parque La Merced) is the Palacio Legislativo, where congress meets. It was here in December 2009 that congress voted against reinstating ousted president Manuel Zelaya.

Iglesia La Merced   CHURCH
(Map p362; Calle Bolívar) In 1847, the convent of La Merced was converted to house Honduras' first university; the country's national gallery was established there in 1996, but moved to Comayagua in 2015. The well-restored building is itself a work of art, and as impressive as the paintings inside.

Museo del Hombre   MUSEUM
(Map p362; www.museodelhombre.com; Av Miguel de Cervantes; L10; ⊙9am-1pm & 3-5pm Mon-Sat) Located in a beautiful colonial-era structure, the Museo del Hombre displays mostly contemporary Honduran art, much of which

Honduras Highlights

1 Copán ruins (p380)
Marvelling at the intricate stone carvings and epic ancient structures, which trace back to an extraordinary Maya empire.

2 Río Cangrejal (p398)

Cruising down this spectacular river on a raft and taking in some of Central America's best white water.

3 Trujillo (p400)
Discovering this forgotten

Caribbean town, with its lovely beaches, quirky history and charming locals.

4 Lago de Yojoa (p369)
Searching for a quetzal in the cloud forests that rise above

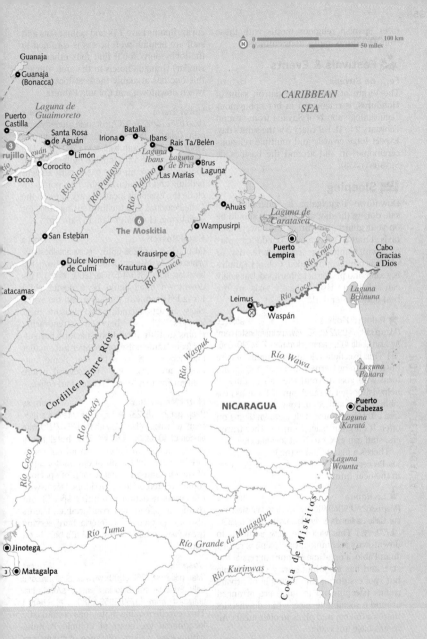

the stunningly undisturbed
natural world.

5 Roatán (p402)
Snorkeling wrecks and reefs
then exploring the remote far
east of this fascinating island.

6 The Moskitia (p351)
Going into the wild on an
upriver adventure into Central
America's last untamed
wilderness.

7 Utila (p408) Immersing
yourself in this diver's paradise,
with affordable prices, great
parties and dramatic reefs all
around.

fuses Spanish religious motifs with those from Honduras' indigenous cultures.

✨ Festivals & Events

Feria de Suyapa
CULTURAL

The Virgin of Suyapa, the patron saint of Honduras, is celebrated in her eponymous Tegucigalpa suburb of Suyapa from around February 2 to 11. February 3 is the saint's day. Expect huge crowds and multiple religious ceremonies in and around the Basílica de Suyapa (p353).

🛏 Sleeping

Downtown Tegucigalpa is generally quite safe during the day, although you should be on your guard at all times and always take taxis at night. Comayagüela is a dodgier part of town: wandering around here, day or night, is not recommended. Colonia Palmira is a safer and pricier neighborhood, but safety can still be an issue – again, taxis are the best option after dark.

⭐ Palmira Hostel
HOSTEL $

(Map p358; ☑ 9972-9666; www.palmirahostel.com; Av Juan Lindo 412; hammock/dm/r L110/220/660; 🛜) This excellent, clean and highly secure hostel is run by Hernán, an English-speaking local who goes beyond the call of duty to help visitors get as much out of Tegus as possible. There's a kitchen, communal area and free afternoon tours of downtown Tegus on offer. It's a great place to meet other travelers; staff can give excellent local advice.

There's a plan to move the hostel to Av de los Próceres and rename it Hostel Proceres in the near future.

⭐ La Ronda
HOSTEL $

(Map p362; ☑ 9949-9108; www.larondahostel.com; cnr Calle La Ronda & Av Máximo Jeréz; dm L330, r L770; 🛜) This welcome new addition to downtown's accommodation scene is run by Juan Pablo, a one-time Honduran reggaetón star, and has a cool and artsy vibe. Simple but spotless dorms and a couple of private rooms (sleeping up to four) are arranged around a sociable terrace, while downstairs there's a full bar and plans to offer meals. All rooms have hot water.

Hotel Granada No 2
HOTEL $

(Map p362; ☑ 2237-7079; hotelgranadateguci galpa@yahoo.com; Subida Casamata 1326; s/d/tr L500/580/680; @🛜) This simple but good-value place has all the essentials, including clean rooms, comfortable beds and tight se-

curity. Rooms have TVs and ceiling fans and staff are helpful; wi-fi access is confined to the lobby only. You'll find four other (very similar) Granada hotels in the area, though this one has arguably the best location between downtown and Colonia Palmira.

Hotel Iberia
PENSION $

(Map p362; ☑ 2237-9267; consuelo.gabrie@yahoo. com; Calle Los Dolores; s/d/tr without bathroom L180/250/360, d with bathroom L280; 🛜) The rooms here are a reasonable budget option, though they are all very basic, with ancient bedding and no natural light. Plus points include the excellent location very close to the Calle Peatonal, and the little sitting areas for socializing. Hot water 6am to 8am only.

Hotel Boston
HOTEL $

(Map p362; ☑ 2238-0510; nuevohotelboston@ yahoo.es; Av Máximo Jérez 321; s/d/tw/q incl breakfast from L365/475/536/1200; @🛜) This downtown hotel could be a poster child for faded grandeur, though it still has some classy aspects, including two pleasant guest lounges. Choose between street-facing rooms that are incredibly spacious but suffer from traffic noise, or cheaper but smaller and darker options to the rear. Some mattresses are *very* soft – try several before committing to a room. Free tea and coffee.

Hotel MacArthur
HOTEL $$

(Map p362; ☑ 2237-9839; www.hotelmacarthur. com; Av Lempira 454; s/d with fan L890/1110, with air-con L1110/1380; ❄🛜♨) This hotel has a strong Honduran flavor, with an enjoyably old-fashioned lobby full of old photographs of the city and a large selection of spacious rooms located off long corridors. Decor-wise the accommodation is nothing special, but rooms are clean and comfortable. There's also an inexpensive cafeteria here serving breakfast, and one of the capital's best hotel pools.

Casa Bella
HOTEL $$$

(Map p358; ☑ 2262-6000; www.casabellahn.com; Calle Principal s/n, Colonia Palmira; s/d/ste incl breakfast from L1750/1950/2180; P❄❄♨) This excellent-value hotel has a fantastic location in the heart of Colonia Palmira, within easy walking distance of many restaurants and bars. Its rather kitsch public areas give way to surprisingly tasteful modern rooms, featuring attractive, dark wood furniture and local handicrafts. Suites are enormous, and all rooms have fridges, safes and cable TV. Decent discounts available on weekends.

Hotel Edén
HOTEL $$$

(Map p358; ☑ 2222-0711; www.hoteledenhn.com; 4a Av, Colonia Palmira; s/d incl breakfast from L1080/1450; ☎) This quirky but central place has 14 comfortable rooms, many of which enjoy brightly painted murals on the walls (even if they don't always compensate for the lack of light or space). The welcome is warm, however, and there's a makeshift 'gym' to pass the time, as well as a pleasant terrace area upstairs.

Econo B&B
B&B $$$

(Map p358; ☑ 2221-5949; www.econobb.com; Av San Carlos 437, Colonia Palmira; s/d with breakfast L1320/1540; ❄☎☀) This curious place is more of a self-contained compound than a B&B, but as such it's a real retreat from the capital's streets and totally secure. Behind its totally unmarked gates (ring the bell by the green gate opposite a bar called Cho-my's) you'll find spacious if rather randomly furnished family-sized rooms. The included breakfast is a lackluster affair, however.

 Eating

There's a dearth of choice downtown, where fast-food joints rule the streets. For more choice head up to Colonia Palmira, where the food is pricier but the quality and variety far greater.

★ Baleadas Express
FAST FOOD $

(Map p358; Av La Paz & Av Juan Lindo, Texaco; baleadas L20-45; ☉ 7am-11pm) As hard as it is to imagine a gas station fast-food outlet being one of the best eating options in the city, within 24 hours in Tegus you will almost certainly meet a local who will wax lyrical about the fantastic *baleadas* (thick flour tortillas containing fried beans, cheese, meat, eggs and other fillings) served up here.

Govinda
VEGETARIAN $

(Map p362; Paseo La Leona & Av Paulino Valladares; set meal L65; ☉ 11am-3pm Mon-Sat; ☑) A pleasingly bizarre vegetarian restaurant with strong Indian influences, Govinda makes for a great meat-free and superb-value lunch stop in downtown Tegus. Get the set meal (which changes daily) served up downstairs, then head upstairs to the terrace to eat; at the highest point there's even a hammock for a postprandial nap, along with some good city views.

Pupusería El Patio
HONDURAN $

(Map p358; Blvr Morazán, Colonia Palmira; pupusas L30-50; ☉ 11am-1:30am) On weekends this beer hall of a place can be a riot, with tables overflowing with bottles and families belting out the karaoke. *Pupusas* (cornmeal stuffed with cheese or refried beans), tacos and other typical Honduran fare are the main items on the menu – groups should go for the Plato de Variedad, which introduces all of the Honduran staples and serves three to four people.

Food Stands
HONDURAN $

(Map p362; Av Paulino Valladares; snacks L20–50; ☉ 11am-3pm daily) At the side of Iglesia Los Dolores, these stands offer a variety of tempting cheapie lunchtime street-food dishes, including *pupusas* and *baleadas*.

★ Galeano Cafe
CAFE $$

(Map p358; ☑ 2263-8096; Plaza San Martín, Colonia Palmira; paninis L135-145; ☉ 7am-9pm Mon-Sat, 9am-7pm Sun; ☎) This very hip cafe rocks both an industrial and upcycling look, with brushed concrete fittings and salvaged wood furniture. It's an absolute lifeline though, as it does great coffee, enormous smoothies served up in glass jars, crepes and panini – try the delicious *pero aguacatero* – as well as breakfasts and pastries. Upstairs is a terrace and Tegus' hippest clothing store as well.

Café Paradiso
CAFE $$

(Map p362; ☑ 2222-3066; www.paradisoblog.word press.com; Av Miguel Paz Barahona 1351; mains L100-220; ☉ 10am-10pm Mon-Sat; ☎☑) An intimate, bohemian hangout, this is the place to find Tegus' creative types. The decor (with an excess of curios and lots of paintings) and layout (multiple rooms set off a central covered patio) are unusual. Food-wise, you can snack on a pastry for just L35 or feast on a filet mignon for L195.

★ Café Honoré
INTERNATIONAL, DELI $$$

(Map p358; ☑ 2239-7566; 5a Calle/República de Argentina 1941, Colonia Palmira; sandwiches/mains from L140/280; ☉ 8:30am-10pm Mon-Wed, to 11pm Thu-Sat; ☎) This is a mecca for the Honduran elite, but if you're yearning for gourmet treats this is the place. The deli section has Parma ham and French cheese while the large street terrace, complete with mod-Asian decor, makes a great place to blow the budget on a pricey gourmet sandwich, burger, salad or pasta dish. Honoré also delivers to wherever you're staying.

Tegucigalpa

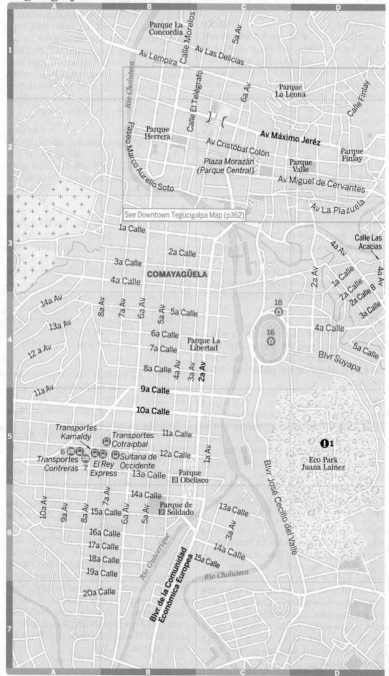

Parque La Concordia

Calle Morelos

5a Av

Av Las Delicias

Av Lempira

Río Choluteca

Calle El Telégrafo

6a Av

Parque La Leona

Calle Finlay

Av Máximo Jeréz

Paseo Marco Aurelio Soto

Parque Herrera

Av Cristóbal Colón

Plaza Morazán (Parque Central)

Parque Valle

Parque Finlay

Av Miguel de Cervantes

Av La Plazuela

See Downtown Tegucigalpa Map (p362)

1a Calle

2a Calle

Calle Las Acacias

3a Calle

4a Calle

COMAYAGÜELA

4a Av

2a Av

1a Calle

2a Calle

2a Calle B

3a Calle

14a Av

8a Av

7a Av

6a Av

5a Av

5a Calle

4a Calle

13a Av

6a Calle

5a Calle

12 a Av

7a Calle

Parque La Libertad

Blvr Suyapa

11a Av

8a Calle

4a Av

2a Av

9a Calle

10a Calle

Transportes Kamaldy

Transportes Cotraipbal

11a Calle

1a Av

6

Transportes Contreras

El Rey Express

7

Sultana de Occidente

12a Calle

Eco Park Juana Lainez

13a Calle

Parque El Obelisco

14a Calle

10a Av

9a Av

8a Av

7a Av

6a Av

5a Av

15a Calle

Parque de El Soldado

13a Calle

3a Av

16a Calle

14a Calle

17a Calle

Río Guacerique

18a Calle

15a Calle

Río Choluteca

19a Calle

20a Calle

Blvr de la Comunidad Económica Europea

Blvr José Cecilio del Valle

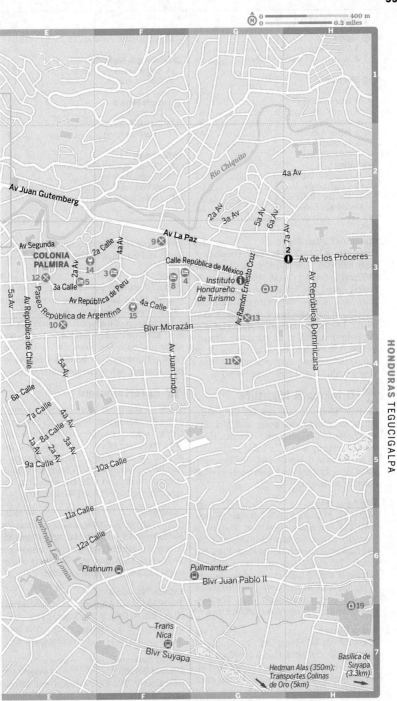

0   400 m
0   0.2 miles

E   F   G   H

1

Río Chiquito

4a Av

Av Juan Gutemberg

2a Av
3a Av
5a Av
6a Av
7a Av

Av La Paz

2

9

Av Segunda

COLONIA
PALMIRA

2a Calle
4a Av

Calle República de México

2
1   Av de los Próceres

12
2a Av

14
3a Calle
5

3

8
4

Instituto
Hondureño
de Turismo

17

Av Ramón Ernesto Cruz

Av República Dominicana

3

Av República de Peru
Av República de Argentina

4a Calle

15
10

Blvr Morazán

13

Av Paseo República de Chile
5a Av

Av Juan Lindo

11

6a Calle

7a Calle

4a Av
8a Calle
3a Av
1a Av
2a Av

9a Calle

10a Calle

Quebrada Las Lomas

11a Calle

12a Calle

Platinum

Pullmantur

Blvr Juan Pablo II

19

Trans
Nica

Blvr Suyapa

Hedman Alas (350m);
Transportes Colinas
de Oro (5km)

Basílica de
Suyapa
(3.3km)

E   F   G   H

Tegucigalpa

⊙ Sights
1 Monumento a La Paz.............................D5
2 Monumento a Simón Bolívar................H3

⊜ Sleeping
3 Casa Bella F3
4 Econo B&B...F3
5 Hotel Edén...E3
6 Hotel Palace...A5
7 Hotel Unión..A5
8 Palmira Hostel......................................F3

⊗ Eating
9 Baleadas Express F3
10 Café Honoré E4
11 Claudio's Italian Bistro G4
12 Galeano Cafe E3

13 Pupusería El Patio G4

⊙ Drinking & Nightlife
14 Angry Beaver E3
15 Glenn's Pub F3

⊗ Entertainment
Cinemark ....(see 19)
16 Estadio Nacional Tiburcio
    Carías Andino....................................C4

⊜ Shopping
17 Centro Comercial Novacentro G3
18 Mercado Mayoreo C4
Metromedia...................................(see 19)
19 Multiplaza Mall....................................H7

Claudio's Italian Bistro   ITALIAN $$$
(Map p358; ☎2235-7738; Av Ramón Ernesto Cruz; mains L230-335; ⊙ noon-9:30pm Sun-Wed, noon-10:30pm Thu-Sat; 🖘) Claudio's attracts a well-heeled crowd and makes for a good break from local cuisine. There's superb pizza and a variety of pasta dishes, seafood and grilled meats. The downstairs wine shop and dining room give way to an attractive alfresco terrace upstairs, and even though the decor can be tacky (those candlesticks!), it's otherwise a sophisticated and friendly option.

🍸 Drinking & Nightlife

Colonia Palmira is your best bet for a night out, with several bars along Blvr Morazán and Paseo de Republica de Argentina. However, as security issues have dogged the city in recent years, Tegus' nightlife generally starts directly after work and tends to wind down by midnight.

Tito Aguacate   BAR
(Map p362; Av Cristóbal Colón & Matute; ⊙11am-9pm) This legendary downtown dive bar is a scruffy haunt for hard drinkers and the odd hipster. It's been around since 1945, but women have only recently been admitted. A *tapa* is served with every drink. Be sure to try the famous hangover cure *calambre* (gin, apple wine, sugar and lime). The sign says 'New Bar' but everyone calls it Tito's.

Angry Beaver   PUB
(Map p358; 2a Av; ⊙6pm-1am; 🖘) An atmospheric pub run by a Honduran/Canadian couple, with a fine choice of beer (including Newcastle Brown Ale and various craft beers) and welcoming staff. There's a great

jukebox, subdued lighting and a good mix of locals and expats at the bar.

Glenn's Pub   PUB
(Map p358; 4a Calle, Colonia Palmira; ⊙6pm-2am Mon-Sat; 🖘) A long-standing 'secret' among *capitalinos,* this intimate, very sociable bar caters to a mix of free-spirited 20-somethings and hardened local drinkers. The action spills out onto the sidewalk on weekend nights. The owner is a hard-rock fan, so expect a soundtrack of endless guitar solos.

☆ Entertainment

There's a small but vibrant arts-and-music scene in Tegucigalpa. Spanish speakers can check out www.agendartehonduras.com for a round-up of cultural events; also ask at your hostel for tips. The Museo para la Identidad Nacional (p353) frequently holds cultural events and exhibits, including free jazz concerts at 5pm each Wednesday.

Cinemark   CINEMA
(Map p358; ☎2231-2044; www.cinemarkca.com; Blvr Juan Pablo II, Multiplaza Mall; tickets from L85) A modern multiscreen cineplex inside the Multiplaza Mall that mainly shows Hollywood films with Spanish subtitles.

**Estadio Nacional
Tiburcio Carías Andino**   SPECTATOR SPORT
(Map p358; 9a Calle, at Blvd Suyapa) This stadium across the river from Comayagüela hosts soccer games and other sporting matches.

**Teatro Nacional
Manuel Bonilla**   PERFORMING ARTS
(Map p362; ☎2222-4366; Av Miguel Paz Barahona) Built in 1912, Honduras' National Theater

hosts a variety of performing arts, including plays and concerts. The theater's interior was inspired by the Athens Theatre of Paris, making it a very enjoyable place to attend a performance.

🛍 Shopping

Honduran handicrafts are sold at small stores on Av Miguel de Cervantes, east of Plaza Morazán. Other than that there's little of interest for shoppers in Tegus, with most shops concentrated in various large malls around town.

Centro Comercial Novacentro   MALL
(Map p358; ☑ 2280-2999; www.novacentrolospro ceres.com; btwn Blvr Morazán & Av La Paz; ☺ 9am-11pm) This big new mall is the current local favorite, and it's easy to see why: as well as having high security and a great range of shops, it's very central and easy to access. In addition to lots of clothing, coffee shops and eating options, there are ATMs and outlets from all the local cell-phone companies.

Mercado Mayoreo   MARKET
(Map p358; Estadio Nacional; ☺ 8am-5pm Fri, 6am-3pm Sat) Every Friday and Saturday, this cheap, colorful market sets up shop near the Estadio Nacional. There's a dazzling array of produce and stalls, hawking everything from birdcages to vegetables – and some great little *pupusa* cafes, too.

Metromedia   BOOKS
(Map p358; Blvr Juan Pablo II, Multiplaza Mall; ☺ 10am-7pm Mon-Sat) Sells English-language books and magazines; there's a cafe, too.

Multiplaza Mall   MALL
(Map p358; www.multiplaza.com; Blvr Juan Pablo II; ☺ 10am-8pm Mon-Sat, noon-6pm Sun) This convenient shopping complex for travelers is located southwest of Colonia Palmira, with lots of shopping choice, ATMs and a cinema.

ℹ Information

DANGERS & ANNOYANCES
➡ Tegucigalpa has a very high crime rate. Even in daylight, the city can be dangerous, so keep your wits about you.

➡ Keep valuables out of sight and avoid walking on side streets alone. Beware of pickpockets.

➡ Comayagüela, a poorer and dirtier city across the river, is controlled by gangs. Some bus lines have terminals here, but otherwise there's no reason to visit.

➡ Only use ATMs with armed guards outside or those inside malls.

➡ It's best to avoid city buses (prone to 'taxing' by gangs) and most *colectivos* (shared taxis). At night, unless you're walking a short distance on busy streets, take taxis.

EMERGENCY & MEDICAL SERVICES
Ambulance (☑ 195)
Police (☑ 199)
Honduras Medical Center (☑ 2280-1500; www.hmc.com.hn; Av Juan Lindo; ☺ 24hr) One of the best private hospitals in the country, with English-speaking doctors and state-of-the-art equipment.
Police (☑ 2222-8736, 199; 5a Av; ☺ 24hr)

MONEY
ATMs are dotted about the city: at the airport, on the northeast corner of Parque Central, in the **Hedman Alas bus terminal** (☑ 2516-2273; www.hedmanalas.com; Blvd Centro America, Colonia Tres Caminos) and in the shopping malls.
Banco Atlántida (Parque Central; ☺ 9am-4pm Mon-Fri, 9am-2pm Sat) Has a 24-hour ATM.
Citibank (Blvr Morazán, Centro Comercial Plaza Criolla; ☺ 8am-4pm Mon-Fri, 9am-1pm Sat) One of several banks here.
HSBC (Blvr Morazán; ☺ 8am-5pm Mon-Fri, 9am-1:30pm Sat) Has an ATM.

POST
Downtown Post Office (Map p362; cnr Av Miguel Paz Barahona & Calle El Telégrafo; ☺ 8am-5pm Mon-Fri, 8am-1pm Sat)

TOURIST INFORMATION
Instituto Hondureño de Turismo (IHT; Map p358; ☑ 2222-2124; www.letsgohonduras.com; cnr Av Ramón Ernesto Cruz & Calle República de México, 1st fl; ☺ 9am-5pm Mon-Fri) Helpful tourist office, with good general information and lots of glossy leaflets – but don't expect too much practical information. You'll need a photo ID to access it.
Immigration Office (☑ 2234-1996, 2234-1998; www.inm.gob.hn; Blvd Communidad Económica Europea, Colonia Las Torres; ☺ 8:30am-4:30pm Mon-Fri) Opposite the City Mall and near the airport, the Immigration Office extends visas (US$20 for 30 days) and handles other immigration matters.

ℹ Getting There & Away

AIR
The **Aeropuerto Internacional Toncontín** (TGU; ☑ 2234-0106; www.interairports.hn; CA-5) is 6.5km south of central Tegucigalpa. A taxi from the center of town costs around L120, though

Downtown Tegucigalpa

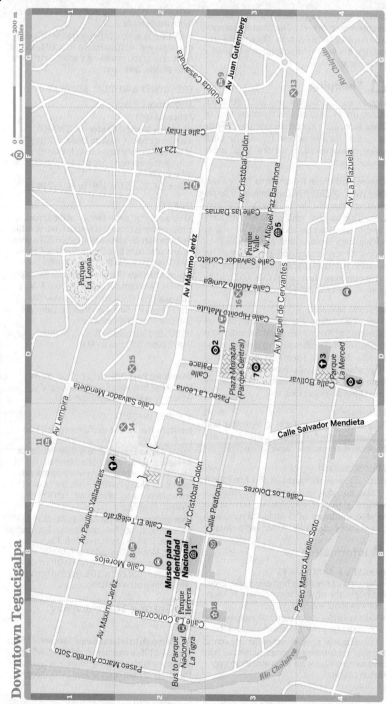

Río Chiquito

Río Choluteca

0   200 m
0   0.1 miles

Museo para la Identidad Nacional 1

Bus to Parque Nacional La Tigra

Parque La Leona

Parque La Merced

Parque Herrera

Parque Valle

Plaza Morazán (Parque Central)

Av Máximo Jeréz

Av Juan Gutemberg

Av Cristóbal Colón

Av Miguel Paz Barahona

Av Miguel de Cervantes

Av La Plazuela

Av Lempira

Av Paulino Valladares

Paseo Marco Aurelio Soto

124 Av

Calle Finlay

Subida Casamata

Calle las Damas

Calle Salvador Corleto

Calle Adolfo Zuñiga

Calle Hipólito Matute

Calle Salvador Mendieta

Calle Palace

Paseo La Leona

Calle Los Dolores

Calle Bolívar

Calle Salvador Mendieta

Calle El Telégrafo

Calle Peatonal

Av Cristóbal Colón

Calle Morelos

Calle Concordia

Calle La

Paseo Marco Aurelio Soto

1   2   3   4   5   6   7   8   9   10   11   12   13   14   15   16   17   18

Downtown Tegucigalpa

⊙ Top Sights
1 Museo para la Identidad
Nacional B2

⊙ Sights
2 Centro de la Cultura Garinagu
de Honduras D3
3 Iglesia La Merced D4
4 Iglesia Los Dolores.............................. C1
5 Museo del Hombre E3
6 Palacio Legislativo D4
7 Plaza Morazán...................................... D3

⊜ Sleeping
8 Hotel Boston....................................... B2
9 Hotel Granada No 2 .... G3
10 Hotel Iberia.. C2
11 Hotel MacArthur C1
12 La Ronda F2

⊗ Eating
13 Café Paradiso G3
14 Food Stands C2
15 Govinda D2
16 Restaurante Duncan Maya E3

⊚ Drinking & Nightlife
17 Tito Aguacate D3

⊛ Entertainment
18 Teatro Nacional Manuel
Bonilla.. A3

going into the city from the airport costs around
L220 to L250.

DESTINATION	COST (L)
La Ceiba	1800
Roatán	2400
Utila	2900

Aerolíneas Sosa (☑2233-5107, airport 2234-0137; www.aerolineasosahn.com; Blvr Morazán, Centro Comercial Los Proceres; ⊙8am-5pm Mon-Fri, 8am-noon Sat)

American Airlines (☑2216-4800; Hotel Marriott, Blvd Juan Pablo II; ⊙8am-5:30pm Mon-Fri, 9am-noon Sat)

Avianca (☑2281-8222; www.avianca.com; Metrópolis, Blvr Suyapa; ⊙8am-5pm Mon-Sat, 9am-2pm Sun)

CM Airlines (☑2547-2425; www.cmairlines.com)

Lanhsa Airlines (☑airport 2234-0804; www.lanhsa.com; Aeropuerto Internacional Toncontín)

BUS

Frustratingly, there's no central bus station in Tegus, meaning that bus lines are scattered all over the city. Unfortunately many bus depots are

in Comayagüela, the least safe area of town – though a spate of recent gang attacks has led to several companies relocating to safer areas in eastern Tegus, and now few 1st-class bus companies run their services from there.

In general you'll need to know which bus you want to take rather than simply turning up at a bus terminal and waiting, so calling ahead is always a smart move.

International & Long-Distance Buses

There are five international bus companies:
Hedman Alas (p361) Connects Tegus with San Salvador and Guatemala City. Two departures offices: one in Comayagüela and a far nicer terminal located behind Multiplaza Mall in the southeast of the city.

Platinum (Map p358; ☑2225-5415; www.platinumcentroamerica.com; Juan Manuel Gálvez 1521) Goes to El Salvador, Guatemala and Nicaragua.

Pullmantur (Map p358; ☑2232-0216; www.pullmantur.com; Blvr Juan Pablo II, Hotel Marriott) Connects Tegus with San Salvador and Guatemala City.

Tica Bus (☑2291-0022; www.ticabus.com; Centro Comercial Plaza Toncontín) Goes to El Salvador, Guatemala and Nicaragua and the Mexican border, and has connections to Costa Rica and Panama.

Trans Nica (Map p358; ☑2239-7933; www.transnica.com; Blvr Suyapa, Hotel Alameda) Heads to Managua and on to San José in Costa Rica.

Long-distance buses for domestic services include the following:
Colinas de Oro (☑9523-1637; Centro Comercial la Alhambra, Colonia Kennedy)
Contreras (Map p358; ☑2238-8984)
Cotraipbal (Map p358; ☑2237-1666)
Cristina (☑2225-1446; www.transportescristina.com; Blvd F.F.A.A.)
El Rey Express (Map p358; ☑2237-8561)
Hedman Alas (p361)
Kamaldy (Map p358; ☑2220-0117)
Sultana de Occidente (Map p358; ☑2238-8507; www.sultanaexpress.webs.com)
Viana (☑2225-6583; www.vianatransportes.com; Blvr Fuerzas Armadas)

ⓘ Getting Around

TO/FROM THE AIRPORT

Local buses run from the airport to Comayagüela, but it's far safer to catch a taxi due to security concerns on city buses; or grab a **colectivo van** (L12), which connects the airport with a stop on Calle Morelos, five blocks west of Parque Central.

BUS

City buses vary from cheap, former US school buses (L7) to faster minibuses known as *rapiditos* (L11), both of which can be dirty and dangerous. Theft is common and gangs sometimes target buses. Stick to taxis.

CAR & MOTORCYCLE

Care hire rates start at L700 per day. **National/Alamo** (☎ 2239-1537, airport 2233-4962; www.alamo.com; Blvr San Juan Bosco; ☺ 8am-6pm Mon-Sat) and the other major international companies can be found at the airport – as well as local agency **Econo Rent-a-Car** (☎ 2235-2105, airport 2291-0108; www.econorentacarhn.com; Calle El Trapiche; ☺ 7am-7pm Mon-Fri, 7am-5pm Sat & Sun).

TAXI

Taxis cruise all over town; a ride costs L60 to L120 depending on the distance. It's always best to call a trusted taxi company rather than stopping one on the street. **Call Taxi** (☎ 8952-8461, 8803-2941) and **Taxi Express** (☎ 9600-1707) are both reputable companies.

There are a couple of useful downtown taxi *colectivo* stops: one on Calle Morelos that is particularly helpful for the airport, and another between Parque Valle and Parque La Merced that runs to the Mercado Jacaleapa terminal (where buses depart for El Paraíso and Danlí). They each charge L12.

Around Tegucigalpa

The gorgeous area around Tegucigalpa features one of Honduras' most impressive national parks, as well as several attractive mountain towns perfect for day trips. Among them is Santa Lucía, a charming old colonial mining town with a spectacu-

BUSES FROM TEGUCIGALPA

International Buses

DESTINATION	COST (L)	DURATION (HR)	BUS LINE	FREQUENCY
Guatemala City (Guatemala)	880	12	Tica Bus	1 daily, 6am
	1205	14	Hedman Alas	1 daily, 5:30am
Managua (Nicaragua)	476	8	Tica Bus	1 daily, 9:30am
	651	7-8	Trans Nica	1 daily, 5am
San Salvador (El Salvador)	440	6½	Tica Bus	1 daily, 6am

Domestic Buses

DESTINATION	COST (L)	DURATION (HR)	BUS LINE	FREQUENCY
Agua Caliente	360	9-10	Sultana de Occidente	hourly until 1pm
Comayagua	50	2	Contreras	12 daily
Copán Ruinas	790	7	Hedman Alas	3 daily
El Paraíso	83	2	Colinas de Oro	every 40min
La Ceiba	274	8	Cristina	8 daily
	725	7½	Viana	3 daily
	274	8	Hedman Alas	3 daily
	274	8	Kamaldy	3 daily
Las Manos*	97	2½	Colinas de Oro	2 daily
San Pedro Sula	210	4	Cristina	10 daily
	178	4	El Rey Express	10 daily
	120	4	Sultana de Occidente	7 daily
	600	4	Viana	5 daily
Santa Rosa de Copán	248	7	Sultana de Occidente	hourly 6am-1:30pm
Tela	227	5½	Cristina	8 daily
Trujillo	280	10	Cotraipbal	2 daily

*Nicaraguan border; last bus from border to Ocotal (Nicaragua) at 4pm

lar vista over the capital, 14km to the east. There's a striking 18th-century *iglesia* (church) and historic streets to explore.

◉ Sights

Parque Nacional La Tigra   NATIONAL PARK
(☑ Jutiapa 2265-1891, Rosario 2265-3167; www.latigra.hn; L300; ⊙8am-4pm, last entrance 2pm) A short distance northeast of the capital, Parque Nacional La Tigra covers 238 sq km of rugged forest, with cloud forest and dry pine forest, numerous rivers and waterfalls and a large and varied (but exceedingly shy) population of mammals, including pumas, peccaries, armadillos and agoutis (rabbit-sized rodents). Somewhat easier to spy are the park's numerous birds – 350 species in all – making La Tigra the country's best birdwatching spot after Lago de Yojoa.

If you're lucky, you may even spot a quetzal, a distinctive, aqua-colored bird with long tail feathers. Impossible to miss is the park's exuberant flora: lush trees, vines, lichens, large ferns, colorful mushrooms, bromeliads and what seems like a million orchids.

⊨ Sleeping

★ Cabaña Mirador El Rosario   GUESTHOUSE $$
(☑ 2767-2141; r L750) This spot is perched on the mountainside and offers great views, lovely rooms, laundry, homemade jams and chutneys and easy access to the national park. The catch: there are only two rooms, so call ahead. Vegetarian meals are served (breakfast L60, dinner L120). Staff will pick you up in San Juancito for L200 (no arrivals after 10pm).

ⓘ Getting There & Away

The Jutiapa entrance is closest to the capital (22km to the northeast). In Tegucigalpa, buses (L22, one hour, hourly 7am-5pm Monday to Friday, 8am, 10am, noon, 1pm and 3pm Saturday & Sunday) leave from Parque Herrera for Aldea El Chaparro, a 15-minute walk from the visitor center. Buses return from El Chaparro at hourly intervals, with the last bus back at 4pm on the weekend.

WESTERN HONDURAS

The heartland of Honduras, this mountainous, forested region encompasses some of the nation's most outstanding sights. The top attraction is easily the excellent Maya ruins of Copán, closely followed by the colonial charm of towns such as Copán Ruinas and Gracias.

Hikers will love the spectacular trails inside the Montaña de Celaque cloud forest, while there's dazzling birdlife and wonderful scenery around idyllic Lago de Yojoa, which has in the past few years established itself as a major stop on the Central American backpacker trail.

Big, booming San Pedro Sula is the economic powerhouse of the nation and a travel hub; though as it has little to offer visitors other than a fearsome reputation as one of the world's most dangerous cities, few travelers hang around.

Comayagua
POP 80,000
Comayagua was the first capital of Honduras and an important religious and political center for over three centuries, until power shifted to Tegucigalpa in 1880. The town's rich past is evident in its fine old churches, an impressive cathedral and its colonial plazas. A very Catholic city, it's *the* place in Honduras to witness Easter celebrations. The rest of the year, it's a pleasant stopover between Tegucigalpa and northern Honduras, though there's little to detain you for longer.

On the outskirts of the town is a huge air base used by the US military. Known as La Palmerola (or Soto Cano), it formed a base for US forces in the 1980s when the Contra war was raging in Nicaragua. Today about a thousand soldiers are stationed here, and you'll often see off-duty soldiers relaxing in town.

◉ Sights

Sights are clustered around the beautiful Parque Central.

Cathedral   CHURCH
(Parque Central; ⊙7am-8pm) Comayagua's impressive cathedral is the largest colonial-era place of worship in Honduras. Built between 1685 and 1715, it's adorned with intricate wooden carvings and gold-plated altars. The cathedral's most interesting feature is its ancient Moorish clock, dating to around 1100AD, which was originally located in the Alhambra in Granada, Spain. In 1620 it was donated to the town by King Phillip III. Look out for the older Roman-style 'IIII' (rather than 'IV') on the clock's face.

Drop by the tourist office and staff from there will accompany you up the bell tower for a closer look; the clock strikes every 15 minutes.

Iglesia La Merced
CHURCH

(1a Av NE; ⊗8am-6pm) Comayagua's first *iglesia* was La Merced. Building started in 1550; it was consecrated as a cathedral in 1561. The plaza out the front is very pretty.

Museo Regional de Arqueología
MUSEUM

(6a Calle NO; L88; ⊗8:30am-4pm) This fine museum is housed in a former presidential palace, which adds to its appeal. Inside you'll find some ancient Lenca artifacts, including a stela, polychrome ceramics, jade jewelry and petroglyphs. Descriptions are in Spanish only.

Parque Nacional Montaña de Comayagua
NATIONAL PARK

(PANACOMA; L66) Spanning more than 300 sq km of primary and secondary forest, PANACOMA (which is managed by Ecosimco) has two main hiking trails leading through the cloud forest, from near the small village of Río Negro, 42km north of Comayagua, to waterfalls. The first trail is to Cascada de los Ensueños, a 75m-high waterfall about an hour's hike through mostly secondary forest. The second trail veers off the first just before reaching Los Ensueños, and leads to another waterfall, El Gavilán.

Sleeping

Hotel America Inc
HOTEL $

(⊋2772-0630; www.hotelamericainc.com; cnr 1a Av NO & 1a Calle NO; r with fan/air-con from L495/595; ❋ 🞉 🞉) A welcoming place in the market area, this modern hotel has a fancy lobby and a wide selection of rooms. The cheaper options are plain but serviceable; the newer ones have refurbished bathrooms and good-quality furnishings. The pool is tiny (around 8m).

Hotel Antigua Comayagua
HISTORIC HOTEL $$

(⊋2772-0816; www.hotelantiguacomayagua.com; cnr 6a Calle NO & 2a Av NO; s/d incl breakfast L860/985; ❋ 🞉 🞉) This is the best option in town: a super-secure, beautifully cared-for property with a wonderful pool and spacious, smart rooms, many of which have balconies. The hotel has its own nightclub as well, which can mean some noise on the weekend, however. It's just around the corner from Parque Central.

Eating

Cafe Tío Juan
CAFE $

(Parque Central; snacks L40-80; ⊗7am-9pm; 🞉) This cute and friendly coffee joint on the main plaza offers you good coffee, inspirational wall quotes and delicious slices of banana bread. There are also a few tables on the street outside – perfect for people-watching over an espresso.

Ricardo's
HONDURAN $$$

(Parque Central; mains L140-300; ⊗7:30am-10pm; 🞉) Right on the Parque Central, this classy restaurant offers the best view in town from its terrace tables and its myriad atmospheric dining rooms bursting with curios and character. It's quite pricey, but the set lunch (L81) is excellent value, and the seafood and grilled meats are of a surprisingly high standard.

Drinking & Nightlife

La Gota de Limón
BAR

(5a Calle NO; ⊗10:30am-7pm Sun-Wed, to 2am Thu-Sat) An upmarket bar-lounge that operates as an (underused) cafe in the day. On weekend nights it morphs into one of the town's best bars, drawing a fashionable crowd with DJs playing a mix of salsa, merengue and Latin hits. There's usually no cover charge.

Orientation

Heading north into town from the main San Pedro Sula–Tegucigalpa highway, you'll pass through the market area after 750m, then hit the Parque Central in another 250m.

Streets are defined according to the compass: NO for *noroeste* (northwest), NE for *noreste* (northeast), SO for *suroeste* (southwest) and SE for *sureste* (southeast).

Information

Banco Atlántida (1a Av NO; ⊗8am-5pm Mon-Fri, 9am-1:30pm Sat) Has an ATM.

Banco Credomatic (Parque Central & 1a Av NO; ⊗8am-noon & 1-4pm Mon-Fri)

Ecosimco (Ecosistema Montaña de Comayagua; ⊋2772-4681; ecosimco@yahoo.com.mx; Edifico Pasaje Andara Flores, Calle del Comercio; ⊗9am-noon & 1-5pm Mon-Fri) Manages the Montaña de Comayagua National Park (it's where you can pay your entry fee). It's 500m north of town – look for the big green gates.

ℹ Getting There & Away

Comayagua is connected to Tegucigalpa (L50, two hours, every 20 minutes) by very regular buses, including those run by **Transportes Catrachos** (☎2772-0260; cnr 1a Calle SO & 1a Av NO), **Transportes Contreras** (☎2772-4618; Av 3 SO) and El Rey Express; pick up El Rey buses on the highway on the south side of town. All buses running between San Pedro Sula and Tegucigalpa pass by the entrance to Comayagua on the main highway.

Transportes Catrachos and El Rey Express also operate buses to San Pedro Sula (L85, three hours, every 30 minutes). Buses to Marcala (L50, 1½ hours) leave just outside the **Transportes Rivera bus terminal** (cnr 2a Calle SO & 1a Ave NO), departing hourly from 6am until 1pm, and again at 3pm.

La Esperanza

POP 22,000 / ELEV 1770M

Up in the highlands, slow-paced La Esperanza is known for its markets. Indigenous influence is strong here – you will see many women wearing the distinctive, colorful Lenca headdress. For these reasons – and not its muddy streets – it's a more interesting stopover than Marcala. As the highest town in Honduras (1770m), it can get decidedly chilly here, too.

◉ Sights

Two blocks west of the pretty Parque Central, the Casa de la Cultura (Av Morazán; ☺noon-4pm Mon-Fri) FREE has a couple of rooms devoted to Lenca culture, including some excellent ceramics and weavings. Continuing up the hill from here you'll soon reach La Gruta (☺9am-4pm), a small cave now converted into a chapel.

🛏 Sleeping

Hotel & Comedor Martiner   HOTEL $
(☎2783-0931; Av España; r L250) A block and a half east of the *parque,* this budget hotel

has clean rooms with cable TV, but there's little more to recommend it, though the roof terrace is cool for hanging out with a view. Rooms don't get much natural light; it's a place for those on a serious budget only. Has a little *comedor* for meals.

★Posada Papa Chepe   HOTEL $$
(☎2783-0443;   posadapapachepe@gmail.com;
Parque Central; s/d/tr/q L700/800/900/1000;
📶) An unexpected charmer on La Esperanza's Parque Central, Papa Chepe's features a wonderfully planted courtyard heaving with plants and flowers surrounded by a series of well-appointed rooms with high ceilings and good hot-water showers (a necessity in this climate). There's a small restaurant at the back, a coffee shop with decent espresso and arts and crafts for sale.

✖ Eating

Restaurants tend to be fairly samey here, though do look out for local dishes containing *choros* (wild mushrooms).

La Casa Vieja   BURGERS $$
(Parque Central; mains L130-250; ☺11am-10pm Tue-Thu, to 11pm Fri & Sat, to 9pm Sun; 📶) Famous for its burgers – the king of which is La Big Daddy (made with a pound of beef) – La Casa Vieja also does chicken wings and breaded shrimp. It's a cool space, with a wood-beamed roof and friendly service.

La Hacienda Lenca   HONDURAN $$
(Av España; mains L80-250; ☺9am-10pm) A block east of Parque Central, this curious place is definitely a winner when it comes to kitsch and mystifying interior design. The waitstaff are super friendly and the food is decent, though you'll find little out of the ordinary on the typically Honduran menu.

ℹ Information

For cash, there's a **Banco Atlántida** (Av Los Proceres) one block north of Parque Central.

BUSES FROM LA ESPERANZA

DESTINATION	COST (L)	DURATION	FREQUENCY
Gracias	90	2½hr	5 daily
Marcala	50	1½hr	6 daily
San Juan	40	1¼hr	hourly
San Pedro Sula	125	4hr	every 40min
Santa Rosa de Copán	90	3½hr	1 daily
Tegucigalpa	130	4hr	every 40min

ⓘ Getting There & Away

The bus situation in La Esperanza can be confusing. The main 'terminal' for Tegucigalpa, San Pedro Sula and Santa Rosa de Cópan (via Gracias) is 800m east of the center, past the bridge. Other (mainly local) services (including those for Marcala) leave from around *mercado quemado* ('burned market'), which is a couple of blocks northeast of the Parque Central. Tickets are sold on board.

The road between Gracias and La Esperanza is now paved and served by very regular minibuses (you may have to change in San Juan en route).

Marcala

POP 20,000

Marcala is a highland town with a strong indigenous heritage. It lies at the southern end of Honduras' 'Ruta Lenca' – a collection of Lenca villages and stronghold of Lencan culture. The town itself is tranquil but unremarkable, but it sits pretty in prime coffee country – there are several opportunities to see the world's favorite bean being harvested and prepared. Several hikes in the surrounding area take in picturesque waterfalls and caves.

🏃 Activities

The hike to **La Estanzuela** – a pretty waterfall and swimming spot – via the impressive cavern **La Cueva del Gigante** is a popular excursion.

Cooperativa RAOS   ECOTOUR
(☑ 2764-3779, 9987-8920; www.cooperativaraos.org; ⊙ 8am-4pm Mon-Fri, to noon Sat) Cooperativa RAOS, on the road toward La Esperanza, is Honduras' first organic farming cooperative. It now represents over 200 small producers. *Finca* (farm) tours (per person L100 to L300) are a great way to learn about organic coffee cultivation and talk to the farmers.

🛏 Sleeping

La Casona   HOTEL $
(☑ 9696-7269; s/d L375/475; 🛜) The best option in this small town, La Casona is tucked away in a large lot hidden behind a computer school (look for the latter's large sign), a block or so from the church. If you stay here be sure to ask for a room at the front of the building, as these all have terraces. There's also hot water.

Hotel y Cafetería Roxana   HOTEL $
(☑ 2764-5866; r L180-280) This unappealing-looking concrete hotel with pink accents isn't going to win any architectural awards, but its rooms are doable for a night and very cheap, all with private hot-water bathrooms and cable TV, and some with a balcony. Meals are also offered in the downstairs *comedor* (mains L50). The hotel is located opposite the post office, close to the market.

🍴 Eating

Casa Gloria   HONDURAN $$
(Parque Central; mains L60-170; ⊙ 8am-9pm; 🛜) Attractive colonial-style place that offers buffet dining – *pollo asada* (grilled chicken), *bistek* (steak) and some veggie options – during the day and service with a smile. The premises are rather faded, but decorated with some fine Lenca ceramics and art.

ⓘ Information

For cash head to **Banco Atlántida** (⊙ 8am-4:30pm Mon-Fri, to noon Sat), at the entrance to town, which has an ATM.

ⓘ Getting There & Away

Buses leave from various points, but all pass the Texaco gas station at the east end of the main road in and out of town.

Foreign travelers are not permitted entry to El Salvador at the nearby border-crossing of Sabanetas (locals are allowed to pass through, though). Save yourself a frustrating journey and use alternative crossings.

BUSES FROM MARCALA

DESTINATION	COST (L)	DURATION	FREQUENCY
Comayagua	60	2½hr	8 daily
La Esperanza	50	1½hr	6 daily
San Pedro Sula	125	5hr	1 daily
Tegucigalpa	110	3½hr	hourly

Lago de Yojoa

Largely undeveloped and ringed by dense tropical forest, Lago de Yojoa is exceptionally scenic. Thanks to the indefatigable efforts of a local microbrewery owner to promote the region, the lake is now *the* most popular spot for breaking the journey between the Bay Islands and Nicaragua.

Lago de Yojoa's birdlife is world-class: the latest species count is up to 485 – over half the total in Honduras – including the elusive quetzal. You can also hike to remote waterfalls and the summit of Santa Bárbara, visit coffee plantations, go tubing and zip lining or row on the lake itself. (As it's very shallow, with many reeds close to shore, swimming here is not great.)

Peña Blanca is the main transportation hub near the lake; it's a bustling but uninteresting commercial town. Los Naranjos, an otherwise unremarkable village some way down a poorly maintained road, is where most travelers base themselves at D&D Brewery.

🏃 Activities

Boat trips on the lake are an essential experience, involving an early start and paddling along the totally undeveloped western side of the lake. Here the magnificent birdlife includes toucans and fish eagles; you may well also see large iguanas and monkeys. Expect to pay L300 per person for a two-hour tour in a rowing boat.

A **three-waterfall hike** runs through the foothills of Parque Montaña Nacional de Santa Bárbara – a delightful day-hike through coffee country and traditional settlements. The main attraction here is a stunning series of falls, dubbed **La Escalada de los Gigantes** (Giants' Stairs) by locals, from where there are sweeping views. D&D Adventures charges L600 for this hike, including transportation.

★ D&D Adventures　　　ADVENTURE TOUR
(🖉 9994-9719;　www.ddadventures.com;　D&D Brewery, Los Naranjos; day trips from L600) Run by D&D Brewery, this excellent outfit has enthusiastic, English-speaking guides and is the best way to explore the more remote areas around Lago de Yojoa. Trips include a fantastic Waterfall Trail Day Hike that takes you through the foothills of the Parque Nacional Montaña de Santa Bárbara and visits

three remote waterfalls. Birdwatching, kayaking and caving are also offered.

🛏 Sleeping

★ D&D Brewery　　　　　LODGE $
(🖉 2544-0052, 9994-9719; www.ddbrewery.com; Los Naranjos; camping/dm per person L80/150, s/d/cabin from L280/340/840; ❄ 🛜 ⛱) 🏊 Having created Honduras' most pioneering and ethically run hotel and brewery, American Bobby Durrette is now busy attracting backpackers to Lago de Yojoa (thus far with considerable success). The simple but spotless and comfortable rooms set amid the thick jungle are great, though D&D's trump card is its superb microbrewery, with several fantastic craft beers (including a porter) on tap.

The lodge does not have lake views, but acts as an excellent base to set up all manner of trips, from hard-core hiking to genteel birdwatching. The passionate staff members are all local and enjoy great benefits including health care, generous wages and on-the-job training. They love their work and this shines through during any visit.

El Cortijo del Lago　　　　HOTEL $
(🖉 2608-5527, 9906-5333; www.elcortijodellago. com; dm/s/d L250/550/625; ❄ 🛜) This lakeside hotel is one of the only places in the area to get right down to the lakeshore itself. The spacious dorm has air-con and the rooms share an atmospheric, screened-in communal area with lake views. The freestanding *cabaña* is the best room and well worth requesting when you book. Victoria the parrot will keep you entertained.

Finca Paradise　　　　CABAÑAS $$$
(🖉 9995-1875, 9502-8189; r/cabin L880/2200) This beautiful coffee plantation is a magical place to stay. The simple rooms have hot water and are very clean, but the real attraction here are the two treehouse-style cabins that sleep six people each. The structures are fairly simple (and definitely not for the vertiginous), have wraparound balconies and are perfect for enjoying the sounds of the forest.

🍴 Eating

El Dorao Cafe　　　　　CAFE $
(Peña Blanca; panini L40-60; ⏱ 7am-7pm; 🛜) An unbelievable find in sleepy Peña Blanca, this smart and cool place has fused local coffee-growing expertise with the needs of the cosmopolitan city dweller. The result is a wonderful cafe serving up excellent coffee,

gorgeous cakes (try the passion-fruit cheese-cake) and a daily changing range of panini. It's on the left immediately after the turnoff toward Los Naranjos.

★ **Restaurante El Estoraque**　　SEAFOOD $$
(mains L140-170; ⊘9am-9pm; 🐱) On the main road 3km before you enter Peña Blanca from La Guama, this locally famous place does superb fish, caught fresh every morning from the lake. Simply choose how you'd like it cooked and it'll be prepared to order, alongside delicious *tajadas* (soft plantain chips) with their own dressing, rice and beans and a selection of excellent *encurtido* (pickles).

❶ Getting There & Away

The small town of Peña Blanca acts as a transportation hub for the lake.

From San Pedro Sula get an El Mochito–bound chicken bus from the main terminal to the village of Los Naranjos (L50, two hours, every 30 minutes). The bus stops within 300m of the D&D Brewery.

From Tegucigalpa, there's a direct daily bus to Los Naranjos and Peña Blanca from the Mercado Mama Chepa in Comayagüela, which leaves at 1pm daily (L145, four hours). Ask for the bus going to Las Vegas, Santa Barbara and tell the driver where you wish to get off. Alternatively get a San Pedro Sula–bound bus to La Guama (L44, three hours, more than 20 daily). From there, take another bus to Peña Blanca (L10, 15 minutes, every 15 minutes) from where you can either get a bus or *mototaxi* to Los Naranjos, 6km away.

Around Lago de Yojoa

If you like the great outdoors, the gorgeous region around Lago de Yojoa will keep you busy for days. Here the rolling, verdant landscape conceals rushing rivers, extraordinary waterfalls, spectacular caves, important archaeological sites and extremely rich flora and fauna, all of which can be explored on your own or with the passionate, English-speaking guides of D&D Adventures (p369).

◉ Sights

Parque Nacional Cerro Azul Meámbar　　NATIONAL PARK
(☑8881-2553; L154) East of Lago de Yojoa, this well-maintained national park boasts kilometers of trails leading to waterfalls, caves and untouched cloud forest. There's also a visitors center, lodge and restaurant here. The entrance is via a turnoff from La Guama on the main CA-5 highway. Frequent pick-ups head to Santa Elena; from there, walking to the park's PANACAM Lodge takes about one hour.

Parque Nacional Montaña de Santa Bárbara　　NATIONAL PARK
FREE Parque Nacional Santa Bárbara is an isolated national park containing Honduras' second-highest peak, Montaña de Santa Bárbara (2744m), plus extensive cloud forest rich in orchids and epiphytes. It's a wonderful place to explore, and though it's a tough hike to the summit you've a very good chance of seeing quetzals on the mountainside – for many the main reason to visit.

Pulhapanzak　　WATERFALL
(www.pulhahn.com; L100; ⊘6am-6pm) This magnificent 43m waterfall on the Río Lindo is just 17km north of Lago de Yojoa (and also an easy day trip from San Pedro Sula). Surrounded by lush forest, it's a privately run beauty spot, where guides will lead you along a path directly behind the waterfall. There's good swimming and zip lining (L500) right across the main body of the falls. Take dry clothes if you do the cave tour, and be aware that it can get crowded here on weekends.

Cuevas de Taulabé　　CAVE
(☑9545-0095; 140km down the CA-5 Hwy from Tegucigalpa; L88; ⊘8am-4pm) Around 20km south of the Lago de Yojoa is the entrance to the Cuevas de Taulabé, a network of underground caves with unusual stalactite and stalagmite formations. Admission includes a guide – but a tip may get you to some of the less-visited areas. So far, the caves have been explored to a depth of 12km with no end in sight. The first section of the caves has lights and a (sometimes slippery) cement pathway: wear appropriate shoes.

Parque Eco-Arqueológico Los Naranjos　　NATIONAL PARK
(☑9654-0040; L120; ⊘8am-4pm) On the northwest side of the lake, this park was first occupied around 1300 BC, and is thought to be the largest Preclassic-era Lenca archaeological site. The ruins themselves are not terribly interesting: they're made of clay, so have been only semi-excavated, to protect them from environmental damage. The main reason to visit, however, is the wildlife. The park has 6km of trails that wind through the forest over hanging bridges and

on a lakeside boardwalk, providing fantastic opportunities for birdwatching.

🛏 Sleeping

Nearly all visitors to this area stay at D&D Brewery (p369), though there are several alternatives in and around the small town of Peña Blanca. There's also Panacam Lodge, located within the Parque Nacional Cerro Azul Meámbar.

Panacam Lodge   LODGE $$
(☑ 8881-2553, in Tegucigalpa 9865-9082; www.pan acam.com; Parque Nacional Cerro Azul Meámbar; s/d/tr/q incl breakfast L1100/1320/1540/1760) This high-quality lodge makes an excellent base for hiking and birdwatching inside the Parque Nacional Cerro Azul Meámbar. Rooms are a combination of cabins and smaller accommodations within the main building. It's also possible to camp here (per person L180). There's food available and the setting is wonderful, surrounded as it is by the sights and sounds of the jungle.

ℹ Information

Parque Nacional Cerro Azul Meámbar Visitors Center (☑ 2608-5510, in Tegucigalpa 2773-2027)

ℹ Getting There & Away

To reach the Pulhapanzak waterfall from San Pedro Sula, take an El Mochito chicken bus (L50, one hour) and get off at San Buenaventura, from where it's a well-marked 15-minute walk. Less frequent – but direct – Pulhapanzak Express buses also go directly to the entrance. The last bus back passes through San Buenaventura around 4pm. The El Mochito bus also passes through Los Naranjos, meaning it's easy to reach the falls from D&D Brewery.

To get to Parque Nacional Cerro Azul Meámbar, there are buses from Peña Blanca to La Guama (L20, 20 minutes, every half hour). In La Guama you then need to take a minibus bound for Santa Helena and pay the driver 200L for the trip up into the park.

San Pedro Sula

POP 719,000
The business and industrial capital of Honduras, San Pedro generates almost two-thirds of the country's GDP, with thousands employed in giant *maquila* (clothes-weaving) factories. It's wealthier and more sophisticated than Tegucigalpa, despite its horrendous reputation for gang violence.

Indeed, it has been named the world's most violent city (outside of a war zone) many times, most recently in 2015. Let's be clear, though – most crime here is gang-on-gang, and it's very rare for tourists to be targeted or caught up in violence. Some areas are violent, but you probably won't see them: the city remains doable for travelers for a day or two.

Despite this, few linger long here: there are few sights, there's little cultural life, and the sultry climate can be oppressive. Since San Pedro's international airport is Honduras' main entry point and its bus station a crucial travel hub, though, you're very likely to pass through.

◉ Sights

The heart of the city around the Parque Central is run-down but full of life.

Cathedral   CHURCH
(Parque Central; ⊙ 8am-6pm) San Pedro's cathedral is a mock-colonial structure that actually dates from 1949. It faces the once-majestic (and now decrepit) art deco **Palacio Municipal** on the other side of the square.

Museo de Antropología e Historia de San Pedro Sula   MUSEUM
(☑ 2557-1874; cnr 3a Av NO & 4a Calle NO; adult/child L40/20; ⊙ 9am-4pm Mon & Wed-Sat, to 3pm Sun) This fine museum walks visitors through the history of the Valle de Sula from its pre-Columbian days to the modern era.

Parque Nacional Cusuco   NATIONAL PARK
(L220; ⊙ 8am-4:30pm) Just 45km from San Pedro Sula, but remarkably difficult to access, Parque Nacional Cusuco is a cloud forest nestled in the impressive Merendón mountain range. The park has abundant wildlife, including parrots, toucans and a large population of quetzals, best spotted from April to June. Its highest peak is Cerro Jilinco (2242m). The visitors center (where guides can be hired) is the starting point for five different hiking trails. Two trails – Quetzal and Las Minas – pass waterfalls and swimming holes.

🛏 Sleeping

Aging budget hotels are mostly in the downtown area south of Parque Central, an area that is dodgy after dark. Hostels and guesthouses tend to be in the more suburban areas of the city, and some way from downtown. Hot water is not that common in many budget places.

La Hamaca
HOSTEL $

(☑ 2510-5174, 9868-3270; www.lahamacahostel. com; 10 Calle btwn 26 & 27 Av, Colonia Figueroa; dm with/without air-con L390/300, r with/without bathroom L1050/910; ✳@☎) This excellent party hostel is a five-minute taxi ride from the bus station. It's run by a dynamic team of young Hondurans (all fluent English speakers), who give superb up-to-date travel advice. Rooms and dorms are spacious, if a little aged, and there's a terrific lounge, games room, kitchen and garden. It's definitely a social place, but parties move elsewhere after 11pm.

Dos Molinos B&B
B&B $

(☑ 2550-5926; www.dosmolinos.hostel.com; cnr 13a Calle & 8a Av, Barrio Paz Barahona; dm L280, s/d/tr incl breakfast L430/650/780; ✳☎) Accommodations here are definitely on the musty side, but the welcome could not be warmer: Blanca and Luis are exceptionally kind hosts and, though they speak little English, quickly make guests feel right at home. All rooms, including the 'dorms' (actually just a twin and triple whose beds are sold individually) have fans and their own cold-water bathrooms.

★ La Madrugada
HOSTEL $$

(☑ 2540-1309, 2553-1089; www.lamadrugadahostel. com; 8 Calle btwn 8 & 9 Av, Barrio Guamilito; dm/ s/d/tr/q L260/780/1030/1290/1550; ✳☎) This new hostel downtown takes up an entire block – it's the impressive conversion of a mansion that retains some original features, including beautifully tiled floors. Dorms are spacious, bright and enjoy generous bathrooms with hot water, while private rooms each sleep up to four. There's a pleasant bar and social area, a pool table and an expansive outside area.

Hotel Guacamaya Inn
HOTEL $$

(☑ 2556-8406, 2556-9083; www.guacamayainn. com; Colonia Los Arcos; s/d L1300/1565; ✳☎) This friendly and good-value hotel is well located a short walk from a huge mall, meaning that there are several eating and drinking options nearby. The red accented rooms are large, clean and comfortable and feature desks and good bathrooms.

✖ Eating

San Pedro Sula has a wide range of culinary choices. Upmarket places, as well as US fast food franchises, are mainly located on Circunvalación. There's also a whole bunch of cheap and cheerful *comedores* at Mercado Guimilito.

Plaza Típica
HONDURAN $

(3a Av NO; meals L50-100; ☺6am-4:30pm) Just north of the Parque Central, this open-sided food court is your best bet for an inexpensive daytime meal. There are around 25 stands rustling up delicious *carne asada* (grilled meat), *tapado* (seafood soup with coconut) and amazing tropical fruit juices.

Café Skandia
CAFETERIA, INTERNATIONAL $$

(Gran Hotel Sula, Parque Central; mains from L120; ☺6am-midnight; ☎) An absolute institution in the city center, this classic 1950s-style cafe looks like it's been transplanted from an ocean liner with its marine-blue color scheme and vintage chrome-and-white-leather seats. There's a vast window that overlooks the hotel's palm-fringed pool. On the menu are steaks, burgers, salads, sandwiches, milkshakes and lots of dessert action.

Donde Ofelia
MEXICAN $$

(☑ 9982-6864; 10 Calle & Av 25; mains L100-200; ☺5:30-11pm Tue-Sun) You're literally caged in at this family-run, semi-open-air place that takes its security very seriously. Another quirk is that you're given an order form when you arrive and you make your order yourself from the long list of traditional Mexican dishes – including *sopa azteca* (tortilla soup) and tacos – all of which make a welcome change from local cooking.

☕ Drinking & Nightlife

The *zona viva*, which hugs the inside of the Circunvalación between 7a Calle SO and 11a Calle SO, is home to the main concentration of bars and clubs.

Doghouse
PUB

(Jardines del Valle; ☺4-11pm Mon-Fri, to 1am Sat; ☎) This intimate bar in the buzzing Jardines del Valle district looks like a log cabin. It's very popular with visiting gringos, as the beers are cheap and you can make requests on the YouTube jukebox. Open-mike comedy night is Wednesdays; trivia night (in English and Spanish) is Thursdays.

ℹ Information

BAC/Bamer (5a Av NO btwn 1a & 2a Calles NO; ☺9am-5pm Mon-Fri, to noon Sat) With ATM.

Banco Atlántida (Parque Central; ☉8:30am-5pm Mon-Fri, 9am-1pm Sat) Has an ATM.

Mesoamérica Travel (☎2558-6447; www.mesoamerica-travel.com; cnr 8a Calle & 32a Avenida NO) Professional agency that does interesting upscale tours throughout Honduras and other countries in Central America, including national park trips.

Post Office (cnr 9a Calle & 3a Av SO; ☉7:30am-5pm Mon-Fri, 8am-noon Sat)

Tourist Police (☎2550-0001; cnr 12a Av NO & Blvr Morazan; ☉24hr) No English is spoken here.

DANGERS & ANNOYANCES

➡ San Pedro Sula's crime rate is one of the highest in the world. Mostly it involves gangs and travelers rarely get caught up in big trouble. However, do be very cautious.

➡ Avoid being flashy with your belongings and dress with restraint (save the shorts for the beach).

➡ Downtown is dodgy after nightfall. Use taxis to get around – don't risk the local buses at any time of day.

BUSES FROM SAN PEDRO SULA

International Buses

DESTINATION	COST (L)	DURATION (HR)	BUS LINE	PHONE	FREQUENCY
Antigua (Guatemala)	1320	9	Hedman Alas	☎2516-2273	1 daily
Guatemala City (Guatemala)	1188	8	Hedman Alas	☎2516-2273	1 daily
	660	8	Fuentes del Norte	☎9843-0507	1 daily
	1452	8	Platinum	☎2516-2167	1 daily
Léon (Nicaragua)	704	10	Tica Bus	☎2220-0579	1 daily
Managua (Nicaragua)	704	12	Tica Bus	☎2220-0579	1 daily
San Salvador (El Salvador)	550	7	Congolón	☎2553-1174	1 daily
	1012	7	Platinum	☎2516-2167	1 daily

Domestic Buses

DESTINATION	COST (L)	DURATION (HR)	BUS LINE	PHONE	FREQUENCY
Agua Caliente	240	5	Congolón	☎2553-1174	every 2hr
Comayagua	85	2½	Diaz	☎2505-9955	hourly
Copán Ruinas	154	3	Casasola	☎2516-2031	7 daily
	440	3	Hedman Alas	☎2516-2273	2 daily
El Mochito	55	2	Tima	☎2659-3161	every 30min
La Ceiba	150-500	3-4	7 bus lines incl Hedman Alas, Viana, Diana Express		every 15-30min
Puerto Cortés	66	1hr-1½	Impala	☎2665-0606	every 15min
Pulhapanzak & Lago de Yojoa	44	2	Etul	☎2516-2011	every 20min
	44	2	Pulhapanzak Express	No phone	9 daily
Santa Rosa de Copán	100	3	Toritos y Copanaecos	☎2516-2045	every 30min
Tegucigalpa	150-650	4-4½	6 bus lines incl El Rey Express, Hedman Alas, Sultana, Viana		every 15-30min
Tela	155	1½	7 bus lines incl COTUC, Mirna, Tela Express		every 15-30min
Trujillo	230	7	Cotuc	☎2520-7497	8 daily
	250	6½	Cotraipbal	☎9908-1509	9 daily

ⓘ Getting There & Away

AIR

San Pedro Sula's modern **Aeropuerto Internacional Ramón Villeda Morales** (SAP; ☎ 6689-3261) is served by daily direct flights to many major cities in Central America and several US cities. Domestically there are connections to Tegucigalpa, La Ceiba, Puerto Lempira and the Bay Islands (usually via La Ceiba). The airport is on SPS-Tela Hwy CA-13, about 14km southeast of the city center.

International Airlines

American Airlines (☎ 2553-3506, airport 2668-3244; www.aa.com; cnr Av Circunvalación & 5a Calle SO, Edificio Banco Ficohsa) Flies to/from Miami.

Avianca (☎ 2550-8222; www.avianca.com; Av Circunvalación, Colonia Trejo, Edif Yude Canahuati) Connects San Pedro with Guatemala City, Miami, New York, San José and San Salvador.

Copa (☎ airport 2668-3212; www.copa.com) Flies to/from Panama City.

Maya Island Air (☎ 2668-0569; www.maya islandair.com) Flies to/from Belize.

United (☎ 2501-0481; www.united.com) Flies to/from Houston and Newark.

Domestic Airlines

Aerolíneas Sosa (☎ 2550-6545, airport 2668-3128; www.aerolineasosa.com; 1a Calle SO btwn 7a & 8a Av SO)

CM Airlines (p363)

BUS

All buses depart from designated bays in the modern, well-organized **Terminal Gran Central Metropolitana** (☎ 2516-1616; Av Circunvalación), 6km south of the Parque Central. There's also a large mall and food court here. The terminal entrance has a handy directory; **Hedman Alas** (☎ 2516-2273; www.hedman alas.com; 3a Calle NO & 8a Av NO) buses have their own terminal at the rear. The magazine *Honduras Tips* has bus information; the website www.horariodebuses.com is an excellent online resource.

To head into town from here, use taxis from the official rank, not freelance drivers.

ⓘ Getting Around

BUS

It's best not to use local buses as they are subject to frequent robberies and 'taxing' by gangs.

CAR & MOTORCYLCE

Car rental agencies in San Pedro Sula with airport offices:

Econo Rent-A-Car (☎ 2668-1884; www.econo rentacarhn.com)

Hertz (☎ 2580-9191; www.hertz.com)

Thrifty (☎ 2668-2427; www.thrifty.com)

TAXI

Average fares around town are L50 to L120. From the bus station to the center is around L100; to the airport about L300. Fares rise substantially after 9pm.

Copán Ruinas

POP 10,000

The town of Copán Ruinas, often simply called Copán, is a beautiful place, paved with cobblestones and lined with white adobe buildings with red-tiled roofs. It's also one of the most charming and traveler-oriented places in Honduras, with a friendly local population, English spoken widely and some great hotels and restaurants. Many people come here just to see the famous nearby Maya ruins (p380), but with plenty of other attractions in the town and nearby, there's reason enough to linger.

◉ Sights

Though the archaeological site is the main attraction of the Copán region, there are other fine places to visit in the area, including several museums in and around town.

Memorias Frágiles   GALLERY
(☎ 2651-3900; Palacio Municipal, Parque Central; ⊙8am-5pm Mon-Fri) **FREE** This fascinating photo exhibition was a gift from Boston's Peabody Museum; it features a collection of rare photos detailing the first archaeological expeditions to Copán at the turn of the 20th century. Many of these proved essential in later restoration work, as the photos showed the site decades beforehand, and offered clues to how the various stone hieroglyphs had lain.

It's located inside the **Palacio Municipal** (City Hall), behind the second door on the left as you enter (you may have to ask for the key).

Macaw Mountain Bird Park   ZOO
(☎ 2651-4245; www.macawmountain.org; L220; ⊙9am-5pm) 🐾 Around 2.5km outside Copán Ruinas is an extensive private reserve aimed at saving Central American macaws. There are plenty of them here, along with toucans, motmots, parrots, kingfishers and orioles, all flying around in spacious, humanely constructed cages. In the 'Encounter Center' un-

Copán Ruinas

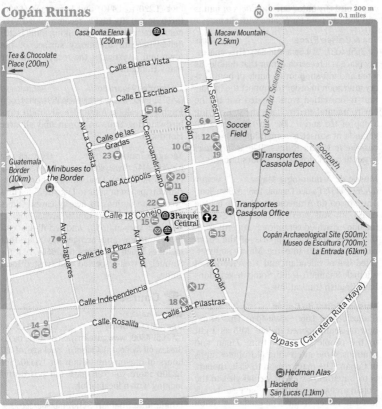

Casa Doña Elena (250m)

Macaw Mountain (2.5km)

Tea & Chocolate Place (200m)

Calle Buena Vista

Calle El Escribano

Av Sesesmil

Quebrada Sesesmil

Av Copán

Soccer Field

Footpath

Av Centroamericano

Calle de las Gradas

Av La Cuesta

Guatemala Border (10km)

Minibuses to the Border

Calle Acrópolis

Transportes Casasola Depot

Calle 18 Conejo

Parque Central

Transportes Casasola Office

Av los Jaguares

Calle de la Plaza

Av Mirador

Copán Archaeological Site (500m); Museo de Escultura (700m); La Entrada (61km)

Calle Independencia

Av Copán

Calle Las Pilastras

Calle Rosalila

Bypass (Carretera Ruta Maya)

Hedman Alas

Hacienda San Lucas (1.1km)

HONDURAS COPÁN RUINAS

Copán Ruinas

⊙ Sights
1 Casa K'inich B1
2 Iglesia Católica Copán Ruinas C3
3 Memorias Frágiles B3
4 Museo de Arqueología Maya B3
5 Museo Digital de Copán B2

⊕ Activities, Courses & Tours
Basecamp Tours .... (see 8)
6 Guacamaya Spanish Academy C2
7 Ixbalanque Spanish School A3
Yaragua Tours .... (see 13)

⊟ Sleeping
8 Café ViaVia B3
9 Hostel Iguana Azul A4
10 Hotel & Hostal Berakah B2
11 Hotel La Posada B2
12 Hotel Mary C2

13 Hotel Yaragua C3
14 La Casa de Café A4
15 Lauro's Hotel B3
16 Terramaya B1

⊗ Eating
17 Café San Rafael C3
Café ViaVia .... (see 8)
18 Carnitas Nia Lola B3
19 Casa Ixchel C2
Comedor Mary .... (see 12)
20 El Rincón Colombiano B2
21 Twisted Tanya's C2

⊖ Drinking & Nightlife
Café ViaVia .... (see 8)
22 Café Welchez B2
23 Sol de Copán B2

caged birds fly onto your shoulders or hands and you can pose for photos with them.

Tea & Coffee Place HOUSE
(☑ 2651-4087; ☺ 4-6pm Mon-Sat) This charming place is a research center that doubles as a tea and gift shop for a couple of hours every afternoon in order to support the important reforestation work carried out by the environmental charity based here. Enjoying a cup of tea and a cake on the wonderful veranda at sunset is something of a rite of passage in Copán Ruinas. Take a *mototaxi* to get here; ask for David Sedat's house.

Museo de Arqueología Maya MUSEUM
(☑ 2651-4437; Parque Central; L66; ☺ 9am-9pm) The Museo de Arqueología Maya is a little dated but still worth a visit. The exhibits include excavated ceramics, fragments from the altars and the supports of the Maya ruins, an insight into the Maya's sophisticated use of calendars and a re-creation of a female shaman's tomb. Some descriptions have English translations.

Museo Digital de Copán MUSEUM
(Parque Central; L66; ☺ 8am-4pm) This brand new museum opened in late 2015 as a gift to the people of Copán from Japan and contains some interesting old photographs of Copán. The main reason to visit, though, is to watch the excellent virtual visit to the Copán archaeological site, which can be enjoyed in either Spanish or English at 10am and 3pm each day.

Iglesia Católica Copán Ruinas CHURCH
(Parque Central) Copán's pretty parish church dominates the town's main plaza. It's illuminated at night.

Casa K'inich MUSEUM
(☑ 2651-4105; off Av Centroaméricano; L20; ☺ 8am-noon & 1-5pm Tue-Sun) Casa K'inich includes an interactive re-creation of the ancient football game practiced by the Copán residents more than a millennia ago. Displays are in three languages: English, Spanish and Ch'orti'. Kids might get a kick out of the stela with a cutout hole to poke their heads through.

🏃 Activities

Basecamp Tours ADVENTURE TOUR
(☑ 2651-4695; www.basecamphonduras.com; Calle de la Plaza) Located inside Café ViaVia, this outfit offers a range of original and adventurous tours around the local area on foot (L220 to L440) and horseback (L330, three hours). Its highly recommended two-hour 'Alternative Copán' walking tour (L220) delves beneath the glossy surface of the town and investigates the reality of life for many Hondurans.

Alexander Alvarado BIRDWATCHING
(☑ 9751-1680; alexander.alvarado469@gmail.com) English speaking Alexander Alvarado runs birdwatching tours in Copán and all over Honduras.

Yaragua Tours ADVENTURE TOUR
(☑ 2651-4147; www.yaragua.com; cnr Calle de la Plaza & Av Copán) Leads hikes, horseback-riding trips, excursions to Lago de Yojoa and even some outings to nearby caves. Offers guided tours of the Copán archaeological site (per person L770) and a full-day coffee plantation and archaeology tour that includes lunch (per person L1650). Ask for Samuel, a well-respected and trusted local guide.

📚 Courses

Guacamaya
Spanish Academy LANGUAGE COURSE
(☑ 2651-4360; www.guacamaya.com; Calle de las Gradas, off Av Copán) Offers a package of 20 hours of one-on-one tuition for L3520. For L2200 more you can have full board and lodging with a local family.

Ixbalanque Spanish School LANGUAGE COURSE
(☑ 2651-4432; www.ixbalanque.com; Av los Jaguares) Offers 20 hours of one-on-one instruction in Spanish for L5720 per week, including a homestay with a local family that provides three meals a day.

🛏️ Sleeping

★ Hotel Mary HOTEL $
(☑ 2651-4673; www.comedormary.com; Av Sesesmiles; s/d L600/700) One of the best deals in town, this beautifully presented place has very sweet rooms that are brightly painted and well maintained. There's hot water, ceiling fans, attractive traditional bed covers and a pretty garden to boot.

Hostel Iguana Azul HOSTEL $
(☑ 2651-4620; www.iguanaazulcopan.com; Calle Rosalila; dm/s/d L175/350/400; 🖭) This colonial-style home has eight comfy bunk beds in two rooms and a shared bathroom with hot water; three private rooms sleep two. There's also a pretty back garden. The communal

area has books and lots of travel information, and there's a fridge but no kitchen. This is backpacking elegance at its finest: even a room-cleaning service is included.

Hotel & Hostal Berakah
HOSTEL $

(✒ 9951-4288, 2651-4771; www.hotelberakahcopan. hostel.com; Av Copán; dm/d/tw incl breakfast L180/400/440) One of the few true hostels in Copán Ruinas, Berakah is very well set up for backpackers, with a range of different rooms and clean, modern bathrooms. Dorms are rather cramped but a great deal, while the next-door house that functions as a second site for the hostel has a well-equipped kitchen, a pool table and more dorms.

Café ViaVia
HOTEL $

(✒ 2651-4652; www.viaviacafe.com/en/copan/ hotel; Calle de la Plaza; s/d/q from L220/330/440; ☎) This small, Belgian-run, European-style hotel has five spotless rooms with private hot-water bathrooms, tiled floors, desks and great beds. There are hammocks, a small garden and enough space to chill out. It's a great place to come for tourist information, and also has an art gallery and lively bar attached, which – be aware – can get noisy.

Lauro's Hotel
HOTEL $

(✒ 2651-4068; www.lauroshotel.com; Calle 18 Conejo; s/d with fan L420/595, r with air-con L800; ✴☎) Half a block from Parque Central, this is a well-managed hotel with a choice of spotless rooms, some with air-con. The owners have gone a bit overboard on the beige color scheme, but otherwise it's a fine choice. Rooms on the upper floors are more pricey and have views of the town.

Hotel Yaragua
HOTEL $

(✒ 2651-4147; www.yaragua.com; cnr Av Copán & Calle de la Plaza; s/d L300/400; ✴☎) The bright-yellow paint job and jungly patio area give this place a cheery feel. Rooms are smallish but comfortable and you can't beat the central location. There's hot water and a shared balcony; air-con costs an extra L100 per day.

Casa Doña Elena
GUESTHOUSE $$

(✒ 2651-4029; www.casadonaelena.com; Av Centroaméricano; s/d/tr L484/792/1100; ✴☎) This family-run hilltop place enjoys some great views of the town and surrounding valley and has a beautifully tended garden shared by its seven individually named rooms. The rooms themselves are simple, but spacious

and clean, with fans (air-con costs L220 extra per day) and TV. It's a 10-minute sturdy uphill walk from the center of town.

Hotel La Posada
HOTEL $$

(✒ 2651-4059; www.laposadacopan.com; Av Centroaméricano; s/d incl breakfast L575/800; ☎) Good value, tranquil and comfortable, La Posada is only half a block from the plaza. Its 19 rooms are set around two leafy patios, are comfortable and clean and have hot-water bathroom, fan and TV.

★ La Casa de Café
B&B $$$

(✒ 2651-4620; www.casadecafecopan.com; Calle Rosalila; s/d incl breakfast L1250/1520; ✴☎) This impeccably decorated B&B has rooms adorned with carved wooden doors and Guatemalan masks. The setting is stunning – the view from the lawn over the copious and delicious breakfast service is of morning mists rising around the Guatemalan mountains in the distance. American owner Howard is a mine of local information and the feeling is very much one of being his personal guests.

La Casa de Café operates an excellent restaurant, open all day. There's also an upscale house and town house available across the street (L2000 to L2600 a night, rates negotiable for longer stays).

Terramaya
BOUTIQUE HOTEL $$$

(✒ 2651-4623; www.terramayacopan.com; Av Centroaméricano; s/d incl breakfast from L2090/2350; ✴☎) This comfortable, stylish newcomer hovers somewhere between a B&B and a boutique hotel, offering six smartly appointed rooms, a lovely backyard garden and a candlelit terrace with misty-eyed mountain views. Two upstairs rooms offer spectacular balconies with vistas out to the ruins and the mountains beyond.

✖ Eating

Casa Ixchel
CAFE $$

(Av Sesesmiles; mains L100-200; ☉8am-6pm; ☎) There's a friendly welcome at this serious coffee lover's place, where locally grown Casa Ixchel Arabica coffee is the fuel of choice and the espresso machine is rarely out of use. There's a great little back patio for eating and drinking in the sunshine, and a brunchy menu for tasty breakfasts and light lunches.

Comedor Mary
COMEDOR $$

(Hotel Mary, Av Sesesmiles; mains L115-250; ☉7am-9pm; ☎) This charming space comprises a

HONDURAS COPÁN RUINAS

garden for alfresco dining and a dining room full of dark wood furniture where excellent *pupusas* are served up. *Comida típica* is also redefined here (try the *lomito de res a la plancha*, a grilled beef tenderloin); service is uncharacteristically friendly and the atmosphere is upscale.

Café ViaVia INTERNATIONAL $$
(www.viaviacafe.com/en/copan; Calle de la Plaza; breakfast L60-80, mains L80-180; ⊙7am-10pm; 🖥🍴) This terrific restaurant serves breakfast, lunch and dinner in a convivial atmosphere, with tables overlooking the street and a replica of Altar Q from the Acrópolis at the Copán Site behind the bar. The organically grown coffee it prepares is excellent, the bread is homemade and there's always a good selection of vegetarian and meat-based dishes on offer.

★Café San Rafael CAFE, DELI $$$
(Av Centroaméricano; meals L150-335; ⊙11am-11pm Tue-Sat, 8am-6pm Sun & Mon; 🖥) This smart cafe serves organic coffee grown at the *finca* (ranch) of the same name, though it's most famous locally for the various cheeses produced here (platters L120 to L500). Breakfasts (L180) are a filling splurge, while the toasted sandwiches (try the excellent steak and provolone) are a great lunch option. The whole place is gorgeous, overlooking a beautifully maintained lawn, and service is friendly.

El Rincón Colombiano COLOMBIAN $$$
(Calle Acrópolis; mains L150-300; ⊙10:30am-10pm Tue-Sun; 🖥) The 'Colombian Corner' has a great rooftop terrace that's perfect for a light lunch (L140) or an atmospheric dinner, complete with fairy lights. Dishes include *ajiaco* (a chicken soup from Bogotá) and *albóndigas en salsa napolitana de cerveza* (meatballs in a Neopolitan beer sauce), although top billing goes to Solomito de Res – beef medallions in a Dutch cheese sauce with sautéed vegetables.

Twisted Tanya's INTERNATIONAL $$$
(☎2651-4182; www.twistedtanyas.com; Parque Central; 2-/3-course meals L380/420; ⊙11am-11pm Mon-Sat; 🖥) Set upstairs, with views over Parque Central and beyond, Tanya's serves up some good versions of Italian and Asian-influenced dishes. Moroccan-style lampshades add an artistic flourish. Happy hour runs from 5pm to 6pm, when there's also a range of good-value, cheaper set

plates (L150 to L220). It can be loud here, so don't come for an intimate dinner.

Carnitas Nia Lola HONDURAN $$$
(Av Centroaméricano; mains L180-355; ⊙7am-10pm; 🖥) Two blocks south of the plaza, this open-air restaurant has a beautiful view toward the mountains over corn and tobacco fields. It's a relaxing place with simple and economical food; the specialties are charcoal-grilled chicken and beef. Happy hour starts at 6:30pm.

🍷 Drinking & Nightlife

★Sol de Copán BAR, BREWERY
(Av Mirador; mains L130-180; ⊙2-10pm Tue-Sat; 🖥) A terrific, German-owned microbrewery in a large basement. The owner, Thomas, is friendly and highly attentive, making sure everyone's regularly topped up with pilsner or lager. Delicious German sausages are served, too. If you're lucky Thomas might show you some of his fermenting vats out the back. *Baleadas* (L65 to L90) are also available.

Café ViaVia BAR
(www.viaviacafe.com/en/copan; Calle de la Plaza; ⊙7am-10pm; 🖥) The bar here is the liveliest in town, with a highly sociable vibe, drink specials, occasional gigs and DJs playing Latin and pop tunes on weekends. Definitely a good place to meet both locals and backpackers.

Café Welchez CAFE
(☎2651-4202; near Parque Central; mains L100-150; ⊙6:30am-9:30pm; 🖥) This very pleasant two-floor place does excellent coffee and cake and has a charming terrace with Parque Central views. Good breakfasts (L100 to L150) are available here, including French toast, eggs Benedict and a 'full American.' Sandwiches, soups and salads complete the offerings.

ℹ Information

Police (☎2651-4060; Calle de la Plaza; ⊙24hr) It's 300m west of the park.

Post Office (Calle de la Plaza; ⊙8am-noon & 1-5pm Mon-Sat) A few doors from the plaza.

MONEY

US dollars can be changed at most banks, though Guatemalan quetzals can at present only be changed on the black market. The following banks have ATMs that accept foreign cards.

BAC (Parque Central; ⊙9am-5pm Mon-Fri, to noon Sat) Exchanges US dollars and has a 24-hour ATM.

BAC/Bamer (Parque Central; ◷8am-5pm Mon-Fri, 8:30am-1pm Sat) Has an ATM that accepts Visa and MasterCard.

Banco Atlántida (cnr Calle Independencia & Av Copán) Changes US dollars and has an ATM.

Banco Credomatic (Calle de la Plaza) On the plaza.

Banco de Occidente (cnr Calle 18 Conejo & Av Copán) On the plaza; changes US dollars and gives cash advances on Visa and MasterCard.

❶ Getting There & Away

An airport opened here in 2015, but at the time of writing was served only by the occasional charter flight.

BUS

Casasola (☑2651-4078; Av Sesesmiles) buses arrive and depart from an open-air **bus depot** (☑2651-4078) at the entrance to town, where destinations include San Pedro Sula (L140, three hours, five daily) and Santa Rosa de Copán (L100, three hours, hourly), from where you can connect easily to Tegucigalpa.

Minibuses to/from the Guatemalan border (L20, 20 minutes, every 20 minutes) run between 6am and 5pm from near the town's cemetery at the end of Calle 18 Conejo. On the Guatemala side, buses to Esquipulas and Chiquimula leave the border regularly until about 5pm.

Both Basecamp Tours (p376) and Hotel Berakah (p377) run popular shuttle buses between Copán Ruinas and Antigua (L550, six hours) via Guatemala City (L550, five hours). Shuttles also run to El Salvador, stopping at Santa Ana (L640, 4½ hours) and San Salvador (L880, five hours); there's one shuttle to Managua in Nicaragua (L2200, 12 hours) and also one to La Ceiba (L880, six hours). You can book via Basecamp or other travel agencies.

Hedman Alas (☑2651-4037; Km 62 Carretera a San Lucas) has a modern terminal just south of town, where you can get 1st-class buses to San Pedro Sula (L395, three hours) at 11am each day (and also at 2pm on Saturday, Sunday and Monday).

Around Copán Ruinas

The forested hills around Copán Ruinas include a few interesting sights that are well worth visiting while you're staying in the town.

◉ Sights

Los Sapos ARCHAEOLOGICAL SITE
(Hacienda San Lucas; L30) The *sapos* (toads) are old Maya stone carvings, set in a location with a beautiful view over the town. The site

is connected with Maya fertility rites. You can get there on horseback in about half an hour, or walk it in about an hour, all uphill. From Los Sapos you can walk to Stela 10 – if you plan on doing that, stop by Café ViaVia (p378) for a free map, as the trail is not well marked.

Los Sapos is on the grounds of Hacienda San Lucas, a century-old farmhouse that has been converted into a B&B and restaurant. There are walking trails here, too.

✦ Activities

Finca El Cisne HORSEBACK RIDING
(☑2651-4695; www.fincaelcisne.com; horseback riding tour incl accommodations, 3 meals & thermal baths from L1800) Visiting this working farm 24km from Copán Ruinas is more like an agri-eco experience than a tour. Founded in the 1920s and still operating, the *finca* mainly raises cattle and grows coffee and cardamom. Full-day and overnight packages include guided horseback riding through the forests, and tours of the coffee and cardamom fields and processing plants.

Luna Jaguar Spa Resort SPA
(www.lunajaguarsparesort.com; L250; ◷8am-5pm) Directly across the river from the hot springs is this high-concept Maya day spa – perhaps what the Maya kings would have done to relax if they had the chance. Thirteen 'treatment stations' (offering hot tubs, herbal steam baths and so on) are scattered around the hillside, connected by a series of stone pathways.

Aguas Termales HOT SPRING
(L250; ◷10am-10pm) This set of hot springs is 24km north of Copán Ruinas, an hour's drive through fertile mountains and coffee plantations. There are a couple of artificial pools, or else you can sit in the river, where the boiling-hot spring water mixes with the cool river water. Bring warm clothes if you come in the evening.

🛏 Sleeping

★**Hacienda San Lucas** HISTORIC HOTEL **$$$**
(☑2651-4495; www.haciendasanlucas.com; s/d/ tr incl breakfast L2860/3300/3960; 🛜) ✿ This magical place some 3km south of town enjoys sweeping views from its wonderfully maintained gardens. It's a rustic experience – so despite the price tag, don't come expecting luxury. The rooms have stone floors, terracotta roofs, wooden furniture and are stuffed with locally made

handicrafts, while the onsite restaurant is superb. The Los Sapos archaeological site is on the property.

✗ Eating

★ **Hacienda San Lucas** HONDURAN $$$
(☑ 2651-4495; www.haciendasanlucas.com; 3-/4-course meal L550/620) Set on farmland overlooking the town and archaeological site, this wonderful place has some of the best food in the region; the romance of dining by candlelight in the restored farmhouse can't really be exaggerated. Cuisine draws heavily on traditional ingredients and techniques and comes accompanied by fine South American wines. Reservations should be made two days in advance.

❶ Getting There & Away

Access from Copán Ruinas is easy and cheap using the town's *mototaxis*.

Copán Archaeological Site

One of the most important of all Maya civilizations lived, prospered, then mysteriously crumbled around the Copán archaeological site, a Unesco World Heritage Site. During the Classic period (AD 250–900), the city at Copán Ruinas culturally dominated the region. The architecture is not as grand as what's across the border in Tikal, but the city produced remarkable sculptures and hieroglyphics, and these days you'll often be virtually alone at the site, which makes it all the more haunting.

The ruins are a pleasant 1km stroll outside of Copán. A visitors center, an excellent sculpture museum and a cafe and gift shop are close to the main entrance. The guides at the Asociación de Guías Copán (p384) really know their stuff and hiring one is a worthwhile investment.

History

Pre-Columbian History

People have been living in the Copán valley since at least 1200 BC; ceramic evidence has been found from around that date. Copán must have had significant commercial activity since early times, as graves showing marked Olmec influence have been dated to around 900 to 600 BC.

In the 5th century AD one royal family came to rule Copán, led by a mysterious king named Mah K'ina Yax K'uk' Mo' (Great

Sun Lord Quetzal Macaw), who ruled from AD 426 to 435. Archaeological evidence indicates that he was a great shaman, and later kings revered him as the semi-divine founder of the city. The dynasty ruled throughout Copán's florescence during the Classic period (AD 250 to 900).

We know little about the subsequent kings who ruled before AD 628. Only some of their names have been deciphered: Mat Head, the second king (no relation to Bed Head); Cu Ix, the fourth king; Waterlily Jaguar, the seventh; Moon Jaguar, the 10th; and Butz' Chan, the 11th.

Among the greatest of Copán's kings was Smoke Imix (Smoke Jaguar; r 628–695), the 12th king. Smoke Imix built Copán into a major military and commercial power in the region. He may have taken over the nearby princedom of Quiriguá, as one of the famous stelae at that site bears his name and image. By the time he died in 695, Copán's population had grown substantially.

Smoke Imix was succeeded by Uaxaclahun Ubak K'awil (18 Rabbit; r 695–738), the 13th king, who willingly took the reins of power and pursued further military conquest. In a war with King Cauac Sky, his neighbor from Quiriguá, 18 Rabbit was captured and beheaded. He was succeeded by K'ak' Joplaj Chan K'awiil (Smoke Monkey; r 738–49), the 14th king, whose short reign left little mark on Copán. Smoke Monkey's son, K'ak' Yipyaj Chan K'awiil (Smoke Shell; r 749–63), was, however, one of Copán's greatest builders. He commissioned the city's most famous and important monument, the great Escalinata de los Jeroglíficos (Hieroglyphic Stairway), which immortalizes the achievements of the dynasty from its establishment until 755, when the stairway was dedicated. It is the longest inscription ever discovered in the Maya lands.

Yax Pasaj Chan Yopaat (Sunrise or First Dawn; r 763–820; also known as Yax Pac, Yax Pasaj Chan Yoaat and Yax Pasah), Smoke Shell's successor and the 16th king, continued the beautification of Copán. The final occupant of the throne, U Cit Tok', became ruler in 822, but it's not known when he died.

Until recently, the collapse of the civilization at Copán had been a mystery. Now, archaeologists have begun to surmise that near the end of Copán's heyday the population grew at an unprecedented rate, straining agricultural resources. In the end, Copán was no longer agriculturally self-sufficient

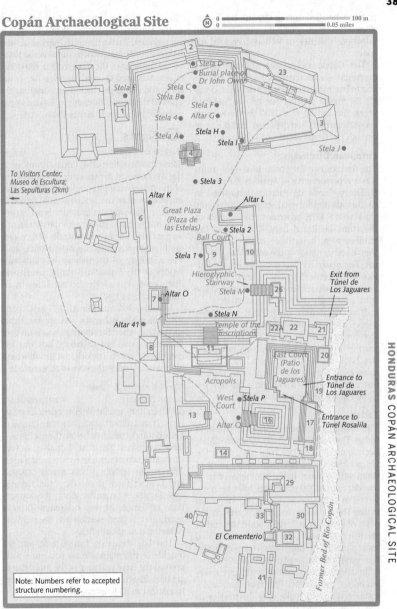

Copán Archaeological Site

- 2
- Stela D
- Burial place of Dr John Owen
- 23
- Stela E
- Stela C
- Stela B
- Stela F
- Stela 4
- Altar G
- Stela A
- Stela H
- Stela I
- 1
- 3
- Stela J
- 4
- To Visitors Center; Museo de Escultura; Las Sepulturas (2km)
- Stela 3
- Altar K
- Altar L
- Great Plaza (Plaza de las Estelas)
- 6
- Stela 2
- Ball Court
- Stela 1
- 9
- 10
- Hieroglyphic Stairway
- Stela M
- 26
- Exit from Túnel de Los Jaguares
- 7
- Altar O
- Stela N
- Altar 41
- Temple of the Inscriptions
- 22A
- 22
- 21
- 8
- 11
- East Court (Patio de los Jaguares)
- 20
- Acropolis
- 19
- Entrance to Túnel de Los Jaguares
- West Court
- Stela P
- Entrance to Túnel Rosalila
- 13
- Altar Q
- 16
- 17
- 18
- 14
- 29
- 40
- 33
- 30
- El Cementerio
- 32
- 41
- Former Bed of Río Copán

Note: Numbers refer to accepted structure numbering.

and had to import food from other areas. The urban core expanded into the fertile lowlands in the center of the valley, forcing both agricultural and residential areas to spread onto the steep slopes surrounding the valley. Wide areas were deforested, resulting in massive erosion that further decimated food production and brought flooding during rainy seasons. Interestingly, this environmental damage of old is not too different from what is happening today – a disturbing trend, but one that meshes with the Maya belief that life is cyclical and history repeats itself. Skeletal remains of people who died during Copán's final years show marked evidence of malnutrition and infectious diseases, as well as decreased life spans.

The Copán valley was not abandoned overnight – agriculturists probably continued to live in the ecologically devastated valley for maybe another one or two hundred years. But by the year 1200 or thereabouts even the farmers had departed, and the royal city of Copán was reclaimed by the jungle.

European Discovery

The first known European to see the ruins was a representative of Spanish King Felipe II, Diego García de Palacios, who lived in Guatemala and traveled through the region. On March 8, 1576, he wrote to the king about the ruins he found here. Only about five families were living here at the time, and they knew nothing of the history of the ruins. The discovery was not pursued, and almost three centuries went by before another Spaniard, Colonel Juan Galindo, visited the ruins and made the first map of them.

It was Galindo's report that stimulated John L Stephens and Frederick Catherwood to come to Copán on their Central American journey in 1839. When Stephens published the book *Incidents of Travel in Central America, Chiapas and Yucatán* in 1841, illustrated by Catherwood, the ruins first became known to the world at large.

Today

The history of Copán continues to unfold today. The remains of 3450 structures have been found in the 27 sq km surrounding the Grupo Principal (Principal Group), most of them within about half a kilometer of it. In a wider zone, 4509 structures have been detected in 1420 sites within 135 sq km of the ruins. These discoveries indicate that at the peak of civilization here, around the end of the 8th century AD, the valley of Copán had more than 27,500 inhabitants – a population figure not reached again until the 1980s.

In addition to examining the area surrounding the Grupo Principal, archaeologists continue to make new discoveries in the Grupo Principal itself. Five separate phases of building on this site have been identified; the final phase, dating from AD 650 to 820, is what we see today. But buried underneath the visible ruins are layers of other ruins, which archaeologists are exploring by means of underground tunnels. This is how they found the Templo Rosalila

(Rosalila Temple), a replica of which is now in the Museo de Escultura. Below Rosalila is yet another, earlier temple, Margarita, and below that, Hunal, which contains the tomb of the founder of the dynasty, Yax K'uk' Mo' (Great Sun Lord Quetzal Macaw). Two of the excavation tunnels, including Rosalila, are open to the public, though you'll need to pay a second entry fee to access them.

◉ Sights

Museo de Escultura
MUSEUM

(Museum of Sculpture; L154) Copán is unique in the Maya world for its sculpture and some of the finest examples are on display at this impressive museum, which is fully signed in English. Entering the museum is an experience in itself: you go through the mouth of a serpent and through its entrails before suddenly emerging into the bright main hall. The highlight of the display is a full-scale replica of the Rosalila Temple, which was discovered in nearly perfect condition by archaeologists in 1989.

Rosalila, dedicated in AD 571 by Copán's 10th ruler, Moon Jaguar, was apparently so sacred that when Structure 16 was built over it, Rosalila was not destroyed but was left completely intact. The original Rosalila temple remains inside the core of Structure 16.

Túnel Rosalila & Túnel de los Jaguares
ARCHAEOLOGICAL SITE

(L330) In 1999, archaeologists opened up two tunnels that allow visitors to get a glimpse of pre-existing structures below the visible surface structures. The first, Rosalila, is very short and takes only a few visitors at a time. The famous temple is only barely exposed, and behind thick glass. The other tunnel, Los Jaguares, running along the foundations of Temple 22, was originally 700m in length, but a large section has been closed, reducing it to about 80m.

The Los Jaguares Tunnel exits on the outside of the main site, so you must walk around the base and rear of the main site to get back in again. While fascinating, it's hard to justify the L330 extra you pay to get in.

◎ The Principal Group

The Principal Group of ruins is about 400m beyond the visitors center across well-kept lawns, through a gate in a fence and down shady avenues of trees. A group of resident macaws loiter along here. The ruins themselves have been numbered for easy identification and a well-worn path circumscribes the site.

The visitors center at the entrance to the ruins houses the ticket office and a small exhibition about the site and its excavation. Nearby are a cafeteria, and souvenir and handicrafts shops. There's a picnic area along the path to the Principal Group of ruins.

It's a good idea to visit the site with a guide, who can help to explain the ruins and bring them to life. Guides work for the co-operative Asociación de Guías Copán (p384) and charge L660 for groups of up to five. You can find them at the entrance to the parking lot. These prices are just for the main site – guides for the tunnels, Las Sepulturas or Museo de Escultura charge an additional L200 to L300 per site.

Stelae of the Great Plaza   ARCHAEOLOGICAL SITE
The path leads to the Gran Plaza (Great Plaza; Plaza de las Estelas) and the huge, intricately carved stelae portraying the rulers of Copán. Most of Copán's best stelae date from AD 613 to 738. All seem to have originally been painted; a few traces of red paint survive on Stela C. Many stelae had vaults beneath or beside them in which sacrifices and offerings could be placed.

Many of the stelae on the Gran Plaza portray King 18 Rabbit, including stelae A, B, C, D, F, H and 4. Perhaps the most beautiful stela in the Gran Plaza is Stela A (AD 731); the original has been moved inside the Museo de Escultura, and the one outdoors, like many here, is a reproduction. Nearby and almost equal in beauty are Stela 4 (AD 731); Stela B (AD 731), depicting 18 Rabbit upon his accession to the throne; and Stela C (AD 782), with a turtle-shaped altar in front. This last stela has figures on both sides. Stela E (AD 614), erected on top of Estructura 1 (Structure 1) on the west side of the Great Plaza, is among the oldest.

At the northern end of the Gran Plaza at the base of Estructura 2, Stela D (AD 736) also portrays King 18 Rabbit. On its back are two columns of hieroglyphs; at its base is an altar with fearsome representations of Chac, the rain god. In front of the altar is the burial place of Dr John Owen, an archaeologist with an expedition from Harvard's Peabody Museum who died during excavation work in 1893.

On the east side of the plaza is Stela F (AD 721), which has a more lyrical design than other stelae here, with the robes of the main figure flowing around to the other side of the stone, where there are glyphs. Altar G (AD 800), showing twin serpent heads, is among the last monuments carved at Copán. Stela H (AD 730) may depict a queen or princess rather than a king. Stela I (AD 692), on the structure that runs along the east side of the plaza, is of a person wearing a mask. Stela J (AD 702), further off to the east, resembles the stelae of Quiriguá in that it is covered in glyphs, not human figures.

Ball Court &
Hieroglyphic Stairway   ARCHAEOLOGICAL SITE
South of the ball court is Copán's most famous monument, the Escalinata de los Jeroglíficos (Hieroglyphic Stairway; AD 743), the work of King Smoke Shell. Today it's protected from the elements by a canvas roof. The flight of 63 steps bears a history (in several thousand glyphs) of the royal house of Copán; the steps are bordered by ramps inscribed with more reliefs and glyphs. The story told on the inscribed steps is still not completely understood because the stairway was partially ruined and the stones jumbled, but archaeologists are using 3D-scanning technology to make a digital version of the original, with the hope of one day reading it in its entirety.

At the base of the Hieroglyphic Stairway is Stela M (AD 756), bearing a figure (probably King Smoke Shell) dressed in a feathered cloak; glyphs tell of the solar eclipse in that year. The altar in front shows a plumed serpent with a human head emerging from its jaws.

Beside the stairway, a tunnel leads to the tomb of a nobleman, a royal scribe who may have been the son of King Smoke Imix. The tomb, discovered in June 1989, held a treasure trove of painted pottery and beautiful carved-jade objects that are now in Honduran museums.

Acrópolis   ARCHAEOLOGICAL SITE
The lofty flight of steps to the south of the Hieroglyphic Stairway mounts the Templo de las Inscripciones (Temple of the Inscriptions). On top of the stairway, the walls are carved with groups of hieroglyphs. On the south side of the Temple of the Inscriptions is the Patio Occidental (West Court), with the Patio Oriental (East Court), also called the Patio de los Jaguares (Court of the Jaguars) to its east. In the West Court, check out Altar Q (AD 776), among the most famous sculptures here; the original is inside

HONDURAS COPÁN ARCHAEOLOGICAL SITE

EL BOSQUE & LAS SEPULTURAS

Excavations at El Bosque and Las Sepulturas have shed light on the daily life of the Maya in Copán during its golden age. **Las Sepulturas**, once connected to the Gran Plaza by a causeway, may have been the residential area where rich and powerful nobles lived. One huge, luxurious residential compound seems to have housed some 250 people in 40 or 50 buildings arranged around 11 courtyards. The principal structure, called the **Palacio de los Bacabs** (Palace of the Officials), had outer walls carved with the full-sized figures of 10 men in fancy feathered headdresses; inside was a huge hieroglyphic bench. To get to Las Sepulturas you have to go back to the main road, turn right, then right again at the sign (2km from the Gran Plaza).

The walk to get to **El Bosque** is the real reason for visiting it, as it's removed from the main ruins. It's a one-hour (5km) walk on a well-maintained path through foliage dense with birds, though there isn't much of note at the site itself save for a small ball court. Still, it's a powerful experience to have an hour-long walk on the thoroughfares of an ancient Maya city all to yourself. To get to El Bosque, go right at the hut where your ticket is stamped. Be sure to slather on the insect repellent before you set off.

the Museo de Escultura. Around its sides, carved in superb relief, are the 16 great kings of Copán, ending with its creator, Yax Pasaj Chan Yopaat. Behind the altar is a sacrificial vault in which archaeologists discovered the bones of 15 jaguars and several macaws that were probably sacrificed to the glory of Yax Pasaj Chan Yopaat and his ancestors.

This group of temples, known as the **Acrópolis**, was the spiritual and political core of the site – reserved for royalty and nobles, a place where ceremonies were enacted and kings buried.

The East Court also contains evidence of Yax Pasaj Chan Yopaat – his **tomb**, beneath Estructura 18. Unfortunately, the tomb was discovered and looted long before archaeologists arrived. Both the East and West Courts hold a variety of fascinating stelae and sculptured heads of humans and animals. To see the most elaborate relief carving, climb Estructura 22 on the northern side of the East Court. This was the **Templo de Meditación** (Temple of Meditation) and has been heavily restored over recent years.

🏃 Activities

Asociación de Guías Copán TOUR
(☑ 2651-4018; guiascopan@yahoo.com) The local guides association has an office in the parking lot; it's well worth hiring a professional to make sense of the ruins. The standard tour of the site (L660) takes 90 minutes, while a tour including the tunnels costs L925 for up to five people. Horseback riding and tours of two other smaller sites are also offered.

ⓘ Getting There & Away

The Copán archaeological site is a couple of kilometers from Copán Ruinas proper and can be walked easily enough. An alternative is to take a *mototaxi* from the town (per person L30).

Gracias

POP 12,800

Gracias is a small, tranquil cobblestone town that's one of the prettiest and most historic settlements in Honduras. For a brief time in the 16th century, it was the capital of all Spanish-conquered Central America and traces of its former grandeur remain in its centuries-old buildings, colonial churches and impressive fort. It's been in a state of slow but charming decline ever since, and today the pace of life here rarely moves beyond walking.

Founded in 1526 by Spanish Captain Juan de Chávez, its original name was Gracias a Dios (Thanks to God). Eventually the town's importance was eclipsed by Antigua (Guatemala) and Comayagua.

The area around Gracias, including Parque Nacional Montaña de Celaque, is mountainous and beautiful, much of it forested, and the main reason to come to Gracias is to explore the undulating countryside around the town itself.

⊙ Sights

Gracias is a charming place to wander around, even if its actual sights are limited. As well as the famous fortress, the town has several colonial *iglesias*, including **San Mar-**

cos on the Parque Central (whose facade, oddly, does not face the plaza).

Most of the area's other attractions, including some fine hot springs, are a few kilometers out of town.

Iglesia de la Merced
CHURCH

(⊙ hours vary) One block north of Parque Central, this striking white stone church has an intricately carved facade and three bell towers. It's currently under renovation in a project funded by the Spanish government, with completion due in 2018. Sporadic concerts and recitals are held here – ask locally if there's anything on while you're in town (otherwise the facade is all you'll see).

Fuerte de San Cristóbal
FORTRESS

(⊙ 8am-4pm) **FREE** Built in response to the tumultuous times of the 18th century, the striking Fuerte de San Cristóbal has fantastic views of Gracias and the San Marcos church below. Beyond that, there's not much else to see up there, save for the **tomb of Juan Lindo**, a Honduran who was the former president of both El Salvador (1841–42) *and* Honduras (1847–52).

Jardín Botánico
GARDENS

(⊙ 8am-5pm Mon-Sat, to noon Sun) **FREE** The city's botanical garden is at the southern end of town, five blocks south of the old Mercado Municipal, and takes up half a city block. Local flora can be admired all year long from a paved path that meanders through the park. Enter through the Museo Casa Galeano.

Museo Casa Galeano
MUSEUM

(📞 2625-5407; L30; ⊙ 9am-6pm) This museum is located in a fascinatingly ancient colonial house desperately in need of a renovation (check out those walls!). But while its setting is interesting, its contents (a fossilized turtle, old coins) are pretty mediocre and labeling is only in Spanish.

🏃 Activities

Marco Aurelio (📞 2656-0627; guiamarcolencas@yahoo.com), the owner of Cafetería Artesenías El Jarrón, can arrange and/or guide hikes in Celaque (L450 to L1200), trips to La Campa (from L850), **horseback-riding** trips, **bike rental** (per hour L30) and tent rental (per night L80).

If you need a guide, ask for Ángel at El Jardín, who does various tours, or for Carlos at Finca Bavaria (p386), who specializes in birdwatching. Good tours can also be organized at the Hotel Guancascos.

🛏 Sleeping

★ Hotel Guancascos
HOTEL **$**

(📞 2656-1219; www.guancascos.com; dm/s/d from L220/550/600; @ 🛜) 🅿 This memorable, Dutch-run place boasts immaculately clean and good-value rooms set off shady paths that meander through the hotel's leafy plot, perched on the hillside under the town's fortress. All plants are labeled, and woodpeckers and hummingbirds are frequently seen. Rooms 13 and 14 share a gorgeous patio area with stellar town views, while the five-bed dorm is great value.

The in-house restaurant is one of the best in town. Tourist information is excellent, tours are available and it's all operated on environmentally friendly principles.

Casa de Mia
HOTEL **$**

(📞 2656-0349; s/d L400/600; ❄ 🛜) This new place has very well-presented and spacious modern rooms, all with fresh linen, air-conditioning, attractive wooden furniture and a picture or two gracing the walls. There's free drinking water and hot water to boot, making it a great budget option. It's just south of the market area and 200m southwest of Parque Central.

El Jardín
HOSTEL **$**

(📞 2656-1244; jardincafegracias@gmail.com; dm/r L220/660; 🛜) The two private rooms and two four-bed dorms here offer good value for money, despite both being rather spartan and not being very centrally located. As it's little known to travelers, you may find yourself alone in the dorms. Ángel, the owner, offers birdwatching, hiking and rappelling tours, and visits to a local opal mine. There's an onsite restaurant.

Hotelito Josue
PENSION **$**

(📞 2656-0076; r with/without TV L300/400; 🛜) A simple place with functional, smallish twin and double rooms off a long flower-filled patio, all with a cold-water bathroom. The family owners are friendly and also run a *lavandería* (laundromat) here. Rooms without TVs are L50 cheaper. Located in the market district, a couple of blocks west of Parque Central.

Hotel Real Camino Lenca
HOTEL **$$$**

(📞 2656-1932; www.realcaminolencahotel.com; s/d/tr incl breakfast L1100/1222/1700; ❄ 🛜) A small, smart and heavily designed place, the Camino Lenca has slick rooms leading off a plant-filled atrium inside a colonial-era building. The rooms themselves are comfortable and have extras such as massage showers and large flatscreen TVs, though many lack natural daylight. There's a popular bar on the rooftop and a restaurant downstairs.

✕ Eating

Cafetería Artesenías El Jarrón HONDURAN $
(Parque Central; mains L60-120; ⊙7am-8pm; 🖊) Bustling, atmospheric place that does a lot of lunchtime trade: the buffet (L70 to L90) is a great deal, with lots of veggie dishes. You sit at polished log tables, and there's a garden patio at the rear. Lencan handicrafts and ceramics are also sold here and tours can be arranged.

Jardín Café INTERNATIONAL $$
(📞2656-1244; mains L130-170; ⊙11am-9pm Mon-Thu, noon-1am Fri & Sat; 🖥🖊) At the northern end of the town, this cute little place is a welcome new addition to the eating options in Gracias. While it's not particularly atmospheric here, the food is great: try the delicious *sandwich graciano* (a steak fajita sandwich with fries). Also on offer are burgers and a selection of vegetarian dishes.

Restaurante Guancascos INTERNATIONAL, HONDURAN $$
(Hotel Guancascos; meals L85-210; ⊙7am-9pm; 🖥) A wonderful terrace restaurant at the Hotel Guancascos (p385), from where you can gaze over Gracias' terracotta-tiled rooftops and the Lencan highlands. Great for breakfast (L70 to L90), a filling sandwich, a veggie plate or pan-fried fish. There's efficient service, excellent fresh juices and wine by the glass.

🍷 Drinking & Nightlife

★Kandil BAR
(⊙11:30am-10pm Tue-Sun; 🖥) Flying the flag for contemporary aesthetics in the rustic Lencan hills, Kandil is a beautifully designed place where modish decor juxtaposes with colonial-style tradition. You can sit either inside its sleek main dining room or outside in the shady courtyard. It's famous for its cocktails and pizza, but the real fun is just lounging with the arty crowd that hangs here.

There's mainly electronic and indie tunes on the stereo, and occasionally independent films are shown. You'll find it two blocks north of Parque Central.

Plaza Cafe COFFEE
(Parque Central; drinks & snacks L20-60; ⊙7am-8:40pm; 🖥) Occupying the two-story hexagonal structure in the middle of the town's central square, this is the best place in town for an espresso, cappuccino, flavored coffee or *granita* (iced fruit drink) and a doughnut – the coffee comes from the nearby Finca Santa Elena. The upstairs seating area is a great place for people-watching.

Finca Bavaria BAR
(⊙6pm-midnight) Set on a neglected 35,000-sq-m *finca de café* (coffee plantation) a couple of blocks north of Parque Central, this place has a raucous bar that's popular with backpackers and full of local characters. It's also one of the cheapest sleeping options in town, though its rooms (single/double L350/400) are very basic and suffering from damp – come here for a drink rather than a bed.

🛍 Shopping

Ensaladas Dulces Lorendiana FOOD
An incredible find, this little store has shelves stacked floor-to-ceiling with hundreds (thousands?) of jars filled with pickled vegetables, chutneys and fruit wines, all prepared by the owner. A take-out portion costs L25. It's 250m southwest of the Parque Central.

ℹ Information

Banco Atlantida (⊙9am-5pm Mon-Fri) One block west of Parque Central. Has an ATM.

Banco de Occidente (Parque Central; ⊙9am-5pm Mon-Fri) With ATM.

Farmacia Alessandra (📞2656-1275; ⊙7:30am-12:30pm & 1:30-8pm)

Hospital Dr Juan Manuel Galvez (📞2656-1100; Carretera a Santa Rosa de Copán; ⊙24hr) This very basic hospital is near the entrance to town, across from a Texaco station.

Post Office (⊙8am-noon & 2-5pm Mon-Fri, 8-11am Sat) One block southeast of Parque Central.

ℹ Getting There & Away

Most buses leave from the terminal, which is on the ring road just northwest of the fortress. It's a busy and confusing place, and you'll have to ask which of the myriad repurposed American school buses (aka 'chicken buses') to get on (tickets are sold on board). Destinations include San Juan, Santa Rosa de Copán, San Pedro Sula and La Esperanza.

HONDURAS GRACIAS

Change at Santa Rosa de Copán for Copán Ruinas and at La Esperanza for Comayagua.

DESTINATION	COST (L)	DURATION	FREQUENCY
La Esperanza	90	2½hr	5 daily
San Juan	40	1hr	8 daily
San Pedro Sula	150	4hr	4 daily
Santa Rosa de Copán	50	1½hr	every 30min

Around Gracias

The rolling green countryside around Gracias includes two very popular thermal springs, several traditional Lenca villages and some superb canyon scenery, where zip lining is available in the village of La Campa.

🏃 Activities

★ Canopy Extremo ADVENTURE SPORTS
(☏ 9696-2967, 9854-4351; La Campa; L660) Canopy Extremo runs exciting zip-lining trips in the countryside around the small village of La Campa. Some six lines soar over the valleys here, with enormous drops below them. Safety is well respected, instructors speak English and the entire course takes just over two hours to complete. It's important to call ahead so that you're expected, and it's also a good idea to request the free pick-up from your hotel in Gracias.

Centro Turístico Terma del Río HOT SPRING
(L100; ⊙ 7am-9pm) Located 7km from town on the road to Santa Rosa de Copán, Centro Turístico Terma del Río hot spring is more relaxed than its 'presidential' counterpart. Catch any bus heading to Santa Rosa to get here.

Aguas Termales Presidente HOT SPRING
(L30; ⊙ 6am-11:30pm) The hot springs at Aguas Termales Presidente are one of Gracias' main attractions. About 6km southeast of town, the hot springs have several pools at various temperatures. The springs are very popular on the weekend and in the evenings, so try to avoid going at these times. To get here take a *mototaxi* from Gracias (L80) and either negotiate a waiting fee or try to flag one heading back once you're done.

🛏 Sleeping

Hostal JB GUESTHOUSE $
(☏ 9925-6042; La Campa; r L350-500) One of the best places to stay on the Ruta Lenca, this is more like a huge house with five rooms for rent. All have new queen-size beds with thick comforters and hot-water bathrooms; guests share a fully equipped kitchen and a spacious living room with sofas, folk art and high wood-beamed ceilings. It's at the hairpin turn just before the church.

Hotel Vista Hermosa HOTEL $
(☏ 2625-4770; La Campa; r L350-500) The hotel does have some pretty views (as the name indicates) and is clean and polished, although it lacks the old-time charm of the rest of the village.

❶ Getting There & Away

Both thermal springs are best reached by *mototaxi* (L80) from Gracias. Buses head from Gracias to La Campa (L25, one hour, four daily) and normally continue on to San Manuel Colohete (L35, two hours), a further hour away.

HONDURAS AROUND GRACIAS

NUEVA OCOTEPEQUE

Dust-blown Nueva Ocotepeque is a crossroads town, with a lot of traffic to the nearby borders at Agua Caliente (Guatemala) and El Poy (El Salvador). It's not a pleasant place, and you're strongly advised to avoid spending the night here. If you do, take care after dark.

Few travelers stay here but there are some adequate hotels, including the good-value Hotel Turista (☏ 2653-3639; Av General Francisco Morazán; d without bathroom L290, s/d L320/450; ☞).

Two long-distance bus companies serve Nueva Ocotepeque: Congolón (☏ 2653-3064) is half a block south of the Parque Central, while Sultana (☏ 2653-2405) is two blocks north of the *parque*. Buses to Agua Caliente and El Poy depart from the Transportes San José terminal two blocks north of the *parque*.

For Tegucigalpa, take a San Pedro Sula bus and transfer. For Santa Rosa de Copán, take any San Pedro Sula bus.

EXPLORING AROUND GRACIAS

Several small towns near Gracias are also worth a visit. **La Campa**, a traditional village 16km south of town, has to be one of the most scenic settlements in Honduras, set below towering mountains and bordering a dramatic canyon. There are several ceramic workshops here and it's possible to hike to the Camapara peak (six hours round-trip; ask at one of the local hotels for a guide).

About 16km past La Campa, **San Manuel Colohete** is another attractive little mountain town; its beautiful, restored colonial church is famous for its 400-year-old fresco paintings.

One of Honduras' most impressive national parks, **Parque Nacional Montaña de Celaque** (L132) boasts El Cerro de las Minas, the country's highest peak (2849m), which is covered in lush forest. The park contains the headwaters of several rivers, a majestic waterfall visible from the entire valley, and very steep slopes, including some vertical cliffs. The park is rich in plant and animal life: pumas, ocelots and quetzals live here, but they are rarely seen. More commonly sighted are butterflies, monkeys and reptiles.

NORTHERN HONDURAS

The lush, tropical northern region of Honduras has seduced visitors for centuries with its natural wonders and easy Caribbean vibe. Between the beaches are mangrove swamps and jungle reserves that scream out to be explored. Rafting the white waters of the Río Cangrejal is *the* big-ticket experience, but there's also fine hiking in Parque Nacional Pico Bonito and the unique flavor and rhythms of the coast's Garifuna villages. Finally, isolated Trujillo, the last stop before the Moskitia, is a charming slice of the old Caribbean, with some wonderful beaches nearby and superb mountain scenery behind it.

Despite all the region has to offer, many visitors simply travel through en route to the Bay Islands or Belize, and see nothing more than the drab charms of Puerto Cortés, Tela or La Ceiba. More than anywhere else, northern Honduras is a place where you should avoid the towns and make a beeline for the countryside.

Omoa

POP 30,000

Omoa feels like the end of the road, and indeed this unremarkable town 18km west of Puerto Cortés sees few visitors. Despite this fact, it's an attractive little resort on a broad curving bay that makes for great sunsets, even if, due to coastal erosion, the brown-sugar beach is minimal. There's a historic fort and a clutch of seafood restaurants along the seafront.

◎ Sights

Fortaleza de San Fernando de Omoa　FORT
(☑ 2658-9167; L88; ◷ 8am-4pm Mon-Fri, 9am-5pm Sat & Sun) Omoa's claim to historical fame is this colossal Spanish fortress. Built in brick and coral between 1759 and 1777 under orders from King Fernando VII of Spain, the fortress was intended to protect the coast from rampant Caribbean piracy, though in 1779 it was captured by the British. Despite that, it's in excellent condition today and the fine visitors center and museum provide a satisfying historical background.

🛏 Sleeping & Eating

Roli's Place　HOSTEL $
(☑ 2658-9082; www.omoa.net/roli.html; campsites/hammock/dm per person L80/80/100, s/d without bathroom L150/200, s/d with bathroom L220/250; ❋🤶) Excellent Swiss-owned hostel on a big grassy plot – a lovely place to hang out, and just 70m from the beach. The well-furnished double rooms, complete with cable TV, are a steal; there's also a decent dorm and a shady campground. Freebies include ocean-going kayaks, bikes and drinking water. Be aware that it's not a party hostel and there are numerous rules.

Hotel Michelle　HOTEL $$
(☑ 2658-9104; www.hotelmichelle.ca; s/d/q L500/700/800; ❋🤶) Right on the beach, this Honduran/Canadian-owned place is good value, with five neat, very well-priced rooms, a small pool and a bar. Some rooms have hot water and meals are available on request. Air-con is optional, so you can save some money if you can survive with just a fan.

Burgers & Mariscos   HONDURAN, SEAFOOD **$$**
(Carretera a Guatemala; mains L70-200; ☺8am-9pm) It's a long haul on foot (about a 15-minute walk from Roli's) but this excellent option on the main highway scores highly for good-value food, including excellent burgers, fresh seafood and tasty *tamarindo* juice.

ℹ Getting There & Away

There are hourly connections (L20, 30 minutes) to/from Puerto Cortés; some buses will branch off the highway and drop passengers at the beach, which is about 1.5km from the highway.

Roli's Place runs shuttles on demand to La Ceiba or Puerto Barrios in Guatemala.

Puerto Cortés

POP 126,000

Honduras' main port is a thoroughly depressing and ugly town – if you've just arrived from Guatemala or Belize, things only get better from here. There's nothing of interest to travelers beyond the ferry to Belize. If you need to overnight for the ferry, Omoa is a far more attractive base, though most people head straight for San Pedro Sula.

✯ Festivals & Events

Garifuna Day   CULTURAL
(☺Apr 12) This annual holiday for Garifuna communities commemorates the day in 1797 when the Garifuna arrived in Honduras.

🛏 Sleeping

Hotel El Centro   HOTEL **$**
(☑2665-1160; 3a Av, btwn 2a & 3a Calles E; r with fan/air-con from L450/650; P❄🗺) This hotel is a secure and clean option in the center of town: a good choice for backpackers.

Prince Wilson Hotel   HOTEL **$$**
(☑2665-6512; s/d with air-con L600/800; ❄🗺) This decent place is your best bet for the ferry, as it's right by the dock. Rooms are clean and comfortable, and staff are helpful. It's easily the best and most secure option.

ℹ Getting There & Away

BOAT
Two different companies run a weekly ferry to Belize. Bizarrely, they both leave at the same time on the same day (11am Monday). Both ferries leave from the same dock next door to

Restaurant El Delfin in Barra la Laguna, 3km southeast of the center. If arriving in Puerto Cortés by bus, ask the driver to let you off at the Laguna intersection, then cross the street and walk toward the bridge, where you'll find the ticket office and immigration authorities.

D-Express (☑2665-0726, 9991-0778) runs to Big Creek and Placencia (both L1320). **Starla International** (☑9545-9322) calls at Dangriga (L1210) and Belize City (L1760). For both services you'll need to be at the dock by 10am to complete paperwork and then board.

Note that it may be cheaper and easier for you to get to Belize via the Guatemalan port of Puerto Barrios.

BUS
Buses for San Pedro Sula (L38, one hour, every 15 minutes until 5:30pm) leave from a terminal on 4a Av between 3a and 4a Calles. Buses for the Guatemalan border at Corinto leave roughly hourly (L60 to L80, two hours) via Omoa (L20, 30 minutes).

Tela

POP 87,600

Tela is a run-down urban resort whose beaches are, sadly, full of trash and in many places simply unsafe even during daytime. Its town center is fairly unattractive and definitely not safe after dark, while its hotels and restaurants are mediocre and overpriced.

Yet despite all that, many people pass through and even stay a night or two here to visit the fantastic Lancetilla Jardín Botánico, the largest botanical garden in the Americas. The two nearby nature reserves – Jeannette Kawas and Punta Izopo – are both wonderful excursions as well, and within easy striking distance of the town.

Tela is crammed with Honduran vacationers during **Semana Santa** (Holy Week before Easter), but the rest of the year things are pretty *tranquilo*.

◉ Sights

The main attraction of Tela itself is its **beaches**, which stretch for miles around the bay. Most are littered, but west of town in front of Hotel Villas Telamar there's a pale, powdery stretch that is kept impeccably clean. Beach beds can be rented by nonguests, but only when occupancy is low at the resort. Beaches further afield, while much cleaner, can be risky to visit.

🏃 Activities

Eco di Mare Tours
TOUR

(☑ 9932-3552, 9727-1007; www.ecodimaretours. edicypages.com; cnr 4a Av NE & 10 Calle NE, in front of Bank Atlántida parking lot) This tour agency offers trips to Lancetilla Jardín Botánico, Parque Nacional Jeannette Kawas and Punta Izopo, as well as various activities, including sport fishing and banana boating. Day trips start at L680 per person.

Garífuna Tours
BOAT TOUR

(☑ 2448-1069; www.garifunatours.com; 9a Calle NE, at 5a Ave NE) A professional, long-established agency that offers tours, including full-day boat excursions to Parque Nacional Jeannette Kawas (from L860), full-day kayaking in Punta Izopo (L860) and trips to Cayos Cochinos (L1080). As the name suggests, the agency also offers excellent tours to the various Garifuna villages, including a popular motorcycle tour (L1740). Tours require a minimum of six people.

🛏 Sleeping

M@ngo Hotel
HOTEL $

(☑ 2448-0388; www.hotelmangotela.com; cnr 5a Av & 8a Calle NE; s/d/tr L475/584/704; ❋ 🛜) This is a great budget option, and the closest Tela has to a hostel. It's centrally located, clean and safe. Though the rooms are pretty ordinary and subject to sonic-boom blasts of cheesy merengue and rabid reggaetón from the store opposite, it's a pleasant and friendly place. Bikes are rented out here (L175 per day), which makes exploring easy.

Hotel Bertha
PENSION $

(☑ 2448-3020; 2a Av NE & 7a Calle NE; r with fan/ air-con from L230/400; ❋) A classic old-school *pensión* in a quiet location. What's great about this place is that the friendly family

owners aren't doing anything fancy, but provide very decent, clean rooms, all with en suite bathrooms (cold water) at affordable prices. Don't expect a particularly warm welcome, though. It's a five-minute walk inland from the beach.

★ Maya Vista Hotel y Restaurante
HOTEL $$

(☑ 2448-1497; www.mayavista.com; 8a Calle NE, btwn 9a & 10a Av NE; s/d/tr L1300/1350/1750; ❋ 🛜 🛏) Easily the best place to stay in Tela, this architecturally interesting place on a hilltop in the middle of town has a fine selection of rooms with tasteful decor, many of which enjoy sweeping views over Tela and the sea. There is also a very good, though pricey, restaurant on site (mains L230 to L345), which specializes in burgers and seafood.

🍴 Eating

Auto Pollo Al Carbón
FAST FOOD $

(11a Calle NE, at 2a Av NE; chicken L38-165; ⏰ 7am-11pm) Roast chicken served under a corrugated-iron roof in a cute red-and-white-painted open-air shack, a wishbone's throw away from the Caribbean. You can grab a quarter-chicken and a salad here for just L38.

Luces del Norte
SEAFOOD $$

(cnr 11a Calle NE & 5a Av NE; mains L140-350; ⏰ 7am-9pm; 🛜) Boasting attractive wooden Caribbean-style premises, this is a popular restaurant locally renowned for its seafood. It also serves up a variety of pasta dishes, omelets and filling breakfasts (around L120 to L150).

Pizzería Bella Italia
ITALIAN $$

(☑ 2448-1055; cnr 4a Av NE & Calle Peatonal; mains L100-300; ⏰ 4:30-10pm Thu-Sun; 🛜) You're paying for the seafront location (as well

---

DIG THAT BEAT: INSIDE GARIFUNA DANCING

Shaking to live Garifuna music is a highlight of the north coast. Musicians create a throbbing, pared-down sound using large drums, a turtle shell, maracas and a big conch shell. Words are chanted; the audience responds and dancers begin to move their hips in physics-defying loops to the *punta*, a traditional Garifuna dance.

During mid-July every year, the **National Garifuna Dance Festival** takes place in the small town of Baja Mar, near Puerto Cortés. All towns and villages have annual fiestas, and cultural events and gatherings of one kind or another happen throughout the year. **Garifuna Day** (p389), a big holiday for all the Garifuna communities, commemorates the day in 1797 when the Garifuna arrived in Honduras.

Near Trujillo, the towns of Santa Fe and Santa Rosa de Aguán have their festivals on July 15 to 30 and August 22 to 29, respectively. The last three days are usually the most frenetic.

the armed security guard) at this rather pricey Italian place. Pizza – from personal to 16-piece *gigantes* – is decent enough, but the specialty is the *panzerotti*, a variation of calzone stuffed with salami, ham, mushrooms and more. Kitschy decor completes the scene.

ⓘ Information

Banco de Occidente (Parque Central; ⊘8am-5:30pm Mon-Fri, 8:30am-1pm Sat) With ATM.

Fundación Prolansate (☑2448-2042; www. prolansate.org; cnr 7a Av & 8a Calle NE; ⊘8am-5:30pm Mon-Thu, to 4:30pm Fri) Promotes sustainable tourism in Tela and has information on Lancetilla Botanical Garden and Parque Nacional Jeannette Kawas. Can organize educational visits.

Post Office (4a Av; ⊘8am-4pm Mon-Fri, 8am-noon Sat)

Tourist Police (☑9713-6731; cnr 11a Calle NE & 4a Av NE; ⊘24hr)

DANGERS & ANNOYANCES

Tela is a poor city and not a safe place after dark. Avoid walking any distance at night, particularly anywhere poorly lit or along the beach after nightfall.

Don't take anything of value to the beach. During the day, also avoid walking alone beyond the Hotel Villas Telamar Resort on the western end of the beach and the La Ensenada Beach Resort pier on the eastern end.

ⓘ Getting There & Away

Slow 'chicken' buses leave Tela every 20 minutes for La Ceiba (L50, 2½ hours, 4am to 6pm) from the long-distance terminal at the corner of 9a Calle NE and 9a Av NE. For quicker direct buses, take a taxi to the gas station on the highway, from where buses to La Ceiba (L80) and San Pedro Sula (L155) depart regularly.

Transportes Tela Express (2a Av NE) operates nine daily direct buses (seven on Sunday) to San Pedro Sula (L160, two hours) from its terminal. **Hedman Alas** (☑2448-3075; Hotel Villas Telamar; ⊘8am-5pm) has a daily connection to San Pedro Sula (L265, two hours) and also to La Ceiba (L295, two hours).

Local buses to the Garifuna villages near Tela depart from a dirt lot on the corner of 11a Calle and 8a Av.

Around Tela

The region surrounding the town of Tela is a fascinatingly diverse place. Within a relatively small area you'll find some great beaches, several nature reserves, thriving Garifuna villages and one of the world's largest botanical gardens.

◉ Sights

Refugio de Vida
Punta Izopo   WILDLIFE RESERVE
(L66) Rivers entering the Punta Izopo Wildlife Refuge spread out into a network of canals that channel through the tangle of mangrove forest. Monkeys, turtles and even crocodiles live here, as well as many species of birds. Gliding silently through the mangrove canals, you can often get close to many forms of wildlife. Tela tour agencies organize kayak trips to Punta Izopo. Alternatively, you can set up a kayak trip yourself in the village of El Triunfo de la Cruz.

Parque Nacional
Jeannette Kawas   NATIONAL PARK
(L120) This national park a short distance outside Tela has several white-sand beaches, including the pretty Playa Cocalito. Offshore coral reefs make for reasonable snorkeling, and howler monkeys, boa constrictors and toucans live in the forest. You can arrange day trips, which include hiking, snorkeling and hanging out on the beach. Tela's two main travel agencies run tours here.

Garifuna Villages

Several idyllic villages populated by the Garifuna are within easy reach of Tela. Each has rustic (sometimes stilted) houses right on the beach, with fishing canoes resting on the sand and the azure waters of the Caribbean lapping against the shore.

◉ Sights

The closest village is attractive little La Ensenada, 3km east along the arc of the beach from Tela, just before you reach the point. Hotel Laguna Mar (☑9811-5558; La Ensenada; d L600; Ⓟ❋), just 100m from the beach, has meticulously maintained gardens and neat little rooms. Seafood restaurants in La Ensenada tend to only open on the weekend.

Larger El Triunfo de la Cruz can be reached by regular buses that depart from near Tela's market. It's the most developed of the Garifuna villages, lacking the peaceful ambiance of the other settlements.

West of Tela it's 8km to Tornabé, a large Garifuna settlement where you can set up

HONDURAS AROUND TELA

boat tours. Past Tornabé, the beach road continues for several more kilometers to **Miami**, a beautiful village of *palapa*-roofed (thatched) huts on a narrow sandbar; it's the most traditional and least changed of the villages on this strip. Boats can be hired here (L1800 for up to seven people) for trips into Parque Nacional Jeannette Kawas.

ⓘ Getting There & Away

Buses to the Garifuna villages depart from the local bus terminal in Tela. There are two routes: one heading west to Tornabé; another heading east to El Triunfo de la Cruz. Buses on both routes depart hourly from around 7am to 5pm Monday to Saturday; the fare ranges from L14 to L20, and journeys take about 30 to 45 minutes to reach the villages.

If you're driving or cycling, you can get to Tornabé by the beach road heading west from Tela. Be careful where you cross the sandbar at the Laguna de los Micos between San Juan and Tornabé – vehicles regularly get stuck in the sand here. You may need a 4WD vehicle to get past Tornabé to Miami. You can also get to Tornabé from the highway: the turnoff, 5km west of Tela, is marked by a sign to 'The Last Resort.' To drive to La Ensenada or El Triunfo de la Cruz, take the highway to the turnoff for El Triunfo de la Cruz, 5km east of Tela. After 1km the road forks: go left to La Ensenada, or right to El Triunfo de la Cruz.

Lancetilla Jardín Botánico

Lancetilla Botanical Garden & Research Center GARDENS
(☑2408-7806; www.esnacifor.hn; L178; ☺7am-5pm) One of the largest tropical botanical gardens in the world, spanning some 1680 hectares and generating 60% of Tela's fresh water, the Lancetilla Botanical Garden & Research Center was founded by the United Fruit Company in 1926 and is still an active center for scientific study today. The gardens are a delight to visit – a tropical wonderland of plant species, 1200 in all, from all corners of the globe. There are 636 species of Asiatic fruit trees, including many varieties of lychee, mango, durian, mangosteen and jackfruit.

Birdlife also thrives at Lancetilla – hundreds of species have been spotted. Each year on December 14 and 15 the Audubon Society conducts a 24-hour bird count; you can participate if you're here then. Migratory species are present from November to February.

Well-marked trails wind through the main garden and arboretum areas, although guided tours (in Spanish only) are available for L100 per hour. Last entry is at 3:30pm.

Rather charming accommodations are available on the site, with cabins (☑2408-6715; tw/cabin L345/460; ☒) with three individual beds and private bathrooms. Book through the visitors center (☑2408-6715; ☺7am-4pm).

ⓘ Getting There & Away

Lancetilla is 6km southwest of the center of Tela. A good way to get here is by bicycle (which you can rent in Tela); about 4km from town there's a turnoff from the highway that leads to the main gardens. Taxis charge L120 each way.

La Ceiba
POP 204,000

La Ceiba is known as Honduras' good-time town: 'Tegucigalpa thinks, San Pedro Sula works and La Ceiba parties,' so the saying goes. Certainly this port city's buzzing nightlife makes it a mecca for fiesta-hungry Hondurans, though nearly all the action is over the estuary in Barrio La Isla, the city's *zona viva* (nightlife district). Elsewhere, expect searing heat and punishing humidity (and take care after dark).

There's otherwise very little of interest in Ceiba itself: local beaches are polluted and unsafe and the downtown has a crumbling, neglected air (though it's still streets ahead of Tela on the charm front). Despite this, most travelers will find themselves here at some point as Ceiba is the transportation hub for the Bay Islands, as well as a great base for exploring the Pico Bonito National Park, the idyllic Cayos Cochinos and the world-class white water on the Río Cangrejal.

◉ Sights

Catedral de San Isidro CHURCH
(Parque Central) The city's most recognizable building, this imposing structure on the Parque Central dates from the early 20th century.

Parque Swinford GARDENS
(Av La República, btwn 7a & 8a Calles; ☺6am-6pm) FREE Parque Swinford is a lush, tropical botanical oasis in the heart of La Ceiba, complete with a restored train carriage from the area's railway heyday.

Activities

Omega Tours
ADVENTURE TOUR
(📞 9631-0295, 9745-6810; www.omegatours.info; Omega Lodge, 9km down road to Yaruca) Set up by a former international kayaker, Omega offers white-water rafting (from L950), kayak and canoe trips, horseback riding, mountain biking and jungle- and river-hiking tours. All trips include a free night at its jungle lodge.

Jungle River Tours
ADVENTURE TOUR
(📞 9681-6466, 2416-5009; www.jungleriverlodge.com) Located at Banana Republic Guest House, this agency organizes white-water rafting and canopy tours (L880), mountain biking (L440) and other trips.

Tourist Options
HIKING, DIVING
(📞 9978-8868, 9982-7534; www.hondurastouristoptions.com; Av La República) This travel agency runs trips to Garifuna villages, hikes to Pico Bonito and day trips to Cayos Cochinos (from L880 per person). It also runs diving trips, day trips to Trujillo and birdwatching tours.

Festivals & Events

Carnaval
CULTURAL
(🕐 late May) The city reaches its good-time peak at Carnaval, when it's crammed with revelers. Saturday is the biggest day, with parades, costumes, music and celebrations in the streets.

Sleeping

Accommodations are fairly uninspiring in La Ceiba, though there is an excellent new hostel. Staying in the center is convenient, although it is eerily quiet at night (when you shouldn't walk the streets). There are far better options outside the city amid the tropical jungle by the Río Cangrejal.

★ 1877 Hostel
HOSTEL $
(📞 9613-3842, 9829-5997; www.1877hostel.com; Av Morazán; dm L265, r from L770; ❄️ 🛜) This superb new hostel is easily the best place to stay in town. The converted house is spacious, and rooms – which run from mixed and female dorms to private rooms that sleep up to four – are all spotless, featuring brand-new beds and great bathrooms. There's a large kitchen and a pleasant communal area outside where the owners are planning to put in a bar.

The whole property is very secure and located right next to the Uniplaza mall and several restaurants.

Hotel El Estadio
HOSTEL $
(📞 3187-6027; www.backpackershuttle.com; Calle Estadio; dm/s/d L180/375/440; ❄️ 🛜) This simple hostel offers very cheap rooms and is well set up for travelers, even if it's rather dark and rooms are pretty aged. Both of the four-bed dorms are small; one of them is for women only. Towels and linens are included. Private rooms are more spacious. Hammocks (L100) are also available. Local tours are offered, including to the Moskitia.

Hotel Catracho
HOTEL $
(📞 2440-2312; www.hotelcatracho.com; 12a Calle, Barrio El Iman; s with fan/air-con L350/450, d with fan/air-con L450/600; ❄️ 🛜) This hotel's functional and rather aged rooms are not a bad deal, with fresh linen provided (though the fan rooms have only cold-water bathrooms) – however, natural light is lacking in most. It's in a quiet but central neighborhood with several eating options within easy walking distance. The wi-fi works in the lobby only.

Hotel Las Hamacas
HOTEL $$
(📞 2440-5299; www.web.hotellashamacas.com; Carratera a Trujillo; r incl breakfast from L800; ❄️ 🛜) This place is a little out of the center, but it's well located for connections to the Bay Island ferries. For your money you get a good range of facilities, including a big pool, spacious rooms decked out in tropical colors, modern bathrooms and a good restaurant. The hotel can also arrange local tours, including trips to Cayos Cochinos.

It's located on the eastern edge of the city, on the main road heading toward Sambo Creek.

Eating

There are some good eating options in La Ceiba, and you'll have the choice of great seafood pretty much everywhere you go. La Línea, a strip where La Ceiba's old railway runs on Av La República, is where you can find street food – including delicious baleadas (tortillas stuffed with refried beans and other fillings) – 24 hours a day.

Pupusaría Universitaria
HONDURAN $
(1a Calle, near Av 14 de Julio; pupusas L25, mains L130-150; 🕐 10am-10pm Sun-Fri) This excellent budget haunt inside a clapboard-and-bamboo building serves up big flavors at moderate rates, including: pupusas (cornmeal mass stuffed with cheese or refried beans), tacos and succulent pinchos (kebabs). It's popular

La Ceiba

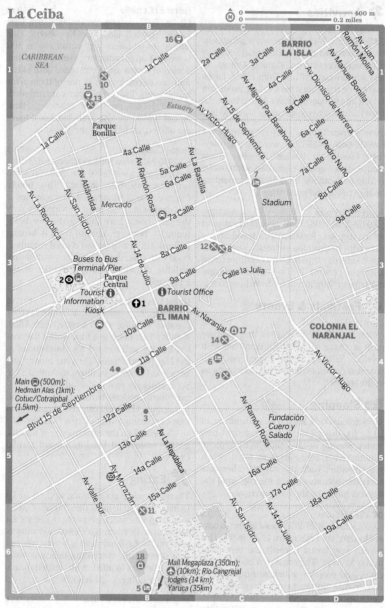

with a young crowd of students, and the staff are friendly.

★ **Ki'boc Café** HONDURAN, INTERNATIONAL **$$**
(4a Av, btwn Calles 8a & 9a; mains L70-150; ⊙7am-7pm Mon-Fri, 8am-7pm Sat, 8am-noon Sun; 🛜)

This friendly place is about as bohemian as Ceiba gets, with a civilized and artsy feel, welcoming staff and organic coffee. The filling breakfasts are the best in town (the *chilaquiles* are a real treat), while the rest of the menu is classic Honduran. There's a

La Ceiba

◎ **Sights**
1 Catedral de San Isidro.........................B3
2 Parque Swinford..................................A3

◆ **Activities, Courses & Tours**
3 Jungle River Tours..............................B5
4 Tourist Options B4

◎ **Sleeping**
5 1877 Hostel.......................................B6
6 Hotel Catracho...................................C4
7 Hotel El Estadio..................................C2

✗ **Eating**
8 Al Corral C3
9 Cafeto...C4
10 Chef Guity B1
11 El Jardín de Susana B6
12 Ki'boc Café...C3
13 Pupusaría Universitaria A1
14 Xpats Bar & Grill...............................C4

◎ **Drinking & Nightlife**
15 La Casa del Jaguar A1
16 La Palapa..B1

◎ **Shopping**
17 Souvenirs El Buen Amigo C4
18 Uniplaza Mall B6

book exchange, a little terrace and an air-conditioned interior with paintings and mismatched decor.

Al Corral BARBECUE **$$**
(☑9960-9855; 4a Av, btwn Calles 8a & 9a; mains L110-225; ☺6-11pm) It's all about meat at this popular grill place beloved by local families. Indeed, the meats are grilled right in front of you in the courtyard dining room, which is decorated with an eclectic mix of cow skulls and antique sewing machines. Some menu highlights include grilled pork ribs, beef kidneys, chorizo or just a vast grill platter (L650 to L750) for four.

Cafeto CAFE **$$**
(Calle 13 & Av Ramon Rosa; breakfasts L80-150; ☺7am-5pm Mon-Fri, to noon Sat; ☎) This curious little coffee shop within La Ceiba's bustling Medicentro Hospital is actually a good place to start the day: it has good espresso, fresh fruit-juice smoothies and a range of breakfast options, including Honduran, American, Mexican and Spanish (though they're served only until 10am). If the door is locked, enter through the hospital.

Chef Guity SEAFOOD **$$**
(off 1a Calle; mains L120-300; ☺11am-10pm Tue-Sun) This Garifuna-style restaurant in the *zona viva* is famous for its seafood, including conch, fish, lobster and crab, but particularly for *tapado* (a fish stew in coconut sauce). It's located on the river just where it flows into the open sea.

★**El Jardín de Susana** HONDURAN **$$$**
(☑2440-0061; Calle 15 & Av Morazán; mains L250-280; ☺10am-2:30pm & 5-10pm Wed-Mon) Totally unsigned (look for the green house with tables in the courtyard), Susana's Garden cooks up a storm and is a local institution these days. Famous particularly for its salad bar (yes, those are fresh vegetables, you are not hallucinating), this might well be the only place ever to serve zucchini in the entire country. Mains are meaty and delicious.

Xpats Bar & Grill INTERNATIONAL **$$$**
(12a Calle, Barrio El Imán; mains L140-300; ☺4pm-midnight Mon-Thu, 4pm-2am Fri, 11am-2am Sat; ☎🅿) This classic expat hangout certainly lives up to its name, attracting a loyal crowd of gringos who come for US sports on the TV and a familiar line-up of barbecued meats and a few veggie options. There are drinks and food specials virtually every day.

🍷 Drinking & Nightlife

★**La Casa del Jaguar** BAR
(off 1a Calle; ☺5-11pm Mon-Sat) This is one of Ceiba's more interesting drinking establishments, a curious, enclosed beach bar with a tree-house feel and lots of nooks, crannies and corners to get cozy in. It's famous locally for the owner's homemade liquors – he dubs it (with a wink) 'the only organic bar in Honduras.' The crowd is bohemian and parties on the weekend go late.

La Palapa BAR, CLUB
(Av 15 de Septiembre; ☺11am-11pm Sun-Wed, to 2am Thu-Sat) This huge, upmarket, two-story, thatched-roof bar-restaurant just off the beach is a *zona viva* mainstay. It draws a wealthy and hedonistic party crowd, though many come here for the excellent seafood as much as to dance it all off afterward. Of the two dance floors, the upstairs one is free, while the downstairs one has a varying cover charge.

HONDURAS LA CEIBA

🛍 Shopping

Uniplaza Mall MALL
(www.uniplaza.net; ⊙8am-9pm Mon-Sat) Centrally located and full of restaurants, and with several secure ATMs, this mall is a useful place for travelers.

Mall Megaplaza MALL
(Carretera a Muelle Cabotaje; ⊙10am-9pm) Modern mall with a cinema, food court, internet cafes, banks and ATMs.

Souvenirs El Buen Amigo ARTS, CRAFTS
(Av Naranjal s/n, Barrio El Iman; ⊙8am-6:30pm Mon-Sat) This small family run place sells Honduran *artesanías* (handicrafts), including Lencan pottery, wood carvings and hammocks. It's a good spot to pick up souvenirs.

ℹ Information

Banco Atlántida (Av San Isidro; ⊙9am-noon & 1pm-5pm Mon-Fri) Has an ATM.

Fundación Cuero y Salado (FUCSA; ☑2443-0117; Calle 11, btwn Av San Isidro & Av La República; ⊙8am-5pm Mon-Fri, 8-11am Sat) Manages the Cuero y Salado Wildlife Reserve.

Hospital Eurohonduras (☑2440-0927; Av Atlántida; ⊙24hr) Between 1a Calle and the beach.

Immigration Office (☑2442-0638; 1a Calle, cnr Av 14 de Julio; ⊙7:30am-3:30pm Mon-Fri)

Post Office (cnr Av Morazán & 14a Calle; ⊙8am-4pm Mon-Fri, 8am-noon Sat)

Tourist Office (☑2440-3044; 9a Calle; ⊙8am-4:30pm Mon-Fri) The friendly and helpful English-speaking staff here offer lots of brochures and free maps of the city. There's also a kiosk (☑2440-1562; ⊙8am-6pm Mon-Sat) on the Parque Central and a desk at the airport.

ℹ Getting There & Away

AIR

La Ceiba's Aeropuerto Golosón is 10km west of La Ceiba, on the highway to Tela. Flights leave frequently for San Pedro Sula, Tegucigalpa, the Bay Islands and the Moskitia.

AeroCaribe (☑2442-1088, 3364-7688; www.aerocaribehn.com; airport) Flies to Guanaja and several destinations in the Moskitia, including Puerto Lempira, Palacios and Brus Laguna.

Aerolíneas Sosa (☑2443-1399, airport 2440-0692; www.aerolineasosa.com; Av San Isidro btwn 8a & 9a Calles) Regular connections to Roatán, Utila and Puerto Lempira.

Avianca (☑2443-2683; www.avianca.com; airport) Flies to Roatán, San Pedro Sula and Tegucigalpa.

Lanhsa (☑2442-1283; www.lanhsa.com; airport) Connects Ceiba with Roatán, Guanaja, Puerto Lempira and Tegucigalpa.

BOAT

Ferries to the Bay Islands operate from the Muelle de Cabotaje pier, about 8km east of town. From the bus terminal or from town, taxis charge about L100. A *colectivo* (L20) goes from the town

BUSES FROM LA CEIBA

DESTINATION	COST (L)	DURATION	BUS LINE	FREQUENCY
Antigua (Guatemala)	1230	11hr	Hedman Alas	2 daily
Copán Ruinas	745	7hr	Hedman Alas	2 daily
La Unión-Cuero y Salado	30	1½hr	Main Terminal	every 45min Mon-Sat, hourly Sun
Nueva Armenia	30	1½hr	Main Terminal	6-8 daily
Sambo Creek/Corazal	20	1hr	Main Terminal	every 35min
San Pedro Sula	145	3½hr	Diana Express	6 daily
	138	3½hr	Catisa-Tupsa	hourly 5am-6pm
	425	3hr	Hedman Alas	4 daily (via San Pedro Sula airport)
	470	3hr	Viana	4 daily
Tegucigalpa	265	7hr	Kamaldy	4 daily
	715	6½hr	Viana	4 daily
	750	6½hr	Hedman Alas	3 daily
Tela	75	2hr	Kamaldy	4 daily
	54	2hr	Main Terminal	every 25min
Trujillo	138	3hr	Cotuc/Cotraipbal	hourly
Yaruca/Río Cangrejal	20	30min	Main Terminal	5 daily, or any Las Mangas bus

center from 7a Calle; there's no *colectivo* on the way back. To get to the ferry pier from the center of La Ceiba, take a bus from Av La República.

The modern, comfortable **Galaxy Wave** (☑ 2445-1775; www.roatanferry.com) sails twice daily to Roatán at 9:30am and 4:30pm (1st/ normal class L836/726, 1¾ hours). There are two separate ferries connecting La Ceiba to Utila; they've been locked in a price war of late, making tickets very cheap at the time of writing. Your choice is between the far nicer and more modern **Utila Dream** (☑ 9450-8133; www.utilaferry.com; Muelle de Cabotaje; one-way L200; ☺ 9:30am & 4pm daily), which takes 45 minutes, and the rather shabbier **Utila Princess** (☑ 2425-3190; www.utilaprincess.com; Muelle de Cabotaje; one-way L114; ☺ ticket office 7am-4pm, sails 9:20 & 4pm daily), which takes one hour.

Sea sickness can affect passengers on all the above services – plan accordingly as bags are not provided.

BUS
The main bus terminal is at Mercado San José, about 1.5km west of central La Ceiba. Local buses run between this terminal and the central plaza (L8), or you can take a *colectivo* taxi (L20). Buses marked 'Terminal' head to the station from the bus stop at Av La República between 7a Calle and 8a Calle.

La Ceiba is a big transportation hub, and there are even services connecting Ceiba to Antigua in Guatemala, as well as shuttles to/from Copán Ruinas – inquire at 1877 Hostel (p393). Most non-luxury buses use the main terminal – **Diana Express** (☑ 2509-4886; www.transportediana express.jimdo.com), **Catisa-Tupsa** (☑ 2441-2539) and **Kamaldy** (☑ 2441-2028; www.trans porteskamaldy.com) all have offices there – but there are some exceptions. The **Viana** (☑ 2441-2230; www.vianatransportes.com; Blvr 15 de Septiembre) bus terminal is another 500m further west along the same road; you'll find **Hedman Alas** (☑ 2441-5347; www.hedmanalas. com) across the street. **Cotuc/Cotraipbal** (☑ 2441-2199) buses for Trujillo leave from terminals on Carretera a Tela.

❶ Getting Around
There are numerous car rental agencies in La Ceiba. The airport is the best place to compare prices. Agencies include **Avis** (☑ 2441-2802; www.avis.com.hn) and **Econo Rent-A-Car** (☑ 2441-5080, 2441-5079; www.econorenta carhn.com; ☺ 8am-5pm).

Colectivo taxis in La Ceiba charge a standard L20 per person, going up a bit after 8pm.

TO/FROM THE AIRPORT
Any non-express bus heading west from the main bus terminal in La Ceiba can drop you at the airport. *Colectivo* taxis from the Parque Central pass the airport (L20); you must wait for the taxi to fill up. A normal taxi costs around L150.

Taxis in the official rank outside the airport charge about L200 to La Ceiba; if you go to the main road and flag down a *colectivo* it's L20 per person.

Around La Ceiba
The area around La Ceiba is a knock-out, and by far the best reason to visit the city. Indeed, many travelers prefer to stay in the surrounding areas rather than in La Ceiba proper, all the better to enjoy the Parque Nacional Pico Bonito, the stunning Río Cangrejal, the beautiful beaches of Cayos Cochinos or the wildlife of Refugio de Vida Silvestre Cuero y Salado.

Río Cangrejal
Surging through the jungle, the turquoise Río Cangrejal is rightly renowned as Central America's premier rafting experience. Even if you've zero intention of dipping an oar in its foaming waters, the region makes a stunning base for all manner of adventure sports, birdwatching or just chilling by the river. The scenery is spectacular, the air is mountain-fresh and there are some excellent places to stay strung out along the riverside.

🏃 Activities
Most visitors are here to raft or kayak the Cangrejal, but there's also mountain biking, horseback riding, swimming and great rainforest hiking. You can book with the lodge you're staying at, or with a travel agency in La Ceiba.

Canopy Tours
Jungle River Tours (p393) operates an eight-cable circuit (per person L88) that lasts two hours and includes a 200m slide across the river.

Hiking
Just uphill from the Jungle River Lodge, right by the Centro de Visitantes (visitors center), a rope bridge extends over the Cangrejal to the other side of the river, allowing hiking access into the heart of Parque Nacional Pico Bonito. Omega Lodge (p398) also has several well-marked trails on its grounds.

Guaruma Servicios HIKING

(☑ 2442-2673; www.guaruma.org) ✐ A worthwhile operation dedicated to boosting opportunities for the local community through sustainable tourism. It's based at the small village of Las Mangas in Río Cangrejal.

Horseback Riding

Horseback riding is offered at Omega Lodge for L1600 per half-day. All the horses live at the lodge and are very well cared for.

White-Water Rafting

The Río Cangrejal offers superb white-water rafting. The scenery is immense, with the river coursing through rainforest that's part of the Parque Nacional Pico Bonito. You've a good chance of seeing herons, kingfishers and toucans.

There are two main sections of the Cangrejal: the upper part is hard-core, offering real Class IV and V thrills, rapids and speed. After very heavy rain it may not be possible to raft here. The lower section offers year-round Class III rafting, with the river surging around giant boulders.

Whichever section you choose you'll need an experienced, competent guide – accidents have occurred in the upper section of the Cangrejal after heavy rainfall, when conditions can be particularly treacherous. Always check out the situation first with your tour operator (you can book through your lodge).

🛏 Sleeping & Eating

La Moskitia Adventuras Lodge LODGE $

(☑ 2441-3279; www.lamoskitia.hn; road to Yaruca Km 9; dm/d L200/500; 🛜) Impressive riverside lodge with a stunning position overlooking the roaring Cangrejal – you'll be mesmerized by the view. Accommodation and restaurant prices are geared to backpacker budgets, and professionally organized rafting, hiking and zip-line tours are offered.

Guaruma Community Lodge CABIN $

(☑ 9572-8393; www.guaruma.org; 12km down road to Yaruca; d/tr/q L400/450/500) These well-constructed, clean cabins in the village of Las Mangas channel funds back into the community, and are a chance to spend time with locals rather than stay ensconced in a lodge. Good-value meals (L80 to L110), bike rental (per day L100) and guides are available.

★ Omega Lodge LODGE $$

(☑ 9631-0295; www.omegatours.info; road to Yaruca Km 9; s/d without bathroom L440/880,

cabins L2090; @ 🛜 ⊠) ✐ A beautifully conceived and constructed ecolodge, Omega is surrounded by thick jungle, which means it doesn't have views. But it *is* very thoughtfully conceived: solar power, a chemical-free pool and ecofriendly waste-management are all at the heart of the lodge's philosophy. The owners pioneered rafting on the Río Cangrejal and offer many excellent trips. Food is outstanding, with plentiful vegetarian choices.

Jungle River Lodge LODGE $$

(☑ 2416-5009, 9681-6466; www.jungleriverlodge. com; road to Yaruca Km 7; dm/d/tr L270/880/990, meals from L100; 🛜) Jungle River Tours' lodge is perched on a ledge with a simply magnificent perspective of the Río Cangrejal valley – the outdoor bar-restaurant here has to have one of Honduras' greatest vistas. Accommodations are far more prosaic, varying from functional dorms to attractive rooms, some with private hot-water bathrooms. There are natural swimming pools below and all kinds of tours can be booked (canopy tours, hiking and white-water rafting).

ℹ Getting There & Away

Most lodges here will arrange for transportation from La Ceiba, including pick-ups at the airport, bus station or the Muelle de Cabotaje (the ferry pier). As all the lodges are on the main road, you can also get on a bus to Yaruca or Las Mangas (L20, 30 minutes) at the main terminal in La Ceiba.

Parque Nacional Pico Bonito

Looming over La Ceiba, the densely forested mountain of Pico Bonito forms one of Honduras' best-known national parks (L160). It harbors some abundant wildlife, including jaguars, armadillos and monkeys.

There are two entrances. El Pino is a village about 15km west of La Ceiba on the highway to Tela. Guides can be arranged here for the moderately difficult three-hour hike to Cascada Zacate waterfall (per person incl park entrance fee L160). If you want to stay here you'll find rustic cabins at the Centro Ecoturístico Natural View (☑ 2368-8343; r L350).

The other entrance is by the Río Cangrejal, where a visitors center (10km down road to Yaruca; ⊙ 7am-4pm) was recently built, along with a suspension bridge over the roaring river (L20 to access for photos). (Conveniently, it's on the same road as the

Río Cangrejal river lodges.) From the visitors center there's a lovely trail (three hours' round-trip) through lush mountainside forest to **El Bejuco waterfall**.

❶ Getting There & Away

Any bus headed toward Tela or San Pedro Sula can drop you at El Pino (L20, 30 minutes). To get to the Río Cangrejal side, jump on a bus to Yaruca or Las Mangas (L20, 30 minutes) at the main terminal in La Ceiba.

Cayos Cochinos

The idyllic white sands of the Cayos Cochinos (Hog Islands), just 17km from the mainland, can easily be visited as a day trip from the La Ceiba region. Access is by motorized canoe from Nueva Armenia or Sambo Creek, east of La Ceiba. There's a L220 entrance fee to enter the Cayos Cochinos.

The two Hog Islands, the 13 tiny coral cays and the seas around them comprise a marine reserve – it's illegal to anchor on the reef, and commercial fishing is prohibited. Consequently, the reefs are pristine and fish abundant. Diving and snorkeling are excellent around the islands, with black coral reefs, wall diving, cave diving, seamounts and a plane wreck. The islands are also known for their unique pink boa constrictors and the strength of the local Garifuna culture.

🛏 Sleeping & Eating

Most people visit Cayos Cochinos for the day, but if you want to play Robinson Crusoe there are informal and extremely rustic cabañas (L150 to L500) available on Chachauate Cay; ask around on the beach. There are also two comfortable, modern cabins with private bathrooms at **Laru Beya** (☑9918-8931; www.cayoscochinoshonduras.webs.com; dm L250) at the east end of the main island.

Day-trip packages will include either a picnic lunch or a BBQ on the beach. There aren't many other eating options save a few shacks selling fish and seafood, or the restaurant at Laru Beya.

❶ Getting There & Away

It's possible to go independently to the cays, although you won't save much money, and local boat operators are unlikely to have a radio or life jackets.

Lots of La Ceiba tour operators offer tours to the cays: this is the best way to visit. Agencies charge around L900 per person (minimum six people) for a full-day trip. You can also visit on a day trip from Roatán.

Sambo Creek

Some 21km east of La Ceiba, Sambo Creek is a thriving Garifuna fishing village. It's a slightly scruffy but fascinating place where you'll see women in striking attire and traditional headdresses. A *punta* (traditional Garifuna dance) party is never far away. The beach is a lovely stretch of sand, which most of the year is pretty clean, though trash washes up after storms.

🏃 Activities

Sambo Creek Canopy Tour & Spa   ADVENTURE SPORTS
(☑3355-5481; canopy tour & spa L880) Sambo Creek Canopy Tour has a massive, 18 zip-line canopy cruise that includes a dip in its hot springs and mud baths. If you want to skip the canopy, the baths alone are L500. It's 500m east of the Hotel Canadien turnoff on the main highway.

🛏 Sleeping & Eating

Centro Turístico Sambo Creek   PENSION $
(☑9587-0874; mauricioelvir@yahoo.com; per person L220) 🥾 Run by the La Ceiba–based travel agency Tourist Options, this cheap place right on the beach is a great place to lay your head in Sambo Creek if your budget is tight.

Villa Helen's   GUESTHOUSE $$
(☑2408-1137; www.villahelens.com; r L880-990, cabins from L1210; ❀🛜❄) The best deal in town, this hotel boasts a tropical bar and restaurant as well as gorgeous gardens and a decent pool. The rooms are fairly basic but come with hot-water bathrooms and small refrigerators. There are also seven cabins, most of which come with living rooms and kitchens.

Kay's Place   HONDURAN $$
(meals from L170; ⊙9:30am-10pm) This beachside restaurant does good fish, seafood and meat grills, as well as serving up cocktails to beach bums. There's often live Garifuna music here.

❶ Getting There & Away

There are buses from La Ceiba's main bus terminal to Sambo Creek (L20, one hour) leaving every 30 minutes throughout the day.

Refugio de Vida Silvestre Cuero y Salado

On the coast about 30km west of La Ceiba, this wetland reserve protects varied and abundant wildlife: manatees are the most famous (and the hardest to see), but there are also howler and white-faced monkeys, sloths, agoutis (rabbit-sized rodents), iguanas, caimans and around 200 bird species.

The small town of **La Unión** is the gateway to Cuero y Salado. From there, you catch a train to a **visitors center**, where a L220 entrance fee is collected and tours can be organized. Two-hour guided **canoe tours** (L150 for two people, plus L220 per guide) are by far the best way to explore the reserve.

For further information, contact Fundación Cuero y Salado (p396) in La Ceiba.

⊙ Getting There & Away

To get to the reserve, take a bus to La Unión from La Ceiba's main terminal (L30, 1½ hours, every 45 minutes). From La Unión, jump on the *trencito* (railcar) for the 9.5km ride (L260, hourly 7am to 2pm) on an old banana railroad to the visitors center. The last railcar returns from the visitors center at 2:30pm; the final bus from La Unión to La Ceiba is at 4pm.

Alternatively, book a tour with a travel agency in La Ceiba.

Trujillo

POP 62,500

Isolated, plucky Trujillo is the end of the line for the Honduran mainland: beyond it lies the virtually roadless jungle of the Moskitia, so there's a frontier-town vibe about the place. The town's setting is magnificent, with soaring mountains in the distance and the wide arc of the Bahía de Trujillo, a brilliant blue expanse of water that has seen the sails of Columbus and many a famous buccaneer, spread out before it. Trujillo boasts some interesting history, excellent nearby beaches and a slow-moving Caribbean air you won't find anywhere else on Honduras' northern coastline.

For years the town has been talked up as Honduras' next big tourism thing, and the completion of a ship terminal means that occasionally the town is swamped by cruise travelers, but thankfully not often: the rest of the year things carry on as they always have done in this delightful, semi-forgotten place.

⊙ Sights

You can sense the town's tumultuous history during a quick stroll around Trujillo's historical core and cobblestone streets. Many fine Caribbean-style wooden houses remain around the Parque Central, and of course there's the fascinating old fort, which offers sweeping views over the bay.

Trujillo also has a fine shoreline, though a lot of trash washes up on its beaches. The best beaches are a few kilometers west of town. Just off the coast, 2km east of Casa Kiwi on the road to Puerto Castillo, is the wreck of a sunken ship that's good for **snorkeling**; close to the shore, it's easily accessible from the beach.

Around 5km east of Trujillo, **Laguna de Guaimoreto** functions as a wildlife refuge and has a complex system of canals and mangrove forests that provide shelter to abundant bird, plant and animal life (including the elusive manatee). Thousands of migratory birds refuel here between November and February. You can hire rowing boats or canoes (and even someone to paddle for you) by the old bridge between Trujillo and Puerto Castillo. Expect to pay around L250 for a two-hour excursion.

★**Fortaleza Santa Bárbara de Trujillo**   FORT
(L66; ⊙9am-5pm) High above the waves, gazing over the Caribbean toward the European motherland, this 17th-century Spanish fortress could not have a more evocative position. Though its ruined remains are not that impressive visually, it's still an inspirational spot to reflect on the forces and characters that shaped the history of the American continent. Fifteen cannons face the sea, and a plaque marks the place where North American wannabe conqueror William Walker was executed. The onsite museum has colonial and Garifuna artifacts.

Iglesia   CHURCH
(Parque Central) The main church in Trujillo dates from 1832 and stands proudly on the Parque Central.

Grave of William Walker   CEMETERY
Just west of town, where the Río Cristales flows into the sea, is the town cemetery. Here lies the grave of William Walker, who died in Trujillo shortly after his ill-fated bid to conquer Central America.

Trujillo

Trujillo

◎ **Top Sights**
1 Fortaleza Santa Bárbara de
 Trujillo...B2

◎ **Sights**
2 Iglesia...B2

▣ **Sleeping**
3 Hotel Emperador A2

✕ **Eating**
4 Café & Sabores A2
5 Cafe Vino Tinto..................................A2
6 Carivida Club Café.............................B1
7 Chico's Place.....................................A2

◎ **Drinking & Nightlife**
8 Cafe Ares A2

ins sleeping up to four people each face the best beach in Trujillo and are surrounded by luscious gardens. There's a restaurant here, and a menagerie, including a rescued capuchin and a white-faced monkey.

The friendly Canadian owners will make you feel right at home. They can also arrange horseback riding and rent paddle boards. It's a couple of kilometers west of Trujillo on the coastal road.

✕ Eating

Café & Sabores HONDURAN $
(Calle Principal; baleadas L16-30, mains L90; ⊙6am-9pm Mon-Sat, to 1pm Sun; ✳🛜) This agreeably old-fashioned diner-like cafe is a good spot for breakfast (L70) and always has five or six set-lunch choices. Excellent *licuados* (fresh-fruit drinks) are L20 to L30, and its *baleadas* (thick flour tortillas stuffed with various fillings) are famous. There's an air-conditioned room at the rear.

★ **Carivida Club Café** INTERNATIONAL $$
(☑9763-5201; mains L150-250; ⊙7am-10pm, until late Fri & Sat; 🛜) It's obvious just from looking at this sleek addition to the seafront that this sophisticated beach lounge is offering something very different to the competition: low lighting, minimalist decor, contemporary wooden furniture – and no headache-inducing music to talk over. It feels almost surreal after any time spent traveling in Honduras. Food is excellent, cocktails are strong and the vibe is cool.

🛏 Sleeping

Hotel Emperador PENSION $
(☑2434-4446; r with/without air-con L600/300; ✳🛜) Owned by a rather eccentric local historian, this hotel has 10 functional rooms to the side of a remarkable Caribbean building, which dates back to 1787. Check out the time-warp atmosphere in the adjoining cafe while you're here.

Casa Alemania HOTEL $$
(☑2434-4466; hotelcasaalemania77@gmail.com; s/d/tw/tr/apt incl breakfast L595/952/1190/1428/2328; ✳🛜🏊) Jovial German owner Gunter Wassmus' surprisingly large hotel sits by a scrappy beach just east of central Trujillo. Rooms are modern, well-appointed and fine value, with good-quality bedding and mattresses, even if some of them feel rather cobbled together. More rooms were being built during our last visit, bringing the total number to 50. Bicycles and kayaks are also rented.

★ **Tranquility Bay** CABAÑAS $$$
(www.tranquilitybayhonduras.com; cabañas L1958; ✳🛜) This fantastic place is definitely a splurge (though in low season room prices tumble by almost half), but it's well worth it: spacious, attractive and clean wooden cab-

HONDURAS TRUJILLO

There's a movie night on Monday and live music on Thursday, and the American management is passionate about getting things right. Look no further for a cool place to hang out in Trujillo.

Cafe Vino Tinto   HONDURAN $$
(mains L120-250; ☺8am-10pm; 🌐) Just below the plaza, this atmospheric little restaurant serves up wonderful sea views, along with pizzas, burgers, quesadillas and fresh fish and seafood. Red wine is available by the glass (L60) and you may be lucky enough to meet English owner Jon, a passionate local historian and a mine of information about the town's history and the neighboring Moskitia.

Chico's Place   SEAFOOD $$$
(mains L175-660; ☺10am-7pm Fri-Sun; 🌐) This place right on the beach enjoys a great reputation locally for its superb seafood. It's busy each weekend, with visitors searching for the quintessential Caribbean beach-bar experience – the waves practically crash at your feet. For the works, order the huge seafood platter (L990).

🍷 Drinking

Cafe Ares   COFFEE
(☺8am-6pm Mon-Sat, 9am-6pm Sun; 🌐) On the hillside just below the Parque Central, this pleasant hut with log columns has gorgeous views out to sea and – most importantly – is your one-stop shop for good coffee and wi-fi.

ℹ️ Information

Banco Atlántida (Parque Central; ☺8am-4:30pm Mon-Fri, 8:30am-noon Sat) Has a 24-hour ATM.

Banco Occidente (Calle 2a & Calle Principal; ☺8am-noon & 1:30pm-5pm Mon-Fri)

Post Office (4a Calle; ☺8am-4pm Mon-Fri, 8-11am Sat)

Tourist Office (📞2434-3140; Parque Central; ☺8am-4pm Mon-Fri) English-speaking staff can help you here.

ℹ️ Getting There & Away

Note that the highway between Trujillo and La Ceiba passes a notorious drug-smuggling route into the Moskitia. It's lined with many police checkpoints.

BOAT

A ferry from the pier connects Trujillo to Guanaja (L800, 1½ hours), one of the Bay Islands, but its timetable is rather vague. On days when it runs, it leaves Trujillo at around 1pm, though its frequency changes according to demand. At the time of research it was generally leaving at least every other day. In the other direction, the boat leaves Guanaja at around 8am, arriving in Trujillo by around 10am.

There are no scheduled departures to the Moskitia region from Trujillo, but fishing and cargo boats do sail there occasionally from the town's pier, so it's worth asking around if you're planning a trip there.

BUS

Two bus companies, **Cotuc** (📞2444-2181) and **Cotraipbal** (📞2434-4932), operate from two small bus terminals 1km and 2km west of the Parque Central respectively, with direct (speedy) and ordinary services. There's another small terminal closer to town, where local chicken buses and the services through Olancho depart.

From the two terminals, buses leave for San Pedro Sula (L220, six hours, nine daily) via La Ceiba (L138, three hours) and Tela (L190, five hours); most leave during the morning, with the last bus at 3pm. There are also three daily buses to Tegucigalpa (L360, 10 to 11 hours) from here.

Local buses go from a stop by the old cemetery to the Garifuna villages of Santa Fe, San Antonio and Guadalupe.

BAY ISLANDS

Spectacular diving and snorkeling draw visitors from around the world to the three Bay Islands (Islas de la Bahía) – Roatán, Utila and Guanaja – located between 25km and 50km off the north coast of Honduras. Their reefs are part of the second-largest barrier reef in the world, and teem with fish, coral, sponges, rays, sea turtles and even whale sharks.

Diving here is very affordable, but lodging and food on the islands are more expensive than on the mainland. Utila is the most affordable island (and very popular with backpackers), while Roatán has better beaches and a beautiful forested interior. Diving is also good on Guanaja, though prices there are prohibitive for most travelers.

The rainy season here runs roughly from October or November to February. March and August are the hottest months; at other times sea breezes temper the heat.

Roatán

POP 65,000

Roatán is the largest and most developed of the Bay Islands. Long and thin (50km long, but only 2km to 4km wide), the island

Bay Islands

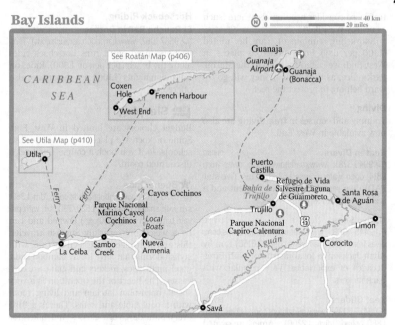

is (like neighboring Utila) a real diving and snorkeling mecca – virtually its entire coastline is fringed by an astonishingly diverse coral reef teeming with tropical fish. On land, exquisite white-sand beaches like West Bay, a mountainous interior of pine-forested hills and the remote wild east of the island (once a pirate hangout) beg to be explored.

Roatán attracts a far more midrange crowd than Utila, with few budget options for sleeping and eating. The vast majority of backpackers base themselves in West End, where there's at least a smattering of hostels and affordable eating options.

Unsurprisingly, this natural beauty hasn't been ignored by property developers and tour operators: a slew of resort hotels, a shopping mall and a cruise-ship terminal have opened in recent years.

West End

Curled around two small turquoise bays and laced with coconut palms, West End is a super-chill diving village close to the western tip of the island. It's the one place in Roatán where independent travelers – rather than package tourists – dominate, and its quirky 'high street' is lined with sea-facing restaurants, boutiques selling sarongs and jewelry, reggae bars and (of course) dive schools.

Even though most accommodations and eating options are geared toward the midrange market, you'll find some good budget places here, plus there's always a community of backpackers to socialize with.

⊙ Sights

Roatán Marine Park WILDLIFE RESERVE
(☑ 2445-4206; www.roatanmarinepark.com)
Originally set up in 2005 with the aim of protecting the reef system around the West End and Sandy Bay, the Roatán Marine Park now covers the whole island. This nonprofit organization campaigns strongly to conserve the marine environment – Roatán's reefs are under enormous pressure, both from construction and the sheer amount of visitors. Four boats patrol the shoreline; people fishing illegally (using nets, harpoons or traps) have been jailed.

The park office rents out snorkeling equipment (L100 per day).

🏃 Activities

Beaches & Snorkeling

Half Moon Bay, which forms the northern part of the West End, is a lovely sandy bay with shallow, sheltered water. Snorkeling is good, but it's some distance out to the reef from the shore and there's a lot of boat traffic, so consider heading elsewhere (such as nearby West Bay).

Snorkeling equipment can be rented (L100 per day) from numerous places in West End: we suggest you go to the Marine Park office, as then your money will go toward helping to protect the reef.

Diving

Training and courses in **free-diving** are also now available in West End.

Roatán Divers   DIVING
(☑ 9949-3781; www.roatandiver.com; dives from L814, open water course L5280) This five-star PADI dive resort has new equipment and a welcoming atmosphere.

Native Sons   DIVING
(☑ 2445-4003; www.roatandivingnativesons.com; dives from L770, open water course L6160) Run by Alvin Jackson, a local instructor with three decades of experience. Very popular with backpackers.

Reef Gliders   DIVING
(☑ 8413-5099; www.reefgliders.com; dives from L880, shark dive L2200) American-owned school that's particularly conscious of diver safety and marine conservation.

Ocean Connections   DIVING
(☑ 9901-3646; www.ocean-connections.com; dives from L880, open water course L7810) Offers a range of training with small classes, and also runs fun dives. Ocean Connections also operates a dive shop in West Bay.

West End Divers   DIVING
(☑ 9565-4465; www.westenddivers.com; dives from L880, open water course L7500) Always popular, this dive shop caters to a younger crowd. It takes safety and service very seriously, as well.

Tyll's Dive   DIVING
(☑ 9698-0416; www.tyllsdive.com; dives from L990, open water course L7040) A relaxed, friendly dive shop on the main drag.

Deep-Sea Submarine

Roatán Institute of Deep Sea Exploration   ADVENTURE TOUR
(☑ 3359-2887; www.stanleysubmarines.com; dives from L11,000) Karl Stanley takes passengers to depths of up to 300m, 450m or 600m in his small, yellow submarine. Since light doesn't penetrate to those depths, those who dare to take the ride can witness some extraordinary marine life, including elusive six-gilled sharks.

Horseback Riding

El Rancho Barrio Dorcas   HORSEBACK RIDING
(☑ 9687-1067; www.barriodorcasranch.com) This well-organized outfit runs horseback rides along the beach (per person L800). Rides on full-moon nights (L1000 per person) are also offered.

🛌 Sleeping

Budget choices are limited in West End. Some inexpensive places are linked to dive schools, so if you book a course you'll get a discounted room.

★ Buena Onda   HOSTEL $
(☑ 9770-0158; www.hbuenaonda.com; dm L360, s/d with shared bathroom L520/790, s/d with private bathroom L650/900; 🛜) Owned and run by a welcoming, worldly Spanish traveler, this excellent place is perfectly set up, with stylish dorms that have lovely bamboo beds, good mattresses, lockers and giant art canvasses. The heart of the operation is a very social, open-plan kitchen and living room with a pool table and sofas. There's a BBQ every Saturday, yoga classes and bikes for hire as well.

Chillies   HOSTEL $
(☑ 2445-4003; www.hotelchilliesroatan.com; Half Moon Bay; dm/d L270/550, cabins L800; 🛜) Run by a welcoming local family, this is an ever-popular choice, not least for its great location right on Half Moon Bay Beach. Budget rooms and dorms in the main building are on the small side, but are kept clean and tidy. Couples may prefer to pay extra for one of the pretty cabins at the rear of the property.

Georphi's Tropical Hideaway   CABINS $
(☑ 2445-4104; www.georphis.com; dm from L220, r with/without bathroom L700/500, cabins from L800; ❄🛜) This sprawling collection of colorful hexagonal wooden cabins in tree-shaded grounds is in the middle of West End and moments from the sea. The attractive, screened cabins are sturdy (though basic) structures – some with kitchen – that all have a private patio with hammocks. Shared kitchens are minuscule but functional, and there's 24-hour hot water.

Posada Arco Iris   HOTEL $$
(☑ 2445-4264; www.roatanposada.com; s/d/tr with fan L925/1056/1188, apt from L1450; ❄@🛜) A fine choice in a shady setting behind Half Moon Bay, this Argentine-owned place has very well-presented rooms and apartments

with kitchens, all brightened up with weavings and tribal art. You'll pay more for aircon and an ocean view, but for groups it can work out to be reasonably affordable. Free kayak use for guests.

Posada Las Orquideas HOTEL $$
(☑2445-4387; www.posadalasorquideas.com; s/d with fan L924/1056, with kitchen L1056/1188; P❄@) This tasteful and well-run place is at the very end of West End (if you turn right at the roundabout coming into town). Rooms are smart and spacious, with those on the 3rd floor commanding higher prices due to their better sea views. There's a jetty that's exclusively for guests, though the water in Gibson Bay is brackish.

Land's End Resort HOTEL $$
(☑9979-9324; www.landsendroatan.com; r/bungalow incl breakfast from L1320/1760; ❄🔊🏊) This lovely, upmarket hotel facing the ocean has a few cheaper rooms that lack ocean views but still represent decent value. The hotel has its own saltwater infinity pool, a bar-restaurant and easy reef access via a ladder into the sea; it's just a 10-minute walk from the West End action. As an added bonus, wild deer roam the grounds.

Casa del Sol HOTEL $$
(☑9961-5260; www.casadelsolroatan.com; r L880-1430, studio with kitchen L1300; ❄@🔊) Right by the entrance to West End, this place has a selection of rooms with Mexican-style colors and hand-painted porcelain sinks in the bathrooms. The studios sleep four and have big bathtubs. Air-con costs L100 extra.

🍴 Eating

Food in West End is pricey. Staying in a place with a kitchen will cut costs, especially if you're part of a group.

For cheap eats look out for **baleada vendors** at various spots along the main strip: they serve up the wheat-flour tortillas at L20 to L40 per hit.

¿Por qué no? BREAKFAST, GERMAN $$
(mains L110-275; ⏰8am-3pm Sun-Fri, dinner by reservation; 🔊) This pleasant cafe with tables on the veranda overlooking the sea does good breakfasts (L80 to L200), pastries and coffee, which brings in a brisk trade each morning. Later on in the day, it's the German-led menu of sausages, potato salad, sauerkraut and schnitzel that's the draw.

ROA Juice Bar & Salads HEALTH FOOD $$
(mains L110-175; ⏰8am-3pm Mon-Sat; 🔊🍴) Something a little different is on offer at this innovative shack created from reclaimed wood-pallet boxes. The young staff will prepare a range of fresh fruit juices and smoothies for you, to accompany various salads and wraps. It's a perfect spot for a light lunch.

Rudy's HONDURAN, INTERNATIONAL $$
(www.roatangeorphis.com/restaurant; breakfasts L70-110, sandwiches L110-140; ⏰7am-3pm Sun-Fri; 🔊) Right on the beach, Rudy's is popular for its breakfasts, with lots of fruit, granola and pancake options on the menu. Also on the menu is the local cure-all fruit *noni*, said to heal anything from arthritis to high blood pressure. *Noni* smoothies are mixed with orange juice to disguise the taste; the shots, which come unadulterated, are only for the brave!

Creole's Rotisserie Chicken HONDURAN $$
(mains L100-210; ⏰noon-9pm Tue-Sat) A low-key island institution, Creole's offers excellent island-style roast chicken (a quarter-chicken is L70), plus shrimp and fish mains. Choose from eight different *fixins* (side dishes) – including coconut rice, carrot salad, coleslaw and red beans – to accompany your main. Round it off with a slab of rum cake and you're set. Dining is on an open-sided deck facing the beach.

★Roatán Oasis INTERNATIONAL $$$
(☑9484-6659; mains L285-525; ⏰5-9pm Mon-Sat; 🔊) A total revolution in the limited food scene of Roatán, the gorgeous Oasis is all about seasonal and locally sourced produce, and may be one of the few places in Honduras where you can find oysters. Come in good time for the three-course set meal (available from 5pm to 7pm), an amazing value at L440 – it features many of the menu's standout dishes.

The charming staff are passionate and efficient, and the entire place so riotously popular that reservations are always a good idea. It's on the main road toward West Bay, a 10-minute walk from West End.

Cannibal Café MEXICAN, INTERNATIONAL $$$
(mains L65-290; ⏰10am-10:30pm Mon-Sat; 🍴) Seriously large tacos are a specialty at this relaxed Mexican-food eatery. Everything on the menu can be made vegetarian. It also offers wine by the glass or bottle.

Roatán

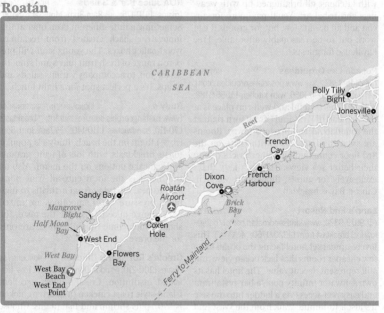

🍷 Drinking & Nightlife

The West End drag is lined with bars where live music or DJs play come dusk. Partying is limited, with most visitors getting up to dive the next day, but it's the liveliest place on the island.

Cafe Escondido　　　　　　　　　BAR
(⊙7:45am-3pm Thu-Sat & Mon, 6-10pm Thu-Sat) Located above West End Divers, this fine cafe-bar has a lovely, breezy upper deck with fine harbor views, magazines for browsing and sofas for lounging. Sip an espresso during the day or slug on a beer and take it all in. There's live music (funk, reggae and acoustic) on Sunday evenings.

Blue Marlin　　　　　　　　　　　BAR
(www.bluemarlinroatan.com; ⊙noon-midnight Mon-Thu, to 2am Fri & Sat, to 10pm Sun) Highly sociable and welcoming bar-restaurant with superb sunset views from the rear deck. Draws a good mix of locals, expats and visitors. There's live music on Fridays and karaoke on Thursdays. Happy hour (4pm to 6pm) features two-for-one cocktails.

Sundowners　　　　　　　　　　　BAR
(⊙11am-9:30pm) This open-sided beachfront bar is *the* expat hangout in Roatán. There's always a crop of grizzly old characters hog-

ging the bar stools from lunchtime onward; backpackers also gather here, despite the dated music. Filling bar grub is served.

ℹ️ Information

There are several ATMs in West End.

ℹ️ Getting There & Away

From the airport, private taxis charge L350 to West End. If you walk to the highway outside the airport, transportation is cheaper: *colectivos* charge L50.

From the ferry terminal, official taxis ask for L500 to West End. A cheaper alternative is to walk 150m to the main road and catch a *colectivo* to Coxen Hole (L50), then another to West End (L35).
Captain Van's (📞2445-5040; www.captain vans.com; ⊙8am-4pm) This reliable (if pricey) West End agency rents scooters (L860 per day), motorcycles (L1200) and cars (from L1200).

Far East

East of Oak Ridge a dirt road snakes across a wildly beautiful landscape, with the forested spine of the island rising above some isolated bays, beaches and mangroves. There are turnoffs for the Garifuna settlement of **Punta Gorda** and the old pirate stronghold of **Port Royal**, but the main attraction is stun-

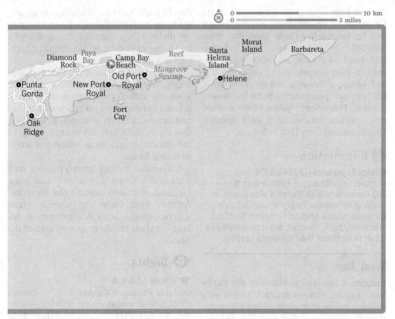

ning Camp Bay Beach on the north shore – a wonderful, virtually undeveloped strip of pale sand. Continue a little further east and you enter the dense pines of the Port Royal National Park.

✖ Eating

La Sirena SEAFOOD $$$
(☑ 3320-6004, 8867-5227; Camp Bay; meals L150-300; ⊙ 11am-8pm) This truly remote and rather makeshift restaurant is housed in a fairly run-down wooden building standing on stilts over the water. Inside, however, you'll be served some of Roatán's best seafood, so it's well worth the long and rough drive from the east of the island.

French Harbour

An important port, French Harbour has a large fishing, shrimp and lobster fleet, but otherwise there's little of interest other than the quirky appeal of Arch's Iguana Farm (☑ 2455-7743; www.archsiguanaandmarinepark. com; L200; ⊙ 9am-4pm) in French Cay, just outside of town. Less a farm than the house of a serious iguanaphile, everywhere you look you see iguanas, some 4000 in all – on the driveway, in the trees, under bushes, everywhere.

Sandy Bay

Located about 4km northeast of West End, Sandy Bay is a quiet little community popular with expats. Here the Carambola Botanical Gardens (☑ 2445-3117; www.caram bolagardens.com; L200; ⊙ 8am-5pm) covers a protected hillside, with several nature trails filled with orchids, spice plants, an 'iguana wall' and lots of wandering agoutis (rodent-like animals). As the name suggests, there's a decent beach here. It's a chilled-out alternative to far busier West End.

🛏 Sleeping & Eating

★ **Roatán Backpackers Hostel** HOSTEL $
(☑ 9714-0413; www.roatanbackpackers.com; dm/r/apt from L265/660/770; 🔊🏊) This recent addition to Roatán's backpacker accommodations is run by the tireless and super-friendly Mel, who ensures that all new arrivals quickly feel at home. The well-organized hostel has multiple room categories, a communal kitchen and a pool and sunbathing patio – complete with its own waterfall. Sandy Bay Beach is just a short walk away. Highly recommended.

Sunken Fish
INTERNATIONAL $$$

(☑ 2407-2070; www.tranquilseas.com; Tranquil Seas Eco-Lodge & Dive Center, Sandy Bay; meals L180-380; ⊘ 7:30am-10pm) The in-house restaurant of a lodge and dive center, the Sunken Fish is open to the public all day and enjoys a fantastic setting overlooking the sea – one particularly apt for impressive sunsets. The eclectic menu offers seafood and Garifuna cuisine, along with Spanish, Honduran and even Thai influences.

ⓘ Information

Clinica Esperanza (☑ 2445-3234; www. clinicaesperanza.org; ⊘ 7:30am-6pm Mon-Fri) Known locally as 'Hospital Miss Peggy,' in honor of its founder, Peggy Stranges, this is the most reliable medical facility on Roatán. It offers very basic services, but is considered by locals to be better than the island hospital.

West Bay

Imagine a paradisical vision of the Caribbean: a quiet, white-sand beach fringed with coconut palms and an azure sea filling the horizon. West Bay is that vision (though not when a cruise ship is in town).

Two decades ago this was still a virgin beach, and backpackers reveled in its unadulterated natural majesty. But times have changed, and a line of uninspiring resort hotels lurk behind the palms and coastal pines. But if you head to the far (southern) end of the kilometer-long beach, close to the volcanic rocks where large black iguanas hide out, there are still few better places in Honduras to indulge in some serious beach time.

It's essential to time your visit carefully, however: when a cruise ship moors up to 5000 people can be disgorged on poor old West Bay, and sunbeds that normally go for L100 will get jacked up to L500.

There are no beachside places here that are geared to backpackers' wallets. Bring your own packed lunch, or else try the little row of shops directly behind the beach, where you'll find **Java Vine** (www.javavine. com; sandwiches from L130; ⊘ 7:30am-5pm Mon-Fri, 8am-2pm & 3-5pm Sat & Sun; ☏), a good place for sandwiches, cake, coffee and wine.

Utila

POP 3500

Utila is a charming island that has enjoyed a reputation for years as *the* place to learn to dive in Latin America. While it may no longer be an incredible bargain due to new taxes on diving, Utila remains diving-obsessed and is one of Honduras' most popular backpacker haunts.

Utila is small (about 13km long and 5km wide) and focused almost entirely on Utila Town, the island's only settlement, which is set on a curving bay with two small beaches and dozens of hotels, restaurants, bars and dive shops. With only a few roads, much of the island is impenetrable wilderness accessible only by sea.

Utila earns its keep mainly from its reef, with over a dozen dive schools and some excellent dive sites around the shoreline. Another huge draw: the juvenile whale sharks – gentle giants measuring up to 6m long – that are regularly spotted around the island.

◎ Sights

★ Whale Shark & Oceanic Research Center
AQUARIUM

(☑ 2425-3760; www.wsorc.com; Main St E; ⊘ 9am-4pm Mon-Sat) **FREE** This excellent place dedicated to whale shark research has numerous displays about the sharks' biology. The real reason to visit, however, is to join one of the regular snorkeling trips (L1000, 7:30am to noon) and track down these glorious creatures yourself. Once the whale sharks are found, everyone dons snorkeling gear and jumps into the ocean with them – an unforgettable experience.

Iguana Research & Breeding Station
WILDLIFE CENTER

(☑ 2425-3946; www.utila-iguana.de; L60; ⊘ 9:30am-noon & 1:30-5pm Mon-Fri) Up the hill from the town center, this great place studies and protects the highly endangered Utila iguana *(Ctenosaura bakeri)*, which is known locally as 'the swamper.' Visitors get to see plenty of these fascinating, spiny-tailed critters. Four excellent naturalist-themed tours of the island (to bat caves and beyond) are offered; there are volunteer opportunities available as well.

Bando Beach
BEACH

(L66) Utila Town's privately run beach is a bit of an underwhelming affair, but at least you're in an enclosed space with sun loungers and access to a bar for cool drinks. Turn right from the harbor and head to the very end of Main St; go over the bridge and it's on the right.

🏃 Activities

Diving

Utila has some superb dive sites. The north side of the island offers spectacular wall diving, with bountiful pelagic life including rays and sharks, and usually excellent visibility. It's great for drift- and deep-diving.

The southern sites are more suited to beginners, with shallower water, though the coral is in a less pristine condition. The seamount **Black Hills** often offers the most prolific marine life, including schools of horse-eyed jacks, while the wreck *Halliburton 211* is a deep-dive thrill.

Utila is rightly famous for the magnificent **whale sharks** that gather here all year. An encounter with one of these creatures will be the highlight of any visit – but as the whale sharks in Utila are juveniles, diving with them is not permitted (though snorkeling is).

Most dive shops start a course every day or two, and many offer instruction in various languages. Prices hardly vary at all, so take a good look around and talk to the instructors before you decide to sign up. Safety and conservation are key concerns; stick with dive shops that are members of UDSEC. Most schools offer free or discounted accommodations if you take a course. PADI open-water dive courses take three or four days and range in price from L6000 to L6500 (including a L58-per-day reef fee, which goes toward the upkeep of the buoys and coral).

Free-diving courses are now available at Free Dive Utila.

Alton's Dive Center
DIVING
(📞 2425-3704; www.diveinutila.com) Friendly and welcoming, this locally owned PADI dive school has up-to-date gear and cheap accommodations right on the dock. It attracts a younger backpacker crowd of serious divers. It's 300m east of the main intersection.

Ecomarine
DIVING
(Gunter's Dive Shop; 📞 2425-3350; www.ecomarineutila.com) The longest-established dive shop on the island, located a 10-minute walk west of the dock. Low-key and unpretentious, with small classes and solid PADI instruction. The backpacker lodge across the street is free for students.

Utila Dive Centre
DIVING
(UDC; 📞 2425-3326; www.utiladivecentre.com) The largest diving operation in Utila, UDC is very serious about safety. The school offers five dive boats, lots of tech-diving and rebreather courses and instruction. Students are separated from certified divers and accommodations at the Mango Inn (p412) are excellent.

Captain Morgan's Dive Centre
DIVING
(📞 2425-3349; www.divingutila.com; next to Pirate Bay Inn, Main St) Right opposite the dock, Captain Morgan's trump card is that it offers more trips to the north coast and its immense drop offs than any other dive center. There's an outdoor teaching area, small beach and new wet suits. Accommodations are in a good new hotel, the Pirate's Bay Inn, a short walk away.

Underwater Vision
DIVING
(📞 2425-3103; www.utilascubadiving.com) Friendly and sociable dive school that offers professional tuition in English, Spanish, German, French, Swedish and Italian. Discounted accommodations are in great dorms in the classy Trudy's (p411) hotel, which doubles as a useful meeting point and has a good place to swim at the small beach.

Parrots Diving Center
DIVING
(📞 2425-3772; www.parrotsdivecenter.com) A proudly local diving center that employs only local instructors, Parrots is popular with budget travelers and has some of the lowest prices on Utila. It's also a very well-run place, with a commendable community outreach program designed to make a difference to the island. Divers stay for free at the Parrots Inn.

Bay Islands College of Diving
DIVING
(BICD; 📞 2425-3291; www.dive-utila.com) Busy, well-established shop with an onsite pool, free accommodations and gym use; diving tours are limited to small groups. The onsite recompression chamber is the only one on the island. Located west of the dock.

Utila Water Sports
DIVING
(📞 2425-3264; www.utilawatersports.com) Small groups and new gear are key attractions at this professional school, located at the upmarket Palms Hotel. Most courses are SSI, not PADI. It's some way east of the main intersection.

Free Dive Utila
ADVENTURE SPORTS
(📞 9730-3424; www.freediveutila.com; Main St E) This very highly regarded operation – the first school of its kind in Central America – teaches free-diving (diving without any

Utila

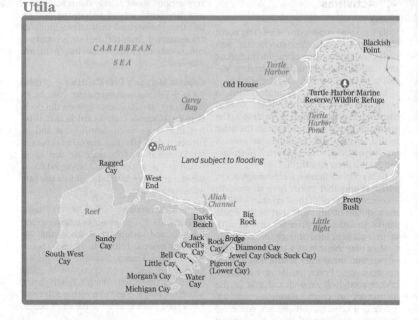

HONDURAS UTILA

breathing apparatus). A 2½-day course costs US$225 and features two classroom sessions and two diving sessions.

Snorkeling

Utila offers exceptional snorkeling, though you'll have to make a bit of an effort to access a good reef. Many dive shops rent snorkel gear (per day around L150), and most dive schools allow snorkelers to tag along on dive boats for a small fee (around L100).

Otherwise there's some snorkeling at Chepes Beach, at the western end of Main St, but the water is very shallow close to shore – pick your way carefully across the sandy bottom for access to deeper water.

Nature Tours

Few visitors make it much beyond Utila Town and the reefs offshore, but the swampy interior of the island is fascinating to explore.

Kanahau (☑ 9874-3344; www.kanahau.com) is an Utilan research and conservation organization based in Pumpkin Hill. Visitors are welcome to join scientists on study tours (L500, four to six hours) to view wildlife, including the critically-endangered Utilan iguana, agouti (a large rodent), bats and lizards.

The Iguana Research & Breeding Station (p408) offers tours (L240 to L400) to bat caves and a dead lagoon and a kayaking trip through the mangroves.

Kayaking, Canoeing & Paddle Boating

Paddling from Utila Town to Rock Harbour is a wonderful day trip. The route goes via Oyster Bed Lagoon and Lower Lagoon and along a mangrove canal. There's a good beach at Rock Harbour that's very private. Many dive schools offer free kayaks for customers, or you can rent them at Gunter's Dive Shop. Paddle boards can be hired at Rico's Cafe, east of the dock.

For guided excursions, Kayak Utila (☑ 3300-9537; half-day trips from L800) is highly recommended, with trips to the cays and north coast and multiday tours on offer.

Boat Trips

Many local fishers have signs in their windows for boat tours; prices start at L1000 per boat. They can take you to Water Cay, to Rock Harbour via the mangrove canal, through the lagoon and other places.

Bush's Bay Island Charters   BOAT
(☑ 3145-7139; utilarooster14@hotmail.com; Main St E) This well-established local company runs regular day trips to Water Cay (L300 per person including hammocks and a beer cooler). It's the go-to place for people want-

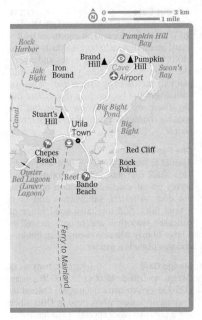

ing to organize boat charters or sport fishing in and around Utila. Cayos Cochinos trips are always regularly arranged.

🛏 Sleeping

Expect to be greeted at the pier by a bunch of brochure-carrying touts giving you the hard sell. Many dive shops have good, cheap (or free) accommodations if you sign up for a course, though such offers only apply on days when you're diving or on the course.

★ The Venue   HOSTEL $
(📞 9505-5760; www.thevenueutila.com; dm L450; 🛜) This great new place just a stone's throw from the town beach brings a new meaning to the term 'party hostel' – by doubling as a popular restaurant and bar, the Venue is never short of folks to hang out with. The smallish rooms all have two bunk beds in them and share a bathroom. The setup is simple, but magical.

Under the fantastic *champa* (thatched big top) there's a full restaurant and bar, where drinking starts early in the day. As a party venue staff also organize kayak tours, Sunday hog-roasts and even trips to Cayos Cochinos. Definitely a great place to meet other backpackers, even if you're not staying here.

★ Rubi's Inn   HOTEL $
(📞 2425-3240; rubisinn@yahoo.com; Main St E; r from L440; ❄🛜) Owned by a charming local couple, this small hotel has 12 spotless, spacious rooms with polished floors and fresh linen in a wooden waterfront building. Rooms on the upper deck overlook the sea, but expect to pay twice as much if you have a view. There's a private dock for swimming and sunbathing, hammocks for chilling in and a guests' kitchen.

Air-con is available but adds L100 to the price. Book ahead by phone.

Sea Side Utila Hostel   HOTEL $
(📞 2425-3150; Main St W; r with/without air-con L660/330; ❄🛜) A 10-minute walk west of the dock, this well-maintained place has a tranquil location close to Chepes Beach. Rooms have two double beds and are available either with air-con or a fan (a far cheaper option). There's also a guests' kitchen. You'll enjoy the sweeping Caribbean views from the shared balcony.

Tony's Place   GUESTHOUSE $
(📞 2425-3376; off Cola de Mico; s/d L150/300; 🛜) With eight basic but clean rooms, stacked on two floors on the same site as the owner's house, this is a good-value budget option. To get here from the dock, walk directly uphill, then look out for the white-and-green building diagonally opposite the Mango Inn.

Hotel Trudy   HOTEL $$
(📞 2425-3103; www.utilascubadiving.com; Main St E; dm L180, r/ste L770/1550; 🛜) A delightful base, this locally owned place has a fantastic oceanfront plot to enjoy, with a small beach-volleyball court and a cafe that makes for a relaxing and sociable stay. Dorms are small but have polished wooden floors and sea views from the communal balcony. The shared bathrooms have hot water. Divers with Underwater Vision get discounted rates.

Bayview Hotel   GUESTHOUSE $$
(📞 2425-3114; bayviewinternet@yahoo.com; Main St W; r L880; ❄🛜) Owned by a welcoming Utilan family who have relatives in the USA, this traditional guesthouse has an enviable waterfront location (with private dock for chilling on) near Chepes Beach. The fine-value rooms are plain but spacious, with firm mattresses; all have bathrooms with hot water, and some have a fridge.

Utila Cay Rentals
CABINS $$$

(☑ 2408-3100; www.utilacaysrentals.com) Barry Jackson runs this local rental agency, which manages Sandy Cay and Little Cay, two tiny coral islets off the coast of Utila with perfect white-sand beaches and little else. Prices are affordable: generally about US$140 per night for Sandy Cay and US$155 per night for Little Cay.

Mango Inn
HOTEL $$$

(☑ 2425-3326; www.mango-inn.com; Cola de Mico; dm L220, r from L1500; ❄ 🔊 ☒) Linked to Utila Dive Center, this excellent place is straight up the hill from the pier. Well-constructed timber accommodations are scattered around a garden shaded by mango trees; the pool area and cafe are just great. Backpacker dorms (which cannot be booked ahead) are very decent value indeed: their shared hot-water bathrooms are far better than average.

✖ Eating

Utila Town has a good selection of eating options for such a small settlement. Several places to stay also have kitchens where you can cook. Poorly stocked supermarkets dot Main St.

Bush's Supermarket
SUPERMARKET $

(Main St E; ☉ 6:30am-6pm Mon-Sat, to noon Sun) Opens early so you can get your day's supplies before you hop on a dive boat. There's relatively little available here, but by local standards the selection is enormous. The attached cafeteria run by Carmela is famous for its cinnamon rolls.

Rio Coco Cafe
CAFE $$

(Main St E; breakfasts L90-140; ☉ 7am-2pm Mon-Fri, 8am-1pm Sat, closed Dec; 🔊) 🍴 This is the best place for good coffee in Utila, with a range of Honduran roasts that can be produced hot or iced. Housed in a cute blue-and-white timber house on the seafront, Rio Coco offers good breakfasts and simple lunches as well – and part of the profits go back to the local community.

RJ's
CARIBBEAN $$

(Main St E; mains L150-200; ☉ 5-9pm Wed, Fri & Sun) Ask anyone on the island where you can find Utila's best food and they'll tell you RJ's without hesitation. While that may be due more to the local taste for traditional Caribbean cooking than anything else, this friendly place does excellent pork and seafood dishes, all accompanied by a sea of trimmings. Note the odd opening hours, and come early.

Hotspot Cafe
CAFE $$

(Main St W; mains L80-130; ☉ 6am-5pm Mon-Sat; 🔊) With real coffee and an enormous whiteboard menu that includes breakfasts (L60 to L100), smoothies, burgers, wraps and a popular steak sub, this cute yellow-and-white painted shack lives up to its name – it heaves with divers and backpackers throughout the day. There are relatively few tables, but the sociable counter is a great place to meet new people.

Che Pancho
CAFE $$

(Main St E; meals L115-140; ☉ 8am-6pm; 🔊🖉) This small cafe has a garden location and serves up an excellent selection of salads, hot dogs, schnitzel, sandwiches and even a tuna fillet. Add to that a good range of pancakes, smoothies and juices – as well as a large library where you can swap books – and this place is a winner.

Mango Café
PIZZA, INTERNATIONAL $$

(Mango Inn, Cola de Mico; pizza L150-180, mains L125-300; ☉ 6am-2pm & 5-10pm; 🔊) Owned by Andrea, an Italian who's lived in Utila since the 1990s, this place specializes in authentic thin-crust pizza from a purpose-built brick oven. The menu runs from egg sandwiches and burritos to seared tuna, coconut shrimp and wine-poached snapper fillet; there's always a daily special, too. If you eat here you're welcome to use the hotel pool and sunbeds.

Munchies
INTERNATIONAL $$

(Main St W; mains L100-190; ☉ 7am-9pm Wed-Mon; 🖉) Situated in a landmark Utilan building dating from 1864, this restaurant's front porch offers the best perch in town for people-watching. It offers friendly service, good vegetarian options, big breakfasts, chicken wings and espresso (when the machine is working). In the mornings you'll often see local iguanas on the back porch.

Mango Tango
INTERNATIONAL $$$

(mains L190-275; ☉ 8am-9:30pm Mon-Fri, 11am-9:30pm Sat & Sun; 🔊) Housed in the bright-yellow Mariposa building near the main dock, Mango Tango has some of the best food in town. Try a lion-fish burger, tuna ravioli or filet mignon from the interesting international menu, or just have one of the small but good-value set breakfasts (L80) – while enjoying the best sea view in town from the breezy terrace.

Birdhouse CARIBBEAN $$$
(📞9695-6257; Main St W; mains L150-300; ⏰11am-2:30pm & 5-11pm Wed-Mon; 🐾) This friendly new addition to Utila's seafront is a colorful and chilled out bar-restaurant. The house specialty is rotisserie chicken, each serving of which comes with a pick of delicious side dishes, such as rice and beans, coleslaw and potato salad. Saturday sees comforting soups served up for the hungover.

🍷 Drinking & Nightlife

The party scene is strong in Utila, which at times feels like a cool college town revolving around a small diving university. Unfortunately most of the unique (if rough) local dance halls have closed in recent years.

Skid Row BAR
(Main St W; ⏰10am-11pm) Everything a hard-drinking bar should be, with a leaky tin roof, concrete floor, pool table, dart board, an excess of wizened characters and a long-suffering bartender. All visitors are cordially invited to take up the 'Giufity Challenge' – downing shots of a Garifuna herb-enhanced moonshine. Decent pub grub, including Tex-Mex dishes and burgers, is also available, as is delivery.

Treetanic BAR
(Cola de Mico; ⏰8pm-midnight, to 1am Wed & Fri) Owned by Neil, an eccentric American artist, this psychedelic mango-treetop bar is somewhere you just have to see while visiting Utila. It always draws a cast of local characters and is definitely one of the more fun places on the island.

La Cueva BAR
(Main St W; ⏰11am-midnight) A dive bar that packs in a curious mix of local characters, hard drinkers and members of the international wandering class. Try the banana-infused rum.

Tranquila Bar BAR
(Main St W; ⏰4pm-1am Sun, Mon & Wed, to 4am Tue & Thu-Sat) Jutting out over the bay, this rather uninspiring bar is nevertheless a key evening hangout and one of the main social hubs for backpackers on the island – more for its prime location and late opening hours than for the appalling music (hard rock, bland Top 40 pap), which everyone moans about.

ℹ️ Information

Morgan's Travel (📞2425-3161; www.utilamorganstravel.com) Arranges plane tickets off the island and taxis to and from the airport. Next to the pier.

Utila Community Clinic (📞2425-3137; Main St W; ⏰8am-noon & 1-2pm Mon-Fri) Run by English-speaking Dr Raissa Canales, who has specialist training in diving injuries. There's also a pharmacy onsite.

World Wide Travel (📞9891-1960; Main St E) This efficient and friendly agency can book you tickets on all flights in Honduras, but is particularly useful for getting you onto the various charter flights to the other Bay Islands, which cannot normally be booked online.

ℹ️ Getting There & Away

AIR

Utila has an airstrip, but no terminal; buy tickets at World Wide Travel or Morgan's Travel in town. Planes serving Utila range from small 20-seaters to tiny five-seaters – and they all fill up fast, so book a spot as early as possible.

Flights between Utila and Roatán save time you would otherwise spend changing ferries in La Ceiba, though at present there are scheduled flights only on Saturdays with **CM Airlines** (📞9522-5304; www.cmairlines.com). **Aerolíneas Sosa** (www.aerolineasosahn.com) flies between Utila and La Ceiba at 6am on Tuesday, Thursday and Saturday; CM Airlines flies only on Saturdays.

From La Ceiba you can continue to San Pedro Sula or Tegucigalpa. Flights to La Ceiba cost around L2000 and take 15 minutes.

BOAT

There are currently two boats connecting the mainland and Utila – the *Utila Dream* and the *Utila Princess* – and nearly all visitors arrive on them. At the time of writing the two companies were trapped in a fierce price war for customers, which has led to historically cheap prices for the journey. This is unlikely to last though, and so while in early 2016 you could do the crossing for as little as L114 on the *Utila Princess*, prices may well have risen by the time you read this.

The **Utila Dream** (📞2425-3191; www.utilaferry.com; one-way L200) is the new kid on the block, and operates the most modern boat with the most professional staff, generally offering the most comfortable experience. The **Utila Princess** (📞2425-3390; one-way L114; ⏰ticket office 8-11am & 2-4:30pm), by contrast, is a converted cargo boat; for years it was the only way to reach Utila for those without the money to fly. At the time of writing, it was the most economical of the two.

Both boats have similar timetables, and run twice a day in each direction. The *Utila Dream* leaves Utila daily at 6:25am and 2pm, and leaves La Ceiba at 9:30am and 4pm, while the *Utila Princess* leaves Utila daily at 6am and 2pm, and leaves La Ceiba at 9:20am and 4pm. Crossings take between 45 minutes and one hour. Arrive 30 minutes before your boat's departure.

There are no scheduled boat links between Utila and Roatán, though there are a good number of charters that make the run – ask at local travel agencies. The team behind the *Utila Dream* have announced that they plan to include a scheduled boat between Utila and Roatán, but nothing was final at the time of research.

❶ Getting Around

You can walk the entirety of Utila's Main St in about 20 minutes.

Bikes are available from many places by the hour/day/week for L25/100/600, though they're generally poorly maintained rust buckets. The best of a fairly bad bunch can be had at **Utila Bike Rental** (☑ 8818-5633; Main St E; ☺ 6am-6pm Sun-Fri).

THE MOSKITIA

The Moskitia, that vast part of Honduras you see on maps with very few roads, is one of the region's last frontiers of untamed wilderness. Huge expanses are virtually untouched jungle, and when combined with magnificent wetland and savanna habitats it's no wonder Moskitia is often dubbed Central America's Amazon.

Manatees, tapirs and jaguars all still thrive here – they have learned to be circumspect around humans, and are not easy to spot. Crocodiles can be seen in the waters, while the birdlife, including macaws and fish eagles, is outstanding.

A visit to this region is not for the fainthearted – access is tricky and conditions on the ground rustic at best, making visiting as part of a tour the safest and easiest approach. Expect to up your normal budget considerably if you come here, and be sure to bring cash with you: there are no ATMs in this part of the country.

Laguna de Ibans

The small traditional coastal communities around Laguna de Ibans are likely to be your first overnight stop if you enter the Moskitia via the overland route. Pick your base from a cluster of small settlements – Cocobila, Raista and Belén. All have good budget accommodations and are a short walk apart.

The quiet Miskito village of Raista is possibly the nicest of the three, with wooden houses on stilts. There are beach walks (though trash spoils the scene), and wildlife-spotting hikes can be arranged to look for nesting sea turtles and crocs in the lagoon (no swimming here, folks!). If you get the chance, take in Plaplaya, a lovely, traditional Garifuna village a short boat ride from Raista, where giant leatherback sea turtles nest and are released by volunteers between April and July.

🛏 Sleeping & Eating

Your only eating options are at hotels.

Raista Eco Lodge LODGE $
(☑ 2433-8220, 8926-5635; Raista; per person L220) A pioneer of ecotourism to the Moskitia, Raista Eco Lodge has rustic but comfortable rooms, mosquito nets and good home-cooking (meals around L100). The Bodden family, who run the place, are friendly and knowledgeable and can arrange tours and onward transportation.

❶ Getting There & Away

There's an airstrip in Belén, with daily flights to and from Trujillo (L2400). *Lanchas* (small motorboats) to Batalla (L250, two hours), for overland connections to Trujillo, stop in all three villages at ungodly times, between 3am and 3:30am. Heading inland, you can arrange transportation to Las Marías (round trip L4500, five to six hours). Heading west, an early-morning *lancha* takes passengers to Palacios in time to catch the first speedboat to Iriona.

Reserva de la Biosfera del Río Plátano

The Río Plátano Biosphere Reserve is a magnificent nature reserve, declared a World Heritage Site in 1980. A vast, unspoiled and untamed wilderness, it's home to extraordinary animal life, including a number of endangered species. The best time to visit is from November to July, though bird-watchers should come in February and March, when many migratory birds are here.

One of the best places to organize tours is in Las Marías, a village in the heart of the reserve with around 100 Miskito and Pech families. There is no running water or electricity here, though there are a few generators.

Short trails around the village are good for birding, but for longer trips it's essential to hire a guide and arrange camping equipment and food. Guides do not speak English. Bookings are difficult to organize in advance and not really necessary.

🕿 Tours

Popular short tours in the reserve include a twilight crocodile-spotting walk and a day trip by boat to see some petroglyphs. Arduous longer trips into primary rainforest include a two-day hike up wildlife-rich **Cerro Baltimore** and a three-day expedition to the summit of **Pico Dama** (840m), both of which require several guides.

🛏 Sleeping & Eating

Several basic lodgings, including Hospedaje Doña Justa, will cook you simple meals on request. There are no other eating options.

Hospedaje Doña Justa   HOTEL $
(☑ 9966-9234; Las Marías; r without bathroom per person L150, meals L60) Super friendly, the Doña Justa is a thatch-roofed building with several airy rooms overlooking a huge flower garden. Each room is well-kept and has decent beds with mosquito nets. There's a big patio with lots of hammocks, perfect for whiling away an afternoon with a book. Meals are prepared upon request.

ℹ Getting There & Away

There are no scheduled *lanchas* (small motorboats) between Las Marías and Raista, but if you hang around for a few days you'll probably get lucky; expect to pay L700 per person (one-way). A round-trip chartered boat ride from Raista costs around L4500 for up to three people (five to six hours); the boat operator will wait in Las Marías for two nights for the round-trip leg. It's also possible to set up dug-out canoe trips and hikes between the coast and Las Marías.

Palacios

Palacios is a tense, rather lawless place known as a drug-running stronghold. Do not venture outside at night, and take care at any time of day.

🛏 Sleeping & Eating

There is just one *comedor* in town, which serves up very cheap meals.

Hotel Moskitia   HOTEL $
(☑ 9996-5648; r L600) This is Palacios' best sleeping option, though it's still pretty basic. The modern rooms are clean and many come with lake-view balconies.

ℹ Getting There & Away

Colectivo canoes will run you across the lake from Batalla (L60, five minutes).

Brus Laguna

Beside the lagoon of the same name, Brus Laguna is an accessible entry point to the Moskitia, as it has an airport. You can head to Raista or even straight to Las Marías from here. There are a couple of internet places here, but no bank. Note that there's now a large US DEA (Drug Enforcement Agency) and Honduran military presence in the area due to increased narco activities.

🛏 Sleeping & Eating

There are only three hotels here. For the best of a bad bunch, check out Villa Biosfera. There's a town *comedor* for basic meals and a couple of stores for very basic self-catering.

Villa Biosfera   CABIN $
(☑ 9919-9925; s/d without bathroom L200/375) This hut on stilts is the best option in Brus Laguna, but is nothing special. Expect neat, if not clean, rooms that have fans and mosquito nets. The bathrooms are not a highlight.

ℹ Getting There & Away

AeroCaribe (☑ 2442-1088; www.aerocaribehn.com) connects La Ceiba with Brus Laguna (L2660) daily. From Batalla, *lanchas* (small motorboats) head to Brus Laguna between 3pm and 5pm (L400, four hours).

Puerta Lempira

POP 8900

Despite being not much more than an overgrown village, Puerto Lempira is the largest town in the Moskitia. Situated on the inland side of the Laguna de Caratasca, it's not that interesting, though it has good air connections, a hospital and erratic internet access.

Possible day trips from Puerto Lempira include the serene Miskito village of **Mistruk**, 18km south of town on the banks of the Laguna de Tansing, which can be reached on a bike.

🏃 Activities

La Ruta Moskitia   ADVENTURE TOUR
(☑ 3391-3388; www.larutamoskitia.com) A collective of community owned ecotourism

HONDURAS PALACIOS

enterprises within the region that together arrange tours and ensure that money remains in local communities.

🛏 Sleeping & Eating

Puerto Lempira has an extremely basic array of eating options, which are mostly street-food stands. For something better, head to Hotel Pinares, which has a good restaurant.

Hotel Pinares HOTEL $
(📞 2433-6681; Av 10; r L500-800; ❄ ⛲) Right on the lagoon, this is the most comfortable place to stay in Puerto Lempira, with breezy rooms surrounding a plant-filled courtyard, a good pool and an onsite restaurant that's one of the few good places to eat in town.

Hotel Yu Baiwan HOTEL $$
(📞 2433-6348, 9568-2142; off Calle Principal; s/d L650/750; ❄) The best deal in town, the Yu Baiwan has plenty of space, firm beds, clean linens, cable TV and friendly service. To get here, look for a narrow cement passageway off Calle Principal, a half-block from the pier.

ℹ Information

Jon Tompson (📞 9758-8996; jontompson 2002@yahoo.com) Jon Tompson, owner of the popular Vino Tinto bar and restaurant in Trujillo, has traveled widely in the Moskitia and may be able to help you set up your trip. He organizes his own informal expeditions there, and can arrange for travelers to continue into Nicaragua, something that is not normally possible.

ℹ Getting There & Away

CM Airlines (www.cmairlines.com; L3050) and **Aerolíneas Sosa** (📞 2433-6558; www. aerolineasosa.com; L2800; ⏱ 8:30am-5:30pm Mon-Fri, to noon Sat & Sun) both fly between La Ceiba and Puerto Lempira several times a week. It's possible to travel overland (and over water) between Brus Laguna and Puerto Lempira but you'll be crossing one of the Americas' principal cocaine smuggling routes – we don't recommend you try. Note that foreigners are not permitted to enter Nicaragua at the nearby border post of Leimus.

SOUTHERN HONDURAS & ISLA DEL TIGRE

Honduras touches the Pacific with a 124km coastline on the Golfo de Fonseca. This perpetually and often infernally hot coastal plain is dominated by agribusinesses: sugarcane, African Palm plantations and shrimp farms.

While it's a much-traveled region (the Interamericana crosses through Honduras here), there's little of interest to travelers – except perhaps Isla del Tigre, which has some charm.

Isla del Tigre is an inactive volcanic island off the southern coast of Honduras, with a highest point of 783m. It's a dramatic place covered in thick forest and with some decent beaches that attract droves of locals but very few foreigners.

Its main town is **Amapala**, a scruffy fishing village with picturesque, crumbling clapboard architecture. Black-sand **Playa Negra**, in the north of the island, is arguably the island's best beach, though there are several other totally undeveloped stretches elsewhere here.

🛏 Sleeping

Accommodations in Isla del Tigre are more expensive than on the mainland. There are few budget options, but on lovely Playa Grande, 4km south of Amapala, the good-value Hotel y Restaurante Dignita is a good bet.

Hotel y Restaurante Dignita HOTEL $$
(📞 2795-8707; s/d L550/700) This is one of the nicer hotels on Playa Grande, with clean and spacious rooms – some with great sea views. The restaurant (mains L120 to L250) is famous for its excellent seafood dishes; guests sit at long wooden tables just a few feet from the ocean. It's perfect for throwing back a couple of beers over a plate of *ceviche*.

🍴 Eating

Isla del Tigre's Playa Grande offers a plethora of eateries, with Dignita being the most popular for its seafood.

ℹ Getting There & Away

If you're only passing through southern Honduras, it's less than three hours by bus between the borders of El Salvador and Nicaragua. Heading east to Nicaragua you're sure to pass through the large city and transportation hub of Choluteca, which has little to detain you, though there are plentiful banks and facilities.

If you are headed to Isla del Tigre, small *colectivo* boats (L20, 20 minutes) depart from the town of Coyolito, 30km from the Interamericana, but you'll have to wait until the boat fills up with 10 passengers. Otherwise you can pay L100 for a private boat trip (the preferred, hassle-free choice).

Buses go to Coyolito from the town of San Lorenzo (L24, one hour, every 40 minutes until 5:30pm) from the terminal behind San Lorenzo's prefabricated market, or from a dusty turnoff 2km north of town. San Lorenzo can be reached by buses that run by Blanquita or San Benito from Tegucigalpa (L87, two hours, every 40 minutes).

❶ Getting Around

Minibuses (L10) from Amapala circuit halfway around the island past beaches. You can also grab a *mototaxi*.

UNDERSTAND HONDURAS

Honduras Today

Welcome to Central America's bad boy: Honduras has for years been the regional cautionary tale about what goes wrong when corruption, drugs and poverty intersect. But this ever-plucky nation refuses to be pigeonholed and has been fighting back steadily against its dangerous international reputation. Murder rates – while still sky-high – are dropping, security is better than it has been for years and things are finally looking up for one of the region's least appreciated destinations.

Crime & Emigration

The original banana republic, Honduras has been ignored or kicked about for most of its existence. But in 2012 the nation finally became newsworthy – the United Nations announced the country had become the murder-rate capital of the world. (Hondurans joked with gallows humor that at last they had won something.) Not surprisingly, crime levels and the deeply interconnected issues of gang and drug cartel activity have grown to dominate the country's collective consciousness.

By 2015, Honduras lost its dubious title of the murder-rate capital of the world to neighboring El Salvador, though by any standards, the security situation in the country remains dire. It's not only the day-to-day threat of attack or robbery that Hondurans have to consider as they go shopping, drive

a car or board a bus. Extortion or 'war taxing' practiced by gangs in poor barrios hikes up costs for the whole nation: street vendors have to pay to pitch a stall and transportation companies have to pay so their buses can pass through gang-controlled territory. Sky-high crime rates curb inward investment, so prospective employers avoid Honduras because of huge security costs. Armed guards stand in front of just about everything. Tourism suffers, and even the Peace Corps pulled out in 2012, citing safety concerns.

Given the status quo, many have voted with their feet and sought a new life in the USA or elsewhere. An estimated million Hondurans live north of the border; according to *La Prensa* newspaper their remittances home for 2014 were some US$3.4 billion, or about 17% of the Honduran economy. There's barely a family in the whole nation that does not have a member in 'El Norte.'

Politics

Following a win at the polls in late 2013, National Party of Honduras candidate Juan Orlando Hernández assumed the Honduran presidency in 2014. A conservative, Hernández (known to locals by his initials JOH) has been credited with seeing murder rates drop but he has also been powerless to make any serious inroads on that age-old Honduran issue of corruption, even being indirectly implicated in it himself. Indeed, the perceived corruption of the political elite has led to a recent series of large anti-government protests, which climaxed in mid-2015 following a scandal that saw the National Party of Honduras allegedly receiving millions in bribes. With the next elections not until 2018, Hernández has tried to placate the popular anger about corruption in the country by setting up a national commission to investigate graft. Long-suffering Hondurans have little faith in elected power structures, but look with some hope instead to the slowly improving security situation and remain hopeful that the worst of the violence is now behind them.

History

Honduras has had a rough deal over the centuries. Things got off to a sparkling start when the Maya civilization emerged in Copán, but then the Spaniards came and trampled all over the territory. Marauding pirates added to the mix in the 17th century.

Independence brought a brief respite, but for virtually the entire 20th century Honduras was dominated by distant, powerful forces as giant US fruit companies and, later, the US military set up shop in the nation.

Early History

The earliest humans are thought to have arrived in Honduras around 9000 BC, though almost nothing is known about their lives other than that they were hunter-gatherers. By around 2000 BC settlements started cropping up across the land.

It was over a millennia more before the Maya site of Copán Ruinas began to flourish, as sculptors carved stone stelae unequaled in the Maya world and mathematicians and astronomers calculated uncannily accurate calendars and planetary movements. For hundreds of years, a good slice of the Maya Classic Period (AD 250 to 900), the city dominated the region culturally, until its decline in the 9th century AD.

Spanish Colonization

Columbus, on his fourth and final voyage, landed near present-day Trujillo in 1502, naming the place Honduras ('depths' in Spanish) for the deep waters off the north coast.

He established a town (Trujillo), Honduras' first capital in 1525, but the gleam of silver from the interior soon caught the eye of the conquistadors: in 1537 Comayagua, midway between the Pacific and Caribbean coasts, became their new capital.

Indigenous people put up fierce resistance to the invasion, although this was weakened by their vulnerability to European-introduced diseases. The sternest resistance was from Lempira (chief of the Lenca tribe, who's considered a national hero), who led a force of 30,000 against the Spanish before he was assassinated. By 1539 resistance was largely crushed.

British Influence

By the beginning of the 17th century, Spanish colonists were coming under regular attack from rival imperial forces – especially the British. Merchants from Britain, attracted by the mahogany and hardwoods of the Honduran Caribbean coast, established settlements there and on the Bay Islands.

Britain eventually ceded control of the Caribbean coast to the Spanish, but continued to influence the region. In 1797, slaves rebelled on the Caribbean island of St Vincent. The British shipped thousands to the island of Roatán, where they mixed with indigenous people. Eventually these people, the Garifuna, crossed to the mainland and founded settlements along the coast.

Independence

After gaining its independence from Spain in 1821, Honduras was briefly part of independent Mexico and then a member of the Central American Federation. The Honduran liberal hero General Francisco Morazán was elected president in 1830. The union was short-lived, however, and Honduras declared itself a separate independent nation in 1838.

Liberal and conservative factions wrestled and power alternated between civilian governments and military regimes – such that the country's constitution would be rewritten 17 times between 1821 and 1982. Honduras has also experienced literally hundreds of coups, rebellions and power seizures since achieving independence.

The 'Banana Republic'

Around the end of the 19th century, US traders marveled at the rapid growth of bananas on the fertile north coast (just a short sail from southern USA). US entrepreneurs bought land for growing bananas, and three companies – including the Standard (later United Fruit) company – bought up huge chunks of land.

Bananas provided 11% of Honduras' exports in 1892, 42% in 1903 and 66% in 1913. The success of the industry made the banana companies extremely powerful within Honduras, with policy and politicians controlled by their interests.

20th-Century Politics

The USA increasingly came to influence Honduran affairs. In 1911 and 1912, US marines were dispatched to the nation to 'protect US investments.'

A two-month strike in 1954 – in which as many as 25,000 banana workers and sympathizers participated – remains a seminal moment in Honduran labor history. Unions were recognized, and workers gained rights that were unheard of in neighboring Central American countries.

From the late 1950s the military steadily began to take a much more important role in the country's governance, via coups and political pressure. Long periods of military rule alternated with civilian presidents throughout the 1960s and 1970s. This cycle was finally ended with the 1981 democratic presidential elections.

The 1980s

During the 1980s Honduras was surrounded by revolutions and conflict. In July 1979 the revolutionary Sandinista movement in Nicaragua overthrew the Somoza dictatorship, and Somoza's national guardsmen fled into Honduras. Civil war broke out in El Salvador in 1980 and internal conflict worsened in Guatemala.

Honduras became the focus of US policy and strategic operations in the region, backed up by General Gustavo Álvarez, who supported an increasing US military presence. Under Ronald Reagan huge sums of money and thousands of US troops were funneled into Honduras; refugee camps of Nicaraguans in Honduras were used as bases for a US-sponsored covert war against the Nicaraguan Sandinista government, known as the Contra War.

Public alarm grew as hundreds of leftists in Honduras 'disappeared' and the US militarization of Honduras ramped up. By 1984 General Álvarez was exiled by fellow officers, and the Honduran government suspended US training of the Salvadoran military within its borders.

In Washington, the Reagan administration was rocked by revelations it had illegally used money from arms sales to Iran to support anti-Sandinista Contras. Large demonstrations followed in Tegucigalpa, and in November 1988 the government refused to sign a new military agreement with the USA. With the election of Violeta Chamorro as president of Nicaragua in 1990, the Contra War ended.

Modern Currents & Coups

Through the presidential administrations of Rafael Leonardo Callejas Romero (1990–94) and Carlos Roberto Reina Idiaquez (1994–98), Honduras struggled economically. Then in 1998 Honduras was dealt a devastating blow as Hurricane Mitch killed thousands and caused widespread devastation (estimated at US$3 billion), setting the economy back years.

In 2001, Ricardo Maduro from the National Party was elected president, largely on the back of his promises to reduce crime. But despite pouring huge resources into the problem, crime levels rose inexorably. In January 2006, José Manuel Zelaya Rosales, a cowboy-hat-wearing rancher from Olancho, was elected president. He aligned himself closely with other Latin American left-wing

THE FOOTBALL WAR

The sporting rivalry between Honduras and El Salvador spilled off the pitch and onto the battlefield in the 1969 Guerra de Fútbol – the notorious Football War.

Tensions did not suddenly break out on the stadium terraces. In the 1950s and 1960s, a flagging economy forced 300,000 Salvadorans to seek better conditions in Honduras. However, the Honduran economy was itself ailing, and Salvadorans began to be targeted as scapegoats. In June 1969, Honduran authorities started throwing Salvadoran immigrants out of the country. A stream of Salvadoran refugees followed, alleging Honduran brutality.

In the same month, the two countries were playing World Cup qualifying matches against each other. At the game in San Salvador, Salvadorans attacked Honduran fans, defiling the Honduran flag and mocking the anthem. Across the border, angry Hondurans then turned on Salvadoran immigrants. Tempers frayed further and the El Salvador army invaded Honduran territory on July 14, capturing Nueva Ocotepeque. Honduras retaliated with air strikes. A ceasefire was called after only six days, but around 2000 Hondurans lost their lives, while thousands of Salvadorans fled home.

READING UP

Want more background? Leaf your way through the following books:

➡ *Enrique's Journey* (by Sonia Nazario) A runaway from Tegucigalpa searches for his mother in the USA.

➡ *Bananas: How the United Fruit Company Shaped the World* (by Peter Chapman) Great insight on the banana giant's impact on Central America.

➡ *The Mosquito Coast* (by Paul Theroux) A vivid fictional account of life in the jungle.

➡ *The United States, Honduras, and the Crisis in Central America* (by Donald E Schulz and Deborah Sundloff Schulz) Discusses the role of the US in Central America during the region's tumultuous civil wars.

➡ *Prisión Verde* (by Ramón Amaya-Amador) Life on a banana plantation by a political writer.

➡ *El Humano y la Diosa* (The Human and the Goddess), *Los Barcos* and *The Big Banana* (by Roberto Quesada) One of Honduras' leading novelists.

➡ The works of Juan Ramón Molina (1875–1908) – perhaps the country's best-loved poet.

leaders (such as Hugo Chávez) but in 2009 his plan to rewrite the constitution – thereby making himself eligible for a second term – provoked a political crisis. The Supreme Court ordered Zelaya be removed from office and despite global indignation – many countries viewed his expulsion as a coup – he was dispatched to exile in the Dominican Republic.

Democratic elections duly followed, and Nationalist party candidate Porfirio 'Pepe' Lobo, a center-right conservative with strong backing from the nation's oligarchy, was voted in. Another rancher from Olancho, Pepe left his sombrero back on the farm, but the chaos continued. Lobo's presidency saw the country rack up foreign debts of over US$5 billion, while ongoing financial turmoil left state workers, including teachers and the military, unpaid.

Culture

Honduras is a complex ethnic, religious and cultural melting pot that you need to understand in order to make the most of any journey here. The legacy of its rich and turbulent history can be seen everywhere, from the Garifuna settlements of former slaves (who remain quite apart from the rest of the population) to the Bay Islands' distinctly British feel. For many, the natural world is the main reason to visit Honduras, and few wildlife lovers leave disappointed.

The National Psyche

Generalizations don't – and shouldn't – come easily for a country with such wide-ranging cultures. The *ladino* (someone of mixed indigenous and European parentage) business employee will have a different outlook to the Garifuna fisher, who may not have much in common with a Lencan subsistence farmer. However, Hondurans are less likely to reach a collective flashpoint than their neighbors, at least historically.

It's this easygoing nature that probably defines the national psyche more than anything else. Other Central Americans, particularly those from El Salvador, tend to view it as laziness, which is a tad harsh. For Western visitors this lack of a sense of urgency can be occasionally frustrating, but it is important to remember that attitudes toward service are very different to, say, the USA. For Hondurans, a steady, laid-back demeanor is the way things are done. A sense of reserve is often maintained – few Hondurans are in-your-face loud and assertive.

Lifestyle

Lifestyles in Honduras vary as widely as the country's shockingly unequal social spectrum. The fortunate economic elite often lead an Americanized lifestyle, driving SUVs and shopping in air-conditioned malls. Far more commonly, Hondurans are forced to scratch out a living. Poverty is perhaps at its most shocking in poor urban barrios, where there's a constant threat of violence.

Lack of opportunities have forced many to seek jobs in the USA, which has an estimated one million Hondurans, over 60% of them undocumented.

Hondurans are hugely family-oriented. They often have a wider family network than many Europeans or North Americans are used to – aunts, uncles, grandparents, cousins and even more distant relatives often play a significant role in family life.

Another attitude in Honduran society is machismo. Women are often still treated as second-class citizens. Women's wages are much lower than men's and reported levels of domestic abuse are disturbing.

People

Around 90% of Hondurans are mestizo, with a mixture of Spanish, indigenous and African heritage.

One of the most ethnically diverse regions of Honduras is the Moskitia, home to Miskito and Pech people, as well as tiny numbers of Tawahka (less than 3000) around the Río Patuca.

Over 50,000 Garinagu (Afro-Carib Garifuna people) live on Honduras' north coast, spread between the Moskitia and the Guatemalan border. Thousands of other people with African ancestry also live on the north coast and Bay Islands.

The indigenous Tolupanes (also called Jicaque or Xicaque) live in small villages dotting the departments of Yoro and Francisco Morazán. Some 38,000 Ch'orti' Maya are found around Copán Ruinas, while the large Lenca group (as many as 300,000) live in southwestern Honduras.

Many of Honduras' elite are of white (Spanish and European) stock, but there are also small numbers in the Bay Islands who trace their (distant) routes back to Britain.

Honduras also has perhaps 100,000 people of Arab descent, mainly Catholic and Orthodox Christians originally from Palestine and the Levant.

Religion

Honduras has traditionally been an overwhelmingly Roman Catholic country, but this has changed considerably in the few decades with the rise of the evangelical movement. Unlike neighboring Guatemala,

few indigenous customs or beliefs have been integrated into Christian worship. There are also small numbers of Orthodox Christians, Jews and Muslims. Tegucigalpa and San Pedro Sula both have synagogues and mosques.

Arts

The Garifuna are known for their incredible dances. If you get a chance to see a performance by the Ballet Folklórico Garífuna, don't miss it.

Musician/politician Aurelio Martínez (who was a deputy in Honduras' Congress for four years) is the star of the *punta* (traditional Garifuna music and dance) scene; his *Garífuna Soul* and *Laru Beya* albums receive rave reviews all over the world.

There's a thriving visual arts scene. Julio Visquerra (b 1943) paints in a style that's been called 'magical realist'; José Antonio Velásquez (1906–83) was a renowned primitist painter. Urban Maeztro is the pseudonym of a Honduran street artist who makes provocative, Banksy-style work. Lovers of graphic novels should check out Honduran Independent Comics (www.hiccomics.com).

Landscape & Wildlife

Honduras is a country of breathtaking natural beauty, with a huge range of bird, mammal, reptile and plant species. However, illegal logging, under-resourced authorities and construction projects are putting this under threat. While the environment has plenty of

BIRDS IN HONDURAS

Over 700 bird species have been recorded in Honduras. The Lago de Yojoa is an avian mecca, and national parks and reserves provide excellent opportunities for spotting toucans, parrots and raptors. Quetzals are found in cloud-forest national parks, including Cusuco, Celaque and La Tigra.

Migratory birds flock to wetlands and lagoons along the north coast from November to February. A successful breeding and reintroduction program has resulted in the scarlet macaw, the Honduran national bird, recolonizing the Copán valley, where there's also an excellent bird park.

defenders, they face a tough struggle against developers, corruption and plain ignorance.

The Land

Countries don't come that big in Central America, but Honduras weighs in as the second-largest (after Nicaragua), with an area of 112,090 sq km. Its coastline includes a 644km Caribbean stretch and 124km on the Pacific side, as well as the Bay Islands and other islets. The fertile north is by far the most developed – its banana plantations have long been a mainstay of the economy.

Much of the Honduran interior is mountainous, with peaks reaching 2849m. There are many fertile highland valleys, but no active volcanoes. Extensive wetland areas, swamps and mangrove forests are dotted along the north coast.

Flora & Fauna

There is a dazzling array of plant species and wildlife in Honduras. Jaguars, tapirs, crocodiles and the mighty Ceiba tree are found in tropical zones; in the cloud forests rare butterflies flit among the orchids and magnificent pines; while whale sharks and sea turtles thrive in the country's turquoise Caribbean waters.

It is the sheer variety of habitats here that allows so many different species to thrive. Honduras has mangroves, freshwater lakes, oceans, lagoons, cloud forests, pine forests and tropical rainforests (considerably more than does Costa Rica).

Much of the habitat is under threat from deforestation. Endangered species include the scarlet macaw (the national bird), Utilan iguana, manatee, quetzal, jaguar and tapir. Their future depends on just how much protection Honduras' protected areas can really offer.

Environmental Issues

Deforestation is the most pressing environmental issue facing Honduras today.

NATIONAL PARKS & PROTECTED AREAS

Almost a fifth of Honduran territory is officially protected as a national park or reserve, but all too often the government lacks the resources – or the political will – to stop development and deforestation.

Important protected areas, including marine reserves, include:

Lancetilla Botanical Garden (p392) This botanical gardens has more than 1200 plant species and hundreds of bird species. Near Tela.

Parque Nacional Cusuco (p371) A cloud forest with a large population of quetzals. Near San Pedro Sula.

Parque Nacional Jeannette Kawas (p391) Habitats include mangrove swamps, a small tropical forest, beaches and offshore reefs. Near Tela.

Parque Nacional Montaña de Celaque (p388) An elevated plateau that includes Honduras' highest peak. Near Gracias.

Parque Nacional Pico Bonito (p398) High biodiversity, dense forests and many waterfalls. Near La Ceiba.

Refugio de Vida Punta Izopo (p391) Includes tropical wet forest, mangroves and wetlands. Near Tela.

Refugio de Vida Silvestre Cuero y Salado (p400) The largest manatee reserve in Central America. Monkeys and birdlife also abound. Near La Ceiba.

Reserva de la Biosfera del Río Plátano (p414) A World Heritage Site, the Río Plátano covers 5251 sq km of lowland tropical rainforest. In the Moskitia.

Roatán Marine Park (p403) Protects the entire coastline of the island and includes some outstanding coral formations. In Roatán.

Tawahka Asangni Biosphere Reserve Tropical rainforest on the ancestral lands of the Tawahka people. In the Moskitia.

Turtle Harbor Marine Reserve On the northern coast of Utila, Turtle Harbor is a marine park popular with divers.

Though Honduras' forests are the densest in Central America, they're disappearing fast – around 2% are lost each year. Talks were held in January 2013 between the EU and Honduras to establish a Voluntary Partnership Agreement so that only legally obtained timber could be exported to Europe. However, illegal timber exports to the USA and Caribbean islands continue.

Activists who oppose loggers, developers or ranchers are regularly threatened, and even killed. In 2015, Honduras was named the 'deadliest country in the world to be a land and environmental defender' by environmental NGO Global Witness. The Punta Sal reserve near Tela is now the Parque Nacional Jeannette Kawas, named after the campaigner who opposed construction plans for years and was murdered in 1995. In 2014 alone, 12 campaigners met with violent deaths.

There are myriad other environmental concerns. Honduras lost two-thirds of its mangrove forests between 1980 and 2003, mostly for shrimp farms. Mining activity is polluting the Lago de Yojoa – the largest source of fresh water in the country – with heavy metals. Vast plantations of African palms are spreading along the north coast, a monocultural environment that provides little in the way of habitat for wildlife.

SURVIVAL GUIDE

ⓘ Directory A–Z

ACCOMMODATIONS

Hotels vary wildly in Honduras depending where you are. In most towns you can get a decent, functional clean room with a bathroom and a fan for around L300 to L500. In the big cities it's very important to choose a hotel in a relatively secure neighborhood, and these places tend to cost more (L400 to L700), as do accommodations in the Bay Islands.

You'll find hostels with dorm beds where travelers gather, including Tegucigalpa, Copán Ruinas, Utila, Roatán, La Ceiba and San Pedro Sula. Costs vary considerably for dorms, from L175 to L300 a bed.

Honduras is pretty cheap overall, certainly compared to Guatemala and Nicaragua; however, Honduran tourism has had a tough few years so many smaller backpacker places have closed and often the only decent (and secure) options are a little pricier than usual.

Note that, as elsewhere in Central America, a *sencilla* (single) usually indicates that the room has one double bed, while a *doble* has two beds – save money and sleep next to a friend.

In resort areas like the Bay Islands, prices peak around Christmas and New Year and during Semana Santa (Easter week).

Air-conditioning is an expensive luxury, particularly in the Bay Islands. Free wi-fi is almost totally ubiquitous in hostels and hotels.

There are no organized campsites in Honduras, though camping is possible in several national parks.

CHILDREN

Like most of Latin America, Honduras is very open and welcoming of children and there's no taboo about bringing children to restaurants or performances.

Travelers will be hard-pressed to find child-specific amenities like car seats, high chairs and bassinets, except perhaps in top-end hotels and resorts. Disposable diapers, wipes, formula and other basics, however, are available in most large supermarkets.

CLIMATE

Confusingly, there are two rainy seasons in Honduras. On the north coast, it rains year-round, but the wettest months are from September to February. During this time floods can occur, impeding travel and occasionally causing severe damage. The south and west of the country has a different, distinct rainy season between May and October.

The mountainous interior is much cooler than the humid coastal lowlands. Altitude affects temperatures greatly: in places like Tegucigalpa (975m) and Gracias (803m) the heat rarely gets too oppressive.

Hurricane season is June to November.

CUSTOMS REGULATIONS

Customs officers are pretty lax; while police and customs officers are entitled to search you at any time, especially in border areas, they rarely do. Even searches at the airport tend to be perfunctory, though you have to submit your luggage to an x-ray upon entering and exiting Honduras. The exception is if something about your appearance or demeanor suggests to the officer you may be carrying drugs.

Beyond drugs, travelers are not allowed to remove any ancient artifact or endangered animal or plant, whether live or a product made from these. It's smart to keep receipts for any item you buy, and especially for anything that might be confused for being a restricted product, such as an especially good Maya replica.

EMBASSIES & CONSULATES

Most embassies are in Tegucigalpa. British citizens are represented by their embassy in Guatemala; the nearest Dutch and Canadian embassies are in Costa Rica, and the nearest Australian, Irish and New Zealand embassies in Mexico City.

Belizean Embassy (☑ 2238-4614; consulado belice@yahoo.com; Av República de Chile, Centro Comercial Hotel Honduras Maya)

Canadian Embassy (☑ +506 2242-4400; www. canadainternational.gc.ca/costa_rica; 3rd fl, Bldg 5, Oficentro Ejecutivo La Sabana, San José, Costa Rica; ☺ 8am-noon & 12:30-4pm Mon-Thu, 7:30am-1pm Fri)

Dutch Embassy (☑ +506 2296-1490; http:// costarica.nlembajada.org; 3rd fl, Bldg 3, Oficentro Ejecutivo La Sabana, La Sabana, San José, Costa Rica)

El Salvadoran Embassy (☑ 2232-4947; http:// embajadahonduras.rree.gob.sv; Diagonal Aguán 2952, Colonia Altos de Miramontes)

French Embassy (☑ 2232-5444; www.amba france-hn.org; Av Juan Lindo)

German Embassy (☑ 2275-9292; www.teguci galpa.diplo.de; Av República Dominicana 925)

Guatemalan Embassy (☑ 2232-5018; www. honduras.minex.gob.gt; Calle Londres, Bloque B, 2nd Fl, Office 0440, Colonia Lomas del Guijarro Sur)

Nicaraguan Embassy (☑ 2231-1966; www. cancilleria.gob.ni; Av Choluteca, Bloque M-1, No 1130, Colonia Lomas de Tepeyac)

UK Embassy (☑ +502 2380-7300; embassy@ intelnett.com; Nivel 11, Edificio Torre Internacional, 16 Calle 0-55, Guatemala City, Guatemala)

US Embassy (☑ 2236-9320; http://honduras. usembassy.gov; Av La Paz)

INTERNET ACCESS

Wi-fi is fairly ubiquitous in Honduras, with nearly every hotel and hostel offering it for free (even if, in many cases, the signal doesn't always reach every room). Many public squares and other government institutions offer free access (though these services are rarely very reliable), as do many restaurants, bars and cafes. Many

hotels offer terminals from which guests can access the internet.

LEGAL MATTERS

There are tourist police in towns including San Pedro Sula and Tela, but as very few officers speak English don't expect too much help. Police officers in Honduras aren't immune to corruption – if you have any problem with the police, contact your embassy immediately.

LGBT TRAVELERS

Honduras is rather a contradictory place for gay people. While on the one hand same-sex marriage and adoption are both banned in the constitution, it is also illegal to discriminate against people on the grounds of their sexuality. Gay people are visible in society here, though open displays of affection between gay or lesbian couples are unusual, and even risky in some situations. Despite that, there are small yet active gay and lesbian communities in all major cities, though most socializing takes place online.

MONEY

It's relatively easy to access money in Honduras: all big towns and cities have plentiful ATMs. Credit cards are usually accepted in hotels.

ATMs

➡ There are cash machines in cities and towns throughout the country, though don't rely on them working in small towns.

➡ ATM robberies are common: never use them at night, unless you're in a secure environment such as a mall. Even in daytime we recommend using ATMs that have armed guards on patrol outside.

Bargaining

Crafts are fairly rare in Honduras, so you won't find many opportunities to haggle while shopping. Prices for many services are fixed, so there shouldn't be any need to bargain: in large cities, for example, both *colectivos* and private taxis have a single fixed price for rides around town. Ask at your hotel what taxis should cost – if you get in knowing what the price should be, most drivers won't argue.

Cash

➡ The unit of currency in Honduras is the lempira (L), which is divided into 100 *centavos*.

➡ Over the last decade the lempira has been steadily sliding against the US dollar. Many establishments give prices in US dollars, and are happy to accept payment in it too.

➡ Banks will exchange US dollars and occasionally euros. Bring your passport and go in the morning.

➡ Your hotel may let you pay in US dollars (worth doing to avoid the bank queues), or even

HONDURAS SURVIVAL GUIDE

SLEEPING PRICE RANGES

The following price ranges refer to a double room with bathroom. Taxes are included in the price.

$	less than L700
$$	L700–1400
$$$	more than L1400

exchange them for you, as may some places in the more touristy areas.

Credit Cards

→ Visa and MasterCard are accepted at most midrange and top-end hotels, as well as at some hostels, but expect a 5% to 10% credit card surcharge (which makes using them quite expensive in the long run).

→ Cash advances on cards are available at most banks in case of emergency.

Exchange Rates

The US dollar and (to a lesser extent) the euro are the only foreign currencies that are easily exchanged in Honduras; away from the borders you will even find it difficult to change the currencies of neighboring countries.

Taxes

Restaurants and hotels are supposed to always include VAT in their prices, but it is not always included in hotel-room prices, so be sure to ask when booking. Many hotels will give you a room without VAT charged as long as you do not require a receipt.

Traveler's Checks

Traveler's checks are extremely difficult to cash or use anywhere in Honduras. Most banks, hotels and other retailers want nothing to do with them.

Tipping

Cafes & Comedores Tipping is not common in *comedores*, cafes or simple restaurants, but is appreciated.

Restaurants Upmarket restaurants will automatically add a 10% service charge to your bill.

OPENING HOURS

Businesses are generally open during the following hours.

Banks 8:30am to 4:30pm Monday to Friday and 8:30am to noon Saturday

Bars noon to midnight daily

Restaurants 7am or 8am until 9pm daily

Shops 9am to 6pm daily

POST

Post offices in most Honduran towns typically are open Monday to Friday 8am to 5pm (often with a couple of hours off for lunch between noon and 2pm) and on Saturday from 8am to noon. Delivery takes 10 to 14 days for most international destinations, longer for Australia. Despite the apparently long delivery times for postal items, Honducor, the Honduran postal service, is considered relatively reliable.

For more secure delivery try FedEx, DHL, Express Mail Service (EMS) or Urgent Express; all have offices in Tegucigalpa, San Pedro Sula and other major cities.

PUBLIC HOLIDAYS

New Year's Day January 1

Day of the Americas April 14

Semana Santa (Holy Week) Thursday, Friday and Saturday before Easter Sunday

Labor Day May 1

Independence Day September 15

Francisco Morazán Day October 3

Día de la Raza (Columbus Day) October 12

Army Day October 21

Christmas Day December 25

SAFE TRAVEL

→ Be very cautious in cities, especially San Pedro Sula and Tegucigalpa, which both have gang problems (though travelers are rarely targeted). Walking in the center in daytime is usually fine.

→ Don't show off your belongings, never walk alone or down side streets in unfamiliar areas, and always keep an eye out for people approaching you: daylight robbery in the street is common.

→ Avoid travel at night, though always take a cab if you have to go out.

→ Small towns are generally much safer than big cities. Watch yourself on the north coast, especially on the beach.

→ It's best not to walk alone on city beaches in Tela or La Ceiba, by day or night.

SMOKING

Honduras has excellent anti-smoking laws, and all restaurants and most hotels are smoke-free areas.

TELEPHONE

The country code for Honduras is ☎ 504 and the international access code is ☎ 00. There are no area codes, and all telephone numbers in the country (both cell and landlines) have eight digits.

TIME

Honduras is GMT minus six hours. There are no daylight savings, as day and night are more

---

EATING PRICE RANGES

The following price ranges refer to the typical cost of a main course.

$	less than L100
$$	L100–200
$$$	more than L200

or less equal year-round. The 24-hour clock is sometimes used.

TOURIST INFORMATION
There are currently very few tourist information offices in Honduras, and those that exist offer limited practical advice. The national office is the Instituto Hondureño de Turismo (p361) in Tegucigalpa. Much better information can be gotten from hostels and travel agencies.

TRAVELERS WITH DISABILITIES
Honduras lacks facilities for disabled travelers, other than in upmarket hotels and resorts. Wheelchair-bound visitors will find it difficult to negotiate towns because of poor-quality sidewalks and cobblestones. Public transportation is not geared to less-able travelers, though the ferries to Roatán do offer wheelchair access.

VISAS
Citizens of the EU, Australia, Canada, Japan, New Zealand and the United States normally receive free, 90-day tourist cards when entering the country. This also applies to nationals of the countries signed up to the CA-4 border agreement – Guatemala, Nicaragua, Honduras and El Salvador.

Other nationalities, including most Asian and African countries, have to apply for a visa in advance from a Honduran embassy, and pay a fee of US$30.

Once inside Honduras you can apply for a one-time 30-day extension (L500) at the main immigration office in Tegucigalpa (travelers have reported problems gaining extensions in other offices). Or, just take a trip outside the CA-4 border agreement area (Belize and Costa Rica are nearest) for at least three days, then get a new 90-day visa upon re-entering Honduras.

VOLUNTEERING
A number of organizations offer volunteer opportunities in Honduras, on projects ranging from building homes to teaching English.

The website www.travel-to-honduras.com has a long list of groups that run volunteer programs here, from large operations like Casa Alianza (www.casa-alianza.org) to the tiny Utila Iguana Conservation Project (p408).

WEIGHTS & MEASURES
The metric system is used in Honduras.

WOMEN TRAVELERS
Honduras is still a male-dominated society. Personal safety is the biggest concern for female travelers. Most women do not feel threatened while traveling alone in Honduras, but it certainly pays to adopt an assertive demeanor.

As elsewhere, you'll probably attract less attention if you dress modestly. On the Bay Islands, where lots of foreign tourists congregate, things are more relaxed, though topless bathing is most definitely out. It's best to head to clubs and bars only with male company, or in a group.

WORK
Most independent travelers who stay in Honduras to work do so on the Bay Islands; dive instructors are almost exclusively foreigners, and many people completing dive-master training raise a little extra cash working as waiters or bartenders in West End, West Bay or Utila. Most do not have work permits and leave every three to six months to get a new tourist visa.

ⓘ Getting There & Away
Flights, tours and rail tickets can be booked online at www.lonelyplanet.com/bookings.

AIR
Frequent direct flights connect Honduras with other Central American capitals and destinations in the USA. There are no direct flights to Europe.

Airports & Airlines
San Pedro Sula's airport is the busiest and largest in the country, followed by that of the capital Tegucigalpa. Roatán is the only other airport that takes international flights, including to Atlanta, Houston and Miami in the US.

Honduras has no national airline. Airlines flying to Honduras include **Aeroméxico Connect** (www.aeromexico.com), **American Airlines** (www.aa.com), **Avianca** (www.avianca.com), **Copa** (www.copa.com), **Delta** (www.delta.com), **Spirit Airlines** (www.spirit.com), **TAG** (www.tag.com.gt), **Tropic Air** (www.tropicair.com) and **United** (www.united.com).

LAND
Border Crossings

Border crossings include Corinto and El Florido (Guatemala), El Amatillo and El Poy (El Salvador), and Guasaule and Las Manos (Nicaragua).

Guatemala

To Guatemala, the main crossings are at El Florido, Agua Caliente and Corinto. There's no official fee to leave Honduras or enter Guatemala but immigration officials often ask for a dollar or two.

The 24-hour border at Agua Caliente is a half-hour bus ride from Nueva Ocotepeque. Buses connect the Honduran and Guatemalan immigration posts, which are 2km apart. From the Guatemalan side buses go to Esquipulas, where you can connect to Guatemala City or Flores.

The 24-hour border at El Florido is 9km west of Copán Ruinas and connected by very regular minibus services (L20, 20 minutes, every 20 minutes). If you're on a trans-border bus or shuttle bus you'll have to get off and clear customs and immigration on both sides of the frontier. Money changers will approach you, usually offering decent rates. There's also a bank on the Guatemalan side.

The Guatemalan border at Corinto (open 6am to 9pm) is a 51km bus ride southwest of Omoa (L45, 1½ hours, every hour). Buses to the border leave from the main highway and will drop you at a set of *comedores*. From there, walk through immigration procedures. Microbuses waiting on the Guatemalan side connect to Puerto Barrios.

El Salvador

To El Salvador, the main crossings are El Poy and El Amatillo; the crossing at Sabanetas near Marcala is *not* open for foreigners.

The El Salvador border at El Poy (open 24 hours) is a short bus ride from Nueva Ocotepeque (L15, 15 minutes, every 20 minutes to 7pm). On both sides, the bus drops you about 100m from the border, from where you walk across and catch a bus onward. On the Salvadoran side, buses leave frequently for San Salvador and La Palma.

There are buses from Choluteca in Honduras' south to the Salvadoran border at El Amatillo (L52, two hours, every 20 minutes until 6:30pm).

Nicaragua

Crossings to Nicaragua are at Guasaule, El Espino and Las Manos.

In southern Honduras, buses run from Choluteca to the Nicaraguan border at Guasaule (L30, 45 minutes, every 20 minutes 6am to 6pm).

For the El Espino border you'll have to travel via San Marcos de Colón, from where there's very regular transportation (L18, 15 minutes).

For Las Manos, buses run from Tegucigalpa (L88, 2½ hours, three daily).

Bus

There are five main luxury-class international bus companies serving Honduras from neighboring countries: Platinum, Pullmantur, Tica Bus, Hedman Alas and Trans Nica. Three other companies (Rutas Orientales, Fuente del Norte and Sultana) offer less pricey alternatives.

The two hubs for international departures are San Pedro Sula and Tegucigalpa. From these two cities you can get to San Salvador (El Salvador); Guatemala City, Antigua and Santa Elena/Flores (Guatemala); Managua (Nicaragua); San José (Costa Rica); and Panama City (Panama).

It's also possible to take local buses, crossing the border on foot and picking up another bus on the other side. This is a cheaper but far slower way to travel.

SEA

The only scheduled international passenger boat services to/from Honduras are the two small boats that run (on the same day at the same time!) weekly from Puerto Cortés to Belize.

If you arrive or depart from Honduras by sea, be sure to clear your paperwork (entry and exit stamps, if necessary) immediately with the immigration office in Puerto Cortés.

Getting Around

AIR

Domestic air travel in Honduras is fairly pricey, though the safety record is generally good. There are connections from La Ceiba, Tegucigalpa and San Pedro Sula to Utila and Roatán, and also between the three major cities themselves. Routes also open up the Moskitia and the Bay Island of Guanaja from La Ceiba. A small airstrip has opened in Copán Ruinas, though at present it is only taking charter day trip flights from Roatán.

AeroCaribe (2442-1088; www.aerocaribehn.com)

Aerolíneas Sosa (La Ceiba 2442-1512, Roatán 2407-0248, San Pedro Sula 2407-0249, Tegucigalpa 2235-5107; www.aerolineasosa.com)

Avianca (☑ San Pedro Sula 2570-8222, Tegucigalpa 2281-8222; www.avianca.com)

CM Airlines (☑ La Ceiba 9450-6477, Roatán 2445-0106, San Pedro Sula 2668-0068, Tegucigalpa 2233-5050; www.cmairlines.com)

Lanhsa Airlines (☑ La Ceiba 2442-1283, Puerto Lempira 9450-1025, San Pedro Sula 2668-0472, Tegucigalpa 2234-0804; www.lanhsa.com)

BICYCLE

On the mainland there are few opportunities to rent bikes, as heavy traffic, bad roads and the ever present danger of being robbed are big deterrents. Tela is an exception: M@ngo Hotel (p390) rents out bikes here, which can be a good way to explore the area around the town.

Bikes really come into their own on the Bay Islands, particularly little Utila, where there is very little traffic – riding around here is both safe and fun.

BOAT

Three passenger ferries operate between La Ceiba and the Bay Islands. There is no scheduled ferry service between the three islands, though there are regular charters between Utila and Roatán during the high season. There's a regular ferry between Trujillo and Guanaja, the third of the Bay Islands.

In the Moskitia, almost all transportation is by water. There are also water taxis on Roatán from West End to West Bay, and from Coyolito on the Golfo de Fonseca over to the Isla del Tigre.

BUS

Buses are a cheap and easy way to get around Honduras, though there are also some very fancy (and consequently far more costly) services. The first buses of the day often start very early in the morning; the last bus usually departs in the late afternoon. Buses on major highways run later.

On major bus routes, you'll often have a choice between taking a *directo* (direct) or a *parando* (an ordinary bus that makes many stops). Micro-buses or *rapiditos* are minivan-like buses.

City buses are not recommended due to safety issues – gangs 'tax' transportation companies and occasionally assault drivers.

CAR & MOTORCYCLE

Driving on the highway in Honduras is like playing in the advanced level of a video game. Many locals drive at insane speeds (to avoid the perceived threat of carjacking), but it's perfectly safe to drive in Honduras as long as you're mindful of your speed and drive defensively.

The main highways are paved, mostly in reasonable condition; most are also toll roads, which means regular but meager payments (around L20) for drivers. Away from the highways, roads tend to be quite rough and sometimes they're unsurfaced: conditions can vary wildly according to rainfall and the time of year, ranging from acceptable to impassable. Always check with locals on your route before you head off, and bear in mind that many navigation systems will send you along the most direct route, rather than the best road – getting local knowledge is always key.

Rental cars are available in Tegucigalpa, San Pedro Sula, La Ceiba and on Roatán. Prices start at L650 a day for an economy car. Motorcycles and scooters can be rented on Utila and Roatán.

TAXI

Taxis are everywhere in Honduran towns. It's very common to share a ride in many places, so each passenger pays around L20. If you want a private ride, rates start at about L60. Fares increase at night.

In the major cities, *colectivos* (shared taxis) ply a number of prescribed routes, costing around L15 to L25 per passenger.

Three-wheeled *mototaxis* (tuk-tuks) are very common in small towns and villages, but they're not allowed to operate in big city centers. Expect to pay about half what you would in a taxi: typically a ride around town costs L10 per person.

Nicaragua

🔊505 / POP 6.1 MILLION

Includes ➡

Managua	431
Granada	444
Masaya	455
Isla de Ometepe	458
San Juan del Sur	464
León	469
Cosigüina Peninsula Beaches	477
Estelí	479
Matagalpa	488
Bluefields	491
Pearl Lagoon	494
Corn Islands	495
Bilwi (Puerto Cabezas)	499
San Carlos	501
Río San Juan	503

Best Places to Eat

➡ El Tercer Ojo (p450)

➡ Café La Nicaragüita (p475)

➡ Barrio Café (p465)

➡ Café Campestre (p463)

Best Places to Sleep

➡ Surfing Turtle Lodge (p477)

➡ Casa Oro Hostel (p465)

➡ Finca Magdalena (p462)

Why Go?

Affable Nicaragua embraces travelers with offerings of volcanic landscapes, colonial architecture, sensational beaches and pristine forests that range from breathtaking to downright incredible. Want 90-octane waves and beach-blanket-bohemia days on lost beaches? Nicaragua's got you covered with two long coastlines of peaced-out surf camps, hippie enclaves and remote fishing villages that are only now entering the tourist game.

Or are you thinking about diving into history, tromping through colonial villages and exploring the region's unique cultural patrimony? Well, Nicaragua's got that, too. Colonial cities like León and Granada offer crimson-hued snapshots of the past, while remote Caribbean fishing villages provide glimpses into present-day life in this diverse, proud and optimistic nation. Beyond that there are volcanoes to be climbed (and surfed down), lagoons to be explored, islands to be discovered – welcome to Nicaragua.

When to Go
Managua

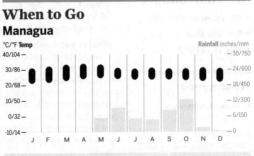

Nov–May High season means dry weather, sunny days, but slightly bigger crowds.

Mar–Nov It's rainy, but green, and you get the biggest, brawniest waves for Pacific Coast surf safaris.

Sep–Nov Hotels are cheaper, but the tail end of hurricane season can screw up your plans.

AT A GLANCE

Currency Córdoba (C$)

Language Spanish

Money ATMs are widespread in most midsize towns in Nicaragua.

Visas Generally not required for stays up to three months.

Time GMT minus six hours

Area 129,494 sq km

Capital Managua

Emergency ☑115 (fire), ☑118 (police), from cell phones ☑911

Exchange Rates

Australia	A$1	C$21.18
Canada	C$1	C$22.35
Costa Rica	₡100	C$5.34
Euro	€1	C$32.36
Japan	¥100	C$27.02
New Zealand	NZ$1	C$20.20
UK	UK£1	C$40.73
US	US$1	C$28.65

Set Your Budget

➡ **Hostel Bed** US$7–20

➡ **Evening Meal** US$2–6

➡ **Bus Ticket** US$1–4

Resources

➡ **Vianica.com** (www.vianica.com)

➡ **Intur** (www.visitanicaragua.com/ingles)

➡ **Latin American Network Information Center** (www.lanic.utexas.edu/la/ca/nicaragua)

Connections

Nicaragua's border with Honduras can be crossed at Las Manos, El Espino or El Guasaule. From Costa Rica, you can enter by road at Peñas Blancas or by boat via Los Chiles. From Potosí, you can hop on a small boat to El Salvador. For more detailed information, see Survival Guide p514.

ITINERARIES

One Week

If you've got limited time in Nicaragua, a trip through the southwest is big on awesome and small on hours in the bus. Kick off your trip in charismatic Granada. Spend three nights taking in the wonderful streetscapes, and visiting the museums and churches. From here, you can head out for day trips or overnighters to the lush crater at Laguna de Apoyo, the lyrical artisan villages known as Pueblos Blancos, or to the Mombacho and Masaya volcanoes and protected wild preserves.

Two Weeks

Next head down the highway to San Jorge, from where you'll take the ferry across to the out-of-this world Isla de Ometepe with its twin volcanoes and endless outdoor activities. From there, it's across the isthmus to the Southern Pacific Beaches. Most people begin and end their beach time in the funked-out international beach village of San Juan del Sur, but definitely plan on spending a night or two on the surf beaches north and south of here. If you are headed north from here, you won't want to miss a stop off in León.

Essential Food & Drink

➡ **Where to eat** Budget eateries – generally *comedores* or *cafetines*, *fritangas* and market stalls – serve a limited range of filling dishes and set meals from US$2 to US$5.

➡ **What to eat** Gallo pinto (mixed rice and beans) is a staple. On the coasts, you can sample wonderful seafood, while the interior has some of the best grass-fed beef in Central America. Be sure to keep an eye out for local specialties, including *nacatamales* (banana-leaf packed with cornmeal and other goodness), *baho* (steamed beef, plantains and yucca), *rondón* (coconut seafood stew served in the Caribbean) and *quesillo* (cheese and onions wrapped in a corn tortilla and topped with sour cream).

➡ **What to drink** Fresh fruit juices are everywhere. Flor de Caña is the national rum, while local beers include Toña and Victoria, both light pilsners.

MANAGUA

POP 2,223,375

Simply put, Managua is a shambles. It is chaotic and broken, poetic and mesmerizing, all at the same time.

And while most travelers are now skipping the city altogether – instead arranging quick airport transfers from nearby Granada – stay a day or two and you will see that big, bad Managua ain't so bad after all, and that this truly is the heartstring that holds the nation's culture and commerce together.

Aside from diving into the whir of a magnificent beehive of honking horns, sprawling markets, garbage and rancor, this low-rise city with improbable trees, remarkable street art and spirited monuments also gives you easy access to nearby lagoons, nature reserves, a smattering of fun beaches like Pochomil and hot springs.

History

A fishing encampment as early as 6000 years ago, Managua has been an important trading center for at least two millennia. When Spanish chronicler Fernández de Oviedo arrived in 1528, he estimated Managua's population at around 40,000; most of these original inhabitants fled to the Sierritas, the small mountains just south, shortly after the Spanish arrived. The small town, without even a hospital or school until the 1750s, didn't really achieve any prominence until 1852, when the seemingly endless civil war between Granada and León was resolved by placing the capital here.

The clever compromise might have worked out better had a geologist been at hand: Managua sits atop a network of fault lines that have shaped its history ever since. The late 1800s were rocked by quakes that destroyed the new capital's infrastructure, with churches and banks crumbling as the ground flowed beneath their feet. In 1931 the epicenter was the stadium – dozens were killed during a big game. In 1968 a single powerful jolt right beneath what's now Metrocentro mall destroyed an entire neighborhood.

And on the evening of December 23, 1972, a series of powerful tremors rocked the city, culminating in a 6.2 quake that killed 11,000 people and destroyed 53,000 homes. The blatant siphoning of international relief funds by President Somoza touched off the Sandinista-led revolution, which was followed by the Contra War, and the city center, including the beautiful old cathedral, was never rebuilt. Rather, it was replaced by a crazy maze of unnamed streets, shacks that turned to shanties that turned to homes and later buildings. There are some efforts to resurrect the old city center – the restoration of the waterfront Malecón is certainly a promising development – but most new construction now happens on the outskirts of the city center.

◉ Sights & Activities

◉ Plaza de la Revolución & Malecón

This quiet collection of pre-earthquake and post-revolutionary monuments, parks, museums and government offices was once the pulsing heart of Managua. Then came the 1972 earthquake, and two decades of war and privation, and the center was all but abandoned. Slowly, it is being resuscitated. At the time of writing, the Malecón (pier) was just re-emerging as a family-friendly destination, complete with new restaurants and activities for kids.

★ **Antigua Catedral**   CATHEDRAL
(Map p438; 14 Av Sureste) The hollow shell of Managua's Old Cathedral remains Managua's most poignant metaphor, shattered by the 1972 earthquake – and, despite promises, never restored. Though still beautiful and serene, attended by stone angels and dappled in golden light, it is empty and off-limits: the cathedral without a heart, in the city without a center.

Plaza de la Revolución   PARK
(Map p438) Inaugurated in 1899 by national hero and original anti-American General José Santos Zelaya, this open plaza has been the scene of countless protests, parades, romances and more. On the northeast of the plaza rests the tomb of Sandinista commander Carlos Fonseca.

Malecón   WATERFRONT
(Map p438) The *malecón* (pier) has been perked up by the newly renovated Puerto Salvador Allende tourist complex at its base. Still, it can be a bit depressing on off days, especially if you're pondering how we could let Lago de Managua (also known as Lake Xolotlán) become one of the most polluted bodies of water in Central America (foreign governments are helping to clean up the

Nicaragua Highlights

1 Isla de Ometepe
(p458) Scrambling to the summits for views to everywhere and beyond on this lush and lovely island.

2 Corn Islands
(p495) Swimming through crystal-clear Caribbean waters.

3 Granada
(p444) Savoring the colonial delights and spirited streets of this colorful city.

4 León (p469)
Finding out why the revolution wasn't televised in the bohemian bars of this buzzing city.

5 Southern Pacific Coast (p464)
Charging the big waves and relaxing in chill surf towns.

6 Reserva Natural Laguna de Apoyo
(p452) Swimming in clear waters, or lazing about in a hammock.

7 Río San Juan
(p503) Boarding a riverboat to explore the abundant birdlife of this picturesque river.

8 Matagalpa
(p488) Discovering the heart of the hardworking highlands in this earthy town.

lake). The area has always drawn local families on weekends.

Puerto Salvador Allende PORT
(Map p438; Malecón; 🚲) Thanks to a recent (and much-needed) overhaul to Managua's previously barren port area, this breezy lakefront complex is now a destination for tourists and locals alike. With around 20 dining venues – ranging from casual food stands to more elegant restaurants – plus playgrounds for children and pathways for strolling, it's a good bet in the afternoon or evening, especially around sunset when the views over the lake are particularly lovely.

👁 Barrio Martha Quezada & Around

Parque Histórico Nacional Loma de Tiscapa PARK
(Map p438) Home to what's easily Managua's most recognizable landmark, Sandino's somber silhouette, this national historic park was once the site of the Casa Presidencial, where Sandino and his men were executed in 1934; what looks like a dilapidated parking structure was for decades one of Nicaragua's most notorious prisons.

You can see Sandino, hastily erected by the departing Frente Sandinista de Liberación Nacional (FSLN; Sandinista National Liberation Front) government after its electoral loss in 1990, from almost anywhere in town; begin your ascent at the Crowne Plaza. You'll pass **Monumento Roosevelt** (Map p438), constructed in 1939, with lovely lake views (today it's a memorial to those killed in the revolution).

The top of Loma de Tiscapa is actually the lip of Volcán Tiscapa's beautiful little crater lake, with incredible views of the city, both cathedrals and Volcán Momotombo, plus **Canopy Tiscapa** (Map p438; ☑ 8872-2555; canopytiscapa@yahoo.com; Lomo de Tiscapa; per person US$17.25; ⊘ 9am-5pm Tue-Sun), a small but fun 1.2km, three-platform, 25-minute tour. Keep in mind that, despite a vigorous clean-up campaign, the lake is polluted with untreated sewage.

National Assembly Pedestrian Walk AREA, PUBLIC ART
(Map p438; Av Central) East of the National Assembly along Av Central is a pedestrian walk with open-air exhibits on Nicaragua's history, featuring everything from historic photos of Sandino to evocative pictures of pre-earthquake Managua. It's a great path to take if you're walking from Barrio Martha Quezada to the lakefront, especially if you're interested in Nicaragua's political and literary histories.

👁 Other Neighborhoods

Huellas de Acahualinca ARCHAEOLOGICAL SITE
(Map p436; ☑ 2266-5774; US$4; ⊘ 9am-4pm) Discovered by miners in 1874, these fossilized tracks record the passage of perhaps 10 people – men, women and children – as well as of birds, raccoons and deer across the muddy shores of Lago de Managua some 6000 years ago. Despite early speculation that they were running from a volcanic eruption, forensics specialists have determined that these folks were in no hurry –

WHERE THE STREETS HAVE NO NAME: NAVIGATING MANAGUA

Like other Nicaraguan cities and towns, Managua has few street signs and only the major roads are named. Large buildings, *rotondas* (traffic circles) and traffic lights serve as de facto points of reference, and locations are described in terms of their direction and distance, usually in *cuadras* (blocks), from these points. Just to complicate matters, many of these references no longer exist, so you may get addresses that begin with something like '*de donde fue Sandy's*' (from where Sandy's used to be...).

In addition, in Managua a special system is used for the cardinal points, whereby *al lago* (to the lake) means 'north' while *arriba* (up) is 'east' and *abajo* (down) is 'west,' the latter expressions deriving from the sun's movement. South is just plain old *sur*. Thus you might hear: '*del antiguo Cine Dorado, una cuadra al lago, dos cuadras arriba*,' meaning from the old Dorado Cinema, one block north, two blocks to the east.

Confused? You get used to it. Places in Managua give the address in Spanish – but we use the cardinal points N (*norte*; north), S (*sur*; south), E (*este*; east) and O (*oeste*; west) – so you can ask locals or just let the cab driver figure it out. Cuadra is abbreviated to 'c' in addresses for listings.

and, interestingly, were fairly tall, between 145cm and 160cm.

Catedral Metropolitana CATHEDRAL
(Map p438; www.catedralmga.blogspot.com; ⊙9am-7pm) Just north of the Metrocentro mall is an unforgettable Managua landmark that's practically new (the doors opened in 1993). It's an architectural marvel that leaves most visitors, well, scratching their heads. It's not a mosque, really: the 63 cupolas (or breasts, or eggs; speculation continues) symbolize Nicaragua's 63 Catholic churches, and also provide structural support during earthquakes – a good thing, since it sits astride a fault line.

🎓 Courses

Viva Spanish School LANGUAGE COURSE
(Map p438; 📱2270-2339; www.vivaspanishschool. com; Metrocentro 5 c E, Del Edificio Banco Produz-camos, 2 c S; lessons per hour US$10) Highly recommended by long-term volunteers and NGO workers, classes here start at US$175 for a 20-hour week. Homestays can be arranged for an additional US$140 per week.

La Academia Nicaragüense de la Danza COURSE
(Map p438; 📱2277-5557; UCA, 50m N, Av Universitaria) Offers a huge range of dance classes (salsa, merengue, reggaetón, folk, ballet, flamenco and bellydancing, to name a few).

Alianza Francesa COURSE
(Map p438; 📱2267-2811; www.alianzafrancesa.org. ni; Planes de Altamira, de la Embajada de México ½ c N) Offers classes in painting, drawing, French, German and Portuguese, along with occasional art exhibits and poetry readings.

✨ Festivals & Events

Carnaval Alegría por la Vida STREET CARNIVAL
(⊙early Mar) The 'Joy for Life' festival is Managua's version of Carnaval, featuring a lively parade of costumed performers, live music, food, dancing, and the crowning of a festival queen. There's a different theme each year.

Day of the Revolution CULTURAL
(⊙ Jul 19) You'll understand why people still love President Daniel Ortega when you see the master work a crowd of 100,000 red-and-black-flag-waving faithful during the Día de la Revolución (Day of the Revolution).

Festival of Santo Domingo de Guzman RELIGIOUS
(⊙Aug 1-10) Managua's *fiestas patronales* (patron saint parties) feature a carnival, sporting events, *hípicos* (horse parades) and a procession of *diablitos,* which takes Santo Domingo to his country shrine at the Sierritas de Managua, followed by music and fireworks.

La Purísima RELIGIOUS
(⊙end Nov–mid-Dec) The Feast of the Immaculate Conception is celebrated throughout Nicaragua, with festivities culminating on December 8. In Managua, the celebration is particularly colorful, with massive altars to the Virgin Mary set up along the blocks of Av Bolivar leading to the lake. After dark, the avenue turns into a huge street party with food stands and live music.

🛏️ Sleeping

Most budget travelers stay in Barrio Martha Quezada, which has about 10 square blocks of fairly strollable streets, and adjacent Bolonia (though note that crime is an issue, especially after dark) – due to easy access to the Tica bus station, the neighborhood is popular with foreigners passing through.

Other options include chain hotels along the Carretera a Masaya and nearby smaller guesthouses on the suburban-feeling side streets; this area is closer to the UCA bus terminal, with frequent connections to León and Granada.

Managua Backpackers Inn HOSTEL $
(Map p438; 📱2267-0006; www.managuahostel. com; Monte de Los Olivos, 1 c N (lago), 1 c O y ½ c N, Casa #56, Carretera a Masaya; dm/d from US$10/32; 🅿️❄️@🛜🏊) In the quiet suburb of Los Robles, this shoestring hostel is minutes away from the Metrocentro mall and endless nightlife and restaurant options. Rooms are basic but breezy, open and comfortable. And all the hostel amenities are here – common room with DVD player, good-sized pool, well-stocked kitchen and plenty of tourist info.

Pandora Hostel HOSTEL $
(Map p438; 📱7524-5303; www.pandorahostel. com; Tica Bus, 1 c S, 1 c E; dm/d US$12/30; ❄️🛜) Clean, friendly and around the corner from the Tica Bus terminal, this brand-new hostel is a great choice for an affordable overnight. There's a bar onsite, and the hostel can arrange an airport shuttle if you ask ahead.

Managua

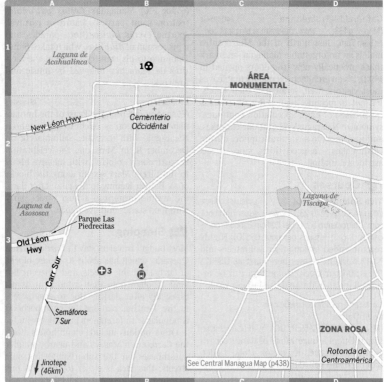

ÁREA MONUMENTAL

Laguna de Acahualinca

New Léon Hwy

Cementerio Occidental

Laguna de Asososca

Parque Las Piedrecitas

Old Léon Hwy

Carr Sur

Semáforos 7 Sur

Jinotepe (46km)

Laguna de Tiscapa

ZONA ROSA

Rotonda de Centroamérica

See Central Managua Map (p438)

Managua

Sights
1 Huellas de Acahualinca B1

Shopping
2 Mercado Roberto Huembes E4

Information
3 Hospital Alemán-Nicaragüense B3

Transport
4 Mercado Israel Lewites (Bóer) B3
5 Mercado Mayoreo H3
6 Mercado Roberto Huembes E4

Hostal Dulce Sueño HOTEL $
(Map p438; 2228-4195; www.hostaldulcesueno. com; Tica Bus, 70m E; s/d from US$12/18; 🖥) This simple guesthouse has spotless, no-frills rooms, and a central patio with a TV and a shared kitchen. It's a few steps from the Tica Bus terminal, but this block is reputedly quite dangerous at night.

Casa Vanegas HOTEL $
(Map p438; 2222-4043; casavanegas1@hot mail.com; Tica Bus, 1 c O; s/d from US$15/22; 🖥) Clean and secure, this friendly family-run spot, just steps from Tica Bus, is convenient if you have an early bus to catch. Casa Vanegas offers decent-sized, unexciting rooms around a small patio plus hammocks, a spacious lounge area, and laundry facilities.

La Bicicleta Hostal HOSTEL $$
(Map p438; 2225-2557; www.labicicletahostal. com; Restaurante La Marsellaise, 2½ c abajo; dm/d US$18/42; 🖥🖥) At this cool and sustainably built new hostel, dorms and guest rooms are named after bicycles – try the Tándem for two people, or the Tricíclo if you're traveling in a group of three. There's a lovely garden area with hammocks for relaxing, plus free wi-fi and an open kitchen for guest use.

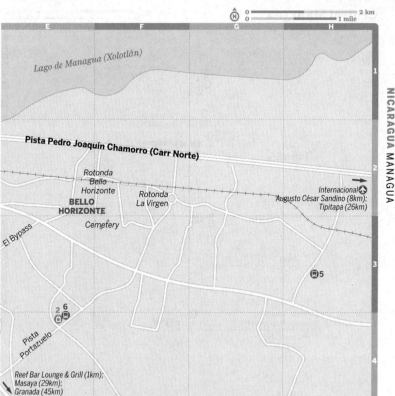

0   2 km
0   1 mile

Lago de Managua (Xolotlán)

Pista Pedro Joaquín Chamorro (Carr Norte)

Rotonda
Bello
Horizonte
Rotonda
La Virgen

BELLO
HORIZONTE

Cemetery

El Bypass

Internacional
Augusto César Sandino (8km);
Tipitapa (26km)

5

2 6

Pista
Portazuelo

Reef Bar Lounge & Grill (1km);
Masaya (29km);
Granada (45km)

Hotel Brandt's   HOTEL $$

(Map p438; ☑ 2277-1884; www.hotelbrandt.com; Los Robles de San Juan, Zona Hippos, 1 c S, 1 c O; r US$84; ❋ ☎) This reasonably priced hotel in the relatively upscale Los Robles neighborhood has clean, modern, airy rooms that sleep up to four people. It's not a charming B&B, but it's a reliable favorite for business travelers passing through, and the buffet breakfast is above par. It's tucked away a few blocks behind the Metrocentro shopping mall.

🍴 Eating

With an abundance of cheap eateries catering to office workers, Barrio Martha Quezada is a great place to get a taste for Nicaraguan cuisine. Most of Managua's popular restaurants are located around Carretera a Masaya to the south of the Metrocentro mall.

Doña Pilar   NICARAGUAN $

(Map p438; Tica Bus, 1 c O, ½ c N; dishes US$3-6; ☺6-9pm Mon-Sat) Doña Pilar's been here for years, and this popular evening *fritanga* (sidewalk grill) is a neighborhood institution, both for its juicy, crispy BBQ chicken and the range of ever-so-slightly greasy tacos and enchiladas. It's a great introduction to typical Nicaraguan cuisine, with huge side servings of *gallo pinto* (rice and beans), chopped pickled cabbage and plantain chips.

Ananda   VEGETARIAN $

(Map p438; frente Estatua de Montoya; mains US$2-5; ☺8am-3pm Mon-Sat; ☑) Enjoy freshly prepared vegetarian plates and a wide range of *licuados* (fruit and veggie juices and smoothies) on this spacious patio overlooking lush gardens. There's a lunch buffet from 11am to 3pm.

Central Managua

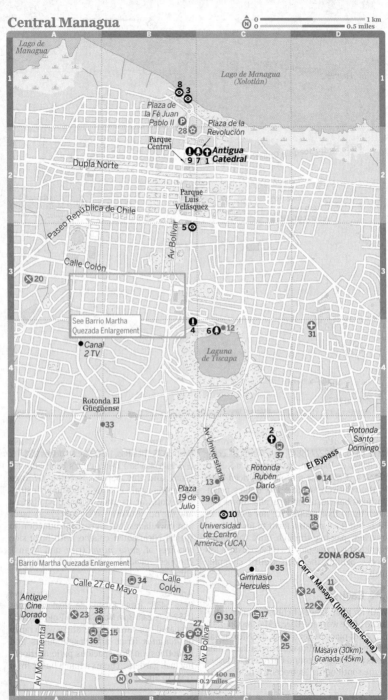

Lago de Managua

Lago de Managua (Xolotlán)

Plaza de la Fé Juan Pablo II

Plaza de la Revolución

Parque Central

Antigua Catedral

Dupla Norte

Parque Luis Velásquez

Paseo República de Chile

Av Bolívar

Calle Colón

See Barrio Martha Quezada Enlargement

Canal 2 TV

Laguna de Tiscapa

Rotonda El Güegüense

Av Universitaria

Rotonda Santo Domingo

Rotonda Rubén Darío

El Bypass

Plaza 19 de Julio

Universidad de Centro América (UCA)

ZONA ROSA

Barrio Martha Quezada Enlargement

Calle 27 de Mayo

Calle Colón

Antigue Cine Dorado

Gimnasio Hercules

Carr a Masaya (Interamericana)

Av Monumenta

Av Bolívar

Masaya (30km); Granada (45km)

Central Managua

◎ **Top Sights**
1 Antigua Catedral.....................................C2

◎ **Sights**
2 Catedral Metropolitana........................C5
3 Malecón...B1
4 Monumento Roosevelt.........................B4
5 National Assembly
  Pedestrian Walk..................................B3
6 Parque Histórico Nacional
  Loma de Tiscapa..................................C4
7 Plaza de la Revolución..........................C2
8 Puerto Salvador Allende......................B1
9 Tomb of Carlos Fonseca.......................B2
10 UCA..C6

◎ **Activities, Courses & Tours**
11 Alianza Francesa...................................D6
12 Canopy Tiscapa C4
13 La Academia Nicaragüense
  de la Danza C5
14 Viva Spanish School.............................D5

◎ **Sleeping**
15 Casa Vanegas...B7
  Hostal Dulce Sueño......................(see 15)
16 Hotel Brandt's D5
17 La Bicicleta Hostal................................C7
18 Managua Backpackers Inn...................D6
19 Pandora Hostel B7

◎ **Eating**
20 Ananda..A3
21 Cafetín Mirna A7
22 Cocina Doña Haydee D6
23 Doña Pilar..A7
24 La Terraza Peruana...............................D6
25 Pan e Vino...C7

◎ **Drinking & Nightlife**
26 El Grillito B7

◎ **Entertainment**
27 La Casa de los Mejía Godoy.................B7
28 Teatro Nacional Rubén
  Darío...B2

◎ **Shopping**
29 Librería Hispamer.................................C5
30 Plaza Inter C7

◎ **Information**
31 Hospital Bautista...................................D4
32 Intur Central...B7

◎ **Transport**
33 American Airlines...................................A5
34 Central Line..B6
35 Delta Airlines..C6
36 Tica Bus..A7
37 Transnica...C5
38 Transporte del Sol.................................A7
39 UCA Minivans..C5

Cafetín Mirna   NICARAGUAN $
(Map p438; Tica Bus, 1 c O, 1 c S; mains US$2-6; ☺8am-5pm Mon-Sat) Come here for a big breakfast with fluffy pancakes, fabulous fresh juices and a good lunch buffet, too – it's a local tradition.

Cocina Doña Haydee   NICARAGUAN $$
(Map p438; www.lacocina.com.ni; Carretera a Masaya Km 4.5; mains US$5-10; ☺breakfast, lunch & dinner) This traditional Nicaraguan eatery does classic dishes, well presented and carefully prepared, from *gallo pinto* and *guiso de chilote* (cheese soup with baby corn) to steak with all the trimmings. There are takeaway locations in the food court at Plaza Inter and Metrocentro shopping malls, too.

La Terraza Peruana   PERUVIAN $$
(Map p438; www.aterrazaperuana.com; de la Pasteleria Sampson, 100m al lago; mains US$5-12; ☺noon-11pm Tue-Sun) A casual but refined Peruvian restaurant set on a cool front balcony overlooking a leafy side street, La Terraza has a huge menu that takes you from coastal to high Andean cuisine. With advance notice you can order such Peruvian classics as *cuy* (roasted guinea pig). Don't miss a cocktail from the pisco list.

Pan e Vino   ITALIAN $$
(Map p438; ☎2278-4442; www.paneevino.online.com.ni; Enitel Villa Fontana, 200m N; mains US$7-14; ☺noon-3pm & 6-11pm Mon-Sat) Getting the thumbs up from Italian expats, this stylish yet unpretentious place does good-sized pasta plates and crunchy-crusted pizzas. It has a small but decent selection of Italian, Spanish and Chilean wines to linger over. Check the website: staff will happily deliver food to your hotel.

🍷 Drinking & Nightlife

There are bars all over town. Some of the better ones can be found in Barrio Martha Quezada, around the Metrocentro mall and at the Rotonda Bello Horizonte. Take a cab home!

El Grillito   BAR
(Map p438; Intur, ½ c N; ☺noon-late) There are a few little outdoor bars like this in the

area, but this one consistently gets a good crowd. A range of snacks and more substantial meals (mains US$3 to US$6) are on the menu and the music volume is conversation-friendly. There's a second location a block south.

Reef Bar Lounge & Grill LOUNGE
(Galeria Santo Domingo; ⊘6pm-3am Wed-Sat) This popular bar and lounge in the emerging *zona viva*, the nightlife zone behind the Santo Domingo mall, is a favorite pre-dance spot for scenesters.

☆ Entertainment

There are dozens of venues around town that occasionally have live music, folkloric dance, alternative theater, poetry readings and other cultural offerings. Thursday editions of *La Prensa* and *El Nuevo Diario* have good listings. You can also take a walk through the UCA (Universidad Centro America; Map p438; www.uca.edu.ni; Rotonda Rubén Darío, 500m O) to see what's on.

La Casa de los Mejía Godoy LIVE MUSIC
(Map p438; ☑2222-6110; www.losmejiagodoy. com; frente Hotel Crowne Plaza; cover charge from US$10) Living legends Carlos and Luis Enrique Mejía Godoy, whose folk-music explorations into the heart of Nicaraguan culture have become church hymns and revolutionary standards since they first started laying down riffs in the 1960s, have moved from their original intimate venue to larger premises, complete with a restaurant and bar (open 8am to 4:30pm Monday to Tuesday, and to 1am Wednesday to Saturday). Make reservations if you're planning on seeing the Godoy Brothers play.

Teatro Nacional Rubén Darío THEATER
(Map p438; ☑2266-3630; www.tnrubendario.gob. ni; Área Monumental) One of the few Managua buildings to survive the 1972 earthquake, this groovy theater often has big-name international offerings on the main stage. It's worth trying to catch some experimental jazz or performance art in the smaller Sala Experimental Pilar Aguirre.

🛍 Shopping

Mercado Roberto Huembes HANDICRAFTS
(Map p436) This is more than just the southbound bus terminal: it has the best selection of souvenirs in Managua, from all over the country. It's also one of the most dangerous

places to wander around, so see if you can get a local guide or friend to take you.

Librería Hispamer BOOKS
(Map p438; www.hispamer.com.ni; UCA, 1 c E, 1 c N; ⊘9am-7pm Mon-Fri, to 5pm Sat) This bookstore on the edge of the UCA campus has a good selection of Nicaraguan and Latin American literature, history and poetry.

Plaza Inter MALL
(Map p438; www.plazaintermall.com.ni; ⊘11am-9pm) Adjacent to Barrio Martha Quezada, it's convenient, with a cinema (with subtitled movies), lots of discount shops, a couple of department stores and a solid food court that's bustling with Nicaraguan families at mealtimes.

🛈 Orientation

Managua's spread-out collection of barrios (neighborhoods) sits on the southern shore of Lago de Managua (Xolotlán). The former center on the lakeshore is now largely derelict, having been left vacant after the 1972 quake, but has several visitor attractions. South of here, Volcán Tiscapa and its crater lake is the city's main landmark. To its west is the pyramidal Hotel Crowne Plaza and the Barrio Martha Quezada, home of many of the city's budget accommodations, while to the south is a thriving commercial zone running along the city's main thoroughfare, Carretera a Masaya.

Managua's central market, Mercado Roberto Huembes, lies 2km southeast of Metrocentro; other major markets (and adjacent bus terminals) are at the western (Bóer), northern (Oriental, confusingly) and eastern (Mayoreo) ends of town.

🛈 Information

DANGERS & ANNOYANCES

Managua has a bad reputation for being a dangerous city, and with fairly good reason. But by using common sense and general caution, you can avoid problems.

➡ Don't flash expensive items. Keep your phone in your pocket or bag.

➡ Look at the map before venturing out on a walk.

➡ Make ATM transactions during daylight hours.

➡ Ask your hotel or hostel to call you a taxi instead of hailing one in the street.

➡ Carry only as much money as you'll need for the day.

➡ If you find yourself surrounded by abandoned houses and businesses, turn around and go back the way you came.

EMERGENCY

Ambulance (Cruz Roja; ☎128)
Fire (emergency ☎115; ☎2222-6406)
Police (emergency ☎118; ☎2249-5714)

INTERNET ACCESS

Internet access is fast and plentiful, averaging US$1 per minute at cafes all over town. Wi-fi can be found in most hotels and, increasingly, at cafes and restaurants.

MEDICAL SERVICES

Managua has scores of pharmacies – some open 24 hours (just knock) – and the nation's best hospitals.

Hospital Alemán-Nicaragüense (Map p436; ☎2249-3368; Carretera Norte, Km 6) Has some German-speaking staff and modern equipment.

Hospital Bautista (Map p438; ☎2264-9020; www.hospitalbautistanicaragua.com; Casa Ricardo Morales Avíles, 2c S, 1½ c E, Barrio Largaespada) Your best bet, with some English-speaking staff.

NATIONAL BUS SERVICES FROM MANAGUA

DESTINATION	COST (US$)	DURATION	DEPARTURES	FREQUENCY	LEAVES FROM
Boaco	2.20	3hr	4am-6:30pm	every 15min	Mayoreo
Carazo (serving Diriamba & Jinotepe)	1.40	1hr	4:30am-6:20pm	every 20min	Bóer
Chinandega/El Viejo	2.70	3hr	5am-6pm	every 30min	Bóer
Chinandega minibus	3	2hr	4am-6pm	when full	Bóer
Estelí	3	2hr	5:45am-5:45pm	hourly	Mayoreo
Granada	0.75	1hr	4am-6pm	every 15min	Huembes
Granada minibus	1.25	1hr	6am-8pm	when full	UCA
Jinotega	3.50	4hr	4am-5:30pm	hourly	Mayoreo
Jinotepe minibus	1.15	1hr	5am-8pm	when full	UCA
Juigalpa	2	4hr	3:15am-10pm	every 20min	Mayoreo
La Paz Centro	1.60	1½hr	6:15am-8pm	every 30min	Bóer
León expreso (via New Hwy & La Paz Centro)	1.85	1½hr	10am-6:30pm	every 2hr	Bóer
León ordinario (via Old Hwy)	1.50	2hr	5am-7pm	every 20min	Bóer
León minibus	2.75	1½hr	4am-6pm	when full	Bóer
León minibus	2.75	1½hr	5am-9:15pm	when full	UCA
Masatepe minibus	1.10	1hr	6:30am-6:30pm	every 20min	Huembes
Masaya	0.50	1hr	5:30am-9pm	every 30min	Huembes
Masaya minibus	0.90	½hr	6am-9pm	when full	UCA
Matagalpa	2.25	2¾hr	3am-6pm	hourly	Mayoreo
Mateare	0.30	40min	5:50am-6:30pm	every 2hr	Bóer
Naindame	1	1½hr	11am-3:30pm	every 20min	Huembes
Ocotal	4.25	3½hr	5am-5pm	hourly	Mayoreo
Pochomil/Masachapa	1.30-1.60	2hr	6am-7pm	every 20min	Bóer
Río Blanco	5	4hr	9:15am-12:15pm	hourly	Mayoreo
Rivas expreso	3.25	1½hr	4am-6pm	every 30min	Huembes
Rivas ordinario	2	2hr	4am-6pm	every 30min	Huembes
San Carlos	7.50	9hr	5am-6pm	6 daily	Mayoreo
San Juan del Sur	3.25	2½hr	5am-6pm	2 daily	Huembes
San Marcos minibus	1	1hr	4am-6pm	when full	Huembes
Somoto	4	4hr	5am-6pm	8 daily	Mayoreo
Ticuantepe minibus	0.40	40min	4am-6pm	when full	Huembes

Hospital Metropolitano Vivian Pellas (☑ 2255-6900; www.metropolitano.com.ni; Carretera a Masaya Km 9.75) State-of-the-art facility.

MONEY

Managua has scores of banks and ATMs, most on the Visa/Plus system. BAC, with machines at Metrocentro mall, Managua International Airport and Plaza España, accepts MasterCard/Cirrus debit cards and gives US dollars and córdobas. Any bank can change US dollars.

TELEPHONE

You can purchase a chip to make your cell phone function on local networks, or make phone calls from your hotel. Call centers and internet cafes are also fairly plentiful downtown.

TOURIST INFORMATION

Intur Central (Nicaraguan Institute of Tourism; Map p438; ☑ 2254-5191; www.visitanicaragua.com/ingles; Crowne Plaza, 1 c S, 1 c O; ☉ 8am-5pm Mon-Fri) The flagship office of Nicaragua's official tourist-info organization has heaps of flyers. There's another office in the international terminal at the airport.

Marena Central (Ministry of the Environment & Natural Resources; ☑ 2263-2830; www.marena.gob.ni; Carretera Norte Km 12.5) Bring ID to the inconveniently located headquarters (out past the airport) to access maps, flyers and management plans for most of Nicaragua's 82 protected areas.

❶ Getting There & Away

AIR

Managua International Airport (Augusto C Sandino; MGA; www.eaai.com.ni; Carretera Norte, Km 13) is a small, manageable airport located about 30 to 45 minutes from most hotels. **Intur** (airport; ☉ 8am-10pm) has an office inside the international terminal, next to the luggage belt in the arrivals area, where English-speaking staff can recommend hotels, confirm flights and share flyers.

The smaller, more chaotic domestic terminal is adjacent to the main building. The following airlines fly from Managua:

American Airlines (Map p438; ☑ 2255-9095; www.aa.com; Plaza España, 3 c S) Daily flights to Miami.

Delta Airlines (Map p438; ☑ 2254-8130; www.delta.com; Seminole Plaza, 3½ c S) Daily flights to Atlanta.

La Costeña (☑ 2263-2142; www.lacostena.com.ni; Managua International Airport) The domestic carrier has regular service to Bluefields, the Corn Islands, Las Minas, Puerto Cabezas and Waspán.

BUS

Managua is the main transportation hub for the country, with several major national bus and van terminals, plus a handful of international bus lines (most grouped in Barrio Martha Quezada).

International Buses

Central Line (Map p438; ☑ 2254-5431; www.transportescentralline.com; Calle 27 de Mayo, 4½ c O, Esso) offers one daily bus to San José, Costa Rica (US$29, eight hours), with stops in Granada and Rivas.

Tica Bus (Map p438; ☑ 8739-5505; www.ticabus.com) is located in a terminal in the heart of Barrio Martha Quezada.

➡ Costa Rica (US$29 to US$46, 10 hours, four daily) Goes to San José.

➡ Guatemala (US$63 to US$80, 30 hours, two daily) To Guatemala City.

➡ Honduras (US$25, seven hours, one daily) To Tegucigalpa.

➡ Panama City (US$74 to US$110, 34 hours, six daily) To Panama City via San José.

➡ San Salvador (US$40 to US$57, 11 hours, two daily)

Transnica (Map p438; ☑ 2270-3133; www.transnica.com) has offices over on the other side of the *laguna*.

➡ Costa Rica (US$29, nine hours, four daily) To San José. There's a luxury bus (US$38) that leaves daily at 1pm.

➡ Honduras (US$30, 10 hours, one daily) For Tegucigalpa.

Transporte del Sol (Map p438; ☑ 2422-5000; www.busesdelsol.com) has two daily buses leaving for San Salvador (US$50) and two for Guatemala City (US$78).

National Buses & Minivans

Buses leave from three main places: Mercado Roberto Huembes for Granada, Masaya and southwest Nicaragua; Mercado Israel Lewites, commonly known as Bóer, for León and the northern Pacific; and Mercado Mayoreo for the Caribbean coast and the northern highlands. Some also leave from the Mercado Oriental, mainly to rural destinations not covered here.

It's faster, more comfortable and a bit more expensive to take minivans from UCA (pronounced 'ooka') or *expreso* (express) versus *ordinario* (regular) services.

Shuttle Buses

With frequent, inexpensive public minibuses running to León, Granada and other popular destinations, Managua's shuttle-bus scene is not huge. The biggest draws here are safety and the direct airport departure, meaning you don't have to cab into town to catch an onward bus. **Paxeos** (☑ 2552-8291; www.paxeos.com) serves Granada (US$40), León (US$70) and many other destinations (prices quoted are for up to three people). **Adelante Express** (☑ 8850-6070; www.adelanteexpress.com) offers similar services.

Around Managua

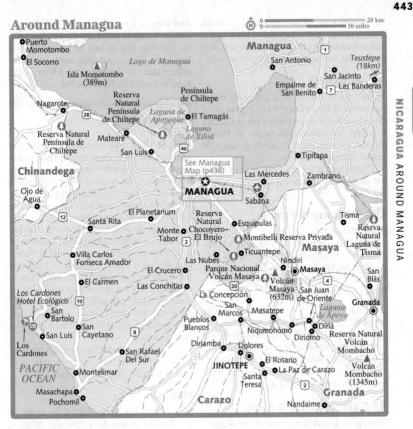

Getting Around

TO/FROM THE AIRPORT

The airport is 11km from town and has its special, more expensive taxis (US$20 to US$25 to most destinations in Managua), which are private – unlike many taxis in Managua, they don't stop to pick up additional passengers along the route. You might also arrange pick-up with your hotel for a more competitive price.

BUS

Local buses are frequent and crowded. They're also known for their professional pickpockets, but stay alert and you'll be fine. Routes run every 10 minutes from 4:45am to 6pm, then every 15 minutes until 10pm. Buses do not generally stop en route – look for the nearest bus shelter. The fare is US$0.25.

CAR & MOTORCYCLE

Driving in Managua is not recommended at night – even if you have a rental car, consider getting a taxi, and make sure your car is in a guarded lot. Night drivers should keep their windows rolled up and stay alert.

TAXI

→ Most taxis in Managua are *colectivos*, which pick up passengers as they go. There are also more expensive private taxis based at the airport, shopping malls, Mercado Roberto Huembes and other places. These are safer, but regular taxis also always congregate close by.

→ Licensed taxis have red plates and the driver's ID above the dash; if yours doesn't, you're in a pirate taxi. This is probably OK, but don't go to the ATM, and beware of scams no matter what kind of taxi you're in. Managua taxis are unmetered and notorious for ripping off tourists. Always negotiate the fare before getting in.

→ At night, take only licensed taxis – there has been an increase in reports of taxi drivers robbing passengers after dark.

Around Managua

Masachapa & Pochomil

The twin towns of Masachapa and Pochomil are so close together that they might as well be one. You arrive in Masachapa, a small fishing village with a handful of bars, hotels and restaurants on the beach. Some will rent surfboards and arrange boating excursions.

🏃 Activities

There's great surfing – a left-point break just north of Montelimar, and a hollow right reef break to the south; beach-break Quizala is closer to Masachapa. South of Pochomil there are scores of smallish, predictable peaks, perfect to learn on.

There's a surprisingly clean river between Masachapa and Pochomil that makes for a fun dip.

🛏 Sleeping & Eating

Hotel Altamar HOTEL $$
(📞 8692-7971; Centro Turístico Pochomil, terminal de buses, 1 c E; d US$45; 🅿️ ❄️) One of the best deals in Pochomil, Altamar has good ocean views and small, spotless rooms. There's a decent restaurant onsite, too.

Casa del Titito HOTEL $$
(📞 8484-7724; www.casadeltitito.com; San Rafael del Sur, Pochomil; d US$60; 📶 ❄️) Right on the beach and featuring an outdoor pool, this easygoing hotel is a good midrange pick with a complimentary Nicaraguan breakfast. French, English, and Spanish are spoken.

❶ Getting There & Away

Buses arrive first at Masachapa – if you're planning on staying here, get off at the *empalme* (T intersection).

Buses run from Pochomil and Masachapa to Managua's Mercado Israel Lewites (US$1.30 to US$1.60, two hours) roughly every 30 minutes from 8am to 6pm.

GRANADA & THE MASAYA REGION

This geographically rich area boasts a number of Nicaragua's most vaunted attractions, including the spellbinding colonial town of Granada and the handicraft center of Masaya. The area is also rich in biodiversity. Wildlife abounds on the flanks of Volcán Mombacho, and Parque Nacional Volcán Masaya is one of the country's most visibly active craters. Lush tropical forest surrounds the banks of the crystalline Laguna de Apoyo, and Las Isletas on Lago de Nicaragua make for another fine swim setting.

Just west of Granada, the Pueblos Blancos (White Villages) stand amid a highland coffee-growing region rich in pre-Columbian traditions. These charming towns are an excellent place to observe some of Nicaragua's most beautiful craftwork in the making.

Granada
POP 123,000

Granada drips with photogenic elegance, a picture postcard at every turn. It's no wonder many travelers use the city as a base, spending at least a day bopping along cobblestone roads from church to church in the city center, then venturing out into the countryside for trips to nearby attractions.

Just out of town, half-day adventures take you to an evocative archipelago waterworld at Las Isletas and fun beaches at the Peninsula de Asese. Volcán Mombacho has walking trails and a butterfly sanctuary, not to mention a few hot springs dotted around its foothills. The Laguna de Apoyo is another must-see: its clear turquoise waters and laid-back waterfront lodges offer a splendid natural respite.

Culturally curious travelers might consider a trip to community-tourism operations in nearby villages such as Nicaragua Libre.

History

Nicknamed 'the Great Sultan,' in honor of its Moorish namesake across the Atlantic, Granada was founded in 1524 by Francisco Fernández de Córdoba, and is one of the oldest cities in the New World. It was constructed as a showcase city, the first chance that the Spanish had to prove they had more to offer than bizarre religions and advanced military technology. The city still retains an almost regal beauty, each thick-walled architectural masterpiece faithfully resurrected to original specifications after every trial and tribulation.

A trade center almost from its inception, Granada's position on the Lago de Nicaragua became even more important when the Spanish realized that the Río San Juan was navigable from the lake to the sea. This made Granada rich – and vulnerable. Between 1665 and 1670, pirates sacked the city three times.

Undaunted, Granada rebuilt and grew richer and more powerful, a conservative cornerstone of the Central American economy. After independence from Spain, the city challenged the colonial capital and longtime Liberal bastion León for leadership of the new nation.

Tensions erupted into full-blown civil war in the 1850s, when desperate León contracted the services of American mercenary William Walker and his band of 'filibusterers.' Walker defeated Granada, declared himself president and launched a conquest of Central America – and failed. Walker was forced into a retreat after a series of embarrassing defeats, and as he fell back to his old capital city, he set it afire and left in its ashes the infamous placard: 'Here was Granada.'

The city rebuilt – again. And while its power has waned, its importance as a tourist center and quick escape from bustling Managua keeps the city of Granada vibrant.

◉ Sights

Convento y Museo San Francisco   CHURCH
(☑2552-5535; Costado Norte de Plaza de Leones, 1 c E; US$2; ◷8am-4pm Mon-Fri, 9am-4pm Sat & Sun) One of the oldest churches in Central America and the most striking building in Granada, Iglesia San Francisco boasts a robin's egg-blue birthday-cake facade and houses both an important convent and one of the best museums in the region. Originally constructed in 1585, it was subsequently burned to the ground by pirates and later William Walker, rebuilt in 1868 and restored in 1989.

Casa de los Leones & Fundación Casa de los Tres Mundos   BUILDING
(Parque Central, 50m N; ◷8am-7pm Mon-Fri, to 6pm Sat & Sun) Founded in 1986 by Ernesto Cardenal, the Fundación Casa de los Tres Mundos moved to elegant 1720 Casa de los Leones in 1992. At the entrance, a board lists special events: poetry readings, classical ballet, folkloric dance and free movies. During regular business hours, your entrance fee buys you a look at a beautiful mansion and a few art displays.

Iglesia La Merced   CHURCH
(Calle Real & Avenida 14 de Septiembre; bell tower US$1; ◷11am-6pm) Perhaps the most beautiful church in the city, this landmark was built in 1534. Most come here for the spectacular views from the bell tower – especially picturesque at sunset.

Originally completed in 1539, it was razed by pirates in 1655 and rebuilt with its current baroque facade between 1781 and 1783. Damaged by William Walker's forces in 1854, it was restored with the current elabo-

rate interior in 1862. Today Catholics come here to see an important image of the Virgen de Fatima.

Catedral de Granada   CATHEDRAL
(Parque Colón; ◷hours vary) The Cathedral of Granada, on the east side of the plaza, was originally built in 1583 but has been destroyed countless times since. This most recent version, built in 1915, has four chapels; a dozen stained-glass panels are set into the dome.

★Museo de Chocolate   MUSEUM
(☑2552-4678; www.chocomuseo.com; Calle Atravesada, across from Bancentro; chocolate workshop adult/child US$21/12; ◷7am-6:30pm; ▣) **FREE** Granada's new chocolate museum is excellent if you're traveling with children: the 'beans to bar' chocolate workshop, where participants learn to roast and grind cocoa beans, and mold their very own Nicaraguan chocolate bar, is hands-on fun for all ages. The museum is located at the **Mansión de Chocolate hotel** (www.mansiondechocolate.com; d from US$104; ▣▣▣), which also has a chocolate-oriented spa and a popular buffet breakfast (US$6), plus a great swimming pool you can use for an extra US$5.

🎓 Courses

Granada is a popular spot for learning Spanish and there are many reputable schools and private teachers.

Casa Xalteva   LANGUAGE COURSE
(☑2552-2993; www.casaxalteva.org; Calle Real Xalteva, Iglesia Xalteva, 25m N; 1 week from US$160; ◷8am-5pm Mon-Fri) Next to the church of the same name, Casa Xalteva also runs a program providing breakfast and education for street kids.

Alianza Francesa de Granada   LANGUAGE COURSE
(www.alianzafrancesagranada.org; Calle El Arsenal s/n; prices vary; ◷9am-9:30pm Mon-Fri) French and Spanish language courses, plus French-inspired cultural events.

👣 Tours

For a classic Granada tour, take a **horse-drawn carriage** (rides 30min/1hr US$5/10) from Parque Central for an hour-long whirl past churches, the cemetery, the *malecón* (waterfront promenade) and more with a Spanish-speaking guide. The guide will wait while you take the other classic Granada trip: a boat ride through Las Isletas.

Granada

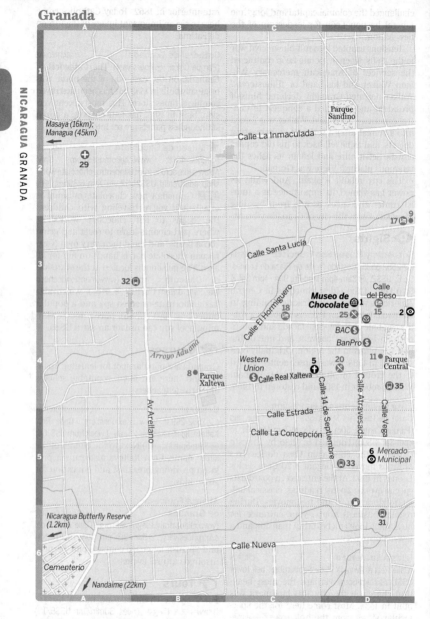

Masaya (16km);
Managua (45km)

Parque
Sandino

Calle La Inmaculada

29

Calle Santa Lucía

32

17 9

Calle El Hormiguero

Calle
del Beso

*Museo de
Chocolate* 1

18

25   15   2

BAC

BanPro

Arroyo Aduana

Western
Union

11 Parque
Central

8 Parque
Xalteva

5

Calle Real Xalteva

20

35

Calle Estrada

Calle La Concepción

Av Arellano

Calle 14 de Septiembre

Calle Atravesada

Calle Vega

6 Mercado
Municipal

Nicaragua Butterfly Reserve
(1.2km)

33

Calle Nueva

31

Cementerio

Nandaime (22km)

Corazón Trips TOUR
(☎ 2552-8852; www.hotelconcorazon.com; Calle
Santa Lucia 141) Located inside the Hotel Con
Corazón, this nonprofit tour operator offers
well-organized trips including bike tours,
cooking classes and trips to Mombacho.

Leo Tours Comunitarios TOUR
(☎ 8422-7905; leotoursgranada@gmail.com; Calla
la Calzada, Parque Central, 1½ c E; ⏰ 8am-9pm)
Enthusiastic locally owned business that offers all the usual options – Las Isletas boat
tours (US$15), Mombacho (US$29) and a

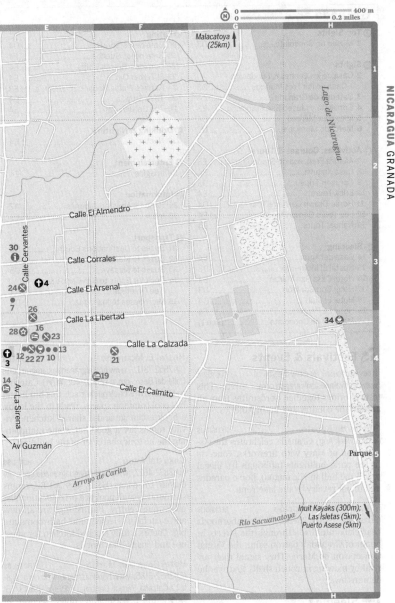

0 ———————————— 400 m
0 ———————————— 0.2 miles

Malacatoya
(25km) ↑

Lago de Nicaragua

Calle El Almendro

Calle Cervantes

30 ❶

24 ✕

7 ●

Calle Corrales

❶ **4**

Calle El Arsenal

26 ✕

Calle La Libertad

28 ✿   **16** ✕ **23**
           📷

Calle La Calzada

3 ❶   **12 22 27 10** ● ● **13**

21 ✕

34 ☕

14 🍴

Av La Sirena

19 🛍

Calle El Caimito

Av Guzmán

Parque

Arroyo de Carita

Río Sacuanatoya

Inuit Kayaks (300m);
Las Isletas (5km);
Puerto Asese (5km)

---

full-day trip to Masaya (US$39) – as well as some interesting visits to local communities.

Nahual Tours TOUR
(☎ 2552-3779; www.nahualtours.com; Calle La Calzada, Parque Central 1 c E) Runs daily shuttles to and from the Monkey Hut at Laguna de Apoyo (one way/round-trip US$5/10), as well as a standard range of tours and activities.

Inuit Kayaks KAYAKING
(☎ 2552-6695; Centro Turístico; per person US$25-35) Inuit Kayaks runs several guided tours around Las Isletas.

Granada

⊙ Top Sights
1 Museo de Chocolate.............................. D3

⊙ Sights
2 Casa de los Leones & Fundación
   Casa de los Tres Mundos D3
3 Catedral de Granada E4
4 Convento y Museo San Francisco........E3
5 Iglesia La Merced.................................C4
6 Mercado Municipal...............................D5

⊕ Activities, Courses & Tours
7 Alianza Francesa de Granada E3
8 Casa Xalteva...B4
9 Corazón Trips.......................................D3
10 Erick Tours...E4
11 Horse-Drawn Carriage Tour.................D4
12 Leo Tours Comunitarios.......................E4
13 Nahual Tours E4

⊜ Sleeping
14 Casa del Agua.......................................E4
15 Hostal El Momento D3
16 Hotel Casa San Martín E4
17 Hotel Con Corazón D3
18 Hotel El Club C4
19 Hotel La Pérgola...................................F4
   Mansión de Chocolate .... (see 1)

⊗ Eating
20 Café de las Sonrisas.............................D4
21 Cafe de los Sueños...............................F4
22 Comidas Típicas y Más.........................E4
23 El Tercer Ojo...E4
24 Kathy's Waffle House............................E3
25 Taco Stop..D4
26 The Garden Café...................................E4

⊖ Drinking & Nightlife
27 Nectar E4

⊗ Entertainment
28 Imagine...E4

ⓘ Information
29 Hospital Amistad Japonés....................A2
30 Intur...E3

ⓘ Transport
31 Buses to Destinations South D6
32 Buses to Managua................................B3
33 Buses to Masaya D5
34 Dock for Boats to San Carlos & Isla
   de Ometepe......................................H4
35 Microbuses to Managua.......................D4

✷ Festivals & Events

International Poetry Festival CULTURAL
(www.festivalpoesianicaragua.com; ⊙Feb) This festival brings together wordsmiths from all around the country and Latin America.

Fiestas de Agosto RELIGIOUS
(⊙3rd week Aug) Granada celebrates the Assumption of Mary with fireworks, concerts in the park, bullfights (although it's illegal to kill the bull in Nicaragua), horse parades and major revelry by the lakefront.

Inmaculada Concepción RELIGIOUS
(Purísimas; ⊙Nov 28–Dec 7) Neighborhoods bear elaborate floats through the streets in honor of Granada's patron saint, the Virgen Concepción de María. They signal their arrival by blowing in conch shells to drive the demons away.

⊨ Sleeping

There's a huge range of sleeping options in Granada, from budget-friendly hostels and guesthouses to some of the nicest hotels in this part of Nicaragua.

Hostal El Momento HOSTEL $
(☑2552-7811; www.hostelgranadanicaragua.com; Calle del Beso; dm/d US$10/40; @🛜) Catering to the mature backpacker set, this hip hostel has cool common spaces, iPads in the lobby, a book exchange and a shared kitchen. Private rooms are a good bet, some maintaining the historic character of the building.

Casa del Agua HOTEL $$
(☑8872-4627; www.casadelaguagranada.com; Av Guzmán s/n; d from US$38; @🛜▨) Big rooms surround a small pool in a prize location just off Parque Central. Furnishings are all new and tastefully selected, and bathrooms are big. There's a fully stocked kitchen for guest use and onsite bike rentals.

Hotel Casa San Martín HOTEL $$
(☑2552-6185; www.hotelcasasanmartin.com; Calle La Calzada, Parque Central, 1 c E; s/d US$43/55; ❄🛜) In a reasonably quiet section of Granada's popular pedestrian promenade, this guesthouse has understated charm. Rooms vary, but each is special – either for spaciousness, views, furnishings or atmosphere – making this a solid midrange bet.

Hotel El Club
HOTEL $$

(2552-4245; www.elclub-nicaragua.com; Calle Libertad de la Piedra Bocona, 1 c O; d from US$42; ✳🛜❄) This corner hotel, located in a pretty colonial building, can be noisy at night. But it's decent value, with a small pool and a nice cocktail bar.

Hotel La Pérgola
HOTEL $$

(2552-4221; www.lapergola.com.ni; Calle El Caimito, alcaldía, 3 c E; r from US$50; P✳🛜) This cozy hotel with its little center courtyard, spacious rooms and big, firm beds is a decent bet. Note: there's no hot water.

Hotel Con Corazón
HOTEL $$$

(2552-8852; www.hotelconcorazon.com; Calle Cervantes, Parque Central, 3 c N; s/d/tr/q US$62/73/94/121; ✳@🛜❄) 🍴 An elegant nonprofit hotel that directs earnings to the development of local educational programs.

The rooms are simple and pleasing, spacious enough without being luxurious. The building itself blends modern and traditional styles to perfection, with much of the decoration coming from recycled materials made by local craftspeople. Ask about volunteer ops here.

It has salsa classes on Monday nights that are open to the public.

🍴 Eating

Granada is full of restaurants serving a wide variety of cuisines, and new options are opening all the time. The city has excellent street food too. Look for it around Parque Central and Mercado Municipal (Calle Atravesada) in the morning, and just before sunset, at *fritangas* (grills) set up around town. Two supermarkets are convenient stops for self-caterers.

BOAT TOUR OF LAS ISLETAS

An easy morning or afternoon trip from Granada takes you by boat to this miniature archipelago of 365 tiny tropical islands. Along the way you'll spot rare birds, colorful flowers and some interesting indigenous fauna – keep your eye out for osprey, kingfishers, caimans and howler monkeys (along the mainland). The privately owned islands that would make a tremendous evil lair are highlights, as well as lunch at the handful of island hotels and restaurants.

There's even a Spanish fortress. Castillo San Pablo was built in 1784 and has great views of Granada and Volcán Mombacho, plus a fine swimming hole nearby.

Most tours also pass Isla de los Monos (Monkey Island). The spider- and capuchin-monkey residents are friendly (they were brought here by a veterinarian living on a nearby island), but may run off with your picnic lunch.

Formed 10,000 years ago when very visible Volcán Mombacho exploded into its current ragged silhouette, these islands were once one of the poorest neighborhoods in Granada, and some are still home to impoverished families, who in general have no official property rights. They are being gradually supplanted by the beautiful homes of folks such as the Pellas (Flor de Caña owners) family, former president Chamorro, and lots of expats.

Most tour companies run trips to Las Isletas, or do it yourself with Inuit Kayaks (p447), about 1km from the Centro Turístico entrance, an outfitter that runs several guided kayak tours. Touts will offer to hook you up with a boat tour as soon as you enter the Centro Turístico. If you're on your own or in a small group, wait around until a larger group forms (unless you want to pay for the whole boat yourself – around US$20 for a one-hour tour); the boat operators will offer discount seats just to fill their boat up. For the best birdwatching, arrange your trip the day before to leave at dawn. Sunset is also quite nice, but the tour is quicker, with less exploration of the further-afield corners of the island group.

A turnoff to the right, just after Inuit Kayaks (look for the sign saying 'Marina Cocibolca'), takes you to the other side of the Peninsula de Asese to Puerto Asese, where you can hire boats to tour the *isletas* on this side. This is a less popular option, so chances of forming an impromptu group are slimmer. The advantage of a tour here is that there are fewer power lines and other boats, so it's a more tranquil experience, but it involves a fair bit of time in open water.

There are numerous restaurants in the island chain. Ask your boat operator to include a stop at one, where a large meal of locally caught fish will cost around US$7.50.

★ **The Garden Café**   CAFE **$**
(www.gardencafegranada.com; Calle La Libertad,
Parque Central, 1 c E; mains US$4-8; ⊘7am-9pm;
❄♪) 𝐷 This lovely cafe, set on a colonial-
style patio around a gorgeous courtyard
garden, offers great breakfasts, healthy sandwiches and salads, plus a daily special featuring a traditionally home-cooked Nicaraguan
dish (on the day we visited, it was *carne
tapada*, stewed beef cooked with carrots,
potatoes and chayote). It also has cocktails,
sangria and wine, plus an excellent fair-trade
store onsite.

Kathy's Waffle House   BREAKFAST **$**
(www.kathyswafflehouse.com; Calle El Arsenal;
dishes US$3-5; ⊘7am-2pm) Drop into Kathy's,
a long-time breakfast institution for tourists
and locals alike, for waffles, pancakes, bot-
tomless coffee and great views of Convento
San Francisco from the front porch.

Taco Stop   TEX-MEX **$**
(www.tacostopnicaragua.com; Ex Cine Karawala,
Calle Atravesada, Parque Central 1 c O, ½ c N; mains
US$3-8; ⊘10:30am-midnight Sun-Tue, to 3am Wed
& Thu, to 5am Fri & Sat; 🕾) Located inside the
shell of a vintage movie theater, this fast-
food-style *taquería* (taco stall) is casual but
stylish. Grab a burrito to go, or sit down for
a spicy Mexican stew and cold beer. The
tortillas are made in-house; there's even a
small salsa bar. Be warned – the salsa verde
is made with locally grown jalapeños and
has a real kick.

Café de las Sonrisas   NICARAGUAN **$**
(www.tioantonio.org; Iglesia de la Merced, 50m al
lago; dishes US$2.50-4; ⊘7am-4pm Mon-Fri, to
3pm Sat) Practice your international communication at this nonprofit cafe run by staff
who are hearing-impaired. It has a picture-
gram menu, sign charts and basic, hearty
and wholesome Nicaraguan fare.

★ **El Tercer Ojo**   FUSION **$$**
(☑2552-7774; www.eltercerojonicaragua.com;
Calle La Calzada, Catedral, 1½ c E; meals US$6-14;
⊘11am-11pm; 🕾♪) Hip and lively, with si-
lent movies projected on the wall at night,
El Tercer Ojo (the Third Eye) is your go-to
for sushi, Indian and Thai food. The expan-
sive menu also features panini and salads,
including several vegetarian and gluten-
free options. Come for the daily happy hour
(5pm to 8pm), or later for live music – check
the online schedule.

Cafe de los Sueños   INTERNATIONAL **$$**
(☑2552-7272; Calle La Calzada, frente Centro
Escolar Carlos A Bravo; dishes US$4-8; ⊘11am-
10:30pm) A few steps from the loudest stretch
of Calle La Calzada, this adorable cafe and
eatery does good salads, freshly grilled fish,
and a few international dishes such as Mexican-style tacos and savory crepes.

Comidas Tipicas y Más   NICARAGUAN **$$**
(Calle La Calzada, Iglesia, 1 c E; dishes US$4-6;
⊘6pm-late Thu-Tue) Typical Nicaraguan food
on the main pedestrian street. Dishes here
cost more than at your local *comedor* (basic
eatery), but it has a sweet patio setting and
the food is carefully prepared. Try the *indio
viejo* (beef stew; US$2.50), *nacatamales*
(banana-leaf-wrapped bundles of cornmeal,
meat, vegetables and herbs; US$2) or quesa-
dillas (US$2.50).

🍷 Drinking & Nightlife

Granada hops most nights, but Thursday
to Saturday is when the real action takes
place. Most people start or end the night
at one of the bars along Calle La Calzada,
known for outdoor drinking and prime
people-watching.

Lakeside Centro Turístico, though it's not
what it used to be, is home to a few discos
and bars. Always take cabs between the Cen-
tro Turístico and central Granada at night.

Nectar   LOUNGE
(Calle La Calzada, Parque Central, 1½ c E; dishes
US$4-6; ⊘11am-11:30pm) A small lounge-bar
with a good list of cocktails (come for happy
hour) and some cozy sitting areas. In high
season it often gets visiting DJs and live
bands to liven the place up. Some delicious
light meals and snacks make up the small,
creative menu.

☆ Entertainment

For a city of this size and popularity, there
aren't as many cultural offerings as you'd ex-
pect in Granada, though live music and film
screenings happen on and around Calle La
Calzada on weekends.

Imagine   LIVE MUSIC
(www.imaginerestaurantandbar.com; Calle La Lib-
ertad s/n; ⊘5-11pm) Just like John Lennon
would have liked it, this chilled-out bar fea-
tures live music most days of the week.

ℹ Information

DANGERS & ANNOYANCES

There have been some reports of robberies on the road leading down to the lake and south into the Centro Turístico – take a cab after dark. Many assaults have been reported by tourists who attempt to cycle to Peninsula de Asese.

INTERNET ACCESS

Most hotels, and many restaurants and cafes, have wi-fi. You'll also spot a few internet cafes near the main plaza.

LAUNDRY

Most hotels and hostels offer laundry services.

MEDICAL SERVICES

Hospital Amistad Japonés (☑ 2552-2719; Calle La Inmaculada, Esso station, 2km O) The most frequently recommended private hospital is out of town, on the road to Managua.

MONEY

Several banks are within a block of Parque Central.

BAC (Calle La Libertad, Parque Central, 1 c O)

BanPro (Calle Consulado, Parque Central, 1 c O)

Western Union (Calle Real Xalteva) International money transfers.

POST

Post Office (Calle Atravesada, Bancentro, ½ c S) Opposite the ex–Cine Karawala, now the home of Taco Stop.

TOURIST INFORMATION

Check at hostels and tour operators for the latest tourist info.

Intur (☑ 2552-6858; www.visitanicaragua.com/ingles; Calle Corrales) The Granada branch of the national tourist office has up-to-date transportation schedules, a reasonable city map, and lots of information and flyers.

ℹ Getting There & Away

BOAT

Traditionally, twice-weekly ferries have left Granada's ferry terminal for Isla de Ometepe. But service was suspended indefinitely at the time of writing due to low water levels on Lago de Nicaragua. Check www.ometepenicaragua.com/ferryboat.php for updates on services.

Puerto Asese (☑ 2552-2269), about 2km southeast of town, has boats for the Las Isletas and Parque Nacional Archipiélago Zapatera.

BUS

For most international services, you'll need to go to nearby Managua. If you're headed south to Costa Rica, though, you can get on a passing Transnica (☑ 2270-3133; www.transnica.com) or Tica Bus (☑ 8739-5505; www.ticabus.com) – check their websites for more information.

Granada doesn't have one central bus terminal. Buses to Managua (US$0.75, one hour, 4am to 7pm, every 20 to 30 minutes), arriving at Managua's Mercado Roberto Huembes, depart from the lot just north of the old hospital on the western edge of town. Microbuses to Managua (US$1.25, one hour, 5am to 7:30pm, every 15 to 30 minutes), arriving at UCA in Managua, leave from the convenient lot just south of the Parque Central on Calle Vega. Buses to Masaya (US$0.50, 30 minutes, 5am to 6pm, every 20 to 30 minutes) leave from two blocks west of the Mercado Municipal, around the corner from Palí.

Buses to destinations south leave from a block south of the market, across from the Shell petrol station.

Carazo (US$0.75, 45 minutes, 6am to 5:05pm, every 20 minutes) For San Marcos, Diriamba (with connections to the Carazo beaches) and Jinotepe.

Catarina & San Juan de Oriente (US$0.60, 30 minutes, 6am to 6pm, every 30 to 60 minutes)

Rivas (US$1.25, 1½ hours, 5:45am to 3:10pm, nearly hourly) Early-afternoon buses will allow you to make the last boat to Isla de Ometepe.

Shuttle Bus

Considering that Managua is a one-hour, one-dollar hop in a minibus (and that León buses leave from the spot where you arrive) and that other destinations are nearly equally accessible, shuttle service is not so popular here. If you have your heart set on shuttle travel, try to get a group together or you may find yourself paying for the entire trip (in either case a taxi may work out way better).

Erick Tours (☑ 8974-5575; www.ericktours nicaragua.com; Parque Central 3 c al lago; tour prices vary) Airport transfers.

Nahual Tours (p447) Has two daily shuttles to Laguna de Apoyo (one-way/round-trip US$5/10).

TAXI

Taxis are plentiful. Always agree on a fare before getting into the taxi, which should be less than US$1 per person if you're getting into a shared taxi anywhere in the city.

It's inexpensive and convenient to take taxis to other destinations, including Masaya and Laguna de Apoyo, keeping in mind that fares vary according to gas prices and your bargaining skills. You can always ask your hotel or hostel to call you a taxi and settle on a price before you're picked up.

Around Granada

Reserva Natural Volcán Mombacho

◉ Sights

Reserva Natural Volcán Mombacho   NATURE RESERVE
(☑ 2552-5858; www.mombacho.org; El Guanacaste, Carretera Granada-Nandaime Km 50; park entrance per car/pedestrian US$20/5, mariposario US$2; ◷ 8am-5pm Fri-Sun, by reservation other days for groups of 10 or more) It's been a few decades since this 1345m volcano, the defining feature of the Granada skyline, has acted up, but it is still most certainly active and sends up the periodic puff of smoke. It's easy to get to the crown of cloud forest, steaming with fumaroles and other bubbling volcanic activity beneath the misty vines and orchids. Most visitors come here on guided tours from Granada.

Reserva Natural Volcán Mombacho is managed by the Fundación Cocibolca, which since 1999 has been building trails and running an eco-mobile (think refurbished military jeeps seating 25) on the 40% grade up to 1100m. Get there early to take the short trail through the organic coffee farm, or check out the mariposario (butterfly garden) and orchid garden (free with entrance), close to the parking lot.

At the top you can find three species of monkey, 168 species of bird and more than 100 types of orchids as part of the jungle canopy that this park is intent on preserving. There is a choice of several trails, including Sendero del Cráter, a 1.5km jaunt to the fumaroles, plus great views of Granada and Las Isletas, and Sendero la Puma, a steeper 4km trek around the lip of the crater, with even better views. Guides, many of whom speak English, are available at the entrance and cost US$12 to US$22 per group of up to seven. Guides are required for a trek up Sendero el Tigrillo, a heart-pumping two-hour tromp up to two overlooks.

The park is open to the public with regular hours on Friday, Saturday and Sunday. However, groups of 10 or more can make arrangements to visit on other days. Time your arrival to coincide with an eco-mobile departure, at 8:30am, 10am and 1pm.

If you have a 4WD, you can drive up the volcano for an extra US$22 – plus US$5 for every adult and US$3 for every child in the car.

There are several attractions in the immediate vicinity, including a pair of interesting rural communities. Inside the reserve but hidden away on a farm, and thus more easily accessible on a separate day trip from Granada, the beautifully maintained, 45°C (113°F) hot springs of Aguas Termales de Calera are replete with sulfur, calcium and other minerals quasi-scientifically proven to keep you radiant and healthy. Look for the excursion listed at outfitters in Granada; expect to pay around US$25 per person, including round-trip transportation.

❶ Getting There & Away

Public transportation is inconvenient: most visitors drive themselves here or come on an organized tour from Granada.

You can also take any Nandaime bus from Granada and ask to be let off at the entrance. From here, you'll walk two steep kilometers (stay left where the road splits) to the spot where the eco-mobiles pick up passengers for the uphill drive.

Reserva Natural Laguna de Apoyo

Set in a picturesque valley brimming with wildlife, the lovely Apoyo crater lake is another one of Nicaragua's many natural wonders. Dry tropical rainforest along the surrounding slopes contains much biodiversity, including howler monkeys and many species of bats. But the real attraction is the pristine water of the lagoon, a massive, mineral-infused pool that is without doubt the best swim in the country.

🏃 Activities

There's a free beach at the bottom of the road; look for the trail just to the right of the T intersection. Otherwise, pay for a day pass at one of the hotels for access to their beaches, docks and kayaks (US$5 to US$7). Scuba-diving classes are available through Hotel SelvAzul (☑ 8631-1890; www.hotelselvazul.com; Triangulo, 500m N; 1 tank dive US$40, introductory course US$60).

🛏 Sleeping & Eating

You can easily visit Laguna de Apoyo as a day trip from Granada, but it's wonderful to wake up here, and there are several good places to stay – including a number of rental houses that are ideal if you're staying for more than a night or two. Check online, and

ALTERNATIVE DAY TRIPS FROM GRANADA

There are several great day trips from Granada. Here are two off-the-beaten-track options.

Nicaragua Libre (☑ 2552-0238; www.ucatierrayagua.org; Entrada de Monte Verde, 500m SE; per person guided tour US$3; ⊙ tours by reservation) This small rural community at the base of Volcán Mombacho is part of the UCA community-tourism project. It offers guided trips through organic coffee farms, horseback rides to San Juan de Oriente and walks to Mombacho. A concerted effort has been made to rescue the art of traditional handicrafts here; look for young artisans selling their work.

Aguas Agrias – La Nanda Community (☑ 8439-9658; www.ucatierrayagua.org/aguas-agrias; Carretera Granada-Nandaime, entrada a Monte Verde 12km E; guided tours US$3-5; ⊙ tours by reservation) This rural community, located just south of Mombacho volcano, is an off-the-beaten-path destination where local guides lead two-hour hikes through a traditional plantation. The unusual volcanic landscape, dotted with a series of refreshing lagoons – some of which you can swim in – makes for an interesting excursion. The community is run by the Union of Cooperative Agriculturalists 'UCA Tierra y Agua.'

shop around, as there were new properties opening at the time of writing.

The Monkey Hut　　　　　　HOSTEL $
(☑ 8887-3546; www.themonkeyhut.net; Triangulo, 450m N; dm/d/cabin US$14/39/59; [P][☎]) This popular waterfront property (US$6 day use for nonguests) features a small beach on the edge of the lake, terraced lounge and picnic areas, a dock with plenty of kayaks, a cocktail bar and cafe, and a pizzeria. Overnight guests also have access to a kitchen and outdoor grills; choose between dorms, private rooms or a freestanding cabin.

Hostel Paradiso　　　　　　HOSTEL $
(☑ 2520-2878; www.hostelparadiso.com; Triangulo, 300m E; dm US$10, s/d without bathroom US$15/25, d/tr US$32/40; [P][✳][@][☎]) A great pick for budget travelers, this lakefront hostel has a large terrace, private dock, kayaks and shared kitchen, plus a good restaurant and bar. Day passes cost US$7 per person. The hostel runs a shuttle to and from Granada for US$3 each way; check the website for details.

❶ Getting There & Away

Many hotels and hostels on the lake offer daily shuttle transportation to and from Laguna de Apoyo from Granada (from US$3 one way), including options for day visitors and overnight guests. Check for details and times on the websites of the Monkey Hut and Hostel Paradiso, or walk around Granada and see what's on offer.

Outside the posted shuttle times, you could also arrange a taxi from Granada (US$12 to US$15), Masaya (US$10 to US$12) or Managua (US$30 to US$40) to the door of your hotel or destination in Laguna de Apoyo.

Both of these options are generally preferable to taking public transportation. Laguna de Apoyo is close to Granada and Masaya, but most buses don't go close to the hotels; they usually drop passengers off near the crater rim. The half-hour, 2km descent isn't a bad walk, but going uphill again is hard work, especially on a hot day.

The main entrance is from a road off the Carretera a Masaya at Km 37.5. Buses run every half-hour between Masaya and the crater rim (US$0.50, 6am to 6pm). Only three buses, which read 'La Laguna,' descend all the way to the waterfront (US$0.70, 5:30am, 10:30am and 3:30pm).

Often directions given are from El Triangulo – the T intersection where the road splits once it hits the waterfront, either heading to the right (south) or left (north).

Pueblos Blancos

This charming mountainous region a short distance from both Masaya and Granada has a refreshing climate and is dotted with pretty villages famed for their skilled craftspeople and colorful traditions. Named after the pale white stucco homes that once dominated the area, the Pueblos Blancos (White Towns) are extremely compact, with villages practically growing into one another, which makes them easy to visit on a day trip.

The gorgeous village of Catarina is known for its mirador (lookout point), which offers sweeping views of Laguna de Apoyo, Lago de Nicaragua and the city of Granada.

Nearby, sleepy San Juan de Oriente may be home to fewer than 3000 people, but it is the most important center of artisanal pottery in Nicaragua. At workshops all over town, you can watch the artists at work.

Masaya

Masaya

◎ Top Sights
1 Mercado de Artesanías de
 Masaya...D3

◎ Sights
2 Iglesia de San Jerónimo......................C2
3 Malecón & Laguna de Masaya...........A3

◎ Sleeping
4 Hotel Maderas Inn C2

◐ Information
5 Intur...D3

◐ Transport
6 Bus Terminal.......................................F3
7 Minivans to Managua..........................D3

Rarely visited by tourists, the friendly village of **Diria** is the gateway to the **Mirador el Boquete**, an alternate lookout over Laguna de Apoyo.

Buses to these villages (US$0.60 to US$1.20, 30 minutes, every 20 to 30 minutes until 5pm) leave regularly from one block south of the market in Granada.

Carazo Towns

Southwest of the Pueblos Blancos, in Carazo department, **San Marcos** and the 'twin cities' of **Jinotepe** and **Diriamba** are set in a citrus- and coffee-cultivation area. The three towns celebrate a distinctive religious and folklore ritual known as 'Toro Guaco,' in which the Nicarao town of Jinotepe and Diriamba, its Chorotega rival before the European conquest, commemorate their relationship. Jinotepe's patron is Santiago (St James), whose day is July 25; Diriamba's is San Sebastián (January 20). These two towns, along with San Marcos, carry out ceremonial visits to each other, livened up with striking costumes and masks displayed in dances, mock battles and plays satirizing their Spanish invaders. The pantomime figure of 'El Güegüense' is a symbol of Nicaraguan identity.

Buses to Diriamba, Jinotepe and San Marcos depart from one block south of the market in Granada (US$1, 45 minutes, hourly until 6pm). There are extremely frequent departures from Masaya and Managua, as well.

Masaya

POP 166,500

Coming from Granada, Masaya may seem a bit down at heel. This is a very workaday little town, unexceptional but for two things – a wonderful, crumbling *malecón* (waterfront walkway) and the famous artisan market, Mercado de Artesanías de Masaya, where you can stock up for every birthday, Christmas and anniversary for the rest of your life without buying two of the same thing. Nicaraguan tourists, by the way, always make sure their visit coincides with one of Masaya's many spectacular festivals, and there are cultural exhibitions and dances every Thursday evening.

Masaya is 29km southeast of Managua and 16km northwest of Granada. The city sits at the edge of Laguna de Masaya, beyond which rises Volcán Masaya, which can be visited on day trips from here or Granada.

◉ Sights & Activities

One of the best ways to see the town is in a **horse-drawn carriage**, which costs about US$3 per person for the grand tour.

★ Mercado de
Artesanías de Masaya   MARKET
(Mercado Viejo; cnr Calle San Miguel & Av El Progreso; ⊘ 9am-6pm) Showcasing the highest-quality crafts in the country, this historic marketplace, a black-basalt Gothic structure with a Spanish-fortress motif that includes turrets, towers and oversized gates, dates from 1888. It's one-stop shopping for Nicaraguan crafts of all kinds and is a popular stop on organized tours. Not to be confused with the section of artisan products inside the Mercado Municipal Ernesto Fernández.

Fortaleza De Coyotepe   FORT
(US$0.70; ⊘ 8am-5pm) Built in 1893 atop Cerro de los Coyotes, this fortress saw the last stand of Benjamín Zeledón, the 1912 hero of resistance to US intervention. The marines managed to take the fortress – as witnessed by a young man named Sandino, who vowed his revenge. In the end, it was the Guardia Nacional's last stronghold, overrun during the Sandinistas' 1979 offensive.

Malecón & Laguna de Masaya   WATERFRONT
Seven blocks west of the Parque Central is an inspiring view in a region famed for them: the view across Laguna de Masaya to the smoking Santiago crater. The attractive, if crumbling, *malecón* was constructed in 1944, when you could still swim, drink or fish in the impressive lagoon. There's a humble collection of restaurant-bars down by the water.

★✦ Festivals & Events

San Lázaro   RELIGIOUS
(⊘ week before Palm Sunday) One of Nicaragua's more unusual religious festivals pays homage to San Lázaro, a folk saint who bestows blessings upon dogs. Locals dress their pets to the nines; festivities include a procession of costumed canines.

San Jerónimo   RELIGIOUS
(⊘ Sep 30) Officially it's eight days of festivities. The patron saint (in the guise of a bearded *campesino* named 'Tata Chombó,' or 'Doctor of the Poor') is taken from the Iglesia de San Jerónimo (cnr Av San Jerónimo & Calle Palo Blanco) altar and carried around Masaya during traditional dance performances. A mock battle ends with peacemaking ceremonies to commemorate the September peace treaties of 1856, 1912 and 1979.

Fireworks, marimbas, parades, drag queens and more make this a fiesta to remember.

🛏 Sleeping

There aren't any great hotels here – it's better to sleep in nearby Granada. Most lodging is clustered about four blocks north of Parroquia de la Asunción, along Av Zelaya (also called Calle Central).

Hotel Maderas Inn   HOTEL **$$**
(☑ 2522-5825; www.hotelmaderasinn.com; Calle Central, Cuerpo de Bomberos, 2c S; d with fan/aircon US$20/45; ❉ 🐾) This family-run inn is simple and a bit smoky, but there are firm mattresses and service is fairly friendly. Ask for a room upstairs.

🍴 Eating

Inexpensive *comedores* (basic eateries) cling to the outside of the Mercado Municipal Ernesto Fernández, just outside the bus terminal. *Vigorón* (mashed yucca topped with coleslaw and pork rinds), fruit salad and *gallo pinto* (blended rice and beans) can be had for around US$1; a sit-down meal with a drink costs around US$2 to US$3. There are also snack stalls on the Parque 17 de Octubre and in the Mercado Artesanías.

❶ Information

Intur (☑ 2522-7615; www.visitanicaragua.com/ingles; Av El Progreso, Mercado Artesanías, ½ c S) This well-funded office has maps and information.

❶ Getting There & Away

Minivans to Managua's Universidad Centro America (US$0.90, 30 minutes) leave the park in front of Iglesia de San Miguel (when full). Other buses (US$0.50) and minivans arrive and depart from the bus station at the eastern side of the Mercado Municipal.

Note that buses don't leave on a regular schedule that you'd want to plan your whole day around (so treat any schedule as a guideline), but they do come and go all day.

Parque Nacional Volcán Masaya

The Spaniards said this was the gate to hell, and put the Bobadilla cross (named for the priest who planted it) atop a now sadly inaccessible cliff. Volcán Masaya (☑ 2528-1444; Carretera a Masaya Km 23; US$4; ⊘ 9am-4:45pm) is the most heavily venting volcano in Nicaragua, and in a more litigious nation there is no way you'd be allowed to drive up to the lip of a volcanic cone as volatile as the Santiago crater. In 2001, an eruption hurled heated rocks 500m into the air, damaging cars and narrowly missing people. At the time of writing, the park was closed until further notice due to dangerous volcanic activity. But if it's open, you should definitely go if you can.

◉ Sights & Activities

Nicaragua's largest national park is built around Volcán Masaya and its system of calderas and craters – including the enormous and ancient crater called El Ventarrón, with a barely perceptible rim that runs from Ticuantepe to Masatepe – and around the Laguna de Masaya.

Try to arrive in the afternoon, when the crater's thousands of *chocoyos* (parakeets) return to their nests in the crater walls, apparently unharmed by the billowing toxic gases. There's always lava bubbling at the bottom (you probably won't see it, though),

BUS SERVICES FROM MASAYA

DESTINATION	COST (US$)	DURATION	DEPARTURES (DAILY)
Carazo (San Marcos, Diriamba & Jinotepe)	0.30-0.50	1¼hr	5am-6pm, every 30min
Catarina, Diriomo & Diriá	0.30-0.50	40min	6am-5pm, every 20min
Catarina, San Juan de Oriente, Niquinohomo, Masatepe & San Marcos	0.50	1¼hr	5am-6pm, every 30min
Granada	0.50	40min	5am-6pm, every 30min
Laguna de Apoyo entrance	0.40	20min	5am-5pm, at least hourly
Managua	0.50	1hr	5am-5pm, every 20min
Matagalpa	3	3hr	5:30am & 6am
Ticuantepe	0.60	45min	6am-5pm, every 20min

and a column of sulfurous gases rising above.

A few outfitters in Granada offer a night tour (US$28 to US$35 per person, four hours) that involves walking through lava tubes and watching what seems to be millions of bats flying in and out of caves. Round-trip transportation is included with those packages, but if you're already at the volcano, you can also join a shorter night tour (US$10) that runs from the visitors center.

If you can't come at night, a day tour is an option. Most tour outfits in Granada come here as part of a Masaya day trip (around US$15 to US$20 per person), which includes the markets and Catarina overlook, though time at the volcano itself is fairly limited.

Have more time to spend? Explore the park's 20km of hiking trails. Shorter, mostly accessible treks require guides (US$0.70 to US$2 per person), which you pay for with your admission (tips are additional). Sendero Los Coyotes (1.5km) meanders through lava-strewn fields and dry tropical forest; Sendero El Comalito (2km) takes you to a smaller cone surrounded by fumaroles; and Sendero Las Cuevas (1.5km to 6km, depending on which paths you take) lets you explore the very cool lava tunnels of Tzinancanostoc, with bats.

There are also longer hikes (5km to 6km) to lookout points and large rocks that don't require guides (although you could certainly arrange them). If you speak Spanish, have a wander around the attractive museum (free admission) at the visitors center, with impressive natural-history displays and beautiful murals, and a butterfly garden.

The park entrance is 7km north of Masaya. You pay for your entry and guided hikes at the entrance gate, and you'll receive a handy brochure with a map and useful information in Spanish and English. It's 5km of paved road to the crater and Plaza de Oviedo, which honors the intrepid priest who went down into the volcano with a sample dish, to find out whether or not the lava was (as he suspected) pure gold. It wasn't, but folks were still impressed enough with the feat to name the parking lot after him. Park officials limit your time here to just five minutes.

❶ Getting There & Away

Many travelers come here on organized tours with transportation included.

Any Managua-bound bus from Masaya or Granada can drop you at the entrance, but it's a steep, hot climb to the crater; hitchhiking is definitely possible, if you're up for it. Alternatively, consider taking a round-trip taxi from Masaya (around US$10) or Granada (around US$15 to US$20), including an hour's wait at the top.

SOUTHWESTERN NICARAGUA

Packed with attractions, the southwest offers up some of Nicaragua's hallmark vistas and adventures. Surfers have been hitting this coastline for years, drawn by perfect, uncrowded waves and chilled-back surfing encampments found to the north and south of San Juan del Sur. No trip to the southwest would be complete without a few days on Isla de Ometepe.

Rivas

POP 50,600

Rivas has its fans – people say it's authentic and lively. But with the beaches, lake and Ometepe beckoning, few travelers pause here long enough to find out. Nearby San Jorge, with easy access to the ferries to Ometepe, is preferable for an overnight.

◉ Sights

Museo de Antropología e Historia MUSEUM
(☑2563 3708; mercado, 1 c S, 1 c E; US$1; ⊙9am-noon Mon-Sat) If you have just two hours in town, this is the place to go. Inside you'll find some moth-eaten taxidermy, a wall of myths and legends and, best of all, a well-signed (in both English and Spanish) collection of pre-Columbian artifacts, many of them recently discovered by the Santa Isabela Archaeological Project.

🛏 Sleeping & Eating

Hospedaje Lidia GUESTHOUSE $
(☑2563-3477; Texaco ½ c O; d US$25, s/d without bathroom US$10/18; 🖎) The location isn't too desirable, but this no-frills, family-run operation offers decent budget lodging, with well-scrubbed rooms and a better-than-average room-to-bathroom ratio.

Vila's Rosti-Pizza PARRILLA $$
(costado sur, Parque Central; dishes US$5-10; ⊙10am-midnight) This centrally located eatery is one of the better dining picks in

town. Come for steaks, burgers and people-watching from the front tables: the entire town crosses the Parque Central at least once during the course of a meal.

ℹ Information

Intur (📞 2563-4914; rivas@intur.gob.ni; Texaco station, ½ c O; ◷ 9am-6pm Mon-Fri) There's a decent selection of flyers here on Rivas, San Juan del Sur and Ometepe.

ℹ Getting There & Away

Rivas is a transportation hub. The **bus terminal** (📞 8669-0330) is adjacent to the *mercado* (market). You can catch more luxurious long-distance buses (most headed to and from Managua, not Granada) at the **long-distance bus stop** (Panamericana, or Pan-American Hwy) just north of the exit to San Jorge. If you're headed south to Costa Rica, catch a **Transnica** (📞 2563-5397; www.transnica.com) bus or **Tica Bus** (📞 8877-1407; www.ticabus.com) on its way to San José (US$29 to US$40) from Managua.

A few buses per day offer onward service to El Ostional.

San Jorge

This relaxed spot, 6km east of Rivas, is where most travelers head to cross over to Isla de Ometepe. The center of town is 1km from the ferry dock, but it's more convenient to stay near the lake.

🛏 Sleeping

Hotel Hamacas   HOTEL **$$**
(📞 2563-0048; www.hotelhamacas.com; ferry terminal, 100m O, 25m S; s/d with fan US$25/30, with air-con US$35/40; P🅿❄🛜🏊) Cute little brick rooms painted in cheerful colors make this hacienda-style hotel the most atmospheric offering in town. Rooms surround a leafy courtyard, with the requisite hammocks strung up around the porch areas.

ℹ Getting There & Away

The road from Rivas to San Jorge ends at the ferry terminal, where there's regular boat service to Isla de Ometepe. Eighteen boats make the trip from San Jorge to Isla de Ometepe (US$1.50 to US$3, one hour) each day between 7am and 5:45pm.

Buses leave for Rivas (US$0.25) almost hourly from the ferry terminal, passing by the Parque Central.

Taxis charge about US$5 to US$6 for a ride between the Rivas bus terminal and the San Jorge ferry terminal.

Isla de Ometepe

POP 29,800

Ometepe never fails to impress. Its twin volcanic peaks, rising out of Lago de Nicaragua, have captured the imagination of everyone from precolonial Aztecs (who thought they'd found the promised land) to Mark Twain (who waxed lyrical about it in his book *Travels with Mr Brown*) – not to mention the relatively few travelers who make it out here. The island's fertile volcanic soil, clean waters, wide beaches, wildlife population, archaeological sites and dramatic profile are quickly propelling it up traveler tick lists.

More than 1700 petroglyphs have been found on Ometepe, making this a DIY-ers fantasy island.

To get to Isla de Ometepe from this side of the mainland, you'll need to first pass through rough-and-tumble Rivas, then get a boat from San Jorge.

🏃 Activities

Ometepe is great for hiking, exploring and swimming. However, the terrain is rough, signage minimal and trails hard to follow. After various tourists got lost and died climbing volcanoes solo, authorities have made local

BUSES FROM RIVAS

DESTINATION	COST (US$)	DURATION	FREQUENCY
Granada	1.25	1½hr	hourly, departs through early evening
Managua	2	2½hr	4:30am-6pm, every 30min
Salinas & Tola beaches	2	1½hr	6-8 daily
San Jorge	0.30	20min	every 30min
San Juan del Sur	1	45min	almost hourly
Southern beaches (San Juan del Sur, Playa el Coco, La Flor and El Ostional)	2.50	2-3hr	4 daily

guides mandatory for these trips. Guides can be hired at tour operators in Moyogalpa and Altagracia or through hotels.

Both of the volcanoes are challenging. Volcán Maderas is the more accessible of the two, a tough, muddy scramble through cloud forest to the crater, where there's a greenish lake below. It's about eight hours there and back. There are several routes to the top; the trails leaving from Finca Magdalena, Mérida and El Porvenir are the most used.

Volcán Concepción is a pretty serious 10- to 12-hour hike, the last bit up steep and slippery volcanic scree. Be prepared for intense heat (sun, not lava), and also for chills at the summit. The two main trails leave from points near Altagracia and Moyogalpa.

On the Maderas side, there are also several trails to see petroglyphs. The petroglyphs near the hotel of El Porvenir are a 45-minute horseback ride from Santo Domingo; ask hotel staffers for directions. Others are found at El Socorro, Finca Magdalena and El Corozal. On the south side of Maderas, an impressive 35m-high waterfall is located a couple of hours' hike above San Ramón.

There are great beaches and swimming spots all around the island; check out Punta Jesús María, Playa Venecia and the Isla de Quiste, a beautiful islet not far from Charco Verde. The most popular beach, Playa Santo Domingo, is on the isthmus connecting the two volcanoes, and has plenty of places to stay and eat. Many of the sleeping options have horses, bikes or kayaks to hire at reasonable rates.

🕭 Tours

Inexpensive local guides are highly recommended during hikes, for safety, to increase your chances of spotting wildlife and for enhanced insight into the island's culture. Guides basically live off your tips, so be generous. Any hotel can arrange a guide.

Moyogalpa
POP 10,500

Moyogalpa is home to the ferry terminal for hourly boats from the mainland, and, as such, the nerve center for Ometepe's nascent tourist industry. There are several hotels and restaurants here, and many of the island's tour companies; it's also base camp for the climb up Volcán Concepción. But it's not exactly an island paradise you'll want to linger in: you're only passing through.

🛏 Sleeping

Hotel Teosintal HOTEL $
(☏ 2569-4105; muelle, 2 c E, 1½ c S; d US$20; 🛜) This basic but clean hotel offers fair rooms for the price.

Hospedaje Soma GUESTHOUSE $$
(☏ 2569-4310; www.hospedajesoma.com; frente del Instituto J.R. Smith; d US$10, r with/without bathroom US$35/25, 2-person cabins with air-con/fan US$60/50; ❊🛜) Book ahead if you're hoping to score a room at this relaxed but professionally run guesthouse, set a 10-minute walk from the ferry dock. Choose between a dorm, private room or cabin, all scattered around a large and beautiful tropical garden. The owners are helpful with planning excursions around the island.

Cornerhouse B&B B&B $$
(www.thecornerhouseometepe.com; muelle, 1 c O; s/d/tr US$25/35/45; 🛜) There are just four rooms at this sweet B&B, a block uphill from the port – and they're available only on a first-come, first-serve basis (no reservations), so you'll have to try your luck when you get off the boat. Breakfast at the lovely Cornerhouse cafe downstairs is included in the price.

🍴 Eating

Cornerhouse CAFE $
(www.thecornerhouseometepe.com; muelle 1 c E; mains US$3-7; ⏰7am-5pm Mon-Fri, to 3pm Sat; 🛜🍴) Easily the most stylish eating venue on this corner of the island. Breakfast is served all day at this rustic-chic cafe just uphill from the port; the menu features eggs Benedict with roasted tomatoes and fresh basil. There are also gourmet sandwiches and salads, including a great one with papaya and toasted almonds, and wi-fi. It's part of the Cornerhouse B&B.

Los Ranchitos INTERNATIONAL $
(muelle, 2 c E, ½ c S; mains US$4-6; ⏰7am-9:30pm) One of the better-looking restaurants in town, with open walls, thatched roofs and a pressed-dirt floor. The menu's your fairly standard range of meat, chicken and seafood, with some good pizza and pasta options thrown in.

Moyogalpa to Altagracia

Around 5km south of Moyogalpa, and easily reached by bicycle, is the remarkable Punta Jesús María, a narrow sandbar that juts out

Isla de Ometepe

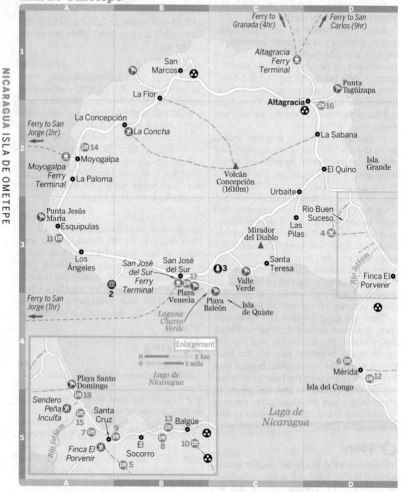

into the lake, forming a natural pier perfect for swimming and picnics.

A kilometer or so down the road from the turnoff to Punta Jesús María is the town of Esquipulas, followed by the turnoff to Finca Samaria (☎8824-2210; Cementerio Esquipulas, 30m al lago; dm/d US$9/23; ☎), a beautiful farmstay option a 500m walk down a dirt road – take a left just before you hit the water.

About halfway between Esquipulas and San José del Sur, look for the turnoff to the Museos el Ceibo (☎8874-8706; www.museoselceibo.com; one/both museums US$5/8;

⊘8am-5pm), 2km down a shady lane off the main road. These are the best museums on the island, with archaeological and coin museums.

Around 10km from Moyogalpa on the Altagracia road, you'll find the Reserva Charco Verde (US$0.75). There is a hiking trail through the woods, and you'll likely see monkeys and plenty of birds. The lovely Playa Bancón looks across at Isla de Quiste.

There are three places to stay here; bookings are often necessary. Hotel Finca Venecia (☎8887-0191; d US$25, cabins with fan/air-con from US$30/50; P❄☎) is a decent bet on

Isla de Ometepe

⊙ **Sights**
1 Cascada San Ramón...........................E5
2 Museos El Ceibo................................A3
3 Reserva Charco Verde.......................C3

⊙ **Activities, Courses & Tours**
4 Ojo de Agua..D3

⊖ **Sleeping**
5 Albergue Ecológico El Porvenir..........B5
6 Caballito's Mar..................................D4
7 El Encanto...A5
8 El Zopilote Finca Ecológica................B5
9 Finca del Sol.....................................B5
10 Finca Magdalena..............................B5
11 Finca Samaria..................................A3
12 Hacienda Mérida..............................D4
13 Hospedaje Así es Mi Tierra...............B5
14 Hospedaje Soma..............................A2
15 Hotel Casa Istiam............................A5
16 Hotel Castillo...................................D2
17 Hotel Charco Verde...........................B3
18 Hotel Villa Paraíso............................A5

⊗ **Eating**
Café Campestre.........................(see 13)

sheltered beach. It's 1km off the paved road some14km from Moyogalpa.

Altagracia

POP 7000

With more natural protection from Concepción's occasional lava flow than Moyogalpa, this is the original indigenous capital of Ometepe, and still the island's most important town. For travelers, there's not much to see here, but it can be a convenient base for exploring the surrounding area – and a good place to crash if your boat gets in late from Granada.

🛏 Sleeping & Eating

Hotel Castillo   HOTEL **$**

(☑2569-4403; www.hotelcastillo-ometepe. blogspot.com; iglesia, 1 c S, ½ c O; dm/s/d from US$6/8/15; ❋@🛜) Nothing fancy going on here, but it's fairly clean and brightly painted, with a couple of common areas. Spend a few more dollars for air-con (provided it's working). The restaurant (dishes US$3 to US$5) is good, and serves real coffee. You can arrange tours here, and rent bikes.

Hospedaje Kencho   HOTEL **$**

(☑8944-4087; Casa Cural, 1 c S; r per person without bathroom US$3, s/d with fan US$5/7, r with air-con

---

this side of the island. The grouping of 20 cabins and four basic rooms sits near the beach. A couple of hundred meters east of these, **Hotel Charco Verde** (☑2560-1271; www.charcoverde.com.ni; Charco Verde, San José del Sur; 2-/3-person cabins from US$48/70; ❋🛜) has modern cabins (ask for a lake view) and standard rooms.

A few kilometers away, **Hotel El Tesoro del Pirata** (☑8927-2831; Valle Verde; d with fan/air-con US$25/35; ❋🛜🏊) is an away-from-it-all spot with functional concrete *cabañas* (cabins) dotted among the trees on a lovely

from US$30; ✻) A budget-friendly option with slightly run-down rooms. Everything is clean, however, and the owners are helpful. Travelers rave about the daily specials on offer at the hotel's onsite restaurant.

Playa Santo Domingo & Santa Cruz

Windswept sandy beaches and many of the island's finest accommodations lie southeast of Altagracia, on the long and lovely lava isthmus that cradles Playa Santo Domingo.

Heading south to Santa Cruz along the island's main road, the beach gets progressively less crowded. Santa Cruz itself has a few places to eat and sleep, and the views are gorgeous.

🏃 Activities

The main attraction is the beach, a 30m to 70m (depending on lake levels) expanse of gray volcanic sand that retreats almost to the sea wall at the height of the rainy season.

You can hire bikes and horses from Hotel Finca Santo Domingo and other local businesses.

Ojo de Agua   SWIMMING
(US$3; ☉dawn-dusk) Take a pleasant stroll through banana plantations to the well-signed, shady swimming hole about 1.5km north of Playa Santo Domingo. The mineral-infused water here bubbles up from 35 small underground springs; with an average temperature of 22°C to 28°C (71°F to 82°F), it makes for a refreshing dip.

🛏 Sleeping & Eating

Hotel Casa Istiam   HOTEL $
(☎8844-2200; d from US$20; ✻🛜) About halfway between Playa Santo Domingo and Santa Cruz, with the beach right across the road and the Río Istiam out back, this basic hotel has a decent restaurant that's open to the public.

Finca del Sol   LODGE $$
(☎8364-6394; www.hotelfincadelsol.com; Santa Cruz; 2-person cabins from US$49; 🛜) 🍃 Quiet, ecofriendly cabins with private porches, free bicycle rental, boxed lunches on request, a breakfast made of tropical fruit grown in the garden – and the whole place powered by solar energy? We think we've found paradise on this corner of the island. You can even walk to the beach from here. It's located in the village of Santa Cruz.

El Encanto   HOTEL $$
(☎8867-7128; www.goelencanto.com; Santa Cruz; d/cabin from US$35/70) Set on a banana farm, rooms here are simply but pleasantly decorated, with big, screened windows and clean, modern bathrooms. Hammocks out front of your room have great lake views. The restaurant gets raves for its mix of Nica classics and international food, including curries, wholemeal bread and several vegetarian options.

Hotel Villa Paraíso   CABIN $$
(☎2569-4859; www.villaparaiso.com.ni; d/cabin from US$35/75; 🅿✻@🛜) The nicest rooms in Santo Domingo are found at this friendly beachfront hotel. The elegant *cabañas* have air-con, direct TV and private terraces. The excellent staff will arrange tours and there's a fantastic restaurant.

Santa Cruz to Balgüe

The northern slopes of Volcán Maderas are one of the island's hot spots: many of the nicest accommodations and dining options are located here, and it's a lovely area for horseback riding, hiking, or just relaxing.

🛏 Sleeping

★**Finca Magdalena**   HOSTEL $
(☎8418-5636; www.fincamagdalena.com; hammocks or campsites per person US$4, dm/d US$12/23, cabins US$46; @) 🍃 This Ometepe mainstay on the slopes of Volcán Maderas is a classic backpacking spot. Rooms and dorms on this working coffee *finca* are set in a rickety old wooden farmhouse and are due for a revamp, but really – with sweeping views of the lake and Volcán Concepción, lush surroundings and good food – you can probably rough it for a few days.

Note that it's a 1.5km climb to the *finca* from the bus stop.

El Zopilote Finca Ecológica   HOSTEL $
(☎8961-8742; www.ometepezopilote.com; 200m up trail from road; hammock/dm US$4/7, 2-person cabins from US$16; 🛜) 🍃 A hippie-style hideaway where many people stay longer than they'd planned. This organic farm offers a range of accommodations scattered around a lush hillside on a sizable working farm. Dorms are basic and cabins are rustic (but fun!) – there's a cool common area, a yoga space, and an organic restaurant.

To reach this place on the inland side of the road, follow the trail to the left of the converted school bus/organic market, then go 200m right to the clutch of traditionally constructed thatched-roof huts on the grassy hillside. You'll see signs.

Hospedaje Así es Mi Tierra GUESTHOUSE $
(☑ 8493-0506; www.mitierraometepe.com; r US$20) At the southern end of town is a sweet little family-run affair offering basic but functional rooms. The best part is a jungle trail that leads down to a pebble beach, complete with an open-air bungalow that's just waiting for you to kick back in a hammock and pop open a *cerveza* (beer).

✕ Eating

★Café Campestre INTERNATIONAL $$
(☑ 8571-5930; www.campestreometepe.com; dishes US$3-8; ☉11:30am-9pm; 🛜🚲) This popular cafe employing local ingredients from the adjacent organic farm has something for everyone: good coffee, freshly baked breads, huge salads and international dishes from hummus platters to Thai curries. There's even kid-friendly amenities and free wi-fi.

Santa Cruz to Mérida & San Ramón

Although more heavily populated than the rest of the southern part of the island, this stretch of road still feels wild and untamed. As with the rest of the island, road conditions are laughable (except in the wet season, when they're no joke) and bus service is patchy at best.

◉ Sights

Cascada San Ramón WATERFALL
(US$3) This stunning 40m waterfall is one of the jewels of the island. The trail begins at the Estación Biológica de Ometepe; it's a steep, four-hour round-trip on an easy-to-follow trail that's lost some of its charm since lots of trees were cut down. But it's still mossy and beautiful at the top, and fabulous for a dip on a hot day.

🏃 Activities

Being relatively sheltered, this side of the island is perfect for kayaking. An obvious destination is Isla del Congo, now called Isla de los Monos (Monkey Island), home to the descendants of four spider monkeys. Spider monkeys aren't present anywhere else on the island (howler and white face monkeys are), so these creatures are pretty

much alone. Don't get too close – these little guys bite. Hacienda Mérida is the closest place to the island that rents kayaks.

The other classic kayaking trip is to the Río Istiam, a swampy inlet that's home to turtles, caimans, the occasional howler monkey and an array of birdlife. Caballito's Mar is the closest kayak-rental place to the entrance of the river and it has guides who know where all the wild things are.

🛏 Sleeping & Eating

★Hacienda Mérida HOTEL $$
(☑ 8868-8973; www.hmerida.com; campsites or hammock per person US$5, dm US$8, r with/without lake view US$35/25; 🅿️@) On the south side of Mérida, this is by far the nicest budget option around (with some very nice midrange rooms thrown in), offering every activity you could possibly want – volcano hikes, kayaking, excellent mountain bikes, sailing, swimming etc. The superstar rooms here are upstairs, with awesome lake views and a shared balcony featuring king-sized hammocks.

Caballito's Mar HOSTEL, GUESTHOUSE $$
(☑ 8842-6120; www.caballitosmar.com; dm/r/ cabin US$8/25/35) About 1km before Mérida, look for a sign to this simple little guesthouse-hostel right on the beach, with great lake views from the waterfront bar-restaurant. Choose between basic dorms, private rooms and cabins. This is the best place to start kayak tours of the Río Istiam (US$25 per person) or DIY trips to nearby Isla del Congo.

Albergue Ecológico El Porvenir LODGE $$
(☑ 8438-4851; www.hotel-elporvenir-isladeom etepe.com; s/d from US$11/23; 🅿️) At the foot of Volcán Maderas, this sunny lodge and restaurant has it all – great volcano views and petroglyphs amid attractive gardens, a restaurant serving good-value meals, and simple but spacious guest rooms. You can arrange everything here from horseback riding to guided hikes.

ℹ Getting There & Away

The most convenient way to get to Isla de Ometepe is the 17km boat ride from San Jorge to Moyogalpa or San José del Sur. There are 18 departures per day (US$1.50 to US$3, one hour) between 7am and 5:45pm. Most are ferries headed to Moyogalpa, though some smaller boats go to San José del Sur instead. Between November and February winds can make the sea rough, particularly in the afternoon; consider taking the ferry.

Ferries also run from Altagracia to Granada and San Carlos, although at the time of writing these services had been suspended until further notice. (Updates will be posted on the bottom of the Ferry Schedules page on www.ometepe nicaragua.com.) If service is running again and you're thinking about doing the Granada–Altagracia run one way only, it's best to leave from Granada – you travel in the day, get some views and arrive late afternoon. Leaving Altagracia for Granada you travel at night and arrive in the early hours of the morning.

Most boats can transport bikes and other equipment without a problem. If you're loading your car onto the ferry, you might have to wait, depending on availability; otherwise, no reservations are required. Passengers pay on the boat.

❶ Getting Around

The southern loop between Moyogalpa and Altagracia, the island's two major towns, is a beautifully paved road. The condition of all other roads varies. The island is bigger than it looks and very few destinations are really walkable. The lack of traffic makes hitchhiking a problem (although any passing pick-up will almost certainly give you a ride) – but you'll also be happy if you have your own rental car or motorbike.

BUS

There's only one main road on the island; this simplifies things. Take a good look at a map before boarding any buses, though, and consult the latest bus schedules at www.ometepenicara gua.com. Bus service is solid (fares US$0.25 to US$1, depending on how far you're going), but the terrible roads in the southern part of the island take their toll on buses and schedules change frequently. Between Moyogalpa and Altagracia there are hourly buses; fewer run on Sunday. All buses from Moyogalpa to the Maderas side of the island stop in Altagracia about one hour later, then head down the isthmus past Playa Santo Domingo.

At Santa Cruz, buses go right (south) to Mérida and San Ramón, and left (east) to Balgüe, perhaps continuing to La Palma. Buses do not serve the southeastern portion of the island, between San Ramón and La Palma, at all.

CAR & MOTORCYCLE

Moyogalpa is the place to rent cars and motorbikes; you'll also find places to rent motorbikes (around US$25 per day) on the other side of the island, around Playa Santo Domingo.

Car rentals are trickier. There aren't a lot of cars available, and one can run you as much as US$100 a day. If you want to drive a car around

Ometepe, you're probably better off bringing one from the mainland.

TAXI

Taxis are rare and expensive, and they're all minivans, jeeps or pick-ups with 4WD. They meet all ferries, but otherwise you should have your hotel make arrangements with a driver at least a few hours in advance.

From Moyogalpa, expect to pay at least US$20 to Altagracia, US$20 to Playa Santo Domingo, US$25 to Balgüe, US$30 to Mérida and US$45 to San Ramón, though your drivers might quote you higher prices – and on an island as remote as this, you won't have a lot of options other than to pay what they request.

SOUTHERN PACIFIC COAST

Southwestern Nicaragua's Pacific beaches offer amazing surf, sand and sun. To get to the Tola beaches – El Astillero down to Playa Gigante – you'll need to pass through Rivas and Tola, then head toward the beach. There is only extremely rough 4WD access on the coast between Veracruz and El Astillero. San Juan del Sur serves as the access point for the beaches between Playa Marsella in the north downward to El Ostional.

San Juan del Sur

POP 15,500

Easygoing San Juan del Sur is the hub for exploration of Nicaragua's toned-and-tanned southern Pacific beaches. The town itself, with its clapboard Victorian houses, a towering statue of Christ on a neighboring hillside and a steady influx of young and beautiful international travelers and surfers, is quite fun, with a good range of dining, drinking, shopping and nightlife venues.

And while the once-sleepy fishing village doesn't sit on an amazing stretch of coastline – you need to head just north or south for that – its half-moon, brown-sugar beach is pretty for a sunset stroll. Top it all off with a string of world-class surfing enclaves located within easy distance of town, and you have all the workings to kick off an amazing adventure in paradise.

🏊 Activities

The best surfing is generally April to December, but waves are less crowded in the low season. There's a beach break on bigger swells at the northern end of the beach, but most surfers hire boats or stay at the beaches north and south of town. Casa Oro Hostel runs a daily shuttle to Playa Maderas.

Several outfitters in San Juan del Sur rent bicycles. The hike to the lookout at Cristo de la Misericordia (Christ of Mercy statue; US$2; ☺8am-5pm) statue, perched high above town, is also a popular excursion.

★**Da Flying Frog**   CANOPY TOUR
(☑8613-4460; www.daflyingfrog.com; per person US$30; ☺8am-4pm Mon-Sat; 🅵) This popular and professionally run canopy tour is fun for the whole family. With 17 platforms and 2.5km of cables, it's one of the biggest zip lines in Nicaragua. Getting to and from the rural site, outside of town on the road to Playa Maderas (transportation provided, if you need it) is a great opportunity for monkey- and bird-watching, too.

Good Times Surf Shop   SURFING
(☑8675-1621; www.goodtimessurfshop.com; btwn El Gato Negro y Barrio Café; ☺7:30am-7pm) Rents gear and organizes shuttles, surf lessons and day trips to nearby breaks.

Rancho Chilamate   HORSEBACK RIDING
(☑8849-3470; www.ranchochilamate.com; Escamequita; daytime/sunset ride US$75/79) Excellent horseback riding tours at a beautiful ranch located a 20-minute drive south of San Juan del Sur (round-trip transportation provided). Daily rides last around three hours and happen at low tide. Riders must be at least 18 years old.

🎓 Courses

APC Spanish School   LANGUAGE COURSE
(☑8450-8990; www.spanishschoolapcsjds.com; Casa de Cultura, Av del Mar s/n, BDF Bank, 20m S; per person per week from US$120, with lodging from US$195) This fun language-learning operation offers accommodations, tours, a cultural center and volunteer opportunities.

Spanish Corner School   LANGUAGE COURSE
(☑2568-2142; www.spanishcornerschool.com; Royal Chateau Hotel, 1 c N; classes per 1hr/10hr/20hr US$9/80/125; ☺8am-10pm) Spanish lessons with an emphasis on Nicaraguan history and culture.

🛏 Sleeping

★**Casa Oro Hostel**   HOSTEL **$$**
(☑2568-2415; www.casaeloro.com; Av del Cine, Parque Central, 1 c O, 50m N; dm/d from US$10/32; 🅿@🛜) This backpacker standby has all the amenities – a great information center, free breakfast, communal kitchen, lounge space, free wi-fi (with complimentary iPads), rooftop bar with ocean views – and good vibes 24/7. Dorm beds and rooms are only available by walk-in: first-come, first-served. Casa Oro also runs the most popular and reliable beach shuttles; check the website for the latest schedules.

Buena Onda
Backpackers Hostel   HOSTEL **$$**
(☑8743-2769;   www.sanjuandelsurbackpackers. com; Casa de Dragon, 50m a mano izquierda, Barrio Frente Sur; d with/without view US$26/21; 🛜) A few minutes' climb from the center of San Juan del Sur, in the hilltop neighborhood known as Barrio Frente Sur, this quiet hostel with a mellow atmosphere has beautiful views – especially from the rooftop terrace (and the vantage point of a hammock). Some rooms have ocean views, too. There's also a communal kitchen.

Rositas Hotel   HOTEL **$$**
(☑8326-7733; www.rositashotel.com; mercado, 1½ c O; d/tr/q from US$33/39/45) This classic hotel has dated and rather quirky guest rooms, but it's a great deal. The location is just half a block from the beach, and the hotel features a breezy common area on the 2nd level. Choose between a 'quiet' room or one with a nice balcony over the street.

El Coco Azul   HOTEL **$$$**
(☑2568-2697; www.elcocoazul.com; Av del Parque; Calle Iglesia; d with/without bathroom US$60/50; 🛜) This petite, boutique-style hotel, cheerfully painted in blue and white, is youthful and affordable. The place has plenty to offer: a location just a stone's throw from the beach, inviting common areas and clean, airy guest rooms, each with a private balcony.

Royal Chateau Hotel   HOTEL **$$$**
(☑2568-2551; www.hotelroyalchateau.com; mercado, 1 c E; d from US$75; 🅿❄🛜) The phrase 'royal chateau' gives you the wrong idea – this is more like a motel with a tropical spin – but this place is good value, with bright and spacious modern rooms set around a palm-studded parking area. If your legs can take the climb, go for a top-floor room – highlighted by naive art – for sweeping bay views.

🍴 Eating

★**Barrio Café**   INTERNATIONAL **$**
(www.barriocafesanjuan.com;   Av del Cine & Calle Central; dishes US$3-8; ☺6:30am-10pm)

San Juan del Sur

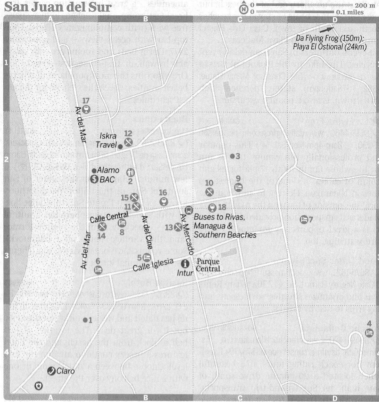

Da Flying Frog (150m);
Playa El Ostional (24km)

Excellent coffee; gourmet breakfasts; killer *ceviche;* an all-Nica staff; potent, fruity rum cocktails – what's not to like? This breezy cafe is on a centrally located corner just a block from the beach. There's a nice boutique hotel attached.

Asados Juanita NICARAGUAN **$**
(Av Mercado; mains US$3-5; ☺6-10pm Mon-Sat) Follow the plumes of smoke to this hugely popular outdoor *fritanga* (grill) where you'll choose between steak or chicken, sweet or savory plantains, and *gallo pinto*. Eat in, or take away – it's delicious and inexpensive.

El Gato Negro CAFE **$**
(UNO Station, 2½ c O; sandwiches & light meals US$4-7; ☺7am-3pm; ☎) 🖉 This hippie-dippy cafe offers the standard range of coffees, juices and fruit plates, plus crepes, bagels and other breakfast-oriented specials. The main draw is the ample lounge space and leafy back patio – both great places to meet

other travelers – and the excellent selection of new and used books.

Super Frutto ICE CREAM **$**
(Hotel Estrella, ½ c E; ice cream US$2-3) Arguably the best frozen treat in all of Nicaragua. Super Frutto does terrific Italian-style gelato, all made in-house. Note: in the heat, you're better off avoiding cones.

Taco Stop TEX-MEX **$**
(www.tacostopnicaragua.com; Av del Cine; mains US$3-7; ☺8:30am-5:30am) This centrally located branch of Nicaragua's modern taco chain offers tacos, quesadillas, burritos, salads and soups – you can eat in-house or take it to go. Note the hours: it's almost never closed. There's a rival taco shop on the other end of the same block.

G&G Gourmet INTERNATIONAL **$$$**
(☎7789-7460; www.ggsanjuan.com; mercado, 25m S; mains US$9-13; ☺6:30-10pm Tue-Sat) A step

San Juan del Sur

Activities, Courses & Tours
1 APC Spanish School.............................A4
2 Good Times Surf Shop.......................B2
3 Spanish Corner School......................C2

Sleeping
4 Buena Onda Backpackers
   Hostel... D4
5 Casa Oro Hostel................................B3
6 El Coco Azul.......................................B3
7 Pelican Eyes Resort.........................D3
8 Rositas Hotel.....................................B3
9 Royal Chateau Hotel.........................C2

Eating
10 Asados Juanita.................................C2
11 Barrio Café.......................................B2
12 El Gato Negro...................................B2
13 G&G Gourmet...................................B3
14 Super Frutto.....................................B3
15 Taco Stop...B2

Drinking & Nightlife
16 Bar Republika...................................B2
17 Howler Bar.. A1
   La Cascada .... (see 7)
18 San Juan del Sur Cervecería.............C2

up from most of the offerings in this laid-back beach town, the refined G&G, owned by a Guataleman-Argentinian couple, offers a short menu of gourmet menu items, including shrimp marinated in passion fruit, seafood risotto, and the excellent pasta *vongole* (homemade pasta with fresh clams, garlic, white wine and cream). The chocolate volcano dessert is locally famous. Make reservations.

Drinking & Nightlife

San Juan del Sur Cervecería   BEER HALL
(www.sjdsbrewers.com; Av Mercado; ⊘11am-2am Wed-Mon) Nicaragua's first craft brewery is – unsurprisingly – a huge hit. Established by American beer enthusiasts, the sleek industrial space is a great place to try the house brews on tap, like the chocolatey 'Pelibuey' porter or the rose-hued 'Jamaica' tart wit. There's live music some nights, brunches on the weekend and a free **brewery tour** on Sundays at noon.

Howler Bar   BAR
(beachfront; ⊘11am-2am) Across from the beach, indoor-outdoor Howler Bar offers a little of everything under an open-air thatched-roof *palapa*: fresh smoothies and

Latin American food, live music, cinema nights and cultural events, craft cocktails and late-night dancing. The bartenders are famous for their *micheladas* (beer cocktails).

Bar Republika   BAR
(Calle Central; dishes US$3-8; ⊘8:30am-late) When you're tired of Toña and rum, this hipster-friendly French-style bar should be your first stop: it does martinis, White Russians and gin and tonics – to name just a few – and offers food specials from tacos and burgers to salads and pitas with hummus. Also open for breakfast.

La Cascada   BAR
(www.pelicaneyesresort.com; Pelican Eyes Resort; ⊘7am-10pm) The hilltop bar and restaurant at **Pelican Eyes** (☎2563-7000, ext 310; www.pelicaneyesresort.com; d from US$170, villa for 4 US$490; ❋🖤🗯) is a lovely spot for sunset drinks – happy-hour specials often include access to the small but scenic swimming pool. There's live music and entertainment on Wednesday nights and other times, too; check local listings.

ℹ Information

Don't walk alone on the beach at night. When heading home from the bars, walk in a large group or jump in a cab.
BAC (Hotel Casa Blanca, Av del Mar) There's a MasterCard-friendly ATM at Hotel Casa Blanca.
Claro (Av del Mar s/n) Pick up a SIM card for your cell phone here.
Intur (☎2568-3022; Calle Iglesia, frente Parque Central) Well stocked with brochures.
Police (☎2453-3732, 8453-3732; final, Av del Mar)

ℹ Getting There & Away

Several outfitters in San Juan del Sur offer shuttle service to beaches north and south. Casa Oro Hostel's (p465) daily shuttles for instance, make the trip to Playa Maderas (round-trip US$5) four times daily, to Playa Hermosa (round-trip US$8) twice daily, and to Playa Remanso (round-trip US$8) once daily. Have a stroll around town to see who's advertising shuttle services to other beaches in the region, including popular destinations like Playas Marsella and Majagual.

BUS

There is regular bus service from the bus stop in front of the market to destinations including the following:
Rivas (US$1, 45 minutes, 6am to 6pm, roughly every 30 to 60 minutes) Here you'll

make connections to onward destinations like Granada and Managua.

Southern beaches (US$1.50, 20 minutes to one hour, three to four times daily) Service to Playa Remanso, Playa El Coco, Refugio de Vida Silvestre La Flor and Playa El Ostional. Departure times change occasionally; stop into a hostel in San Juan del Sur to see or ask about the latest posted times. Bus service to the beaches south of town is regular, but depends on road conditions – if you're here in the wet season, you may find it drastically reduced (or even cancelled).

Shuttle Bus

Several travel agencies and outfitters in town, like **Iskra Travel** ([𝒥] 2568-2054; www.iskra travel.com; UNO Station, 2½ c O; shuttle to San Jorge or Granada US$30, shuttle to Managua US$40; ⊙ 9am-6pm), offer shuttle services to Managua, Granada, Masaya, San Jorge (for the ferry to Ometepe), the border of Costa Rica, and other destinations. Book in advance.

CAR

Alamo ([𝒥] 2277-1117; www.alamonicaragua. com; Av del Mar) rents sedans and 4WD vehicles. You'll probably want the latter, especially if you're heading to the beaches north of town.

TAXI

Taxis congregate close to the market. In theory, each driver has a list of set rates for destinations outside of town, but you'll hear a small range of prices. Get together with other travelers for the best deal.

Beaches North of San Juan del Sur

The gorgeous beaches north of San Juan del Sur – Maderas, Majagual, Marsella and Ocotal – are magnets for surfers and sunbathers alike. The scene is rapidly developing: yoga retreats and boutique hotels are popping up along the coast, and the breaks can get crowded during high season.

Playa Maderas

A good-time-vibes backpacker and surfer hangout, this stunning beach – with rocky expanses that offer excellent tide pooling and wide, wonderful sandy stretches for sunbathing – is famed for having one of the best beach breaks in the country. The surf break here, sometimes called Los Playones, is a slow wave in fairly deep (2m) water, good for beginners, with two right and two left breaks that get hollow on a rising tide.

🛏 Sleeping & Eating

Matilda's Hostal   HOSTEL **$**
([𝒥] 8456-3461; www.hostalmatilda.com; Playa Maderas; dm/s/d from US$10/15/25) A basic but beloved family-run complex, Matilda's rents surfer huts and basic rooms.

Casa Maderas Ecolodge   LODGE **$$**
([𝒥] 8786-4897; www.casamaderas.com; empalme Playa Maderas–Marsella, 200m N; dm/s/d/tr US$18/38/42/48; 🛜 🏊) 𝒫 A budget pick near both Playa Maderas and Playa Marsella, this lodge-style hostel is set on 3 hectares of lush, jungle-like terraced gardens. Choose between dorm beds draped in mosquito nets or cozy cabins on the hillside. The food's only so-so, and it's not exactly on the beach – it's a 10-minute walk away – but it's fair value.

Tacos Locos   MEXICAN **$$**
(beachfront, Playa Maderas; dishes US$6-14) A breezy taco shop overlooking the beach; it's also a good place to seek shelter from the sun on a hot day.

ⓘ Getting There & Away

Most travelers drive their own 4WD vehicles to these beaches or take a shuttle service from San Juan del Sur.

The Casa Oro (p465) shuttle (US$5, four daily) drops passengers off at Playa Maderas, a short walk away from Majagual.

Hiring a cab from San Juan del Sur is a third option. Expect to pay anywhere from US$10 to US$30 per carload; you can pre-arrange this with your hotel or hostel, or negotiate with the licensed taxi drivers parked near the market.

Beaches South of San Juan del Sur

Heading south from San Juan del Sur toward the border of Costa Rica, a string of low-key beach villages offer surf breaks, sea-turtle-watching opportunities, and calm waters for snorkeling. There's an interesting wildlife refuge, but you'll also see plenty of monkeys in the trees if you just keep your eyes open while traveling along the hilly forested road. Several segments of *Survivor* were filmed in Playa Hermosa; today, it's a private beach with an admission fee.

Playa Hermosa

Playa Hermosa is famous for great surfing – there are five breaks on this beach alone – and a cool, lost-in-paradise vibe. It's a privately owned beach, so you'll need to pay an entrance fee of US$10 at Playa Hermosa Ecolodge. Here, at the lodge and surf camp, you can also arrange activities like horseback riding, sailing, fishing, ziplining and the like.

Just south of Playa Hermosa (and north of Playa El Coco) are the increasingly popular beaches and surf breaks of Playa Yankee and Playa Escameca.

Playa El Coco

This is a world-class beach – a spectacular stretch of sparkling sand punctuated by cliffs so pretty that they grace about half of the country's tourist literature. Prices here are steep for the area.

🛏 Sleeping & Eating

La Veranera GUESTHOUSE **$$$**
(☑ 8328-6260; www.laveranera.net; Calle Playa el Coco; d from US$90, q with shared bathroom US$80; ❀ 🛜 ☲) This sweet beachfront B&B has just four fan-cooled guest rooms, all with access to a pretty swimming pool. There's a simple onsite bar and restaurant. Though comparatively pricey, the one quad room that sleeps four (with shared bathroom) is a good budget pick. Note that air-conditioning costs US$10 extra per night.

Puesta del Sol SEAFOOD **$$$**
(www.playaelcoco.com.ni/restaurante; Parque Maritimo El Coco, beachfront; mains US$9-20; ⊙ 7am-late; 🛝) A beachfront eatery serving breakfast as well as lunchtime specials like *ceviche,* seafood stew and seafood risotto. There's also a children's menu. The cuisine and service are hit or miss, but the sunset views are sublime.

Refugio de Vida Silvestre La Flor

One of the principal laying grounds for endangered olive ridley and leatherback turtles, this wildlife refuge (locally called by its shorter name, 'La Flor') is 20km south of San Juan del Sur. It's easy to visit on a guided tour from San Juan del Sur or from Playa Hermosa Ecolodge in Playa Hermosa.

When there aren't any turtles around, the park still has an attractive, undeveloped beach, a couple of monkeys onsite and a few short trails; there's a decent beach break (right and left) at the northern end. (But during turtle season there's no surfing as the beach is off-limits.)

You can camp at the reserve (US$20 per tent). The closest hotels are in Playa El Coco.

Playa El Ostional

This fishing village, practically a stone's throw from the Costa Rican border, has an attractive brown-sugar beach that's often totally empty. These calm waters are great for snorkeling and swimming; the beach is a lovely spot to get away from it all while still remaining in easy distance of San Juan del Sur. As the tide rolls in, fisherfolk push their colorful wooden boats out into the surf – a prime photo opportunity.

🛏 Sleeping

Manta Raya Hospedaje GUESTHOUSE **$$**
(☑ 8353-7091; beachfront, north end; s/d/tr US$15/25/35) The rooms here are quite basic – a bed, fan and lamp – but some come with ocean views (and a slight breeze).

ⓘ Getting There & Away

Although there is regular bus service between San Juan del Sur and El Ostional (US$1.50, one hour, four daily), you'll need to walk several kilometers from the bus stop to many of the beaches. Playa El Coco, La Flor and Playa El Ostional are all close to the road. Driving is also a convenient option.

LEÓN & NORTHWESTERN NICARAGUA

This is Nicaragua at its fieriest and most passionate. The regional capital of León is – and will always be – a hotbed of intellectualism and independence. Just out of León, more than a dozen volcanic peaks wait to be climbed (or surfed). This region has some of the best beach accommodations – and best surfing – in the country. And the virgin wetlands of the Reserva Natural Isla Juan Venado are not to be missed. Further afield, you'll find the biggest mangrove forest in Central America, awe-inspiring beauty at Reserva Natural Volcán Cosigüina and unique windows into everyday Nicaraguan life in the little towns along the way.

León

POP 201,100
Intensely political, buzzing with energy and, at times, drop-dead gorgeous (in a

crumbling, colonial kind of way), León is what Managua should be – a city of awe-inspiring churches, fabulous art collections, stunning streetscapes, cosmopolitan eateries, fiery intellectualism, and all-week, walk-everywhere, happening nightlife. Many people fall in love with Granada, but most of them leave their heart in León.

History

León was originally founded in 1524 by Francisco Hernández de Córdoba near the foot of Volcán Momotombo. After a series of natural disasters, the Spanish abandoned the site in 1610 to rebuild the city near the important indigenous settlement of Subtiava, where it remains.

León served as the nation's capital for most of the colonial period and also served as the ecclesiastical center for the entire region, resulting in an impressive legacy of many fine churches and colonial buildings. The Universidad Autónoma de Nicaragua (UNAN), Nicaragua's first university, was founded here in 1912.

Traditionally León has been the most politically progressive of Nicaraguan cities. During the revolution, virtually the entire town fought against Somoza. Dramatic murals around town serve as reminders of that period and the city remains a strong Sandinista heartland.

◉ Sights

Catedral de León   CATHEDRAL
(Parque Central; ⊘ 8am-noon & 2-4pm Mon-Sat) Officially known as the Basílica de la Asunción, León's cathedral is the largest in Central America, its expansive design famously (and perhaps apocryphally) approved for construction in much more important Lima, Peru. Leónese leaders originally submitted a more modest but bogus set of plans, but architect Diego José de Porres Esquivel, the Capitan General of Guatemala (also responsible for San Juan Bautista de Subtiaba, La Recolección and La Merced churches, among others), pulled the switcheroo and built this beauty instead.

Museo Rubén Darío   MUSEUM
(www.rubendario.enriquebolanos.org; cnr Calles Central Rubén Darío & 4a Av SO; by donation; ⊘ 8am-noon & 2-5pm Tue-Sat, 8am-noon Sun) Nicaragua's most famous poet, Rubén Dario, lived in this house for the first 14 years of his life – indeed, he started writing poetry right here at age 12. That first poem is on display here, as are various personal effects. Of all the museums and monuments dedicated to the poet that are scattered across his doting homeland, this colonial house seems like the one where you'd be most likely to run into his ghost.

★ Museo de Arte Fundación Ortiz-Gurdián   MUSEUM
(Parque Central, 2c W; US$0.80; ⊘ 10:30am-6:30pm Tue-Sat, 9am-6pm Sun) Probably the finest museum of contemporary art in all of Central America, the Ortiz-Gurdián Collection has spilled over from its original home in Casa Don Norberto Ramiréz, refurbished in 2000 to its original Creole Civil style, with Arabic tiles and impressive flagstones. The collection includes works by Picasso, Chagall, Miró and a number of noted Nicaraguan artists.

Museo de Leyendas y Tradiciones   MUSEUM
(☑ 2315-4678; 4a Calle SO, frente Ruinas San Sebastián; US$2; ⊘ 8am-5pm) León's most entertaining and eclectic museum, the Museum of Myths & Traditions is now housed in La XXI (the 21st Garrison). What makes this museum unmissable is the striking contrast of its main subjects: a quirky collection of life-sized papier-mâché figures from Leónese history and legend, handmade by founder Señora Toruña (who is also represented in glorious papier-mâché), and murals graphically depicting methods the Guardia Nacional used to torture prisoners.

Iglesia de la Recolección   CHURCH
(1a Av NE, 2a Calle NE; ⊘ hours vary) Three blocks north of the cathedral, the 1786 Iglesia de la Recolección is considered the city's most beautiful church, a Mexican-style baroque confection of swirling columns and bas-relief medallions that portray the life of Christ. Dyed a deep yellow, accented with cream and age, the lavishly decorated facade may be what makes the cover of all the tourist brochures, but be sure to stop inside and admire the slender mahogany columns and ceiling decorated with harvest motifs.

Museo Historico de la Revolución   MUSEUM
(Parque Central; US$2; ⊘ 8am-5pm) León is the heart and soul of liberal Nicaragua. Stop into this museum for an overview of the Nicaraguan revolutionaries who stood up against the Somoza dictatorship, tracing national history from the devastating earthquake of 1972 to the Sandinista overthrow.

📖 Courses

Hostels are the best places to inquire about private Spanish tutors (who charge from around US$7 per hour).

León Spanish School   LANGUAGE COURSE
(☑8183-7389; www.leonspanishschool.org; La Casa de Cultura, 1a Calle NO, Iglesia de La Merced, 2c O; 20hr course with/without homestay US$250/150) Based in La Casa de Cultura, this is a professional operation with plenty of cultural activities and out-of-town excursions.

👉 Tours

Volcano surfing is all the rage around León, which involves riding a 'sandboard' (something like a modified snowboard) or toboggan down black-gravel slopes. Agencies around town offer excursions to Cerro Negro, Volcán Cosigüina and other area volcanoes.

Tierra Tour   ADVENTURE TOUR
(☑2315-4278; www.tierratour.com; Iglesia de la Merced, 1½ c N) A well-established operator with locations in both León and Granada. Full- and half-day tours go to the volcanoes (including both trekking and sandboarding excursions) and pretty much anywhere you'd want to go in the region, from León Viejo to Reserva Natural Isla Juan Venado. Also offers daily shuttles to and from Granada, as well as to Antigua and El Salvador.

Tierra Tour also arranges passage on the daily boat across the Gulf of Fonseca to El Salvador.

Get Up Stand Up   SURFING
(☑5800-2394; www.gsupsurf.com; del Banco Procredit, ½ c S; ◷9am-9pm) This cool surf shop – the only one in León – runs daily shuttles to and from Las Peñitas and arranges lessons and gear rental in conjunction with Bigfoot Beach Hostel (p477). The indie brand also designs and prints its own T-shirts. It's a great stop for information if you're considering a surf excursion.

Quetzaltrekkers   ADVENTURE TOUR
(☑2311-7388; www.leon.quetzaltrekkers.org; Mercantil, ½ c O) 🍃 Profits from this outstanding operator go to Las Tías, a charity that helps children from underprivileged areas learn to build their own lives, and other worthy causes; volunteers are very welcome.

🎉 Festivals & Events

Every Saturday, from early afternoon till midnight, the Parque Central comes alive for the Tertulia Leónesa, inviting everyone outside to eat, drink and dance to music played by local combos. León also plays host to a number of lively annual celebrations.

THE CITY OF CHURCHES

With more than 16 places to pray, including several more in Barrio Subtiaba, the city tourist board is lobbying to have León officially declared 'The City of Churches.'

The 1639 Iglesia de San Francisco (Parque Central, 2c O, ½ c N; ◷hours vary) is one of the oldest in the city – a national heritage site with lots of gold, a gorgeous nave and a rather rococo interior. It was abandoned between 1830 and 1881, then refurbished with two elaborate altarpieces for San Antonio and Nuestra Señora de la Merced (Our Lady of Mercy). The attached Convent San Francisco (◷hours vary), founded in 1639, was badly damaged during the 1979 battle for León. Check out what used to be the convent at Hotel El Convento next door.

Nuestra Señora de Guadalupe (7a Calle SE & Av Central), built in 1743, is León's only church that's oriented north–south; it's historically connected to the city by the 1850 Puente Guadalupe, built across the Río Chiquito. And don't let the dumpy, modernist, neoclassic exterior of 1625 Capilla San Juan de Dios (cnr 1a Calle SO & 3rd Av SO) fool you – when it's open, the interior is one of the city's prettiest, with lots of precious wood and a very human scale.

For something completely different, swing by ultra-Gothic 1884 Iglesia Zaragoza (Parque Central, 4 c O, 2c N; ◷hours vary), one of the best spots for film students to stage a vampire flick. They could also use one of the several ruined churches around town, including Ruinas Veracruz and Ruinas Iglesia Santiago in Barrio Subtiaba, and Ruinas San Sebastian (Parque Central, 3 c S), near La XXI (the 21st Garrison).

NICARAGUA LEÓN

Olla Quemada (100m);
Barrio Subtiava (1km);
Bautista de Subtiaba (1.1km);
Poneloya (20km)

Museo de
Arte Fundación
Ortiz-Gurdián

Parque
Central

C Central Rubén Darío

Nuestra
Señora de
Guadalupe
(450m)

Dilectus (1km)

Río Chiquito

Semana Santa   RELIGIOUS
(⊘ late Mar or early Apr) The Leónese Semana
Santa is something special, with Barrio Subtiaba's colorful sawdust 'carpets,' temporary
and beautiful images that the funeral procession for Jesus walks over, and a sand-castle
competition in Poneloya.

Masacre del 23 Julio 1959   CULTURAL
(⊘ Jul 23) One afternoon in 1959, local schoolchildren staged a demonstration against Somoza. As they chanted 'Freedom! Freedom!,'
the Guardia Nacional fired into the crowd,
killing four students and wounding several others. Those wounded, some in wheel-

Leyendas y Tradiciones (p470) on a parade from the cathedral to Barrio Subtiaba.

Día de la Purísima Concepción RELIGIOUS
(☉ Dec 7) Known simply as 'La Purísima' and observed throughout the country, this lively celebration of Nicaragua's patron saint is the occasion for the *La Gritería* (a shouting ritual that honors the Virgin Mary), enjoyed here with unusual vigor.

🛏 Sleeping

Bigfoot Hostel HOSTEL $
(☎ 2315-3863; www.bigfoothostelleon.com; del Banco Procredit, ½ c S; dm/d from US$8/26; ❄ 🛜 🏊) With kitchen access, a miniature swimming pool and freshly made mojitos on offer, it wouldn't really matter what the rooms were like, but they're a good deal. There's a good travelers' vibe at this party hostel – staff swear the party shuts down at 10pm – and a sweet little cafe-bar out front.

Lazybones Hostel HOSTEL $
(☎ 2311-3472; www.lazyboneshostelnicaragua.com; 2a Av NO, Parque Rubén Darío, 2½ c N; dm US$8, r with/without bathroom US$30/20; 🅿 @ 🛜 🏊) This quiet, less party-oriented spot has trim grounds, excellent rooms and dorms, and a laid-back atmosphere. The age-old patio and sitting areas are every bit as lovely as those in some midrange hotels, and the bar, good-sized pool and yummy breakfasts make this a good deal.

Hostal Las Vacaciones GUESTHOUSE $
(☎ 8552-1568; Iglesia La Recolección, 200m E; s/d US$20/25; 🛜) This popular guesthouse is perfectly located and affordably priced, offering hostel-style accommodations and comfortable private rooms. Amenities include a shared kitchen, bicycle rental and leafy terrace space.

Tortuga Booluda HOSTEL $
(☎ 2311-4653; www.tortugabooluda.com; 1a Calle SO, Catedral, 4½ c O; dm/r US$8/24; @ 🛜) More small hotel than hostel, the 'Lazy Turtle' does, however, offer all the hostel amenities, namely a great kitchen, book exchange, free coffee, pool table, some good chill-out areas and a sociable atmosphere. Rooms are simple but stylish, and dorms are spacious enough. Note that you can't reserve dorm beds – they're first-come, first-served.

Vía Vía HOSTEL $
(☎ 2311-6142; www.viaviacafe.com; del Banco Pro-Credit, ½ c S; dm/s/d US$7/19/29; 🛜) The Vía

chairs, still lead a parade, right after every single marching band from the area has announced that their generation will not forget.

Carnaval Mitos y Leyendas CULTURAL
(Nov 1) This Halloween-esque fiesta features the papier-mâché crew from the Museo de

León

⦿ **Top Sights**
1 Museo de Arte Fundación Ortiz-
    Gurdián.. B4

⦿ **Sights**
2 Capilla San Juan de Dios...................... B5
3 Catedral de León.................................. D4
4 Convent San Francisco........................ B4
5 Iglesia de la Recolección..................... D3
6 Iglesia Zaragoza................................... A3
7 Museo de Leyendas y Tradiciones....... C5
8 Museo Historico de la Revolución........ C4
9 Museo Rubén Darío.............................. B4
10 Puente Guadalupe............................... D6
11 Ruinas San Sebastián......................... C6

🏃 **Activities, Courses & Tours**
12 Get Up Stand Up...................................E3
13 León Spanish School........................... B4
14 Quetzaltrekkers................................... C3
15 Tierra Tour... C3

🛏 **Sleeping**
16 Bigfoot Hostel......................................E3
17 Casona Colonial................................... D2
18 Hostal Las Vacaciones.........................F3
19 Lazybones Hostel................................. C3
20 Tortuga Booluda.................................. A5
21 Vía Vía..E3

🍴 **Eating**
22 Café La Nicaragüita............................. C3
23 CocinArte... B5
24 La Unión Supermercado...................... D4
25 Mercado Central.................................. D4
26 Pan y Paz... E4
27 Paz de Luna Café................................. D2
28 Supermercado La Colonia................... A4
29 Taquezal... C4

🍷 **Drinking & Nightlife**
30 Bohemios Bar-Disco............................ C4

🎭 **Entertainment**
31 Alianza Francesa................................. D2
32 Teatro Municipal José de la Cruz
    Mena.. C5

ℹ **Information**
33 Beni Tours.. D3
34 Intur... C3
35 Oficina de Información Turistica
    León.. C4

🚌 **Transport**
36 Gekko Explorer.................................... E3
37 Nica Time... C3
38 Ruta del Golfo...................................... B5
39 Tierra Tour... C3

Vía chain of hostels, which stretches from Kathmandu to Buenos Aires, consistently comes up with the goods. This is no exception, offering beautiful, colonial-style rooms with great bathrooms, and spacious six-bed dorms with their own bathrooms. The patio area is lush and there's an atmospheric cafe-bar area out front.

Casona Colonial HISTORIC HOTEL **$$**
(☑ 2311-3178; www.casonacolonialguest.com; 4a Calle NE, Parque San Juan, ½ c O; s/d from US$20/25; ❂❋🛜) With more character than many in this price range, the medium-sized rooms here are long on colonial atmosphere without all the costly little extras. Beds are big, with lavish bedheads, and the occasional chip in the paintwork or tear in the wallpaper adds to (rather than detracts from) the charm.

🍴 Eating

The best place to eat on the cheap or buy fresh veggies is the **Mercado Central** (Parque Central, 2c E; ⊘ 6am-5pm), with several inexpensive eateries serving *comidas corrientes* (set meals). After hours, two of the best *fritangas* (grills) in town set up right

outside, on the street behind the cathedral, where you can enjoy a huge meal for around US$2. **La Unión Supermercado** (1a Calle NE; ⊘ 8am-10pm Mon-Sat, to 8pm Sun) is a big supermarket option for self-caterers, though **La Colonia** (www.lacolonia.com.ni; La Casa de Cultura, 2c O; ⊘ 9am-9pm) is more upscale.

★ **Pan y Paz** CAFE **$**
(☑ 8631-2760; www.panypaz.com; esquina de los bancos, 1½ c E; mains US$3-6; ⊘ 7am-9pm Mon-Sat; 🛜) Run by a European couple, this fabulous French bakery specializes in homemade breads. Grab a table on the breezy interior courtyard and choose from a menu of freshly baked pastries and gourmet salads and sandwiches. Later in the day, try the cheese plate; it even has Argentine wines by the glass. An added bonus: the prices are more than fair.

Paz de Luna Café CAFE **$**
(☑ 2311-2581; www.pazdelunabb.com; Iglesia La Recolección, 1½ c N; mains US$3-6) At this sleek, hipster-friendly coffee shop – think black-and-white tiled floors, a gilded chandelier, fruit crates repurposed as furniture – a wall-sized chalkboard menu spells out the

long menu of coffee drinks, breakfasts (both traditionally Nicaraguan and otherwise), crêpes, panini, omelets, salads and pastas.

★ **Café La Nicaragüita** INTERNATIONAL **$$**
(Iglesia La Merced, 2 c N, ½ c O; mains US$4-8; ☺noon-9pm Thu-Tue) This friendly little restaurant uses fresh and local produce to make a solid range of menu items: sandwiches, salads, burgers, pastas, steaks and fajitas, to name a few, plus a few Nicaraguan small plates (like *tostones*, or fried plantain slices) for good measure. Also on the chalkboard: fresh fruit smoothies and icy rum-based cocktails, from mojitos to daiquiris (US$2).

CocinArte VEGETARIAN **$$**
(☏8854-6928; www.cocinarterestaurant.com; 4a Calle SO, frente El Laborío; mains US$4-7; ☺noon-10pm Wed-Mon; 🖉) León's vegetarian hot spot. This colorful eatery offers meat-free versions of dishes from around the world in the elegant but relaxed surrounds of an old colonial house. There are a few meat dishes (cooked in separate pans and served with separate cutlery) to keep the carnivores happy, and a leafy patio; the most popular tables are on the front porch.

Taquezal NICARAGUAN **$$**
(1a Calle SO, Parque Central, ½ c O; dishes US$4-7; ☺4pm-late) With a grand, high-ceilinged dining room kept cool by a battalion of ceiling fans, this is one of León's most atmospheric eating spots. The food is good and there's a cozy, candlelit rear patio.

🍸 Drinking & Nightlife

León's university students fuel the party. There are plenty of other places to get your drink on – 1a Calle west of the park is a particularly good area to go bar-hopping. Many hostels have lively bars that attract both travelers and locals.

There are some discos just outside of town on the bypass road, but also a few good dance floors right in the center of town.

Olla Quemada BAR
(Colegio La Salle, 150m O) This hot spot features a line-up of live music, indie films, Latin dance nights and a good mix of locals and travelers all week.

Bohemios Bar-Disco CLUB
(1a Av NO, Parque Central, ½ c N; ☺9pm-3:30am Wed-Sat) In the unsigned orange building in front of the basketball court, this is your classic Latin disco – plenty of rum, reg-

gaetón and *bacchata* (romantic Dominican dance music).

☆ Entertainment

Teatro Municipal José de la Cruz Mena PERFORMING ARTS
(www.teatrojcmena-nicaragua.com; 2a Av SO, Parque Central, 1 c O, 1 c S; ☺hours vary) Check the board in front of this attractive 1885 theater to see what's on here and around town during your visit. It's been impressively restored, and for less than US$3 you may be able to catch anything from Salvadoran rock groups to art films to the national ballet on the very accessible stage. There's also an online schedule.

Alianza Francesa PERFORMING ARTS
(☏2311-0126; www.alianzafrancesa.org.ni; 1a Av NE, Iglesia de la Recolección, 1½ c N; ☺8am-noon & 2-5pm Mon-Fri) Often screens art-house movies in French and Spanish and sponsors concerts. Drop in for its monthly program.

ℹ️ Information

Most budget spots have wi-fi and do laundry.
BAC (1a Calle NE, La Unión, 10m E)
Clean Express Lavandería (cnr Av Central & 4a Calle NE; ☺7am-7pm) DIY machine wash (US$2) and dry (US$1.25 per 20 minutes) your clothes, or pay a little extra to have it done for you.
Hospital San Vicente (☏2311-6990) Out past the main bus terminal, the region's largest hospital is a 1918 neoclassical beauty that attracts architecture buffs as well as sick tourists.
Intur (☏2311-3382; www.intur.gob.ni; 2a Av NO, Parque Rubén Darío, 1½ c N) Helpful (if they're not too busy) staff have lots of flyers and a reasonable city map. For really tricky questions, the hostels are often better informed.
Marena (Ministry of the Environment & Natural Resources; ☏2311-3776; www.marena.gob. ni; frente Shell station; ☺10am-6pm Mon-Fri) Inconveniently located across from the Shell station at the southern entrance to the León bypass road, it administers three volcanic national reserves – Telica-Rota, Pilas-El Hoyo and Momotombo – and nonvolcanic Isla Juan Venado. It offers general information. Your best bet is going directly to the Isla Juan Venado ranger station in Las Peñitas or with a private tour.
Oficina de Información Turística León (☏2311-3528; Av Central, Parque Central, 25m N; ☺8:30am-noon & 2-6pm Mon-Fri, 9am-5pm Sat & Sun) Just steps from the cathedral, this tourist office is an excellent source of information. If you

speak a little Spanish, the youthful staff can help you plan your travels; if not, it's still one-stop shopping for tours and activities, since many operators post their latest offerings and promotions here.

ⓘ Getting There & Around

The city is strollable, but big enough that you may want to take taxis, particularly at night.

The one-way streets and (relative) lack of traffic make León a good cycling city. You can rent bikes for around US$5 to US$7 per day from hostels.

BUS

National Buses

Most buses leave from León's chaotic **main bus terminal** (☑ 2311-3909; 6a Calle NE, Palí, 1½km E), which has a fun market area nearby (watch your wallet). If you're heading south, you'll invariably pass through Managua.

International Buses

There are several international-bus agencies running through Nicaragua, but the main terminal and booking centers are in Managua. Buses headed south stop first in Managua, with an often lengthy wait between connections – it's better to make your own way there and take the bus from Managua.

Buy bus tickets to Costa Rica and Honduras online, or at **Beni Tours** (☑ 2315-2349; ⊘ 9am-6pm Mon-Fri). If you're heading north for Guatemala or El Salvador, area travel agencies can help you book tickets.

Shuttle Buses

Shuttle services are a good (and secure) way to go between León and various key destinations. Many tour operators in town offer trips, most leaving around 8:30am to 9:30am, in air-conditioned vans. Be sure to book ahead. If you're headed to less popular destinations, be aware that most shuttles don't leave without at least four passengers.

Tierra Tour (☑ 2315-4278; www.tierratour. com; 1a Av NO, Iglesia de la Merced, 1½ c N) and **Nica Time** (☑ 8404-9638; agencianicatime@ gmail.com) go to Granada, Managua and San Juan del Sur. **Gekko Explorer** (☑ 001-305-560-5354; www.gekkotrailsexplorer.com; Procredit Bank, 25m S) goes to Chinandega, plus international destinations like Antigua, Guatemala.

If you're headed to El Salvador, try Gekko Explorer or Tierra Tour. The latter offers a package combining the boat ride from Potosí, Nicaragua to La Union, El Salvador with a night at a beachfront hostel (US$80 per person).

BOAT

A convenient (and beautiful) way to get to El Salvador is the shuttle and boat trip organized by **Ruta del Golfo** (☑ 2315-4099; www.ruta delgolfo.com; Vapues, costado norte, Iglesia El Laborío; border crossing to El Salvador from US$99; ⊘ 9am-6pm); advance booking required. The trip involves a pick-up in León and 4WD transfer to Potosí via Chinandega, then a boat trip across the Gulf of Fonseca to La Unión. Travel time is about five hours, with two to three departures weekly, but factor in another couple of hours for the border crossing itself. Tierra Tour also handles the trip.

NATIONAL BUS SERVICES FROM LEÓN

DESTINATION	COST (US$)	DURATION	FREQUENCY
Chinandega (bus)	0.80-1	1½hr	4:30am-8pm, every 20min
Chinandega (microbus)	1.20	50min	4:30am-8pm, departs when full
Estelí	2.70	2½-3hr	5:20 am-3:30pm, 4 daily
Granada (microbus)	3	2-3hr	hourly
La Paz Centro	0.75	40min	every 45min
Managua (microbus)	2.75	1¼hr	4:30am-7pm, departs when full
Managua (Carr Nueva, via La Paz Centro) *expreso*	1.80	1¼hr	5am-4pm, almost hourly
Managua (Carr Vieja, via Puerto Sandino) *ordinario*	1.50	1¾hr	5am-6:30pm, every 20min
Masaya	2.90	2½hr	hourly
Matagalpa	3	2½hr	4:30am-2:45pm, 3 daily
Nagarote	1	1hr	hourly
Rota (Cerro Negro)	0.75	2¼hr	5:50am-3:20pm, 3 daily
Salinas Grandes	0.80	2hr	5:15am-4pm, 4 daily

Poneloya & Las Peñitas Beaches

The most accessible beaches from León are Poneloya and Las Peñitas, both an easy 20-minute bus ride from Mercadito Subtiaba in León. The road splits at the sea: go right for Poneloya proper, left for more developed La Peñitas and Reserva Natural Isla Juan Venado.

Several wilder, less accessible beaches further south are a bit more difficult to reach, including **Salinas Grandes**, with regular bus service from León and its own access to Reserva Natural Isla Juan Venado. A group of three even less explored beaches can be reached from the fractured but passable Carretera Vieja to Managua: **Puerto Sandino**, **El Velero** and **El Tránsito**.

◎ Sights

Reserva Natural Isla Juan Venado NATURE RESERVE
(US$4.50) This 18km-long, sandy barrier island (in some places only 300m wide) has swimming holes and lots of wildlife, including nesting turtles and mosquitoes galore. On one side of the uninhabited island you'll find long, wild, sandy beaches facing the Pacific, on the other, red and black mangroves reflected in emerald lagoons.

⌂ Sleeping & Eating

For the widest variety of sleeping options, head to Las Peñitas. There's also a famous hostel, Surfing Turtle Lodge, off the coast of Poneloya. Many visitors also visit these beaches on day trips from León.

Bigfoot Beach Hostel HOSTEL $
(☑ 8410-0409; www.bigfoothostellaspenitas.com; del la Policia, 250m S; dm US$5, d/tr with shared bathroom US$15/20; ☞ ☜) The beachfront sister of the popular Bigfoot Hostel (p473) in León, this youth-oriented spot has a swimming pool, a beach-volleyball court, a bar-restaurant with daily happy hour specials, even tent rental (US$3 per person). The hostel offers surf lessons in conjunction with Get Up Stand Up (p471) in León, and runs a convenient daily shuttle to and from town.

★ Surfing Turtle Lodge LODGE $$
(☑ 8640-0644; www.surfingturtlelodge.com; Isla Los Brasiles, Poneloya; dm US$10-12, r US$35-45, cabin US$60; ☞) ⌀ Getting to this Utopian-like island paradise is half the fun. From Chepe's Bar in Poneloya, you catch a small boat (US$1) to the 7km-long island known as Isla Los Brasiles, then walk 15 minutes (or get a lift in a horse-drawn carriage, on request) to this beachfront hideout. There's good surf right out front, and bonfires at night.

Lazy Turtle HOTEL $$
(☑ 8546-7403; www.thelazyturtlehotel.com; d/ste US$35/50) Facing the calm waters of the tidal bay, this relaxed *hotelito* (little hotel) is a hit with travelers. Simple but relatively modern rooms and suites come with drinking water – a nice touch – and the onsite restaurant is well known for its Mexican-inspired cuisine and burgers (including a good veggie burger).

Bomalu GUESTHOUSE $$
(☑ 7532-5546; www.bomalunicaragua.com; cruce Peñitas–Poneloya, 900m S; d without bathroom US$20, d with air-con US$38; ✸ ☞ ☜) This mellow beachhouse-style spot, located right on the sand, has seven affordable guest rooms (most of which share a few bathrooms). Guests rave about the outdoor lounge space and the excellent restaurant, which is open to the public and specializes in seafood. The hotel offers transportation to León for US$4 per person.

Dulce Mareas PIZZA $$
(mains US$3-8; ◎ 8am-9pm Wed-Sun) It's known for pizzas baked in a clay-brick oven, but this sweet beachfront eatery also does breakfast and lunch – plus coffee, desserts and cold cocktails, all with a view of the water. You can also rent out rooms (double US$40).

❶ Getting There & Away

Buses to Poneloya and Las Peñitas (US$0.50, 40 minutes) depart hourly, 6am to 6pm, from El Mercadito in Subtiaba. Day-trippers take note: the last bus returns around 6pm, too.

Another option: Bigfoot Hostel (p473) runs a daily shuttle to Bigfoot Beach Hostel in Las Peñitas.

Cosigüina Peninsula Beaches

The Cosigüina peninsula is well on its way to becoming an island, worn away on two sides by brilliant estuaries and fringed with sandy beaches, ranging from the pearl-grays of Jiquilillo to coal-black at Playa Carbón.

These aren't the easiest beaches to visit, but you'll be rewarded with impressive stretches of sand interrupted only by fishing villages, sea turtles and mangrove swamps. The surfing is great but largely unexplored, and hotels are relatively few and far between.

Playa Aserradores

This long, smooth stretch of sand has excellent surfing: the main attraction here is a serious wave, best for experienced surfers. There are other activities on offer here, too, from fishing and kayak tours to horseback riding and bicycle rental. It's also a quiet place to just relax by the sea.

🛌 Sleeping & Eating

Hotel Chancletas HOTEL $$$
(📞 8868-5036; www.hotelchancletas.com; Playa Asserradores; dm US$10, tr with/without bathroom US$100/45; P❄🛜) Perched up on a grassy hillside overlooking Aserradores' famous break, this relaxed surfers' spot has nice rooms and a variety of activities on offer. There's surfboard rental, too, and a restaurant open for breakfast, lunch and dinner.

Playa Jiquilillo

This endless pale-gray beach frames what you thought existed only in tales that begin 'You should have seen it back when I was first here...' The picture-perfect fishing village fronts a dramatic rocky point, where tide pools reflect the reds and golds of a huge setting sun, Cosigüina's ragged bulk rising hazy and post-apocalyptic to the north.

The region remains largely undeveloped, despite its beauty and accessibility, because a devastating 1992 tsunami wiped this village out completely.

🛌 Sleeping & Eating

Rancho Tranquilo HOSTEL $
(📞 8968-2290; www.ranchotranquilo.wordpress.com; Los Zorros Jiquilillo; dm/s/d US$7/20/22; P) This collection of bungalows and a small dorm on its private stretch of beach is a great budget choice. There's a cool bar and common area, and vegetarian dinners (US$2 to US$4.50) are served family-style. Check online for information on the area's turtle rescue program.

Rancho Esperanza GUESTHOUSE $$
(📞 8879-1795; www.rancho-esperanza.com; Jiquilillo; dm US$8, 2-person cabañas with/without bathroom US$35/25) 🌿 This quiet and ecofriendly collection of simple bamboo huts – which are scattered across a grassy field just slightly removed from the beach – offers volunteer opportunities in community projects related to education and environmental issues. There's also a small library of English-language books and a good breakfast (served all day).

Corinto

Nicaragua's only deep-water port was originally a much older town, Puerto El Realejo; founded in 1522, it was subsequently attacked by such famous pirates as William Dampier and John Davis. As time passed and sand filled in the estuary, the barrier island of Punto Icaco became the port, where Corinto was founded in 1858.

This was where US president Ronald Reagan mined in 1983, after which Congress passed a law specifically forbidding the use of taxpayer dollars for overthrowing the Nicaraguan government. Thus began the Iran-Contra affair.

Corinto's 19th-century wooden row houses, narrow streets and broad beaches score high on the 'adorability potential' scale, although actual adorability ratings are much lower. It's a bit sad: although some 65% of the nation's imports and exports flow through, very little of the money stays here. Cruise ships arrive throughout the year, but passengers are whisked away to more scenic spots.

Reserva Natural Estero Padre Ramos

A few minutes north of Los Zorros is the community of Padre Ramos, one of the small towns inside the federally protected wetlands of Reserva Natural Estero Padre Ramos. The river delta is part of the largest remaining mangrove forests in Central America, and is key in the proposed **Reserva Biologica Golfo de Fonseca** (Gulf of Fonseca Biological Corridor), a wetlands conservation agreement between Nicaragua, Honduras and El Salvador.

There's not much tourist infrastructure here, but hotels in the area offer boat, kayak and birding tours for around US$10 to US$40 per person. Sea turtles lay their eggs here between July and December, peaking in October and November.

ℹ Getting There & Away

Buses and minivans ply the routes between Chinandega and Corinto, but service to northern beaches is infrequent: at the time of writing, there was only one daily bus from Chinandega to Aserradores, departing from Chinandega's Mercadito at 12:30pm (US$1, 1½ hours).

Many travelers drive here: you'll want a 4WD vehicle for the bumpy ride from the well-signed exit off the Chinandega–Potosí Hwy.

NORTHERN NICARAGUA

You've officially escaped Central America's backpacker superhighway and arrived in a place where colorful quetzals nest in misty cloud forests, and Nicaragua's best coffee and tobacco are cultivated with both capitalist zeal and collective spirit. With a little time and commitment you'll duck into ancient, crumbling cathedrals, get pounded by countless waterfalls, explore recently discovered canyons, and pay tribute to the pirates, colonists, revolutionaries, artists and poets who were inspired by these fertile mountains and mingled with the humble, open-hearted people who've lived here for generations.

Estelí

POP 122,900

A Sandinista stronghold, a university town, a market center for the thousands of farmers that populate its surrounding hills: Estelí has a multifaceted soul. On weekdays you can wake up with sunrise yoga before Spanish class; on Saturday you can mingle with farmers at the massive produce market, then see them again at midnight, dancing like mad in a *ranchero* bar. And we haven't even mentioned the world-class cigars and the zeal with which a city with socialist roots has taken to slot machines. You don't have to be a Che Guevara devotee to dig this town.

Set on the Pan-American Hwy close to the Honduran border, Estelí was a strategic gateway that saw heavy fighting and helped turn the revolution and, later, the Contra War. It's no surprise then, that Estelí has remained one of the Sandinistas' strongest support bases.

◉ Sights

Although Estelí's most impressive attractions are in the surrounding mountains, the 1823 Catedral has a wonderful facade and is worth a wander. Keep an eye out for the interesting murals that crop up about town, many of which were painted by participants in the Funarte children's mural workshop (www.funarte.org.ni).

★ **Galería de Héroes y Mártires**   MUSEUM
(☑2714-0942, 8419-3519; http://galleryofheroes andmartyrs.blogspot.com; Av 1a NE & Calle Transversal, ½ c N; by donation; ◉9:30am-4pm Tue-Fri) Be sure to stop by this moving gallery devoted to fallen revolutionaries, with displays of faded photos, clothes and weaponry. Check out the exhibit (with English signage) on Leonel Rugama, the warrior-poet.

Opening hours are irregular; if there's no one around swing by later.

Catedral   CHURCH
The 1823 cathedral has a wonderful facade and is worth a wander. A number of interesting murals can be seen in the surrounding blocks, although most of the original revolutionary works have long disappeared.

Murals   PUBLIC ART
You'll still see some murals around the streets of Estelí, and although many of the original revolutionary pieces have been lost to development, there are also new works that keep the tradition alive. Many of the modern pieces were painted by children through the Funarte (www.funarte.org.ni) program.

🎓 Courses

CENAC Spanish School   LANGUAGE COURSE
(☑2713-5437; www.spanishschoolcenac.com; Panamericana, btwn Calles 5a SE & 6a SE; per week with/without homestay US$195/120) Professionally run Spanish school with classes for all levels.

Horizonte Nica   LANGUAGE COURSE
(☑2713-4117; www.escuelahorizonte.edu.ni; Av 2a SE, Calle 9a SE, ½ c S; per week with/without homestay US$220/150) This well-established program uses its extensive contacts with local development groups to get students involved in the community.

Estelí

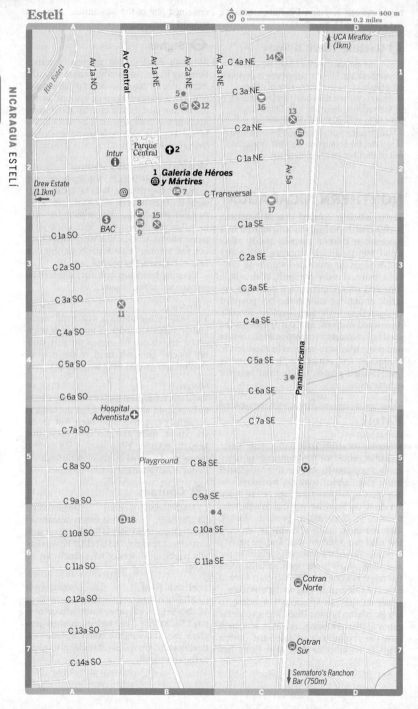

Estelí

⊙ **Top Sights**
1 Galería de Héroes y
  Mártires.. B2

⊙ **Sights**
2 Catedral... B2

⊕ **Activities, Courses & Tours**
3 CENAC Spanish School.......................... C4
4 Horizonte Nica B6
5 Tree Huggers.. B1

⊕ **Sleeping**
6 Hospedaje Luna B1
7 Hotel Los Altos....................................... B2
8 Hotel Nicarao.. B2

9 Iguana Hostel.. B3
10 Sonati..C2

⊗ **Eating**
11 Buffet Castillo B3
12 Café Luz.. B1
13 El Quesito C1
14 Restaurante Tipiscayán........................ C1
15 Rincón Pinareño B3

⊙ **Drinking & Nightlife**
16 Aroma's Ole... C1
17 Mocha Nana Café................................... C2

⊛ **Shopping**
18 Calzado Figueroa....................................B6

Tours

Estelí produces and rolls some of the world's finest tobacco. Seeds are original Cuban stock, as are the curing and rolling techniques you can witness firsthand in the warehouse-like factories. Fumes can get intense, but you'll acclimatize. Tobacco is harvested March through April and *puros* (cigars) are rolled always and forever.

While the tobacco industry is a massive employer in the region and a major contributor to the local economy, conditions for workers vary dramatically. Some factories have airy and spacious rolling areas while others are your classic sweatshop.

Many of the major producers have special tax status and are unable to sell cigars from their factories. It is not possible to send cigars home via the postal service in Nicaragua.

Local tour guide **Leo Flores** (☑8415-2428; leoafl@yahoo.es) is well connected in the industry and can get you access to a wide variety of factories and plantations. You can also organize a tour with Tree Huggers to watch the rolling process at Cuban-owned **Tabacalera Santiago**, which costs US$8 (plus a suggested US$2 donation to the organization's Library Bus), and includes transportation and a local guide. The tour offers insights into the entire cigar-making process and visitors are free to talk to the staff as they roll 60 varieties of stogie. Cigars are available for purchase at the end of the tour.

It's also possible to contact some factories and arrange a visit directly. Factory visits are easiest to schedule during the week, when plantation access is more flexible.

★**Tree Huggers**   CULTURAL TOUR
(☑8496-7449; http://treehuggers.cafeluzyluna.org; Av 2a NE & Calle 3a NE; ⊙8am-8pm) ✐ This friendly and vibrant tour office is the local specialist for trips to Miraflor and Tisey, but also offers other interesting community tourism trips throughout the region and a great-value cigar tour. Friendly staff dispense a wealth of impartial information for independent travelers. Profits support local social projects.

Drew Estate   TOUR
(www.cigarsafari.com; Barrio Oscar Gamez 2) Estelí's most innovative cigar company offers all-inclusive, multiday 'Cigar Safari' tours aimed at serious cigar enthusiasts.

🛏 Sleeping

Iguana Hostel   HOSTEL **$**
(☑8824-2299; Av Central, Transversal, 75m S; dm/s/d US$7/12.50/14) Cheap and cheerful, the Iguana has a central location and everything budget travelers need: spacious rooms, a guest kitchen and hammocks in the courtyard. The dorms are particularly good value – they have just a couple of comfortable beds in each.

Hospedaje Luna   HOSTEL **$$**
(☑8405-8919, 8441-8466; www.cafeluzyluna.org; cnr Av 2a NE & Calle 3a NE; dm/s/d/tr US$10/20/28/33; ☎) ✐ With a central location, spotless rooms, a courtyard common area and a wealth of information on Estelí

and the surrounding area, this nonprofit hostel is the budget traveler's favorite. There is a small kitchen for guest use and fast wi-fi throughout. Profits are donated to community projects in Miraflor, which also welcome volunteers.

Sonati
HOSTEL **$$**
(📱 2713-6043; hostal.esteli@sonati.org; Catedral, 3½ c E; dm US$8-9, s/d/tr from US$15/20/28; 🛜) 🌿 This chilled hostel feels a lot like a house share, with plenty of communal space, a spacious common kitchen and a pleasant rear garden. Rooms are neat and you could get lost in some of the huge bathrooms. The management offers tours and hikes in the area and organizes volunteer placements with local organizations. Profits go toward local environmental education projects.

Hotel Nicarao
GUESTHOUSE **$$**
(📱 2713-2490; hotelnicarao79@yahoo.es; Av Central, Calle Transversal, ½ c S; s/d from US$13/23, without bathroom US$10/20; 🛜) This charming garden gem doesn't look too inviting from the street, but inside you'll find pleasant rooms at exceptional value set around a spacious courtyard with sofas and rocking chairs.

★ Hotel Los Altos
BOUTIQUE HOTEL **$$$**
(📱 2713-5264; hotel_losaltosesteli@hotmail.com; Calle Transversal, Av 1NE, 50m E; s/d/t incl breakfast US$55/60/70; ❄️🛜) In a meticulously restored colonial house right in the center of town, Los Altos manages to be both stylish and unpretentious. The welcoming lobby has a high, wild-cane ceiling, wrought-iron chandeliers and classic Spanish tiles. Rooms are all different but all feature bright tile floors, elegant wooden furniture and spacious work desks. Breakfast is served in the charming internal courtyard.

🍴 Eating

El Quesito
NICARAGUAN **$**
(cnr Calle 2a NE & Av 4a NE, Del Asoganor, 1 c N; breakfast US$0.70-2.50, mains US$4.50; ⏰ 6:30am-8pm) Pull up a handmade wooden chair at this rustic corner diner and enjoy homemade yogurt flavored with local fruits, *quesillos* and *leche agria* (sour milk) – yes, what most of us pour down the sink is a delicacy in Nicaragua! It also prepares excellent, nongreasy Nica breakfasts and good meals.

Buffet Castillo
NICARAGUAN **$**
(📱 2713-0337; Parque Central, 4 c S, ½ c O; meals US$2-4; ⏰ 7am-6pm Mon-Sat) Often packed at lunchtime, this spacious diner offers up restaurant-quality meals, including ribs, fried fish and jalapeño chicken, at a budget price. The original branch across the road is still open if you can't find a seat in the new building.

Café Luz
INTERNATIONAL **$$**
(📱 8405-8919; www.cafeluzyluna.org; cnr Av 2a NE & Calle 3a NE; snacks US$2-4, mains US$6.50-9; ⏰ 8am-11pm; 🛜🌿) 🌿 Bored of Nica grub? Pop into this hip coffee house where the burritos and fajitas have some kick and the organic salads arrive on your table direct from the growers in Miraflor. The diverse menu includes many vegetarian options. It's also the best place in the center for a social drink in the evening.

Restaurante Tipiscayán
NICARAGUAN **$$**
(📱 2713-7303; cnr Calle 4a NE & Av 4a NE; mains US$3.50-10; ⏰ noon-10pm Thu-Tue) The family of San Juan de Limay soapstone sculptor Freddy Moreno serves good-quality traditional fare, including great quesadillas and Nica-style tacos in an elegant space full of art. Also serves good coffee and traditional drinks such as *pinolillo* (a chilled beverage of maize and cacao).

Rincón Pinareño
CUBAN **$$**
(📱 2713-4369; Av 1a SE & Calle 1a SE; mains US$5.50-17, sandwiches from US$3.50; ⏰ noon-10pm) A tasty Cuban diner with a lovely 2nd-floor veranda serving deliciously messy pressed sandwiches, tasty smoked chicken, pork chops and ribs. Also a popular spot for dessert.

🍷 Drinking & Nightlife

★ Semaforo's Ranchon Bar
BAR
(Panamericana & Hospital, 300m S; ⏰ 6pm-4am Thu-Sun) Get down with the good working people of Estelí, Tisey and Miraflor at a proper *ranchero* bar. This indoor/outdoor club with the *palapa* (thatched) roof and bandstand brings terrific live music to a crowd that's here to dance in their boots and cowboy hats. You will see asses (aged 18 to 60) shimmy and shake.

Aroma's Ole
CAFE
(cnr Calle 3a NE & Av 4a NE; ⏰ 10am-10pm Mon-Sat, 7am-10pm Sun) It's a bit out of the way, but this stylish, street-side cafe serves up great coffee using freshly roasted beans from Dipilto, one of the country's best growing regions. There's also a small selection of

wines and a menu of light meals and more hearty fare.

Mocha Nana Café   CAFE
(☑ 2713-3164; Calle Transversal, Av 4a SE, ½ c E; drinks US$1-2.50; ☺ 11am-9pm) Where Estelí intellectuals gather to sip caffeine, debate politics and culture, and munch tasty waffles. On Friday evenings there is often live music by local bands (cover US$2.50).

🔒 Shopping

The must-have souvenir of Estelí is a box of cigars, best purchased after a cigar tour. The region is also known for reasonably priced custom leather: saddles, boots and wallets are available at the many workshops located along Av 1a SO.

Calzado Figueroa   SHOES
(☑ 8946-4341; Av 1a SO & Calle 9a SO, 30m S; ☺ 8am-7pm Mon-Sat, to noon Sun) Get in touch with your inner cowboy with some genuine, handcrafted, Cuban-heel riding boots (from US$80 to US$100) at this high-quality leather workshop. Peruse the large selection or order a tailor-made pair and watch the entire boot-making process.

ℹ️ Information

BAC (Av 1a NO, Calle Transversal, 50m S) Reliable ATM.

Estelí@Net (Calle Transversal, Av Central, 20m O; internet per hour US$0.50; ☺ 8am-8pm) Also offers international calls.

Hospital Adventista (☑ 2713-3827, 8851-5298; Av Central, Calle 6a SO, ½ c S; ☺ 24hr) Private clinic with a variety of specialists.

Intur (☑ 2713-6799; Plaza Plator, Parque Central, ½ c O; ☺ 8am-4pm) Official tourist office with an abundance of regional brochures, but not a lot of expertise.

Lavanderia Express (☑ 2714-1297; Av 2a SE, Calle 1a SE, 30m S; per pound US$0.80; ☺ 9am-5pm) Economical wash and dry laundry service.

Police (☑ 2713-2615; Panamericana, Calle 8a SE)

ℹ️ Getting There & Away

Estelí has two bus terminals: the blue-collar **Cotran Norte** (☑ 2713-2529) has plenty of slot machines and a soft-rock soundtrack, while **Cotran Sur** (☑ 2713-6162; Panamericana) is more refined. Both are located at the southern end of the city on the Panamericana.

BUSES FROM ESTELÍ

Buses from Cotran Norte

DESTINATION	COST (US$)	DURATION (HR)	FREQUENCY (DAILY)
Jalapa	3.50	2¾	4:10am, noon
Jinotega (via Concordia, San Rafael)	1.80	2	5:45am, 8:15am, 9:15am, 2:15pm, 3:45pm, 4:45pm
León (bus)	2.80	2½	3:10pm
León (microbus)	3	2	departs when full around 6am and 1pm
Masaya	3	3	2pm & 3pm
Ocotal	1.80	1½	6am-11am, hourly
San Juan de Limay	1.80	2½	5:30am, 7am, 10am, 12:15pm, 2pm, 3pm
Somoto	1.15	1½	5:30am-6:10pm, hourly
Yali (via Miraflor)	2	2½	6am, 9:15am, 12:30pm, 3:45pm

Buses from Cotran Sur

DESTINATION	COST (US$)	DURATION (HR)	FREQUENCY
León	2.80	2½	5am, 5:45am & 6:45am Mon-Sat, 6:45am Sun
Managua (expreso)	3	2½	hourly from 4:45am-9:45am & 12:15pm-3:15pm (from 6:45am Sun)
Managua (ordinario)	2.25	3½	3:30am-6pm, half-hourly
Matagalpa (ordinario)	1.25	1¾	5:15am-5:40pm, half-hourly
Tisey	1	1½	6:30am, 1:30pm Thu-Tue

Área Protegida Miraflor

Miraflor is not your average tourist destination. Part nature reserve, part rural farming community, it's challenging to get to and even more difficult to define. There are no big hotels or restaurants here, just a loose collection of like-minded farmers with an interest in tourism and the environment.

Its namesake is a small mountain lake around which the Área Protegida Miraflor (declared a reserve in 1999) unfurls with waterfalls, blooming orchids, coffee plantations, swatches of remnant cloud forest home to hold-out monkey troops, hiking trails and dozens of collective-farming communities that welcome tourists. Yes, nature is glorious here, but the chance to participate in rural Nicaraguan life – making fresh tortillas, milking cows, harvesting coffee, riding horses through the hills with local *caballeros* (horsemen) – is unforgettable.

Advanced reservations are essential to ensure visitor income is distributed evenly among participating farmers and your hosts are prepared for your arrival.

🏃 Activities

Miraflor has three climate zones (ranging from 800m to 1400m) and is home to over 200 species of orchid and 307 bird species, linked by 20km of trails and rutted roads. The *zona bajo* (low zone), around Coyolito, is a tropical, oak savannah ecosystem; the *zona intermedia* (intermediate zone), which includes Sontule, has some remnant cloud forests and tons of orchid varieties; in the *zona alta* (high zone), you'll find coffee farms, more swatches of cloud forest, and some excellent quetzal and monkey viewing near Ceballa in Los Volcancitos.

Local guides (US$15 for solo travelers, US$20 for groups of two to four) are both inexpensive and a great resource. They know all the best hikes and climbs and can share insights into Miraflor's unique history and local daily life. If you plan on exploring much beyond your homestay, guides become essential – paths are poorly marked and cross private farms where permission must sometimes be negotiated. Horses are also available (around US$15 per day) and are a good choice if you plan on visiting various different communities.

Dedicated coffee tours with tasting sessions (US$70 for up to 10 participants) can be arranged with advanced notice. Other specialized tours include orchid hikes (US$35 for up to 10 participants) and bird-watching trips (US$35 to US$50 for up to six participants).

Some landowners charge admission to visit sights or pass through their property, so bring plenty of change.

UCA Miraflor (Unión de Cooperativas Agropecuarias de Miraflor; ☎ 2713-2971; www.ucamiraflor.com; Gasolinera Uno Norte, 2 c E, ½ c N; ⊗ 8am-noon & 1-5:30pm Mon-Fri, 8am-3pm Sat) 🖉 in Estelí manages the reserve and can help you plan a visit, hook you up with an English-speaking guide and book family homestays. Alternatively, Tree Huggers (p481) provides detailed, impartial advice on planning a trip, and can also make reservations.

🍴 Sleeping & Eating

There are several choices of accommodations within the reserve, all of which should be booked through UCA Miraflor or Tree Huggers (p481) in Estelí.

Farmhouse rooms allow the most interaction with local families; *cabañas* have more privacy. Both options are rustic and some accommodations have pit latrines. Expect to pay around US$28 per person, including three meals.

If creature comforts are important, Finca Neblina del Bosque (☎ 8701-1460; www.neblinadelbosque.com; Ceballal; cabañas per person incl meals US$30-40), owned by a Nica-German couple, is the most comfortable option in Miraflor (though it has decidedly less rural farming flavor).

ℹ Getting There & Away

For Coyolito (US$0.70, one hour) and La Pita (US$1, 1¾ hours), buses leave Estelí from the Pulpería Miraflor (near the Uno gas station on the Panamericana north of town) at 5:45am and 1pm daily, returning from La Pita at 7:30am and 2:30pm.

There is one direct bus daily (except Sunday) from Estelí to Ceballal (US$1.50, two hours) via Sontule and La Perla, leaving from the Cotran Norte at 2:15pm and returning from Ceballal at 6:45am.

Alternatively, for Ceballal take the Estelí–Yali (via Miraflor) bus at 6am, noon or 3:45pm from Cotran Norte to La Rampla (US$1, two hours), from where it's a 1km walk uphill to the beginning of the accommodations. The bus continues onto Puertas Azules, from where it's a 20-minute walk to La Perla and a 1¾-hour walk to Sontule.

It's also possible to walk up the hill from La Pita to Cebollal in around 45 minutes, but it's a steep climb.

Área Protegida Cerro Tisey-Estanzuela

Smaller, drier and less populated but every bit as gorgeous as Área Protegida Miraflor, this *other* protected area, just 10km south of Estelí, has also jumped on the tourism bandwagon. You won't see the same species diversity in Tisey (which is what locals call the region), but those rugged, pine-draped mountains, red-clay bat caves, waterfalls and marvelous vistas that stretch to Lago de Managua – and even El Salvador on clear days – are worth the trip.

It's possible to visit Tisey on a day trip from Estelí; however, the reserve's attractions are spread out all over its 93 sq km and public transportation is limited so you'll see more if you spend the night.

◉ Sights

The main entrance to Tisey is accessed from the dirt road beside Hospital San Juan de Dios in Estelí. In the park's lower elevations, just 5km from Estelí, is the inspiring Salto Estanzuela (US$1), a gushing 36m waterfall that careens over a bromeliad-studded cliff and breaks into a half-dozen foaming threads that feed a perfect swimming hole. Locals descend in hordes during Semana Santa.

After the falls, the road begins to climb high into the mountains before arriving at the Eco-Posada, where you'll find a handful of Spanish-speaking guides for hire (US$20 to US$25 per day).

A short walk further along the road is the entrance to Alberto Gutiérrez' singular Galería del Arte el Jalacate (by donation), where you can see his charming murals carved into the cliff-face. About 3km further is the cute hamlet of La Garnacha, known for a chapel that housed huddled refugees of a Contra invasion during the war, and a dairy cooperative (8658-1054; garnacha turistica@yahoo.es; Comunidad La Garnacha) that produces artisanal, Italian-style goat cheese.

⬒ Sleeping & Eating

The one *comedor* (basic eatery) in La Garnacha serves excellent *comida típica* (regional specialties; dishes US$3 to US$5) made

from local ingredients, including organic salads and, of course, cheese.

Eco-Posada LODGE $
(8658-4086; r per person US$7, cabañas US$18; P) This place offers comfortable *cabañas* with flush toilets and front porches slung with hammocks overlooking a small creek lined with flowers and fruit trees, as well as spartan, tin-roofed rooms with shared bathrooms. Cheap meals are available in the attached *comedor*.

Cabañas La Garnacha LODGE $$
(8658-1054; garnchaturistica@yahoo.es; La Garnacha; r per person US$10, cabañas US$25-30) These cute *cabañas* with hot water are run by the community and overlook a small lake. There are also cheaper, hotel-style rooms with tiled bathrooms by the entrance. Reserve in advance.

ⓘ Getting There & Away

Tisey is served by two buses a day (US$1, 1½ hours), which are marked 'La Tejera' and leave from Estelí Cotran Sur at 6:30am and 1:30pm. The buses pass Salto Estanzuela and Eco-Posada before arriving at the La Garnacha turnoff, a 1.5km walk from the community. Buses return to Estelí from the La Garnacha turnoff at 8:30am and 3:30pm. On Wednesday there is no service.

In the dry season, you may be able to charter a taxi from Estelí (about US$50 for five to six hours), but the road is in fairly poor condition and most drivers don't want to rough up their sedans. Alternatively, Tree Huggers (p481) offers round-trip transportation in pick-ups for US$60, which is a good option for day-trippers.

Salto Estanzuela is about a 90-minute walk or 40-minute bicycle ride from the Hospital San Juan de Dios in Estelí. Expect to pay around US$15 each way in a taxi.

Somoto
POP 37,000
Diminutive Somoto has not always been a shoe-in on the itineraries of visitors to northern Nicaragua. In fact, until 2003 this was just another sleepy colonial town in the Honduran shadow, famed for its donkeys and *rosquillas* (crusty cornbread rings). Then two Czech scientists stumbled onto a rift in the rugged, overgrown clay earth outside town and, just 75 million years after these charcoal granite cliffs pierced the earth's surface, Europeans 'discovered' Cañón de Somoto (Somoto Canyon), where the Río Coco is born.

Of course, the locals living nearby have known about it all along and formerly referred to the site as 'La Estrechura' (The Narrows), while it's said that the area's original inhabitants, the Chorotegas, referred to the region as Tepezonate (Mountain of Water).

⊙ Sights

★ **Monumento Nacional
Cañon de Somoto**   NATIONAL PARK
(Carrertera Somoto–El Espino Km 229.5; US$2) The Coco (or Wangki), Central America's longest river, runs all the way to the Caribbean, but its first impression may be its most spectacular. Gushing from underground, it has carved solid rock into this 3km-long gorge that drops 160m, and at times is just a hair under 10m wide. Protected as Monumento Nacional Cañon de Somoto, the canyon is an unmissable experience.

☞ Tours

★ **Somoto Canyon Tours**   ADVENTURE TOUR
(☑ 8610-7642; www.somotocanyontours.org; Carretera Somoto–El Espino Km 229.5) 🏃 A well-run community tourism organization based in the village of Sonis, right by the entrance to the Cañon de Somoto. It specializes in natural adventures in the canyon, including an overnight option where you'll sleep in tents under the stars, but also organizes **horseback riding** and other **hikes** in the region. Highly recommended.

🛏 Sleeping & Eating

Sonis Homestay   HOMESTAY $
(☑ 8610-7642; www.somotocanyontours.org; Carretera El Espino Km 229.5, Sonis; dm/r US$7/15) 🏃 If you are in Somoto only to see the canyon, consider staying with one of the local families in the village of Sonis (right at the canyon entrance) as part of their community tourism project. Accommodations are in purpose-built *cabañas* right next to family homes.

Quinta San Rafael   LODGE $$$
(☑ 8449-1766; info.canondesomoto@gmail.com; entrada Cañon de Somoto; house for up to 12 visitors US$250, cabaña for 6-8 visitors US$120) With a privileged location down in the valley just before the entrance to the canyon, this spacious rural property offers the most comfortable accommodations for miles around. The main house has two floors, with an open fireplace in the lounge and kitchen area and a wonderful deck with panoramic views of the mountains. There are also several smaller *cabañas*.

**Bar y Restaurant
El Almendro**   NICARAGUAN $$
(☑ 2722-2152; Parque Central, 2 c S; mains US$8-9; ⊙ noon-10pm) This bar-restaurant feels like something from the Wild West, but the food is actually pretty good. Choose from fish, chicken or beef in a variety of sauces served with all the usual extras.

ⓘ Getting There & Away

The bus terminal is on the Panamericana, six blocks from the town center.

Jinotega

POP 46,000

Hidden in a cat's eye of a valley, Jinotega, the 'City of Mists,' is enclosed on all sides by mountains dappled in cloud forests, crowned with granite ridges and pocked with deep gorges.

While coffee tourism percolates in Matagalpa, Jinotega, which brims with adventure and promise, still sees far more foreign-aid workers than tourists. So walk these cobbled streets, visit nearby Lago de Apanás and hike into the misty mountains, where you can harvest coffee with locals and stroll through primary forest. Just make sure to get to Cerro La Cruz on a clear day to glimpse the cat's eye in all her jade glory.

And that City of Mists moniker is no joke. The average temperature is just 20°C (68°F)

BUSES FROM SOMOTO

DESTINATION	COST (US$)	DURATION	FREQUENCY
El Espino (Honduran border)	0.50	40min	5:15am-5:15pm, hourly
Estelí	1.15	1¾hr	5:20am-5pm, every 40min
Managua (*expreso*)	4	4hr	5am, 6:15am, 7:30am, 2pm, 3:15pm
Managua (*ordinario*)	3	4½hr	4am-5pm, almost hourly
Ocotal	0.60	1hr	5:15am-4:30pm, every 45min

and the town can get 2600mm of rain annually. Bring rain gear and a fleece for the cool evenings.

⊙ Sights

★ Cerro La Cruz
RELIGIOUS SITE

A steep yet worthwhile hour's hike from the cemetery and embedded in a boulder-crusted ridge is the town cross, originally placed here in 1703 by Franciscan Fray Margíl de Jesús. The view of Jinotega and the layered Cordillera Isabelía from up here is unreal. Take the center path through the cemetery and begin the sweaty climb. When you emerge from the trees and come to a plateau, hug the ridge tightly and keep climbing.

Catedral San Juan
CHURCH

The beauty of Jinotega's cathedral (c 1805) is in the sanctuary, where you'll marvel at the chestnut and gold-leaf altar and pristine white arches and rows of heavenly saints, sculpted with so much life and light they make spiritual peace contagious. Opposite the church is the terrific, split-level Parque Central shaded by palms and towering laurel trees.

⊨ Sleeping

Hotel Primavera
GUESTHOUSE $

(☑2782-2400; Parque Central, 5 c N, 1 c E; s/d US$8/12.50, without bathroom US$4.70/9.35) The cleanest cheapie in town has new tiles in the rooms, cable TV and decent mattresses, and is owned by a lovely family who hang out in the lobby. The door shuts at 10pm sharp,

so make arrangements if you intend to stay out late.

Hotel Sollentuna Hem
HOTEL $

(☑2782-2334; solentunahem@gmail.com; Parque Central, 4 c N; s/d US$13.50/16; P 🕸) A favorite among travelers, this small, welcoming hotel has a variety of good-value rooms with cable TV and hot water. Ask to take a look around, as some are better than others.

★ Hotel Café
HOTEL $$$

(☑2782-2710; www.cafehoteljinotega.com; Gasolinera Uno, 1 c O, ½ c N; s/d incl breakfast US$50/60; P ❄ 🕸) The most comfy sleep in Jinotega is located at this three-star property. Most (but not all) of the rooms are flooded with natural light, which reflects pastel paint jobs. Service is professional and courteous. The marble baths and hyper-speed laundry service are nice, too.

✗ Eating & Drinking

★ La Casa de Don Colocho
BAKERY $

(☑2782-2584; Parque Central, 3 c E, 3 c S; pastries US$0.60-1.10, coffee US$1-1.50; ☺8am-6pm Mon-Sat; 🖪) A bakery every town would love. The cinnamon rolls are dense and sugary and the pineapple triangles are addictive – and those are just two of the dozens of items this place turns out daily. The ovens begin to open at around 1pm, except on weekends. Plan your visit accordingly.

Soda El Tico
NICARAGUAN $

(☑2782-2059; Parque Central, 1 c E, ½ c S; buffet meals US$4, mains US$6; ☺7:30am-10pm) By far the most appetizing restaurant in town,

BUSES FROM JINOTEGA

DESTINATION	COST (US$)	DURATION	FREQUENCY	DEPARTS FROM
Esteli	1.80	2hr	5:15am, 7am, 9am, 1pm, 2:45pm & 3:30pm	Cotran Norte
Managua	3.40	3½hr	4am to 4pm, 10 daily. Goes via a new road & does not enter Matagalpa.	Cotran Sur
Matagalpa	1	1¼	5am to 6pm, half-hourly	Cotran Sur
Pantasma (via Asturias)	2	1½hr	4am to 4:30pm, hourly	Cotran Norte
Pantasma (via San Gabriel)	1.8	1½hr	5:30am to 4:30pm, hourly	Cotran Norte
San Rafael del Norte (ordinario)	0.80	40min	6am to 6pm, half-hourly	Cotran Norte
San Rafael del Norte (expreso)	1	30min	6am to 6pm, half-hourly	Cotran Norte
Yalí	2	2hr	6am, 8:30am, 10am, noon & 2:30pm	Cotran Norte

Soda El Tico is a classic steam-table buffet with steak, pork loin and grilled chicken served with a tasty salad bar. You can also order a variety of snacks and specialties from the menu.

★ Bar Jinocuba
BAR
(Alcaldía, 5 c N; ⊗ 3-11pm Mon-Thu, to midnight Fri-Sun; 🕾) A groovy bohemian bar (and guaranteed *ranchero*-free zone) with occasional, hip live-music performances and cultural events. The young owners are very knowledgeable about tourism in the region and can hook you up with independent English-and German-speaking guides to explore the surrounding mountains. Also serves Cuban and international meals.

Café Flor de Jinotega
CAFE
(☑ 2782-2617; Cotran Norte, 1½ c N; espresso drinks US$0.50-0.75; ⊗ 8am-6pm) Quite simply the best cup of coffee in town, and possibly on all of the Ruta de Café. Relax at one of the see-through tables filled with three kinds of coffee beans and get to know what good java is. Staff can also arrange guides and transportation to visit nearby coffee farms.

La Taverna
BAR
(Parque Central, 2 c O; ⊗ noon-midnight) The coolest dive bar in the northern highlands has timber tables, a dark wood interior, a lively late-night crowd and tasty beef fajitas (US$5).

ⓘ Getting There & Away

There are two bus terminals. **Cotran Norte**, on the edge of the market, is little more than a chaotic parking lot. A wonderful contrast, the brand-new **Cotran Sur** (🕾) sits near the town's southern entrance and is the best terminal in the region: it has shops, departure announcements and even a waiting lounge with wi-fi.

Matagalpa

POP 89,100 / ELEV 902M

If you love coffee, mountains and urbanity, then have your cake and eat it in Matagalpa, a town where, for decades, an ever-increasing number of Liberal coffee patriarchs and subsistence Sandinista farmers have rubbed shoulders during city festivals and at market. Growth has sent Matagalpa sprawling into the foothills, up crumbling streets lined with shacks and onto graded plateaus laid out in tony subdivisions. Just glance skyward from nearly every city street and you'll see pristine boulder-strewn peaks.

When you've sipped your last cup of city, head for the hills, where you can hike through primary forest to gushing waterfalls, pick coffee, explore mineshafts and listen to *ranchero* troubadours jam under a harvest moon.

If you're looking for a base from which to explore the best the region has to offer or just want to hang around in an accessible, authentic city, it's hard to beat Matagalpa.

◉ Sights

★ Casa Museo
Comandante Carlos Fonseca
MUSEUM
(Parque Rubén Darío, 1 c E; by donation; ⊗ 9am-5pm Mon-Fri, to noon Sat) **FREE** Commander Carlos Fonseca, the Sandinista equivalent of Malcolm X (read: bespectacled, goateed, intense, highly intelligent and charismatic), grew up desperately poor in this humble abode with his single mother and four siblings, despite the fact that his father was a coffee magnate. Now it's a tiny but enthralling museum that follows his evolution as a leader from childhood until his death.

Museo de Café
MUSEUM
(Av José Benito Escobar, Parque Morazán, 1 c S; ⊗ 8am-12:30pm & 2-5pm Mon-Fri, to noon Sat) **FREE** Recently overhauled, this absorbing museum features large, glossy, printed displays in Spanish and English on the roots of regional *café* and modern coffee production in the region, as well as old coffee processing machinery. Particularly interesting are the panels on the hardy immigrants who set up the first plantations in the region. Well worth a visit before any trip into the surrounding countryside.

🏃 Activities

Café Girasol
HIKING
(☑ 2772-6030; www.familiasespeciales.org; contiguo Puente Salida Managua; ⊗ 7am-6pm) 🖉 A charitable setup that accepts volunteers, Café Girasol sells detailed leaflets (US$1) for a number of self-guided walks in the Matagalpa area that vary in length from four to eight hours. While you're here be sure to sample the excellent coffee and homemade yogurt – the profits support projects for children with disabilities.

It's located by the main bridge, a couple of blocks southwest of the market.

BOSAWÁS

If you are the kind of traveler that relishes dropping off the radar, the Reserva de Biosfera Bosawás is the place for you. The largest rainforest in the Americas after the Amazon, it's a magical place of spectacular forested peaks and fast-flowing rivers that rush past tiny indigenous villages. With no roads, no hotels and no electricity, it's a tough place to visit, but the potential for adventure is enormous.

The easiest way into the reserve is via the town of Wiwili on the Río Coco in northern Jinotega department. There is no public transportation on the river, but if you're not in a hurry, it's possible to travel all the way to the Caribbean using the boats of local traders and organizations. Once you get into the reserve proper, the only places to stay are in indigenous Mayanga and Miskito villages, where you can often arrange some sort of accommodations. It can get cold at night, so bring warm clothes as well as plenty of food, water purification tablets and a flashlight.

📖 Courses

Escuela de Español Colibrí   LANGUAGE COURSE
(www.colibrispanishschool.com; Parque Morazán, 1 c S, ½ c E; tuition per hour US$11-12) This popular school inside Matagalpa Tours offers one-on-one Spanish classes, plenty of cultural activities and volunteer placements for students. Packages that include 20 hours of classes per week plus a homestay with a local family and all meals cost US$344.

🏃 Tours

⭐ **Matagalpa Tours**   ADVENTURE TOUR
(📱 8647-4680, 2772-0108; www.matagalpatours. com; tours from US$15; ⏰ 8am-12:30pm & 2-6pm Mon-Fri, 8am-4pm Sat) Matagalpa Tours offers nearly a dozen interesting and enriching ways to get into this city and the surrounding countryside. In Matagalpa proper it offers urban walking tours and rents out bicycles, but its best work is done around the local mountains, where it offers both day trips and multiday excursions, including an informative tour of local coffee farms.

🛏 Sleeping

Hotel El Castillo   HOTEL $
(📱 2772-0034;   hotelelcastillomt@gmail.com; Parque Morazán, 3 c E; s/d/tr US$15/17/24; 🛜) Set on a hillside with great views, this family-run hotel is only three blocks from the cathedral. Rooms at the front of the building have small private balconies overlooking the city and are outstanding value; the view-less rooms at the back feel too enclosed and are not particularly inviting. Add US$2 for breakfast.

Martina's Place   HOSTEL $$
(📱 2772-3918;   www.martinasplace-hostal.com; Cancha El Brigadista, 1½ c E; dm/s/d with shared bathroom US$8/14/28, s/d US$15/30; 🛜) A homey new hostel offering neat and comfortable private rooms and a massive dorm in a convenient location. The mattresses are comfortable and the owners extremely helpful, but the best reason to set up here is the spacious garden area – complete with BBQ and outdoor kitchen. That and the pet rabbit, George.

Buongiorno Principessa   GUESTHOUSE $$
(📱 2772-2721;   buongiornoprincipessa35@gmail. com; Colonia Lainez; dm/r incl breakfast US$12/30; 🛜) This laid-back guesthouse in a narrow lane is an excellent-value base for exploring town. Dorms feature good mattresses and are not overcrowded, while private rooms are bright and welcoming. The included breakfast is top quality but the highlight is the fine rooftop terrace offering 360-degree views around town.

Hostal Don Guillermo   HOTEL $$
(📱 2772-3182;   www.hoteldonguillermomatagalpa. com; Claro, ½ c E; s/d US$30/35; 🛜) With a great location, elegant furnishings and a relaxed atmosphere, this small hotel offers some of the best value in town. The rooms are bright and spacious and the ample bathrooms have piping-hot water and good pressure. Breakfast is served in the small, plant-filled courtyard. A top choice.

Maria's B&B   HOTEL $$
(📱 2772-3097; www.mariasbnb.com; BanPro, 1 c E, ½ c N; r US$46-66; 🅿 ❄ 🛜) A fantastic addition to the local hotel scene, this intimate place right in the center of town has just half a dozen bright, spotless and comfortable rooms surrounding inviting common areas. Guests can access the open-plan kitchen. Service is warm and welcoming, particularly

from Doña Chepa, who will cook your breakfast to order each morning.

Eating

Look to the smoky booths that set up at sunset just north of Palí supermarket and the cathedral for the regional specialty, *güirílas*. Made with a fresh corn masa, they are sweeter and thicker than your average tortilla.

Rincón Don Chaco   NICARAGUAN $

(Av José Beníto Escobar, Parque Morazán, 2 c S; batidos US$1-1.80, burgers US$1-2, mains US$4.30-4.80; ⊙ 7:30am-5pm Mon-Fri, to 3pm Sun) A fresh-pressed, Formica diner with amazing *batidos* (fruit shakes made with milk or water). The pineapple and celery in orange juice is an instant classic, while the coconut in milk is also worth a try. There are also tasty veggie burgers and other snacks as well as a small selection of main meals available.

Taquero   NICARAGUAN, MEXICAN $

(Parque Darío, 1 c S, 1½ c O; meals US$3-7; ⊙ 5:30pm-midnight) Part *fritanga* (grill), part Mexican diner, this hugely popular hybrid serves up surprisingly good grub until late. Ignore the tasteless stuffed iguanas on the wall and pick between impossibly tender BBQ beef, tangy chicken and ribs from the grill, or hit the menu for quality tacos, burritos and quesadillas.

★ La Vita é Bella   ITALIAN $$

(☑ 2772-5476; Parque Morazán, 2½ c E, 1½ c N; pastas US$3-4, mains US$5-8; ⊙ noon-10pm, closed Tue; ☑) This local institution serves up flavorful authentic Italian dishes at low prices in a relaxed bistro atmosphere. The thin-crust pizza is some of the best in Nicaragua and the pasta dishes are also full of flavor. Vegetarians can take their pick from a wide selection of menu items. The only downer: canned mushrooms. Come early to get a table.

Drinking

Artesanos   BAR

(☑ 2772-2444; Parque Morazán, 1 c S, ½ c E; ⊙ 9am-midnight) Hands down the grooviest bar-cafe in town. There's an all-dark-wood dining room, a large patio, great coffee, and a young, hipster crowd who drink and groove to electronica and Latin rhythms till closing time.

Selección Nicaraguense   CAFE

(www.sn.com.ni; Parque Darío; ⊙ 8am-10pm; ⊛) Pretty slick for the northern highlands, this modern cafe serves up good hot and cold coffee-based drinks using single-origin beans from around the region. Enjoy a cup in the fancy air-con lounge space or in the

BUSES FROM MATAGALPA

Buses from Cotran Sur

DESTINATION	COST (US$)	DURATION	FREQUENCY
Chinandega	3.40	3½hr	5am & 2pm
Ciudad Darío	0.85	1hr	5:30am, 7:30am, 10:25am, 11am, 11:25am, 12:55pm
Estelí	1.20	2¼hr	5:20am-5:40pm, half-hourly
Jinotega	0.80	1hr	5am-6pm, half-hourly
León	3	2½hr	6am, 9:30am, 3pm, 4pm
Managua (expreso)	3	2¼hr	5:20am-5:20pm, hourly
Managua (ordinario)	2.10	2¾hr	3:35am-6:05pm, half-hourly
Masaya	3	3hr	2pm & 3:30pm (no buses Thu or Sun)

Buses from Cotran Norte

DESTINATION	COST (US$)	DURATION	FREQUENCY (DAILY)
Cerro Colorado (via Yucul)	2	2hr	5:30am-4pm, hourly
El Cuá	2.30	4hr	6am, 7am, 9am, 10:30am, noon, 1:30pm
Esquipulas	1.50	1½hr	5:40am, 7am, 8am, 9am, noon, 1:30pm, 3pm, 4:30pm, 5:30pm
San Ramón	0.40	30min	5am-7pm, half-hourly

large patio out the back. Also sells bags of coffee to go – whole or ground.

🔒 Shopping

Telares de Nicaragua HANDICRAFTS
(☑2772-0108; Parque Morazán, 1 c S, ½ c E; ⊘8am-5pm Mon-Fri, to 2pm Sat) 🌿 In the Matagalpa Tours building, this fair-trade outlet sells brightly colored fiber arts from indigenous artisans in El Chile, corn-husk dolls, beaded jewelry, baskets and a selection of the smooth, black local pottery, which is mixed with volcanic ash and fired at extreme temperatures.

ℹ️ Information

BAC (Parque Morazán, ½ c S) ATM serves Visa and MasterCard networks.
Clinica Santa Fe (☑2772-5113, emergency 8419-6283; catedral, 3 c N, ½ c E; ⊘24hr) Professional private clinic.
Copymat Cyber (Parque Morazán, 1 c S; per hour US$0.40; ⊘7am-9pm) Cheap and speedy internet access.
Intur (☑2772-7060; inturmatagalpa@gmail.com; Av Martínez, Parque Morazán, 3 c S; ⊘8am-noon & 1-5pm Mon-Fri) Provides general tips on attractions in the area.
Lavandería Cuenta Conmigo (☑2772-6713; Parque Morazán, 2 c E, 3½ c N; per load small/large US$2.90/4.30; ⊘8am-5pm Mon-Fri) Wash your clothes and support mental-health programs at this pioneering nonprofit laundry service.
Police (☑2772-3870, emergency 118; Parque Morazán)

ℹ️ Getting There & Away

There are two main bus terminals in Matagalpa. Clean and fairly well-organized **Cotran Sur** (☑2772-4659), about 800m west of Parque Rubén Darío, generally serves Managua, Jinotega and most points south.

Disorienting by comparison, **Cotran Norte** (Cotramusun) is next to the northern market and goes to mostly rural destinations in the north.

CARIBBEAN COAST

An overland ramble to Nicaragua's Caribbean coast would be the perfect terrain for an epic novel. Your settings would include wide, muddy rivers surrounded by thick jungle, a fascinating tropical port town and an expanse of mangrove-shrouded black water, home to more than a dozen ethnic fishing enclaves. And we haven't even got to the pristine offshore islands ringed by white sand with a turquoise trim.

Your cast will feature tough and insightful characters from English-speaking Creole towns and indigenous Miskito, Mayangna, Rama and Garifuna communities. And there will be plenty of action too, with scuba diving, epic treks through dense rainforest, beachcombing, and fishing in the mangroves.

But even the most skilled author would struggle to capture the essence of the region, a vibrant mix of indigenous, African and European cultures that you'll only really get a feel for if you check it out for yourself.

Bluefields

POP 54,900

With brick streets etched into a series of jade peninsulas, Bluefields (the city) stretches into Bluefields (the bay) like many fingers. In between is a series of docks, floating restaurants, shipwrecks, and fish and produce markets. The city was once full of old wood Victorian charm before Category IV Hurricane Juana wiped it off the map in 1988. Today's Bluefields is rather overindulgent in new concrete boxes, especially in the loud knot of streets downtown that eventually give way to poor tin-roof neighborhoods that ramble over nearby hillsides and inland along polluted brackish creeks.

Named after the Dutch pirate Blewfeldt, who made his base here in the 1700s, the capital of the Región Autónoma Atlántico Sur (South Atlantic Autonomous Region; RAAS) is the beating heart of Creole culture, famed for its distinctive music, colorful dances and delicious cuisine, considered by many as the best in the country. And while it is not your typical Caribbean dream destination, if you give it a chance and get to know some of the town's colorful locals, Bluefields' decaying tropical charm will definitely grow on you. Still, you probably won't linger too long. After all, you are just a boat ride away from the intriguing Pearl Lagoon basin, the spectacular Pearl Keys and those luscious Corn Islands.

◎ Sights & Activities

★**Museo Historico Cultural de la Costa Caribe** MUSEUM
(CIDCA; Iglesia Morava, 2 c S; admission US$2; ⊘9am-noon & 2-5pm Mon-Fri) Learn about the Caribbean region's diverse cultures with a visit to this fascinating museum that contains an interesting mix of historical items

from the pre-Columbian era and British rule, including a sword belonging to the last Miskito king and artifacts left by the Kukra indigenous group.

Rama Cay   ISLAND
Located inside Bluefields' bay, this barbell-shaped island is home to around 800 people – around half of all remaining Rama Indians. Isolated by the dominant Miskito culture, they still speak their own language and use their traditional government structures. It's a crowded place and a trip here is a cultural experience rather than a relaxing Caribbean island excursion.

Visits can be organized through the GTRK office (p493) in Bluefields, which can arrange transportation and also lodging.

Moravian Church   CHURCH
This large concrete church is Bluefield's most iconic building and was constructed to the exact specifications of the 1849 wooden original, destroyed in Hurricane Juana. Like all churches of the order it has a red tin roof and all-white exterior.

👉 Tours

Rumble in the Jungle   FISHING
(☑ 8832-4269; www.rumbleinthejungle.net; Casa Rosa, Loma Fresca; packages per day from US$375) The only sportfishing outfitter in the area, Rumble in the Jungle is run out of hotel Casa Rosa. Owner Randy Poteet knows all the best fishing spots and offers lagoon, river and blue-water options around Bluefields, Pearl Lagoon and beyond.

✨ Festivals & Events

★ Palo de Mayo   CULTURAL
(Maypole Festival; ⊘ May) Nicaragua's best street party simmers along throughout May with a series of neighborhood parties and cultural events, but the highlights are the energetic Carnival on the last Saturday of the month and the closing Tulululu march on the 31st.

🛏 Sleeping

Bluefields Bay Hotel   GUESTHOUSE $
(Tia Irene; ☑ 2572-2143; Barrio Pointeen, frente Nicafish; r with/without air-con US$20/15; ❄) Run in conjunction with a local university, this laid-back guesthouse by the bay has a variety of recently renovated rooms offering excellent value and a great walk-anywhere location. The attached open-air restaurant is

built right over the water; the food is hit or miss, but it's a fine place for a drink while watching the *pangas* (small motorboats) come and go.

Guesthouse Campbell   GUESTHOUSE $
(☑ 8827-2221; Galileo, 2½ c S; r with/without air-con US$11/20; ❄) A bit out of the way but great value, this family-run guesthouse has clean, comfortable rooms with fresh paint jobs, private bathroom and cable TV.

Hotel Jackani   GUESTHOUSE $$
(☑ 2572-0440; hoteljackani@gmail.com; Frente Policia, Barrio Punta Fria; s/d/tw/tr incl breakfast US$30/40/50/60; ❄ 🛜) This new family-run hotel in front of the police station is already very popular with travelers thanks to its spotless rooms and warm welcome. Guests also appreciate the included breakfast, fast internet and the large balcony out front with views over to the bay.

Casa Rosa   LODGE $$$
(☑ 8832-4269; Loma Fresca; r/ste US$55/75; ❄ 🛜) Perched on a tributary of the Río Escondido in the breezy Loma Fresca neighborhood, this Nica-American sportfishing resort is a 10-minute taxi ride from the commercial heart of town, but looks and feels a million miles away. Most guests come to fish, but the clean and comfortable wooden rooms with air-con, wi-fi, cable TV and a river serenade would work for anyone.

🍴 Eating

Bluefields' favourite snack is the *paty* – a savory spiced meat pastry sold for US$0.30 by roaming vendors all over town.

★ Cevicheria El Chino   SEAFOOD $
(frente Colegio Bautista; ceviche US$2; ⊘ 7am-9pm) Don't leave Bluefields without trying El Chino's marvelous *ceviche* prepared fresh every day and served in small polystyrene cups, alongside an array of auto parts at this unremarkable grocery shop. Choose from shrimp, fish, oyster or mixed and watch out for the outrageously spicy homemade 'Ass in Space' chili sauce – made with pounds of habanero chilies.

There's no sign and the owner tells us plenty of readers walk right by with their heads in their guidebook. It's the only store on the block in front of the Baptist School.

Comedor de Las Platas   NICARAGUAN $
(contiguo Galileo; meals incl drink US$3; ⊘ noon-8pm) A quiet *comedor* serving budget lunch-

es during the day, this local institution transforms into the best *fritanga* (grill) in town in the evenings, serving up delicious *fritos* – greasy fried chicken on piles of plantain chips with pickles. Come early.

★ **Galeria Aberdeen** CAFE $$
(Los Pipitos; ☎2572-2605; Mercado, 1½ c O; light meals US$4-7) Feeling just a tad too chic for grimy Bluefields, this light-filled, split-level cafe serves real coffee (US$1 to US$2.50) in addition to panini, pasta dishes, salads and other meals you won't find anywhere else. Also has a great selection of desserts and a fridge full of imported beers. The walls are covered with works by local artists and it hosts regular cultural events.

Luna's Ranch NICARAGUAN $$
(Loma Fresca, frente Urracan; mains US$5-9; �}11am-10pm) There are many reasons to visit this impressive thatched restaurant on the Loma Fresca hill, such as occasional live concerts and the interesting collection of images of the old Bluefields, including many of the devastation wrought by the hurricane. But the biggest attraction is the generous portions of mouthwatering seafood. It's a 10-minute taxi ride (US$0.50) from downtown.

Drinking & Nightlife

★ **Four Brothers** CLUB
(Parque Reyes, 6 c S; �} 8pm-4am Thu-Sun) Dance up a storm to dancehall, country and reggae on the wooden dance floor at this legendary disco ranch, comfortable in the knowledge that your dignity is protected by the extremely low-wattage lighting. It doesn't get going until after midnight. Go in a group: it sometimes gets a little rough later on.

Midnight Dream (LaLa's) BAR
(Iglesia, 2 c N; �}11am-midnight) With an open-air deck that feels like it is floating on the bay and ridiculously loud reggae numbers, this atmospheric spot is where cool cats go to drink and get their groove on.

Information

BanCentro (Iglesia, ½ c S) Has a Visa/Plus ATM.
Clinica Bacon (☎2572-2384; Iglesia, 1 c S, ½ c O) Private clinic with a range of specialists and a laboratory.
Cyberzone (Galileo 20m N; per hour US$0.35; �}8am-7pm Mon-Sat) Fast internet connection.

Fadcanic (☎2572-2386; wawashang@fadcanic.org.ni; Barrio Punta Fria, oficinas del PNUD; �}9am-5pm Mon-Fri, 9am-noon Sat) Organizes visits to the Kahka Creek reserve and Wawashang Education Center. It also sells great products from the agricultural school in the office.
Gobierno Territorial Rama-Kriol (GTRK; ☎2572-1765, 8622-8407; www.rama-territory.com; Parque Reyes, 2 c S; �}8am-5pm) The official representatives of the vast territory south of Bluefields belonging to the indigenous Rama and Creole populations. Staff here can help arrange transportation and accommodations in villages throughout the region, including Monkey Point, Rama Cay, Tik Tik Kaanu and Bang Kukuk.
Intur (☎2572-0221; Iglesia, 2 c S, Punta Fria; �}8am-5pm Mon-Fri) Tourist office with some basic information about traveling in the region. There is also a small kiosk at the airport to orientate new arrivals.
Police (☎2572-2448; Barrio Punta Fria)

Getting There & Away

AIR
Take a taxi (US$0.50) to the Bluefields Airport, where **La Costeña** (☎2572-2500, 2572-2750; Aeropuerto; �}6am-5pm) has daily flights to Managua and Great Corn Island, and flies to Bilwi three days a week.

Bilwi (one way/return US$96/148, 50 minutes, 11:10am Monday, Wednesday and Friday)
Corn Island (one way/return US$64/99, 20 minutes, 7:25am and 3:05pm)
Managua (one way/return US$82/127, 70 minutes, 8:45am, 1:10pm and 4:15pm)

BOAT
There are a couple of scheduled boat services to Corn Island departing on Wednesday. The government-run Río Escondido (US$10, five hours) has the most reliable schedule, departing from the Muelle Municipal (Municipal Dock) at 9am on the dot. Larger and more comfortable but slightly slower, the **Captain D** (☎8850-2767; seat/bunk US$10/12) leaves around noon. If it arrives fully loaded from Rama it may depart from Bluff as it is unable to enter Bluefields. Its schedule often changes, so call to check.

There are also a number of cargo boats making the trip on irregular schedules.

Transporte Vargas (☎2572-0724, 2572-1510; contiguo Muelle Municipal; �}5am-4pm) at the Muelle Municipal has collective *pangas* to El Rama (US$9.50, two hours) with guaranteed departures at 5:30am and then further services when boats fill up. There are usually departures at around noon and 3pm. Transporte Vargas also runs boats to Tasbapauni and Orinoco in the greater Pearl Lagoon area.

Transporte Jipe (☑ 2572-1879; contiguo Mercado; ☺ 5am-4pm) next to the market also runs *pangas* to El Rama (US$9.50, two hours, 5:30am and 3pm).

For Pearl Lagoon (US$6, one hour) *pangas* leave from the dock next to the Muelle Municipal at 8:30am, 11am, 2pm and 3:30pm. Note that schedules are flexible – if a boat fills up, it will leave early. *Pangas* crossing the bay to El Bluff (US$2, 30 minutes) leave from behind the market when full.

Pearl Lagoon

At last, you've arrived in the real Caribbean. Here are dirt roads and palm trees, reggae music, and an English-speaking Creole community that fishes the local waters for shrimp, fish and lobster, and still refers to Spanish-speaking Nicaraguans as 'the Spaniards.' You can feel the stress roll off your shoulders as soon as you get off the boat from Bluefields. And the best part is that despite its obvious charms, this town still sees very few tourists – which means you may well be the only foreigner buzzing through the mangroves and jungle that surround Pearl Lagoon (the bay). The bay is a timeless expanse of black water and home to more than a dozen ethnic fishing villages.

If your Caribbean dream is tinted turquoise, you can easily arrange a tour of the nearby Pearl Keys, where you'll find sugar-white beaches that double as turtle hatcheries, and swaying coconut palms that lull you into inner peace. Of course, nothing tops off a day on the water like cold beer, lobster with coconut sauce and heavy doses of reggae music, all of which are available among Pearl Lagoon's collection of restaurants and bars sprinkled along traffic-free roads patrolled by fishers, their families and free-roaming horses.

◎ Sights & Activities

The town is laid out along two main north–south roads: Front Rd, on the water, and another road a block inland.

At the southern end of the inland road you'll find the **Moravian Church**, with its characteristic red tin roof. Take the path opposite the church due west and walk through town until you reach the savannah, a striking flat ecosystem with several freshwater creeks and interesting birdlife. Keep on the concrete path and after around

2km (30 minutes) you will reach the humble Miskito fishing communities of **Awas** and **Raiti Pura**, where the grassy shore is perfect for a picnic. The water here is shallow and great for swimming.

You can also make the journey by bike; Queen Lobster Tours rents bikes for US$1 per hour.

⚲ Tours

Fuel costs make up the lion's share of any boat charter. Plan on paying around US$60 to US$80 per day for the boat and captain plus fuel. If you're on a budget, look for a boat with a small engine: it will take longer but you'll save plenty. Note that small engines are only an option when the weather is calm.

While fluctuations in fuel prices affect prices dramatically, a ballpark price for one-day trips to the keys is around US$180 to US$200 for a small group. For larger groups, budget around US$45 per visitor. All tours include transportation and lunch on one of the islands.

★ **Captain Sodlan McCoy**   BOAT TOUR
(☑ 8410-5197, 8368-6766; Up Point) Anyone can take you to the Pearl Keys, but few know the area even half as well as Captain Sodlan McCoy, a colorful, no-nonsense fisherman who has been visiting the islands since he was a boy. A trip with Sodlan is much more than sightseeing, it's a cultural experience. He also offers bird-watching, fishing and community trips.

To find him turn right out of the dock and head to the end of the path.

Kabu Tours   ECOTOUR
(☑ 8714-5196; www.kabutours.com) A community-run venture set up by the Wildlife Conservation Society (p495) to offer an alternative source of income to turtle fishers from the community of Kakabila. It offers overnight and multiday trips to the Pearl Keys, including turtle spotting and snorkeling. It also runs fascinating cultural tours to communities in the Pearl Lagoon basin. See the website for a list of packages.

Queen Lobster Tours   BOAT TOUR
(☑ 8499-4403, 8662-3393; www.queenlobster.com; Muelle, 200m N) Professionally run eco-tourism outfit specializing in overnight trips to the Pearl Keys, as well as inventive activities around town such as traditional cooking classes.

🛏 Sleeping

Slilma Guesthouse
GUESTHOUSE $

(☑2572-0523; slilma_gh1@yahoo.com; Enitel, 1 c S, 1 c E; r with air-con US$30-35, r with fan US$15-20, r without bathroom US$10; ❄) Take the first left after the cell tower to find this budget guesthouse offering small but very clean rooms with small TVs and the cleanest shared bathrooms in the Atlantic region. There are also more spacious rooms with air-con and private bathrooms upstairs.

Comfort Zone
GUESTHOUSE $

(☑8829-7113; Muelle, 2 c S, ½ c E; r with air-con US$35, s/d/tr with fan US$11/14.50/18; ❄) Next to the family store, these tiled rooms with flatscreen TV, small desks, fans and private bathroom are a good deal, and the owners couldn't be more accommodating.

Queen Lobster
BUNGALOW $$

(☑8662-3393; Front Rd, Muelle 200m N; s/d/tr US$30/40/50; 🛜) An innovative small hotel offering two beautifully crafted bamboo and thatch huts on stilts over the water with private bathrooms, and hammocks on the porch. The attached restaurant is one of the best in town serving fantastic seafood dishes, but the owners plan to close it down to make space for more rooms.

Green Lodge
HOTEL $$

(☑2572-0507; Front Rd, Muelle 75m S; s/d with air-con US$30/35, r without bathroom US$7-14; ❄🛜) Half a block from the dock, this long-running hotel is a fine choice. The cheaper rooms upstairs in the family home are a little cramped, but those in the new wing are clean, spacious and comfortable. Owner Wesley Williams is a knowledgeable source of information on local history and culture.

🍴 Eating

Pearl Lagoon is a great place to try traditional Creole cuisine, either in one of the town's restaurants or with a fresh cooked meal out in the open during a boat trip.

Coconut Delight
BAKERY $

(Miss Betty's; Muelle, 30m S; bakery items from US$0.25-US$1; ⊙8am-8pm Mon-Sat) Follow the sweet smells to this pink wooden hut to discover Caribbean baking at its finest. Tear into hot coconut bread, *toto* (sticky ginger bread), journey cakes, fluffy soda cakes and even vegetarian *paty* served with a smile by jolly giant and all-round-nice-guy Mr Byron.

★ Casa Ulrich
INTERNATIONAL $$

(☑8603-5173; Up Point, Muelle 350m N; mains US$5.50-12.50; ⊙7am-10pm; 🛜) Local boy and Swiss-trained chef Fred Ulrich has returned to Pearl Lagoon after a long absence working in resorts all over the Americas and has invested in his own hotel and restaurant right by the water. Everything on the menu is top-notch, but make sure to try the tender fillet steaks that arrive at your table on a sizzling platter or the delicate shrimp pasta.

ℹ Information

Western Union (frente Muelle, Tienda Miss Isabel; ⊙9am-5pm Mon-Fri) Receive international transfers here. It will also give a cash advance on a credit card for a percentage fee.

Wildlife Conservation Society (WCS; ☑2572-0506; www.wcs.org; Muelle, 20m S, Pearl Lagoon; ⊙9am-5pm Mon-Fri) A conservation organization working to protect endangered marine turtles on the Pearl Keys. Swing by the office to find out more about its programs.

ℹ Getting There & Away

Boats run to Bluefields (US$6, one hour) at 6:30am and 1pm. Sign up the day before for the early boat.

Every Monday, Wednesday, Thursday and Saturday, a *panga* makes the run to Orinoco and Marshall Point from Bluefields via Pearl Lagoon (US$12, two hours, 9am); it returns to Pearl Lagoon and Bluefields the following day. This boat can also drop travelers at the communities of Kakabila, Brown Bank and La Fe. There are *pangas* from Bluefields to Tasbapauni (US$12, 2½ hours) that pass Pearl Lagoon every day at 11am. Times are liable to shift depending upon the season, so you'll need to ask about departure times at the dock.

One bus (US$6.30, five hours) a day leaves Pearl Lagoon at 5am for El Rama, from where you can connect to services to Managua and San Carlos.

Corn Islands

The Caribbean coast's biggest tourist draw is actually 70km offshore on a pair of enchanting islands with horseshoe bays, crystalline coves and underwater caves. Great Corn is larger and peopled by a Creole population that lives in colorful wooden houses, many of which are sprinkled along the main road that encircles the island. And though tourism is the second-largest industry, behind lobster fishing, you won't see mega-developments here.

Little Corn, a tiny, jungled, car-less jewel, actually attracts more tourists, with most visitors heading for funky, creative beachside *cabañas* that are the perfect setting for Robinson Crusoe 2.0. The dive sites are more diverse on Little Corn, the jungle is thick and the food is outrageously good, which explains why so many ignore the larger island and indulge in car-free tranquillity. But there is a catch: during high season there can be more foreigners than locals.

Great Corn Island

POP 7100

Large enough to get lost in humble hillside and beachfront neighborhoods that are poor but still full of spirit, and small enough to find your way home again, Great Corn is on the shortlist for most authentic Caribbean island. Here are barefoot bars, commercial fishing wharfs, pick-up baseball games on the beach, smiling young lobster divers catch-in-hand, an ever-present armada of elders sitting in rocking chairs on creaky front porches and elegant virgin beaches backed by picturesque headlands. It's a place where reggae and country music can coexist without irony. Where fresh lobster is a staple ingredient rather than a luxury. And the longer you stay, the less you want to leave.

◉ Sights

Great Corn measures about 6 sq km and is looped by one main road – which has several spur roads that lead to various beaches and neighborhoods. Long Bay is where you'll find the island's best stretch of golden sand. It arcs from a pile-up of local fishing *pangas* and lobster traps to a wild, jungle-covered headland. If you're looking for a place to snooze and swim in absolute tranquillity, this is your destination. Southwest Bay beckons with another outstanding wide beach. The water here is calmer but the area is more developed and less rustic.

Walk up the dirt trail behind the Sunrise Hotel in South End past the banana groves and you will be rewarded with panoramic views from Mt Pleasant as the sun plunges beneath the Caribbean Sea. Or make your way to Quinn Hill, where Spanish artist Rafael Trénor has installed a cube (the lower half is buried to make it look like a pyramid) symbolizing one of the earth's eight vortex points as part of his Soul of the World Project (www.souloftheworld.com).

Next to the stadium, the Culture House (Mt Pleasant, contiguo Alcaldía; ☺ 8am-8pm Mon-Fri) museum won't hold your attention very long with its pictures of old beauty queens, preserved lobsters and collection of John Grisham novels. But there are a couple of pre-Columbian pots and if you come in the evening, you can watch the local youth band jam in the music room.

🏃 Activities

The tourist office (p497) is able to organize guides (US$15 to US$30 per person) for hikes all over the island, including to the wild Bluff Point.

There's terrific snorkeling along the reef off the Sally Peachie coast. Among the other highlights for snorkelers are the remains of a Spanish Galleon off Waula Point – there's not much left, you'll mostly just be checking out some old cannons and an anchor, but it's still neat – and a more complete wreck of a steamship full of fish in shallow water off Sally Peachie. Mr Dorsey at Yellowtail (p497) offers highly recommended guided snorkeling tours. Paraiso Club (☑ 2575-5111; www.paraisoclub.com; Waula Point; cabañas s/d US$54/70, bungalow s/d US$66/84, all incl breakfast; ❄ 🗢) rents snorkel gear and also arranges chartered snorkeling tours (US$25 per person) and fishing trips (US$40 per person).

There are two new dive shops on the island, which has helped put Big Island firmly back on the dive map. New dive sites are being discovered all the time, leading to an ever expanding list of attractions for divers of all skill levels.

🛏 Sleeping

G&G HOTEL $
(☑ 2575-5017; martinez-downs69@hotmail.com; contiguo Pasenic, Brig Bay; r with/without air-con US$25/15; ❄) If you don't need to be right by the water's edge, save your cash for lobster and beers and check into this modern hotel in town, which offers outstanding value on clean and spacious rooms. It's within walking distance of a fairly inviting stretch of beach and the main dock.

Mi Mundo HOSTEL $$
(☑ 8526-6379; www.mimundocornislandhostel.com; Brig Bay; dm US$10-12, r US$30-40; ❄ 🗢) A budget traveler's dream, this welcoming new hostel is literally built over the water. It offers a range of comfortable rooms and

dormitories and has a breezy common area and communal kitchen upstairs with fantastic views over the brilliant turquoise Caribbean. Management offers great local advice and rents snorkel gear in order to explore the reef, which is right on the doorstep.

Hospedaje Los Escapados GUESTHOUSE $$
(www.losescapadosecocabanas.com; Sally Peachie; s/d/tr from US$36/49/71.50; 🛜) Perched up on the hillside in Sally Peachie, this small guesthouse offers something different with four large luxury tents with polished wooden floors and fantastic private bathrooms set among lush tropical gardens. The tents can be totally opened out at the front to catch the fresh breeze and each has its own wooden deck with sea views.

Yellowtail GUESTHOUSE $$
(📞8909-8050; Sally Peachie; r US$25) This relaxed place has just two cabins with fridge, cooker and private bathroom in a lovely part of the island. Owner Dorsey offers guided snorkeling tours around the reef in front of the guesthouse.

⭐ **Arenas Beach Resort** HOTEL $$$
(📞2575-5223; www.arenasbeachhotel.com; Southwest Bay; s/d bungalow US$67/84, s/d US$87/109; ❄) Great Corn Island's most professionally managed resort. Choose from colorful wooden bungalows with sea views from the hammocks on the balconies, or modern rooms with fantastic bathrooms (and hairdryers!) in the main building. The white-sand beach comes raked and dotted with cushy lounge chairs surrounding a bar in a wooden boat.

✖ Eating

Island Bakery & Sweets BAKERY $
(Sally Peachie; ⏰7am-6pm Mon-Sat) Head to this good old-style Caribbean bakery and indulge in all kinds of delicious sweet snacks including fantastic cinnamon rolls, coconut pies and cakes. There's also a good variety of natural drinks – try the ginger and pineapple.

Victoria's NICARAGUAN $
(Sally Peachie; dishes U$1.35-5; ⏰6:30am-9pm) Pull up a plastic chair on the roadside porch at this friendly shop/bar/restaurant hybrid in Sally Peachie and enjoy delicious local-style fast food and ice-cold beers. Among the options are *fritos* (fried chicken or pork and cabbage salad on heaps of fried green plantain chips) and Nica-style tacos. A very local experience.

Sea Side Grill SEAFOOD $$
(North End; mains US$7-14; ⏰7am-9pm) A friendly waterside restaurant that serves up consistently excellent seafood dishes served with a choice of three sides as well as lobster burgers and other light meals. The open-air dining area catches a good breeze and is inviting enough to keep you there for a few beers after you've finished your meal. With two hours' notice, staff will cook *rundown* (seasoned fish or meat cooked in coconut milk with root vegetables) to order.

ℹ Information

BanPro (Brig Bay) ATM and currency conversion available on the main road, just southwest of the airport.

Cyber Comisariato (📞2575-5268; Entrada Picnic Center; internet per hour US$0.70; ⏰7am-8pm)

Hospital (📞2575-5236; Alcaldía, 500m E) This 24-hour public clinic offers emergency services.

Police (📞2570-1440; contiguo Aeropuerto) Up on the hill between the airport and the stadium.

Tourist Office (📞ext 29, 2575-5091; lgarcia@intur.gob.ni; contiguo Estadio; ⏰8am-noon & 1:30-5pm Mon-Fri) Friendly tourist office inside the *alcaldia* building.

ℹ Getting There & Away

Great Corn's small airport is served by La Costeña, which runs flights to Bluefields (one way/return US$64/99, 20 minutes), with continuing service to Managua (one way/return US$107/164, 70 minutes) at 8:10am, 12:45pm and 4:10pm.

Several regular boats make the five- to six-hour trip to Bluefields via El Bluff. The government-run *Rio Escondido* (US$10) leaves on Thursday at 9am and is the most punctual service. More comfortable but slightly less reliable is the *Captain D* (seat/bunk US$10/12), a large cargo ship that leaves at 11pm on Saturday. It also runs once a month from Corn Island to Bilwi (US$22, 10 hours), usually leaving Thursday in the evening.

There are a number of other less comfortable fishing and cargo boats that make the Bluefields run and there is usually always at least one departure on Sunday nights. Bring a hammock or you will be trying to get comfortable on the cold steel deck.

Little Corn Island

POP 500

This jade *isleta* is a dreamy escape with imaginative bungalow properties encamped on otherwise virgin beaches. Even if cars were allowed (which they aren't), they wouldn't be able to maneuver the thin concrete and muddy jungle paths that wind beneath the mango, coconut and breadfruit trees, and into the thick forest that buffers the northern and eastern coasts.

The northern end of the island is the most secluded, has the best beaches and is the perfect setting for your Crusoe homage. Locals live, drink, dine, shoot pool and dance in the Village, which is set on a serene harbor sheltered from the north winds. The rugged, windy eastern coast makes for a transcendent afternoon of beachcombing: gorgeous white-sand beaches are framed by boulders, driftwood, headlands and coconut groves.

◉ Sights & Activities

The island's best and most picturesque beaches are on opposite ends of the island. Unfortunately, at the time of research, many of the beaches on the windward side had lost a fair bit of their sand to erosion, although locals say that with an extended set of good north winds the sand should pile up again.

From Casa Iguana you can stroll south along the windward shore, scramble over the rocks and arrive on **Big Fowl House Beach** `FREE`, then **Jimmy Lever Beach**. Or walk 2km (20 minutes) north from the Village through the jungle to **Otto Beach**. Then navigate the rugged northern shore until you find the spectacular **Goat Beach**, framed by two headlands.

On the way back, don't forget to head up to the **lighthouse**, a steel tower jutting 6m above the mango trees, where you can glimpse the island's curves and coves, and catch an outrageous sunset.

There is great snorkeling on the east and north sides of the island. Many hotels in these areas rent snorkeling gear, as do the dive shops. If you want a guide, ask in the Village for **Aqua Boy** (☑ 8573-2875, 8422-4500; Front Rd, Village; snorkeling US$20) or on the windward side for **Schweizer** (☑ 8367-0939; snorkeling US$20).

Up the hill from the school, **Alfonso** (☑ 8732-6398; School, 300m N; fishing per person US$60) organizes fishing trips in his boat.

Kite Little Corn   KITESURFING
(www.kitelittlecorn.com; Stedman's Hotel; ⊗ 8am-6pm) Soar over the turquoise waters of Little Island with this new kitesurfing school run by Nacho, an affable Spaniard who is pas-

sionate about the sport. Located on the windy side of the island inside Stedman's Hotel, it offers two-day intensive courses (US$300) and group tuition (US$35 per hour).

Dive Little Corn   DIVING
(☑ 8856-5888; dlcshopstaff@gmail.com; Village; 1/10 dives US$35/280; ⊗ 8am-6pm) Little Corn's original dive shop is owned and managed by Casa Iguana and provides a high level of service. It offers open water (US$330) and advanced open water (US$270) courses.

🛏 Sleeping

You can stay either in the Village, which is convenient and offers the most restaurant and nightlife options, or in one of the more secluded slices of paradise. Most businesses have signs in the Village telling you which path to take.

Lighthouse Hotel   HOSTEL $$
(☑ 5723-2477; www.thelighthouselci.com; dm/cabaña US$17/50; 🛜) On the highest point of the island, this welcoming new hotel has cute wooden *cabañas* with fantastic views over the windward side waters. Both the private *cabañas* and dorms are simple but comfortable and the onsite bar-restaurant serves great food and has become something of a hot spot for drinks. A fine choice if you don't need to be right on the sand.

Casa Iguana   LODGE $$
(www.casaiguana.net; cabañas s/d US$30/35, casitas US$65-75) This gathering of freshly painted wooden *cabañas* (smaller, with shared bathrooms) and *casitas* (larger, with private bathrooms) arranged on a rocky cliff just above the beach is hugely popular. The location and views are tremendous and the restaurant serves first-class fare; however, the constant stream of expat staff means it doesn't have much local flavor.

Ensueños   BUNGALOW $$
(www.ensuenos-littlecornisland.com; cabañas from US$30, casas US$70-100) Surrounded by forest and fruit orchards, and perched on a golden crescent of sand and a sheltered turquoise cove, this enchanting hotel features a variety of different rustic candelit *cabañas* by the waterside and three delightful solar-powered *casas* with small kitchens a bit further back.

Elsa's Place   HUT $$
(☑ 8848-8136, 2575-5014; elsasplace@yahoo.com; cabañas US$30-60, r without bathroom US$15-25) Miss Elsa sticks to a winning formula:

cheap, comfortable rooms right by the water. There is a variety of simple but neat wooden bungalows with private bathrooms and some basic cheapies out the back. Probably the best deal on this stretch.

Derek's Place BUNGALOW $$$

(www.dereksplacelittlecorn.com; cabañas US$60-100) The dreamiest beach bungalows on the island are found spread out over a lovely grassy promontory covered with coconut palms that feels far from the crowds. The *cabañas* are thatched, geometrically inspired and fashioned from bamboo, wood, old bottles, recycled shipping line and other natural materials. There's dedicated hammock space, snorkel gear for rent and a small, friendly dive shop onsite.

🍴 Eating

Most restaurants are located in the Village, although almost all hotels also serve meals.

El Bosque NICARAGUAN $

(breakfast US$3.50, mains US$4.30-7) A simple sand-floored *comedor* surrounded by greenery, El Bosque serves up good breakfasts and filling portions of local specialties to hungry travelers.

Rosa's NICARAGUAN, VEGETARIAN $

(breakfast US$3.50, meals US$4.30-7; ⊘6:30am-9:30pm; 🍴) This humble *comedor* on the trail between the Village and Iguana Beach is a fine spot for breakfast and also has vegetarian pastas and coconut curries, as well as other typical local dishes.

★Habana Libre CUBAN $$

(📞2572-9086; mains US$8-12; ⊘noon-10pm) Long considered the Corn Islands' best restaurant, this Cuban-run kitchen serves up outstanding plates of fish, shrimp, roast pork and *ropa vieja* (a Cuban shredded-beef delicacy) on a swank dining patio. But the absolute star of the show is the lobster in jalapeño sauce – don't leave the island without trying it.

Comedor Bridget NICARAGUAN $$

(📞8437-7295; meals US$7-9.50; ⊘7am-10pm) Pull up a chair on the porch of this converted family home and order the superb salt-dusted, lightly fried fish and a cold beer. It also serves great-value lobster, shrimp and fried-chicken dishes. It's your number one choice for no-nonsense authentic local dining.

🍷 Drinking & Nightlife

Tranquilo Cafe CAFE

(⊘8am-late; 🛜) Feeling homesick? Head to this hip open-air cafe for great burgers, buffalo wings and bruschetta with an indie-rock soundtrack. It's the most popular haunt among travelers for an evening drink and hosts regular bonfire parties and other events. It might feel a bit too gringo for some.

Aguila's BAR

(⊘11am-1am) Little Corn Island's most popular after-hours hangout. The sweaty pool hall is a hotbed of hustling and competition, and the music thumps in the open-air dance hall just above the beach. It's not the slightest bit classy, but it's good fun.

ℹ Getting There & Away

Collective *pangas* to Little Corn (US$5.20, 40 minutes) leave from the pier on Great Corn at 10am and 4:30pm; if you're staying on the northern end of Little Corn, you should take the morning boat. Boats leave Little Corn at 7am and 1:30pm from the main pier. If you're taking the morning flight to Managua, it's best to travel the day before. It can get very rough and you may get soaked. Bring garbage bags to cover your luggage. For a smoother ride, it's possible to ride on the large cargo ships (US$2 to US$3, 1¼ hours) that supply the *islita*, but there are only a handful of departures each week.

Bilwi (Puerto Cabezas)

POP 48,500

This impoverished Caribbean port town and ethnic melting pot sprawls along the coast and back into the scrubby pines on wide brick streets and red-earth roads, full of people and music, smiles and sideways glances. Old wooden churches, antique craftsman homes and ramshackle slums are knitted together with rusted sheet-metal fencing, coconut palms and mango trees. In a single stroll you'll eavesdrop on loud jagged Miskito banter, rapid-fire español and lovely, lilting Caribbean English. Sure, this city has systemic problems (poverty, decay, crime), and its ramshackle infrastructure lags behind the rest of the country. But with tasty seafood, great-value historic lodging options, and seaside indigenous communities a boat ride away, it can also be as alluring as a sweet, yet slightly sketchy, new friend.

◉ Sights & Activities

There is next to no tourism in Bilwi; missionaries and aid workers still far outnumber travelers here.

Beaches around Bilwi are nobody's idea of the Caribbean dream. La Bocana, an old pirate hangout at the river mouth north of town, has a stretch of decent beach, but crooks still dig it here. Come with a local.

★ Casa Museo Judith Kain   MUSEUM
(☎ 2792-2225; Parque Central, 4 c N, 1 c O; ⊕ 8am-5pm Mon-Fri) **FREE** Set in the former home of a prolific local painter, this museum provides a window into what it was like to live in Bilwi in the good old days. There are B&W photos, old dugout canoes, terrific local handicrafts and an antique collection (the sewing machines are especially cool); dozens of Kain's paintings are also on display. It's attached to one of the best hotels in town.

☞ Tours

Amica   CULTURAL TOUR
(Association of Indigenous Women on the Atlantic Coast; ☎ 2792-2219; asociacionamica@yahoo.es; Parque Central, 3 c S; ⊕ 8am-noon Mon, 2-5:30pm Mon-Fri, 8am-noon Sat) 🏄 Your ticket into the area's natural reserves and indigenous communities is through Amica. In addition to working to stop domestic violence and promote family planning and indigenous rights, it can arrange forest treks, canoe tours and fishing trips in the mangroves. It also offers overnight visits to the Miskito Keys (US$600, eight visitors) and guides (US$6) to visit communities around town.

🛏 Sleeping

Casa Museo Judith Kain   HOTEL $
(☎ 2792-2225;   www.casamuseojudithkain.com; Parque Central, 4 c N, 1 c O; r/tw with fan US$13/16, r/tw/tr with air-con US$24/28/32; 🅿 ❋ 🛜) In a town with an abundance of great-value lodging, this may be the best of the bunch. Rooms set in two superb old craftsman gems are su-

per clean and charming with high, beamed ceilings, hot water, porches and balconies sprinkled with wooden rockers overlooking gardens full of birds. No wonder it's always booked up.

El Cortijo II   GUESTHOUSE $$
(☎ 2792-2340; cortijoarguello@yahoo.com; Parque Central, 3 c N, 1 c E; s/d US$18/21.50, with balcony US$21.50/25; ❋ 🛜) This 60-year-old craftsman gem is your Caribbean grandma's house. Rooms are spotless with worn wooden floors and high ceilings. The common living room is filled with gorgeous antiques – including old hand-blown glass buoys – and if you reserve ahead, you may snag a room with a private sea view balcony, steps from a creaky wooden walk that leads to the rolling sea. Nice!

🍴 Eating & Drinking

Most local lobster is exported, but when it's in season you'll find it at around US$7.50 a plate – often the same price as chicken or fish! If you're pinching pennies, head to the market, where you'll find some stalls selling tasty fried fish.

★ Restaurante Faramhi   SEAFOOD $$
(☎ 2792-1611; frente Aeropuerto; mains US$7.50; ⊕ 11am-10pm) Close to the airport, this popular restaurant serves easily the best food in town. It's a very Bilwi kind of place: the open-air dining area features seashell light shades, a random disco light and a country music soundtrack. The menu reflects the town's multiethnic roots with typical seafood plates starring alongside an ensemble of good Chinese dishes.

Wachi's Pizza   PIZZA $$
(Parque Central, 2 c E; pizzas US$4.50-13; ⊕ noon-9pm) Being the only real pizzeria within a 200km radius, this place would run a brisk trade even if it wasn't up to scratch – fortunately it is, with generous sized pies sporting good thick crusts and tasty toppings served on a pleasant porch overlooking the Caribbean.

BUSES FROM BILWI (PUERTO CABEZAS)

DESTINATION	COST (US$)	DURATION	FREQUENCY (DAILY)
Managua	25.20	20-24hr	10am & 1pm
Rosita	7.50	6-10hr	6am & 7pm
Siuna	10	10-12hr	7am
Waspám	6	6hr	5:30am & 7pm

Kabu Yula BAR
(Parque Central, 5 c S; ⊘2pm-2am) A two-story open-air bar with unbroken sea views, the 'sea dog' is the perfect place for an afternoon tipple.

ⓘ Getting There & Away

AIR
Although you can hop on a super-long-distance (and rather painful) bus from Managua or (occasionally) catch a boat from Corn Island, most people come by plane. **La Costeña** (☑2792-2282; Aeropuerto; ⊘8am-noon & 3-6pm) offers regular flights to Managua and Bluefields. Book tickets in advance. Departure tax is US$2. Flights include:

Bluefields (one way/return US$96/148, 50 minutes, 11:20am Monday, Wednesday and Friday)

Managua (one way/return US$97/149, 1½ hours, 7:40am, noon and 3:40pm Monday to Saturday, 7:40am and noon Sunday)

BOAT
The only regular boat service to/from Bilwi is the **Captain D** (☑8850-2767), which runs between Corn Island and Bilwi (US$22, 10 to 12 hours) about once a month depending on demand. Call to check the schedule.

BUS
Buses depart from the bus terminal, 2km west of town.

SAN CARLOS & AROUND

The steamy riverside town of San Carlos is a key hub for river transportation, and launchpad for a number of highly appealing attractions, including the Archipiélago de Solentiname, several wildlife reserves and the fabulously unlikely Spanish castle at El Castillo.

San Carlos

POP 12,200

The capital of the isolated Río San Juan department is the gateway to some of Nicaragua's most compelling countryside but is itself a curious place with a bit of an identity crisis. During the day it is a busy international port filled with herds of travelers in transit, which explains the bustling and festive *malecón* (waterfront) lined with restaurants. But when night falls, and the magnificent views disappear with the setting sun, it re-verts to a rather lackluster small town where gossiping is the main form of entertainment.

Most travelers burn their San Carlos hours by exploring the old Spanish fortress, planning river and island adventures, stocking up on córdoba and checking emails one last time before they drop off-grid for a while.

⊙ Sights

San Carlos is less a tourist destination and more a place to wait for your ship, or *panga* (small motorboat), to come in, but there is beauty here – particularly on the grounds of **Centro Cultural Jose Coronel Urtecho**, which is set within the crumbling walls of **Fortaleza de San Carlos** (⊘9am-5pm) FREE. It's no El Castillo, but it was built in 1724 and has amazing lake and Río San Juan views from several lookout points linked by garden trails. The cultural center has some interesting displays on local culture, biology and history. It even has a map of the Nicaraguan canal that never was, c 1791. There's another old **Spanish observation post**, with cannons, at Restaurant Mirador.

🛏 Sleeping & Eating

The cheapest eats in town are at the cluster of bus-terminal *comedores* (basic eateries), the best of which is **Comedor Alondra** (Terminal de buses; meals incl beverage US$3).

Gran Lago Hotel HOTEL $$
(☑2583-0075; www.grandhotelsnicaragua.com; Parque Central, 1 c O, 1 c S; s/d/tr incl breakfast US$36/40/60; ❀🛜) Right on the edge of the lake with views over to the Archipiélago de Solentiname, this small hotel has a variety of rooms split over two levels. Those downstairs are a bit closed in and dark but the bigger upper-floor rooms get plenty of light and views of the lake. The small rear deck is a lovely place to hang out with a book.

Posada Doña Juanita GUESTHOUSE $$
(☑2583-0024; posada_juanita@hotmail.com; Del Hospital 2 c N, 1 c O, ½ c N; s/d incl breakfast US$35/45) It's a bit of a hike from the center but the rooms in this cute guesthouse on the 2nd floor of a family home are bright, spacious and comfortable. Prices include a quality breakfast.

Restaurante Kaoma NICARAGUAN $$
(☑2583-0293; Parque Central, 1½ c S; mains US$7-11; ⊘8am-midnight) A beautiful terrace restaurant with old wooden floors, beamed

ceilings and massive lake views. The extensive menu includes tender beef dishes and fish, which comes sautéed in a buttery garlic sauce or stuffed with shrimp.

ℹ Information

Banpro (Malecón) ATM inside the second pavilion on the *malecón*.

Hospital Felipe Moncada (☑ 2583-0244) About 1km north of town.

Intur (☑ 2583-0301; riosanjuan@intur.gob.ni; contiguo a Migración; ◷ 8am-4pm) Not visitor focused but offers some basic travel advice.

Marena (☑ 2583-0296; ◷ 8am-4pm) Processes fishing licenses, technically required for all fishing on the Río San Juan, but unless you are in your own boat your captain/tour operator should organize these.

Migración (☑ 2583-0263; Malecón; ◷ 8am-5pm) Processes entry/exit formalities for those traveling along the Río Frio to Costa Rica.

Telecentro (Parque Central; per hour US$0.70; ◷ 8am-5:30pm Mon-Fri) Internet by the park.

ℹ Getting There & Away

AIR

With the completion of the new paved road linking San Carlos and Managua, flights to and from the region are now infrequent and often sell out, so book well in advance.

The San Carlos airport is a 3km, US$1 cab ride from downtown San Carlos. **La Costeña** (☑ 2583-0048; frente Cementerio; ◷ 8am-noon & 3-5pm) operates compact, 12-seat planes on Thursday and Sunday leaving San Carlos for San Juan de Nicaragua (one way/return US$55/85, 30 minutes) at 12:55pm. Going the other direction, flights for Ometepe (one way/return US$55/85, 20 minutes) and Managua (one way/return US$76/116, 50 minutes) depart at 2:15pm – although the schedule is flexible and you may be sent on a scenic flight down the river to San Juan before heading to Managua directly from there; make sure to check in early.

BOAT

Collective riverboat services to Boca de Sábalos (US$2.85, two hours) and El Castillo (US$3, three hours) leave from the **Muelle Municipal** (Municipal Dock), half a block west of the *mercado* (market), at 8am, noon, 2:30pm and 3:30pm Monday through Saturday, 8am and 1:30pm on Sunday. Express boats to Sábalos (US$4.15, 1½ hours) and El Castillo (US$5.20, two hours) leave at 6:30am, 10am and 4pm.

At the time of research, the government-run ferry linking San Carlos with San Miguelito, Altagracia (Isla de Ometepe) and Granada was out of service due to low water levels on the approach

to San Carlos. There were no immediate plans to reactivate the service. If it returns to operation it is likely to run on the same schedule, leaving San Carlos from the Muelle Municipal at 2pm Tuesday and Friday. Check the latest with the **EPN** (☑ 2583-0256; Muelle Municipal) in San Carlos.

Boats to the Islas Solentiname leave from the public dock next to Migracíon.

BUS

Buses leave from the bus terminal in San Carlos for the following destinations:
➠ **Boca de Sábalos** (US$2.20, two hours, 7am, 9am, 11am, 2pm, 4:30pm and 7pm)
➠ **El Rama** (US$5.50, seven hours, 9am)
➠ **Juigalpa** (US$4, four hours, 10am, 11.10am, 12:40pm and 1:30pm) Managua-bound buses will also drop passengers in Juigalpa.
➠ **Managua** (US$5.50, six hours, 2am, 6:30am, noon, 2:30pm, 6pm, 9pm and 10:30pm)
➠ **San Miguelito** (US$2, two hours) Direct buses leave at 12:20pm and 1pm, but you can hop on any Managua- or Juigalpa-bound bus and get off at the San Miguelito turnoff.

Minivans for the border crossing at Las Tablillas (US$2.20, 30 minutes) depart when full from the terminal from 3am to 5:30pm.

Alternatively **Agua Trails** (☑ 8859-1481; www.aguatrails.com) runs a shuttle service to La Fortuna in Costa Rica.

Islas Solentiname

If you're the type who likes islands draped in jungle, surrounded by crystalline waters that reflect the forest, sun and sky, and populated by farmers and fishers who share their wealth and also happen to be terrific artists and craftspeople, you do not want to miss this oft-overlooked archipelago. And we haven't even mentioned the gators, monkeys, orchids and migratory waterfowl, the sensational offshore fishing, the mind-blowing sunsets and the spectacular starlight. Almost forgotten for 500 years, and nearly destroyed in a single day, the Archipiélago de Solentiname does not seem entirely of this world.

◉ Sights & Activities

Solentiname comprises 36 islands; the largest are Mancarrón, San Fernando (also called Isla Elvis Chavarría) and Venada (Isla Donald Guevara). The first two have the principal facilities for travelers. Mancarrón also has the islands' most famous sight, the simple yet beautiful adobe church that was the spiritual and communal center of Cardenal's community. Near here is an interesting archaeological exhibition, while a short walk away is El Refugio, the main community on the island, where you can wander among the local homes watching artisans create brightly painted balsa carvings.

San Fernando has an excellent museum, with informative displays on the pre-Columbian residents of the archipelago, as well as a gallery that showcases the work of some of the islands' best artists. There are many petroglyphs scattered around the islands, which make appealing destinations for hikes – there are also caves to explore on Isla Venada. Fishing is good around here, and Isla Zapote has fantastic bird-watching possibilities. Otherwise, the islands are just great for taking it easy.

🛏 Sleeping & Eating

Most accommodations are grouped on Mancarrón and San Fernando, although there is also a family homestay on Isla Venada.

Hotel Sueño Feliz GUESTHOUSE $
(☑ 8478-5243; esperanzosales.29@gmail.com; El Refugio; r per person with/without breakfast US$10/8) A simple guesthouse set in the home of a friendly local artisan family. It offers three simple rooms with peach paint jobs in the main house as well as a log-and-concrete *cabaña* out the back that sleeps up to six. Affordable meals are available and it offers a full range of tours around the archipelago.

★ Hotel La Comunidad GUESTHOUSE $$
(☑ 2277-3495, 8966-7056; contiguo Muelle; r per person with/without meals US$40/20) 🍴 This pair of charming solar-powered wooden houses overlooking the bay is easily the best deal on Mancarrón, with breezy hammock-strung balconies, spacious rooms and huge bathrooms with outdoor showers. Some even have bidets (no joke!). Guests can use the wi-fi at the library, and hotel profits support the local school. If there is no one around, ask for Ernesto at the library.

Albergue Celentiname GUESTHOUSE $$
(☑ 8465-2426, in Costa Rica 506-7096-8676; hotel celentiname.blogspot.com; r per person incl full board US$40) Tucked into a flowering garden that feels like something out of a tropical utopia is this secluded guesthouse, a gorgeous 10-minute walk from the main dock on the extreme northern end of the west-coast trail. Basic but neat wooden *cabañas*

come with two beds and a terrace with lake and garden views.

ℹ Getting There & Around

Transol (☑ 8828-3243, 8555-4739; www. transol.com.ni; ⏱ 24hr) runs a daily fast boat service (US$10, 90 minutes) between San Carlos and the islands, leaving from the dock next to Migración in San Carlos at 3pm and returning at 9am. This is by far the fastest and most comfortable way to get to the archipelago.

If you're on a tight budget and have a flexible itinerary, slow public boats (US$4, two to three hours) run on Tuesday and Friday leaving Mancarrón at 5am and stopping about 30 minutes later at San Fernando before continuing on to San Carlos. They return to Solentiname from the dock next to Migración in San Carlos at 1pm.

If that doesn't work with your schedule, you can hire a private boat (seating at least six) between San Carlos and the islands for US$120 to US$150.

Río San Juan

You simply must see this river. It surges purposefully through rolling green hills, thick jungle and wetlands on its irrepressible march to the Caribbean.

Not that you'll be sitting around all day admiring its beauty. This river demands action. After all, it was once the domain of indigenous traders, Spanish conquistadors, British pirates, gold hunting travelers and even Mark Twain. Follow their example and penetrate the vine-hung wilderness of jaguars and macaws that is the Reserva Biológica Indio-Maíz, troll for tarpon, search for alligators in the moonlight and then make a toast to your adventures while overlooking the remains of a 16th-century Spanish fort. All of which will cost you. But it's worth it to fully experience this spectacular and unforgettable waterway.

Boca de Sábalos

It feels like that thick jungle looming on its edges is about to reclaim this muddy, dusty town set at the confluence of the Río San Juan and Río Sábalos (Tarpon River). And therein lies its appeal. When you lounge on the terrace of your hotel, lodge or guesthouse at sunset, you'll watch birds fish and ride end-of-the-day thermals as you hear that familiar, primordial roar of the howler monkeys.

Río Sábalos effectively splits the town in half, with the inexpensive *hospedajes* and main road on one side, and a smaller community, threaded by a slender footpath past rustic homes and gardens, on the other. It's two córdobas (US$0.10) to cross the canal in a dugout canoe.

🛏 Sleeping

⭐ Sábalos Lodge   LODGE $$
(☑ 8823-5555, 8823-5514; www.sabaloslodge. com; Muelle, 1km E; bungalows US$35-75) This collection of stilted bungalows set in one meandering riverside row achieves the *Robinson Crusoe* ideal. Each one has an indoor-outdoor living room with hammocks, a bed swathed in mosquito netting, and an outdoor shower. The best part: each bungalow has its own personalized view of the river and offshore island, which is alive with birds at sunset. Meals run US$9 to US$12.

The best deal is the family *cabaña* (US$75), which can fit four to five guests.

Hotel Sábalos   HOTEL $$
(☑ 8659-0252; www.hotelsabalos.com.ni; frente Muelle; s/d US$22/38, with river view US$27/42, all incl breakfast; 🛜) Perched on stilts over the water at the mouth of the Río Sábalos, this charming hotel has comfortable wooden rooms with hot water, and rocking chairs on the wide veranda. It also has the only real restaurant in Sábalos (mains US$6 to US$7) serving quality meals with a river view. Staff will run across the river from the dock in their boat.

ℹ Getting There & Away

Boca de Sábalos is pretty much the last town on the river accessible by road and has fairly frequent bus services, which makes it a convenient place to spend the night if you miss the last boat downstream from San Carlos.

Boat services from Boca de Sábalos:

El Castillo (US$0.55, one hour, 10am, 2pm, 4:30pm and 5:30pm Monday to Saturday, 10am and 2:30pm Sunday; express US$1, 30 minutes, 7:30am and 11am)

San Carlos (US$3.50, 2½ hours, 6am, 7am, 8am and 3pm Monday to Saturday, 6am and 3pm Sunday; express US$4.75, one hour, 6am and noon)

Buses from San Carlos cross the Río Sábalos on a sketchy-looking barge (you want to get off before it drives on!) and continue right on into town.

Bus departures from Sábalos:

Buena Vista (US$1.50, one hour, 11am and 4pm) Returning at 6am and 1pm.

San Carlos (US$2.50, two hours, 4am, 6am, 7am, 1pm, 3pm and 4pm)

El Castillo

Cute, compact and crowned with its stunning 17th-century Spanish fortress, it's no surprise that diminutive El Castillo is the Río San Juan's showpiece destination. It's laced with pebbled-concrete walking paths that wind up, down and around the hill, shaded by mango, coconut, orange and almond trees, and cradled by the Río San Juan – wide and foaming with two sets of rapids that proved to be the bane of British pirates for centuries. A town this civilized means that the jungle has been tamed here, so don't expect the howlers to sing you to sleep. The good news is that you are just 15 minutes by boat from Nicaragua's best-preserved lowland rainforest, the Reserva Biológica Indio-Maíz.

🧭 Tours

⭐ Nena Tour   ADVENTURE TOUR
(☑ 2583-3010; www.nenalodge.com) A fantastic tour operator based at Nena Lodge offering the full range of hikes in the Reserva Indio-Maíz plus canoe tours on the nearby Río Juana (US$15 per person, three hours) and a night alligator tour (US$45 for up to four passengers). Also rents an inflatable raft to run the rapids in front of town (US$20 for up to three participants).

🛏 Sleeping & Eating

Casa de Huesped
Chinandegano   GUESTHOUSE $
(☑ 2583-3011; Muelle, 240m E; s/d US$12/18, without bathroom US$8/15; 🛜) This creaky wooden house done up with potted tropical plants and a shabby-chic dining area is built right over the river and is the best cheapie in town. The wooden and bamboo rooms are breezy and have high ceilings. Get the corner room if you can. Or just come for lunch or dinner.

Hotel Tropical   HOTEL $$
(☑ 5772-5283; Muelle 130m E; r incl breakfast US$25; ❄) Lie back and listen to the rushing water of El Castillo outside your window at this small hotel above Restaurant Vanessa. While the wooden rooms with air-con, cable TV and tiled bathrooms are a fine deal, the best thing is the breezy wooden porch perched right above the rapids.

TRIPS AROUND EL CASTILLO

Conveniently located at the dock, El Castillo's tourist office (☎8526-9267; frente muelle; ◷8am-6pm) sources local guides for a variety of tours. It helps to make reservations a day in advance. Some menus of guided hikes and *panga* trips:

Reserva Biológica Indio-Maíz, Río Bartola (US$75 for up to five people, four hours) Take a private *panga* to the Río Bartola entrance of the Indio-Maíz reserve, then hike 3km through primary forest, where you'll be dwarfed by 500-year-old giants, taste medicinal plants, and spot tree frogs, green iguanas and three types of monkey (spider, white-faced and howler). After the hike you'll motor up Río Bartola, where you'll swim in a crystal-clear river surrounded by jungle.

Reserva Biológica Indio-Maíz, Aguas Frescas (US$85 for up to five people, five hours) Virtually identical to the Bartola trip in terms of scenery but the Aguas Frescas trail is a slightly longer and more challenging hike.

Reserva Biológica Indio-Maíz, Caño Sarnoso (US$120 for up to five people, five hours) This boat trip travels further down the Río San Juan to observe the ruins of the old steamboats and abundant wildlife around the El Diamante rapids, including crocodiles and birdlife. It can also be combined with one of the trails within the reserve.

The tourist office also organizes a night caiman-watching tour (US$45 for up to four visitors).

You don't have to go through the tourist office, which can seem less than helpful at times. There are several private operators with signs up around town offering similar tour rosters.

❶ Getting There & Away

From El Castillo, collective boats leave for San Carlos (US$3, three hours) via Boca de Sábalos (US$0.50, 30 minutes) at 5am, 6am, 7am and 2pm. On Sunday there are only two services at 5am and 2pm. Fast *pangas* to San Carlos (US$5, two hours) via Boca de Sábalos (US$1, 15 minutes) leave at 5:30am, 9am and 11am.

Slow boats to San Juan de Nicaragua (US$10, seven to eight hours) pass El Castillo around 9am on Tuesday, Thursday and Friday. Express services (US$20, four to five hours) pull into the dock at around 8:15am on Tuesday and Friday.

UNDERSTAND NICARAGUA

Nicaragua Today

Like him or loathe him, President Daniel Ortega's reelection in 2011 delivered something that Nicaragua had lacked for a long time: a sense of stability. After years of devastation from civil war, the country's infrastructure slowly started rebuilding. Gone were the transportation strikes, debilitating power rationing and unpredictable rallies. But as he prepares to run for a third consecutive term in 2016, Ortega's anti-poverty platform has raised questions – behind Haiti, Nicaragua remains the second-poorest country in the Western Hemisphere.

Traditionally, Nicaraguan presidents have only been permitted to serve two five-year terms. But 2014 saw a landmark moment in Congress: the decision to abolish term limits, as well as to dispense a long-time rule requiring a presidential candidate to garner at least 35% of the vote. Riots and protests in opposition to the policy change prompted violent conflicts between police and the public.

The implications for Daniel Ortega, of course, are significant – at the time of writing, he was preparing for a third run in November 2016. Third *official* run, that is: Ortega also served as president from 1985 to 1990, but Nicaragua's Supreme Court, in a controversial ruling, decided that the term didn't count toward his term limit.

History

Early History

Pre-Hispanic Nicaragua was home to several indigenous groups, including the ancestors of today's Rama, who live on the Caribbean coast, and the Chorotegas and Nicaraos, on the Pacific side. The latter spoke a form of Náhuatl, the language of the Aztecs. Many Nicaraguan places retain their Náhuatl names.

By 1500 BC Nicaragua was broadly settled, and though much of this history has been lost, at least one ancient treaty between the Nicarao capital of Jinotepe and its rival Chorotegan neighbor, Diriamba, is still celebrated as the Toro Guaco.

European Arrival

Although Columbus stopped briefly on the Caribbean coast in 1502, it was Gil González de Ávila, sailing north from Panama in 1522, who would really make his mark here. He found a chieftain, Cacique Nicarao, governing the southern shores of Lago de Nicaragua and the tribe of the same name. The Spaniards thus named the region Nicaragua.

Nicarao subjected González to hours of inquiry about science, technology and history. González famously gave Nicarao an ultimatum: convert to Christianity, or else. Nicarao's people complied, a move that in the end only delayed their massacre at the hands of the Spanish; other native groups were thus warned.

Six months later González made Cacique Diriangén the same offer; Diriangén went with 'or else.' His troops were outgunned and eventually destroyed but inspired further resistance. After conquering four Pacific tribes – 700,000 Chorotega, Nicarao, Maribios and Chontal were reduced to 35,000 in 25 years – the nations of the central highlands halted Spanish expansion at the mountains, with grim losses.

Colonial Settlement

The main Spanish colonizing force arrived in 1524, founding the cities of León and Granada. Both were established near indigenous settlements, whose inhabitants were put to work.

The gold that had attracted the Spaniards soon gave out, but Granada and León remained. Granada became a comparatively rich colonial city, with wealth due to surrounding agriculture and its importance as a trading center. It was also a center for the Conservative Party, favoring traditional values of monarchy and ecclesiastical authority. Originally founded on Lago de Managua, León was destroyed by volcanic eruptions in 1610 and a new city established some

30km northwest. León in time became the center for radical clerics and intellectuals, who formed the Liberal Party and supported the unification of Central America and reforms based on the French and American Revolutions.

The difference in wealth between the two cities, and the political supremacy of León, led to conflicts that raged into the 1850s, at times erupting into civil war. The animosity stopped only when the capital was moved to the neutral location of Managua.

Zelaya's Coup & US Intervention

In 1893 a Liberal general named José Santos Zelaya deposed the Conservative president and became dictator. Zelaya soon antagonized the US by seeking a canal deal with Germany and Japan. Encouraged by Washington, which sought to monopolize a transisthmian canal in Panama, the Conservatives rebelled in 1909.

After Zelaya ordered the execution of two US mercenaries accused of aiding the Conservatives, the American government forced his resignation, sending marines as a coercive measure. Thus began a period of two decades of US political intervention in Nicaragua. In 1925 a new cycle of violence began with a Conservative coup.

The Conservative regime was opposed by a group of Liberal rebels including Augusto C Sandino, who recruited local peasants in the north of the country and eventually became leader of a long-term rebel campaign resisting US involvement.

Sandino & the Somoza Era

When the US marines headed home in 1933, the new enemy became the new US-trained Guardia Nacional, whose aim was to put down resistance by Sandino's guerrillas, as is documented in Richard Millett's comprehensive study *Guardians of the Dynasty: A History of the US-Created Guardia Nacional de Nicaragua and the Somoza Family*. This military force was led by Anastasio Somoza García.

Somoza engineered the assassination of Sandino after the rebel leader was invited to Managua for a peace conference. National guardsmen gunned Sandino down on his way home. Somoza, with his main enemy out of the way, set his sights on supreme power.

Overthrowing Liberal president Sacasa a couple of years later, he established himself as president, founding a family dynasty that would rule for four decades.

After creating a new constitution to grant himself more power, Somoza García ruled Nicaragua for the next 20 years, sometimes as president, at other times as a puppet president, amassing huge personal wealth in the process (the Somoza landholdings attained were the size of El Salvador).

After his assassination in León, Somoza was succeeded by his elder son, Luis Somoza Debayle. In 1967 Luis died, and his younger brother, Anastasio Somoza Debayle, assumed control, following in his father's footsteps by expanding economic interests throughout Nicaragua.

Rising Opposition

In 1961 Carlos Fonseca Amador, a prominent figure in the student movement that had opposed the Somoza regime in the 1950s, joined forces with Colonel Santos López (an old fighting partner of Sandino) and other activists to form the Frente Sandinista de Liberación Nacional (Sandinista National Liberation Front; FSLN). The FSLN's early guerrilla efforts against Somoza's forces ended in disaster for the fledgling group, but over the years it gained support and experience, turning it into a formidable opponent.

On December 23, 1972, at around midnight, an earthquake devastated Managua, leveling more than 250 city blocks. The *Guardian* newspaper reported that, as international aid poured in, the money was diverted to Anastasio Somoza and his associates, while the people who needed it suffered and died. This dramatically increased opposition to Somoza among all classes of society.

By 1974 opposition was widespread. Two groups were widely recognized – the FSLN (Sandinistas) and the Unión Democrática de Liberación, led by Pedro Joaquín Chamorro, popular owner and editor of the Managua newspaper *La Prensa,* which had long printed articles critical of the Somozas.

In December 1974, the FSLN kidnapped several leading members of the Somoza regime. The government responded with a brutal crackdown in which Carlos Fonseca was killed in 1976.

Revolution & the FSLN

For a Nicaraguan public tired of constant violence, the last straw was the assassination of Chamorro. As street violence erupted

and a general strike was called, business interests and moderate factions in the Frente Amplio Opositor (Broad Opposition Front; FAO) unsuccessfully attempted to negotiate an end to the Somoza dictatorship.

By mid-1978 many major towns were rising up against government forces. The Guardia Nacional's violent reprisals garnered further support for the Sandinistas.

The FAO threw in its lot with the Sandinistas, whom they now perceived as the only viable means with which to oust the dictatorship. This broad alliance formed a revolutionary government provisionally based in San José, Costa Rica, which gained recognition and arms from some Latin American and European governments.

Thus the FSLN was well prepared to launch its final offensive in June 1979. The revolutionary forces took city after city, supported by thousands of civilians. On July 17, as the Sandinistas were preparing to enter Managua, Somoza fled the country. He was assassinated by Sandinista agents a year later in Asunción, Paraguay. The Sandinistas marched victorious into Managua on July 19, 1979.

They inherited a shambles. Poverty, homelessness, illiteracy and inadequate health care were just some of the problems. An estimated 50,000 people had been killed in the revolutionary struggle, and perhaps 150,000 more were left homeless.

Trying to salvage what it could of its influence over the country, the USA (under President Jimmy Carter) authorized US$75 million in emergency aid to the Sandinista-led government.

However, by late 1980 it was becoming concerned about the increasing numbers of Soviet and Cuban advisers in Nicaragua and allegations that the Sandinistas were supplying arms to leftist rebels in El Salvador.

The Contra War

After Ronald Reagan became US president in January 1981, relations between Nicaragua and the US began to sour. Reagan suspended all aid to Nicaragua and, according to the Report of the Congressional Committees Investigating the Iran-Contra Affair, by the end of the year had begun funding the counterrevolutionary military groups known as Contras, operating out of Honduras and Costa Rica, despite the US maintaining formal diplomatic relations with Managua.

Most of the original Contras were ex-soldiers of Somoza's Guardia Nacional, but as time passed, their ranks filled with disaffected local people. Honduras was heavily militarized, with large-scale US-Honduran maneuvers threatening an invasion of Nicaragua. The Sandinistas responded by instituting conscription and building an army that eventually numbered 95,000. Soviet and Cuban military and economic aid poured in, reaching US$700 million in 1987.

A CIA scheme to mine Nicaragua's harbors in 1984 resulted in a judgment against the US by the International Court of Justice. The court found that the US was in breach of its obligation under customary international law not to use force against another State and ordered it to pay repatriations to the Nicaraguan government; the Reagan administration rejected the findings and no payments were ever made.

Shortly afterward, the *New York Times* and *Washington Post* reported the existence of a CIA-drafted Contra training manual promoting the assassination of Nicaraguan officials and other strategies illegal under US law, causing further embarrassment for the Reagan administration.

Nicaraguan elections in November 1984 were boycotted by leading non-Sandinistas, who complained of sweeping FSLN control of the nation's media. The Sandinistas rejected the claims, announcing that the media was being manipulated by Contra supporters (*La Prensa* eventually acknowledged receiving CIA funding for publishing anti-Sandinista views). Daniel Ortega was elected president with 63% of the vote, and the FSLN controlled the National Assembly by a similar margin.

In May 1985 the USA initiated a trade embargo of Nicaragua and pressured other countries to do the same. The embargo lasted for five years, helping to strangle Nicaragua's economy.

With public opinion in the US growing wary of the war, the US Congress rejected further military aid for the Contras in 1985. According to the congressional report into the affair, the Reagan administration responded by continuing to fund the war through a scheme in which the CIA illegally sold weapons to Iran and diverted the proceeds to the Contras. When the details were leaked, the infamous Iran-Contra affair blew up.

After many failed peace initiatives, the Costa Rican president, Oscar Arías Sánchez, finally came up with an accord aimed at ending the war. It was signed in Guatemala City in August 1987 by the leaders of Costa Rica, El Salvador, Nicaragua, Guatemala and Honduras. Less than a year later, the first cease-fire of the war was signed by representatives of the Contras and the Nicaraguan government at Sapoa, near the Costa Rican border.

Polls & Peace

By the late 1980s the Nicaraguan economy was again desperate. Civil war, the US trade embargo and the inefficiencies of a centralized economy had produced hyperinflation, falling production and rising unemployment. As it became clear that the US Congress was preparing to grant the Contras further aid, Daniel Ortega called elections that he expected would give the Sandinistas a popular mandate to govern.

The FSLN, however, underestimated the disillusionment and fatigue of the Nicaraguan people. Economic problems had eclipsed the dramatic accomplishments of the Sandinistas' early years: redistributing Somoza lands to small farming cooperatives, reducing illiteracy from 50% to 13%, eliminating polio through a massive immunization program and reducing the rate of infant mortality by a third.

The Unión Nacional Opositora (UNO), a broad coalition of 14 political parties opposing the Sandinistas, was formed in 1989. UNO presidential candidate Violeta Barrios de Chamorro had the backing and financing of the USA, which had promised to lift the embargo and give hundreds of millions of dollars in economic aid to Nicaragua if UNO won. The UNO took the elections of February 25, 1990, gaining 55% of the presidential votes and 51 of the 110 seats in the National Assembly, compared with the FSLN's 39. Ortega had plenty of grounds for complaint, but in the end he went quietly, avoiding further conflict.

Politics in the 1990s

Chamorro took office in April 1990. The Contras called a heavily publicized ceasefire at the end of June. The US trade embargo was lifted, and foreign aid began to pour in.

Chamorro faced a tricky balancing act in trying to reunify the country and satisfy all interests. Economic recovery was slow; growth was sluggish and unemployment remained stubbornly high. Nevertheless, in 1996, when Nicaragua went to the polls again, the people rejected the FSLN's Ortega and opted for former Managua mayor Arnoldo Alemán of the PLC, a center-right liberal alliance.

Alemán invested heavily in infrastructure and reduced the size of the army by a factor of 10, but his administration was plagued by scandal, as corruption soared and Alemán amassed a personal fortune from the state's coffers, earning himself a place on Transparency International's list of the top 10 corrupt public officials of all time. Meanwhile, however, the Sandinistas had their own image problems, as the ever-present Ortega was accused by his stepdaughter of sexual abuse. In a gesture of mutual self-preservation, Ortega and Alemán struck a sordid little deal, popularly known as *el pacto* (the pact), which *Time* magazine reported was designed to nullify the threat of the opposition, pull the teeth of anti-corruption watchdogs and guarantee Alemán immunity from further investigation.

Sandinista diehards felt betrayed by Ortega's underhanded dealings, but many still believed in their party, and Ortega remained an important figure.

Sandinista 2.0

After losing three successive elections, FSLN leader Ortega returned to power in the November 2006 elections, capitalizing on disillusionment with neoliberal policies that had failed to jump-start the country's economy and an *el pacto*–sponsored law that lowered the threshold for a first-round victory to 35% of the votes (Ortega received 38%).

Taking office in January 2007, Ortega proclaimed a new era of leftist Latin American unity, leaving the USA and some international investors a little jumpy. The early days of Ortega's presidency were a flurry of activity, with Nicaragua's energy crisis seemingly solved via a deal with Venezuela's Hugo Chávez, and Ortega pledging to maintain good relations with the USA while at the same time courting closer ties with US archrival Iran.

But as the Ortega government found its feet, there was no sign of radical land reforms or wave of nationalizations that the business sector had dreaded and some diehard FSLN supporters had hoped for. Ortega for the most part followed the economic course set by the previous government and continued to honor Nicaragua's international financial obligations.

The first test for Nicaraguan democracy under the new Ortega government surfaced in 2008, with countrywide municipal elections. The FSLN claimed victory in over 70% of municipalities, when it had come to power with only 38% of the vote. Opposition forces claimed widespread voter fraud and *La Prensa* labeled the election 'the most fraudulent elections in Nicaraguan history.'

Nevertheless Ortega weathered the storm and by the end of his return term was able to point to solid economic growth alongside the reintroduction of free health care and education among the achievements of his government.

Culture

The National Psyche

Nicaragua has a fierce cultural streak and prides itself on homegrown literature, dance, art, music and cuisine. This spiritual independence is a holdover not only from the revolution and Contra War, but back to Spanish colonization, when indigenous nations won limited autonomy at enormous personal cost.

Nicaragua also still suffers from a bit of post-traumatic stress disorder. Spanish-speakers will hear plenty of stories involving tanks, explosions and aerial bombings, not to mention 'the day the family cow wandered into the minefield' stories. Former Sandinistas and Contras work, play and take Communion together, however, and any tensions you might expect seem to have been addressed and worked through. Opinions differ about the Sandinista years, but both sides will always agree to a good debate. Jump in and you'll learn more about the political scene than you ever would by reading a newspaper or guidebook.

Of course, attitudes differ from place to place. Residents of the English- and Miskito-speaking Atlantic coast rarely consider themselves part of Nicaragua proper, and many would prefer to be returned to the British Empire than suffer further oppression by the 'Spaniards' on the other side of the country. The cattle ranchers of the central highlands resist interference from the federal government, while coffee pickers in Matagalpa or students in León are willing to walk to Managua to complain to the government if they perceive that an injustice has been done.

Lifestyle

Nicaragua is a country in motion. One in five Nicas live outside the country, most in the USA, Costa Rica and Honduras. Waves of migration to the cities, which began in the 1950s, have left more than 55% of the population urban. Most internal immigrants are young women, and most go to Managua; men tend to follow the harvest into rural areas and the surrounding countries. Regular jobs are difficult to find, and more than half of employed Nicaraguans are in the 'informal sector' – street vendors, cleaners, artisans – without benefits or job security.

Despite the country's Catholic background, couples often live together and have children without being married, especially in larger cities. Nicaraguans are generally fairly accepting of the LGBT community, although the community is still fighting for full legal recognition.

Wealth is distributed unequally, with the moneyed elite living much as they would in Miami or elsewhere. For the vast majority of Nicaraguans, however, just putting food on the table is a daily struggle, with 46% living below the poverty line and perhaps a third of the country subsisting on two meals or fewer per day; almost one-fifth of children are at risk of problems relating to malnutrition, while in the Atlantic regions it is more than 30%.

However, when hitting the streets, even the poorest Nicaraguans will generally always appear in clean, freshly pressed clothes, which is why they find 'wealthy' backpackers in smelly rags so amusing.

People

With 6.1 million people spread across 130,000 sq km, Nicaragua is the second-least densely populated country in Central America after Belize. The CIA World Factbook estimates that 69% of the population is *mestizo* (of mixed ancestry, usually Spanish and indigenous people), 17% white, 9% black and 5% indigenous. The most recent census reports that just over 440,000 people describe themselves as indigenous: the Miskito (121,000), Mayangna/Sumo (9800) and Garifuna (3300), all with some African heritage, occupy the Caribbean coast alongside the Rama (4200). In the central and northern highlands, the Cacaopoeras and Matagalpas (15,200) may be Maya in origin, while the Chorotegas (46,000), the Subtiavas (20,000) and the Nahoas (11,100) have similarities to the Aztecs.

European heritage is just as diverse. The Spanish settled the Pacific coast, while a wave of German immigrants in the 1800s has left the northern highlands surprisingly *chele* (white, from *leche*, or milk). And many

of those blue eyes you see on the Atlantic coast can be traced back to British, French and Dutch pirates.

The original African immigrants were shipwrecked, escaped or freed slaves who began arriving soon after the Spanish. Another wave of Creoles and West Indians arrived in the late 1800s to work on banana and cacao plantations in the east. Mix all that together, simmer for a few hundred years and you get an uncommonly good-looking people who consider racism a bit silly.

Religion

Although Nicaragua's majority religion is Catholic, Nicaraguan Catholicism retains many indigenous elements, as the decor and ceremonies of churches such as San Juan Bautista de Subtiava and Masaya's María Magdalena make clear. Liberation theology also made its mark on Nicaraguan Catholicism, influencing priest and poet Ernesto Cardenal to advocate armed resistance to the Somoza dictatorship. Publicly chastised and later defrocked by Pope John Paul II, Cardenal remains a beloved religious leader. Nicaragua's incredible selection of Catholic churches and fascinating *fiestas patronales* remain highlights of the country.

On the Atlantic coast, Moravian missionaries from Germany began arriving in the early 1800s, and today their red-and-white wooden churches are the centerpieces of many Creole and Miskito towns. More recently, more than 100 Protestant sects, most US-based and collectively referred to as *evangelistas,* have converted at least 21% of the population; in fact, many of the foreigners you'll meet in rural Nicaragua are missionaries, who may try to convert you too.

Perhaps most interesting, around 12% of Nicaraguans say they are atheist or agnostic, unusual in Latin America.

Arts

Nicaragua is a bright star in the firmament of Latin American literature, and poetry is the country's most important and beloved art. Rubén Darío (1867–1916), a poet who lived in León, is one of the most renowned authors in the Spanish language, and his writings have inspired literary movements and trends throughout the Latin world. Three outstanding writers emerged soon after Darío, and their works are still popular: Azarías Pallais (1884–1954), Salomón de la Selva (1893–1959) and Alfonso Cortés (1893–1969). In the 1930s the experimental 'Vanguardia' movement came on the scene, led by José Coronel Urtecho, Pablo Antonio Cuadra, Joaquín Cuadra Pasos and Manolo Cuadra. A number of leading personalities in the Sandinista leadership, including Sergio Ramírez, Rosario Murillo and Ernesto Cardenal, made literary contributions as well as political ones.

Landscape

Nicaragua, comprising 129,494 sq km, is the largest country in Central America. It is bordered on the north by Honduras, the south by Costa Rica, the east by the Caribbean Sea and the west by the Pacific Ocean.The country has three distinct geographical regions.

Pacific Lowlands

The western coastal region is a broad, hot, fertile lowland plain broken by 11 major volcanoes. Some of the tallest are San Cristóbal (1745m), northeast of Chinandega; Concepción (1610m), on Isla de Ometepe in Lago de Nicaragua; and Mombacho (1345m), near Granada. The fertile volcanic soil and the hot climate, with its distinct rainy and dry seasons, make this the most productive agricultural area in the country. It holds the country's major population centers. Also in the area are Lago de Nicaragua (also known by its indigenous name, Cocibolca), the largest lake in Central America, studded with more than 400 islands, and the smaller Lago de Managua (Xolotlán).

North-Central Mountains

The north-central region, with its high mountains and valleys, is cooler than the Pacific lowlands and also very fertile. About 25% of the country's agriculture is concentrated here, including most coffee production. The highest point in the country, Pico Mogotón (2438m), is near the Honduran border, in the region around Ocotal.

Caribbean Coast

The Caribbean ('Atlantic') region occupies about half of Nicaragua's area. The 541km coastline is broken by many large lagoons and deltas. Twenty-three rivers flow from the central mountains into the Caribbean, including the Río Coco (685km), Nicaragua's longest river, and the Río San Juan (199km),

which flows from Lago de Nicaragua. These define much of the borders with Honduras and Costa Rica respectively.

The Caribbean region gets an immense amount of rainfall. It is sparsely populated and covered by tropical rainforest. The largest towns are Bluefields and Bilwi (Puerto Cabezas), both coastal ports. Several small islands, including the much-visited Corn Islands (Islas del Maíz), lie off the Caribbean coast, surrounded by coral reefs.

Wildlife

Nicaragua is home to about 1800 vertebrate species, including 250 mammals, and 30,000 species in total, including 688 bird species (around 500 resident and 150 migratory).

Animals are slowly working their way northward, a migration of densities that will one day be facilitated by the Mesoamerican Corridor, a proposed aisle of shady protected rainforest stretching from Panama to Mexico. Other countries in on the agreement are just getting started on the project, but Nicaragua's two enormous Unesco biosphere reserves, Bosawás and Southeast Nicaragua (Río San Juan), make a significant chunk.

Environmental Issues

With a developing economy, poor infrastructure and limited resources, Nicaragua faces a tough task in protecting the environment at the same time as lifting its citizens out of poverty. While there has certainly been progress in recent times, the country still faces a variety of pressing environmental issues.

SURVIVAL GUIDE

❶ Directory A–Z

ACCOMMODATIONS

Outside absolute peak periods in major tourist destinations, it's rarely necessary to reserve accommodations in advance in Nicaragua.

Hospedajes These cheap guesthouses are often family-run and are sometimes the only option in smaller towns.

Hotels Larger, more polished and less personal; they offer facilities including reception and often a restaurant.

Hostels Traveler's hostels with dormitories and common areas are only found in the main tourist areas.

Ecolodges Usually at the higher end of the market, these offer comfortable rooms surrounded by nature.

EMBASSIES & CONSULATES

Most embassies and consulates are located in Managua.

Canadian Embassy (☎2268-0433; http://travel.gc.ca/assistance/embassies-consulates/nicaragua; Los Pipitos, 2 c abajo, Bolonia)

Costa Rican Consulate (☎2251-0429; www.rree.go.cr; Rotonda Rubén Darío, 2 c E, 500m N; ☺8am-3pm)

Dutch Embassy (☎2276-8643; https://netherlands.visahq.com/embassy/nicaragua; Colegio Teresiano, 1 c S, 1 c O)

French Embassy (☎2228-1056; www.ambafrance-ni.org; Iglesia El Carmen, 1½ c O)

German Embassy (☎2266-7500; www.managua.diplo.de; Rotonda El Güegüense, 1½ c N)

Mexican Embassy (☎2278-1859; http://embamex.sre.gob.mx/nicaragua; Altamira d'Este, frente Claro)

US Embassy (☎2266-6010; http://nicaragua.usembassy.gov; Carretera Sur, Km 5.5)

INTERNET ACCESS

Internet access on the Pacific coast is fast (US$0.50 to US$0.70 per hour), cheap and widely available, even in small towns. The Caribbean coast has slightly slower, more expensive internet service, which is not widely available. Top-end hotels mostly have 'business centers' and often connections for laptops and wi-fi in rooms. The computer icon used in our hotel listings signifies that the hotel has a computer with internet access available to guests free of charge.

Public wi-fi in restaurants and cafes is becoming more common, but is still rare outside big cities. If you're staying for a while, consider purchasing a USB modem, which works well in larger cities but is often very slow in rural areas.

Nicaragua's cell data network is continually improving and works fairly well in big cities but can be painfully slow in rural towns where everyone is trying to get online through one tower. Sim cards are cheap and prepaid internet packets are also very affordable.

LEGAL MATTERS

Nicaragua's police force is professional and visible, and very approachable by Central American standards.

For minor traffic violations your driver's license will normally be confiscated and you will need to go to the bank to pay your fine and then to the nearest police station to retrieve your document. This can be a pain if you are only driving through. Some people advocate slipping traffic cops a 100-córdoba (US$4) bill with your ID to smooth out minor traffic violations, but that

SLEEPING PRICE RANGES

Price indicators for sleeping options in our listings denote the cost of a standard double room with private bathroom.

$	Less than US$20
$$	US$20–US$50
$$$	More than US$50

could always backfire. It's best to play it cool and hope they let you off with just a warning.

If you get caught with drugs or committing a more serious crime, it won't be that easy to get away from the law.

LGBT TRAVELERS

While consensual gay sex was recently decriminalized in Nicaragua, attitudes may take a bit longer to change. As in most of Latin America, gay and lesbian travelers will run into fewer problems if they avoid public displays of affection, and ask for two beds and then push them together. That said, lots of Nicaraguan gays and lesbians flaunt their sexuality, so you probably won't have much difficulty figuring out the scene.

There is a small selection of gay and lesbian bars and clubs in Managua and a vaguely tolerant scene in Granada, but apart from that, it's a pretty straight (acting) country.

MONEY

ATMs are widespread in most midsize towns in Nicaragua, but you'll need to stock up on cash before heading to rural areas. Credit cards are widely accepted in larger towns but rarely in rural areas apart from higher-end hotels. US dollars are the alternative currency and widely accepted, but for smaller items using córdobas is cheaper and easier.

It's worth carrying an emergency supply of dollars in case you have problems with your card.

OPENING HOURS

Opening hours vary wildly in Nicaragua as there are many informal and family-run establishments. General office hours are from 9am to 5pm. Some offices and shops, especially in rural areas, close for lunch from noon to 2pm. Government departments usually close slightly earlier and also take a meal break.

Comedores (cheap eateries) usually open for breakfast and lunch while more formal restaurants serve lunch and dinner.

Banks 8:30am–4:30pm Monday to Friday, to noon Saturday

Comedores 6am–4pm

Government Offices 8am–noon & 1–4pm Monday to Friday, 8am to noon Saturday

Museums 9am–noon & 2–5pm
Restaurants noon–10pm
Bars noon–midnight
Clubs 9pm–3am
Shops 9am–6pm Monday to Saturday

PUBLIC HOLIDAYS

New Year's Day (January 1) Shops and offices start closing at noon on December 31.

Semana Santa (Holy Week; Thursday, Friday and Saturday before Easter Sunday) Beaches are packed, hotel rates skyrocket and everything is closed – make sure you have a place to be.

Labor Day (May 1)

Mother's Day (May 30) No one gets away with just a card – more places close than at Christmas.

Anniversary of the Revolution (July 19) No longer an official holiday, but many shops and government offices close anyway.

Battle of San Jacinto (September 14)

Independence Day (September 15)

Día de los Difuntos (November 2) All Souls' Day.

La Purísima (December 8) Immaculate Conception.

Navidad (December 25) Christmas.

SAFE TRAVEL

Despite the fact that Nicaragua has one of the lowest crime rates in Central America, as a 'wealthy' foreigner you will at least be considered a potential target by scam artists and thieves.

➡ Pay extra attention to personal safety in Managua, the Caribbean region, around remote southern beaches and in undeveloped nature reserves.

➡ In larger cities, ask your hotel to call a trusted taxi.

➡ Backcountry hikers should note there may be unexploded ordnance in very remote areas, especially around the Honduran border. If in doubt, take a local guide.

TELEPHONE

Nicaragua's calling code is ☑ 505. There are no area codes within Nicaragua. While less common with the wide adoption of cells, some homes and businesses 'rent' their phone for a fee (usually around US$0.25 per minute) for national calls to landlines and cell phones. Direct calls abroad using the phone network or cell phones are expensive – any internet cafe will offer much cheaper rates.

Cell Phones

Many travelers simply buy a phone upon arrival – prices start at around US$15, and there are phone shops at the airport. You can also buy a SIM card (around US$3.50) and insert it into any unlocked GSM phone. The two phone companies are Claro and Movistar which now have similar levels of coverage. Electronic top-ups are available at *pulperías* (corner stores) and gas stations all over the country.

TOURIST INFORMATION

Intur (Nicaraguan Institute of Tourism; ☑ 2222-3333; www.visitanicaragua.com/ingles), the government tourism office, has branches in most major cities. It can always recommend hotels and activities (but not make reservations) and point you toward guides.

The *alcaldía* (mayor's office) is your best bet in small towns without a real tourist office. Although tourism is not the mayor's primary function, most will help you find food, lodging, guides and whatever else you might need. In indigenous communities, there may not be a mayor, as many still have councils of elders. Instead, ask for the president (or *wihta* in Miskito communities), who probably speaks Spanish and can help you out.

TRAVELERS WITH DISABILITIES

While Nicaraguans are generally accommodating toward people with mobility issues, and will gladly give you a hand getting around, the combination of cobbled streets, cracked sidewalks and stairs in pretty much every building can make life tough.

There are few regular services for disabled travelers and because of difficulties in finding suitable transportation, it's easiest to go through a tour company. Vapues Tours (www.vapues.com) is an experienced local operator, specializing in accessible travel.

There are very few wheelchair-accessible toilets and bathrooms in Nicaragua, so bringing toilet-seat extensions and wall-mountable mobility aids are highly recommended.

VISAS

All visitors entering Nicaragua are required to purchase a Tourist Card for US$10.

Those entering by land also pay a US$2 migration processing fee. Upon departure by land or boat there is another US$2 migration fee, while a small municipal charge – usually around US$1 –

EATING PRICE RANGES

Price indicators for eating options in our listings denote the cost of a typical main course.

$	Less than US$5
$$	US$5–US$10
$$$	More than US$10

may also be levied by the local government depending on the border crossing.

VOLUNTEERING

Nicaragua has a very developed volunteer culture, traceable to the influx of 'Sandalistas' (young foreign volunteers) during the revolution. Many hostels and Spanish schools maintain lists of organizations. Also check out Volunteer South America (www.volunteersouthamerica.net) and Go Abroad (www.goabroad.com).

ⓘ Getting There & Away

Nicaragua is accessible by air via the international airport in Managua, by road using four major border crossings with Honduras and Costa Rica (plus another crossing to Costa Rica at San Pancho – Las Tabillas, which sees few visitors), and by boat between El Salvador and Potosí, and Costa Rica and San Carlos.

Flights, cars and tours can be booked online at lonelyplanet.com/bookings.

AIR

Upon arrival in Nicaragua by air, visitors are required to purchase a tourist card for US$10; make sure to have US currency handy.

It's worth checking fares to neighboring Costa Rica, which is an air-conditioned bus ride away and may be significantly cheaper to fly into.

LAND
Border Crossings

Nicaragua shares borders with Costa Rica and Honduras. Generally, Nicaraguan border crossings are chaotic (there are no signs anywhere), but the procedure is fairly straightforward provided you have your documents in order.

Ocotal to Tegucigalpa, Honduras See the sunny Segovias and the Honduran capital at this major, business-like border. The Las Manos crossing point is efficient, although sometimes crowded.

Somoto to Choluteca, Honduras A high-altitude crossing that comes with an amazing granite canyon. Crossing point El Espino is laid-back and easy.

El Guasaule to Choluteca, Honduras The fastest route from Nicaragua, an easy cruise north from lovely León. The El Guasaule crossing is hot, hectic and disorganized.

Sapoá to Peñas Blancas, Costa Rica The main border crossing is generally easy unless your arrival coincides with an international bus or two, in which case it could take hours. The local municipality charges an additional US$1 fee at this crossing.

Bus

International buses have reclining seats, air-conditioning, TVs, bathrooms and sometimes even food service, and are definitely safer for

travelers with luggage. Crossing borders on international buses is generally hassle-free. At many borders the helper will take your passport, collect your border fees, get your stamp and return your passport to you as you get back on the bus. At the Costa Rican border post at Peñas Blancas you must complete the formalities in person.

There are direct bus services (without changing buses) to Costa Rica, Honduras, El Salvador and Guatemala, and connecting services to Panama and Mexico.

King Quality (www.king-qualityca.com) Luxury buses to Costa Rica, Honduras, El Salvador and Guatemala.

Nica Expreso (www.nicaexpreso.com) Runs from Chinandega (via León) to San José, Costa Rica.

Tica Bus (☑8739-5505; www.ticabus.com) Travels to Costa Rica, Honduras and El Salvador with connecting services to Guatemala, Mexico and Panama.

Transnica (☑2270-3133; www.transnica.com) Serves Costa Rica, Honduras and El Salvador.

Transporte del Sol (☑2422-5000; www.busesdelsol.com) Same-day service to Guatemala and San Salvador.

Car & Motorcycle

To bring a vehicle into Nicaragua, you'll need the originals and several copies of the ownership papers (in your name), your passport and a driver's license.

You'll get a free 30-day permit (lose it and you'll be fined) and you will need to purchase obligatory accident insurance for US$12. You may also be required to pay US$3 to US$4 for the fumigation of your vehicle. Your passport will be stamped saying you brought a vehicle into the country; if you try to leave without it, you'll have to pay import duty. It's possible to extend the vehicle permit twice at the DGA office in Managua before you have to leave the country.

You can now drive across two border crossings to Costa Rica. The most popular is at Sapoá–Peñas Blancas near Rivas; the new crossing at San Pancho-Las Tablillas in the Río San Juan still sees few vehicles.

It's possible to drive across the Nicaragua–Honduras border at El Guasaule, Somoto–El Espino and Ocotal–Las Manos.

ⓘ Getting Around

AIR

The hub for domestic flights is Managua International Airport. Other airports are simple affairs and some are little more than dirt strips outside town (or in Siuna and Waspám, in the middle of town). The airport in San Juan de Nicaragua is located across the bay in Greytown and is one of the few airports in the Americas where you need to take a boat to get on your flight.

There is one domestic carrier, La Costeña (☎ 2263-2142; www.lacostena.com.ni), which services Bluefields, the Corn Islands, Las Minas, Ometepe, Tola, San Carlos, San Juan de Nicaragua (Greytown), Bilwi and Waspám. Many domestic flights use tiny single-prop planes where weight is important and bags necessarily get left behind, so keep all necessities in your carry-on luggage.

Note that La Costeña is one of the few airlines that actually charges more to book online – a US$18 surcharge.

BOAT

Many destinations are accessible only, or most easily, by boat. Public *pangas* (small open motorboats) with outboard motors are much more expensive than road transportation – in general it costs around US$6 to US$8 per hour of travel. In places without regular service, you will need to hire your own private *panga*. Prices vary widely, but you'll spend about US$50 to US$100 per hour for four to six people; tour operators can usually find a better deal. It's easy, if not cheap, to hire boat transportation up and down the Pacific coast. On the Atlantic side, it's much more difficult. While it's not common, boats *do* sink here and tourists have drowned – please wear your life jacket.

River boats on the Río San Juan tend to be slow and fairly cheap. There are often express and regular services – it's worth paying a bit extra for the quicker version.

Following are the major departure points with regular boat service.

Bluefields To Pearl Lagoon, El Rama and Corn Island.

Corn Islands Regular boats run between Great Corn and Little Corn Islands.

El Rama To Bluefields.

San Carlos To the Islas Solentiname, the Río San Juan, the scenic border crossing to Costa Rica and several natural reserves.

Waspám The gateway to the Río Coco.

BUS

Bus coverage in Nicaragua is extensive although services are often uncomfortable and overcrowded. Public transportation is usually on old Bluebird school buses, which means no luggage compartments. Try to avoid putting your backpack on top of the bus, and instead sit toward the back and put it with the sacks of rice and beans.

Pay your fare after the bus starts moving. You may be issued a paper 'ticket' on long-distance buses – don't lose it, or you may be charged again. Some bus terminals allow you to purchase tickets ahead of time, which should in theory guarantee you a seat. While buses sometimes cruise around town before hitting the highway, you're more likely to get a seat by boarding the bus at the station or terminal.

Bus terminals, often huge, chaotic lots next to markets, may seem difficult to navigate, particularly if you don't speak much Spanish. Fear not! If you can pronounce your destination, the guys yelling will help you find your bus – just make sure they put you on an *expreso* (express) and not an *ordinario* (ordinary bus) or you'll be spending more time on the road than you planned.

CAR & MOTORCYCLE

Driving is a wonderful way to see Pacific and central Nicaragua, but it's best to use public transportation on the Caribbean side as roads are, for the most part, terrible.

HITCHHIKING

Hitchhiking is never entirely safe, and we don't recommend it. Travelers who hitchhike should understand that they are taking a small but potentially serious risk.

Nevertheless hitchhiking is very common in Nicaragua, even by solo women – to find a ride, just stick out your thumb. Foreign women, particularly those carrying all their bags, should think twice before hitchhiking solo. Never hitchhike into or out of Managua.

In rural areas where bus service is rare, anyone driving a pick-up truck will almost certainly stop for you. Climb into the back tray (unless specifically invited up front) and when you want to get off, tap on the cabin roof a couple of times.

You should always offer to pay the driver, which will almost always be refused.

LOCAL TRANSPORTATION

In smaller towns there are fewer taxis and more *tuk tuks* (motorized three wheelers) and *triciclos* (bicycle rickshaws). They're inexpensive – around US$0.50 per person to go anywhere in town – and kind of fun.

TAXI

Almost all taxis in Nicaragua are *colectivos* (shared taxi or minibus), which stop and pick up other clients en route to your destination, however it is always possible to pay a bit extra for an express service.

In Managua, always negotiate the fare before getting in. Taxis at major border crossings may also overcharge, given the chance.

Most other city taxis have set in-town fares, usually around US$0.50 to US$0.70, rising slightly at night. Ask a local how much a fare should cost before getting into the cab.

Hiring taxis between cities is a comfortable and reasonable option for midrange travelers. Prices vary widely, but expect to pay around US$10 for every 20km.

Costa Rica

⤷ 506 / POP 4.87 MILLION

Includes ➜

San José. 520

Central Valley
& Highlands. 533

Caribbean Coast 542

La Fortuna &
Volcán Arenal 554

Monteverde &
Santa Elena. 561

Playa Tamarindo. 576

Montezuma 583

Manuel Antonio 593

Southern Costa Rica
& Península de Osa. . .598

Best Places to Eat

➜ Café de los Deseos (p527)

➜ Jalapeños Central (p536)

➜ Como en mi Casa Art Café (p552)

➜ Orchid Coffee (p567)

➜ Cocina Clandestina (p585)

Best Places to Sleep

➜ Camp Supertramp (p581)

➜ Luz en el Cielo (p584)

➜ Flutterby House (p597)

➜ Hostel Pangea (p525)

➜ Aracari Garden Hostel (p543)

➜ Buddha House (p589)

Why Go?

The bellowing of howler monkeys echoes across the tree-tops. Magnificent frigate birds circle high overhead, while less-than-sonorous squawking uncovers a pair of scarlet macaws. Morning breaks in the coastal rainforest. Similar scenes unfold across Costa Rica, from the dry tropical forest along the Pacific coast to the misty cloud forest at higher altitudes. One-third of this country's area is protected, making it a wildlife wonderland.

The flora and fauna are only part of the appeal. Annually Costa Rica attracts more than one million visitors eager to catch a wave, climb a volcano or otherwise partake of paradise.

It's never easy to maintain the delicate balance between preserving natural resources and cashing in on economic opportunity, but Ticos are tireless in their efforts. These peace-loving people are eager to share the staggering scenery, bountiful biodiversity and complete contentment of *pura vida*, the 'pure life' of Costa Rica.

When to Go
San José

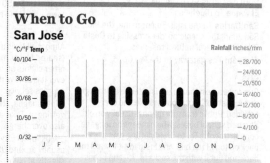

Jan–Apr The 'dry' season sees consistently hot temperatures and sunny skies.

May–Jul Crowds thin out and prices drop during the 'green' rainy season.

Dec The holidays are festive, though accommodation prices skyrocket.

Connections

You can enter overland from Nicaragua (at Peñas Blancas, Las Tablillas or Los Chiles) and from Panama (at Sixaola, Paso Canoas or Río Sereno). For more detailed information, see Survival Guide p618.

ITINERARIES

One Week

From San José, beeline north to La Fortuna. After a refreshing forest hike on the flanks of Volcán Arenal, soak in the country's best hot springs. Then catch a boat across Laguna de Arenal, and a bus to Monteverde, where you might encounter the elusive quetzal on a stroll through the Bosque Nuboso Monteverde.

Next: beach time. Head west to the biggest party town in Guanacaste, Playa Tamarindo, and enjoy the ideal surf, top-notch restaurants and rowdy nightlife.

Two Weeks

In week two, visit waterfalls and linger a bit in chilled-out Montezuma, where you can connect via jet boat to Jacó, another town with equal affection for surfing and partying. Spend half a day busing to Quepos, the gateway to Parque Nacional Manuel Antonio. A full day in the park starts with some jungle hikes and wildlife-watching and ends with a picnic and a dip in the park's perfect waters.

Essential Food & Drink

➜ The Tico diet consists largely of rice and beans and – when it's time to change things up – beans and rice.

➜ Breakfast for Ticos is usually *gallo pinto* (literally 'spotted rooster'), a stir-fry of rice and beans, usually served with eggs, cheese or *natilla* (sour cream).

➜ Most restaurants offer a set meal at lunch and dinner called a *casado*, or a 'married man's' lunch, featuring meat, beans, rice and salad. An extremely popular *casado* is the ubiquitous *arroz con pollo* (chicken and rice).

➜ Seafood is plentiful, fresh and delicious. While it's not traditional Tico fare, you'll find *ceviche* (raw fish or shrimp, marinated in lime juice and served chilled) on most menus.

➜ On the Caribbean coast, the cuisine shows off its Caribbean roots. Don't miss a chance to sample *rondón*, a spicy seafood gumbo.

AT A GLANCE

Currency Costa Rican colón (₡); US dollars (US$) also accepted

Languages Spanish & English

Money ATMs are ubiquitous; credit and debit cards widely accepted

Visas Generally not required for stays less than 90 days

Time GMT minus six; no daylight saving time

Area 51,100 sq km

Capital San José

Emergency 🖉911

COSTA RICA

Exchange Rates

Australia	A$1	₡397
Canada	C$1	₡418
Euro	€1	₡606
Japan	¥100	₡506
New Zealand	NZ$1	₡378
UK	UK£1	₡762
US	US$1	₡536

Set Your Budget

➜ **Dorm bed** US$8 to US$15

➜ **Casado** US$3 to US$8

➜ **Bus fare** US$4 to US$12

➜ **National park admission** US$15

➜ **Zip-line canopy tour** US$40 to US$60

Resources

➜ **Tico Times** (www.ticotimes.net)

➜ **Costa Rica Tourism Board** (www.visitcostarica.com)

➜ **Lonely Planet** (www.lonelyplanet.com)

Costa Rica Highlights

1 **Parque Nacional Tortuguero** (p542) Sliding silently through jungle canals in search of wildlife or volunteering to protect endangered sea turtles.

2 **Puerto Viejo de Talamanca** (p549) Surfing, sampling the culinary scene, lazing on the beach and partying.

3 **La Fortuna** (p554) Hiking the slopes of Volcán Arenal, then soothing your weary muscles with a soak in volcano-heated pools.

4 **Monteverde & Santa Elena** (p561) Spotting the resplendent quetzal through the mist at one of the nearby reserves.

5 **Mal País** (p582) Surfing luscious breaks and feasting on farm-fresh cooking.

6 **Parque Nacional Manuel Antonio** (p593) Watching troops of monkeys, slow-moving sloths and gliding brown pelicans.

7 **Parque Nacional Chirripó** (p601) Climbing atop Costa Rica's tallest peak to watch the sunrise.

8 **Parque Nacional Corcovado** (p606) Hiking the remote coast and rich rainforest in the country's premier wilderness experience.

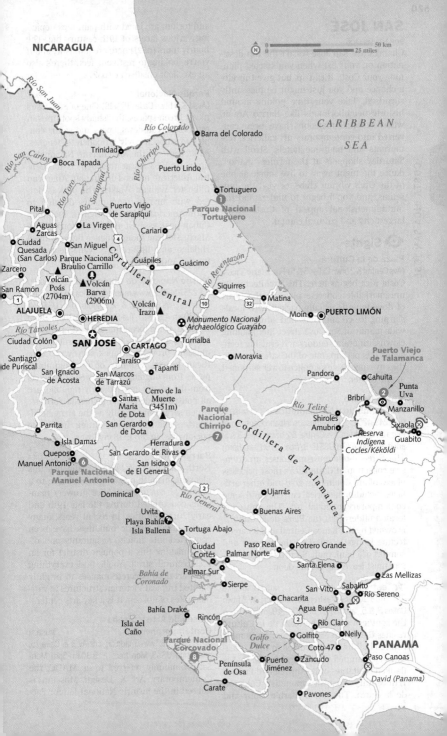

SAN JOSÉ

POP 1.72 MILLION

Chances are San José wasn't the top destination on your list when you started planning your Costa Rica trip, but give this city a chance and you just might be pleasantly surprised. Take your time poking around historic neighborhoods like Barrio Amón, where colonial mansions have been converted into contemporary art galleries, restaurants and boutique hotels. Stroll with Saturday shoppers at the farmers market, dance the night away to live music at one of the city's vibrant clubs, or visit the museums, and you'll begin to understand the multidimensional appeal of Costa Rica's largest city and cultural capital.

◉ Sights

Plaza de la Cultura   PLAZA

(Avs Central & 2 btwn Calles 3 & 5) For many Ticos, Costa Rica begins here. This architecturally unremarkable concrete plaza in the heart of downtown is usually packed with locals slurping ice-cream cones and admiring the wide gamut of San José street life: juggling clowns, itinerant vendors and cruising teenagers. It is perhaps one of the safest spots in the city since there's a police tower stationed at one corner.

Museo de Oro
Precolombino y Numismática   MUSEUM

(☑2243-4202; www.museosdelbancocentral.org; Plaza de la Cultura, Avs Central & 2 btwn Calles 3 & 5; adult/student/child US$11/8/free; ⊙9:15am-5pm) This three-in-one museum houses an extensive collection of Costa Rica's most priceless pieces of pre-Columbian gold and other artifacts, including historical currency and some contemporary regional art. The museum, located underneath the Plaza de la Cultura, is owned by the Banco Central and its architecture brings to mind all the warmth and comfort of a bank vault. Security is tight; visitors must leave bags at the door.

★ Teatro Nacional   NOTABLE BUILDING

(☑2010-1110; www.teatronacional.go.cr; Av 2 btwn Calles 3 & 5; admission US$10; ⊙9am-7pm) On the southern side of the Plaza de la Cultura resides the Teatro Nacional, San José's most revered building. Constructed in 1897, it features a columned neoclassical facade that is flanked by statues of Beethoven and famous 17th-century Spanish dramatist Calderón de la Barca. The lavish marble lobby and auditorium are lined with paintings depicting various facets of 19th-century life. The hourly tours (p521) here are fantastic, and if you're looking to rest your feet, there's also an excellent onsite cafe (p527).

Parque Nacional   PARK

(Avs 1 & 3 btwn Calles 15 & 19) One of San José's nicest green spaces, this shady spot lures in retirees to read newspapers and young couples to smooch coyly on concrete benches. At its center is the Monumento Nacional, a dramatic 1953 statue that depicts the Central American nations driving out American filibuster William Walker. The park is dotted with myriad monuments devoted to Latin American historical figures, including Cuban poet, essayist and revolutionary José Martí, Mexican independence figure Miguel Hidalgo and 18th-century Venezuelan humanist Andrés Bello.

Museo Nacional de Costa Rica   MUSEUM

(☑2257-1433; www.museocostarica.go.cr; Calle 17 btwn Avs Central & 2; adult/child US$8/4; ⊙8:30am-4:30pm Tue-Sat, 9am-4:30pm Sun) Entered via a beautiful glassed-in atrium housing an exotic butterfly garden, this museum provides a quick survey of Costa Rican history. Exhibits of pre-Columbian pieces from ongoing digs, as well as artifacts from the colony and the early republic, are all housed inside the old Bellavista Fortress, which served historically as the army headquarters and saw fierce fighting (hence the pockmarks) in the 1948 civil war.

Barrio Amón   AREA

North and west of Plaza España lies this pleasant, historic neighborhood, home to a cluster of *cafetalero* (coffee grower) mansions constructed during the late 19th and early 20th centuries. In recent years, many of the area's historic buildings have been converted into hotels, restaurants and offices, making this a popular district for an architectural stroll. You'll find everything from art-deco concrete manses to brightly painted tropical Victorian structures in various states of upkeep. It is a key arts center.

Museo de Arte y Diseño
Contemporáneo   MUSEUM

(☑2257-7202; www.madc.cr; cnr Av 3 & Calle 15; admission US$3, Mon free; ⊙9:30am-5pm Mon-Sat) Commonly referred to as MADC, the Contemporary Art & Design Museum is housed in the historic National Liquor Factory building, which dates from 1856. The largest and most important contemporary-art museum in the region, MADC is focused on the works of contemporary Costa Rican, Central American and South American artists, and occasionally features temporary exhibits devoted to interior design, fashion and graphic art.

★Museo de Jade   MUSEUM
(☑2521-6610; www.museodeljadeins.com; Plaza de la Democracia; adult/child US$15/5; ⊗10am-5pm) Reopened in its brand-new home in mid-2014, this museum houses the world's largest collection of American jade (pronounced '*ha*-day' in Spanish). The ample new exhibition space (five floors offer six exhibits) allows the public greater access to the museum's varied collection. There are nearly 7000 finely crafted, well-conserved pieces, from translucent jade carvings depicting fertility goddesses, shamans, frogs and snakes to incredible ceramics (some reflecting Maya influences), including a highly unusual ceramic head displaying a row of serrated teeth.

Parque Metropolitano La Sabana   PARK
Once the site of San José's main airport, this 72-hectare green space at the west end of Paseo Colón is home to a museum (☑2256-1281; www.musarco.go.cr; east entrance of Parque La Sabana; ⊗9am-4pm Tue-Sun; 🖬), a lagoon and various sporting facilities – most notably Costa Rica's national soccer stadium. During the day, the park's paths make a relaxing place for a stroll, a jog or a picnic.

👉 Tours

★Really Experience Community   TOUR
(Triángulo de la Solidaridad Slum Tour; ☑2297-7058; www.elninoylabolacr.org; per person US$12-25) Nonprofit Boy with a Ball wants to be clear: this is a slum tour. It may seem exploitative, but visiting El Triángulo, a squatter development of 2000 people north of San José, is anything but. Promising young residents lead the tours, introducing guests to neighbors and community entrepreneurs. No cameras are allowed, but the conversations make a lasting impression.

Teatro Nacional   CULTURAL TOUR
(☑2010-1143; www.teatronacional.go.cr/Visitenos/turismo; Av 2 btwn Calles 3 & 5; tours US$10; ⊗9am-5pm) On this fascinating tour, guests are regaled with stories of the art, architecture and people behind Costa Rica's crown jewel, the national theater. The best part is a peek into otherwise off-limits areas, such as the Smoking Room, which feature famous paintings, lavish antique furnishings and ornate gold trim.

ChepeCletas   TOUR
(☑8849-8316, 2222-7548; www.chepecletas.com) This dynamic Tico-run company offers cultural walking tours and free cycling tours of San José (tips accepted), a foodie-oriented exploration of the Mercado Central, a bar-hopping tour focused on traditional downtown *cantinas,* and a guided visit to San José's parks and green spaces. It also offers a nighttime biking tour once a week and group rides every Sunday morning.

COSTA RICA SAN JOSÉ

TALK LIKE A TICO

San José is loaded with schools that offer Spanish lessons (either privately or in groups) and provide long-term visitors to the country with everything from dance lessons to volunteer opportunities. Well-established options include the following.

Amerispan Study Abroad (☑in USA & Canada 800-511-0179, worldwide 215-531-7917; www.amerispan.com; with/without homestay from US$380/225)

Costa Rican Language Academy (☑2280-5834, in USA 866-230-6361; www.crlang.co.cr; Calle Ronda, Barrio Dent)

Institute for Central American Development Studies (ICADS; ☑2225-0508; www.icads.org; Curridabat; month-long courses with/without homestay US$1990/915)

Personalized Spanish (☑2278-3254, in USA 786-245-4124; www.personalizedspanish.com; Tres Ríos)

Already speak Spanish? To truly talk like a Tico, check out the Costa Rica Idioms app, available for iOS and Android. It's quite basic but defines local lingo and uses each term in a sentence. *Tuanis, mae!* (Cool, dude!)

San José

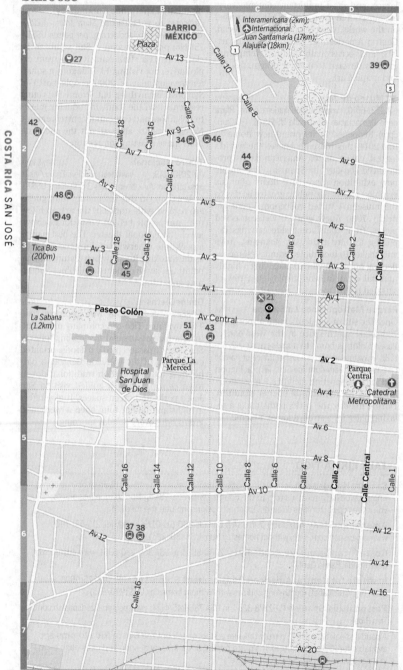

BARRIO MÉXICO

Plaza

Av 13

Calle 10

Interamericana (2km);
Internacional
Juan Santamaría (17km);
Alajuela (18km)

27

39

Av 11

Calle 8

Calle 18

Calle 16

Calle 12

Av 9

Calle 14

Av 7

34   46

42

Av 5

44

Av 9

Av 7

48

Av 5

Calle 6

Calle 4

Calle 2

Calle Central

49

Tica Bus
(200m)

Av 3

Calle 18

Calle 16

Av 3

Av 3

41

45

Av 1

Av 1

La Sabana
(1.2km)

Paseo Colón

21

51   43

4

Av Central

Parque La
Merced

Av 2

Parque
Central

Hospital
San Juan
de Dios

Av 4

Catedral
Metropolitana

Av 6

Calle 16

Calle 14

Calle 12

Calle 10

Calle 8

Calle 6

Calle 4

Calle 2

Av 8

Calle Central

Calle 1

Av 10

Av 12

37 38

Av 12

Calle 16

Av 14

Av 16

Calle 16

Av 20

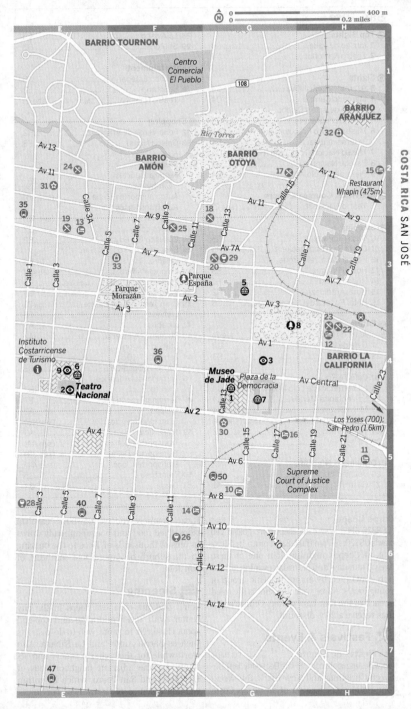

COSTA RICA SAN JOSÉ

San José

◎ Top Sights
1 Museo de Jade G4
2 Teatro Nacional E4

◎ Sights
3 Asamblea Legislativa G4
4 Mercado Central C4
5 Museo de Arte y Diseño
   Contemporáneo G3
6 Museo de Oro Precolombino y
   Numismática E4
7 Museo Nacional de Costa Rica G4
8 Parque Nacional G4
9 Plaza de la Cultura E4

◎ Activities, Courses & Tours
Teatro Nacional .... (see 2)

◎ Sleeping
10 Casa Ridgway G5
11 Costa Rica Backpackers H5
12 Hostel Casa del Parque H4
13 Hostel Pangea E3
14 Hostel Shakti F6
15 Hotel Aranjuez H2
16 Hotel Posada del Museo G5

◎ Eating
Alma de Café .... (see 2)
17 Café de los Deseos G2
18 Café Miel G3
19 Café Rojo E3
20 Café Té Ría G3
21 La Sorbetera de Lolo Mora C4
22 La Ventanita Meraki H4
23 Maza Bistro H4
Restaurante Shakti .... (see 14)
24 Talentum E2
25 Zero Army F3

◎ Drinking & Nightlife
26 Bochinche F6
27 Castro's A1

28 La Avispa E5
29 Stiefel G3

◎ Entertainment
30 El Lobo Estepario G5
31 El Sótano E2
Teatro Nacional .... (see 2)

◎ Shopping
32 Feria Verde de Aranjuez H2
33 Galería Namu F3

◎ Transport
Autotransportes
   Caribeños .... (see 39)
Autotransportes Mepe .... (see 46)
Autotransportes San
   Carlos .... (see 46)
34 Blanco Lobo B2
35 Buses to Heredia E2
36 Buses to Los Yoses & San
   Pedro F4
Empresa Alfaro .... (see 44)
37 Empresarios Unidos B6
38 Expreso Panamá B6
39 Gran Terminal del Caribe D1
40 Lumaca E6
41 Nicabus A3
42 Pulmitan de Liberia A2
43 Station Wagon C4
44 Terminal 7-10 .... C2
45 Terminal Coca-Cola B3
46 Terminal del Atlántico
   Norte B2
47 Terminal Tracopa E7
48 Tralapa A2
Transmonteverde .... (see 46)
49 TransNica A3
Transportes Cobano .... (see 44)
Transportes Deldú .... (see 39)
Transportes Jacó .... (see 44)
50 Transtusa G5
51 Tuasa B4

Carpe Chepe TOUR
(☎8326-6142; www.carpechepe.com; guided pub crawls US$20; ⊙7pm Thu & Sat) For an insider's look at Chepe's nightlife, join one of these lively Thursday- and Saturday-evening guided pub crawls, led by an enthusiastic group of young locals. A free welcome shot is included at each of the four bars visited. Online bookings receive a 20% discount.

✦ Festivals & Events

Las Fiestas de Zapote CULTURAL
(www.fiestaszapote.com; ⊙late Dec–early Jan) Between Christmas and New Year's, this week-long holiday celebration of all things Costa Rican (namely rodeos, cowboys, carnival rides, fried food and booze) annually draws in tens of thousands of Ticos to the bullring in the suburb of Zapote, just southeast of San José.

🛏 Sleeping

You'll find the cheapest sleeps in the city center, with nicer midrange and top-end spots clustered in more well-to-do districts such as Barrio Amón and La Sabana. Also worthwhile for their charm, safety and serenity are the adjacent neighborhoods of Los Yoses and San Pedro, which lie within walking distance of downtown. For tonier options, the upscale suburb of Escazú – a 20-minute bus ride away – is a good choice.

Central San José

★ Hostel Casa del Parque   HOSTEL $
(② 2233-3437; www.hostelcasadelparque.com; Calle 19 btwn Avs 1 & 3; dm US$14, d with/without bathroom US$49/39; ☎) A vintage art-deco manse from 1936 houses this cozy and welcoming spot on the northeastern edge of Parque Nacional. Five large, basic private rooms (two with private bathroom), a new five-bed dormitory and an older 10-bed dormitory upstairs have parquet floors and simple furnishings. Take some sun on the plant-festooned outdoor patio and take advantage of the shared kitchen.

★ Hostel Pangea   HOSTEL $
(② 2221-1992; www.hostelpangea.com; Av 7 btwn Calles 3 & 3A, Barrio Amón; dm US$14, d with/without bathroom US$55/35, ste from US$70; ℗ @ ☎ ⊠) This industrial-strength hostel – 25 dorm beds and 25 private rooms – has been a popular 20-something backpacker hangout for years. It's not difficult to see why: it's smack in the middle of the city and comes stocked with a pool and a rooftop restaurant-lounge with stellar views. Needless to say, it's a party spot.

Costa Rica Backpackers   HOSTEL $
(② 2223-2406, 2221-6191; www.costaricabackpackers.com; Av 6 near Calle 21; dm US$12-16, d without bathroom US$35; ℗ @ ☎ ⊠) This popular hostel has 17 basic but clean dormitories and 14 doubles with shared bathrooms surrounding a spacious hammock-filled garden and a free-form pool. Two bars, a restaurant and ambient chill-out music enhance the inviting, laid-back atmosphere. Other benefits include a communal kitchen and TV lounge, free luggage storage, internet access, an onsite travel agency and low-cost airport transfers ($26).

Hostel Shakti   HOSTEL $
(www.hostelshakti.com; cnr Av 8 & Calle 13; dm/s/d/tr US$18/30/40/60; ℗ ✳ @ ☎) This lovely little guesthouse uses bold colors and natural materials to create an oasis of calm and comfort amid the chaos of San José. Three dorms and four private rooms are dressed up with eclectic furnishings and colorful bedding. There is a fully equipped kitchen, but you might not need it, as the onsite restaurant is healthy, fresh and amazing.

Casa Ridgway   GUESTHOUSE $
(② 2222-1400, 2233-6168; www.casaridgwayhostel.com; cnr Calle 15 & Av 6A; incl breakfast dm US$17, s/d without bathroom US$24/38; ℗ ⊖ ☎) This small, peaceful guesthouse on a quiet side street is run by the adjacent Friends' Peace Center, a Quaker organization promoting social justice and human rights. There is a small lounge, a communal kitchen and a lending library filled with books about Central American politics and society. No smoking or alcohol is allowed, with quiet hours from 10pm to 6am.

★ Hotel Aranjuez   HOTEL $$
(② 2256-1825; www.hotelaranjuez.com; Calle 19 btwn Avs 11 & 13; incl breakfast s US$28-55, d US$48-65, s/d without bathroom US$22/38; ℗ @ ☎) This hotel in Barrio Aranjuez consists of five nicely maintained vintage homes that have been strung together with a labyrinth of gardens and connecting walkways. The 36 spotless rooms come in various configurations, all with lockbox and cable TV. The hotel's best attribute, however, is the lush garden patio, where a legendary breakfast buffet is served every morning.

Luz de Luna   BOUTIQUE HOTEL $$
(② 2225-4919; www.luzdelunahotelboutique.com; Calle 33 btwn Avs 3 & 5; r US$50-80; ☎) A converted old mansion, this new boutique hotel, restaurant and cafe is in a prime location: the heart of Barrio Escalante's Paseo Gastronómico La Luz district and its up-and-coming restaurants. Foodies who like to relax will appreciate this sanctuary and self-described 'lunar complex' for its lush gardens, hardwood floors and occasional pre-Columbian statue.

Hotel Posada del Museo   GUESTHOUSE $$
(② 2258-1027; www.hotelposadadelmuseo.com; cnr Calle 17 & Av 2; s US$50-80, d US$70-90; @ ☎) Managed by an amiable, multilingual couple, this architecturally intriguing, 1928-vintage inn is diagonally across from the Museo Nacional. French doors line the entrances to each of the rooms, no two of which are alike. Some rooms accommodate up to four people, making this a family-friendly option. Light sleepers, take note: the hotel is adjacent to the train tracks.

La Sabana & Around

Gaudy's   HOSTEL $
(② 2248-0086; www.backpacker.co.cr; Av 5 btwn Calles 36 & 38; dm US$13, r with/without bathroom

US$39/32; (P@🛜) Popular among shoestring travelers for years, this homey hostel inside a sprawling modernist house northeast of Parque La Sabana has 13 private rooms and two dormitories. The owners keep the design scheme minimalist and the vibe mellow, with professional service and well-maintained rooms. There's a communal kitchen, a TV lounge, a pool table and a courtyard strung with hammocks.

Mi Casa Hostel
HOSTEL $

(☑ 2231-4700; www.micasahostel.com; incl breakfast dm US$15, r with/without bathroom from US$38/27; P@🛜) This converted modernist home in La Sabana has polished-wood floors, vintage furnishings and 14 eclectic guest rooms to choose from, including one 10-person dorm and another room that's wheelchair-accessible. Mellow communal areas are comfortably furnished, and the shared kitchen is clean and roomy. There is a pleasant garden, a pool table, free internet, and laundry service.

Rosa del Paseo
HOTEL $$

(☑ 2257-3225; www.rosadelpaseo.com; Paseo Colón btwn Calles 28 & 30; s/d/ste from US$75/85/90; P@🛜) 🍴 Don't let the Paseo Colón location and the small facade fool you: this sprawling Victorian-Caribbean mansion (built in 1910 by the Montealegre family of coffee exporters) has 18 rooms reaching way back into an interior courtyard far from the city noise. The hotel still maintains the original tile floors and other historic details, including antique oil paintings and sculptures.

Colours Oasis Resort
HOTEL $$

(☑ 2296-1880, in USA & Canada 866-517-4390; www.coloursoasis.com; cnr Triángulo de Pavas & Blvr Rohrmoser; r US$55-200; 🛜🏊) This longtime LGBT-friendly hotel occupies a sprawling Spanish colonial–style complex in the elegant Rohrmoser district (northwest of La Sabana). Rooms and mini-apartments have modern furnishings and impeccable bathrooms. Facilities include TV lounge, mini-gym, pool, sundeck and Jacuzzi, as well as a new international restaurant, ideal for evening cocktails.

Los Yoses & San Pedro

Locals use several prominent landmarks when giving directions, including Spoon restaurant, the Fuente de la Hispanidad fountain and Más x Menos supermarket.

★ Hostel Bekuo
HOSTEL $

(☑ 2234-1091, in USA 1-813-750-8572; www.hostel bekuo.com; dm US$11-13, d from US$30; 🛜) For pure positive energy, you won't find a nicer hostel anywhere in San José. This restful spot, in a hip area of Los Yoses just a block south of Av Central, feels extremely homey, thanks to frequent backyard BBQs, spontaneous pitchers of free sangria, a living room with piano and guitar, and a kitchen equipped with good knives, appliances and an inviting central work space.

Hostel Urbano
HOSTEL $

(☑ 2281-0707; www.hostelurbano.com; dm US$12-14, d with/without bathroom US$38/32) Within easy walking distance of the university and its associated nightlife, yet right on the bus line into downtown San José, this immaculate new hostel is in a 1950s home, opposite Parque Kennedy in San Pedro. Guests feel instantly welcome, with its open floor plan, spacious backyard, pool table, modern internet facilities and kitchen-dining area that's nice enough to host a dinner party.

Hostel Casa Yoses
HOSTEL $

(☑ 2234-5486; www.casayoses.com; Av 8, Los Yoses; incl breakfast dm US$11-15, d US$42; P@🛜) A mellow spot, this Spanish Revival–style house from 1949 is perched on a hill that offers lovely views of the valley from the front garden. Here you'll find 10 rooms (four of them dorms) of varying decor and style, all of which are spotless, with wood floors and tiled hallways.

Hostel Backpackers San José
HOSTEL $

(☑ 2234-8186; Av Central btwn Calles 29 & 33, Los Yoses; dm/r without bathroom US$14/40, s/d/tr/q with bathroom US$40/55/69/80; P@🛜🏊) This graceful neoclassical home once belonged to José Figueres, the Costa Rican president who abolished the army and granted women the right to vote. While the hostel contains five dormitories, it feels much more like an inn, with seven large private rooms with modern bathrooms, sofas, wi-fi and flat-screen TVs. The owners recently opened a bar facing the street.

Hotel Ave del Paraíso
HOTEL $$

(☑ 2225-8515, 2283-6017; hotelavedelparaiso.com; s/d incl breakfast US$68/79; @🛜) 🍴 Decorated with beautiful mosaic tiles, this hotel run by an artsy family is set back from the busy street just far enough to permit a good night's sleep. There's a bubbling outdoor Jacuzzi tub on the property and a wonderful restaurant and bar, Café Kracovia (p528), owned by the same family. The university is just a two-minute walk north.

Hotel Milvia   B&B $$
(☑ 2225-4543; www.hotelmilvia.com; s/d/tr incl breakfast US$67/78/85; @🛜) Owned by a well-known Costa Rican artist and former museum director, this lovely Caribbean-style building offers a homey retreat from the city. Nine eclectic rooms, all dotted with bright artwork, surround a pleasant courtyard with trickling fountain. An upstairs terrace provides views of the mountains. It's in San Pedro 100m north of Más x Menos.

🍴 Eating

🍴 Central San José

The city's hectic commercial heart has some of the cheapest eats in town. One of the best places for a budget-priced lunch is the **Mercado Central** (Avs Central & 1 btwn Calles 6 & 8; ☺ 6am-6pm Mon-Sat), where you'll find a variety of *sodas* serving *casados,* tamales, seafood and everything in between.

★Café de los Deseos   CAFE $
(☑ 2222-0496;   www.facebook.com/Cafedelos deseos; Calle 15 btwn Avs 9 & 11; mains US$5-12; ☺ 2-10pm Tue-Sat; 🛜) Abuzz with artsy young bohemians, this cozy, colorful Barrio Otoya cafe makes a romantic spot for drinks (from wine to cocktails to smoothies), *bocas* (handmade tortillas with Turrialba cheese, salads, teriyaki chicken, individual pizzas), and tempting desserts. Walls are hung with the work of local artists and rooms are adorned with hand-painted tables, beaded curtains and branches entwined with fairy lights.

La Sorbetera de Lolo Mora   DESSERTS $
(☑ 2256-5000; Mercado Central; desserts US$2-5; ☺ 9:30am-5:45pm Mon-Sat) Head to the main market for dessert at this century-old local favorite that serves up fresh sorbet and cinnamon-laced frozen custard. Do as the locals do and order *barquillos* (cylindrical sugar cookies that are perfect for dipping).

La Ventanita Meraki   FAST FOOD $
(☑ 4034-2655;   www.facebook.com/laventanita meraki; Av 3 & Calle 21, in front of the train station; mains US$5-8; ☺ noon-9pm Tue-Thu, to 2am Fri, 6pm-2am Sat) Ventanita means 'little window' in Spanish and Meraki means 'artistry' in Greek. Put them together and it's an accurate moniker for this new fusion hole-in-the-

wall, a to-go window in front of downtown's train station that serves innovative street food. Expect elaborate spins on typical fare, along with sandwiches like pumpkin butter cheese madness, and Twinkie *frito* (fried Twinkie) for dessert.

Café Té Ría   CAFE $
(☑ 2222-8272;   www.facebook.com/CafeTeRiaen Amon; cnr Av 7 & Calle 13; mains US$6, cakes US$1.50-3; ☺ 10:30am-7:30pm Mon-Fri, noon-7:30 Sat; 🛜☑🍽) This petite, pet-friendly cafe in Barrio Amón is adorned with local art and replete with homey goodness. It's a perfect place to work over a few cups of morning coffee, then stay for lunch. Specials often include a mouthwatering baked trout with capers and a fresh salad. Sandwiches and pastries are also a big hit, and vegetarians are well-served.

Alma de Café   CAFE $
(☑ 2010-1119; www.almadecafe.net; Teatro Nacional; mains US$6-11; ☺ 9am-7pm Mon-Sat, to 6pm Sun) One of the most beautiful cafes in the city, this atmospheric spot evokes early-20th-century Vienna. In other words, a perfect place to sip cappuccino, enjoy a crepe or quiche and take in the lovely ceiling frescoes and rotating art exhibitions. The elaborate coffee cocktails are an excellent midday indulgence.

Talentum   CAFE $
(☑ 2256-6346;   www.galeriatalentum.com; Av 11 btwn Calles 3 & 3A; lunch specials US$8-10; ☺ 11am-7pm Mon & Tue, to 8pm Wed-Fri) This vibrant, quirky cultural space in a renovated mansion runs the gamut from cafe to art gallery. Sporting local artwork inside and out, with cozy seating on vintage couches and an outdoor deck, it's a fun place for a midday break. The ever-changing cultural agenda includes book signings, films, anatomical drawing classes and occasional live music.

Café Miel   CAFE $
(www.facebook.com/cafemielcostarica; Av 9 btwn Calle 11 & 13; coffee US$1-5, pastries US$2; ☺ 9am-6pm Mon-Fri, 2-6pm Sat) This tiny cafe opened to such wild success in 2014 that the owners opened another one right down the street. What's their secret? In addition to adorable and homey interiors, the artisanal products from the cafes' chefs and bakers. The mushroom *empanadas* are divine, as is the locally sourced coffee.

Zero Army
CAFE $

(☑ 2248-2401; www.facebook.com/zeroarmycr; Calle 9 & Av 9; smoothies US$3-4; ⊗ 6:30am-5:15pm Mon-Fri, 9am-2pm Sat) Named for Costa Rica's nonexistent army, this new smoothie and juice bar in the center of Barrio Amón serves fresh fruit drinks in reusable glass bottles. The smoothies are all-natural, highly refreshing and named for Costa Rican destinations. Breakfast wraps are highly recommended.

Café Rojo
CAFE $

(☑ 2221-2425; cnr Av 7 & Calle 3; mains US$7-10, coffee US$1.50-4; ⊗ noon-7pm Mon-Thu, to 8pm Fri & Sat, 10am-7pm Sun; ☑) This quaint new cafe with a towering cactus out front uses the fresh produce of Costa Rica to create innovative lunch specials, such as green plantain balls and pickled beets with chayote puree. Vegans will find plenty to like here, as will coffee enthusiasts. All the flavorings and syrups for drinks are homemade, and the iced ginger coffee is divine.

Maza Bistro
BISTRO $

(☑ 7293-9082; www.facebook.com/Mazacostarica; Calle 19, on Parque Nacional; mains US$8; ⊗ 10am-7pm Mon-Fri; ☑) The furniture here is disorganized, making it tough to get in the door. But maybe the owners are focused on food? Each day, the menu is written on scrolls, often including whatever is organic, fresh and local. Think bowls of veggies and cured trout, homemade honey wine and *tortas* of kale. Terrariums and minirecords as coasters lend some charm.

Restaurante Shakti
VEGETARIAN $

(☑ 2222-4475; cnr Av 8 & Calle 13; mains US$5-10; ⊗ 7:30am-7pm Mon-Fri, 8am-6pm Sat; ☑) This informal neighborhood health-food outpost has simple, organic-focused cooking and freshly baked goods. Favorites include veggie burgers, along with various fish and chicken dishes, but most people come for the vegetarian *plato del día* – only US$6 for soup, salad, main course and fruit drink (or US$8 with coffee and dessert thrown in)!

La Sabana & Around

Supermarkets include **Más X Menos** (☑ 2248-0968; www.masxmenos.co.cr; cnr Autopista General Cañas & Av 5; ⊗ 7am-midnight Mon-Sat, to 10pm Sun; P) and **Palí** (☑ 2256-5887; www.pali.co.cr; Paseo Colón btwn Calles 24 & 26; ⊗ 8am-7pm Mon-Thu, to 8pm Fri & Sat, to 5pm Sun; P).

Soda Tapia
SODA $

(☑ 2222-6734; www.sodatapia.com; cnr Av 2 & Calle 42; mains US$4-10, desserts US$2-7; ⊗ 6am-2am Sun-Thu, 24hr Fri & Sat; P) An unpretentious '50s-style diner with garish red-and-white decor, this place is perpetually filled with couples and families noshing on grilled sandwiches and generous *casados*. If you have the nerve, try the monstrous 'El Gordo,' a pile of steak, onions, cheese, lettuce and tomato served on Spanish bread. Save room for dessert: ice-cream and fruit sundaes are a specialty here.

Las Mañanitas
MEXICAN $$

(☑ 2248-1593; Calle 40 btwn Paseo Colón & Av 3; mains US$6-17; ⊗ 11:30am-10pm Mon-Sat) At this authentic Mexican place near the park, well-rendered specialties include tacos in sets of four – corn tortillas accompanied by chicken, steak, sea bass or *carne al pastor* (spiced pork). Fans of *mole poblano* (central Mexico's famous chili and chocolate sauce) will also want to try it here, as the restaurant's owner hails from Puebla.

Los Yoses & San Pedro

Café Kracovia
CAFE $

(☑ 2253-9093; www.cafekracovia.com; snacks US$4-10, mains US$8-14; ⊗ 10:30am-9pm Mon, to 11pm Tue-Sat; ☎) With several distinct spaces, from a low-lit, intimate downstairs to an outdoor garden courtyard, this hip cafe has something for everyone. Contemporary artwork and a distinct university vibe create an appealing ambiance for lunching on crepes, wraps, salads, daily specials and craft beer. It's 500m north of the Fuente de la Hispanidad traffic circle, where San Pedro and Los Yoses converge.

Él Porton Rojo
PIZZA $$

(☑ 2224-4872; www.facebook.com/PizzaElPorton Rojo; Av 10 & Calle 43; pizzas small US$8-10, large US$16-18; ⊗ noon-3pm & 6-11:30pm Mon-Sat) Serving up some of the best pizza and sangria in the Los Yoses area, this hip restaurant doubles as a gallery. Funky local art sells right off the walls, and a steady influx of customers from Hostel Bekuo (p526) keeps things lively.

Mantras
VEGETARIAN $$

(☑ 2253-6715; www.facebook.com/mantrasveggie cafe; Calle 35 btwn Avs 11 & 13; mains US$8-10; ⊗ 8:30am-5pm; ☑) Widely recognized as the best vegetarian restaurant in San José (if not all of Costa Rica), Mantras draws rave reviews from across the foodie spectrum for meatless main dishes, salads and desserts so delicious that it's easy to forget you're eating healthily. It's in Barrio Escalante, and for Sunday brunch, the line often stretches out the door.

🍷 Drinking & Nightlife

Chepe's artsiest, most sophisticated drinking venues are concentrated north and east of the center, in places like Barrio Amón and Barrio Escalante. For a rowdier, younger scene, head to Barrio la California, the UCR university district, or Calle la Amargura.

★**Stiefel** PUB
(www.facebook.com/StiefelPub; ⊘6pm-2am Mon-Sat) Two-dozen-plus Costa Rican microbrews on tap and an appealing setting in a historic building create a convivial buzz at this pub half a block from Plaza España. Grab a pint of Pelona or Maldita Vida, Malinche or Chichemel; better yet, order a flight of four miniature sampler glasses and try 'em all!

Hoxton Pub PUB
(☑7168-1083; www.facebook.com/hoxtonstag; ⊘9pm-4am Tue-Sat) Good cocktails, great music and a lively dance floor in a cool old Los Yoses mansion just east of Subaru. The place often holds theme nights and brings in good DJs on the weekend. Tuesday's ladies night is the biggest party in town, with ladies paying no cover and drinking free until midnight. Hundreds show up to rage til dawn.

Wilk BREWERY
(www.facebook.com/wilkcraftbeer; Calle 33 & Av 9; ⊘4pm-1am Tue-Sat) This new pub in Barrio Escalante attracts a mixed crowd of Ticos and gringos who share an appreciation for craft brews and seriously delicious burgers (veggie included). The wide selection of craft beer includes all of the inventive concoctions of **Costa Rica Craft Brewing** (☑2249-0919; www.facebook.com/craftbeercostarica; Ciudad Colón; ⊘9am-5pm Mon, to 11pm Tue & Wed, to midnight Thu, noon-5pm Fri, 1pm-midnight Sat, noon-6pm Sun), which is a partner in the pub.

Castro's CLUB
(☑2256-8789; cnr Av 13 & Calle 22; ⊘6pm-3am Sun-Thu, 5pm-4:30am Fri & Sat) Chepe's oldest dance club, this classic Latin American disco in Barrio México draws crowds of locals and tourists to its large dance floor with a dependable mix of salsa, cumbia and merengue.

☆ Entertainment

Pick up *La Nación* on Thursday for listings (in Spanish) of the coming week's attractions. The *Tico Times* 'Weekend' section (in English) has a calendar of theater, music and museum events. The free publication GAM Cultural (www.gamcultural.com) and the website San José Volando (www.sanjosevolando.com) are also helpful guides to nightlife and cultural events.

★**Teatro Nacional** THEATER
(☑2010-1111; www.teatronacional.go.cr; Calles 3 & 5 btwn Avs Central & 2) Costa Rica's most important theater stages plays, dance, opera, symphony, Latin American music and other major events. The main season runs from March to November, but there are performances throughout the year.

LGBT SAN JOSÉ

The city is home to Central America's most thriving gay and lesbian scene. As with other spots, admission charges vary depending on the night and location (from US$5 to US$10). Some clubs close on various nights of the week (usually Sunday to Tuesday) and others host women- or men-only nights; inquire ahead or check individual club websites for listings.

Many clubs are on the south side of town, which can get rough after dark. Take a taxi.

La Avispa (☑2223-5343; www.laavispa.com; Calle 1 btwn Avs 8 & 10; ⊘8pm-6am Thu-Sat, 5pm-6am Sun) A lesbian disco bar that has been in operation for more than three decades, La Avispa (the Wasp) has a bar, pool tables and a boisterous dance floor that's highly recommended by travelers.

Bochinche (☑2221-0500; cnr Calle 11 & Av 10; ⊘8pm-5am Wed-Sat) A club that features everything from classic disco to electronica, as well as special themed nights. As this club is on the south side of town, it can get rough after dark.

El Lobo Estepario

LIVE MUSIC

(📞2256-3934; www.facebook.com/loboesteparioocr; Av 2, cnr opposite La Caja de ANDE; ⏱4pm-12:45am Sun-Thu, to 2am Fri & Sat, closed Mon) This artsy dive attracts some of the top local talent for live-music gigs.

El Sótano

LIVE MUSIC

(📞2221-2302; www.facebook.com/sotanocr; cnr Calle 3 & Av 11; ⏱7pm-2:30am Mon, noon-2:30am Tue-Sat, 2-6pm Sun) One of Chepe's most atmospheric nightspots, Sótano is named for its cellar jazz club, where people crowd in for frequent performances including intimate Tuesday jam sessions. Upstairs, a cluster of elegant high-ceilinged rooms in the same mansion have been converted to a gallery space, stage, and dance floor where an eclectic mix of groups play live gigs.

🛍 Shopping

⭐**Feria Verde de Aranjuez**

MARKET

(www.feriaverde.org; ⏱7am-noon Sat) For a foodie-friendly cultural experience, don't miss this fabulous Saturday farmers market, a weekly meeting place for San José's artists and organic growers since 2010. You'll find organic coffee, artisanal chocolate, tropical-fruit Popsicles, fresh produce, baked goods, leather, jewelry and more at the long rows of booths set up in the park at the north end of Barrio Aranjuez.

Galería Namu

HANDICRAFTS

(📞2256-3412, in USA 800-616-4322; www.galeria namu.com; Av 7 btwn Calles 5 & 7; ⏱9am-6:30pm Mon-Sat year-round, plus 1-4pm Sun Dec-Apr) This fair-trade gallery brings together artwork and cultural objects from a diverse population of regional ethnicities, including Boruca masks, finely woven Wounaan baskets, Guaymí dolls, Bribrí canoes, Chorotega ceramics, traditional Huetar reed mats, and contemporary urban and Afro-Caribbean crafts. It can also help arrange visits to remote indigenous territories in different parts of Costa Rica.

Kiosco SJO

HANDICRAFTS

(📞2253-8426; www.kioscosjo.com; cnr Calle 31 & Av 5; ⏱noon-10pm Tue-Fri, 9am-10pm Sat, 9am-4pm Sun) With a focus on sustainable design by Latin American artisans, this sleek shop in Barrio Escalante stocks handmade jewelry, hand-tooled leather boots and bags, original photography, artisanal chocolates, fashion and contemporary home decor by established regional designers. It's pricey, but rest assured that everything you find here will be of exceptional quality.

ℹ Orientation

San José's center is arranged in a grid with *avenidas* (avenues) running east to west and *calles* (streets) running north to south. Av Central is the nucleus of the downtown area and is a pedestrian mall between Calles 6 and 9.

Slightly further west of downtown is La Sabana, named for its huge and popular park where many *josefinos* spend their weekends jogging, swimming, picnicking or attending soccer matches.

East (and within walking distance) of the center are the contiguous neighborhoods of Los Yoses and San Pedro, the former a low-key residential area with some nice accommodations, the latter home to the tree-lined campus of the UCR, the country's most prestigious university.

You can pick up a free map of the city at the tourist office.

ℹ Information

DANGERS & ANNOYANCES

Though Costa Rica has the lowest crime rate of any Central American country, crime in urban centers such as San José is a problem. The most common offense is opportunistic theft (eg pickpocketing and mugging). Keep a streetwise attitude.

Neighborhoods covered by Lonely Planet are generally safe during the day, though you should be especially careful around the Coca-Cola bus terminal and the red-light district south of Parque Central, particularly at night. Be advised that adjacent neighborhoods can vary greatly in terms of safety; inquire locally before setting out.

EMERGENCY

Fire (📞118)

Red Cross (📞128)

Traffic Police (📞2222-9245, 📞2222-9330)

MEDICAL SERVICES

Clínica Bíblica (📞2522-1000; www.clinica biblica.com; Av 14 btwn Calles Central & 1; ⏱24hr) The top private clinic in the downtown area. Doctors speak English, French and German, and an emergency room is open 24 hours.

Hospital CIMA (📞2208-1000; www.hospital cima.com; Los Laureles) The hospital is 500m west of the Próspero Fernández tollbooth in the area of Guachipelín, on the west side of Escazú. Affiliated with Baylor University Medical Center in the USA, it is one of the most modern hospitals in the greater San José metropolitan area.

POST

Correo Central (Central Post Office; ☎ 2223-9766; www.correos.go.cr; Calle 2 btwn Avs 1 & 3; ⊗ 6:30am-6pm Mon-Fri, to noon Sat) In a gorgeous historic building near the center of town. Express and overnight services.

TOURIST INFORMATION

Instituto Costarricense de Turismo (ICT; ☎ 2222-1090, in USA & Canada 866-267-8274; www.visitcostarica.com; Edificio de las Academias, Av Central btwn Calles 1 & 3; ⊗ 8am-5pm Mon-Fri) The government tourism office provides handy intercity bus schedules and free maps of San José and Costa Rica.

ⓘ Getting There & Away

AIR

All international flights leave from Juan Santamaría (SJO) airport outside Alajuela.

Aeropuerto Internacional Juan Santamaría (☎ 2437-2400; fly2sanjose.com) Handles all international flights and **NatureAir** (☎ 2299-6000, in USA 1-800-235-9272; www.natureair.com) domestic flights in its main terminal. Domestic flights on **Sansa** (☎ 2290-4100; www.flysansa.com) depart from the Sansa terminal.

Aeropuerto Tobías Bolaños (☎ 2232-2820; Pavas) In the San José suburb of Pavas; services private charter and a few national flights.

BUS

Bus transportation in San José can be bewildering. There is no public bus system and no central terminal. Instead, dozens of private companies operate out of stops scattered throughout the city. Many bus companies have no more than a stop (in this case pay the driver directly); some have a tiny office with a window on the street; others operate from bigger terminals servicing entire regions.

Gran Terminal del Caribe (Calle Central) A roomy station north of Av 13; serves destinations on the Caribbean slope, with connections to Tortuguero.

Terminal 7-10 (☎ 2519-9740; www.terminal 7-10.com; 7th Av & Calle 10) A brand new bus terminal serving Nicoya, Nosara, Sámara, Santa Cruz, Tamarindo, Jacó, Cóbano and a few other places.

Terminal Coca-Cola (Av 1 btwn Calles 16 & 18) A well-known, labyrinthine landmark; buses leave from the terminal and the four-block radius around it to points all over Costa Rica, including the Central Valley and the Pacific coast.

Terminal del Atlántico Norte (cnr Av 9 & Calle 12) A small, rather decrepit terminal serving Monteverde, La Fortuna and southern Caribbean coastal destinations.

Terminal Tracopa (☎ 2221-4214; www.tracopacr.com; Calle 5 btwn Avs 18 & 20) On the south end of town; serves southern and southwestern destinations including Golfito, Quepos/Manuel Antonio, and Paso Canoas on the Panama border.

Domestic Bus Companies

Autotransportes Caribeños (☎ 2222-0610; www.grupocaribenos.com; Gran Terminal del Caribe, Calle Central) Northeastern destinations including Puerto Limón, Guápiles, Cariari, Siquirres and Puerto Viejo de Sarapiquí.

Autotransportes Mepe (☎ 2257-8129, 2758-1572; www.mepecr.com; Terminal del Atlántico Norte) Southern Caribbean destinations including Cahuita, Puerto Viejo de Talamanca, Manzanillo, Bribrí and Sixaola.

Autotransportes San Carlos (☎ 2255-4300; Terminal del Atlántico Norte) La Fortuna, Ciudad Quesada and Los Chiles.

Blanco Lobo (☎ 2257-4121; Calle 12 btwn Avs 7 & 9) Puerto Jiménez.

Empresa Alfaro (☎ 2222-2666; www.empresaalfaro.com; Terminal 7-10) Nicoya, Nosara, Sámara, Santa Cruz and Tamarindo.

Empresarios Unidos (☎ 2222-8231; cnr Av 12 & Calle 16) San Ramón and Puntarenas.

Lumaca (☎ 2552-5280, 2537-2320; Av 10 btwn Calles 5 & 7) Cartago.

Pulmitan de Liberia (☎ 2222-0610; Calle 24 btwn Avs 5 & 7) Northwestern destinations including Cañas, Liberia, Playa del Coco and Tilarán.

Station Wagon (☎ 2441-1181; Av 2 btwn Calles 10 & 12) Alajuela and the airport.

Tracopa (☎ 2221-4214; www.tracopacr.com) Southwestern destinations including Ciudad Neily, Dominical, Golfito, Manuel Antonio, Palmar Norte, Paso Canoas, Quepos, San Isidro del General, San Vito and Uvita.

Tralapa (☎ 2248-1925; Av 5 btwn Calles 20 & 22) Several Península de Nicoya destinations, including Playa Flamingo, Playa Hermosa, Playa Tamarindo and Santa Cruz.

Transmonteverde (☎ 2645-7447; www.facebook.com/Transmonteverde; Terminal del Atlántico Norte, cnr Av 9 & Calle 12) Monteverde.

Transportes Cobano (☎ 2221-7479; transportescobano@gmail.com; Terminal 7-10) Montezuma and Mal País.

Transportes Deldú (Gran Terminal de Caribe) Peñas Blancas (Nicaraguan border).

Transportes Jacó (☎ 2290-2922, 2290-7920; www.transportesjacoruta655.com; Terminal 7-10) Jacó.

Transtusa (☎ 2222-4464; www.transtusacr.com; Calle 13A btwn Avs 6 & 8) Cartago and Turrialba.

Tuasa (☎ 2442-6900; Av 2 btwn Calles 12 & 14) Alajuela and the airport.

International Bus Companies

International buses get booked up fast. Buy your tickets in advance – and take your passport.

Expreso Panamá (☏ 2221-7694; www.expresopanama.com; Terminal Empresarios Unidos, cnr Av 12 & Calle 16) Panama City.

Nicabus (☏ 2221-2581; cnr Av 1 & Calle 20) Managua.

Tica Bus (☏ 2296-9788; www.ticabus.com; cnr Transversal 26 & Av 3) Nicaragua, Panama, El Salvador and Guatemala.

TransNica (☏ 2223-4242; www.transnica.com; Calle 22 btwn Avs 3 & 5) Nicaragua and Honduras.

Shuttle Bus Companies

Grayline (☏ 2220-2126; www.graylinecostarica.com) and **Interbus** (☏ 4100-0888; www.

DOMESTIC BUSES FROM SAN JOSÉ

DESTINATION	COMPANY	COST (US$)	DURATION (HR)	FREQUENCY
Cahuita	Mepe	8.95	4	6am, 10am, noon, 2pm, 4pm
Cartago	Lumaca	1.08	1	every 15min
Dominical & Uvita	Tracopa	10.86	4½-5½	6am, 6:30am, 3pm
Golfito	Tracopa	13.85	7	6:30am, 7am, 3:30pm
Jacó	Transportes Jacó	4.45	2½	every 2hr 7am-7pm
La Fortuna	San Carlos	4.70	4	6:15am, 8:40am, 11:30am
Liberia	Pulmitan	7.30	4½	hourly
Los Chiles	San Carlos	4.50	5	5:30am, 3pm
Monteverde/Santa Elena	Transmonteverde	5.23	4½	6:30am, 2:30pm
Montezuma/Mal País	Cobano	15.10	5½-6	6am, 2pm
Nicoya	Alfaro	7.13	5	7:30am, 10am, 1pm, 3pm, 5pm
Palmar Norte	Tracopa	10.86	4½	5am, 7am, 10am, 1pm, 6:30pm
Paso Canoas	Tracopa	15.40	6½	5am, 11am, 1pm, 6:30pm
Peñas Blancas	Deldú	8.62	6	9 daily
Playa Flamingo	Tralapa	11.34	6	8am, 10:30am, 3pm
Playa Sámara	Alfaro	8.26	5	noon
Playa Tamarindo	Alfaro	10.50	5	11:30am, 3:30pm
Playa Tamarindo	Tralapa	12	5	11:30am, 3:30pm
Puerto Jiménez	Blanco Lobo	13	8	8am, noon
Puerto Limón	Caribeños	5.95	3	hourly
Puerto Viejo de Sarapiquí	Caribeños	4.71	2½	13 daily
Puerto Viejo de Talamanca	Mepe	10.60	4½	6am, 10am, noon, 2pm, 4pm
Puntarenas	Empresarios Unidos	5.10	2½	hourly
Quepos/Manuel Antonio	Tracopa	7.60	3½	every 1-2hr
San Isidro de El General	Tracopa	12.70	7	6am, 8:15am, noon, 2:15pm, 4pm
Sixaola	Mepe	13	5½	6am, 10am, 2pm, 4pm
Tilarán	Pulmitan	7.48	4	7:30am, 9:30am, 12:45pm, 3:45pm, 6:30pm
Turrialba	Transtusa	2.75	2	hourly

interbusonline.com) shuttle passengers in air-conditioned minivans from San José to a long list of popular destinations around Costa Rica. They are more expensive than the standard bus services, but they offer door-to-door service and can get you there faster.

❶ Getting Around

TO/FROM THE AIRPORT

In normal traffic, an official taxi from the airport to downtown San José should cost around US$30, as measured on the meter. You can reserve a pick-up with **Taxi Aeropuerto** (☏ 2221-6865). Plan on spending extra for wait time during periods of heavy traffic.

Interbus (p532) runs shuttles in both directions between the airport and San José hotels (US$15 per adult, US$7 per child under 12 years) – good value if you're traveling alone.

Even cheaper are the public buses (US$1.10) operated by Tuasa (p531) and Station Wagon (p531), which pick up passengers at a stop on the main road in front of the airport. Make sure to verify the destination before boarding, as some buses from this stop go to Alajuela, others to San José. On the return trip, board at the Tuasa or Station Wagon terminal in downtown San José (both opposite Iglesia de La Merced near the corner of Av 2 and Calle 12) and be sure to tell the driver that you are getting off at the airport *(Voy al aeropuerto, por favor)*. Most hotels can also arrange for private airport pick-up at reasonable rates.

BUS

Local buses are useful to get you into the suburbs and surrounding villages, or to the airport. Most buses run between 5am and 10pm and cost between US$0.40 and US$1.10.

La Sabana To catch a bus heading west from San José toward La Sabana (US$0.40), head for the convenient downtown stop at the southeast corner of Av 3 and Calle 3.

Los Yoses & San Pedro Catch eastbound buses to Los Yoses and San Pedro (US$0.50) from the northeast corner of Calle Central and Av 9.

Heredia Regular buses (Calle 1 btwn Avs 7 & 9) leave from Calle and Av 7.

TAXI

Marías (meters) are generally used, though a few drivers will tell you they're broken and try to charge you more – especially if you don't speak Spanish. Not using a meter is illegal. The rate for the first kilometer should automatically appear when the meter starts up (at the time of research, the correct starting amount was 610 colones). Make sure the *maría* is operating when you get in, or negotiate the fare up front. Short rides downtown cost US$2 to US$4. There's a 20% surcharge after 10pm that may not appear on the *maría*.

CENTRAL VALLEY & HIGHLANDS

It is on the coffee-cultivated hillsides of the Central Valley that you'll find Costa Rica's heart and soul. This is not only the geographical center of the country, but also its cultural and spiritual core. It is here that the Spanish first settled, here that coffee built a prosperous nation, here that picturesque highland villages still gather for centuries-old fiestas. It is also here that you'll get to fully appreciate Costa Rica's country cooking: artisanal cheeses, steamy corn cakes and freshly caught river trout.

Curvy mountain roads force travelers to slow their roll. Quaint and quirky agricultural towns invite leisurely detours to farmers markets and church processions, a refreshing break from the tourist-industrial complex on the coasts. But it's not all cows

INTERNATIONAL BUSES FROM SAN JOSÉ

DESTINATION	BUS COMPANY	COST (US$)	DURATION (HR)	FREQUENCY
David (Panama)	Tracopa	21	8	7:30am, noon
Guatemala City	Tica Bus	105	48	3am
Panama City	Expreso Panamá	40	14	noon
Panama City	Tica Bus	42-58	16	noon, 11:45pm
Managua (Nicaragua)	Tica Bus	29-42	9	3am, 6am, 7:30am, 12:30pm
Managua (Nicaragua)	TransNica	29-38	8-9	4am, 5am, 9am, noon
Managua (Nicaragua)	Nicabus	29	8	5:30am, 9:30am
San Salvador (El Salvador)	Tica Bus	84	20	3am
Tegucigalpa (Honduras)	TransNica	57	18	4am

Central Valley & Highlands

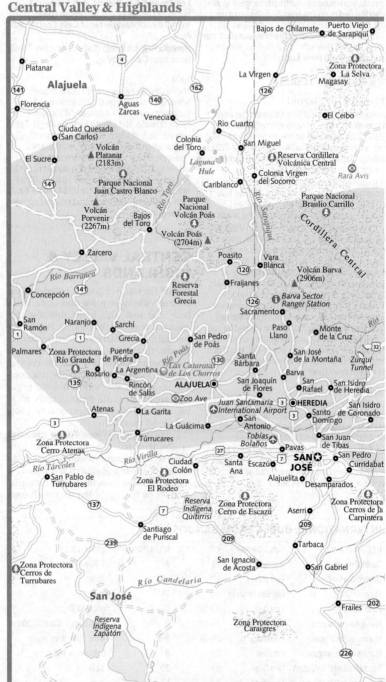

Platanar

Alajuela

④

⑭¹

Florencia

Aguas
Zarcas

⑭⁰

Venecia

Río Cuarto

Bajos de Chilamate   Puerto Viejo
de Sarapiquí

La Virgen

Zona Protectora
La Selva
Magasay

⑫⁶

El Ceibo

Ciudad Quesada
(San Carlos)

Colonia
del Toro

San Miguel

Reserva Cordillera
Volcánica Central

El Sucre

Volcán
Platanar
(2183m)

*Laguna
Hule*

Colonia Virgen
del Socorro

Rara Avis

⑭¹

Parque Nacional
Juan Castro Blanco

Cariblanco

Parque Nacional
Braulio Carrillo

Volcán
Porvenir
(2267m)

Bajos
del Toro

Parque
Nacional
Volcán Poás

Cordillera Central

Zarcero

Volcán Poás
(2704m)

Poasito

Vara
Blanca

Volcán Barva
(2906m)

Río Barranca

⑭¹

⑫⁰

Concepción

Reserva
Forestal
Grecia

Fraijanes

⑫⁶

Barva Sector
Ranger Station

San
Ramón

Naranjo

Sarchí

Sacramento

Paso
Llano

Monte
de la Cruz

Río

Palmares

①

Zona Protectora
Río Grande

Grecia

Puente
de Piedra

San Pedro
de Poás

Río Poás

⑬⁰

Santa
Bárbara

San José
de la Montaña

*Zurquí
Tunnel*

③²

Rosario

La Argentina

*Las Cataratas
de Los Chorros*

ALAJUELA

Barva

⑬⁵

Rincón
de Salas

San Joaquín
de Flores

San
Rafael

San Isidro
de Heredia

Atenas

La Garita

Zoo Ave

Juan Santamaria
International Airport

③

HEREDIA

San Isidro
de Coronado

La Guácima

San
Antonio

③

Santo
Domingo

③

Túrrucares

*Tobías
Bolaños*

Pavas

San Juan
de Tibas

Zona Protectora
Cerro Atenas

Río Virilla

Ciudad
Colón

⑦

⑦

**SAN
JOSÉ**

San Pedro
Curridabat

Río Tárcoles

San Pablo de
Turrubares

Santa
Ana

Escazú

Alajuelita

Desamparados

Zona Protectora
El Rodeo

⑬⁷

*Reserva
Indígena
Quitirrisí*

⑦

Zona Protectora
Cerro de Escazú

Aserrí

Zona Protectora
Cerros de la
Carpintera

Santiago
de Puriscal

⑳⁹

⑳⁹

Tarbaca

②³⁹

San Ignacio
de Acosta

San Gabriel

Zona Protectora
Cerros de
Turrubares

Río Candelaria

San José

*Reserva
Indígena
Zapatón*

Zona Protectora
Caraigres

Frailes

②⁰²

②²⁶

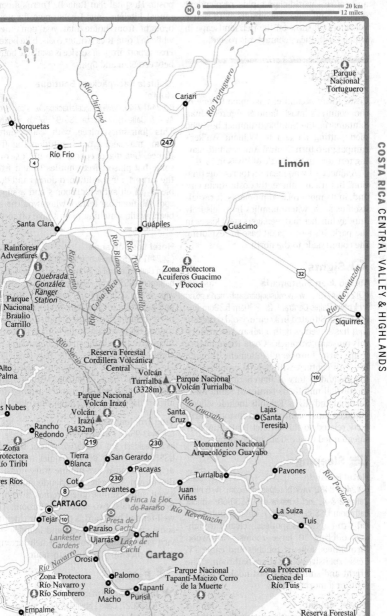

and coffee – world-class rapids, resplendent quetzals and close encounters with active volcanoes all show off the rich landscape in which Costa Rica's character is rooted.

Alajuela

POP 185,000

Costa Rica's second city is home to one of the country's most famous figures: Juan Santamaría, the humble drummer boy who died putting an end to William Walker's campaign to turn Central America into slaving territory in the Battle of Rivas in 1856.

Alajuela is by no means a tourist 'destination.' But it's an inherently Costa Rican city, and, in its more relaxed moments, it reveals itself as such, where families have leisurely Sunday lunches and teenagers steal kisses in the park. It's also a good base for exploring the countryside to the north.

◎ Sights

Museo Juan Santamaría   MUSEUM

(☏ 2441-4775; www.museojuansantamaria.go.cr; Av 1 btwn Calles Central & 2; ⊙ 10am-5:30pm Tue-Sun) FREE Situated in a century-old structure that has served as both a jail and an armory, this museum chronicles Costa Rican history from early European settlement through the 19th century, with special emphasis on the life and history of Juan Santamaría and the pivotal mid-1850s battles of Santa Rosa, Sardinal and Rivas. Exhibits include videos, vintage maps, paintings and historical artifacts related to the conflict that ultimately safeguarded Costa Rica's independence.

🛏 Sleeping

Hotel Pacandé   B&B $

(☏ 2443-8481; www.hotelpacande.com; Av 5 btwn Calles 2 & 4; incl breakfast r US$50-60, without bathroom US$35; P @ ?) This popular, locally run option is spotlessly clean throughout, offering 10 large rooms with wood furnishings, folk-art touches and cable TV. Less-expensive rooms share bathrooms. The bright and sunny breakfast nook is a great spot for a morning brew.

Hostel Maleku   HOSTEL $

(☏ 2430-4304; www.malekuhostel.com; incl breakfast dm US$15, s/d without bathroom US$25/38; @ ?) This super-friendly, family-run backpackers' abode has five spick-and-span rooms tucked into a vintage home between the airport and downtown Alajuela (op-

posite Hospital San Rafael). There's a communal kitchen, plus free storage for items brought from home that you don't need while in Costa Rica (winter coats, bike boxes). Free airport drop-off service is available hourly between 5am and 5pm.

Alajuela Backpackers Boutique Hostel   HOTEL $

(☏ 2441-7149; www.alajuelabackpackers.com; cnr Av 4 & Calle 4; dm/r/ste US$19/55/70; ✳ @ ?) This four-story place with cookie-cutter rooms may feel a tad institutional at first glance, but dig deeper and you'll discover some big pluses: free shuttles to and from the airport, air-conditioned dorms and doubles with en suite bathrooms and a supercool 4th-floor bar terrace where you can sip beers while watching planes take off in the distance.

Hotel Los Volcanes   GUESTHOUSE $$

(☏ 2441-0525; www.hotellosvolcanes.com; Av 3 btwn Calles Central & 2; incl breakfast s/d without bathroom US$40/52, with bathroom US$52/68, with air-con US$72/84; P ⊖ ✳ @ ?) Tranquil and centrally located, this welcoming place in a refurbished 1920s mansion has 15 rooms, from vintage units with period-style furniture and clean, shared bathrooms, to contemporary rooms with flat-screen TV, air-con and safe. There's an enjoyable courtyard in the back, complete with gurgling fountain. The helpful owners arrange free airport drop-off at the end of your stay.

Vida Tropical B&B   B&B $$

(☏ 2443-9576; www.vidatropical.com; Calle 3; incl breakfast s/d US$45/65, without bathroom US$35/50; P @ ? ✿) In a quiet residential neighborhood a five-minute walk north of downtown Alajuela, this friendly house has seven snug, simple guest rooms awash in bright murals; two share a bathroom. The well-tended backyard is perfect for catching some sun in a hammock, and laundry service is available. Owners can help arrange airport pick-up (US$8) at any hour.

🍴 Eating

★ **Jalapeños Central**   MEXICAN $

(☏ 2430-4027; Calle 1 btwn Avs 3 & 5; mains US$4-8; ⊙ 11:30am-9pm Mon-Sat, to 8pm Sun) Offering the best Tex-Mex in the country, this popular, 11-table spot will introduce some much-needed spice into your diet. The simple and fresh burritos, chimichangas and enchiladas come in a meal deal or on their own, and regardless should be devoured alongside a salty margarita.

El Chante Vegano VEGETARIAN $
(☑2440-3528, 8911-4787; www.elchantevegano.com; mains US$7-10; ☺11am-8pm Tue-Sun; ☑) Two brothers, their mom and a girlfriend run this eatery specializing in healthy, organic food. Vegan treats are served on an open-air, street-facing patio, including garbanzo and portobello-mushroom burgers, falafel, textured-soy-protein nachos, pasta, pizza and sandwiches like the Veggie Lú (grilled veggies, avocado and sprouts on homemade bread).

Coffee Dreams Café CAFE $
(☑2430-3970; cnr Calle 1 & Av 3; mains US$5-9; ☺8am-8pm Mon-Sat, 9am-6pm Sun; ☑) For breakfast, *bocas* (appetizers) and a variety of *típico* (traditional Costa Rican) dishes, this centrally located cafe is a reliably good place to dine or enjoy a coffee accompanied by one of its rich desserts.

ⓘ Information

Hospital San Rafael (☑2436-1000; www.hospitalsanrafael.sa.cr; Calle 4) Alajuela's hospital, housed in a three-story complex 300m south of Av 10.

Post Office (☑2443-2653; cnr Av 5 & Calle 1; ☺8am-5:30pm Mon-Fri, to noon Sat)

ⓘ Getting There & Away

A taxi to the airport is about US$8. There is no central bus terminal.

San José via Juan Santamaría International Airport (Station Wagon; US$1.10, 45 minutes, every 10 minutes 4am to 11:30pm) Departs from Av 4, between Calles 2 and 4.

San José (Tuasa West; US$1.10, 45 minutes, every 10 minutes 5am-11pm) Departs from Calle 8, between Avs Central and 1.

Volcán Poás (Coopetransasi; ☑2449-5141; US$4.60 round trip, 90 minutes each way, departs 9am, returns 2:30pm) Departs from Calle 8, between Avs Central & 2.

Parque Nacional Volcán Poás

Just 37km north of Alajuela by a winding and scenic road is Parque Nacional Volcán Poás (☑2482-1226; admission US$15; ☺8am-3:30pm), ideal for those who want to peer into an active volcano without the hardship of hiking one. Volcán Poás (2704m) had its last blowout in 1953, which formed the

enormous crater measuring 1.3km across and 300m deep.

Poás offers the wonderful opportunity to watch the bubbling, steaming cauldron belch sulfurous mud and water hundreds of meters into the air. There are two other craters, as well. In recent years Poás has posed no imminent threat of eruption, though scientists still monitor it closely.

🏃 Activities

From the visitors center there is a paved, wheelchair-accessible 600m path that leads to a crater lookout. Visitors are prohibited from descending into the crater because of the toxic sulfuric-acid fumes that are emitted from the cauldron.

Upon leaving the lookout, you can simply retrace your steps to the parking lot, or continue touring the park on a series of trails that collectively make a 3.6km loop back to the main path. For the longer loop, head east from the crater lookout onto Sendero Botos, a 1.4km, 30-minute trail that takes you through dwarf cloud forest, which is the product of acidic air and freezing temperatures. Here you can wander about looking at bromeliads, lichens and mosses clinging to the curiously shaped and twisted trees growing in the volcanic soil. Birds abound, especially the magnificent fiery-throated hummingbird, a high-altitude specialty of Costa Rica. The trail ends at Laguna Botos, a peculiar cold-water lake that has filled in one of the extinct craters.

From here, continue south on Sendero Canto de Aves, a 1.8km, 45-minute trail through taller forest, which gets significantly less traffic than the other parts of the park and is ideal for birdwatching. Species to look for include the sooty robin, black guan, screech owl and even the odd quetzal (especially from February to April). Although mammals are infrequently sighted in the park, coyotes and the endemic montane squirrel are present.

Return to the main path via the 400m, 10-minute Sendero Escalonia, which will drop you at the restrooms just north of the visitors center.

ⓘ Getting There & Away

Coopetransasi runs a daily bus to the summit (round trip US$4.60, 1½ hours each way), leaving Alajuela at 9am and returning from the mountaintop at 2:30pm. If you're coming from San José, catch a local Tuasa bus (US$1.10,

45 minutes) no later than 8:15am from Tuasa's terminal on Av 2 between Calles 12 and 14, then upon arrival in Alajuela walk one block south to the Volcán Poás bus stop.

Parque Nacional Braulio Carrillo

Enter this under-explored **national park** (☑ 2206-5500; adult/child $12/5; ⊙ 8am-3:30pm) and you will have an idea of what Costa Rica looked like prior to the 1950s, when 75% of the country's surface area was still covered in forest: steep hills cloaked in impossibly tall trees are interrupted only by cascading rivers and canyons. It has extraordinary biodiversity due to the range of altitudes, from steamy 2906m cloud forest alongside Volcán Barva to lush, humid lowlands on the Caribbean slope. Its most incredible feature, however, is that this massive park is only 30 minutes north of San José.

Activities

Quebrada González Sector

Three easy to moderate trails fan out from the **Quebrada González ranger station** (☑ 2206-5500; ⊙ 8am-4pm) between Guápiles and San José. On the north side of Hwy 32, the mostly flat, gravel-paved 1km **Sendero El Ceibo** is the easiest of the three, passing a giant ceibo tree, a scenic overlook and seven other marked points of interest before looping back to the ranger station. Proximity to the highway creates some distracting traffic noise here.

Sendero Botarrama, a slightly more rugged spur trail (expect mud and exposed roots) branches off Sendero El Ceibo and continues another 1km to the junction of the crystal-clear Río Honduras with the Río Sucio (Dirty River), the yellow waters of which carry volcanic minerals.

Back on the south side of Hwy 32, the 1.6km, gravel-paved **Sendero Las Palmas** is another loop trail that climbs moderately into dense rainforest – prime territory for birdwatching.

Barva Sector

Climbing **Volcán Barva** is a strenuous adventure along a remote but reasonably well-maintained trail. Because of its relative inaccessibility, there is a good chance you will be alone.

Begin from the western entrance of the park, north of Heredia. From there a 2.5km signed track climbs to the summit. Trails are often muddy, and you should be prepared for rain at any time of the year.

❶ Getting There & Away

Frequent buses between San José and Guápiles can drop you off at the Quebrada González station, but the return trip is more challenging. While it's possible to flag a bus down on busy Hwy 32, your luck will depend on the driver's discretion and how full the bus is.

Public buses from Heredia (US$1.40, one hour, departing 5:25am and 6:25am) will only get you as far as Paso Llano, 7km from the park entrance at Barva.

Cartago

POP 158,000

After the earthquake rubble was cleared, in the early 20th century, nobody bothered to rebuild Cartago to its former quaint specifications. As in other commercial towns, expect plenty of functional concrete structures. One exception is the bright white **Basílica de Nuestra Señora de los Ángeles** (Calle 15 btwn Avs 0 & 1), which is visible from many parts of the city, standing out like a snowcapped mountain above a plain of one-story edifices.

The city is thrown briefly into the spotlight every August, when pilgrims from every corner of the country descend on the basilica to say their most serious prayers. The remainder of the year, Cartago exists mainly as a commercial and residential center, though the beauty of the surrounding mountains helps take the edge off modern life.

🛏 Sleeping & Eating

Los Ángeles Lodge   B&B **$$**
(☑2551-0957, 2591-4169; hotel.los.angeles@hot mail.com; Av 1 btwn Calles 13 & 15; incl breakfast s US$35-40, d US$50-65; ❀☎) With its balconies overlooking the Plaza de la Basílica, this decent B&B stands out with spacious and comfortable rooms, hot showers and breakfast made to order. There is a decent restaurant on site.

❶ Getting There & Away

BUS

Bus stops are scattered around town.

Orosi (Autotransportes Mata Irola) US$0.95, 35 minutes, departs every 20 minutes between 5:30am and 10:25pm, from Calle 3 between Avs 2 and 4.

San José (Lumaca) US$1.10, 55 minutes, departs every 15 minutes between 5am and 11pm, from the terminal on Calle 6 between Avs 3 and 5.

Turrialba (Transtusa) US$1.60, 1½ hours, departs every 30 minutes from 5:45am to 10:40pm weekdays (less frequently on weekends), from Av 4 between Calles 5 and 7.

TRAIN

Train service runs between San José's Estación del Pacífico and Cartago's downtown **station** (Av 3 btwn Calles 4 & 6). The one-hour trip costs US$1.05. Trains run Monday to Friday only, with a schedule weighted toward morning and afternoon commute hours.

Valle de Orosi

This straight-out-of-a-storybook river valley is famous for mountain vistas, a lake formed by a hydroelectric facility, a truly wild national park and coffee – lots and lots of coffee. A well-paved 32km scenic loop winds through a landscape of rolling hills terraced with coffee plantations and valleys dotted with pastoral villages, all set against the backdrop of two volcanoes, Irazú and Turrialba. If you have a rental car (or a good bicycle) you're in for a treat, though it's still possible to navigate most of the loop via public buses.

The loop road starts 8km southeast of Cartago in **Paraíso**, heads south to **Orosi**, then doubles back northeast and west around the artificial **Lago de Cachí**, passing the historic church at **Ujarrás** en route back to Paraíso. Alternatively, from Orosi you can branch south into Parque Nacional Tapantí-Macizo Cerro de la Muerte, an end-of-the-road national park with superb river and mountain scenery.

◉ Sights & Activities

Iglesia de San José Orosi   CHURCH
Orosi is one of the few colonial-era towns to survive Costa Rica's frequent earthquakes, which have thankfully spared the photogenic village church. Built in 1743, it is the oldest religious site still in use in Costa Rica. The roof of the church is a combination of thatched cane and ceramic tiling, while the carved-wood altar is adorned with religious paintings of Mexican origin.

Parque Nacional Tapantí-Macizo
Cerro de la Muerte   NATIONAL PARK
(adult/6-12yr US$10/5; ☉8am-4pm) This 580-sq-km national park protects the lush northern slopes of the Cordillera de Talamanca, and is the wettest park in the country, getting an average 8000mm of precipitation a year. In 2000 it was expanded to include the infamous Cerro de la Muerte (Mountain of Death). This precipitous peak is the highest point on the Interamericana and the northernmost extent of *páramo,* a highland shrub and tussock-grass habitat – most commonly found in the Andes – that's home to a variety of rare bird species.

Finca Cristina   TOUR
(☑2574-6426, in US 203-549-1945; www.cafe cristina.com; guided tour per person US$15; ☉by

appointment only) Finca Cristina, 2km east of Paraíso on the road to Turrialba, is an organic coffee farm. Linda and Ernie have been farming in Costa Rica since 1977, and a 90-minute tour of their *microbeneficio* (miniprocessing plant) is a fantastic introduction to the processes of organic-coffee growing, harvesting and roasting.

Sleeping & Eating

Montaña Linda   HOSTEL $
(☑ 2533-3640; www.montanalinda.com; dm US$9, s/d/tr without bathroom US$15/22/30, guesthouse s/d/tr US$30/30/35; P@) A short walk southwest of the bus stop, this welcoming, chilled-out budget option has three tidy dorms and eight private rooms surrounding a homey terrace with flowers, hammocks and a wood-heated hot tub. All share a guest kitchen and six bathrooms with hot showers. Owners provide an exceptional information packet highlighting local attractions, including hot springs, waterfalls and more.

Kiri Mountain Lodge   LODGE $
(☑ 2533-2272, 8488-4085; www.kirilodge.net; s/d incl breakfast US$35/45; P?) About 2km before the park entrance, Kiri has six rustic *cabinas* with intermittent wi-fi and hot water, surrounded by 50 mossy hectares of land. Trails wind into the nearby Reserva Forestal Río Macho, and the lodge's **restaurant** (casados US$8-12; ⊙ 7am-8pm) specializes in trout.

❶ Getting There & Around

Autotransportes Mata Irola (☑ 2533-1916) runs buses (US$0.95) every 30 minutes to Paraíso (20 minutes) and Cartago (40 minutes) from multiple stops along Orosi's main street. Transfer in Paraíso for buses to Ujarrás and Cachí (US$1.15).

Turrialba

POP 29,900

When the railway shut down in 1991, commerce slowed down, but Turrialba nonetheless remained a regional agricultural center, where local coffee planters could bring their crops to market. And with tourism on the rise in the 1990s, this modest mountain town soon became known as the gateway to some of the best white-water rafting on the planet. By the early 2000s Turrialba was a hotbed of international rafters looking for Class-V thrills. For now, the Río Pacuare runs on, but its future is uncertain.

✻ Activities

Most organized expeditions from Turrialba head for the Río Pacuare, which arguably offers the most scenic rafting in Central America. The river plunges down the Caribbean slope through a series of spectacular canyons clothed in virgin rainforest, through runs named for their fury and separated by calm stretches that enable you to stare at near-vertical green walls towering hundreds of meters above. The Pacuare can be run year-round, though June to October are considered the best months.

Ecoaventuras   OUTDOORS
(www.ecoaventuras.co.cr) An outdoor adventure company that offers white-water rafting in the Pacuare and Pejibaye rivers, along with horse-riding, mountain-biking and canopy tours. A three-day rafting experience with all meals, accommodations, equipment and an included zip-line tour costs US$360 per person. It's 100m north and 100m west of the Rawlings Factory.

Explornatura   RAFTING
(☑ 2556-0111, in USA & Canada 866-571-2443; www.explornatura.com; Av 4 btwn Calles 2 & 4) Does rafting, mountain-biking and horse-riding tours. A rafting day trip on the Pacuare is US$85 per person, horse riding is US$68 per person and mountain biking costs US$60 per person.

Locos   RAFTING
(☑ 2556-6035, in USA 707-703-5935; www.whiteh2o.com) Locos takes guests on wild rides of varying difficulty down the Ríos Pacuare and Reventazón. The outfit also runs a more relaxing trip down the Río Pejibaye. A day of rafting is typically around US$85 per person (depending on the size of the group).

Sleeping

★ **Casa de Lis Hostel**   HOSTEL $
(☑ 2556-4933; www.hostelcasadelis.com; Av Central near Calle 2; dm US$14, s/d/tr/q US$40/45/60/68, without bathroom US$36/36/48/56; ?) Hands down Turrialba's best value, this sweet, centrally located eight-room place is a traveler's dream come true. Spotless dorms and doubles with comfy mattresses and individual reading lamps are complemented by a fully equipped kitchen, volcano-view roof terrace, pretty back garden, fantastic information displays and a distinctly friendly atmosphere. Laundry service (US$8 per load) is available.

WORTH A TRIP

MONUMENTO NACIONAL ARQUEOLÓGICO GUAYABO

Nestled into a patch of stunning hillside forest 19km northeast of Turrialba is the largest and most important archaeological site in the country. **Guayabo** (☑2559-1220; US$5; ☺8am-3:30pm) is composed of the remains of a pre-Columbian city that was thought to have peaked at some point in AD 800, when it was inhabited by as many as 20,000 people. Today visitors can examine the remains of old petroglyphs, residential mounds, an old roadway and an impressive aqueduct system – built with rocks that were hauled in from the Río Reventazón along a cobbled, 8km road. Amazingly, the cisterns still work, and (theoretically) potable water remains available onsite. In 1973, as the site's importance became evident, Guayabo was declared a national monument, with further protections set forth in 1980. The site occupies 232 hectares, most of which remains unexcavated. It's a small place, so don't go expecting Maya pyramids.

Guided tours are available from **Asociación de Guías U-Suré** (☑8534-1063; guided tour for 1-3 people US$20, for 4-9 US$35, for 10-20 US$50), whose office is directly adjacent to the ticket window.

Getting There & Away

Buses from Turrialba (US$0.95, one hour) depart at 6am, 10:30am, 3pm and 6pm Monday through Friday and at 10:30am, 3pm and 6pm on Saturday and Sunday. Buses return from Guayabo to Turrialba at 7am, 12:30pm and 4pm daily. You can also take a taxi from Turrialba (about US$30 round trip, with one hour to explore the park).

Hotel Interamericano HOTEL $

(☑2556-0142; www.hotelinteramericano.com; Av 1 near Calle 1; s/d/tr/q US$25/35/45/55, without bathroom US$12/20/30/40; ⓟ☜) On the south side of the old train tracks is this basic 20-room hotel, traditionally regarded by rafters as *the* meeting place in Turrialba. The collection of basic rooms includes some with private bathrooms, some without and many that combine bunks with regular beds. The friendly owner provides day care for children who are too young to go rafting.

Hotel Wagelia HOTEL $$

(☑2556-1566; www.hotelwageliaturrialba.com; Av 4 btwn Calles 2 & 4; s/d incl breakfast US$55/80; ⓟ☜) Simple, modern and clean rooms come with cable TV and face a quiet interior courtyard. A restaurant serves Tico specialties, and the pleasant terrace bar is a good place for a drink and wi-fi.

✗ Eating

★Maracuyá CAFE $

(☑2556-2021; Calle 2 north of Av 10; frozen coffee US$4, mains US$6; ☺2-10pm Wed-Mon; ☑) This bright-walled cafe serves up one of the best coffee treats in the country – a frozen caffeine concoction with gooey *maracuyá* (passion fruit) syrup and crunchy seeds. Dishes include veggie wraps, creative salads and Latin American favorites like *patacones* (fried plantains).

La Feria COSTA RICAN $

(☑2556-5550; Calle 6 north of Av 4; mains US$6-15; ☺11am-10pm Wed-Mon, to 3pm Tue; ☑) This unremarkable-looking eatery has friendly service and excellent, reasonably priced home cooking. Sometimes the kitchen gets a bit backed up, but the hearty *casados* (typical dishes with beans, rice, a small salad and a choice of protein) are well worth the wait.

Wok & Roll ASIAN $

(☑2556-6756; Calle 1; mains US$7-19; ☺11am-10pm Wed-Mon) Pan-Asian cuisine, from Singapore-style noodles to Chinese steamed buns, fills the menu at this new eatery near Turrialba's main square. OK, perhaps they're overdoing the fusion thing with the Turri Volcano Roll (made with avocado, cucumber and, yes, Turrialba cheese!), but nobody can argue with tempura ice cream for dessert. Don't miss the homemade mint lemonade and honey-sweetened jasmine tea.

ⓘ Getting There & Away

A modern bus terminal is located on the western edge of town off Hwy 10.

San José via Paraíso and Cartago US$2.70, 1¾ hours, departs hourly from 4am to 9pm.

Siquirres, for transfer to Puerto Limón US$2.25, 1½ hours, departs every 60 to 90 minutes from 5:30am to 6:30pm. Schedules vary slightly on weekends.

CARIBBEAN COAST

While the sunny climate and easy accessibility of the Pacific have paved the way (literally) for development on that rich coast, the Caribbean side has languished in comparison. The same rain-drenched malarial wildness that thwarted the first 16th-century Spaniards from settling here also isolated this region for centuries afterward. Thus, its culture – influenced by indigenous peoples and West Indian immigrants – blended slowly and organically and is distinctly different from that of the rest of Costa Rica.

It still takes a little more effort to travel here to see the nesting turtles of Tortuguero, raft the Río Pacuare or dive the reefs of Manzanillo. Life is more rugged and rustic on this coast, allowing wildlife to thrive. And it's well worth tasting its unique flavors: the *rondón* (spicy seafood gumbo), the lilt of patois, and the uncrowded stretches of palm-lined beaches.

Tortuguero

POP 1500

Located within the confines of Parque Nacional Tortuguero, accessible only by air or water, this bustling little village with strong Afro-Caribbean roots is best known for attracting hordes of sea turtles (the name Tortuguero means 'turtle catcher') – and the hordes of tourists who want to see them. While the peak turtle season is in July and August, the park and village have begun to attract travelers year-round. Even in October, when the turtles have pretty much returned to the sea, caravans of families and adventure travelers arrive to go on jungle hikes and to canoe the area's lush canals.

◉ Sights & Activities

Parque Nacional Tortuguero   PARK
(US$15; ⊙6-7am, 7:30am-noon & 1-4pm) This misty, green coastal park sits on a broad floodplain parted by a jigsaw of canals. Referred to as the 'mini-Amazon,' Parque Nacional Tortuguero's intense biodiversity includes over 400 bird species, 60 known species of frog, 30 species of freshwater fish and three monkey species as well as the threatened West Indian manatee.

Caimans and crocodiles can be seen lounging on river banks, while freshwater turtles bask on logs.

Over 120,000 visitors a year come to boat the canals and see the wildlife, particularly to watch turtles lay eggs. This is the most important Caribbean breeding site of the green sea turtle, 40,000 of which arrive every season to nest. Of the eight species of marine turtle in the world, six nest in Costa Rica, and four nest in Tortuguero. Various volunteer organizations address the problem of poaching with vigilant turtle patrols.

Park headquarters is at **Cuatro Esquinas** (☑2709-8086; ⊙6-7am, 7:30am-noon & 1-4pm), just south of Tortuguero village. Sharks and strong currents make the beaches unsuitable for swimming.

Boating

Four aquatic trails wind their way through Parque Nacional Tortuguero, inviting waterborne exploration. **Río Tortuguero** acts as the entrance way to the network of trails. This wide, beautiful river is often covered with water lilies and is frequented by aquatic birds such as herons, kingfishers and anhingas – the latter of which is known as the snakebird for the way its slim, winding neck pokes out of the water when it swims.

Caño Chiquero and **Canõ Mora** are two narrower waterways with good wildlife-spotting opportunities. According to park regulation, only kayaks, canoes and silent electric boats are allowed in these areas. Caño Chiquero is thick with vegetation, especially red guácimo trees and epiphytes. Black turtles and green iguanas like to hang out here. Caño Mora is about 3km long but only 10m wide, so it feels as if it's straight out of *The Jungle Book*. **Caño Harold** is actually an artificially constructed canal, but that doesn't stop the creatures – such as Jesus Christ lizards and caimans – from inhabiting its tranquil waters.

Canoe rental and boat tours are available in Tortuguero village.

Hiking

Behind Cuatro Esquinas ranger station, the park currently has just one trail on solid ground. Visitors can hike the muddy, 2km out-and-back trail that traverses the tropical humid forest and parallels a stretch of beach. Green parrots and several species of monkey are commonly sighted here. The short trail is well marked. Rubber boots are required and are available for rent at hotels and near the park entrance.

At the time of research, the park was preparing to open a second hiking option, Cerro Tortuguero Trail. To reach the trailhead, guests will take boats to the town of

San Francisco, north of Tortuguero village, where they will disembark at a new ranger station and buy a ticket (prices TBD). The trail then takes visitors 1.8km up a hill for a view of the surrounding lagoon, forest and ocean.

👣 Tours

Leonardo Tours OUTDOORS
(📞8577-1685; www.leonardotours.wordpress.com) With nine years of experience guiding tours in the area, Leonardo Estrada brings extensive knowledge and infectious enthusiasm to his turtle, canoeing, kayaking and hiking tours.

Tinamon Tours TOUR
(📞8842-6561, 2709-8004; www.tinamontours.de) Trained zoologist and 20-plus-year Tortuguero resident Barbara Hartung offers hiking, canoeing, cultural and turtle tours in German, English, French or Spanish.

Ballard Excursions TOUR
(www.tortuguerovillage.com/ballardexcursions) Ross Ballard, a Canadian with deep local roots, leads 3½-hour walking tours focusing on the biology and ecology of the species-rich rainforest at the foot of Cerro Tortuguero, the region's tallest hill.

🛏 Sleeping

★Aracari Garden Hostel HOSTEL $
(📞2767-2246; www.facebook.com/aracarigarden; dm US$10, r US$25-30; 📶) This newly renovated, tangerine-colored hostel on the south side of the soccer field has eight sparkling rooms, relaxing shared spaces and a resident kinkajou that dangles from the property's fruit trees. A stay comes with free coffee, a shared open-air kitchen, laundry ($3 per kg), and all the requisite camaraderie of an intimate, well-run hostel. The ocean is 50m away.

La Casona CABINA $
(📞2709-8092; lacasonadetortuguero@yahoo.com; s/d US$18/25, d with kitchenette US$35; 📶) Eleven cute rooms with rustic touches surround a lovely garden at this family-run spot. The entire place is adorned in art created from recycled materials and driftwood, and a waterfall on the property is home to several baby iguanas. It's on the north side of the soccer field.

Cabinas Tortuguero CABINA $
(📞8839-1200, 2709-8114; www.cabinas-tortugero.com; r $14-30; 📶) Down a side street between the boat landing and the park entrance, you'll find eight quaint bungalows surrounding a tidy garden at this popular budget spot. Under new ownership since 2015, the property also features hammocks for lounging, a shared kitchen and laundry service.

El Icaco HOTEL $
(📞2709-8044; www.hotelelicaco.com; s/d/tr/q US$20/30/35/40; 📶🅿) This simple oceanfront lodging offers clean, brightly painted rooms and friendly service. The beachfront location is ideal, and there are plenty of hammocks from which to enjoy it. The hotel also offers access to an offsite swimming pool along with rental housing for groups and families. Cash only.

★Hotel Miss Junie CABINA $$
(📞2709-8029; www.iguanaverdetours.com; s/d standard US$50/55, superior US$65/75, all incl breakfast; 📶) Tortuguero's longest-established lodging, Miss Junie's place is set on spacious, palm-shaded grounds strewn with hammocks and wooden armchairs. Spotless, wood-paneled rooms in a tropical plantation-style building are tastefully decorated with wood accents and bright bedspreads. Upstairs rooms share a breezy balcony overlooking the canal; the **restaurant** (📞2709-8029; mains US$13-20; ⊙7-9am, noon-2pm & 6-9pm) downstairs is delicious. It's at the northern end of the town's main street.

★Rana Roja LODGE $$
(📞2709-8260, 2223-1926; www.tortuguerorana roja.com; r/cabins per person incl breakfast US$55/70, r per person incl 3 meals US$70; @📶🅿) 🌿 This jungle hideaway is one of Tortuguero's best-value options, especially for solo travelers. Fifteen immaculate rooms and 12 cabins with private terraces and rockers are connected by elevated walkways; all have tile floors, hot showers and awesome views of nature. Free kayaks are available onsite, and guests can make use of the pool at the adjacent **Evergreen Lodge** (📞2222-6841; www.evergreentortuguero.com; 2-night packages per person s/d US$279/229; 📶🅿).

🍴 Eating

★Taylor's Place CARIBBEAN $
(📞8319-5627; mains US$7-14; ⊙6-10pm) Low-key atmosphere and high-quality cooking come together beautifully at this backstreet eatery southwest of the soccer field. The inviting garden setting, with chirping insects

and picnic benches spread under colorful paper lanterns, is rivaled only by friendly chef Ray Taylor's culinary artistry. House specialties include beef in tamarind sauce, grilled fish in garlic sauce, and fruit drinks both alcoholic and otherwise.

Fresh Foods CARIBBEAN $
(☑2767-1063; mains US$7-12, smoothies US$3-4) Next to the Morpho grocery store in the commercial center of the village, this family-owned food stand opened in 2013 to offer breakfast, solid Caribbean meals and giant, delicious smoothies in fishbowl glasses. And after a long day on the canals, a tasty Caribbean-style filet and a passion-fruit drink really nails it.

❶ Information

There are no banks or ATMs in town and only a few businesses accept credit cards, so bring all the cash you'll need.

Tortuguero Info Center (☑2709-8055; tortugueroinfo.tripod.com; ◷8am-6pm) An information center that also sells tours out of **Cabinas Balcon del Mar** (☑2709-8124, 2767-7412).

❶ Getting There & Away

BUS & BOAT

The classic public-transit route to Tortuguero is by bus from San José to Cariari to La Pavona, then by boat from La Pavona to Tortuguero. Alternatively, Tortuguero is accessible by private boat from Moín, near Puerto Limón on the Caribbean coast (p545).

From San José, take the 6:10am, 9am or 10:30am bus to Cariari (US$3.50, three hours) from Gran Terminal del Caribe. In Cariari, you will arrive at a bus station at the south end of town (known as the *estación nueva*). From here, walk or take a taxi 500m north to the *estación vieja* (old station), otherwise referred to as the Terminal Caribeño. Here you can catch a local **Coopetraca** (☑2767-7590) bus (US$2.20, 6am, 9am, 11:30am and 3pm) to La Pavona, where you'll transfer onto the boat (US$3.20 to US$4) to Tortuguero.

On the return trip, boats leave Tortuguero for La Pavona daily at 5:30am, 9am, 11am and 2:45pm, connecting with Cariari-bound buses at the La Pavona dock.

SHUTTLE SERVICE

Caribe Shuttle (☑2750-0626; www.caribeshuttle.com) Provides boat/air-conditioned van service from Tortuguero to Puerto Viejo (US$75, five hours) and Arenal-La Fortuna (US$60, six hours).

Jungle Tom Safaris (☑2221-7878; www.jungletomsafaris.com) Offers one-way shuttles between Tortuguero and San José (US$45). All-inclusive one- and two-night packages (US$99 to US$152) can also include shuttles from Cahuita (US$60), Puerto Viejo (US$60) and Arenal-La Fortuna (US$60), as well as optional tours.

Ride CR (☑2469-2525; www.ridecr.com) Shuttles from Arenal-La Fortuna (US$55).

Puerto Limón

The biggest city on Costa Rica's Caribbean coast, the birthplace of United Fruit and capital of Limón Province, this hardworking port city sits removed from the rest of the country. Cruise ships deposit dazed-looking passengers between October and May. Around here, business is measured by truckloads of fruit, not busloads of tourists, so don't expect any pampering.

A general lack of political and financial support from the federal government means that Limón is not a city that has aged gracefully. It is a grid of dilapidated buildings, overgrown parks and sidewalks choked with street vendors. Crime is a problem: the city, distressingly, has as many homicides annually as San José – even though San José has five times the population. It's worth noting, however, that most of this violence is related to organized crime and does not affect travelers. Despite its shortcomings, Limón can be a compelling destination for adventurous urban explorers.

🛏 Sleeping & Eating

Find cheap eats at the *sodas* in the **central market** (Av 2 btwn Calles 3 & 4; ◷6am-8pm Mon-Fri). You can get groceries at the large **Más X Menos** (cnr Av 3 & Calle 3; ◷6:30am-10pm), or at the **Palí** (cnr Calle 7 & Av 1; ◷7am-9pm Mon-Fri, 8am-7:30pm Sat & Sun) next to the Terminal Caribeño.

Hotel Miami HOTEL $
(☑2758-0490; hmiamilimon@yahoo.com; Av 2 btwn Calles 4 & 5; s/d/tr US$27/37/42, with air-con US$41/58/67; [P][❄][@]) For its location on the main drag, this clean, mint-green place feels surprisingly serene, especially in the rooms in back. All 34 tidy rooms are equipped with cable TV and fan. Rooms with air-conditioning have hot water. Welcoming staff, common balconies overlooking the street and a secure setup add up to the best value in town.

★ Soda El Patty
CARIBBEAN $

(☑2798-3407; cnr Av 5 & Calle 7; patí US$1.50, mains US$4-5; ⊙7am-7pm) This beloved nine-table Caribbean eatery serves up delicious *patí* – flaky beef turnovers stuffed with onion, spices and Panamanian peppers – along with sweet plantain tarts and heaping plates of rice and beans (the spicier, more flavorful version of the country's traditional *casado*). On Fridays, the chef prepares a special, piping-hot cauldron of *rondón* soup.

Macrobiótica Bionatura
VEGETARIAN $

(☑2798-2020; Calle 6 btwn Avs 3 & 4; ⊙8am-6:15pm Mon-Fri, to 5:15pm Sat; 🖉) This macrobiotic grocery store sells healthy vegetarian foods, vitamins, and all things made of soy.

❶ Information

If you're traveling onward to Parismina or Tortuguero, Limón will be your last opportunity to get cash (and phonecards, for the Parismina-bound).

Banco de Costa Rica (☑2758-3166; cnr Av 2 & Calle 1) Exchanges US dollars and has an ATM.

Scotiabank (cnr Av 3 & Calle 2; ⊙9am-5pm Mon-Fri, to 1pm Sat) Exchanges cash and has a 24-hour ATM that dispenses US dollars.

DANGERS & ANNOYANCES

Though police presence has ramped up noticeably, pickpockets can be a problem, particularly in the market and along the sea wall. In addition, people do get mugged here, so stick to well-lit main streets at night, avoiding the sea wall and Parque Vargas. If driving, park in a guarded lot and remove everything from the car.

❶ Getting There & Away

BOAT

Cruise ships dock in Limón, but smaller passenger boats bound for Parismina and Tortuguero use the port at Moín, about 7km west of town.

Tracasa buses to Moín from Puerto Limón (US$0.60, 20 minutes) depart from Terminal Caribeño hourly from 5:30am to 6:30pm (less frequently on Saturday and Sunday). Get off the bus before it goes over the bridge.

ABACAT (Asociación de Boteros de los Canales de Tortuguero; ☑8360-7325) Operates regular services to Tortuguero.

Tropical Wind (☑8327-0317, 8313-7164) Operates almost-daily shuttles between Tortuguero and Moín in high season.

BUS

Buses from all points west arrive at **Terminal Caribeño** (Av 2 btwn Calles 7 & 8), just west of the baseball stadium. Buses to all points south depart from **Autotransportes Mepe Terminal** (☑2758-1572; Calle 6 btwn Avs 1 & 2), on the east side of the stadium.

Manzanillo (US$4.90, two hours) via **Cahuita** (US$2.40, one hour) and **Puerto Viejo de Talamanca** (US$3.70, 1.5 hours) Autotransportes Mepe Terminal, every one to two hours from 5:30am to 6:30pm.

San José (US$7, three hours) Terminal Caribeños, every 30 minutes from 4:30am to 9:30am, then every hour to 4:30pm; later buses on weekends.

Sixaola (US$5.25, three hours) Autotransportes Mepe Terminal, hourly from 5am to 7pm.

Cahuita

POP 11,479

Even as tourism has mushroomed on Costa Rica's southern coast, Cahuita has managed to hold onto its laid-back Caribbean vibe. The roads are made of dirt, many of the older houses rest on stilts and chatty neighbors still converse in Mekatelyu. A graceful black-sand beach and a chilled-out demeanor hint at a not-so-distant past, when the area was little more than a string of cacao farms.

Cahuita proudly claims the area's first permanent Afro-Caribbean settler: a turtle fisherman named William Smith, who moved his family to Punta Cahuita in 1828. Now his descendants, along with those of so many other West Indian immigrants, run the backyard eateries and brightly painted bungalows that hug this idyllic stretch of coast.

Situated on a pleasant point, the town itself has a waterfront but no beach. For that, most folks make the five-minute jaunt up the coast to Playa Negra or southeast into neighboring Parque Nacional Cahuita.

◉ Sights

Parque Nacional Cahuita NATIONAL PARK
(admission US$5) This small but beautiful park – just 10 sq km – is one of the more frequently visited national parks in Costa Rica. The reasons are simple: the nearby town of Cahuita provides attractive accommodations and easy access; more importantly, the white-sand beaches, coral reef and coastal rainforest are bursting with wildlife.

Tree of Life GARDENS
(☑8317-0325, 2755-0014; www.treeoflifecostarica.com; adult/child US$15/7.50; ⊙tour 11am Tue-Sun,

Cahuita

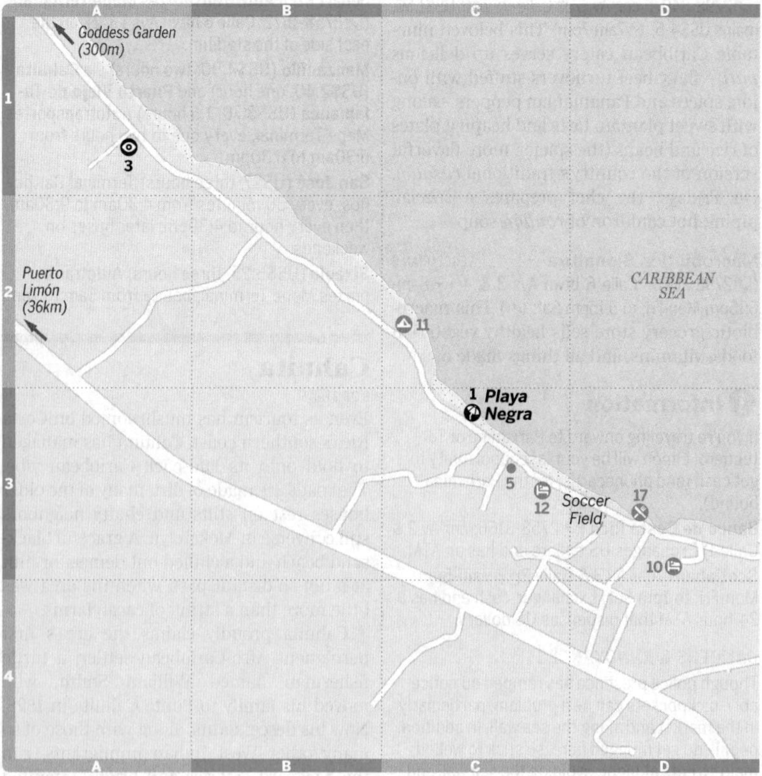

closed May, Jun, Sep & Oct) This lovingly maintained wildlife center and botanical garden 3km northwest of town on the Playa Negra road rescues and rehabilitates animals while also promoting conservation through educational programs. The rotating cast of residents typically includes kinkajous, peccaries, sloths, monkeys and toucans. There's excellent English-language signage throughout. It's also possible to volunteer here; see the website for information.

★Playa Negra BEACH

At the northwest end of Cahuita, Playa Negra is a long, black-sand beach flying the *bandera azul ecológica,* a flag that indicates the beach is kept to the highest ecological standards. This is undoubtedly Cahuita's top spot for swimming and is never crowded. When the swells are big, this place also has an excellent beach break for beginners.

Activities

Hiking

An easily navigable 8km **coastal trail** leads through the jungle from Kelly Creek to Puerto Vargas. At times the trail follows the beach; at other times hikers are 100m or so away from the sand. At the end of the first beach, Playa Blanca, hikers must ford the dark Río Perezoso, or 'Sloth River,' which bisects Punta Cahuita. Inquire about conditions before you set out: under normal conditions, this river is easy enough to wade across, but during periods of heavy rain it can become impassable since it serves as the discharge for the swamp that covers the point.

The trail continues around Punta Cahuita to the long stretch of Playa Vargas. It ends at the southern tip of the reef, where it meets up with a road leading to the Puerto Vargas ranger station. Once you reach the ranger station, it's another 1.5km along a gravel road to the park entrance. From here, you can hike the

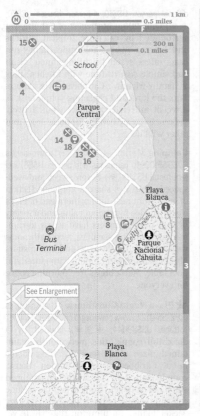

Cahuita

◎ **Top Sights**
1 Playa Negra C3

◎ **Sights**
2 Parque Nacional Cahuita....................E4
3 Tree of Life...A1

◎ **Activities, Courses & Tours**
4 Cahuita Tours.....................................E1
5 Centro Turístico Brigitte....................C3

◎ **Sleeping**
6 Bungalows Aché F3
7 Cabinas Riverside..............................F3
8 Cabinas Secret Garden......................F2
9 Cabinas Smith 1 & 2...........................E1
10 Cabinas Tito......................................D3
11 Camping María...................................C2
12 Playa Negra Guesthouse...................C3

◎ **Eating**
13 Café y Delicias..................................E2
14 Cocoricó...E2
15 Miss Edith's.......................................E1
16 Smoothie Bar & Crêpe Café...............E2
17 Sobre Las Olas D3

◎ **Drinking & Nightlife**
18 Coco's Bar E2

3.5km back to Cahuita along the coastal highway or catch a ride going in either direction.

Swimming

Almost immediately upon entering the park, you'll see the 2km-long **Playa Blanca** stretching along a gently curving bay to the east. The first 500m of beach may be unsafe for swimming, but beyond that, waves are generally gentle. (Look for green flags marking safe swimming spots.) The rocky Punta Cahuita headland separates this beach from the next one, **Playa Vargas**. It is unwise to leave clothing or other belongings unattended when you swim.

☞ Tours

Centro Turístico Brigitte HORSEBACK RIDING
(☎2755-0053; www.brigittecahuita.com; Playa Negra) Behind Reggae Bar in the heart of Playa Negra, this well-signed backstreet spot does it all, but specializes in horseback tours

(three hours to full day, US$60 to US$110) and surf lessons (US$35 including use of board). Brigitte also rents bicycles (US$8) and offers laundry (US$10 a load) and internet (US$2 per hour) services. Check the website or stop by in person for full details.

Also offers a couple of basic wood *cabinas* and two private single rooms, plus a good onsite restaurant.

Cahuita Tours TOUR
(☎2755-0101, 2755-0000; www.cahuitatours.com) One of the most established agencies in town.

Snorkeling House TOUR
(☎8361-1924; www.snorkelinghouse.com) Local tour guide and conservationist Fernando Brown launches his excellent snorkeling tours in Cahuita national park from Miss Edith's (p549), his family's restaurant. The tour includes a couple of stops where reef sharks, rays and numerous fish are often spotted, and concludes with a fresh fruit snack.

⌨ Sleeping

There are two general areas to stay in Cahuita: the town center (which can be a little noisy) or north of town along Playa Negra. If walking between Playa Negra and the center at night, don't carry valuables; better yet, bike or take a taxi, especially if traveling alone.

Central Cahuita

Cabinas Riverside
CABINA $

(☑ 8893-2252; d with/without kitchen US$30/25; P) Managed by friendly Cahuita local Peck Ferguson and family, this tidy budget place just around the corner from Kelly Creek ranger station offers nine simple rooms with mosquito nets and hot showers; five units that are a bit more expensive also come with kitchens. The grassy yard abuts a swampy area perfect for spotting caimans, monkeys and sloths.

Cabinas Secret Garden
CABINA $

(☑ 2755-0581; koosiecosta@live.nl; dm/s/d/tr US$12/18/22/30; P🛜) This tiny place with a lush garden has five tiled units with fans, mosquito nets, and hot-water showers in cubicle-style bathrooms, plus one five-bed dorm with cold showers. There's also a nice shared kitchen with free coffee.

Cabinas Smith 1 & 2
CABINA $

(☑ 2755-0068; s/d/tr with fan US$18/23/30, s/d/tr/q with air-con US$30/35/40/45; P❄🛜) These clean rooms spanning two properties between the main drag and the waterfront are run by a friendly older couple with deep local roots. Eight units adjacent to the owners' home have TV, air-con and wi-fi; five older fan-cooled units around the corner are primarily of interest to the seriously budget-minded. All share a guest kitchen.

Bungalows Aché
BUNGALOW $$

(☑ 2755-0119; www.bungalowsache.com; bungalow s US$45, d US$50-55; P🛜) In Nigeria, Aché means 'Amen,' and you'll likely say the same thing when you see these three spotless polished-wood bungalows nestled into a grassy yard bordering the national park. Each octagonal unit comes with a lockbox, minifridge, kettle and small private deck with hammock. A three-bedroom vacation house (doubles US$70, up to seven people US$120) is available 1km inland.

Playa Negra

Cabinas Tito
BUNGALOW $

(☑ 8880-1904, 2755-0286; www.cahuita-cabinas-tito.com; d with/without hot water US$35/25, ad-

ditional person US$10, 4-person houses US$70; P🛜) Only 200m northwest of Cahuita, yet surrounded by extensive tropical gardens and banana plants, this quiet family-run oasis offers seven brightly painted, clean and simple *casitas* (one with kitchen) plus a family-friendly Caribbean-style house. Tito, the kind and charming young host, is a recent university graduate who's actively seeking to create habitat for birds, frogs and other wildlife.

Camping María
CAMPGROUND $

(☑ 2755-0091; campsites per person US$8, incl tent rental US$10; 🛜) Seven sweet and well-spaced campsites share a gorgeous section of waterfront near the northern end of Playa Negra, shaded by coconut palms and a variety of fruit trees. Campers have access to rudimentary cooking facilities, two bathrooms with cold-water showers and an upstairs library and recreation room with guitar and pool table. María brews free morning coffee for everyone.

★ Playa Negra Guesthouse
BUNGALOW $$

(☑ 2755-0127; www.playanegra.cr; s/d US$64/79, cottages US$89-144; P🛜⊠) Owned by a delightful couple, this meticulously maintained place offers four charming rooms in a Caribbean-style plantation house, complemented by three kitchen-equipped storybook cottages. Tropical accents include colorful mosaics in the bathrooms and cozy wicker lounge furniture on the private verandas. A lovely pool, honor bar and BBQ area are tucked into the well-manicured garden dotted with fan palms.

Eating

Cocoricó
ITALIAN $

(mains US$6-12; ⊙ 5-10pm Wed-Mon) The menu here revolves around pizza, pasta and other Italian-themed mains, but it's better known for its regular movie screenings. Free movies are shown every night, as are two-for-one cocktails from 5pm to 10pm.

Café y Delicias
INTERNATIONAL $

(breakfast US$3-4, dishes US$4-9; ⊙ 6:30am-5pm Mon-Sat, 7am-1pm Sun) Greet the morning with a cup o' joe and a warm cinnamon roll, or unwind in the afternoon with a refreshing *jugo*. Breakfast offerings include French toast and bacon, while the lunch menu revolves around salad, spaghetti and quiche. Hearty sandwiches on homemade whole-grain bread are perfect for beach picnics at the national park.

**Smoothie Bar
& Crêpe Café**   JUICE BAR, CREPERIE $
(juices US$2-4, crepes US$3-7; ⊘7am-5:30pm) At this friendly main-street spot, Sherilyn whips up fresh fruit crepes and juices mixed with water, milk, yogurt or ice cream. There's always an attractively priced juice of the day (US$2), but even better is the *agua de sapo*, a delicious, sinus-clearing Caribbean concoction made with lemon juice, water, brown sugar and loads of fresh ginger.

★ Sobre Las Olas   SEAFOOD $$
(☑2755-0109; pastas US$12-15, mains US$12-25; ⊘noon-10pm Wed-Mon; ⌖) Garlic shrimp, seafood pasta, or fresh grilled fish of the day come accompanied by crashing waves and sparkling blue Caribbean vistas at this sweet spot owned by a lively couple. Cahuita's top option for romantic waterfront dining, it's only a 400m walk northwest of Cahuita, on the road to Playa Negra. Save room for the delicious tiramisu.

★ Miss Edith's   CARIBBEAN $$
(☑2755-0248; mains US$6-24; ⊘7am-8pm; ⌖) This long-time local restaurant serves a slew of Caribbean specialties and a number of vegetarian options. The service may be laid-back, and some dishes aren't spectacular, but the spicy jerk chicken and potatoes stewed in garlic are more than worth the wait.

🍷 Drinking & Nightlife

Coco's Bar   BAR
(www.facebook.com/cocosbar.cahuita; ⊘noon-late) Low-key Cahuita is home to one insanely loud drinking hole: Coco's Bar. You can't miss it at the main intersection, painted Rasta red, gold and green and cranking the reggaetón up to 11. On some nights (usually on weekends) there's also live music.

ℹ Information

Banco de Costa Rica (⊘9am-4pm Mon-Fri) At the bus terminal; has an ATM.
Internet Palmer (per hr US$2; ⊘7am-7:30pm) Internet access in the heart of town.
Kelly Creek Ranger Station (☑2755-0461; admission by donation; ⊘6am-5pm)
Puerto Vargas Ranger Station (☑2755-0302; admission US$5; ⊘8am-4pm Mon-Fri, 7am-5pm Sat & Sun)

ℹ Getting There & Away

Autotransportes Mepe buses arrive and depart at the bus terminal 200 m southwest of Parque Central.

Puerto Viejo de Talamanca

There was a time when the only travelers to the little seaside settlement once known as Old Harbor were intrepid surfers who padded around the quiet, dusty streets, board under arm, on their way to surf Salsa Brava. That, certainly, is no longer the case. This burgeoning party town is bustling with tourist activity: street vendors ply Rasta trinkets and Bob Marley T-shirts, stylish eateries serve global fusion everything and intentionally rustic bamboo bars pump dancehall and reggaetón. The scene can get downright hedonistic, attracting dedicated revelers who arrive to marinate in ganja and *guaro*.

Despite that reputation, Puerto Viejo nonetheless manages to hold on to an easy charm. Stray a couple of blocks off the main commercial strip and you might find yourself on a sleepy dirt road, savoring a spicy Caribbean stew in the company of local families. Nearby, you'll find rainforest fruit and cacao farms set to a soundtrack of cackling birds and croaking frogs, and wide-open beaches where the daily itinerary revolves around surfing and snoozing. So, chill a little. Party a little. Eat a little. You've come to just the right place.

COSTA RICA PUERTO VIEJO DE TALAMANCA

BUSES FROM CAHUITA

DESTINATION	COST (US$)	DURATION (HR)	FREQUENCY (DAILY)
Manzanillo	2.40	1	roughly 2 hourly, 7am-7pm
Puerto Limón	2.40	1½	about every 30min, 6am-8pm
Puerto Viejo de Talamanca	1.50	½	roughly 2 hourly, 7am-7pm
San José	8.90	4	7am, 8am, 9:30am, 11:30am & 4:30pm
Sixaola	3.95	2	hourly, 6am-7pm; passes through Bribrí

Puerto Viejo de Talamanca

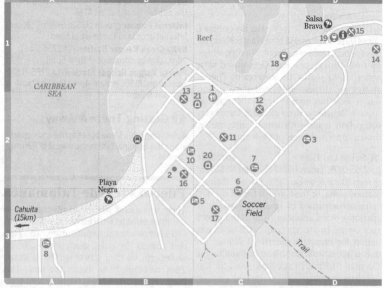

☉ Sights

★ Playa Cocles
BEACH

Playa Cocles, about 2km east of town, has impressive waves for surfers who aren't so keen to break skin and bones on nearby Salsa Brava (Costa Rica's biggest break). It has lefts and rights, which both break close to the steep beach. Conditions are usually best from December to March, and early in the day before the wind picks up.

Jaguar Centro de Rescate
WILDLIFE RESERVE

(☎ 2750-0710; www.jaguarrescue.com; Playa Chiquita; adult/child under 10yr US$20/free; ⊙ tours 9:30am & 11:30am Mon-Sat; 🖐) ⏀ Named in honor of its original resident, this well-run wildlife-rescue center in Playa Chiquita now focuses mostly on other animals, including raptors, sloths and monkeys. Founded by zoologist Encar and her partner, Sandro, a herpetologist, the center rehabilitates orphaned, injured and rescued animals for reintroduction into the wild whenever possible. Volunteer opportunities are available with a three-week minimum commitment.

🏃 Activities

Breaking on the reef that hugs the village is the famed Salsa Brava, a shallow break that is also one of the country's most infamous waves. It's a tricky ride – if you lose it, the waves will plow you straight into the reef – and definitely not for beginners. Salsa Brava offers both rights and lefts, although the right is usually faster. Conditions are best with an easterly swell.

Waves in the area generally peak from November to March, and there is a surfing miniseason from June to July. From late March to May, and in September and October, the sea is at its calmest.

Several surf schools around town charge US$40 to US$50 for two hours of lessons. Stands around town rent boards from about US$20 per day.

Caribbean Surf School
SURFING

(☎ 8357-7703) Lessons by super-smiley surf instructor Hershel Lewis, widely considered the best teacher in the town. Recently he also started teaching paddle boarding.

One Love Surf School
SURFING

(☎ 8719-4654; jewell420@hotmail.com) Julie Hickey and her surfing sons Cedric and Solomon specialize in surf lessons, massage school and yoga classes for women and children.

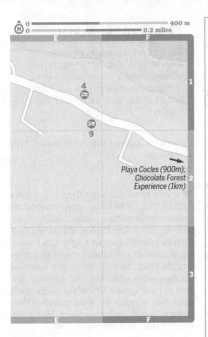

Puerto Viejo de Talamanca

Activities, Courses & Tours
1 Caribbean Surf School........................C2
2 Terraventuras B2

Sleeping
3 Cabinas Tropical.................................D2
4 Escape Caribeño................................E1
5 Hostel Pagalú C3
6 Hotel Pura Vida..................................C3
7 Jacaranda Hotel & Jungle
   Garden..C2
8 Kaya's Place A3
9 La Ruka Hostel E1
10 Lionfish Hostel B2

Eating
11 Bread & Chocolate C2
12 Café Rico..C2
13 Como en mi Casa Art Café................B2
14 De Gustibus D1
15 Laszlo's..D1
16 Sel & Sucre......................................B2
17 Soda Shekiná....................................C3

Drinking & Nightlife
18 Lazy Mon..C1
19 Salsa Brava......................................D1

Shopping
20 Lulu Berlu Gallery C2
21 Organic Market C2

Playa Cocles (900m);
Chocolate Forest
Experience (1km)

Tours

Chocolate Forest Experience   TOUR
(8836-8930, 8341-2034; www.caribeanscr.
com/chocolate-tour; Playa Cocles; guided tours
US$26; tours 10am Mon, 10am & 2pm Tue &
Thu, 2pm Fri & Sat) Playa Cocles–based
chocolate producer Caribeans leads tours
of its sustainably managed cacao forest and
chocolate-creation lab, accompanied by
gourmet chocolate tastings.

Terraventuras   TOUR
(2750-0750; www.terraventuras.com; 7am-
7pm) Offers overnights in Tortuguero, a shaman tour, and a Caribbean cooking class,
along with the usual local tours. Also has its
very own 23-platform, 2.1km-long canopy
tour (US$58), complete with Tarzan swing.

Sleeping

Hostel Pagalú   HOSTEL $
(2750-1930; www.pagalu.com; dm/s/d
US$12/30/33, s/d without bathroom US$25/28;
P) This peaceful, contemporary hostel offers a break from Puerto Viejo's party scene.
Clean, airy dorms and doubles abound in
niceties, including large lockers, charging
stations for MP3 players and bunk-side
reading lamps. There's a shared, open-air

kitchen and a quiet lounge with tables and
hammocks, plus a supply of spring water for
refilling your own reusable bottle.

Cabinas Tropical   CABINA $
(2750-2064; www.cabinastropical.com; s/d/tr
US$40/45/55; P) Ten spacious rooms –
decorated with varnished wood and shiny
tiles – surround a primly landscaped garden
on the eastern end of town. The comfortable quarters are just part of the appeal:
biologist owner Rolf Blancke leads excellent
hikes, birdwatching excursions, and tours
of a nearby fruit and spice farm (per person
US$20 to US$65, minimum two people).

Jacaranda Hotel & Jungle Garden   CABINA $
(2750-0069; www.cabinasjacaranda.net; s/d/
tr/q from US$30/45/50/55; P) In a bloom-
ing garden intersected by mosaic walkways,
this place near the soccer field has 15 simple
wood *cabinas* with spotless ceramic-tile
floors and murals of flowers, along with a
small, shared kitchen and patio. Yoga classes
are available, and the onsite spa offers massage and bodywork.

Hotel Pura Vida
HOTEL $

(☑ 2750-0002; www.hotel-puravida.com; s/d/tr US$55/55/65, without bathroom US$40/45/55; P ☎) This inn opposite the soccer field doubles as a Spanish school and offers solidly midrange amenities. Ten breezy, immaculate rooms come clad in polished wood, bright linens and ceramic-tile floors; many have charming views of the surrounding village. Showers are heated with solar power and there's a lounge with easy chairs and hammocks. Breakfasts, snacks and chilled beers are available.

La Ruka Hostel
HOSTEL $

(☑ 2750-0617; www.facebook.com/laruka.hostel; dm US$10, r with/without bathroom US$45/30; ☎) If the cute painting of the surfing dog doesn't lure you in, the friendly welcome from owners Dannie and Dave will. Just east of town, this hostel has spacious common areas up front, a shared kitchen out back, plus dorm space and a couple of private rooms with shared bath upstairs.

Lionfish Hostel
HOSTEL $

(☑ 2750-2143; www.facebook.com/thelionfish hostel; dm US$7-10, r US$25) Started by local surfers, this new hostel appeals to on-the-go types looking for like-minded adventurers. The dorms are basic and sometimes a bit stuffy, but it's a small price to pay for the bonfires and cookouts that take place out back on weekends. At the time of research, a Jacuzzi was under construction.

Escape Caribeño
BUNGALOW $$

(☑ 2750-0103; www.escapecaribeno.com; s/d/tr garden view US$70/75/85, ocean view US$90/95/105; P ✳ @ ☎) Charming owners keep these 14 spick-and-span bungalows with spotless bathrooms, some on the beach side and others in the garden across the road, 500m east of town toward Playa Cocles. More expensive units are in lovely Caribbean-style structures with stained-glass shower stalls; all units have stocked minifridges, cable TV, fans and hammocks. Breakfast (US$5 to US$9 extra) is also available.

Kaya's Place
GUESTHOUSE $$

(☑ 2750-0690; www.kayasplace.com; s/d without bathroom US$40/43, d/ste US$55/87; P ✳ ☎) Across the road from the beach at Puerto Viejo's western edge, this funky guesthouse has 17 snug, basic rooms, ranging from dim units with shared cool-water showers to more spacious garden rooms with air-con and private bathroom. The property also includes a bungalow, a private cabin and three apartments.

> ### ⓘ BIKE TO THE BEACH
>
> A bicycle is a fine way to get around town, and pedaling out to beaches east of Puerto Viejo is one of the highlights of this corner of Costa Rica. You'll find rentals all over town for about US$5 per day.

✗ Eating

★ Como en mi Casa Art Café
CAFE $

(☑ 6069-6337, 6069-6319; www.comoenmicasa costarica.wordpress.com; cakes US$4, mains US$5-10; ⊙ 7am-4pm Thu-Tue; ☑) Owned by a friendly bohemian expat couple, this charming vegetarian cafe makes everything from scratch, from the jams to the hot sauces to the gluten-free pancakes. The walls are covered in local art and 10% of the coffee profit helps buy supplies for local schools. Oddly enough, you'll find this place above the butcher shop in the center of town.

★ Bread & Chocolate
BREAKFAST $

(☑ 2750-0723; cakes US$4, meals US$6-9; ⊙ 6:30am-6:30pm Wed-Sat, to 2:30pm Sun; ☑) Ever had a completely homemade PB&J (bread, peanut butter and jelly all made from scratch)? That and more can be yours at this dream of a gluten-lover's cafe.

Café Rico
CAFE $

(☑ 2750-0510; caferico.puertoviejo@yahoo.com; breakfast US$3-8; ⊙ 5:30am-1pm; ☎) Home to some of Puerto Viejo's best home-roasted coffee, this cozy garden cafe serves breakfast accompanied by a plethora of other services: free wi-fi, a book exchange, a laundry, and rentals of bikes and snorkeling gear.

Guests who stay in the attached *cabinas* get laundry and rentals free. A room is US$30 to US$50 with a discount for three or more nights.

Soda Shekiná
CARIBBEAN $

(☑ 2750-0549; mains US$7-12; ⊙ 11:30am-9pm Wed-Mon) Delicious traditional Caribbean home cooking can be found at this back-street eatery with wooden slab tables on an open-air terrace, just northwest of the soccer field. Everything is served with coconut rice and beans, salad and caramelized fried bananas.

Sel & Sucre
FRENCH $

(☑2750-0636; meals US$4-10; ☺noon-9:30pm; 🎵) Dark coffee and fresh-fruit smoothies offer a nice complement to the menu of crepes, both savory and sweet. These delights are all prepared by the one and only chef Sebastien Flageul, meaning service can be slow. But it's worth the wait.

At research time, a new hostel was underway upstairs.

De Gustibus
BAKERY $

(☑2756-8397; www.facebook.com/degustibusbakery; baked goods from US$1; ☺6:45am-6pm) This bakery on Puerto Viejo's main drag draws a devoted following with its fabulous focaccia (US$1 a slice), along with slices of pizza, apple strudels, profiteroles and all sorts of other sweet and savory goodies. Eat in, or grab a snack for the beach.

★Laszlo's
SEAFOOD $$

(mains US$16; ☺6-9:30pm) Whaddya get when you take a champion sport fisherman, born and raised in Transylvania, and transplant him to Puerto Viejo by way of New Jersey? Answer: an amazing, eclectic eatery with no sign and no menu that only opens when owner Laszlo catches enough fish. The day's catch comes with garlic and parsley, homemade French fries and grilled veggies. Yum.

🍷 Drinking & Nightlife

Lazy Mon
CLUB

(☺12:30pm-2:30am) Puerto Viejo's most dependable spot for live music, Lazy Mon draws big crowds with reggae at happy hour (4pm to 7pm), then keeps things hopping with more of the same throughout the evening. The ping-pong and pool tables are popular gathering spots, and fire shows take place every Thursday night.

Salsa Brava
BAR

(☑2750-0241; ☺11am-3am) Specializing in fresh seafood and open-grill cooking, this popular spot is the perfect end-of-day cocktail stop – hit happy hour from 4pm to 6pm and you'll also catch two-for-one mojitos for sunset overlooking the Salsa Brava surf break. On Friday and Sunday it brings in DJs for the popular reggae nights.

🛍 Shopping

Lulu Berlu Gallery
CRAFTS

(☑2750-0394; ☺9am-9pm) On a backstreet parallel to the main road, this gallery carries folk art, clothing, jewelry, ceramics, embroidered purses and mosaic mirrors, among many other one-of-a-kind, locally made items. Out back, the popular restaurant Congo Reef opened recently.

Organic Market
MARKET

(☺6:30-11am Sat) Don't miss the weekly organic market, when area vendors and growers sell snacks typical of the region, particularly tropical produce and chocolate. Arrive before 9am or the best stuff will be long gone.

ℹ Information

Banco de Costa Rica (☺9am-4pm Mon-Fri) Two ATMs work on Plus and Visa systems, dispensing both colones and dollars. Sometimes they run out of cash on weekends, and they can be finicky; if one machine won't let you withdraw cash, try the other.

Banco Nacional (☺9am-4pm Mon-Fri, ATM 6am-10pm daily) Just off main street near the bridge into town. Dispenses colones only.

Costa Rica Way (☑2750-3031; www.costaricaway.info; ☺8am-6pm) Has internet access and reliable information on local tours and activities.

Pipens Internet (☑2750-0486; per hr US$2; ☺9am-8pm) Desktops and wireless access. Right next to the bus station.

Puerto Viejo Satellite (www.puertoviejosatellite.com) has information on local lodgings, eating and activities.

DANGERS & ANNOYANCES

Be aware that though the use of marijuana (and harder stuff) is common in Puerto Viejo, it is nonetheless illegal.

As in other popular tourist centers, theft can be an issue. Stay aware, use your hotel safe, and

COSTA RICA PUERTO VIEJO DE TALAMANCA

BUSES FROM PUERTO VIEJO

DESTINATION	COST (US$)	DURATION	FREQUENCY (DAILY)
Bribrí/Sixaola	1.50/3.35	30/90min	roughly hourly 6:30am-7:30pm
Cahuita/Puerto Limón	1.50/3.60	30/90min	roughly hourly 5:30am-6:30pm
Manzanillo	1.30	30min	every 2hr 6:45am-7:45pm (less frequently on weekends)
San José	10.90	5hr	7:30am, 9am, 11am & 4pm daily, plus 1pm Sun

if staying outside of town avoid walking alone late at night.

❶ Getting There & Away

All public buses arrive and depart from the bus stop along the beach road in central Puerto Viejo. The ticket office is diagonally across the street.

Sixaola

POP 11,061

This is the end of the road – literally. Bumpy tarmac leads to an old railroad bridge over the Río Sixaola that serves as the border crossing into Panama. Like most border towns, Sixaola is hardly scenic: it's an extravaganza of dingy bars and roadside stalls selling rubber boots.

There's no good reason to stay in Sixaola, but if you get stuck, head for safe, clean **Cabinas Sanchez** (🏠 2754-2105; d/tr US$20/30; 🌐).

The bus station is just north of the border crossing, one block east of the main drag.

Buses to either San José (US$13.15, six hours, 6am, 8am, 10am and 3pm) or Puerto Limón (US$6.30, three hours, hourly from 5am to 7pm) all stop at Bribrí and Cahuita.

There are also regular buses to Puerto Viejo de Talamanca (US$3.25, one hour, hourly between 5:30am and 7:30pm Monday through Saturday, every two hours on Sunday).

For details on the border crossing, see Border Crossings (p619).

ARENAL & NORTHERN LOWLANDS

You know about the region's main attraction: that now-dormant volcano, surrounded by old lava fields, bubbling hot springs and a stunning lake. Venture further onto the wild rivers and into the tropical jungle of the northern lowlands and you will discover real-life Costa Rica, where agricultural commerce and ecological conservation converge as a work in green progress. Stretching from the borderlands of Nicaragua south to the Cordillera de Tilarán, *fincas* (farms) of banana, sugarcane and pineapple roll across humid plains. Community tourism lives and breathes here, creating added revenue for a historically farm-based economy. You can spot a macaw in the wild, paddle into roaring rapids and cruise inky lagoons, all with

lifelong resident guides, then nest in lodges that double as private rainforest reserves. When the tourist hordes get you down, make your way here for a refreshing blast of rural realism and an invigorating dose of wild beauty.

La Fortuna & Volcán Arenal

Whether you approach from the west or from the east, the drive into the Arenal area is spectacular. Coming from Tilarán in the west, the paved road hugs the northern bank of Laguna de Arenal. The lake and forest vistas are riveting, but pay attention to your driving and watch for potholes and coati jams. On either side of the road – up the green slope and down on the lakeside – lovely inns, hip coffeehouses and eccentric galleries appear like pictures in a pop-up book. Approaching from Ciudad Quesada (San Carlos), you'll have Volcán Platanar as the backdrop, as the road winds through this green, river-rich agrarian region, passing through prosperous towns bright with bougainvillea. If the weather cooperates, the resolute peak of Arenal looms in front of you.

The volcano may be dormant, but plenty of adventure still awaits you here. There are trails to hike, waterfalls to rappel down, and innumerable sloths to spot. No matter what your preferred method of exploring – hiking, biking, horseback riding, zip lining – you can do it here. And when your body says it's had enough, you can ease into a volcano-heated pool to soak your aches and pains away.

◎ Sights

★ **Parque Nacional Volcán Arenal**   PARK
(🏠 2461-8499; adult/child US$15/5; ◎ 8am-4pm) From 1968 until 2010, Volcán Arenal was an ever-active and awe-striking natural wonder, producing menacing ash columns, massive explosions and streams of glowing molten rock almost daily. While the fiery night views are gone for now, this mighty mountain is still a worthy destination. Part of the Área de Conservación Arenal, the park is rugged and varied, with about 15km of well-marked trails that follow old lava flows. Hikers routinely spot sloths, coatis, howler monkeys, white-faced capuchins and even anteaters.

Parque Nacional Volcán Arenal is west of La Fortuna. The main park entrance is on the road to El Castillo (turn off the main road 13km west of town). It's easiest to reach the park by car or on a tour. Otherwise, take any bus to Tilarán and ask the driver to let you off at the turnoff.

Catarata Río Fortuna   WATERFALL
(www.cataratariofortuna.com; admission US$12; ☺8am-5pm) You can glimpse the sparkling 70m ribbon of clear water that pours through a sheer canyon of dark volcanic rock arrayed in bromeliads and ferns with minimal sweat equity. But it's worth the climb down and out to see it from the jungle floor. Though it's dangerous to dive beneath the thundering falls, a series of perfect swimming holes with spectacular views tiles the canyon in aquamarine. This is also the trailhead for the difficult hike to Cerro Chato.

🏃 Activities

Hiking
Although it's no longer active, Volcán Arenal is the big draw here. There is a well-marked trail system within the park, and several private reserves on its outskirts. Waterfalls, lava flows and crater lakes are all worthy destinations, which you can reach without a guide.

Cerro Chato Trail   HIKING
(www.arenalobservatorylodge.com; Arenal Observatory Lodge; day pass per person US$10) The ultimate hike in the national park, the Cerro Chato Trail meanders through pasture before climbing steeply into patches of virgin growth, reaching into misty sky. The trail crests Cerro Chato, Arenal's dormant partner, and ends in a 1100m-high volcanic lake that is perfect for a dip. The hike is only 8km round trip, but it will take two to three hours each way.

Arenal 1968   HIKING
(☎2462-1212; www.arenal1968.com; admission US$12, mountain bike rental US$45; ☺7am-10pm) Right next to the park entrance, you'll find a private network of trails along the original 1968 lava flow. There's a *mirador* (lookout) which on a clear day offers a picture-perfect volcano view. Mountain bikes are available to ride on these trails. It's located 1.2km from the highway turnoff to the park, just before the ranger station.

Hot Springs
Beneath La Fortuna the lava is still curdling and heating countless bubbling springs. There are free, natural hot springs in the area that any local can point you toward. If you're after a more comfortable experience, consider one of the area's resorts.

★Eco Termales Hot Springs   HOT SPRING
(☎2479-8787; www.ecotermalesfortuna.cr; admission US$36; ☺10am, 1pm or 5pm; 🅿) 🚲 Everything from the natural circulation systems in the pools to the soft lighting is understated, luxurious and romantic at this gated, reservations-only complex about 4.5km northwest of town. Lush greenery surrounds the walking paths that cut through these gorgeous grounds. Only 100 visitors are admitted at a time, to maintain the ambiance of serenity and seclusion.

Paradise Hot Springs   HOT SPRING
(www.paradisehotspringscr.com; adult/child US$23/15; ☺11am-9pm) This low-key place has one lovely, large pool with a waterfall and several smaller, secluded pools, surrounded by lush vegetation and tropical blooms. The pools vary in temperature (up to 40°C), some with hydromassage. Paradise is much simpler than the other larger spring settings, but there are fewer people, and your experience is bound to be more relaxing and more romantic.

👉 Tours

★Don Olivo Chocolate Tour   ECOTOUR
(☎6110-3556, 2469-1371; www.facebook.com/tourdechocolatedonolivo; tour US$25; ☺8am, 10am, 1pm & 3pm; 🅿) Let Don Olivo or his son show you around their family *finca,* showing off their sugar cane, oranges and – of course – cocoa plants. The process of turning this funny fruit into the decadent dessert that we all know and love is truly fascinating. Bonus: lots of taste-testing along the way!

Bike Arenal   CYCLING
(☎2479-7150; www.bikearenal.com; Av 319 A, Rte 702; rental per day/week US$25/150, half-/full-day tour US$85/135; ☺7am-6pm) This outfit offers a variety of bike tours for all levels of rider, including a popular ride around the lake and a half-day ride to El Castillo. You can also do versions of these rides on your own. Make advance arrangements for rental and an English-speaking bike mechanic will bring the bicycle to you.

Wildlife Tours

Arenal Oasis   BIRDWATCHING, NIGHT WALK
(☎2479-9526; www.arenaloasis.com; night/bird walks US$40/55; ☺5:45pm) The Rojas Bonilla

family has created this wild frog sanctuary, home to some 28 species of croaking critters. The frogs are just the beginning of this night walk, which continues into the rainforest to see what other nocturnal animals await. If you're more of a morning person, they also do a bird-watching tour. Reservations recommended. Located 3km from La Fortuna's centre; hotel pick-up costs US$10.

Canoa Aventura   CANOEING
(☑2479-8200; www.canoa-aventura.com; canoe trip US$67; ⊙6:30am-9:30pm) 🖊 This long-standing family-run company specializes in canoe and float trips led by bilingual naturalist guides. Most are geared toward wildlife- and bird-watching.

Horseback Riding

Arenal Wilberth Stables   HORSEBACK RIDING
(☑2479-7522; www.arenalwilberthstable.com; per person US$65; ⊙7:30am, 11am & 2:30pm) Three-hour horseback-riding tours depart from these stables, at the foot of Arenal. The ride takes in forest and farmland, as well as lake and volcano views. The stables are opposite the entrance to the national park, but there's an office in town next to Arenal Resort Hostel.

Alberto's Horse Tours   HORSEBACK RIDING
(☑2479-7711, 2479-9043; www.facebook.com/albertoshorses; per person US$85; ⊙8:30am-1:30pm) Alberto and his son lead popular horseback-riding trips to the Catarata de la Fortuna. It's a three- or four-hour trip, but you'll spend about an hour off your horse, when you hike down to the falls for a swim or a photo op. Beautiful setting, beautiful horses. Cash only.

Canopy Tours & Canyoning

Arenal Paraíso Canopy Tours   CANOPY TOUR
(☑2479-1100; www.arenalparaiso.com; tours US$45; ⊙8am-5pm; 🖥) A dozen cables zip across the canyon of the Río Arenal, giving a unique perspective on two waterfalls, as well as the rainforest canopy. Also includes admission to the resort's swimming pool and 13 thermal pools, which are hidden among the rocks and greenery on the hillside

Sky Adventures   CANOPY TOUR
(☑2479-4100; www.skyadventures.travel; adult/child SkyTrek US$77/53, Sky Tram US$44/37, Sky Walk US$37/26, Sky Limit US$77/53; ⊙7:30am-4pm) El Castillo's entry in the canopy-tour category has zip lines (Sky Trek), a floating gondola (Sky Tram) and a series of hanging bridges (Sky Walk). It's safe and well run,

and visitors tend to leave smiling. A unique combo, Sky River Drift combines a zip line with tree-climbing (and jumping) and river tubing. There's also mountain biking on the property.

PureTrek Canyoning   CANYONING
(☑2479-1313, US toll free 1-866-569-5723; www.puretrekcanyoning.com; 4hr incl transportation & lunch US$100; ⊙7am-10pm; 🖥) 🖊 The reputable PureTrek leads guided rappels down three waterfalls, one of which is 50m high. Also included: rock climbing and 'monkey drop,' which is actually a zip line with a rappel at the end of it. High marks for attention to safety and high-quality gear. It gets some big groups, but does a good job keeping things moving.

Check-in at PureTrek headquarters, located in a tree house 6km west of town.

🛏 Sleeping

Sleeping Indian Guesthouse   GUESTHOUSE $
(☑2479-8431, 8446-9149; sleepingindianguesthouse@gmail.com; Av Fort; d US$45; 🛜) Ethnic insensitivities aside, this is a delightful 2nd-story guesthouse just north of the church. Six sweet fan-cooled rooms have lofty ceilings, tile floors, colorful paint jobs and tile windows. The spacious common area includes a fully equipped kitchen, two balconies with volcano views, and a homey living room, well stocked with books, games and funky artwork. The live-in owner is a gracious host.

Arenal Hostel Resort   HOSTEL $
(☑2479-9222; www.arenalhostelresort.com; Av Central; dm/s/d/tr/q US$17/50/60/80/90; P🗙@🛜🏊) 🖊 Offering the best of hostel and resort, this welcoming place is arranged around a landscaped garden, complete with hammocks, small pool, party-place bar and volcano view. All rooms are clean, spacious and air-conditioned, with en suite bathrooms. A word of warning: a recurring complaint is that reservations were 'lost' or clients were 'bumped' to Hostel Backpackers La Fortuna.

Arenal Backpackers Resort   HOSTEL $
(☑2479-7000; www.arenalbackpackersresort.com; Av Central; dm US$14-18, tents s/d US$30/40, s/tw/d US$55/60/70; P🗙@🛜🏊) The original hostel-resort in La Fortuna, this self-proclaimed 'five-star hostel' with volcano views is pretty cushy. Sleep on orthopedic mattresses and take hot showers in your en suite bathroom (even in the dorms). Somewhere between dormitory and hotel is the

covered tent city: raised tents have air mattress and electricity (but no proper walls, so you'll hear your neighbors loud and clear).

Hostel Backpackers La Fortuna HOSTEL $
(☑ 2479-9129; www.hostelbackpackerslafortuna.com; dm/s/d/tr/q US$15/45/50/70/85; P✴@🛜🏊) This is the most 'grown-up' hostel in town. The rooms are done in whites and beiges, and the courtyard is lush, lovely and strung with hammocks. Guests are invited to go down the street to the sister property, Arenal Hostel Resort, to join the party (swimming pool, bar) and then to return here for quiet, comfort and a good night's sleep.

La Choza Inn INN $
(☑ 2479-9361; www.lachozainnhostel.com; Av Fort btwn Calles 2 & 4; dm US$10, s/d US$35/50, air-con US$10, all incl breakfast; P✴@🛜) With all the budget 'resorts' in town, it's refreshing to find a charming, old-fashioned, family-run inn, where kids and puppies interact with the guests and facilities are basic but the staff is always accommodating. Take your pick from the dark, palm-wood dorms or the attractive doubles boasting Arenal views from the balconies.

Hotel Monte Real HOTEL $$
(☑ 2479-9357; www.monterealhotel.com; Av Arenal btwn Calles 3 & 5; r US$85-95, ste US$110, all incl breakfast; P✴🛜🏊) A smart, modern motel property on the edge of town, next to the Río Burio. This excellent location combines the convenience of town with the nature and rusticity of the forest – meaning lovely gardens and wildlife at your doorstep. Spacious rooms have Spanish-tile floors, stained-wood ceilings and sliding glass doors, some with private balcony.

La Fortuna Suites GUESTHOUSE $$
(☑ 8577-1555; www.lafortunasuites.com; d/ste from US$55/95, all incl breakfast; P✴🛜) Here's a chance to luxuriate in some high-end amenities at midrange prices. We're talking high-thread-count sheets and memory-foam mattresses, custom-made furniture and flat-screen TVs, gourmet breakfast on the balcony and killer views. Despite all these perks, guests agree that the thing that makes this place special is the hospitality shown by the hosts. It's 300m west of Parque Central.

🍴 Eating

Rainforest Café CAFE $
(☑ 2479-7239; Calle 1 btwn Avs Central & Arenal; mains US$4-6; ⊗7am-8:30pm; 🛜🅿) We know

it's bad form to start with dessert, but the irresistible sweets at this popular spot are beautiful to behold and delicious to devour. The savory menu features tasty burritos, *casados*, sandwiches etc. There's also a full menu of hot and cold coffee, including some tempting specialty drinks (Mono Loco = coffee, banana, milk, chocolate, cinnamon).

La Central CAFE $
(☑ 2479-8080; cnr Calle 2 & Av Central; breakfast US$3, mains US$4-8; ⊗8am-6pm Wed-Mon; 🛜🅿) A breezy terrace, filled with greenery and art, this is a perfect stop for breakfast or lunch. The place touts natural healthy food, and you'll find lots of vegetarian options – fresh, hearty salads, a tasty veggie burger, and a Middle Eastern spread with hummus and *baba ganoush*. Come later in the day for fresh fruit-juice cocktails and occasional live-music acts.

Soda Viquez SODA $
(☑ 2479-7133; cnr Calle 1 & Av Arenal; mains US$6-10; ⊗7am-10pm; 🅿) Travelers adore the 'local flavor' that's served up at Soda Viquez (in all senses of the expression). It's a super-friendly spot, offering tasty *típico*, especially *casados*, rice dishes and fresh fruit *batidos*. Prices are reasonable, portions ample.

Chifa La Familia Feliz FUSION $$
(☑ 8469-6327; Calle 2; mains US$8-12; ⊗11am-10pm; 🛜🅿🍴) If you're looking for a change of taste – a *real* change from *casados* and pizza – check this out. In case you didn't know, *Chifa* means 'Chinese food' in Peruvian-Spanish. So what we have here is Peruvian Chinese food, which is something special indeed. The chef goes out of his way to welcome and satisfy all comers.

Anch'io Ristorante & Pizzeria ITALIAN $$
(☑ 2479-7024; Av Central; mains US$10-18; ⊗noon-10pm; P🛜🍴) If you have a hankering for pizza, you can't do better than Anch'io, where the crust is crispy thin, the toppings are plentiful, and the pie is cooked in a wood-fired oven. Start yourself off with a traditional antipasto. Accompany with cold beer or a bottle of red. Add super service and pleasant patio seating. And you've got yourself a winner.

🍷 Drinking & Nightlife

El Establo BAR
(☑ 2479-7675; Calle 2; ⊗5pm-2am Wed-Sat) La Fortuna's raucous *sendero* bar with an attached disco fronts the bull ring and attracts

an ever-enthusiastic local following. The age demographic here ranges from 18 to 88. That's almost always a good thing.

ⓘ Information

Centro Medico Sanar (☏2479-9420; cnr Calle 5 & Av Fort; ☺8am-8:30pm) Medical consultation, ambulance services and pharmacy.

Correos de Costa Rica (Av Fort; ☺8am-5:30pm Mon-Fri, 7:30am-noon Sat)

Servicios Contables Mario Esquivel (☏2460-8989, 2479-7027; www.secmesa.com; Calle 1; ☺24hr) Located in the Hotel Las Colinas building, this private clinic is open 24/7 and has English-speaking staff.

ⓘ Getting There & Away

BUS

The **bus terminal** (Av Arenal) is on the river road. Keep an eye on your bags, particularly on the weekend San José run.

Monteverde (US$4, six to eight hours) Take the early bus to Tilarán, where you'll have to wait a few hours for the onward bus to Santa Elena.

San José (Auto-Transportes San José–San Carlos) US$5, two hours, departs 12:45pm and 2:45pm. Alternatively, take the bus to Ciudad Quesada, from where there are frequent departures to San José.

Tilarán With connection to Monteverde (Auto-Transportes Tilarán, departs from the Parque Central) US$3, 3½ hours, departs 8am and 4:30pm.

TAXI-BOAT-TAXI

The fastest route between Monteverde–Santa Elena and La Fortuna is the taxi-boat-taxi combo (formerly known as jeep-boat-jeep, which sounds sexy but it was the same thing). It is actually a minivan with the requisite yellow 'turismo' tattoo, which takes you to Laguna de Arenal, meeting a boat that crosses the lake, where a 4WD taxi on the other side continues to Monteverde. It's a terrific transportation option

that can be arranged through almost any hotel or tour operator (US$25 to US$35, four hours).

This is increasingly becoming the primary transportation between La Fortuna and Monteverde as it's incredibly scenic and reasonably priced.

Tilarán

POP 7300

Near the southwestern end of Laguna de Arenal, the small town of Tilarán has a laid-back, middle-class charm thanks to its long-running status as a regional ranching center. Nowadays, it's also the main commercial center for the growing community of expats that resides along the shores of Laguna de Arenal.

Most visitors, however, are just passing through, traveling between La Fortuna and Monteverde. Because it's situated on the slopes of the Cordillera de Tilarán, this little hub is a much cooler alternative (in climate and atmosphere) than the towns along the Interamericana.

🛏 Sleeping & Eating

Hotel Tilarán   HOTEL $
(☏2695-5043; s/d without bathroom US$14/22, with bathroom US$20/26; ℗) As cheap as they come, rooms are tiny and cleanish. If you can get one of the rooms toward the back, this is a decent budget choice on the western side of Parque Central. There's an appealing retro bar on the street front.

Hotel Guadalupe   HOTEL $$
(☏2695-5943; www.hotelguadalupe.co.cr; s/d incl breakfast US$40/60; ℗❀🐕🏊) This modern hotel attracts traveling business types, who make themselves at home in simple rooms, dressed up with jewel tones and tiled floors. Service is friendly and efficient. There is a decent restaurant onsite, as well as swimming pool, kiddie pool and hot tub.

BUSES FROM TILARÁN

DESTINATION	COMPANY	COST (US$)	DURATION	FREQUENCY
Cañas	Transporte Villana	1	30min	7 daily, 5am-3:30pm
La Fortuna	Transporte Tilarán-San Carlos	5	3½hr	7am, 12:30pm
Puntarenas	Empresa Maravilla	4	2hr	6am, 1pm
San José		7	4hr	5am, 7am, 9:30am & 2pm daily; 5pm Saturday and Sunday only
Santa Elena/Monteverde	TransMonteverde	3	2½hr	7am, 4pm

WORTH A TRIP

CAÑO NEGRO

The **Refugio Nacional de Vida Silvestre Caño Negro** (☎2471-1309; www.ligambiente.com; adult/child US$5/1; ⊙8am-4pm) is a remote, 102-sq-km refuge that has long lured anglers seeking that elusive 18kg snook, and birdwatchers hoping to glimpse rare waterfowl. During the dry season water levels drop, concentrating the birds (and fish) in photogenically (or tasty) close quarters. From January to March, when migratory birds land in large numbers, avian density is most definitely world class.

Thanks to improved roads, tour operators are now able to offer relatively inexpensive trips to Caño Negro from all over the country. However, you don't need them to explore the river. It's much more intriguing and rewarding to rent some wheels (or hop on a bus), navigate the rutted road into the rural flat lands and hire a local guide right in the center of Caño Negro village. It's also a lot cheaper, and it puts money directly into the hands of locals, thus encouraging communities in the area to protect wildlife.

Getting There & Away

Buses arrive and depart from the terminal half a block west of Parque Central. Be aware that Sunday-afternoon buses to San José can sell out as much as a day in advance.

Los Chiles

POP 5550

Seventy kilometers north of Muelle on a smooth, paved road through the sugarcane, and just 6km south of the Nicaraguan border at Las Tablillas, lies the sweltering farming and fishing town of Los Chiles. Arranged with dilapidated grace around a ragged soccer field and along the unmanicured banks of the leisurely Río Frío, the humid lowland village is charming by border-town standards (sex workers and foreboding 'import-export' types notwithstanding). It was originally settled by merchants and fisherfolk who worked on the nearby Río San Juan, much of which forms the Nicaragua–Costa Rica border.

With the opening of the new border crossing at Las Tablillas, international travelers are no longer obligated to pass through Los Chiles, though the scenic boat ride across the border is a pleasant way to go. This is also a good base for enjoying the water route to Caño Negro.

Sleeping & Eating

With the new border crossing at Las Tablillas, it's usually possible to cruise right by Los Chiles without spending the night. If that doesn't work for you, you'll find a limited selection of hotels in town.

Hotel y Cabinas Carolina CABINA $
(☎2471-1151; r from US$30; P❄📶) Not your typical border-town accommodations. This friendly, family-run option gets rave reviews for attentive staff, spotless rooms and excellent local food. It's near the main highway, just a few blocks south of the bus station.

Getting There & Away

BOAT

The boat docks are located about 1km west of the bus terminal. Regular boat transportation is limited to quick shuttles across the Nicaraguan border (US$10 to US$12). With the opening of the land border at Las Tablillas, this river border is pretty sleepy. Boats depart only once a day (supposedly around 1pm). Before hopping on the boat to Nicaragua, you need to stop at the immigration office, across the street from Hotel Tulipán.

BUS

All buses arrive and leave from the terminal behind Soda Pamela, near the intersection of Hwy 35. **Chilsaca** (☎2460-1886; www.chilsaca.com) has 16 daily buses to Ciudad Quesada (US$2.25, two hours) from 4:30am to 6pm; you can transfer here for La Fortuna. Autotransportes San Carlos (p531) has two daily buses to San José (US$6, five hours), departing at 5am and 3pm. There are also three departures to Caño Negro (US$4, 2½ hours), at 5am, 2pm and 5pm. Timetables are subject to change so always check ahead. For information about the border crossing, see Border Crossings (p618).

Valle de Sarapiquí

This flat, steaming stretch of *finca*-dotted lowlands was once part of the United Fruit Company's vast banana holdings. Harvests were carried from the plantations down to Puerto Viejo de Sarapiquí, where they were shipped downriver on boats destined for North America. In 1880 a railway connected rural Costa Rica with the port of Puerto Limón, and Puerto Viejo de Sarapiquí became a backwater. Although it's never managed to recover its former glory as a transport route, the river again shot to prominence as one of the premier destinations in Costa Rica for kayakers and rafters. With the Parque Nacional Braulio Carrillo as its backyard, this is one of the best regions for wildlife-watching, especially considering how easy it is to get here.

🏃 Activities & Tours

White-Water Rafting

Aguas Bravas   RAFTING
(☑ 2766-6525; www.aguasbravascr.com; rafting trips US$75, safari float US$65; ⊗9am-5:30pm) This excellent and well-established rafting outfit has set up shop along the Río Sarapiquí (complete with onsite hostel). Aguas Bravas has two tours on offer: take a gentle safari float to spot birds, iguanas, caimans and other wildlife, or sign up to splash through 14km of 'extreme rapids' on the San Miguel section of the river.

Aventuras del Sarapiquí   RAFTING
(☑ 2766-6768; www.sarapiqui.com; river trips US$60-80) A highly recommended outfitter, offering adventures in land, air and water. Beside white-water rafting (both Class II and III/IV trips), you can also fly through the air on a 14-cable canopy tour. Or, stay down to earth with horseback riding, mountain biking or good old-fashioned hiking.

Sarapiquí Outdoor Center   RAFTING, KAYAKING
(☑ 2761-1123; www.costaricaraft.com; 2/4hr rafting trip US$65/90, guided kayak trips from US$90) Here is the local paddling authority. In addition to its own rafting excursions, it offers kayak rental, lessons and clinics. Indie paddlers should check in for up-to-date river information. If you need somewhere to sleep before you hit the water, you can crash in the simple rooms or pitch a tent here.

Tropical Duckies   KAYAKING
(☑ 8760-3787, 2761-0095; www.tropicalduckies.com; adult/child US$65/50; ⊗departs 9am & 1pm) Highly recommended for beginners and families, this outfit does tours and instruction in inflatable kayaks, which allow for a fun paddle even when the river is low. Paddle on flat moving water or Class III rapids (or somewhere in between). Reserve ahead.

Boat Tours
The boat traffic at the dock in Puerto Viejo is no longer transporting commuters who have somewhere to go. Nowadays, it's used primarily for tourist boats, which cruise the Ríos Sarapiquí and Puerto Viejo, looking for birds and monkeys. On a good day, passengers might spot an incredible variety of water birds, not to mention crocodiles, sloths, two kinds of monkeys and countless iguanas sunning themselves on the muddy riverbanks or gathering in the trees.

Ruta Los Heroes   BOAT TOUR
(☑ 2766-5858; 2hr tour per person US$20; ⊗7am-3pm) The pink building near the dock is a boat-captain cooperative, offering river tours with ecological and historical emphasis. Make arrangements to leave as early as possible to beat the heat and see more wildlife. If the office is closed (as it sometimes is in the low season), you can negotiate directly with the captains you find at the dock.

Farm Tours

Best Chocolate Tour   FOOD, FARM
(☑ 8815-0031, 8501-7951; per person US$30; ⊗tours 8am, 10am, 1pm & 3pm) Where does chocolate come from? This local Chilamate family can answer that question for you, starting with the cacao plants growing on their farm. The two-hour demonstration covers the whole chocolate-making process, with plenty of tasting along the way.

Organic Paradise   FOOD, FARM
(☑ 2761-0706; www.organicparadisetour.com; adult/child US$$35/14; ⊗8am, 10am, 1pm & 3pm) Take a bumpy ride on a tractor-drawn carriage and learn everything you ever wanted to know about pineapples. The two-hour tour focuses on the production process and what it means to be organic, but it also offers real insight into Costa Rican farm culture, as well as practical tips like how to choose your pineapple at the supermarket.

🛏 Sleeping

Isla del Río   HOSTEL $
(☑ 2766-6525; www.aguasbravascr.com; dm US$12, r with/without bathroom US$40/35; P🐾🙢) After riding the rapids, you can hunker down at this riverside hostel, operated by Aguas Bravas. It's a clean, basic set-up with solid wooden beds, clean bathrooms and hearty breakfasts (US$6). There are trails for exploring, as well as an outdoor hangout area where you can lounge in a hammock,

listen to the rushing river and recall your rafting adventure.

Cabinas Laura CABINA **$**
(📞2766-6316; s/d US$25/30; 🅿❄) Located on the road to the pier in Puerto Viejo, this place is quiet and cheap. Rooms are simple but spotless, with new tiles, wooden furnishings and cable TV.

★**Chilamate Rainforest Eco Retreat** LODGE **$$**
(📞2766-6949; www.chilamaterainforest.com; dm US$30-35,s/d/tr/qinclbreakfastUS$90/110/130/155; 🅿🛜) 🍴 Family-run and family-friendly, this is an inviting and truly innovative retreat, where owners Davis and Meghan are dedicated to protecting the environment and investing in community. Built on 20 hectares of secondary forest, the solar-powered cabins are basic but full of character, with hand-crafted furniture and natural air-cooling. The restaurant serves incredible, fresh breakfast and dinner buffets, using local, organic ingredients.

★**Posada Andrea Cristina B&B** B&B **$$**
(📞2766-6265; www.andreacristina.com; d incl breakfast US$58-62; 🅿🛜) On the edge of town and at the edge of the forest, this charming B&B in Puerto Viejo is a gem. The grounds are swarming with birds, sloths and monkeys, not to mention the frogs that populate the pond. Quaint cabins all have high, beamed ceilings, colorful paint jobs and private terraces. Or opt to stay in a funky tree house, built around a thriving Inga tree.

✖ **Eating & Drinking**

Chicharronera Caballo Loco STEAK **$**
(📞8630-2320; www.facebook.com/chicharronera caballoloco; mains US$4-8; ⊙6am-8pm Mon-Sat, 11am-10pm Sun) This is an open-air joint, serving up *chicharones* (fried pork or beef rinds) and other meats just outside the livestock auction mart at the main Puerto Viejo junction. Take your lunch inside to watch the auction action. The livestock sales can attract quite a crowd of *sabaneros* and other local characters, so it's great people-watching (and animal-watching, for that matter).

Restaurante Mar y Tierra COSTA RICAN **$**
(📞8434-2832; mains US$8-10; ⊙8am-10pm) You can't miss this roadside restaurant, set in an A-frame in the middle of La Virgen. The seafood and steak restaurant is popular with both locals and travelers. Try the *arroz Mar y Tierra*, a Tico take on surf and turf.

Bar & Cabinas El Río BAR
(📞2761-0138; ⊙noon-10pm) At the southern end of La Virgen, turn off the main road and make your way down to this atmospheric riverside hangout, set on rough-hewn stilts high above the river. Locals congregate on the upper deck to sip cold beers and nosh on filling Tico fare.

From here, you can you can stumble right into your bed if you stay in one of the A-frame bungalows (with fan/air-con US$15/20) near the road.

ℹ **Getting There & Away**
The **bus terminal** (⊙5am-7pm) is right across from the park in Puerto Viejo de Sarapiquí, near the Hotel El Bambú. Local buses run hourly between La Virgen and Puerto Viejo de Sarapiquí (US$1, 30 minutes) from 6am to 8pm.
Ciudad Quesada (Transportes Linaco) US$3, two hours, departs eight times daily from 4:40am to 6:30pm.
San José (Autotransportes Sarapiquí and Empresarios Guapileños) US$2.50, two hours, departs 5am, 5:30am, 7am, 8am, 11am, 1:30pm, 3pm and 5:30pm.

NORTHWESTERN COSTA RICA

What did you come to Costa Rica for? To lounge on pristine beaches and ride glorious waves? To hike up volcanoes and soak in geothermal springs? To spy on birds and monkeys and get lost among ancient trees? The northwestern corner of Costa Rica packs in all this and more. Unlike any other part of Costa Rica, Guanacaste – in the far northwest – is a wide, flat expanse of grasslands and dry tropical forest, where savanna vistas are broken only by windblown trees. Further east, the Cordillera de Guanacaste rises majestically out of the plains in a line of sputtering, steaming volcanic peaks that beg exploration. Further south, higher altitudes create a misty, mystical cloud forest, teeming with life. What did you come to Costa Rica for? Here it is...

Monteverde & Santa Elena

Spread out on the slopes of the Cordillera de Tilaran, this area is a sprawling chain of villages, farms and nature reserves. The biggest population center – the village of Santa Elena – runs almost seamlessly into

COSTA RICA MONTEVERDE & SANTA ELENA

Monteverde & Santa Elena

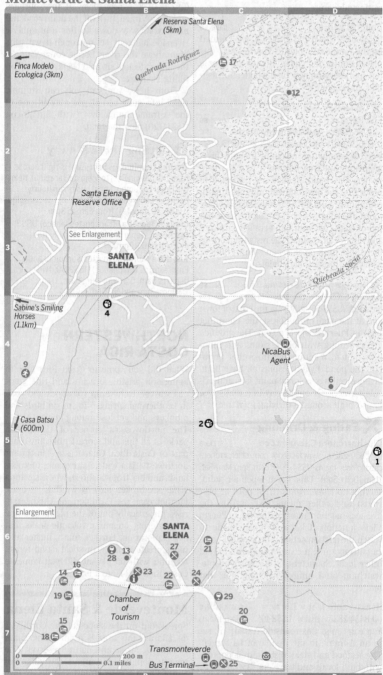

Reserva Santa Elena
(5km)

Quebrada Rodriguez

17

12

Finca Modelo
Ecologica (3km)

Santa Elena
Reserve Office

See Enlargement

SANTA
ELENA

Quebrada Sucia

Sabine's Smiling
Horses
(1.1km)

4

9

NicaBus
Agent

6

Casa Batsu
(600m)

2

1

Enlargement

SANTA
ELENA

27

21

13

28

16

14

23

22

24

19

Chamber
of
Tourism

29

20

15

18

Transmonteverde
Bus Terminal

25

0   200 m
0   0.1 miles

Monteverde & Santa Elena

◎ Sights
1	Bat Jungle	D5
2	Butterfly Garden	C5
3	Monteverde Friends School	F7
4	Monteverde Theme Park	B4

◯ Activities, Courses & Tours
5	Café de Monteverde	E6
6	Centro Panamericano de Idiomas	D4
7	Cerro Amigos	E4
8	Curi-Cancha Reserve	E6
9	Finca El Rodeo	A4
10	Monteverde Cheese Factory	E6
11	Monteverde Institute	E6
12	Original Canopy Tour	D1
13	Selvatura	B6

◉ Sleeping
14	Cabinas & Hotel Vista al Golfo	A6
15	Cabinas Eddy	A7
16	Cabinas El Pueblo	A6
17	Capulín Cabins & Farm	C1
18	Casa Tranquilo	A7
19	Monteverde Backpackers	A7
20	Monteverde Luxury Hostel	C7
	Pensión Santa Elena	(see 27)
21	Santa Elena Hostel Resort	C6
22	Sleepers	B6

⊗ Eating
23	Monteverde Cheese Factory Outlet	B6
24	Orchid Coffee	C6
	Paz y Flora	(see 18)
25	Sabor Tico	C7
26	Stella's Bakery	E6
27	Taco Taco	B6

⊖ Drinking & Nightlife
28	Bar Amigos	B6
29	Monteverde Beer House	C7

its next-door neighbor Cerro Plano and its next next-door neighbor, tiny Monteverde (which borders the namesake reserve).

The Reserva Bosque Nuboso de Monteverde (Monteverde Cloud Forest Reserve) is the most famous one, but there are public and private properties of all shapes and sizes – from tiny family *fincas* to the vast Children's Eternal Rainforest – that blanket this whole area in luscious green. As a result, there are trails to hike, birds to spot, waterfalls to swim and adventures to be had everywhere you turn.

◉ Sights

Reserva Biológica Bosque
Nuboso Monteverde   WILDLIFE RESERVE
(Monteverde Cloud Forest Wildlife Biological Reserve; ☑ 2645-5122; www.reservamonteverde.com; adult/concession/child under 6yr US$20/10/free; ⊙ 7am-4pm) This beautiful reserve came into being in 1972, when the Quaker community, spurred on by the threat of encroaching squatters, joined forces with environmental and wildlife organizations to purchase and protect an extra 328 hectares (811 acres) of land. This fragile environment relies almost entirely on public donations to survive. Today, the reserve totals 10,500 hectares (25,946 acres).

Monteverde Friends School   CULTURAL CENTRE
(www.mfschool.org; Monteverde; per person US$15; ⊙ tours 8am Tue & Fri; ▣) Here's a great way for children to learn about and interact with the local culture: spend some time at the schoolhouse. With advance reservation, visitors can sit in on morning assembly and tour the grounds. Kids are even invited to attend a class (and recess!) with an English-speaking buddy.

Bat Jungle   ZOO
(☑ 2645-7701; www.batjungle.com; Monteverde; adult/child US$13/11; ⊙ 9am-7pm; ▣) The so-called Bat Jungle in Monteverde is a small but informative exhibit, with good bilingual educational displays and a free-flying bat habitat housing almost 100 bats. Make a reservation for your 45-minute tour to learn about echolocation, bat-wing aerodynamics and other amazing flying-mammal facts.

Butterfly Garden   ZOO
(Jardín de Mariposas; ☑ 2645-5512; www.monteverdebutterflygarden.com; Cerro Plano; adult/student/child US$15/10/5; ⊙ 8:30am-4pm; ▣) Everything you ever wanted to know about butterflies, with four gardens representing different habitats and home to more than 40 species. Up-close observation cases allow you to witness the butterflies as they emerge from the chrysalis (if your timing is right). Other exhibits feature the industrious leaf-cutter ant and the ruthless tarantula hawk (actually a wasp that eats tarantulas) and lots of scorpions. Kids love this place, and knowledgeable naturalist guides truly enhance the experience.

Monteverde Theme Park   ZOO
(Monteverde Frog Pond; ☑ 2645-6320; www.monteverdethemepark.com; Santa Elena; per attraction $13-17, canopy tour adult/child $35/20; ⊙ 9am-4:30pm, ranario to 8pm) Formerly known as the Ranario, or Frog Pond, this place added an insect house, a butterfly garden and canopy tour – hence, it's now a theme park. The frogs are still the highlight: about 25 species reside in transparent enclosures lining the winding indoor jungle paths. Sharp-eyed guides point out frogs, eggs and tadpoles with flashlights. Your ticket entitles you to two visits, so come back in the evening to see the nocturnal species.

⚘ Activities

Cerro Amigos   HIKING
Take a hike up to the highest peak in the area (1842m) for good views of the surrounding rainforest and, on a clear day, Volcán Arenal, 20km away to the northeast. Behind Hotel Belmar in Cerro Plano, take the dirt road going downhill, then the next left. The trail ascends roughly 300m in 3km. Note that this trail does not connect to the trails in the Monteverde reserve.

Curi-Cancha Reserve   HIKING, BIRDWATCHING
(☑ 8356-1431, 2645-6915; www.curi-cancha.com; admission US$14, guided hike US$15, natural history tour US$45, bird tour US$60; ⊙ 7am-3:30pm, guided hike 7:30am & 1:30pm) Bordering Monteverde but without the crowds, this lovely private reserve on the banks of the Río Cuecha is popular among birders. There are about 10km of well-marked trails, a hummingbird garden and a view of the continental divide. Make reservations for the guided hikes, including the early-morning bird walks and specialized three-hour natural history walks.

⚘ Courses

Monteverde Institute   LANGUAGE COURSE
(☑ 2645-5053; www.monteverde-institute.org; Monteverde; weeklong courses US$375, homestay incl meals per day US$23) This nonprofit educational institute in Monteverde offers interdisciplinary courses in Spanish, as well as more specialized programs in tropical ecology, conservation and ecotourism, among other topics. Courses are occasionally open to the public, as are volunteer opportunities in education and reforestation.

Centro Panamericano
de Idiomas   LANGUAGE COURSE
(CPI; ☑ 2265-6306; www.cpi-edu.com; Cerro Plano; weeklong classes US$390; ⊙ 8am-5pm) Specializes in Spanish-language education, with courses geared toward families, teenag-

ers, medical professionals and retirees. For fun: optional dance and cooking classes are included with your tuition.

👉 Tours

Adventure Tours

Finca Modelo Ecologica   OUTDOORS
(📞2645-5581; www.familiabrenestours.com; tree-tops/canyoning/combo US$40/70/100; ⊙tree-tops 8am-4pm, canyoning 8am, 11am & 2pm) The Brenes family *finca* offers a number of unique and thrilling diversions. Their masterpiece is the two-hour canyoning tour, which descends six glorious waterfalls, the largest of which is 40m. No experience necessary, just an adventurous spirit. Tree-huggers can climb a 132ft ficus tree, using ropes and rappels to go up and down.

Original Canopy Tour   CANOPY TOUR
(📞2645-5243; www.theoriginalcanopy.com; adult/student US$45/35/25; ⊙7:30am, 10:30am & 2:30pm) The storied zip-line tour that started the trend. With 15 cables, a Tarzan swing and a rappel through the center of an old fig tree, it's a lot more fun than most history museums. Your adrenaline rush may not be as big as at some of the other canopy tours, but you'll enjoy smaller groups and more emphasis on the natural surroundings.

Selvatura   CANOPY TOUR
(📞2645-5929; www.selvatura.com; canopy US$50, walkways US$30, each exhibit US$5-15; ⊙7:30am-4pm) One of the bigger games in town, Selvatura has 3km of cables, 18 platforms and one Tarzan swing over a stretch of incredibly beautiful primary cloud forest. In addition to the cables, it has 3km of 'Treetops Walkways,' as well as a hummingbird garden, a butterfly garden and an amphibian and reptile exhibition.

Food Tours

Café de Monteverde   FOOD
(📞2645-7550; www.lifemonteverde.com; Monteverde; tour per person US$18; ⊙coffee tasting 7:30am-6pm, tours 8am & 1:30pm) 🍴 Stop by the shop in Monteverde to take a crash course in coffee and sample the delicious blends. Or, sign on for the three-hour tour on sustainable agriculture, which visits organic *fincas* implementing techniques like composting and solar energy. Learn how coffee growing has helped to shape this community and how it can improve the local environment.

Monteverde Cheese Factory   FOOD
(La Lechería; 📞2645-7090; www.monteverde cheesefactory.com; Monteverde; tours adult/child

---

WORTH A TRIP

RESERVA SANTA ELENA

The exquisitely misty 310-hectare **Reserva Santa Elena** (📞2645-7107, 2645-5390; www.reservasantaelena.org; adult/student US$14/7, guided hike US$15; ⊙7am-4pm) offers a completely different cloud forest experience to Monteverde. Cutting through the veiled forest, the 10km of dewy trails see much less traffic, retaining a magic that is sometimes missing at Monteverde. Open since 1992, this reserve was one of the first community-managed conservation projects in the country.

There's a **reserve office** (📞2645-5390; www.reservasantaelena.org; Colegio Técnico Profesional; ⊙8am-4pm Wed-Fri) at the Colegio Técnico Profesional in town. The reserve itself is about 6km northeast of the village of Santa Elena. There's a simple restaurant, coffee shop and gift store. Note that all proceeds go toward managing the reserve as well as to environmental-education programs in local schools.

US$12/10; ⊙store 7:30am-5pm Mon-Sat, to 4pm Sun, tours 9am & 2pm Mon-Sat) Until the upswing in ecotourism, Monteverde's number-one employer was the Monteverde Cheese Factory, which was started in 1953 by Monteverde's original Quaker settlers. Learn about the history of the Quakers in Costa Rica and their methods for producing and pasteurizing cheese on a two-hour tour of the factory (reservations required). You can also pop in any time to sample the creamy goodness. Bonus: now there's a **Santa Elena outlet** (ice cream $US2-4; ⊙10am-8pm), right next door to the Catholic church.

Horseback Riding

Sabine's Smiling Horses   HORSEBACK RIDING
(📞2645-6894; www.smilinghorses.com; Monteverde; 2hr/3hr/all-day ride per person US$45/65/105; ⊙tours 9am, 1pm & 3pm) Conversant in four languages (in addition to equine), Sabine will make sure you are comfortable on your horse, whether you're a novice rider or an experienced cowboy. Her longstanding operation in Monteverde offers a variety of treks including a popular waterfall tour (three hours) and a magical full-moon tour (monthly). And yes, the horses really do smile.

Finca El Rodeo
HORSEBACK RIDING

(☑ 2645-6306; www.caballerizaelrodeo.com; Santa Elena; per person $40-60) Based at a local *finca,* this outfit offers tours on private trails through rainforest, coffee plantations and grasslands, with plenty of pauses to spot wildlife and admire the fantastic landscapes. The specialty is a sunset tour to a spot overlooking the Golfo de Nicoya. *¡Que hermoso!*

🛏 Sleeping

★ Casa Tranquilo
HOSTEL $

(☑ 2645-6782; www.casatranquilohostel.com; Santa Elena; dm US$10, d with/without bathroom US$30/22, all incl breakfast; ⓟ@🛜) At Casa Tranquilo, the wonderful Tico hospitality starts first thing in the morning with home-made banana bread. In addition to the excellent breakfast, staff lead free guided hikes, sharing their in-depth local expertise. The rooms are simple and spotless, some featuring skylights and gulf views. Colorful murals adorn the outside, so you'll know you are in the right place.

Pensión Santa Elena
HOSTEL $

(☑ 2645-5051; www.pensionsantaelena.com; Santa Elena; d without bathroom US$28, d with bathroom US$32-38, ste US$45-60, all incl breakfast; ⓟ@🛜) This full-service hostel right in central Santa Elena is a perennial favorite, offering budget travelers top-notch service and *pura vida* hospitality. Each room is different, with something to suit every budget. The 'grand' rooms in the annex feature perks like superior beds, stone showers and iPod docks.

Cabinas Eddy
CABINA $

(☑ 2645-6635; www.cabinas-eddy.com; Santa Elena; d US$40-60, without bathroom US$35; ⓟ@🛜) This budget spot continues to get rave reviews for its amazing breakfasts, attentive service and delightful manager Freddy (son of Eddy). The rooms are spotless, as is the fully equipped communal kitchen. The balcony is a great place to relax with a cup of free coffee and take in the view.

Monteverde Backpackers
HOSTEL $

(☑ 2645-5844; www.monteverdebackpackers.com; Santa Elena; dm US$10-12, d/tr/q US$30/45/55, all incl breakfast; ⓟ@🛜) Small and friendly, Monteverde Backpackers is part of the Costa Rica Hostel Network. The wood-paneled rooms are clean and comfy enough, the showers are hot, the location in Santa Elena is quiet, and management is helpful. Free-

bies include coffee, hammocks and a sunset hike. Breakfast is DIY, so you can make 'em how you like 'em (eggs, that is).

Monteverde Luxury Hostel
HOSTEL $

(☑ 2645-5157; www.monteverdeluxuryhostel.com; Santa Elena; dm US$16, d US$58; ⓟ🛜) Think of a classy mountain lodge with lots of amenities, where you meet cool people and share adventures. That's the concept behind this hostel-lodge. Rooms range from stylish, six-bed dorms to private, semi-luxurious tree-top cabins. All guests are invited to the huge common area to listen to some tunes, access free wi-fi and sip happy-hour cocktails.

Cabinas El Pueblo
CABINA $

(☑ 2645-6192; www.cabinaselpueblo.com; d incl breakfast with/without bathroom from US$32/25; ⓟ@🛜) On a quiet road just steps from Santa Elena town, this pleasant hostel is run by an attentive Tico couple, Marlenny and Freddy. Well-furnished rooms are bright and clean, if cramped. You'll also find a communal kitchen, hammocks and – most importantly – an exceedingly warm welcome. All guests are gifted a treat from the family coffee plantation.

Cabinas & Hotel Vista al Golfo
CABINA $

(☑ 2645-6321; www.cabinasvistaalgolfo.com; Santa Elena; dm US$10, r with/without bathroom from US$30/20, ste US$50, all incl breakfast; ⓟ🛜) Rooms in this bright, kitschy lodge are well kept, the showers are hot and the owners will make you feel right at home. The upstairs balcony rooms have great views of the rainforest and, on a clear day, the Golfo de Nicoya. There's nothing really special going on here, with the exception of an excellent common space, furnished with beanbags, hammock chairs and more awesome views.

Sleepers
HOSTEL $

(☑ 8305-0113; www.sleeperssleepcheaperhostels.com; Santa Elena; dm US$10, s/d US$25/30, all incl breakfast) You can't miss this lime-green and aqua-blue building in central Santa Elena. Downstairs it looks like a friendly restaurant, but it's actually a crowded communal kitchen, where happy travelers prepare and share meals. Upstairs it looks like a modern motel, but it's actually a hostel, where happy travelers surf the web and catch a breeze on the balcony. Rooms are spotless, with en suite bathrooms.

★ Capulín Cabins & Farm
CABINA $$

(☑ 2645-6719; www.cabinascapulin.com; Santa Elena; cabina US$60-90; ⓟ🛜) Observe traditional farm life, hike the trails to spot birds and monkeys, or just swing in a hammock and watch the show in the sky. There are eight comfortable cabins of varying sizes – some with kitchens and some with fantastic views to the gulf. Your Tico farm family hosts could not be more generous in sharing their knowledge of the area.

Santa Elena Hostel Resort   LODGE **$$**
(🖉 2645-7879; www.costaricahostels.net; Santa Elena; dm US$14, d with/without balcony US$58/52; P✳🛜) With fish in the koi pond and monkeys on the rooftops, this newish hostel may seem like paradise. The shady grounds are strung with hammocks for sunny days, while there's a big stone fireplace for cool nights. The rooms are not all that, but they have stained-wood walls and high sloped ceilings. It's worth paying for private balconies with sweet views.

✕ Eating

⭐**Orchid Coffee**   CAFE **$**
(🖉 2645-6850; mains US$4-12; ⊙7am-7pm; 🛜🍴) 🍷 If you're feeling peckish, go straight to this lovely cafe in Santa Elena, filled with art and light. Take a seat on the front porch and take a bite of heaven. It calls itself a coffee shop, but there's a full menu of traditional and nontraditional breakfast items, sweet and savory crepes, interesting and unusual salads, and thoroughly satisfying sandwiches. And coffee, too, but so much more.

Taco Taco   MEXICAN **$**
(🖉 5108-0525; www.facebook.com/tacotacomonteverde; mains US$5-8; ⊙noon-8pm; 🛜) Quick and convenient, this *taquería* offers tasty Tex-Mex tacos, burritos and quesadillas filled with shredded chicken, slow-roasted short rib, roasted veggies and battered mahimahi. The only difficulty is deciding (but you really can't go wrong). The deck in front of Pensión Santa Elena is perfect for people-watching, but the seating supply is limited, especially if you want a shady spot.

Paz y Flora   VEGETARIAN **$**
(🖉 2645-6782; www.pazflorarestaurante.com; mains US$7-10; 🍴🍷) Good for the body, good for the soul and good for the earth. That's what Paz y Flora in Santa Elena strives for in its menu of vegetarian and vegan delights. It's a pretty comprehensive offering, with sandwiches, salads, pasta, rice and *rollitos*. It's all super fresh and deliciously satisfying. Look for the Buddha mosaic and you'll know you're in the right place.

Sabor Tico   SODA **$**
(🖉 2645-5827; www.restaurantesabortico.com; mains US$5-8; ⊙9am-9pm) 🍷 Ticos and travelers alike rave about this local Santa Elena joint. Look for some tasty twists on the standard fare, such as *sopa da olla* (beef soup), *chorreada Tica* (fried corn cakes) and tamales (holiday fare, typically). The *gallos* (soft tortilla with delicious filling of your choice) are a perfect alternative to the more filling *casado* for lunch.

Stella's Bakery   BAKERY **$**
(🖉 2645-5560; Monteverde; mains US$4-8; ⊙6am-10pm; 🛜🍴) A bakery for birdwatchers. Come in the morning for strong coffee and sweet pastries, or come later for sandwiches on homemade bread and rich, warming soup. Whenever you come, keep on eye on the bird feeder, which attracts tanagers, mot-mots and an emerald-green toucanet.

COSTA RICA MONTEVERDE & SANTA ELENA

BUSES FROM SANTA ELENA

DESTINATION	COMPANY	COST (US$)	DURATION	FREQUENCY
Las Juntas*	TransMonteverde	2	1½hr	4:30am
Puntarenas	TransMonteverde	3	3hr	4:30am, 6am, 3pm
Reserva Monteverde		1.20	30min	Departs 6:15am, 7:30am, 1:20pm, 3pm; returns 6:45am, 11:30am, 2pm, 4pm
San José	Tilarán Transportes	5	5hr	6:30am, 2:30pm
Tilarán, with connection to La Fortuna		3	2½hr, 7hr in total	7am, 4pm

* Buses to Puntarenas can also drop you off in Las Juntas.

Drinking & Nightlife

Bar Amigos
BAR

(☑2645-5071; www.baramigos.com; Santa Elena; ☺noon-3am) With picture windows overlooking the mountainside, this Santa Elena mainstay evokes the atmosphere of a ski lodge. But, no, there are DJs, karaoke, billiards and sports on the screens. This is the one consistent place in the area to let loose, so there's usually a good, rowdy mix of Ticos and tourists. The food is also surprisingly good.

Monteverde Beer House
BEER GARDEN

(☑8659-2054; www.facebook.com/monteverde beerhouse; Santa Elena; ☎) It's not a brewery – contrary to the sign – but it does offer a selection of local craft beers. There's a shady deck out back and smiling servers on hand, so it's a perfect atmosphere for kicking back after a day of adventures. The Middle Eastern food (mains US$6 to US$10) is hit or miss, but if you're hungry, go for the shakshuka.

ℹ Information

Chamber of Tourism (☑2645-6565; Santa Elena; ☺9am-noon & 1-7pm) Operated by the local chamber of commerce, this office promotes its member hotels and tour companies, so it's not necessarily an unbiased source.

Consultorio Médico (☑2645-7778; Cerro Plano; ☺24hr) Across the intersection from Hotel Heliconia.

Correos de Costa Rica (Santa Elena; ☺8am-4:30pm Mon-Fri, to noon Sat) Across from the shopping mall.

L@undry Internet (☑2645-7717; Santa Elena; ☺8am-8pm) Check your email while you wait for your clean clothes.

Police (☑2645-6248) In Santa Elena.

ℹ Getting There & Away

BUS

All buses stop at the bus terminal in downtown Santa Elena, where most of the budget digs are, and do not continue into Monteverde. You'll have to walk or take a taxi if that's where you plan to stay. On the trip in, keep an eye on your luggage, particularly on the San José–Puntarenas leg, as well as on the Monteverde–Tilarán run. Keep all bags at your feet and not in the overhead bin. Stories of theft and loss are legion.

If you're traveling to Managua or Grenada in Nicaragua, you can make arrangements to meet the international bus en route on the Interamericana in Lagartos:

Monteverde Experts (☑2645-7263; www. monteverdeexperts.com) Agent for TicaBus.

NicaBus Agent (☑2645-7063)

TAXI-BOAT-TAXI SHUTTLE

The fastest route between Monteverde–Santa Elena and La Fortuna is a taxi-boat-taxi combo (US$25 to US$30, four hours, departs 8am and 2pm), which can be arranged through almost any hotel or tour operator in either town, including **Monteverde Tours** (Desafío Adventure Company; ☑2645-5874; www.monteverdetours. com). A 4WD minivan takes you to Río Chiquito, meeting a boat that crosses Laguna de Arenal, where a van on the other side continues to La Fortuna. This is increasingly becoming the primary transportation between La Fortuna and Monteverde as it's incredibly scenic, reasonably priced and saves half a day of rough travel.

Liberia
POP 53,800

The sunny rural capital of Guanacaste has long served as a transportation hub connecting Costa Rica with Nicaragua, as well as being the standard-bearer of Costa Rica's *sabanero* culture. Even today, a large part of the greater Liberia area is involved in ranching operations, but tourism is fast becoming a significant contributor to the economy. With an expanding international airport, Liberia is a safer and more chilled-out alternative Costa Rican gateway to San José, which means more travelers are spending a night or two in this sweet town, knitted together by corrugated-tin fencing, mango trees and magnolias.

🛏 Sleeping

Hotel Liberia
HOTEL $

(☑2666-0161; www.hotelliberiacr.com; Calle Real btwn Avs Central & 2; dm US$13, s/d torre US$32/45, casona US$38/50; P ☎) It's hard to resist the glorious shady courtyard at this historic guesthouse, which is one of Liberia's best budget options. The most appealing 'casona' rooms are set in the old building, where the high ceilings, tile floors and wooden furniture contribute to an old-fashioned ambiance. Less atmospheric 'torre' rooms and dorms are in the newer concrete building at the back of the courtyard.

Hospedaje Dodero
HOSTEL $

(☑8729-7524; www.hospedajedodero.yolasite.com; Av 11 btwn Calles 12 & 14; d US$25-30; ❄☎) Three things: super clean, super service and close to the bus station. Small, private rooms, mostly with bathrooms. There's a communal outdoor kitchen, overlooking a small yard, filled with flowers and hung with hammock. It's nothing fancy, but it's very friendly.

Liberia

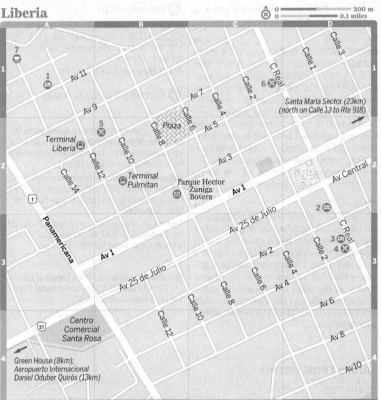

N 0 —— 200 m
   0 —— 0.1 miles

Santa Maria Sector (23km)
(north on Calle 13 to Rte 918)

Terminal
Liberia

Terminal
Pulmitan

Parque Hector
Zuniga
Bovera

Plaza

Panamericana

Av 25 de Julio

Av 25 de Julio

Centro
Comercial
Santa Rosa

Green House (8km);
Aeropuerto Internacional
Daniel Oduber Quirós (13km)

La Posada del Tope   GUESTHOUSE **$**
(2666-3876; www.facebook.com/hotellaposada
deltope; Calle Real btwn Avs 2 & 4; d US$25;
P⊜@🔊) Rooms are in the *'casa real'*
across the street from the wooden lobby. Set
around an awesome garden and furnished
with eclectic art and antiques, this place has
a lot of personality. Rooms are decidedly
basic and not that clean and bathrooms are
shared (mostly), but the price is right. The
bilingual Tico owner, Denis, is a wealth of
information.

✕ Eating & Drinking

Liberia has a good selection of restaurants,
both in town and on the road going out to
the airport. If you're taking the bus, pick up
some snacks for the road at the traditional
covered **market** (Ave 7 btwn Calles 10 & 12;
⊙6am-7pm Mon-Sat, to noon Sun), conveniently
located next to Terminal Liberia.

Liberia

⊜ Sleeping
1	Hospedaje Dodero	A1
2	Hotel Liberia	D2
3	La Posada del Tope	D3

✕ Eating
4	Café Liberia	D3
5	Market	B2
6	Restaurante El Pilon	C1

⊖ Drinking & Nightlife
7	Mariajuana	A1

Restaurante El Pilon   COSTA RICAN **$**
(2666-0616; Calle Central btwn Avs 5 & 7; casados US$5-8; ⊙6:30am-4pm Mon-Sat) A great
little find for fans of *casados*. This local
diner serves at least 10 daily, featuring fresh
pescado (fish), *pollo* (chicken), steak, lamb

and more. Relax around wooden tables in the cool, dark-tiled dining room.

Café Liberia
ORGANIC $$

(☑ 2665-1660; Calle Real btwn Avs 2 & 4; mains US$8-10; ⏰ 11am-9pm Tue-Sun, 3-9pm Mon; ❋ 🖥 ☑) This beautifully restored colonial-era building has heavy wooden furniture and frescoed ceilings, creating a romantic ambiance for rich coffee and gourmet fare. Simple food is taken to new levels: *ceviche* (seafood marinated in lemon or lime juice, garlic and seasonings) is served with irresistible, warm, fresh-baked tortilla chips. It's also an atmospheric setting for live music and other occasional performances.

★ Mariajuana
CAFE

(☑ 2665-7217; www.facebook.com/mariajuanares taurante; ⏰ 3-10:30pm Tue-Sun; 🖥 🍴) There's a great mellow vibe at this alfresco bar, tucked into a big tree-shaded yard at the end of a dead-end street. It's part cafe and part gallery, with wind chimes in the air, African masks on the walls and a menu of coffee drinks, cocktails and bar food (mains US$6 to US$8). No better place in Liberia to spend a hot afternoon.

🛈 Information

Hospital Dr Enrique Baltodano Briceño (☑ 2666-0011, emergencies 2666-0318; Rte 918) Behind the stadium on the northeastern outskirts of town.

Post Office (cnr Av 3 & Calle 8)

🛈 Getting There & Away

AIR

Located 12km west of Liberia, **Aeropuerto Internacional Daniel Oduber Quirós** (LIR; www. liberiacostaricaairport.net) serves as the country's second international airport.

NatureAir (☑ Aeropuerto Internacional Daniel Oduber Quirós 2668-1106, reservations 2299-6000; www.natureair.com; ⏰ 6am-5pm) To/from San José.

Sansa (☑ Aeropuerto Internacional Daniel Oduber Quirós 2668-1017, reservations 2290-4100; www.flysansa.com) To/from San José.

BUS

Buses arrive and depart from **Terminal Liberia** (Av 7 btwn Calles 12 & 14) and **Terminal Pulmitan** (Av 5 btwn Calles 10 & 12).

BUSES FROM LIBERIA

DESTINATION (COMPANY)	COST (US$)	DURATION	TERMINAL	FREQUENCY (DAILY)
Cañas (Reina del Campo)*	2	1½hr	Terminal Liberia	half-hourly, 5:30am-5:30pm
Curubandé	2	40min	Terminal Liberia	6:40am, noon, 5pm
La Cruz/Peñas Blancas (Arrieta)	2.50	1½-2hr	Terminal Liberia	5:30am, 8:30am, 9am, 11am
Nicoya, via Filadelfia and Santa Cruz (La Pampa)	2.50	1½hr	Terminal Liberia	half-hourly, 4:30am-8:20pm
Playa Flamingo (La Pampa)	3	1½hr	Terminal Liberia	6am, 8am, 10am, 11am, 12:30pm, 5pm, 6pm
Playa del Coco (Pulmitan)	1.50	1hr	Pulmitan	hourly 5am-11am, plus 12:30pm, 2:30pm, 6:30pm
Playa Hermosa (La Pampa)	2	1½hr	Terminal Liberia	5 daily, 7:30am-5:30pm
Playa Tamarindo (La Pampa)	3	2hr	Mercado Municipal	7 daily, 3:50am-12:30pm; hourly 2pm-6pm
Puntarenas* (Reina del Campo)	3	3hr	Terminal Liberia	9 daily, 5am-3:30pm
San José (Pulmitan)	6	4hr	Pulmitan	14 daily, 3am-10pm

* It's quicker to jump off the San José–bound bus in your destination.

Parque Nacional Rincón de la Vieja

Given its proximity to Liberia – really just a hop, a skip and a few bumps away – this 141-sq-km national park feels refreshingly uncrowded and remote. The name means 'old lady's nook,' and it's named after the active Volcán Rincón de la Vieja (1895m), the steamy main attraction. The park also covers several other peaks in the same volcanic range, including the highest, Volcán Santa María (1916m). The park exhales geothermal energy. It bubbles with multihued fumaroles, tepid springs and steaming flatulent mud pots, as well as a young and feisty *volcancito* (small volcano). All of these can be visited on foot on well-maintained steep trails. Note the Las Pailas sector is closed on Monday.

🏃 Activities

Hiking

From the Santa María ranger station, there are some 12km worth of hiking trails which take in the hot springs. Since the 2012 eruptions the trek to the summit of Rincón de la Vieja is no longer open to the public.

Sendero Las Pailas HIKING

A circular trail known as Sendero Las Pailas – about 3km in total – takes you east of Las Pailas ranger station, past boiling mud pools *(las pailas)*, sulfurous fumaroles and a *volcancito*. This is the most popular (and most crowded) section of the park, as it's an easy but worthwhile trail with a lot to see.

Catarata La Cangreja HIKING

About 350m west of the Las Pailas ranger station are two waterfall trails. Catarata La Cangreja is the classic, dropping 50m straight from a cliff into a small lagoon where you can swim. Dissolved copper salts give the falls a deep blue color. This trail winds through forest, past truly massive strangler figs, then on to open savannah spiked with yucca on the volcano's flanks, where views stretch as far as the Palo Verde wetlands and the Pacific beyond.

Hot Springs

There's no better way to recover from a grueling hike than by soaking in thermal springs. Many of the springs are reported to have therapeutic properties, which is always a good thing if you've been hitting the *guaro cacique* a little too hard.

In the Sector Santa María, a trail leads 2.8km west through the 'enchanted forest,' past the lovely Catarata Bosque Encantado (Enchanted Forest Falls), to sulfurous hot springs. Don't soak in them for more than about half an hour (some people suggest much less) without taking a dip in the nearby cold springs, 2km away, to cool off. If you want real-deal, volcano-created thermal pools, here they are: it doesn't get more 'natural' than this.

On the fringes of the park, there are several private facilities that have thermal pools with varying temperatures. No hiking required. Many companies and hotels offer tours to these sites from Liberia.

Hot Springs Río Negro HOT SPRING

(📞 2690-2900; www.guachipelin.com; per person US$10; ☉9am-5pm) Set in the dry forest along the Río Negro, this magical place is managed by the Hacienda Guachipelín. Ten natural, stone-crafted hot pools are accessible by a lovely wooded trail, with hanging bridges leading to pools on either side of the raging river. Pools range in temperature from 28°C to 53°C.

🛏 Sleeping & Eating

El Sol Verde CAMPGROUND $

(📞 2665-5357; www.elsolverde.com; campsite US$9, tent houses US$27.50, d/q US$50/70; 🅿🛜) 🍃 The lovely couple here in Curubandé village offer three Spanish-tiled, wood-walled rooms. Alternatively, bed down in the camping area, where there are a few furnished tent houses, a shared outdoor kitchen, solar-heated showers and plenty of space to pitch your own tent. The mural-painted terrace is a lovely place to relax, and you'll find hiking, swimming and wildlife in the immediate vicinity.

Casa Rural Aroma de Campo HOTEL $$

(📞 2665-0008, reservations 7010-5776; www.aromadecampo.com; s/d/tr/q US$55/76/104/123, bungalow $130, all incl breakfast; 🅿🛜❄) Near the village of Curubandé, this serene, epiphyte-hung, hammock-strung oasis has six rooms with polished hardwood floors, open bathrooms, colorful wall art, mosquito nets and classy rural sensibility. Scattered around the property, an additional six prefab bungalows have bold colors and glass walls for better immersion in the forested setting. Delicious meals are served family-style in the courtyard. Warning: the pet parrot is an early riser.

Rinconcito Lodge LODGE $$

(☎2666-2764, 2200-0074; www.rinconcitolodge.com; lodge s/d US$34/47, standard s/d $52/74, superior d $78; P 📶) Just 3km from the Santa María sector of the park, this affordable option has attractive, rustic cabins that are surrounded by some of the prettiest pastoral scenery imaginable. The cheaper rooms are tiny, but they are also just as clean and fresh as you can imagine. The lodge also offers horseback riding and zip-lining tours.

Orientation & Information

The two main entrances to the park each have their own ranger station, where you sign in, pay admission and get free maps. Most visitors enter through **Las Pailas ranger station** (☎2666-5051; www.acguanacaste.ac.cr; adult/child 6-12yr/child 5yr & under US$15/5/ free; ⏲8am-4pm Tue-Sun, no entry after 3pm) on the western flank, where most of the trails begin. The **Santa María ranger station** (☎2666-5051; www.acguanacaste.ac.cr; adult/child US$15/5; ⏲7am-4pm, no entry after 3pm), to the east, is in the Hacienda Santa María, a 19th-century *rancho* that was reputedly once owned by US President Lyndon Johnson. This is your access point to the sulphorous springs.

Getting There & Away

There's no public transportation to the park entrances, but a bus travels from Liberia to Curubandé three times daily in each direction (40 minutes). Any hotel in Liberia can arrange transportation to the park for around US$20 per person. Alternately, you can hire a 4WD taxi from Liberia for about US$40 to Las Pailas, or US$65 to Santa María, each way.

La Cruz

POP 6040

La Cruz is the closest town to the Peñas Blancas border crossing with Nicaragua, and it's the principal gateway to Bahía Salinas, Costa Rica's premier kitesurfing destination. La Cruz itself is a fairly sleepy provincial town set on a mountaintop plateau, with lots of Tico charm and magical views of an epic wind-swept bay. **El Mirador** is a required stop, to stretch your legs and widen your worldview.

Sleeping

Amalia's Inn INN $

(☎2679-9618; s/d US$25/35; P ❄) This yellow stucco house on a cliff isn't a bad place to spend the night. For starters, the shared terracotta terraces have stupendous bay views. Inside, homey rooms are furnished rather randomly, but the brick floors and wooden ceilings are attractive. Walls in the meandering house are hung with modernist paintings by Amalia's late husband, Lester Bounds.

Hotel La Mirada HOTEL $

(☎2679-9702; www.hotellamirada.com; d US$45-65; P ❄ 📶) Just off the Interamericana you'll find the town's spiffiest spot. Family owned and lovingly cared for, rooms are spacious and clean, with high, beamed ceilings and loft sleeping spaces. The biggest rooms have kitchenettes and air-con. Despite the name, there's no view to speak of.

WORTH A TRIP

SANTA ROSA

The **Santa Rosa Sector** (☎2666-5051; www.acguanacaste.ac.cr; adult/child US$15/5, surfing or snorkeling surcharge US$12; ⏲8am-4pm) is the southern sector of the Area de Conservación Guanacaste. Some 30km of hiking trails weave through this tropical dry forest, offering fantastic vistas of the Cordillero Guanacaste and the Valle Naranjo. It's also the site of two historic battles, with the small La Casona museum and Monument de los Heroes to prove it. Along the coast, Playa Naranjo is a legendary surfing beach, while Playa Nancite is a critical nesting site for the olive ridley turtle.

To reach the Santa Rosa sector, turn off the Interamericana at the signed entrance 35km north of Liberia. It's 7km on a paved road to the park headquarters, where you'll also find the museum, campgrounds and a nature trail. From here, a very rough track leads 12km to Playa Naranjo. It's a notoriously bad road, impassable during the rainy season, and requiring 4WD at any time of year.

ℹ Getting There & Away

The bus station is located on the western edge of town, just north of the road to Bahía Salinas. A **Transportes Deldú counter** (📞 2221-2596; www.facebook.com/transportedeldu; ⏱ 7:30am-12:30pm & 1:30-6pm) sells tickets and stores luggage. To catch a TransNica bus to Peñas Blancas at the border and on to Managua in Nicaragua, you'll need to flag down a bus on the Interamericana.

Peñas Blancas US$1, 45 minutes, 10 almost hourly from 5am to 5:30pm.

San José via Liberia US$7, five hours, departs hourly from 5am to 7pm.

For information on the border crossing, see Border Crossings (p618).

PENÍNSULA DE NICOYA

Maybe you've come to the Península de Nicoya to sample the sapphire waters that peel left and right, curling into perfect barrels up and down the coast. Or perhaps you just want to hunker down on a pristine patch of sand and soak up some sun. By day, you might ramble down rugged roads, fording rivers and navigating ridges with massive coastal views. By night, you can spy on nesting sea turtles or take a midnight dip in the luxuriant Pacific. In between adventures, you'll find no shortage of boutique bunks, tasty kitchens and indulgent spas to shelter and nourish body and soul. Whether you come for the thrills or just to chill, the Nicoya peninsula delivers. You'll find that the days (or weeks, or months) drift away on ocean breezes, disappearing all too quickly.

Playa del Coco

Sportfishing is the engine that built this place, while deep-sea diving has become an additional attraction. You'll mingle with the foreign-born anglers and divers at happy hour (it starts rather early). That said, there is an actual Tico community here, and plenty of Tico tourists. Stroll along the grassy beachfront plaza at sunset and gaze upon the wide bay, sheltered by long, rugged peninsular arms, the natural marina bobbing with motorboats and fishing *pangas* (small motorboats). All will be right in your world.

🏃 Activities

Sportfishing, sailing, scuba diving and sea kayaking are popular activities that keep the troops entertained. Sea kayaks are perfect for exploring the rocky headlands to the north and south of the beach.

Pacific Coast
Stand-Up Paddle WATER SPORTS
(📞 8359-5118; www.pacificcoastsuptours.com; lessons US$35, tours US$65-85) Let Jorge and his crew take you out for an amazing day of paddling, exploring hidden coves, spotting dolphins and other sea creatures, and picnicking on a near-private beach. The three-hour tour even allows time for snorkeling. These guys also do surf tours and snorkel tours, all of which are recommended.

Summer Salt DIVING
(📞 2670-0308; www.summer-salt.com; 2 tanks from US$85) This friendly Swiss-run dive shop has professional, bilingual staff. Snorkelers are also welcome on the dive boats

🛏 Sleeping

Garden House at M&M HOSTEL $
(📞 2670-0273; gardenhouse@hotelmym.com; La Chorrera; dm $20-25, d $60; ❄ 🛜 🏊) There are plenty of budget *cabinas* in Coco but this is the only proper hostel. After many changes of name and management, the property is now known as the Garden House, and is operated by the good folks behind Hotel M&M. There are three dorm rooms, a handful of privates and a sweet swimming pool, all within striking distance of the beach.

Villa del Sol HOTEL $$
(📞 2670-0085, in Canada 866-793-9523, in USA 866-815-8902; www.villadelsol.com; La Chorrera; r incl breakfast US$85, apt US$100; 🅿 ❄ @ 🛜 🏊) About 1km north of the town center, this leafy, tranquil property attracts monkeys, iguanas and a good variety of birdlife, in addition to the happy travelers lounging on hammocks. The main building has stylish rooms with sunset-view balconies. In the back building, studio apartments (sleeping four) offer excellent value. Walk to the beach in five minutes or less.

Hotel M&M HOTEL $$
(📞 2670-1212; www.hotelmym.com; s/d/tr incl breakfast US$34/54/70; 🅿 🛜) A romantic beachfront hacienda with an all-wood balcony overlooking the boardwalk. Fan-cooled rooms have ceramic tiled floors, beamed ceilings and cold-water showers. This simple place is one of the only beachfront properties in Coco. And if the beach is not your

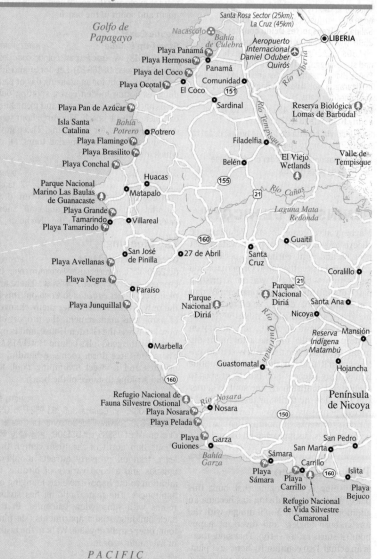

Golfo de
Papagayo

Santa Rosa Sector (25km);
La Cruz (45km)

Nacascolo

Bahía
de Culebra

LIBERIA

Playa Panamá
Playa Hermosa
Playa del Coco
Playa Ocotal
El Coco

Aeropuerto
Internacional
Daniel Oduber
Quirós

Panamá

Comunidad

Sardinal

151

Río Liberia

Reserva Biológica
Lomas de Barbudal

Playa Pan de Azúcar

Isla Santa
Catalina

Bahía
Potrero

Potrero

Playa Flamingo
Playa Brasilito
Playa Conchal

Filadelfia

Río Tempisque

El Viejo
Wetlands

Valle de
Tempisque

Huacas

Belén

155

Parque Nacional
Marino Las Baulas
de Guanacaste

Matapalo

21

Río Cañas

Playa Grande
Tamarindo
Playa Tamarindo

Villareal

160

Laguna Mata
Redonda

Guaitil

Playa Avellanas

San José
de Pinilla

27 de Abril

Santa
Cruz

Coralillo

21

Playa Negra

Paraíso

Parque
Nacional
Diriá

Parque
Nacional
Diriá

Santa Ana

Playa Junquillal

Nicoya

Río Quirimán

Reserva
Indígena
Matambú

Mansión

Marbella

Guastomatal

Hojancha

160

Península
de Nicoya

Refugio Nacional de
Fauna Silvestre Ostional

Río Nosara

Playa Nosara
Playa Pelada

Nosara

150

Playa
Guiones

Garza

San Pedro

San Marta

Bahía
Garza

Sámara

Carrillo

Playa
Sámara

Playa
Carrillo

160

Islita

Playa
Bejuco

Refugio Nacional
de Vida Silvestre
Camaronal

PACIFIC

OCEAN

0   20 km
0   10 miles

Guanacaste

Fortuna
Miravalles
Protection
Zone
Volcán
Tenorio
(1916m)
Parque Nacional
Volcán Tenorio
San Rafael
de Guatuso
Reserva
Indígena
Guatuso
Río Cote

Alajuela

Pijije

Bagaces

Tierras
Morenas

Arenal

Laguna
de Arenal

Venado

Unión

La Fortuna (15km)

Tronadora

Río Tenorio

Río Corobicí

Cañas

Tilarán

Quebrada
Grande

Río Chiquito

Parque Nacional
Volcán Arenal

Reserva
Santa Elena

Parque Nacional
Palo Verde

Bebedero

Reserva
Taboga

Cordillera de Tilarán

Santa
Elena
Monteverde

Reserva Biológica Bosque
Nuboso Monteverde

Río Bebedero

Puerto
Humo

Río Tempisque

Las Juntas de
Abangares

Refugio de
Vida Silvestre
Cipanci

Parque Nacional
Barra Honda

Puente La
Amistad

Quebrada
Honda

Río Lagarto

Barra
Honda

Isla
Chira

Río Grande

Reserva Biológica
de los Pájaros

Rancho
Grande

Río

Golfo de
Nicoya

Isla
Caballo

Carmona

Río Ora

Lepanto

Chacarita

Barranca

Jicaral

Ferry

PUNTARENAS

Mata de
Limón

Cangrejal

Río Juan de León

Playa
Naranjo

Isla San
Lucas

Reserva Biológica
Isla Guayabo

Quebrada Seca

Río Blanco

Bahía
Gigante

Bejuco

Playa San
Miguel

San Francisco
de Coyote

Isla
Gigante

Reserva Biológica
Islas Negritos

La Javilla

Paquera

Playa
Coyote

Río Bongo

Puntarenas

Curú

Refugio Nacional de
Vida Silvestre Curú

Isla
Tortuga

Playa
Caletas

Pochote

Bajos de Arió

Playa Tambor

Tambor

Bahía
Ballena

Playa
Manzanillo

Río Negro

Cóbano

Reserva Absoluta
Nicolás Wessburg

Montezuma

Playa
Santa Teresa

Montezuma-Jacó Passenger Ferry

Mal País

Cabuya

Reserva Natural
Absoluta Cabo Blanco

thing, you're invited to take a dip in the pool at sister property Garden House (p573).

Eating & Drinking

Congo CAFE $
([phone] 2670-1265; www.costaricacongo.com; mains US$6-10; [hours] 8am-7pm; [icons]) Part cafe, part funky retail boutique, Congo's interior is groovy with arched booths, rattan sofas and a deconstructed wood-and-granite coffee bar. They serve all the espresso drinks and an array of healthy sandwiches, salads and breakfasts.

Soda La Teresita COSTA RICAN $
([phone] 2670-0665; mains US$5-10; [hours] 6:30am-9pm Mon-Sat, to 5pm Sun) Located at the crossroads of the main drag and the beach, this place can't be beaten for people-watching in Coco. It's also your best bet for lunch, whether you're hankering for a *torta* (sandwich) or a traditional *casado*. Teresita also cooks up a hearty breakfast.

La Vida Loca BAR
([phone] 2670-0181; www.lavidalocabeachbar.com; [hours] 11am-11pm) Across a creaky wooden footbridge on the south end of the beach is where you'll find this hangout, popular among gringos and Ticos alike. It's a classic beach bar, with pool tables, live music and good vibes. If you're hungry, order up some comfort food such as burgers, nachos, meat loaf, chili dogs, clam chowder and more.

Information

Police Southeast of the plaza, by the beach.
Post Office On the southeast side of the plaza by the beach.

Getting There & Away

All buses arrive and depart from the main terminal, south of town.
Liberia US$2, one hour, departs hourly from 5am to 11pm.
San José Pulmitan (p531), US$10, five hours, departs 4am, 8am and 2pm.

Playa Tamarindo

Well, they don't call it Tamagringo for nothing. Tamarindo's perennial status as Costa Rica's top surf and party destination has made it the first and last stop for legions of tourists. It stands to reason, then, that this is the most developed beach on the peninsula with no shortage of hotels, bars and restaurants.

Despite its party-town reputation, Tamarindo is more than just drinking and surfing. It forms part of Parque Nacional Marino Las Baulas de Guanacaste, and the beach retains an allure for kids and adults alike. Foodies will find some of the best restaurants in the country. Families and students will appreciate the fierce competition that has kept lodging prices reasonably low. And Tamarindo's central location makes it a great base for exploring the northern peninsula.

Sights

Parque Nacional Marino Las Baulas de Guanacaste PARK
([phone] 2653-0470; adult/child US$12/2, turtle tours incl admission US$30; [hours] 8am-noon & 1-5pm, tours 6pm-2am) Las Baulas national marine park encompasses the entire beach at Playa Grande, as well as the adjacent land and 220 sq km of ocean. Playa Grande is one of the world's most important nesting areas for the *baula* (leatherback turtle). In the evenings from October to March, rangers lead tours for visitors to witness this amazing cycle of life. Canoe tours explore the mangroves, which are home to caimans and crocodiles, as well as numerous bird species such as the roseate spoonbill.

Activities

Surfing
Like a gift from the surf gods, Tamarindo is often at its best when neighboring Playa Grande is flat. The most popular wave is a medium-sized right that breaks directly in front of the Tamarindo Diria hotel. The waters here are full of virgin surfers learning to pop up. There is a good left that's fed by the river mouth, though be advised that crocodiles are occasionally sighted here, particularly when the tide is rising (which is, coincidentally, the best time to surf). There can be head-high waves in front of the rocks near Le Beach Club.

More advanced surfers will appreciate the bigger, faster and less crowded waves at neighboring beaches: Playa Langosta, on the other side of the point; Playas Avellanas, Negra and Junquillal to the south; and Playa Grande to the north.

There are countless surf schools offering lessons and board rental in Tamarindo. Surf lessons hover at around US$45 for 1½ to two hours, and most operators will let you keep the board for a few hours beyond that to practice.

PLAYAS AVELLANAS & NEGRA

These popular surfing beaches have some of the best, most consistent waves in the area, made famous in the surf classic *Endless Summer II*.

Playa Avellanas is an absolutely stunning pristine sweep of pale golden sand. Backed by mangroves in the center and two gentle hillsides on either end, there's plenty of room for surfers and sunbathers to have an intimate experience even when there are lots of heads in town.

Playa Negra is also undeniably romantic. Though the sand is a bit darker and the beach is broken up by rocky outcrops, gorgeous dusty back roads link tide pools of expat shredders who picked this place to exist (and surf) peacefully. Though there isn't much local soul here, the beach itself is a beaut.

There is no public transportation between Tamarindo and these beaches, though surf camps often organize trips. You can also catch a ride on the Avellanas Express (p580), which departs Tamarindo at 9am, 11am, 2pm and 3:50pm, with two of these shuttles going all the way to Playa Negra. To return to Tamarindo, the shuttle departs from Playa Negra at 10am and 3pm, and from Avellanas at 10:15am, 11:40am, 3:15pm and 6pm.

Iguana Surf
SURFING

(☑2653-0091; www.iguanasurf.net; board rental US$20, group/semiprivate/private lessons US$45/65/80; ☺8am-6pm) Iguana Surf has been giving lessons for some 25 years, so it probably knows what it's doing. Excellent for couples, families or anyone. The two-hour lesson includes a rash guard and locker, in addition to the surfboard. After your lesson, all gear is half-price.

Learn Improve Surf Company
SURFING

(☑8316-0509; www.learnimprovesurfcompany.com; lessons per person US$30-70) Edgar Sanchez wants to teach you how to surf. This upstart company excels at offering instruction for all ages and abilities. It also takes more advanced wave riders on surf tours to Playa Avellanas and Playa Grande.

Kelly's Surf Shop
SURFING

(☑2653-1355; www.kellysurfshop.com; board rental per day/week US$20/120, group/semiprivate/private lessons US$50/65/90; ☺9am-6pm) One of the best surf shops in the area, Kelly's has a terrific selection of newish boards that it rents by the day or week. Premium boards cost a bit more. Staff are super informative, with lessons, advice and other recommendations to get you out on the waves.

Diving

Tamarindo is a surf town. But that doesn't mean there is nothing to see below the waves. Enticing dive sites in the vicinity include the nearby Cabo Velas and out to the Islas Catalinas.

Freedive Costa Rica
DIVING

(☑8353-1290; www.freedivecostarica.com; Plaza Conchal; free diving US$35-55, snorkeling US$55, spearfishing US$145; ☺9:30am-5:30pm) Owner Gauthier Ghilain claims free diving is 'the most natural, intimate and pure form of communion with the underwater world.' It requires no bulky gear and minimal training. He promises a safe and super-fun environment in which to learn how to explore the deep blue sea in new ways.

Tamarindo Diving
DIVING

(☑8583-5873; tamarindodiving.net; 2-tank dives US$110) It's called Tamarindo Diving, but Davide Gabbi actually takes clients on a boat that departs from Playa Flamingo and heads out to the Islas Catalinas. (It's a trade-off: you'll spend more time on the road but less time on the boat motoring to your destination.) Turtles, dolphins and whales are often spotted from the boat, while eagle rays, sharks and manta rays are lurking below the surface.

Courses

Coastal Spanish Institute
LANGUAGE COURSE

(☑2653-2673; www.coastalspanish.com; per week from US$310) This Spanish school is located right on the beach in downtown Tamarindo (which may make it more difficult to concentrate on your grammar and vocabulary). The place specializes in weekly surf and Spanish packages, which include 20 hours of Spanish classes and six hours of surf instruction, as well as board rental.

Playa Tamarindo

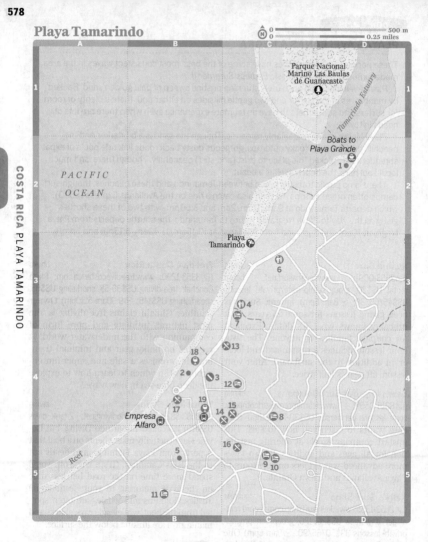

N 0 _____ 500 m
0 _____ 0.25 miles

Instituto de Wayra   LANGUAGE COURSE
(☎2653-0359; www.spanish-wayra.co.cr; per week
from US$320; ⏱7:30am-5:30pm Mon-Fri, 10am-
4pm Sun) A Spanish program that offers small
class sizes and an immersive experience. The
school recommends (and arranges) homestays so students have more opportunities to
practice.

🛏 Sleeping

Tamarindo Backpackers   HOSTEL $
(☎2653-1720; www.tamabackpackers.com; dm
US$15, d from US$50; P❄@🛜🏊) This attractive yellow hacienda has a great vibe that

welcomes all comers. Private rooms (mostly
with shared bathroom) are excellent value,
with Spanish-tiled floors, mural-painted
walls, beamed ceilings and flat-screen TVs.
The dorms are quite clean but otherwise un-
spectacular. Outside, hammocks are strung
in the tropical gardens and around a small
pool. Five-minute walk to the beach.

La Botella de Leche   HOSTEL $
(☎2653-0189; www.labotelladeleche.com; dm
US$13-15, d US$40; P❄@🛜🏊) With a relaxed
vibe, this congenial spot – aka 'the bottle of
milk' – is recommended for its warm and at-

Playa Tamarindo

⊕ Activities, Courses & Tours
1 Asociación de Guías Locales...............D2
2 Coastal Spanish Institute B4
3 Freedive Costa Rica............................B4
4 Iguana Surf C3
5 Instituto de Wayra B5
6 Kelly's Surf Shop................................C3

⊜ Sleeping
7 Blue Trailz Hostel...............................C3
8 Hotel Mahayana.................................C4
9 La Botella de Leche C5
10 Pura Vida Hostel C5
11 Tamarindo Backpackers.....................B5
12 Villas Macondo..................................C4

⊗ Eating
13 El Casado del Carro C4
14 Falafel Bar...C4
15 Green Papaya.....................................C4
16 La Bodega..C5
17 Surf Shack B4

⊙ Drinking & Nightlife
18 El Be!...B4
19 Sharky's B4

tentive management and fully air-conditioned rooms and dormitories. Stenciled walls pretty up the otherwise plain rooms. Facilities include a shared kitchen, surfboard racks, hammocks and a TV lounge.

Blue Trailz Hostel HOSTEL $
(☑2653-1705; dm/r US$15/69; ❉@☎) Across the street from the beach, this immaculate and intimate hostel is popular among the surfer set. Budget travelers appreciate the clean, cool dorms (with air-con) as well as the attentive service from the staff. Guests get reduced rates on boards, bikes, lessons and tours. Sweet.

Pura Vida Hostel HOSTEL $
(☑8747-8780; www.puravidahostel.com; dm US$15-18, d with/without bathroom US$60/50; ❉@☎) Inside this leafy compound are dorms and private rooms accented by trippy murals and mirrored mosaics. The vibe is friendly and super chill, especially in the common *rancho*, furnished with hammocks and rocking chairs. It sometimes organizes open-mike nights and other live music. Also: free bikes and boards.

Hotel Mahayana HOTEL $$
(☑2653-1154; www.hotelmahayana.com; d US$62; P❉☎☀) The Mahayana is a sweet retreat, away from the hustle and bustle of the main drag. Spotless, citrus-painted rooms are fitted with high ceilings, big windows and private terraces (with hammocks). The courtyard contains a small, cool pool and an outdoor kitchen, which is at your disposal.

Villas Macondo HOTEL $$
(☑2653-0812; www.villasmacondo.com; s/d/tr US$50/60/70, with air-con US$75/85/95, apt US$125-170; P❉@☎☀) Although it's only 200m from the beach, this establishment is an oasis of serenity in an otherwise frenzied town – it's also one of the best deals around. Beautiful modern villas with private hammocks and patios surround a solar-heated pool and tropical garden. Larger apartments are equipped with full kitchens, making them ideal for families.

✗ Eating

★La Bodega BREAKFAST, SANDWICHES $
(☑8395-6184; www.labodegatamarindo.com; Nahua Hotel; mains US$6-8; ☉7am-3pm Mon-Sat; ☎☑▦) This delightful shop and cafe specializes in unique combinations of ingredients, focusing on fresh, local and organic. For breakfast, it does amazing things with eggs, while lunch is a daily changing menu of unique sandwiches and salads. Any time of day, you can't go wrong with banana bread or lemon scones and a cup of fresh brewed java.

★Green Papaya MEXICAN $
(☑2652-0863; www.facebook.com/Gr33nPapaya; mains US$5-10; ☉9am-10pm Tue-Sun; ❉☎☑▦) Swing on up to the bar for a breakfast burrito or pull up a tree-stump stool to sample the terrific tacos at this fantastic new addition. The mahimahi tacos are perfection in a tortilla, while non-meat-eaters will appreciate the multiple veggie options. You'll go loco for the Coco Loco dessert. Everything is funky, fresh and friendly – don't miss it.

Surf Shack BURGERS $
(☑2653-2346; www.facebook.com/surfshacktamarindo; mains US$5-10; ☉11am-9pm; ☎▦) If you are craving a big bad burger, Surf Shack has you covered, with a good selection of patties, thick-cut onion rings and irresistible milkshakes. Tin-can walls and surfboard decor create a super laid-back vibe, enhanced by the drinks coming from the bar. It's steps from the beach; the sea breeze is the perfect accompaniment to anything you order.

Falafel Bar
LEBANESE $

(☎2653-1268; www.facebook.com/tamarindo falafelbar; mains US$5-8; ⊙10am-10pm Wed-Mon; 🖉) When you get tired of *casados* (as you do), head to this Middle Eastern cafe for all the faves: shawarma, falafel, tabbouleh, hummus and kebabs. The pita bread is made fresh daily. And now the place has improved on the 'bar' part with the recent acquisition of an alcohol license.

El Casado del Carro
COSTA RICAN $

(casados US$4; ⊙noon-3pm) Doña Rosa has been delivering top-notch *casados* from her late-model Toyota hatchback for more than a decade. Her devoted Tico following lines up daily at noon, and she generally sells out by 2pm. You'll get your meal in a Styrofoam platter (nobody's *perfecto*), usually with yucca or plantains, rice, chicken or beef, and some tasty black beans.

🍷 Drinking & Nightlife

El Be!
BAR

(☎2653-0178; ⊙11am-close) Formerly Le Beach Club, this place has changed languages (and added an exclamation point!) but the cool vibe remains the same. Lounge on beach beds or hammocks and listen to the DJ do his stuff. Happy hour (4pm to 7pm) features drink specials, live jazz music and fabulous sunsets. It's not a bad option for food if you're feeling peckish.

Sharky's
SPORTS BAR

(☎2653-4705; www.sharkysbars.com; ⊙11:30am-2:30am Thu-Tue, 5pm-2:30am Wed) If you're looking for a place to watch the big game, look no further than Sharky's. Besides nine screens showing sports, there are burgers and wings and lots of beer. There's a nightly line-up of fun and games, including karaoke night on Tuesday and ladies' night on Saturday. Get ready to get your drink on.

ℹ Information

Backwash Laundry (⊙8am-8pm Mon-Sat) Get your filthy unmentionables washed, dried and folded.

Coastal Emergency Medical Service

(☎2653-1974, emergency 8835-8074; ⊙24hr) For emergency medical service.

ℹ Getting There & Away

The **Empresa Alfaro** (☎2653-0268; ⊙7:30am-5:30pm Mon-Sat, 9am-3:30pm Sun) office is near the beach, while other buses depart from the bus stop in front of Pacific Park.

Private shuttle buses offer a faster (albeit more expensive) option. **Tamarindo Shuttle** (☎2653-0505; www.tamarindoshuttle.com) provides comfortable and convenient transfers from Tamarindo to destinations around the country, including both airports. **Tropical Tours** (☎2640-1900, 2640-0811; www.tropicaltourshuttles.com) has daily shuttles that connect Tamarindo to San José, as well as several destinations in the southern part of the Nicoya peninsula.

ℹ Getting Around

BOAT

Stop by the **Asociación de Guías Locales** (☎2653-1687; www.sinac.go.cr/AC/ACT/PN MarinoBaulas; boats to Playa Grande US$3, turtle tours US$25-35; ⊙7am-4pm) at the northern end of the beach to hire a boat to cross the estuary to Playa Grande.

BUS

Here's a great service. **Avellanas Express** (US$6; ⊙8am-5pm) runs a surf shuttle to area beaches. There are three different 'lines' from Tamarindo: back and forth to Playa Grande; south to Avellanas and Negra; and north to Conchal and Flamingo. Based at Neptuno Surf Shop.

Playa Sámara

POP 4200

Is Sámara the black hole of happiness? That's what more than one expat has said after stopping here on vacation and never leaving. On the surface it's just an easy-to-navigate beach town with barefoot, three-star appeal. The crescent-shaped strip of pale-gray sand spans two rocky headlands, where the sea is calm and beautiful. But be careful, the longer you stay the less you'll want to leave.

BUSES FROM TAMARINDO

DESTINATION	COMPANY	COST (US$)	DURATION (HR)	DEPARTURES
Liberia		3	2½	12 daily 3:30am-6pm
San José	Alfaro	11	5½	3am & 5:30am
San José	Tralapa	11	5½	7am
Santa Cruz		2	1½	6am, 8:30am & noon

🏄 Activities

No matter what you like to do at the beach, you can probably do it at Playa Sámara. Expert surfers might get bored by Sámara's inconsistent waves, but beginners will have a blast. Otherwise, there's hiking, horseback riding and sea kayaking, as well as snorkeling out around Isla la Chora. Take a break from the beach to explore the forested hillsides on foot or on zip line.

Pato Surf School SURFING

(☑ 8761-4638; www.patossurfingsamara.com; board rental per day US$15, lessons US$30-40) Set right on the beach, Pato offers inexpensive and quality board rental, as well as beginner surf instruction. Pay for a lesson and get free board rental for five days! Also on offer: stand-up paddle rental and lessons; kayak rental and tours; and snorkel gear. Plus, massage on the beach and occasional beach yoga. What else do you want?

🎓 Courses

Centro de Idiomas Intercultura LANGUAGE COURSE

(☑ 2656-3000; www.samaralanguageschool.com; courses per week with/without homestay US$460/315) Centro de Idiomas Intercultura is right on the beach, which makes for a pleasant – if not always productive – place to study. Language courses can be arranged with or without a family homestay. Courses for kids are also available.

🛏 Sleeping

★ Camp Supertramp HOSTEL $

(☑ 2656-0373; campsupertramp.com; campsite US$8, dm US$14-16) There's something truly unique going down at Camp Supertramp, 1.5km west of Sámara and 600m from the beach. The list of things to love is long: Thomas (the owner), Jukebox (his dog), the jungle shower, the fire pit, the 1971 VW bus, the ping-pong table, and more. Sleep in the multilevel Monkey Room or the comfy-bed Delux Dorm. The vibe here is fun-filled and super chill.

El Cactus Hostel HOSTEL $

(☑ 2656-3224; www.samarabackpacker.com; dm US$14, d US$34-48; 🌐🖥) Brightly painted in citrus colors, El Cactus is a great option for Sámara's backpacker set, especially those who prefer serenity over revelry. Fresh rooms have wooden furniture, clean linens and hot-water showers. Hammocks hang

around a small pool, and a fully fitted kitchen is also available. Located on a side street in the center of town, 100m from the beach.

Hotel Matilori HOSTEL $

(☑ 2656-0291; www.hostelmatilori.com; dm/s/d/ tw US$16/30/36/32; 🅿🛜) A terrific-value hostel with private rooms (and shared bathrooms) in the main house and cozy dorm rooms (sleeping four or six) in the newer annex. All the rooms have fresh coats of jewel-toned paints, and guests have use of an updated kitchen and a shady patio. Endearing owners Fran and Jen welcome you with a *cerveza* on arrival!

Casa Paraiso GUESTHOUSE $

(☑ 2656-0741; scodinzolo@libero.it; d US$45; 🛜) There's a lovely little guesthouse tucked in behind Ahora Sí. A handful of simple rooms are brushed in deep blues and inviting pastels, with thematic murals, high ceilings and comfy beds. Ceiling fans will keep you cool while hot-water showers will warm you up.

Las Mariposas HOSTEL $

(☑ 8703-3625, 2656-0314; www.hostelmariposas. com; hammock US$8, dm US$12-15, d without bathroom US$30-38; 🛜) On a rough dirt road near the language school, this fun, friendly hostel guarantees a good time, as long as you're in the right frame of mind. It's got wooden rooms and dorms, plenty of swaying hammocks, paper lantern lighting and a communal kitchen. It's just 60m from the sand.

La Mansion B&B B&B $$

(☑ 2265-0165; www.samarabeach.com/lamansion; s US$40, d US$50-80, ste US$150; 🅿❄🛜) This whitewashed concrete hacienda is on a quiet street, twirling with fans and bursting with colorful knickknacks. There's loads of charm: rooms are spacious and bright, and the breakfast is huge and delicious.

🍴 Eating & Drinking

It's not exactly a party town, but Sámara sees some action at night. All of the beach bars get busy after sunset. Lo Que Hay and Flying Taco (p582) are both technically taco bars, but after hours, the emphasis is on the 'bar.'

★ Lo Que Hay MEXICAN $

(☑ 2656-0811; www.loquehaybeachbar.com; tacos US$2, mains US$5-10; ⏰ 7am-late) This rocking beachside taqueria and pub offers six delectable taco fillings: fish, chorizo, chicken, beef, pork, veggie. The grilled avocados stuffed with *pico de gallo* are choice. Even *sin* tacos, a good time will be had as the bar crowd sips into the wee small hours.

Roots Bakery
BAKERY $

(☑8924-2770; www.facebook.com/rootsbakery cafeEnSamara; items US$3-5; ⊙7am-4pm; 🛜) The carrot cake is really good; and the spinach quiche is better. But the cinnamon buns are otherworldly – so rich and gooey and sweet and chewy that you might have to do penance after you eat one. Required eating.

Roots is on the main drag, opposite the turnoff to Carrillo.

Ahora Sí
VEGETARIAN $

(☑2656-0741; www.ahorasi.isamara.co; mains US$5-11; ⊙8am-10pm; 🅿🛜✏) A Venetian-owned vegetarian restaurant and all-natural cocktail bar. It does smoothies with coconut milk; gnocchi with nutmeg, sage and smoked cheese; soy burgers and yucca fries; wok stir-fries; and thin-crust pizzas. All served on a lovingly decorated tiled patio.

Sámara Organics – Mercado Organico
MARKET $$

(☑2656-3046; www.samaraorganics.com; drinks US$2-5; ⊙7am-8pm) It's not cheap, but self-caterers (and anybody with a dietary restriction) will appreciate this cafe and market, well stocked with organic produce and delicious prepared foods. Come get your healthy food fix.

Flying Taco
BAR

(☑8409-5376; ⊙noon-2am; 🛜) This joint is a laid-back, Tex-Mex beach bar. It's open for lunch – and the grub is recommended – but it's more fun to come at night, when you can also listen to live music, sing karaoke, play poker and drink margaritas. But don't skip the tacos.

ℹ Information

La Vida Verde (Green Life; ☑2656-1051; greenlife@samarabeach.com; per kg US$3; ⊙8am-6pm Mon-Sat) Drop your dirty duds off at this laundry, 75m west of Banco Nacional. Or call ahead for pick-up and delivery.

Post Office (⊙8am-noon & 1:15-5:30pm Mon-Fri) Located in the same building as the police station, on the main road near the beach.

Samara Info Center (☑2656-2424; www.samarainfocenter.com; ⊙9am-9pm) Located on the beach near Lo Que Hay, the Info Center is run by the amiable Brenda and Christopher. It's basically a tour consolidator, but they can help with accommodations, restaurant recom-

mendations, transportation and simply answering questions about Sámara and Carrillo. And they book tours.

ℹ Getting There & Away

Traroc buses go to Nicoya (US$3.60, one hour) 10 times a day from 5:30am to 7pm. Heading in the opposite direction, the same buses go to Playa Carrillo.

Mal País & Santa Teresa

Get ready for tasty waves, creative kitchens and babes in board shorts and bikinis, because the southwestern corner of Península de Nicoya has all that and more. Which is why it's become one of Costa Rica's most life-affirming destinations. Here, the sea is alive with wildlife and is almost perfect when it comes to shape, color and temperature. The hills are dotted with stylish boutique sleeps and sneaky kitchens run by the occasional runaway, top-shelf chef. Sure, there is a growing ribbon of mostly expat development on the coastline, but the hills are lush and that road is still rutted earth (even if it is intermittently sealed with aromatic vats of molasses). The entire area unfurls along one coastal road that rambles from Santa Teresa in the north through Playa El Carmen, the area's commercial heartbeat, then terminates in the fishing hamlet of Mal País.

Surfing is the *raison d'être* for most visits to Santa Teresa and Mal País, and perhaps for the town itself. Most travelers want to do little else, except maybe stretch their muscles with a little yoga. That said, it's a gorgeous, pristine coastline: horseback riding or fishing trips can be easily arranged.

🛏 Sleeping

Don Jon's
BUNGALOW $

(☑2640-0700; www.donjonsonline.com; Santa Teresa; dm US$15-20, bungalows US$45-70, apt US$80-120; 🅿❄🛜) Just past the soccer field, Don Jon's place is the perfect base for surfers and anybody looking to 'relax to the max.' Rustic teak bungalows are creatively decorated and quite appealing, while attractive Spanish-tiled dorms have high-beamed ceilings and plenty of hammocks in the garden.

Casa Zen
GUESTHOUSE $

(☑2640-0523; www.zencostarica.com; Santa Teresa; dm/d/tr/q incl breakfast US$15/35/42/50; 🅿🛜) This lovely Asian-inspired guesthouse is decked out in celestial murals and happy

Buddha sculptures. The colorful but basic rooms share super clean bathrooms and two fully equipped kitchens. Some guests have complained that the thin walls and passing traffic detract from the Zen atmosphere; but we would argue that the noise is just an opportunity to practice more Zen.

Wavetrotter
HOSTEL $

(✉ 2640-0805; www.wavetrottersurfhostel.com; Santa Teresa; dm US$15, r without bathroom US$35; P 🛜) An excellent option for hostel hoppers, not just surfers, Wavetrotter is a simple place, with all-wood six-bed dorms overlooking a vast common area. There are private rooms in the garden, which is also home to howlers and iguanas. There is a huge communal kitchen and – major bonus – the whole place is spotless.

It's one block east of the main road: turn right before Pizza El Pulpo.

Cuesta Arriba
HOSTEL $

(✉ 2640-0607; www.cuestaarriba.com; Santa Teresa; dm US$15, d US$50-60, all incl breakfast; ⊘ 9am-7pm; P ❄ 🛜 🐾) This is a thinking person's hostel, attracting a polished crowd of travelers who appreciate the orderly atmosphere. En suite bathrooms, polished concrete floors, colorful tapestries and mosaic tile embellishments look lovely in both shared and private rooms. Communal areas include a big well-stocked kitchen area, a breezy terrace upstairs and a garden with hammocks.

Malpaís Surf Camp & Resort
LODGE $$

(✉ 2640-0031; www.malpaissurfcamp.com; Mal País; dm US$17, d with/without bathroom US$73/40, villa from US$108; P ❄ @ 🛜 🐾) There are comfortable, private cabanas and more luxurious digs, but the best deal at this surfers' lodge is the open-air *rancho*, with a tin roof and pebble floors, which you can share with three other surfers. Explore the landscaped tropical grounds, swim in the luscious pool, grab a cold beer in the open-air lounge and soak up the good vibes.

🍴 Eating & Drinking

Zwart Cafe
CAFE $

(✉ 2640-0011; Santa Teresa; mains US$4-8; ⊘ 7am-5pm; 🛜) Zwart means 'black' in Dutch, but this shabby-chic, artist-owned gallery and cafe is all white (or mostly, damn dust!). You'll love the surf-inspired Technicolor canvases, the lively outdoor patio and the popular breakfasts, including chocolate chip pancakes and breakfast burritos. At lunch it's all about the burritos. There's a dynamite used bookstore here too.

Roca Mar
BAR

(✉ 2640-0250; Santa Teresa; ⊘ noon-9pm; 🛜) Tucked away at Blue Surf Sanctuary at the northern end of town, this is a pretty perfect beach lounge that attracts a local expat crowd. Beanbags are stuck in the sand, and hammocks are slung in the trees – all perfectly positioned for sunset. On Sunday evenings, it hosts an official Sunset Party – a family-friendly event with live music and fire dancers and such.

ⓘ Getting There & Away

All buses begin and end at Ginger Café, 100m south of Cuesta Arriba hostel, but you can flag the bus down anywhere along the road in Santa Teresa. At Frank's Place, the buses turn left and head inland toward Cóbano.

A direct bus to San José via the Paquera ferry departs at 7:30am and 3:30pm (US$13, six hours). Local buses to Cóbano (US$2, 45 minutes) depart at 7am and noon.

Montezuma Expeditions (✉ 2642-0898; www.montezumaexpeditions.com; Santa Teresa) organizes shuttle-van transfers to San José, Tamarindo and Sámara; Jacó, La Fortuna, Liberia and Monteverde; Manuel Antonio; and Dominical.

Montezuma

Montezuma is an immediately endearing beach town that demands you abandon the car to stroll, swim and (if you can stroll a little further) surf. The warm and wild ocean and that remnant, ever-audible jungle has helped this rocky nook cultivate an inviting, boho vibe. Typical tourist offerings such as canopy tours do a brisk trade here, but you'll also bump up against Montezuma's internationally inflected, artsy-rootsy beach culture in yoga classes, volunteer corps, veggie-friendly dining rooms and neo-Rastas hawking uplifting herbs. No wonder locals lovingly call this town 'Montefuma.'

It's not perfect. The accommodations are particularly poor value, and the eateries can be that way too (though there are some absolute gems). But in this barefoot *pueblo*, which unfurls along several kilometers of rugged coastline, you're never far from the rhythm and sound of the sea, and that is a beautiful thing.

Montezuma

0 — 100 m
0 — 0.05 miles

Montezuma

Sights
1 Playa Montezuma........................ B1

Activities, Courses & Tours
   Montezuma Yoga.......................(see 4)
2 Zuma Tours A2

Sleeping
3 Downtown Montezuma Hostel A3
4 Hotel Los Mangos......................B4
5 Hotel Pargo Feliz.......................B2
6 Luna Llena A2
7 Luz en el Cielo A2

Eating
8 Kalibó.................................A3
9 Orgánico..............................B2

Drinking & Nightlife
10 Chico's Bar............................B2

the right just after the bridge. You'll want proper hiking footwear.

Playa Montezuma　　　　BEACH
The best beach close to town is just north of Cocolores restaurant, where the sand is powdery and sheltered from big swells. This is your glorious sun-soaked crash pad. The water's shade of teal is immediately nourishing, the temperature is perfect and fish are abundant. At the north end of the beach, look for the trail that leads to a cove known as Piedra Colorada. A small waterfall forms a freshwater pool, which is a perfect swimming spot.

**Reserva Natural Absoluta
Cabo Blanco**　　　　NATURE RESERVE
(2642-0093; adult/child US$12/2; 8am-4pm Wed-Sun) Costa Rica's oldest protected wilderness area covers 12 sq km at the tip of the Península de Nicoya. The unique park is covered by evergreen forests, bisected by a hiking trail and flanked by empty white-sand beaches and offshore islands. Follow the **Sendero Sueco** (Swedish Trail), which leads 4.5km down to a magnificent, jungle-backed beach at the tip of the peninsula. Note that the reserve is closed on Monday and Tuesday.

Sights & Activities

★ Montezuma Waterfalls　　　　WATERFALL
(parking US$2) A 40-minute river hike leads to a waterfall with a delicious swimming hole. Further along the trail, a second set of falls offers a good clean 10m leap into deep water. Reach the 'diving platform' from the trail: do not try to scale the slippery rocks! Daring souls can test their Tarzan skills on the rope that swings over a third set. A lot of travelers enjoy these thrills but a few of them have died, so do it at your own risk.

As you head south past Hotel La Cascada, there's a parking area, then take the trail to

Sleeping

★ Luz en el Cielo　　　　HOSTEL, B&B $
(8811-3700, 2642-0030; www.luzenelcielo.com; dm US$18-28, d/q US$90/136; P🐶) In the heart of the jungle but two minutes from

town, this homey hostel and B&B is an inviting retreat. Crowded dorm rooms are super clean with sturdy wood furniture and lockers, while the new 'luxury' dorms are more spacious, with TVs, private balconies and en suite bathrooms. The treetop *cabinas* are also wonderful. Amazing breakfasts (included in rates), enticing hammocks and super friendly staff.

Luna Llena HOSTEL $
(☑2642-0390; www.lunallenahotel.com; dm/s/d without bathroom US$15/28/38, d with bathroom US$55-65; P🖥) On the northern edge of town on a hilltop overlooking the bay is a budget option which is absolutely delightful and truly unique. The rooms are all simple but stylish, colorful and clean; most have balconies. There are two kitchens, a BBQ grill and a breezy communal lounge with rattan chair-swings and stunning ocean views. Wildlife abounds in the surrounding trees.

Hotel Los Mangos HOTEL $
(☑2642-0076; www.hotellosmangos.com; r with/without bathroom US$75/35, bungalows US$90; P🌡🖥🏊) Scattered across mango-dotted gardens, this whimsical hotel has plain, painted-wood rooms in the main building and attractive (though dark) octagonal bungalows that offer more privacy. Monkeys populate the mango trees and yoga classes (☑2642-1311, 8704-1632; www.montezumayoga. com; per person US$14; ⊗classes 8:30am & 6pm daily) are held in the gorgeous, ocean-view yoga pavilion.

Downtown Montezuma Hostel HOSTEL $
(☑8516-6921; www.facebook.com/dtmontezuma; dm US$14, d with/without bathroom US$45/35; 🖥) This funky little two-story hostel has art on all the walls, a clean communal kitchen and plenty of hammocks for your swinging pleasure. Rates all include all-you-can drink coffee and make-your-own pancakes for breakfast. The rooms – four-bed dorms and private doubles – are nothing special, but guests love the fun, friendly vibe. Quiet time after 11pm is strictly enforced.

Hotel Pargo Feliz CABINA $
(☑2642-0064; d US$35-50; 🖥) You can't beat the location of these beachfront *cabinas* in the heart of Montezuma. Rooms are simple, clean and fan-cooled. The communal balcony and garden terrace have relaxing hammocks with sea views, and at night the surf will lull you to sleep.

🍴 Eating & Drinking

Kalibó CAFE $
(☑2642-4545; mains US$3-8; ⊗6am-9pm; 🍴) A tiny place with an open kitchen and half a dozen tables, across from the bus stop. This perfect breakfast stop does homemade pastries, fresh fruit smoothies and strong local coffee. It also serves salads, sandwiches and proper meals. It's a charmer.

★ Cocina Clandestina LATIN AMERICAN $$
(☑8315-8003; www.facebook.com/clandestina montezuma; mains US$8-12; ⊗noon-9pm Tue-Sat; 🖥🍴♿) The secret is out. The hottest new restaurant in Montezuma is this awesome, artistic place in the trees at the butterfly gardens (☑2642-1317; www.montezumagardens. com; admission US$4; ⊗8am-4pm). Look for innovative takes on Central American standards, such as daily changing taco specials and delectable chicken mole enchiladas. Vegetarians are joyfully accommodated with yam and lentil cakes or *chilles rellenos*. The beverage of choice is Butterfly Beer, brewed onsite.

Orgánico VEGETARIAN $$
(☑2642-1322; mains US$8-12; ⊗8am-9pm; 🍴) When it says 'pure food made with love,' it means it – this healthy cafe turns out vegetarian and vegan dishes such as spicy Thai burgers, a *sopa azteca* with tofu, smoothies and more (as well as meaty options too). Avocado ice cream is something everyone should try. There's live music almost nightly, including a wildly popular open mike on Monday nights.

COSTA RICA MONTEZUMA

BUSES FROM MONTEZUMA

DESTINATION	COST (US$)	DURATION	DEPARTURES (DAILY)
Cabo Blanco via Cabuya	1.50	45min	8 buses 5:30am-8pm
Cóbano	2	1hr	8:15am, 10:15am, 12:15pm & 4:15pm
Paquera via Cóbano	3	2hr	3:45am, 6am, 10am, noon, 2pm & 4pm
San José	14	5hr	7:30am & 3:30pm

ⓘ PUNTARENAS–PENINSULA FERRIES

All transportation is geared to the arrival and departure of the Puntarenas ferries. If either the bus or the ferry is running late, the other will wait.

From Paquera

The **Ferry Naviera Tambor** (☑ 2661-2084; www.navieratambor.com; adult/child/bicycle/motorcycle/car US$1.65/1/4.50/7/23) leaves daily at 5:30am, 9am, 11am, 2pm, 5pm and 8pm. The trip to Puntarenas takes about an hour. Buy a ticket at the window, reboard your car and then drive on to the ferry; you can't buy a ticket on board. Show up at least an hour early on holidays and busy weekends. The terminal contains a *soda* where you can grab a bite while waiting for the boat.

Buses meet arriving passengers at the ferry terminal and take them to Paquera, Tambor and Montezuma. They can be crowded, so try to get off the ferry fast to secure a seat. Most travelers take the bus from the terminal directly to Montezuma (US$3, two hours). Many taxi drivers will tell you the bus won't come, but this isn't true. There are no northbound buses.

Getting several travelers together to share a taxi to Montezuma (or wherever) is a good option since the ride will take half as long as the bus. A taxi to Montezuma is about US$12 per person, and to Mal País it's about US$20 – provided you have a full car.

From Playa Naranjo

The **Coonatramar ferry** (☑ 2661-1069; www.coonatramar.com; adult/child/bicycle/motorcycle/car US$2/1/4/6/18) to Puntarenas departs daily at 8am, 12:30pm, 4:30pm and 8:30pm, and can accommodate both cars and passengers. The trip takes 1½ hours. If traveling by car, get out and buy a ticket at the window, get back in your car and then drive on to the ferry. You cannot buy a ticket on board. Show up at least an hour early on holidays and busy weekends, as you'll be competing with a whole lot of other drivers to make it on.

Buses meet the arriving ferry and take passengers on to Jicaral, for travel on to the more northerly parts of the peninsula. If you're headed to Montezuma or Mal País, take the other ferry from Puntarenas to Paquera.

Chico's Bar BAR

(⊙11am-2am) When it comes to nightlife, Chico's is the main (only?) game in town, which means that everybody ends up here eventually – old, young, Ticos, tourists, rowdy, dowdy – especially on Thursday nights, which is reggae night. Snag a table on the back patio for a lovely view of the beach and beyond.

ⓘ Information

The only ATM in town is a BCR *cajero* located across from Chico's Bar. The nearest full-service bank is in Cóbano. For money exchange, tour operators in town will take US dollars, euros or traveler's checks.

ⓘ Getting There & Away

BOAT

Zuma Tours (☑ 2642-0024; www.zumatours.net) operates a fast water shuttle connect-

ing Montezuma to Jacó in an hour. At US$40 or so, it's not cheap, but it'll save you a day's worth of travel. From Montezuma, boats depart at 9:30am daily, and the price includes van transfer from the beach to the Jacó bus terminal. From Jacó, the departure to Montezuma is at 11am. During the high season, it may run an additional shuttle, departing Montezuma at 1:30pm and departing Jacó at 3pm. Book in advance from any tour operator. Also, dress appropriately; you will get wet.

BUS

Buses depart Montezuma from the sandy lot on the beach, across from the soccer field. Buy tickets directly from the driver. To get to Mal País and Santa Teresa, go to Cóbano and change buses.

Montezuma Expeditions (☑ 2642-0919; www.montezumaexpeditions.com; US$40-70) operates daily private shuttles to San José, La Fortuna, Monteverde, Jacó, Manuel Antonio, Dominical, Tamarindo, Sámara and Liberia.

CENTRAL PACIFIC COAST

Stretching from the rough-and-ready port of Puntarenas to the tiny town of Uvita, the central Pacific coast is home to both wet and dry tropical rainforests, sun-drenched sandy beaches and a healthy dose of wildlife. On shore, national parks protect endangered squirrel monkeys and scarlet macaws, while offshore waters are home to migrating whales and pods of dolphins.

With so much biodiversity packed into a small geographic area, it's no wonder the coastal region is often thought of as Costa Rica in miniature. Given its close proximity to San José and the Central Valley and highlands, and its well-developed system of paved roads, this part of the country is a favorite weekend getaway for domestic and international travelers.

While threats of unregulated growth and environmental damage are real, it's also important to see the bigger picture, namely the stunning nature that first put the central Pacific coast on the map.

Puntarenas

POP 8063

The 'Pearl of the Pacific' is a battered port city at the tip of a sandy peninsula (8km long but only 100m to 600m wide). Lively and hot, this provicial capital served as a major coffee port during the 19th century. During the dry season, Tico vacationers pack the beaches. Otherwise, it's the home of rowdy dockworkers and sailors alongside elderly ladies who scrub their sidewalks and keep the bougainvilleas blooming. Most travelers come here just to catch the ferry to the Nicoya peninsula.

🛈 Getting There & Away

BOAT

Car and passenger ferries bound for Paquera and Playa Naranjo depart several times a day

from the **northwestern dock** (Av 3 btwn Calles 31 & 33). If you are driving and will be taking the car ferry, arrive at the dock early to get in line. The vehicle section tends to fill up quickly and you may not make it on. In addition, make sure that you have purchased your ticket from the walk-up ticket window before driving onto the ferry. You will not be admitted onto the boat if you don't already have a ticket.

Schedules change seasonally and can be affected by inclement weather. Check with the ferry office by the dock for any changes. Many of the hotels in town also have up-to-date schedules posted.

Coonatramar (📞2661-1069; www.coonatramar.com; adult/child US$2/1.10, bike/car US$4/18) has daily departures to Playa Naranjo (for transfer to Nicoya and points west) at 6:30am, 10am, 2:30pm and 7:30pm.

Naviera Tambor (📞2661-2084; www.navieratambor.com; adult/child US$1.60/1, bike/car US$4.40/23) has daily departures to Paquera (for transfer to Montezuma and Mal País) at 5am, 9am, 11am, 2pm, 5pm and 8:30pm.

BUS

Buses for San José depart from the large navy-blue building on the north corner of Calle 2 and Paseo de los Turistas. Book your ticket ahead of time on holidays and weekends. Buses for other destinations leave from across the street, on the beach side of the Paseo.

Parque Nacional Carara

Situated at the mouth of the Río Tárcoles, the 52-sq-km park is only 50km southeast of Puntarenas by road or about 90km west of San José via the Orotina highway. Straddling the transition between the dry forests of Costa Rica's northwest and the sodden rainforests of the southern Pacific lowlands, this national park is a biological melting pot of the two. Acacias intermingle with strangler figs, and cacti with deciduous kapok trees, creating heterogeneity of habitats with a blend of wildlife to match, including the scarlet macaw and Costa Rica's largest crocodiles. The park's three trails can easily be explored in

BUSES FROM PUNTARENAS

DESTINATION	COST (US$)	DURATION (HR)	FREQUENCY
Jacó	2.20	1½	8 daily 4:30am-5:30pm
Quepos	3.80	3½	5 daily 4:30am-3pm
San José	5.10	2½	hourly 4am-9pm
Santa Elena, Monteverde	3	3	8:15am & 2:15pm

CROCODILE BRIDGE

If you're driving from Puntarenas or San José, pull over by the Río Tárcoles bridge, also known as Crocodile Bridge. If you scan the sandbanks below the bridge, you'll have a fairly good chance of seeing as many as 30 basking crocodiles. Although they're visible year-round, the best time for viewing them is low tide during the dry season.

half a day; come early to maximize wildlife sightings.

ℹ Information

Carara Ranger Station (⊙7am-3pm Dec-Mar, 8am-4pm Apr-Nov) Info on the park and the possibility to hire guides (US$30, two-person minimum); 3km south of Río Tárcoles.

ℹ Getting There & Away

Any bus traveling between Puntarenas and Jacó can leave you at the park entrance. You can also catch buses headed north or south in front of Restaurante Los Cocodrilos. This may be a bit problematic on weekends, when buses are full, so go midweek if you are relying on a bus ride. If you're driving, the entrance to Carara is right on the Costanera and is clearly marked.

Jacó

POP 9527

Few places in Costa Rica generate such divergent opinions as Jacó. Partying surfers, North American retirees and international developers laud it for its devil-may-care atmosphere, bustling streets and booming real-estate opportunities. Observant ecotourists, marginalized Ticos and loyalists of the 'old Costa Rica' absolutely despise the place for the *exact* same reasons.

Jacó was the first town on the central Pacific coast to explode with tourist development and it remains a major draw for backpackers, surfers, snowbirds and city-weary *josefinos* (inhabitants of San José). Although working-class Tico neighborhoods are nearby, open-air trinket shops and tour operators line the tacky main drag which, at night, is given over to a safe but somewhat seedy mix of binge-drinking students, surfers and scantily clad ladies of negotiable affection.

While Jacó's lackadaisical charm is not for everyone, the surfing is excellent, the restaurants and bars are generally great and the nightlife can be a blast.

🏃 Activities

Surfing

Although the rainy season is considered best for Pacific coast surfing, Jacó is blessed with consistent year-round breaks. Even though more advanced surfers head further south to Playa Hermosa, the waves at Jacó are strong, steady and a lot of fun for intermediate surfers. Jacó is also a great place to learn to surf or start a surf trip as many places offer lessons and it's easy to buy and sell boards here.

If you're looking to rent a board for the day, shop around as the better places will rent you a board for US$15 to US$20 for 24 hours.

Tortuga Surf Camp   SURFING

(☎2463-3348; www.tortugasurfcamp.com; surfing lessons from US$60; ⊙9am-5pm) Regardless of your age or ability, this is one of the top places in Jacó to learn to surf or improve your technique. Michael and his crew are very patient and encouraging.

Hiking

Mt Miros   HIKING

A worthwhile pastime that few tourists are aware of is following the trail up Mt Miros, which winds through primary and secondary rainforest and offers spectacular views of Jacó and Playa Hermosa. The viewpoint is several kilometers uphill. Note that the trailhead is unmarked, so ask a local to point it out to you.

🍴 Tours

Jacó Canyoning   ADVENTURE SPORTS

(☎2643-1834; www.jacocanyoning.com; Av Pastor Díaz; tours US$79-159; ⊙7am-9pm) This experienced, safety-conscious operator arranges some of the most adrenaline-charged excursions in town, from tamer waterfall rappelling to extreme canyoneering, cliff jumping and paddleboarding.

Kayak Jacó   KAYAKING

(☎2643-1233; www.kayakjaco.com; tours from US$75) This reliable, responsible company facilitates kayaking and sea-canoeing trips that include snorkeling excursions to tropical islands, in a wide variety of customized day and multiday trips. Though it does have a presence at Playa Agujas, 250m east of the beach, it's best to phone or email in advance.

Discovery Horseback Tours HORSEBACK RIDING
(☑8838-7550; www.horseridecostarica.com; rides from US$80) Nearby beach and rainforest rides are available through this highly recommended outfit, run by an English couple who offer an extremely high level of service and professionalism and who clearly take excellent care of their horses.

🛌 Sleeping

★ Room 2 Board Hostel & Surf School HOSTEL $
(☑2643-4949, in the USA 323-315-0012; www.room2board.com; dm from US$16, r with/without bathroom from US$62/59; ᴘ❊@☎☀) Now *this* is a hostel. Brand new, spacious and professionally run, it has a buzzy onsite cafe, dedicated staff who arrange tours and surfing lessons, and various configurations of rooms spread across three floors. The hammocks on the roof terrace catch the breeze, dorms come with excellent mattresses, rain showers and lockers, and there are yoga classes and movie screenings.

Buddha House GUESTHOUSE $
(☑2643-3615; www.hostelbuddhahouse.com; Av Pastor Díaz; dm US$18, s with/without bathroom US$70/35, d with/without bathroom US$80/40; ᴘ❊☎☀) Bold colors and modern art create an artistic atmosphere at this 'boutique hostel,' where the best private rooms are spacious suites. Communal areas include a breezy patio, a spotless kitchen and even a small pool, and the staff are lovely. What's less lovely is the noise: the hostel is next to a bar that parties late into the night.

Hotel de Haan HOSTEL $
(☑2643-1795; www.hoteldehaan.com; Calle Bohío; dm US$12, r from US$30; ᴘ@☎☀) A hostel rather than a hotel, this Dutch-Tico outpost is popular with backpackers and surfers on a budget. Basic private rooms have hot-water bathrooms and are tidy but dark; dorms share bathrooms. The open-air kitchen overlooks the pool area, and is a great place to meet and hang out with fellow travelers, which some guests do late into the night.

Las Camas Hostel HOTEL $
(☑8639-4241, 8533-7619; www.lascamashostel.com; Dorado Sol; dm with/without air-con US$13/11, r US$30; ᴘ❊@☎☀) This young backpacker start-up is a highly personable shoestring offering, kind of like a buddy's house. Las Camas puts you minutes away from the beach and the nightlife, yet guests seem content spending more of their time on the expansive rooftop deck. Rooms are a bit rough around the edges, but shabbiness is easy to forgive at this price range.

★ Hotel Perico Azul HOTEL $$
(☑2643-1341; www.hotelpericoazuljaco.com; r/studio/ste US$60/75/160; ᴘ❊☎☀) Tucked away off a quiet side street, this small hotel is difficult to fault. The rooms and apartments are light and spotless, with bright splashes of color, there's a small pool to relax around, staff go out of their way to make you feel welcome, and owner Mike runs the recommended Tortuga Surf Camp (p588); surfing packages can be arranged.

🍴 Eating

★ Side Street Bistro FUSION $
(☑2643-2724; Calle Bribri; sandwiches US$6-10; ⏱11am-4pm Mon, 11am-9pm Tue-Sat, 9am-5pm Sun) Ever since it opened, this little bistro has won over local and visiting fans with fresh, creative sandwiches such as the BBQ-pulled-pork sloppy joe, coffee-and-cacao-rubbed tenderloin and the reuben and the shrimp po'boys. There are local craft beers to wash them all down. And the breakfasts, oh, the breakfasts! Butter pecan waffles, maple bacon whisky eggs Benedict... In a word: awesome.

★ Namaste INDIAN $
(☑8482-6867; Calle Bohío; mains US$6-12; ⏱8am-7pm; ☎☀) You'll find this friendly little place by the delicious smells of Indian spices. Breakfast specials include *shakshuka* (Israeli-style eggs fried up with tomatoes and herbs), while the rest of the day you can feast on falafel, Bombay masala fish, chicken curry, *baba ghanoush* and other flavorful Middle Eastern and Asian dishes. Its smoothies are remarkable, too.

Soda a Cachete COSTA RICAN $
(☑8633-1831; Av Pastor Díaz; meals US$5-9; ⏱8am-8pm) Although many of the local *sodas* have been pushed out by gringo palates, this little place survives through its loyal following, who drop by for huge, excellent breakfasts and set lunches. A few bucks will get you rice, beans, a fish or meat dish of the day and some juice. It's across from the Red Cross.

The Wok
ASIAN $

(☑2643-6168; Av Pastor Díaz; mains US$4-8; ⏰11am-9pm; 🍴) The Wok's pan-Asian menu is courtesy of the Dutch owner who lived in Asia for a while and it's reliably good – especially the stir-fries and the ribs (only available on Wednesdays). The scattered tables facing Jacó's main street also provide primo people-watching. It's next to the Budget car-rental place.

🍷 Drinking & Nightlife

Bar Nirvana
BAR

(☑8429-5255; Av Pastor Díaz; ⏰7pm-2am) Great mojitos and a very chilled-out owner-bartender who built the place from scratch and is happy to chat to you. Good for after-dinner drinks and gets raucous as the night wears on.

Monkey Bar
CLUB

(☑2643-2357; Av Pastor Díaz; ⏰9pm-2:30am Tue-Sun) Attracting a young crowd of locals and visitors, Monkey Bar pumps with good times, reggaetón and pheromones.

ℹ Information

Jacó is the epicenter of Costa Rica's prostitution scene. Assuming that the working girl or guy is over 18 (not always a given), prostitution is legal in Costa Rica, but travelers who wish to explore this dark corner of Costa Rican nightlife should carefully consider the health and safety risks and negative social impacts.

Locals warn against walking alone on the beach at night, as there have been several muggings.

ℹ Getting There & Away

BOAT

Zuma Tours (☑2642-0050, 2642-0024; www.zumatours.net) Runs speedboat transfers from Jacó to Montezuma, with shuttle pick-up in Jacó between 10am and 10:30am, and 11am boat departures from Herradura (US$40, one hour). From Montezuma boats depart at 9:30am. It's also possible to get dropped off in Mal País and Santa Teresa (US$50).

BUS

Gray Line, Easy Ride and Monkey Ride run shared shuttles from Jacó to popular destinations, including Granada, Nicaragua.

Buses originate in Puntarenas or Quepos, so consult your lodgings about the latest schedule and get to the stop early.

Puntarenas US$2.20, 1½ hours, 12 daily between 5am and 7:30pm.

Quepos US$2.70, 1½ hours, 12 daily between 6am and 7pm.

San José US$5.50, 2½ hours, eight daily between 6am and 7pm.

Quepos
POP 12,907

Located just 7km from the entrance to Manuel Antonio, the small, busy town of Quepos serves as the gateway to the national park, as well as a convenient port of call for travelers in need of goods and services. Although the Manuel Antonio area was rapidly and irreversibly transformed following the eco-tourism boom, Quepos has largely retained an authentic Tico feel.

While many visitors to the Manuel Antonio area prefer to stay outside Quepos, accommodations in town are generally very good value, and there's a burgeoning restaurant scene that belies the town's small size. Quepos is also gridded with easy-to-walk streets, which provide the opportunity to interact with the friendly locals.

🏃 Activities

★ Paddle 9
ADVENTURE TOUR

(☑2777-7436; www.paddle9sup.com; tours US$60-150) These new kids on the block are a young, passionate, safety-conscious team who've introduced SUP (stand-up paddle-boarding) to Quepos (the tour leader's a pro) and who delight in showing visitors around the Pacific coast. Apart from their three-hour mangrove or ocean paddleboarding tours, their most popular outing is a seven-hour tour that involves swimming in various waterfalls, with a paddleboarding intro.

Oceans Unlimited
DIVING

(☑2777-3171; www.scubadivingcostarica.com; 2-tank dive US$110) 🤿 This shop takes its diving very seriously, and runs most of its excursions out to Isla Larga and Isla del Caño, which is south in Bahía Drake (connected via a two-hour bus trip). It also has a range of specialized PADI certifications, and regular environmental-awareness projects that make it stand out from the pack.

Unique Tours
ADVENTURE TOUR

(☑8396-0679, 2777-1119; www.costaricaunique tours.com) This established local operator organizes entertaining rafting tours of the Río Savegre, ocean and mangrove kayaking outings and more. But what makes it unique is that it's the only operator to do coastal hikes to Parque Nacional Manuel Antonio. Prices vary depending on group size.

H2O Adventures   ADVENTURE SPORTS

(Ríos Tropicales; ☑2777-4092; www.h2ocr.com) The venerable Costa Rican rafting company Ríos Tropicales has a hugely popular franchise in Quepos called H2O Adventures, which organizes rafting outings on the Naranjo, El Chorro and Savegre rivers, as well as kayaking and tubing outings. Rates for Class II to IV rapids are US$70.

🛏 Sleeping

★Villas Jacquelina   GUESTHOUSE $

(☑8345-1516; www.villasjacquelina.com; Calle 2; r US$35-70, apt US$130; P ❄ 🐾 ⓦ 🏊) By far the best budget option in town, this large, rambling building with various configurations of rooms (with/without bathrooms) is run by the indomitable Steve, an Arizonian transplant with energy to spare and tons of local knowledge, who can help arrange tours. There are large hangout spaces with hammocks, good breakfasts, and a vibe of friendly camaraderie prevails among guests.

Pura Vida Hostel   HOSTEL $

(☑2777-2321; www.puravidahostelmanuelantonio. com; dm US$10-15, r per person US$15-20, all incl breakfast; ❄ @ ⓦ) From the rainbow-hued facade to the interior murals, this place is nothing if not colorful. The rooms have tropical-colored walls, bright linens, tile floors and lockers. Big, shared balconies overlook the jungle-covered hills, where you're likely to spot squirrel monkeys passing through. It's on the southern edge of town on the road to Manuel Antonio.

Hotel Papa's Papalotes   HOTEL $

(☑2777-3774; www.papaspapalotes.com; Av 2; s with/without air-con US$45/35, d with/without air-con US$55/45; ❄ ⓦ) A decent budget choice in central Quepos, with private rooms a better bargain than at some nearby hostels. The decor won't make your social-media posts,

but the place is clean and secure. If you opt for fan-only, you'll be woken up by the dawn chorus of traffic passing along the street; pack earplugs.

🍴 Eating

★Marisquería Jiuberth   SEAFOOD $

(☑2777-1292; mains from US$7; ⓧ11am-10pm) Run by a hardworking fisherman's family, this local institution with brightly tiled floors serves some of the best seafood in town, yet is practically unknown to visitors because it's tucked out of the way. Whether you have the catch of the day, or the moreish, satisfying fish soup, the portions are wonderfully generous and the service attentive. Follow unpaved Calle 2 out of town.

★Brooklyn Bakery   BAKERY $

(Av 3; bagels US$1.50, mains US$5-8; ⓧ7:30am-6pm Mon-Sat; ⓦ 🐾) Real New York–style bagels and lox! (A real rarity in Costa Rica). Rye bread! Iced coffee! This adorable little bakery bakes its fresh wares every morning, as well as serving light bites throughout the day and delicious specials at lunchtime, such as Italian meatball sandwiches and oxtail ravioli.

Soda Come Bien   CAFETERIA $

(☑2777-2550; Av 1; mains US$3.50-8; ⓧ6am-5pm Mon-Sat, to 11am Sun) The daily rotation of delicious cafeteria options might include fish in tomato sauce, *olla de carne* (beef soup with rice) or chicken soup, but everything is fresh, the ladies behind the counter are friendly and the burly portions are a dream come true for hungry shoestringers. Or, pick up a fresh *empanada* before or after a long bus ride.

Farmers Market   MARKET $

(Calle 4; ⓧ4pm Fri-noon Sat) Self-caterers should check out the farmers market near the waterfront, where you can buy directly from farmers, fisherfolk, bakers and other food producers.

BUSES FROM QUEPOS

DESTINATION	COST (US$)	DURATION (HR)	FREQUENCY
Jacó	2.70	1½	10 daily 4:30am-5:30pm
Puntarenas	3.80	3	8 daily 4:30am-5:30pm
San Isidro de El General, via Dominical	3.80	3	5:30am, 11:30am, 3:30pm
San José	7	3½	6 daily 4:30am-4:45pm
Uvita, via Dominical	8	2	6:30am, 9:30am, 5:30pm

Manuel Antonio Area

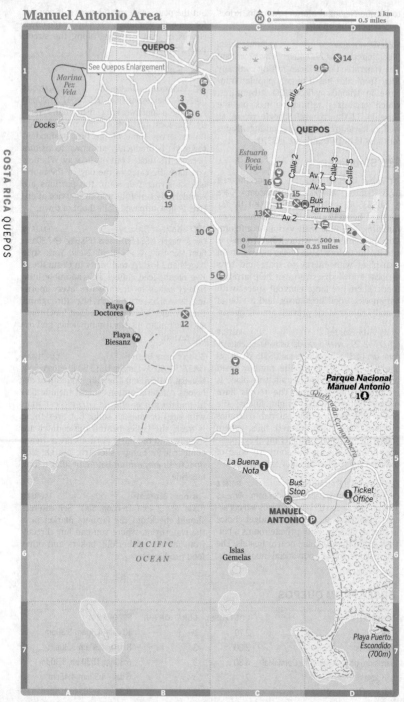

QUEPOS

See Quepos Enlargement

Marina Pez Vela

Docks

8

3

6

19

10

5

QUEPOS

9 ✕ 14

Calle 2

Estuario Boca Vieja

17

16

Av 7

Av 5

Calle 2

Calle 3

Calle 5

15

11

Bus Terminal

13

Av 2

7

2

4

0 ———— 500 m
0 ———— 0.25 miles

Playa Doctores

Playa Biesanz

12

18

Parque Nacional Manuel Antonio 1

Quebrada Camaronera

La Buena Nota

Bus Stop

Ticket Office

MANUEL ANTONIO

PACIFIC OCEAN

Islas Gemelas

Playa Puerto Escondido (700m)

Manuel Antonio Area

◎ Top Sights
  1 Parque Nacional Manuel Antonio.........D4

⊕ Activities, Courses & Tours
  2 H2O Adventures D3
  3 Oceans Unlimited B1
  4 Paddle 9 ....D3

⊜ Sleeping
  5 Backpackers Manuel Antonio..............C3
  6 Hostel Plinio...B1
  7 Hotel Papa's Papalotes.......................D3
  8 Pura Vida Hostel B1
  9 Villas Jacquelina D1
  10 Vista Serena Hostel..............................B3

⊗ Eating
  11 Brooklyn Bakery.....................................C2
  12 Falafel Bar B4
  13 Farmers Market......................................C2
  14 Marisquería Jiuberth.............................D1
    Sancho's..(see 5)
  15 Soda Come Bien.....................................C2

⊙ Drinking & Nightlife
  16 Café Milagro...C2
  17 Cuban Republik Disco Lounge..............C2
  18 El Avión C4
  19 Ronny's Place..B2

⚑ Drinking & Nightlife

Café Milagro
CAFE

(✆2777-1707; www.cafemilagro.com; Calle 4; ⊙7am-5pm Mon-Sat) Café Milagro sources its coffee beans from all over Costa Rica and produces a variety of estate, single-origin and blended roasts to suit any coffee fiend's palate, with 1% of its profits going to environmental causes via international nonprofit 1% for the Planet. Unlike its other, bigger branch en route to Manuel Antonio, this is takeout coffee only (US$3.50 to US$7); no meals.

Cuban Republik Disco Lounge
CLUB

(✆8345-9922; cover charge US$4; ⊙9pm-3am Thu-Sun) Cuban Republik hosts the most reliable party in central Quepos, and it has some kind of drink special nearly every night if you arrive early (before 10:30pm or 11pm). Later, the DJs get loud, the drinks get more pricey. Women get in for free before 11pm on Friday night and it's a nice, mixed Tico and gringo scene.

❶ Getting There & Away

Scheduled private shuttles, operated by Gray Line, Easy Ride and Monkey Ride, run between Quepos/Manuel Antonio and popular destinations such as Jacó (US$35), Monteverde (US$55), Puerto Jiménez (US$79), San José (US$49) and Uvita (US$35).

All buses arrive at and depart from the busy, chaotic main terminal in the center of town. If you're coming and going in the high season, buy tickets for San José in advance at the Transportes Morales ticket office (✆2777-0263; ⊙7-11am & 1-5pm Mon-Sat, 7am-1pm Sun) at the bus terminal; colectivo fares to San José are slightly cheaper and take two hours longer.

Manuel Antonio

As you travel the road between Quepos and Parque Nacional Manuel Antonio, the din from roaring buses, packs of tourists and locals hunting foreign dollars becomes increasingly loud, reaching its somewhat chaotic climax at Manuel Antonio village. Hordes descend on this tiny oceanside village at the entrance to the country's most visited national park. Don't show up all bright-eyed and bushy-tailed, expecting deserted beaches and untouched tropical paradise. Higher primates tend to be the most frequently sighted species, especially during the congested dry season, when tour groups arrive en masse.

But come here in low season or on a Monday, and you'll find a tranquil little village with waves sedately lapping at the white sand. And, when troops of monkeys climb down from the forest canopy to the tropical sands, you can get up close and personal with some marvelous wildlife.

◎ Sights

★Parque Nacional Manuel Antonio
NATIONAL PARK

(✆2777-0644; park entrance US$16; ⊙7am-4pm Tue-Sun) Parque Nacional Manuel Antonio is the country's smallest (just 19.83 sq km) and most popular national park. A clearly marked trail system winds through rainforest-backed white-sand beaches and rocky headlands, the wildlife (iguanas, sloths, monkeys) is plentiful, and the views across the bay to the pristine outer islands are gorgeous.

The downside? The crowds. Get here early (7am) and head for the furthest reaches of the park for a bit of tranquillity and the best chances to spot wildlife.

🏃 Activities

Swimming
There are four beautiful beaches – three within the park and one just outside the park entrance. The beaches are often numbered – most people call Playa Espadilla (outside the park) '1st beach,' Playa Espadilla Sur '2nd beach,' Playa Manuel Antonio '3rd beach,' Playa Puerto Escondido '4th beach' and Playa Playitas '5th beach.' Some people begin counting at Espadilla Sur, which is the first beach in the park, so it can be a bit confusing trying to figure out which beach people may be talking about. Regardless, they're all equally pristine, and provide sunbathing opportunities; check conditions with the rangers to see which ones are safe for swimming.

Hiking
Parque Manuel Antonio has an official road, Sendero El Perezoso, that's paved and wheelchair-accessible and connects the entrance to the network of seven short trails. None of them are strenuous, all are well marked and heavily traversed, though there are some quiet corners near the ends of the trails. Off-trail hiking is not permitted. A new (as yet nameless) trail was added in 2015, its boardwalk parallel to the Sendero Principal; it provides a quieter alternative to the crowds along the main stretch.

🛏 Sleeping

★ **Vista Serena Hostel** HOSTEL $
(☑ 2777-5162; www.vistaserena.com; incl breakfast dm US$11-18, bungalows with/without air-con US$60/50; P@🐕) Perched scenically on a quiet hillside, this memorable hostel allows gringo backpackers to enjoy spectacular ocean sunsets from a hammock-filled terrace and strum the communal guitar. Accommodations range from spartan econo-dorms to plusher dorms to bungalows for those who want a bit more privacy. Super-friendly owners Sonia and Conrad are commendable for their efforts in assisting countless travelers.

★ **Hostel Plinio** HOSTEL $
(☑ 2777-6123; dm/d US$15/60; ⚹🐕) Attuned to backpacker needs, Hostel Plinio ticks most boxes: a convenient location near Quepos, a large pool and ample common areas with hammocks and sofas for socializing, a gracious owner, an efficient tour desk and superior doubles with jungle views for couples wanting more privacy. The downside? The roadside location, meaning some rooms are noisy, and the wi-fi doesn't reach everywhere.

Backpackers Manuel Antonio HOSTEL $
(☑ 2777-2507; www.backpackersmanuelantonio.com; dm/d incl breakfast US$12/35; P⚹@🐕) This locally owned hostel has a very sociable vibe and a good location – relatively near the entrance of the park and walking distance from a good grocery store. The dorms are clean and secure (if small), and there's a grill and pool out back for socializing. Larger rooms, with a bunk and double bed, are good for groups of friends.

🍴 Eating & Drinking

Falafel Bar MEDITERRANEAN $
(☑ 2777-4135; mains US$5-9; ⏲11am-7pm; 🐕) Adding to the diversity of cuisine to be found along the road, this falafel spot dishes up authentic Israeli favorites. You'll also find plenty of vegetarian options, including couscous, fresh salads, stuffed grape leaves, fab fruit smoothies and even french fries for the picky little ones.

Sancho's MEXICAN $
(☑ 2777-0340; mains from US$5; ⏲8am-10pm; 🐕) A great view from the open-air terrace, potent house margaritas, excellent fish tacos and humongous *chile verde* burritos are just some of the draws at this friendly gringo-run joint. A place to knock back a few beers with friends in a convivial, chilled-out atmosphere, rather than woo your date.

Ronny's Place BAR
(☑ 2777-5120; www.ronnysplace.com; ⏲noon-10pm) The insane views at Ronny's Place, of two pristine bays and jungle on all sides, make it worth a detour (just for a drink – don't bother eating here). While plenty of places along this stretch of road boast similar views, the off-the-beaten-path location makes it feel like a secret find. Look for the well-marked dirt road off the main drag.

El Avión BAR
(☑ 2777-3378; ⏲11:30am-late; 🐕) Constructed around a 1954 Fairchild C-123 plane, allegedly purchased by the US government in the '80s for the Nicaraguan Contras but never used, this striking bar-restaurant is a great spot for a beer and stellar sunset-watching.

Skip the food, though, and double-check the check, as complaints have been made about overcharging.

ℹ Information

La Buena Nota (⌨2777-1002; ⊙8am-6pm) At the northern end of the village, this place serves as an informal tourist information center. It sells maps, guidebooks, books in various languages, English-language newspapers, beach supplies and souvenirs; it also rents out body boards. Look for a free copy of the English-language *Quepolandia*, which details everything to see and do in the area.

Ticket Office (⌨2777-5185; park entrance US$16; ⊙7am-4pm Tue-Sun) The park ticket office is around 20m from the park entrance on your left.

ℹ Getting There & Away

The bus stop in Manuel Antonio is at the end of the road into the village that runs along the beach. Buses depart Manuel Antonio beach for San José (US$9.10, three hours) 15 times daily between 4am and 5:30pm. Buy tickets well in advance at the Quepos bus terminal (p593).

Buses for destinations other than San José leave from the main terminal in Quepos.

Local buses (US$0.50, 20 minutes, every 30 minutes) and shared taxis connect Manuel Antonio village with Quepos.

Dominical

Dominical hits a real sweet spot with the travelers who wander up and down its rough dirt road with a surfboard under an arm, balancing the day's activities between surfing and hammock hang time. And although some may decry the large population of expats and gringos who have hunkered down here and the sheer volume of cars on its main street, proud residents are quick to point out that Dominical recalls the mythical 'old Costa Rica' – the days before the roads were all paved, and when the coast was dotted with lazy little towns that drew a motley crew of surfers, backpackers and affable do-nothings alike. Dominical has no significant cultural sights, no paved roads and no chain restaurants, but for those who come here to surf or to swing in a hammock, the place is just right.

◎ Sights

★**Cataratas Nauyaca**   WATERFALL
(⌨2787-0542, 2787-0541; www.cataratasnauyaca.com; horseback tour US$70, hike admission US$5;

⊙tours 8am Mon-Sat) This center, owned and operated by a Costa Rican family, is home to the coast's most impressive waterfalls, which cascade through a protected reserve of both primary and secondary forest. The family runs horseback-riding tours to the falls (reservations required; Dominical pickup available), where visitors can swim in the inviting natural pools. Alternatively, you can hike to the falls in one hour or so if you're in decent shape.

The center is located 10km up the road from Dominical to San Isidro.

★**Alturas Animal Sanctuary**   NATURE RESERVE
(⌨2200-5440; www.alturaswildlifesanctuary.org; minimum donation adult/under 12yr US$25/15; ⊙9-11am & 1-3pm Tue-Sun) Around 1.5km east and uphill from Dominical, this animal sanctuary takes in injured and orphaned animals as well as illegal pets, its mission being to rehabilitate those that can be and reintroduce them to the wild, and look after those that cannot. During the two-hour tour you're introduced to its residents: a macaw missing an eye, monkeys that were caged since infancy, Bubba the famous coatimundi, a caracara with a psychological problem and more. Entertaining, educational and a terrific cause.

⚡ Activities

Dominical owes its fame to its seriously sick point and beach breaks, though surf conditions here are variable. There is a great opportunity to learn surfing in the whitewater beach breaks, but beware of getting in too deep, as you can really get trashed out here if you don't know what you're doing. If you're just getting started, stay in the white water or make for the nearby Playa Dominicalito, which is a bit tamer

★**Sunset Surf**   SURFING
(⌨8917-3143, 8827-3610; www.sunsetsurfdominical.com; Domilocos; all-inclusive packages per week from US$1415; ⊙8am-4:30pm) Operated by Dylan Park, who grew up surfing the waves of Hawaii and Costa Rica, Sunset offers a variety of packages (including one for women only). It has a three-to-one student-instructor ratio and Park is an excellent teacher. Day lessons (from US$55) also available.

Dominical Surf Adventures   RAFTING, SURFING
(⌨2787-0431; www.dominicalsurfadventures.com; ⊙8am-5pm Mon-Sat, 9am-3pm Sun) A bit of

an adventurer's one-stop shop, where visitors can book white-water-rafting, kayaking, snorkeling and dive trips and surf lessons (from US$50) from its humble little desk on the main drag. Rafting trips start at US$80 (for runs on the Class II and III Guabo) and include a more challenging run on the Río Coto Brus' Class IV rapids.

🛌 Sleeping

Montañas de Agua   HOTEL $
(☑ 2787-0200; www.montanasdeagua.com; d with/without air-con US$50/30, apt US$75; 🅿 🌀 🛜) Dominical's best budget option is hidden among the lush foliage at the top of the southern spur road, south of the main drag. Even the cheapest rooms are well maintained and have tile floors, wide-plank ceilings, hot-water showers and small porches strung with hammocks. The grounds are beautiful, the staff are friendly and it's steps from the beach.

Piramys/Cool Vibes Hostel   HOSTEL $
(☑ dorm 8353-6428, private rooms 2787-0196; www.hosteldominical.com; dm/r US$12/32; 🅿 @ 🛜) At this rambling beachfront hostel at the southern end of town, the corrugated-iron roof and tarpaulin protect the open-air dorm with beds draped in mosquito nets. Downstairs, the private rooms are fairly basic but comfortable. A huge, airy lounge has hammocks and TV, and there's a bar, a communal kitchen and surfboards for rent. Dorms are first come, first served.

Albergue Alma de Hatillo   B&B $$
(☑ 8850-9034; www.cabinasalma.com; r US$70-140; 🅿 🌀 @ 🛁) Consisting of immaculate cabins clustered beneath the fruit trees in the village of Hatillo, 6km west of Dominical, this friendly B&B is run by Sabina, a charming Polish woman. Boons? Fresh produce from the property for breakfast and the owner's innate helpfulness. Banes? The location near the highway detracts from the

tranquillity of the yoga classes in the open-air studio.

🍴 Eating & Drinking

El Pescado Loco   SEAFOOD $
(mains US$8-9; ⊘ noon-6pm) This little outdoor shack has only seven menu items, but when it comes to fish and shrimp tacos with chipotle sauce and chunky guacamole, it's totally nailed the flavors. Your quest to find the perfect fish taco may be over. Our only quibble: how about real cutlery instead of disposable?

Del Mar Taco Shop   TACOS $
(tacos US$4; ⊘ 10am-9pm) On the approach to the beach, an American expat cooks up some of the Pacific Coast's best tacos in this casual surfer hangout. We prefer the fish tacos to the shrimp, which are overwhelmed a little by the batter. Chunky burritos are also available and the guacamole is superb.

Cafe Mono Congo   CAFE $
(☑ 8384-2915; mains US$4-9; ⊘ 6:30am-7pm; 🛜 🍴) Perch on a swing at the bar or at a riverside table to enjoy the best espresso in town, hands down. This open-air cafe also dishes up tasty, simple breakfasts and (largely veggie) lunches, using organic local produce. Find it at the junction of the road into town and the main drag – couldn't be simpler.

Café de Ensueños   CAFE $
(meals US$5-9; ⊘ 6am-8pm) Run by a lovely Tico family, this local cafe is tucked away at the end of the southern spur road. Organic coffee drinks, fresh juices and hearty breakfasts are all served alfresco under a covered terrace – an excellent spot for a quiet, unhurried morning. Extra hungry? Go for the gut-busting Special Breakfast.

Tortilla Flats   BAR
(☑ 2787-0033; ⊘ noon-late) The beachfront Tortilla Flats is the de facto place for surfers to enjoy sunset beers after a day in the water

BUSES FROM DOMINICAL

DESTINATION	COST (US$)	DURATION	FREQUENCY (DAILY)
Jacó	2.70	1½hr	10 daily 5am-6pm
Palmar	2	1½hr	4:45am, 10:30am, 3pm
Quepos	5.50	1hr	5:45am, 8:25am, 12:35pm, 12:45pm, 4:35pm, 4:45pm
San José	10.85	4½hr	5:45am, 2pm
Uvita	1	20min	8 daily 4:45am-6:30pm

(skip the food, though). Its open-air atmosphere and easy vibes reflect the clientele, with surf videos on continuous loop, but continents may drift before you get served.

ⓘ Information

There's a **Banco de Costa Rica** (BCR; ☎ 2787-0381; ⊗ 9am-4pm Mon-Fri) on the highway just outside of town, and a postal service upstairs in the same small shopping center.

DANGERS & ANNOYANCES

Waves, currents and riptides in Dominical are very strong, and there have been drownings in the past. Watch for red flags (which mark riptides), follow the instructions of posted signs and swim at beaches that are patrolled by lifeguards. If you're smart, the beach is no problem, but people do die here every year.

Also, Dominical attracts a heavy-duty party crowd, which in turn has led to a burgeoning drug problem.

ⓘ Getting There & Away

Gray Line, Easy Ride and Monkey Ride offer private and shared shuttle services to popular destinations such as Jacó, San José, Monteverde, Tamarindo and Sierpe; Easy Ride has direct services to Granada, Nicaragua.

Buses pick up and drop off passengers along the main road in Dominical.

Uvita

Just 17km south of Dominical, this sweet little village consists of a few dirt roads, lined with farms, guesthouses and tiny shops, a cluster of strip malls by the main Costanera Sur entrance, and a scattering of hotels in the jungle-covered hills above. With its gentle pace of life, it should give you a good idea of what the central Pacific coast was like before the tourist boom. Uvita's main attraction is **Parque Nacional Marino Ballena** (☎ 2743-8236; admission US$6; ⊗ 7am-6pm), a pristine marine reserve famous for its migrating pods of humpback whales and its virtually abandoned wilderness beaches, but there are also good waterfalls nearby and once a year it holds the country's biggest hippie-fest, the **Envision Festival** (www.envisionfestival.com).

Held a short distance from the main entrance to Uvita, the sweet little **farmers market** (⊗ 8am-1pm Sat) is a good place to mingle with locals and longtime expats, and purchase locally grown fruit and vegetables, honey and home-cooked foods.

Uvita is a perfect base for exploring Costanera Sur, which is home to some truly spectacular, and largely empty beaches, as well as an exhilarating natural water slide in the shape of **Cascada Verde** (admission US$2; ⊗ 8am-4pm).

🛏 Sleeping

★ **Cascada Verde**   HOSTEL $
(☎ 2743-8191,8593-9420; www.cascadaverde-costa rica.com; dm/s/d from US$11/22/34; 🅿 @ 🛜) ✈
If you're looking for a quiet retreat in the jungle, this hostel, run by a young German couple, is for you. About 2km uphill from Uvita, it features jaw-dropping jungle views from the dining terrace, a large communal kitchen, plenty of indoor and outdoor spaces for relaxing, appealingly designed rooms with bamboo partitions, and a waterfall a short walk away.

Flutterby House   HOSTEL $
(☎ 8341-1730, 2743-8221; www.flutterbyhouse.com; campsite US$7, dm US$14, d US$40-120; 🅿 @ 🛜)
✈ Is it possible to fall in love with a hostel? If so, the ramshackle collection of colorful *Swiss Family Robinson*–style tree houses and dorms has beguiled us. The place is run by a pair of Californian sisters, and the clientele here tends to be of the barefoot, surfing variety. Socialize at the bar.

Tucan Hotel   HOSTEL $
(☎ 2743-8140; www.tucanhotel.com; campsite/hammock/dm US$10/10/14; d from US$44; 🅿 ❄ @ 🛜) Located 100m inland from the main highway, this cheapie is popular with international travelers of all ages. The rooms are arranged around a semi-open communal area, and there are also simple tents and hammocks, as well as the lofty tree house. Bonuses include a shared kitchen, daily movies at 4pm, an Italian restaurant and a convivial atmosphere.

ⓘ Getting There & Away

Most buses depart from the two sheltered bus stops on the Costanera in the main village.

Dominical US$1, 30 minutes, 10 daily between 4:45am and 5:30pm.

Quepos US$8, two hours, departs 4:40am, 5am, 11am, 1pm and 4pm.

San José US$10.50, 3½ hours, departs 5:30am and 1pm.

Private shuttle companies – Grayline, Easy Ride and Monkey Ride – offer pricier transfers from Uvita to Dominical, San José, Quepos, Jacó, Puerto Jiménez and other popular destinations.

Península de Osa & Golfo Dulce

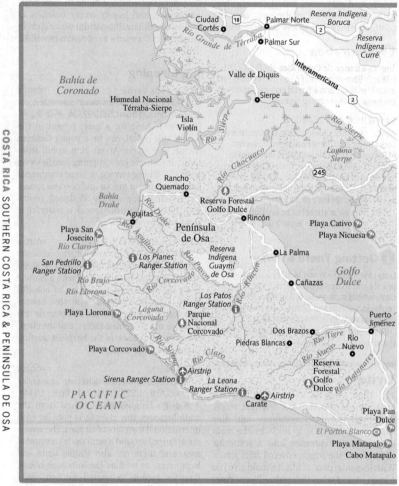

SOUTHERN COSTA RICA & PENÍNSULA DE OSA

From the chilly heights of Cerro Chirripó (3820m) to the steamy coastal jungles of the Península de Osa, this sector of Costa Rica encompasses some of the country's least-explored and least-developed land. Vast tracts of wilderness remain untouched in Parque Internacional La Amistad, and the country's most visible indigenous groups – the Bribrí, Cabécar, Boruc and Ngöbe – maintain traditional ways of living in their remote territories.

Quetzal sightings in the cloud forests are not unusual, and scarlet macaw appearances throughout the coastal region are the norm. Besides the easily spotted birds, and monkeys, sloths and coatis roaming the region's abundant parks and reserves, in Parque Nacional Corcovado there's also the rare chance to spy on slumbering tapir. Meanwhile, the rugged coasts of the Golfo Dulce and Península de Osa captivate travelers with abandoned wilderness beaches, world-class surf and opportunities for rugged exploration. This is the land for intrepid travelers yearning for something truly wild.

Valle de Coto Brus (237)

Puntarenas

Reserva Indígena
Guaymí de Coto Brus

Chacarita

Fila Costeña

Río Esquinas

Parque
Nacional
Piedras
Blancas   Gamba   (2)

Río Claro

Playa San   Refugio Nacional de   Río Claro
Josecito   Fauna Silvestre Golfito

Playa   Golfito   Paso Canoas (18km);
Cacao

Punta
Gallardo

Ferry

Zancudo   Río Coto Colorado
Playa Zancudo

(238)

Bahía de   Valle de Coto
Pavón   Colorado

Playa Río Claro
Backwash   de Pavones   Pavones
Bay   Punta   Reserva Indígena
Banco   Guaymí de
Conte Burica

Río Cotón

Río Coto Brus

San Isidro de El General

With a population of around 45,000, San Isidro de El General is the fastest-growing urban area outside the capital. Little more than a sprawling, utilitarian market town at the crossroads between some of Costa Rica's prime destinations, it's a place where few travelers choose to linger.

'El General' (often referred to as Pérez Zeledón, the name of the municipality) is the region's largest population center and major transportation hub. If you're traveling to the southern Pacific beaches or Chirripó,

a brief stop is inevitable. Some accommodations options just outside the town environs are worthy destinations in their own right.

And – a curious footnote – the women of San Isidro de El General are widely regarded as Costa Rica's finest. Perhaps it's the fresh mountain air and strong coffee?

The heart of San Isidro is the network of narrow streets clustered around the Parque Central.

🛏 Sleeping & Eating

Hotel Chirripó HOTEL $
(☎2771-0529; Av 2 btwn Calles Central & 1; r with/without bathroom US$57/41; P❄🐾📶) Let's put it bluntly: if you're traveling through town, weary and cash-poor, this is *the* choice. Popular with discerning budget travelers, this centrally located hotel is a two-minute stroll from the bus station and filled with bare, whitewashed rooms that are barren but utterly dirt- and grime-free.

Hotel Los Crestones HOTEL $$
(☎2770-1200, 2770-1500; www.hotelloscrestones. com; cnr Calle Central & Av 14; s with/without air-con US$43/36, d with/without air-con US$57/47; P❄📶🐾) This sharp motor court is decked with blooming flowerboxes and climbing vines outside – indeed a welcome sight to the road-weary traveler. Inside, functional rooms feature modern furnishings and fixtures, which are made all the better by the attentive staff who keep this place running efficiently. The restaurant is dire, though.

★Urban Farm Cafe INTERNATIONAL $
(☎2771-2442; Calle Central; mains US$5-7; ⏱7am-7pm Mon-Sat; 📶🐾) With its 'from farm to table' motto, this delightful cafe singlehandedly pushes San Isidro's dining scene up a big notch. Breakfast options range from 'Hawaiian-style' macadamia pancakes with banana to veggie omelettes and bacon wraps, while its lunchtime wraps and salads are just overflowing with fresh vegetables. Wash it down with a delectable fruit smoothie.

La Casa del Marisco SEAFOOD $
(☎8366-1880, 2772-2862; Calle Central; mains US$5-12; ⏱10am-10pm Mon-Sat) Since this unpretentious seafood spot is usually slammed at lunchtime, it's best to come during off hours for its several daily varieties of *ceviche*, fresh fish or shrimp prepared as you like it (plus pastas, burgers, salads and soups). The crowd of local clientele not-so-subtly hints at the choice sustenance served here.

❶ Getting There & Away

In San Isidro the local bus terminal (known as Mercado) is on Av 6 and serves nearby villages. The bus to San Gerardo de Rivas (for Parque Nacional Chirripó; US$3, 1½ hours) departs from the local terminal five times daily from 5:30am.

You will find **Terminal Tracopa** (☑2771-0468) on the Interamericana, just southwest of Av Central. If heading for Paso Canoas, Golfito or Palmar Norte, try to catch a bus that originates from San Isidro, or risk standing room only.

Terminal Quepos (☑2771-4744) is on the side-street west of the Interamericana.

San Gerardo de Rivas

If you have plans to climb Chirripó, you're in the right place – the tiny, tranquil, spread-out town of San Gerardo de Rivas is at the doorstep of the national park. This is a place to get supplies, a good night's rest and a hot shower before and after the trek.

Given how the park authorities have made it very difficult to obtain hiking permits (almost impossible for walk-ins), San Gerardo is doing its best to promote other activities, and its bird-filled alpine scenery makes it a beautiful place to linger. Those who don't have the time or energy to summit Chirripó can go on lovely, less-difficult hikes in its two private nature reserves, and there's rural tourism aplenty, from the local

trout farm to local cheese- and chocolate-makers in nearby Canaan.

The road to San Gerardo de Rivas winds its way 22km up the valley of the Río Chirripó from San Isidro.

❂ Sights

★**Cloudbridge**
Nature Reserve   NATURE RESERVE
(☑in USA 917-494-5408; www.cloudbridge.org; admission by donation; ☉sunrise-sunset) About 2km past the trailhead to Cerro Chirripó you will find the entrance to the mystical, magical Cloudbridge Nature Reserve. Covering 182 hectares on the side of Cerro Chirripó, this private reserve is an ongoing reforestation and preservation project spearheaded by New Yorkers Ian and Genevieve Giddy. A network of trails traverses the property, which is easy to explore independently. Even if you don't get far past the entrance, you'll find two waterfalls, including the magnificent Catarata Pacifica.

Talamanca Reserve   NATURE RESERVE
(www.talamancareserve.com) With over 4000 acres of primary and secondary cloud forest, this private reserve has numerous hiking trails, the longest being a seven-hour trek, and another leading to its 10 waterfalls. Talamanca is doing its best to promote itself as an alternative to Parque Nacional Chirripó, and non-guests are welcome to hike its trails

BUSES FROM SAN ISIDRO DE EL GENERAL

Terminal Tracopa

DESTINATION	COST (US$)	DURATION (HR)	FREQUENCY
Golfito	8.60	3	3-4 daily
Neily	8.60	4	4:45am, 7am, 12:30pm, 3pm
Palmar Norte	6.30	2	4 daily
Paso Canoas	9.25	4½	8am, 10:40am, 4:10pm, 6:30pm, 9:30pm
San José	7.10	3	13, 8:35am-8:30pm
San Vito	7.75	3½	5:30am, 9am, 11am, 2pm, 7pm

Terminal Quepos

DESTINATION	COST (US$)	DURATION (HR)	FREQUENCY (DAILY)
Dominical	3.20	1½	7am, 9am, 11:30am, 3:30pm, 4pm
Puerto Jiménez (via Palmar Norte)	10	5	6:30am, 11am, 3pm
Quepos	5.20	3	7am, 11:30am, 3:30pm
Uvita	3.60	2	9am, 4pm

DON'T MISS

CLIMBING CERRO CHIRRIPÓ

Parque Nacional Chirripó (☑2742-5083; park fee per day US$20; ☺closed Oct & 2nd half of May) While much of the Cordillera de Talamanca is difficult to access, Costa Rica's highest peak, Cerro Chirripó (3820m), is the focus of popular two-day ascents from San Gerardo de Rivas. The only way up the peak is on foot, and although the trekking route is long and challenging, watching the sunrise from such lofty heights, literally above the clouds, is an undeniable highlight of Costa Rica. Most hikers go up to Crestones Base Lodge and summit at sunrise the following day.

Sleeping & Eating

Crestones Base Lodge (dm US$39; ☎) The only accommodations in the park, with room for up to 54 people in dorm-style bunks; the price includes sheets, pillow and blankets. Solar panels provide electric light for limited hours, though showers are cold, and there's a good cafeteria serving three meals per day (US$10 to US$13 per meal). Amazingly, the lodge also has wi-fi. Reservations are essential.

Information

It is essential that you stop at the ranger station (p602) in San Gerardo de Rivas at least one day before you intend to climb Chirripó to register your park permit (bring your reservation and payment confirmation). After you've done that, you have to confirm your Crestones Base Lodge reservation at the consortium office.

Jane & Fraser Tyrell (☑2556-8664, UK 0800 612 8718, US & Canada 888-434-0076; chirripo@costaricarios.com) Jane and Fraser Tyrell specialize in assisting Chirripó-bound hikers with securing park permits and accommodation reservations for Crestones Base Lodge. They charge US$15 per person to make relevant reservations for one night or US$20 for two nights. You'll still have to register your permit with the ranger station the day before the hike.

Getting There & Away

Travelers connect to the trails via the mountain village of San Gerardo de Rivas, which is also home to the ranger station. From opposite the ranger station, in front of Cabinas El Bosque, there is free transportation to the trailhead at 5am. Also, several hotels offer early-morning trailhead transportation for their guests.

---

for a day fee of US$25. ATV tours are available both to guests and non-guests.

🍴 Sleeping & Eating

⭐**Casa Mariposa** HOSTEL **$**
(☑2742-5037; www.hotelcasamariposa.net; dm US$16, d US$40-60; 🅿@) 🧷 Just 50m from the park entrance, this adorable hostel is built into the side of the mountain and is characterized by the warmth and knowledge of owners John and Jill. Traveler-oriented benefits – warm clothes to borrow for the hike, laundry service, assistance with booking the Chirripó lodge and tips on alternative activities in the area – make it ideal.

Casa Hostel Chirripó HOSTEL **$**
(☑2742-5020; www.casachirripo.com; dm US$15, r with/without bathroom US$40/35; ☎) Near the football field, this colorful new hostel offers its guests a free shuttle to the park entrance

at 5am, gives them a space to cook and socialize, and post-hike provides cozy rooms and dorms to lay down their weary heads.

El Urán Hotel y Restaurante HOSTEL **$**
(☑2742-5003; www.hoteluran.com; r per person without bathroom US$22, d US$57, all incl breakfast; 🅿☎) Just 70m below the trailhead, these no-nonsense budget digs are a longtime mecca for hikers heading to/from Chirripó. Budget-friendly rooms are fine for a restful snooze, while the onsite restaurant, grocery store and laundry facility all cater to the shoestring set. Note that it's possible to buy beer here (the *pulpería* doesn't sell alcohol).

⭐**Casa de los Celtas** B&B **$$**
(☑8707-2921, 2770-3524; www.casaceltas.com; r US$60; 🅿☎) Overlooking 4 acres of native greenery and brightened by Sheelagh's orchid collection, this delightful B&B is run by two retired British travelers, whose genuine

warmth and knowledge of the area greatly enhances your stay. Choose between a twin room or a compact, self-contained cottage and feast on Sheelagh's gourmet cooking (three-course dinner US$19). Extensive breakfasts feature plenty of fresh fruit.

❶ Information

Consorcio Aguas Eternas (Consortium Office; ☑ 2742-5097; infochirriposervicios@gmail. com; ⏰ 8am-noon & 1:30-4:30pm) Right by the soccer field, this is the office responsible for the Crestones Base Lodge bookings. If you've had a third party reserve your space for you, you still need to check in here the day before your hike; otherwise, you may only reserve your space via phone or email with a prior reservation code from the park ranger's office.

Ranger Station (Sinac; ☑ 2742-5348; ⏰ 6:30am-noon & 1-4:30pm) The Chirripó ranger station is 1km below the soccer field, at the entrance to San Gerardo de Rivas. If you've made reservations at Crestones Base Lodge and to hike up Cerro Chirripó, you must stop by the day before to confirm your permit. If you haven't booked your park permit in advance, there's a very slim chance of next-day availability.

❶ Getting There & Away

Arriving via public transportation requires a connection through San Isidro. Buses to San Isidro depart from the soccer field six times daily (three daily on Sunday) between 5.15am and 9pm (US$2, 1½ hours).

Palmar

At the intersection of the country's two major highways, this crossroads town serves as a gateway to the Península de Osa and Golfo Dulce. This functional banana-growing settlement makes a convenient base for exploring the Sierpe area if you have a particular interest in pre-Columbian stone spheres

(that the area is newly famous for), and the Festival de la Luz in December is worth stopping for.

Palmar is actually split in two – to get from Palmar Norte to Palmar Sur, take the Interamericana southbound over the Río Grande de Térraba bridge, then take the first right. Most facilities are in Palmar Norte, clustered around the intersection of the Carretera Interamericana and the Costanera Sur – if you're heading to Bahía Drake via Sierpe, this is your last chance to hit an ATM. Palmar Sur is home to the airstrip and a little park with an excellent example of a stone sphere.

❶ Getting There & Away

Buses to San José and San Isidro stop on the east side of the Interamericana. Other buses leave from in front of the Pirola's Pizza and Seafood restaurant or the Tracopa window across the street. Buses to Sierpe depart from in front of the Gollo store.

Sierpe

This sleepy village on the Río Sierpe is the gateway to Bahía Drake, and if you've made a reservation with any of the jungle lodges further down the coast, you will be picked up here by boat. Beyond its function as a transit point, there is little reason to spend any more time here than necessary, though it's well worth taking a peek at one of the celebrated pre-Columbian stone spheres in the main square. If you're visiting the excellent Sitio Arqueológico Finca 6 (☑ 2100-6000; finca6@museocostarica.go.cr; 4km north of Sierpe; admission US$6; ⏰ 8am-4pm Tue-Sun) near Sierpe, it's worth stopping here for lunch. Mangrove cruises can also be arranged here.

BUSES FROM PALMAR

DESTINATION	COST (US$)	DURATION	FREQUENCY (DAILY)
Dominical	2	1½hr	8:20am, 1:20pm, 3:45pm
Golfito	3.20	1½hr	11:20am, 12:30pm
Neily	3.20	1½hr	6 daily 7:30am-5:30pm
Paso Canoas	3.80	2hr	6 daily 10:30am-8:30pm
San Isidro	6.20	2½hr	8:30am, noon, 2:45pm, 5pm
San José	11.50	5½hr	16-19 daily 5:40am- 6:30pm
Sierpe	0.75	40min	7 daily 4:30am-5:30pm

ℹ Information

La Perla del Sur (☑ 2788-1082, 2788-1071; info@perladelsur.net; ⊙ 8am-5pm; 🛜) This info center and open-air restaurant next to the boat dock is the hub of Sierpe – arrange your long-term parking (US$6 per night), book a tour and take advantage of the free wi-fi before catching your boat to Drake. The food is hit and miss, though.

ℹ Getting There & Away

Scheduled flights and charters fly into Palmar Sur, 14km north of Sierpe. If you are heading to Bahía Drake, most upmarket lodges will arrange the boat transfer. Should things go awry or if you're traveling independently, there's no shortage of water taxis milling about – be prepared to negotiate a fair price. Regularly scheduled *colectivo* boats depart Sierpe for Drake at 11:30am (US$15) and 4:30pm (US$20).

Buses to Palmar Norte (US$0.70, 40 minutes) depart from in front of Pulpería Fenix at 5:30am, 8:30am, 10:30am, 12:30pm, 3:30pm and 6pm. A taxi to Palmar costs about US$28.

Bahía Drake

POP 295

One of Costa Rica's most isolated destinations, Bahía Drake *(drah-kay)* is a veritable Lost World, bordered by Parque Nacional Corcovado to the south. In the rainforest canopy, howlers greet the rising sun with their haunting bellows, while pairs of macaws soar between the treetops, filling the air with their cacophonous squawking. Offshore in the bay itself, pods of migrating dolphins flit through turquoise waters near the beautiful Isla del Caño marine reserve.

One of the reasons why Bahía Drake is brimming with wildlife is that it remains largely cut off from the rest of the country. Life is centered around the sedate village of Agujitas, the area's transportation hub, which attracts increasing numbers of backpackers and nature lovers with inexpensive digs and plenty of snorkeling, diving and wildlife-watching opportunities. The more remote corners of Bahía Drake are home to some of Costa Rica's best (and priciest) wilderness lodges.

🏃 Activities

Hiking

The 17km trail connecting Agujitas to San Pedrillo ranger station is an excellent day hike. Along the way are gorgeous beaches, the possibility of a canoe tour with **Río Claro**

Tours (per person US$15), and wildlife to be seen. You can also get a tour operator to drop you by boat at a point of your choosing and walk back to Agujitas.

Swimming & Snorkeling

About 20km west of Agujitas, **Isla del Caño** (admission US$10, diving charge US$4, incl in tour price) is considered the best place for snorkeling in this area. Lodges offer day trips to the island (from US$80 per person), usually including the park fee, snorkeling equipment and lunch on Playa San Josecito. The clarity of the ocean and the variety of the fish fluctuate according to water and weather conditions: it's worth inquiring before booking.

Along the coast between Agujitas and Corcovado, Playa San Josecito and Playa Caletas attract many tropical fish, while Playa Cocalito, a small, pretty beach near Agujitas, is pleasant for swimming and sunbathing.

👉 Tours

⭐**Pacheco Tours** WILDLIFE WATCHING
(☑ 8906-2002; www.pachecotours.com) Very competent all-rounder organizing snorkeling tours to Isla del Caño, day trips to Corcovado, day-long tours combining jungle trekking with waterfall swimming (US$55), and whale-watching excursions.

Corcovado Info Center WILDLIFE WATCHING
(☑ 2775-0916, 8846-4734; www.corcovadoinfocenter.com; whale-watching/Corcovado day tours US$110/90) Leading tours into Corcovado and Isla del Caño, all guides with this outfit are local, bilingual and ICT-certified. It's at the beach end of the main road in Agujitas.

Drake Divers DIVING
(☑ 2775-1818; www.drakediverscr.com; ⊙ 7am-7pm) This outfit specializes in diving at Isla del Caño, charging US$135/180 for two-/three-tank dives. Snorkelers are welcome to come along (US$80). The equipment is not the newest and the boat is not a purpose-built diving boat, but the divemasters are experienced.

🛌 Sleeping & Eating

⭐**Martina's Place** GUESTHOUSE $
(☑ 8720-0801; www.puravidadrakebay.com; dm/s/d from US$11/25/35; 🛜) With a few fan-cooled dorms and rooms inside, this budget spot also provides access to a clean, thoroughly

COSTA RICA BAHÍA DRAKE

equipped communal kitchen and an onsite cafe serving German meatballs! This friendly, economical place in the middle of Agujitas is an excellent spot to meet other budget travelers, tap into Martina's wealth of Corcovado intel and arrange a variety of local tours.

Drake Bay Backpackers   HOSTEL **$**
(📞2775-0726; www.drakebaybackpackers.com; camping per person US$5, dm/s/d from US$13/25/30; **P❋🛜**) This excellent non-profit, off-the-beaten-track hostel is a boon for budget travelers wanting to connect with the local community. Competitively priced local tours can be arranged, there's a nice hangout area, a BBQ patio and even a volleyball court, and homestays (US$30) can be arranged. It's in the village of El Progreso, near the airstrip, straight after the river crossing.

★**Casita Corcovado**   B&B **$$**
(📞2775-0627, 8996-8987; www.casitacorcovado. com; s/d incl breakfast US$57/80; ❂❋🛜) Jamie and Craig's lovely little oceanfront home has three rooms, all sharing a bathroom and with super-comfortable orthopedic beds. Guests have access to two breezy patios and plenty of hammocks, with the amenities of the village at the doorstep, but it's the warmth and helpfulness of your hosts that sets this place apart. Delicious, home-cooked meals are also available.

★**Finca Maresia**   BUNGALOW **$$**
(📞8888-1625, 2775-0279; www.fincamaresia.com; Camino a Los Planes; incl breakfast s US$30-75, d US$40-90) The globe-trotting owners have created this absolute gem of a *finca* hotel that stretches across a series of hills. Budget travelers are drawn by the excellent value-to-price ratio and superb wildlife-watching opportunities. All rooms and the open-air communal area are exposed to an audio track of jungle sounds, and manager Juan is a phenomenal host.

❶ Getting There & Away

BOAT
All of the hotels offer boat transfers between Sierpe and Bahía Drake with prior arrangements. Most hotels in Drake have beach landings, so wear appropriate footwear.

If you have not made advance arrangements with your lodge for a pick-up, two *colectivo* boats depart daily from Sierpe at 11:30am and 4:30pm, and from Bahía Drake back to Sierpe at 7:15am (US$15) and 2:30pm (US$20).

BUS
A bus to La Palma (where you can connect to a bus to Puerto Jiménez) picks passengers up along the beach road and in front of the supermarkets at around 4am and 1:30pm (US$5, two hours). The return journey from La Palma is at 11am and 4:45pm. Double-check departure times locally.

Puerto Jiménez

POP 3036

Sliced in half by the swampy, overgrown Quebrada Cacao, and flanked on one side by the emerald waters of the Golfo Dulce, the vaguely Wild West outpost of Puerto Jiménez is shared equally by local residents and wildlife. While walking through the dusty streets of Jiménez (as it's known to locals), it's not unusual to spot scarlet macaws roosting on the soccer field, or white-faced capuchins traversing the treetops adjacent to the main street.

On the edge of Parque Nacional Corcovado, Jiménez is the preferred jumping-off point for travelers heading to the famed Sirena ranger station, and a great place to organize an expedition, stock up on supplies, eat a hot meal and get a good night's rest before hitting the trails.

Despite the region's largest and most diverse offering of hotels, restaurants and other tourist services, this is very much a close-knit Tico community at its core.

☞ Tours

★**Osa Wild**   TOUR
(📞8709-1083, 8376-1152, 2735-5848; www. osawildtravel.com; Rte 245, downtown Puerto Jiménez; tours from US$30, 1-day Corcovado tour US$85; ☉8:30am-noon & 2:30-7pm) 🌿 Osa Wild is *the* way to connect with Corcovado park and Osa. It's just what the area so desperately needed: a resource for travelers to connect with community-oriented initiatives that go to the heart of the real Osa through homestays, farm tours and sustainable cultural exchanges. It also offers more typical stuff like kayaking tours and guided trips through Corcovado.

Osa Aventura   ADVENTURE TOUR
(📞8372-6135, 2735-5670; www.osaaventura.com) 🌿 Run by Mike Boston, a biologist with a real passion for nature, Osa Aventura aims to introduce travelers to the beauty of rainforest life and to raise awareness of the need to preserve Corcovado's unique envi-

ronment. Adventures vary from three-day treks through Corcovado to a new tour that focuses on Golfo Dulce's rural communities. Custom tours also available.

Surcos Tours TOUR
(☑ 8603-2387, 2227-1484; www.surcostours.com)
🖋 A trio of excellent guides make Surcos the best company tours into Osa that focus on wildlife and birdwatching. Tours vary from day hikes in Corcovado and Matapalo to multiday experiences in Corcovado and specialized birding tours. Arrangements for tours are made through its website.

🛏 Sleeping

Cabinas Back Packer GUESTHOUSE $
(☑ 2735-5181; s/d with air-con US$30/40, without air-con US$17/30; ❈ 🛜) One of the better budget digs – it's squeaky clean, relatively quiet as it's a couple of blocks from the main street, and comes with a front garden strung with hammocks. Rooms share clean bathrooms and there are bicycles for guest use. It also rents tents and camping gear and there's even a brightly tiled kitchen, available for a US$5 fee.

Lunas Hostel HOSTEL $
(☑ 2735-6007; www.lunashostel.com; dm/d US$12/24; ❈ 🛜) A backpacker haven presided over by friendly and helpful owner Alex, who's been a guardian angel to more than one traveler in distress. While the fan-cooled dorms and rooms are can't-swing-a-cat size, the handmade furniture and excellent mattresses are a boon. Shared bathrooms only. Alex can arrange Corcovado tours, though there have been mixed reports about the guide he works with.

Oro Verde Hostel HOSTEL $
(☑ 2735-5241; www.oroverdehostel.com; dm/s/d US$10/15/24; ❈ 🛜) This super-central, rambling hostel offers spacious, spartan and rather anonymous rooms and dorms. However, the hot water is reliable, there's a guest kitchen, and the friendly couple who own the place go out of their way to be helpful. Light sleepers: try to avoid the rooms facing the main drag.

Cabinas Marcelina HOTEL $
(☑ 2735-5286, 2735-5007; www.jimenezhotels.com/cabinasmarcelina; s/d with air-con US$36/50, without air-con US$25/45; 🅿 ❈ 🛜) Marcelina's place is a long-standing favorite among budget travelers looking for a peaceful night's sleep. The concrete building is painted

salmon pink and is surrounded by blooming trees, lending it a homey atmosphere. Rooms have modern furniture, fluffy towels and tile bathrooms. The owner is largely AWOL, though, so this is not the place to book excursions.

★**Cabinas Jiménez** CABINA $$
(☑ 2735-5090; www.cabinasjimenez.com; s/d from US$45/60, cabinas US$80-120; 🅿 ❈ 🛜 🛝) Cabinas Jiménez is hands-down the nicest place to stay in Jiménez proper. All of the rooms come with fridges and jungle scenes painted on the walls, and poolside rooms come with chill-out patios. Pricier *cabinas* have kitchenettes and fantastic views of the lagoon. Bikes and kayaks are free for guests' use, and the bilingual staff is friendly and helpful.

🍴 Eating

★**Restaurante Monka** COSTA RICAN $
(☑ 2735-5051; mains US$5-6; ⊙ 6am-10pm; 🛜 🍴) Bright and airy and the best breakfast spot in town, Monka does excellent smoothies and extensive breakfast platters, from American-style, involving bacon and pancakes, to Mexican-style *huevos rancheros*. The rest of the day you can fill up on good, inexpensive *casados*. Several breakfast options and *casados* are vegetarian.

★**Jardín Dulce** FRENCH $
(mains US$6-8; ⊙ 7am-9pm Tue-Sat; 🛜 🍴) Just across from the soccer field, this delightful garden cafe that doubles as a florist is French-run and serves delicious homemade food. Half the dishes are vegetarian, but you'll also find the likes of quiche lorraine, *croque monsieur* and Lebanese-style chicken. Whatever you do, don't skip the homemade sweets: the fame of its truffles has spead far and wide.

Los Delfines COSTA RICAN $
(☑ 2735-5083; meals US$6-14; ⊙ 10am-10pm) At the end of the beach road that passes the waterfront walk, Los Delfines is the perfect toes-in-the-sand spot for a late *gallo pinto* breakfast or a beer and delish *ceviche* after sunning on the crescent of beach just beyond.

Restaurant Carolina COSTA RICAN $
(☑ 2735-5185; dishes US$3-8; ⊙ 6am-10pm; 🛜) This local favorite on the main drag still attracts its share of expats, nature guides, tourists and locals. Expect Tico standards, fresh-fruit drinks, extensive breakfasts, good

coffee and cold beers that go down pretty easily on a hot day.

ℹ️ Information

The **police** and **post office** (🕐 8am-5pm Mon-Sat) can be found near the soccer field.

Área de Conservación Osa (ACOSA; Osa Conservation Area Headquarters; ☎ 2735-5036; Corcovado park fee per person per day US$15; 🕐 8am-noon & 1-4pm Mon-Fri) Information about Parque Nacional Corcovado, Isla del Caño, Parque Nacional Marino Ballena and Golfito parks and reserves.

Banco Nacional (☎ 2735-5020; 🕐 8:30am-3:45pm Mon-Fri) It has an ATM.

BCR (Banco de Costa Rica; ☎ 2735-5260; 🕐 9am-4pm Mon-Fri) Across from the church; it also has an ATM.

ℹ️ Getting There & Away

BOAT

Several fast **ferries** (☎ 8632-8672, 8656-0926, 8722-3828) travel to Golfito (US$6, 30 minutes), departing at 6am, 8:45am, 11:30am, 2pm and 4:20pm daily. Double-check current schedules, as they change often and without notice.

BUS

Most buses arrive at the peach-colored terminal on the west side of town. All of these pass La Palma (23km away) for the eastern entry into Corcovado.

TAXI

The *colectivo* (shared truck taxi) runs daily to Cabo Matapalo (1½ hours, US$9) and Carate (2½ hours, US$19) on the southern tip of the national park. **Departures** (☎ 8837-3120, 8832-8680) are from Soda Deya at 6am and 1:30pm, returning at 8:30am and 4pm.

Parque Nacional Corcovado

This national park takes up 40% of the Osa Peninsula and is the last great original tract of tropical rainforest in Pacific Central America. The bastion of biological diversity is home to half of Costa Rica's species, including the largest population of scarlet macaws, as well as countless other endangered species, including Baird's tapir, the giant anteater and the world's largest bird of prey, the harpy eagle.

Corcovado's amazing biodiversity as well as the park's demanding, multiday hiking trails have long attracted a devoted stream of visitors who descend from Bahía Drake and Puerto Jiménez to see the wildlife and experience a bona fide jungle adventure.

🏃 Activities

There are three main trails in the park that are open to visitors, as well as shorter trails around the ranger stations. Trails are primitive and the hiking is hot, humid and insect-ridden, but the challenge of the trek and the interaction with wildlife at Corcovado are thrilling. Carry plenty of food, water and insect repellent.

The main route traverses the park from Los Patos to Sirena, then exits the park at La Leona (or vice versa). This allows hikers to begin and end their journey in or near Puerto Jiménez, offering easy access to La Leona and Los Patos.

The most popular section is La Leona to Sirena, with an additional trail section running parallel to the beach trail for those who don't want to expose themselves to the relentless sun. The toughest day is the trek from La Tarde to Sirena via Los Patos – a whopping 30km.

A new El Tigre trail loop has been added that starts in Dos Brazos and dips into the park but doesn't join up with the rest of the trail network; you still have to pay the full park fee to hike it, though.

Hiking is best in the dry season (from December to April), when there is still regular rain but all of the trails are open. It remains muddy, but you won't sink quite as deep.

👉 Tours

All visitors to Corcovado must be accompanied by an ICT-certified guide. Besides their intimate knowledge of the trails, local guides

BUSES FROM PUERTO JIMÉNEZ

DESTINATION	COST (US$)	DURATION (HR)	FREQUENCY (DAILY)
La Palma	2.60	1	at least once hourly
Neily	4.60	3	5:30am, 2pm
San Isidro de General	10	5½	5am, 9am, 1pm
San José	13	8	5am, 9am

are amazingly informed about flora and fauna, including the best places to spot various species. Most guides also carry telescopes, allowing for up-close views of wildlife.

Guides are most often hired through the Área de Conservación Osa park office (p606) in Puerto Jiménez, or through hotels and tour operators. Two recommended local offices are the super-reliable, locally run Osa Wild (p604) in Puerto Jiménez and Corcovado Info Center (p603) in Bahía Drake. Prices vary considerably depending on the season, availability, size of your party and type of expedition you want to arrange. In any case, you will need to negotiate a price that includes park fees, meals and transportation.

Sleeping & Eating

Camping costs US$6 per person per day at the Sirena, La Leona and San Pedrillo ranger stations; facilities include potable water and latrines. Remember to bring a flashlight or a headlamp, as the campsites are pitch black at night. Camping is not permitted anywhere other than the three ranger stations; there are no accommodations at Los Patos.

All visitors are required to pack out all of their trash.

Sirena ranger station serves meals (US$20 to US$25 per meal) by advance reservation only and there are no cooking facilities. All other ranger stations have drinking water, but you have to bring your own provisions.

Information

Information and maps are available at the office of Área de Conservación Osa (p606) in Puerto Jiménez, where you also have to pay your park entry fee of US$15 per day.

Park headquarters are at Sirena ranger station on the coast in the middle of the park. Other ranger stations are located on the park boundaries: San Pedrillo station in the northwest corner on the coast; La Leona station in the southeast corner on the coast (near the village of Carate); there's a new ranger station in Dos Brazos village; and the rebuilt Los Patos ranger station is actually just outside the park boundary, closest to La Tarde.

Getting There & Away

FROM BAHÍA DRAKE
From Bahía Drake, you can walk the coastal trail that leads to San Pedrillo station (about seven hours from Agujitas). Many lodges and tour companies run day tours here, with a boat ride to San Pedrillo (30 minutes to an hour, depending on the departure point) or Sirena (one to 1½ hours).

FROM CARATE
In the southeast, the closest point of access is Carate, from where La Leona station is a one-hour, 3.5km hike west along the beach.

Carate is accessible from Puerto Jiménez via a poorly maintained, 45km dirt road. This journey is an adventure in itself, and often allows for some good wildlife-spotting along the way. A 4WD *colectivo* travels this twice daily for US$9, departing Carate at 8.15am and 3.45pm. Otherwise you can hire a 4WD taxi for around US$90.

FROM LA PALMA
From the north, the closest point of access is the town of La Palma, from where you can catch a bus or taxi south to Puerto Jiménez or north to San José. It's 14km from La Palma to the ranger station at Los Patos.

Golfito

POP 7880

With a long and sordid history, spread-out Golfito is a rough-around-the-edges port that stretches out along the Golfo Dulce. The town was built on bananas – the United Fruit Company moved its regional headquarters here in the '30s. In the 1980s, declining markets, rising taxes, worker unrest and banana diseases forced the company's departure.

In an attempt to boost the region's economy, the federal government built the duty-free Zona Americana in Golfito. This surreal shopping mall Depósito Libre (⊗8am-9pm)

BUSES FROM GOLFITO

DESTINATION	COST (US$)	DURATION (HR)	FREQUENCY (DAILY)
Neily	2.90	1½	hourly 6am-7pm
Pavones	3.80	2½	10am & 3pm
San José, via San Isidro de El General (Tracopa)	14.70	7	5am & 1.30pm
Zancudo	3.80	3	10am & 3pm

attracts Ticos and expats from around the country, who descend on the otherwise decaying town for 24-hour shopping sprees. There are a few other attractions, but Golfito is largely a transportation hub for hikers heading to Corcovado, surfers heading to Pavones and sportfishers.

ⓘ Getting There & Away

Fast ferries travel to Puerto Jiménez from the Muellecito (US$6, 30 minutes), departing at 6am, 8:45am, 11:30am, 2pm and 4:20pm daily. This schedule is subject to change, so it's best to check for current times at the dock; in any event, show up early to ensure a spot.

Most buses stop at the depot opposite the small park in the southern part of town. Tracopa buses depart from the stop in front of Muelle Bananero.

Pavones

POP 2732

Home to the second-longest left-hand surf break on the planet, Pavones is a legendary destination for surfers the world over. As this is Costa Rica's southernmost point, you'll need to work hard to get down here. However, the journey is an adventure in its own right, especially since the best months for surfing coincide with the rainy season.

The village remains relatively off the beaten path, and though both foreigners and Ticos are transforming Pavones from its days as a relative backwater, Pavones' few streets are still unpaved, the pace of life is slow and the overall atmosphere is tranquil and New Agey.

🏃 Activities

Pavones is one of Costa Rica's most famous surf breaks. Conditions are best with a southern swell, usually during the rainy season from April to October, but the rest of the year the waves are ideal for beginners. Sea Kings Surf Shop (☑2776-2015; ☺9am-5pm Mon-Sat) has boards for rent and arranges surfing lessons.

🛏 Sleeping & Eating

★ Rancho Burica   LODGE $
(☑2776-2223; www.ranchoburica.com; dm/r per person US$15/40; ⓟ☀☎) This legendary Dutch-run outpost is literally the end of the road in Punta Banco, and it's where surfers and like-minded spirits gather to socialize

in the evenings. All fan-cooled rooms are en suite, and hammocks are interspersed around the property, which has convivial common areas, a restaurant and a trail to a romantic jungle lookout. The owners are involved in turtle conservation, too.

Cabinas & Café de la Suerte   GUESTHOUSE $
(☑2776-2388; www.cafedelasuerte.com; r US$35-70; ☀☎) Run by a friendly surfer couple (who also run the vegetarian restaurant on the premises), this colorful three-room guesthouse is just 50m from the beach and comes with a hammock-hung terrace shared by the upstairs rooms and a secluded garden corner for the downstairs one. Rooms have fridges. From the supermarket crossroads, follow the beach road to the left.

★Lanzas de Fuego
Surf & Adventure Lodge   LODGE $$
(☑2776-2014, 8634-0739; www.lanzasdefuego. com; r per person US$45; ☀☎) Run by cheerful South African owner Rainy, this hillside lodge organizes multiday surfing, birding and sportfishing packages, with its own boat to whisk surfers to the best hot spots. It's an intimate, friendly place, with three cabins to accommodate eight guests, a huge thatched-roofed hangout space and a restaurant serving wholesome Tico meals. Cross the bridge and carry on until the signpost.

Yoga Farm   LODGE $$
(www.yogafarmcostarica.org; dm/r/cabin incl meals & yoga US$43/50/65) ♪ This tranquil retreat has simple rooms and dorms, three vegetarian meals prepared with ingredients from the organic garden, and daily yoga classes in an open-air studio overlooking the ocean. It's an uphill 15-minute walk from road's end in Punta Banco: take the uphill road and go through the first gate on the left. No wi-fi or phones; rejuvenation is key.

ⓘ Information

We cannot stress this enough: Pavones has no bank or gas station, so make sure you have plenty of money and gas prior to arrival. Very few places accept credit cards and the nearest ATM and gas station are in Laurel, an hour's drive away.

ⓘ Getting There & Away

Two daily buses go to Golfito (US$3.80, two hours). The first leaves at 5:15am, departing from the end of the road in Punta Banco and stopping by the two supermarkets. The second leaves at 12:30pm from the school. You can also pick up the early bus in Pavones; check locally for the current bus stops.

Paso Canoas

The main port of entry between Costa Rica and Panama is hectic, slightly seedy and completely devoid of charm. As you might imagine, most travelers leave Paso Canoas with little more than a passing glance at their passport stamp.

Both **BCR** (Banco de Costa Rica; ☏ 2732-2613; ◷ 9am-4pm Mon-Sat, 9am-1pm Sun) and **Banco Nacional** (◷ ATM 5am-10pm) have ATMs near the **Migración & Aduana office** (☏ 2299-8007, 2732-2150; ◷ 6am-10pm), which is next door to the Tracopa bus terminal. Rates for converting excess colones into dollars are not great. **Báncredito** (◷ 8am-4:30pm) also has an ATM.

Colones are accepted at the border, but are difficult to get rid of further into Panama.

The **Instituto Panameño de Turismo** (☏ 2727-6524; ◷ 6:30am-9:30pm), in the Panamanian immigration post, has basic information on travel to Panama.

ⓘ Getting There & Away

Tracopa buses leave for San José (US$15.40, 7½ hours) at 3:30am, 8am, 11am and 4:30pm. The Tracopa bus terminal (a window really) is north of the border post, on the east side of the main road. Sunday-afternoon buses are full of weekend shoppers, so buy tickets as early as possible. Buses for Neily (US$0.85, 30 minutes) leave from in front of the post office at least once an hour from 5:30am to 6:30pm. Taxis to Neily cost about US$10.

Just across the border, buses run to David, the nearest city in Panama, from where there are onward connections to Panama City and elsewhere. For more information, see Border Crossings (p618).

UNDERSTAND COSTA RICA

Costa Rica Today

Costa Rica acquired a new president – Luis Guillermo Solís – in 2014, although that has not changed the political landscape dramatically. Many Costa Ricans viewed Solís as an agent of much-needed but not-too-radical change when they voted him in, but his government continues to face substantial problems inherited from past administrations: namely, the growing rate of inflation, growing unemployment and severe income inequality.

One notable development: in 2015 Costa Rica became the first country in Central American to recognize same-sex marriage, and Solís has expressed his support, even flying the rainbow flag at the presidential house.

Costa Rica has long had a reputation for being green, but, to paraphrase Kermit: it ain't easy. Back in 2009, then-president Óscar Arias set an ambitious goal that Costa Rica achieve carbon neutrality by the year 2021. Meeting this goal would make Costa Rica the first carbon-neutral country in the world; but the first phase – addressing energy and agriculture – is already behind schedule. Solís has proposed extending the deadline, but by how long?

Meanwhile, the border along the Río San Juan has long caused tension with northern neighbor Nicaragua. In December 2015 the International Court of Justice ruled that Costa Rica has sovereignty over the 3km patch of wetlands in Río San Juan, and Nicaragua promised to abide by the ruling. This development suggests a new era in Tico-Nica relations, although on the ground it feels as tense as ever.

History

Like other Central American countries, Costa Rica's history remains a loose sketch during the reign of its pre-Columbian tribes, and European 'discovery' of the New World was followed by the subjugation and evangelization of Costa Rica's indigenous peoples. But in the mid-20th century Costa Rica radically departed from the standard Central American playbook by abolishing its army, diversifying its economy and brokering peace in the region, paving the way for today's stable and environmentally friendly nation.

Lost World

About 500 years ago, on the eve of European discovery, as many as 400,000 people lived in today's Costa Rica. The Central Valley hosted roughly 20 small tribes, organized into chiefdoms, with a *cacique* (chief) leading a hierarchical society that included shaman, warriors, workers and slaves. To the east, the fierce Caribs dominated the Atlantic coastal lowlands. Adept at seafaring, they provided a conduit of trade with the South American mainland.

Heirs of Columbus

On his fourth and final voyage to the New World in 1502, Christopher Columbus was forced to drop anchor near today's Puerto Limón after a hurricane damaged his ship. Waiting for repairs, Columbus ventured into the verdant terrain and exchanged gifts with welcoming natives. He returned from this encounter claiming to have seen 'more gold in two days than in four years in Spain.'

To the disappointment of his conquistador heirs, the region did not abound with gold and the locals were not so affable. The pestilent swamps, volcano-topped mountains and oppressive jungles made Columbus' paradise seem more like hell for new colonies. Scarce in mineral wealth and indigenous laborers, the Spanish eventually came to regard the region as the poorest and most miserable in all the Americas. It was not until the 1560s that a Spanish colony was established at Cartago.

Central Valley Sunday

Costa Rica's colonial path diverged from the typical Spanish pattern in that a powerful landholding elite and slave-based economy never gained prominence. Instead, modest-sized villages of small-holders developed in the interior Central Valley. In national lore, this relative egalitarianism is touted as 'rural democracy.' Costa Ricans grew corn, beans and plantains for subsistence, and produced sugar, cacao and tobacco for sale. As the 18th century closed, the population topped 50,000.

As Spanish settlement expanded, the indigenous population plummeted. While disease was the main source of death, the Spanish exploited native labor relentlessly. Outside the valley, several tribes managed to prolong their survival under forest cover, staging occasional raids, but eventually they were defeated by military campaigns.

A Sovereign Struggle

In 1821 the Americas wriggled free of Spain's imperial grip. An independent Costa Rica took shape under Juan Mora Fernandez, first head of state (1824–33). In 1824 the Nicoya-Guanacaste province seceded from Nicaragua and joined its more easygoing southern neighbor, defining the territorial borders.

As one empire receded, another rose. In the 19th century, the USA was in an expansive mood and Spanish America looked vulnerable. In 1856 the soldier of fortune William Walker landed in Nicaragua intending to conquer Central America, establish slavery and construct an interoceanic canal. When Walker marched on Costa Rica, he faced a hastily mobilized volunteer army of 9000 civilians. They stopped the Yankee mercenaries at Santa Rosa, chasing them back into Nicaragua.

Coffee Rica

The introduction of the caffeinated red bean transformed the impoverished nation into the wealthiest in the region. When an export market emerged, the government promoted coffee to farmers by providing free saplings. By the end of the 19th century, more than one-third of the Central Valley was dedicated to coffee cultivation, and coffee accounted for more than 90% of all exports.

An elite group of coffee barons monopolized the processing, marketing and financing of the coffee economy, but they lacked the land and labor to monopolize the crop. As such, the coffee economy in Costa Rica created a wide network of high-end traders and small-scale growers (unlike in the rest of Central America, where a narrow elite controlled large estates, worked by tenant laborers). Today Costa Rica has an estimated 130,000 coffee farms.

Banana Boom

The coffee trade unintentionally gave rise to Costa Rica's next export boom – bananas. Getting coffee out to world markets necessitated a rail link from the central highlands to the coast. In 1871 the government contracted the building of the railroad to Minor Keith, nephew of an American railroad tycoon.

The project was a disaster. Malaria and accidents forced a constant replenishing of workers. The government defaulted on funding and construction costs soared over budget. In 1890 the line was finally completed, and running at a loss.

Bananas were first grown along the railroad tracks as a cheap food source for workers. Desperate to recoup his investment, Keith shipped some to New Orleans. Consumers went bananas. *Fincas* (plantations) replaced lowland forests and bananas surpassed coffee as Costa Rica's most lucrative export by the early 20th century.

Joining with another American importer, Keith founded the infamous United Fruit Company, soon the largest employer in Central America. Known as *el pulpo* (the octopus) to locals, United Fruit owned huge swathes of lush lowlands, much of the transportation and communication infrastructure, and bunches of bureaucrats. A wave of migrant laborers arrived from Jamaica, changing the country's ethnic complexion and provoking racial tensions. Although Costa Rica became the world's leading banana exporter, the profits shipped out along with the bananas.

In 1913 a banana blight known as 'Panama disease' shut down many Caribbean plantations and the industry relocated to the Pacific. Eventually United Fruit lost its banana monopoly.

Birth of a Nation

Early Costa Rican politics followed the Central American pattern of violence and dictatorship. Presidents were more often removed at gunpoint than by the ballot box. Although Costa Rica began to implement more equitable policies in the early 20th century, disenfranchised groups resorted to protest politics, forcing the resignation of at least one president.

In the 1940s tension mounted as activists continued to champion the rights of the working class and the poor. Civil war broke out after disputed elections in 1948. Led by coffee grower and utopian democrat José Figueres Ferrer, armed workers battled military forces, and Nicaraguan and US forces joined in the fray. Peace was restored in under two months at the cost of 2000 deaths.

Figueres became head of a temporary junta government. His 1949 constitution granted full citizenship and voting rights to women, blacks, indigenous groups and Chinese minorities. His copious decrees taxed the wealthy, nationalized banks and built a modern welfare state. Most extraordinarily, Figueres abolished the military, calling it a threat to democracy. These actions became the foundation for Costa Rica's unique and unarmed democracy.

The Contra Conflict

The sovereignty of the small nations of Central America was limited by their northern neighbor, as the USA was hostile toward leftist politics. During the 1970s radical socialists forced the military regimes of Guatemala, El Salvador and Nicaragua onto the defensive. When they toppled the American-backed Somoza dictatorship in Nicaragua in 1979, President Ronald Reagan decided to intervene. The Cold War arrived in the hot tropics.

Under intense US pressure, politically moderate Costa Rica was reluctantly dragged in. The Contras set up camp in Costa Rica, from where they staged guerrilla raids and built a secret jungle airstrip to fly in weapons and supplies.

The war polarized Costa Rica. Conservatives pushed to re-establish the military and join the anticommunist crusade. On the opposing side, in May 1984 over 20,000 demonstrators marched through San José to give peace a chance. The debate peaked with the 1986 presidential election. The victor was 44-year-old Oscar Arias Sánchez, an intellectual reformer in the mold of Figueres.

Once in office, Arias affirmed his commitment to a negotiated resolution and reasserted Costa Rican national independence. He vowed to uphold neutrality and kick out the Contras. Soon, the US ambassador quit his post and a public ceremony had Costa Rican schoolchildren planting trees on the secret CIA airfield. Most notably, Arias became the driving force in uniting Central America around a peace plan, which ended the Nicaraguan war. In 1987 he was awarded the Nobel Peace Prize.

Paradise Found

Five hundred years later, the same dense rainforest that conquistadors had cursed revealed a hidden wealth: ecotourism.

After a crash in coffee prices in the 1970s, an unusual alliance was formed between big business and environmentalists. If wealth could not be sustained through the country's exports, then what about imports – of tourists? Costa Rica embarked on a green revolution. By 1995 there were more than 125 government-protected sites. Success encouraged private landholders to build reserves as well.

Tourism now outweighs both agriculture and industry as the biggest slice of the economy. The success of the 'green revolution' has created a new concern, namely the need for sustainable tourism. The increasing number of visitors to Costa Rica has led to more hotels, more transportation and more infrastructure upgrades. This tourist-driven encroachment inevitably places stress on the fragile ecosystem that people are flocking to see.

Culture

People

Most Costa Ricans are mestizo, having a mix of Spanish and indigenous and/or African roots (though the majority of Ticos consider themselves to be white). Indigenous groups comprise only 1% of the population. These groups include the Bribrí and Cabécar, the Brunka, the Guaymí and the Maleku.

Less than 3% of the population is black, concentrated on the Caribbean coast. Tracing its ancestry to Jamaican immigrants who were brought to build railroads in the 19th century, this population speaks Mecatelyu: a creole of English, Spanish and Jamaican English.

Chinese (1% of the population) also first arrived to work on the railroads and since then have had regular waves of immigration. Taiwanese immigration has been particularly strong.

Lifestyle

With the lack of war, long life expectancy and a relatively sturdy economy, Costa Rica enjoys the highest standard of living in Central America. Indeed, Costa Rica often tops lists of the 'happiest' places in the world.

Significantly, life expectancy in Costa Rica is almost the same as in the USA, thanks to a comprehensive socialized health-care system and proper sanitation systems.

Still, the divide between rich and poor is broad. The middle and upper classes largely reside in San José and other major cities. For the vast majority of *campesinos* (farmers) and *indigenas* (people of indigenous origin), life is harder, poverty levels are higher and standards of living are lower. This is especially true along the Caribbean coast, where the descendants of Jamaican immigrants have long suffered from a lack of attention by the federal government.

As in the rest of the world, globalization is having a dramatic effect on Costa Ricans, who are increasingly mobile, international and intertwined in the global economy – for better or for worse.

Landscape

Despite its diminutive size – at 51,000 sq km it is slightly smaller than the USA's West Virginia – Costa Rica's land is an explosion of technicolor, topographical contrasts. On one coast are the breezy skies and big waves of the Pacific. Only 119km away lie the muggy and languid shores of the Caribbean. In

PURA VIDA

Pura vida – pure life – is more than just a slogan that rolls off the tongues of Ticos (Costa Ricans) and emblazons souvenirs; in the laid-back tone in which it is constantly uttered, the phrase is a bona fide mantra for the Costa Rican way of life. Perhaps the essence of the pure life is something better lived than explained, but hearing *'pura vida'* again and again while traveling across this beautiful country – as a greeting, a stand-in for goodbye, 'cool,' and an acknowledgement of thanks – makes it evident that the concept lives deep within the DNA of this country.

The living seems particularly pure when Costa Rica is compared with its Central American neighbors such as Nicaragua and Honduras; there's little poverty, illiteracy or political tumult, the country is crowded with ecological jewels, and the standard of living is high. What's more, Costa Rica has flourished without an army for the past 60 years. The sum of the parts is a country that's an oasis of calm in a corner of the world that has been continuously degraded by warfare. And though the Costa Rican people are justifiably proud hosts, a compliment to the country is likely to be met simply with a warm smile and an enigmatic two-word reply: *pura vida*.

ENDANGERED SPECIES

The number-one threat to most of Costa Rica's endangered species is habitat destruction, followed by hunting and trapping.

➡ The legendary resplendent quetzal – topping every naturalist's must-see list – approaches extinction as its home forests are felled.

➡ A booming pet trade has extirpated the population of large, squawky scarlet macaws.

➡ Sea turtles have suffered from the destruction of beaches, which directly affect their ability to reproduce, as well as from hunting and the harvesting of eggs.

between there are active volcanoes, alpine peaks and crisp high-elevation forest. Few places on earth can compare with this little country's spectacular interaction of natural, geological and climatic forces.

The national-park system protects 35 national parks, covering 11% of the country. Scores of other protected zones include wetlands and mangroves, in addition to a slew of privately owned and operated reserves. Authorities claim that one-third of the country is under conservation. Unfortunately, some of this land is still at risk – partly because the government lacks the funds and infrastructure to enforce its protection policies.

Wildlife

Animals

Poison arrow frogs, giant tarantulas and spider monkeys inhabit our imagination of the tropics. In reality, few places live up to our wild expectations – but Costa Rica does. Considered the world nucleus of wildlife diversity, it has over 615 species per 10,000 sq km. (Compare that to the USA's 104 species.)

Birders have recorded over 850 avian species in Costa Rica. Some 200-plus species of migrating birds come from as far away as Alaska and Australia, so it's not unusual to see your backyard birds feeding alongside trogons and toucans. Because many birds in Costa Rica have restricted ranges, you are guaranteed to find different species everywhere you travel.

Visitors will almost certainly see one of Costa Rica's four types of monkey or two types of sloth, but there are an additional 230 types of mammal awaiting the patient observer. More exotic sightings might include the amazing four-eyed opossum or silky anteater, the elusive tapir or the sly jaguarundi.

Plants

Costa Rica's floral biodiversity is staggering: close to 12,000 species of vascular plants have been described in Costa Rica, and the list gets longer each year. Orchids alone account for about 1400 species.

The diversity of habitats that created this many species is a wonder – one day you're canoeing in a muggy mangrove swamp, and the next day squinting through bone-chilling fog to see orchids in a montane cloud forest. While the country's beaches are beautiful, travelers would be remiss to visit Costa Rica without seeing some of its distinctive plant communities, including rainforests, mangrove swamps, cloud forests and dry forests.

SURVIVAL GUIDE

ℹ Directory A–Z

ACCOMMODATIONS

Accommodations come at every price and comfort level: from luxurious ecolodges and sparkling all-inclusive resorts and backpacker palaces to spartan rooms with little more than a bed and four cinderblock walls. The variety and number of rooms on offer means that advance booking is not usually mandatory, although it's recommended during holiday weeks (Christmas, New Year and Easter).

The term *cabina* (cabin) is a catch-all that can define a wide range of prices and amenities – from very rustic to very expensive. In general, dorm rooms cost between US$12 and US$15, and a budget double costs up to US$40. High-season (December to April) prices are quoted in this book. Many lodges lower their prices during the 'green' season (May to November). Expect to pay a premium during Christmas, New Year and Easter week (Semana Santa). Prices are inclusive of tax and given in US dollars, which is the preferred currency for listing rates in Costa Rica.

Most destinations have at least one campground, which usually includes toilets and cold showers. Campsites are available at many national parks as well; take insect repellent, food

SLEEPING PRICE RANGES

The following price ranges refer to a standard double room with bathroom in high season. Unless otherwise stated a combined tourism and sales tax of 13% is included in the price.

$	less than US$50
$$	US$50–100
$$$	more than US$100

and supplies. Camping prices are generally per person, per night.

If you're traveling in from another part of Central America, you'll notice that prices in Costa Rica are much higher than in the rest of the region.

CHILDREN

Although Costa Rica is in the heart of Central America, it's a relatively easy place for family travel, making the nature of pre-departure planning more similar to North America or Europe than, say, Honduras.

➡ Hydration is particularly crucial in this tropical climate, especially for children who aren't used to the heat and humidity; fortunately, Costa Rica's tap water is safe everywhere (except for the rare exception, usually in remote areas).

➡ If you're traveling with an infant or small child, stock up on formula, baby food and snacks before heading to remote areas, where shops are few and far between.

➡ Many restaurants offers kids' menus but these tend to be international rather than Costa Rican.

➡ Children under the age of 12 receive a 25% discount on domestic-airline flights, while children under two fly free (provided they sit on a parent's lap).

➡ Children (except for those under the age of three) pay full fare on buses.

➡ Car seats for infants are not always available at car-rental agencies, so bring your own or make sure you double (or triple) check with the agency in advance.

CUSTOMS

All travelers over the age of 18 are allowed to enter the country with 5L of wine or spirits and 500g of processed tobacco (400 cigarettes or 50 cigars). Pornography and illicit drugs are prohibited.

EMBASSIES & CONSULATES

Australia and New Zealand do not have consular representation in Costa Rica; their closest embassies are in Mexico City. Most countries are represented in San José. Mornings are the best time to go to embassies and consulates.

Canadian Embassy (2242-4400; www.costarica.gc.ca; Oficentro Ejecutivo La Sabana, 3rd fl, Edificio 5, Sabana Sur; ⊕7:30am-4pm Mon-Thu, to 1pm Fri) Behind La Contraloría.

Dutch Embassy (2296-1490; costarica.nlambassade.org; 3rd fl, Oficentro La Sabana, Edificio 3, Sabana Sur; ⊕7:30am-4:30pm Mon-Thu, to 12:30pm Fri)

French Embassy (2234-4167; www.ambafrance-cr.org; Curridabat; ⊕7:30am-12:30pm Mon-Fri) On the road to Curridabat, 200m south and 50m west of the Mitsubishi agency.

German Embassy (2290-9091; www.san-jose.diplo.de; 8th fl, Edificio Torre Sabana, Sabana Norte; ⊕8am-noon Mon-Fri) Two blocks west of the ICE building.

Guatemalan Embassy (2291-6172, 2220-1297; www.minex.gob.gt; Sabana Sur; ⊕9am-1pm Mon-Fri) Situated 100m south and 50m west of Gimnasio Fitsimons.

Honduran Embassy (2291-5145, 2232-9506; www.embajadahonduras.co.cr; Blvr Rohrmoser; ⊕9am-noon & 1:30-5pm Mon-Fri)

Israeli Embassy (2221-6444; embassies.gov.il; 11th fl, Edificio Colón, Paseo Colón btwn Calles 38 & 40; ⊕9am-noon Mon-Fri)

Italian Embassy (2234-2326, 2224-6574; www.ambsanjose.esteri.it; Los Yoses; ⊕9am-noon Mon-Fri)

Mexican Embassy (2257-0633; embamex.sre.gob.mx/costarica; Av 7 btwn Calles 13 & 15; ⊕9am-6pm Mon-Fri) About 250m south of the Subaru dealership, Los Yoses.

Nicaraguan Embassy (2221-2884, 2221-2957; www.cancilleria.gob.ni/embajadas; Av Central 2540 btwn Calles 25 & 27; ⊕9am-5pm Mon-Fri) In Barrio La California.

Panamanian Embassy (2281-2442; www.embajadadepanamaencostarica.org; Barrio La Granja; ⊕9am-3pm Mon-Fri) In San Pedro.

Spanish Embassy (2222-5745, 2222-1933; www.exteriores.gob.es; Calle 32 btwn Paseo Colón & Av 2; ⊕8am-noon Mon-Fri)

Swiss Embassy (2221-4829; www.eda.admin.ch/sanjose; 10th fl, Edificio Centro Colón, Paseo Colón btwn Calles 38 & 40; ⊕8am-4pm Mon-Thu, to noon Fri)

UK Embassy (2258-2025; www.gov.uk/government/world/organisations/british-embassy-in-costa-rica; 11th fl, Edificio Centro Colón, Paseo Colón btwn Calles 38 & 40; ⊕8:30am-4:15pm Mon-Thu, to 1pm Fri)

US Embassy (2519-2000, 2519-2590; costarica.usembassy.gov; cnr Av Central & Calle 120; ⊕8am-noon & 1-4pm Mon-Fri) Opposite Centro Commercial del Oeste in Pavas.

FOOD & DRINK

The most popular eating establishment in Costa Rica is the *soda*. These are small, informal lunch counters dishing up a few daily *casados* (set meals). Other popular cheapies include the omnipresent fried- and rotisserie-chicken stands.

A regular *restaurante* is usually higher on the price scale and has slightly more atmosphere. Many *restaurantes* serve *casados*, while the fancier places refer to the set lunch as the *almuerzo ejecutivo* (literally 'executive lunch').

For something smaller, *pastelerías* and *panaderías* are shops that sell pastries and bread, while many bars serve *bocas* (snack-sized portions of main meals).

LBGT TRAVELERS

In Costa Rica the situation facing gay and lesbian travelers is better than in most Central American countries and some areas of the country – particularly Quepos and Parque Nacional Manuel Antonio – have been gay vacation destinations for two decades. Homosexual acts are legal, and in 2015 Costa Rica became the first country in Central America to recognise gay relationships. Still, most Costa Ricans are tolerant of homosexuality only at a 'don't ask, don't tell' level. Same-sex couples are unlikely to be the subject of harassment, though public displays of affection might attract unwanted attention.

The undisputed gay and lesbian capital of Costa Rica is Manuel Antonio; while there, look for the gay magazine *Playita*. The monthly newspaper *Gayness* and the magazine *Gente 10* (in Spanish) are both available at gay bars in San José.

Agua Buena Human Rights Association (☏ 2280-3548; www.aguabuena.org) This noteworthy nonprofit organization has campaigned steadily for fairness in medical treatment for people living with HIV/AIDS in Costa Rica.

Center of Investigation & Promotion of Human Rights in Central America (CIPAC; ☏ 2280-7821; www.cipacdh.org) The leading gay activist organization in Costa Rica.

Toto Tours (☏ 800-565-1241, in USA 773-274-8686; www.tototours.com) Gay-travel specialists who organize regular trips to Costa Rica, among other destinations.

MAPS

Unfortunately detailed maps are hard to come by in Costa Rica, so it's best to purchase one before your trip.

➡ The excellent, water-resistant 1:350,000 *Costa Rica Adventure Map* published by National Geographic also has an inset map of San José. Available online or in various book and gift shops in San José.

➡ Another quality option is the 1:330,000 Costa Rica sheet produced by International

Travel Map, which is waterproof and includes a San José inset.

➡ The **Fundación Neotrópica** (☏ 2253-2130; www.neotropica.org) publishes a 1:500,000 map showing national parks and other protected areas; available online and in San José bookstores.

➡ The ICT (Instituto Costarricense de Turismo; p531) publishes a 1:700,000 Costa Rica map with a 1:12,500 Central San José map on the reverse; it's free at the ICT office in San José.

➡ **Maptak** (www.maptak.com) has maps of Costa Rica's seven provinces and their capitals.

➡ Few national-park offices or ranger stations have maps for hikers. Topographical maps are available for purchase from **Instituto Geográfico Nacional** (IGN; ☏ 2257-7798; Calle 9 btwn Avs 20 & 22, San José; ☺7:30am-noon & 1-3pm Mon-Fri).

➡ The *Mapa-Guía de la Naturaleza Costa Rica* is an atlas no longer published by Incafo that included 1:200,000 topographical sheets, as well as English and Spanish descriptions of Costa Rica's natural areas. Out-of-print used copies can be purchased online.

MONEY

Both US dollars and Costa Rican colones are accepted everywhere and dispensed from ATMs across the country. With the exception of the smallest towns and shops in rural areas, credit cards are accepted.

➡ The Costa Rican currency is the colón (plural colones), named after Cristóbal Colón (Christopher Columbus).

➡ Bills come in 1000, 2000, 5000, 10,000, 20,000 and 50,000 notes, while coins come in denominations of five, 10, 20, 25, 50, 100 and 500.

➡ Paying for things in US dollars is common, and at times is encouraged, since the currency is viewed as being more stable than colones.

➡ In US-dollar transactions the change will usually be given in colones.

➡ Newer US dollars (ie big heads) are preferred throughout Costa Rica.

➡ When paying in US dollars at a local restaurant, bar or shop the exchange rate can be unfavorable.

Tipping

Bellhop/Porter	US$1-5 per service
Housekeeping	US$1-2 per day
Restaurants	10% service charge usually included
Taxis	N/A
Tour guides	US$5-15 per person per day

OPENING HOURS

Opening hours vary throughout the year. The following are high-season opening hours; hours will generally decrease in the shoulder and low seasons. Unless otherwise stated, count on sights, activities and restaurants to be open daily.

Banks 9am to 4pm Monday to Friday, sometimes 9am to noon Saturday.

Bars & clubs 8pm to 2am.

Government offices 8am to 5pm Monday to Friday. Often closed between 11.30am and 1.30pm.

Restaurants 7am to 9pm. Upscale places may open only for dinner. In remote areas, even the small *sodas* (inexpensive eateries) might open only at specific meal times.

Shops 8am to 6pm Monday to Saturday.

PUBLIC HOLIDAYS

Días feriados (national holidays) are taken seriously in Costa Rica. Banks, public offices and many stores close. During these times, public transportation is tight and hotels are heavily booked. Many festivals coincide with public holidays.

New Year's Day (January 1)

Semana Santa (Holy Week; March or April) The Thursday and Friday before Easter Sunday is the official holiday, though most businesses shut down for the whole week. From Thursday to Sunday bars are closed and alcohol sales are prohibited; on Thursday and Friday buses stop running.

Día de Juan Santamaría (April 11) Honors the national hero who died fighting William Walker in 1856; major events are held in Alajuela, his hometown.

Labor Day (May 1)

Día de la Madre (Mother's Day; August 15) Coincides with the annual Catholic Feast of the Assumption.

Independence Day (September 15)

Día de la Raza (Columbus Day; October 12).

Christmas Day (December 25) Christmas Eve is also an unofficial holiday.

Last week in December The week between Christmas and New Year is an unofficial holiday; businesses close and beach hotels are crowded.

SAFE TRAVEL

Costa Rica is a largely safe country but petty crime (bag snatchings, car break-ins etc) is common and muggings do occur, so it's important to be vigilant. Many of Costa Rica's dangers are nature-related: rip tides, earthquakes and volcanic eruptions are among them. Predatory and venomous wildlife can also pose a threat, so a wildlife guide is essential if trekking in the jungle.

TELEPHONE SERVICES

➡ Cell service now covers most of the country and nearly all of the country that is accessible to tourists.

➡ Public phones are found all over Costa Rica, and chip or Colibrí phonecards are available in 1000-, 2000- and 3000-colón denominations.

➡ Chip cards are inserted into the phone and scanned. Colibrí cards (more common) require you to dial a toll-free number (🖉 199) and enter an access code. Instructions are provided in English or Spanish.

➡ The cheapest international calls from Costa Rica are direct-dialed using a phonecard. To make international calls, dial 🖉 00 followed by the country code and number.

➡ Pay phones cannot receive international calls.

➡ To call Costa Rica from abroad, use the country code (🖉 +506) before the eight-digit number.

➡ Due to the widespread popularity of voice-over IP services such as Skype, and more reliable ethernet connections, traveling with a smartphone or tablet can be the cheapest and easiest way to call internationally.

Cell Phones

➡ 3G and 4G systems available, but those compatible with US plans require expensive international roaming.

➡ Prepaid SIM cards are cheap and widely available.

➡ Of the four cellular providers (Claro, Kolbi, Movistar, TuYo), Kolbi has the best coverage in remote areas (such as the Península de Osa) and Movistar has the worst.

TIME

Costa Rica is six hours behind GMT, so Costa Rican time is equivalent to Central Time in North America. There is no daylight-saving time.

TOILETS

➡ Public restrooms are rare, but most restaurants and cafes will let you use their facilities, sometimes for a small charge – never more than 500 colones.

➡ Bus terminals and other major public buildings usually have toilets, also at a charge.

➡ Don't flush your toilet paper. Costa Rican plumbing is often poor and has very low pressure.

⇒ Dispose of toilet paper in the rubbish bin inside the bathroom.

TOURIST INFORMATION

The government-run tourism board, the ICT (p531), has an office in the capital; English is spoken. The ICT can provide you with free maps, a master bus schedule, information on road conditions in the hinterlands, and a helpful brochure with up-to-date emergency numbers for every region.

TRAVELERS WITH DISABILITIES

Independent travel in Costa Rica is difficult for anyone with mobility constraints. Although Costa Rica has an equal-opportunity law, the law applies only to new or newly remodeled businesses and is loosely enforced. Therefore, very few hotels and restaurants have features specifically suited to wheelchair use. Many don't have ramps, and room or bathroom doors are rarely wide enough to accommodate a wheelchair.

Streets and sidewalks are potholed and poorly paved, making wheelchair use frustrating at best. Public buses don't have provisions to carry wheelchairs, and most national parks and outdoor tourist attractions don't have trails suited to wheelchair use. Notable exceptions include Parque Nacional Volcán Poás (p537) and the **Parque Nacional Rincón de la Vieja** (✆ 661-8139), Sector Las Pailas.

Download Lonely Planet's free Accessible Travel guide from http://lptravel.to/Accessible Travel.

VISAS

Passport-carrying nationals of the following countries are allowed 90 days' stay with no visa: Argentina, Australia, Canada, Chile, Iceland, Ireland, Israel, Japan, Mexico, New Zealand, Panama, South Africa, the US and most Western European countries.

Most other visitors require a visa from a Costa Rican embassy or consulate.

For the latest info on visas, check the websites of the **ICT** (✆ 2222-1090, in USA & Canada 866-267-8274; www.visitcostarica.com) or the **Costa Rican Embassy** (www.costarica-embassy.org).

Extensions

⇒ Extending your stay beyond the authorized 30 or 90 days is time consuming; it's easier to leave the country for 72 hours and then re-enter.

⇒ Extensions can be handled by the **migración** (Immigration; ✆ 2220-0355; ⏱ 8am-4pm) in San José, opposite Channel 6, about 4km north of Parque La Sabana.

⇒ Requirements for extensions change, so allow several working days.

VOLUNTEERING

Costa Rica offers a huge number of volunteer opportunities. Word of mouth is a powerful influence on future volunteers, so a majority of programs in Costa Rica are very conscientious about pleasing their volunteers. Almost all placements require a commitment of two weeks or more.

Forestry Management

Cloudbridge Nature Reserve (www.cloud bridge.org) Trail building, construction, tree planting and projects monitoring the recovery of the cloud forest are offered to volunteers, who pay for their own housing with a local family. Preference is given to biology students, but all enthusiastic volunteers can apply.

Tropical Science Center (www.cct.or.cr) This longstanding NGO offers volunteer placement at Reserva Biológica Bosque Nuboso Monteverde. Projects can include trail maintenance and conservation work.

Fundación Corcovado (www.corcovado foundation.org) An impressive network of people and organizations committed to preserving Parque Nacional Corcovado.

Monteverde Institute (www.monteverde-institute.org) A nonprofit educational institute offering training in tropical biology, conservation and sustainable development.

DISCOUNT CARDS

Note that discount cards are not universally accepted at museums and parks.

CARD	DISOUNTS	REQUIREMENTS	COST	APPLY
Costa Rica Discount+	car rental, activities & hotels	buy online and print	US$50 for 6 days	http://costarica discount.com
International Student Identity Card (ISIC)	museum & tour discounts	full-time student	US$25, depending on country of origin	www.isic.org
International Student Exchange (ISE)	museum & tour discounts	full-time student btwn 12yr and 26yr	US$25	www.isecard.com

Organic Farming

Finca La Flor de Paraíso (www.la-flor.org) Offers programs in a variety of disciplines from animal husbandry to medicinal-herb cultivation.

Punta Mona (www.puntamona.org) An organic farm and retreat center that is centred on organic permaculture and sustainable living.

Rancho Margot (www.ranchomargot.com) This self-proclaimed life-skills university offers a natural education emphasizing organic farming and animal husbandry.

Reserva Biológica Dúrika (www.durika.org) A sustainable community on an 8500-hectare biological reserve.

WWOOF Costa Rica (www.wwoofcostarica. org) This loose network of farms is part of the large international network of Willing Workers on Organic Farms (WWOOF). Placements are incredibly varied. WWOOF Mexico, Costa Rica, Guatemala and Belize have a joint $33 membership, which gives potential volunteers access to all placement listings.

Wildlife Conservation

Be aware that conservationists in Costa Rica occasionally face harassment or worse from local poachers and that police are pretty ineffectual in following up incidents.

Earthwatch (www.earthwatch.org) This broadly recognized international volunteer organization works in sea-turtle conservation in Costa Rica.

Profelis (www.grafischer.com/profelis) A feline conservation program that takes care of confiscated wild cats, both big and small.

Reserva Playa Tortuga (www.reservaplaya tortuga.org) Assist with olive ridley turtle conservations efforts near Ojochal.

Sea Turtle Conservancy (www.conserve turtles.org) From March to October this Puerto Limón organization hosts 'eco-volunteer adventures' working with sea turtles and birds.

ⓘ Getting There & Away

AIR

The US Federal Aviation Administration has assessed Costa Rica's aviation authorities to be in compliance with international safety standards.

DEPARTURE TAX

➡ There is a US$29 departure tax on all international outbound flights, payable in dollars or colones, though most carriers now include it in the ticket price.

➡ There is a US$7 land exit fee payable at immigration posts at land border crossings.

➡ **Aeropuerto Internacional Daniel Oduber Quirós** (LIR; www.liberiacostaricaairport.net) This airport in Liberia also receives international flights from the USA, the Americas and Canada. It serves a number of American and Canadian airlines and some charters from London, as well as regional flights from Panama and Nicaragua.

➡ **Aeropuerto Internacional Juan Santamaría** (☑ 2437-2400; fly2sanjose.com) International flights arrive here, 17km northwest of San José, in the town of Alajuela.

BORDER CROSSINGS

Costa Rica shares land borders with Nicaragua and Panama. There is no fee for travelers to enter Costa Rica; however, a Costa Rica land exit fee of US$7 is payable at immigration by credit or debit card only (no cash).

Nicaragua

There is a brand new border crossing at **Los Chiles–Las Tablillas**, thanks to the new bridge that crosses the Río San Juan just north of the Nicaraguan border.

➡ The Los Chiles–Las Tablillas border crossing is open from 8am to 4pm daily.

➡ Hourly buses connect Los Chiles and Las Tablillas (US$1, 15 minutes). There are also direct buses from San José and Ciudad Quesada (San Carlos).

➡ After walking across the border, you'll go through Nicaraguan immigration. The entrance fee is US$12, payable in US dollars or cordobas.

➡ After exiting immigration, you can catch a boat up the river or hop on a bus or a *colectivo* to San Carlos (US$2.20, 30 minutes).

➡ If you are entering Costa Rica from Nicaragua, you can take an hourly bus to Los Chiles or Ciudad Quesada, or catch the direct bus to San José, which departs at 2:30pm.

➡ It's also still possible to cross this border by boat, which is a slower but more pleasant way of doing it. There is only one round trip per day (US$10 to US$12, departing Los Chiles 1pm or when there's sufficient demand). You'll avoid the Costa Rica land exit fee, but you'll still have to pay US$12 to enter Nicaragua.

Situated on the Interamericana, **Sapoá–Peñas Blancas** is the most heavily trafficked border station between Nicaragua and Costa Rica.

➡ The Sapoá–Peñas Blancas border crossing is open from 6am to 10pm Monday to Saturday, and until 8pm Sunday.

➡ Waiting times at this border can be several hours. Plan on at least an hour's wait.

➡ **Tica Bus** (☑ in Managua 222-6094, in Panama City 262 2084), **Nica Bus** (☑ in Managua 228-1374) and **TransNica** (☑ 2223-4242; www. transnica.com) all have daily buses that serve points north and south. Regular buses depart Peñas Blancas, on the Costa Rican side, for La Cruz, Liberia and San José.

➡ Note that Peñas Blancas is only a border post, not a town, so there is nowhere to stay.

Panama

Note that Panama is GMT minus five hours, one hour ahead of Costa Rica.

At the time of writing, entry to Panama required proof of US$500 (per person), proof of onward travel from Panama and two photocopies of your passport. Travelers have reported being turned away from Panamanian border crossings even with onward bus tickets, so our tip is to reserve an airline ticket online (for a flight originating in Panama), print the itinerary, and let the reservation expire without actually booking it.

The Carretera Interamericana (Pan-American Hwy) at **Paso Canoas** is by far the most frequently used entry and exit point with Panama, and is open 6am to 10pm Monday to Friday, and to 8pm on weekends.

➡ The border crossing in either direction is generally straightforward, if slow.

➡ Get an exit stamp from Costa Rica at the immigration office before entering Panama; do the same on the Panamanian side when entering Costa Rica.

➡ There is no charge for entering Costa Rica. Entry to Panama costs US$1.

➡ Northbound buses usually stop running at 6pm. Travelers without a private vehicle should arrive during the day.

➡ Those with a private vehicle are likely to encounter long lines.

➡ Tica Bus travels from Panama City to San José (US$42 to US$58, 15 hours) daily and crosses this border post. In David, Tracopa has one bus daily from the main terminal to San José (nine hours). In David you'll also find frequent buses to the border at Paso Canoas (US$2.60, 1½ hours) that leave every 10 minutes from 4am to 8pm.

Situated on the Caribbean coast, **Guabito–Sixaola** is a fairly tranquil and hassle-free border crossing.

➡ If you are coming from Bocas del Toro, you first have to take the frequent boat to Almirante (US$2), then a public bus or shuttle to Changuinola (40 minutes), from where you can take a quick taxi to the border or to the bus station (US$5).

➡ One daily bus travels between Changuinola and San José at 10am (US$16, eight hours). Otherwise, you can walk over the border and catch one of the hourly buses that go up the coast from Sixaola.

Río Sereno–San Vito is a rarely used crossing in the Cordillera de Talamanca. The border is open 8am to 4pm on the Costa Rican side and 9am to 5pm on the Panamanian side. The small village of Río Sereno on the Panamanian side has a hotel and a place to eat; there are no facilities on the Costa Rican side.

➡ Regular buses depart Concepción and David in Panama for Río Sereno. Local buses (US$1.60, 40 minutes, 11 daily) and taxis (US$30) go from the border to San Vito.

➡ For travelers departing Costa Rica, there is a US$7 exit tax, payable at a kiosk at the border crossing.

ℹ Getting Around

AIR

➡ Costa Rica's domestic airlines are Nature Air and Sansa. Sansa is linked with Grupo TACA.

➡ Both airlines fly small passenger planes, and you're allocated a baggage allowance of no more than 12kg.

➡ Space is limited and demand is high in the dry season, so reserve and pay for tickets in advance.

➡ In Costa Rica schedules change constantly and delays are frequent because of inclement weather. You should not arrange a domestic flight that makes a tight connection with an international flight.

➡ Domestic flights (excepting charter flights) originate and terminate at San José.

BICYCLE

With an increasingly large network of paved secondary roads and heightened awareness of cyclists, Costa Rica is emerging as one of Central America's most comfortable cycle-touring destinations. That said, many roads are narrow and winding and there are no designated cycle lanes, so there's an element of risk involved.

Mountain bikes and beach cruisers can be rented in towns with a significant tourist presence, for US$10 to US$20 per day. A few companies organize bike tours around Costa Rica.

BOAT

In Costa Rica there are some regular coastal services and safety standards are generally good.

➡ The Coonatramar Ferry (p586) links the port of Puntarenas with Playa Naranjo four times daily. The Ferry Naviera Tambor (p586) travels between Puntarenas and Paquera every two hours, for a bus connection to Montezuma.

➡ Zuma Tours (p590) runs a daily water taxi between Montezuma and Jacó.

➡ On the Golfo Dulce a daily passenger ferry links Golfito with Puerto Jiménez on the Península de Osa. On the other side of the Península de Osa, water taxis connect Bahía Drake with Sierpe.

➡ On the Caribbean coast there is a bus and boat service that runs several times a day, linking Cariari and Tortuguero via La Pavona.

→ Boats ply the canals that run along the coast from Moín to Tortuguero, although no regular service exists.

BUS

Local Bus

→ Local buses are a cheap and reliable way of getting around Costa Rica. The longest domestic journey out of San José costs less than US$20.

→ San José is the transportation center for the country, though there is no central terminal. Bus offices are scattered around the city: some large bus companies have big terminals that sell tickets in advance, while others have little more than a stop – sometimes unmarked.

→ Buses can be very crowded but don't usually pass up passengers on account of being too full. Note that there are no buses from Thursday to Saturday before Easter Sunday.

→ There are two types of bus: *directo* and *colectivo*. The *directo* buses should go from one destination to the next with few stops; the *colectivos* make more stops and are very slow going.

→ Trips longer than four hours usually include a rest stop as buses do not have toilets.

→ Space is limited on board, so if you have to check luggage be watchful. Theft from overhead racks is rampant, though it's much less common than in other Central American countries.

→ Bus schedules fluctuate wildly, so always confirm the time when you buy your ticket. If you are catching a bus that picks you up somewhere along a road, get to the roadside early.

→ For information on departures from San José, pay a visit to the ICT (p531) office to pick up the reasonably up-to-date copy of the master schedule, which is also available on its website.

ℹ️ ONWARD TICKETS

→ Officially, travelers are required to have a ticket out of Costa Rica before they are allowed to enter. This is rarely and erratically enforced.

→ Those arriving overland with no onward ticket can purchase one from international bus companies in Managua (Nicaragua) and Panama City (Panama).

Shuttle Bus

The tourist-van shuttle services (aka gringo buses) are a pricier alternative to the standard intercity buses. Shuttles are provided by **Gray Line** (www.graylinecostarica.com), **Easy Ride** (www.easyridecr.com), **Monkey Ride** (www.monkeyridecr.com) and **Interbus** (www.interbus online.com).

→ All four companies run overland transportation from San José to the most popular destinations, as well as directly between other destinations (see the websites for the comprehensive list).

→ These services will pick you up at your hotel, and reservations can be made online, or through local travel agencies and hotel owners.

→ Popular destinations they serve include Quepos, Monteverde/Santa Elena, Manuel Antonio, Jacó, Dominical, Uvita, Puerto Jiménez, Arenal, Montezuma and Mal País.

→ Easy Ride offers international services directly from Jacó, Tamarindo and Liberia to Granada and Managua in Nicaragua and from Monteverde to Managua.

CAR & MOTORCYCLE

→ Drivers in Costa Rica are required to have a valid driver's license from their home country. Many places will also accept an International Driving Permit (IDP), issued by the automobile association in your country of origin. After 90 days, however, you will need to get a Costa Rican driver's license.

→ Gasoline (petrol) and diesel are widely available, and 24-hour service stations are along the Interamericana. At the time of research, fuel prices averaged US$1.01 per liter.

→ In more remote areas, fuel will be more expensive and might be sold at the neighborhood *pulpería* (corner store).

→ Spare parts may be hard to find, especially for vehicles with sophisticated electronics and emissions-control systems.

TAXI

Taxis are considered a form of public transportation in remote areas. They can be hired by the hour, half-day or full day, or you can arrange a flat fee for a trip. Meters are not used on long trips, so arrange the fare ahead of time. Fares can fluctuate due to worse-than-expected road conditions and bad weather in tough-to-reach places.

Panama

☑507 / POP 3.7 MILLION

Includes ➡

Panama City 623
Panama Canal. 642
Pacific Coast
& Highlands. 646
David 654
Boquete 657
Parque Nacional
Volcán Barú 662
Bocas del
Toro Province 664
Colón 677
Comarca de
Guna Yala. 681
Darién Province 684

Why Go?

Consider Panama a place of discovery: explore the ruins of Spanish forts on the Caribbean coast or boat deep into indigenous territories in a dugout canoe. With a spate of deserted islands, chill Caribbean vibes on one side and monster Pacific waves on the other, Panama offers the best of all beach worlds. Panama City – culturally diverse, driven, rough-edged yet sophisticated – is among Latin America's most vibrant and outward-looking capitals, with English widely spoken. In the last century, the canal defined Panama, but it's what lies just beyond that may define this one. The canal expansion spells growth and even more glitz, but for now you can still pick an empty islet and play survivor for a day.

Best Places to Eat

➡ El Último Refugio (p671)
➡ Mercado de Mariscos (p635)
➡ Mare Bonita (p650)
➡ Boquete Fish House (p661)
➡ Coco Hill (p676)

Best Places to Sleep

➡ Bambuda Lodge (p675)
➡ Magnolia Inn (p632)
➡ Hibiscus Garden (p652)
➡ Lost & Found Hostel (p664)
➡ Eco Venao (p651)

When to Go
Panama City

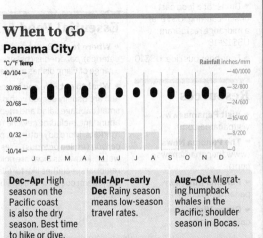

| Dec–Apr High season on the Pacific coast is also the dry season. Best time to hike or dive. | Mid-Apr–early Dec Rainy season means low-season travel rates. | Aug–Oct Migrating humpback whales in the Pacific; shoulder season in Bocas. |

PANAMA

AT A GLANCE

Currency US dollar ($)

Language Spanish

Money ATMs widely available. Credit cards accepted in some areas.

Visas Generally not required for stays of 90 days.

Time GMT minus five hours

Area 74,340 sq km

Capital Panama City

Police ☑104

Exchange Rates

Australia	A$1	US$0.74
Canada	C$1	US$0.78
Euro zone	€1	US$1.13
Japan	¥100	US$0.94
New Zealand	NZ$1	US$0.70
UK	£1	US$1.42

Set Your Budget

➡ Air-conditioned dorm bed: US$13

➡ Dinner at a food cart or self-catering: US$5; at a midrange restaurant: US$12–18

➡ Four-hour bus ride: US$10

Resources

➡ **Visit Panama** (www.visitpanama.com)

➡ **The Panama News** (www.thepanamanews.com)

➡ **Panama Info** (www.panamainfo.com)

➡ **Casco Viejo** (www.cascoviejo.org)

Connections

The principal crossing to Costa Rica is on the Interamericana at Paso Canoas. Guabito on the Caribbean side and Río Sereno in the highlands are less chaotic border posts. For more detailed information, see Survival Guide p705.

ITINERARIES

One Week

Charge the capital, seek out a rainforest adventure and end with a Caribbean getaway on this one-week itinerary. Start by imbibing the rush of Panama City. Visit Panamá Viejo, destroyed in a massive pirate raid. Pedal along Cinta Costera, the coastal beltway, to Casco Viejo, the cobblestone neighborhood with plaza cafes and rooftop bars. Day trip to nearby Miraflores Locks to witness mammoth ships squeezing through the canal. At nearby Parque Nacional Soberanía you can climb a canopy tower to search for toucans and sloths, or you can kayak Lago Gatún alongside howler monkeys and sunbathing crocodiles. Next, fly to Bocas del Toro for four days of chill Caribbean vibes. Snorkel the aquamarine waters with tropical fish and coral reefs, and explore Isla Colón by quad bike. Alternatively, escape to Isla Bastimentos, with thatched resorts and jungle lodges. For a dose of culture, take a chocolate tour on the mainland or visit indigenous groups on other islands with a community tourism initiative.

Two Weeks

Got a second week? Head over the continental divide to highland Boquete to explore coffee farms and cloud forests before hitting the great beaches of the Pacific coast and circling back to the capital.

Essential Food & Drink

➡ **Where to eat** Budget eateries like *cafeterías* (simple eateries), *panaderías* (bakeries), stands and market stalls sell a range of filling dishes and set meals from US$3 to US$6.

➡ **What to eat** Rice and beans are a staple in Panama and are usually served with *patacones* (fried plantains), a small cabbage salad and meat. Seafood is inexpensive and abundant, including *ceviche* (marinated raw fish) at fish markets. More adventurous palates shouldn't miss *pulpo al carbón* (grilled octopus). Fresh tropical juices and coconut water (known as *pipa*) are sold on the street. Don't miss regional specialties like *tortilla de maíz* (fried cornmeal cake), Caribbean coconut rice and bottled D'Elida's hot pepper sauce.

PANAMA CITY

POP 880,700

The most cosmopolitan capital in Central America, Panama City is both vibrant metropolis and gateway to tropical escapes. Many worlds coexist here. Welcoming both East and West, Panama is a regional hub of trade and immigration. The resulting cultural cocktail forges a refreshing 'anything goes' attitude, more dynamic and fluid than its neighbors.

Unflinchingly urban, the capital rides the rails of chaos, with traffic jams, wayward taxis and casinos stacked between chic clubs and construction sites. A center of international banking and trade, the sultry skyline of shimmering glass and steel towers is reminiscent of Miami. In contrast, the peninsula of Casco Viejo has become a thriving colonial neighborhood where cobblestones link boutique hotels with underground bars and crumbled ruins with pirate lore.

Escape is never far. Day trip to sandy beaches (Pacific or Caribbean), admire the canal, or explore lush rainforests of howler monkeys, toucans and sloths.

History

Panama City was founded in 1519 by the Spanish governor Pedro Arias de Ávila (Pedrarias), not long after conquistador Vasco Núñez de Balboa first saw the Pacific. Although the Spanish settlement quickly became an important center of government and church authority, the city was ransacked and destroyed in 1671 by the English pirate Captain Henry Morgan, leaving only the stone ruins of Panamá Viejo.

Three years later, the city was reestablished about 8km to the southwest in the area now known as Casco Viejo. Although the peninsular location was well defended, the Spanish overland trade route faded upon the destruction of the Caribbean port at Portobelo in 1746.

Panama gained independence from Spain in 1821 and became part of Gran Colombia; a decade later the regional confederation dissolved and Panama belonged to Colombia. Panama City subsequently declined in importance, though it would return to prominence in the 1850s when the Panama Railroad was completed, and gold seekers on their way to California flooded across the isthmus by train.

Panama declared its independence from Colombia on November 3, 1903, and Panama City was firmly established as the capital. Since the Panama Canal was completed in 1914, the city has emerged as a center for international business and trade.

The city's greatest modern setback occurred in 1989, when the USA invaded to oust dictator (and former US collaborator) Manuel Noriega from power. The capital suffered damage both from the invasion itself and from the subsequent looting, with residential blocks of Chorrillo destroyed by combat-ignited fire.

Following the handover of the Panama Canal from the US to Panama in 1999, and the subsequent closure of US military bases in the country, Panama City has taken charge of its own destiny. Today, Panama City is by far the wealthiest city in Central America. With a spate of foreign investment and the Panama Canal expansion, the city is poised to continue its transformation.

◉ Sights

◎ Casco Viejo

Following the destruction of the old city by Captain Henry Morgan in 1671, the Spanish moved their city 8km southwest to a rocky peninsula at the foot of Cerro Ancón. The new location was easier to defend as the reefs prevented ships from approaching the city except at high tide. The new city was also easy to defend, as a massive wall surrounded it, which is how Casco Viejo (Old Compound) got its name.

In 1904, when construction began on the Panama Canal, all of Panama City existed where Casco Viejo stands today. However, as population growth and urban expansion pushed the boundaries of Panama City further east, the city's elite abandoned Casco Viejo and the neighborhood rapidly deteriorated into a slum.

Today, Casco Viejo's crumbling facades have been mostly replaced by immaculate renovations. Declared a Unesco World Heritage Site in 2003, the area is getting international recognition. The newly restored architecture gives a sense of how magnificent the neighborhood must have looked in past years. Some developers, committed to mitigating the effects of gentrification here, are creating one affordable unit for each high-end one constructed, and are working on interesting local cultural initiatives. Yet the consensus is that most of the neighborhood's former occupants have already been relegated to the periphery.

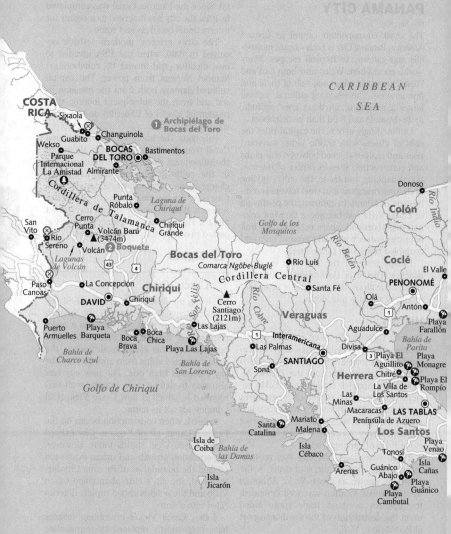

Panama Highlights

❶ Archipiélago de Bocas del Toro (p664) Whiling the days away sipping coconuts and snorkeling at laid-back resorts.

❷ Boquete (p657) Fueling up for highland adventures with local mountain-grown coffee in the town of eternal spring.

❸ Panama City (p623) Spending the day admiring the faded glory of the old city, Casco Viejo, then reveling till sunrise on Calle Uruguay.

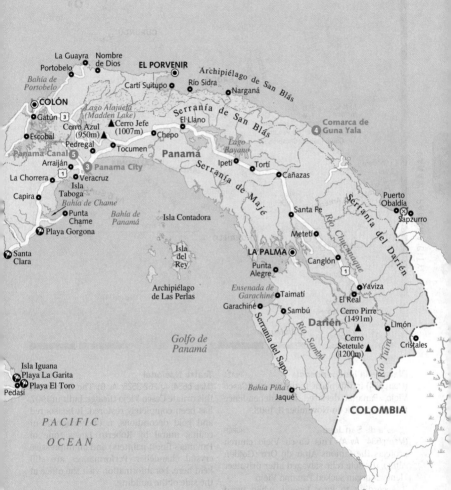

Panama City

0 ——————— 100 km
0 ——————— 50 miles

La Guayra   Nombre
Portobelo   de Dios   **EL PORVENIR**   Archipiélago de San Blás
*Bahía de
Portobelo*   Cartí Suitupo   Río Sidra
COLÓN   Narganá
Gatún [3]   *Lago Alajuela
             (Madden Lake)*   Serranía de San Blás
Cerro Azul   ▲Cerro Jefe   El Llano   Comarca de
Escobal   (950m) (1007m)   [4] Guna Yala
             ▲   Chepo
Pedregal   *Lago
Panama Canal [5] Tocumen   Bayano*
Arraiján   **Panama**   Serranía de Majé
             [1] [3] **Panama City**   Ipetí   Tortí
La Chorrera   Veracruz   Cañazas   Puerto
Capira   Isla   Obaldía
                 Taboga   *Bahía de Chame*   Serranía del Darién ⊗
                 Punta   Sapzurro
                 Chame   *Bahía de   Isla Contadora   Santa Fe
                 Playa Gorgona Panamá*   Metetí
                                                                    Río Chucunaque
▲Santa   Isla   **LA PALMA** ⊙ Canglón
  Clara   del   [1]
                            Rey   Punta
                                          Alegre   Yaviza
                            Archipiélago   El Real
                            de Las Perlas *Ensenada de   Cerro Pirre
                                           Garachiné* Taimatí   (1491m)   Limón
                                          Garachiné   ▲
                                                  Sambú   **Darién** Cerro Cristales
                            *Golfo de   Setetule ▲
                            Panamá*   (1200m)
                                                         Serranía del Sapo
Isla Iguana   Río Sambú Río Tuira
Playa La Garita
Playa El Toro   *Bahía Piña*
Pedasí   Jaqué   **COLOMBIA**

PACIFIC

OCEAN

[4] Comarca de Guna Yala
(p684) Cruising white-sand
cays, swimming in clear waters
and soaking up sunrise on a
sailboat.

[5] Panama Canal (p642)
Laying eyes on this awe-
inspiring, engineering marvel
in the midst of an expansion.

Panama City

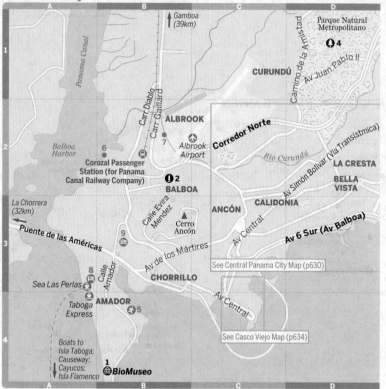

Plaza de la Independencia   PLAZA

(Map p634) In this plaza, in the heart of Casco Viejo, Panama declared its independence from Colombia on November 3, 1903.

Iglesia de San José   CHURCH

(Map p634; Av A) This Casco Viejo church protects the famous Altar de Oro (Golden Altar), the sole relic salvaged after privateer Henry Morgan sacked Panamá Viejo.

According to local legend, when word came of Morgan's impending attack, a priest attempted to disguise the altar by painting it black. The priest told Morgan that the famous altar had been stolen by another pirate, and even convinced Morgan to donate handsomely for its replacement. Morgan is said to have told the priest, 'I don't know why, but I think you are more of a pirate than I am.' Whatever the truth, the baroque altar was later moved from the old city to the present site.

Teatro Nacional   THEATER

(Map p634; ☎ 262-3525; Av B) The interior of this ornate Casco Viejo theater, built in 1907, has been completely restored. It boasts red and gold decorations, a once-magnificent ceiling mural by Roberto Lewis (one of Panama's finest painters) and an impressive crystal chandelier. Performances are still held here. For information visit the office at the side of the building.

Plaza de Francia   PLAZA

(Map p634) At the tip of the southern point of Casco Viejo, this beautiful plaza pays homage to the French role in the construction of the canal. Its large stone tablets and statues are dedicated to the memory of the 22,000 workers who died trying to create the canal.

Paseo las Bóvedas   WATERFRONT

(Map p634) This esplanade runs along the top of the sea wall built by the Spanish to protect the city. From here, you can see the Puente de

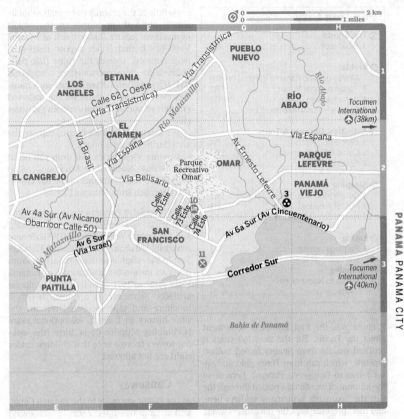

las Américas arching over the waterway and the ships lining up to enter the canal.

Museo del Canal Interoceánico   MUSEUM
(Canal Museum; Map p634; ☎ 211-1649; www.museodelcanal.com; Calle 6a Oeste, Casco Viejo; US$2; ◷ 9am-5pm Tue-Sun) This impressive museum is housed in a beautifully restored building that once served as the headquarters for the original French canal company. The Panama Canal Museum (as it's more commonly known) presents excellent exhibits on the famous waterway, framed in their historical and political context. Signs are in Spanish, but English-speaking guides and audio tours (US$5) are available.

Palacio de las Garzas   HISTORIC BUILDING
(Presidential Palace; Map p634; Av Alfaro) The Palacio de las Garzas is named after the great white herons *(garzas blancas)* that reside here. The president of Panama lives on the upper floor.

Museo de Arte Religioso Colonial   MUSEUM
(Museum of Colonial Religious Art; Map p634; ☎ 228-2897; www.inac.gob.pa/museos; cnr Av A & Calle 3a Este, US$1; ◷ 9:20am-4pm Tue-Sat) Housed beside the ruins of the Iglesia y Convento de Santo Domingo, the Museo de Arte Religioso Colonial has a collection of colonial-era religious artifacts, some dating from the 16th century.

Just inside the ruins' doorway, the Arco Chato is a long arch that stood here unsupported for centuries. It even played a part in the selection of Panama over Nicaragua as the site for the canal since its survival was taken as proof that the area was not subject to earthquakes. It collapsed in 2003 but has since been rebuilt.

◉ Panamá Viejo

Founded on August 15, 1519, by Spanish conquistador Pedro Arias de Ávila, the city of

Panama City

◉ Top Sights
  1 BioMuseo B4

◉ Sights
  Museo de Sitio Panamá Viejo ...... (see 3)
  2 Panama Canal Murals B2
  3 Panamá Viejo G2
  4 Parque Natural Metropolitano D1

◉ Activities, Courses & Tours
  5 Bicicletas Moses B4
  6 Canal & Bay Tours B2
  7 Ecocircuitos B2

◉ Sleeping
  8 Country Inn & Suites A3
  9 Hostal Amador Familiar B3
  10 Hostal Casa Margarita F2

◉ Eating
  11 Parillada Jimmy G3

◉ Shopping
  Mercado Nacional de
  Artesanías .... (see 3)

Panamá was the first European settlement along the Pacific. For the next 150 years it profited mainly from Spain's famed bullion pipeline, which ran from Peru's gold and silver mines to Europe via Panamá. Because of the amount of wealth that passed through the city, the Spaniards kept many soldiers here, and their presence kept the buccaneers away.

In 1671, 1200 pirates led by Captain Henry Morgan ascended the Río Chagres and proceeded overland to Panamá. Although the city was not fortified, it was protected on three sides by the sea and marshes, and on the land side was a causeway with a bridge to allow tidal water to pass underneath. But to the bewilderment of historians, when Morgan and his men neared the city, the Spanish soldiers left this natural stronghold and confronted the buccaneers in a hilly area outside town.

It was the first of many mistakes in battle. After the Spanish force fell to pieces nearly everything of value was either plundered and divvied up or destroyed by fire.

For the next three centuries, the abandoned city served as a convenient source of building materials. By the time the government declared the ruins a protected site in 1976 (Unesco followed suit in 1997), most of the old city had already been dismantled and overrun.

So little of the original city remains that its size, layout and appearance are the subject of much conjecture. Today, much of Panamá Viejo lies buried under a poor residential neighborhood, though the ruins (Map p626; ☑226-8915; www.panamaviejo.org; adult/child US$12/5; ⊙ 8:30am-4:30pm Tue-Sun) are a must-see, even if only to stand on the hallowed grounds of one of Central America's greatest cities.

For safety reasons it's best to explore the area during daylight hours.

Panamá Viejo buses will drop you off at the Mercado Nacional de Artesanías (p638) behind the first remnants of the old city as you approach from Panama City.

Museo de Sitio Panamá Viejo   MUSEUM
(Map p626; ☑226-8915; www.panamaviejo.org; Av 6 Sur, Panamá Viejo; adult/child US$12/5; ruins only adult/child US$8/free; ⊙ 8:30am-4:30pm Tue-Sun) In the original settlement, this museum hosts an impressive scale model of Panamá Viejo prior to 1671 as well as a few colonial artifacts. Signs are in Spanish, though a brochure and tape recording recount the site's history in English. An optional extra is climbing Mirador de la Torre (the lookout tower) though note that children under eight are not allowed.

◉ Causeway

At the Pacific entrance to the Panama Canal, a 2km palm-tree-lined *calzada* (causeway) connects the four small islands of Naos, Culebra, Perico and Flamenco to the mainland. The Causeway is popular in the early morning and late afternoon, when residents walk, jog, skate and cycle its narrow length.

The Causeway also offers sweeping views of the skyline and the old city, with flocks of brown pelicans diving into the sea. Some people come here simply to savor the pleasant breeze at one of the many restaurants and bars.

If you don't have your own vehicle, it's most convenient to take a taxi to the Causeway (US$4 to US$8). Any of the restaurants or bars can call one for you.

★ BioMuseo   MUSEUM
(Museum of Biodiversity; Map p626; www.bio museopanama.org; adult/child US$22/11; ⊙ 10am-4pm Tue-Fri, to 5pm Sat & Sun) Celebrating Panama as the land bridge that has permitted astonishing biodiversity in the region, this museum is a visual feast. World-renowned

architect Frank Gehry, who created the Guggenheim Museum in Bilbao (Spain), designed this landmark museum of crumpled multicolor forms. Exhibits are world-class, with botanical gardens in the works. Audio guides come in five languages. It's located on the Causeway.

◉ Parque Natural Metropolitano

On a hill north of downtown, the 265-hectare Parque Natural Metropolitano (Map p626; ✔info 232-5516; www.parquemetropolitano.org; Av Juan Pablo II; US$5; ⊙8am-5pm Mon-Fri, to 1pm Sat) protects vast expanses of tropical semideciduous forest within the city limits. It serves as an incredible wilderness escape from the trappings of the capital. Two main walking trails, the Nature Trail and the Tití Monkey Trail, join to form one long loop, with a 150m-high *mirador* (lookout) offering panoramic views of Panama City, the bay and the canal, all the way to the Miraflores Locks.

Mammals in the park include *tití* monkeys, anteaters, sloths and white-tailed deer, while reptiles include iguanas, turtles and tortoises. More than 250 bird species have been spotted here. Fish and shrimp inhabit the Río Curundú along the eastern side of the park.

The park was the site of an important battle during the US invasion to oust Noriega. Also of historical significance, concrete structures just past the park entrance were used during WWII as a testing and assembly plant for aircraft engines.

The park is bordered to the west and north by Camino de la Amistad and to the south and east by Corredor Norte; Av Juan Pablo II runs right through the park.

Pick up a pamphlet for a self-guided tour in Spanish and English at the visitors center (Map p630; ✔232-5516; ⊙8am-5pm Mon-Fri, to 1pm Sat), 40m north of the park entrance.

◉ Other Neighborhoods

★ Museo de Arte Contemporáneo   MUSEUM
(Map p630; ✔262-3380; www.macpanama.org; Av de los Mártires, Ancón; adult/child US$5/1.50; ⊙9am-4pm Mon-Fri, to noon Sat, to 3pm Sun) This wonderful privately owned museum features the best collection of Panamanian art anywhere, an excellent collection of works on paper by Latin American artists, and the occasional temporary exhibition by a foreign or national artist.

Panama Canal Murals   PUBLIC ART
(Map p626; Balboa; ⊙7:30am-4:15pm Mon-Fri) FREE The story of the monumental effort to build the Panama Canal is powerfully depicted in murals by notable artist William B Van Ingen of New York. The murals are mounted in the rotunda of the Panama Canal Administration Building. The paintings have the distinction of being the largest group of murals by an American artist on display outside the USA.

It's closed on weekends, but guards may allow visits between 10am and 2:30pm if you ask politely.

🎓 Courses

Casco Antiguo
Spanish School   LANGUAGE COURSE
(Map p634; ✔228-3258; www.cascospanish.com; Calle 4a Oeste; 1-week 20hr intensive US$249) This reader-recommended Spanish school sits in the heart of Casco Viejo. In addition to private and group lessons, it also offers accommodations and activities.

Institute for Spanish
Language Studies   LANGUAGE COURSE
(ILERI; ✔260-4424; www.isls.com/panama; Camino de la Amistad, El Dorado; per week from US$255) Located in the suburban El Dorado neighborhood, this language school offers four hours of one-on-one instruction per day, five days a week. Also has homestay options.

👉 Tours

Barefoot Panama   TOUR
(Map p634; ✔6780-3010; www.barefootpanama.com; Av A s/n; city tour per person US$85) Prompt and professional, this tiny American-run agency based in Casco Viejo does a great tour of Panama City that takes in everything from history to flora and fauna. There are also day trips to San Lorenzo and Gamboa, with visits to a Wounaan indigenous village.

City Sightseeing Panama   BUS TOUR
(Map p630; ✔392-6000; www.city-sightseeing.com; Av Justo Arosemena & Calle 29 Este, Calidonia; 24hr ticket adult/child US$29/15) A good way to get your bearings, these red double-deckers loop the city. Stops include Multicentro Mall, Calle Uruguay, Casco Viejo and the Amador Causeway. Service is hop on, hop off, so you can explore the sights all you want with hourly pick-ups. Departures run between 9am and 4pm, except for the night tour. Tickets are good for 24 or 48 hours.

PANAMA PANAMA CITY

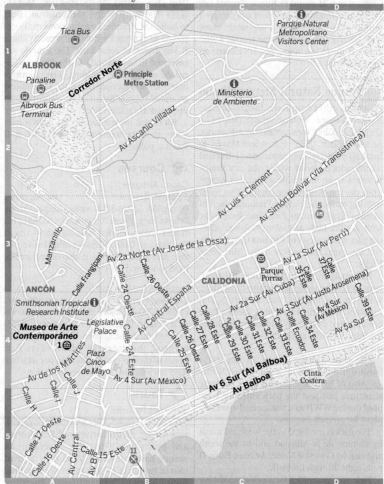

The outfit also offers a tour of the canal zone.

✨ Festivals & Events

Carnaval CULTURAL
(⊙ Feb/Mar) Carnaval in Panama City is celebrated with merriment and wild abandon in the days preceding Ash Wednesday. From Saturday until the following Tuesday, work is put away and masks, costumes and confetti come out, and for 96 hours almost anything goes.

Panama Jazz Festival MUSIC
(www.panamajazzfestival.com; ⊙ mid-Jan) A blast, the Panama Jazz Festival is gaining momentum as one of the biggest musical events in Panama, drawing hundreds of thousands of spectators for a week of events held all over the city. Open-air events are usually free, while big-draw theater spectacles require tickets.

🛏 Sleeping

Panama City offers every kind of accommodation. A glut of options means that many

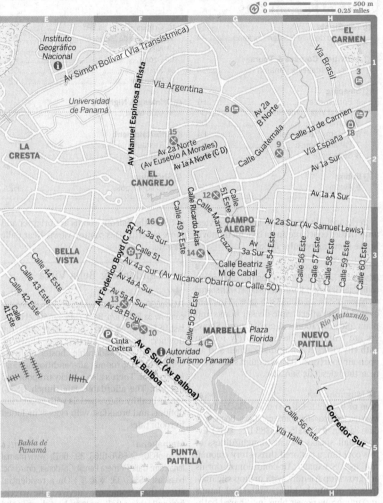

high-end hotels offer deals that bring them into the midrange.

Boutique lodgings are on the rise. Post urban renewal, old-world charmer Casco Viejo is an excellent place to stay, with many restaurants and cafes within walking distance.

Fast-paced modern Panama is best experienced in the overlapping neighborhoods of Bella Vista, Marbella and El Cangrejo. For those who prefer the quiet life, outlying neighborhoods have excellent B&B options. These include the former US-occupied neighborhoods of Albrook, Ancón and Amador, located in the Canal Zone.

Casco Viejo

★ **Luna's Castle** HOSTEL $
(Map p634; ☎ 262-1540; www.lunascastlehostel.com; Calle 9a Este; dm/d/tr incl breakfast US$16/34/51; @ 🕏) Housed in a creaky, colonial mansion, Luna's masterfully blends Spanish-colonial architecture with funky, laid-back backpacker vibes and great service. Shell out the extra dollar for a dorm with air-conditioning. A bit loony and very friendly, it's the kind of hostel people keep talking about long after their trip.

Central Panama City

◎ Top Sights
1 Museo de Arte Contemporáneo A4

◎ Activities, Courses & Tours
2 City Sightseeing Panama C4

◎ Sleeping
3 Baru Lodge H1
4 Hostel Villa Vento Surf G4
5 Mamallena D3
6 Panama Hat Hostel................................. F4
7 Panama House H2
8 Saba Hotel G1

◎ Eating
9 Avatar G2

10 Crêpes & Waffles................................... F4
11 Mercado de Mariscos B5
12 Niko's Café G2
13 Ozone.. F3
14 Sukhi...G3
15 Wine Bar F2

◎ Drinking & Nightlife
16 Club Moat F3

◎ Entertainment
17 Restaurante-Bar
 Tinajas... F3

◎ Shopping
18 Exedra Books...H2

Perks include free bikes, laundry service, an activities concierge and a basement movie house showing popular flicks.

Hospedaje Casco Viejo HOSTEL $
(Map p634; ☑ 211-2027; www.hospedajecascoviejo. com; Calle 8a Oeste; dm/d incl breakfast with shared bathroom US$14/28, d US$33; ⓟ@⑳) This renovated hostel offers triple-decker bunks and plain, pleasant rooms at great prices. Showers are temperate. There's a lovely rooftop with city views, a communal kitchen and an open-air courtyard. It's on a quiet side street near the Iglesia de San José.

★ Magnolia Inn INN $$
(Map p634; ☑ 202-0872, in USA 1-786-375-9633; www.magnoliapanama.com; cnr Calle Boquete & Calle 8a Este; dm US$15, r US$88-135; ⑳⑳) Every detail speaks to the thoughtfulness of this cool inn, a restored three-story colonial run by US expats. Air-conditioned dorms are grown-up friendly, with orthopedic mattresses, quality bedding, individual lamps and numerous power plug-ins. Shared bathrooms are immaculate and service is top-notch. Ample doubles with city views come stocked with minifridges, flat-screen TVs and coffee makers. There's also a kitchen.

Casa Nurrati BOUTIQUE HOTEL $$
(Map p634; ☑ 262-2315; http://casanurratti.com; Av B; d/tr incl breakfast US$80/120; ⑳⑳) A minimally boutique offering above an Italian restaurant, this small lodging features 12 white rooms, many of them small, accessed via elevator. It's low-lit and simply decorated, with recycled pallets, themed photography and polished-cement floors. For a bit extra

(US$20) the balcony rooms are brighter and more cheerful. Has rooftop views. Near Calle 8a Este.

Calidonia & Bella Vista

★ Panama Hat Hostel HOSTEL $
(Map p630; ☑ 269-3315; www.thepanamahathostel. com; Av 5a B Sur s/n, Bella Vista; dm/d incl breakfast US$25/50; ⑳⑳⑳) Let's start with the downer: there's no kitchen use. However, this small retro-adorable hostel delivers with sparkling rooms, air-conditioning and fresh decor. There's also a backyard pool and hot tub. The affordable cafe (lunch US$5) serves healthy daily specials with vegetarian options, and breakfast with eggs is included in room rates.

Mamallena HOSTEL $
(Map p630; ☑ 6676-6163, 393-6611; www.mamal lena.com; Calle Primera Perejil, Calidonia; dm/d incl breakfast US$13/33; ⑳@⑳) On a residential street that's somehow survived the wrecking ball, this small, homey hostel nails the mark on service. Amenities include 24-hour desk service, pancake breakfasts and DVD library. High-ceilinged dorms have air-con at night and the cute motel-style doubles offer considerable privacy. The onsite travel agency offers sailing to San Blás and popular day trips.

Saba Hotel HOTEL $$
(Map p630; ☑ 201-6100; www.thesabahotel.com; Vía Argentina s/n, Bella Vista; s/d US$63/68; ⑳@⑳) Modern and cheerful, the Saba is great value in Bella Vista. With lots of glass and bamboo, there's a sustainable theme

that's probably more stylish than substantive. You can get a carrot juice at the detox bar or just order room service while watching your flat-screen TV. Service is great and there's a restaurant.

El Cangrejo & San Francisco

Panama House
B&B **$**

(Map p630; ☑ 263-4366; www.panamahousebb. com; Calle 1a de Carmen 32, El Carmen; dm/d with shared bathroom incl breakfast US$15/45, d/tr incl breakfast US$55/65; P ✱ @ 🛜) In a cozy colonial near Vía Brasil, this congenial home is lovely and sought-after. Fresh rooms have safe boxes, high ceilings, warm light and tiled bathrooms with scalloped sinks. Mattresses are a bit slim. Guests of all ages congregate in the communal kitchen or lounge area or on the lush hammock patio.

Hostel Villa Vento Surf
HOSTEL **$**

(Map p630; ☑ 6101-4841, 397-6002; Calle 47 No 7, Marbella; dm/d/tr incl breakfast US$17/35/45; ✱ @ 🛜 🏊) This relaxed hostel with pleasant staff sits in a suburban-style home around the corner from the nightlife hot spot of Calle Uruguay. Young internationals come for the swimming pool or the easy-access partying, though it's relatively calm (all laptops engaged). Bunks crowd larger dorms, but air-con keeps them cool. Breakfast is pancakes and coffee.

Baru Lodge
B&B **$$**

(Map p630; ☑ 393-2340; www.barulodge.com; Calle 2a Norte H-7, El Carmen; s/d incl breakfast US$60/75; ✱ @ 🛜) Tasteful and cordial, this inn sits on a residential street central to the action. Rooms are sleek and modern, with subdued colors and soft lighting. The English-speaking owner makes guests right at home. Cable TV, fast wi-fi and air purifiers are among the perks. The garden patio has wicker seating, where continental breakfasts are served.

Hostal Casa Margarita
B&B **$$**

(Map p626; ☑ 394-5557; www.hostalcasamargarita. com; Casa 97, Calle Los Claveles, San Francisco; s/d/tr incl breakfast US$70/80/95; P ✱ @) Irresistibly cozy and chic, this stucco house features seven smart, impeccable but simple rooms with colorful touches, flat-screen TVs and minifridges. A huge garden and breakfast patio provide ample space to lounge or dally over a complete breakfast that includes fresh fruit. Guests also have access to the kitchen, but the real treasures here are the warm hosts.

Canal Zone

Hostal Amador Familiar
INN **$**

(Map p626; ☑ 314-1251; www.hostalamador familiar.com; Casa 1519, Calle Akee, Balboa; dm incl breakfast US$17, d with fan/air-con US$33/39; P ✱ @ 🛜) If you like quiet, this big, red

PANAMA **PANAMA CITY**

THE JAZZ SOLUTION

Once a down-and-out section of the city with crumbling architecture and serious poverty, Casco Viejo is coming into a new chapter. Making a strong push toward revitalization, the neighborhood is home to dozens of new restaurants, cafes, shops and renovated historical buildings. In the midst of this architectural revival, another less tangible one struggles to take place: that of the Panamanian music community.

Jazz great and native Panamanian Danilo Perez returned here to the musical conservatory where he learned his first notes to establish **Fundación Danilo Perez** (Map p634; ☑ 211-0272; www.fundaciondaniloperez.com; 1069 Av A), a musical foundation that has generated over US$1 million in youth scholarships. It also sponsors the **Panama Jazz Festival** (p630), a wildly popular citywide event featuring artists from all over the world.

In an interview with *El Casqueño*, Perez says, 'Through the discipline of music we can create relevant leaders and good citizens. We can solve many of society's problems.' Youth are chosen from inner-city Panama and all parts of the country, including Colón and the Comarca de Guna Yala. Some grants take students as far as Boston, to the Berklee College of Music and the New England Conservatory. Many come back to the music conservatory to teach others and complete the cycle of community participation.

The Panama Jazz Festival is held every January, with a week of events in theaters around the city, culminating in a free Saturday concert in the Casco's Plaza de la Independencia. The foundation in Casco Viejo also houses a library and music museum and is open to the public (admission is free).

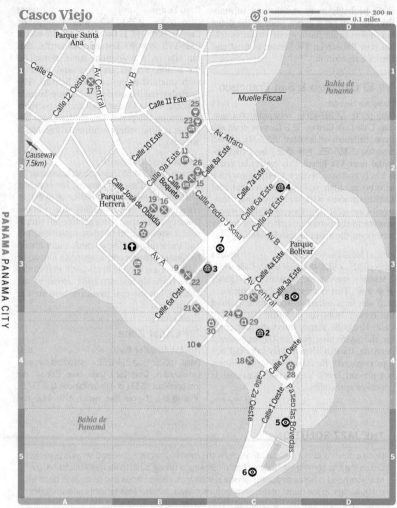

Casco Viejo

canal house offers cheap accommodations. Tiled high-ceilinged rooms with rod-iron beds are worn out but clean. Dorms are dark and less appealing and service is, sadly, lax. Highlights are the pleasant dining patio and open-air kitchen. Guests must take a taxi to the center (US$7); it's just off the Causeway.

Country Inn & Suites   HOTEL **$$**
(Map p626; ☎211-4500; www.countryinns.com/panamacanalpan; cnr Avs Amador & Pelicano, Amador; d US$66; ❚❋❂) They say there are only two lodgings overlooking the canal: one is the prison holding Noriega, the other is this

chain hotel. Though reminiscent of a retirement community in Panama City, Florida, it's well run and good value, with Causeway access and a huge swimming pool. Rooms boast private balconies overlooking the Puente de las Américas.

Dos Palmitos   B&B **$$**
(☎391-0994, 6051-4723; www.panamabedand breakfast.com; Calle Victor Hugo 0532B, Cerro Ancón; s/d incl breakfast US$75/88; ❋@☎) If your attraction to Panama is more about wildlife than wild life, check out this tucked-away French B&B. There are just four rooms, dec-

Casco Viejo

◉ Sights
1 Iglesia de San José B3
2 Museo de Arte Religioso Colonial C4
3 Museo del Canal Interoceánico C3
4 Palacio de las Garzas C2
5 Paseo las Bóvedas C5
6 Plaza de Francia C5
7 Plaza de la Independencia C3
8 Teatro Nacional C3

◉ Activities, Courses & Tours
9 Barefoot Panama B3
10 Casco Antiguo Spanish School B4

◉ Sleeping
11 Casa Nurrati B2
12 Hospedaje Casco Viejo B3
13 Luna's Castle B2
14 Magnolia Inn B2

◉ Eating
15 Aki B2

16 Barrio Pizza B2
17 Café Coca Cola A1
18 Café Per Due C4
19 Crave B2
20 Granclement C3
21 Madrigal B3
22 Super Gourmet B3

◉ Drinking & Nightlife
23 Bar Relic B2
24 Duke's Bar C4
25 La Rana Dorada B1
26 Tántalo Bar B2

◉ Entertainment
27 Fundación Danilo Perez B3
28 Platea C4
Teatro Nacional .... (see 8)

◉ Shopping
29 Karavan C4
30 Papiro y Yo C4

PANAMA PANAMA CITY

orated with retro posters and vintage newsclips and featuring immaculate wooden floors, king-size beds and wicker furniture. The backyard terrace offers birdwatching and abundant breakfasts featuring homemade bread and fresh juice. Also offers transportation and tours.

It's on the quiet Cerro Ancón – a good place to take a walk, but for everything else you'll need a taxi.

✖ Eating

✖ Casco Viejo

★ **Mercado de Mariscos**   MARKET $

(Map p630; Av Balboa; mains US$3-14; ⊗ from 6am) Above a bustling fish market, this unassuming restaurant is *the* place to get your seafood fix. Come early as service at peak time is painfully slow. Gems include whole fried fish and cavernous bowls of 'Get Up Lazarus' soup (a sure hangover cure).

Outside, stands ladle out delicious US$3 plastic cups of *ceviche* (seafood marinated in lime, garlic and seasonings), including classic concoctions, Mediterranean style (with olives) and curry.

Crave   CAFE $

(Map p634; ☑ 209-0094; Calle José de Obaldía s/n; mains US$8-13; ⊗ 11:30am-11:30pm Mon-Sat, 10am-4pm Sun) A refreshing casual option serving fresh cafe fare that's artfully

prepared. Think handcut fries, fish tacos and burgers served with crispy Brussels sprouts or pots of delicious pickled vegetables. There's a range of boutique beers, and cocktails are prepared with house-made infusions and sugarcane. Also does Sunday brunch.

Barrio Pizza   PIZZA $

(Map p634; ☑ 399-3521; www.barriopizza.com; Av Central s/n; mains US$8-12; ⊗ 11am-11pm; ✳ ♠) Happiness is blistering wood-fired pizza baked to order and topped with truffle oil, roasted eggplant or meatballs. The simple menu also has Caesar salads, wine and beer. Come early for a seat.

Aki   JAPANESE $

(Map p634; ☑ 6938-8473; Calle 8a Este s/n; mains US$9-12; ⊗ noon-midnight Sun-Fri, 3pm-midnight Sat) Duck into this dark nook for delicious fusion-style sushi. Spicy tuna on crispy rice squares hits the spot. Cocktails are innovative and well prepared. For a bargain, check out the weekday lunch special (US$6).

Café Per Due   ITALIAN $

(Map p634; ☑ 228-0547; Av A; mains US$5-12; ⊗ 9am-10pm Tue-Sun, closed Dec; ☑) Our pick for a quick bite, this casual Italian-run eatery serves scrumptious thin-crust pizzas. Check out the bacon and blue cheese or the fresh tomato, basil and garlic. Mozzarella is not skimped on. For privacy, try the tiny brick courtyard with a couple of tables.

Café Coca Cola
PANAMANIAN $

(Map p634; Av Central; plates US$3-8; ☺7:30am-11pm; ✳) A neighborhood institution, this old-school diner comes complete with chess-playing señoras and no-nonsense waitresses. Televisions broadcasting soccer matches seal its status as working-class hangout. Of course, the real reason you're here is to eat out on hearty platefuls of rice, beans and the featured meat of the day without breaking the bank.

Granclement
GELATERIA $

(Map p634; Av Central; gelato US$3.50-5; ☺11:30am-8pm Mon-Thu, to 11pm Fri, to 9pm Sat, 12:30-8pm Sun) Pure pleasure defines these intense tropical-fruit gelatos and rich, creamy flavors such as coffee, orange-chocolate and ginger. A few scoops of these fussy French creations will sweeten a leisurely stroll through the Casco.

★Super Gourmet
DELI $

(Map p634; Av A; mains US$3-9; ☺8am-5pm Mon-Sat, 10am-4pm Sun; ✦) Stocking gourmet goods that range from wine to wasabi peas, this is the perfect pre-picnic stop. You can also grab soup, natural juices or a baguette deli sandwich with roasted chicken and peppers, pastrami or three cheeses. For breakfast, eggs on English muffins or *arepas* (savory corn cakes) hit the spot.

★Madrigal
SPANISH $$$

(Map p634; ✆211-1956; www.andresmadrigal.com; Av A; mains US$26-30; ☺noon-2:30pm Mon-Fri, 6:30-10:30pm Mon-Sat) Pure delight, this upscale eatery from Michelin-starred chef Andrés Madrigal has a fetish for details. Start with sea-bass *ceviche* with coconut foam, slivers of hot pepper and passionfruit mousse and you'll wonder if anything has ever tasted this good. *Ropa vieja* (shredded beef) is done to perfection and the seafood soup is earthy and satisfying. Great service.

🍴 El Cangrejo & San Francisco

Niko's Café
CAFETERIA $

(Map p630; Calle 51 Este, El Cangrejo; mains US$3-8; ☺24hr) The creation of a Greek immigrant who once sold food from a cart, Niko's has become one of Panama City's most successful chains, with locations throughout the city (this one's near Vía España). These sprawling 24-hour cafeterias serve hearty portions of inexpensive food ranging from made-to-order breakfasts to Panamanian dishes and desserts.

★Avatar
INDIAN $$

(Map p630; ✆393-9006; www.avatarindiancuisine.com; cnr Vías Argentina & España, El Cangrejo; mains US$9-16) Serving rich kormas, fragrant rice and complex curries in a swanky piano bar, Avatar is sheer delight for spice enthusiasts. Southern Indian cuisine is the house specialty, though if you want it really hot you will have to insist. On weekdays, lunch is 25% off.

Wine Bar
ITALIAN $$

(Map p630; Av Eusebio A Morales, El Cangrejo; mains US$7-17; ☺5pm-1am) Some say this Italian bistro with an encyclopedic wine list is the best dinner value in town. It's certainly popular among the local cognoscenti. You can order off two menus: Wine Bar for a bite with wine, or Pomodoro (open for lunch) for pizzas and satisfying pasta. Or grab a plate of soft and hard cheeses and enjoy the patio.

Parillada Jimmy
PARRILLA $$

(Map p626; ✆226-1096; Av Cincuentenario, San Francisco; mains US$9-18; ☺11:30am-11:30pm) The long, open porch with high ceilings and wrought-iron chandeliers lend a farmhouse feel to this Panama City institution. An open grill sears some serious cuts of beef, chicken and country-style sausage. Located in the San Francisco district just east of the Multiplaza Mall, Parillada Jimmy packs in lunchtime diners and an after-work crowd.

★Maito
PANAMANIAN $$$

(✆391-4657; www.maitopanama.com; Av 3m Sur, San Francisco; mains US$8-27; ☺noon-3pm Mon-Fri, 7-11pm Mon-Sat) With style and pedigree, Maito toys with the classics, folding in everyday Caribbean, Latin and Chinese influences. While results are mixed, it's still worthwhile. Start with a watermelon Waldorf salad. Ribs glazed in passion fruit are tender but lack the crispness of the duck chow mein. Seafood risotto in squid ink proves divine. There's garden seating and impeccable service.

🍴 Bella Vista

Crêpes & Waffles
CREPERIE $

(Map p630; ✆269-1574; Av 5a B Sur; mains US$5-10; ☺noon-10pm Mon-Sat, 9am-10pm Sun; ✆) Ideal for an afternoon pick-me-up or a quick bite before clubbing, this salad bar and crêpe factory has something for everyone. Spinach, ricotta and tomato is a good standby, but the sweet crêpes, with fillings such as cheese, apples, chocolate and caramel, are delectable. There's also a salad bar.

Sukhi
THAI $

(Map p630; ☑ 395-6081; Calle Beatriz M de Cabal; mains US$8-13; ⊙ 11:30am-10pm Mon-Sat) A casual and cheerful cafe offering lovely – though not the most authentic – Southeast Asian food. Portions run small. Start with the fried calamari with ginger-cilantro dipping sauce. Flavors pop in the green-bean green curry, while *ladna* (noodles in gravy) comes in fragrant beef broth with broccoli rabe. Service is good and the price is right.

Ozone
INTERNATIONAL $$

(Map p630; Calle Uruguay; mains US$10-22; ⊙ 11am-3pm & 6-11pm) Packed with worker bees at midday, Ozone is a local fixture serving enormous, fragrant portions of good food from 110 countries. There are even kosher and halal options. It's too bad the ambiance is wanting – the dark location was once a garage. It's also hard to find – look closely for the sign.

🍷 Drinking & Nightlife

Bars and clubs open and close with alarming frequency in Panama City, though generally speaking, nightlife is stylish, sophisticated and fairly pricey. The well-to-do denizens of the capital love a good scene, so it's worth scrubbing up, donning some nice threads and parting with a bit of dough. You might regret blowing your budget the next morning, but that's the price you pay to party with the beautiful people.

Big areas for nightlife include Casco Viejo, San Francisco and Bella Vista's Calle Uruguay. The current boom in craft beer has people hitting small breweries, a novelty for Panama.

For the latest on what's happening in the city, *La Prensa* (www.prensa.com) has weekend listings in the Thursday and Friday editions or on its website; look for the 'De Noche' section.

Doors usually open at 11pm. Bars and clubs close between 2am and 3am, except for casinos, which now can't serve alcohol. Remember to bring ID. Most clubs have a cover charge of US$10 to US$25; this varies greatly depending on the place, the date and the time.

La Rana Dorada
MICROBREWERY

(Map p634; Av Alfaro, Casco Viejo; ⊙ noon-12:30am Sun-Wed, to 3am Thu-Sat) Replete with shiny brass fixings and wooden stools, this is a wonderful, award-winning brewpub of small craft beers, served alongside tasty thin-crust pizzas or brats (mains US$3 to US$9). After-work happy hour is just catching on, but it goes gangbusters here. A second location is on Vía Argentina.

Tántalo Bar
COCKTAIL BAR

(Map p634; cnr Calle 8a Este & Av B, Casco Viejo; cover US$5-10; ⊙ rooftop deck 5pm-2am) Though it serves casual lunches, this ultra-hip cafe-bar is best known for sunset happy hours on its rooftop deck. Pair your cocktail with good, fusion-style tapas. Cover is charged after 10pm, but to get a spot on the tiny roof deck, show up around 7pm. Wednesday is salsa night.

Bar Relic
BAR

(Map p634; www.relicbar.com; Calle 9a Este, Casco Viejo; ⊙ 9pm-2am Tue-Sat) Wildly popular with travelers and hip young Panamanians, this cavernous hostel bar is a hit. Service is friendly and patrons easily mingle in the ample courtyard with shared picnic tables. Not only are you partying outside (a rarity in Panama City) but you're next to the historical wall of the city.

Upstairs in the hostel there's a calmer, more grown-up option for cocktails.

Duke's Bar
GAY & LESBIAN

(Map p634; ☑ 6597-6200; Edificio Cuatro Casas 3, Calle 4a Oeste, Casco Viejo; ⊙ 6:30pm-1am Tue-Sat) A new addition to Casco Viejo, this elegant, low-lit bar caters to the gay and lesbian crowd, late 20s and up, though it's friendly to all.

Cayucos
CAFE

(Causeway) This open-air resto-bar sits on the water with excellent views of the city. While not exactly a bar, it has the perfect ambiance for the first cold beer of the evening or a leisurely drink on the weekend.

Club Moat
GAY & LESBIAN

(Map p630; ☑ 6747-2544; Calle Aquilino de la Guardia 12, El Cangrejo; ⊙ 10pm-3am) 🌈 The hot spot of the moment is this multistory club with *musica electronica,* dancing and drinks. All-you-can-drink specials (US$12) are dangerous. Ideal for late at night.

☆ Entertainment

If you're not looking to get blotto, there are numerous ways to spend a moonlit (or rainy) evening in the city. A good place to start is the arts section in the Sunday edition of *La Prensa* or the back pages of the *Panama News*.

Restaurante-Bar Tinajas
DANCE

(Map p630; ✆ 263-7890; www.tinajaspanama.com; Av 3a A Sur, Bella Vista; entry US$5; ⊙ Mon-Sat) A good place to see traditional Panamanian folk dancing, this dinner show is a classic. Sure, it's touristy, but it's nicely done just the same. Shows are held Wednesday to Saturday at 9pm with a US$12 minimum per person for drinks and food. Reservations recommended. It's near Av Frederico Boyd.

Platea
JAZZ

(Map p634; ✆ 228-4010; Calle 1 Oeste) A tiny jazz club on the tip of the peninsula.

Teatro Nacional
THEATER

(Map p634; ✆ 262-3525; Av B, Casco Viejo) Casco Viejo's lovely 19th-century playhouse stages ballets, concerts and plays.

🛍 Shopping

⭐ Karavan
ARTS

(Map p634; ✆ 228-7177; www.karavan-gallery.com; Calle 3a Oeste, Casco Viejo; ⊙ 10am-6pm Mon-Sat, 11am-3:30pm Sun) An excellent place to find original Guna embroidery with modern designs and Congo art from Portobelo, with artisans working onsite. Karavan commissions local artists and works closely to develop new talent.

Mercado Nacional de Artesanías
MARKET

(National Artisans Market; Map p626; Panamá Viejo; ⊙ 9am-4pm Mon-Sat, to 1pm Sun) A great place to shop for memorable souvenirs.

Papiro y Yo
FASHION

(Map p634; ✆ 211-3830; info@papiroyyo.com; cnr Calle 4a Oeste & Av A, Casco Viejo; ⊙ 10am-7pm Mon-Sat) An innovative boutique selling *mola* (traditional Guna embroidery) designs reimagined on gorgeous Italian silk. It also sells stylish jewelry and baskets crafted from recycled materials.

Exedra Books
BOOKS

(Map p630; ✆ 264-4252; cnr Vías España & Brasil, El Carmen; ⊙ 9:30am-9:30pm Mon-Sat, 11am-8:30pm Sun) Easily one of Central America's best bookstores.

ℹ Orientation

Panama City stretches about 20km along the Pacific coast, from the Panama Canal at its western end to the ruins of Panamá Viejo to the east.

Near the canal are Albrook Airport, the Causeway and the wealthy Balboa and Ancón suburbs, first built for US canal and military workers. The colonial part of the city, Casco Viejo, juts into the sea on the southwestern side of town. In the south, the Causeway has numerous restaurants, bars and fine vantage points on the edge of the ocean.

The main drag is Av Central, which runs through Casco Viejo to Parque Santa Ana and Plaza Cinco de Mayo; between these two plazas, the avenue is a pedestrian-only shopping street. At a fork further east, the avenue becomes Av Central España; the section that traverses the El Cangrejo business and financial district is called Vía España. The other part of the fork becomes Av Simón Bolívar and, finally, Vía Transístmica as it heads out of town and across the isthmus toward Colón.

MAPS

Instituto Geográfico Nacional (Tommy Guardia; Map p630; ✆ 236-2444; La Cresta; ⊙ 8am-4pm Mon-Fri) Has an excellent collection of maps for sale. Just off Av Simón Bolívar near Av Arturo del Valle, opposite the Universidad de Panamá.

ℹ Information

DANGERS & ANNOYANCES

Casco Viejo is the focus of an ambitious urban-renewal program. Always exercise caution, though, and stay where it's well lit and where there are plenty of people around. Generally speaking, the tip of the peninsula southeast of Calle 10 Este and Calle 11 Este is safe for tourists and patrolled by police officers. Inland (north of Parque Herrera and Parque Santa Ana) there are high-density slums. Other high-crime areas include Curundú, Chorrillo, Santa Ana, San Miguelito and Río Abajo.

Calle Uruguay, the clubbing hub of the city, also attracts opportunists. Don't take your full wallet out at night. We have heard reports of women approaching male travelers for a hug and taking their wallets.

Taxis generally allow unrelated passengers to share the cab, but robberies do occasionally occur. It's best not to get into a taxi that already has a passenger. If you speak Spanish, you can offer a slightly higher fare to keep your taxi to yourself. Evaluate any taxi you hail before getting in (check for door handles and taxi licensing numbers). It's very common for taxi drivers to refuse fares to destinations simply for their own convenience.

There are occasional reports of robbery near the ruins of Panamá Viejo – don't go after sunset, and always keep an eye out.

Panama has become stringent about drug control, which sometimes means roadblock checks of drivers and their passengers. Always have your passport with you.

When walking the streets of Panama City, be aware that drivers do not yield to pedestrians. Sometimes it's best to approach intersections like Panamanians – look both ways, then run like hell.

EMERGENCY

Police (☑104)

INTERNET ACCESS

Most lodgings and restaurants have wi-fi, as do some public places.

MEDICAL SERVICES

Centro Médico Paitilla (☑265-8800, 265-8883; cnr Calle 53 Este & Av Balboa, Paitilla) This medical center has well-trained physicians who speak both Spanish and English.

Centro Metropolitano de Salud (☑512-6600; Calle Principal 237, Los Ríos; ☺7:30am-noon & 1-3pm Mon-Fri) Offers yellow-fever vaccinations with international certificate (required for travel to Colombia if returning) for a minimal charge. In the Canal Zone.

MONEY

ATMs are abundant throughout the city. The Banco Nacional de Panamá counter at Tocumen International Airport is one of the few places in Panama City that exchanges foreign currency.

Panacambios (☑223-1800; ground fl, Plaza Regency Bldg, Vía España, El Cangrejo; ☺8am-5pm Mon-Fri) Buys and sells international currencies.

POST

Many hotels sell stamps and some will mail guests' letters.

Post Office (Map p630; ☑512-7657; www.correospanama.gob.pa; Av Central s/n, Calidonia; ☺7am-5:45pm Mon-Fri, to 4:45pm Sat) Full postal services and express mail.

TELEPHONE

Purchase SIM cards at any cell-phone shop or kiosk. They come with minimal credit that can be topped up at the same shop.

TOURIST INFORMATION

Autoridad de Turismo Panamá (ATP; Panama Tourism Authority; Map p630; ☑526-7000; www.visitpanama.com; 29th fl, Edificio Bisca, cnr Av Balboa & Aquilino de la Guardia, Bella Vista; ☺8:30am-3pm Mon-Fri) Panama's tourism bureau is headquartered in a high-rise next to the Hilton hotel. Help is limited here; it's mostly geared toward high-end tourism. There's also an ATP booth in Casco Viejo.

Ministerio de Ambiente (Map p630; ☑500-0855, 315-0855; www.miambiente.gob.pa; Calle Broberg 804, Cerro Ancón, Albrook; ☺8am-4pm) Formerly known as ANAM, the Ministry of the Environment can occasionally provide maps and information on national parks. However, it is not set up to provide much assistance to tourists.

❶ Getting There & Away

AIR

International flights arrive at and depart from **Tocumen International Airport** (☑238-2700; www.tocumenpanama.aero; Av Domingo Díaz), 35km northeast of the city center. From **Albrook Bus Terminal**, near Albrook Airport, airport buses (US$1.25, one to 1½ hours) marked 'Tocumen Corredor' depart every 15 minutes to Tocumen airport.

Domestic flights depart from **Albrook Airport** (Aeropuerto Marcos A Gelabert; Map p626; ☑315-0403), aka Aeropuerto Marcos A Gelabert, in the former Albrook Air Force Station near the canal.

Air Panama (☑316-9000; www.airpanama.com; Albrook Airport) covers domestic routes and has its own travel agency. International carrier **Copa Airlines** (☑217-2672; www.copaair.com; Av Central s/n, Casco Viejo; ☺8am-5pm Mon-Fri, 9am-1pm Sat) now flies to domestic destinations.

Flights within Panama are inexpensive and short – few are longer than an hour. However, if traveling to Darién Province, Isla Contadora or the Comarca de Guna Yala, it's quite possible that the plane may make multiple stops. Prices vary according to season and availability.

BOAT

Barcos Calypso (☑314-1730; Balboa Yacht Club, Amador Causeway; round-trip US$14) Departures to Isla Taboga at 8:30am weekdays, plus 3pm Friday, and at 8am, 10:30am and 4pm weekends.

Sea Las Perlas (Map p626; ☑391-1424; www.sealasperlas.com; Balboa Yacht Club, Amador Causeway; adult/child one way US$45/35) This catamaran ferry service departs for Isla Contadora daily at 7am, returning at 3:30pm. There's an 11am departure on Sunday. The journey takes 1¾ hours.

Taboga Express (Map p626; ☑6234-8989; www.tabogaexpress.com; Balboa Yacht Club, Amador Causeway; adult/child round-trip US$16/8) This new catamaran is your fastest option to Taboga (30 minutes one way). Departs daily at 8am, 9:30am, 11am, 3pm and 4:30pm. With four returns daily.

BUS

Albrook Bus Terminal (Gran Terminal; Map p630; ☑303-3030, 303-6255; www.grantnt.com), near Albrook Airport, is a convenient and modern one-stop location for most buses leaving Panama City. The terminal includes a food court, banks, shops, a sports bar, a storage room, bathrooms and showers. A mall, complete with supermarket and cinema, is next door.

Passengers must buy a *tarjeta* (multiuse card) to pay the US$0.10 terminal tax at the entry turnstile. You can try offering another passenger cash to swipe their card for you. The *tarjeta* also allows access to the bus-station bathrooms.

For assistance, go to the Information booth.

All local buses are on the new **Metrobus** (p641) system with designated bus stops and clean, new buses. Cash is not accepted. Passengers must buy *tarjetas* (US$2) at a special kiosk in Albrook terminal or at designated locations (such as supermarkets or main bus stops, all listed on the website). If you don't have a *tarjeta*, try offering another passenger reimbursement for swiping their card.

Both **Panaline** (Map p630; ☑ 227-8648; www.viajeros.com/panaline; Albrook Bus Terminal) and **Tica Bus** (Map p630; ☑ 314-6385; www.ticabus.com; Albrook Bus Terminal) serve San José (Costa Rica); see their websites for hours.

Canal Zone buses depart from the Albrook terminal for Balboa and Clayton, Miraflores Locks, and Gamboa, leaving every 45 minutes. In transition, these buses will soon be run by Metrobus with the same card system.

CAR & MOTORCYCLE

Rental rates start at US$20 per day for the most economical cars, including unlimited kilometers. Insurance is extra.

Tolls are your responsibility and carry heavy fines if unpaid. Make sure your dashboard toll sticker has credit before using it: use the ID number to refill the account in any supermarket.

Budget (☑ 263-8777; www.budgetpanama. com; Tocumen International Airport)

Hertz (☑ 301-2611; www.hertzpanama.com.pa; Tocumen International Airport)

National (☑ 275-7100; www.nationalpanama. com; Tocumen International Airport)

TRAIN

The **Panama Railway Company** (PCRC; ☑ 317-6070; www.panarail.com; Carretera Gaillard, Corozal; one way adult/child US$25/15) operates a glass-domed train that takes passengers on a lovely ride from Panama City to Colón on weekdays, departing at 7:15am and returning at 5:15pm. The train follows the canal, at times en-

BUSES FROM PANAMA CITY

DESTINATION	COST (US$)	DURATION (HR)	FREQUENCY
Aguadulce	6.35	3	33 daily
Antón	4.70	2	every 20min
Cañita	3	2½	11 daily
Chame	2.60	1¼	37 daily
Changuinola	29	10	8pm daily
Chitré	10	4	hourly
Colón	3.50	2	every 20min
David	15-19	7-8	15 daily
El Copé	6.50	4	9 daily
El Valle	4.25	2½	hourly
Las Tablas	10	4½	hourly
Macaracas	10	5	5 daily
Paso Canoas	17-22	8	5 daily
Penonomé	5.25	2½	48 daily
Pesé	9.65	4½	6 daily
San Carlos	3.25	1½	25 daily
San José (Costa Rica)	60	16	2 daily
Santiago	9	4	20 daily
Soná	10	6	6 daily
Villa de los Santos	9	4	18 daily
Yaviza	16	6-8	8 daily

From the Airport

Tocumen International Airport (☑ 238-2700; www.tocumenpanama.aero; Av Domingo Díaz) is 35km northeast of the city center. The cheapest way to get into the city is to exit the terminal, cross the street (to the bus shelter) and catch a bus to the city. The 10-minute walk might seem longer with luggage. Taxis (around US$30) can be hired at the Transportes Turísticos desk at the airport exit; they're much faster than the bus. Beside the desk is a taxi stand with posted prices. Don't be distracted by touts offering rides at ridiculously high prices; they take their cut from the taxis.

Albrook Airport (p639), north of Cerro Ancón, handles domestic flights. The easiest way to get from the airport to downtown is by taxi; the ride should cost between US$5 and US$8.

From the Bus Terminal

All long-distance buses arrive at **Albrook Bus Terminal** (p639); from here there are connections throughout the city. Routes (such as Vía España and Panamá Viejo) are displayed in the front window; fares are US$0.35. If you arrive after dark, it is recommended that you take a taxi (US$3 to US$7) to your destination.

gulfed by dense vine-strewn jungle. If you want to relive the heyday of luxury train travel for an hour or two, this is definitely the way to do it.

Note that the Panama City terminus is actually located in the town of Corozal, a 15-minute cab ride from the capital.

❶ Getting Around

BICYCLE
You can rent bicycles in some hostels and at the Causeway. **Moses** (Map p626; ☑ 211-2718; Amador Causeway; ☺ 9am-7pm Sat & Sun) operates a booth with rentals starting at US$4 per hour for mountain bikes. You can also rent tandems and rickshaw bikes.

BUS
Panama City has almost finished phasing out its *diablos rojos* (red devils) for modern, safe, air-conditioned Metrobus buses. Rides cost US$0.35 to $1.25, with the higher cost for *corredor* (highway) routes.

Buses run along the three major west–east routes: Av Central–Vía España, Av Balboa–Vía Israel and Av Simón Bolívar–Vía Transístmica. The Av Central–Vía España streets are one way going west for much of the route; eastbound buses use Av Perú and Av 4 Sur – these buses will take you into the banking district of El Cangrejo. Buses also run along Av Ricardo J Alfaro (known as Tumba Muerto).

Metrobuses stop at official bus stops and Albrook Bus Terminal near Albrook Airport.

SUBWAY
Panama City's new transportation system is known as **El Metro** (www.elmetrodepanama.

com; fare US$0.35-1.35; ☺ 5am-10pm). The main line connects Albrook with Vía Transístmica, Vía España and Calidonia. It will eventually extend to Tocumen International Airport and branches will go to the suburbs. The main terminal is across from Albrook Bus Terminal. Fares are paid with the same card used for the Metrobus system.

TAXI
Taxis are plentiful but problematic. Some drivers do not travel (or even know) the whole city, so don't be surprised if they leave you standing on the sidewalk upon hearing your destination.

Taxis are not metered, but there is a list of standard fares that drivers are supposed to charge, measured by zones. One zone runs a minimum of US$2; Canal Zone destinations run up to US$6. An average ride, crossing a couple of zones, would cost US$3 to US$6, more for additional passengers or if it's late. Always agree on a fare before you get into the cab, or better yet, ask your hotel to estimate the fare to your destination and then simply hand the driver the money upon arriving. Taxis can also be rented by the hour.

Watch out for unmarked large-model US cars serving hotels as cabs. Their prices are up to four times that of regular street taxis.
America Libre (☑ 223-7342)
Radio Taxi America (☑ 221-1932)
Taxi Unico Cooperativa (☑ 221-3611)

AROUND PANAMA CITY

No visit to Panama City would be complete without taking a day trip to its famous waterway – just remember that the Canal Zone is much, much more than just the canal. The rainforest surrounding the canal is easily accessed and one of the best places to view a variety of Central American wildlife.

Panama Canal

One of the world's greatest human-made marvels, the Panama Canal stretches 80km from Panama City on the Pacific side to Colón on the Atlantic side, cutting right through the continental divide. Around 14,000 vessels pass through each year, and ships worldwide are built with the dimensions of the canal's locks (305m long and 33.5m wide) in mind.

The canal has three sets of double locks: Miraflores and Pedro Miguel on the Pacific side and Gatún on the Atlantic. Between the locks, ships pass through a huge artificial lake, Lago Gatún, created by the Gatún Dam across the Río Chagres, and the Culebra Cut, a 14km cut through the rock and shale of the isthmian mountains. With the passage of each ship, a staggering 197 million L of fresh water is released into the ocean.

The canal annually brings in US$2 billion in revenue. Ships pay according to their weight. The highest toll currently paid by the largest ships reaches US$450,000; the lowest amount was US$0.36, paid in 1928 by Richard Halliburton, who swam through.

An expansion that will double the capacity of the canal was due to open in mid-2016.

◉ Sights

Miraflores Visitors Center MUSEUM
(☑276-8325; http://visitcanaldepanama.com; adult/child US$15/10; ☺9am-5pm) The easiest and best way to visit the Panama Canal is to head to the Miraflores Visitors Center, located just outside Panama City. This modern visitors center features a large four-floor interactive museum, several viewing platforms and an excellent restaurant serving sumptuous buffet spreads with panoramic views of canal transit. Tip: the best time to view big liners passing through is from 9am to 11am and from 3pm to 5pm, when they are more frequent.

To get there, take any Paraíso or Gamboa bus from the Albrook Bus Terminal in Panama City. Buses pass along the canalside highway to Gamboa and will let you off at the 'Miraflores Locks' sign (US$0.35) on the highway, 12km from the city center. It's about a 15-minute walk to the locks from the sign. Otherwise, you can take a taxi; drivers will typically wait 30 minutes at the locks and then drive you back to the capital. Expect to pay no more than US$30 round-trip; agree on the price beforehand.

Pedro Miguel Locks CANAL
[FREE] North past the Miraflores Locks, the Pedro Miguel Locks can be seen from the highway to Gamboa. One hundred meters beyond the locks there's a parking strip from where onlookers can watch ships transit the canal.

✦ Activities

Canal & Bay Tours BOAT TOUR
(Map p626; ☑209-2002; www.canalandbaytours. com; partial/full transit US$125/170) Offers partial canal transits (4½ hours), which pass through the Pedro Miguel and Miraflores Locks, every Saturday morning. On one Saturday every month full transits (10 hours) run from Balboa on the Pacific coast to Cristóbal on the Caribbean coast, passing all three sets of locks. Check the website for dates of upcoming transits. While the guiding is good, readers have complained about logistical snafus.

★ Yala Tours ADVENTURE TOUR
(☑232-0215, 6641-6676; www.yalatourspanama. com) This small Swiss-run operation provides specialized trips throughout Panama, including day trips to Gamboa and the Canal Zone. A highlight is kayaking Río Chagres and Lago Gatún while watching canal ships mow through. Also offers a canal boat tour in Lago Gatún, wildlife-watching and hiking in Parque Nacional Soberanía, and cultural visits to an Emberá village.

EcoCircuitos ADVENTURE TOUR
(☑315-1488; www.ecocircuitos.com; Albrook Plaza, 2nd fl, No 31, Ancón) 🌿 A reputable, sustainable operator offering conventional tours to the Panama Canal and canal transits, tours of Parque Nacional Soberanía, birdwatching on Pipeline Rd and fun kayaking trips on Lago Gatún.

Around the Canal

The Canal Zone is home to a number of impressive attractions, especially if you're into wildlife-watching, hiking and birdwatching. On a day trip from Panama City, you could visit the Miraflores Locks and finish at the Parque Nacional Soberanía and the Panama Rainforest Discovery Center. With prior arrangements, you could also take an organized tour of Isla Barro Colorado, one of the

Panama Canal

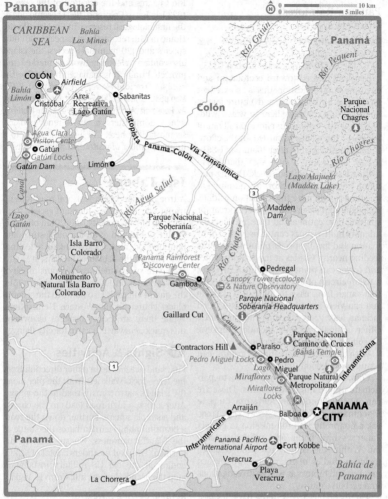

world's most famous tropical research stations, or an Emberá or Wounaan indigenous village on the shores of the Río Chagres.

Parque Nacional Soberanía

Parque Nacional Soberanía PARK
(www.miambiente.gob.pa; US$5) This 22,104-hectare park is one of the most accessible tropical rainforests in Panama. It extends much of the way across the isthmus, from Limón on Lago Gatún to just north of Paraíso. It features hiking trails, the Río Chagres, part of Lago Gatún and a remarkable variety of wildlife. Leaflets and information about the park, including a brochure for self-guided walks along the nature trail, are available from park headquarters near Gamboa.

Known residents include 105 species of mammal, 525 species of bird, 55 species of amphibian, 79 species of reptile and 36 species of freshwater fish. Hiking trails in the park include a section of the old Sendero Las Cruces (Las Cruces Trail) and the 17km Pipeline Rd, providing access to Río Agua Salud, where you can walk upriver for a swim under a waterfall.

In order to fully appreciate the wildlife here, it's wise to hire a guide. Charges vary.

Panama Rainforest Disovery Center

Panama Rainforest Discovery Center PARK
(☑306-3133, 6450-6630; www.pipelineroad.org; adult/child US$30/4, night walk donation US$35; ☺6am-4pm) Geared toward ecotourism and environmental education, this is an excellent facility for birdwatchers and nature-lovers. Since you are probably here to watch wildlife, it's worth making an effort to roll out of bed early. You will be rewarded for the effort. In fact, those arriving after 10am pay US$10 less in admission, a sure sign that you're getting less bang for your buck. During premium hours, just 25 visitors are admitted at one time to minimize the impact on wildlife.

A 32m-high observation tower is great for spotting blue cotinga and toucans. The sustainably built visitors center provides information and has 13 species of hummingbirds feeding nearby. Guides at the visitors center and tower can point out wildlife. Currently, a 1.2km circuit of forest trails offers options that range from easy to difficult. Lake-side you can view aquatic birds such as wattled jacanas, least grebes, herons and snail kites. Other animals around include monkeys, crocodiles, coatis and butterflies.

With advance reservations, groups can set up special night tours.

Contact the center if you'd like to participate in bird migration counts. These are run by the **Fundación Avifauna Eugene Eisenmann** (☑306-3133; www.avifauna.org. pa), a nonprofit with the mission to protect Panama's bird fauna and rainforest habitat. Within the center, scientific research includes studies of migratory birds, green macaws and raptors as well as investigations into carbon capture.

There's no bus access to the park. It's best to negotiate a taxi, rent a car or go with an organized tour. The center is located 1.6km from the entrance to Pipeline Rd. You must pass the town of Gamboa, at the end of Gaillard Rd, and follow the signs.

Nearby Emberá and Wounaan indigenous villages can be visited by prior arrangement from the dock at Lago Gatún.

Monumento Nacional Isla Barro Colorado

This lush island in the middle of Lago Gatún is the most intensively studied area in the neotropics. Formed by the damming of the Río Chagres and the creation of the lake, in 1923 Isla Barro Colorado (BCI) became one of the first biological reserves in the New World. Home to 1316 recorded plant species, 381 bird species and 120 mammal species, the island also contains a 59km network of marked and protected trails. It is managed by the **Smithsonian Tropical Research Institute** (STRI; Map p630; ☑212-8000; www.stri.org; Tupper Bldg, Av Roosevelt, Ancón; ☺8:30am-4:30pm Mon-Fri), which administers a world-renowned research facility here. The island is open to a limited number of visitors on guided tours.

Isla Taboga

A tropical island with just one road and no traffic, Isla Taboga is a pleasant escape from the rush of Panama City, only 20km offshore. With the addition of an annual festival and boutique lodgings, it's growing as a destination. Named the 'Island of Flowers,' it is covered with sweet-smelling blossoms much of the year. First settled by the Spanish in 1515, the quaint village is also home to the second-oldest church in the Western Hemisphere. While there are better beaches elsewhere, this quick getaway is a salve for city living.

◉ Sights & Activities

Fine sand beaches lie in either direction from the ferry dock. Walk left from the pier along the island's narrow main road to the village. After a fork, a high road leads to the church and a simple square. Further down the road, a beautiful public garden bares the statue of the island's patroness, Nuestra Señora del Carmen. The road meanders a total of 5.2km, ending at the old US military installation atop the island's highest hill, Cerro El Vigia.

Refugio de Vida Silvestre Islas Taboga y Urabá WILDLIFE RESERVE
This wildlife reserve was established to protect key avian habitat. Taboga and nearby Urabá are home to one of the world's largest breeding colonies of brown pelicans, with up to 100,000 individuals – about half of the world population of this species. The reserve covers about a third of Taboga as well as the entire island of Urabá, just off Taboga's southeast coast. May is the height of nesting season, but pelicans are seen from January to June.

Iglesia de San Pedro CHURCH
Founded in 1550, La Iglesia de San Pedro is the second-oldest church in the Western

Hemisphere; inside is a handsome altar and lovely artwork.

Festivals & Events

Nuestra Señora del Carmen FIESTA
(⊙16 Jul) Island patroness Nuestra Señora del Carmen is honored with a seafaring procession each year. Seemingly everyone partakes in games, fire-breathing or dancing.

Fiesta del Mar FIESTA
(www.fiestadelmarpanama.com; ⊙Jan) Only in its second year, this festival highlights local culture, with live Panamanian calypso music, dancing, a pageant and food events. Held at the end of January, it draws 4000 guests to this tiny island.

Sleeping & Eating

Zoraida's Cool GUESTHOUSE $
(⊘6471-1123; d/tr US$40/45) Overlooking the bay, this turquoise house is run by Rafael, the widow of Zoraida. Rooms are small and mattresses plastic-wrapped, but it's the cheapest digs around. The clincher is a hammock deck that's ideal for a snooze with Pacific views. Turn left as you exit the dock and walk for a few minutes until you see a sign leading you up the hill.

Cerrito Tropical B&B $$
(⊘390-8999, 6489-0074; www.cerritotropical panama.com; d incl breakfast US$88, 2-person apt US$95-130; ❋🛜) This smart Canadian and Dutch–owned B&B occupies a quiet nook atop a steep road. Rooms are stylish, and some are more spacious than others and not all feature TVs. Management can arrange tours such as fishing, hiking and whalewatching, and daytime packages including lunch and showers for nonguests. Taxi from the pier, or make the steep walk, going right uphill at the end of Calle Francisco Pizarro.

★Calaloo SEAFOOD $
(⊘6000-5172; mains $7-10; ⊙9am-5pm Mon-Thu, to 8pm Fri-Sun, by reservation if closed; 🅿) This cute, colorful eatery offers the standard fare of fish and chips in addition to veggie options. It's a great place to have a beer and watch the village hubbub. Service is notably slow, but crazy weekend crowds way outnumber the cooks. Just be patient. It's run by the folks from Cerrito Tropical B&B.

Donde Pope Si Hay PANAMANIAN $
(mains US$4-9; ⊙8am-8pm) A simple cement eatery serving fresh fish, cold green coconut water and *patacones* (fried plantains); there is nothing mysterious about Pope beyond its name.

ⓘ Information

For more information, visit the excellent English-language site www.taboga.panamanow.com.

ⓘ Getting There & Away

The scenic boat trip to Isla Taboga is part of the island's attraction. Ferries land at a pier near the north end of the island. Schedules can change, so check online for updates. Note that the police check ferry passengers for drugs upon arrival.

Barcos Calypso (⊘314-1730; round-trip US$14) ferries depart from Isla Naos on the Causeway in Panama City. The easiest way to reach the dock is by taxi (US$7). Trips take 45 minutes and depart Panama City at the following times:

DEPARTURE	TIME
Mon & Fri	8:30am, 3pm
Tue, Wed & Thu	8am, 10:30am
Sat & Sun	4pm

Return ferries from Isla Taboga:

DEPARTURE	TIME
Mon-Thu	4pm
Fri	9:30am, 4:30pm
Sat & Sun	9am, 3pm, 5pm

The new **Taboga Express** (⊘6234-8989; www.tabogaexpress.com; adult/child round-trip US$16/8; 🛜) catamaran takes 30 minutes and is killing the competition with good reason: it's fast. It leaves daily from Panama City's Balboa Yacht Club on the Causeway at 8am, 9:30am, 11am, 3pm and 4:30pm.

Return catamarans depart Isla Taboga at 8:45am, 10:15am, 2:30pm, 4pm and 5pm.

Archipiélago de las Perlas

Named for the large pearls found in its waters, the Archipiélago de las Perlas comprises 90 named islands and more than 100 unnamed islets, each surrounded by travel-magazine-worthy white-sand beaches and turquoise waters. Home to the palatial mansions of the rich and powerful, Isla Contadora is the best known. Popular US TV show *Survivor* filmed its 2003 season on an unnamed island in the chain. Real-estate developments, which would add luxury homes and resorts to areas with poor longtime settlements, are increasingly under fire.

Activities

Coral Dreams
DIVING

(☑ 6536-1776; www.coral-dreams.com; 1hr dive $95, 3hr snorkeling $65) This small PADI-certified outfit with experienced instructors is located in front of the Contadora airport. Snorkeling tours go to Isla Mogo (Survivor Island). It also runs whale-watching trips (July to October) with a hydrophone to hear whale calls, and rents snorkel equipment.

Survivor Las Perlas
ADVENTURE TOUR

(☑ 6738-1708; http://ecotourspanama.net/survivor lasperlas; 3-day camping tours per person US$249) Welcome to the wild side, where you can explore uninhabited islands in the archipelago, snorkel reefs and camp in hammocks on desolate beaches on a guided group trip. Scavenger hunts are part of the fun. The trip visits islands Mogo Mogo and Chapera, featured in the *Survivor* reality TV series. Meals and local boat transportation included. The tour is run by Panama Travel Unlimited.

Sleeping

★ B&B Gerald's Place
B&B $$

(☑ 250-4159; www.island-contadora.com; d incl breakfast US$96; ✳ 🛜) With a good location near the ferry landing, Gerald's is central and comfortable, with consistently good service. Rooms may lack views, but are modern and well equipped, with flat-screen TVs and air-con.

Perla Real
B&B $$$

(☑ 250-4095, 6513-9064; www.perlareal.com; d/tr/ste incl breakfast US$127/145/165; ✳ 🛜) Looking more Santa Fé than tropical, this comfortable inn is one of the best options on the island. Spacious rooms have French doors and prim decor, with painted ceramic sinks, stenciled walls and soft cotton bedding. Ideal for long stays, suites come with an equipped kitchen and living space. The quiet residential area is a 10-minute walk from the beaches.

Getting There & Away

Most visitors travel to Isla Contadora, served from Panama City by **Air Panama** (☑ 316-9000; www.airpanama.com) and **Sea Las Perlas** (☑ 391-1424; www.sealasperlas.com; adult/child one way US$45/35) ferry service.

PACIFIC COAST & HIGHLANDS

Between Chiriquí Province and Panama City, the regions of Coclé, Veraguas and Península de Azuero have long been overshadowed by the flash of the capital, the coolness of the highlands and the lure of the Caribbean. But for Panama's heart and soul, this may be the best place to look.

Dominated by agriculture, these are friendly provinces of laid-back colonial towns, farms and hillside villages. Founded by the Spanish four centuries ago, traditions live on in original colonial architecture, dazzling festivals and exquisite handicrafts.

Highlights include Santa Catalina, one of the best surf destinations in Central America, as well as the scenic mountain towns of Santa Fé and El Valle. The Pedasí coast is an up-and-coming destination for off-the-beaten-track beaches and surf.

El Valle

POP 7600

Officially known as El Valle de Antón, this picturesque town is nestled in the crater of a huge extinct volcano, and ringed by verdant forests and jagged peaks. El Valle is a popular weekend getaway for urban dwellers in need of fresh air and scenery and it's a North American retirement community. With an extensive network of trails, this is a superb place for walking, hiking or horseback riding. Nearby forests offer excellent birdwatching, and the valleys of El Valle are home to an impressive set of waterfalls as well as the increasingly rare golden frog.

Sights & Activities

Chorro El Macho
WATERFALL

(Manly Falls; admission US$5; ⊙8am-5pm) The most famous waterfall in the El Valle area is 35m-high Chorro El Macho, which is located about 2km north of town; it's a 10-minute walk from the road and the entrance to the **Canopy Adventure** (☑ 6613-7220, 264-5720; www.canopytower.com/canopy-adventure; canopy rides US$65; ⊙8am-4pm) tour. Below the falls you'll find a large rocky swimming pool surrounded by rainforest and fed by river water. There is also a series of short hiking trails that wend their way into the surrounding forest.

As its somewhat humorous name implies, this towering waterfall is quite forceful and makes for some excellent photographs. El Valle's famed canopy tour offers an unforgettable aerial view of Chorro El Macho.

El Níspero ZOO
(983-6142; adult/child US$5/2; 7am-5pm) About 1km north of Av Central, El Níspero is a zoo set in the forest. It is home to everything from tapirs and capuchin monkeys to jaguars and more than 50 species of bird. It is also the best place to see Panama's endangered *ranas doradas* (golden frogs), strikingly colored, very photogenic amphibians housed in the **El Valle Amphibian Conservation Center** (EVACC; http://amphibianrescue. org/evacc; 9am-5pm Wed-Mon) FREE onsite.

Aprovaca Orquídeas GARDENS
(983-6472; http://aprovaca.com; adult/child US$2/0.75; 9am-4pm) For the best selection of *orquídeas* (orchids) in the region, visit this idyllic not-for-profit garden run by the local association of orchid growers at the eastern end of town. Volunteers work to maintain the lovely flowers inside the greenhouse and the grounds, and they welcome visitors to show off the more than 100 species of orchids cultivated here. Orchids are temperamental bloomers; check out the display room near the entrance to see what's flowering at the moment.

Pozos Termales HOT SPRING
(Calle Los Pozos; admission US$3; 8am-4:30pm) Pozos Termales thermal baths complex features a series of pools of varying temperatures and alleged curative properties. Post-soak, there are buckets for applying healing mud to your skin. The next step is to take the requisite photo and then head to the showers. The baths are a 10-minute walk southwest of the center at the end of Calle Los Pozos, near Río Antón.

🛌 Sleeping

Bodhi Hostel HOSTEL $
(908-7120, 6429-4143; http://bodhihostels.com; Av Central; dm/d incl breakfast US$15/35; @ 🛜) A welcome arrival to El Valle's budget accommodations scene, this central hostel counts six private rooms with shared showers, and a massive, bright and airy dorm with 27 beds in triple-deck bunks. Dorms are curtained and have lockers; the artwork is by volunteers. The Buddha theme, bafflingly prevalent in Panama, is present here.

La Casa de Juan GUESTHOUSE $
(6453-9775,6807-1651; www.lacasadejuanpanama. blogspot.com; Calle Cocorron No 4; campsites per tent US$5, dm/s/d US$10/20/25; P 🛜) This massive, bare-bones setup with 17 rooms overflows with disused ATVs, outdoor weight-lifting equipment and farm implements, but it is an acceptable (just) budget hostel-style option. Though decrepit, the house is relatively clean and Señor Juan is a social host also offering great local advice and guided walks.

⭐ **Cabañas Potosí** CABIN $$
(6946-6148, 983-6181; www.elvallepotosi.com; Calle La Reforma No 84; campsites US$15, d/tr US$59/69; P 🛜) 🧴 A very welcoming place and good for a peaceful sleep, Cabañas Potosí is situated just over 1km southwest of the town center. The park-like grounds offer lovely views of the peaks that ring the valley, including La India Dormida. The four concrete cabins each have three beds, a fridge and use of one of two outdoor communal kitchens.

⭐ **Golden Frog Inn** INN $$
(Villa Rana Dorada; 6565-8307, 983-6117; www. goldenfroginn.com; d/ste incl breakfast from US$77/150; P ❄ 🛜 🐕) Attentive and relaxing, this deluxe Canadian-Panamanian-owned lodge with six very different rooms and suites is the perfect place to laze after a long day of play. Start with the swimming pool and migrate to the open-air living spaces and large library. The expansive grounds include orchids and fruit trees; adjoining trails mean you can hike from right out the door.

🍴 Eating

El Quijote SPANISH $$
(983-6210, 6095-0124; Calle El Hato No 1; mains US$5-9; 8am-10pm Tue-Sun) This 'spit' (ie grill) restaurant is a local favorite, noted for its well-prepared Spanish dishes such as *pulpo a la plancha* (grilled octopus), paella and the unusual *migas*, a dish of herbed breadcrumbs often served with ribs. El Quijote is a simple affair, almost like a *fonda* (cheap restaurant), with an incongruous little fountain in the center adding a dash of color.

L'Italiano PIZZA $$
(6682-9398, 908-7378; www.facebook.com/ L-italiano-660035177397679; Av Central; mains US$11-14; 11am-9pm Wed-Sun) They say that this restaurant and pizzeria with just 40

MAMALLENA ECOLODGE

At this mellow ecolodge (☑ 6673-0752, 6781-7545; http://mamallenaecolodge.com; Camino a La Laguna; dm/d without bathroom US$13/40, 2-person cabins with/without bathroom US$60/45, all incl breakfast) on a sprawling 174-hectare farm, accommodations are in a comfortable Swiss-style home and riverfront cabins in a stunning highland setting. You can hike the area and swim in a pleasing river pool. The Welsh and US hosts recycle and use organic permaculture to revitalize once-abandoned fruit orchards. Guests can cook for themselves or sign up for good-value shared dinners (with vegetarian options).

There's a full bar that's enhanced with local herbs and chili peppers. Pancake breakfasts are included.

Mamallena Ecolodge is a 1½-hour drive from Panama City and 30 minutes from El Valle (Coclé Province). From Panama City coordinate a transfer or bus to Coronado where you can catch the La Laguna *colectivo* (US$1.20, 30 minutes) to a crossroads 3km from the lodge. Arrange ahead for pick-ups from here.

covers inside and out has the best pizza in El Valle. With an Italian owner and chef at the oven it certainly tastes like the real thing. Along with some 15 different pizzas (US$6.50 to US$13), there are a number of pasta dishes (US$11 to US$13) and more complex mains on offer.

ℹ Getting There & Away

To leave El Valle, hop aboard a bus traveling along Av Central; on average, buses depart every 30 minutes. Final destinations are painted on windshields of the bus. If your next destination isn't posted, catch a bus going in the same direction and transfer.

To reach El Valle from the Interamericana, disembark from any bus at San Carlos, about 3km beyond the turning for El Valle. Minibuses collect passengers at the station here and travel to El Valle (US$1.50, one hour, every 30 minutes). Last departure is 4pm weekdays and 7pm at weekends. From Panama City the trip to El Valle takes 2½ hours (US$4.50).

Chitré

POP 48,480

One of Panama's oldest settlements, the hot city of Chitré is hardly geared up for travelers, but it's an agreeable stop on the way down to the peninsula's beaches. The capital of Herrera Province, it's the largest city on the Península de Azuero, and the cultural and historic capital of the region.

⌂ Sleeping & Eating

Miami Mike's   HOSTEL $
(☑ 6603-9711, 910-0628; www.miamimikeshostel.com; Av Herrera & Calle Manuel Maria Correa; dm

US$11, s/d US$17/22; 🛜) It certainly ain't the Ritz, but the price, location and warm welcome make this 1st-floor walk-up a serious option. The four rooms are themed (Rebel, Che, Bob Marley, Marilyn Monroe), with colorful murals; one has its own bathroom. There's a good communal kitchen but the best 'extra' is the spectacular roof terrace, with 360-degree views and a bar.

Host Mike Wilson is a font of knowledge and can advise on excursions throughout the area. Fans keep you cool here.

Hotel Rex   HOTEL $
(☑ 996-4310, 996-2408; www.facebook.com/Hotel-Rex-Chitre-Panama-121877944544889; Calle Melitón Martín s/n; d/tr US$44/66; ✳🛜) With a prime location on Parque Union and good dining downstairs, Rex is a solid choice. Its 33 clean tile rooms have brick walls, cable TV, fresh towels and water thermoses. Ask for a room on the 2nd floor where there's a large communal veranda overlooking the cathedral and main square.

★ Salsa y Carbon   PARRILLA $$
(☑ 996-6022; www.salsaycarbon.com; cnr Calles Julio Botello & Francisco Corro; mains US$8-14; ⏲11am-10pm) This open-air Colombian thatched BBQ house grills some of the best steak and ribs in the region. Meat and chicken are exceptionally tender and served with salad and *arepas* (maize flatbreads). The covered outside seating catches cool breezes and is a delight.

ℹ Getting There & Around

Chitré is a center for regional bus transportation. Buses arrive and depart from **Terminal de**

Transportes de Herrera (☑ 996-6426), 1km south of downtown, near Vía Circunvalación. The terminal has a 24-hour restaurant and a car rental agency. To get there, **Radio Taxi** (☑ 996-4442) charges US$2. The 'Terminal' bus (US$0.30) leaves from the intersection of Calle Aminta Burgos de Amado and Av Herrera.

Tuasa (☑ 996-2661) and **Transportes Inazun** (☑ 996-4177) buses depart from Chitré's Terminal de Transportes de Herrera for Panama City (US$9.10, four hours, every 40 minutes from 6am to 11pm). Other buses departing from Chitré operate from sunrise to sunset.

To get to David (US$9.50), take a bus to Santiago (US$3.25, every half hour) and then catch a *directo* (direct bus). Buses leave from the gas station at the intersection of the Interamericana and the Carretera Nacional.

Pedasí

POP 2410

Unpretentious and picturesque, Pedasí's streets are lined with tiled colonials and leafy spaces. For years this sleepy retreat came to life only at festival times. But outsiders are discovering the big appeal of small-town life and wilderness beaches.

◉ Sights & Activities

Snorkeling and diving around nearby islands, which are surrounded by large coral reefs, are major attractions. Sportfishers can land wahoo, tuna, mahimahi, amberjack and Pacific mackerel. For guided trips (from about US$200 for two passengers), ask at **Pedasí Sports Club** (☑ 6749-4308, 995-2894; www.pedasisportsclub.com; Av Central s/n; ⊙ 9am-6pm Mon-Sat) or **Pedasí Tours** (☑ 995-2466; www.pedasitours.com; Av Central; ⊙ 9am-6pm Mon-Sat).

Isla Cañas   WILDLIFE RESERVE
(admission US$10) Isla Cañas is one of a handful of places that olive ridley sea turtles nest in high numbers (the others are two beaches on the Pacific side of Costa Rica and two beaches in Orissa on the Bay of Bengal in India). Endangered species including the hawksbill, loggerhead sea, leatherback and green turtle nest here too.

Bring a mosquito net and lots of insect repellent, long pants, a windbreaker or bug jacket and mosquito coils if you have them.

Refugio de Vida Silvestre
Isla Iguana   WILDLIFE RESERVE
(US$10) This 55-hectare wildlife reserve is centered on a deserted island ringed by coral fields. The water is shallow enough for snorkeling; the reef fish are enormous; and humpback whales can be spotted in the surrounding waters between June and November.

🛏 Sleeping

Dim's Hostal   GUESTHOUSE $
(☑ 6274-4156, 995-2303; reservacionesdimshostal@gmail.com; Av Central s/n; s/d incl breakfast US$33/49; P ✳ 🛜) Dim's has a family atmosphere and a coveted backyard patio, complete with breakfast tables, hammocks and a mango tree. The nine rooms vary in quality – some are quite cramped and have dull tile floors – but the owners are delightful and service-oriented.

Doña María B&B   B&B $
(☑ 995-2916; www.donamariabnb.com; Av Central s/n; d/tr incl breakfast US$50/65; P ✳ 🛜) Ideal for couples, this caring family-run lodging has six nice rooms above a family home, featuring tiles, firm queen-sized beds with plush quilted covers, and cable TV. The patio has soft sofas that look out onto the main street and a stack of magazines to peruse. An annex features three additional rooms in back, one of which has disabled access.

★ **La Rosa de los Vientos**   B&B $$
(☑ 6530-4939, 6778-0627; www.bedandbreakfastpedasi.com; Via Playa del Toro; d/tr/q incl breakfast US$60/75/85; P 🛜) With the feel of a rural hacienda, this lovely red-tile Spanish colonial just up from the beach has three smart rooms with colorful weavings, antique tiles and ocean views. It's designed to be eco-friendly, so there is no air-con, but fans do the trick. Multilingual owners Isabelle and Robert offer warm hospitality.

🍴 Eating

Fonda Mama Fefa   PANAMANIAN $
(Calle Los Estudiantes s/n; set meals US$2.50-3; ⊙ 5am-2pm Mon-Sat) Matriarch of creole cooking, Mama Fefa usually runs out of lunch by noon (though you can linger longer). Cheap and cheerful, these huge *comidas típicas* (regional specialties) include meat or fish, rice, salad and a drink. Devotees share the space at a few outdoor tables. Take the side street opposite the landmark supermarket for two blocks. It's on the right.

Pasta e Vino   ITALIAN $
(☑ 6695-2689; mains US$7-11; ⊙ 6-10pm Wed-Sun) This unadorned Italian-owned restaurant

offers pastas, salads and a decent wine list. Food is simple but authentic, such as the pesto with black olives and fresh cheese. It's all about service, expertly executed by hosts Danilo and Elena. Look for a yellow house three blocks past the main plaza on the road to Playa El Toro.

Smiley's Restaurant NORTH AMERICAN $
(☑ 995-2863, 6510-9652; www.facebook.com/ smileys.restaurante; Av Central s/n; mains US$4-12; ⊙ noon-9:30pm Tue-Sun) Catering largely to expats, this friendly bar-restaurant serves up grilled fish, pasta dishes such as lasagna, and deli sandwiches including minced BBQ pork with coleslaw. There's also good live music on Tuesday and Friday nights, sports matches on the tube, and an extensive drinks menu to match. Check the Facebook page for daily specials.

★**Mare Bonita** FUSION $$
(☑ 6200-0124; www.facebook.com/pages/Restau rante-Mare-Bonita/372368832954808; Calle Las Tablas; mains US$10-15; ⊙ 5-10pm) Considered by many to be the best restaurant in Pedasí, it's certainly the most inventive. Chilean chef Luis Morales keeps the menu in a state of flux, offering teriyaki chicken and Thai-style pork one week, and gourmet hamburgers and fired fish *ceviche* the next. The long, narrow dining room done up in sky-blue has an Asian feel to it.

❶ Information

ATP (☑ 995-2339; azuero@atp.gob.pa; ⊙ 8am-4pm Mon-Sat) Helpful but slow, the ATP office lies one block past the main road in the north of town. It has a list of boat contacts for Isla Cañas.

Banco Nacional de Panama (☑ 995-2257; Av Central s/n; ⊙ 8am-3pm Mon-Fri, 9am-noon Sat) Has an ATM (one of two in town on Av Central) near the entrance to town.

❶ Getting There & Away

Buses to Las Tablas leave every hour between 6am and 4pm (US$2.40, one hour) from next to El Pueblo supermarket. Buses to Playa Venao (US$2, 30 minutes) leave at 7am, noon and 2pm. Buses to Cañas (US$2.40, 45 minutes) depart at 7am and noon.

Sunset Coast

The Sunset Coast is the name given to the west side of Península de Azuero facing the Gulfo de Montijo and Pacific Ocean. The sobriquet is accurate for it is the only place in Panama from which you can watch the sun go down from a beach.

Here you'll find long, sandy beaches virtually empty of holiday makers, excellent surfing and the chance to see three species of turtles hatching. There are nature walks in the mangroves and Parque Nacional Cerro Hoya is just down the road.

DON'T MISS

LAS FIESTAS DE AZUERO

Famous throughout Panama, the traditional festivals of Azuero were created around customs from early Spanish settlers. This is a side of Panama that few foreigners ever get to see. While you may lose a day from a *seco* (alcoholic drink made from sugarcane) hangover, taking part in the wilder side of the peninsula is more than worth the suffering. Some of the best-known festivals include the following:

Carnaval The four days before Ash Wednesday in Chitré, Parita, La Villa de los Santos and especially Las Tablas

Semana Santa March/April in Pesé and La Villa de los Santos

Feria Internacional de Azuero Late April/early May in La Villa de los Santos

Fiesta de Corpus Christi Forty days after Easter in La Villa de los Santos

Fiesta de San Juan Bautista June 24 in Chitré

Patronales de San Pablo & San Pedro June 29 in Pedasí and La Arena

Feria de la Mejorana Late September in Guararé

Festival de la Virgen de las Mercedes Late September in Guararé

Foundation of Chitré Day October 19 in Chitré

El Grito de La Villa November 10 in La Villa de los Santos

The gateway to the Sunset Coast is Santiago, about 60km north of Mariato. Other important settlements include Malena and Torio, 11km and 15km south of Mariato respectively.

🏃 Activities

Malena Beach
Conservation Association   WILDLIFE WATCHING
(Asociación Conservacionista de Playa Malena; 📋 6676-0220, 6685-8908; Playa Malena; donation US$15) Between late June and into January, you can find three species of turtles on the beaches of Malena, and volunteers of the Malena Beach Conservation Association work toward their preservation. Chairperson Ana González and her community volunteers take visitors on turtle watches; peak season for laying and hatching is October.

The organization also offers accommodations, horseback riding (US$10 per hour), boat tours and nature walks.

Centro AAPEQ   WILDLIFE WATCHING
(📋 6389-5249, 6491-9365; tortugas.aapeq@gmail.com; Rusia de Quebra) This association based near Morillo focuses its attention on the conservation of turtles and reforestation of the Mata Oscura mangrove. The affable couple in charge can take you on a tour (US$10) through the mangroves or through the forest up to a waterfall, where you can you see strawberry poison-dart frogs. Kayaks are available as well.

🛏 Sleeping & Eating

Hostal Iguana Verde   HOSTEL $
(📋 6676-0220, 6685-8908; r US$20) The chairperson of the Malena Beach Conservation Association rents out a handful of fancooled rooms on the main road in Malena. They are simple but clean, and are a short distance from the beach.

Heliconia Bed & Breakfast   B&B $$
(📋 6676-0220, 6370-2857; http://hotelheliconiapanama.com; Palmilla; s/d incl breakfast US$50/89; P ❄ 🛜 🛁) 🎋 The Sunset Coast's anchor tenant, Heliconia Bed & Breakfast in Palmilla, just north of Malena, is an excellent retreat thoughtfully crafted by two extremely knowledgeable Dutch biologists, who also offer recommended area tours. Heliconia counts four smart rooms set within 8 hectares of botanical gardens, a lovely lounge and terrace, and an above-ground pool.

Shaka Bar   INTERNATIONAL $$
(📋 6627-9787; mains US$8-15; ⏱ 5:30pm-midnight Thu-Sun) Entertainment central on the Sunset Coast and the watering hole of choice for both local expats and visiting surfers, Shaka is also a restaurant (food available till 9:30pm) serving cheeseburgers and fish-and-chips. Visit at least once when in the area.

❶ Getting There & Away

Up to 10 buses a day link Santiago with Torio (US$4.25, 1½ hours), via Mariato, between 6am and 5pm. The buses at noon and 2pm carry on as far as Rusia de Quebra, where **Centro AAPEQ** is located.

Playa Venao
POP 2500

A long, protected beach, Playa Venao – officially Venado but mispronounced and misspelled as 'Venao' – recently transformed from a wild beach to a 'go to' destination. Surfers lay the first claim to its waters; waves are consistent and break in both directions.

🛏 Sleeping & Eating

★ Eco Venao   LODGE $
(📋 832-0530; www.ecovenao.com; campsites per person US$6, dm/d without bathroom US$11/30, 2-person cabins US$40, 6-person houses US$200; P ❄ 🛜) 🎋 On the north side of the main road, North American–owned Eco Venao offers a cool mountain ambiance. Perfect for surfers and adventurers, its 20 excellent options range from low to high end, offering something for everyone. The lush 57-hectare property means mini-adventures are close at hand, from howler monkey visits and a playground to a short waterfall hike.

Selina Hostel Playa Venao   HOSTEL $$
(📋 202-5919; www.selinahostels.com; campsites per person US$18, dm US$14-20, d with/without bathroom from US$70/45, d deluxe US$99-119; P 🛜 🛁) This beachside branch of a hostel chain consists of 16 colorful thatched bungalows in rows running down to a pool and the beach. The 38 rooms come in every possible shape and size, from a mixed dorm with 12 beds to a private double with bathroom and balcony.

Our favorite is deluxe double room 204. The hostel's nerve center is the beachside bar and its pool tables, where surfers will regale you with tales of their exploits; escape to the recycled van with the thatched roof opposite. Selina rents boards for US$10/75 per day/week and organizes turtle-watching tours to Isla Cañas (US£$90 per person).

★ **Coleos Cafe** CAFE $

(☑ 6289-2820; www.facebook.com/Coleos-cafe-855109761222106; mains US$8; ⊙ 9am-10pm) This wonderful little place just up from the beach serves homemade pasta dishes, delicious hummus plates, sandwiches (US$5 to US$7) and a wide range of delectable breads, brownies and cookies. Enjoy breakfast (US$5 to US$9) on the tiny terrace.

🛈 Getting There & Away

The Playa Venao turnoff is 33km southwest of Pedasí (2km past the turn for Resort La Playita). The Cañas–Pedasí bus (US$2) passes by between 7am and 9am and makes the return journey between noon and 12:30pm and 2pm and 2:30pm. Confirm exact times with your hotel. You can also take a taxi from Pedasí (from US$18).

Santa Catalina

POP 300

Santa Catalina is one of Central America's top surf spots. The fishing village has a laid-back feel, with limited dining and nonexistent nightlife. Enjoy it while it's still remote, undeveloped and home to some seriously wicked surf. Santa Catalina is the main springboard for day and overnight trips to Isla de Coiba and its national park.

🏃 Activities

The best waves are generally from December to April, though there's surf here year-round. Unlike the Caribbean, the Pacific offers fairly consistent sets, though a good swell will really give a boost to the surfing here. Be advised that many of the breaks in the area are over rocks, and can easily snap your board if you don't know what you're doing. Most of the accommodations in town rent boards and offer surfing lessons.

★ **Dream Diving** DIVING

(☑ 6765-0631; www.dreamdivingpanama.com; ⊙ 8am-4:30pm) 🌊 This excellent dive shop just at the turnoff to the beach is run by a very eco-minded Colombian and offers snorkeling trips to Coiba (US$90) and two-/three-tank dives for US$130/160.

Surf & Shake SURFING

(☑ 6451-9939; www.surfandshake.com; ⊙ 9am-6pm) On the road to the beach just 150m in from the main street, Surf & Shake rents boards and sells leashes, boards and surf wear, as well as tasty fruit shakes. Run by German surfers, it's also a good spot for surf info.

🛏 Sleeping

Oasis Surf Camp CABIN $

(☑ 6670-5636, 6671-7049; www.oasissurfcamp.com; camping with/without tent per person US$12/7, dm US$15, d with fan/air-con US$45/55, ste US$135; P❄🛜) This Italian-owned surf camp has long been a staple of Santa Catalina, and its beachfront setting is one of the best. Bright, colorful cabins overlooking the black-sand beach have adequate facilities including hot showers and ample hammocks. The suite is a two-bedroom wooden house with wicker furniture, a kitchen and great balcony views. The dorm has five beds.

Boarder's Haven GUESTHOUSE $

(☑ 6572-0664; www.labuenavidahotel.com; s/d/tr US$25/30/35; ❄🛜) The ideal choice for those on a shoestring budget, this tiny guesthouse has just seven single beds in three rooms with real mattresses, shared bathrooms and a petite kitchen that's fully equipped. The brightly colored (and named) rooms have air-con and a ceiling fan. It sits on the main road in the center of town.

★ **Hibiscus Garden** RESORT $

(☑ 6615-6097; www.hibiscusgarden.com; Playa Lagartero; dm/s/d with shared bathroom US$15/30/35, s/d/q with private bathroom from US$45/55/80; P❄🛜) On Playa Lagartero, 11km northeast of Santa Catalina, these relaxed German-owned and Italian-run lodgings fuse modern with rustic, with stylish installations and minimal fuss. There's playful mosaics done by volunteers throughout, while the 14 rooms have recycled driftwood beds and private hammock terraces. An open-air dorm catches the breeze and views. The 6km-long beach is calm, secluded and very swimmable.

★ **La Buena Vida** CABIN $$

(☑ 6635-1895, 6572-0664; www.labuenavidahotel.com; 2-person villas US$66-88, 4-person studio US$110; P❄🛜) 🌊 These lovely villas spilling down a leafy hillside along the main road in the center of Santa Catalina will whisk you away from it all. Each is themed and decorated with colorful mosaics and tiles crafted by the American owners. 'Gecko' is the most deluxe, while 'Butterfly' offers the delicious option of showering outdoors. 'Bird' has two floors.

✘ Eating

La Vieja Panaderia   BAKERY **$**
(The Old Bakery; ☑6900-5776; sandwiches & salads US$5-7.50, pizza US$6.50-8.50; ☺6:30am-3pm & 6-10pm Thu-Tue) This Italian-run local institution is a bakery by day and a pizzeria after dark. Come before 9:30am as bread (US$1.50 to US$2) sells out and breakfasts (think omelets and pancakes) are slow to get served. There's also great coffee, lunch boxes to go, cakes and delectable muffins. The eight pizzas on offer are tasty and authentic.

La Buena Vida   NORTH AMERICAN **$**
(☑6635-1895, 6572-0664; www.labuenavida.biz; mains from US$7; ☺6am-2pm) If you're hitting the water early, this will be the first spot open for a bite. Great options include breakfast burritos and Greek scrambles with feta, olives, tomatoes and eggs. This funky tiled cafe perched above the main street also sells fresh fruit drinks and a lunchtime selection of salads, tacos and sandwiches on homemade bread.

Pizzeria Jammin   PIZZA **$**
(☑6604-3910; pizzas US$6.50-11; ☺from 6:30pm) A Santa Catalina mainstay, this open-air *rancho* (small house-like building) offers delicious thin-crust pizzas baked in a stone oven. Nightlife tends to concentrate here – perhaps it's the cheep beer, though there's also good wine and picnic tables conducive to sharing. It gets crowded, so arrive early in the evening. You'll find it on the road to the hotels facing the beach.

La Moncheria Heladería   ICE CREAM **$**
(☑6849-1796; www.facebook.com/pages/La-Moncheria-Santa-Fe/864661973552320; ☺3-10pm) This *gelataria* on a narrow dirt road on the way to La Punta surfing beach serves just about the best ice cream in Panama.

ⓘ Getting There & Around

To reach Santa Catalina from Panama City, take a bus to Santiago, then another to Soná where buses leave for Santa Catalina (US$4.65, 1½ hours) at 5:30am, 8:40am, 11:20am, 1:35pm, 2:40pm and 4:45pm. If you miss the bus, hire a taxi from Soná to Santa Catalina from US$45. Direct Panama City–Soná buses run every two hours.

From Santa Catalina, seven buses serve Soná daily, leaving at 6:15am, 7am, 8am, 10:20am, 1:15pm, 3pm and 6pm. In Santa Catalina, the bus stops at the intersection with the beach road. If you're staying outside the town center, most lodgings are a 1km walk on mostly flat but unshaded

---

WORTH A TRIP

ISLA DE COIBA

With the exception of Ecuador's Galápagos Islands and Isla de Coco in Costa Rica, few destinations off the Pacific coast of the Americas are as exotic as this **national park** (Coiba National Park; www.coibanationalpark.com; US$20) covering the 503-sq-km Isla de Coiba. Although just 20km offshore in the Golfo de Chiriquí, Coiba is a veritable lost world of pristine ecosystems and unique fauna.

Isolated for the past century due to its status as a notorious penal colony, Coiba offers travelers the chance to hike through primary rainforest and snorkel and dive in a marine park with increasingly rare wildlife. However, with virtually no tourist infrastructure in place, you're going to have to plan hard (and pay top dollar) to really see it up close.

Coiba was declared a national park in 1992, and in 2005 Unesco made it a World Heritage Site.

---

terrain. Note that there are never taxis in town, unless, of course, someone is arriving from Soná.

Santa Fé

POP 3050

This tiny mountain town 53km north of Santiago lies in the shadow of the continental divide. At an altitude of 500m, Sante Fé is cooler than the lowlands, and much of the surrounding forest is as it was when the Spanish founded the town in 1557.

Santa Fé has fresh, clean air and bucolic surroundings, yet it sees few foreign visitors. With the lush mountainsides, waterfalls, mountain streams and accessible swimming spots of Santa Fé National Park on the town's doorstep, this is an ideal destination for hikers, birdwatchers and those simply wanting to soak up the beauty of the highlands.

⊙ Sights & Activities

Río Bulaba   RIVER
There's a lovely swimming hole on this river about a 20-minute walk from town. Head northeast along the road past the Coffee Mountain Inn on the way to El Pantino. The swimming hole is about 600m from there.

Here a local named William rents **inner tubes** (US$8) and life jackets, which allow you to float idly down the river; it eventually merges with Río Santa Maria. He can also arrange a taxi return.

Cerro Tute   MOUNTAIN

With excellent open views of the valley, Cerro Tute is home to the area's famed bird life and features a cliff blasted with up currents that seem to prevent anyone falling off. An extensive trail network winds through primary and secondary rainforest. It's a few kilometers south of town, on the western side of the Santiago–Santa Fé road; count on five hours there and back.

🛏 Sleeping & Eating

★Hostal La Qhia   GUESTHOUSE $

(🖉6592-5589, 954-0903; www.panamamountain house.com; dm US$12, d & tr with shared/private bathroom US$39/44; 🅿🛜) Surrounded by lush gardens and hammocks, this original bamboo-and-stone chalet makes a great base camp for mountain adventures around Santa Fé. The three clean, snug rooms all feature crisp bedding; the ones upstairs are complete charmers. Dorms with six beds and a room with private bathroom occupy a small cement addition with an outdoor kitchen.

Hotel Anachoreo   HOTEL $

(🖉6911-4248; www.anachoreo.com; s/d/tr/q incl breakfast US$44/55/66/77; 🅿🛜) Hugging the hillside with panoramic views, this Dutch-Cambodian enterprise is a small hotel boasting four ample rooms with high ceilings and queen-size beds, and tubs in the bathrooms. There's also a new communal kitchen. Fragrant flower, herb and vegetable gardens flank the property on all sides; hammocks abound. The multilingual owner gives local 4WD tours and offers directions for hiking trails.

Restaurante Hermanos
Pineda   PANAMANIAN $

(🖉954-0777; mains US$6-12; ⊙7am-9pm) This welcoming, family-run place just up from the town center serves Panamanian favorites (think beans and lots of fried stuff) and has also branched out to pizza (US$5 to US$12). The large open veranda looking out onto the main road is a plus, as is the large map of the national park in front.

❶ Getting There & Away

Buses from Santa Fé to Santiago (US$2.90, 1½ hours) depart from the **bus station** every 30

minutes from 4am to 6pm, stopping at the more central **bus stop** en route. Note that if you are trying to reach the surf town of Santa Catalina in one day, you must leave Santa Fé by 9am to make all the bus connections in time.

CHIRIQUÍ PROVINCE

Chiriquí claims to have it all: Panama's tallest mountains, longest rivers and most fertile valleys. The province is also home to spectacular highland rainforests and the most productive agricultural and cattle-ranching regions in the country. As a result, *los chiricanos* (natives of Chiriquí) take a particular pride in their province and wave the provincial flag – in every sense – at the slightest opportunity.

It's also a land of immense beauty. On the coast, the pristine Golfo de Chiriquí boasts long sandy beaches and a rich diversity of marine life. The mist-covered mountains near the town of Boquete, a favorite of North American and European retirees, is a good base for adventures such as white-water rafting and hiking the flanks of Panama's highest point, Volcán Barú (3475m). Boquete is also the center of Panama's coffee industry, which means that a potent cup of shade-grown arabica is never more than a cafe away.

David

POP 144,860

Although it feels more like an overgrown country town, David is Panama's second-largest city and the capital of Chiriquí Province. It's more a center of agricultural industry than a cultural hub; you will be disappointed if you have museums, clubs and fine dining in mind. Yet, with foreign capital flowing into Chiriquí, David is rapidly gaining wealth and importance, and is poised to boom.

Halfway between Panama City and San José (Costa Rica), David is an important transportation hub.

🛏 Sleeping

★Bambu Hostel   HOSTEL $

(🖉730-2961; www.bambuhostel.com; Calle de la Virgencita; dm US$11-14, d with/without bathroom US$35/30; 🅿❄🛜🏊) This chilled-out house run by friendly New York City musician Greg has a regular air-conditioned dorm

David

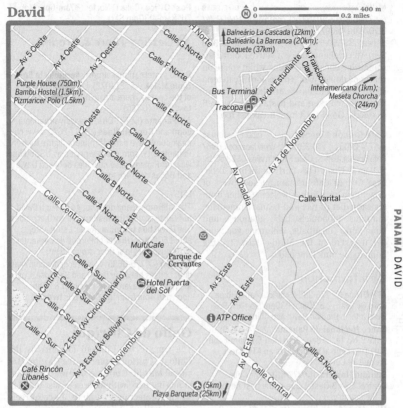

Calle G Norte

Calle F Norte

Av 5 Oeste

Av 4 Oeste

Av 3 Oeste

Calle E Norte

Balneário La Cascada (12km);
Balneário La Barranca (20km);
Boquete (37km)

Av del Estudiante

Av Francisco Clark

Bus Terminal

Interamericana (1km);
Meseta Chorcha
(24km)

Tracopa

Purple House (750m);
Bambu Hostel (1.5km);
Pizmaricer Polo (1.5km)

Av 2 Oeste

Calle D Norte

Av 1 Calle C Norte

Calle C Norte

Calle B Norte

Av 3 de Noviembre

Calle A Norte

Av 1 Este

Calle Central

Av Obaldía

Calle Varital

MultiCafe

Parque de
Cervantes

Calle A Sur

Av Central

Calle B Sur

Calle C Sur (Av Cincuentenario)

Av 2 Este (Av Bolivar)

Calle D Sur

Av 3 Este (Av Bolivar)

Av 3 de Noviembre

Hotel Puerta
del Sol

Calle 5 Este

Av 6 Este

ATP Office

Av 8 Este

Calle Central

Calle B Norte

Café Rincón
Libanés

(5km)
Playa Barqueta (25km)

PANAMA DAVID

with six beds and a thatched 'jungle house' on stilts out back, with 10 beds and mosquito nets. The seven doubles have air-con and include electric hot-water showers. The sprawling garden has a swimming pool, a cheap beer bar and the requisite hammocks. Wonderful.

Purple House HOSTEL **$**
(📞 774-4059; www.purplehousehostel.com; cnr Calle C Sur & Av 6 Oeste; dm US$9, d with/without bathroom US$27/25, all incl breakfast; 🅿 ❄ 🛜) Peace Corp veteran Andrea pioneered David's first hostel and has served as able den mother of this five-room place ever since. Guests have use of a communal kitchen, cable TV and a vertical fountain for cooling off. Tiled dorm rooms with six and 10 beds are clean (and purple) without air-con. Doubles offer optional add-ons such as air-con (US$5).

Hotel Puerta del Sol HOTEL **$**
(📞 775-1662, 774-8422; www.hotelpuertadelsol. com.pa; Av 3 Este; d/tr US$45/54; 🅿 ❄ 🛜) A very secure budget choice, this central hotel offers 86 tasteful tiled rooms with wood furnishings. Rooms are on the small side, but the setting is pleasant. Amenities include hot-water showers, cable TV and a full-service restaurant open daily till 10pm (Sunday lunch only, till 3pm).

🍴 Eating

Pizmaricer Polo PANAMANIAN **$**
(📞 6406-9088; www.facebook.com/pages/Maris queria-Pizmaricer-polo/298511190316835; Calle de la Virgencita; mains US$4.25-8) A very basic restaurant – a *fonda* almost – in the hostel district, Pizmaricer Polo almost exclusively serves seafood, with a few pork dishes thrown in to keep ichthyophobes happy. The *ceviche* is a cut above and the whole fried fish is the best (and probably cheapest) in town.

MultiCafe CAFETERIA $
(☑774-6180; www.facebook.com/pages/Multi-Café/
317029381703197; cnr Calle A Norte & Av 2 Este;
dishes US$2.50-5; ☉7am-9pm Mon-Sat, to 3pm
Sun) An excellent choice if you're looking for
something cheap and filling while you're on
the hoof downtown. This colorful cafeteria
south of the landmark cathedral has trays of
local beef, chicken and pasta dishes as well
as salads. Good for a local breakfast too.

Café Rincón Libanés MIDDLE EASTERN $$
(☑774-2700, 730-3911; www.facebook.com/
CafeRinconLibanes; Calle F Sur; mains US$8.50-18;
☉11am-11:30pm) This fairly authentic 'Leba-
nese Corner Cafe' restaurant southwest of
downtown provides a welcome relief from
a steady diet of rice and beans. Homemade
hummus, tabbouleh, baba ghanoush and
lamb *kofta* (meatballs) will make you won-
der if you're in the Middle East. Try the
homemade pink lemonade.

❶ Information

ATP Office (☑775-2839; chiriqui@atp.gob.pa;
Calle Central; ☉8:30am-4:30pm Mon-Fri) Pro-
vides information on David and Chiriquí Province.
Banco Nacional de Panamá (☑774-6400;
Calle B Norte; ☉8am-3pm Mon-Fri, 9am-noon
Sat) This central branch with an ATM faces
Parque de Cervantes.
Chiriquí Hospital (☑777-8814; cnr Calle
Central & Av 3 Oeste) One of the best hospitals
in the country.
Ministerio de Ambiente (fax 774-6671; ☉8am-
4pm Mon-Fri) Provides tourist information and
advice, and camping permits for national parks.
It's 4.5km south of David's center.

Post Office (Calle C Norte; ☉7am-6pm Mon-
Fri, 8am-4:30pm Sat)

❶ Getting There & Around

AIR

David's international airport, **Aeropuerto En-
rique Malek** (☑721-1072), is about 5km south
of the center. There are no buses to the airport;
take a taxi (US$5).
Air Panama (☑721-0841; www.flyairpanama.
com) and **Copa Airlines** (☑217-2672; www.co
paair.com) have daily 45-minute flights to/from
Panama City, some as low-priced as US$60 one
way. Air Panama also now flies between David
and Bocas del Toro town.

BUS

The Interamericana does not go through David
but skirts around its western and northern sides.
The David **bus terminal** (Av del Estudiante) is
about 500m northeast of Parque de Cervantes.
Most buses begin service around 6am.
Tracopa (☑775-0585; www.tracopacr.com) has
direct buses between David and San José, Costa
Rica (US$21, seven hours), daily at 8:30am,
noon and 4pm from the David bus terminal.

Golfo de Chiriquí

The gem of the Chiriquí lowlands is the
Golfo de Chiriquí, home to the Parque Na-
cional Marino Golfo de Chiriquí, a nation-
al marine park with an area of just over 147
sq km, protecting 25 islands, 19 coral reefs
and abundant wildlife. The marine park
also protects the 30-sq-km Isla Boca Brava,
a lovely little island with hiking trails and
beautiful outer beaches. It's home to howler

BUSES FROM DAVID

DESTINATION	COST (US$)	DURATION	FREQUENCY
Boquete	1.75	1hr	every 20min to 9:30pm
Caldera	2.40	45min	hourly until 7:30pm
Cerro Punta	3.50	2¼hr	every 20min to 6pm
Changuinola	9.70	4½hr	half-hourly to 6:30pm
Guadalupe	3.50	2½hr	every 20min to 6pm
Horconcitos	2	45min	11am & 5pm
Las Lajas	5	1½hr	4 daily
Panama City	18	7-8hr	every 45min 6:45am-8pm
Paso Canoas	2.10	50min	every 15min to 9:30pm
Puerto Armuelles	4	2½hr	every 15min to 9pm
Santiago	9	3hr	hourly until 9pm
Río Sereno	5.10	2½hr	every 30min to 5pm
Volcán	3	1½hr	every 20min to 8pm

PANAMA GOLFO DE CHIRIQUÍ

monkeys, several types of nesting sea turtles and 280 recorded bird species. It is reached from the mainland village of Boca Chica.

Visitors can surf, kayak the calm interior waters, snorkel, watch wildlife under the rainforest canopy or fish for big game.

🛏 Sleeping

Hotel Boca Brava   HOTEL $
(☑851-0017, 6929-2996; http://hotelbocabrava. com; Isla Boca Brava, Boca Chica; s/d without bathroom US$35/40, d/ste with bathroom from US$50/75; ❄) An unexpected budget option on Isla Boca Brava, this hotel with 15 rooms, ranging from rustic to deluxe, is ideal for mingling with fellow travelers, though we have received some complaints from readers about the quality of the accommodations. Doubles are snug; the cheapest fan-cooled 'economy' doubles have shared bathroom.

At the other end of the spectrum are the delightful bay-view cottage (US$60) and two-bedroom suite (US$75) with air-conditioning. The aerie-like bar and restaurant (mains from US$5 to US$8) occupies a cool space on an overhanging deck with expansive water views. It's the perfect setting for a sundowner. The hotel can arrange excursions such as snorkeling, whale-watching and birdwatching.

ℹ Getting There & Away

To reach Boca Chica from David, take any of the frequent Interamericana buses heading east to the Horconcitos turnoff (US$2, one hour). From there a van (US$3, 50 minutes) leaves four to five times daily for Boca Chica. At the Boca Chica dock, hire a water taxi (US$3 per person) to take you 200m to the Isla Boca Brava dock at Hotel Boca Brava.

Playa Las Lajas

POP 1520

With one of the longest beaches in Panama, 12km-long palm-fringed Playa Las Lajas seems to stretch forever. The beach gathers serious crowds at weekends, but during the week it often lies empty, so you can savor the glorious expanse all by yourself.

🛏 Sleeping & Eating

Nahual Eco Hostel   HOSTEL $
(Hospedaje Ecológico Nahual; ☑6620-6431; www. nahualpanama.com; dm US$10, s/d with bathroom US$30/40, without bathroom US$15/25; ℗☎) With *ranchos* (small house-like buildings)

and attractive cabins, this fun, Italian-run place is the best bargain lodging in Las Lajas. It sits across the road from the beach in a leafy garden and is 100% chemical free. There are six rooms, four with bathrooms and two (one a six-bed dorm) with shared facilities. The excellent vegan cafe-restaurant, open daily to 10pm, serves homemade pasta.

Naturalmente   B&B $
(☑6211-1787, 727-0656; www.naturalmente panama.com; d incl breakfast US$45-65; ℗☎❄) The three fan-cooled thatched cabins with little terraces at this delightful B&B accommodate between two and four people. It's at the northern end of Las Lajas town – not at the beach – but there's a small above-ground pool in the gardens. The Mediterranean restaurant (mains from US$9.50 to US$13) is one of the best eateries on the gulf.

ℹ Getting There & Away

To reach Las Lajas, take any bus from David (US$2.75, 90 minutes) that travels to the Las Lajas turnoff, 76km east on the Interamericana. The town of Las Lajas is 3km south of the Interamericana and the beach a further 9km south. At the turnoff, a taxi (US$7) will take you to where the road meets the sea. Turn right and proceed 1.5km until you reach the resort.

Boquete

POP 19,000

Boquete is known for its cool, fresh climate and pristine natural surroundings. Flowers, coffee, vegetables and citrus fruits flourish in its rich soil, and the friendliness of the locals seems to rub off on everyone who passes through.

Boquete gained a deluge of expats after the American Association for Retired Persons (AARP) named it a top retirement spot. Until you see the gated communities and sprawling estates dotting the hillsides up close though, you'd be hard-pressed to see what the fuss is about. Downtown Boquete, with its broken pavements, dirty sidewalks and single span across the Río Caldera is not the idyllic mountain town many expect.

The surrounds, however, are another matter. Boquete is one of the country's top destinations for outdoor-lovers. It's a hub for hiking, climbing, rafting, visiting coffee farms, soaking in hot springs, studying Spanish or canopy touring. And, of course, there's nothing quite like a cup of locally grown coffee.

Boquete

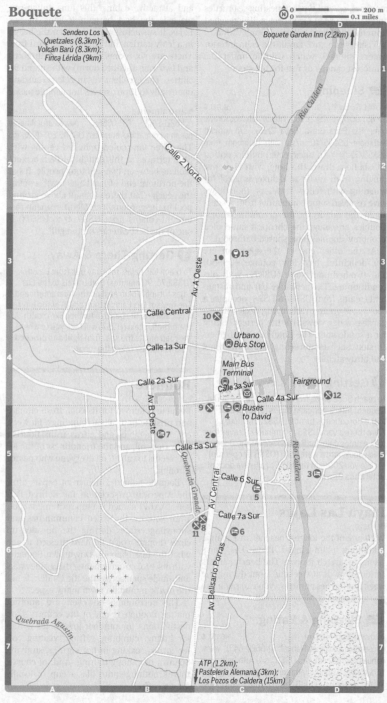

0   200 m
0   0.1 miles

Sendero Los
Quetzales (8.3km);
Volcán Barú (8.3km);
Finca Lérida (9km)

Boquete Garden Inn (2.2km)

Río Caldera

Calle 2 Norte

Av A Oeste

1 ● 🍴13

Calle Central   10 ❌

Calle 1a Sur

Urbano
Bus Stop

Main Bus
Terminal

Calle 2a Sur

Calle 3a Sur   Fairground

Av B Oeste   Calle 4a Sur   ❌12

9 ❌   4

Buses
to David

🏠7   2 ●

Calle 5a Sur   Río Caldera

Quebrada Grande   3 🏠

Av Central

Calle 6 Sur

5

Calle 7a Sur

❌8   Calle 7a Sur

11   🏠6

Av Belisario Porras

Quebrada Agustín

ATP (1.2km);
Pastelería Alemana (3km);
Los Pozos de Caldera (15km)

Boquete

⊕ Activities, Courses & Tours
1 ATV Adventures Boquete....................C3
   Boquete Outdoor
      Adventures ....(see 2)
   Boquete Tree Trek......................(see 2)
2 Habla Ya Language Center.................C5

⊜ Sleeping
3 El Oasis...D5
4 Mamallena Boquete Hostel................C5
5 Pensión Marilós.....................................C5
6 Pensión Topas......................................C6
7 Refugio del Río B5

⊗ Eating
8 Boquete Fish House C6
9 El Sabrosón #3.....................................C5
10 Gelateria La Ghiotta C4
11 Mike's Global Grill C6
12 Pizzeria Ricos Little Italy....................D4

⊕ Drinking & Nightlife
13 Boquete Brewing Company...............C3

🏃 Activities

Hiking

With its breathtaking vistas of mist-covered hills and nearby forests, Boquete is one of the most idyllic regions for hiking and walking. Several good paved roads lead out of town into the surrounding hills, passing coffee farms, fields, gardens and virgin forest.

Although many visitors will be content with picturesque strolls along the river, the more ambitious can climb Volcán Barú (p662). There are several entrances to the Parque Nacional Volcán Barú, but the most accessible trail starts near Boquete.

It's possible to access the Sendero Los Quetzales (p662) from Boquete, though the trail is uphill from here; you'll have an easier time if you start hiking from Cerro Punta above Volcán. Landslides have affected the trail in the past. Ask locals about conditions before heading out.

Sendero El Pianista HIKING
(Pianist Trail) This day-hike wends its way through dairy land and into humid cloud forest. You need to wade across a small river after 200m, but then it's a steady, leisurely incline for 2km before you start to climb a steeper, narrow path. Using a guide is highly recommended and should cost US$35/60 for a half-/full day.

The path leads deep into the forest, but you can turn back at any time. To access the

trailhead from Boquete, head north on the right bank of the river and cross over two bridges. Immediately before the third bridge, about 4km out of town, a track leads off to the left between a couple of buildings. The trail is not especially difficult but it isn't always well maintained. In April 2014 two Dutch nationals died while hiking here, though the cause of their deaths remains a mystery. Don't go alone and always let the people at your hostel or hotel know your plans.

White-Water Rafting

Adventure seekers shouldn't miss the excellent white-water rafting that's within a 1½-hour drive of Boquete. Ríos Chiriquí and Chiriquí Viejo both flow from the fertile hills of Volcán Barú, and are flanked by forest for much of their lengths. In some places, waterfalls can be seen at the edges of the rivers, and both rivers pass through narrow canyons with awesome, sheer rock walls.

The Río Chiriquí is most often run from May to December, while the Chiriquí Viejo is run the rest of the year. Rapids are III and III-plus, and tours last four to five hours.

When booking a trip, inquire if the outfitter uses a safety kayak for descents and if guides are certified in swift-water rescue. These should be minimum requirements for a safe trip.

Boquete Outdoor Adventures ADVENTURE SPORTS
(☑ 6630-1453, 720-2284; www.boqueteoutdoor adventures.com; Plaza Los Establos, Av Central; ☺8am-7:30pm) This highly recommended outfitter run by veteran outdoorsman Jim Omer offers quality rafting trips (from US$65 to US$75) and tailored vacations that are ideal for families. The sportfishing adventures on the Golfo de Chiriquí are value-priced (from US$600/1200 inshore/offshore for four passengers). Guides are bilingual and the company uses local service providers. Excellent source of information.

Also offers birdwatching (half-/full day US$40/80) and, from July to October, whale-watching (US$75) tours.

👉 Tours

ATV Adventures Boquete ADVENTURE TOUR
(☑ 6678-5666; www.facebook.com/atv4x4boquete; Av Central; ☺9am-7pm) Offers tours of Boquete and surrounds on 4WD ATVs (quad bikes) and side-by-side UTVs. Prices start at US$70 for ATVs and US$100 for UTVs per two people for the 1½-hour Scenic Tour.

Longer trips include the 3½-hour Coffee Tour (US$120/200) and a five-hour Hot Springs Tour (US$160/375).

Boquete Tree Trek   CANOPY TOUR
(☑ 720-1635; www.boquetetreetrek.com; Plaza Los Establos, Av Central; canopy tours US$65; ☺ 8am & 1pm) Travelers love this four-hour canopy tour with 12 zip lines, 14 platforms, a rappel and a Tarzan-swing in secondary forest. Tours depart daily at 8am and 1pm. The lines pick up some serious speed, so you might want to consider going heavy on the handbrake. Also sells other tours, and includes transportation from the center.

Kotowa Coffee Estate Tour   TOUR
(☑ 6634-4698, 720-3852; http://coffeeadventures. net; tours US$35; ☺ 2pm Mon-Sat) The 3½-hour tours of this gourmet coffee-grower's estate is said to be the most comprehensive in the area. Guests learn about the estate's history (beginning with a Canadian's arrival in 1918), get a full tour of the production facilities and processing mill, and have a tasting session. Reservations required.

🎓 Courses

Habla Ya Language Center   LANGUAGE COURSE
(☑ 730-8344; www.hablayapanama.com; Plaza Los Establos, Av Central; ☺ 8am-5:30pm Mon-Fri, 9am-1pm Sat, 1-5pm Sun) Habla Ya offers both group and private Spanish lessons. A week of group lessons (20 hours) starts at US$195. The language school is also well connected to local businesses, so students can take advantage of discounts on everything from accommodations to tours and participate in volunteer projects.

🎉 Festivals & Events

Feria de las Flores y del Café   FERIA
(http://feriadeboquete.com; ☺ Jan) The town's annual Flower & Coffee Fair is held over 10 days each January. While there's coffee in the name, it's strangely missing from exhibits, though you will find plenty of rum and children's carnival rides. Book accommodations well ahead.

Boquete Jazz & Blues Festival   JAZZ
(☺ Feb) Local and international talent converge on Boquete for four days in February for the biggest annual music event in Chiriquí Province.

Feria de las Orquídeas   FERIA
(☺ Apr) Showing more than 150 varieties, the orchid fair is held for 10 days every year. It's

not all flowers; sundown brings rock concerts and dancing.

🛏 Sleeping

Mamallena Boquete Hostel   HOSTEL $
(☑ 6723-2014, 730-8342; www.mamallenaboquete. com; Av Central; dm US$14, d/tr/q with bathroom US$38/55/65, r without bathroom US$33; 🅿 🛜) Facing the central plaza, this turquoise ex-boardinghouse is backpacker central, complete with kitchen, laundry and free pancake breakfasts. For its huge capacity, it feels rather cozy. Three eight-bed dorms boast orthopedic mattresses while 13 of the 16 private rooms have their own bathrooms. There's a sheltered patio area with grill. Service-oriented, it runs tours and shuttles to Bocas and Santa Catalina.

Pensión Topas   GUESTHOUSE $
(☑ 720-1005; www.facebook.com/pages/Pension-Topas-Boquete-Panama/877290745620094; Av Belisario Porras; s/d with bathroom US$29/42, without bathroom US$16/26; 🅿 🛜 🏊) Built around a small organic garden, this blue-and-orange lodging run by an eccentric German features Tintin murals, a collection of a half-dozen motorbikes and eight tidy rooms. A shady outdoor patio provides ample shared space, and perks include a swimming pool and cable TV. Best rooms are the two on the 2nd floor of the outbuilding, which has a balcony.

Refugio del Río   HOSTEL $
(☑ 6676-5786, 720-2088; www.facebook.com/hostal refugiodelrio; Av B Oeste; dm US$13-15, d with/without bathroom US$40/31, cabins US$42; 🅿 @ 🛜) With the comfy feel of a large home, this budget stop features a huge guest kitchen and a good location. Some 13 sprawling rooms are pleasant and well furnished, but could be tidier. The dormitory features a row of a dozen single beds with snug covers but saggy mattresses. Reserve ahead for the cool three-person tree-house cabin overlooking the stream.

Pensión Marilós   GUESTHOUSE $
(☑ 720-1380; marilos66@hotmail.com; cnr Av A Este & Calle 6 Sur; s/d with bathroom US$15/20, without bathroom US$10/15; 🅿) With the feel of a well-worn family home, Marilós offers a central location at bargain rates. Its half-dozen rooms are decorated with assorted knickknacks and doodads reminiscent of the guest bedroom at grandma's house. There's a parrot that's in and out of its cage, ready to greet you at the entrance.

El Oasis HOTEL $$
(☑720-1586; www.oasisboquete.com; Av Buenos Aires; d incl breakfast US$88; P@🖥) Although it's within walking distance, El Oasis is across the Río Caldera from Boquete proper and is a good deal quieter than staying in town; the river's just meters away. The 18 rooms and suites are immaculate and cozy; at times the place feels more like a B&B than a hotel. The garden restaurant serves good soups.

Boquete Garden Inn INN $$
(☑720-2376; www.boquetegardeninn.com; Palo Alto; d incl breakfast US$79-119; P🖥) On the edge of the Río Palo Alto, this garden inn with a dozen rooms in six red-mud cottages is run by a welcoming Briton. The grounds overflow with blossoming tropical flowerbeds, and birds abound (95 species spotted). Rooms – there are five types – with canopy beds are lovely and modern. Service stands out.

Lounging around the patio bar decorated with traditional Panamanian masks proves a fine cap on the day, especially from 6pm to 7pm when drinks are complimentary.

✖ Eating & Drinking

Mike's Global Grill INTERNATIONAL $
(☑730-9360, 6865-8873; www.mikesglobalgrill.com; Av Central Oeste; mains US$7-12; ⊙8am-10pm Mon-Thu, 8am-11pm Fri & Sat, 9am-10pm Sun) This homesick restaurant is the love child of Mike and Heidi who met – where else? – at the South Pole. To further the wanderlust theme, dishes range from Asian fusion to North American chili and British fish and chips. The ambiance is chilled, with a long bar and sofas. Breakfast daily, and live music on Thursday, Friday and Saturday nights.

El Sabrosón #3 CAFETERIA $
(☑720-2147; Av Central; mains US$3-6; ⊙6:30am-10pm Mon-Fri, to 11pm Sat & Sun) Our favorite of the three branches of this much-loved local institution cooks up cheap and filling Panamanian cuisine served cafeteria-style, and has tables on a terrace overlooking the main drag. Although Boquete is rapidly being colonized by gringo-friendly boutique eateries, this is one local institution that remains true to its roots.

Pizzeria Ricos Little Italy PIZZA $
(☑720-1291, 6390-2415; opposite Calle 4a Sur; pizzas small US$7-10, large US$13-20; ⊙11am-9pm Tue-Sun) Enjoy the real McCoy at this hole-in-the-wall pizzeria with six tables. It's just across the bridge and facing the fairgrounds.

Gelateria La Ghiotta ICE CREAM $
(☑6107-1465; cnr Av Central & Calle Central; 1/2/3 scoops US$1.75/2.75/3.75; ⊙11am-8pm Thu-Tue) Great selection of Italian ice cream at this central and very friendly little *gelateria*. Choose from 10 flavors, including *guanabana* (soursop), pineapple and coffee.

★**Boquete Fish House** SEAFOOD $$
(☑6521-2120, 6918-7111; www.facebook.com/BoqueteFishHouseRestaurant; Av Central; mains US$10-14; ⊙noon-8pm Mon-Sat) One of our favorite places in Boquete for a tasty, inexpensive meal is this fish house along the Quebrada Grande. It offers sea bass prepared in eight different ways – from the delightful version that's steamed and wrapped in lettuce leaves to the pedestrian-but-tasty fish and chips. There are meat and vegetarian choices as well.

★**Il Pianista** ITALIAN $$
(☑720-2728; Palo Alto; mains US$12-17.50; ⊙noon-10pm Tue-Sun) This Italian restaurant and pizzeria has riverstone walls and just a few tables along one of Boquete's hillside roads. Sicilian Giovanni cooks while his Panamanian wife, Doris, serves. A bottle of wine and pizza or calzone make the perfect leisurely lunch, but don't come in a rush: service can be slow. Local buses go past, or follow signs for Boquete Garden Inn; it's just above it.

Boquete Brewing Company MICROBREWERY
(☑6494-4992; www.boquetebrewingcompany.com; Av Central; ⊙4-10pm) US-style craft-beer bars and pubs are all the rage in Panama these days; there are five in the capital, so why should Boquete be left out? This place has eight beers and two hard ciders on tap at any given time, and they range from the sublime (hard lemonade) to the ridiculous (watermelon ale). Cheers!

❶ Information

ATP (☑720-4060; chiriqui@atp.gob.pa; Hwy 43; ⊙8am-4pm) About 1.5km south of Boquete on the road to David, the large ATP office sits atop a bluff overlooking town. Here you can pick up maps and obtain information on area attractions. There's a coffee shop on the ground floor and an exhibition upstairs detailing the history of the region (in Spanish only).

Banco Nacional de Panama (☑720-1328; Av Central; ⊙8am-3pm Mon-Fri, 9am-noon Sat) Has an ATM.

Centro Medico San Juan Bautista (☑720-1881; Calle 2 Norte) For medical care.

Global Bank (📞720-2329; Av Central; ⊗8am-3pm Mon-Fri, 9am-noon Sat) Bank with ATM.

Post Office (⊗7am-6pm Mon-Fri, to 5pm Sat) In the former train station on the central plaza.

ℹ️ Getting There & Around

The **main bus terminal** is on the main road near the main plaza. Buses to David (US$1.75, one hour, every 30 minutes) depart from the **south side of Boquete's main plaza** every 30 minutes from 5am to 6:30pm. From David they run from 6am to 9:30pm. Hourly buses run to the town of Caldera (US$2, 45 minutes).

Shuttle vans departing from in front of the **Mamallena Boquete Hostel** (p660) link Boquete with Bocas del Toro (US$30 including boat, four hours) and Santa Catalina (US$35, five hours).

Boquete's small size lends itself to easy exploration. The *urbano* (local) buses that wind through the hills cost US$0.50. They depart **on the main road one block north of the plaza**. Taxis charge US$2 to US$3 for most places around town.

For scooter (US$25 per hour) or bike rentals (about US$3), check out local travel agencies and hostels. Cars can be rented at **Dollar** (📞721-1103; Plaza Los Establos, Av Central; ⊗8am-5pm), and are a great option to explore more of the local area.

Parque Nacional Volcán Barú

This 143-sq-km national park (admission US$5) is home to Volcán Barú, Panama's only volcano and the dominant geographical feature of Chiriquí Province. Volcán Barú is no longer active, but it apparently once was, and counts not one but seven craters. At 3474m its summit, the highest point in Panama, affords views of both the Pacific and Caribbean coasts when clear.

The national park is also home to the Sendero Los Quetzales (p662), one of the most scenic treks in the entire country. As its name implies, the trail is one of the best places in Central America to spot the rare resplendent quetzal, especially during the dry season (from February to May). However, even if the Maya bird of paradise fails to show, the park is home to more than 250 bird species as well as pumas, tapirs and the agouti paca, a large spotted rodent also called *conejo pintado* (painted rabbit).

🏃 Activities

Volcán Barú HIKING

For views from the summit of both the Pacific and Caribbean coasts, climbing Volcán Barú is a goal of many visitors. It might not be worth it in poor weather, as the going is strenuous and rough, and there is little to see in cloud cover. You can enter the national park on the eastern (Boquete) and western (Volcán) sides of the volcano.

The eastern summit access from Boquete is the easier, but it involves a strenuous uphill hike along a 13.5km road that goes from the park entrance – about 8km northwest of the center of town – to the summit. The road is paved to the ranger station and several kilometers beyond. If you drive or taxi as far up as possible and then walk the rest of the way, it takes about five or six hours to reach the summit from the park gate; walking from town would take another two or three hours each way.

We recommend you hike at night, starting at 11pm or midnight and arriving at dawn to see the sunrise. But for this you'll need to hire a guide and be prepared for the cold. Another option is to spend the night. Camping will also allow you to be at the top during the morning, when the views are best.

The western access is just outside the town of Volcán, on the road to Cerro Punta. The rugged 16.5km-long road into the park (requiring a 4WD vehicle) goes only a short way off the main road to the foot of the volcano. The view of the summit and the nearby peaks from this entrance are impressive, and there's a lovely loop trail that winds through secondary and virgin forest. The ascent takes eight to 10 hours.

⭐**Sendero Los Quetzales** HIKING

One of Panama's most beautiful trails runs between Cerro Punta and Boquete, crisscrossing the Río Caldera. You can hike from either direction, but west to east offers more downhill: the town of Cerro Punta is almost 1000m higher than Boquete. The 8km route takes between four and six hours. Getting to and from the trailhead takes another couple of hours either side (about 23km in total). A guide is recommended.

A 4WD taxi can take you to the trailhead on the Cerro Punta side for about US$25 per person; a *colectivo* (shared taxi) will cost US$6. Taxi drivers know the area as Respingo. Road conditions may be very poor due to landslides. The trail is 5km uphill from the main road and 2km from the last paved road. When you exit the trail, it's another 8km along the road to Boquete, though you may be able to catch a taxi along the road. In total, the hike is about 23km, so plan accordingly if you intend to walk the length of the trail.

Buses run from David to Cerro Punta (US$3.50, 2¼ hours); last departure 6pm. Consider leaving your luggage at one of the hotels in David to save yourself the hassle of backtracking. Take only the bare essentials with you on the walk, and a little cash for a good meal and/or lodging when you arrive in Boquete.

Be aware that conditions can change any time, especially after heavy rain. We recommend that you hike the trail with a guide; there's talk that this may become a requirement. In recent times many travelers have gotten lost on this stretch and resources for rescue are practically nonexistent.

Sleeping

Parque Nacional Volcán Barú Camping   CAMPGROUND $
(campsites US$5) Camping is possible in the park and on the trail to the summit from the Boquete side, along the Sendero Los Quetzales at a picnic spot called Mirador La Roca or at the ranger station at the entrance to the Sendero Los Quetzales on the Cerro Punta side.

Information

Admission to the park is paid at either of the trailheads leading to the summit or at the ranger station on the Cerro Punto side of the Sendero Los Quetzales. The best time to visit is during the dry season, especially early in the morning when wildlife is most active.

Be advised that overnight temperatures can drop below freezing, and it may be windy and cold during the day, particularly in the morning. Dress accordingly and bring a flashlight (torch).

Getting There & Away

The trailhead leading to the summit of Volcán Barú is best accessed from the town of Boquete, while the Sendero Los Quetzales is best approached from Cerro Punta. A taxi will cost US$30 and US$25 respectively.

Cerro Punta

POP 7750

Lying at 800m, this tranquil highland town is reminiscent of an alpine village. As you near Cerro Punta, the region takes on an almost European look, with meticulously tended vegetable plots and chalet-like houses with steep-pitched roofs. It's unsurprising to learn that a Swiss colony was founded here many decades ago and the hamlet just south is called Nueva Suiza (New Switzerland).

Visitors come to Cerro Punta primarily during the dry season (from mid-December to April) to access the two nearby national parks: Volcán Barú and La Amistad. The town itself makes a charming stop, however, especially since the area is known for its succulent strawberries, available much of the year at roadside stands.

Sleeping & Eating

Hotel Cerro Punta   HOTEL $
(6546-7334, 771-2020; www.hotelcerropunta. com; s/d US$24/36; P ⊛) This friendly hotel located on the main road offers a row of 10 concrete rooms that are a bit tired and beat up. But they overlook a grassy backyard, and the private hot-water bathroom will be the last you'll see for a while if you're on your way to Volcán Barú or La Amistad national parks. Decent and good value in-house restaurant.

Getting There & Away

Buses run from David to Cerro Punta (US$3.50, 2¼ hours, every 20 minutes), stopping at Volcán and Bambito along the way, and carrying on to Guadalupe. If you're coming from Costa Rica, catch this bus at the turnoff from the Interamericana at La Concepción.

If you're driving, the main road continues through Cerro Punta and ends at Guadalupe, 3km further. Another road takes off to the left heading for the Las Nubes entrance to Parque Internacional La Amistad, just under 7km to the northwest.

Parque Internacional La Amistad

The 4000-sq-km Parque Internacional La Amistad, a favorite of hikers and naturalists alike, covers portions of both Chiriquí and Bocas del Toro Provinces. Although the lion's share of the park lies in the latter, the Chiriquí side, with its entrance at Las Nubes, is more accessible.

Activities

Most of the park is inaccessible terrain high up in the Talamanca mountains. It's worth making the trek, though, as the park is home to a recorded 90 mammal species and all six cat species. More than 450 bird species have also been recorded here, including quetzals and harpy eagles.

Lost World Tours   ADVENTURE TOUR
(6432-8182, 6920-3036; www.thelostand foundhostel.com; 2-/4-person hikes per person US$500/400) The La Amistad Trek goes from

WORTH A TRIP

LOST & FOUND HOSTEL

The only cloud-forest lodge in Panama, the **Lost & Found Hostel** (☑ 6432-8182; www.thelostandfoundhostel.com; Valle de la Mina; dm/d/tr without bathroom US$15/35/50, breakfast US$4-$6, lunch US$5-6, dinner US$6-8; @ 🛜) is a backpacker community perched on a steep hill reached on foot and facing a gaping mountain panorama. There are two dorms (with another on the way) of between 10 and 15 bunk beds, and four basic but clean private rooms. Shared bathrooms are stall-style and well maintained.

The new kitchen is stocked with basic provisions for sale, and you can also order meals. There's a mini-pub, lounge and movie-room loft, set well away from sleepers.

The Canadian owners have plotted every detail, from two tricked-out treasure hunts that take visitors mucking through rivers and labyrinths, to an eight-hour maze of trails through La Fortuna Forest Reserve that go as high as 2200m. Activities are varied and well priced, and as many as three excursions depart each day. A highlight is the Lost World Tour (US$40), which takes hikers to an impressive waterfall and visits an indigenous community. You can also tour the trails on horseback (US$40) and visit a local coffee producer (US$25). The hostel's mascot is Rocky, a resident kinkajou who lives in and out of his cage and cannot be released into the wild. We love the viewing tower and the new mini zip line that's free for guests.

Given the isolation, it's necessary to call or email reservations 24 hours in advance. To reach here take the bus from David (US$3.50, one hour) and ask to be dropped off at Km 42 near the large Lost & Found billboard. Follow the trail to the right of the provisions shop upward for about 20 minutes. You can also take a bus from Bocas del Toro Province, starting in Changuinola or Almirante (around US$7). Special shuttle buses link the Mamallena Hostel in Boquete with Lost & Found for US$15.

Guadalupe through the rainforest of the continental divide and across the lowlands to Norteño in Bocas del Toro Province. The trek lasts from three to four days, depending on the group, and is led by a bilingual former Peace Corps volunteer and a local indigenous guide. Accommodation is in Ngöbe-Buglé villages and food is local.

The terrain is very steep and rugged and the weather can be unpredictable; tours are only recommended for those with considerable hiking experience.

🛏 Sleeping

Las Nubes Ranger Station CABIN **$**
(☑ 775-3163, 774-6671; dm US$15) The basic ranger station at Las Nubes has a dormitory cabin with bunk beds. Due to its popularity among international school groups, reservations are advisable. Guests have kitchen access; stock up on provisions in Cerro Punta. Bring your own bedding; a mosquito net is a good idea. To reserve, call the Ministerio de Ambiente in David or the Co-op Restaurant at the park entrance.

❶ Information

Admission to the park (US$5) is paid at the Las Nubes park office, 6km northwest of Cerro Punta. Camping permits (US$10 per person) are payable at the Las Nubes ranger station.

If you plan to spend much time at Las Nubes, be sure to bring a jacket or sweater. At 2280m above sea level, this area of the park has a cool climate; temperatures are usually around 24°C (75°F) in the daytime but can drop as low as 3°C (38°F) at night.

❶ Getting There & Away

The Las Nubes entrance is about 6km northwest from Cerro Punta; a sign on the main road in Cerro Punta marks the turnoff. A taxi should cost US$7.

BOCAS DEL TORO PROVINCE

With its Caribbean islands dotting a shock of blue waters, Bocas del Toro is all that's tropical. This is Panama's principal tourist draw and it will no doubt provide some of your most memorable experiences. The archipelago consists of six densely forested islands, scores of uninhabited islets and the Parque Nacional Marino Isla Bastimentos, Panama's oldest marine park.

The longtime base of Chiquita Banana, the mainland boasts the Parque Internacional La Amistad, shared with Costa Rica. It's also home to diverse wildlife such as the elusive jaguar, traditional Ngöbe-Buglé settlements, and the Naso, one of few remaining American tribes with its own monarch.

Most visitors come for a hefty dose of sun and surf. Few are disappointed with the Bocas cocktail of water fun and thatched luxury, but there's a lot, lot more to what might be Panama's most beautiful corner.

Isla Colón

POP 9000

The archipelago's most developed island is home to the provincial capital of Bocas del Toro. From the mid-1990s, foreign investors flooded the island, creating hotels, restaurants and condos while infrastructure for water, trash and sewage lagged far behind. Today, the island, which runs on diesel, struggles to find a balance between satisfying development and serving community needs.

Activities

Diving & Snorkeling

Although experienced divers accustomed to crystal-clear Caribbean diving may be disappointed with the archipelago – nearly 40 rivers discharging silt into the seas around the archipelago reduce visibility dramatically – it still has much to offer. The islands' emerald-green waters are home to the usual assortment of tropical species and with a little luck you might see barracuda, stingrays, dolphins and nurse sharks. The better sites include Dark Wood Reef, northwest of Bastimentos; Hospital Point, a 15m wall off Cayo Nancy; and the base of the buoy near Punta Juan north of Isla Cristóbal.

A two-tank dive will cost between US$70 and US$75. Certification courses start at US$250. A number of reliable suppliers offer good-value snorkeling and diving trips out of Bocas.

Boat Tours

The most popular tours in the area are all-day snorkeling trips, which are perfect for nondivers who want a taste of the area's rich marine life. A typical tour costs US$25 per person, and goes to Dolphin Bay, Cayo Crawl, Red Frog Beach (US$3 entry) and Hospital Point.

A trip to the distant Cayos Zapatillas costs US$30 (plus an additional US$5 for admission to the marine park), and includes lunch, beach time and a jungle hike on Cayo Zapatilla Sur.

Many 'tours' are really little more than boat transportation to a pretty spot. If you have your own snorkel gear (or if you rent it), you can also charter motor boats. Agree on a price before you go.

Surfing

Beginner surfers looking for a bit of reef experience should check out Playa Punch (Playa Paunch; Map p666), which offers a good mix of lefts and rights. Although it can get heavy when big, Punch generally offers some of the kindest waves around.

Just past Punch en route to Playa Bluff is a popular reef break known as Dumpers. This left break can get up to 3m and should only be ridden by experienced surfers; wiping out on the reef here is dangerous. There is also an inner break known as Inner Dumps, which also breaks left but is more forgiving than its outer mate.

Be careful walking out on the reefs as they are sharp and full of sea urchins – don't go barefoot. If you wipe out and get cut up, be sure to properly disinfect your wounds. Be aware that seawater in the Caribbean does not help the healing process; the warm water temperature means the ocean is full of live bacteria.

The island's most infamous surf spot is Playa Bluff (p667), which throws out powerful barreling waves that break in shallow water along the beach and have a reputation for snapping boards (and occasionally bones). The waves close quickly, but the tubes here are truly awesome, especially when the swells are strong.

Kayaking

Sea kayaking is a great way to travel between islands. You will need to be wary of boat traffic, though, and the occasional swell. Some dive shops and hostels rent kayaks.

Cycling

Whether you're heading along the paved road to Boca del Drago or taking a dirt track to Playa Bluff, a bike can seriously increase your mobility. Note that the bike ride to Boca del Drago from Boca town is taxing; if you're unsure of your fitness level, head for Punta Bluff instead. Bikes are available from some hostels as well as from Ixa's Bike World (Map p669; Av H; per hour US$1, per half-/ full day US$7/10; ⊗8am-6pm) and Bocas Bicis

Archipiélago de Bocas del Toro

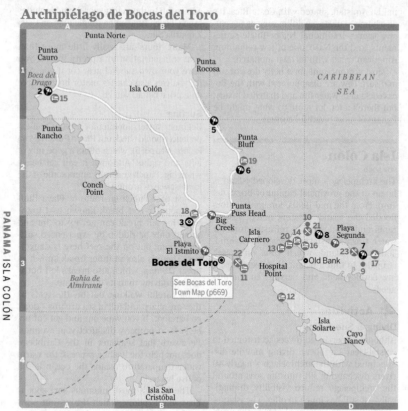

Archipiélago de Bocas del Toro

◉ Top Sights

1 Parque Nacional Marino Isla
Bastimentos E4

◉ Sights

2 Boca del Drago A1
3 Finca Los Monos Botanical
Garden...B3
4 Nivida Bat Cave.....................................E3
5 Playa Bluff C2
6 Playa Punch...C2
7 Red Frog Beach.....................................D3
8 Wizard Beach..D3

◎ Activities, Courses & Tours

Bastimentos Alive......................(see 16)
9 Bastimentos Sky Zipline
Canopy Tour....................................D3
10 Up in the Hill D3

◎ Sleeping

11 Aqua Lounge...C3
12 Bambuda Lodge C3
13 Beverly's Hill C3
14 Bubba's House C3
15 Cabañas Estefany.................................A1
Gran Kahuna Beach Hostel ....(see 11)
16 Hostal Bastimentos.............................D3
17 Palmar Tent Lodge D3
18 Sand Dollar Beach Bed &
Breakfast..B2
19 Tesoro Escondido C2
Tierra Verde ....(see 11)
20 Tío Tom's Guesthouse C3

◎ Eating

Chavela.......................................(see 16)
21 Coco Hill D3
22 Leaf Eaters Cafe C3
23 Nacho Mama's.......................................D3

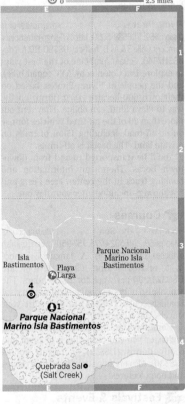

bit tricky at first, but you'll get the hang of it. It's best to go early in the morning.

Bocas del Toro Town

POP 7400

Colorful and full of Caribbean-style clapboard houses, Bocas del Toro (better known simply as Bocas town) was built by the United Fruit Company in the early 20th century. Today it is a relaxed community of West Indians, Latinos and resident gringos, with a friendly atmosphere that is contagious. It's an easy place to get stuck into and an even easier one in which to linger.

Bocas serves as a convenient base for exploring the archipelago; *taxis marinos* (water taxis) can whisk you away to remote beaches and snorkeling sites for just a few dollars. The real allure here, though, is simply to be able to slow down and soak up the Caribbean vibes.

◉ Sights

Finca Los Monos
Botanical Garden   GARDENS
(Map p666; ☑ 6729-9943, 757-9461; www.bocas deltorobotanicalgarden.com; garden/birdwatching tours US$15/25; ☉ garden tours 1pm Mon & 8:30am Fri, birdwatching tours 6:30am & 5pm upon request) One of the joys of visiting Bocas is touring the 'Monkey Farm' botanical garden a couple of kilometers northwest of the center. Painstakingly carved out of 10 hectares of secondary rainforest over almost two decades, it contains hundreds of species of local and imported trees and ornamental plants and is teeming with wildlife.

Co-owner and guide Lin Gillingham will point out howler and white-faced capuchin monkeys, sloths and various bird species. Tours must be booked in advance; garden tours depart regularly while birding tours are on demand.

Playa Bluff   BEACH
(Map p666) This lovely beach is pounded by intense waves. Though you wouldn't want to get into the water here without a board, the soft, yellow sand and palm-fringed shores are pristine. The beach is 8km from Bocas town, alongside the road after you round Punta Bluff. It serves as a nesting area for sea turtles from May to September.

Boca del Drago   BEACH
(Dragon's Mouth; Map p666) Boca del Drago, in the northwest of Isla Colón, is one of the best beaches on the island, though the surf can be rough at times. Just offshore from the

---

(Map p669; Av E; per hour/day low season US$1.50/5, high season US$2/10; ☉ 9am-7pm) in Boca town. Flying Pirates (p668) rents ATVs (quad bikes).

Hiking

If you're looking to seriously get off the beaten path, there is a network of undeveloped hiking trails that fan out across Isla Colón. One of the more popular hikes starts at the end of the coastal road in Mimbi Timbi to the northeast and carries on west along the coast to Boca del Drago. You will need about six hours of daylight to complete the hike, and you must carry in all your water. The trail winds past caves, caverns and plenty of vine-entangled jungle. A bike will help speed things up a bit, though you'll be carrying it part of the way, especially if it's been raining recently.

Fishing

The best option for aspiring anglers on a budget is to go surf casting with the local water-taxi drivers. The hand lines can be a

beach is a patchy coral-and-sand sea bottom that offers good snorkeling when the sea is calm and the water clear.

🏃 Activities

Dragon Tours
BOAT TOUR

(Map p669; ☑ 6499-6317, 757-7010; www.dragontours.net; cnr Calle 3 & Av C; per person incl lunch US$39-48) This perennially popular charter company sails its purpose-built 63ft catamaran complete with water slide to various islands on day trips, which always include lunch (BBQ, pizza etc).

La Buga
DIVING

(Map p669; ☑ 6781-0755, 757-9534; www.labuga panama.com; Calle 3; ⊙ 8am-8pm) A very well regarded dive shop, La Buga leads two to three dive trips a day. Highlights include night dives and visits to the caves off Bastimentos (US$90). It also offers surfboard rentals and surf lessons, stand-up paddles (US$15 per hour per day) and kayak rentals. While you explore your options, grab a bite at the cute cafe attached.

Anaboca
TOUR

(La Asociación Natural Bocas Carey; ☑ 6553-6566, 6996-0608; www.anaboca.org; per person US$20) 🗡 This nonprofit run by the local community addresses marine-turtle conservation. In season (April to August), certified guides offer nighttime tours to view turtle hatching on Playa Bluff. You can also arrange overnight community stays, a good idea if you are there to watch hatching in the wee hours.

Mono Loco Surf School
SURFING

(Map p669; ☑ 760-9877; http://monolocosurf school.com; Calle 2; 3hr lessons US$50; ⊙ 9am-6pm) Recommended surf shop and school run by a group of serious surfing dudes. Also rents boards (half/full day US$15/20).

Bocas Sailing
BOAT TOUR

(Map p669; ☑ 6464-4242, 757-7048; www.bocas sailing.com; Calle 3; per person US$48; ⊙ 9:30am-4:30pm) Including affordable overnight adventures and options for snorkeling, fishing and dolphin-watching, Bocas Sailing has

---

ℹ️ BOCAS CONFUSION

Note that the town, the archipelago and the province all share the name Bocas del Toro. To avoid confusion, we refer to the provincial capital as 'Bocas town' or simply 'Bocas.'

---

popular tours on a 42ft catamaran that are kid-friendly, too.

Flying Pirates
ADVENTURE SPORTS

(Map p669; ☑ 6689-5050; http://flyingpiratesbocas.com; cnr Calle 3 & Av B; half-day US$90-110, full day US$117-140; ⊙ 9am-7pm) One of the best ways to explore Isla Colón is by ATV (quad bike), and the people at Flying Pirates, based on their own 600-hecatre *finca* (farm) on the way to Playa Bluff, can oblige. They rent out more than 30 of the fat-tired vehicles for use on or off-road, including 15km of trails on private land. The beach is off-limits.

You'll be transported to and from downtown Bocas. There's an information and booking truck in the center. Free beers and hot showers included after your day out.

🎓 Courses

Spanish by the Sea
LANGUAGE COURSE

(Map p669; ☑ 6592-0775, 757-9518; www.spanish bythesea.com; Calle 4) A language school in a relaxed setting. Group lessons are US$225/300 per week for 20/30 hours. The school also offers a popular six-hour survival Spanish course (US$45) to kick-start your travels. Has a branch in Boquete.

Homestays can be arranged (US$25 per night), or you can bunk down in clean and comfy dorms (US$12) or private rooms (US$30). Also organizes parties, dance classes and open lectures.

🎉 Festivals & Events

Feria del Mar
FERIA

(⊙ Sep) The weeklong 'Sea Fair' is held on Playa El Istmito, a few kilometers northwest of downtown Bocas.

Día de la Virgen del Carmen
RELIGIOUS

(⊙ Jul) *Bocatoreños* make a pilgrimage to the cave at La Gruta in the middle of the Isla Colón for Mass in honor of the Virgen del Carmen on the third Sunday in July.

Fundación de la Provincia de Bocas del Toro
CULTURAL

(⊙ Nov 16) Celebrating the foundation of the province in 1903, this is a day of parades and other events; it's a big affair, attracting people from all over the province.

🛏️ Sleeping

IN BOCAS TOWN

Hostel Heike
HOSTEL $

(Map p669; ☑ 757-9708; www.hostelheike.com; Calle 3; dm with/without air-con US$13/11, d/tr incl

Bocas del Toro Town

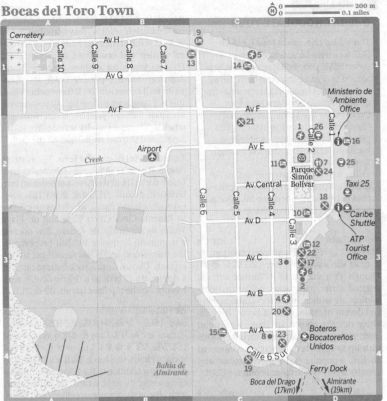

Bocas del Toro Town

🟠 Activities, Courses & Tours

1 Bocas Bicis	D2
2 Bocas Sailing	D3
3 Dragon Tours	C3
4 Flying Pirates	C3
5 Ixa's Bike World	C1
6 La Buga	D3
7 Mono Loco Surf School	D2
8 Spanish by the Sea	C4

🛏 Sleeping

9 Cocomo	C1
10 Hostal Hansi	D3
11 Hostel Heike	C2
12 Hotel Bocas del Toro	D3
13 Hotel Lula's	C1
14 Mondo Taitú	C1

15 Residencial Dos Palmas	C4
16 Selina Hostel Bocas del Toro	D2

🍴 Eating

17 Buena Vista Bar & Grill	D3
18 Cafe del Mar	D2
19 El Último Refugio	C4
20 Om Café	C4
21 Pizzeria Alberto	C2
22 Raw Fusion	D3
23 Super Gourmet	C4
24 Taco Surf	D2

🍸 Drinking & Nightlife

25 Barco Hundido	D2
26 Bookstore Bar	D2
Selina Bar	(see 16)

breakfast US$24/36; ❄ @ 🛜) Aglow with colorful murals and natural woods, Heike is the perfect spot for chilling in an old Caribbean-style house right in the center of town. The

nine rooms include dorms with up to 10 beds; a sprawling roof deck with hammocks is the perfect spot for a cold beer and a good book. Free purified water and hot drinks.

DON'T MISS

OREBA CHOCOLATE TOUR

This guided **chocolate tour** (📞 6649-1457; www.oreba.bocasdeltoro.org; per person US$35) leaves Bocas and takes you around an organic chocolate farm, run by the indigenous Ngöbe-Buglé community, on the mainland near Almirante. Tour the farm, see tree sloths, sample chocolate – classified as some of the highest grade cacao in the world – and enjoy a traditional lunch. Book direct or through **Super Gourmet** (p671).

The trip (two-person minimum) is guided in Spanish and English. The price does not include the boat trip from Bocas to Almirante (US$12 round trip).

Mondo Taitú
HOSTEL $

(Map p669; 📞 760-8136; www.mondotaitu.com; Av G; dm/d with shared bathroom US$10/24; @ 🛜) Though it's a shadow of its former self, the original surfer backpacker hostel in Bocas soldiers on, with a chilled social atmosphere and decent nightlife right at home. It's definitely not the choice for those who mind (real) grunge. The 13 rooms include dorms with up to eight beds. There's a communal kitchen, a popular bar, a movie lounge and laundry facilities. Surfboards rent for US$15.

Hostal Hansi
GUESTHOUSE $

(Map p669; 📞 757-9085; http://hostalhansi.bocas.com; cnr Av D & Calle 2; s with shared bathroom US$13, s/d/tr US$18/33/39; 🛜) This cat-mad German-owned guesthouse prides itself on having a quiet interior, hot showers and some strict rules. The 15 rooms have fans and are spotless and comfortable. Doubles sport their own balcony. Guests can cook in an ample kitchen, where fridge space is organized by room number. The Teutonic regimentation may not be to everyone's taste. Strictly no bookings.

Residencial Dos Palmas
HOTEL $

(Map p669; 📞 757-9906; www.facebook.com/Residencial-Dos-Palmas-1619749634947555; Calle 6 Sur; d/tr US$30/35; ❄️) Boasting as being '100% *bocatoreño*,' Dos Palmas offers eight basic wooden rooms with old-fashioned furnishings and bright turquoise walls. Run by a friendly matriarch, it's not some cookie-cutter lodging, though some might find it a little stuffy. It sits above the water and boasts exceptional views of the bay from the back terrace. Don't miss sunset!

Cocomo
B&B $$

(Map p669; 📞 757-9259; www.cocomoonthesea.com; cnr Av H & Calle 6; s/d/tr incl breakfast US$65/85/95; ❄️ 🛜) A colorful clapboard house with a tropical garden and waterfront hammock deck, Cocomo wants for nothing. Run by North American tourism pioneer Doug, this four-room B&B knows service. If the weather's bad, this is a snug spot to hole up. All-you-can-eat breakfast includes pastries, cereal, fruit and omelets. There's a laundry service, free use of kayaks and you can swim right off the dock.

Selina Hostel Bocas del Toro
HOSTEL $$

(Map p669; 📞 202-7966; www.selinahostels.com; Calle 1; dm US$14-18, d with/without bathroom from US$60/45, d deluxe US$75-108; @ 🛜) This ever-expanding hostel chain, which has properties in Panama City's Casco Viejo and on Playa Venao on Península de Azuero, has opened a mammoth turquoise 196-bed property on the waterfront, and it has something for everybody. Choose from a rock-bottom bunk in a dorm with 12 beds to a deluxe double with balcony on the top floor (room 312 or 313).

★ Hotel Lula's
B&B $$

(Map p669; 📞 6629-0836, 757-9057; www.lulabb.com; cnr Av H & Calle 6; d/tr/q incl breakfast US$77/88/99; ❄️@ 🛜) A place of porches and rocking chairs, this lovely B&B is a stylish and welcoming addition to the Bocas accommodations scene. Its eight rooms are immaculate, with air-con, fans, wooden ceilings and floors, and a snug design. The hosts, two affable guys from Atlanta, Georgia, give first-rate service, in addition to big Southern breakfasts.

★ Hotel Bocas del Toro
INN $$$

(Map p669; 📞 6673-9018, 757-9018; www.hotelbocasdeltoro.com; Calle 2; d incl breakfast from US$129; ❄️@ 🛜) Our favorite place to stay in Bocas town, this three-story waterfront inn has 11 spacious all-hardwood rooms that feature firm beds with luxurious linens and a warm decor; some have seafront balconies. Perks include concierge service and amenities such as Silico Creek coffee produced by a Ngöbe-Buglé community. There's a fun street-side bar and an excellent deck-side restaurant overlooking the harbor.

AROUND THE ISLAND

★ Tesoro Escondido
CABIN $

(Map p666; 📞 6711-9594; www.bocastesoroescondido.com; d/tr from US$45/55, 2-/3-/4-person cabins US$85/100/115; 🏊) Exuding a very homespun charm, this colorful seafront lodge with eight rooms, three thatched cottages and a suite works its magic. Mosaic tables and recycled-bottle construction in the showers lend a bohemian air; the hammock-strewn upstairs balcony is a treat; and rooms 7 and 8, accessed by a stepped tree trunk, are awesome.

Cabañas Estefany
CABIN $

(Map p666; ☑6582-9912,6956-4525; www.cabanas turisticasestefany.com; dm US$12, d with kitchen US$35, 6-person cabin US$80-100; @) Though it's a far cry from luxury, 11-room Cabañas Estefany is one of the few budget beach lodgings on Isla Colón. Its wooden *cabañas* (cabins) are bare-bones and bathrooms have cold-water showers. Secure a room with a fan as it can get quite buggy. The rooms on the 1st floor have balconies and ocean views.

Sand Dollar Beach Bed & Breakfast
B&B $$

(Map p666; ☑6627-5906,757-9671; www.sanddollar beachbb.com; Sand Dollar Beach; d incl breakfast US$99-132, ste US$149-200; ❄️🛜) Vaguely reminiscent of a US antebellum plantation, this B&B in a yellow clapboard manor about 3km west of Bocas town counts four lovely rooms, a suite named after flowers and a separate apartment for families. The wrap-around verandas on two floors give views of the beach across the road and are the ultimate in relaxation.

🍴 Eating

⭐Taco Surf
MEXICAN $

(Map p669; ☑6951-5739; www.tacosurfbocas.com; Calle 2; mains US$3.50-8.50; ⊗noon-9pm Thu-Tue; 🐾) Just opposite the main plaza, this small garden eatery owned by an affable couple from San Diego serves Baja California–style Mexican food, with fish tacos, California burritos, nachos and specialty fries seasoned with herbs. There are at least six vegetarian choices on the menu. The margaritas – especially the passion fruit and sweet basil – are to die for.

Cafe del Mar
CAFE $

(Map p669; ☑6212-8712; www.facebook.com/ Cafe-del-Mar-822286594497665; Calle 1; dishes US$5-9; ⊗8am-4pm Tue-Sun; 🐾) This eatery the size of a large closet serves excellent all-natural wraps, sandwiches and burgers. Preservatives of all sorts are banned, and there are plenty of choices for vegetarians. Eat in or take-out. Great coffee (US$1.50 to US$3), too.

Pizzeria Alberto
PIZZA $

(Map p669; ☑757-9066; Calle 5; pizzas US$8.50-14; ⊗5-10pm Fri-Wed) Sardinian-run Alberto's is a favorite local haunt, where pizzas with toppings such as artichokes, olives and Gorgonzola satisfy big appetites.

Raw Fusion
ASIAN $

(Map p669; ☑6938-8473; www.facebook.com/ RawFusionBocas; Calle 3; mains US$7-10; ⊗3-10pm Tue-Sun) Just a little plank restaurant on the water, but the Asian-fusion offerings are spot on. Sake accompanies fresh tofu spring rolls and amazing tuna tapas. The salads are wonderful, and service is friendly and attentive. At night candles are lit and the full bar, specializing in original martinis (from US$7), starts humming.

Super Gourmet
SUPERMARKET $

(Map p669; ☑757-9357; www.supergourmetbocas. com; Calle 3; ⊗9am-7pm Mon-Sat) This treasure trove of a grocery store stocks special treats such as rotisserie chicken, Mexican food, wine and frozen bagels. It also has a section of sustainable local gifts, which include handmade soaps and outstanding local Bocas chocolate, as well as kosher foodstuffs.

Om Café
INDIAN $$

(Map p669; ☑6127-0671; http://omcafebocas.com; Calle 3; mains US$8-15; ⊗4-10pm Mon-Fri year-round, 4-10pm Sat Dec-Apr; 🐾) Guaranteed to make you sweat, this welcoming and very attractive upstairs Indian cafe cooks up classic curries, korma and thalis. Service can be slow, so order one of the original cocktails to keep you company, such as the Tipsy Turban (US$6), a dizzy mix of passion fruit or lime juice, rum and sugar. Good selection of vegetarian dishes.

Buena Vista Bar & Grill
NORTH AMERICAN $$

(Map p669; ☑757-9035; www.buenavistabocas. com; Calle 3; mains US$8.50-18; ⊗noon-10pm Wed-Mon) This long-established but peripatetic establishment serves some of the best burgers, tacos and wraps in town, and dinner ups the ante with a surf-and-turf menu. Run by a welcoming Panamanian-American couple, it's a good bet for a decent bite and may be the only spot around for swift service. Haven/heaven for hungry expats.

⭐El Último Refugio
CARIBBEAN $$

(Map p669; ☑6726-9851; www.ultimorefugio. com; Calle 6 Sur; mains US$11-16; ⊗6-10pm) One of the best restaurants in Bocas town, this mellow North American–run place on the edge of the sea specializes in Caribbean and seafood dishes, with fare such as red curry calamari and miso-crusted grouper on the chalkboard. Service is friendly and the tranquil location makes it a great spot for a quiet, romantic dinner.

🍸 Drinking & Nightlife

Selina Bar
CLUB
(Map p669; ☎202-7966; www.selinahostels.com; Calle 1) The bar at this new landmark hostel is open daily, with happy hour between 7pm and 8pm, but most people make it here between 10pm and 2am on a Friday, when all the stops are pulled out and it's party time.

Bookstore Bar
BAR
(Map p669; ☎6452-5905; www.facebook.com/pages/Bocas-BookstoreBar-aka-Loco-Daves/1396790643908649; Calle 2; ⊗2pm-2am Mon-Fri, 6pm-2am Sat & Sun) Just what its name suggests: this cavernous spot is both a place selling books and one selling drinks, though most punters seem more interested in the latter. Run by a couple of affable North Americans, it's mecca for gringos at the start (and sometimes at the end) of an evening. Live music on Tuesdays from 9pm.

Barco Hundido
BAR
(Map p669; Calle 1; ⊗8pm-midnight) At some point you'll probably find yourself at this open-air bar, affectionately known as the 'Wreck Deck' after the sunken banana boat that rests in the clear Caribbean waters in front. A short boardwalk extends from the bar to an island seating area – including swings; perfect for stargazing.

🛈 Information

ATP Tourist Office (Autoridad de Turismo Panama; Map p669; ☎757-9642; bocasdeltoro@atp.gob.pa; Calle 1; ⊗8:30am-3:30pm Mon-Fri) In a large government building on the eastern waterfront.

Banco Nacional de Panamá (☎758-3850; cnr Calle 4 & Av E; ⊗8am-3pm Mon-Fri, 9am-2pm Sat) Exchanges traveler's checks and has a 24-hour ATM.

Bocas del Toro Hospital (☎757-9201; Av G; ⊗24hr) The island's only hospital has a 24-hour emergency room. New Taiwan-funded facility under construction to the northwest.

Ministerio de Ambiente Office (Map p669; ☎757-9442, 758-6822; Calle 1; ⊗9am-5pm Mon-Fri) Can answer questions about national parks or other protected areas.

Post Office (Map p669; Calle 3; ⊗8am-3pm Mon-Fri, to 1pm Sat) In the town hall, overlooking Parque Simón Bolívar from the north.

DANGERS & ANNOYANCES
The surf can be dangerous and there are frequent riptides – use caution when going out into the waves.

Unlike in most other places in Panama, tap water is not safe to drink in the archipelago unless it is filtered. Bocas town has a water-treatment plant, but locals say the tap water is not to be trusted. It's certainly fine for brushing your teeth, but for drinking purchase bottled water or purify your own.

The archipelago is generally a conservative place and local law bans men (and women) from walking the streets shirtless. Even if you are on your way to the beach, wear a shirt or you might be sent back to your hotel by the police.

No matter what age you are, you will almost certainly be offered drugs for sale while walking the streets of downtown Bocas. Do not even think about it; Panama takes its drug laws very seriously indeed.

🛈 Getting There & Away
All arrivals must pay US$3 tourist tax when arriving at any port in Bocas del Toro.

AIR
Air Panama (☎757-9841; www.flyairpanama.com) Flies to Panama City (from US$123, one hour) twice daily sometimes via Changuinola (US$63) as well as to David (US$63). Office at the **airport** (Map p669).

Nature Air (☎in US 800-235-9272; www.natureair.com) Flies from San José, Costa Rica (from US$130, 1½ hours), on Monday, Wednesday and Thursday.

BOAT
If you don't fly into Bocas you'll have to take a water taxi (US$6) from Almirante on the mainland. On the waterfront, **Taxi 25** (Map p669) makes the half-hour trip between 6am and 6:30pm every 30 minutes.

Caribe Shuttle (Map p669; ☎757-7048; www.caribeshuttle.com) runs a combination boat-bus trip (US$39) to Puerto Viejo in Costa Rica twice daily. There's also an option to go on to Cahuita (US$38) or San Jose (US$75). It provides a hotel pick-up but you must reserve one day in advance.

🛈 Getting Around
A cross-island bus goes to Boca del Drago (US$2.50, one hour) from Parque Simón Bolívar, with six departures between 5:30am and 8:30pm. It doubles up as a school bus, so afternoon trips may be delayed.

To reach nearby islands, you can hire boaters operating motorized boats and canoes along the waterfront. As a general rule, you should always sort out the rate beforehand, and clarify if it is for one way or round trip. Always pay on the return leg – this guarantees a pick-up – though most boaters will want some money upfront to buy petrol. Though rates vary, you will get a better deal if you speak Spanish, are with a group and arrange for a pick-up.

Boteros Bocatoreños Unidos (Map p669; ☑757-9760; Calle 3; ☺6:30am-11pm) runs to destinations including Isla Carenero (US$1), Isla Bastimentos and Isla Solarte (US$5) and Red Frog Beach (US$8). Scheduled boats leave for Almirante (20 minutes, US$6) every half hour. Staff is trained in safe boating and sustainable tourism practices.

Isla Carenero

POP 350

A few hundred meters southeast from Isla Colón lies the often-overlooked Isla Carenero. This tiny island takes its name from 'careening,' which in nautical talk means to lean a ship on one side for cleaning or repairing. In October 1502, Columbus' ships were careened and cleaned on this cay while the admiral recovered from a bellyache.

In recent times many hotels have been added, and nature isn't as wild here as it is on the more remote islands. Yet Carenero remains a nice alternative if you're seeking peace and quiet. It's also a good place for an easily accessible, leisurely lunch.

🛏 Sleeping & Eating

Aqua Lounge   HOSTEL $
(Map p666; www.bocasaqualounge.info; dm/d/tr incl breakfast US$12/28/42; � ☜) Rough, rustic and grungy, this 12-room backpacker palace is a matchstick construction on the dock facing Bocas town. And guests just can't get enough – from the hugely popular US$1-a-bottle bar (open late; party night is Wednesday) to the wraparound dock with swimming platform and swings.

Fan-cooled dorms have up to a dozen beds; choose the one with four on the upper floor. Wi-fi at the bar.

Gran Kahuna Beach Hostel   HOSTEL $
(Map p666; ☑757-9551; www.grankahunabocas. com; dm/d US$14/55; ❄ @ ☜) Wildly popular, this waterfront surfer inn is adorable, with yellow cement cabins, six bright rooms and six-bed dorms, and even a picket fence. It offers a huge flat-screen TV, a communal kitchen and an onsite bar. Cleanliness is impressive; not so the cavalier service – you might have to urge the desk person away from their nails to check in.

★Tierra Verde   HOTEL $$
(Map p666; ☑757-9903; www.hoteltierraverde. com; s/d/tr incl breakfast US$65/75/85, ste US$150-175; ❄ @ ☜) This family-run three-story hotel sits back from the beach amid shady palms and flowers. Designed in a contemporary island style, the six spacious all-wood rooms on two floors and the suite at the top feature large windows that allow in ample light. There's hot water and the option of airport pick-ups (US$10). Go for rooms 4 or 5 for their ocean views.

★Leaf Eaters Cafe   VEGETARIAN $
(Map p666; ☑757-9543; www.facebook.com/bocasleafeaters; dishes US$6-10; ☺10am-4pm Mon-Sat; ☑) This vegetarian and vegan lunch place has upped stakes from its old location and settled almost opposite above the water on Isla Carenero. It serves quirky and remarkably flavorful vegetarian dishes such as 'hippie bowls' (brown rice with vegetables and dressing) along with cheese paninis, bean tacos, scrumptious shiitake burgers and chocolate-banana smoothies. Bright and cheery decor and friendly atmosphere.

❶ Getting There & Away

Isla Carenero is a quick and easy US$1 boat ride from the waterfront in Bocas town. Oddly, there is no public pier. Water taxis dock at the small marina on the tip of the island. From here, there is a track that leads to the little town and continues across the island.

Isla Bastimentos

POP 1950

Although it's just a 10-minute boat ride from the town of Bocas del Toro, Isla Bastimentos is like a different world. Some travelers say this is their favorite island in their favorite part of Panama. The northwest coast of the island is home to palm-fringed beaches that serve as nesting grounds for sea turtles, while most of the northern and southern coasts consists of mangrove islands and coral reefs that lie within the boundaries of the Parque Nacional Marino Isla Bastimentos.

The main settlement on Bastimentos is Old Bank. It has a prominent West Indian population whose origins are in the banana industry. The island is also home to the Ngöbe-Buglé village of Quebrada Sal (Salt Creek).

⊙ Sights

Bastimentos has some amazing beaches, but be careful when swimming as the surf can really pick up on the northern coast.

Wizard Beach
BEACH

(Playa Primera; Map p666) The most beautiful beach on Isla Bastimentos is awash in powdery yellow sand and backed by thick vine-strewn jungle. It's connected to Old Bank via a wilderness path, which normally takes 20 minutes or so but can be virtually impassable after heavy rains. The path continues along the coast to Playa Segunda (Second Beach) and Red Frog Beach.

Red Frog Beach
BEACH

(Map p666; admission US$3) Small but perfectly formed, Red Frog Beach is named after the *rana rojo* (strawberry poison-dart frog), an amphibian you're most unlikely to encounter here due to development, local kids trapping them to impress tourists, and a tidal wave of day-trippers in season. From Bocas town, water taxis (US$4) head to the public dock next to a small marina on the south side of the island, from where the beach is an easy 15-minute walk.

★ Parque Nacional Marino Isla Bastimentos
PARK

(Map p666; admission US$10) Established in 1988, this 132-sq-km marine park was Panama's first. Protecting 130 islands of the Bocas del Toro archipelago, including the coral-fringed Cayos Zapatillas, and the wetlands in the center of Isla Bastimentos, the marine park is an important nature reserve for mangroves, monkeys, sloths, caiman, crocodile and 28 species of amphibians and reptiles.

Get up-to-date park information from the ATP (p672) or Ministerio de Ambiente (p672) offices in Bocas del Toro town. To camp out anywhere in the park, you are required to first obtain a permit (US$10) from the latter.

Nivida Bat Cave
CAVE

(Bahía Honda; Map p666; admission US$5) One of Bastimentos' most fascinating natural wonders, Nivida is a massive cavern with swarms of nectar bats and a subterranean lake. The cave lies within the borders of the Parque Nacional Marino Isla Bastimentos and half the fun is getting here. But it's next to impossible to do it on your own. An organized tour from Old Bank costs US$35 per person.

The tour involves a 25-minute boat ride from Old Bank to the channel entrance. You'll then spend a similar amount of time gliding though mangroves and lush vegetation. From the dock it's then a half-hour hike to the cave. Wear sturdy shoes or boots; you will be provided with headlamps at the cave entrance.

⚡ Activities

★ Up in the Hill
TOUR

(Map p666; ☑6607-8962, 6570-8277; www.upinthehill.com; Old Bank; drinks & snacks US$2.50-4) It's worth the hot 20-minute haul up to this organic farm at the highest point on Isla Bastimentos for the views, and to see chocolate being grown and turned into one of the world's favorite comestibles. There's a cafe serving chocolate drinks, coffee from Boquete and homemade hibiscus tea, and a shop with its own line of coconut-based natural body products.

Bastimentos Sky Zipline Canopy Tour
ADVENTURE SPORTS

(Map p666; ☑6987-8661, 836-5501; www.redfrogbeach.com/bocas-del-toro-zipline.html; per person US$55; ◷10am, 1pm & 3:30pm) Seven zip lines, a swaying sky bridge and a vertical rappel are highlights of this attraction, brought to you by a well-known Costa Rican zip-line designer, in the hills just south of Red Frog Beach. Tours last two hours.

Bastimentos Alive
ADVENTURE TOUR

(Map p666; ☑6514-7961, 6945-6167; www.bastimentosalive.com; Old Bank; trek with/without BBQ US$45/35; ◷11am) This new but already well-regarded tour operator leads daily treks

DON'T MISS

GEMS OF THE ARCHIPELAGO

Tired of the crowds? Find adventure by hiring a boat to try out these excursions:

Cayo Crawl Get lost in these mangrove-dotted channels – also called Coral Cay – near Isla Bastimentos.

Cayos Zapatillas Set out for the pristine white-sand beaches and virgin forests on these two uninhabited islands southeast of Isla Bastimentos.

Dolphin Bay Spot dolphins frolicking at this densely populated breeding ground south of Isla San Cristóbal.

Cayo Swan Spot red-billed tropic birds and white-crowned pigeons in this cay near Isla de los Pájaros, north of Isla Colón.

BAMBUDA LODGE

Beg, borrow and/or steal to stay at **Bambuda Lodge** (Map p666; ☑ 6962-4644, 6765-4755; http://bambuda.net; dm US$16, d US$69-99, d with shared bathroom US$59, incl breakfast; ✳ @ 🛜 ☒), the archipelago's most attractive budget resort. Most visitors to Isla Solarte are day-trippers on boat tours, but the options for staying overnight include this destination budget lodge. It's a carefully crafted all-wood complex with 11 rooms set up in lush rainforest, with trails and overlooking a coral reef. There's a lovely pool on the slope and a new 60m-long water slide from reception straight down into the ocean. A chilled, welcoming retreat.

Owned and operated by two friends from Toronto who can't do enough for you, Bambuda counts two fan-cooled dorms with 10 beds each and nine private rooms, four of them quite luxurious and with their own bathrooms. The open-sided bar and dining room serves set meals (US$8 to US$12) and the grounds, set on 6 hectares with 40 different tropical fruit trees (mango, star fruit, custard apple etc), are breathtaking with 10km of trails fanning out in several directions. There's snorkeling equipment as well kayaks and canoes available.

Isla Solarte is a quick and easy boat ride (US$3) from the waterfront in Bocas town.

through the jungle, with stops at Red Frog Beach and the organic Up in the Hill farm at the highest point on the island. Lunch and a Caribbean-style BBQ at the end of the tour are included. It's a 7½-hour day (six without the BBQ). Add US$10 for transfer from Bocas town.

🛏 Sleeping

Bubba's House
GUESTHOUSE **$**
(Map p666; ☑ 6403-9447, 6589-8872; www.bubbashouse.com; Old Bank; dm US$16, d US$38-45; ✳🛜) This attractive wooden guesthouse on the waterfront is the best place to stay in Old Bank, and it attracts a lively and interesting crowd. The 11 colorful rooms with painted floors include privates as well as en suite dorms for up to six guests. The back-deck bar and restaurant has a great collection of musical instruments. The welcoming hosts are Argentinian.

Tío Tom's Guesthouse
GUESTHOUSE **$**
(Map p666; ☑ 757-9831; www.tiotomsguesthouse.com; Old Bank; d US$38, 2-person bungalow US$48; 🛜) This rickety wooden guesthouse perched over the sea has been offering cheap, clean and unfussy rooms for years. A highlight is the waterfront deck strewn with hammocks. There are five rooms for two or three people and a separate bungalow; all have private bathrooms. The German owner offers hearty meals (dinner US$8), organizes diving tours and rents kayaks.

Hostal Bastimentos
HOSTEL **$**
(Map p666; ☑ 6795-8093, 757-9053; www.hostalbastimentos.com; Old Bank; dm US$8-10, d US$15-20, d/tr with air-con US$45/50; ✳@🛜) On a hill off the main path, this sprawling yellow

clapboard house has a bright selection of 28 rooms and hammock decks. Spaces are creaky but serviceable; private rooms with air-con also have fridges and balconies with great views. Backpacker-ready, it includes two kitchens, and a common room with a bar, TV and dartboard.

★ Palmar Tent Lodge
CAMPGROUND **$$**
(Map p666; ☑ 838-8552; www.palmartentlodge.com; Red Frog Beach; dm tents US$15, d/tr tents from US$50/60, 2-person bungalows US$85) On the edge of the jungle and facing celebrated Red Frog Beach, Palmar has introduced glamping to Bocas del Toro and the archipelago will never be the same. Accommodations are in solar-powered circular tents for two to three, with all the comforts (including large lock boxes for valuables); in an eight-bed dorm; and in a luxurious two-story thatched 'jungalow' for two.

The huge open-sided restaurant-bar is the place to be most nights (and days, come to think of it). The fun and well-informed owners, two mates from Washington, DC, offer a laundry list of tours and excursions and there are yoga classes (US$6) twice daily onsite. Water-taxi shuttles (US$4 one way) link the lodge with Bocas town twice a day. No internet.

Beverly's Hill
CABIN **$$**
(Map p666; ☑ 757-9923; www.beverlyshill.blogspot.com; Old Bank; s/d without bathroom US$17/35, d with bathroom US$60-70; 🛜) 🌿 These thatched cabins occupy a lush green garden replete with red frogs, incongruous in the center of Old Bank. The seven immaculate rooms feature fans, firm mattresses and hot-water showers; hammocks abound. The onsite

ADVENTURES IN NASO COUNTRY

On the border of Parque Internacional La Amistad and a proposed Naso *comarca* (autonomous region), **Soposo Rainforest Adventures** (☑ 6631-2222, 6875-8125; www.soposo.com; day tour per person US$90, 2-/3-day package incl lodging, meals & tours US$140/275) is a unique jungle lodging and sustainable tour operator, and a recommended step off the well-worn trail. Guests stay in stilted thatched huts, eat traditional foods and immerse themselves in Naso culture.

The project, spearheaded by an ex–Peace Corps volunteer and her Naso husband, has been lauded by travelers. It was created to offer the Naso people an alternative income, bolster cultural self-esteem and protect natural resources in the face of a massive hydroelectric project, which is changing the nature of the area. A highlight is a three-day trip up the Río Teribe to the village of the Naso monarch.

From Changuinola, it's a 30-minute taxi ride to the village of El Silencio, from where there's river access to the lodging.

composting and water filtration system makes this one of the most environmentally friendly hotels on the island.

✖ Eating

Nacho Mama's TEX-MEX **$**
(Map p666; ☑ 6539-5151; Red Frog Beach; tacos US$5-6, with drink US$12; ⊙11am-5pm Tue-Sun) Pitched on the shifting sands of Red Frog Beach, this one-hit wonder does a thriving business dispensing tacos with fish, shrimp, ceviche and chicken throughout the day. But never on a Monday. And never nachos.

Chavela SEAFOOD **$**
(Map p666; ☑ 6502-0024; www.facebook.com/barrestaurantechavela; Old Bank; mains US$4-12; ⊙6-10pm) Attractive little eatery in a lime-green shack at the bottom of the landmark Hostel Bastimentos. Chavela serves cheap-as-chips burgers but emphasizes seafood in all its guises, from *ceviche de pulpo* (raw octopus cured in lime juice) and fish tacos to barracuda steak.

Coco Hill VEGETARIAN **$$**
(Map p666; Old Bank; dishes US$7.50-16; ⊙10am-10pm Wed-Mon) Close to the island's highest point, Australian Michelle concocts some pretty exotic meatless dishes at her vegetarian, vegan and gluten-free restaurant and bar. It might seem a bit of a hike, but who can resist red-pepper soup, mixed mezze plates, and Kahlua and rum brownies? The blackboard menu changes daily. Cocktails are made with fresh fruit juices.

❶ Information

There have been reports of muggings on the trail between Old Bank and Red Frog Beach. Never go on any trail after dark and never go alone. Carry only essentials such as a towel and water, never valuables.

❶ Getting There & Away

A water taxi to Old Bank costs US$3. It's US$4 to the public dock for Red Frog Beach. To Isla Solarte it's US$5. You'll pay from US$10 to US$25 one way to locations further south on the island.

Almirante

POP 12,730

A clutch of stilted homes on the water, this unkempt village has seen better days, but it remains the springboard for the Archipiélago de Bocas del Toro so is always busy.

Taxi 25 runs a water shuttle to Bocas town (US$6, 30 minutes); a taxi between the bus terminal and the dock should cost no more than US$1.

An air-conditioned bus to Changuinola (US$1.45) leaves every 15 minutes between 6am and 8pm and takes 45 minutes. Taxis to Changuinola (from US$20) can be bargained, particularly if you start your walk from the dock to the bus terminal.

Changuinola

POP 42,000

Headquarters of the Chiriquí Land Company, the company that produces Chiquita bananas, Changuinola is a hot and rather dusty town surrounded by a sea of banana plantations. Although there is little reason to spend any time here, overland travelers linking to Costa Rica will have to pass through.

🛏 Sleeping & Eating

Hotel Semiramis   HOTEL **$**
(☑ 758-6006; Av 17 de Abril; d/tr US$33/35; ❄ 🛜)
This shiny tiled hotel at the southern end of
the main street is the best in town. There's
air-con, hot water and 20 proper rooms –
but not all have windows.

Cotty's   PANAMANIAN **$**
(☑ 760-0161; Av 17 de Abril; meals US$2.50; ⊘ 24hr)
On the main road, this clean cafeteria-style
restaurant with folkloric murals on the walls
prepares unfussy Panamanian fare. A plate
of curried chicken and rice (US$2) is gratify-
ing and quick.

ⓘ Getting There & Away

Buses for Costa Rica leave from the terminal
just south of the Delta gas station. Other buses depart from Terminal Urraca (☑ 758-8115),
with departures between 6am and 7pm.

COLÓN PROVINCE

With an edgy reputation more true crime
than travel, Colón rarely makes travel wish
lists, but there is more to this Caribbean
province than its downtrodden capital.
Think pristine beaches and lowland rainforests, colonial splendors and modern engineering marvels. Portobelo, with its growing
music and art scene, shows the best of vibrant
Congo culture, while the luxury train between
Panama City and Colón remains one of the
greatest rail journeys in the Americas.

Colón

POP 35,000
With its colonial grandeur crumbling and its
neighborhoods marginalized, Colón is the city
that Panama forgot, in spite of vigorous development meant to court Caribbean cruise
ships. Prior to 1869, the railroad connecting
Panama City and Colón was the only rapid
transit across the continental Western Hemisphere. A last whiff of prosperity was seen
during the construction of the Panama Canal.

On the city's edge, the Zona Libre (Free
Zone) was created in 1948. Generating some
US$5 billion in annual commerce, little ben-
efit seems to trickle down to locals. From
close up, it's an island of materialism floating in a sea of unemployment and poverty.

Recent improvements in city safety are attributed to tighter gang control and an arms
for food program that got many guns off the
streets. The improved Ruta 3 between Panama City and Colón is now a four-lane highway, resulting in much quicker travel times.

🛏 Sleeping & Eating

Meryland Hotel   HOTEL **$**
(☑ 441-7055; www.hotelmeryland.com; cnr Calle 7
& Av Santa Isabel; s/d US$45/60; 🅿 ❄ @ 🛜) A
massive stone building, this business hotel
fronts an attractive city park in a comparatively safe part of Colón. Small tiled rooms
with gold tones and wrought-iron furniture
have air-con, cable TV and hot-water bathrooms, though you're paying for security, not
luxury. The restaurant saves you the trouble
of having to leave the hotel at night.

Arrecifes   SEAFOOD **$$**
(☑ info 441-9308; Calle 3 at Paseo Gorgas; mains
US$10-15; ⊘ noon-8pm Mon-Sat) Local business
owners lunch at this nondescript port build-
ing cooking up great Caribbean seafood in
the gated port area. Expect no frills and
no water views, just generous portions of
criollo-style seafood, stewed in onions, pep-
pers and tomatoes, and whole fried snapper.

BUSES FROM CHANGUINOLA

DESTINATION	COST (US$)	DURATION	FREQUENCY
Almirante (with boat connections to Isla Colón)	145	45min	every 30min
Altos del Valle (Bosque Protector de Palo Seco)	7.25	2¼hr	every 30min
David	9.70	4¾hr	every 30min
El Silencio (Parque Internacional La Amistad)	1.25	30min	every 20min
Guabito-Sixaola	1	30min	every 30min
Las Tablas (Las Delicias)	2	1½hr	hourly
Panama City	29	12hr	daily 7am
San José (Costa Rica)	16	6hr	daily 10am

ℹ Orientation

The Zona Libre occupies the southeastern corner of the city, while the cruise-ship port, Colón 2000, is located just north of it. If you turn left on Calle 13, you'll pass the passenger train terminal, which lies 200m before the port of Cristóbal.

ℹ Information

Apart from the cruise port on the eastern side of the city and the bustling Zona Libre (free-trade zone), Colón has a dangerous reputation. Violent crime rates have lowered, but visitors should exercise caution when walking around, even during the day. Paseo de Washington, the renovated waterfront area, and Av Bolívar are safe to peruse by day. Always travel by taxi at night.

ℹ Getting There & Away

BUS

From Panama City, express and regular buses for Colón leave every 30 minutes from the Albrook Bus Terminal.

Colón's **Terminal de Buses** (cnr Calle Terminal & Av Bolívar) serves towns throughout Colón Province with hourly departures.

If you are headed east of Colón from Panama City, these buses can be boarded at Sabanitas, the turnoff for Portobelo, thus avoiding a trip into Colón. Be aware that buses may be standing room only, particularly on weekends.

DESTINATION	COST (US$)	DURATION
Escobal (near Parque National San Lorenzo)	1.25	35min
La Guayra	3	2hr
Nombre de Dios	3.80	2½hr
Panama City	3.50	1-1.5hr
Portobelo	1.60	1½hr

TRAIN

One of the best ways to fully appreciate the canal's expanse is to travel from Panama City to Colón along the historic **Panama Railroad** (☑ 317-6070; www.panarail.com; one way adult/child US$25/15; ⊙ daily departures from Panama City at 7:15am, Colón at 5:15pm). Note that the Panama City terminus is actually located in the town of Corozal, a 15-minute drive from the capital.

ℹ Getting Around

While in Colón, it's not a good idea to walk around unknown neighborhoods. Fortunately, taxis congregate at the bus terminal, train station and the Zone Libre, and fares across the city are usually under US$2.

A round-trip taxi for three to four passengers runs around US$60 to Fuerte San Lorenzo and US$30 to Gatun Locks; fewer passengers should

negotiate a better fare. From the terminal you can also take a bus to Gatun Locks (US$1).

Around Colón

Agua Clara Visitor Center   VIEWPOINT

(☑ 276-8325; www.micanaldepanama.com; adult/child US$15/10; ⊙ 8am-3:15pm) This new observation center offers an exclusive panoramic view of the Panama Canal expansion. Visits take slightly over an hour. Covered decks view Lago Gatún and the locks; there is also a theater with videos in English, exhibits, a cafe and a gift shop. With no onsite museum, the focus here is really about getting a good look at the expansion. A short rainforest trail has sloths and monkeys. Exhibits close at 4pm but visitors must enter by 3:15pm.

The turnoff is just past the railroad tracks, to the left; for the locks, continue straight at the turnoff. The center is accessible to travelers with disabilities.

Gatún Locks   CANAL

(US$5; ⊙ 8am-4pm) The Gatún Locks, 10km south of Colón, raise southbound ships 29.5m from Caribbean waters to Lago Gatún. Just the size of them is mind-boggling. In *The Path Between the Seas*, David McCullough notes that if stood on its end, a single lock would have been the tallest structure on earth at the time it was built, taller by several meters than even the Eiffel Tower. Each chamber could have accommodated the *Titanic* with room to spare.

Workers poured a record-setting 1.82 million cu meters of concrete to construct the Gatún Locks. The concrete was brought from a giant mixing plant to the construction site by railroad cars that ran on a circular track. Huge buckets maneuvered by cranes carried the wet concrete from the railroad cars and poured it into enormous steel forms. Locomotives moved the forms into place. This protracted process continued virtually uninterrupted for four years until the Gatún Locks were completed.

A viewing stand opposite the control tower offers a prime view of the locks in action. The two-hour process is the most interesting stage of the canal transit and the English brochure clearly describes what you're watching.

Once the ships pass through the locks, they travel 37km to the Pedro Miguel Locks, which lower southbound ships 9.3m to Lago Miraflores, a small body of water between two sets of Pacific locks. Ships are then lowered to sea level at the Miraflores Locks.

Buses to the Gatún Locks leave the Colón bus terminal hourly (US$1.25, 20 minutes). If you arrive by taxi you can stop here before heading on to Gatún Dam – another 2km away. A taxi ride from Colón to the locks and dam and back should cost US$60 per party, but agree on a price before leaving.

Parque Nacional San Lorenzo NATIONAL PARK
Centered on the ruins of the crumbling Spanish colonial fortress of Fuerte San Lorenzo, the 9.6-sq-km Parque Nacional San Lorenzo includes the former US military base of Fuerte Sherman, as well as 12 different ecosystems including mangroves, marshlands, semi-deciduous forests and humid rainforests.

Portobelo

POP 4600

This Caribbean fishing village is so laid-back and languorous, it is incredible to ponder that it was once the greatest Spanish port in Central America. Mules once carried Peruvian gold and Oriental treasures to Panama City via the fortresses at Portobelo. Though English privateers destroyed them several times throughout their history, many of these atmospheric colonial fortresses still stand. Throughout the village, homes are situated among these atmospheric ruins.

Today, Portobelo's residents scratch out a living fishing, tending crops or raising livestock. Though economically depressed, Portobelo is experiencing something of a cultural revival, with interest surging in Congo art and dancing. There are also nice beaches, accessed by boat, and worthwhile diving and snorkeling.

Sights

Fuerte San Jerónimo FORT
Fuerte San Jerónimo, close to Portobelo center, was the largest fortress ever built to protect the bay. Eighteen cannon embrasures face the mouth of the bay, some exactly where the Spanish troops left them in 1821, the year Panama declared independence. Beyond the impressive gateway, there's the remains of the officers' quarters, barracks and a guardroom.

If you're short on time, San Jerónimo is the more complete of Portobelo's accessible forts and makes for the best visit.

Real Aduana de Portobelo HISTORIC BUILDING
(US$5; ⊙8am-4pm) The handsome, two-story Royal Customs House of Portobelo was origi-

nally built in 1630 to serve as the *contaduría* (counting house) for the king's gold. Now the two main rooms house permanent exhibitions, including replicas of Spanish-colonial rifles, sketches of Portobelo's forts, 20th-century black-and-white photos of the town and a few dozen rusty cannonballs. There's also an informative video (in English too).

Iglesia de San Félipe CHURCH
This 1814 Catholic church is the home of Portobelo's famed Black Christ. Believers attribute miracles to the 1.5m statue that was found floating in the bay, and it's celebrated every October with the popular Festival de Cristo Negro. The church was the last structure built by the Spanish before they withdrew from Panama.

Activities

Scubaportobelo DIVING
(☑261-3841; www.scubapanama.com) Outfitter Scubaportobelo offers all-inclusive scuba packages. It's located on the road into town, on the left.

Festivals & Events

Festival de Cristo Negro FESTIVAL
(Black Christ Festival; ⊙Oct 21) Every October, pilgrims from all over Panama arrive in Portobelo to partake in this festival, which honors a miracle-giving 1.5m-high statue of the Black Christ housed in the Iglesia de San Félipe. After the sun sets, the statue is paraded down the streets, while pilgrims bedecked in purple robes and thorned crowns dance and drink until the wee hours.

PORTOBELO'S TOP FIVE ESCAPES

➡ Hire a water taxi to explore the awesome mangroves east of Isla Grande (p680).

➡ Snorkel around Spanish cannons encrusted in the coral landscape.

➡ Kayak up the tranquil Río Claro.

➡ Watch a sunset from Fuerte San Fernando.

➡ Join a Congo dance workshop (☑6693-5690; Calle Principal, Casa Artesanal; per person US$20; ⊙10am-2pm Fri-Sun) and sweat to cool African rhythms.

Festival de Diablos y Congos   FESTIVAL

(🕓 Feb/Mar) The most intriguing local tradition is Festival de Diablos y Congos, a festival of rebellion and ridicule that mocks the colonial Spaniards. During the festivity, participants assume the role of escaped slaves and take 'captives.' It is held two weeks after Carnaval, sometimes coinciding with March 20, Portobelo's patron saint day. The tradition of Los Congos (named for its participants) dates from the slave-trading days when blacks escaped into the jungle and formed communities of exiles.

🛏 Sleeping & Eating

El Castillo   HOSTEL $

(📱 6738-1561; eponango@hotmail.com; dm/d with shared bathroom US$10/18) This worn seafront restaurant and hostel indeed resembles a castle – one drawn by Miyazaki. Still, its French-speaking Vietnamese host, Richard, is welcoming and it has that tumble-down charm. Rooms are basic, with mosquito nets and fans. The restaurant (mains US$12 to US$25) is open from 9am to 11pm and offers some appealing options for vegetarians, including Thai curry.

⭐La Morada de la Bruja
Portobelo   BOUTIQUE HOTEL $$

(📱 6759-6987, 6528-0679; www.lamoradadelabruja portobelo.com; r US$60-75, 4-person loft US$100, 2-bedroom house US$225; 🅿❄🛜) Quite extraordinary, this chill photographer's home has been adapted for guests but maintains a very personal touch. A small apartment and two ample waterfront houses sport modern, artful decor and a grassy seafront perfect for lounging. The bright, open interiors showcase photography and local Congo art. There are also kayaks for rent and boat services for excursions to remote beaches.

Coco Plum   HOTEL $$

(📱 448-2102; www.cocoplum-panama.com; s/d/tr US$55/65/75; 🅿❄) An attractive, motel-style lodging, the friendly Coco Plum has been around for years. On the waterfront, the feel of the place is ocean kitsch, replete with nets, shells and pastels, but the effect is cozy. The attached bar-restaurant (mains US$8 to US$16) is popular with travelers – check out the octopus in coconut milk or seafood stew.

ℹ️ Information

ATP (📱 448-2200, 6485-7028; 🕓 8am-4pm) Just off the main road through town, ATP has good information. Only Spanish is spoken.

ℹ️ Getting There & Away

Buses to Portobelo (US$1.60, 1½ hours, every 30 minutes) depart from Colón's Terminal de Buses from 6:30am to 6pm. **Buses to Colón** leave from a bus stop on the main road through town.

From Panama City you can avoid Colón. Take the Colón bus and get off at El Rey supermarket in Sabanitas, 10km before Colón. Next, catch the bus coming from Colón to Portobelo when it passes through Sabanitas (US$1.40, 1¼ hours). Since it's often full, take as little luggage as possible.

Isla Grande

Palm trees and white-sand beaches form the backdrop to this lovely little island, just 15km from Portobelo. A popular getaway for Panama City folk fleeing the urban grind, Isla Grande is an ideal setting for snorkeling, scuba diving or simply soaking up the island's relaxed vibe. There are no roads, just a path along the eastern island perimeter. A few hundred people of African descent live on Grande, most of whom eke out a living from fishing and coconuts – you'll get a taste of both when you sample the fine island cuisine.

🏃 Activities

This 5km-long, 1.5km-wide island has two trails, one that loops the shoreline and another slippery cross-island trail. The lovely beaches on the northern side of the island can be reached by boat or on foot.

Some fine snorkeling and dive sites are within a 10-minute boat ride of the island. For diving, contact a Portobelo-based operator (p679). Diving is limited to between April and December, when seas are calmer.

Boat taxis can also take you further afield to explore the mangroves east of Isla Grande or snorkeling off the coast of the nearby islets.

🎉 Festivals & Events

Isla Grande Carnaval   FESTIVAL

(🕓 Feb-Mar) Isla Grande celebrates Carnaval in rare form: women wear traditional *polleras* (festive dresses), while men wear ragged pants tied at the waist with old sea rope, and everyone dances to African-influenced Conga drums and song. There are also satirical songs about current events and a lot of joking in the Caribbean calypso tradition.

🛏 Sleeping & Eating

Macondo Hostel   HOSTEL **$**

(☑ 6102-6262; dm/d US$15/35; ☜) Follow the signposted path a block inland to this agreeable, breezy two-story hostel set under the rainforest canopy. Bunks occupy dark and ample rooms with fans. It's good value for budget travelers, with shady, pleasant shared spaces and hammocks. And if you want to party during the day, you'll probably find company.

Sister Moon   CABAÑAS **$$**

(☑ 6948-1990; www.hotelsistermoon.com; d/tr/q with fan US$77/116/153, d with air-con US$140, day pass US$20; ❉☜☜) Your best bet for island lodging is this lovely clutch of hillside cabins surrounded by swaying palms and crashing waves. With no beach, guests sunbathe on attractive waterfront decks, though the surf can be rough. Perks include private balconies with porch hammocks. Showers are tiny. It also rents attractive houses at Brother Sun next door.

Hotel Congo Restaurante   SEAFOOD **$$**

(☑ 6296-8624; mains US$15) Set at the end of a pier, this shady, open-air restaurant and bar serves some of the best fare on the island. Spanish-run, a welcome Mediterranean influence employs olive oil and caramelized onions in fragrant seafood dishes. Meanwhile, the onsite budget hotel is undergoing serious renovations, though some rooms are open to the public. Located mid-island.

❶ Getting There & Away

Isla Grande is a 10-minute boat ride from La Guayra, a tiny coastal hamlet that is connected to Colón via frequent bus connections. Boats arriving at Isla Grande dock in front of Hotel Isla Grande.

Buses to La Guayra leave from the Colón bus terminal (US$3, 1½ hours). From Panama City, take a Colón-bound bus to Sabanitas and change buses next to El Rey supermarket for La Guayra. Buses return from La Guayra at 8am, 9am and 1pm.

Panama City tour operators bring day-trippers from Panama City.

In La Guayra, boats at the dock go to the island (or beyond). Each leaves when full. The 10-minute boat ride costs US$3 to US$5 per person; secure parking costs US$5 per day.

COMARCA DE GUNA YALA

Imagine a turquoise tropical archipelago with one island for every day of the year. With white sand and waving palms, these Caribbean islands cheat no one's version of paradise. The Comarca is home to the Guna, the first group in Latin America to gain indigenous autonomy. Though they have had contact with Europeans since Columbus sailed these waters in 1502, clan identity is paramount, and many make tenacious efforts to preserve a traditional way of life.

In 2009 the road to Cartí was completed, making the region more accessible than ever and opening up options for day trips. Still off the beaten track, this narrow, 226km-long strip on the Caribbean coast stretches from the Golfo de San Blás to the Colombian border.

Community islands are acre-sized cays packed with bamboo huts, livestock and people. Visitors often prefer the more remote outer islands with few inhabitants. Most areas require landing fees.

History

Although the Guna have lived in eastern Panama for at least two centuries, scholars fiercely debate their origins. Language similarities with people who once lived several hundred kilometers to the west would indicate that the Guna migrated eastward. However, oral tradition has it that the Guna migrated to San Blás from Colombia after the 16th century, following a series of devastating encounters with other tribes armed with poison-dart blowguns.

Regardless of the Guna's origins, scholars agree that life on the islands is relatively new for them. Historians at the end of the 18th century wrote that the only people who used the San Blás islands at that time were pirates, Spaniards and the odd explorer. However, the Guna flourished on the archipelago due to the abundance of seafood. They supplemented this with food crops, including rice, yams, yucca, bananas and pineapples, grown on the nearby mainland.

Today, there are an estimated 50,000 Guna; almost 32,000 live on the district's islands, 8000 live on tribal land along the coast and many live outside the district. So communal are the island-dwelling Guna that they inhabit only 49 of the nearly 400 cays; the rest are mostly left to coconut trees, sea turtles and iguanas.

🏊 Activities

Most lodgings offer complete packages, where a fixed price gets you a room, three meals a day and boat rides to neighboring islands for swimming, snorkeling and lounging on the beach. If you seek community life, you can also arrange visits to more populated islands. Before swimming off the shores of a heavily populated island, consider that all waste goes here, unfiltered in most cases.

Snorkeling is good in places, but many coral reefs are badly damaged. You can often rent snorkeling equipment from your hotel; serious snorkelers should bring their own gear. Jaunts to hike the mainland jungles are arranged with a guide. Most travelers are content with simply soaking up the Caribbean sun.

🛏 Sleeping & Eating

Carefully selecting your accommodations on the islands is key, since their remoteness makes it difficult to change your mind. Camping on an uninhabited island isn't wise, because you run the risk of encountering drug traffickers in the night. The Guna do not allow the Panamanian coast guard or US antidrug vessels to operate in the archipelago, so the uninhabited islands are occasionally used by Colombian traffickers running cocaine up the coast.

There is only a handful of lodgings on the islands and none on the mainland. Most of these are basic but comfortable. Most densely populated islands in the district have a store

selling basic items, as well as pay phones for domestic and international calls. The phones are public, but there's usually a Guna standing nearby charging a telephone tax of US$1 per call or more. Cell phones work in some areas.

Since there are almost no restaurants, each lodging provides meals for guests. They are usually seafood based, with lobster available at an extra cost. Quality varies, as some of the fishing stocks have been depleted, but there is always rice and a healthy supply of fresh coconuts. Always ask before taking a coconut – they are among the region's main sources of income.

Cabañas Tigre CABIN $
(☑ 6099-2738; cabins with/without bathroom US$25/15) The best feature here is the relaxed reception – guests have their own ample space but also get to see a fair amount of typical village life, with locals who are more open and relaxed toward travelers than they are elsewhere. They also recycle. Pleasant bamboo-and-thatch *cabañas* have cement floors, colorful hammocks and shared facilities, and are near the beach.

The ocean here is crystal clear and fairly placid, perfect for kayaking (from December to June) or snorkeling. Snorkel gear, meals (US$3 to US$7) and transfers to Cartí (US$30) are extra.

RESPONSIBLE TRAVEL IN GUNA YALA

When visiting the Comarca de Guna Yala, consider how your visit may affect the community. Tourism revenue can play a vital role in the development of the region, particularly if you are buying locally produced crafts or contracting the services of a Guna guide. However, Western interests have already caused irreversible damage to the region. Be aware of your surroundings and remain sensitive about your impact.

One look at the paradisiacal setting, the rainbow flag and the distinctive Guna dress and you might feel transported into the pages of *National Geographic*. Don't snap that shutter just yet, though. If the Guna appear unfriendly, consider their predicament. When cruise ships visit, the number of people on an already congested island can triple. Then, nearly two-thirds of the populace (the tourists) turns paparazzi on the other third (the Guna). It's an unsavory scene repeated again and again. To rein in the situation, the Guna charge fees for photographs taken of them as well as visitation fees for each island. If you can't afford the photo fee, tuck away your camera and strike up a conversation instead.

Remain mindful of the way you dress. Guna men never go shirtless and Guna women dress conservatively, with their cleavage, their belly and most of their legs covered. Arriving in Guna villages in a bikini or shirtless is interpreted as a sign of disrespect.

Trash is a problem on the islands, and there is no effective plan for its management. For the Guna, the cost of removal to the mainland is too high, and there is no designated site or 'culture' of waste management, since all refuse was relatively innocuous until outside influence prevailed. You may see litter and burning piles of plastics. With no current solution to the issue, do what you can to pack out your own garbage, if necessary, and try to consume fresh products with minimal packaging – ie choose coconut water over cola.

Cabañas Miro
CABAÑAS **$**

(☑ 6769-5801; r per person incl 3 meals US$25) For shoestringers who want nothing more than some thatch over their head and sand beneath their toes, this is it. However, it's about to get a bit more crowded, with seven new cabins under construction. There is little to do here, but dining outdoors around the picnic table provides the perfect opportunity to mix with fellow travelers.

Cartí Homestay
HOSTEL **$$**

(☑ 6734-3454, 6517-9850; www.cartihomestay kunayala.blogspot.com; Carti Suitupo; r per person incl 3 meals & tour US$50; @) Catering to backpackers, Cartí Homestay is the best place to meet young Gunas and strike up a conversation, though the inflatable Jägermeister bottle in the corner is a good indicator of the kind of cultural interactions you might expect. The English-speaking hosts also offer cabin lodgings on a more remote island and coordinate speedboats to Puerto Obaldia for Colombia-bound travelers.

★ De Mar Achu
CABAÑAS **$$**

(☑ 6513-6597, 6595-6806; camping/cabins US$55/80 per person incl transfer, tour & 3 meals) This clutch of pleasant cabins is one of the best deals around, with prices cut in half for stays longer than one night. Cabins are well spaced for privacy, with options for families or couples. There are spacious new cement bathhouses, volleyball and hammocks. Shady camping is also all-inclusive and well priced. Offers community visits to Río Sidra and snorkeling excursions.

Cabañas Naranjo Chico
CABAÑAS **$$**

(☑ 6686-7437, 6086-7716; www.sanblaskunayala. com; r per person with/without bathroom incl 3 meals, transfer & tours US$110/85) Six cabins offer quiet and a lovely swimming beach. Those with shared bathrooms have sand floors, newer cabins with private bathrooms are set on stilts over the water. All have solar power. The del Valle family are prompt with response times for reservations, which is rare in these parts. Transfers leave the river port near Carti.

Achutupu Dumat
CABAÑAS **$$**

(Wissudub; ☑ 6846-5217; argeliomorales2347@ gmail.com; Chichime Cays; per person camping/dm/private r incl 3 meals & transfer to Carti US$70/80/90) Host Argelio Morales offers shady camping and six thatched cabins with electricity, plus one tour per day. As at other island destinations, trash is building up here – guests are required to pack out their own. Campers are supplied with tents and camping equipment. If you have your own, ask for a discount.

🛍 Shopping

Molas are the most famous of Panamanian traditional handicrafts. Made of brightly colored squares of cotton fabric sewn together, the finished product reveals landscape scenes, birds, sea turtles, fish and beasts – often surrounded by a mazelike geometric pattern. Traditional geometric designs are usually valued more than modern ones. Craftsmanship varies considerably. The simplest are sold for upwards of $10; elaborate designs are works of art valued at several hundred dollars. You can find *molas* on the islands (or, rather, the *mola* sellers will find you).

ℹ Information

Flights are limited, so book as far in advance as possible. You should also reserve your hotels in advance, especially since package deals are the norm in the Comarca. There's no cash machine, so visit an ATM *before* reaching the islands.

From May through November temperatures are generally lower. When there's no breeze and the mercury rises, humidity sets in and life on the San Blás islands can cease to be paradise. During January and February the trade winds arrive.

In the Comarca it helps to have a good command of Spanish as few Guna outside the tourist centers speak English. In fact, many older Guna do not speak Spanish. In more remote areas your guide or boat operator may have to do the talking for you. A few words of Guna will win you friends and favors wherever you go.

The Guna are very particular about what foreigners do on their islands. As a result, tourists must register and pay a visitation fee, between US$3 and US$12 per person, on nearly every island. You're expected to pay regardless of whether you stay for a week or only half an hour. On smaller, privately owned islands, you must seek out the owner, obtain permission to stay and pay a fee of around US$7 per person.

Visitors are expected to pay to take photographs of the Guna people (around US$1 per subject or photo). If you want to take someone's photo, ask his or her permission first. You may not be required to pay for a photograph taken of an artisan from whom you buy crafts, but it depends on the person. Some islands may charge you US$50 just for possessing a video camera.

You must carry your passport to enter the region.

GUNA LIVING 101

Lodging considerations in the Comarca de Guna Yala are vastly different from those on the mainland. Here, a spot in a thatched hut with a sand floor can cost anywhere between US$50 and US$150 per night. So what's the difference?

Often it has more to do with access, ambiance and organization than anything else. Densely populated community islands are more likely to have budget options, but they will not live up to your image of a remote tropical paradise. Resort islands generally have a bigger price tag, but they may not offer many opportunities to interact with locals. When planning, consider why you're going and the following:

Space Does the island have shade? Privacy? Are there pleasant areas to swim or do you have to take a boat to reach swimming and snorkeling sites?

Access Is the island too remote, requiring expensive transfers to do anything?

Hospitality Ask other travelers about their experience.

Water Is it potable? Consider bringing a filter.

Bathrooms Are there modern installations or does the toilet sit at the end of a dock?

Safety Do excursion boats have life vests and good motors?

Lodgings generally include three meals (but not drinks), one outing per day (snorkeling or a community visit, for example) and transportation to or from the airport or Cartí, but do confirm ahead. Fees for drinking water and visits to Guna islands may be separate. It is always wise to bring snacks, insect repellent, a first-aid kit and a flashlight. Rates are generally lower from April to November.

When booking, remember that internet access is not prevalent and any cell-phone number is only good until that phone accidentally falls into the ocean. But approach your hosts with good humor and patience, and they will probably reciprocate in spades.

Getting There & Away

AIR

Air Panama (316-9000; www.airpanama.com) has daily flights to Playón Chico, Ogobsucum and Achutupu. Flights depart from Albrook Airport in Panama City and take 30 minutes to an hour. Ticket prices vary according to season and availability.

Book as far in advance as possible, as demand far exceeds supply. Note that planes may stop at several islands in the archipelago, loading and unloading passengers or cargo before continuing on.

CAR

The El Llano–Cartí road is the only road that leads into the district. It connects the town of El Llano, on the Interamericana 70km east of Panama City, to the San Blás coastal hamlet of Cartí. The road begins near El Llano at the turnoff for Nusagandi.

It's best to take a shared 4WD with a powerful engine, a winch and good tires. Ask your Panama City hostel to arrange transportation. **Tito** (6151-8827), **Kuna Yala Expeditions** (6708-5254; eliasperezmartinez@yahoo.com) and driver **Germain Perez** (6734-3454; www.cartihomestaykunayala.blogspot.com) also provide transfers.

BOAT

Sailboats travel to Colombia via the archipelago, but most board in Colón Province. Lodgings in Panama City have more information about these privately run trips.

The popular new **San Blas Adventures** (www.sanblasadventures.com; per person all-inclusive US$375) four-day service takes backpackers between Cartí and La Miel (the Colombian border), visiting Guna communities, camping on beaches and snorkeling along the way. Fiberglass boats have outboard engines. It's a good alternative to the sailboat crossing, avoiding cramped overnight quarters and rough seas. See the website for useful planning details.

DARIÉN PROVINCE

One of the world's richest biomes is the 5760-sq-km Parque Nacional Darién, where the primeval meets the present with scenery nearly unaltered from one million years ago. Even today in the Darién, the Emberá and Wounaan people maintain many of their traditional practices and retain generations-old knowledge of the rainforest. In a stroke of irony, much of the Darién has remained untouched because of its volatile reputation.

The road to Yaviza – the most accessible part of the province – has scenes of habitat destruction. Cruising the waterways and hiking trails are the only ways to explore the slow-paced interior Darién and the Pacific coast, where Emberá, Wounaan and African-Darienita cultures coexist.

The region's issues are complex. Police checkpoints are frequent because of narco-trafficking. The Darién is not for everyone, but with careful planning and the right destinations, it offers opportunities for intrepid travelers to discover something truly wild.

History

Living within the boundaries of the Darién, the group commonly known as the Chocóes emigrated from Colombia's Chocó region long ago. Anthropologists use two linguistic groups – the Emberá and the Wounaan – though with the exception of language, the groups' cultural features are virtually identical. Both groups prefer to be thought of as two separate peoples.

Before the introduction of guns, the Emberá and Wounaan were experts with the *boroquera* (blowgun), using envenomed darts with lethal toxins from poisonous frogs and bullet ants. Many scholars believe that they forced the Guna out of the Darién and into the Caribbean coastal area they now inhabit.

The Emberá and Wounaan are known for their incredibly fine dugout canoes. Known as *piraguas,* they have shallow bottoms that are ideal for the dry season, when rivers run low. The Panama Canal Authority has long employed Emberá and Wounaan craftsmen to make the *piraguas* that are used by officials to reach the upper parts of the canal's watershed. Until the late 1990s, the US Air Force solicited Emberá and Wounaan help with jungle living. Many of them trained US astronauts and air-force pilots at Fuerte Sherman, near Colón, in tropical-wilderness survival.

Today, the majority of the nearly 10,000 Emberá and Wounaan in Panama live deep in the rainforests of the Darién, particularly along the Ríos Sambú, Jaqué, Chico, Tuquesa, Membrillo, Tuira, Yapé and Tucutí.

☞ Tours

The Darién is the only major part of Panama where a guide is necessary, and one is required in the national park. You can hire Spanish-speaking guides locally for about US\$25 to US\$35 per day. However, transportation costs can be very expensive. Tour operators can take care of all arrangements without a language barrier, teach you about the incredible local ecology, cook for you and humor you when you have blisters. Another option is to go with an independent naturalist guide.

★ **Jungle Treks** ADVENTURE TOUR
(☑ 6438-3130; www.jungletreks.com) Run by a veteran naturalist guide, this recommended outfitter specializes in boutique, expedition-style travel for groups of six or more. Destinations include the interior and Pacific coast. Check the website for set dates. Custom trips have a three-day minimum. Fluent in English.

Ecocircuitos ECOTOUR
(Map p626; ☑ 315-1488; www.ecocircuitos.com; Albrook Plaza, 2nd fl, No 31, Ancón, Panama City) 🍃 A great outfitter offering four-day trips to Parque Nacional Darién with visits to an Emberá community. It's a member of APTSO (Asociación Panameño de Turismo Sostenible), Panama's sustainable-tourism alliance. English is spoken.

Panama Exotic Adventures TOUR
(☑ in Panama City 223-9283; www.panamaexotic adventures.com) With an ecolodge in Metetí and longtime experience in the region, this dedicated French-run operator offers three-to eight-day trips with hands-on visits to indigenous communities, kayaking and outings. Ask about tailor-made trips.

Ancon Expeditions TOUR
(☑ 269-9415; www.anconexpeditions.com) Ancon travels to its own private lodge in Punta Patiño on the Pacific coast and further afield. Special programs for birdwatchers and hikers are excellent.

ℹ️ Information

Information on the Darién rapidly becomes outdated. Always seek updates, ideally from a guide who leads frequent trips to the area.

In Yaviza, the Sede Administrativa Parque Nacional Darién can provide some information on the park and potentially help you find guides (usually rangers with days off). Travelers must register here to visit the park and check in with the police before heading out into the jungle. There are also police checkpoints along the road to Yaviza and at ports.

Panama City's **Instituto Geográfico Nacional** (p638) sells topographical maps for some regions of the Darién.

Darién Province

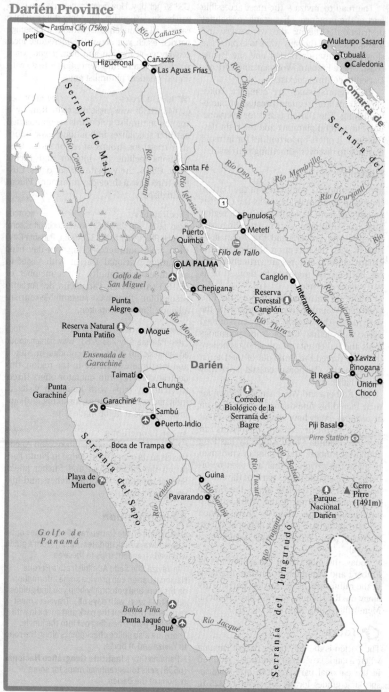

Panama City (75km)
Río Cañazas
Ipetí
Tortí
Higueronal
Cañazas
Las Aguas Frías
Mulatupo Sasardí
Tubualá
Caledonia
Comarca de
Serranía de Majé
Río Congo
Río Chucunaque
Serranía del
Río Cucunatí
Río Iglesias
Santa Fé
Río Oso
Río Membrillo
Río Ucurganti
1
Punulosa
Metetí
Puerto
Quimba
Filo de Tallo
Río
LA PALMA
Canglón
Interamericana
Río Chucunaque
Golfo de
San Miguel
Chepigana
Reserva
Forestal
Canglón
Punta
Alegre
Río Tuira
Reserva Natural
Punta Patiño
Mogué
Río Mogué
Yaviza
Pinogana
Ensenada de
Garachiné
Darién
El Real
Unión
Chocó
Taimatí
La Chunga
Punta
Garachiné
Garachiné
Corredor
Biológico de la
Serranía de
Bagre
Sambú
Piji Basal
Puerto Indio
Pirre Station
Boca de Trampa
Serranía del Sapo
Guina
Río Balsas
Playa de
Muerto
Río Venado
Río Sambú
Pavarando
Río Tucutí
Parque
Nacional
Darién
Cerro
Pirre
(1491m)
Golfo de
Panamá
Río Uruganti
Serranía del Jungurudó
Bahía Piña
Punta Jaqué
Jaqué
Río Jacqué

DANGERS & ANNOYANCES

The greatest hazard in the Darién is the difficult environment. Trails, when they exist at all, are often poorly defined and are never marked. Many large rivers that form the backbone of the Darién transportation network create their own hazards. Any help at all, let alone medical help, is very far away. If you get lost, you are done for. To minimize these risks, it's recommended that you explore the Darién either as part of an organized tour or with the help of a qualified guide.

Dengue and malaria are serious risks. Consult your doctor before you go about necessary medication, and cover up as much as possible, especially at dawn and dusk. Areas of the Parque Nacional Darién are prime territory for the deadly fer-de-lance snake. The chances of getting a snakebite are remote, but do be careful and always wear boots on treks. Although they don't carry Lyme disease, ticks are widespread. Bring tweezers and a few books of matches to ensure you're able to remove the entire tick, if it's burrowed well into your skin.

The US State Department warns travelers against visiting remote areas of the Darién off the Interamericana. This blanket advisory includes the entirety of Parque Nacional Darién, although certain destinations may be OK to visit.

Particularly treacherous, however, are the areas between Boca de Cupe and Colombia, the traditional path through the Darién Gap. As there's only minimal police presence, you're on your own if trouble arises.

Although the no-go zones in the Darién are well removed from the traditional tourist destinations, their dangers cannot be underestimated. Narcotraffickers who utilize these jungle routes don't appreciate encountering travelers. In the past, former Colombian guerrillas or runaways took refuge here. Missionaries and travelers alike have been kidnapped and killed in the southern area of the Darién.

Despite all this, parts of the Darién can be visited safely.

ℹ Getting There & Away

The Interamericana terminates 266km from Panama City in the frontier town of Yaviza, and the vast wilderness region of the Darién lies beyond. The highway starts again 150km further on in Colombia. This break between Central and South America is known as the Darién Gap – literally the end of the road.

There are buses on Sunday, Tuesday and Thursday from Panama City to Yaviza between 3:30am and 7am (US$16, 4½ hours). Be sure to tell the bus driver your destination.

With irregular frequency, **Air Panama** (☎316-9000; www.airpanama.com) has flights to Jaqué and Puerto Obaldía.

ℹ Getting Around

In the vast jungles of Darién Province, rivers are often the only means of travel, with *piraguas* (long canoes; mostly motorized) providing the transportation.

Transportation to interior destinations like El Real and La Palma leaves from Puerto Quimba, near the Interamericana city of Metetí, and Yaviza. In La Palma, you can hire motorized boats to the Río Mogué and the Río Sambú. From El Real, travelers can access Piji Basal or Parque Nacional Darién.

Metetí

Located 1km southeast of a police checkpoint, Metetí is the Darién's fastest-growing locality, with the best infrastructure in the region. The surroundings are being quickly deforested, though interesting ecolodges are found on the outskirts. Travelers come to link to La Palma and interior Darién via a scenic boat ride.

🛏 Sleeping & Eating

Hotel Felicidad HOTEL **$**
(☑ 299-6544; www.hotelfelicidad.com; d US$25; ❄) Bleach-scented with clean cement rooms, friendly service and flowery gardens. Avoid rooms without an outside window as they tend to be musty.

Filo de Tallo LODGE **$$$**
(☑ 6673-5381; www.panamadarien.com; 4-day package per person from US$1050) 🌿 Perched upon a grassy knoll on the outskirts of Metetí, this handsome ecolodge is run by Panama Exotic Adventures. Thatched bamboo huts feature firm beds draped in mosquito netting and attached bathrooms with pastel river stones and handcarved basins. Enjoy wine and good international-Panamanian meals in the open-air living and dining area with a stunning panorama of the region.

Once a shooting range for the Noriega camp, the transformation of this space to ethno-adventure tourism couldn't be stranger. Activities include kayaking and visiting a Wounaan village. While the lodge occupies a deforested sector just on the tip of the Darién, it is one of the best lodgings in the region and provides a good dose of indigenous culture. It is also certified as carbonneutral by Forest Finance. Packages include all meals and activities and transportation to/from Panama City.

ℹ Getting There & Away

From Panama City, buses to Yaviza stop in Metetí (US$15, four hours) on Sunday, Tuesday and Thursday.

For boats to La Palma or Sambú, take the turnoff for Puerto Quimba, a port on the Río Iglesias. A passenger pick-up shuttles between Metetí and Puerto Quimba every 30 minutes from 6am until 9pm (US$2), or take a taxi (US$10). The paved road between Metetí and Puerto Quimba is about 20km long.

From Puerto Quimba, unscheduled boats to La Palma (20 minutes) leave when full between 7:30am and 6:30pm (US$4). A one-way charter may also be an option. Passengers must register at the police checkpoint next to the ticket counter.

Boats also go to Sambú on Monday, Wednesday and Friday (US$24, 2½ hours).

Yaviza

POP 4500

Part bazaar and part bizarre, this concrete village is the end of the road. Here the Interamericana grinds to a halt and beyond lies the famous Darién Gap. Rough edged and misshapen, it's hardly a destination in its own right unless you have cockfighting in mind. For travelers, it is an essential check-in stop for entry to Parque Nacional Darién.

🛏 Sleeping

Hospedaje Sobia Kiru HOTEL **$**
(☑ 299-4409; d US$25; ❄) A two-story turquoise house with clean rooms and blessed air-conditioning, Hospedaje Sobia Kiru is on a side street across from the port, next to the Cable Onda office. Ask for Leticia.

Ya Darien GUESTHOUSE **$**
(☑ 6653-0074; d US$25; ❄) Has tidy rooms with cold-water showers; the help may be slow as molasses, but it works.

ℹ Information

Note that you must write to **SENAFRONT** (Servicio Nacional de Fronteras; ☑ in Panama City 527-1000; www.senafront.gob.pa) in Panama City ahead of time in Spanish with details of your itinerary in order to travel in the area. The office can also suggest local guides.

ℹ Getting There & Away

Buses from Panama City go to Yaviza (US$16, 4½ hours) on Sunday, Tuesday and Thursday.

Public boats to El Real go sporadically when full (US$5). The cost of a private boat charter to

---

ⓘ GETTING TO COLOMBIA

The Interamericana stops at the town of Yaviza and reappears 150km further on, far beyond the Colombian border. Overland crossings through the Darién Gap on foot are not recommended.

The Caribbean crossing between Puerto Obaldía (Panama) and Capurganá (Colombia) has become a better option than in the past. Air Panama flies to Puerto Obaldía. From here, there are no buses. You must boat or walk to the Colombian village of Sapzurro. On foot, this takes about 2½ hours, but the track is indistinct in places, and sporadic regional insecurity makes boating the better option. Just on the border, the Panamanian village of La Miel is building a hostel and features a gorgeous beach (it's 20 minutes on foot from Sapzurro).

From Sapzurro, ferries go to Capurganá; alternatively, it's a two-hour walk. As the security situation constantly changes, it's best to get an update with solid information about the route beforehand.

Sailing or boating to Colombia is by far the safest option after flying.

More of a tour than just transportation, the popular San Blas Adventures (☑ 6696-1554, 6731-2530; http://sanblasadventures.com; 4-day trip US$375) takes backpackers from Panama to Colombia, passing through the San Blás Islands and coastal Darién, camping and snorkeling on the way. On the Panamanian side, the trip starts in Cartí and ends in Sapzurro (Colombia). Travel is on a covered boat with outboard motors. There are regular set departures and the website features useful details for planning.

El Real (US$60 to US$90 one way) depends on motor size and fuel costs.

El Real

Riverside El Real, also known as El Real de Santa María, dates from the conquistador days when it was merely a fort beside Río Tuira. The settlement prevented pirates from sailing upriver to plunder Santa María, where gold from the Cana mines was stored. Today, El Real is one of the largest towns in the Darién, though it's still very much a backwater settlement.

El Real is the last sizable settlement before the national park. Those heading up to Rancho Frío should either hire a local guide or be part of a tour – the Ministerio de Ambiente (p639) will not let you proceed unescorted. Before your arrival, send a letter of intent to SENAFRONT (p688) and contact the Panama City office of the Ministerio de Ambiente to pay the park entry fee (foreigners US$15) and lodging fees.

🛌 Sleeping

Fonda Doña Lola   PANAMANIAN **$**
(meals US$3-5) A cheap eatery serving rice and meat dishes with fried plantains.

ⓘ Getting There & Away

Veteran boatman **Chicho Bristan** (☑ 6913-0321, 299-6566; round-trip for 3 passengers

US$60) offers charter trips between El Real and Yaviza or Puerto Quimba. When your boat arrives at El Real, register with SENAFRONT at the stand in front of the boat landing.

Pick-up trucks transfer passengers to Piji Basal (US$25) and Pirre 1 (US$30), a 1½-hour hike from Rancho Frío, the entry point to Parque Nacional Darién.

Rancho Frío

Thirteen kilometers south of El Real, as the lemon-spectacled tanager flies, is the Rancho Frío sector of Parque Nacional Darién. It's home to Pirre Station (Pirre 2), not be confused with the station at the top of Mt Pirre near Cana. Rare bird species represented here include the crimson-bellied woodpecker, the white-fronted nunbird and the striped woodhaunter. It's a riveting spot for birdwatchers.

The excellent trail network includes a two-day trek to Mt Pirre ridge and a one-hour walk through thick jungle to a series of cascades. Neither should be attempted without a guide as they are unmarked, and if you get lost out here you're finished.

Visitors must write to SENAFRONT (p688) in Panama City in Spanish of their travel intentions in the Darién and carry photocopies of the letter with them. It may be examined at checkpoints. Depending on the security situation, SENAFRONT may require visitors to go with a guide.

SURVIVING THE DARIÉN

Parque Nacional Darién is the most ecologically diverse land-based national park in Central America, but with its serious risks and poisonous snakes, it isn't for all. Yet as a destination it is fascinating and fulfilling – provided you take the necessary precautions and are prepared.

Security

The jungle is an ideal hideout for rogue elements and a transit point for illegal migrants. The Panamanian police take defending this area very seriously and it is unwise to go against their recommendations.

Established routes are recommended both for your safety and for legal reasons. The police have been known to detain those on unauthorized routes and suspect them of illegal activity – even if they are with a guide.

Safety

Solo travel here is not recommended. Since trails are unmarked, it is easy to get lost. No one is likely to come to your aid, but you might come across poisonous snakes and scorpions – who could end your trip (or your time on Earth) unexpectedly.

Preparations

Though it's remote, the Darién is not cheap. Travelers should make a careful budget, noting that even those who loathe taking tours generally do so here. Decide whether going with an independent guide and paying all the fuel and food costs separately will really work out to your advantage – especially since the cost of fuel can be astronomical. Those who contract a local guide should speak Spanish, otherwise the whole endeavor is prone to frustrating misunderstandings. Keep your baggage to a minimum on any jungle trek. Insect repellent, sunblock, a hat and rain gear are essential. Food can only be found in the few towns; it's not available at the ranger stations. Bring some drinking water and a means of purifying water. Visit during the dry season (mid-December through mid-April); otherwise, you'll be slogging your way through thick mud and swatting at moth-size mosquitoes. Engines break, flights are postponed; in

🛏 Sleeping

Barracks CABIN $

(Rancho Frío; per person US$15) At Pirre Station, these barracks have fold-out cots for visitors, a small outdoor dining area beside a very basic kitchen, a *palapa* (open-sided shelter) with a few chairs and a number of flush toilets and cold-water showers. Pay the Ministerio del Medio Ambiente directly in Panama City, if possible.

❶ Getting There & Away

Pirre Station can only be reached by hiking (four hours), or a combination of boating and hiking or 4WD transportation (from US$30) and hiking from El Real or Piji Basal. Transportation only goes as far as Pirre 1, a 1½-hour hike from Rancho Frío. For those hiking, the road offers minimal indications. It is best to go with a guide.

La Palma

POP 4200

The provincial capital of Darién Province, La Palma is a one-street town located where the wide Río Tuira meets the Golfo de San Miguel. Pastel stilt houses lord over the muddy waterfront, a scene abuzz with commerce, bars and evangelist messages.

Most travelers pass through La Palma to take a boat ride to somewhere else, like the Ancon nature reserve and lodge at Reserva Natural Punta Patiño or the Emberá villages lining the banks of the Río Sambú. If you have time, check out the ruins of 17th-century Spanish forts, five minutes away by boat (US$30).

Every facility of interest to the traveler is located on the main street, which is within 300m of the airstrip. There's a bank, a hospital and a police station as well as three hotels, three bars and several food stands. Those who intend to go further inland should talk to the police here first.

🛏 Sleeping & Eating

Hotel Biaquira Bagara HOTEL $

(☑ 299-6224; d with/without bathroom US$25/17; ❄ 🛜) Simple and sweet, Hotel Biaquira Bagara has hardwood decks, wicker furniture and firm beds.

short, travel delays are about as common as raindrops in the Darién. Go with extra food and cash, a flashlight, matches, good personal equipment and flexibility in your schedule.

Guides

Guides are now required for the Parque Nacional Darién. A naturalist guide will have a different skill set from that of a *guía local* (local or community guide). Consider your needs and criteria.

The following are essential attributes in a guide:

➡ Experience in the area

➡ Extensive local contacts and problem-solving skills

➡ A planned itinerary with realistic travel times and contracted transportation

➡ Good equipment (tents etc) if you do not have your own

➡ Any necessary permits

The following are desirable attributes:

➡ Skill at spotting animals

➡ Knowledge of local history, animals and plants

➡ Knowledge of English (or another language)

➡ First-aid kit and skills

➡ Handheld radio and/or cell phone for areas with coverage

Fellow travelers can provide guide references, but it is important to meet your guide beforehand – particularly if you're traveling solo.

Find out ahead of time if gas, transportation, food and fees are included. Don't assume that a local guide is experienced – some have sold trips despite never having set foot in the national park. The **Sede Administrativa Parque Nacional Darién** (☎299-4495; Interamericana, Ministerio de Ambiente bldg; park entry US$15; ⊗8am-4pm Mon-Fri) keeps a list of community guides.

★**Restaurante Lola** PANAMANIAN **$**
(☎6721-8632; mains US$5-15; ⊗7am-7pm Mon-Sat) A clean and cheerful cafe serving shrimp or fish *criollo*-style (with a flavorful sauce) in addition to grilled meats.

❶ Getting There & Away

Boats to Puerto Quimba (US$4, 20 minutes) leave when full, running between 5:30am and 5pm. Puerto Quimba has buses to Metetí, where other buses go to Panama City or Yaviza.

To charter a private boat and a guide, look in the vicinity of the dock for a responsible captain with a seaworthy motorboat (US$120 to US$300 per day, gas included).

Reserva Natural Punta Patiño

On the southern shore of the Golfo de San Miguel, 25km from La Palma, is this private 263-sq-km **wildlife preserve** owned by Ancon and managed by the organization's for-

profit arm, Ancon Expeditions. It contains species-rich primary and secondary forest, and is one of the best places in Panama to spot harpy eagles. Even if the big bird doesn't show, there's a good chance of seeing everything from three-toed sloths to capybaras, the world's largest rodent.

The only way to reach the preserve is by boat or plane. Landing on the tiny strip of ocean-side grass that's called a runway in these parts is definitely part of the experience.

❶ Getting There & Away

The Ancon Expeditions tour includes the round-trip airfare between Panama City and Punta Patiño, lodging, food and activities. This can also be combined with a trip up the Río Mogué to the Emberá village of Mogué and a guided hike to a harpy eagle's nest. Punta Patiño is also a destination on Ancon's highly recommended two-week Darién Explorer Trek.

Independent travelers can hire boats in La Palma to reach Punta Patiño. Notify Ancon Expeditions in advance to reserve a cabin.

Sambú

Riverside Sambú is an interesting stop, populated by Emberá and *cimarrón* people (the ancestors of the latter escaped the slave trade by living in the jungle). Urban by Darién standards, it has an airstrip, a hospital and a pay phone. Given the ease of flying in here, it makes a good launching point for visiting riverside Emberá and Wounaan communities and absorbing the slow jungle pace.

From Sambú, visitors can plan enjoyable trips to Puerto Indio (with permission from the Emberá and Wounaan) and visit petroglyphs or mangrove forests. Bocaca Verano is a lagoon with crocodiles and prolific birdlife. Local guide Lupicinio, found in front of Sambú Hause hotel, guides hiking excursions to see harpy eagles and tours to Bocaca Verano in the dry season.

For boat tours, Juan Murillo (☑6940-7765; gulf fishing US$90) takes visitors fishing in the Golfo de San Miguel in his 75HP boat.

🛏 Sleeping & Eating

Mi Lindo Sueño HOTEL $
(☑333-2512; r without bathroom US$15) A perfectly acceptable option, sitting alongside the airstrip. Rooms have fans. Note that the phone number is that of a public phone outside the hotel.

Sambú Hause GUESTHOUSE $$
(☑6672-9452, 268-6905; www.sambuhausedarien panama.com; s/d incl meals US$75/125) The only jungle B&B around, Sambú House is a North American–owned, attractive yellow clapboard run by friendly Mabel. Cozy but simple, this might be the only place to get pancake breakfasts in the Darién. You can also arrange cultural tours here.

Comidas Benedicta PANAMANIAN $
(meals US$4) You can get cheap and tasty meals at Comidas Benedicta, where Anthony Bourdain dined when in Sambú.

❶ Getting There & Away

At the time of writing, there were only charter flights to Sambú. A *panga* (small motorboat) from Puerto Quimba (US$24) goes to Sambú in the early morning on Monday, Wednesday and Friday, with one stop in La Palma.

Return trips are not scheduled far in advance; ask around to confirm a date. From Puerto Quimba there is a bus service to Metetí (US$2) and on to Panama City.

UNDERSTAND PANAMA

Panama Today

The fastest-growing economy in Latin America, Panama owes much of its prosperity to the Panama Canal. The 80km belt of locks links the Atlantic to the Pacific, and east with west.

A canal expansion was due to open in mid-2016 on the heels of the canal's 100-year anniversary – slightly behind schedule and way over budget. The expanded canal is expected to shift trade patterns, upsetting the prosperity of North American west-coast ports.

Detractors fear that the project – along with the tab for the new US$1.2 billion Panama City subway system, the US$200 billion beltway in Bahía de Panamá, a new international airport and other projects – will shackle Panama with serious debt.

While poverty has reduced by 10% in the last decade, Panama still has the second-worst income distribution in Latin America. Hopes are high that the country's investments in infrastructure will pay off. But with US$23 billion of national debt, many Panamanians are weary of the national spend now, pay later approach. More and more, disgruntled citizens have been protesting about the privatization of public resources, high-level corruption and unchecked development. For Panama, it's time to put the people first.

History

The waistline of the Americas, Panama has played a strategic role in the history of the Western Hemisphere, from hosting the biological exchange of species to witnessing clashes between cultures. Once an overland trade route linking ancient Peru and Mexico, post–Colombian conquest Panama became the conduit for exported Inca treasures. Set amid two oceans, transit is a longtime theme here. As the Panama Railroad once brought prospectors to the California gold rush, the Panama Canal has become the roaring engine of global commerce.

Lost Panama

The coastlines and rainforests of Panama have been inhabited by humans for at least 10,000 years. Indigenous groups including the Guna, the Ngöbe-Buglé, the Emberá, the Wounaan, the Bribrí and the Naso were living on the isthmus prior to the Spanish arrival. However, the historical tragedy of Panama is that despite its rich cultural history, there are virtually no physical remains of these great civilizations.

What is known about pre-Columbian Panama is that early inhabitants were part of an extensive trading zone that extended as far south as Peru and as far north as Mexico. Archaeologists have uncovered exquisite gold ornaments and unusual life-size stone statues of human figures as well as distinctive types of pottery and metates (stone platforms that were used for grinding corn).

Panama's first peoples lived beside both oceans and fished in mangrove swamps, estuaries and coral reefs. It seems only fitting that the country's name is derived from an indigenous word meaning 'abundance of fish.'

New World Order

In 1501 the discovery of Panama by Spanish explorer Rodrigo de Bastidas marked the beginning of the age of conquest and colonization in the isthmus. However, it was his first mate, Vasco Núñez de Balboa, who earned lasting fame following his discovery of the Pacific Ocean 12 years later.

On his fourth and final voyage to the New World in 1502, Christopher Columbus saw 'more gold in two days than in four years in Spain' in present-day Costa Rica. Although his attempts to establish a colony at the mouth of the Río Belén failed due to fierce local resistance, Columbus petitioned the Spanish Crown to have himself appointed as governor of Veraguas, the stretch of shoreline from Honduras to Panama.

Following Columbus' death in 1506, King Ferdinand appointed Diego de Nicuesa to settle the newly claimed land. These various attempts would miserably fail. Much to the disappointment of conquistadors, Panama was not rich in gold. Add tropical diseases, inhospitable terrain and less than welcoming natives, and it's easy to see why early Spanish colonies struggled and often failed.

In 1513, Balboa heard rumors about a large sea and a wealthy, gold-producing civilization across the mountains – likely the Inca Empire of Peru. Driven by ambition, Balboa scaled the continental divide and on September 26, 1513, became the first European to set eyes on the Pacific Ocean. He claimed the ocean and all the lands it touched for the king of Spain.

The Empire Expands

In 1519 a cruel and vindictive Spaniard named Pedro Arias de Ávila (called Pedrarias by contemporaries) founded the city of Panamá on the Pacific, near present-day Panama City. The governor ordered the beheading of Balboa in 1517 on a trumped-up charge of treason. He is also remembered for murderous attacks against the indigenous population, whom he roasted alive or fed to dogs.

Pedrarias nonetheless established Panamá as an important Spanish settlement, a commercial center and a base for further explorations, including the conquest of Peru. From Panamá, vast riches of Peruvian gold and Oriental spices were transported across the isthmus by foot. This famous trade route, known as the Sendero Las Cruces (Las Cruces Trail), can still be walked.

As the Spaniards grew plump on the wealth of plundered civilizations, the world began to notice the prospering colony, especially the English privateers lurking in coastal waters. In 1573 Sir Francis Drake destroyed the Nombre de Dios settlement and set sail for England with a galleon laden with Spanish gold.

The Spanish responded by building large stone fortresses at San Lorenzo and Portobelo. Still, Welsh buccaneer Sir Henry Morgan overpowered Fuerte San Lorenzo and sailed up the Río Chagres in 1671. After crossing the isthmus, Morgan destroyed the city of Panamá, burning it to the ground to return to the Caribbean coast with 200 mules loaded with Spanish loot.

The Spanish rebuilt the city a few years later on a cape several kilometers west of its original site. The ruins of the old settlement, now known as Panamá Viejo, and the colonial city of Casco Viejo are within the city limits of the present-day metropolis.

British privateering continued. After Admiral Edward Vernon destroyed the fortress of Portobelo in 1739, the Spanish abandoned the Panamanian crossing in favor of sailing the long way around Cape Horn to the west coast of South America.

The End of Empire

Spain's costly Peninsular War with France from 1808 to 1814 – and the political turmoil, unrest and power vacuums that the conflict caused – led Spain to lose all its colonial possessions in the first third of the 19th century.

Panama gained independence from Spanish rule in 1821 and immediately joined Gran Colombia, a confederation of Colombia, Bolivia, Ecuador, Peru and Venezuela – a united Latin American nation that had long been the dream of Simón Bolívar. However, internal disputes led to the formal abolition of Gran Colombia in 1831, though fledgling Panama retained its status as a province of Colombia.

Birth of a Nation

Panama's future forever changed when world powers caught on that the isthmus was the narrowest point between the Atlantic and Pacific Oceans. In 1846 Colombia signed a treaty permitting the USA to construct a railway across the isthmus, granting free transit and the right to protect the railway with military force. At the height of the California gold rush in 1849, tens of thousands traveled from the USA's east coast to the west coast via Panama in order to avoid hostile tribes in the central states. Colombia and Panama grew wealthy from the railway, and the first talks of a canal across Central America began to surface.

The idea of a canal across the isthmus was first raised in 1524 when King Charles V of Spain ordered a survey to determine the feasibility of a waterway. Later, Emperor Napoleon III of France also considered the idea. Finally, in 1878, French builder Ferdinand de Lesseps, basking in the glory of the recently constructed Suez canal, was contracted by Colombia to build the canal, bringing his crew to Panama in 1881. Much like Napoleon, Lesseps severely underestimated the task, and over 22,000 workers died from yellow fever and malaria in less than a decade. In 1889 insurmountable construction problems and financial mismanagement drove the company bankrupt.

The USA saw the French failure as a business opportunity. In 1903 Philippe Bunau-Varilla, one of Lesseps' chief engineers, agreed to sell concessions to the USA, though the Colombian government refused. Bunau-Varilla approached the US government to back Panama if it declared independence from Colombia.

On November 3, 1903, a revolutionary junta declared Panama independent, and the US government immediately recognized its sovereignty – the first of a series of American interventions. Although Colombia sent troops by sea to try to regain control, US battleships prevented them from reaching land. Colombia only recognized Panama as a legitimately separate nation in 1921, when the US compensated Colombia with US$25 million.

The USA & the Canal

Following independence, Bunau-Varilla was appointed Panamanian ambassador to the USA, with his first act of office paving the way for future American interventions. Hoping to profit from the sale of canal concessions to the USA, Bunau-Varilla arrived in Washington, DC, before Panama could assemble a delegation. On November 18, 1903, Bunau-Varilla and US Secretary of State John Hay signed the Hay-Bunau-Varilla Treaty, which gave the USA far more than had been offered in the original treaty. In addition to owning concessions to the canal, the USA was also granted 'sovereign rights in perpetuity over the Canal Zone,' an area extending 8km on either side of the canal, and a broad right of intervention in Panamanian affairs.

Despite opposition from the tardy Panamanian delegation as well as lingering questions about its legality, the treaty was ratified, ushering in an era of friction between the USA and Panama. Construction began again on the canal in 1904 and despite disease, landslides and harsh weather, the world's greatest engineering marvel was completed within a decade. The first ship sailed through the canal on August 15, 1914.

In the following years, the US military repeatedly intervened in political affairs. In response to growing Panamanian disenchantment, the Hay-Bunau-Varilla Treaty was replaced in 1936 by the Hull-Alfaro Treaty. The USA relinquished its rights to use its troops outside the Canal Zone and to seize land for canal purposes, and the annual sum paid to Panama for use of the Canal Zone was raised. However, a wave of Panamanian opposition to US occupation grew. Tensions reached a boiling point in 1964 during a student protest that left 27 Panamanians dead and 500 injured. Today, the event is commemorated as Día de Los Mártires (National Martyrs' Day).

As US influence waned, the Panamanian army grew more powerful. In 1968 the Guardia Nacional deposed the elected president and took control of the government. Soon after, the constitution was suspended, the national assembly was dissolved, the press censored and the Guardia's General Omar Torrijos Herrera emerged as the new leader. Though he plunged Panama into debt with a massive public works program, Torrijos did convince US president Jimmy Carter to cede control of the canal. The resulting Torrijos-Carter Treaty guaranteed full Panamanian control of the canal as of December 31, 1999, as well as a complete withdrawal of US military forces.

The Rise & Fall of Noriega

Still feeling triumphant from the recently signed treaty, Panama was unprepared for the sudden death of Torrijos in a plane crash in 1981. Two years later, Colonel Manuel Antonio Noriega seized the Guardia Nacional, promoted himself to general and made himself the de facto ruler of Panama. Noriega, a former head of Panama's secret police, a former CIA operative and a graduate of the School of the Americas, quickly began to consolidate his power. He enlarged the Guardia Nacional, significantly expanded its authority and renamed it the Panama Defense Forces. He also created a paramilitary 'Dignity Battalion' in every city, town and village, its members armed and ready to inform on any of their neighbors showing less than complete loyalty to the Noriega regime.

Things went from bad to worse in early 1987 when Noriega was publicly accused of involvement in drug trafficking with Colombian drug cartels, murdering his opponents and rigging elections. Many Panamanians demanded Noriega's dismissal, protesting with general strikes and street demonstrations that resulted in violent clashes with the Panama Defense Forces. In February 1988, Panamanian President Eric Arturo Delvalle attempted to dismiss Noriega, but was forced to flee Panama. Noriega subsequently appointed a president more sympathetic to his cause.

Noriega's regime became an international embarrassment. In March 1988, the USA imposed economic sanctions against Panama, ending a preferential trade agreement, freezing Panamanian assets in US banks and refusing to pay canal fees. A few days after the sanctions were imposed, an unsuccessful military coup prompted Noriega to step up violent repression of his critics. After Noriega's candidate lost the presidential election in May 1989, the general declared the election null and void. Meanwhile, Guillermo Endara, the winning candidate, and his two vice-presidential running mates, were badly beaten by Noriega's thugs, with the entire bloody scene captured by a TV crew and broadcasted internationally. A second failed coup in October 1989 was followed by even more repressive measures.

On December 15, 1989, Noriega's legislature declared him president, and his first official act of office was to declare war on the USA. The following day an unarmed US marine dressed in civilian clothes was killed by Panamanian soldiers while leaving a restaurant in Panama City.

The US reaction was swift and unrelenting. In the first hour of December 20, 1989, Panama City was attacked by aircraft, tanks and 26,000 US troops. The invasion, intended to bring Noriega to justice and create a democracy better suited to US interests, left more than 2000 civilians dead, tens of thousands homeless and destroyed entire tracts of Panama City.

On Christmas Day, Noriega sought asylum in the Vatican embassy. US forces surrounded the embassy and pressured the Vatican to release him. They bombarded the embassy with blaring rock music. Mobs of angry Panamanians surrounded the embassy, calling for Noriega to be ousted.

After 10 days of psychological warfare, the Vatican embassy persuaded Noriega to give himself up by threatening to cancel his asylum. Noriega surrendered to US forces on January 3, and was flown to Miami where he was convicted of conspiracy to manufacture and distribute cocaine.

After his US prison sentence ended in 2007 he was extradited to Paris in April 2010. A retrial found Noriega guilty and sentenced him to seven years in prison, but he was conditionally released in order to serve 20 years in Panama, starting in December 2011, where he is incarcerated today.

Modern Struggles

After Noriega's forced removal, Guillermo Endara, the legitimate winner of the 1989 election, was sworn in as president, and Panama attempted to put itself back together. The country's image and economy were in shambles, and its capital had suffered damage from both the invasion and the widespread looting that followed. Unfortunately, Endara proved to be an ineffective leader whose policies cut jobs and cost his administration its early popularity. He was voted out of office in 1994 with single-digit approval ratings.

In the 1994 election, the fairest in recent Panamanian history, Ernesto Pérez Balladares became president. Under his direction, the Panamanian government implemented a program of privatization that focused on infrastructure improvements, health care

PANAMA UNDERSTAND PANAMA

and education. Although Pérez Balladares allocated unprecedented levels of funding, he was viewed as corrupt. In the spring of 1999, voters rejected his attempt to change constitutional limits barring a president from serving two consecutive terms.

In 1999 Mireya Moscoso, the widow of popular former president Arnulfo Arias, and Panama's first female leader and head of the conservative Arnulfista Party (PA), took office. Moscoso's ambitious plans never materialized. As Panama celebrated its centenary in 2003, unemployment reached 18%. Moscoso was accused of wasteful spending – as parts of the country went without food, she paid US$10 million to bring the Miss Universe pageant to Panama. She was also accused of looking the other way during Colombian military incursions into the Darién.

Martín Torrijos, a member of the Revolutionary Democratic Party (PRD) and the son of former leader Omar Torrijos, took over in 2004. Although there is still debate regarding the success of his administration, he did implement much-needed fiscal reforms, including an overhaul of the nation's social security system. Furthermore, his proposal to expand the Panama Canal was overwhelmingly approved in a national referendum on October 22, 2006.

Current Climate

On May 3, 2009, Panama bucked the Latin American leftist trend by electing conservative supermarket magnate Ricardo Martinelli president. Part of the conservative Democratic Change (CD) party, Martinelli was a pro-business choice who created an investment boom by slashing trade barriers and red tape. During his tenure, ambitious public projects like Central America's first subway system became the order of the day and Panama's 8% growth rate sparkled as the best in Latin America.

Eventually the honeymoon ended and the success story turned part pulp fiction, part political thriller. Martinelli's former vice president and dark-horse opposition leader Juan Carlos Varela was elected president in 2014 on promises to play by the book and implement constitutional checks and balances. Martinelli faces charges of corruption in a US$45 million program to feed poor schoolchildren. There was also a wire-tapping scandal involving political foes. Remember those colossal infrastructure projects? Now US$1.2 billion of contracts have come under scrutiny

and some project directors with government contracts have been arrested. Martinelli maintains his innocence from Miami, where he fled via private jet to a luxury condo that was made famous in the film *Scarface*.

In Panama, the future remains uncertain, but it is very unlikely to be dull.

Culture

The National Psyche

Panamanian identity is in many ways elusive. Perhaps it's only natural given the many years that Panama has been the object of another country's meddling. From the US-backed independence of 1903 to the strong-armed removal of Noriega in 1989 – with half-a-dozen other interventions in between – the USA has left a strong legacy in the country.

Nearly every Panamanian has a relative or at least an acquaintance living in the USA, and parts of the country seem swept up in mall fever, with architectural inspiration straight out of North America. Panamanians (or at least the ones who can afford to) deck themselves out in US clothes, buy US-made cars and take their fashion tips straight from Madison Ave.

Others are quite reticent to embrace the culture from the north. Indigenous groups like the Emberá and Guna struggle to keep their traditions alive as more and more of their youth are lured into the Western lifestyles of the city. On the Península de Azuero, where there is a rich Spanish cultural heritage exemplified by traditional festivals, dress and customs, villagers raise the same concerns about the future of their youth.

Given the clash between old and new, it's surprising the country isn't suffering from a serious case of cognitive dissonance. However, the exceptionally tolerant Panamanian character weathers many contradictions – the old and the new, the grave disparity between rich and poor, and the stunning natural environment and its rapid destruction.

Much of the famous Panamanian tolerance begins in the family, which is the cornerstone of society and plays a role in nearly every aspect of a person's life. Whether among Guna sisters or Panama City's elite, everyone looks after each other. Favors are graciously accepted, promptly returned and never forgotten.

This mutual concern extends from the family into the community, and at times the whole country can seem like one giant extend-

PANAMA UNDERSTAND PANAMA

ed community. In the political arena, the same names appear time and again, as nepotism is the norm rather than the exception. Unfortunately, this goes hand-in-hand with Panama's most persistent problem: corruption.

Panamanians view their leaders' fiscal and moral transgressions with disgust, and they are far from being in the dark about issues. Yet they accept things with patience and an almost fatalistic attitude. Outsiders sometimes view this as a kind of passivity, but it's all just another aspect of the complicated Panamanian psyche.

Lifestyle

In spite of the skyscrapers and gleaming restaurants lining the wealthier districts of Panama City, nearly a third of the country's population lives in poverty. Furthermore, almost a quarter of a million Panamanians struggle just to satisfy their basic dietary needs. The poorest tend to live in the least populated provinces: Darién, Bocas del Toro, Veraguas, Los Santos and Colón. There is also substantial poverty in the slums of Panama City, where an estimated 20% of the urban population lives. Countrywide, 9% of the population lives in *barriados* (squatter) settlements.

For *campesinos* (farmers), life is hard. A subsistence farmer in the interior might earn as little as US$8 per day, far below the national average of US$12,000 per capita. In the Emberá and Wounaan villages of Darién, traditional living patterns persist much as they have for hundreds of years. Thatched hut communities survive on subsistence agriculture, hunting, fishing and pastoralism. The life expectancy in these frontier villages is about 10 years below the national average. The majority of the Emberá and Wounaan communities lack access to clean water and basic sanitation.

The middle and upper class largely reside in and around Panama City with a level of comfort similar to their counterparts in Europe and the USA. They live in large homes or apartments, have a maid, a car or two, and for the lucky few a second home on the beach or in the mountains. Cell phones are de rigueur. Vacations are often enjoyed in Europe or the USA. Most middle-class adults can speak some English and their children usually attend English-speaking schools.

People

The majority of Panamanians (65%) are *mestizo*, which is generally a mix of indigenous and Spanish descent. In truth, many non-black immigrants are also thrown into this category, including a sizable Chinese population – some people estimate that as much as 10% of the population is of Chinese ancestry. There are several other large groups: about 9% of Panamanians are of African descent, 7% of European descent, 7% of mixed African and Spanish descent, and 12% are indigenous. Generally, black Panamanians are mostly descendants of English-speaking West Indians, such as Jamaicans and Trinidadians, who were originally brought to Panama as laborers.

Of the several dozen native tribes that inhabited Panama when the Spanish arrived, few remain. The Guna live on islands along the Caribbean coast in the autonomous region of the Comarca de Guna Yala. Considered the most politically organized, they regularly send representatives to the national legislature. The Emberá and Wounaan inhabit the eastern Panamá province and the Darién; Panama's largest tribe, the Ngöbe-Buglé live in the provinces of Chiriquí, Veraguas and Bocas del Toro. The Teribe inhabit Bocas del Toro Province, while the Bribrí are found along the Talamanca Reserve. Despite modernizing influences, each of Panama's indigenous groups maintains its own language and culture.

Religion

Religion in Panama can best be observed by walking the streets of the capital. Among the scores of Catholic churches, you'll find breezy Anglican churches filled with worshippers from the West Indies, synagogues, mosques, a shiny Greek Orthodox church, an impressive Hindu temple and a surreal Baha'i House of Worship (the headquarters for Latin America).

Freedom of religion is constitutionally guaranteed in Panama, although the preeminence of Roman Catholicism is also officially recognized, with 85% of the population describing themselves as Catholic. Schoolchildren have the option to study theology, though it is not compulsory. Protestant denominations account for 12% of the population, Muslims 4.4% and Baha'i 1.2%. Approximately 3000 Jews (many of them recent immigrants from Israel), 24,000 Buddhists and 9000 Hindus also live in Panama.

The various indigenous tribes of Panama have their own belief systems, although these are fading quickly due to the influence of Christian missionaries. As in other parts of Latin America, the evangelical movement is spreading like wildfire.

698

Although Catholics are the majority, only about 20% of them attend church regularly. The religious orders aren't particularly strong in Panama either – only about 25% of Catholic clergy are Panamanian, while the rest are foreign missionaries.

Arts

Panama's all-embracing music scene includes salsa, Latin and American jazz, traditional music from the central provinces, reggae, reggaetón and Latin, British and American rock 'n' roll. Their biggest export is world-renowned salsa singer Rubén Blades, who even ran for president in 1994, finishing third. The jazz composer and pianist Danilo Pérez is widely acclaimed by critics, while Los Rabanes produces classic Panamanian rock. Heavy on the accordion, Panamanian folk music (called *típico*), is well represented by Dorindo Cárdenas, the late Victorio Vergara (whose band lives on as Nenito Vargas y los Plumas Negras) and the popular brother-sister pair of Samy and Sandra Sandoval. These days reggaetón (also known as *punta*) permeates all social levels in Panama. Key artists include Danger Man, who died in gang violence; balladeer Eddie Lover; and the artist known as Flex, who has also been very successful in Mexico.

Several of Panama's best novels were written mid-20th century. *El Ahogado* (The Drowned Man), a 1937 novel by Tristán Solarte, blends elements of the detective, gothic and psychological genres with a famous local myth. *El Desván* (In the Garret), a 1954 novel by Ramón H Jurado, explores the emotional limits of the human condition. *Gamboa Road Gang*, by Joaquín Beleño, is about the political and social events surrounding the Panama Canal. Today's notable authors include poet and novelist Giovanna Benedetti, historical novelist Gloria Guardia and folk novelist Rosa María Britton.

North American novelist Cristina Henríquez, who is half-Panamanian, offers insight into Panamanian identity from a sometimes displaced point of view. Her 2010 novel *The World in Half* was followed in 2014 by *The Book of Unknown Americans,* a love story that weaves in the experiences of diverse Latin immigrants to the United States.

The first prominent figure on Panama's art scene, French-trained Roberto Lewis (1874–1949) painted allegorical images in public buildings; look for those in the Palacio de las Garzas in Panama City. In 1913 Lewis became the director of Panama's first art academy, where he and his successor, Humberto Ivaldi (1909–47), educated a generation of artists. Among the school's students were Juan Manuel Cedeño and Isaac Benítez, and mid-20th-century painters Alfredo Sinclair, Guillermo Trujillo and Eudoro Silvera. More recent artists of note include Olga Sinclair and Brooke Alfaro.

Sports

Owing to the legacy of US occupation, baseball is the national pastime. Although Panama has no professional teams, amateur leagues play in stadiums throughout the country. In the US major leagues, Mariano Rivera, the record-setting pitcher for the New York Yankees, is a national hero. The batting champ Rod Carew, another Panamanian star, was inducted into the Hall of Fame in 1991. Former NY Yankee Roberto Kelly is also fondly remembered.

Boxing is another popular spectator sport, and a source of local pride since Panama City native Roberto Durán won the world championship lightweight title in 1972. A legend, he went on to become the world champion in each of the welterweight (1980), light middleweight (1983) and super middleweight (1989) categories. Currently, Panama also has three reigning world boxing champions.

Panama's first Olympic gold came in 2008 when Irving Saladino won the long jump in Beijing.

Landscape & Wildlife

The Land

Panama is both the narrowest and the southernmost country in Central America. The long S-shaped isthmus borders Costa Rica in the west and Colombia in the east. Its northern Caribbean coastline measures 1160km, compared to a 1690km Pacific coastline in the south, and its total land area is 74,340 sq km. By comparison, Panama is slightly bigger than Ireland or Austria.

The Panama Canal, which is about 80km long, effectively divides the country into eastern and western regions. Two mountain ranges run along Panama's spine in both the east and the west. The highest point in the country, Chiriquí's Volcán Barú, is also the country's only volcano.

PANAMA UNDERSTAND PANAMA

Like all Central American countries, Panama has large, flat coastal lowlands, with huge banana plantations. There are about 480 rivers in Panama and 1518 islands near its shores. The two main island groups are the San Blás and Bocas del Toro Archipelagos on the Caribbean side, but most of the islands are on the Pacific side.

Wildlife

Panama's position as a narrow land bridge between two huge continents has given it a remarkable variety of plant and animal life. Species migrating between the continents have gathered in Panama, which means that it's possible to see South American armadillos, anteaters and sloths alongside North American tapirs, jaguars and deer. With its wide variety of native and migratory species, Panama is one of the world's best places for birdwatchers.

Panama has more than 978 recorded bird species and more than 10,000 plant species, in addition to 125 animal species found only here. The country's 105 rare and endangered species include scarlet macaws, harpy eagles (the national bird of Panama), golden frogs, jaguars and various species of sea turtle. Panama is one of the best places to see a quetzal. Five species of sea turtle can be seen here, while among the primates there are capuchins, tamarins and squirrel, spider and howler monkeys.

Tropical rainforest is the dominant vegetation in the canal area, along the Caribbean coast and in most of the eastern half of the country. The Parque Nacional Darién protects much of Panama's largest tropical rainforest region. Other vegetation zones include Pacific coast grasslands, highland mountain forest, cloud forest on the highest peaks and mangrove forest on both coasts.

National Parks & Reserves

Panama has 16 national parks and more than two dozen officially protected areas. About a third of Panama is set aside for conservation, while about 40% of land remains covered by forest. Panama also has more land set aside for habitat protection than any other Central American country, and its forests contain the greatest number of species of all New World countries north of Colombia. Yet all of these statistics do not account for the fact that protected lands are, in fact, often poorly protected.

In many of the national parks and protected areas, mestizo and indigenous villages are scattered about. In some scenarios, these communities help protect and maintain parks and wildlife. Headquartered in Panama City, the Ministerio de Ambiente (www.miambiente.gob.pa), Panama's Ministry of the Environment, runs the nation's parks. To enter a national park, travelers must pay US$5 (US$20 if it's a national marine park) at a regional office or ranger station in the park being visited. Permits to camp or stay at a ranger station (US$5 to US$10) can generally be obtained in these places as well.

PANAMA UNDERSTAND PANAMA

PANAMA'S NATIONAL PARKS & RESERVES

A few highlights include the following:

Parque Internacional La Amistad (International Friendship Park; entry US$5, campsites US$10; ⊙8am-4pm) Home to several indigenous groups, pristine rainforest and abundant wildlife.

Parque Nacional Darién (p691) Unesco World Heritage Site with 5760 sq km of world-class wildlife-rich rainforest.

Parque Nacional Isla de Coiba (p653) Includes the 493-sq-km Isla de Coiba, regarded by scientists as a biodiversity hot spot.

Parque Nacional Marino Golfo de Chiriquí (p656) Protects 25 islands and numerous coral reefs.

Parque Nacional Marino Isla Bastimentos (p674) An important nature reserve for many species of Caribbean wildlife, including sea turtles.

Parque Nacional Soberanía (p643) A bird-watcher's paradise in lush rainforest.

Parque Nacional Volcán Barú (p662) Surrounds Panama's only volcano and highest peak, 3475m Volcán Barú.

Parque Natural Metropolitano (p629) Tropical semi-deciduous forest in the city limits.

Environmental Issues

Unfortunately, deforestation is one of the country's gravest environmental problems. Additionally, with Panama's national parks grossly understaffed, illegal hunting, settling and logging take place even inside parks.

Another major concern is mining. Roughly 26% of Panama is mined or under mining concessions, bringing concerns of contaminated water sources, and the destruction of forest and human habitats. In spite of objections by prominent environmental groups, the government has approved and expedited large-scale mining projects, most notably a US$6.2 billion project – an investment greater than the initial expansion of the Panama Canal – to extract gold and copper.

A major victory for community interests was the 2012 passing of law 415, which prohibits extraction in indigenous territories and requires their approval for hydroelectric projects. The change came after a shutdown of Ngöbe-Buglé community protests in February 2012 left two protesters dead.

SURVIVAL GUIDE

ℹ Directory A–Z

ACCOMMODATIONS

Book lodgings two to six months ahead during super-peak times such as the week preceding Easter, the November festivals and the weeks surrounding Christmas and New Year. More popular hostels and small hotels usually require reservations in high season.

Hotels Abound in midrange and high-end categories.

B&Bs A midrange phenomenon most common in the capital, Boquete and Bocas.

Hostels Cheap and spreading in Panama, ranging from quiet digs to party central.

Lodges Running the gamut from rustic to high end, these are good places to commune with nature, mostly in the highlands.

ACTIVITIES

Bird-Watching

With more than 900 bird species in Panama, all you need to do to spot feathered friends is get a good pair of binoculars and hit the trails. Two popular spots include Pipeline Rd in Parque Nacional Soberanía and Burbayar Lodge in Panamá Province. **Panama Audubon Society** (ℐ 232-5977; www.audubonpanama.org), located in Panama City, organizes the annual Christmas bird count on Pipeline Rd, and runs birdwatching expeditions throughout the country.

Diving & Snorkeling

Panama's underwater world spans two great oceans, and abounds with colorful coral gardens, towering rock shelves, sunken wrecks and a rich diversity of marine life. Fans of multicolored reef fish and bathtub-warm water should head for the Caribbean, while more advanced divers in search of enormous pelagic animals and remote dive sites should head to the Pacific. Three major spots in Panama that have a deserved reputation for fine scuba diving are the Archipiélago de Bocas del Toro, the Caribbean town of Portobelo and the Pacific-coast Isla de Coiba.

The Guna prohibit dive operators from working in the Comarca de Guna Yala, but the snorkeling is some of the best in Panama.

Fishing

With 1518 islands, 2988km of coast and 480 rivers, there's no problem finding a fishing spot in Panama. Possibilities include deep-sea fishing, fishing for bass in Lago Gatún on the Panama Canal, trout fishing in the rivers running down Volcán Barú, and surf casting on any of Panama's Pacific and Caribbean beaches.

Hiking

Panama offers everything from dry tropical rainforests and highland cloud forests to humid jungles and blistery mountain peaks.

Starting near the capital on the shores of the canal, Parque Nacional Soberanía contains a section of the historic Sendero Las Cruces. Closer to Panama City, Parque Natural Metropolitano boasts a number of short but rewarding hikes in plush rainforest that skirts the capital.

Popular highland retreats include Boquete; El Valle, nestled into the extinct volcano now known as Valle de Antón; and Santa Fé, surrounded by rivers, waterfalls and cloud forests. All feature hikes in a pristine mountain setting.

Chiriquí is home to two of Panama's most famous hikes: Volcán Barú and Sendero Los Quetzales in Parque Nacional Volcán Barú. While Los Quetzales is more scenic in poor weather, ascents up Barú, which is Panama's highest peak, can offer views of both oceans on a clear day.

Recommended remote destinations include the Las Nubes sector of the Parque Internacional La Amistad. With trails only accessible with a guide, it is as rugged and uncharted as Central America gets.

Surfing

The country's top surfing destination is the Caribbean archipelago of Bocas del Toro, which attracts strong winter swells and surfers from around the world. Although it remains an off-the-beaten-path destination, Santa Catalina on the Pacific coast has some of the most challenging breaks in Central America. There is also uncrowded surfing on the laid-back Caribbean island of Isla Grande and at Playa Venao on the Península de Azuero

White-Water Rafting & Kayaking

Whether you take to the water by raft or kayak, Panama boasts some excellent opportunities for river running. The best-known white-water runs are on the Ríos Chiriquí and Chiriquí Viejo, with Class III-plus rapids. The unofficial river-running capital of Panama is the highland town of Boquete. Sea-kayaking centers are Bocas del Toro and Chiriquí Provinces.

CUSTOMS REGULATIONS

You may bring up to 10 cartons of cigarettes and five bottles of liquor into Panama tax free. If you try to leave Panama with products made from endangered species – such as jaguar teeth, ocelot skin and turtle shell – you'll face a steep fine and jail time.

ELECTRICITY

The electrical current is 120V in Panama City and 110V, 60Hz elsewhere. Plugs are two pronged, as in the US and Canada.

EMBASSIES & CONSULATES

More than 50 countries have *embajadas* (embassies) or *consulados* (consulates) in Panama City. With the exception of those of the US and France, most embassies are located in the Marbella district of Panama City.

Ireland, Australia and New Zealand have no consulates or embassies in Panama.

Canadian Embassy (☏294-2500; www.canadainternational.gc.ca/panama; Piso 11, Tower A, Torre de las Americas, Punta Pacifica)

Colombian Embassy (☏392-5586; http://panama.consulado.gov.co; 1st fl, Condominio Posada del Rey, Vía Italia, Punta Paitilla; ⊙7:30am-1:30pm Mon-Fri)

Costa Rican Embassy (☏264-2980; www.embajadacostaricaenpanama.com; 30th fl, Edificio Bisca, cnr Aquilino de la Guardia & Av Balboa, Bella Vista)

Costa Rican Consulate (☏774-1923; www.embajadacostaricaenpanama.com; 3rd fl, Edificio Omega, Av Samuel Lewis, Obarrio; ⊙8am-3pm Mon-Fri)

French Embassy (☏211-6200; www.ambafrance-pa.org; Plaza de Francia, Las Bóvedas, Casco Viejo)

German Embassy (☏263-7733; www.panama.diplo.de; Piso PH, World Trade Center, Calle 53 Este, Marbella; ⊙9am-noon Mon-Fri)

Netherlands Consulate (☏280-6650; http://panama.nlambassade.org; No 23, 23rd fl, Tower 1000, Calle Hanono Missri, Punta Paitilla; ⊙9am-3pm Mon-Fri)

SLEEPING PRICE RANGES

The following price ranges refer to a double room with bathroom in high season or a hostel dorm bed. Unless otherwise stated, tax is included in the price.

$	less than US$60
$$	US$60–130
$$$	more than US$130

UK Embassy (☏297-6550; www.gov.uk/government/world/panama; 4th fl, Humbolt Tower, Calle 53 Este, Marbella; ⊙7:30am-4:30pm Mon-Thu, to 12:30pm Fri)

US Embassy (☏317-5000; www.panama.usembassy.gov; Av Demetrio Basillo Lakas 783, Clayton; ⊙8am-5:30pm Mon-Thu, to noon Fri)

FOOD & DRINK

Food

Panama's national dish is *sancocho* (chicken and vegetable stew). *Ropa vieja* (literally 'old clothes'), a spicy shredded beef combination served over rice, is also common. Rice is the staple of Panama.

Breakfast staples and snacks are *tortillas de maíz* (thick, fried cornmeal cakes) and *hojaldras* (deep-fried mass of dough served hot and covered with sugar). For lunch, simple *comida corriente* is an inexpensive set meal of beef, chicken or fish served with rice, black beans, fried plantain, chopped cabbage and maybe an egg or an avocado.

Specialties include *carimañola*, a yucca roll filled with chopped meat then deep-fried. The most common snack is the *empanada* (turnover filled with ground meat and fried). *Tamales* (cornmeal with a few spices and chicken or pork, wrapped in banana leaves and boiled) are another favorite. Seafood is abundant and includes shrimp, Caribbean king crab, octopus, lobster and *corvina* (sea bass). Along the Caribbean coast you'll also find a West Indian influence to the dishes, such as coconut rice and coconut bread, or seafood mixed with coconut milk.

In Panama City you'll often see vendors pushing carts and selling *raspados*, cones filled with shaved ice topped with fruit syrup and sweetened condensed milk.

Drink

Fresh fruit drinks, sweetened with sugar and mixed with water or milk, are called *chichas*, and are extremely popular. *Chicheme* is a concoction of milk, sweet corn, cinnamon and vanilla.

Coffee is traditionally served very strong and offered with cream or condensed milk. Milk is pasteurized and safe to drink. Espresso drinks are available only in major cities and tourist destinations.

EATING PRICES RANGES

The following price ranges refer to a main dish.

$	less than US$12
$$	US$12–18
$$$	more than US$18

The national alcoholic drink is made of *seco*, milk and ice. *Seco*, like rum, is distilled from sugarcane, but it doesn't taste anything like the rum you know. This is the drink of *campesinos* (farmers). Popular in the central provinces, *vino de palma* is fermented sap extracted from the trunk of a palm tree called *palma de corozo*. By far the most popular alcoholic beverage in Panama is *cerveza* (beer).

INTERNET ACCESS

Most cities and towns in Panama have inexpensive internet cafes. Public wi-fi access is increasingly common in bus terminals, plazas, libraries and restaurants. Hotels and hostels in more tourist-oriented areas have wi-fi and some computer terminals for use; the Guna Yala and Darién regions are exceptions.

LEGAL MATTERS

The legal drinking age in Panama is 18, which is strictly enforced in Panama City and generally ignored elsewhere.

Remember that you are legally required to carry identification at all times. This should be a photographic ID, preferably a passport. Although this may seem like an inconvenience, police officers reserve the right to request documentation from tourists at all times, and several readers have been forced to spend the night in prison for failure to produce proper ID.

It is illegal for men and women to walk around topless, even if you are on your way to the beach. This rule is strictly enforced in Bocas del Toro town on Isla Colón, and you can expect to be stopped on the streets by police officers if you don't cover up.

In Panama penalties for possession of even small amounts of illegal drugs are much stricter than in the USA, Europe, Australia and almost everywhere else. Defendants often spend years in prison before they are brought to trial and, if convicted (as is usually the case), can expect sentences of several more years. Most lawyers won't accept drug cases because the outcome is certain: conviction.

If you are jailed, your embassy will offer only limited assistance. This may include a visit from an embassy staff member to make sure your human rights have not been violated, letting your family know where you are and putting you in contact with a lawyer (whom you must pay yourself). Embassy officials will not bail you out.

LGBT TRAVELERS

Panamanians are more out than ever, though this openness is much more prevalent in the capital than anywhere else. More than in other parts of Central America, you will probably meet openly gay locals, though the culture is generally discreet. Gay unions are still not legal here, but many think this may change relatively soon. Perhaps it's a legacy of *machismo*, but, according to locals, discrimination is more prevalent against lesbians.

Panama City has a bathhouse and a few gay and lesbian clubs and bars. Outside the capital, gay bars are hard to come by and discrimination is more widespread. In most instances, gays and lesbians just blend in with the straight crowd at the hipper places and avoid village beer halls and other conventional lairs of homophobia.

Gay Pride is held annually in downtown Panama City, usually in June. The parade is sponsored by Asociación Hombres y Mujeres Nuevos de Panamá, Panama's first and only lesbian and gay association.

MAPS

At **Instituto Geográfico Nacional** (p638) in Panama City, you can buy topographical maps of selected cities and regions. Various free tourist publications distributed in Panama also have maps, though hiking maps are rarely available at national-park ranger stations.

MONEY

Panama uses the US dollar as its currency. The official name for it is the balboa, but it's exactly the same bill. People use the terms *dólar* and balboa interchangeably.

Panamanian coins are of the same value, size and metal as US coins, though both are frequently used. Coins include one, five, 10, 25 and 50 *centavos* (or *centésimos*) – 100 *centavos* equal one balboa (dollar). Most businesses won't break US$50 and US$100 bills, and those that do may require you to present your passport.

ATMs

Throughout Panama, ATMs are readily available except in the most isolated places. Look for the red *'sistema clave'* signs to find an ATM. They accept cards on most networks (Plus, Cirrus, MasterCard, Visa and Amex).

These places have no banks, and it's a long way to the nearest ATM: Santa Catalina, Santa Fé, Boca Brava, Isla Contadora, Isla Grande, Portobelo, Isla de Coiba and the Darién.

Credit Cards

Although they are widely accepted at travel agencies, upscale hotels and many restaurants, credit cards can present difficulties elsewhere.

In short, carry enough cash to get you to the next bank or ATM.

Tipping

Restaurants Tipping should be 10%; check to see if it's included in the bill.

Taxis Tipping is optional, but you can round up a dollar or two, especially at night.

Guides It is customary to tip US$7 to US$10 per person for day tours; tip on the high end for naturalist guides.

OPENING HOURS

Opening hours vary throughout the year. The following are high-season hours.

Banks 8:30am to 1pm or 3pm, some open Saturday morning.

Bars and clubs Bars from 9pm, clubs from 11pm to 3am or 4am.

Government offices 8am to 4pm Monday to Friday.

Malls and shops 10am to 9pm or 10pm.

Offices 8am to noon and 1:30pm to 5pm Monday to Friday.

Restaurants 7am to 10am, noon to 3pm and 6pm to 10pm, later in Panama City; often closed Sunday.

Supermarkets 8am to 9pm, some open 24 hours.

PUBLIC HOLIDAYS

New Year's Day January 1

Martyrs' Day January 9

Good Friday, Easter March/April

Workers' Day May 1

Founding of Old Panama (Panama City only) August 15

Hispanic Day October 12

National Anthem Day November 1

All Souls' Day November 2

Independence Day November 3

First Call for Independence November 10

Independence from Spain November 28

Mothers' Day December 8

Christmas Day December 25

SAFE TRAVEL

Crime is a problem in parts of Panama City, though the city's better districts are safer than in many other capitals. The city of Colón has street crime, so consult hotel staff on areas to avoid.

Parts of Darién Province bordering Colombia are still a staging ground for narcotraffickers and human traffickers. Always register with SENAFRONT (border control) in Panama City before traveling and preferably go with a guide.

There have been cases of drug trafficking on boats traveling the Caribbean from Colombia north to Panama, and to a lesser extent on the Pacific side.

THE TRANSPANAMA TRAIL

This cross-country circuit (www.transpanama.org) runs from the border of Costa Rica toward Panama City, but you can hike any three-day stretch for a good taste of Panama's rugged backcountry. More information is available on the website, where you can also download GPS tracks for free.

Hiking Safety

Though it's tropical, Panama runs the gamut from hot to cold and hiking is not easy here. Always ask local outfitters or rangers about trail conditions before heading out, and ensure you go adequately prepared. Carry plenty of water, even on short journeys, and always bring food, matches and adequate clothing – jungles *do* get quite a bit colder at night, particularly at higher elevations.

Hikers have been known to get lost in rainforests, even seemingly user-friendly ones such as Parque Nacional Volcán Barú and the Sendero Los Quetzales. Landslides, storms and vegetation growth can make trails difficult to follow. In some cases, even access roads can deteriorate enough for transportation to leave you a few miles before your intended drop-off point. This is just the reality of the jungle. Many hikers have gotten lost, and there is no official rescue organization to help. If you are heading out without a guide, let your plans be known at your hotel and tell them the number of days you will be gone.

Never walk in unmarked rainforest; if there's no trail going in, you can assume that there won't be one when you decide to turn around and come back out. Always plan your transportation in advance – know where and when the last bus will pass your terminus, or arrange for a taxi pick-up with a responsible, recommended transporter.

Police

Police corruption is not as big a problem in Panama as it is in some other Latin American countries. However, it's not unheard of for a police officer to stop a motorist for no obvious reason, invent a violation, and levy a fine to be paid on the spot. Showing confusion will sometimes fluster the officer into letting you go. If there has been a violation, offer to go to the police station to pay.

Some cities in Panama have tourist police – a division created to deal specifically with travelers. Identifiable by armbands on their uniform, officers in this division may be more helpful.

Swimming Safety

Unfortunately, drownings occur every year in Panamanian waters, about 80% of them caused by rip currents. A rip is a strong current that pulls the swimmer out to sea. It occurs when two currents that move parallel to the shore meet, causing the opposing waters to choose the path of least resistance, which is the path out to sea.

Some tips:
➡ If you are caught in a rip, stay calm and swim parallel to the shore to get out of it – rip currents dissipate quickly.
➡ It is most important to remember that rip currents will pull you out but not under.
➡ When the current dissipates, swim back in at a 45-degree angle to the shore to avoid being caught by the current again.
➡ Do not try to swim directly back in, as you would be swimming against the rip and would only exhaust yourself.
➡ If you feel a rip while you are wading, try to come back in sideways, thus offering less body surface to the current. If you cannot make headway, walk parallel to the beach until you get out of the rip.

TELEPHONE

Panama's country code is ☑ 507. To call Panama from abroad, use the country code before the seven-digit Panamanian telephone number. There are no local area codes in Panama.

Pay phones have been replaced with internet calling services. If you are traveling for an extended period, it may be useful to get a SIM card (US$5) if you have an unlocked cell phone. Otherwise, kiosks in malls sell pay-per-use phones for as little as US$20, and many come with minutes loaded.

TOURIST INFORMATION

Autoridad de Turismo Panamá (ATP; Panama Tourism Authority; ☑ 526-7000; www.visit panama.com) is the national tourism agency. Outside the flagship Panama City office, ATP runs offices in Bocas del Toro, Boquete, Colón, David, Paso Canoas, Penonomé, Portobelo, Santiago, Villa de los Santos, Las Tablas, El Valle and Pedasí. There are smaller information counters in Casco Viejo, and in both Tocumen International Airport and Albrook domestic airport.

ATP has a few useful maps and brochures but often has a problem keeping enough in stock for distribution to tourists. Most offices are staffed with people who speak only Spanish. Some employees really try to help, but others are just passing the time. As a general rule, you will get more useful information if you have specific questions.

TRAVELERS WITH DISABILITIES

Panama is generally not wheelchair friendly, though high-end hotels provide wheelchair-accessible rooms. There are parking spaces for people with disabilities and some oversized

bathroom stalls. Outside the capital, adequate infrastructure is lacking.

VISAS

Every visitor needs a valid passport and an onward ticket to enter Panama, but further requirements vary by nationality and change occasionally. Anyone planning a trip to Panama is well advised to check online to obtain the latest information on entry requirements. Ticketing agents of airlines that fly to Panama and tour operators can often provide this information. Some tips:
➡ Tourist-card fees are included in the price of your air ticket.
➡ Visitors generally get a 90-day stamp in their passport upon entering Panama.
➡ After 90 days, visas and tourist cards can be extended at *migración* (immigration) offices.
➡ Travelers entering Panama overland will probably be asked to show an onward ticket and potentially proof of sufficient funds (US$500) or a credit card.

At the time of research, people holding passports from the following countries needed to show only their passports to enter Panama: Argentina, Austria, Belgium, Chile, Colombia, Costa Rica, Czech Republic, Denmark, El Salvador, Finland, France, Germany, Greece, Guatemala, Holland, Honduras, Hungary, Ireland, Israel, Italy, Luxembourg, Paraguay, Poland, Portugal, Singapore, South Korea, Spain, Sweden, Switzerland, the UK and Uruguay.

People from the following countries need a passport and a tourist card: Antigua, Australia, Bahamas, Barbados, Belize, Canada, China, Dominican Republic, Granada, Guyana, Jamaica, Japan, New Zealand, Taiwan, Thailand, Tobago, Trinidad, the USA and Venezuela.

Citizens from countries not on this list will need to obtain a visa, available at Panamanian embassies or consulates. Contact the one nearest you or call **Migración y Naturalización** (Immigration Office; ☑ 507-1051, 507-1800; www.migracion. gob.pa; cnr Av Cuba & Calle 28 Este, Calidonia; ☉7:30am-3:30pm Mon-Fri) in Panama City.

ⓘ Getting There & Away

AIR

Panama has four international airports, but you're likely to arrive at one of the following two:
Tocumen International Airport (☑ 238-2700; www.tocumenpanama.aero; Av Domingo Díaz) In Panama City.
Aeropuerto Enrique Malek (☑ 721-1072) In David.

Airlines with international flights to Panama:
Air Panama (☑ 316-9000; www.airpanama.com)
American Airlines (☑ 264-8999; www.aa.com)
Avianca (☑ 264-5919; www.avianca.com)

Copa (📋217-5656; www.copaair.com; ⊘8am-5pm Mon-Fri)
Delta Airlines (📋238-4793; www.delta.com)
Iberia (📋227-2322; www.iberia.com)
Taca Airlines (📋238-4116; www.taca.com)
Viva Colombia (📋800-157-1073; www.viva colombia.co)

At all three border crossings, you can take a local bus up to the border on either side, cross over, board another local bus and continue on your way. Be aware that the last buses leave the border crossings at Guabito and Río Sereno at 7pm and 5pm, respectively; the last bus leaves Paso Canoas for Panama City at 9:30pm.

Two companies, **Panaline** (📋256-8721; www.viajeros.com/panaline) and **Tica Bus** (📋227-3318; www.ticabus.com), operate daily *directo* (direct) buses between San José (Costa Rica) and Panama City, departing from **Albrook Bus Terminal** (p639). Both recommend making reservations a few days in advance.

Costa Rica

The most heavily trafficked border crossing to/from Costa Rica is at Paso Canoas (open 7am to 7pm), 53.6km northwest of David on the Interamericana. Some tips:

➤ The best place to sleep before crossing is David.

➤ Ensure that you have both entry and exit stamps put in your passport.

➤ Allow one to 1½ hours for the formalities on both sides. Buses from David depart frequently for the border (US$2.10, 50 minutes, every 15 minutes) from 4:30am.

➤ On the Costa Rican side, you can catch regular buses to San José or other parts of the country.

➤ From David, there are also taxis to Paso Canoas (US$35).

The least trafficked crossing into Costa Rica is the border post at Río Sereno (open 9am to 5pm Monday to Saturday, to 3pm Sunday), located 35km northwest of Volcán. Buses to the border depart from David and travel via La Concepción, Volcán and Santa Clara (US$5.10, 2½ hours, every half hour). On the Costa Rican side of the border, you can take a 15-minute bus or taxi ride to San Vito, where you can catch buses to regional destinations.

The Caribbean border post at Guabito/Sixaola (open 8am to 5pm), 16km northwest of Changuinola, sees less traffic than Pacific-side routes, though most travelers find it hassle-free. Buses from Changuinola depart frequently for the border (US$1, 20 minutes, every half hour) from 6am to 7pm. On the Costa Rican side of the border, you can catch regular buses on to Puerto Limón and San José, as well as regional destinations.

Colombia

It's possible to cross to Colombia by sea, though it can be a rough crossing. Multiday motorboat and sailboat trips depart from Colón Province or the Comarca de Guna Yala.

Driving to Panama from the USA or Canada may take from a week to considerably longer depending on the stops. Driving at night is not recommended. Central American roads are narrow, rarely painted with a center stripe, often potholed and subject to hazards such as cattle and pedestrians in rural areas.

To drive to Panama, get insurance in advance, have your papers in order (including a *permiso de salida* – exit permit – from the country of the car's origin) and never leave your car unattended (fortunately, guarded lots are common in Latin America). US license plates are attractive as souvenirs, so display these from inside the car.

If you are bringing a car into Panama, you must pay US$15 for a *tarjeta de circulación* (vehicle control certificate) and another US$1 to have the car fumigated. You will also need to show a driver's license, proof of ownership and Panamanian insurance papers – insurance is best bought upon entering the country at an insurance dealer near *aduana* (customs). Copy the insurance policy and have it officially stamped.

Your passport will be stamped to show that you have paid and followed procedures when you brought the vehicle into the country. A car visa is only valid for one month and can be renewed for up to three months. Overstaying will cost you another US$300 to US$500, payable only before expiration.

❶ Getting Around

Panama's domestic destinations are served by **Air Panama** (📋316-9000; www.airpanama.com) and **Copa Airlines** (📋217-5656; www.copaair.com; ⊘8am-5pm Mon-Fri). Domestic flights depart Panama City from Albrook Airport. Located near the Costa Rican border, David's Aeropuerto Enrique Malek frequently handles flights to and from San José.

Book ahead in high season, when demand for flights to destinations like Bocas overflows. Always confirm bookings.

SPEAK PANAMEÑO

You can express your appreciation with *chévere* ('cool'); *buena leche* is 'good luck'; *una pinta* means 'a beer' while *vaina* just means 'thing.'

ⓘ DEPARTURE TAX

Panama levies a US$40 departure tax for passengers on international flights; this is included in the price of the ticket.

BICYCLE

If you can get over the heat, you can cycle through Panama easily enough, with lodgings within a day's ride. Cycling within larger Panamanian cities – particularly Panama City – is not for the faint of heart. Roads tend to be narrow, and vehicles drive aggressively. Also, frequent rains reduce motorists' visibility and bicycle-tire grip.

Outside the cities, Panama's Interamericana boasts the best quality in Central America, although sections have an extremely narrow shoulder. Roads in many of the provinces (especially in Veraguas and Colón) are in poor shape – plan accordingly and bring lots of spare parts.

BOAT

Boats are the chief means of transportation in several areas of Panama, particularly in Darién Province, the Archipiélago de las Perlas, and the San Blás and Bocas del Toro island chains.

The tourist mecca of Bocas del Toro on Isla Colón is accessible from Almirante by frequent water taxis.

Colombian and Guna merchant boats carry cargo and passengers along the San Blás coast between Colón and Puerto Obaldía, stopping at up to 48 of the islands to load and unload passengers and cargo. However, these boats are often dangerously overloaded. Taking passage on a sailboat, or the four-day motorboat service to Colombia, is a wiser option.

Since there aren't many roads in the eastern part of Darién Province, boat travel is often the most feasible way to get from one town to another, especially during the rainy season. The boat of choice here is the *piragua* (long canoe), carved from the trunk of a giant ceiba tree. The shallow hulls of these boats allow them to ride the many rivers that comprise the traditional transportation network of eastern Panama. Many are motorized.

BUS

You can take a bus to just about any community in Panama that is reachable by road. Some of the buses are full-size Mercedes-Benzes equipped with air-con, movie screens and reclining seats. These top-of-the-line buses generally cruise long stretches of highway.

Most common are small Toyota Coaster buses, affectionately called *chivas*. Use these to visit towns on the Península de Azuero and along the Interamericana.

Panama City is phasing out its converted school buses, known as *diablos rojos* (red devils). Replacing them is the Metrobus system. Riders can obtain swipe cards at Albrook Bus Terminal or main bus stops. Official bus stops are used and the transportation is air-conditioned.

CAR & MOTORCYCLE

To rent a vehicle in Panama, you must be 25 years of age or older and present a passport and driver's license – if you are over 21 and can present a valid credit card, some agencies will waive the age requirement. Even with an international agency, you are usually renting through their subsidiaries and will not get any support from them outside Panama.

Prices for rentals in Panama run from US$35 per day for an economy car to US$110 per day for a *cuatro por cuatro* (4WD). When you rent, carefully inspect the car for minor dents and scratches, missing radio antennae, hubcaps and the presence of a spare tire. Damage *must* be noted on your rental agreement; otherwise you may be charged for it when you return the car.

There have been many reports of theft from rental cars. You should never leave valuables in an unattended car, and you should remove all luggage from the trunk when you're checking into a hotel overnight – most hotels provide parking areas for cars.

Signs can be confusing or wholly absent. In Panama, there are many poor secondary roads, and even paved roads often resemble a lunar landscape.

HITCHHIKING

Hitchhiking is not uncommon as you arrive in rural areas, but it's not as widespread in Panama as elsewhere in Central America; most people travel by bus, and visitors would do best to follow suit. Hitchhiking is never entirely safe in any country, and we don't recommend it. Travelers who hitch should understand that they are taking a small but potentially serious risk.

TAXI

Taxis are cheap and plentiful, though not all drivers have a good grasp of locations. Some tips:
➡ Before even getting into a taxi, state your destination and settle on a rate. Panamanian taxis don't have meters, but there are standard fares between neighborhoods of Panama City.
➡ Get informed. Ask the staff at your accommodations for typical rates between city sectors; these usually go up after dark.
➡ Taxis can be scarce late at night and around the holidays. At these times, it's best to call for a radio taxi.
➡ More expensive 'sedan' taxis operate from upscale hotels. They charge double what you'd pay a hailed cab.

TRAIN

The train trip between Panama City and Colón is scenic.

Understand Central America

CENTRAL AMERICA TODAY 708

Transportation and tourism are economic highlights, while energy security (or lack thereof) is a concern. Poverty and violence continue to cast a long, dark shadow over the region.

HISTORY 710

Central America is a little region with a big history, from the mysterious Maya to the Spanish conquistadors to the 20th-century struggles for peace and prosperity.

PEOPLE & CULTURE 717

In a region dominated by mestizo peoples, minority groups of European, African and indigenous descent have played a prominent role in the history and culture.

Central America Today

The outlook for Central America today depends greatly on where one is standing. From the southern part of the region, the future looks bright, with mostly stable politics and expanding economic opportunities in tourism and transportation. Things look bleaker from the northern countries, where many citizens are struggling to break out of an interminable cycle of violence and poverty, with the only escape often being emigration.

Best on Film

Ixcanul (dir Jayro Bustamante; 2015) Multi-award-winning film about a young Kaqchikel girl's coming of age in Guatemala.

Mosquito Coast (dir Peter Weir; 1986) Harrison Ford and River Phoenix star as members of an American family in search of a simpler life in Central America. Set in Honduras; filmed in Belize.

Curse of the Xtabai (dir Matthew Klinck; 2012) Belizeans are quite proud of this feature-length horror film, the first to be 100% filmed and produced in Belize using local scenery, cast and crew.

Hands of Stone (dir Jonathan Jakubowicz; 2016) The anticipated biopic of Panamanian boxing legend Roberto Durán, starring Robert De Niro.

Best in Print

A Mayan Life (Gaspar Pedro Gonzáles; 1995) The first published novel by a Maya author is an excellent study of rural Guatemalan life.

The Country Under My Skin (Gioconda Belli; 2003) An enthralling autobiography detailing the Nicaraguan poet's involvement in the Nicaraguan revolution.

Empire of Blue Water (Stephen Talty; 2008) An intriguing pirate history and a New York Times bestseller.

Canals: Bigger & Deeper

The Panama Canal is surely one of the region's biggest success stories, hauling in US$2 billion annually and fueling the fastest-growing economy in Latin America. And now it's about to get even bigger. One of the world's largest transportation projects, the US$17-billion expansion will double the capacity and triple the traffic in the canal by adding a third lane and digging deeper to accommodate bigger vessels. A financial boon for Panama, the expanded canal is expected to be completed in 2016, just on the heels of its 100th anniversary.

Meanwhile, up the road, Nicaragua is supposedly starting its own big dig – a US$50-billion waterway connecting the Atlantic and the Pacific. At 277km long, the Nicaragua Canal would be nearly four times longer than its Panamanian predecessor. The Chinese-funded project has come under fire for its unrealistic price tag and timeline, as well as unaddressed environmental and logistical concerns. Construction is scheduled to begin in late 2016, but as this date keeps getting shifted back, some wonder if President Ortega and his Chinese partners really intend to follow through on this project.

Politics of Petroleum

Initiated by former Venezuelan president Hugo Chávez in 2005, PetroCaribe is an alliance that grants its 17 member countries extremely favorable terms in their purchase of oil from Venezuela. The PetroCaribe initiative has undoubtedly benefited its members, which include Belize, El Salvador, Honduras and Nicaragua.

But PetroCaribe has come under scrutiny in Venezuela, which faces its own economic crisis, especially with plunging oil prices. Meanwhile, Chávez's party (and that of his successor, President Nicolas Maduro) lost its majority in the Venezuelan National Assembly in 2015. Although Maduro has reiterated his commitment to the agreement, the opposition party is calling for its review and reform.

Member countries – including our friends in Central America – have started to contemplate life without PetroCaribe. In Belize, for example, Prime Minister Barrow brought forward elections to 2015, anticipating the political ramifications of a halt in that revenue stream. Many others are keeping a careful watch on domestic Venezuelan politics.

Keeping the 'Eco' in Ecotourism

Much of Central America has embraced tourism as a promise of prosperity, offering employment, investment and an endless stream of cold hard cash. It's the number-one industry in Belize and Costa Rica and plays a smaller but increasingly significant role in Nicaragua and Panama. But all these countries face the ongoing challenge of balancing the demands of a thriving tourist sector with its environmental impacts.

It's already an old story in Costa Rica, where debates rage around paving roads, building on beaches and chopping down trees. Once-remote destinations like Monteverde and Bahía Salinas will see big increases in visitors as their main access routes get paved in coming years, calling into question their off-the-beaten-track appeal. In Belize, Norwegian Cruise Line has been granted permission to develop an island near Placencia, a project which will expose the entire region to cruise-ship traffic and other environmental impacts. Nicaragua and Panama do not get nearly the number of visitors as their neighbors, but as tourism grows, they too will have to find a way to manage it.

Most residents of these countries are proud of their natural heritage and recognize that the goals of environmental conservation and economic prosperity are not mutually exclusive. But the best way to pursue those goals is anything but clear.

Poverty & Violence

Throughout Central America, far too many people continue to suffer from poverty and violence. Even the most prosperous nations (Costa Rica and Panama) have poverty rates hovering around 25%, with a wide disparity between the richest and poorest citizens. Other countries are faring much worse, with some 46% of the population living below the poverty line in Nicaragua, 54% in Guatemala – and 60% in Honduras. Unemployment and income inequality are ongoing challenges throughout Central America.

Meanwhile, violence continues to plague poverty-stricken barrios and rural villages, especially in Guatemala, El Salvador and Honduras. In recent years, the latter two countries have been vying for the dubious title of 'murder capital of the world.' Crime levels, gang violence and drug-cartel activity are intricately connected and seemingly insurmountable problems – which many residents believe they can avoid only by seeking refuge in 'El Norte' (the USA and Canada).

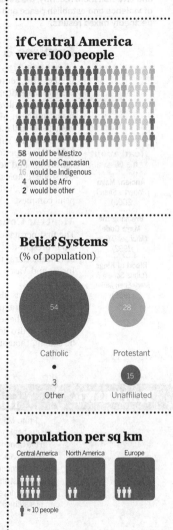

POPULATION: **44,459,300**

AREA: **521,875 SQ KM**

GDP PER CAPITA: **PANAMA US$20,900; NICARAGUA US$5000**

LITERACY RATE: **COSTA RICA 97.8%; HONDURAS 88.5%**

if Central America were 100 people

58 would be Mestizo
20 would be Caucasian
16 would be Indigenous
4 would be Afro
2 would be other

Belief Systems
(% of population)

54 Catholic
28 Protestant
3 Other
15 Unaffiliated

population per sq km

Central America   North America   Europe

≈ 10 people

History

In the pre-Columbian era, the mighty Maya empire stretched across the Central American isthmus. After this heyday, the region endured conquistadors and colonialism, subjugation and civil war. More recently, the seven spunky nations have striven to overcome this legacy of violence and establish peace and prosperity in their corner of the planet – though with decidedly mixed results.

Empires & Nations

Meet the Maya

In the 16th century, marauders from across the ocean transformed Central America, vanquishing one of Mesoamerica's greatest pre-Columbian civilizations: the Maya. The Maya civilization once extended from southern Mexico to Nicaragua, from Honduras to El Salvador, with its heartland in the high plains of Guatemala and lowlands of Belize and the Yucatan.

The Maya perfected a hieroglyphic writing system, practiced precise astronomy and advanced mathematics, and designed and built grandiose stone temples and palaces. They endured for nearly three millennia, reaching a high stage around 1000 AD, before capitulating to the European conquest.

Meet the Conquistadors

The first permanent Spanish settlement in Central America was in Panama (present-day Darién) in 1510, which served as base for fellow sons of Extremadura: the Pizarro brothers, who trooped south to assault the Incas; and Vasco Núñez de Balboa, who ventured west to gaze on the Pacific.

Panama was also the launch site for Gil González Dávila, who sailed north to Nicaragua, where he betrayed the local *cacique* (tribal leader) Nicarao and beheaded his rival conquistador Francisco Hernández de Córdoba. Pedro de Alvarado, meanwhile, never found the jade kingdom he sought, though he did manage to get appointed military governor of

Read about the Maya

Ancient Maya
(Robert J Sharer; 2006)

Breaking the Maya Code
(Michael D Coe; 1992)

Blood of Kings
(Linda Schele & Mary Ellen Miller; 1986)

TIMELINE	1100 BC	AD 250–AD 1000	1000–1600
	Proto-Maya settlements begin to appear in the Copán Valley in Guatemala. By 1000 BC settlements on the Pacific coast show early signs of developing a hierarchical society.	The Classic period of the Maya civilization is characterized by the construction of cities and temples and other artistic and intellectual achievements. The population reaches around 400,000.	During the Postclassic Period, the Maya civilization continues to develop, although populations are not as concentrated. Highlands Maya organize into competing kingdoms, establishing groupings that survive today.

Guatemala, which he tyrannized for 15 years – until, in battle against desperate natives, his horse rolled over and killed him in the saddle.

Spanish Rule

By the middle of the 16th century, the days of vainglorious conquistadors had passed, and the Spanish Crown now imposed imperial bureaucracy. Alvarado's fiefdom was reorganized into the Kingdom of Guatemala, under the Viceroy of New Spain. For most of the next 300 years, this included present-day states of Central America and Mexico's Chiapas. The capital was located in Santiago (now Antigua), in southwest Guatemala. Meanwhile, present-day Panama was also under Spanish rule, but part of the Viceroyalty of Peru, with its capital in Lima.

The Crown's hold was not complete, however. In northeast Honduras (present-day Belize), upstart British squatters built a haven for pirates, smugglers and poachers, who withstood all of the king's eviction efforts.

Independence in the Americas

In 1821, the Americas wriggled free of Imperial Spain's grip. Mexico declared independence for itself, as well as for Central America. The Central American colonies then declared independence from Mexico for themselves. With an empire up for grabs, the region descended into conflict.

The newly liberated colonies considered their fate: stay together in a United States of Central America or go their separate national ways? At first, they came up with something in between – the Central American Federation (CAF). But it could neither field an army nor collect taxes. Accustomed to being in charge, Guatemala attempted to dominate the CAF, thus hastening its demise. One by one, the constituent parts became independent nation-states.

Gods & Monsters

Maya Mysticism

In the world of the Maya, even the king listened to the high priest. Priests provided counsel, managed the seasonal calendar, kept records of the kingdom, educated noble sons and planned religious feasts. Why were the priests so influential? Because they could talk to the gods – and there were a *lot* of gods to talk to. More than 250, in fact: gods for life, death, rain, thunder, east, west, fighting, loving, hunting, fishing, mountains, rivers, heroes, demons, medicine, corn and even chocolate. They inhabited the three realms of the Maya: the twinkling heavens above, all things living and earthly, and the ominous multi-level underworld.

Joyce Kelly's *An Archaeological Guide to Northern Central America* (1996) offers the best descriptions of the Maya sites of Belize, Guatemala and Mexico.

1502	1510-27	1540	1638
Christopher Columbus sails down the Caribbean coastline looking for a sailing route to the Pacific Ocean. First recorded contact between indigenous inhabitants and Europeans.	The first permanent Spanish settlement in Central America is in Panama (present-day Darien), later serving as a base for Gonzalo Davila, who sails north to Nicaragua. Pedro Alvarado is named military-governor of Guatemala.	The Spanish establish the Kingdom of Guatemala, which includes most of Central America: Costa Rica, Nicaragua, Honduras, El Salvador, Guatemala and the Mexican state of Chiapas.	British Baymen 'settle' Belize when former pirate Peter Wallace lays the foundations for a new port at the mouth of the Belize River, on the site of today's Belize City.

Catholicism

Impressive Cathedrals

Catedral de Santiago (p115; Antigua, Guatemala)

Catedral de León (p470; Nicaragua)

Iglesia La Merced (p445; Granada, Nicaragua)

Iglesia San Francisco (p445; Granada, Nicaragua)

Catedral de Comayagua (p365; Honduras)

When the Europeans arrived, they brought their own supernatural conduits. In the ensuing clash of divine powers, the Maya gods were obliterated. Henceforth, there could be only one deity in Central America: the Catholic god. An advanced guard of Jesuits, Franciscans and Dominicans penetrated the heathen wilds, established religious outposts and suppressed false idols. Bishop Diego de Landa, converter-in-chief, confiscated all sacred texts – which contained the accumulated knowledge of the Maya culture – and burned them to ash. Local temples and ritual sites were ransacked, abandoned and reclaimed by the dense rainforest. In their place rose new, baroque-style monuments in the lush mountain valleys, proclaiming the victory of the new god.

As with the Maya, Spain's conquering chiefs and high priests shared a vision of power and reverence while enjoying lives of privilege and status. The Catholic Church long monopolized religious conviction in Central America, serving as a complement to political power.

Evangelical Protestantism

Today, a new contest for Central American souls is under way, as Evangelical Protestantism woos worshipers away from Catholicism. The region's first born-again political leader was Guatemala's General Efraín Ríos Montt (also known for his killing sprees against indigenous peoples). In Guatemala, Honduras, El Salvador and Belize, Protestants now comprise at least one-third of the population. Media-savvy ministers and North American missionaries hasten the conversion rate. Maya pyramids and Catholic cathedrals have made room for Protestant mega-churches, such as the Friends of Israel Bible Baptist Tabernacle in San Salvador, which draws more than 50,000 churchgoers each Sunday.

Paradise & Plunder

New World Economy

The pre-Columbian economy rested on agriculture and trade. The Maya built terraced fields in the steep mountains, raised platforms in the swampy lowlands, and slashed and burned the thick forests. They grew corn, tubers, beans, squash and peppers. They tamed the wild fruits of the forest: papaya, mango, banana and cacao. They fished the rivers and lakes with nets – and with cormorants on a leash – and they hunted down tasty forest creatures such as peccary, deer and monkey. But the tropical terrain made grand-scale agriculture impractical, and the region was notably lacking in precious metals.

The Spanish were undeterred, and instead harnessed the region's main economic resource – people. The Crown authorized the creation

1797	1821	1853–56	1903–14
After a slave rebellion on St Vincent, thousands of Garifuna people are sent to the island of Roatán, eventually migrating to mainland Honduras and southern Belize as well.	Central America becomes independent from Spain and briefly joins the Mexican Empire, and then the United Provinces of Central America.	Tennessee-born conquistador William Walker attempts to conquer Central America. His Yankee mercenaries are defeated during a march on Costa Rica, and the self-declared president of Nicaragua is executed by a Honduran firing squad.	With the support of the US, Panama declares itself independent from Colombia, and canal concessions are granted to the US. The Panama Canal is completed a decade later.

of feudal-style agricultural estates, the notorious *economienda*, whereby powerful colonial overlords exploited an indigenous labor force. They produced New World luxuries for Old World aristocrats – indigo from El Salvador, cacao from Guatemala, tobacco from Chiapas. The *economienda* system, however, did not take hold in Costa Rica, the poorest region of colonial Central America, where private family farms prevailed over corporate feudal estates.

Coffee Rica

In 1843 the merchant vessel HMS *Monarch* arrived in London from Puerto Limón carrying bulging sacks of roasted red beans. The riches that Costa Rica had long promised had finally been uncovered, as the volcanic soil and moist climate of the Central Valley highlands proved ideal for coffee cultivation. The drink's quick fix made it popular with working-class consumers in the industrializing North. Thousands of coffee saplings were quickly planted along shady hillsides in Guatemala, Nicaragua and Honduras. The Central American coffee boom was on.

Costa Rica went from the most impoverished to the wealthiest country in the region. The aroma of riches lured a wave of enterprising German immigrants to Central America. Across the region, powerful cliques of coffee barons reaped the rewards from the caffeine craze.

The coffee processing cooperative Coopedota, located in Costa Rica's Valley of the Saints, launched the country's first carbon-neutral coffee.

Banana Boom

In Costa Rica, getting coffee out to world markets required rail links from the central highlands to the coast. Meanwhile, the California gold rush prompted a Panamanian rail link between the Atlantic and Pacific. US companies undertook the railroad construction projects, both of which were disastrous due to malaria and yellow fever. Local recruits gave way to US convicts, to Chinese indentured servants, and to freed Jamaican slaves.

In Costa Rica, bananas were planted along the tracks as a cheap food source for the workers. As an experiment, would-be railroad tycoon Minor Cooper Keith shipped a few bananas to New Orleans, and he struck gold – or rather, yellow. Northern consumers went crazy for the elongated finger fruit.

By the 1900s bananas had replaced coffee as the region's most lucrative export. The United Fruit Company converted much of Central America into a corporate fiefdom, controlling transportation, communication, postal service, labor markets and export markets – as well as more than a few politicians.

1949	1960–90	1963	1972
Costa Rican president José Figueres implements a new constitution, which grants voting rights to minorities and women and abolishes the military.	US-backed military dictators rule much of the region. Crackdowns on impoverished and indigenous peoples lead to the formation of active left-wing guerrilla groups in Guatemala, El Salvador, Honduras and Nicaragua.	The first federally protected nature reserve, Cabo Blanco, is established in Costa Rica, eventually leading to the creation of the national park system.	Jacques Cousteau takes his research ship *Calypso* to the Great Blue Hole – bringing unprecedented publicity to Belize and boosting its popularity as a destination for divers and snorkelers.

Dictatorship & Democracy

A Democratic Oasis

After independence, politics in Central America usually featured a few elite families competing for control of state patronage, through shifting alliances of army officers and coffee barons. Presidents were more often removed at gunpoint than by the ballot box. Across the region – including Costa Rica, El Salvador, Honduras and Guatemala – the polarized left and right tangled for power through coups and electoral fraud.

In Costa Rica, the unsustainable situation came to a head in the 1940s, when economic and ethnic tensions spiraled into civil war. Armed workers battled military forces, and Nicaraguan and US forces joined the fray. Peace was restored two months – and 2000 deaths – later. Out of the chaos came a coffee grower and utopian democrat, José Figueres, who became the unlikely leader of a temporary junta government. He taxed the wealthy, nationalized the banks and built a modern welfare state. His 1949 constitution granted voting rights to women, as well as full citizenship to black, Indian and Chinese minorities. Most extraordinarily, Figueres abolished the military, calling it a threat to democracy. His transformative regime became the foundation for Costa Rica's uniquely unarmed democracy.

Cold War in the Hot Tropics

US claims of hegemony over the Western Hemisphere were as old as the Monroe Doctrine. But, especially from the mid-20th century, the US routinely acted to constrain the autonomy of Central America's nation-states, seeking to influence political choices, economic development and foreign policies. After all, it's a direct drive down the US Army-constructed Pan-American Hwy.

In the 1950s Guatemala's democratically elected President Jacobo Árbenz vowed to nationalize the vast unused landholdings of the United

A SAINT FOR THE PEOPLE

In the late 20th century, a wave of 'liberation theology' washed over the region, setting populist priests against rapacious dictators. Subversive clerics were feared by the ruling class, which mobilized its coercive agents to quell the criticism. The most notorious episode in this conflict was the assassination of the Archbishop of San Salvador, Óscar Romero, who was gunned down while saying Mass in 1980.

The heinous crime made Romero a martyr: the UN marked his death date, 24 March, as the Day of Truth and Dignity for Victims of Human Rights Atrocities, and the Vatican bestowed sainthood on the bishop in 2015.

1981	1983-9	1979-87	1980-92
After years of anti-colonial and pro-independence political movements, Belize receives formal international recognition of its independence from Great Britain.	Former CIA operative Manual Noriega seizes power in Panama. His authoritarian regime is corrupt and murderous, ending only when the US invades Panama and imprisons Noriega.	Guerrilla groups known as the Sandinistas overthrow the dictatorial Somoza regime in Nicaragua. The US-backed Contras launch a counter-revolution, ushering in an era of civil war that polarizes the region.	After years of strife, El Salvador descends into all-out civil war between a US-backed military and various guerrilla groups. After 12 years of fighting and some 75,000 deaths, a compromise is finally reached.

Fruit Company (offering as compensation the property value declared on its tax returns). Democracy be damned, United Fruit appealed to its friends in Washington; in 1954, a CIA-orchestrated coup forced President Árbenz from office. His successor, Colonel Castillo Armas, was hailed as an anti-communist hero, treated to a ticker-tape parade in New York City and honored with a Doctor of Law degree from Columbia University. Three years later, Armas was gunned down in the presidential palace; soon after United Fruit's confiscated lands were finally returned.

Armas was succeeded by a series of military presidents. More support came from the US government – in the form of money and counter-insurgency training. Violence became a staple of political life, land reforms were reversed, voting was made dependent on literacy (disenfranchising around 75% of the population), the secret police force was revived and military repression was common. In 1960 left-wing guerrilla groups began to form, and the Guatemalan civil war was on.

Gradually, guerrilla warfare spread. By the 1970s radical socialists had forced military oligarchies around the region onto the defensive. In Nicaragua, the rebellious Sandinistas toppled the American-backed Somoza dictatorship. Alarmed by the Sandinistas' Soviet and Cuban ties, the US decided it was time to intervene. The organizational details of the counter-revolution were delegated to junior officer Oliver North, who secretly aided and abetted the Contra rebels to incite civil war in Nicaragua.

The conflict polarized the region. When civil war erupted in El Salvador after the assassination of Archbishop Romero, the US pumped huge sums into a moribund military, effectively prolonging that conflict as well. Throughout the 1980s, government-sponsored death squads decimated villages, while guerrilla groups did their best to undermine elections and stifle the economy. Meanwhile, Honduras became a base for the US-sponsored covert war in Nicaragua.

The young president of Costa Rica, Oscar Arias Sánchez, was the driving force in uniting Central America around a peace plan, which finally ended the Nicaraguan war. For his efforts, Arias became the first Central American to be awarded a Nobel Peace Prize. Within a few years, peace treaties were also signed in El Salvador and Guatemala.

From Colonialism to Neocolonialism

While civil wars raged around the region, two countries remained relatively peaceful, albeit under the control of greater powers.

In Belize, it was not the Spanish, but rather the British who took hold, logging the forests, growing fruit and sugarcane, and dubbing the colony 'British Honduras'. While an independence movement gathered force throughout the second half of the 20th century, full independence was put off until a nagging security matter was resolved: namely, the Guatemalan

The US Army's School of the Americas, originally based in Panama, trained some of the worst human-rights abusers in Latin America – including Manuel Noriega. For information on the school's history visit www.soaw.org.

1987 Costa Rican president Óscar Arias Sánchez wins the Nobel Peace Prize for his work on the Central American peace accords, which brought about greater political freedom throughout the region.

1991 Guatemala recognizes Belize's independence, but the exact border remains in dispute.

1992 K'iche' political activist Rigoberta Menchú wins the Nobel Peace Prize for her work promoting indigenous rights in Guatemala.

1996 Peace accords are signed in Guatemala, bringing to an end the 36-year civil war, in which an estimated 200,000 people died.

constitution explicitly included Belize as part of its territorial reach. Only British troops at the border stopped the larger country from following through on that.

It was not until 1981 that Belize was at last declared an independent nation-state within the British Commonwealth. Even Guatemala recognized Belize as a sovereign nation in 1991, although to this day it maintains its territorial claim.

Meanwhile, at the southern end of the isthmus, Panama was still a province of Colombia at the start of the 20th century. When a military junta declared Panama independent, the US government immediately recognized the sovereignty of the new country – backing it up with battleships when Colombia tried to regain control. In return, Panama granted the US concession to the canal, as well as a broad right of intervention into Panamanian affairs.

In the years following the completion of the canal, Panamanians became increasingly disenchanted with US intervention and occupation. As the northern giant gradually ceded its rights, the Panamanian military grew more powerful. When Manuel Noriega came to power in the 1980s he expanded the military and brutally squashed all dissent; drug trafficking, election rigging and murder all played a role in his regime. The US finally intervened in 1989, invading Panama City and arresting Noriega. A decade later the US rescinded control of the canal and withdrew all troops, finally leaving Panama to negotiate its own uncertain future.

Imperfect Democracy

Today, a new era of democratization has unfolded, as both right-wing and left-wing dictatorships have stepped aside to allow contested elections. A sign of the times: a former Salvadoran guerrilla organization managed to transition to mainstream politics, even fielding a successful presidential candidate.

The systems are not perfect. As recently as 2009, democratically elected Honduran President Manuel Zelaya was ousted by the military (on orders from the Supreme Court). In 2014 the Nicaraguan Congress made the controversial decision to abolish term limits – just in time for President Daniel Ortega to run for his third term. Central American politics are plagued by corruption and greed...but then again, what democracy isn't?

Guatemala recognized Belize's independence only in 1991, but the exact border remains in dispute. An agreement to take the matter to the International Court of Justice was signed in 2008.

1999	2012
The US ends nearly a century of occupation of Panama by closing all of its military bases and rescinding control of the canal.	Despite end-of-the-world predictions from non-Maya people, Baktun 13 ends without major incidents and a new Great Cycle of the Maya Long Count calendar begins.

People & Culture

At the crossroads of continents, Central America has been influenced not only by its North and South American neighbors, but even more so by its European colonizers and African immigrants. With populations descended from these four corners – as well as prominent indigenous groups – the region's culture is a rich and fascinating blend.

The Peoples of Central America

Central America may appear homogeneous at first glance, but this mostly Latin American region is a patchwork of European-, Amerindian- and African-descended groups – most of which have intermingled and intermixed with each other. Some 78% of the regional population are in fact mestizo (Spanish-Amerindian mix) or Caucasian (European). Most of the remaining population is made up of dozens of distinct indigenous groups, from the once-mighty Maya to the barely-surviving Maleku. A small but significant percentage is descended from African slaves and immigrant workers.

Mestizo

Mestizos are people of mixed Spanish and indigenous Amerindian descent. They are the largest ethnic group in Central America, comprising about 58% of the regional population; they're also the largest ethnic group in every Central American country except Costa Rica. (El Salvador has the region's highest percentage of mestizos, at 86%.) But even Belize – which was not settled by the Spanish – has a large and growing mestizo population, due to the influx of refugees from neighboring countries.

While not uniform, the mestizo culture defines the region, which is predominantly Catholic and Spanish-speaking.

THE FIRST MESTIZOS

In 1511, the Spanish ship *Valdivia* was wrecked at sea when a reef ripped through its hull. About 15 survivors drifted for several days before making it to shore in northern Belize, where they were promptly apprehended by anxious Maya. Just to be on the safe side, the locals sent 10 of the Spaniards to the gods and kept five for themselves.

One of the captives was conquistador Gonzalo Guerrero, a skilled warrior – and apparently not a bad diplomat, either. Guerrero managed to win his freedom and a position of status with the Maya chief at Chetumal. He became a tribal consultant on military matters and married the chief's daughter; their three children are considered the first mestizos (mixed-race Spanish and indigenous people) in the New World.

Eight years later Hernán Cortés arrived in the Yucatán and summoned Guerrero to serve him in his campaign of conquest. But Guerrero had 'gone native', with facial tattoos and body piercings. He turned down the offer, saying instead that he was a captain of the Maya. Cortés moved on in his search for gold and glory. Guerrero, meanwhile, organized Maya defenses in the wars that followed. It would take the Spanish more than 20 years to finally defeat the Maya of Yucatán and Belize.

Caucasian

Approximately 20% of the Central American population is Caucasian – mostly of Spanish origin, descending from conquistadors and colonists who settled here, beginning in the 16th century.

Costa Rica has an unusually high percentage of Caucasians – 66% – due to the limited intermixing between Spanish farmers and indigenous groups there. Europeans continued to descend on Costa Rica throughout the 19th century. Even now, the numbers continue to grow, with the recent influx of retirees and other immigrants from North America.

Guatemala, Nicaragua and Panama all have smaller but still significant Caucasian populations – 12% to 18% – mostly descended from Spanish settlers. In the late 19th and early 20th centuries, the government of Nicaragua gave away land to German and French immigrants who were willing to cultivate it, which contributed to its 17% Caucasian population.

In the 20th century Central America became a refuge for alternative thinkers seeking a peaceful place to live according to beliefs that were unwelcome in North America. Belize has a small but visible population of Mennonites (of German/Dutch descent) who settled here in the 1950s and 1960s in attempt to preserve their traditional way of life and strict moral code. A few years later a group of Quakers fled the US to avoid conscription into the military; they settled in Monteverde, Costa Rica and eventually founded the famous cloud-forest reserve.

Maya Linguistic Groups

Kiche' (1.6 million) – Guatemalan highlands

Yucatec (1.2 million) – Mexico & Belize

Q'equchi' (one million) – Guatemala & Belize

Ch'orti' (51,000) – Guatemala & Honduras

Indigenous

The Maya are the most famous indigenous group in Central America, but there are dozens of lesser known Amerindian groups. These native peoples make up 16% of the overall regional population.

Maya

The Maya are the largest indigenous group in Central America, with an estimated population of seven million. From 2000 BC to AD 1500, the Maya civilization spanned the northern part of Central America, building great cities, undertaking elaborate rituals and engaging in violent warfare. Contemporary Maya culture does not bear much resemblance to its ancient counterpart, but it does retain some unique remnants of the heritage, including traditional clothing, religious practices and – most significantly – language.

Throughout Central America, there are some 32 distinct linguistic groups that comprise the modern-day Maya population. The largest concentration is in Guatemala, where Maya peoples represent nearly 40% of the population. There are also significant populations in Mexico, Belize, Honduras and El Salvador.

Other Indigenous Groups

In pre-Columbian Central America, the southern part of the region was inhabited by many distinct indigenous groups that were unrelated to the Maya. Dozens of them endure to this day, although they all face challenges in preserving their culture, language and identity in this era of increasing global uniformity.

The largest populations include the Ngöbe-Buglé and the Guna in Panama; the Lenca in Honduras and El Salvador; the Miskito in coastal Honduras and Nicaragua; and the Bribrí and Cabécar in Costa Rica.

Afro Central American

From their earliest arrivals in the New World, the Spanish brought African slaves to trade and to work. In the 19th century many other Afro peoples arrived from Jamaica and other parts of the Antilles. African laborers, both immigrants and slaves, played a crucial role in the development of the region – felling forests, building railroads and dredging canals. Nowadays, their descendants make up about 4% of the Central American population, and they are concentrated mainly on the Caribbean coast.

Kriol

Creoles are mixed-race people who are the descendants of African slaves and European baymen, loggers and colonists. There are significant Creole populations in Belize (called Kriol, 25%) and Nicaragua (9%), most of whom are descendants of escaped or shipwrecked slaves. Racially mixed and proud of it, Creoles speak a fascinating and unique version of English: it sounds familiar at first but it is not easily intelligible to a speaker of standard English.

In the 1780s, after much conflict, the Spanish and the British reached an agreement allowing Brits to cut logwood and mahogany in Belize. In return, Britain agreed to abandon the Mosquito Coast of Nicaragua. Thousands of settlers – many of African descent – migrated to Belize to work in the labor-intensive logging industry. After several generations of mixing with the loggers and other colonists, the Kriols became the most populous ethnic group in Belize.

Afro-Panamanians & Costa Ricans

In the second half of the 19th century, both Costa Rica and Panama undertook railroad construction projects to facilitate the transportation of produce and people. In Panama the goal was to move people across the isthmus and on to California during the gold rush. In Costa Rica, the goal was to transport coffee from the dense interior out to Puerto Limón, so it could be shipped out to the world. In both cases, construction laborers were recruited from around the Antilles (especially Jamaica).

Many of these Afro-descended laborers stayed on to work on the banana plantations that sprang up alongside the railroads. Because the plantations were US-owned, the workers had little contact with local Spanish-speaking populations, so retained their customs and language. Nowadays, some 8% of the population in Costa Rica has African roots. Descended mainly from Jamaican workers, they are concentrated on the Caribbean Coast and most speak an English dialect.

In the early 20th century the French commenced construction of the Panama Canal and continued to import labor, bringing thousands of workers from the French Antilles. Some scholars estimate that around 20,000 Afro-Antilleans remained in Panama after the completion of the canal. Nowadays, Afro-Panamanians make up about 15% of the population.

One of the highlights of visiting San Blás, Panama is witnessing firsthand the vibrancy of the Guna's unique culture.

Garifuna

In the 17th century, shipwrecked African slaves washed ashore on the Caribbean island of St Vincent. They hooked up with the indigenous population of Caribs and Arawaks and formed a whole new ethnicity, now known as the Garifuna (plural Garinagu). When St Vincent changed hands, the Garinagu were deported and shuffled around to various islands; their population dwindled until a small group finally arrived on the Honduran coast. From here, these people of mixed Native American and African heritage began to spread along the Caribbean coast of Central America.

Nowadays there are significant populations of Garifuna peoples in Honduras, Belize and Guatemala, with smaller numbers in Nicaragua. Many still speak the Garifuna language, which is a combination of Arawak and African languages. While the Garinagu make up a small percentage of the population (6% in Belize, 1% in Honduras) their cultural influence is disproportionately large. They have a strong sense of community and ritual, in which drumming and dancing play important roles. In 2001 Unesco declared Garifuna language, dance and music to be a 'Masterpiece of the Oral and Intangible Heritage of Humanity' – one of the first recipients of this honor, which is the cultural equivalent of the World Heritage list.

Central American Lifestyles

In Central America, the contrast between urban and rural lifestyles is pretty stark, encompassing jobs, income, education and more. For better or for worse, some things like family and church remain constant – though which church may be a subject for debate these days.

Family

The family unit in Central America remains the nucleus of life. Extended families often live near each other and socialize together. Those with relatives in positions of power – nominal or otherwise – don't hesitate to turn to them for support. Favors are graciously accepted, promptly returned and never forgotten. Despite modernizing influences – education, cable TV, contact with foreign travelers, time spent abroad – traditional family ties remain strong at all levels of society. Old-fashioned gender roles are strong too, although this is changing in Costa Rica, Nicaragua and Panama.

Despite the closeness, many families have at least one member who has emigrated to the United States to work. Remittances from abroad are a major source of income for families across the region.

Religion

Religion continues to be a major force in the lives of Central Americans, though the once staunchly Catholic region is changing. Ever since the arrival of the Spanish – and with them missionaries, priests and papal decrees – Central America has been dominated by Catholicism. Today, about 54% of the region's population are practicing Catholics.

But the 20th century brought a new set of missionaries – this time evangelical Protestants from North America – commonly known as evangelicos. The fiery services and paradisaical promises have particular appeal among the rural poor. Some 28% of the region's population have been wooed into joining the faith.

Urban vs Rural

Central America is characterized by vast discrepancies in levels of healthcare, education, wealth and modernity. These differences often line up along the urban rural divide. In capital cities, well-heeled residents drive high-end cars, own vacation properties and travel overseas. Meanwhile, just an hour's drive away, an indigenous family might paddle a dugout canoe and practice subsistence agriculture.

Even in the region's most prosperous countries (Costa Rica and Panama), somewhere around 25% of the population lives below the poverty level. In the poorest countries (Guatemala and Honduras), the number is more than 50%. The vast majority of the destitute live in rural areas, many representing indigenous groups. Across the region, the rural poor have significantly lower standards of living, fewer opportunities for education and less-than-adequate healthcare. The region has seen waves of outgoing migration, as the sons and daughters of farmers seek out better lives in the cities.

The middle and upper classes reside mainly in urban areas, especially in capital cities, where they enjoy a lifestyle that is similar to their counterparts in North America or Europe.

Arts & Culture

You probably didn't come to Central America for high culture: art museums and symphony halls are few on the ground. To discover the richness of Central America's arts, you have to look in unexpected places – gritty dance clubs and dark alleys, rural villages and women's cooperatives. In Central America, anyone and everyone is an artist, or a musician, or a poet. Art is all around you, so keep your eyes open.

Street Art

Throughout Central America, the art scene is vibrant and visible, as some of the most poignant contemporary work takes the form of street art – murals and mosaics that grace decrepit buildings and brighten city streets. Often these paintings record historic events and raise awareness of social issues, a tradition that dates to a time when a large percentage of the population was illiterate. Interestingly, the street art is most vibrant in war-torn countries such as El Salvador, Guatemala and Nicaragua.

In El Salvador, the best examples are in Perquín, La Palma and Suchitoto, as well as the capital. In 1997 national icon Fernando Llort created a colorful, folkloric ceramic-tile mural entitled *Harmonia de Mi Pueblo*. A tribute to persevering Salvadorans and a celebration of peace, the artwork was mounted on the facade of the Catedral Metropolitana in San Salvador. Artists and residents were shocked and outraged when the local archbishop had the mural removed in 2012, without consulting the government or the artist.

Paintings cover the walls in many Nicaraguan cities, especially the Sandinista strongholds of León and Estelí. The latter is home to a new movement of *muralistas*, who use more recognizable graffiti techniques to convey their social commentary.

Urban Maeztro is the pseudonym of a Honduran street artist who makes provocative, overtly political work, decrying the violence that pervades Tegucigalpa.

The most famous Guatemalan artist is Efraín Recinos, whose murals grace the National Music Conservatory. He's also a celebrated architect and sculptor. Not exactly a street artist, Recinos was awarded Guatemala's highest honor, the Order of the Quetzal, in 1999.

INDIGENOUS ARTS & CRAFTS

Souvenir hunters will be delighted by the wealth of handicrafts and folk art that is available in Central America, much of it produced by indigenous groups in the region.

Especially in the highlands of Guatemala, the Maya weave festive, colorful clothing and textiles. The *huipil* (a women's tunic) is often a true work of art – a multicolored web of stylized animal, human, plant and mythological shapes. Many women still use the pre-Hispanic backstrap loom to make these creations.

Panama's indigenous groups produce high-quality woodcarvings, textiles, ceramics, masks and other handicrafts. The Emberá and Wounaan are renowned for their woven baskets, some of which are highly decorated with bright colors and natural motifs, made from the nahuala bush and chunga palm. The Guna are known for their *molas* (the embroidered panels used by women in their traditional dress). Ocú and Penonomé people produce superior panama hats.

In Costa Rica, indigenous crafts include intricately carved and painted masks made by the Boruca, as well as handwoven bags and linens and colorful Chorotega pottery.

Poetry

In Central America, peasants can be poets, and poets can do politics. Poetry is beloved throughout the region, especially in the countries that have seen the most violence and poverty – always good inspiration for verse.

Guatemala's first great literary figure was poet and Jesuit priest Rafael Landivar, whose collection of poetry was published in 1781. The literary spokesperson of the Guatemala people is Miguel Ángel Asturias (1899–1974). His masterpiece novel, *Men of Maize*, won him the Nobel Prize for Literature in 1967, but before that he was a poet-diplomat and an outspoken political commentator.

In Nicaragua, any *campesino* (farmer) can tell you who the greatest poet in history is: Rubén Darío, voice of the nation and founder of the *modernismo* literary movement. Nicaragua is also home to the peculiar cultural archetype of 'warrior poets,' folks who choose to use both the pen and the sword. The best known example is Gioconda Belli, who was working undercover with the Sandinistas when she won the prestigious Casa de las Americas international poetry prize.

Speaking of warrior poets, Salvadoran poet Roque Dalton was exiled for his radical politics – and eventually executed for allegedly playing double agent. His notable works include *Taberna y Otros Lugares* (1969), a political vision in verse.

Music

At the intersection of Latin beats and Caribbean cool, there is the *música* of Central America. You'll hear calypso, reggae, soca and salsa around the region, but you'll also discover lesser-known, uniquely Central American musical genres that incorporate the best of the more mainstream styles.

The marimba is a percussion instrument that resembles a xylophone, except it's made of wood and so produces a mellower sound. The instrument is usually played by three men; there's a carnival-like quality to its sound and compositions. Marimba music is used during Maya religious ceremonies, and it's considered the national instrument in Guatemala. But it's also popular in Costa Rica and Nicaragua, where groups like La Cuneta Son Machín have updated marimba folk music with a *cumbia*-rock beat.

Musicians and linguists speculate that the name *punta*, a traditional Garifuna drumming style, comes from the word *bunda*, which means 'buttocks' in many West African languages. The word derivation is not certain, but it is perhaps apt. Played at any celebration, this music inspires Garifuna peoples across Central America to get up and shake their *bunda*.

In the 1970s Belizean musician Pen Cayetano traveled around Central America and came to the realization that Garifuna traditions were in danger of withering away. He wanted to inspire young people to embrace their own culture, so he invented a cool and contemporary genre by adding electric guitar to traditional *punta* rhythms – and so *punta* rock was born. Since the 1980s, *punta* rock has become popular across the region (and across ethnic groups), though especially in Belize and Honduras.

Once the music of the urban poor in Panama, reggaetón nowadays permeates all countries and social strata in Central America (and beyond). Taking cues from hip hop, especially the rap-like vocals, this unique genre also incorporates musical influences from Jamaican dance-house, Trinidadian soca and Puerto Rican salsa. Reggaetón is wildly popular across the region, especially in Panama, Costa Rica and Guatemala.

Panamanian songwriter and salsa star Rubén Blades attracted 18% of the vote when he ran for president. Will he try again in 2019?

Survival Guide

DIRECTORY A–Z 724

Accommodations 724

Children 725

Customs
Regulations 725

Discount Cards 725

Electricity 725

Embassies
& Consulates 725

Food & Drink 726

Health 726

Insurance 727

Internet Access 728

Legal Matters 728

LGBT Travelers 728

Maps 728

Money 729

Opening Hours 729

Post 729

Public Holidays 729

Safe Travel 730

Smoking 731

Telephone 731

Time 731

Toilets 731

Tourist
Information 732

Travelers with
Disabilities 732

Visas 732

Volunteering 732

Women Travelers 733

Work 733

TRANSPORTATION . . 734

GETTING THERE
& AWAY 734

Entering the Country 734

Air 734

Land 735

Sea 736

GETTING AROUND 736

Air 736

Bicycle 737

Boat 737

Bus .737

Car & Motorcycle 738

Hitchhiking 738

LANGUAGE 739

Glossary 744

Food & Drink Glossary 746

Directory A–Z

Accommodations

The cost of accommodations varies from country to country. Nicaragua, Honduras and Guatemala are the cheapest countries, while Mexico, Belize, Panama and Costa Rica (and many beach destinations) are more expensive. Features such as a private bathroom, hot water and aircon will drive up the price.

Reservations are necessary in tourist areas during peak season, particularly during Semana Santa (Easter Week) and the week between Christmas and New Year, when locals are also traveling around the region.

Prices do change; use any prices listed as a gauge only.

Camping

If you plan on camping, it's best to bring your own gear. Organized campgrounds aren't common. Facilities at campgrounds vary widely, so make sure you know ahead of time if fire pits, latrines and water will be available.

Some hostels have dedicated camping areas. Some national parks and reserves (particularly in Costa Rica) also have basic camping facilities, but they can get crowded. In some places it's also feasible to ask to camp on private land.

Guesthouses & Hotels

Guesthouses are generally small, family-run lodgings. Most rooms have a fan and shared bathroom (though you may need to bring your own towel and soap). Conditions are highly variable, ranging from nice rooms with a shared bathroom to rooms with a dumpy bed, smeared mosquito remains on the walls, and a smelly leaky-faucet shower down the hall.

In hotels, rooms with air-con and TV usually cost at least $20 more than a room with a fan. Breakfast is not usually included in the overnight rate.

'Hot water' can be lukewarm and working only at certain hours of the day. Be sure to inquire if your water is unexpectedly cold, as it may just be a matter of turning on the hot water heater. Beware of the electric shower – it's a cold-water showerhead juiced by an electric heating element. Don't touch it, or anything metal, while in the shower or you may get a shock.

Used toilet paper should be placed in the receptacle provided, and *not* flushed down the toilet.

We've done our best to avoid listing places used by the 'hourly' crowd. If you stumble on some we've included, please let us know.

Hammocks & Cabins

Sleeping in a hammock can make for a breezier night than sleeping in a stuffy room. Many beach towns have hammock rooms or areas for the same price as a dorm. *Cabañas* (or *cabinas; cabins*) provide memorable stays on the beach or in the jungle. Amenities vary – many are simple thatched-roof huts with a dirt or sand floor.

Homestays

Spanish-language schools arrange homestays in towns where the language-school scene is strong, including Antigua and Quetzaltenango (Guatemala), Granada (Nicaragua), Copán (Honduras) and Bocas del Toro (Panama). A similar option is *turismo rural* – community tourism initiatives with rural homestays.

Homestays usually offer private sleeping quarters in a local home, with bathroom facilities shared with the family. Meals are often included. It's usually an affordable room-and-board option, with the added benefit of giving you plenty of opportunities to practice your Spanish.

Hostels

Hostels are found throughout Central America and serve all ages. Many hostels offer a few private rooms in addition to dormitories with bunk beds (which generally cost around US$10 to US$15 per person).

Children

Central America is a safe and exciting destination for families with children. Beaches on two coastlines, wildlife-rich forests and endless opportunities for adventure guarantee to thrill kids of all ages.

➡ Be sure children are up to date on all routine immunizations. Some recommended vaccines may not be approved for children, so be careful they do not drink tap water or consume any questionable food.

➡ For more ideas about family travel, see Lonely Planet's *Travel with Children*. For information on climate around the region, see the Directory section of our individual country content.

Customs Regulations

All visitors leaving and entering a Central American country go through customs. Be prepared for bag checks at both airports and land borders. Most are just a quick gaze-and-poke, more of a formality than a search – but not always. Be polite with officials at all times.

Discount Cards

A member card from **Hostelling International** (HI; www.hihostels.com) isn't terribly useful in Central America, except in Mexico and Costa Rica where some hostels offer minimal discounts to cardholders. Those going on to South America, however, may want to invest in the membership, as the card is more commonly accepted there.

Carriers of the **International Student Identity Card** (ISIC; www.isic.org) can get very good discounts on travel insurance, as well as discounted air tickets.

Electricity

Most countries in Central America use plug type A or B, the same as is used in the United States. In Belize, you may come across type G plugs. Voltage varies between 110v and 220v. For more information see www.worldstandards.org.

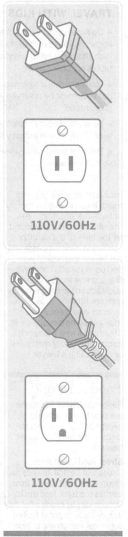

110V/60Hz

110V/60Hz

Embassies & Consulates

For embassy phone numbers and addresses, see the Directory section of each individual country.

As a visitor in a Central American country, it's important to realize what your own country's embassy can and can't do. Generally speaking,

TRAVEL WITH KIDS

➡ Do not expect all the amenities that are available at home, as you're unlikely to find conveniences such as high chairs in restaurants, cribs at hotels, or changing tables in public toilets.

➡ Many car rental agencies offer child seats (for a fee), but they must be reserved in advance and quality is not guaranteed.

➡ Formula, diapers and other baby necessities are widely available in grocery stores.

➡ Discreet public breastfeeding is common, though less so in urban areas.

your embassy will not help much if you're even remotely at fault in a situation – remember that you are bound by the laws of the country you are in. Your embassy will not be sympathetic if you end up in jail after committing a crime locally, even if such actions are legal in your own country.

In an emergency, you may get some assistance in obtaining a new passport, contacting family members or contacting a lawyer.

Food & Drink

Reservations for eating here are practically unheard of, except at high-end restaurants in the biggest tourist centers.

Street Food Urban areas throughout Central America have cheap street food, served from *carritos* (carts) or food trucks. Options vary by country, but may include tacos, *pupusas* (grilled corn meal with cheese or bean filling) or *churrasco* (BBQ meat) with rice and beans.

Comedores A simple diner serving set meals – almost every town has one. Also known as *sodas* in Costa Rica.

Restaurantes A more formal dining experience than the *comedor*, with a wider menu and probably a selection of wines and beers.

Health

The most critical health concern in Central America is mosquito-borne illnesses, and all travelers should take precautions to prevent mosquito bites: strong insect repellent with DEET is essential. At the time of research, pregnant women (and women who are trying to get pregnant) are advised against traveling to Central America due to the outbreak of the Zika virus.

There are no required vaccinations for Central America, except if you are coming from a yellow-fever–infected country in Africa or South America – then you must have a yellow fever vaccine. Among others recommended are typhoid, rabies and hepatitis A and B. Visit your doctor well ahead of your trip, since most vaccines don't produce immunity until at least two weeks after they're given. Ask your doctor for an International Certificate of Vaccination (aka 'the yellow booklet'), which will list all the vaccinations you've received. This is mandatory for countries that require proof of yellow-fever vaccination.

Before You Go
HEALTH INSURANCE

Find out in advance if your insurance plan will make payments directly to providers or reimburse you later for overseas health expenditure. If the latter, be sure to collect receipts.

If your travel insurance does not cover you for medical expenses abroad, consider buying supplemental insurance. Check lonely planet.com/travel-insurance for more information.

US travelers can find a list of recommended doctors abroad and emergency evacuation details on the website of the **US State Department** (http://travel.state.gov). Click on International Travel, then Before You Go, then Your Health Abroad.

RESOURCES

It's usually a good idea to consult the health sections of your government's travel advice before departure. Other resources:

World Health Organization (www.who.int/ith) Publishes a superb book called *International Travel and Health*, which is revised annually and available on its website at no cost. The website lists updated risks and worldwide vaccination certificate requirements.

MD Travel Health (www.mdtravelhealth.com) Provides complete travel health recommendations for every country, updated daily.

In Central America
AVAILABILITY & COST OF HEALTH CARE

Good medical care is available in most of the region's capital cities, but options are limited elsewhere. In general, private hospitals are more reliable than public facilities, which may experience significant shortages of equipment and supplies.

Many doctors and hospitals expect payment in cash, regardless of whether you have travel health insurance. If you develop a life-threatening medical problem, you'll probably want to be evacuated to a country with state-of-the-art medical care. Since this may cost tens of thousands of dollars, take out travel insurance that covers medical expenses before your trip.

Many pharmacies are well supplied, but important medications may not be consistently available. Be sure to bring along adequate supplies of all prescription drugs.

INSECT-BORNE DISEASES

All travelers are advised to take precautions against insect-borne diseases, including malaria, chinkunguyna, dengue and Zika. Many of these illnesses cannot be prevented with vaccines or medication, so the most effective prevention is to avoid bug bites:

➡ Use an insect repellent that contains 20% or more DEET.

➡ Treat clothing, bedding and camping gear with permethrin, which binds tightly to clothing.

➡ Cover exposed skin with long sleeves, pants and hats.

➡ Sleep in places with screened windows or use a bed net.

TAP WATER

Tap water is not safe to drink in many parts of Central America. Vigorous boiling for one minute is the most effective means of water purification. At altitudes greater than 2000m (6500ft), boil for three minutes.

Another option is to disinfect water with iodine pills. Instructions are usually enclosed and should be carefully followed. Or else you can add 2% tincture of iodine to one liter of water (five drops to clear water, 10 drops to cloudy water) and let it stand for 30 minutes. If the water is cold, longer times may be required. The taste of iodinated water may be improved by adding vitamin C (ascorbic acid). Iodinated water should not be consumed for more than a few weeks. Pregnant women, those with a history of thyroid disease and those allergic to iodine should not drink iodinated water.

A number of water filters are on the market. Those with smaller pores (reverse osmosis filters) provide the broadest protection, but they are relatively large and also readily plugged by debris. Those that have somewhat larger pores (microstrainer filters) are ineffective against viruses, although they do remove other organisms. Manufacturers' instructions must be carefully followed.

Insurance

A travel insurance policy covering theft, loss, accidents and illness is highly recommended. Some policies compensate travelers for misrouted or lost luggage. Also check that the coverage includes worst-case scenarios: ambulances, evacuations or an emergency flight home. Some policies specifically exclude 'dangerous activities', which can include scuba diving, motorcycling or even trekking. Be sure to read the small print.

There is a wide variety of policies available. Policies handled by student-travel organizations usually offer good value. If a policy offers lower and higher

RECOMMENDED VACCINATIONS

VACCINE	RECOMMENDED FOR	DOSAGE	SIDE EFFECTS
chicken pox	travelers who've never had chicken pox	2 doses; 1 month apart	fever, mild case of chicken pox
hepatitis A	all travelers	1 dose before trip; booster 6-12 months later	soreness at injection site, headaches, body aches
hepatitis B	long-term travelers in close contact with the local population	3 doses over 6-month period	soreness at injection site, low-grade fever
measles	travelers born after 1956 who've had only 1 measles vaccination	1 dose	fever, rash, joint pains, allergic reactions
rabies	travelers who may have contact with animals and may not have access to medical care	3 doses over 3- to 4-week period	soreness at injection site, headaches, body aches
tetanus-diphtheria	all travelers who haven't had a booster within 10 years	1 dose lasts 10 years	soreness at injection site
typhoid fever	all travelers	4 capsules by mouth; 1 taken every other day	abdominal pain, nausea, rash
yellow fever	required for travelers arriving from a yellow-fever–infected area in Africa or South America	1 dose lasts 10 years	headaches, body aches; severe reactions are rare

medical-expense options, the low-expenses policy should be OK for Central America – medical costs are not nearly as high here as elsewhere.

If you are robbed (p730) and need to make a claim, you must report the loss or theft to local police within 24 hours. Make a list of stolen items and their value. At the police station, you need to complete a *denuncia* (statement), a copy of which is given to you for your insurance claim.

Worldwide travel insurance is available at www. lonelyplanet.com/travel-insurance. You can buy, extend and claim online anytime – even if you're already on the road.

Internet Access

Internet access is widely available. Wi-fi is available at all but the most basic places to stay, as well as at some cafes and restaurants. Many hostels also have guest computers.

Internet cafes are less prevalent than they used to be; rates range from US$0.50 per hour in cities and touristy destinations to US$6 in remote areas.

Either Alt + 64 or Alt-G + 2 is the command to get the @ symbol on Spanish-language keyboards.

Legal Matters

It is advisable (and sometimes required) to carry a passport or photo ID at all times.

Costa Rica, Guatemala and Honduras have dedicated tourist police working in the big cities. In some countries the police force has a reputation for corruption, but it is unlikely that you will be stopped and hassled or asked for a bribe. Law enforcement is generally professional, visible and effective. Throughout the

region, police checkpoints and vehicle searches are not uncommon.

Marijuana and cocaine are illegal everywhere in the region and penalties are severe. Recent reforms to drug laws in Mexico stipulate that first-time offenders are not punished for possession of a small amount of drugs for personal use. Allowable amounts are strictly enforced, and offenders will generally be arrested and prosecuted.

In many countries, you are presumed guilty until found innocent. If you are accused of a serious crime, you will be taken to jail. In this case, your embassy will offer only limited assistance. This may include a visit from an embassy staff member to make sure your human rights have not been violated, contacting your family and putting you in touch with a lawyer (whom you must pay yourself).

LGBT Travelers

Central America can be an unwelcoming place for gay men and lesbians, but there are some bright spots. Same-sex marriage was legalized in Mexico in 2009 and in Costa Rica in 2013. The current president of Costa Rica, Luis Guillermo Solís, has been unusually vocal in his support for gay rights, and even flew the rainbow flag at the presidential house.

Advocacy groups in other Central American countries are eager to follow suit. Consensual gay sex has been decriminalized all around the region, with the exception of Belize. Gay and lesbian travelers can actually be barred from entering Belize, though we are not aware of any such incidents.

That said, official and unofficial harassment is possible anywhere in Central America. In general, public displays of affection will not

be tolerated and gay men (and possibly women) could find themselves the target of verbal or physical abuse. Discretion is definitely the rule in Central America, especially in the countryside. Lesbians are generally less maligned than gay men so women traveling together should encounter few, if any, problems.

Where to Go

There is usually at least one gay bar in big cities, which makes meeting people easier. Some of the more public gay and lesbian scenes:

Costa Rica There is a thriving scene in San José (p520) and in Manuel Antonio (p593).

El Salvador The charming mountain town of San Vicente (p324) is a popular gay destination.

Guatemala Travelers will find a small and subdued gay scene in both Antigua (p114) and Guatemala City (p101).

Mexico The biggest and best gay scene in the region is at the bars and clubs in Cancún (p50) and Playa del Carmen (p59).

Nicaragua Travelers will find a few gay-specific bars in Managua (p431).

Panama Bars come and go, but the gay scene in Panama City (p623) is surprisingly limited. The normally discreet population is more open during **Carnaval** (☺Feb/Mar) festivities, which usually feature a gay float in the parade.

Maps

The best map of the region is the fold-up color 1:1,100,000 *Central America Travel Reference Map* (US$13), produced by **International Travel Maps & Books** (www.itmb.ca) in Canada.

ITMB also publishes separate maps covering each of the Central American countries and various regions of Mexico, as well as several maps of South America.

Money

ATMs

➡ Bring an ATM (or debit) card. ATMs are available in most cities and large towns and are almost always the most convenient, reliable, secure and economical way of getting cash. Many ATMs are connected to the MasterCard/Cirrus or Visa/Plus networks.

➡ The exchange rate from ATMs is usually as good as (if not better than) that at any bank or legal money changer.

➡ Notify your bank of your travel plans so international transactions are not rejected.

Black Market

The *mercado negro* (black market) – also known as *mercado paralelo* (parallel market) – is generally limited to money changers at borders, who may or may not be legal. They are known to slip in torn bills or to short-change on occasion, though they accept local currencies that banks elsewhere sometimes don't take. Such unofficial exchange rates for the US dollar can be lower than official bank rates.

Cash

It's a good idea to always have a small amount of US dollars handy – enough to get a room, a meal and a taxi, at least – because they can be exchanged or even spent practically anywhere. It's particularly useful when crossing the border or when an ATM isn't available. Central American currencies don't always fly in the next country; plan ahead before you head to remote areas and take more than enough cash.

Getting change for bigger notes in local currency is a daily concern. Notes worth even US$20 can sometimes be difficult to change.

Credit & Debit Cards

➡ American Express, Visa and MasterCard are the most widely accepted credit cards in Central America. Some card companies also charge a fee (from 2% to 10%) for international transactions. Some banks issue cash advances on major credit cards.

➡ Although credit cards are widely accepted, it is not always economical to use them. In Costa Rica, for example, many hotels offer a discount for cash payment.

Money changers

Change traveler's checks or foreign cash at a bank or a *casa de cambio* (currency exchange office). Rates between the two are usually similar, but in general *casas de cambio* are quicker, less bureaucratic and open longer or on weekends. Street money changers, who may or may not be legal, will only handle cash.

Sometimes you can also change money unofficially at hotels or in shops that sell imported goods (electronics dealers are an obvious choice). Compare exchange rates and commission fees first. Big cities tend to offer better exchange rates.

Don't accept torn notes, as most locals won't when you try to use them.

Traveler's Checks

Traveler's checks are not nearly as convenient as ATM cards and you may have difficulty cashing them – even at banks. If you must, use only widely accepted brands, such as American Express, Visa, Thomas Cook and Citibank. To facilitate replacement, keep a record of check numbers and the original bill of sale separately in a safe place.

In some countries, such as Honduras, traveler's checks are nearly impossible to cash and banks and *casas de cambio* charge high commissions. Check if there's a fixed transaction fee (regardless of the value of the checks) or a percentage fee (from 3% up to 10%).

Opening Hours

Standard opening hours can be found in the Directory section of each individual country.

Post

International postal rates can be quite expensive. Generally, important mail and parcels should be sent by registered or certified service; otherwise they may go missing. Sending parcels can be awkward, as often a customs officer must inspect the contents before a postal clerk can accept them, so don't seal them until the packages have been inspected. The place for posting parcels overseas is sometimes different from the main post office.

UPS, FedEx, DHL and other shipping and private courier services are available in some countries, providing an efficient but expensive alternative.

Public Holidays

New Year's Day January 1 (region-wide)

Martyrs' Day January 9 (Panama)

Baron Bliss Day March 9 (Belize)

Good Friday March or April (region-wide)

Holy Saturday March or April (region-wide)

Easter Monday March or April (region-wide)

Juan Santamaría Day April 11 (Costa Rica)

Day of the Americas April 14 (Honduras)

Labor Day May 1 (region-wide)

Sovereign's Day May 24 (Belize)

Mother's Day May 30 (Nicaragua)

Army Day June 30 (Guatemala)

Feast of San Salvador August 6 (El Salvador)

Mother's Day August 15 (Costa Rica)

Assumption Day August 15 (Guatemala)

Founding of Old Panama August 15 (Panama City only)

National Day September 10 (Belize)

Battle of San Jacinto September 14 (Nicaragua)

Independence Day September 15 (Costa Rica, El Salvador, Guatemala, Honduras, Nicaragua)

Independence Day September 21 (Belize)

Francisco Morazán Day October 3 (Honduras)

Columbus Day October 12 (Belize, Costa Rica, Honduras, Panama)

Revolution Day (Día de la Revolución) October 20 (Guatemala)

Army Day October 21 (Honduras)

All Souls Day November 2 (El Salvador, Guatemala, Nicaragua, Panama)

Independence Day November 3 (Panama)

First Call for Independence November 10 (Panama)

Garifuna Settlement Day November 19 (Belize)

Independence from Spain November 28 (Panama)

Immaculate Conception December 8 (Nicargua)

Mothers' Day December 8 (Panama)

Christmas Day December 25 (region-wide)

Safe Travel

➡ Parts of Honduras, El Salvador and Guatemala are plagued by high crime rates and gang activity. It doesn't usually involve foreign visitors, but some have been victims of grab-and-run theft, assault, rape, carjacking and murder.

➡ Capital cities tend to have the highest rates of crime.

➡ Many sexual assaults occur on isolated beaches.

➡ Avoid night buses (with the possible exception of Mexico and Panama), as highway robberies often happen at night.

➡ It's wise to seek updates from other travelers, tourist offices, police, guesthouse owners and Lonely Planet's **Thorn Tree** (www.lonelyplanet.com/thorntree).

Darién Province

Certain parts of Darién Province (p684), on the Panama-Colombia border, are restricted. Travel requires special permission from Servicios Nacional de Fronteras (SeNaFront) in Panama City. The US Department of State warns travelers against visiting this remote area, due to the potential dangers.

Drugs

➡ Avoid any conversation with someone who offers you drugs.

➡ If you are in an area where drug trafficking is prevalent, ignore it and do not show any interest whatsoever, since drugs are sometimes used to set up travelers for blackmail and bribery.

Natural Hazards

Central America is prone to a wide variety of natural disasters, including earthquakes, hurricanes, floods and volcanic eruptions. General information about natural-disaster preparedness is available from the **US Federal Emergency Management Agency** (www.fema.gov).

Police & Military

Corruption is a very serious problem among Latin American police, who are generally poorly paid and poorly supervised. In many countries, they are not reluctant to plant drugs on unsuspecting travelers or enforce minor regulations to the letter in the hope of extracting *coimas* (bribes).

➡ If you are stopped by someone claiming to be a plainclothes policeman, never get into a vehicle with them. Don't give them any documents or show them any money and don't take them to your hotel. If the police appear to be the real thing, insist on going to a police station on foot.

➡ Military checkpoints are frequent in places such as Chiapas, Panama's Darién Province and El Salvador. Most involve routine passport checks.

➡ In police stations, English-speaking interpreters are a rarity. Some cities have a tourist police service that may be more helpful.

Robbery & Theft

Thefts take place, particularly in larger cities and transit points such as bus stations. Most is of the pickpocket or grab-and-run variety. Be wary of offers of food, drinks, sweets or cigarettes from strangers on buses, trains or in bars, as they could be laced with sedatives.

If you are the victim of a robbery, go to the police to report the theft and to get a police statement to present to your insurance company. Say '*Quiero poner una acta de un robo*' (I want to report a robbery). You may have to write up the report yourself, then present it for an official stamp and signature.

Photocopies or photos of original passports, visas and air tickets and careful records of credit-card numbers are invaluable during replacement procedures. Replacement passport applications are usually referred to the home country, so it helps to have someone back home with a copy of passport details.

To protect yourself:

➡ Don't use an iPhone or laptop in public places, as it may attract the attention of thieves.

➡ Wear a money belt to keep a bigger stash of money or your passport out of sight. Keep small amounts of cash in your pockets but use zip pockets.

➡ Purses or bags can be slashed or grabbed. Use a cheap, nondescript bag for walking around cities.

➡ Be wary of anyone pointing out a spilled substance (mustard, dog feces) on your clothes. It's a classic pickpocketing ploy: one thief helps to clean the victims, the other robs them.

➡ Avoid night buses.

➡ It's worth splurging on taxis after dark, particularly in cities. Don't wander alone down empty city streets or in isolated areas.

➡ When possible, keep valuables sealed in a signed envelope in a hotel safe.

➡ Keep doors and windows locked.

➡ Don't camp overnight on beaches or in the countryside unless you can be sure it's safe.

➡ Get local safety news from guesthouse owners, tourist offices and other travelers.

➡ Don't resist a robbery. Many thieves are armed.

Swimming Safety

Hundreds of people drown each year at Central America's beaches. Of these, 80% are caused by riptides – strong currents that pull the swimmer out to sea. They can occur even in waist-deep water. The best advice: ask about conditions before entering the water. If it's dangerous, don't tempt the ocean.

Smoking

Smoking regulations vary widely from country to country. In Belize and Nicaragua, there are few restrictions, and smoking in bars and restaurants is generally permitted. In Costa Rica and Panama, it is banned in all enclosed spaces, as well as outdoor public places. The other countries' laws are somewhere in between, but generally ban smoking in enclosed public areas.

Telephone

Internet cafes with net-to-phone (VOIP) service provide the cheapest way to make international calls, with rates varying between US$0.10 and US$0.50 per minute to the USA and Europe.

From traditional landlines, the most economical way of calling abroad is by phone cards purchased at kiosks or corner stores. You can also try direct-dial lines, accessed via special numbers and billed to an account at home. It is sometimes cheaper to make a collect or credit-card call to Europe or North America than to pay for the call where you are.

Many towns and cities have a telephone office with phone booths for local and international calls. Rates can be high. Avoid credit-card phones in Mexico and the black 'press button' phones in Guatemala, which charge extortionate rates.

Cell Phones

Cell (mobile) phones are widely used around Central America's bigger towns and cities. Calling a cell phone is always more expensive than calling a landline.

If you plan to carry your own cell phone, a GSM tri- or quad-band phone is your best bet. Another option is purchasing a prepaid SIM card in-country. You will need a compatible GSM phone that's SIM-unlocked. Or else you can purchase a cheap local cell phone, available in kiosks from around US$20.

Time

Most of Central America is on Central Standard Time (GMT/UTC minus six hours). The exception is Panama, which is on Eastern Standard Time (GMT/UTC minus five hours).

Toilets

The toilets of Central America are fine; it's just the plumbing that has issues. Nowhere in the region should you deposit toilet paper or anything else in the toilet unless a sign specifies that it's OK to do so. Wastebaskets are generally provided for that purpose.

Some public toilets have attendants who charge a small fee (US$0.10 or so) and provide paper. It's a good idea to keep a spare roll of toilet paper handy while traveling.

Tourist Information

Travelers will find a tourist office in the capital city of each country; some countries have them in outlying towns as well. If you're a student, look for student travel agencies in the capital cities of Costa Rica and Panama and in Cancún, Mexico.

Check www.visitcentro america.com (in Spanish only), which has standard tourist-board coverage of all countries.

Travelers with Disabilities

Central America generally isn't well equipped for those with disabilities: services such as specially equipped phones, toilets or anything in braille are rare to the point of nonexistence. Expensive international hotels are more likely to cater to guests with disabilities than cheap hotels; air travel or pre-arranged transportation will be more feasible than most local buses; off-the-beaten-track destinations will be less accessible than well-developed ones.

Belize and Costa Rica are better equipped for travelers with disabilities than other Central American countries (due in part to the many elderly travelers who arrive on cruise ships). In both countries, it's possible to find hotels and attractions that can accommodate wheelchairs, especially in the most popular tourist spots. Some of Costa Rica's well-known national parks are also wheelchair-accessible, including Parque Nacional Volcán Poás and (soon) Parque Nacional Rincon de la Vieja.

It's not region-specific, but **Access-Able Travel Source** (www.access-able.com) is an excellent resource to consult for more information.

Resources

Download Lonely Planet's free *Accessible Travel* guide from http://lptravel.to/AccessibleTravel.

Visas

At present citizens of the USA, EU, Canada, Australia, New Zealand and many other nations can arrive in all Central American countries (including Mexico) without arranging a visa beforehand. Check ahead from your country before planning your trip, as this may change.

Many countries charge an entry or tourist fee upon arrival – from US$5 to US$20.

Note that, if you need a visa for a certain country and arrive at a land border without one, you will probably have to return to the nearest town that has a consulate and obtain a visa. Airlines will not normally let you board a plane to a country for which you don't have the necessary visa. Also, a visa in itself may not guarantee entry: in rare cases, you may still be turned back at the border if you don't have sufficient funds for your visit or an onward or return ticket (p735).

Requirements for Entry

Checking passports is a routine procedure upon arriving in a country, but some officials may ask about your financial resources either verbally or on the application form. If you lack 'sufficient

funds' for your proposed visit, officials may limit the length of your stay. (US$500 per month for your planned stay is generally considered sufficient; traveler's checks, and sometimes a credit card, should qualify toward the total amount.)

Several Central American countries require you to have an onward ticket (p735) leaving the country.

Visa Extensions

Once you are inside a country, you can always apply for an extension at the country's immigration office *(migración)*. There's usually a limit to how many extensions you can receive; if you leave the country and re-enter, your time starts over again.

Volunteering

'Voluntourism' is a recent travel trend that allows travelers to learn more about a place they visit and – ideally – 'give back' to the host community.

Some international organizations make arrangements for volunteers, which can be an expensive endeavor. You can also find local volunteer opportunities once in the country (although advance arrangements are still recommended). Be aware that most volunteer opportunities require a minimum time commitment; volunteers usually pay a fixed fee to cover room and board.

On offer are programs to teach English, pick up trash, work on farms, construct

VIVA EL CA-4!

Guatemala, Honduras, El Salvador and Nicaragua's 'CA-4 Border Control' agreement allows free travel for up to 90 days within this sub-region for citizens of the four countries and many foreign nationals (including residents of the USA, Canada, the UK and Australia).

On paper, at least, you should only have to pay a tourist fee once to enter these four countries. Yet border patrols may also charge you a few dollars for 'paperwork'; if they insist, you won't have much alternative but to pay.

homes, maintain trails, monitor turtle nesting beaches, care for rescue animals and assist at medical clinics. Volunteer opportunities are often in isolated locations, and they may involve long hours and grueling work. But the work can also be tremendously rewarding.

For more information on volunteering, get a copy of Lonely Planet's *Volunteer: A Traveller's Guide to Making a Difference Around the World.*

International Volunteer Organizations

Some of these international organizations offer the chance to get college credit or take Spanish classes as a part of the volunteer opportunity.

Amigos de las Américas (www.amigoslink.org) Youth-oriented summer programs range from working in a national park to helping with community development in Costa Rica, Mexico, Nicaragua and Panama.

Habitat for Humanity (www.habitat.org) Join an eight-day 'Global Village' trip to Central America to help with home construction, clean air and water projects or community development.

Idealist (www.idealist.org) A forum for advertising volunteering opportunities, internships and jobs around the world.

International Volunteer Programs Association (www.volunteerinternational.org) Does not run its own programs, but partners with other associations

to recruit volunteers and ensure a rewarding experience.

ResponsibleTravel (www.responsibletravel.com) UK-based, ecofriendly tour operator with many volunteer trips.

STA Travel (www.statravel.com) A worldwide student-travel agent that offers trips with a volunteering element.

Transitions Abroad (www.transitionsabroad.com) Has numerous volunteer links; look on its website under Central America.

Women Travelers

Women traveling solo through Central America typically find that popular perceptions overestimate the dangers they face. The biggest adjustment is getting used to the vocal male population, many of whom hoot, hiss and whistle. Ignore this behavior and most of the time you will be simply left alone.

Of course, women should take all the normal precautions they would in any new territory or big city. Dress according to local norms to avoid unwanted attention (often this means avoiding shorts). Talk to locals to find out which areas may be dangerous. Certain bars and soccer games tend to be testosterone-fueled territory where a woman's presence will invite attention.

Locals, particularly families, will often go out of their way to help a single female traveler. Keep in mind, though, that it's more typical for Latin American women to socialize with other women,

and women in Central America's more conservative societies rarely have male friends – so befriending someone's husband can attract resentment. Socializing with men here in general is a little unusual – it's probable that they will think you want more than friendship.

In the case of sexual assault, it's best to contact your embassy and see a doctor.

Work

According to law you must have a permit to work in Central America. In practice people may get paid under the table or through some bureaucratic loophole, if they can find suitable work. Many travelers work short-term jobs (through the aforementioned loophole) in restaurants, hostels or bars geared to international travelers, for subsistence wages. Before taking such a job, consider volunteering instead, as many of these jobs could just as well be performed by locals.

Teaching English is another option, though bear in mind that wages do not match international standards. Big cities offer the best possibilities for schools or private tutoring. Many schools will require Teaching English as a Foreign Language (TEFL) teaching certificates.

Some international organizations publish job opportunities.

Transportation

GETTING THERE & AWAY

Most visitors reach Central America by air or overland from Mexico. Flights, cars and tours can be booked online at lonelyplanet.com/bookings.

Entering the Country

Make sure your passport is valid for at least six months beyond the projected end of your trip and has plenty of blank pages for stamp-happy officials. Always keep it with you while traveling between destinations.

Air

All Central American countries have international airports. Other than flights from South America (p735), nearly all arriving flights go via US gateways (particularly Hous-ton, Miami or New York's JFK) or Mexico City.

International Airports

BELIZE

Philip SW Goldson International Airport (BZE; Belize City; www.pgiabelize.com)

COSTA RICA

Aeropuerto Internacional Juan Santamaría (SJO; San José; ☎2437-2400; fly2sanjose.com)

Daniel Oduber Quirós International Airport (LIR; Liberia; www.liberiacostaricaairport.net)

EL SALVADOR

Aeropuerto Internacional Comalpa (SAL; San Salvador; ☎2339-8264; www.aeropuertoelsalvador.gob.sv)

GUATEMALA

Aeropuerto Internacional La Aurora (GUA; Guatemala City; ☎2260-6257)

Aeropuerto Internacional Mundo Maya (FRS; Flores)

HONDURAS

Aeropuerto Internacional Ramón Villeda Morales (SAP; San Pedro Sula; ☎6689-3261)

Aeropuerto Internacional Toncontín (TGU; Tegucigalpa ☎2233-5107, airport 2234-0137; www.aerolineasosahn.com)

Roatán Airport (RTB; Roatán; ☎2445-1880)

MEXICO

Aeropuerto Internacional de Cancún (CUN; Cancun; ☎998-848-72-00; www.asur.com.mx)

NICARAGUA

Augusto C Sandino (MGA; Managua; www.eaai.com.ni)

PANAMA

Tocumen International Airport (PTY; Panama City; ☎238-2700; www.tocumenpanama.aero)

CLIMATE CHANGE & TRAVEL

Every form of transportation that relies on carbon-based fuel generates CO_2, the main cause of human-induced climate change. Modern travel is dependent on planes, which might use less fuel per kilometer per person than most cars but travel much greater distances. The altitude at which aircraft emit gases (including CO_2) and particles also contributes to their climate change impact. Many websites offer 'carbon calculators' that allow people to estimate the carbon emissions generated by their journey and, for those who wish to do so, to offset the impact of the greenhouse gases emitted with contributions to portfolios of climate-friendly initiatives throughout the world. Lonely Planet offsets the carbon footprint of all staff and author travel.

Aeropuerto Enrique Malek
(DAV; David; ☑721-1072)

Departure Tax

All seven Central American countries levy departure taxes on air passengers, ranging from US$29 to US$40, although they are usually included in the price of the ticket. If you're staying on the ground, you will still have to pay a land departure fee when leaving Belize (US$18.75) and Costa Rica (US$7).

Tickets

Central America's slender isthmus shape makes 'open-jaw' tickets – flying into one place (say Cancún or Guatemala City) and out from another (eg Panama City) – an attractive option, and the good news is that it's often not much more expensive than a round-trip ticket. If you're flexible on where you start and end, shop around: discount fares come and go.

You might think going to a hub city, such as San Salvador on Avianca, would save money, but sometimes it's *more* expensive. The reason – in the confusing world of airline ticket pricing – is that airlines are trying to compete with more direct options. Again, shop around.

High-season rates (generally July and August, Christmas to New Year, and around Semana Santa) can be considerably more expensive.

Student travel agencies such as **STA Travel** (www.statravel.com) offer student discounts for those under 26.

If you're flying from Europe or Australia, chances are you can get a free stopover in a US gateway city such as Los Angeles or Miami.

ROUND-THE-WORLD TICKETS

Round-the-world (RTW) tickets are an option if coming from the US or Europe, but a lack of flight connections between Australasia and Central America have all but taken Latin America off

ONWARD TICKET REQUIREMENTS

If you're planning on flying into one country and back from another, note that immigration officials may require proof of onward or continuing travel. The restriction mainly ensures that nonresidents don't stay long-term without permission.

Showing 'continuing travel' to another country (say, a flight home) and explaining how you'll get there is almost always enough. Most travelers are never asked. It's still a good idea to ask the airlines, as they can be fined for bringing in a passenger without proper documentation. Also, it may be worth showing a print-out of a 'bus reservation' for leaving the country.

This requirement also may pop up at land borders. Crossing into Costa Rica, for instance, it's sometimes necessary to purchase a bus ticket at the border for leaving Costa Rica – even if you don't plan to use it. For private cars entering, no onward ticket is required but proper documentation for the vehicle is needed.

RTW ticket options from that part of the world.

FROM SOUTH AMERICA

Avianca (El Salvador; www.avianca.com) and Copa Airlines (Panama; www.copaair.com) airlines connect Central American cities to and from Argentina, Bolivia, Brazil, Chile, Colombia, Ecuador and Peru. The Chilean airline LAN (www.lan.com) also offers many connections between Central and South America.

If you're planning to visit both Central America and South America on a trip, note that some airlines allow a free stopover in Central America. Panama City is often the cheapest link to and from South America, especially Colombia, Ecuador and Venezuela (unsurprisingly, given their distance from Panama).

Note that many South American countries require onward air tickets upon arrival.

Land

From Mexico
BUS

It's possible to take a bus from the USA or Canada

into Mexico and directly into Central America. The three most convenient land borders between Mexico and Central America are at the Chetumal–Corozal (Belize) border in Quintana Roo (Yucatán Peninsula); the Ciudad Cuauhtémoc–La Mesilla (Guatemala) border; and the Ciudad Hidalgo–Ciudad Tecún Umán (Guatemala) border in Chiapas state (about 38km to the south of Tapachula).

Another popular border crossing is by boat across the Río Usumacinta at the Frontera Corozal–Bethel (Guatemala) border, south of Palenque.

CAR & MOTORCYCLE

Most people driving to Central America do so from the USA (or Canada). Buying a car in the region (including Mexico) is very complicated: you're better off bringing your car (with all the ownership papers) from your home country.

A drive through Central America will likely offer an amazing trip, but it's unlikely to save you money. In addition to fees, there's paperwork, tolls, parking concerns and other red tape. Border crossings are a particular hassle. You'll also need to be prepared to stop for passport checks at military checkpoints. Also, highway robberies aren't unknown, so avoid driving at night.

Prior to departure, purchase liability insurance that is valid in Mexico, such as **Oscar Padilla Mexican Insurance** (☏in North America 800-466-7227800-466-7227 FREE; www.mexicaninsurance.com). Make sure you bring your documentation, as you'll have to show it at the border. Mandatory insurance is for sale at the border as you enter Belize, Nicaragua, Costa Rica and Panama. Insurance is not required in El Salvador, Guatemala or Honduras.

Drive the Americas (www.drivetheamericas.com) is an excellent resource, with trip planning tips, vehicle recommendations, vehicle sales, roadtripper profiles and active forums for asking and answering questions.

A few other pre-trip considerations:

➡ You will need a valid driver's license from your home country.

➡ Unleaded gas (petrol) is now available throughout Central America.

➡ Make sure that your car's shock absorbers and suspension are in good shape for the bumpy roads.

➡ A spare fuel filter – and other spare parts – could be invaluable.

➡ Check with a national tourist board or consulate for any changes to the rules on bringing a car into Mexico, or Central America, before showing up in your vehicle.

From South America

There are no road connections between South America and Central America (via Panama). Instability in the Panama–Colombia border region, plus the difficulty of travel, have essentially made the trip over the Darién Gap on foot an impossibility. All visitors to the Darién must register with the police.

Sea

Unless you're a yachtie or on a cruise ship, options for boat travel heading to/from the region are limited. The most popular route is taking a (shared) chartered sailboat between the Archipiélago de San Blas, Panama and Cartagena in Colombia (per person US$550). The five-day trip usually includes a few days on the islands and two days' transit to/from Colombia. There is also a shorter route to/from the border town of La Miel, Colombia and nearby Sapzurro, Colombia (per person US$400). For more information about this journey, contact the following.

Blue Sailing (☏in Cartagena 57-5-668-6485, in USA 203-660-8644; www.bluesailing.net) This company keeps the schedule for more than a dozen boats that sail between Colombia and Panama. Look online to see photos of the boats, to learn about the captains and to book the trips.

Captain Jack's (www.sailcolombiapanama.com) Captain Jack's Hostel in Portobelo, Panama books trips on boats traveling out of Portobelo or Carti and El Porvenir.

Casa Viena (☏in Cartagena 57-5-664-6242; www.casaviena.com) A Cartagena hostel that helps with boat trips to Panama.

Sailing Koala (☏in Cartagena 57-312-670-7863, in Panama 507-6047-9283; www.sailingkoala.com) A recommended sailing operation.

Mamallena Tours (www.mamallena.com) This tour company – based at the hostels of the same name in Panama City and Cartagena – organizes sailing trips between the two countries, via San Blas.

Note that cargo boats are a risky business; smuggling is common on the Colón–Cartagena cargo route.

GETTING AROUND

Buses are the cheapest and most accessible way to get around Central America, particularly along the Pan-American Hwy (also called the Panamericana or Interamericana), which runs through all of the countries except Belize.

Air

Many flights connect the region by international carriers as well as the national airlines. Some smaller domestic airlines provide services, too. Occasionally it will be necessary to change planes in the carrier's hub city (eg a Managua–Panama City flight may change planes up north in San Salvador).

Cost is an obstacle. Despite relatively short distances, individual one-way and round-trip tickets within Central America (whether bought abroad or within the region) can be very expensive.

➡ Flights can sometimes be overbooked; reconfirm your ticket before arriving at the airport.

➡ Airfares can vary wildly – depending on the length of stay, time of year and special promotions – so treat high-season fares as a rough gauge only in identifying potential routes.

➡ Note that San Salvador and San José are the most popular hubs. Occasionally a promotional return flight may be even cheaper than a one-way fare.

➡ Worthwhile domestic flights include Managua to the Corn Islands (about US$165 return), which saves a two-day bus/boat trip each way. Flights within Panama and Costa Rica can also be cheap.

Bicycle

Long-distance cycling in the region can be dangerous, as few drivers are accustomed to sharing narrow streets in cities, or often-shoulderless two-lane highways, with bicycles. That said, cycling is on an upswing, with mountain rides and coffee-plantation tours (including guide and bike) available all over Central America.

You can rent bicycles in several cities and traveler hangouts, such as San Cristóbal de las Casas (Mexico), Flores (Guatemala), Granada (Nicaragua), La Fortuna (Costa Rica) and Panama City. There are many mountain-bike tours available (notably in cooler locales such as Guatemala's highlands and San Cristóbal de las Casas). Consider the seasons if you're planning to cycle a lot. The dry season (roughly December to April) should spare you from getting soaked.

If you're planning to cycle across borders, keep a document proving your ownership of the bike handy for immigration officials.

Check out El Pedalero (www.elpedalero.com) to read cyclist Gareth Collingwood's adventures and tips on cycling around Latin America.

Boat

Key domestic water journeys include the ride down the Río Dulce in Guatemala, or down the Río Escondidas to Bluefields, Nicaragua, and then out to the Corn Islands in the Caribbean.

Other Caribbean islands reached by boat include the Bay Islands in Honduras; Caye Caulker and Ambergris Caye in Belize; and Cozumel and Isla Mujeres in Mexico. And of course, the Panama Canal is one of the world's most important waterways, connecting the Caribbean and the Pacific.

Traveling by boat is not an uncommon way to get around the region, including several border crossings:

➡ Travelers between Palenque, Mexico and Flores, Guatemala cross the Río Usumacinta near Frontera Corozal, Mexico and Bethel, Guatemala.

➡ There is a regular water taxi between Punta Gorda, Belize and Puerto Barrios (and sometimes Lívingston), Guatemala.

➡ There's a river border crossing between San Carlos, Nicaragua and Los Chiles, Costa Rica, though nowadays most folks use the new bridge at Las Tablillas.

Bus

Some of the most memorable moments of your trip will come from bus rides. Bus service is well developed throughout the region, though not always comfortable. While some buses are air-conditioned with reserved seats that may recline, many others are colorfully repainted former US school buses (aka 'chicken buses'), with a liberal policy toward lugging merchandise (though it's unlikely you'll have to share your seat with a chicken).

Avoid night buses throughout the region (with the possible exception of Mexico and Panama), as these have been popular targets for highway robbers.

First-class and some 2nd-class buses depart on scheduled times from a *terminal de autobuses* (long-distance bus station); others leave from parking-lot bus terminals once they are full (these stop to collect more passengers all along the way – so you're likely to be able to get a lift from the highway if need be). Be aware that many cities have more than one bus station. Bus companies can have their own terminals as well. Departure frequency varies.

Luggage may be stored in a lower compartment or piled on the roof of the bus. Keep an eye on your luggage if you can, particularly on

SAMPLE BUS FARES

Remember that bus connections and border-crossing formalities can add extra time to the trip.

ORIGIN	DESTINATION	DURATION (HR)
Cancún, Mexico	Belize City	9-10
Flores, Guatemala	Guatemala City	8-10
Guatemala City	Copán Ruinas, Honduras	5
Managua, Nicaragua	San José	9
San Cristóbal de las Casas, Mexico	Antigua, Guatemala	11
San José, Costa Rica	Panama City	14
San Salvador, El Salvador	Tegucigalpa, Honduras	8
Tegucigalpa, Honduras	Managua, Nicaragua	8

the easily accessible racks in a packed bus. Always keep your valuables tucked away on your person. Watch out for pickpockets on crowded buses and in bus stations.

In some places, travel agents run private shuttle services (mostly vans with air-con) to popular destinations. They're more comfortable and more expensive than public buses.

Colectivos & Minibuses

Connecting hub towns with smaller ones on short-haul trips is an array of minibuses (called *rapidito* in Honduras, *chiva* in Panama, and *colectivo* in Costa Rica and Mexico). When available, these are cheaper than 1st-class buses and run frequently. The catch: they also make frequent stops and the driver knows no word for 'full'.

Car & Motorcycle

Driving Licenses

To drive in Central America, you must have a valid driver's license from your home country or an International Driving Permit (IDP), which is issued by automobile associations worldwide.

Be prepared for police checkpoints – always stop and have your papers handy.

Rental

Central America is relatively easy to explore by private vehicle. This option would be more popular if it weren't for the cost (rental, insurance and fuel). Rentals range from about US$15 per day in Nicaragua to US$55 per day in Belize, but 4WD vehicles are more expensive (generally US$30 to US$80). If your goal in renting a car is to reach some otherwise unreachable areas (such as isolated beaches south of Tulum in Mexico and around Costa Rica's Península de Nicoya), it's worth paying for a 4WD: paved roads only go so far.

Mandatory insurance is a huge add-on to the cost of a car rental in most Central American countries, and your insurance policy back home is not accepted here. The (usually) mandatory Collision Damage Waiver (CDW) can double your daily rate, while many companies will give a hard sell for more expensive comprehensive insurance. If your credit card provides insurance on car rentals, be sure to bring the documentation to prove it; in most cases, you'll still have to pay for the CDW.

➡ As of March 2016, the price of gas ranges from about US$0.60 (in Panama) to US$1.15 (in Belize) per liter.

➡ In many cases it's cheaper to arrange (even same-day) rentals with major car-rental agencies on their websites; during research in Tulum we saved 50% on the quoted local fare by going to an internet cafe next door and booking a car online!

➡ To rent a car, you'll need a passport and a driver's license. Some agencies rent to those 21 and over, others to only those 25 and over.

➡ All of Central America drives on the right-hand side of the road.

➡ Rented cars are usually not allowed to leave the country – though Budget, for example, allows travel from Guatemala to Mexico, Honduras and El Salvador, with some restrictions.

➡ Scooters and bigger motorcycles are available in some places, the latter usually costing about the same price as a compact car.

Hitchhiking

Hitchhiking (*tomando un jalón* – literally 'taking a hitch') is never entirely safe in any country in the world, and Lonely Planet does not recommend it. However, it is common in parts of Central America. Travelers who hitchhike should understand that they are taking a small but potentially serious risk.

If you do get a ride, it is polite to offer to pay gas money, even though the driver may turn it down.

Language

Latin American Spanish is the language of choice for travelers in all of Central America except for Belize (where English is the official language, but both Spanish and a local Creole are also widely spoken). Maya and Náhuatl are the most common of a number of indigenous languages spoken throughout the region.

Latin American Spanish pronunciation is easy, as most sounds are also found in English. Note that kh is a throaty sound (like the 'ch' in the Scottish *loch*), v and b are similar to the English 'b' but softer (between a 'v' and a 'b'), and r is strongly rolled. There are some variations in spoken Spanish across Central America, the most notable being the pronunciation of the letters *ll* and *y*. In our pronunciation guides they are represented with y because they are pronounced as the 'y' in 'yes' in most of Central America. In some parts of the region, though, you may hear them pronounced like the 'lli' in 'million'. If you read our colored pronunciation guides as if they were English, you'll be understood. The stressed syllables are indicated with italics in our pronunciation guides.

Where both polite and informal options are given in this section, they are indicated by the abbreviations 'pol' and 'inf'. The masculine and feminine forms are indicated with 'm' and 'f' respectively.

WANT MORE?

For in-depth language information and handy phrases, check out Lonely Planet's *Latin American Spanish Phrasebook*, *Mexican Spanish Phrasebook* and *Costa Rican Spanish Phrasebook*. You'll find them at **shop.lonelyplanet.com**, or you can buy Lonely Planet's iPhone phrasebooks at the Apple App Store.

BASICS

Hello.	Hola.	o·la
Goodbye.	Adiós.	a·dyos
How are you?	¿Qué tal?	ke tal
Fine, thanks.	Bien, gracias.	byen gra·syas
Excuse me.	Perdón.	per·don
Sorry.	Lo siento.	lo syen·to
Please.	Por favor.	por fa·vor
Thank you.	Gracias.	gra·syas
You are welcome.	De nada.	de na·da
Yes.	Sí.	see
No.	No.	no

My name is ...
Me llamo ... me ya·mo ...

What's your name?
¿Cómo se llama usted? ko·mo se ya·ma oo·ste (pol)
¿Cómo te llamas? ko·mo te ya·mas (inf)

Do you speak English?
¿Habla inglés? a·bla een·gles (pol)
¿Hablas inglés? a·blas een·gles (inf)

I don't understand.
Yo no entiendo. yo no en·tyen·do

ACCOMMODATIONS

I'd like a single/double room.
Quisiera una kee·sye·ra oo·na
habitación a·bee·ta·syon
individual/doble. een·dee·vee·dwal/do·ble

How much is it per night/person?
¿Cuánto cuesta por kwan·to kwes·ta por
noche/persona? no·che/per·so·na

Does it include breakfast?
¿Incluye el een·kloo·ye el
desayuno? de·sa·yoo·no

air-con	aire acondicionado	ai·re a·kon·dee·syo·na·do
bathroom	baño	ba·nyo
bed	cama	ka·ma
campsite	terreno de cámping	te·re·no de kam·peeng
guesthouse	pensión	pen·syon
hotel	hotel	o·tel
youth hostel	albergue juvenil	al·ber·ge khoo·ve·neel
window	ventana	ven·ta·na

DIRECTIONS

Where is ...?
¿Dónde está ...?　　don·de es·ta ...

What's the address?
¿Cuál es la dirección?　kwal es la dee·rek·syon

Could you please write it down?
¿Puede escribirlo, por favor?　pwe·de es·kree·beer·lo por fa·vor

Can you show me (on the map)?
¿Me lo puede indicar (en el mapa)?　me lo pwe·de een·dee·kar (en el ma·pa)

at the corner	en la esquina	en la es·kee·na
at the traffic lights	en el semáforo	en el se·ma·fo·ro
behind ...	detrás de ...	de·tras de ...
in front of ...	enfrente de ...	en·fren·te de ...
left	izquierda	ees·kyer·da
next to ...	al lado de ...	al la·do de ...
opposite ...	frente a ...	fren·te a ...
right	derecha	de·re·cha
straight ahead	todo recto	to·do rek·to

EATING & DRINKING

Can I see the menu, please?
¿Puedo ver el menú, por favor?　pwe·do ver el me·noo por fa·vor

What would you recommend?
¿Qué recomienda?　ke re·ko·myen·da

Do you have vegetarian food?
¿Tienen comida vegetariana?　tye·nen ko·mee·da ve·khe·ta·rya·na

I don't eat (red meat).
No como (carne roja).　no ko·mo (kar·ne ro·kha)

That was delicious!
¡Estaba buenísimo!　es·ta·ba bwe·nee·see·mo

Cheers!
¡Salud!　sa·loo

The bill, please.
La cuenta, por favor.　la kwen·ta por fa·vor

KEY PATTERNS

To get by in Spanish, mix and match these simple patterns with words of your choice:

When's (the next flight)?
¿Cuándo sale (el próximo vuelo)?　kwan·do sa·le (el prok·see·mo vwe·lo)

Where's (the station)?
¿Dónde está (la estación)?　don·de es·ta (la es·ta·syon)

Where can I (buy a ticket)?
¿Dónde puedo (comprar un billete)?　don·de pwe·do (kom·prar oon bee·ye·te)

Do you have (a map)?
¿Tiene (un mapa)?　tye·ne (oon ma·pa)

Is there (a toilet)?
¿Hay (servicios)?　ai (ser·vee·syos)

I'd like (a coffee).
Quisiera (un café).　kee·sye·ra (oon ka·fe)

I'd like (to hire a car).
Quisiera (alquilar un coche).　kee·sye·ra (al·kee·lar oon ko·che)

Can I (enter)?
¿Se puede (entrar)?　se pwe·de (en·trar)

Could you please (help me)?
¿Puede (ayudarme), por favor?　pwe·de (a·yoo·dar·me) por fa·vor

Do I have to (get a visa)?
¿Necesito (obtener un visado)?　ne·se·see·to (ob·te·ner oon vee·sa·do)

I'd like a table for ...	Quisiera una mesa para ...	kee·sye·ra oo·na me·sa pa·ra ...
(eight) o'clock	las (ocho)	las (o·cho)
(two) people	(dos) personas	(dos) per·so·nas

Key Words

appetisers	aperitivos	a·pe·ree·tee·vos
bottle	botella	bo·te·ya
bowl	bol	bol
breakfast	desayuno	de·sa·yoo·no
children's menu	menú infantil	me·noo een·fan·teel
(too) cold	(muy) frío	(mooy) free·o
dinner	cena	se·na
food	comida	ko·mee·da

English	Spanish	Pronunciation
fork	tenedor	te·ne·dor
glass	vaso	va·so
hot (warm)	caliente	kal·yen·te
knife	cuchillo	koo·chee·yo
lunch	comida	ko·mee·da
main course	segundo plato	se·goon·do pla·to
plate	plato	pla·to
restaurant	restaurante	res·tow·ran·te
spoon	cuchara	koo·cha·ra
with	con	kon
without	sin	seen

Meat & Fish

beef	carne de vaca	kar·ne de va·ka
chicken	pollo	po·yo
duck	pato	pa·to
lamb	cordero	kor·de·ro
lobster	langosta	lan·gos·ta
pork	cerdo	ser·do
shrimps	camarones	ka·ma·ro·nes
tuna	atún	a·toon
turkey	pavo	pa·vo
veal	ternera	ter·ne·ra

Fruit & Vegetables

English	Spanish	Pronunciation
apple	manzana	man·sa·na
apricot	albaricoque	al·ba·ree·ko·ke
artichoke	alcachofa	al·ka·cho·fa
asparagus	espárragos	es·pa·ra·gos
banana	plátano	pla·ta·no
beans	judías	khoo·dee·as
beetroot	remolacha	re·mo·la·cha
cabbage	col	kol
carrot	zanahoria	sa·na·o·rya
celery	apio	a·pyo
cherry	cereza	se·re·sa
corn	maíz	ma·ees
cucumber	pepino	pe·pee·no
grape	uvas	oo·vas
lemon	limón	lee·mon
lentils	lentejas	len·te·khas
lettuce	lechuga	le·choo·ga
mushroom	champiñón	cham·pee·nyon
nuts	nueces	nwe·ses
onion	cebolla	se·bo·ya
orange	naranja	na·ran·kha
peach	melocotón	me·lo·ko·ton

English	Spanish	Pronunciation
peas	guisantes	gee·san·tes
pepper (bell)	pimiento	pee·myen·to
pineapple	piña	pee·nya
plum	ciruela	seer·we·la
potato	patata	pa·ta·ta
pumpkin	calabaza	ka·la·ba·sa
spinach	espinacas	es·pee·na·kas
strawberry	fresa	fre·sa
tomato	tomate	to·ma·te
watermelon	sandía	san·dee·a

Other

bread	pan	pan
butter	mantequilla	man·te·kee·ya
cheese	queso	ke·so
egg	huevo	we·vo
honey	miel	myel
jam	mermelada	mer·me·la·da
oil	aceite	a·sey·te
pasta	pasta	pas·ta
pepper	pimienta	pee·myen·ta
rice	arroz	a·ros
salt	sal	sal
sugar	azúcar	a·soo·kar
vinegar	vinagre	vee·na·gre

Drinks

English	Spanish	Pronunciation
beer	cerveza	ser·ve·sa
coffee	café	ka·fe
(orange) juice	zumo (de naranja)	soo·mo (de na·ran·kha)
milk	leche	le·che
red wine	vino tinto	vee·no teen·to
tea	té	te
(mineral) water	agua (mineral)	a·gwa (mee·ne·ral)
white wine	vino blanco	vee·no blan·ko

SIGNS

Abierto	Open
Cerrado	Closed
Entrada	Entrance
Hombres/Varones	Men
Mujeres/Damas	Women
Prohibido	Prohibited
Salida	Exit
Servicios/Baños	Toilets

EMERGENCIES

Help!	*¡Socorro!*	so·ko·ro
Go away!	*¡Vete!*	ve·te

Call ...!	*¡Llame a ...!*	ya·me a ...
a doctor	*un médico*	oon me·dee·ko
the police	*la policía*	la po·lee·see·a

I'm lost.
Estoy perdido/a.   es·toy per·dee·do/a (m/f)

Where are the toilets?
¿Dónde están los   don·de es·tan los
baños?   ba·nyos

I'm ill.
Estoy enfermo/a.   es·toy en·fer·mo/a (m/f)

I'm allergic to (antibiotics).
Soy alérgico/a a (los   soy a·ler·khee·ko/a a (los
antibióticos).   an·tee·byo·tee·kos) (m/f)

SHOPPING & SERVICES

What time does it open/close?
¿A qué hora abre/   a ke o·ra ab·re/
cierra?   sye·ra

I'd like to buy ...
Quisiera comprar ...   kee·sye·ra kom·prar ...

I'm just looking.
Sólo estoy mirando.   so·lo es·toy mee·ran·do

Can I look at it?
¿Puedo verlo?   pwe·do ver·lo

I don't like it.
No me gusta.   no me goos·ta

How much is it?
¿Cuánto cuesta?   kwan·to kwes·ta

That's too expensive.
Es muy caro.   es mooy ka·ro

Can you lower the price?
¿Podría bajar un   po·dree·a ba·khar oon
poco el precio?   po·ko el pre·syo

There's a mistake in the bill.
Hay un error   ai oon e·ror
en la cuenta.   en la kwen·ta

QUESTION WORDS

How?	*¿Cómo?*	ko·mo
What?	*¿Qué?*	ke
When?	*¿Cuándo?*	kwan·do
Where?	*¿Dónde?*	don·de
Which?	*¿Cuál? (sg)*	kwal
	¿Cuáles? (pl)	kwa·les
Who?	*¿Quién?*	kyen
Why?	*¿Por qué?*	por ke

ATM	*cajero*	ka·khe·ro
	automático	ow·to·ma·tee·ko
market	*mercado*	mer·ka·do
post office	*correos*	ko·re·os
tourist office	*oficina*	o·fee·see·na
	de turismo	de too·rees·mo

TIME & DATES

What time is it?
¿Qué hora es?   ke o·ra es

It's (10) o'clock.
Son (las diez).   son (las dyes)

It's half past (one).
Es (la una) y media.   es (la oo·na) ee me·dya

morning	*mañana*	ma·nya·na
afternoon	*tarde*	tar·de
evening	*noche*	no·che
yesterday	*ayer*	a·yer
today	*hoy*	oy
tomorrow	*mañana*	ma·nya·na

Monday	*lunes*	loo·nes
Tuesday	*martes*	mar·tes
Wednesday	*miércoles*	myer·ko·les
Thursday	*jueves*	khwe·ves
Friday	*viernes*	vyer·nes
Saturday	*sábado*	sa·ba·do
Sunday	*domingo*	do·meen·go

January	*enero*	e·ne·ro
February	*febrero*	fe·bre·ro
March	*marzo*	mar·so
April	*abril*	a·breel
May	*mayo*	ma·yo
June	*junio*	khoon·yo
July	*julio*	khool·yo
August	*agosto*	a·gos·to
September	*septiembre*	sep·tyem·bre
October	*octubre*	ok·too·bre
November	*noviembre*	no·vyem·bre
December	*diciembre*	dee·syem·bre

TRANSPORTATION

Public Transportation

boat	*barco*	bar·ko
bus	*autobús*	ow·to·boos
plane	*avión*	a·vyon
train	*tren*	tren

NUMBERS

1	*uno*	oo·no
2	*dos*	dos
3	*tres*	tres
4	*cuatro*	*kwa*·tro
5	*cinco*	*seen*·ko
6	*seis*	seys
7	*siete*	*sye*·te
8	*ocho*	*o*·cho
9	*nueve*	*nwe*·ve
10	*diez*	dyes
20	*veinte*	*veyn*·te
30	*treinta*	*treyn*·ta
40	*cuarenta*	kwa·*ren*·ta
50	*cincuenta*	seen·*kwen*·ta
60	*sesenta*	se·*sen*·ta
70	*setenta*	se·*ten*·ta
80	*ochenta*	o·*chen*·ta
90	*noventa*	no·*ven*·ta
100	*cien*	syen
1000	*mil*	meel

first	*primero*	pree·*me*·ro
last	*último*	*ool*·tee·mo
next	*próximo*	*prok*·see·mo

airport	*aeropuerto*	a·e·ro·*pwer*·to
aisle seat	*asiento de pasillo*	a·*syen*·to de pa·*see*·yo
bus stop	*parada de autobuses*	pa·*ra*·da de ow·to·*boo*·ses
cancelled	*cancelado*	kan·se·*la*·do
delayed	*retrasado*	re·tra·*sa*·do
ticket office	*taquilla*	ta·*kee*·ya
timetable	*horario*	o·*ra*·ryo
train station	*estación de trenes*	es·ta·*syon* de *tre*·nes
window seat	*asiento junto a la ventana*	a·*syen*·to *khoon*·to a la ven·*ta*·na

A ... ticket, please.	*Un billete de ..., por favor.*	oon bee·*ye*·te de ... por fa·*vor*
1st-class	*primera clase*	pree·*me*·ra *kla*·se
2nd-class	*segunda clase*	se·*goon*·da *kla*·se
one-way	*ida*	*ee*·da
return	*ida y vuelta*	*ee*·da ee *vwel*·ta

What time does it arrive/leave?
¿A qué hora llega/sale? a ke *o*·ra *ye*·ga/*sa*·le

Does it stop at ...?
¿Para en ...? *pa*·ra en ...

Which stop is this?
¿Cuál es esta parada? kwal es *es*·ta pa·*ra*·da

Could you tell me when we get to ...?
¿Puede avisarme cuando lleguemos a ...? *pwe*·de a·vee·*sar*·me *kwan*·do ye·*ge*·mos a ...

I want to get off here.
Quiero bajarme aquí. *kye*·ro ba·*khar*·me a·*kee*

How much is it (to the airport)?
¿Cuánto cuesta ir (al aeropuerto)? *kwan*·to *kwes*·ta eer (al a·e·ro·*pwer*·to)

Please take me to (this address).
Por favor, lléveme a (esta dirección). por fa·*vor* *ye*·ve·me a (*es*·ta dee·rek·*syon*)

Driving & Cycling

I'd like to hire a ...	*Quisiera alquilar ...*	kee·*sye*·ra al·kee·*lar* ...
4WD	*un todoterreno*	oon to·do·te·*re*·no
bicycle	*una bicicleta*	*oo*·na bee·see·*kle*·ta
car	*un coche*	oon *ko*·che
motorcycle	*una moto*	*oo*·na *mo*·to

child seat	*asiento de seguridad para niños*	a·*syen*·to de se·goo·ree·*da* *pa*·ra *nee*·nyos
diesel	*petróleo*	pet·*ro*·le·o
helmet	*casco*	*kas*·ko
mechanic	*mecánico*	me·*ka*·nee·ko
petrol/gas	*gasolina*	ga·so·*lee*·na
service station	*gasolinera*	ga·so·lee·*ne*·ra
truck	*camion*	ka·*myon*

Is this the road to ...?
¿Se va a ... por esta carretera? se va a ... por *es*·ta ka·re·*te*·ra

Can I park here?
¿Puedo aparcar aquí? *pwe*·do a·par·*kar* a·*kee*

The car has broken down.
El coche se ha averiado. el *ko*·che se a a·ve·*rya*·do

I had an accident.
He tenido un accidente. e te·*nee*·do oon ak·see·*den*·te

I've run out of petrol/gas.
Me he quedado sin gasolina. me e ke·*da*·do seen ga·so·*lee*·na

I have a flat tyre.
Se me pinchó una rueda. se me peen·*cho* *oo*·na *rwe*·da

GLOSSARY

alcaldía – mayor's office

apartado – post-office box

artesanía – handicraft

Av – abbreviation for avenida (avenue)

ayuntamiento – municipal government

bahía – bay

bajareque – traditional wall construction, where a core of stones is held in place by poles of bamboo or other wood then covered with stucco or mud

balneario – public beach or swimming area

barrio – district; neighborhood

Black Caribs – see *Garífuna*

caballeros – literally 'horse-men,' but corresponds to the English 'gentlemen'; look for the term on bathroom doors

cabaña – cabin or bungalow

cabina – see *cabaña*; also a loose term for cheap lodging in Costa Rica (in some cases it refers to cabins or bungalows, in others it refers merely to an economical hotel room)

cajero automático – automated teller machine (ATM)

calle – street

callejón – alley; small, narrow or very short street

calzada – causeway

camión – truck; bus

camioneta – pick-up truck

campesino – farmer

Carretera Interamericana – Interamerican Hwy, or In-ter-americana (also referred to as the Pan-American Hwy, or Pan-americana); the nearly continuous highway running from Alaska to Chile (it breaks at the Darién Gap in Panama)

casa de cambio – currency exchange office

casa de huéspedes – guest-house

cascada – waterfall

catedral – cathedral

cay – small island of sand or coral fragments; also caye, cayo

cayuco – dugout canoe

cenote – large, natural limestone cave used for water storage or ceremonial purposes

cerro – hill

cerveza – beer

Chac – Maya rain god; his like-ness appears on many ruins

chac-mool – Maya sacrificial stone sculpture

chamarra – thick, heavy woolen blanket (Guatemala)

chapín – citizen of Guatemala; Guatemalan

chicken bus – former US school bus used for public transportation

cine – movie theater

ciudad – city

cofradía – Maya religious brotherhood, particularly in highland Guatemala

colectivo – shared taxi or minibus that picks up and drops off passengers along its route

colón – national currency of Costa Rica

comedor – basic and cheap eatery, usually with a limited menu

conquistador – any of the Spanish explorer-conquerors of Latin America

Contras – counterrevolu-tionary military groups fighting against the Sandinista govern-ment in Nicaragua throughout the 1980s

cordillera – mountain range

córdoba – national currency of Nicaragua

corte – piece of material 7m to 10m long that is used as a wraparound skirt

costa – coast

criollo – Creole; born in Latin America of Spanish parentage; on the Caribbean coast it refers to someone of mixed African and European descent; see also *mestizo* and *ladino*

cuadra – city block

cueva – cave

damas – ladies; the usual sign on bathroom doors

edificio – building

entrada – entrance

expreso – express bus

faja – waist sash that binds garments and holds what would otherwise be put in pockets

finca – farm; plantation; ranch

fritanga – sidewalk barbecue, widely seen in Nicaragua

fuerte – fort

Garífuna – descendants of West African slaves and Carib In-dians, brought to the Caribbean coast of Central America in the late 18th century from the island of St Vincent; also referred to as *Black Caribs*

Garinagu – see *Garífuna*

gibnut – small, brown-spotted rodent similar to a guinea pig; also called *paca*

golfo – gulf

gringo/a – mildly pejorative term used in Latin America to describe male/female foreigners, particularly those from North America; often applied to any visitor of European heritage

gruta – cave

hacienda – agricultural estate or plantation; treasury, as in Departamento de Hacienda (Treasury Department)

hospedaje – guesthouse

huipil – long, woven, white sleeveless tunic with intricate, colorful embroidery (Maya regions)

iglesia – church

indígena – indigenous

Interamericana – see *Carretera Interamericana*

invierno – winter; Central America's wet season, which ex-tends roughly from April through mid-December

isla – island

IVA – *impuesto al valor agre-gado;* value-added tax

ladino – person of mixed indig-enous and European parentage, often used to describe a *mestizo* who speaks Spanish; see also *mestizo* and *criollo*

lago – lake

laguna – lagoon; lake

lancha – small motorboat

lempira – national currency of Honduras

malecón – waterfront promenade

mar – sea

marimba – xylophonelike instrument

mercado – market

Mesoamerica – a geographical region extending from central Mexico to northwestern Costa Rica

mestizo – person of mixed ancestry, usually Spanish and indigenous; see also *criollo* and *ladino*

metate – flat stone on which corn/maize is ground

migración – immigration; immigration office

milpa – cornfield

mirador – lookout

mola – colorful hand-stitched appliqué textile made by Kuna women

muelle – pier

municipalidad – town hall

museo – museum

Navidad – Christmas

oficina de correos – post office

ordinario – slow bus

paca – see *gibnut*

PADI – Professional Association of Diving Instructors

palacio de gobierno – building housing the executive offices of a state or regional government

palacio municipal – city hall; seat of the corporation or municipal government

palapa – thatched, palm-leaf-roofed shelter with open sides

Panamericana – see *Carretera Interamericana*

panga – small motorboat

parada – bus stop

parque – park; sometimes also used to describe a plaza

parque nacional – national park

peña – folkloric club; evening of music, song and dance

pensión – guesthouse

petén – island

playa – beach

pozo – spring

propina – tip; gratuity

pueblo – small town or village

puente – bridge

puerta – gate; door

puerto – port; harbor

pulpería – corner store; minimart

punta – point; traditional Garífuna dance involving much hip movement

quebrada – ravine; brook

quetzal – national currency of Guatemala, named after the tropical bird

rancho – thatched-roof restaurant

río – river

Ruta Maya – Maya Route, describing travels to the Maya sites of Mexico, Guatemala and Belize (chiefly), but also El Salvador and Honduras

s/n – sin número (without number); used in addresses

sacbé (pl **sacbeob**) – ceremonial limestone avenue or path between Maya cities

salida – exit

santo – saint

Semana Santa – Holy Week, the week preceding Easter

sendero – path or trail

sierra – mountain range; saw

stela, stelae – standing stone monument of the ancient Maya, usually carved

supermercado – supermarket; anything from a corner store to a large, Western-style supermarket

templo – temple; church

terminal de autobus – bus terminal

Tico/a – male/female inhabitant of Costa Rica

tienda – small shop

típica – see *típico*

típico – typical or characteristic of a region, particularly used to describe food; also a form of Panamanian folkloric music

traje – traditional handmade clothing

turicentro – literally 'tourist center'; outdoor recreation center with swimming facilities, restaurants and camping (El Salvador)

venado – deer; venison

verano – summer; Central America's dry season, roughly from mid-December to April

volcán – volcano

Zapatistas – members of the left-wing group Ejército Zapatista de Liberación Nacional (EZLN), fighting for indigenous rights in Chiapas, Mexico

FOOD & DRINK GLOSSARY

aguardiente – clear, potent liquor made from sugarcane; also referred to as *caña*

aguas de frutas – fruit-flavored water drink

batido – milkshake made with fresh fruit and milk or water

bocas – savory side dishes or appetizers

bolitas de carne – snack of mildly spicy meatballs

cafetería – informal restaurant with waiter service

cafetín – small *cafetería*

caña – see *aguardiente*

carne ahumada – smoked, dried (jerked) meat

ceviche – raw seafood marinated in lemon or lime juice, garlic and seasonings

chicha – heavily sweetened, fresh fruit drinks

chicharrón – pork crackling

cocina – literally 'kitchen'; small, basic restaurant, or cookshop, usually found in or near municipal markets

comedor – cheap, basic eatery, usually with a limited menu

comida a la vista – meal served buffet- or cafeteria-style

comida corriente or corrida; casado – set meal of rice, beans, plantains and a piece of meat or fish

comida típica – typical local-style meal or food

empanada – turnover stuffed with meat or cheese, baked

or fried, sometimes with fruit filling as a dessert.

fritanga – sidewalk barbecue, widely seen in Nicaragua

gallo pinto – common meal of mixed rice and beans

garnaches – fried corn tortillas, served open faced or wrapped, with chicken, fish or beef, shredded cabbage and sometimes cheese

gaseosa – soft drink

guacamole – a dip of mashed or chopped avocados

guaro – local firewater made with sugarcane (Costa Rica)

horchata – sweet rice milk drink with cinnamon

huevos fritos/revueltos – fried/scrambled eggs

licuado – fresh fruit drink, blended with milk or water

menú del día – fixed-price meal of several courses

mondongo – tripe soup

pan de coco – coconut bread

panadería – bakery

patacones – fried green plantains cut in thin pieces, salted, pressed and then fried

plato del día – plate (or meal) of the day

pico de gallo – fresh salsa

pipa – coconut water, served straight from the husk

plátano maduro – ripe plantains baked or broiled with butter, brown sugar and cinnamon; served hot

plato típico – meal typical or characteristic of a place or region

pupusa – cornmeal pocket filled with cheese or refried beans, or a mixture of both (El Salvador)

raspados – shaved ice flavored with fruit juice

refresco – soda, or soft drink; in Costa Rica a drink made with local fruits

rellenitos – refried black beans in mashed plantain dumplings

ropa vieja – literally 'old clothes'; spicy shredded beef

rotisería – restaurant selling roast meats

salbutes – see *garnaches*

sancocho – a spicy stew usually made with chicken

seco – alcoholic drink made from sugarcane

soda – place that serves a counter lunch; soda or soft drink (Panama)

tamales – spiced ground corn with chicken or pork, boiled in banana leaves

tapado – rich Garífuna stew made from fish, shrimp, shellfish, coconut milk and plantain, spiced with coriander

tortilla de maíz – a fried cornmeal cake in Panama

vegetariano/a – male/female vegetarian

Behind the Scenes

SEND US YOUR FEEDBACK

We love to hear from travelers – your comments keep us on our toes and help make our books better. Our well-traveled team reads every word on what you loved or loathed about this book. Although we cannot reply individually to your submissions, we always guarantee that your feedback goes straight to the appropriate authors, in time for the next edition. Each person who sends us information is thanked in the next edition – the most useful submissions are rewarded with a selection of digital PDF chapters.

Visit **lonelyplanet.com/contact** to submit your updates and suggestions or to ask for help. Our award-winning website also features inspirational travel stories, news and discussions.

Note: We may edit, reproduce and incorporate your comments in Lonely Planet products such as guidebooks, websites and digital products, so let us know if you don't want your comments reproduced or your name acknowledged. For a copy of our privacy policy visit lonelyplanet.com/privacy.

OUR READERS

Many thanks to the travelers who used the last edition and wrote to us with helpful hints, useful advice and interesting anecdotes:

Adam O'Rahilly, Andree-Anne Roberge, Angela Jaeger, Axel Lilja, Ben Johnson, Ben Martin, Chelsea Madden, Daniel Ulbrich, David Herrero, Dominik Boerner, Eirik Rye, Emilie Jaspers, Hannah Woloschuk, Jim Latham, Jodie Knutsen, Jordi Galdon, Justin Nelson, Karina McAuley, Katy Haydn-Smith, Laura Farrell, Loes Verbeeck, Marie Christiansen, Mark Candey, Mat Bowman, Neil Rear, Nicqui Walker, Pat Westcott, Snorre Sæveraas, Stefanie Harris, Uwe Lask

AUTHOR THANKS

Steve Fallon

Muchas gracias to those who offered assistance, ideas and/or hospitality along the way, especially to my ATV-cruising partner, Carla Rankin, of Bocas del Toro town. Other helpful folk I met along the way included Juan José Calvache in Panama City; Loes Roos and Kees Groenendijk on Isla de Coiba and the Veraguas Sunset Coast; Alberto Young Lim in El Valle; Jane Walker and Barry Robbins in Boquete; and Brian and Amy Wilcox on Isla San Cristóbal. Thanks to co-author Carolyn McCarthy for all the right contacts and to editor Bailey Johnson, who got me out of a mess more than once. My great love goes to my partner, Michael Rothschild, who can't believe I'm still alive after my encounter with that green-and-black poison-dart frog.

Bridget Gleeson

Thank you to La Esperanza Granada for providing such a positive first impression of Nicaragua, and to all the local families I worked with there, years ago, for their kindness and patience as I learned Spanish. Thanks to the staff at Rosita's in San Juan del Sur for helping me out of a jam, and to all the travelers and Lonely Planet readers I met on the road – your advice and perspective helped me, and your enthusiasm for Nicaragua inspired me.

Paul Harding

Many people in Belize helped with advice, information or just a good chat over a cold Belikin. Thanks in particular to Vitali and Nick around Belmopan; Mike, James and Daniel in San Ignacio; Eric and friends in Hopkins; and Ernesto and Aurora in Maya Center. Big thank you to Bailey at Lonely Planet and my legendary co-author Alex. Most of all, and as always, thanks to Hannah and Layla at home for your love and patience.

John Hecht

Thanks to the countless number of good people in the Yucatán who helped make this wonderful journey so special. Special gratitude goes out to co-author Lucas Vidgen, Yurij Gabassi and my wife, Lau, who looked after two hyperactive kitties while I was gone.

Tom Masters

A big debt of thanks to all those who helped me in Honduras, particularly Hernan, Margarita and Antonio in Tegucigalpa, Tesla and Meme in San Pedro, Bobby and Walter at D&D Brewery, Howard in Copán Ruinas, Froni in Gracias, Milady in Utila and Ginny and Jon in Trujillo. Thanks also to Joe Kellner who accompanied me for much of the journey and was such a fearless companion and intrepid driver on some crazy roads.

Tom Spurling

Thanks to Bailey for offering me another job. Thanks to the Writer Tech Team for telling me things I should have read in the manual. Thanks to Jorge and to Chobe for the *guanaco* spirit. Thanks to my family for not letting me go. To my two Lexton buddies, Muzza and

Matpat, well represented, gents. Thanks also to Tom Turtle for living the dimly lit dream. And to Cesar, Manolo, Rene, and all who work for El Salvador. Keep fighting the good fight!

Lucas Vidgen

Thanks first and foremost to the Mexicans and Guatemalans for making such enjoyable countries to travel and work in. Specifically, Andres and Sylvia were a huge help in San Cristóbal, and the Campeche section wouldn't have been the same without Alonso Escobar and his compadre César. Thanks also to Johann in Guate for all the inside juice and a great night out, Denis in Rio Dulce and Charlie in Monterrico. To all the readers who wrote in with tips and info – gracias! And, as always, thanks to América, Sofía and Teresa for being there, and being there when I got back.

Mara Vorhees

Muchas gracias to my many co-authors and many more amigos down in Central America. Special thanks to my consultant on Central American history and politics, who also happens to be my best friend and favorite travel companion. *¡Qué suerte!*

ACKNOWLEDGEMENTS

Climate map data adapted from Peel MC, Finlayson BL & McMahon TA (2007) 'Updated World Map of the Köppen-Geiger Climate Classification', Hydrology and Earth System Sciences, 11, 163344.

Chichén Itzá illustration pp62–3 by Michael Weldon

Tikal illustration pp204–5 by Michael Weldon.

Cover photograph: Red-eyed tree frog, Costa Rica, Dirk Ercken / Shutterstock ©

THIS BOOK

This 9th edition of Lonely Planet's *Central America on a Shoestring* guidebook was researched and written by Steve Fallon, Bridget Gleeson, Paul Harding, John Hecht, Tom Masters, Tom Spurling, Lucas Vidgen and Mara Vorhees. Additional research for Mexico was provided by Lucas. Additional research for Nicaragua and Belize was provided by Alex Egerton. Additional research for Costa Rica was provided by Ashley Harrell

and Anna Kaminski. Additional research for Panama was provided by Carolyn McCarthy. Additional research for Guatemala was provided by Daniel C Schechter. The previous edition was written by Carolyn McCarthy, Sandra Bao, Greg Benchwick, Joshua Samuel Brown, Alex Egerton, John Hecht, Daniel C Schechter, Tom Spurling, Iain Stewart, Lucas Vidgen and Mara Vorhees. This guidebook was produced by the following:

Destination Editors Bailey Johnson, Clifton Wilkinson

Product Editor Grace Dobell

Senior Cartographers Mark Griffiths, Corey Hutchison, Alison Lyall

Book Designer Mazzy Prinsep

Assisting Editors Michelle Bennett, Andrea Dobbin, Ali Lemer, Katie O'Connell, Gabrielle Stefanos, Ross Taylor

Cover Designer Campbell McKenzie

Thanks to Kate James, Elizabeth Jones, Kirsten Rawlings, Luna Soo, Angela Tinson, Tony Wheeler, Amanda Williamson

Index

A

accommodations 36-7, 724-5, *see also individual locations*
language 739-40
activities 39-43, *see also individual activities, individual locations*
Actun Tunichil Muknal 264
adventure sports, *see individual sports*
Afro Central American people 718-20
Agua Azul 93
Ahuachapán 317-18
air travel 734-5, 736
Alajuela 536-7
Alegría 325-6
Almirante 676
Altagracia 461-2
Altun Ha 17, 249, **17**
Amapala 416
Ambergris Caye 243-9, **244**
amusement parks
  Parque Acuático Xocomil 166
  Parque Chatún 181
  Parque de Diversiones Xetulul 166
animals, *see also* wildlife-watching, wildlife centers & reserves
  butterflies 266
  flamingoes **41**
  howler monkeys 249
  turtles 42, 56-7, 170, 651
  whale-sharks 57
Antigua 114-27, **116-17**, **41**
  accommodations 121-2
  activities 119
  courses 119-20
  drinking & nightlife 124-5
  festivals & events 121

Map Pages **000**
Photo Pages **000**

food 122-4
information 126
LGBT travelers 125
shopping 125-9
sights 115-19
tours 120-1
travel to/from 127-8
travel within 126-7
Apaneca 318-19
aquariums 408
archaeological museums
  CCIT 207-8
  Centro Cultural Kumool 149
  Museo Arqueológico de Campeche 80-1
  Museo El Baúl 167
  Museo Lítico 208
  Museo Nacional de Antropología David J Guzmán 293
  Museo Nacional de Arqueología y Etnología 105
  Museo Regional de Arqueología 366
  Museo Santa Bárbara 196
archaeological sites 180
  Acrópolis (Copán Site) 383-4
  Actun Tunichil Muknal 264
  Altun Ha 17, 249, **17**
  Ball Court & Hieroglyphic Stairway (Copán Site) 383
  Cahal Pech 260
  Calakmul 82
  Caracol 265-6
  Casa Blanca 316
  Ceibal 193-5
  Cerro Maya 252
  Chichén Itzá 72-4
  Chuitinamit 138
  Cihuatán 304
  Cobá 68
  Copán 16, 380-4, **38**

Dzibilchaltún 75
Edzná 82
Ek' Balam 75
El Baúl Hilltop Site 167-8
El Bosque 384
El Mirador 211-13
El Zotz 212
Huellas de Acahualinca 434-5
Joya de Cerén 304
K'um'arkaj 147-8
La Blanca 212
Lamanai 249-50
Las Piedras 168
Las Sepulturas 384
Los Sapos 379
Lubaantun 279
Mixco Viejo 172
Monumento Nacional Arqueológico Guayabo 541
Museo Cultura Cotzumalguapa 168
Naranjo 212
Nim Li Punit 279
Palenque 13, 89-91, **90**
Parque Arqueológico Takalik Abaj 166-7
Piedras Negras 212
Quiriguá 183-4
Río Azul 212
Ruinas de Quelepa 328-9
Ruinas de San Andrés 304
San Bartolo 212
Santa Rita 252
Sitio Arqueológico Finca 6 602
Stelae of the Great Plaza 383
Tazumal 316
Tikal 10, 202-10, **204-5**, **10**, **204-5**
Tulum 66
Túnel Rosalila & Túnel de los Jaguares 382
Uaxactún 210-11
Uxmal 75, **21**

Xunantunich 266
Yaxchilán 88-9
Yaxhá 211
Zaculeu 161
Archipiélago de Bocas del Toro 10, **10-11**
Archipiélago de las Perlas 645-6
area codes, *see also* telephone services
  Belize 284
  Costa Rica 616
  El Salvador 348
  Guatemala 225
  Honduras 425
  Mexico 96
  Nicaragua 513
  Panama 704
Área Protegida Cerro Tisey-Estanzuela 485
Área Protegida Miraflor 484-5
Arenal 554-61
art galleries, *see* galleries
arts 721-2, *see also individual countries*
Ataco 319-20
ATMs 728
  Belize 283
  Costa Rica 615
  El Salvador 347
  Guatemala 223
  Honduras 424
  Mexico 96
  Nicaragua 512
  Panama 702
Awas 494

B

Bahía de Jiquilisco 327
Bahía Drake 603-4
Balgüe 462-3
bargaining 21
bathrooms 731
Bay Islands 12, 402-14, **403**, **12**

beaches
Bando Beach 408
Big Fowl House Beach 498
Boca del Drago 667-8
Cabañas Playa Blanca 57
Cosigüina Peninsula 477-9
Goat Beach 498
Isla Martín Pérez 332
Jimmy Lever Beach 498
Las Flores 331
Las Peñitas 477
Otto Beach 498
Playa Aserradores 478
Playa Avellanas 577
Playa Bluff 667
Playa Brava 332
Playa Cocles 550
Playa Del Carmen 59-64, 60
Playa del Coco 573-6
Playa El Coco 469
Playa El Cuco 331
Playa El Ostional 469
Playa El Tunco 15, 306, 15
Playa El Zonte 306
Playa Esteron 331
Playa Hermosa 468
Playa Jaguey 331
Playa Jiquilillo 478
Playa Las Lajas 657
Playa Las Tunas 331
Playa Maderas 468
Playa Majahual 332
Playa Montezuma 584
Playa Negra (Cahuita) 546
Playa Negra (Isla del Tigre) 416
Playa Norte 57
Playa Sámara 580-2
Playa Santo Domingo 459, 462
Playa Tamarindo 576-80, 578
Playa Venao 651-2
Playa Venecia 459
Poneloya 477
Punta Jesús María 459
Red Frog Beach 674
Tela 389
Wizard Beach 674
Belize 45, 230-85, 232-3
accommodations 230, 282
border crossings 98, 277, 285
budget 231

climate 230
consulates 282-3
culture 281-2
drinks 231
economy 280
embassies 282-3
environment 282
food 230, 231
highlights 232-3, 232-3
history 280-1
internet access 283
itineraries 231
LGBT travelers 283
measures 285
money 230, 231, 283
opening hours 283
public holidays 283-4
tourist information 284
travel seasons 230
travel to/from 285
travel within 285
visas 284
volunteering 284-5
websites 231
weights 285
Belize City 234-8, 235, 236
Belmopan 255-9
Bermudian Landing 249
bicycle travel 737, see cycling
Big Falls 279
Bilwi (Puerto Cabezas) 499-501
Biotopo del Quetzal 172-3
Biotopo Monterrico-Hawaii 170
birds 421
birdwatching 40, see also wildlife-watching
Belize 251, 254
Costa Rica 555-6, 564, 605
El Salvador 310-11
Guatemala 170, 172-3, 201-2, 208, 219
Honduras 365, 376
Mexico 75
Nicaragua 484
Panama 644, 689-90, 700
Bluefields 491-4
Blue Hole National Park 259
Blue Hole Natural Monument 246
boat trips 736, 737
Belize 239, 245, 270
Costa Rica 542, 560, 586
Guatemala 170-1, 192

Honduras 369, 390, 410
Nicaragua 446, 449, 494
Panama 642, 665, 668
Boca de Sábalos 503-4
Bocas del Toro Province 664-77, 666-7, 10
Bocas del Toro town 667-73, 669
Bolas de Fuego 27
books 420, 708, see also individual countries
Boquete 657-62, 658
border crossings 732, 735-6
Belize 98, 227, 285
Costa Rica 618-19, 705
El Salvador 227, 349-50, 427
Guatemala 98, 182, 227, 285, 349, 427
Honduras 227, 350, 427, 514
Mexico 98, 227, 285
Nicaragua 427, 514, 618-9
Panama 619, 689, 705
Brus Laguna 415
budget 19, 36-8, see also individual countries
bus travel 735, 737-8
business hours 729

C
Cahal Pech 260
Cahuita 545-9, 546-7
Calakmul 82
Campeche 79-82, 80-1
Cancún 50-6, 54
accommodations 53
activities 50, 53
drinking & nightlife 55
food 53, 54
shopping 55
sights 50
travel to/from 55-6
canoeing, see also kayaking
Costa Rica 543, 556, 613
Honduras 410
canopy tours
Belize 280
Costa Rica 556, 565
El Salvador 318
Guatemala 208
Honduras 397, 399
Nicaragua 465
Panama 660, 674
canyoning
Costa Rica 556, 565, 588
car travel 735-6, 738

Caracol 265-6
Carazo Towns 454
Caribbean Coast 491-501, 542-54
Cartago 539
Catarina 453
cathedrals, see churches & cathedrals
caves
Actun Tunichil Muknal 264
Blue Hole National Park 259
Centro Turístico Cueva de las Minas 181
Cuevas de Ak'tun Kan 196
Cuevas de Taulabé 370
Nivida Bat Cave 674
Nohoch Che'en Caves Branch Archaeological Reserve 255
Caye Caulker 17, 239-43, 240, 17
Cayos Cochinos 399
Ceibal 193-5
cell phones 731
cemeteries 400
cenotes
Cenote Azul 69
Cenote Choo-Ha 68
Cenote Multún-Ha 68
Cenote Sagrado 73
Cenote Tamcach-Ha 68
Cenote X'Kekén 71
Cristalino Cenote 61
Central Pacific Coast 587-97
Central Valley & Highlands (Costa Rica) 533-41, 534-5
Cerro El Pital 338
Cerro Punta 663
Cerro Tute 654
Chalatenango 336-7
Chalchuapa 316
Champerico 167
Changuinola 676-7
Chiapas 82-93, 51, 84-5, see also Mexico's Yucatán & Chiapas
Chichén Itzá 72-4, 62-3
Chichicastenango 144-7, 145, 29
children, travel with 725
Costa Rica 614
El Salvador 348
Guatemala 221-2
Honduras 423
Chiquimula 179-80
Chiriquí Province 654-64

INDEX C-D

Chitré 648-9
chocolate tours
 Belize 260, 276
 Costa Rica 551, 555, 560
 Panama 670
Chuitinamit 138
churches & cathedrals 471
 Antigua Catedral
  (Managua) 431
 Basílica de Esquipulas
  181
 Basílica de Suyapa 353
 Catedral de Granada
  445, **2**, **12**
 Catedral de León 470
 Catedral de San Isidro
  392
 Catedral de Santa
  Ana 312
 Catedral de Santiago 115
 Catedral (Estelí) 479
 Catedral San Juan 487
 Catedral Metropolitana
  (Managua) 435
 Catedral Metropolitana
  (San Salvador) 290
 Catedral Nuestra Señora
  de la Paz 329
 Cathedral (Comayagua)
  365-6
 Cathedral (San Pedro
  Sula) 371
 Convento y Museo San
  Francisco 445
 Iglesia Católica Copán
  Ruinas 376
 Iglesia de Chalatenango
  337
 Iglesia de la Merced
  (Gracias) 385
 Iglesia de la
  Recolección 470
 Iglesia de San Félipe 679
 Iglesia de San Francisco
  119
 Iglesia de San José 626
 Iglesia de San José
  Orosi 539
 Iglesia de San Pedro
  644-5
 Iglesia de Santo Tomás
  144
 Iglesia El Calvario 293,
  313
 Iglesia El Carmen 313
 Iglesia El Rosario 290

Iglesia La Merced
 (Comayagua) 366
Iglesia La Merced
 (Granada) 445
Iglesia La Merced
 (Tegucigalpa) 353
Iglesia Los Dolores 353
Iglesia Parroquial
 Santiago Apóstol 137
Iglesia (Trujillo) 400
Iglesia y Convento de
 Nuestra Señora de la
 Merced 115
Moravian Church
 (Bluefields) 492
Moravian Church (Pearl
 Lagoon) 494
Nuestra Señora de
 Asunción 317
St John's Cathedral 234
Templo de San
 Bernardino 71
Templo El Calvario 173
cigar tours 481
Cihuatán 304
Cinquera 339
climate 18, 25-7, **18**, see
 also individual countries
Cobá 68-9
Cobán 173-7, **174-5**
coffee 319
coffee tours
 Costa Rica 539-40, 565
 Guatemala 174
 Nicaragua 484
 Panama 660
Colón 677-8
Colón Province 677-81
Comarca de Guna Yala
 681-4
Comayagua 365-7
consulates 725-6
 Belize 282-3
 Costa Rica 614
 El Salvador 345-6
 Guatemala 222
 Honduras 424
 Mexico 95-6
 Panama 701
Copán Ruinas 16, 374-9,
 375
Copán Archaeological Site
 380-4, **381**, **16**
Corinto 478
Corn Islands 495-9
Corozal 252-4, **253**
Corral de Mulas 327
Costa Maya 15

Costa Rica 46, 516-620,
 518-19
 accommodations 516,
  613-14
 border crossings 618-9
 budget 517
 children, travel with 614
 climate 516
 consulates 614
 culture 612
 customs regulations 614
 disabilities, travelers
  with 617
 discount cards 617
 drinks 517, 615
 embassies 614
 food 516, 517, 615
 highlights 518-19, **518-19**
 hiking 542, 546-7
 history 609-12
 itineraries 517
 landscape 612-13
 LGBT travelers 529, 615
 maps 615
 money 517, 615-16
 opening hours 616
 public holidays 616
 safety 616
 telephone services 616
 time 616
 toilets 616-17
 tourist information 617
 travel to/from 517, 618-19
 travel within 619-20
 visas 617
 volunteering 617-18
 websites 517
 wildlife 613
Cotton Tree Chocolate
 Factory 276
courses, see drumming
 courses, painting
 classes, language
 courses, individual
 locations
crocodiles 588
Crooked Tree Wildlife
 Sanctuary 251
culture 717-22
 Belize 281-2
 Costa Rica 612
 El Salvador 342-3
 Guatemala 217-18
 Honduras 420-1
 Mexico 94
 Nicaragua 509-11
 Panama 696-8
customs regulations 725,
 see also individual
 countries

cycling 43
 Costa Rica 555
 Guatemala 130, 221
 Honduras 385
 Mexico 66, 68, 75
 Panama 665-7

D
dancing classes
 Belize 247
 Guatemala 109, 154
 Honduras 390
 Mexico 61, 78
 Nicaragua 435, 467
dangers, see safety
Dangriga 267-9, **268**
Darién Province 684-92,
 686-7
 safety 690-1, 730,
David 654-6, **655**
Día de los Muertos (Day of
 the Dead) 27
Diria 454
Diriamba 454
disabilities, travelers
 with 732
 Costa Rica 617
 El Salvador 348
 Guatemala 226
 Honduras 426
 Nicaragua 513
 Panama 704
discount cards 725,
 see also individual
 countries
diving & snorkeling 42-3
 Belize 239, 243-4, 270-1,
  272
 Costa Rica 547, 573, 577,
  590, 603
 El Salvador 293
 Guatemala 143
 Honduras 393, 403-4,
  409-10
 Mexico 50, 57, 58-9,
  66, 70
 Nicaragua 498
 Panama 646, 649, 652,
  665, 668, 679
Dominical 595-7
drinking & nightlife, see
 individual locations
drinks 726, 740-1
driving, see car travel
drugs 730, see also legal
 matters
drumming courses 270, 276
Dzibilchaltún 75

Map Pages **000**
Photo Pages **000**

E

ecotourism 709
  Costa Rica 540, 555
  Honduras 368, 415-16
  Nicaragua 494
Edzná 82
Ek' Balam 75
El Castillo 504-5
El Castillo de San Felipe 186-7
El Día de Todos los Santosa 164
El Estor 187-8
El Mirador 211-13
El Oriente 179-93
El Petén 193-212, **194-5**
El Real 689
El Refugio 503
El Remate 201-2
El Salvador 45, 286-350, **288-9**
  accommodations 286, 345
  arts 342, 343
  books 343
  border crossings 349-50
  budget 287
  children, travel with 348
  climate 286, 345
  consulates 345-6
  culture 342-3
  customs regulations 346
  disabilities, travel with 348
  drinks 287
  economy 339-40
  embassies 345-6
  emergencies 346
  environment 343-50
  festivals & events 294
  food 286, 287
  health 346
  highlights 288-9
  history 340-2
  internet access 346
  itineraries 287
  LGBT travelers 347
  money 287, 347
  opening hours 347
  politics 339-40
  public holidays 347
  religion 342-3
  safety 345
  telephone services 348
  tourist information 348
  travel seasons 286
  travel within 350
  travel to/from 349-50
  visas 346

volunteering 293-4, 335, 348
websites 287
El Triunfo de la Cruz 391
El Valle 646-8
El Zotz 212
electricity 725
embassies, see consulates
emergencies 742, see also individual countries
environmental issues
  deforestation 220-1, 282, 344-5, 700-6
  endangered species 282, 613
  invasive species 94
  mining 344-5, 700-6
Esquipulas 180-3
Estelí 479-83, **480**
etiquette 20
events, see festivals & events
exchange rates
  Belize 230
  Costa Rica 517
  El Salvador 287
  Guatemala 100
  Honduras 352
  Mexico 49
  Nicaragua 430
  Panama 622

F

farms
  Arch's Iguana Farm 407
  Costa Rica 560
festivals & events 25-7, see also individual countries
  Azuero 650
  Bolas de Fuego 27
  Carnaval 393
  Carnaval Mitos y Leyendas 473
  Día de la Purísima Concepción 473
  Día de los Muertos (Day of the Dead) 27
  El Día de Todos los Santosa 164
  Envision Festival 597
  Festival de la Luz 602
  Garifuna Day 389, 390
  Garifuna Settlement Day 27, 267
  Las Fiestas de Zapote 524
  Masacre del 23 Julio 1959 472-3
  National Garifuna Dance Festival 390

Palo de Mayo 492
Panama Jazz Festival 630, 633
Quema del Diablo 145
San Jerónimo 455-6
San Lázaro 455
Semana Santa 26, 472
films 708
Finca El Paraíso 187
Finca Ixobal 195
Finca Santa Leticia 318
fishing
  Belize 239, 272, 276
  Guatemala 105
  Honduras 390
  Nicaragua 492
  Panama 649, 667, 700
Flores 196-201, **199**
food 726, see also individual locations
  language 740-1
forts
  El Castillo de San Felipe 186-7
  Fortaleza De Coyotepe 455
  Fortaleza de San Carlos 501
  Fortaleza de San Fernando de Omoa 388
  Fortaleza Santa Bárbara de Trujillo 400
  Fortress (Laguna Bacalar) 69
  Fuerte de San Cristóbal 385
  Fuerte de San Miguel 80-1
  Fuerte San Jerónimo 679
Fray Bartolomé de las Casas 179
free-diving, see diving & snorkeling

G

galleries
  El Arbol de Dios 290
  Galería Pop-Wuj 144
  Image Factory 234
  La Antigua Galería de Arte 119
  Memorias Frágiles 374
  Museo de Arte 151
  Museo de Arte de El Salvador 290
  Museo del Hombre 353-6
  Museo Nacional de Arte Moderno 105

Pen Cayetano Studio Gallery 267
gardens, see parks & gardens
Garifuna people 390, 719-20
Garifuna Settlement Day 27, 267
Garifuna Villages 391-2
Gatún Locks 678-9
gay travelers, see LGBT travelers
Glover's Reef Atoll 270
Golfito 607-8
Golfo de Chiriquí 656-7
Golfo de Fonseca Islands 332
Golfo Dulce **598-9**
government travel advice 731
Gracias 384-7
Granada 12, 444-51, **446-7**
  accommodations 448-9
  courses 445
  drinking & nightlife 450
  entertainment 450
  festivals & events 448
  food 449-50
  history 444-5
  sights 445
  tourist information 451
  tours 445-7
  travel to/from 451
Great Corn Island 496-7
Guanacaste National Park 257
Guatemala 44, 99-229, **102-3**
  accommodations 99, 221
  activities 221
  arts 218-19
  border crossings 98, 182
  budget 100
  children, travel with 221-2
  climate 99
  consulates 222
  culture 217-18
  disabilities, travelers with 226
  drinks 100
  economy 213-14
  embassies 222
  environment 219-29
  food 99, 100
  health 222
  highlights 102-3
  history 214-16
  internet access 222
  itineraries 100

Guatemala *continued*
  language 100
  legal matters 222-3
  LGBT travelers 223
  money 100, 223
  national parks &
    reserves 220
  opening hours 223
  politics 213-14
  public holidays 224
  religion 218
  safety 224-5
  telephone services 225
  time 100
  tourist information 226
  travel seasons 99
  travel to/from 227
  travel within 227-9
  visas 226
  volunteering 226
  websites 100
  women travelers 226
  work 226
Guatemala City 101-14,
  104, **108-9**
  accommodations 106-7
  drinking & nightlife
    107-10
  food 107
  information 110-11
  shopping 110
  sights 101-6
  travel to/from 111-13
  travel within 113-14

H
health 726-7, *see also
  individual countries*
Highlands (Guatemala)
  127-65
Highlands (Costa Rica)
  533-41, **534-5**
highlights 8-17, **8-9**
hiking 39-40
  Costa Rica 537, 538, 555,
    564, 571, 588, 594,
    603, 606
  El Salvador 310-11, 323,
    329, 337
  Guatemala 138, 139, 149,
    153, 164, 221
  Honduras 366, 368, 369,
    371, 393, 397
  Nicaragua 458-9, 484,
    496

Map Pages **000**
Photo Pages **000**

Panama 659, 662-3,
  667, 700
history 710-16
  Belize 280-1
  Cold War 714-15
  Copán Site 380
  Costa Rica 609-12
  democracy 716
  dictatorships 714
  El Salvador 340-2
  football 419
  Guatemala 214-16
  Honduras 417-20
  independence 711
  Maya 710
  Mexico 94
  Neocolonialism 715-16
  Nicaragua 505-9
  Panama 692-6
  religion 711-12
  Spanish settlement
    710-11
hitchhiking 738
holidays 729-30
Honduras 45, 351-428,
  354-5
  accommodations 423
  border crossings 227,
    350, 427, 514
  budget 352
  children, travel with 423
  climate 351, 423
  consulates 424
  culture 420-1
  customs regulations 423
  disabilities, travelers
    with 426
  drinks 352
  embassies 424
  food 351, 352
  highlights 354-5
  history 417-20
  internet access 424
  itineraries 352
  legal matters 424
  LGBT travelers 424
  measures 426
  money 352, 424-5
  opening hours 425
  post 425
  public holidays 425
  safety 425
  smoking 425
  telephone services 425
  tourist information 426
  travel seasons 351
  travel to/from 426-7
  travel within 427-8
  visas 426

volunteering 426
websites 352
weights 426
women travelers 426
work 426
Hopkins 270-2
horseback riding
  Costa Rica 547, 556,
    565-6, 589
  Guatemala 221
  Honduras 379, 385,
    398, 404
  Nicaragua 465
hot springs & spas
  Aguas Termales (Copán
    Ruinas) 379
  Aguas Termales
    Presidente 387
  Centro Turístico Terma
    del Río 387
  Costa Rica 571
  Eco Termales Hot
    Springs 555
  Luna Jaguar Spa Resort
    379
  Paradise Hot Springs 555
  Parque Nacional Rincón
    de la Vieja 571
  Pozos Termales 647
Huehuetenango 161-3, **162**
Hummingbird Hwy 259-60

I
immigration 734
indigenous peoples 718-20,
  *see also individual
  groups*
insurance 727-8
internet access 728
internet resources 19
Isla Bastimentos 673-6
Isla Boca Brava 656-7
Isla Cañas 649
Isla Carenero 673
Isla Colón 665-77
Isla Conchagüita 332
Isla Cozumel 64-6, **65**
Isla de Coiba 653
Isla de Ometepe 16,
  458-64, **460**, **16**
Isla del Tigre 416-17
Isla Espíritu Santo 327
Isla Grande 680-1
Isla Madre Sal 327
Isla Martín Pérez 332
Isla Meanguera 332
Isla Méndez 327
Isla Montecristo 326
Isla Mujeres 56-8

Isla Taboga 644-5
Isla Venada 503
Isla Zacatillo 332
Isla Zapote 503
Islas Solentiname 502-3
itineraries 28-35, **28**, **30**,
  31, **32**, **34-5**, *see also
  individual countries*

J
Jacó 588-90
Jinotega 486-8
Jinotepe 454
Joya de Cerén 304
Juayúa 320-2

K
kayaking, *see also
  canoeing*
  Costa Rica 560, 588-9
  Honduras 410
  Nicaragua 447, 463
  Panama 665, 701
kitesurfing 239, 498
Kriol people 719
K'um'arkaj 147-8

L
La Blanca 212
La Campa 388
La Ceiba 392-7, **394**
La Costa del Bálsamo 306-9
La Cruz 572-3
La Democracia 168-9
La Ensenada 391
La Esperanza 367-8
La Fortuna 554-8
La Garnacha 485
La Laguna de Alegría 325
La Libertad 305-6
La Palma 338-9, 690-1
La Unión 330-1
Lago de Atitlán 15, 128-65,
  129, **15**
Lago de Coatepeque 311
Lago de Izabal 184-8
Lago de Yojoa 369-70
Lagos de Montebello 88
Laguna Bacalar 69-70
Laguna de Ibans 414
Laguna de Olomega 329
Lamanai 249-50
Lancetilla Botanical Garden
  & Research Center 392
landscape
  Costa Rica 612-13
  Honduras 421-3
  Nicaragua 511

language 21, 739-46
language courses
  Costa Rica 521, 538,
    564-5, 577-8, 581
  El Salvador 335, 346-7
  Guatemala 119-20, 130,
    139-40, 149, 153-4, 171
  Honduras 376
  Mexico 59
  Nicaragua 435, 445, 465,
    479-80, 489
  Panama 629, 668
Lanquín 177-8
Las Isletas 449
Las Peñitas 477
legal matters 728, *see also*
  individual countries
León 469-76, **472-3**
  accommodations 473-4
  courses 471
  drinking & nightlife 475
  entertainment 475
  festivals & events 471-3
  food 474-5
  history 470
  sights 470
  tourist information 475-6
  tours 471
  travel to/from 476
LGBT travelers 728
  Belize 283
  Costa Rica 615
  El Salvador 347
  Guatemala 223
  Honduras 424
  Mexico 96
  Nicaragua 512
  Panama 702
Liberia 568-70, **569**
libraries 293
lifestyle 720-1
literature 420, 708
Little Corn Island 497-9
Lívingston 189-93
Los Chiles 559
Los Cóbanos 306
Los Planes de Renderos
  305
Lubaantun 279

M
Mahahual 70
Mal País 582-3
Managua 431-44, **436-7**,
  438, **443**
  accommodations 435-7
  activities 431
  courses 435

drinking & nightlife
  439-40
entertainment 440
festivals & events 435
food 437-9
history 431
shopping 440
sights 431
tourist information
  440-2
travel to/from 442
travel within 434, 443
Mancarrón 502
Mapa en Relieve 101
maps 728
Marcala 368
markets
  Chichicastenango 144
  Guatemala City 105, 110
  Mercado de Artesanías
    de Masaya 455
  Panama City 638
  Quetzaltenango (Xela)
    159
  San Salvador 301
Masachapa 443-4
Masaya 455-6, **454-5**
Masaya region 444-57
massages
  Belize 245
  El Salvador 331
  Guatemala 142
Matagalpa 488-91
Maya people 718
medical services 726-7
meditation
  Guatemala 142
  Honduras 384
Mérida (Mexico) 74-9,
  76-7, 23
Mérida (Nicaragua) 463-4,
  464
Mestizos 717
Metapán 314-16
Metetí 688
Mexico's Yucatán &
  Chiapas 44, 48-98,
  51, **52-3**
  accommodations 48, 95
  border crossings 98,
    227, 285
  budget 49
  climate 48, 95
  consulates 95-6
  culture 94
  customs regulations 95
  discount cards 95
  drinks 49
  economy 94
  embassies 95-6

emergencies 96
food 48, 49
highlights 51
history 94
itineraries 49
LGBT travelers 96
money 49, 96
opening hours 96
public holidays 96
safety 95
tourist permits 96-7
travel seasons 48
travel to/from 97-8
travel within 98
visas 97
volunteering 59, 97
websites 49
Miami (Honduras) 392
military 730
Mirador el Boquete 454
Miramundo 338
Misol-Ha 93
Mixco Viejo 172
monasteries 115, 118-19
money 19, 728-9, *see also*
  individual locations
Monterrico 169-72
Monteverde 561-8,
  562-3, 14
Montezuma 583-7, **584**
Monumento Nacional Isla
  Barro Colorado 644
Morazán 332-4
Moskitia, the 414-16
motorcycle travel 735-6, 738
Mountain Pine Ridge 265-6
Moyogalpa 459
Mt Pleasant 496
museums
  BioMuseo 628-9
  Cacaopera Museum 333
  Casa de los Venados 71
  Casa de Montejo 74-5
  Casa del Tejido
    Antiguo 118
  Casa K'inich 376
  Casa MIMA 101
  Casa Museo Comandante
    Carlos Fonseca 488
  Casa Museo Judith
    Kain 500
  Centro de Textiles del
    Mundo Maya 83
  Centro Monseñor
    Romero 292
  Cojolya Association of
    Maya Women
    Weavers 137
  Culture House (Great
    Corn Island) 496

El Campamento
  Guerrillero Simulado
  333
Galería de Héroes y
  Mártires (Estelí) 479
George Price Center for
  Peace &
  Development 257
Gran Museo del Mundo
  Maya 74
Gulisi Garifuna Museum
  267
Miraflores Visitors
  Center 642
Museo Balam 163
Museo Capitán
  Dulché 57
Museo Casa Galeano 385
Museo de Antropología e
  Historia 457
Museo de Antropología e
  Historia de San Pedro
  Sula 371
Museo de Arqueología
  Maya 376
Museo de Arte
  Contemporáneo 629
Museo de Arte
  Fundación
  Ortiz-Gurdián 470
Museo de Arte Religioso
  Colonial 627
Museo de Arte y Diseño
  Contemporáneo 520-1
Museo de Café 488
Museo de Chocolate 445
Museo de Escultura 382
Museo de Jade 521
Museo de la Arquitectura
  Maya 80
Museo de la Medicina
  Maya 83
Museo de la Palabra y La
  Imagen 290-2
Museo de la Revolución
  Salvadoreña 333
Museo de Leyendas y
  Tradiciones 470
Museo del Canal
  Interoceánico 627
Museo del Ferrocarril 101
Museo de Oro
  Precolombino y
  Numismática 520
Museo de Paleontología,
  Arqueología y
  Geología 180
Museo de Sitio Panamá
  Viejo 628
Museo Digital de Copán
  376
Museo Historico Cultural
  de la Costa Caribe
  491-2

INDEX M-P

museums *continued*
Museo Historico de la
Revolución 470
Museo Ixchel 105
Museo Ixkik' 151
Museo Juan Santamaría
536
Museo Maya de Cancún
50
Museo Nacional de
Costa Rica 520
Museo Nacional de
Historia 101
Museo Nacional de
Historia Natural Jorge
Ibarra 106
Museo para la Identidad
Nacional 353
Museo Popol Vuh 105
Museo Regional del
Oriente 329
Museo Rubén Darío 470
Museum of Belize 234
music 21, 722
Belize 281
Garifuna 390
Guatemala 154, 158, 218
Panama 633, 698

N
Naranjo 212
national parks & reserves
220, 344, 422, *see also*
parks & gardens
Área Protegida Cerro
Tisey-Estanzuela 485
Área Protegida Miraflor
484-5
Biotopo Cerro Cahuí
201-2
Biotopo Chocón
Machacas 192
Biotopo del Quetzal 172-3
Blue Hole National
Park 259
Cloudbridge Nature
Reserve 600
Coiba National Park 653
Guanacaste National
Park 257
Isla de Coiba 653
Monumento Nacional
Cañon de Somoto 486
Monumento Nacional Isla
Barro Colorado 644
Parque Arqueológico
Takalik Abaj 166-7

Map Pages **000**
Photo Pages **000**

Parque Eco-Arqueológico
Los Naranjos 370
Parque Internacional La
Amistad 663-4
Parque Nacional Braulio
Carrillo 538
Parque Nacional Cahuita
545
Parque Nacional Carara
587-8
Parque Nacional Cerro
Azul Meámbar 370
Parque Nacional
Chirripó 601
Parque Nacional
Corcovado 606-7
Parque Nacional Cusuco
371
Parque Nacional Darién
691
Parque Nacional El
Imposible 323-4
Parque Nacional
Jeannette Kawas 391
Parque Nacional La
Tigra 365
Parque Nacional Los
Volcanes 310-11
Parque Nacional Manuel
Antonio 13, 593,
13, **33**
Parque Nacional Marino
Ballena 597
Parque Nacional Marino
Golfo de Chiriquí
656-7
Parque Nacional Marino
Isla Bastimentos 674
Parque Nacional Marino
Las Baulas de
Guanacaste 576
Parque Nacional
Montaña de Celaque
388
Parque Nacional
Montaña de
Comayagua 366
Parque Nacional
Montaña de Santa
Bárbara 370
Parque Nacional Pico
Bonito 398-9
Parque Nacional Rincón
de la Vieja 571-2
Parque Nacional San
Lorenzo 679
Parque Nacional
Soberanía 643
Parque Nacional Tapantí-
Macizo Cerro de la
Muerte 539
Parque Nacional
Tortuguero 542

Parque Nacional Volcán
Arenal 554
Parque Nacional Volcán
Barú 662-3
Parque Nacional Volcán
Masaya 456-7
Parque Nacional Volcán
Poás 537-8
Parque Nacional Walter T
Deininger 305
Refugio Nacional de
Vida Silvestre Caño
Negro 559
Reserva Biológica
Bosque Nuboso
Monteverde 14
Reserva Biológica Indio-
Maíz, Aguas Frescas
505
Reserva Biológica
Indio-Maíz, Caño
Sarnoso 505
Reserva Biológica Indio-
Maíz, Río Bartola 505
Reserva de Biosfera
Bosawás 489
Reserva de la Biosfera
del Río Plátano 414-15
Reserva de la Biosfera
Ría Celestún 75
Reserva Natural Absoluta
Cabo Blanco 584
Reserva Natural Estero
Padre Ramos 478-9
Reserva Natural Isla
Juan Venado 477
Reserva Natural Laguna
de Apoyo 452-3
Reserva Natural Volcán
Mombacho 452
Reserva Santa Elena 565
Río Blanco National
Park 280
Shipstern Conservation
Management Area 254
Talamanca Reserve
600-1
natural hazards 730
Nebaj 149-50
Nicaragua 45, 429-515,
432-3
accommodations
429, 511
border crossings 427, 514
budget 430
climate 429
consulates 512
culture 509-11
disabilities, travelers
with 513
embassies 512
festivals 455
food 429

history 505-9
internet access 512
itineraries 430
legal matters 512
LGBT travelers 512
money 430, 512
opening hours 512
public holidays 512-13
safety 513
telephone services 513
tourist information 513
travel to/from 430, 514
travel within 514
visas 513
volunteering 513
nightlife, *see individual
locations*
Nim Li Punit 279
Northern Honduras
388-402
Northern Lowlands 554-61
Northern Nicaragua 479-91
Northwestern Costa Rica
561-73
Northwestern Nicaragua
469-79
Nueva Ocotepeque 387

O
Omoa 388-9
opening hours 729,
*see also individual
countries*
Orange Walk 250-2

P
paddle boating 410
painting classes 435
palaces
Palacio del
Ayuntamiento 115
Palacio de los Capitanes
Generales 115
Palacio Nacional de la
Cultura 101
Palacio Nacional 292
Palacios 415
Palenque 13, 89-93, **90**,
13, **29**
Palmar 602
Panajachel 129-37, **132-3**
Panama 46, 621-706,
624-5
accommodations 621,
700
activities 700-1
arts 698
border crossings 619,
689, 705

budget 622
climate 621
consulates 701
culture 696-8
customs regulations 701
disabilities, travelers with 704
drinks 622, 701-2
electricity 701
embassies 701
environment 698-706
food 621, 622, 701
highlights 624-5
history 692-6
internet access 702
itineraries 622
legal matters 702
LGBT travelers 702
money 622, 702-3
opening hours 703
politics 692
public holidays 703
religion 697-8
safety 703-4
sports 698
telephone services 704
tourist information 704
travel seasons 621
travel to/from 704-6
travel within 705-6
visas 704
websites 622
Panama Canal 642, 708, **643**
Panama City 14, 623-41. **626-7**, **630-1**, **634**, 14
accommodations 630-5
courses 629
drinking & nightlife 637
entertainment 637-8
festivals & events 630
food 635-7
information 638-9
shopping 638
sights 629
tours 629-30
travel to/from 639-41
travel within 641-2
Panchimalco 305
paragliding 119, 130
parks & gardens, *see also* national parks & reserves
Aprovaca Orquídeas 647
Carambola Botanical Gardens 407
Cerro Tzankujil 142
Finca Los Monos Botanical Garden 667

Green Iguana Conservation Project 260
Jardín Botánico Dr Alfredo Barrera Marín 58
Jardín Botánico (Gracias) 385
Jardín Botánico La Laguna 290
Lancetilla Botanical Garden & Research Center 392
Orquigonia 173
Parque Balboa 305
Parque Histórico Nacional Loma de Tiscapa 434
Parque Metropolitano La Sabana 521
Parque Minerva 105
Parque Nacional Las Victorias 173
Parque Nacional (San José) 520
Parque Natural Metropolitano 629
Parque Santa Lucía 74
Parque Swinford 392
Plaza de la Revolución 431
Tree of Life 545
Turicentro Agua Fría 337
Parque Arqueológico Takalik Abaj 166-7
Parque Internacional La Amistad 663-4
Parque Nacional Braulio Carrillo 538
Parque Nacional Carara 587-8
Parque Nacional Corcovado 606-7
Parque Nacional El Imposible 323-4
Parque Nacional La Tigra 365
Parque Nacional Los Volcanes 310-11
Parque Nacional Manuel Antonio 13, 593, **13**, **33**
Parque Nacional Marino Isla Bastimentos 674
Parque Nacional Montaña de Comayagua 366
Parque Nacional Pico Bonito 398-9
Parque Nacional Rincón de la Vieja 571-2
Parque Nacional San Lorenzo 679
Parque Nacional Soberanía 643

Parque Nacional Volcán Barú 662-3
Parque Nacional Volcán Masaya 456-7
Parque Nacional Volcán Poás 537-8
Parque Nacional Walter T Deininger 305
Paso Canoas 609
passports 734
Pavones 608-9
Pearl Lagoon 494-5
Pedasí 649-50
Pedro Miguel Locks 642
Península de Nicoya 573-86, **574-5**
Península de Osa 598-609, **598-9**
Perquín 333-4
Piedras Negras 212
Placencia 272-6, **273**
planning
basics 18-19
Belize 45, 230-1
budgeting 19, 36-8
calendar of events 25-7
Costa Rica 46, 516-17
El Salvador 45, 287-8
Guatemala 44, 99-100
Honduras 45, 350-1
websites 19
Mexico 44, 48-9
Nicaragua 45, 429-30
Panama 46, 620-1
travel seasons 18, 25-7
Playa Del Carmen 59-64, **60**
Playa del Coco 573-6
Playa Las Lajas 657
Playa Sámara 580-2
Playa Tamarindo 576-80, **578**
Playa Venao 651-2
Pochomil 443-4
poetry 722
police 728, 730
El Salvador 301
Guatemala 111, 126, 159, 200
Honduras 424
Nicaragua 512
Panama 703
politics 708-9
Poneloya 477
Portobelo 679-80
postal services 729, *see also individual countries*
poverty 709
public art 721

Murals (Estelí) 479
National Assembly Pedestrian Walk 434
Panama Canal Murals 629
public holidays 729-30, *see also individual countries*
Pueblos Blancos 453-4
Puerta Lempira 415-16
Puerto Barrios 188-9
Puerto Cortés 389
Puerto Jiménez 604-6
Puerto Limón 544-5
Puerto Morelos 58-9
Puerto Viejo de Talamanca 549-54, **550-1**
Punta de Manabique 189
Punta Gorda 276-9, **277**
Punta San Juan 327
pura vida 612

Q
Quema del Diablo 145
Quepos 590-3
Quetzaltenango (Xela) 151-61, **152**, **156-7**
Quezaltepeque 290
Quiriguá 183-4

R
rafting 43
Costa Rica 540, 560, 591, 595-6
El Salvador 314-15
Honduras 398
Panama 659, 701
Raiti Pura 494
Rama Cay 492
Rancho Frío 689-90
Refugio de Vida Silvestre Cuero y Salado 400
Refugio de Vida Silvestre La Flor 469
religion 720, *see also individual countries*
reserves, *see* national parks & reserves
Reserva de la Biosfera del Río Plátano 414-15
Retalhuleu 165-6
Río Azul 212
Río Blanco National Park 280
Río Bulaba 653-4
Río Cangrejal 397-8
Río Dulce 184-6
Río San Juan 503-5
Rivas 457-8

Roatán 402-8, **406-7**
  Far East 406-7
  French Harbour 407
  Sandy Bay 407-8
  West Bay 408
  West End 403-6
robbery 730-1
round-the-world tickets 735
Ruinas de Quelepa 328-9
Ruinas de San Andrés 304
Ruta de las Flores 16, 316-22

S
safety 730-1, *see also individual countries*
sailing
  Belize 239, 244, 245
  Guatemala 184
  Panama 668
Salamá 172
Sambo Creek 399
Sambú 692
San Antonio 280
San Bartolo 212
San Carlos 501-2
San Cristóbal de las Casas 82-7, **86-7**
San Fernando 503
San Gerardo de Rivas 600-2
San Ignacio 260-5, **262**
San Isidro de El General 599-600
San Jorge 458
San José 520-33, **522-3**
  accommodations 524-7
  drinking & nightlife 529
  entertainment 529-30
  festivals & events 524
  food 527-9
  shopping 530
  sights 520-1
  tourist information 530-1
  tours 521, 524
  travel to/from 531-3
  travel within 533
San Juan de Oriente 453, **466**
San Juan del Sur 464-8, **33**
San Manuel Colohete 388
San Marcos 454
San Marcos La Laguna 141-3

San Miguel 327-30, **328**
San Pedro 243-9, **244**
San Pedro Columbia 279
San Pedro La Laguna 139-41
San Pedro Sula 371-4
San Ramón 463-4
San Salvador 290-304, **291**, **292-3**, **296**, **298**
  accommodations 294-7
  activities 293-4
  drinking & nightlife 300
  entertainment 300
  food 297-300
  information 301-2
  shopping 300-1
  sights 290-3
  travel to/from 302
  travel within 302-4
San Vicente 324-5
Santa Ana 311-14, **312**
Santa Catalina 652-3
Santa Cruz 462
Santa Cruz del Quiché 147-9
Santa Cruz La Lagun 143-4
Santa Elena 196-201, 561-8, **562-3**
Santa Fé 653-4
Santa Lucía 364-5
Santa Lucía Cotzumalguapa 167-8
Santa Rosa Sector 572
Santa Tecla 309-10
Santa Teresa 582-3
Santiago Atitlán 137-9
Sarteneja 254-5
Sayaxché 193
Semuc Champey 178-9
Sierpe 602-3
Sipacate 169
Sittee Point 270-2
Sixaola 554
smoking 731
snorkeling, *see* diving & snorkeling
Somoto 485-6
Sonsonate 322
Southern Costa Rica 598-609
Southern Honduras 416-17
Southern Pacific Coast 464-9
Southwestern Nicaragua 457-64
Spanish language 739-46, *see also language courses*
spas, *see* hot springs & spas

stand-up paddleboarding 573
street art, *see* public art
Suchitoto 334-6
Sunset Coast 650-1
surfing 42
  Costa Rica 550, 576-7, 581, 588, 595-6, 608
  El Salvador 305, 306, 308, 331
  Guatemala 169
  Nicaragua 465
  Panama 652, 665, 668, 700-1
swimming 731
  Costa Rica 547, 594, 603
  Honduras 368
  Mexico 61, 68, 71
  Nicaragua 462

T
Tacuba 322-3
Tazumal 316
Tegucigalpa 353-65, **358-9**, **362**
  accommodations 356-7
  drinking & nightlife 360
  entertainment 360-1
  festivals & events 356
  food 357-60
  information 361
  shopping 361
  sights 353-6
  travel to/from 361-3
  travel within 363-4
Tela 389-91
telephone services 731, *see also individual countries*
theft 730-1
Tikal 10, 202-10, **204-5**, **11**, **204-5**
Tilarán 558-9
time 731, 742
tipping 21
  Belize 283
  Costa Rica 616
  El Salvador 347
  Guatemala 223
  Honduras 425
  Panama 703
Tobacco Caye 270
Todos Santos Cuchumatán 163-5
toilets 731
Toledo 279-80
Tornabé 391
Tortuguero 542-4

tourist information 732, *see also individual locations*
tours
  Belize 260-1, 276
  Costa Rica 521, 539-40, 543, 551, 555, 560, 565, 590, 590-1, 604-5
  El Salvador 318, 323
  Guatemala 174, 208
  Honduras 369, 376, 393, 397, 399, 410, 415-16
  Nicaragua 465, 481, 484, 486, 489, 500
  Panama 642, 646, 659-60, 663-4, 674-5, 685
transportation 734-8
  language 742-3
travel seasons 18, 25-7, *see also individual countries*
travel to/from Central America 734-6
travel within Central America 736-8
trekking, *see* hiking
Trujillo 400-2, **401**
Tulum 66-8
Turrialba 540-1

U
Uaxactún 210-11
Uspantán 150-1
Usulután 326-7
Utila 408-14, **410-11**
Uvita 597
Uxmal 75

V
vacations 729-30
vaccinations 727
Valladolid 70-2
Valle de Orosi 539-40
Valle de Sarapiquí 559-61
violence 709
visas 732, *see also individual countries*
Volcán Arenal 554-8, **4**
volcanoes
  Cerro de Oro 138
  El Salvador 315
  Parque Nacional Los Volcanes 310-11
  Santiaguito 153
  Volcán Barú 662-3
  Volcán Chaparrastique 329
  Volcán Izalco 310
  Volcán San Pedro 139
  Volcán Santa María 153

Volcán Tajumulco 153
Volcán Tolimán 138
volunteering 732-3
  Belize 284-5
  El Salvador 293-4, 335, 348
  Guatemala 226
  Mexico 59, 97

W
walking, *see* hiking
waterfalls
  Agua Azul 93
  Cascada de los Ensueños 366
  Cascada San Ramón 463
  Catarata Río Fortuna 555
  Cataratas Nauyaca 595
  Chorro El Macho 646
  La Escalada de los Gigantes 369
  Los Siete Altares 190
  Misol-Ha 93
  Montezuma Waterfalls 584
  Pulhapanzak 370
  Salto Estanzuela 485
water sports, *see individual sports*
weather 18, 25-7, **18**
websites 19, *see also individual locations*
Western Belize 255-67, **256-7**

wetland reserves
  Refugio de Vida Silvestre Cuero y Salado 400
whale sharks 409
white-water rafting, *see* rafting
wildlife, *see* animals
wildlife centers & reserves, *see also* aquariums
  Alturas Animal Sanctuary 595
  Biotopo Monterrico-Hawaii 170
  Crooked Tree Wildlife Sanctuary 251
  Iguana Research & Breeding Station 408
  Isla Cañas 649
  Jaguar Centro de Rescate 550
  Monkey Bay Wildlife Sanctuary 255
  Panama Rainforest Discovery Center 644
  Parque Hawaii 170
  Refugio de Vida Punta Izopo 391
  Refugio de Vida Silvestre Isla Iguana 649
  Refugio de Vida Silvestre Islas Taboga y Urabá 644
  Refugio de Vida Silvestre La Flor 469
  Reserva Biológica Bosque Nuboso Monteverde 564

  Reserva Natural Punta Patiño 691
Roatán Marine Park 403
Tortugario Monterrico 170
wildlife-watching 40
  Costa Rica 555-6, 603
  Guatemala 201-2
  Mexico 56-7, 57, 75
  Panama 643, 651
women travelers 733
  Guatemala 226
  Honduras 426
work 733
World Heritage Sites
  Antigua 114-27, **116-17**
  Casco Viejo 623, 626-7
  Coiba National Park 653
  Copán Archaeological Site 16, 380-4
  Isla de Coiba 653
  Joya de Cerén 304
  Parque Nacional Darién 691
  Quiriguá 183-4
  Reserva de la Biosfera del Río Plátano 414-15
  Tikal 10, 202-10, **204-5**, 10, **204-5**

X
Xunantunich 266

Y
Yaviza 688-9
Yaxchilán 88-9
Yaxhá 211
yoga
  Belize 245
  Costa Rica 585, 608
  Guatemala 142
  Yucatán 48-9, 5-82, **51**, **52-3**, *see also* Mexico's Yucatán & Chiapas

Z
Zaculeu 161
ziplining
  Belize 266, 280
  El Salvador 318
  Honduras 387
zoos, *see also* aquariums, wildlife centers & reserves
  Bat Jungle 564
  Belize Zoo 255
  Butterfly Garden 564
  El Níspero 647
  La Aurora Zoo 106
  Macaw Mountain Bird Park 374-6
  Monteverde Theme Park 564

Map Legend

Sights
- Beach
- Bird Sanctuary
- Buddhist
- Castle/Palace
- Christian
- Confucian
- Hindu
- Islamic
- Jain
- Jewish
- Monument
- Museum/Gallery/Historic Building
- Ruin
- Shinto
- Sikh
- Taoist
- Winery/Vineyard
- Zoo/Wildlife Sanctuary
- Other Sight

Activities, Courses & Tours
- Bodysurfing
- Diving
- Canoeing/Kayaking
- Course/Tour
- Sento Hot Baths/Onsen
- Skiing
- Snorkeling
- Surfing
- Swimming/Pool
- Walking
- Windsurfing
- Other Activity

Sleeping
- Sleeping
- Camping

Eating
- Eating

Drinking & Nightlife
- Drinking & Nightlife
- Cafe

Entertainment
- Entertainment

Shopping
- Shopping

Information
- Bank
- Embassy/Consulate
- Hospital/Medical
- Internet
- Police
- Post Office
- Telephone
- Toilet
- Tourist Information
- Other Information

Geographic
- Beach
- Gate
- Hut/Shelter
- Lighthouse
- Lookout
- Mountain/Volcano
- Oasis
- Park
- Pass
- Picnic Area
- Waterfall

Population
- Capital (National)
- Capital (State/Province)
- City/Large Town
- Town/Village

Transport
- Airport
- Border crossing
- Bus
- Cable car/Funicular
- Cycling
- Ferry
- Metro station
- Monorail
- Parking
- Petrol station
- Subway/Subte station
- Taxi
- Train station/Railway
- Tram
- Underground station
- Other Transport

Note: Not all symbols displayed above appear on the maps in this book

Routes
- Tollway
- Freeway
- Primary
- Secondary
- Tertiary
- Lane
- Unsealed road
- Road under construction
- Plaza/Mall
- Steps
- Tunnel
- Pedestrian overpass
- Walking Tour
- Walking Tour detour
- Path/Walking Trail

Boundaries
- International
- State/Province
- Disputed
- Regional/Suburb
- Marine Park
- Cliff
- Wall

Hydrography
- River, Creek
- Intermittent River
- Canal
- Water
- Dry/Salt/Intermittent Lake
- Reef

Areas
- Airport/Runway
- Beach/Desert
- Cemetery (Christian)
- Cemetery (Other)
- Glacier
- Mudflat
- Park/Forest
- Sight (Building)
- Sportsground
- Swamp/Mangrove